American Casebook Series
Hornbook Series and Basic Legal Texts
Black Letter Series and Nutshell Series

of

WEST PUBLISHING COMPANY
P.O. Box 64526
St. Paul, Minnesota 55164–0526

Accounting

FARIS' ACCOUNTING AND LAW IN A NUTSHELL, 377 pages, 1984. Softcover. (Text)

FIFLIS' ACCOUNTING ISSUES FOR LAWYERS, TEACHING MATERIALS, Fourth Edition, 706 pages, 1991. Teacher's Manual available. (Casebook)

SIEGEL AND SIEGEL'S ACCOUNTING AND FINANCIAL DISCLOSURE: A GUIDE TO BASIC CONCEPTS, 259 pages, 1983. Softcover. (Text)

Administrative Law

AMAN AND MAYTON'S HORNBOOK ON ADMINISTRATIVE LAW, Approximately 750 pages, 1993. (Text)

BONFIELD AND ASIMOW'S STATE AND FEDERAL ADMINISTRATIVE LAW, 826 pages, 1989. Teacher's Manual available. (Casebook)

GELLHORN AND LEVIN'S ADMINISTRATIVE LAW AND PROCESS IN A NUTSHELL, Third Edition, 479 pages, 1990. Softcover. (Text)

MASHAW, MERRILL, AND SHANE'S CASES AND MATERIALS ON ADMINISTRATIVE LAW—THE AMERICAN PUBLIC LAW SYSTEM, Third Edition, 1187 pages, 1992. (Casebook)

ROBINSON, GELLHORN AND BRUFF'S THE ADMINISTRATIVE PROCESS, Third Edition, 978 pages, 1986. (Casebook)

Admiralty

HEALY AND SHARPE'S CASES AND MATERIALS ON ADMIRALTY, Second Edition, 876 pages, 1986. (Casebook)

MARAIST'S ADMIRALTY IN A NUTSHELL, Second Edition, 379 pages, 1988. Softcover. (Text)

SCHOENBAUM'S HORNBOOK ON ADMIRALTY AND MARITIME LAW, Student Edition, 692 pages, 1987 with 1992 pocket part. (Text)

Agency—Partnership

DEMOTT'S FIDUCIARY OBLIGATION, AGENCY AND PARTNERSHIP: DUTIES IN ONGOING BUSINESS RELATIONSHIPS, 740 pages, 1991. Teacher's Manual available. (Casebook)

FESSLER'S ALTERNATIVES TO INCORPORATION FOR PERSONS IN QUEST OF PROFIT, Third Edition, 339 pages, 1991. Softcover. (Casebook)

HENN'S CASES AND MATERIALS ON AGENCY, PARTNERSHIP AND OTHER UNINCORPORATED BUSINESS ENTERPRISES, Second Edition, 733 pages, 1985. Teacher's Manual available. (Casebook)

REUSCHLEIN AND GREGORY'S HORNBOOK ON THE LAW OF AGENCY AND PARTNERSHIP, Second Edition, 683 pages, 1990. (Text)

SELECTED CORPORATION AND PARTNERSHIP STATUTES, RULES AND FORMS. Softcover. Revised 1991 Edition, 953 pages.

STEFFEN AND KERR'S CASES ON AGENCY-PARTNERSHIP, Fourth Edition, 859 pages, 1980. (Casebook)

STEFFEN'S AGENCY-PARTNERSHIP IN A NUTSHELL, 364 pages, 1977. Softcover. (Text)

Agricultural Law

MEYER, PEDERSEN, THORSON AND DAVIDSON'S AGRICULTURAL LAW: CASES AND MATERIALS, 931 pages, 1985. Teacher's Manual avail-

Agricultural Law—Cont'd
able. (Casebook)

Alternative Dispute Resolution
KANOWITZ' CASES AND MATERIALS ON ALTERNATIVE DISPUTE RESOLUTION, 1024 pages, 1986. Teacher's Manual available. (Casebook) 1990 Supplement.

NOLAN–HALEY'S ALTERNATIVE DISPUTE RESOLUTION IN A NUTSHELL, 298 pages, 1992. Softcover. (Text)

RISKIN AND WESTBROOK'S DISPUTE RESOLUTION AND LAWYERS, 468 pages, 1987. Teacher's Manual available. (Casebook)

RISKIN AND WESTBROOK'S DISPUTE RESOLUTION AND LAWYERS, Abridged Edition, 223 pages, 1987. Softcover. Teacher's Manual available. (Casebook)

RISKIN'S DISPUTE RESOLUTION FOR LAWYERS VIDEO TAPES, 1992. (Available for purchase by schools and libraries.)

American Indian Law
CANBY'S AMERICAN INDIAN LAW IN A NUTSHELL, Second Edition, 336 pages, 1988. Softcover. (Text)

GETCHES AND WILKINSON'S CASES AND MATERIALS ON FEDERAL INDIAN LAW, Second Edition, 880 pages, 1986. (Casebook)

Antitrust—see also Regulated Industries, Trade Regulation
BARNES AND STOUT'S ECONOMIC FOUNDATIONS OF REGULATION AND ANTITRUST LAW, 102 pages, 1992. Softcover. Teacher's Manual available. (Casebook)

FOX AND SULLIVAN'S CASES AND MATERIALS ON ANTITRUST, 935 pages, 1989. Teacher's Manual available. (Casebook) 1993 Supplement.

GELLHORN'S ANTITRUST LAW AND ECONOMICS IN A NUTSHELL, Third Edition, 472 pages, 1986. Softcover. (Text)

HOVENKAMP'S BLACK LETTER ON ANTITRUST, Second Edition approximately 325 pages, April 1993 Pub. Softcover. (Review)

HOVENKAMP'S HORNBOOK ON ECONOMICS AND FEDERAL ANTITRUST LAW, Student Edition, 414 pages, 1985. (Text)

POSNER AND EASTERBROOK'S CASES AND ECONOMIC NOTES ON ANTITRUST, Second Edition, 1077 pages, 1981. (Casebook) 1984–85 Supplement.

SULLIVAN'S HORNBOOK OF THE LAW OF ANTITRUST, 886 pages, 1977. (Text)

Appellate Advocacy—see Trial and Appellate Advocacy

Architecture and Engineering Law
SWEET'S LEGAL ASPECTS OF ARCHITECTURE, ENGINEERING AND THE CONSTRUCTION PROCESS, Fourth Edition, 889 pages, 1989. Teacher's Manual available. (Casebook)

Art Law
DUBOFF'S ART LAW IN A NUTSHELL, Second Edition, approximately 325 pages, 1993. Softcover. (Text)

Banking Law
BANKING LAW: SELECTED STATUTES AND REGULATIONS. Softcover. 263 pages, 1991.

LOVETT'S BANKING AND FINANCIAL INSTITUTIONS LAW IN A NUTSHELL, Third Edition, 470 pages, 1992. Softcover. (Text)

SYMONS AND WHITE'S BANKING LAW: TEACHING MATERIALS, Third Edition, 818 pages, 1991. Teacher's Manual available. (Casebook)

    Statutory Supplement. *See Banking Law: Selected Statutes*

Bankruptcy—see Creditors' Rights

Business Planning—see also Corporate Finance
PAINTER'S PROBLEMS AND MATERIALS IN BUSINESS PLANNING, Second Edition, 1008 pages, 1984. (Casebook) 1990 Supplement.

    Statutory Supplement. *See Selected Corporation and Partnership*

Civil Procedure—see also Federal Jurisdiction and Procedure
AMERICAN BAR ASSOCIATION SECTION OF LITIGATION—READINGS ON ADVERSARIAL JUSTICE: THE AMERICAN APPROACH TO ADJUDICATION, 217 pages, 1988. Softcover. (Coursebook)

CLERMONT'S BLACK LETTER ON CIVIL PROCEDURE, Third Edition, approximately 350 pages, May, 1993 Pub. Softcover. (Review)

COUND, FRIEDENTHAL, MILLER AND SEXTON'S

Civil Procedure—Cont'd

CASES AND MATERIALS ON CIVIL PROCEDURE, Fifth Edition, 1284 pages, 1989. Teacher's Manual available. (Casebook)

COUND, FRIEDENTHAL, MILLER AND SEXTON'S CIVIL PROCEDURE SUPPLEMENT. 476 pages, 1991. Softcover. (Casebook Supplement)

FEDERAL RULES OF CIVIL PROCEDURE—EDUCATIONAL EDITION. Softcover. 761 pages, 1992.

FRIEDENTHAL, KANE AND MILLER'S HORNBOOK ON CIVIL PROCEDURE, Second Edition, approximately 1000 pages, May 1993 Pub. (Text)

KANE AND LEVINE'S CIVIL PROCEDURE IN CALIFORNIA: STATE AND FEDERAL 1992 Edition, 551 pages. Softcover. (Casebook Supplement)

KANE'S CIVIL PROCEDURE IN A NUTSHELL, Third Edition, 303 pages, 1991. Softcover. (Text)

KOFFLER AND REPPY'S HORNBOOK ON COMMON LAW PLEADING, 663 pages, 1969. (Text)

LEVINE, SLOMANSON AND WINGATE'S CALIFORNIA CIVIL PROCEDURE, CASES AND MATERIALS, 546 pages, 1991. Teacher's Manual available. (Casebook)

MARCUS, REDISH AND SHERMAN'S CIVIL PROCEDURE: A MODERN APPROACH, 1027 pages, 1989. Teacher's Manual available. (Casebook) 1991 Supplement.

MARCUS AND SHERMAN'S COMPLEX LITIGATION–CASES AND MATERIALS ON ADVANCED CIVIL PROCEDURE, Second Edition, 1035 pages, 1992. Teacher's Manual available. (Casebook)

PARK AND MCFARLAND'S COMPUTER-AIDED EXERCISES ON CIVIL PROCEDURE, Third Edition, 210 pages, 1991. Softcover. (Coursebook)

SIEGEL'S HORNBOOK ON NEW YORK PRACTICE, Second Edition, Student Edition, 1068 pages, 1991. Softcover. (Text) 1992 Supplemental Pamphlet.

SLOMANSON AND WINGATE'S CALIFORNIA CIVIL PROCEDURE IN A NUTSHELL, 230 pages, 1992. Softcover. (Text)

Commercial Law

BAILEY AND HAGEDORN'S SECURED TRANSACTIONS IN A NUTSHELL, Third Edition, 390 pages, 1988. Softcover. (Text)

EPSTEIN, MARTIN, HENNING AND NICKLES' BASIC UNIFORM COMMERCIAL CODE TEACHING MATERIALS, Third Edition, 704 pages, 1988. Teacher's Manual available. (Casebook)

HENSON'S HORNBOOK ON SECURED TRANSACTIONS UNDER THE U.C.C., Second Edition, 504 pages, 1979, with 1979 pocket part. (Text)

MEYER AND SPEIDEL'S BLACK LETTER ON SALES AND LEASES OF GOODS, Approximately 300 pages, 1993. Softcover. (Review)

NICKLES' BLACK LETTER ON COMMERCIAL PAPER, 450 pages, 1988. Softcover. (Review)

NICKLES, MATHESON AND DOLAN'S MATERIALS FOR UNDERSTANDING CREDIT AND PAYMENT SYSTEMS, 923 pages, 1987. Teacher's Manual available. (Casebook)

NORDSTROM, MURRAY AND CLOVIS' PROBLEMS AND MATERIALS ON SALES, 515 pages, 1982. (Casebook)

NORDSTROM, MURRAY AND CLOVIS' PROBLEMS AND MATERIALS ON SECURED TRANSACTIONS, 594 pages, 1987. (Casebook)

RUBIN AND COOTER'S THE PAYMENT SYSTEM: CASES, MATERIALS AND ISSUES, 885 pages, 1989. Teacher's Manual Available. (Casebook)

SELECTED COMMERCIAL STATUTES. Softcover. 1897 pages, 1992.

SPEIDEL, SUMMERS AND WHITE'S COMMERCIAL LAW: TEACHING MATERIALS, Fourth Edition, 1448 pages, 1987. Teacher's Manual available. (Casebook)

SPEIDEL, SUMMERS AND WHITE'S COMMERCIAL PAPER: TEACHING MATERIALS, Fourth Edition, 578 pages, 1987. Reprint from Speidel et al., Commercial Law, Fourth Edition. Teacher's Manual available. (Casebook)

SPEIDEL, SUMMERS AND WHITE'S SALES: TEACHING MATERIALS, Fourth Edition, 804 pages, 1987. Reprint from Speidel et al., Commercial Law, Fourth Edition. Teacher's Manual available. (Casebook)

SPEIDEL, SUMMERS AND WHITE'S SECURED

LAW SCHOOL PUBLICATIONS—Continued

Commercial Law—Cont'd

TRANSACTIONS: TEACHING MATERIALS, Fourth Edition, 485 pages, 1987. Reprint from Speidel et al., Commercial Law, Fourth Edition. Teacher's Manual available. (Casebook)

STOCKTON AND MILLER'S SALES AND LEASES OF GOODS IN A NUTSHELL, Third Edition, 441 pages, 1992. Softcover. (Text)

STONE'S UNIFORM COMMERCIAL CODE IN A NUTSHELL, Third Edition, 580 pages, 1989. Softcover. (Text)

WEBER AND SPEIDEL'S COMMERCIAL PAPER IN A NUTSHELL, Third Edition, 404 pages, 1982. Softcover. (Text)

WHITE AND SUMMERS' HORNBOOK ON THE UNIFORM COMMERCIAL CODE, Third Edition, Student Edition, 1386 pages, 1988. (Text)

Community Property

MENNELL AND BOYKOFF'S COMMUNITY PROPERTY IN A NUTSHELL, Second Edition, 432 pages, 1988. Softcover. (Text)

VERRALL AND BIRD'S CASES AND MATERIALS ON CALIFORNIA COMMUNITY PROPERTY, Fifth Edition, 604 pages, 1988. (Casebook)

Comparative Law

BARTON, GIBBS, LI AND MERRYMAN'S LAW IN RADICALLY DIFFERENT CULTURES, 960 pages, 1983. (Casebook)

FOLSOM, MINAN AND OTTO'S LAW AND POLITICS IN THE PEOPLE'S REPUBLIC OF CHINA IN A NUTSHELL, 451 pages, 1992. Softcover. (Text)

GLENDON, GORDON AND OSAKWE'S COMPARATIVE LEGAL TRADITIONS: TEXT, MATERIALS AND CASES ON THE CIVIL LAW, COMMON LAW AND SOCIALIST LAW TRADITIONS, 1091 pages, 1985. (Casebook)

GLENDON, GORDON AND OSAKWE'S COMPARATIVE LEGAL TRADITIONS IN A NUTSHELL. 402 pages, 1982. Softcover. (Text)

Computers and Law

MAGGS, SOMA AND SPROWL'S COMPUTER LAW—CASES, COMMENTS, AND QUESTIONS, 731 pages, 1992. Teacher's Manual available. (Casebook)

MAGGS AND SPROWL'S COMPUTER APPLICATIONS IN THE LAW, 316 pages, 1987. (Coursebook)

MASON'S USING COMPUTERS IN THE LAW: AN INTRODUCTION AND PRACTICAL GUIDE, Second Edition, 288 pages, 1988. Softcover. (Coursebook)

Conflict of Laws

CRAMTON, CURRIE AND KAY'S CASES–COMMENTS–QUESTIONS ON CONFLICT OF LAWS, Fourth Edition, 876 pages, 1987. (Casebook)

HAY'S BLACK LETTER ON CONFLICT OF LAWS, 330 pages, 1989. Softcover. (Review)

SCOLES AND HAY'S HORNBOOK ON CONFLICT OF LAWS, Student Edition, 1160 pages, 1992. (Text)

SIEGEL'S CONFLICTS IN A NUTSHELL, 470 pages, 1982. Softcover. (Text)

Constitutional Law—Civil Rights—see also First Amendment and Foreign Relations and National Security Law

ABERNATHY'S CIVIL RIGHTS AND CONSTITUTIONAL LITIGATION, CASES AND MATERIALS, Second Edition, 753 pages, 1992. (Casebook)

BARNES AND STOUT'S THE ECONOMICS OF CONSTITUTIONAL LAW AND PUBLIC CHOICE, 127 pages, 1992. Softcover. Teacher's Manual available. (Casebook)

BARRON AND DIENES' BLACK LETTER ON CONSTITUTIONAL LAW, Third Edition, 440 pages, 1991. Softcover. (Review)

BARRON AND DIENES' CONSTITUTIONAL LAW IN A NUTSHELL, Second Edition, 483 pages, 1991. Softcover. (Text)

ENGDAHL'S CONSTITUTIONAL FEDERALISM IN A NUTSHELL, Second Edition, 411 pages, 1987. Softcover. (Text)

FARBER AND SHERRY'S HISTORY OF THE AMERICAN CONSTITUTION, 458 pages, 1990. Softcover. Teacher's Manual available. (Text)

FISHER AND DEVINS' POLITICAL DYNAMICS OF CONSTITUTIONAL LAW, 333 pages, 1992. Softcover. (Casebook Supplement)

GARVEY AND ALEINIKOFF'S MODERN CONSTITUTIONAL THEORY: A READER, Second Edition, 559 pages, 1991. Softcover. (Reader)

LOCKHART, KAMISAR, CHOPER AND SHIFFRIN'S CONSTITUTIONAL LAW: CASES–COMMENTS–QUESTIONS, Seventh Edition, 1643 pages,

Constitutional Law—Civil Rights—Cont'd
1991. (Casebook) 1992 Supplement.

LOCKHART, KAMISAR, CHOPER AND SHIFFRIN'S THE AMERICAN CONSTITUTION: CASES AND MATERIALS, Seventh Edition, 1255 pages, 1991. Abridged version of Lockhart, et al., Constitutional Law: Cases–Comments–Questions, Seventh Edition. (Casebook) 1992 Supplement.

LOCKHART, KAMISAR, CHOPER AND SHIFFRIN'S CONSTITUTIONAL RIGHTS AND LIBERTIES: CASES AND MATERIALS, Seventh Edition, 1333 pages, 1991. Reprint from Lockhart, et al., Constitutional Law: Cases–Comments–Questions, Seventh Edition. (Casebook) 1992 Supplement.

MARKS AND COOPER'S STATE CONSTITUTIONAL LAW IN A NUTSHELL, 329 pages, 1988. Softcover. (Text)

NOWAK AND ROTUNDA'S HORNBOOK ON CONSTITUTIONAL LAW, Fourth Edition, 1357 pages, 1991. (Text)

ROTUNDA'S MODERN CONSTITUTIONAL LAW: CASES AND NOTES, Fourth Edition, approximately 1100 pages, April, 1993 Pub. (Casebook)

VIEIRA'S CONSTITUTIONAL CIVIL RIGHTS IN A NUTSHELL, Second Edition, 322 pages, 1990. Softcover. (Text)

WILLIAMS' CONSTITUTIONAL ANALYSIS IN A NUTSHELL, 388 pages, 1979. Softcover. (Text)

Consumer Law—see also Commercial Law

EPSTEIN AND NICKLES' CONSUMER LAW IN A NUTSHELL, Second Edition, 418 pages, 1981. Softcover. (Text)

SELECTED COMMERCIAL STATUTES. Softcover. 1897 pages, 1992.

SPANOGLE, ROHNER, PRIDGEN AND RASOR'S CASES AND MATERIALS ON CONSUMER LAW, Second Edition, 916 pages, 1991. Teacher's Manual available. (Casebook)

Contracts

BARNES AND STOUT'S THE ECONOMICS OF CONTRACT LAW, 127 pages, 1992. Softcover. Teacher's Manual available. (Casebook)

CALAMARI AND PERILLO'S BLACK LETTER ON CONTRACTS, Second Edition, 462 pages, 1990. Softcover. (Review)

CALAMARI AND PERILLO'S HORNBOOK ON CONTRACTS, Third Edition, 1049 pages, 1987. (Text)

CALAMARI, PERILLO AND BENDER'S CASES AND PROBLEMS ON CONTRACTS, Second Edition, 905 pages, 1989. Teacher's Manual Available. (Casebook)

CORBIN'S TEXT ON CONTRACTS, One Volume Student Edition, 1224 pages, 1952. (Text)

FESSLER AND LOISEAUX'S CASES AND MATERIALS ON CONTRACTS—MORALITY, ECONOMICS AND THE MARKET PLACE, 837 pages, 1982. Teacher's Manual available. (Casebook)

FRIEDMAN'S CONTRACT REMEDIES IN A NUTSHELL, 323 pages, 1981. Softcover. (Text)

FULLER AND EISENBERG'S CASES ON BASIC CONTRACT LAW, Fifth Edition, 1037 pages, 1990. (Casebook)

HAMILTON, RAU AND WEINTRAUB'S CASES AND MATERIALS ON CONTRACTS, Second Edition, 916 pages, 1992. Teacher's Manual available. (Casebook)

KEYES' GOVERNMENT CONTRACTS IN A NUTSHELL, Second Edition, 557 pages, 1990. Softcover. (Text)

SCHABER AND ROHWER'S CONTRACTS IN A NUTSHELL, Third Edition, 457 pages, 1990. Softcover. (Text)

SUMMERS AND HILLMAN'S CONTRACT AND RELATED OBLIGATION: THEORY, DOCTRINE AND PRACTICE, Second Edition, 1037 pages, 1992. Teacher's Manual available. (Casebook)

Copyright—see Patent and Copyright Law

Corporate Finance—see also Business Planning

HAMILTON'S CASES AND MATERIALS ON CORPORATION FINANCE, Second Edition, 1221 pages, 1989. (Casebook)

OESTERLE'S THE LAW OF MERGERS, ACQUISITIONS AND REORGANIZATIONS, 1096 pages, 1991. (Casebook) 1992 Supplement.

Corporations

HAMILTON'S BLACK LETTER ON CORPORATIONS, Third Edition, 732 pages, 1992. Softcover. (Review)

HAMILTON'S CASES AND MATERIALS ON CORPORATIONS—INCLUDING PARTNERSHIPS AND

Corporations—Cont'd

LIMITED PARTNERSHIPS, Fourth Edition, 1248 pages, 1990. Teacher's Manual available. (Casebook) 1990 Statutory Supplement.

HAMILTON'S THE LAW OF CORPORATIONS IN A NUTSHELL, Third Edition, 518 pages, 1991. Softcover. (Text)

HENN'S TEACHING MATERIALS ON THE LAW OF CORPORATIONS, Second Edition, 1204 pages, 1986. Teacher's Manual available. (Casebook)

Statutory Supplement. *See Selected Corporation and Partnership*

HENN AND ALEXANDER'S HORNBOOK ON LAWS OF CORPORATIONS, Third Edition, Student Edition, 1371 pages, 1983, with 1986 pocket part. (Text)

SELECTED CORPORATION AND PARTNERSHIP STATUTES, RULES AND FORMS. Revised 1991 Edition, 953 pages. Softcover.

SOLOMON, SCHWARTZ AND BAUMAN'S MATERIALS AND PROBLEMS ON CORPORATIONS: LAW AND POLICY, Second Edition, 1391 pages, 1988. Teacher's Manual available. (Casebook) 1992 Supplement.

Statutory Supplement. *See Selected Corporation and Partnership*

Corrections

KRANTZ' THE LAW OF CORRECTIONS AND PRISONERS' RIGHTS IN A NUTSHELL, Third Edition, 407 pages, 1988. Softcover. (Text)

KRANTZ AND BRANHAM'S CASES AND MATERIALS ON THE LAW OF SENTENCING, CORRECTIONS AND PRISONERS' RIGHTS, Fourth Edition, 619 pages, 1991. Teacher's Manual available. (Casebook)

Creditors' Rights

BANKRUPTCY CODE, RULES AND OFFICIAL FORMS, LAW SCHOOL EDITION. 910 pages, 1992. Softcover.

EPSTEIN'S DEBTOR-CREDITOR LAW IN A NUTSHELL, Fourth Edition, 401 pages, 1991. Softcover. (Text)

EPSTEIN, LANDERS AND NICKLES' CASES AND MATERIALS ON DEBTORS AND CREDITORS, Third Edition, 1059 pages, 1987. Teacher's Manual available. (Casebook)

EPSTEIN, NICKLES AND WHITE'S HORNBOOK ON BANKRUPTCY, Approximately 1000 pages, January, 1992 Pub. (Text)

LOPUCKI'S PLAYER'S MANUAL FOR THE DEBTOR-CREDITOR GAME, 123 pages, 1985. Softcover. (Coursebook)

NICKLES AND EPSTEIN'S BLACK LETTER ON CREDITORS' RIGHTS AND BANKRUPTCY, 576 pages, 1989. (Review)

RIESENFELD'S CASES AND MATERIALS ON CREDITORS' REMEDIES AND DEBTORS' PROTECTION, Fourth Edition, 914 pages, 1987. (Casebook) 1990 Supplement.

WHITE AND NIMMER'S CASES AND MATERIALS ON BANKRUPTCY, Second Edition, 764 pages, 1992. Teacher's Manual available. (Casebook)

Criminal Law and Criminal Procedure—see also Corrections, Juvenile Justice

ABRAMS' FEDERAL CRIMINAL LAW AND ITS ENFORCEMENT, 866 pages, 1986. (Casebook) 1988 Supplement.

BUCY'S WHITE COLLAR CRIME, CASES AND MATERIALS, 688 pages, 1992. Teacher's Manual available. (Casebook)

DIX AND SHARLOT'S CASES AND MATERIALS ON CRIMINAL LAW, Third Edition, 846 pages, 1987. (Casebook)

GRANO'S PROBLEMS IN CRIMINAL PROCEDURE, Second Edition, 176 pages, 1981. Teacher's Manual available. Softcover. (Coursebook)

HEYMANN AND KENETY'S THE MURDER TRIAL OF WILBUR JACKSON: A HOMICIDE IN THE FAMILY, Second Edition, 347 pages, 1985. (Coursebook)

ISRAEL, KAMISAR AND LAFAVE'S CRIMINAL PROCEDURE AND THE CONSTITUTION: LEADING SUPREME COURT CASES AND INTRODUCTORY TEXT. 802 pages, 1992 Edition. Softcover. (Casebook)

ISRAEL AND LAFAVE'S CRIMINAL PROCEDURE—CONSTITUTIONAL LIMITATIONS IN A NUTSHELL, Fourth Edition, 461 pages, 1988. Softcover. (Text)

JOHNSON'S CASES, MATERIALS AND TEXT ON CRIMINAL LAW, Fourth Edition, 759 pages, 1990. Teacher's Manual available. (Casebook)

JOHNSON'S CASES AND MATERIALS ON CRIMI-

Criminal Law and Criminal Procedure—Cont'd

NAL PROCEDURE, 859 pages, 1988. (Casebook) 1992 Supplement.

KAMISAR, LAFAVE AND ISRAEL'S MODERN CRIMINAL PROCEDURE: CASES, COMMENTS AND QUESTIONS, Seventh Edition, 1593 pages, 1990. (Casebook) 1992 Supplement.

KAMISAR, LAFAVE AND ISRAEL'S BASIC CRIMINAL PROCEDURE: CASES, COMMENTS AND QUESTIONS, Seventh Edition, 792 pages, 1990. Softcover reprint from Kamisar, et al., Modern Criminal Procedure: Cases, Comments and Questions, Seventh Edition. (Casebook) 1992 Supplement.

LAFAVE'S MODERN CRIMINAL LAW: CASES, COMMENTS AND QUESTIONS, Second Edition, 903 pages, 1988. (Casebook)

LAFAVE AND ISRAEL'S HORNBOOK ON CRIMINAL PROCEDURE, Second Edition, 1309 pages, 1992 with 1992 pocket part. (Text)

LAFAVE AND SCOTT'S HORNBOOK ON CRIMINAL LAW, Second Edition, 918 pages, 1986. (Text)

LOEWY'S CRIMINAL LAW IN A NUTSHELL, Second Edition, 321 pages, 1987. Softcover. (Text)

LOW'S BLACK LETTER ON CRIMINAL LAW, Revised First Edition, 443 pages, 1990. Softcover. (Review)

SALTZBURG AND CAPRA'S CASES AND COMMENTARY ON AMERICAN CRIMINAL PROCEDURE, Fourth Edition, 1341 pages, 1992. Teacher's Manual available. (Casebook) 1992 Supplement.

SUBIN, MIRSKY AND WEINSTEIN'S THE CRIMINAL PROCESS: PROSECUTION AND DEFENSE FUNCTIONS, Approximately 450 pages, February, 1993 Pub. Softcover. Teacher's Manual available. (Text)

VORENBERG'S CASES ON CRIMINAL LAW AND PROCEDURE, Second Edition, 1088 pages, 1981. Teacher's Manual available. (Casebook) 1990 Supplement.

Domestic Relations

CLARK'S HORNBOOK ON DOMESTIC RELATIONS, Second Edition, Student Edition, 1050 pages, 1988. (Text)

CLARK AND GLOWINSKY'S CASES AND PROBLEMS ON DOMESTIC RELATIONS, Fourth Edition. 1150 pages, 1990. Teacher's Manual available. (Casebook) 1992 Supplement.

KRAUSE'S BLACK LETTER ON FAMILY LAW, 314 pages, 1988. Softcover. (Review)

KRAUSE'S CASES, COMMENTS AND QUESTIONS ON FAMILY LAW, Third Edition, 1433 pages, 1990. (Casebook)

KRAUSE'S FAMILY LAW IN A NUTSHELL, Second Edition, 444 pages, 1986. Softcover. (Text)

KRAUSKOPF'S CASES ON PROPERTY DIVISION AT MARRIAGE DISSOLUTION, 250 pages, 1984. Softcover. (Casebook)

Economics, Law and—see also Antitrust, Regulated Industries

BARNES AND STOUT'S CASES AND MATERIALS ON LAW AND ECONOMICS, 538 pages, 1992. Teacher's Manual available. (Casebook)

GOETZ' CASES AND MATERIALS ON LAW AND ECONOMICS, 547 pages, 1984. (Casebook)

MALLOY'S LAW AND ECONOMICS: A COMPARATIVE APPROACH TO THEORY AND PRACTICE, 166 pages, 1990. Softcover. (Text)

Education Law

ALEXANDER AND ALEXANDER'S PUBLIC SCHOOL LAW, Third Edition, 880 pages, 1992. Teacher's Manual available. (Coursebook)

ALEXANDER AND ALEXANDER'S THE LAW OF SCHOOLS, STUDENTS AND TEACHERS IN A NUTSHELL, 409 pages, 1984. Softcover. (Text)

YUDOF, KIRP AND LEVIN'S EDUCATIONAL POLICY AND THE LAW, Third Edition, 860 pages, 1992. (Casebook)

Employment Discrimination—see also Gender Discrimination

ESTREICHER AND HARPER'S CASES AND MATERIALS ON THE LAW GOVERNING THE EMPLOYMENT RELATIONSHIP, Second Edition, 966 pages, 1992. (Casebook) Statutory Supplement.

JONES, MURPHY AND BELTON'S CASES AND MATERIALS ON DISCRIMINATION IN EMPLOYMENT, (The Labor Law Group). Fifth Edition, 1116 pages, 1987. (Casebook) 1990 Supplement.

PLAYER'S FEDERAL LAW OF EMPLOYMENT DIS-

LAW SCHOOL PUBLICATIONS—Continued

Employment Discrimination—Cont'd
CRIMINATION IN A NUTSHELL, Third Edition, 338 pages, 1992. Softcover. (Text)

PLAYER'S HORNBOOK ON EMPLOYMENT DISCRIMINATION LAW, Student Edition, 708 pages, 1988. (Text)

PLAYER, SHOBEN AND LIEBERWITZ' CASES AND MATERIALS ON EMPLOYMENT DISCRIMINATION LAW, 827 pages, 1990. Teacher's Manual available. (Casebook) 1992 Supplement.

Energy and Natural Resources Law—see also Oil and Gas

LAITOS' CASES AND MATERIALS ON NATURAL RESOURCES LAW, 938 pages, 1985. Teacher's Manual available. (Casebook)

LAITOS AND TOMAIN'S ENERGY AND NATURAL RESOURCES LAW IN A NUTSHELL, 554 pages, 1992. Softcover. (Text)

SELECTED ENVIRONMENTAL LAW STATUTES—EDUCATIONAL EDITION. Softcover. 1296 pages, 1992.

Environmental Law—see also Energy and Natural Resources Law; Sea, Law of

BONINE AND MCGARITY'S THE LAW OF ENVIRONMENTAL PROTECTION: CASES—LEGISLATION—POLICIES, Second Edition, 1042 pages, 1992. (Casebook)

FINDLEY AND FARBER'S CASES AND MATERIALS ON ENVIRONMENTAL LAW, Third Edition, 763 pages, 1991. Teacher's Manual available. (Casebook)

FINDLEY AND FARBER'S ENVIRONMENTAL LAW IN A NUTSHELL, Third Edition, 355 pages, 1992. Softcover. (Text)

PLATER, ABRAMS AND GOLDFARB'S ENVIRONMENTAL LAW AND POLICY: NATURE, LAW AND SOCIETY, 1039 pages, 1992. Teacher's Manual available. (Casebook)

RODGERS' HORNBOOK ON ENVIRONMENTAL LAW, 956 pages, 1977, with 1984 pocket part. (Text)

SELECTED ENVIRONMENTAL LAW STATUTES—EDUCATIONAL EDITION. Softcover. 1296 pages, 1992.

Equity—see Remedies

Estate Planning—see also Trusts and Estates; Taxation—Estate and Gift

LYNN'S INTRODUCTION TO ESTATE PLANNING IN A NUTSHELL, Fourth Edition, 352 pages, 1992. Softcover. (Text)

Evidence
BERGMAN'S TRANSCRIPT EXERCISES FOR LEARNING EVIDENCE, 273 pages, 1992. Teacher's Manual available. (Coursebook)

BROUN AND BLAKEY'S BLACK LETTER ON EVIDENCE, 269 pages, 1984. Softcover. (Review)

BROUN, MEISENHOLDER, STRONG AND MOSTELLER'S PROBLEMS IN EVIDENCE, Third Edition, 238 pages, 1988. Teacher's Manual available. Softcover. (Coursebook)

CLEARY, STRONG, BROUN AND MOSTELLER'S CASES AND MATERIALS ON EVIDENCE, Fourth Edition, 1060 pages, 1988. (Casebook)

FEDERAL RULES OF EVIDENCE FOR UNITED STATES COURTS AND MAGISTRATES. Softcover. 549 pages, 1992.

FRIEDMAN'S THE ELEMENTS OF EVIDENCE, 315 pages, 1991. Teacher's Manual available. (Coursebook)

GRAHAM'S FEDERAL RULES OF EVIDENCE IN A NUTSHELL, Third Edition, 486 pages, 1992. Softcover. (Text)

LEMPERT AND SALTZBURG'S A MODERN APPROACH TO EVIDENCE: TEXT, PROBLEMS, TRANSCRIPTS AND CASES, Second Edition, 1232 pages, 1983. Teacher's Manual available. (Casebook)

LILLY'S AN INTRODUCTION TO THE LAW OF EVIDENCE, Second Edition, 585 pages, 1987. (Text)

MCCORMICK, SUTTON AND WELLBORN'S CASES AND MATERIALS ON EVIDENCE, Seventh Edition, 932 pages, 1992. Teacher's Manual available. (Casebook)

MCCORMICK'S HORNBOOK ON EVIDENCE, Fourth Edition, Student Edition, 672 pages, 1992. (Text)

ROTHSTEIN'S EVIDENCE IN A NUTSHELL: STATE AND FEDERAL RULES, Second Edition, 514 pages, 1981. Softcover. (Text)

Federal Jurisdiction and Procedure
CURRIE'S CASES AND MATERIALS ON FEDERAL COURTS, Fourth Edition, 783 pages, 1990. (Casebook)

CURRIE'S FEDERAL JURISDICTION IN A NUTSHELL, Third Edition, 242 pages, 1990.

Federal Jurisdiction and Procedure—Cont'd
Softcover. (Text)

FEDERAL RULES OF CIVIL PROCEDURE—EDUCATIONAL EDITION. Softcover. 761 pages, 1992.

REDISH'S BLACK LETTER ON FEDERAL JURISDICTION, Second Edition, 234 pages, 1991. Softcover. (Review)

REDISH'S CASES, COMMENTS AND QUESTIONS ON FEDERAL COURTS, Second Edition, 1122 pages, 1989. (Casebook) 1992 Supplement.

VETRI AND MERRILL'S FEDERAL COURTS PROBLEMS AND MATERIALS, Second Edition, 232 pages, 1984. Softcover. (Coursebook)

WRIGHT'S HORNBOOK ON FEDERAL COURTS, Fourth Edition, Student Edition, 870 pages, 1983. (Text)

First Amendment
GARVEY AND SCHAUER'S THE FIRST AMENDMENT: A READER, 527 pages, 1992. Softcover. (Reader)

SHIFFRIN AND CHOPER'S FIRST AMENDMENT, CASES—COMMENTS—QUESTIONS, 759 pages, 1991. Softcover. (Casebook) 1992 Supplement.

Foreign Relations and National Security Law
FRANCK AND GLENNON'S FOREIGN RELATIONS AND NATIONAL SECURITY LAW, 941 pages, 1987. (Casebook)

Future Interests—see Trusts and Estates

Gender Discrimination—see also Employment Discrimination
KAY'S TEXT, CASES AND MATERIALS ON SEX-BASED DISCRIMINATION, Third Edition, 1001 pages, 1988. (Casebook) 1992 Supplement.

THOMAS' SEX DISCRIMINATION IN A NUTSHELL, Second Edition, 395 pages, 1991. Softcover. (Text)

Health Law—see Medicine, Law and

Human Rights—see International Law

Immigration Law
ALEINIKOFF AND MARTIN'S IMMIGRATION: PROCESS AND POLICY, Second Edition, 1056 pages, 1991. (Casebook)

Statutory Supplement. *See Immigration and Nationality Laws*

IMMIGRATION AND NATIONALITY LAWS OF THE UNITED STATES: SELECTED STATUTES, REGULATIONS AND FORMS. Softcover. 519 pages, 1992.

WEISSBRODT'S IMMIGRATION LAW AND PROCEDURE IN A NUTSHELL, Third Edition, 497 pages, 1992. Softcover. (Text)

Indian Law—see American Indian Law

Insurance Law
DEVINE AND TERRY'S PROBLEMS IN INSURANCE LAW, 240 pages, 1989. Softcover. Teacher's Manual available. (Coursebook)

DOBBYN'S INSURANCE LAW IN A NUTSHELL, Second Edition, 316 pages, 1989. Softcover. (Text)

KEETON'S COMPUTER-AIDED AND WORKBOOK EXERCISES ON INSURANCE LAW, 255 pages, 1990. Softcover. (Coursebook)

KEETON AND WIDISS' INSURANCE LAW, Student Edition, 1359 pages, 1988. (Text)

WIDISS AND KEETON'S COURSE SUPPLEMENT TO KEETON AND WIDISS' INSURANCE LAW, 502 pages, 1988. Softcover. Teacher's Manual available. (Casebook)

WIDISS' INSURANCE: MATERIALS ON FUNDAMENTAL PRINCIPLES, LEGAL DOCTRINES AND REGULATORY ACTS, 1186 pages, 1989. Teacher's Manual available. (Casebook)

YORK AND WHELAN'S CASES, MATERIALS AND PROBLEMS ON GENERAL PRACTICE INSURANCE LAW, Second Edition, 787 pages, 1988. Teacher's Manual available. (Casebook)

International Law—see also Sea, Law of
BERMANN, DAVEY, FOX AND GOEBEL'S CASES AND MATERIALS ON EUROPEAN COMMUNITY LAW, Approximately 1200 pages, 1993. (Casebook) Statutory Supplement. *See European Economic Community: Selected Documents*

BUERGENTHAL'S INTERNATIONAL HUMAN RIGHTS IN A NUTSHELL, 283 pages, 1988. Softcover. (Text)

BUERGENTHAL AND MAIER'S PUBLIC INTERNATIONAL LAW IN A NUTSHELL, Second Edition, 275 pages, 1990. Softcover. (Text)

EUROPEAN ECONOMIC COMMUNITY: SELECTED DOCUMENTS. Approximately 550 pages,

International Law—Cont'd
1993. Softcover

FOLSOM'S EUROPEAN COMMUNITY LAW IN A NUTSHELL, 423 pages, 1992. Softcover. (Text)

FOLSOM, GORDON AND SPANOGLE'S INTERNATIONAL BUSINESS TRANSACTIONS—A PROBLEM-ORIENTED COURSEBOOK, Second Edition, 1237 pages, 1991. Teacher's Manual available. (Casebook) 1991 Documents Supplement.

FOLSOM, GORDON AND SPANOGLE'S INTERNATIONAL BUSINESS TRANSACTIONS IN A NUTSHELL, Fourth Edition, 548 pages, 1992. Softcover. (Text)

HENKIN, PUGH, SCHACHTER AND SMIT'S CASES AND MATERIALS ON INTERNATIONAL LAW, Second Edition, 1517 pages, 1987. (Casebook) Documents Supplement.

INTERNATIONAL LITIGATION AND ARBITRATION: SELECTED TREATIES, STATUTES AND RULES. Approximately 275 pages, 1993. Softcover

INTERNATIONAL ORGANIZATIONS IN THEIR LEGAL SETTING: SELECTED DOCUMENTS. Approximately 500 pages, March, 1993 Pub. Softcover

JACKSON AND DAVEY'S CASES, MATERIALS AND TEXT ON LEGAL PROBLEMS OF INTERNATIONAL ECONOMIC RELATIONS, Second Edition, 1269 pages, 1986. (Casebook) 1989 Documents Supplement.

KIRGIS' INTERNATIONAL ORGANIZATIONS IN THEIR LEGAL SETTING, Second Edition, approximately 1150 pages, March, 1993 Pub. Teacher's Manual available. (Casebook) Statutory Supplement.

LOWENFELD'S INTERNATIONAL LITIGATION AND ARBITRATION, Approximately 875 pages, 1993. (Casebook) Statutory Supplement. *See International Litigation: Selected Documents*

WESTON, FALK AND D'AMATO'S INTERNATIONAL LAW AND WORLD ORDER—A PROBLEM-ORIENTED COURSEBOOK, Second Edition, 1335 pages, 1990. Teacher's Manual available. (Casebook) Documents Supplement.

Interviewing and Counseling

BINDER AND PRICE'S LEGAL INTERVIEWING AND COUNSELING, 232 pages, 1977. Softcover. Teacher's Manual available. (Coursebook)

BINDER, BERGMAN AND PRICE'S LAWYERS AS COUNSELORS: A CLIENT-CENTERED APPROACH, 427 pages, 1991. Softcover. (Coursebook)

SHAFFER AND ELKINS' LEGAL INTERVIEWING AND COUNSELING IN A NUTSHELL, Second Edition, 487 pages, 1987. Softcover. (Text)

Introduction to Law—see Legal Method and Legal System

Introduction to Law Study

HEGLAND'S INTRODUCTION TO THE STUDY AND PRACTICE OF LAW IN A NUTSHELL, 418 pages, 1983. Softcover. (Text)

KINYON'S INTRODUCTION TO LAW STUDY AND LAW EXAMINATIONS IN A NUTSHELL, 389 pages, 1971. Softcover. (Text)

Judicial Process—see Legal Method and Legal System

Jurisprudence

CHRISTIE'S JURISPRUDENCE—TEXT AND READINGS ON THE PHILOSOPHY OF LAW, 1056 pages, 1973. (Casebook)

SINHA'S JURISPRUDENCE (LEGAL PHILOSOPHY) IN A NUTSHELL. Approximately 350 pages, 1993. Softcover. (Text)

Juvenile Justice

FOX'S JUVENILE COURTS IN A NUTSHELL, Third Edition, 291 pages, 1984. Softcover. (Text)

Labor and Employment Law—see also Employment Discrimination, Workers' Compensation

FINKIN, GOLDMAN AND SUMMERS' LEGAL PROTECTION OF INDIVIDUAL EMPLOYEES, (The Labor Law Group). 1164 pages, 1989. (Casebook)

GORMAN'S BASIC TEXT ON LABOR LAW—UNIONIZATION AND COLLECTIVE BARGAINING, 914 pages, 1976. (Text)

LESLIE'S LABOR LAW IN A NUTSHELL, Third Edition, 388 pages, 1992. Softcover. (Text)

NOLAN'S LABOR ARBITRATION LAW AND PRAC-

Labor and Employment Law—Cont'd

TICE IN A NUTSHELL, 358 pages, 1979. Softcover. (Text)

OBERER, HANSLOWE, ANDERSEN AND HEINSZ' CASES AND MATERIALS ON LABOR LAW—COLLECTIVE BARGAINING IN A FREE SOCIETY, Third Edition, 1163 pages, 1986. Teacher's Manual available. (Casebook) Statutory Supplement. 1991 Case Supplement.

RABIN, SILVERSTEIN AND SCHATZKI'S LABOR AND EMPLOYMENT LAW: PROBLEMS, CASES AND MATERIALS IN THE LAW OF WORK, (The Labor Law Group). 1014 pages, 1988. Teacher's Manual available. (Casebook) 1988 Statutory Supplement.

WOLLETT, GRODIN AND WEISBERGER'S COLLECTIVE BARGAINING IN PUBLIC EMPLOYMENT, (The Labor Law Group). Fourth Edition, approximately 600 pages, April, 1993 Pub. (Casebook)

Land Finance—Property Security—see Real Estate Transactions

Land Use

CALLIES AND FREILICH'S CASES AND MATERIALS ON LAND USE, 1233 pages, 1986. (Casebook) 1991 Supplement.

HAGMAN AND JUERGENSMEYER'S HORNBOOK ON URBAN PLANNING AND LAND DEVELOPMENT CONTROL LAW, Second Edition, Student Edition, 680 pages, 1986. (Text)

WRIGHT AND GITELMAN'S CASES AND MATERIALS ON LAND USE, Fourth Edition, 1255 pages, 1991. Teacher's Manual available. (Casebook)

WRIGHT AND WRIGHT'S LAND USE IN A NUTSHELL, Second Edition, 356 pages, 1985. Softcover. (Text)

Legal History—see also Legal Method and Legal System

PRESSER AND ZAINALDIN'S CASES AND MATERIALS ON LAW AND JURISPRUDENCE IN AMERICAN HISTORY, Second Edition, 1092 pages, 1989. Teacher's Manual available. (Casebook)

Legal Method and Legal System—see also Legal Research, Legal Writing

ALDISERT'S READINGS, MATERIALS AND CASES IN THE JUDICIAL PROCESS, 948 pages, 1976. (Casebook)

BERCH, BERCH AND SPRITZER'S INTRODUCTION TO LEGAL METHOD AND PROCESS, Second Edition, 585 pages, 1992. Teacher's Manual available. (Casebook)

BODENHEIMER, OAKLEY AND LOVE'S READINGS AND CASES ON AN INTRODUCTION TO THE ANGLO-AMERICAN LEGAL SYSTEM, Second Edition, 166 pages, 1988. Softcover. (Casebook)

DAVIES AND LAWRY'S INSTITUTIONS AND METHODS OF THE LAW—INTRODUCTORY TEACHING MATERIALS, 547 pages, 1982. Teacher's Manual available. (Casebook)

DVORKIN, HIMMELSTEIN AND LESNICK'S BECOMING A LAWYER: A HUMANISTIC PERSPECTIVE ON LEGAL EDUCATION AND PROFESSIONALISM, 211 pages, 1981. Softcover. (Text)

KEETON'S JUDGING, 842 pages, 1990. Softcover. (Coursebook)

KELSO AND KELSO'S STUDYING LAW: AN INTRODUCTION, 587 pages, 1984. (Coursebook)

KEMPIN'S HISTORICAL INTRODUCTION TO ANGLO-AMERICAN LAW IN A NUTSHELL, Third Edition, 323 pages, 1990. Softcover. (Text)

MEADOR'S AMERICAN COURTS, 113 pages, 1991. Softcover. (Text)

REYNOLDS' JUDICIAL PROCESS IN A NUTSHELL, Second Edition, 308 pages, 1991. Softcover. (Text)

Legal Research

COHEN AND OLSON'S LEGAL RESEARCH IN A NUTSHELL, Fifth Edition, 370 pages, 1992. Softcover. (Text)

COHEN, BERRING AND OLSON'S HOW TO FIND THE LAW, Ninth Edition, 716 pages, 1989. (Text)

COHEN, BERRING AND OLSON'S FINDING THE LAW, 570 pages, 1989. Softcover reprint from Cohen, Berring and Olson's How to Find the Law, Ninth Edition. (Coursebook)

Legal Research Exercises, 4th Ed., for use with Cohen, Berring and Olson, 253 pages, 1992. Teacher's Manual available.

ROMBAUER'S LEGAL PROBLEM SOLVING—ANALYSIS, RESEARCH AND WRITING, Fifth Edition, 524 pages, 1991. Softcover. Teacher's Manual with problems availa-

Legal Research—Cont'd

ble. (Coursebook)

STATSKY'S LEGAL RESEARCH AND WRITING: SOME STARTING POINTS, Fourth Edition, approximately 270 pages, 1993. Softcover. Teacher's Manual available. (Coursebook) Student Workbook.

TEPLY'S LEGAL RESEARCH AND CITATION, Fourth Edition, 436 pages, 1992. Softcover. (Coursebook)

   Student Library Exercises, Fourth Edition, 276 pages, 1992. Answer Key available.

Legal Writing and Drafting

CHILD'S DRAFTING LEGAL DOCUMENTS: PRINCIPLES AND PRACTICES, Second Edition, 425 pages, 1992. Softcover. Teacher's Manual available. (Coursebook)

DICKERSON'S MATERIALS ON LEGAL DRAFTING, 425 pages, 1981. Teacher's Manual available. (Coursebook)

FELSENFELD AND SIEGEL'S WRITING CONTRACTS IN PLAIN ENGLISH, 290 pages, 1981. Softcover. (Text)

GOPEN'S WRITING FROM A LEGAL PERSPECTIVE, 225 pages, 1981. (Text)

MARTINEAU'S DRAFTING LEGISLATION AND RULES IN PLAIN ENGLISH, 155 pages, 1991. Softcover. Teacher's Manual available. (Text)

MELLINKOFF'S DICTIONARY OF AMERICAN LEGAL USAGE, 703 pages, 1992. Softcover. (Text)

MELLINKOFF'S LEGAL WRITING—SENSE AND NONSENSE, 242 pages, 1982. Softcover. Teacher's Manual available. (Text)

PRATT'S LEGAL WRITING: A SYSTEMATIC APPROACH, Second Edition, approximately 550 pages, April, 1993 Pub. Teacher's Manual available. (Coursebook)

RAY AND COX'S BEYOND THE BASICS: A TEXT FOR ADVANCED LEGAL WRITING, 427 pages, 1991. Softcover. Teacher's Manual available. (Text)

RAY AND RAMSFIELD'S LEGAL WRITING: GETTING IT RIGHT AND GETTING IT WRITTEN, 250 pages, 1987. Softcover. (Text)

SQUIRES AND ROMBAUER'S LEGAL WRITING IN A NUTSHELL, 294 pages, 1982. Softcover. (Text)

STATSKY AND WERNET'S CASE ANALYSIS AND FUNDAMENTALS OF LEGAL WRITING, Third Edition, 424 pages, 1989. Teacher's Manual available. (Text)

TEPLY'S LEGAL WRITING, ANALYSIS AND ORAL ARGUMENT, 576 pages, 1990. Softcover. Teacher's Manual available. (Coursebook)

WEIHOFEN'S LEGAL WRITING STYLE, Second Edition, 332 pages, 1980. (Text)

Legislation—see also Legal Writing and Drafting

DAVIES' LEGISLATIVE LAW AND PROCESS IN A NUTSHELL, Second Edition, 346 pages, 1986. Softcover. (Text)

ESKRIDGE AND FRICKEY'S CASES AND MATERIALS ON LEGISLATION: STATUTES AND THE CREATION OF PUBLIC POLICY, 937 pages, 1988. Teacher's Manual available. (Casebook) 1992 Supplement.

NUTTING AND DICKERSON'S CASES AND MATERIALS ON LEGISLATION, Fifth Edition, 744 pages, 1978. (Casebook)

STATSKY'S LEGISLATIVE ANALYSIS AND DRAFTING, Second Edition, 217 pages, 1984. Teacher's Manual available. (Text)

Local Government

FRUG'S CASES AND MATERIALS ON LOCAL GOVERNMENT LAW, 1005 pages, 1988. (Casebook) 1991 Supplement.

MCCARTHY'S LOCAL GOVERNMENT LAW IN A NUTSHELL, Third Edition, 435 pages, 1990. Softcover. (Text)

REYNOLDS' HORNBOOK ON LOCAL GOVERNMENT LAW, 860 pages, 1982 with 1990 pocket part. (Text)

VALENTE AND MCCARTHY'S CASES AND MATERIALS ON LOCAL GOVERNMENT LAW, Fourth Edition, 1158 pages, 1992. Teacher's Manual available. (Casebook)

Mass Communication Law

GILLMOR, BARRON, SIMON AND TERRY'S CASES AND COMMENT ON MASS COMMUNICATION LAW, Fifth Edition, 947 pages, 1990. (Casebook)

GINSBURG, BOTEIN AND DIRECTOR'S REGULATION OF THE ELECTRONIC MASS MEDIA: LAW

Mass Communication Law—Cont'd

AND POLICY FOR RADIO, TELEVISION, CABLE AND THE NEW VIDEO TECHNOLOGIES, Second Edition, 657 pages, 1991. (Casebook) Statutory Supplement.

ZUCKMAN, GAYNES, CARTER AND DEE'S MASS COMMUNICATIONS LAW IN A NUTSHELL, Third Edition, 538 pages, 1988. Softcover. (Text)

Medicine, Law and

FISCINA, BOUMIL, SHARPE AND HEAD'S MEDICAL LIABILITY, 487 pages, 1991. Teacher's Manual available. (Casebook)

FURROW, JOHNSON, JOST AND SCHWARTZ' HEALTH LAW: CASES, MATERIALS AND PROBLEMS, Second Edition, 1236 pages, 1991. Teacher's Manual available. (Casebook)

FURROW, JOHNSON, JOST AND SCHWARTZ' BIOETHICS: HEALTH CARE LAW AND ETHICS, Reprint from Furrow et al., Health Law, Second Edition. Softcover. Teacher's Manual available. (Casebook)

FURROW, JOHNSON, JOST AND SCHWARTZ' THE LAW OF HEALTH CARE ORGANIZATION AND FINANCE, Reprint from Furrow et al., Health Law, Second Edition. Softcover. Teacher's Manual available.

FURROW, JOHNSON, JOST AND SCHWARTZ' LIABILITY AND QUALITY ISSUES IN HEALTH CARE, Reprint from Furrow et al., Health Law, Second Edition. Softcover. Teacher's Manual available. (Casebook)

HALL AND ELLMAN'S HEALTH CARE LAW AND ETHICS IN A NUTSHELL, 401 pages, 1990. Softcover (Text)

JARVIS, CLOSEN, HERMANN AND LEONARD'S AIDS LAW IN A NUTSHELL, 349 pages, 1991. Softcover. (Text)

KING'S THE LAW OF MEDICAL MALPRACTICE IN A NUTSHELL, Second Edition, 342 pages, 1986. Softcover. (Text)

SHAPIRO AND SPECE'S CASES, MATERIALS AND PROBLEMS ON BIOETHICS AND LAW, 892 pages, 1981. (Casebook) 1991 Supplement.

Military Law

SHANOR AND TERRELL'S MILITARY LAW IN A NUTSHELL, 378 pages, 1980. Softcover. (Text)

Mining Law—see Energy and Natural Resources Law

Mortgages—see Real Estate Transactions

Natural Resources Law—see Energy and Natural Resources Law, Environmental Law

Negotiation

GIFFORD'S LEGAL NEGOTIATION: THEORY AND APPLICATIONS, 225 pages, 1989. Softcover. (Text)

TEPLY'S LEGAL NEGOTIATION IN A NUTSHELL, 282 pages, 1992. Softcover. (Text)

WILLIAMS' LEGAL NEGOTIATION AND SETTLEMENT, 207 pages, 1983. Softcover. Teacher's Manual available. (Coursebook)

Office Practice—see also Computers and Law, Interviewing and Counseling, Negotiation

HEGLAND'S TRIAL AND PRACTICE SKILLS IN A NUTSHELL, 346 pages, 1978. Softcover (Text)

MUNNEKE'S LAW PRACTICE MANAGEMENT: MATERIALS AND CASES, 634 pages, 1991. Teacher's Manual available. (Casebook)

Oil and Gas—see also Energy and Natural Resources Law

HEMINGWAY'S HORNBOOK ON THE LAW OF OIL AND GAS, Third Edition, Student Edition, 711 pages, 1992. (Text)

KUNTZ, LOWE, ANDERSON AND SMITH'S CASES AND MATERIALS ON OIL AND GAS LAW, Second Edition, approximately 1000 pages, 1993. Teacher's Manual available. (Casebook) Forms Manual. Revised.

LOWE'S OIL AND GAS LAW IN A NUTSHELL, Second Edition, 465 pages, 1988. Softcover. (Text)

Partnership—see Agency—Partnership

Patent and Copyright Law

CHOATE, FRANCIS AND COLLINS' CASES AND MATERIALS ON PATENT LAW, INCLUDING TRADE SECRETS, COPYRIGHTS, TRADEMARKS, Third Edition, 1009 pages, 1987. (Casebook)

HALPERN, SHIPLEY AND ABRAMS' CASES AND MATERIALS ON COPYRIGHT, 663 pages, 1992. (Casebook)

Patent and Copyright Law—Cont'd

MILLER AND DAVIS' INTELLECTUAL PROPERTY—PATENTS, TRADEMARKS AND COPYRIGHT IN A NUTSHELL, Second Edition, 437 pages, 1990. Softcover. (Text)

NIMMER, MARCUS, MYERS AND NIMMER'S CASES AND MATERIALS ON COPYRIGHT AND OTHER ASPECTS OF ENTERTAINMENT LITIGATION—INCLUDING UNFAIR COMPETITION, DEFAMATION, PRIVACY, ILLUSTRATED, Fourth Edition, 1177 pages, 1991. (Casebook) Statutory Supplement. See *Selected Intellectual Property Statutes*

SELECTED INTELLECTUAL PROPERTY AND UNFAIR COMPETITION STATUTES, REGULATIONS AND TREATIES. Softcover.

Products Liability

FISCHER AND POWERS' CASES AND MATERIALS ON PRODUCTS LIABILITY, 685 pages, 1988. Teacher's Manual available. (Casebook)

PHILLIPS' PRODUCTS LIABILITY IN A NUTSHELL, Third Edition, 307 pages, 1988. Softcover. (Text)

Professional Responsibility

ARONSON, DEVINE AND FISCH'S PROBLEMS, CASES AND MATERIALS IN PROFESSIONAL RESPONSIBILITY, 745 pages, 1985. Teacher's Manual available. (Casebook)

ARONSON AND WECKSTEIN'S PROFESSIONAL RESPONSIBILITY IN A NUTSHELL, Second Edition, 514 pages, 1991. Softcover. (Text)

LESNICK'S BEING A LAWYER: INDIVIDUAL CHOICE AND RESPONSIBILITY IN THE PRACTICE OF LAW, 422 pages, 1992. Softcover. Teacher's Manual available. (Coursebook)

MELLINKOFF'S THE CONSCIENCE OF A LAWYER, 304 pages, 1973. (Text)

PIRSIG AND KIRWIN'S CASES AND MATERIALS ON PROFESSIONAL RESPONSIBILITY, Fourth Edition, 603 pages, 1984. Teacher's Manual available. (Casebook)

ROTUNDA'S BLACK LETTER ON PROFESSIONAL RESPONSIBILITY, Third Edition, 492 pages, 1992. Softcover. (Review)

SCHWARTZ, WYDICK AND PERSCHBACHER'S PROBLEMS IN LEGAL ETHICS, Third Edition, approximately 400 pages, 1993. (Coursebook)

SELECTED STATUTES, RULES AND STANDARDS ON THE LEGAL PROFESSION. Softcover. 940 pages, 1992.

SMITH AND MALLEN'S PREVENTING LEGAL MALPRACTICE, 264 pages, 1989. Reprint from Mallen and Smith's Legal Malpractice, Third Edition. (Text)

SUTTON AND DZIENKOWSKI'S CASES AND MATERIALS ON PROFESSIONAL RESPONSIBILITY FOR LAWYERS, 839 pages, 1989. Teacher's Manual available. (Casebook)

WOLFRAM'S HORNBOOK ON MODERN LEGAL ETHICS, Student Edition, 1120 pages, 1986. (Text)

WYDICK AND PERSCHBACHER'S CALIFORNIA LEGAL ETHICS, 439 pages, 1992. Softcover. (Coursebook)

Property—see also Real Estate Transactions, Land Use, Trusts and Estates

BARNES AND STOUT'S THE ECONOMICS OF PROPERTY RIGHTS AND NUISANCE LAW, 87 pages, 1992. Softcover. Teacher's Manual available. (Casebook)

BERNHARDT'S BLACK LETTER ON PROPERTY, Second Edition, 388 pages, 1991. Softcover. (Review)

BERNHARDT'S REAL PROPERTY IN A NUTSHELL, Second Edition, 448 pages, 1981. Softcover. (Text)

BOYER, HOVENKAMP AND KURTZ' THE LAW OF PROPERTY, AN INTRODUCTORY SURVEY, Fourth Edition, 696 pages, 1991. (Text)

BROWDER, CUNNINGHAM, NELSON, STOEBUCK AND WHITMAN'S CASES ON BASIC PROPERTY LAW, Fifth Edition, 1386 pages, 1989. Teacher's Manual available. (Casebook)

BRUCE, ELY AND BOSTICK'S CASES AND MATERIALS ON MODERN PROPERTY LAW, Second Edition, 953 pages, 1989. Teacher's Manual available. (Casebook)

BURKE'S PERSONAL PROPERTY IN A NUTSHELL, Second Edition, approximately 400 pages, May, 1993 Pub. Softcover. (Text)

CUNNINGHAM, STOEBUCK AND WHITMAN'S HORNBOOK ON THE LAW OF PROPERTY, Second Edition, approximately 900 pages, May, 1993 Pub. (Text)

DONAHUE, KAUPER AND MARTIN'S CASES AND MATERIALS ON PROPERTY, AN INTRODUCTION TO THE CONCEPT AND THE INSTITUTION, Third

Property—Cont'd

Edition, approximately 1000 pages, 1993. Teacher's Manual available. (Casebook)

HILL'S LANDLORD AND TENANT LAW IN A NUTSHELL, Second Edition, 311 pages, 1986. Softcover. (Text)

JOHNSON, JOST, SALSICH AND SHAFFER'S PROPERTY LAW, CASES, MATERIALS AND PROBLEMS, 908 pages, 1992. Teacher's Manual available. (Casebook)

KURTZ AND HOVENKAMP'S CASES AND MATERIALS ON AMERICAN PROPERTY LAW, Second Edition, approximately 1350 pages, March, 1993 Pub. Teacher's Manual available. (Casebook)

MOYNIHAN'S INTRODUCTION TO REAL PROPERTY, Second Edition, 239 pages, 1988. (Text)

Psychiatry, Law and

REISNER AND SLOBOGIN'S LAW AND THE MENTAL HEALTH SYSTEM, CIVIL AND CRIMINAL ASPECTS, Second Edition, 1117 pages, 1990. Teacher's Manual available. (Casebook) 1992 Supplement.

Real Estate Transactions

BRUCE'S REAL ESTATE FINANCE IN A NUTSHELL, Third Edition, 287 pages, 1991. Softcover. (Text)

MAXWELL, RIESENFELD, HETLAND AND WARREN'S CASES ON CALIFORNIA SECURITY TRANSACTIONS IN LAND, Fourth Edition, 778 pages, 1992. Teacher's Manual available. (Casebook)

NELSON AND WHITMAN'S BLACK LETTER ON LAND TRANSACTIONS AND FINANCE, Second Edition, 466 pages, 1988. Softcover. (Review)

NELSON AND WHITMAN'S CASES AND MATERIALS ON REAL ESTATE TRANSFER, FINANCE AND DEVELOPMENT, Fourth Edition, 1346 pages, 1992. (Casebook)

NELSON AND WHITMAN'S HORNBOOK ON REAL ESTATE FINANCE LAW, Second Edition, 941 pages, 1985 with 1989 pocket part. (Text)

Regulated Industries—see also Mass Communication Law, Banking Law

GELLHORN AND PIERCE'S REGULATED INDUSTRIES IN A NUTSHELL, Second Edition, 389 pages, 1987. Softcover. (Text)

MORGAN, HARRISON AND VERKUIL'S CASES AND MATERIALS ON ECONOMIC REGULATION OF BUSINESS, Second Edition, 666 pages, 1985. (Casebook)

Remedies

DOBBS' HORNBOOK ON REMEDIES, Second Edition, approximately 1000 pages, April, 1993 Pub. (Text)

DOBBS' PROBLEMS IN REMEDIES. 137 pages, 1974. Teacher's Manual available. Softcover. (Coursebook)

DOBBYN'S INJUNCTIONS IN A NUTSHELL, 264 pages, 1974. Softcover. (Text)

FRIEDMAN'S CONTRACT REMEDIES IN A NUTSHELL, 323 pages, 1981. Softcover. (Text)

LEAVELL, LOVE AND NELSON'S CASES AND MATERIALS ON EQUITABLE REMEDIES, RESTITUTION AND DAMAGES, Fourth Edition, 1111 pages, 1986. Teacher's Manual available. (Casebook)

O'CONNELL'S REMEDIES IN A NUTSHELL, Second Edition, 320 pages, 1985. Softcover. (Text)

SCHOENBROD, MACBETH, LEVINE AND JUNG'S CASES AND MATERIALS ON REMEDIES: PUBLIC AND PRIVATE, 848 pages, 1990. Teacher's Manual available. (Casebook) 1992 Supplement.

YORK, BAUMAN AND RENDLEMAN'S CASES AND MATERIALS ON REMEDIES, Fifth Edition, 1270 pages, 1992. Teacher's Manual available. (Casebook)

Sea, Law of

SOHN AND GUSTAFSON'S THE LAW OF THE SEA IN A NUTSHELL, 264 pages, 1984. Softcover. (Text)

Securities Regulation

HAZEN'S HORNBOOK ON THE LAW OF SECURITIES REGULATION, Second Edition, Student Edition, 1082 pages, 1990. (Text)

RATNER'S SECURITIES REGULATION IN A NUTSHELL, Fourth Edition, 320 pages, 1992. Softcover. (Text)

RATNER AND HAZEN'S SECURITIES REGULATION: CASES AND MATERIALS, Fourth Edition, 1062 pages, 1991. Teacher's Manual available. (Casebook) Problems and Sample Documents Supplement.

Statutory Supplement. *See Securities*

Securities Regulation—Cont'd
Regulation, Selected Statutes

SECURITIES REGULATION, SELECTED STATUTES, RULES, AND FORMS. Softcover. Approximately 1375 pages, 1993.

Sports Law

CHAMPION'S SPORTS LAW IN A NUTSHELL,. Approximately 300 pages, January, 1993 Pub. Softcover. (Text)

SCHUBERT, SMITH AND TRENTADUE'S SPORTS LAW, 395 pages, 1986. (Text)

Tax Practice and Procedure

GARBIS, RUBIN AND MORGAN'S CASES AND MATERIALS ON TAX PROCEDURE AND TAX FRAUD, Third Edition, 921 pages, 1992. Teacher's Manual available. (Casebook)

MORGAN'S TAX PROCEDURE AND TAX FRAUD IN A NUTSHELL, 400 pages, 1990. Softcover. (Text)

Taxation—Corporate

KAHN AND GANN'S CORPORATE TAXATION, Third Edition, 980 pages, 1989. Teacher's Manual available. (Casebook) 1991 Supplement.

SCHWARZ AND LATHROPE'S BLACK LETTER ON CORPORATE AND PARTNERSHIP TAXATION, 537 pages, 1991. Softcover. (Review)

WEIDENBRUCH AND BURKE'S FEDERAL INCOME TAXATION OF CORPORATIONS AND STOCKHOLDERS IN A NUTSHELL, Third Edition, 309 pages, 1989. Softcover. (Text)

Taxation—Estate & Gift—see also Estate Planning, Trusts and Estates

MCNULTY'S FEDERAL ESTATE AND GIFT TAXATION IN A NUTSHELL, Fourth Edition, 496 pages, 1989. Softcover. (Text)

PEAT AND WILLBANKS' FEDERAL ESTATE AND GIFT TAXATION: AN ANALYSIS AND CRITIQUE, 265 pages, 1991. Softcover. (Text)

PENNELL'S CASES AND MATERIALS ON INCOME TAXATION OF TRUSTS, ESTATES, GRANTORS AND BENEFICIARIES, 460 pages, 1987. Teacher's Manual available. (Casebook)

Taxation—Individual

DODGE'S THE LOGIC OF TAX, 343 pages, 1989. Softcover. (Text)

GUNN AND WARD'S CASES, TEXT AND PROBLEMS ON FEDERAL INCOME TAXATION, Third Edition, 817 pages, 1992. Teacher's Manual available. (Casebook)

HUDSON AND LIND'S BLACK LETTER ON FEDERAL INCOME TAXATION, Fourth Edition, 410 pages, 1992. Softcover. (Review)

MCNULTY'S FEDERAL INCOME TAXATION OF INDIVIDUALS IN A NUTSHELL, Fourth Edition, 503 pages, 1988. Softcover. (Text)

POSIN'S FEDERAL INCOME TAXATION, Second Edition, approximately 650 pages, May, 1993 Pub. Softcover. (Text)

ROSE AND CHOMMIE'S HORNBOOK ON FEDERAL INCOME TAXATION, Third Edition, 923 pages, 1988, with 1991 pocket part. (Text)

SELECTED FEDERAL TAXATION STATUTES AND REGULATIONS. Softcover. 1686 pages, 1993.

Taxation—International

DOERNBERG'S INTERNATIONAL TAXATION IN A NUTSHELL, 325 pages, 1989. Softcover. (Text)

KAPLAN'S FEDERAL TAXATION OF INTERNATIONAL TRANSACTIONS: PRINCIPLES, PLANNING AND POLICY, 635 pages, 1988. (Casebook)

Taxation—Partnership

BERGER AND WIEDENBECK'S CASES AND MATERIALS ON PARTNERSHIP TAXATION, 788 pages, 1989. Teacher's Manual available. (Casebook) 1991 Supplement.

BISHOP AND BROOKS' FEDERAL PARTNERSHIP TAXATION: A GUIDE TO THE LEADING CASES, STATUTES, AND REGULATIONS, 545 pages, 1990. Softcover. (Text)

BURKE'S FEDERAL INCOME TAXATION OF PARTNERSHIPS IN A NUTSHELL, 356 pages, 1992. Softcover. (Text)

SCHWARZ AND LATHROPE'S BLACK LETTER ON CORPORATE AND PARTNERSHIP TAXATION, 537 pages, 1991. Softcover. (Review)

Taxation—State & Local

GELFAND AND SALSICH'S STATE AND LOCAL TAXATION AND FINANCE IN A NUTSHELL, 309 pages, 1986. Softcover. (Text)

HELLERSTEIN AND HELLERSTEIN'S CASES AND MATERIALS ON STATE AND LOCAL TAXATION, Fifth Edition, 1071 pages, 1988. (Case-

LAW SCHOOL PUBLICATIONS—Continued

Taxation—State & Local—Cont'd
book)

Torts—see also Products Liability

BARNES AND STOUT'S THE ECONOMIC ANALYSIS OF TORT LAW, 161 pages, 1992. Softcover. Teacher's Manual available. (Casebook)

CHRISTIE AND MEEKS' CASES AND MATERIALS ON THE LAW OF TORTS, Second Edition, 1264 pages, 1990. (Casebook)

DOBBS' TORTS AND COMPENSATION—PERSONAL ACCOUNTABILITY AND SOCIAL RESPONSIBILITY FOR INJURY, 955 pages, 1985. Teacher's Manual available. (Casebook) 1990 Supplement.

KEETON, KEETON, SARGENTICH AND STEINER'S CASES AND MATERIALS ON TORT AND ACCIDENT LAW, Second Edition, 1318 pages, 1989. (Casebook)

KIONKA'S BLACK LETTER ON TORTS, 339 pages, 1988. Softcover. (Review)

KIONKA'S TORTS IN A NUTSHELL, Second Edition, 449 pages, 1992. Softcover. (Text)

PROSSER AND KEETON'S HORNBOOK ON TORTS, Fifth Edition, Student Edition, 1286 pages, 1984 with 1988 pocket part. (Text)

ROBERTSON, POWERS AND ANDERSON'S CASES AND MATERIALS ON TORTS, 932 pages, 1989. Teacher's Manual available. (Casebook)

Trade Regulation—see also Antitrust, Regulated Industries

MCMANIS' UNFAIR TRADE PRACTICES IN A NUTSHELL, Third Edition, approximately 450 pages, 1993. Softcover. (Text)

SCHECHTER'S BLACK LETTER ON UNFAIR TRADE PRACTICES, 272 pages, 1986. Softcover. (Review)

WESTON, MAGGS AND SCHECHTER'S UNFAIR TRADE PRACTICES AND CONSUMER PROTECTION, CASES AND COMMENTS, Fifth Edition, 957 pages, 1992. Teacher's Manual available. (Casebook)

Trial and Appellate Advocacy—see also Civil Procedure

APPELLATE ADVOCACY, HANDBOOK OF, Second Edition, 182 pages, 1986. Softcover. (Text)

BERGMAN'S TRIAL ADVOCACY IN A NUTSHELL, Second Edition, 354 pages, 1989. Softcover. (Text)

BINDER AND BERGMAN'S FACT INVESTIGATION: FROM HYPOTHESIS TO PROOF, 354 pages, 1984. Teacher's Manual available. (Coursebook)

CARLSON'S ADJUDICATION OF CRIMINAL JUSTICE: PROBLEMS AND REFERENCES, 130 pages, 1986. Softcover. (Casebook)

CARLSON AND IMWINKELRIED'S DYNAMICS OF TRIAL PRACTICE: PROBLEMS AND MATERIALS, 414 pages, 1989. Teacher's Manual available. (Coursebook) 1990 Supplement.

CLARY'S PRIMER ON THE ANALYSIS AND PRESENTATION OF LEGAL ARGUMENT, 106 pages, 1992. Softcover. (Text)

DESSEM'S PRETRIAL LITIGATION IN A NUTSHELL, 382 pages, 1992. Softcover. (Text)

DESSEM'S PRETRIAL LITIGATION: LAW, POLICY AND PRACTICE, 608 pages, 1991. Softcover. Teacher's Manual available. (Coursebook)

DEVINE'S NON-JURY CASE FILES FOR TRIAL ADVOCACY, 258 pages, 1991. (Coursebook)

GOLDBERG'S THE FIRST TRIAL (WHERE DO I SIT? WHAT DO I SAY?) IN A NUTSHELL, 396 pages, 1982. Softcover. (Text)

HAYDOCK, HERR, AND STEMPEL'S FUNDAMENTALS OF PRE-TRIAL LITIGATION, Second Edition, 786 pages, 1992. Softcover. Teacher's Manual available. (Coursebook)

HAYDOCK AND SONSTENG'S TRIAL: THEORIES, TACTICS, TECHNIQUES, 711 pages, 1991. Softcover. (Text)

HEGLAND'S TRIAL AND PRACTICE SKILLS IN A NUTSHELL, 346 pages, 1978. Softcover. (Text)

HORNSTEIN'S APPELLATE ADVOCACY IN A NUTSHELL, 325 pages, 1984. Softcover. (Text)

JEANS' HANDBOOK ON TRIAL ADVOCACY, Student Edition, 473 pages, 1975. Softcover. (Text)

LISNEK AND KAUFMAN'S DEPOSITIONS: PROCEDURE, STRATEGY AND TECHNIQUE, Law School and CLE Edition. 250 pages, 1990. Softcover. (Text)

MARTINEAU'S CASES AND MATERIALS ON APPELLATE PRACTICE AND PROCEDURE, 565 pages, 1987. (Casebook)

Trial and Appellate Advocacy—Cont'd

SONSTENG, HAYDOCK AND BOYD'S THE TRIALBOOK: A TOTAL SYSTEM FOR PREPARATION AND PRESENTATION OF A CASE, 404 pages, 1984. Softcover. (Coursebook)

WHARTON, HAYDOCK AND SONSTENG'S CALIFORNIA CIVIL TRIALBOOK, Law School and CLE Edition. 148 pages, 1990. Softcover. (Text)

Trusts and Estates

ATKINSON'S HORNBOOK ON WILLS, Second Edition, 975 pages, 1953. (Text)

AVERILL'S UNIFORM PROBATE CODE IN A NUTSHELL, Second Edition, 454 pages, 1987. Softcover. (Text)

BOGERT'S HORNBOOK ON TRUSTS, Sixth Edition, Student Edition, 794 pages, 1987. (Text)

CLARK, LUSKY AND MURPHY'S CASES AND MATERIALS ON GRATUITOUS TRANSFERS, Third Edition, 970 pages, 1985. (Casebook)

DODGE'S WILLS, TRUSTS AND ESTATE PLANNING–LAW AND TAXATION, CASES AND MATERIALS, 665 pages, 1988. (Casebook)

McGOVERN, KURTZ AND REIN'S HORNBOOK ON WILLS, TRUSTS AND ESTATES–INCLUDING TAXATION AND FUTURE INTERESTS, 996 pages, 1988. (Text)

MENNELL'S WILLS AND TRUSTS IN A NUTSHELL, 392 pages, 1979. Softcover. (Text)

SIMES' HORNBOOK ON FUTURE INTERESTS, Second Edition, 355 pages, 1966. (Text)

TURANO AND RADIGAN'S HORNBOOK ON NEW YORK ESTATE ADMINISTRATION, 676 pages, 1986 with 1991 pocket part. (Text)

UNIFORM PROBATE CODE, OFFICIAL TEXT WITH COMMENTS. 863 pages, 1991. Softcover.

WAGGONER'S FUTURE INTERESTS IN A NUTSHELL, 361 pages, 1981. Softcover. (Text)

Water Law—see also Energy and Natural Resources Law, Environmental Law

GETCHES' WATER LAW IN A NUTSHELL, Second Edition, 459 pages, 1990. Softcover. (Text)

SAX, ABRAMS AND THOMPSON'S LEGAL CONTROL OF WATER RESOURCES: CASES AND MATERIALS, Second Edition, 987 pages, 1991. Teacher's Manual available. (Casebook)

TRELEASE AND GOULD'S CASES AND MATERIALS ON WATER LAW, Fourth Edition, 816 pages, 1986. (Casebook)

Wills—see Trusts and Estates

Workers' Compensation

HOOD, HARDY AND LEWIS' WORKERS' COMPENSATION AND EMPLOYEE PROTECTION LAWS IN A NUTSHELL, Second Edition, 361 pages, 1990. Softcover. (Text)

LITTLE, EATON AND SMITH'S CASES AND MATERIALS ON WORKERS' COMPENSATION, 537 pages, 1992. Teacher's Manual available. (Casebook)

WEST'S LAW SCHOOL ADVISORY BOARD

CURTIS J. BERGER
Professor of Law, Columbia University

JESSE H. CHOPER
Dean and Professor of Law,
University of California, Berkeley

DAVID P. CURRIE
Professor of Law, University of Chicago

YALE KAMISAR
Professor of Law, University of Michigan

MARY KAY KANE
Professor of Law, University of California,
Hastings College of the Law

WAYNE R. LaFAVE
Professor of Law, University of Illinois

RICHARD C. MAXWELL
Professor of Law, Duke University

ARTHUR R. MILLER
Professor of Law, Harvard University

GRANT S. NELSON
Professor of Law, University of California, Los Angeles

ROBERT A. STEIN
Dean and Professor of Law, University of Minnesota

JAMES J. WHITE
Professor of Law, University of Michigan

CHARLES ALAN WRIGHT
Professor of Law, University of Texas

*

INTERNATIONAL ORGANIZATIONS IN THEIR LEGAL SETTING

Second Edition

By

Frederic L. Kirgis, Jr.
Law School Association Alumni Professor
Washington and Lee University School of Law

AMERICAN CASEBOOK SERIES®

WEST PUBLISHING CO.
ST. PAUL, MINN., 1993

American Casebook Series, the key symbol appearing on the front cover and the WP symbol are registered trademarks of West Publishing Co. Registered in the U.S. Patent and Trademark Office.

COPYRIGHT © 1977, 1981 WEST PUBLISHING CO.
COPYRIGHT © 1993 By WEST PUBLISHING CO.
610 Opperman Drive
P.O. Box 64526
St. Paul, MN 55164–0526

All rights reserved
Printed in the United States of America

Library of Congress Cataloging-in-Publication Data

Kirgis, Frederic L.
    International organizations in their legal setting /
by Frederic L. Kirgis, Jr. — 2nd ed.
      p.   cm. — (American casebook series)
    Includes index.
    ISBN 0–314–01643–0
    1. International agencies. I. Title. II. Series.
JX1995.K56 1993
341.2—dc20   92–37615
                                                                              CIP

ISBN 0–314–01643–0

   Kirgis, Int'l Orgs. 2d Ed.

To
my wife, Carol

*

Preface

It is only a modest exaggeration to say that there is an international organization for practically every field of human endeavor. To list only the fields encompassed by the United Nations and its related organizations (the specialized agencies, the General Agreement on Tariffs and Trade and the International Atomic Energy Agency), included would be international peacekeeping and peacemaking, human rights, labor relations, food production and distribution, education, promotion of science and cultural activities, health, economic development, monetary affairs, international trade, civil aviation, postal services, telecommunications, meteorology, maritime commerce, protection of intellectual property, and nuclear energy. Organizations not formally related to the United Nations account for a great many additional subject areas.

To deal with these matters, international organizations range all the way from the multilateral body with aspirations for universal membership and a very broad range of interests (the United Nations), to the specialized U.N. agencies (each with wide membership but a relatively narrow focus), to organizations with select membership but relatively wide interests (e. g. the Council of Europe or the Organization of American States), to agencies that are restricted both as to membership and subject matter (e. g. International River Commissions or the U.S.-Canadian International Joint Commission). Some organizations are strictly intergovernmental in that they accept only states (nations) as members, while others accept or are composed entirely of nongovernmental entities.

No attempt is made in these materials to cover all international organizations, or even to cover all of the subject areas mentioned above. The materials do attempt to delve into the legal and quasi-legal issues surrounding some important common characteristics of intergovernmental organizations, with the emphasis in the first five chapters on organizations having wide membership.

Many of the issues in the first four chapters are constitutional or procedural in nature; that is, they have to do with the powers of, and restrictions upon, the organizations or their members as set forth in the constituent instruments (variously called charters, articles of agreement or something similar) of the organizations, and as developed in practice by the organizations themselves. For example, virtually all organizations face potential problems relating to their basic legal characteristics in international law and in the municipal (domestic) law of their member states. Recurring issues arise concerning eligibility for membership or participation, rights of members and termination of membership. To varying extents, organizations have developed legislative or quasi-legislative powers and dispute-settlement mechanisms raising common problems relating to relinquishment of sovereign prerogatives by members, fairness and effectiveness of decision-making, and so forth. Enforcement measures of uneven fairness and utility have been developed to try to keep members in step. All of these problems are examined comparatively, identifying and contrasting the ways in which representative, significant intergovernmental organizations deal with them on paper and in practice. More emphasis is placed on the United Nations, particularly in Chapter 4 on enforcement measures, than in the first edition. The reason, of course, is the U.N.'s much more prominent role in 1993 than in 1977 when the first edition was completed.

Chapter 5 continues the emphasis on the U.N., in the peacekeeping and peacemaking context. Here, the U.N.'s role has grown exponentially, raising new prospects and problems.

Considerable attention is given to two early, precedent-setting U.N. peacekeeping operations, in the Middle East and the Congo (now Zaîre), in order to set the stage for examination of some of the more recent efforts. Space limitations precluded any attempt to cover all of the significant, recent peacekeeping operations. Yugoslavia was chosen because it appeared to be symptomatic of the kinds of issues likely to arise from the ethnic conflicts of the 1990s and the breakup of states, and because of the magnitude and complexity of the U.N. operation. Liberia and Somalia were chosen because they presented more contained, yet important, sets of issues: regional peacekeeping in Liberia, and U.N. involvement in a conflict in Somalia that was as noninternational as one could expect to find in the 1990s. Nicaragua provided an example of successful U.N. peacekeeping, supplemented by U.N. involvement in the democratic process.

The Nicaragua case study leads to a more general examination in Chapter 5 of U.N. participation in national elections, and to consideration of the Secretary-General's role as a peacemaker.

Chapter 5 includes a substantial section on humanitarian intervention, another burgeoning U.N. field in the 1990s. That in turn leads to an examination of peace enforcement as well as Secretary-General Boutros Boutros-Ghali's provocative ideas about preventive deployment, and to questions about the U.N.'s possible role in endowing some nonstate entities with a form of international personality.

Chapter 6 turns to a broad treatment of human rights. Once again, the United Nations gets quite a bit of attention, but no useful examination of human rights could be made without virtually equal time for the work of two regional organizations: the Organization of American States and the Council of Europe. In all these human rights systems, tensions exist between domestic jurisdiction and international supervision. Chapter 6 tends to this, and looks at the mechanisms by which the three organizations try to vindicate human rights without losing the cooperation of their member states. As with most of the rest of the materials, attention is paid particularly to procedural and "constitutional" issues, though substantive human rights are not ignored.

Chapters 4 and 5, and to a lesser extent the other chapters as well, deal with some situations that were ongoing when this was written. These include situations in Iraq, Libya, the former Yugoslavia and Somalia. There is a risk, of course, in including ongoing situations in a casebook that the publisher has to put between two nonremovable covers on a date that bears no particular relationship to unfolding events. Yet the desirability of presenting materials of current significance seemed clearly to justify the inclusion of these case studies. Instructors may wish to supplement some of the materials to take account of events occurring after the book has been published.

The organizations to be studied vary throughout the book, according to the issue at hand. One organization that was included in the first edition, but not in the second, is the European Community. The need to devote more attention to the United Nations, and the futility of trying to do justice to the greatly expanded supranational powers and activities of the EC in what could only be a single chapter, led to the conclusion that coverage of the EC had best be left to books devoted entirely to it.

Aside from the United Nations, the selection of organizations has been made by weighing a number of variables such as the significance of the organization in terms of its area of endeavor and its influence within that area (hence, for example, the two regional organizations mentioned above in relation to human rights); the extent to which its rules and/or practice concerning a specific issue are representative of methods adopted by other organizations or, if unique, represent efforts to deal effectively with a significant problem; and the availability of source materials concerning the actual practice of the organizations. The emphasis is on recent practice, which means that relatively little material from the first edition is retained here (even though the approach of Chapters 1 through 4 and Chapter 6 is quite similar to the approach of the same chapters in the first edition).

The eclectic approach of this book means that the student will not be immersed in the law or practice of any one organization, unless the instructor elects to use the book for a course solely in United Nations law—as, I think, one easily could. If the book is used for a comparative study of international organizations, I would hope that the student will gain insights into the role of law and of legal concepts in an ongoing process extending into several of the areas of human endeavor outlined at the beginning of this Preface. If the book is used for a comparative study of how international organizations deal with human rights issues—as could be done by concentrating on the ILO, the U.N.'s humanitarian activities and Chapter 6—I hope it will yield insights into the current state of the international legal process in a particularly important, and rapidly developing, field.

Before we turn briefly to some editorial matters, let it be known that one cannot so much as leaf through these materials—especially in Chapters 2, 3 and 4—without being struck with some nagging questions about the basic relationship between law and international organizations: do legal principles and legal arguments really influence the ways in which international organizations conduct their affairs? How can legal arguments be distinguished, if at all, from political preferences in international bodies representing heterogeneous and often conflicting interests and values? If legal principles get trampled by an international organization or by some of its members in their dealings with it, does anybody other than the short-term losing side really care?

These are serious questions that cannot be ignored. They do not have easy answers. It is my hope, however, that they will not produce in the student (or teacher) total cynicism about law and legal methodology as an ordering force and mechanism for change within international organizations. Law is after all an imperfect tool at all levels; it can be and is manipulated in state and county legislative and administrative bodies as well as in the United Nations, and it can be tempered by political considerations in the United States Supreme Court as it is in the International Court of Justice. Yet society—including informed international society—should care about evaluating the extent to which law, or at least legal thinking (stressing such things as making consistent decisions on similar facts, giving reasoned arguments based on principles other than mere promotion of one's self-interest, and the like) can influence institutional behavior, and should care about enhancing that role whenever it can be done. Surely organizations directly concerned with human well-being and survival on an international scale are important enough to merit our serious attention in these respects.

This is a "casebook" only in a loose sense. Relatively few judicial opinions exist dealing with the important, recurring legal or quasi-legal problems of international organizations. A great deal of the law of these organizations stems from the actual practice of their principal organs—secretariats, plenary bodies such as the U.N. General Assembly, and select "upper chambers" such as the Security Council. Consequently this book is sprinkled with excerpts from reports and debates of those organs, together with the resolutions and other instruments they have produced, and such relevant judicial opinions as do exist.

The Supplement to the book contains introductory descriptions of the organizations covered in the main volume, along with edited documents serving as source materials for many of the issues raised in the book. The Preface to the Supplement explains the basis for deciding which documents to put in the Supplement and which to include in the main volume. Whenever a reference is made in the main volume to a document the student needs to consult in the Supplement, the item is italicized. For example, mention in the main volume of U.N. Charter *article 2(7)* would indicate to the reader that the italicized provision is to be found in the Supplement and should be consulted at that point.

No materials have been included unless I thought they raised interesting and important questions. Rather than leave the questions entirely to the imagination of the instructor or student, I have included those I had in mind. Instructors using this book will undoubtedly think of other questions, or will reformulate some of the questions I have asked, or will prefer to ignore at least some of my questions. However that may be, the questions will have served their purpose if they operate with some regularity to focus students' thought about the materials and if they serve to give direction to class discussions. Many of the questions, or course, have no right answers in any absolute sense, but they do call for reasoned, careful responses that draw on the materials presented.

This is a teaching book, rather than a compendium or bibliography. Even as to the limited range of issues covered, no effort has been made to set forth all source materials that might be relevant. Rather, the attempt has been to select excerpts from constituent instruments, debates, reports, opinions and scholarly analyses that pose as clearly and concisely as possible the issues to be examined. Sometimes original source materials have been shunned, if a summary would do essentially as well with a substantial saving of words. Citations are limited to those materials that would be particularly useful to a student who wishes either to clear up a point or to dig deeply into the subject area. (Useful books on the law of international organizations include The United Nations in the International Legal Order (O. Schachter & C. Joyner eds. 1993), and A Handbook on International Organizations (R.-J. Dupuy ed. 1988). Somewhat dated, but still useful, is D. Bowett, The Law of International Institutions (4th ed. 1982).)

Most footnotes and string citations from source materials have been omitted. When footnote references have been retained, the original numbering has been retained. My own footnotes are designated by letters, "a" to "z." Omissions other than footnotes and citations are indicated by three asterisks.

FREDERIC L. KIRGIS, JR.

Lexington, Virginia
January 1993

*

Symbols and Abbreviations

United Nations documents present a formidable array of symbols with meanings that do not always leap out at the reader. Some of the more commonly-encountered symbols are explained below.

Symbols for principal organs:

A	General Assembly (also GA)
S	Security Council (also SC)
E	Economic and Social Council (also ECOSOC or ESC)
T	Trusteeship Council
ST	Secretariat

Symbols for subsidiary U.N. bodies:

C	Committee
AC	Ad Hoc Committee
PC	Preparatory Committee
CN	Commission
CONF	Conference

Symbols relating to the document itself:

Res.	Resolution
Doc.	Document
L.	Limited distribution
PV	Provisional version, usually to be reissued later after any corrections
Add.	Addendum
Rev.	Revision
Supp.	Supplement

Meeting records:

OR	Official Records
SR	Summary Records

To make matters more confusing, these symbols are surrounded by numbers. Some examples:

G.A. Res. 2749, 25 GAOR Supp. 21, U.N.Doc. A/8021: General Assembly Resolution number 2749, which may be found in Supplement number 21 to the General Assembly Official Records for the 25th session. The parallel citation for that Supplement is A/8021: document number 8,021 of the General Assembly.

Beginning with the General Assembly's 31st session (1976), documents are numbered by session, rather than consecutively from the General Assembly's inception. The first numbers for each session are reserved for the supplements to the Official Records. Thus the 21st supplement to the General Assembly Official Records for the 45th ses-

xi

sion would be U.N. Doc. A/45/21. Mimeographed documents for the 45th session (not supplements to the Official Records) would have higher numbers, e.g. A/45/120.

U.N. Doc. A/C.6/45/15: the 15th document issued during the 45th session by the General Assembly's 6th Committee (its Legal Committee).

U.N. Doc. E/AC.12/L.43/Add.3: the third addendum to the 43rd document issued in a limited distribution series by the 12th Ad Hoc Committee of the Economic and Social Council.

U.N. Doc. S/8365: document number 8,365 issued by the Security Council.

U.N. Doc. A/CONF.48/14: the 14th document issued by the 48th Conference convened by the General Assembly.

There are other U.N. bodies that are not separate entities from the United Nations, but that have lives (and abbreviated names) of their own:

ICJ	International Court of Justice
ILC	International Law Commission
UNICEF	United Nations Children's Fund
UNCITRAL	United Nations Commission on International Trade Law
UNCTAD	United Nations Conference on Trade and Development
UNDP	United Nations Development Program
UNEP	United Nations Environment Program
UNITAR	United Nations Institute for Training and Research
UNRWA	United Nations Relief and Works Agency
WFC	World Food Council

The specialized agencies have their own document symbols, which are too varied to be set forth here. They normally indicate the specialized agency by its initials, and then contain letters and numbers indicating the issuing organ and the number of the particular document in the series. The specialized agencies are:

FAO	Food and Agriculture Organization
IBRD	International Bank for Reconstruction and Development (World Bank)
ICAO	International Civil Aviation Organization
IDA	International Development Association (an affiliate of the World Bank)
IFAD	International Fund for Agricultural Development
IFC	International Finance Corporation (an affiliate of the World Bank)
ILO	International Labor Organization

IMO	International Maritime Organization (formerly Inter-Governmental Maritime Consultative Organization)
IMF	International Monetary Fund
ITU	International Telecommunication Union
UNESCO	United Nations Educational, Scientific and Cultural Organization
UNIDO	United Nations Industrial Development Organization
UPU	Universal Postal Union
WHO	World Health Organization
WIPO	World Intellectual Property Organization
WMO	World Meteorological Organization

There are currently two agencies related to the United Nations that are not technically specialized agencies, but that are treated for most purposes as though they were:

GATT	General Agreement on Tariffs and Trade
IAEA	International Atomic Energy Agency

Abbreviations for some other significant international organizations include:

EC	European Communities (European Economic Community, European Coal and Steel Community, European Atomic Energy Community)
EFTA	European Free Trade Association
IEA	International Energy Agency
ICSID	International Centre for Settlement of Investment Disputes (an affiliate of the World Bank)
CSCE	Conference on Security and Co-operation in Europe
OAS	Organization of American States
OAU	Organization of African Unity
OECD	Organization for Economic Cooperation and Development

Other abbreviations that may be unfamiliar include:

U.N.C.I.O.	United Nations Conference on International Organization (preparation of the U.N. Charter, San Francisco, 1945)
U.N.T.S.	United Nations Treaty Series
L.N.T.S.	League of Nations Treaty Series
U.S.T.	United States Treaties and Other International Agreements
T.I.A.S.	Treaties and Other International Acts Series (U.S.)
C.T.I.A.	Consolidated Treaties & International Agreements (U.S.)
Bevans	Bevans, Treaties and Other International Agreements of the U.S.A., 1776–1949

Acknowledgments

Two research assistants, Jane Quirion and Patti McNerney, have been very helpful, particularly in connection with Chapter 6. In addition, I have received indispensable assistance from the students in International Organizations classes at Washington and Lee and elsewhere. They have revealed inadequacies in earlier versions of these materials, and have made helpful suggestions on a number of occasions.

The staff of the Washington and Lee University Law Library, under the leadership of Sally Wiant, has been unfailingly helpful. I am especially indebted to Macy Brittigan Coffey, for maintaining her good humor as I pestered her for documents—sometimes quite obscure—not only from the U.N., but from other organizations that do not have the document distribution service the U.N. has. She consistently came up with the documents I needed.

I have also had the benefit of working in the libraries of the United Nations and the International Maritime Organization as I prepared these materials. The staffs of both libraries found, or pointed me to, several of the documents that appear in this book.

The Frances Lewis Law Center, the research arm of the Washington and Lee University School of Law, has covered the compensation of my research assistants and the expense of my trips to the U.N. library, for which I am most grateful.

When I have needed secretarial help, the staff of the Law School Word Processing Center at Washington and Lee, led by Darlene Moore, has responded promptly and accurately. They have made my job as painless as any large writing project could be.

Acknowledgments for permission to use copyrighted materials appear with the materials in the body of the book. I am grateful to the publishers and other copyright holders who have granted me permission to use their materials.

*

Summary of Contents

	Page
PREFACE	v
SYMBOLS AND ABBREVIATIONS	xi
ACKNOWLEDGMENTS	xv
TABLE OF CASES	xxxiii

Chapter 1. Legal Status of International Organizations and of Associated Persons and Premises 1
Sec.
1. Introduction 1
2. International Legal Capacity 7
3. The Status of International Organizations in the Domestic Law of the United States 19
4. The Status of Persons and Premises Associated With International Organizations 54

Chapter 2. Membership and Participation in International Organizations 137
1. Introduction 137
2. Admission to Membership 138
3. Observer Status and Nonvoting Participation 166
4. Representation 176
5. Decision–Making Procedures 188
6. Voluntary Withdrawal and Withholding of Support 238

Chapter 3. Rule Making and Dispute Settlement 274
1. Rule–Making Powers 274
2. Dispute–Settlement and Interpretive Powers 388

Chapter 4. Enforcement Techniques 522
1. Introduction 522
2. Nonsanctions 524
3. Sanctions 554

Chapter 5. The Evolving United Nations: Peacekeeping, Peacemaking and Humanitarian Intervention 716
1. Peacekeeping and Peacemaking 716
2. Humanitarian Intervention 852
3. Beyond Peacekeeping 881
4. Nonstates, The U.N. and International Personality 889

Chapter 6. Protecting Basic Human Rights in the United Nations and in Regional Organizations 891

Sec.
1. Introduction 891
2. The United Nations 892
3. The Inter-American System 975
4. The European System 1030

INDEX 1101

Table of Contents

	Page
PREFACE	v
SYMBOLS AND ABBREVIATIONS	xi
ACKNOWLEDGMENTS	xv
TABLE OF CASES	xxxiii

Chapter 1. Legal Status of International Organizations and of Associated Persons and Premises 1

Sec.
1. Introduction 1
   El–Erian, First Report on Relations Between States and Inter-Governmental Organizations 1
2. International Legal Capacity 7
   A. "International Personality" 7
      Reparation for Injuries Suffered in the Service of the United Nations 7
   B. Treaty–Making Capacity 14
      P. Szasz, The Law and Practices of the International Atomic Energy Agency 17
      Memorandum, U.N. Office of Legal Affairs 17
3. The Status of International Organizations in the Domestic Law of the United States 19
   A. Legal Capacity and Federal Jurisdiction 19
      International Refugee Organization v. Republic S.S. Corp. 21
   B. Privileges and Immunities of Organizations 26
      1. The United Nations 26
         United Nations Conference on International Organization .. 28
         Foreign Sovereign Immunities Act of 1976 30
         Memorandum, U.N. Office of Legal Affairs 32
      2. Specialized Agencies 35
         Articles of Agreement of the International Bank for Reconstruction and Development 39
         Lutcher S.A. v. Inter–American Development Bank 39
         Mendaro v. World Bank 43
4. The Status of Persons and Premises Associated With International Organizations 54
   A. Introduction 54
   B. Mission Premises 56
      1. Protection From Demonstrations 56
         Report of the Committee on Relations With the Host Country ... 56
         Act for the Prevention and Punishment of Crimes Against Internationally Protected Persons 59
      2. Eviction 61
         767 Third Avenue Associates v. Permanent Mission of Zaire ... 61

Sec.		Page
4.	The Status of Persons and Premises Associated With International Organizations—Continued	
	3. Execution Against a Mission's Bank Account	68
	Foxworth v. Permanent Mission of Uganda	68
C.	Civil Suit Against a Delegate to the U.N. or a U.N. Official: Jurisdiction and Immunity	70
	Diplomatic Relations Act	72
D.	Governmental Measures Restricting U.N.–Related Persons and Missions	79
	1. Imprisonment of a Staff Member	79
	Statement of U.N. Legal Counsel on the Meaning of "Officials" of the United Nations	80
	Memorandum of U.N. Legal Counsel on the Right to Visit Staff Members in Custody	81
	Report by the U.N. Secretary–General on Detention of Staff Members	82
	2. Experts on Missions	84
	Applicability of Article VI, Section 22, of the Convention on the Privileges and Immunities of the United Nations (The Mazilu Case)	86
	3. U.S. Security Measures	92
	a. Abuse of Privileges of Residence	92
	Debate in the Committee on Relations With the Host Country	92
	b. Travel Restrictions	98
	Note Verbale by the U.N. Secretary–General to the Permanent Representative of the United States	99
	Report of the U.N. Committee on Relations With the Host Country	101
	c. Size of a Mission	103
	d. The Attempt to Close an Observer Mission	104
	United States v. Palestine Liberation Organization	106
	e. The Denial of a Visa to a U.N. Invitee	113
	U.S. State Department's Statement on Denial of a Visa to Yasir Arafat	114
	Memorandum by the United States Representative at the United Nations (Lodge)	117
	Annex to Letter from Hammarskjöld to Lodge	118
	Statement by the U.N. Legal Counsel on the U.S. Denial of a Visa to Yasir Arafat	119
E.	The U.N. Administrative Tribunal and Rights of Staff Members	121
	The Chinese Translators Case	123

Chapter 2. Membership and Participation in International Organizations 137

1. Introduction 137

Sec.		Page
2.	Admission to Membership	138
	A. The United Nations	138
	1. "Statehood" and Conditions Attached to a Vote for Admission	138
	United Nations Conference on International Organization	138
	Conditions of Admission of a State to Membership in the United Nations	140
	2. Ability and Willingness to Carry Out Charter Obligations	144
	3. The Admission Procedure: Article 4(2)	148
	B. The Specialized Agencies	149
	1. The Soviet Union's Application to the ILO	150
	Report of the Special Study Mission on International Organizations and Movements	150
	2. Namibia's Application to the ILO	153
	Opinion of the ILO Legal Adviser on the Possible Admission of Namibia	153
	Response of the Council for Namibia	156
	3. Palestine's Application to WHO	158
	Criteria for Statehood Under International Law: The Case of the Palestine Liberation Organization	160
	World Health Assembly Debate	162
	4. The European Economic Community and FAO	164
3.	Observer Status and Nonvoting Participation	166
	A. The United Nations	166
	1. The General Assembly	166
	General Assembly Debate	168
	2. The Security Council	170
	Security Council Debate	170
	Security Council Debate	173
	B. U.N.–Related Organizations	175
4.	Representation	176
	A. The General Assembly	176
	1. China	176
	M. Whiteman, Digest of International Law	177
	Resolution on Representation of China	179
	2. Cambodia/Kampuchea	181
	General Assembly Debate	181
	B. Other U.N. Organs and Related Organizations	184
	Resolution on Representation of a Member State	184
	Food and Agriculture Organization Decision on Representation of China	186
5.	Decision–Making Procedures	188
	A. The Security Council	188
	1. Russia as Successor to the Soviet Union's Veto Power	188
	Whiteman, Digest of International Law	190

Sec.				Page
5.	Decision–Making Procedures—Continued			
		2. Procedural Issues		191
			Repertoire of the Practice of the Security Council 1946–1951	194
			Security Council Debate	196
		3. A Short–Handed Security Council		202
			Opinion of U.N. Legal Counsel on the Inability of the General Assembly to Elect a Non–Permanent Member of the Security Council	202
		4. Future Composition and Structure		206
			General Assembly Debate on Security Council Composition and Structure	206
	B.	The General Assembly and Other Broadly Representative U.N. Bodies		211
		1. Decision–Making Techniques		211
			Opinion of U.N. Office of Legal Affairs on Majority Required for Adoption by the General Assembly of a Draft Resolution Before It	212
			Jenks, Unanimity, the Veto, Weighted Voting, Special and Simple Majorities and Consensus as Modes of Decision in International Organisations	214
			Koh & Jayakumar, Negotiating Process of UNCLOS III	217
		2. Restructuring Proposals		223
			Executive Summary of "A Successor Vision: The United Nations of Tomorrow"	226
			Nordic Memorandum on Reform of United Nations Governance and Finance	230
		3. The U.N. Budget Process		233
	C.	U.N.–Related Organizations		235
		Jenks, Unanimity, the Veto, Weighted Voting, Special and Simple Majorities and Consensus as Modes of Decision in International Organisations		236
6.	Voluntary Withdrawal and Withholding of Support			238
	A.	The United Nations		239
		M. Whiteman, Digest of International Law		239
		Schwelb, Withdrawal From the United Nations: the Indonesian Intermezzo		244
		Certain Expenses of the United Nations		248
	B.	U.N.–Related Organizations		254
		M. Whiteman, Digest of International Law		254
		M. Whiteman, Digest of International Law		258
		Letter From the U.S. Secretary of State to the Director General of the International Labor Organization		260
		Letter From the U.S. Secretary of State to the Director General of UNESCO		264
		Reply From the Director General of UNESCO		265
		Letter From the Assistant Secretary of State for International Organization Affairs to the Director General of UNESCO		266
		FAO Conference Resolution on Provision of Technical Assistance to the Palestinian People		270

TABLE OF CONTENTS

	Page
Chapter 3. Rule Making and Dispute Settlement	274

Sec.
1. Rule–Making Powers 274
    A. The International Labor Organization 276
        Valticos, The International Labour Organization 276
        Memorandum by the International Labor Office 278
        Convention Concerning Equal Remuneration for Men and Women Workers for Work of Equal Value 281
        Recommendation Concerning Equal Remuneration for Men and Women Workers for Work of Equal Value 282
        Convention Concerning Safety and Health in Construction 285
        Recommendation Concerning Safety and Health in Construction 288
        International Labor Office, the International Labour Code, 1951 291
        E. Luard, International Agencies: The Emerging Framework of Interdependence 293
    B. The International Monetary Fund 295
        IMF Executive Board Decision on Surveillance Over Exchange Rate Policies 298
    C. The International Civil Aviation Organization 302
        T. Buergenthal, Law–Making in the International Civil Aviation Organization 302
        Milde, Interception of Civil Aircraft vs. Misuse of Civil Aviation . 309
    D. The International Maritime Organization 318
        C. Henry, the Carriage of Dangerous Goods by Sea 319
        International Convention for the Prevention of Pollution by Ships 326
        Convention on the Law of the Sea 329
    E. The United Nations 333
        1. The General Assembly as a Participant in the Shaping of International Law 334
            a. Theory and Practice 334
                J. Castañeda, Legal Effects of United Nations Resolutions 335
                Schwebel, The Effect of Resolutions of the U.N. General Assembly on Customary International Law 337
                Higgins, The Role of Resolutions of International Organizations in the Process of Creating Norms in the International System 341
                Schreuer, Recommendations and the Traditional Sources of International Law 345
            b. The Law of Expropriation 351
                Declaration on Permanent Sovereignty Over Natural Resources 352
                Charter of Economic Rights and Duties of States 355
                TOPCO/Calasiatic v. Libyan Arab Republic 357
            c. Use of Shared Natural Resources 360
                F. Kirgis, Prior Consultation in International Law 361
        2. The General Assembly in a Quasi–Constitutive Role .. 365
            a. Israel 366
                Resolution on Palestine 368

TABLE OF CONTENTS

Sec.   Page

1. Rule–Making Powers—Continued
    - b. Palestine 372
        - Comment, Following in Another's Footsteps: The Acquisition of International Legal Standing by the Palestine Liberation Organization 373
        - Palestinian Proclamation of Independence 375
        - Khalidi, The Resolutions of the 19th Palestine National Council 377
        - Resolution on Proclamation of the State of Palestine ... 378
    - c. Namibia 380
        - Resolution Establishing the Council for South West Africa (Namibia) 381
        - Decree for the Protection of the Natural Resources of Namibia 383
        - Report on Human Rights Provisions in the Constitution of Namibia 386
        - Report on the Implementation of Security Council Resolution 435 387

2. Dispute–Settlement and Interpretive Powers 388
    - A. The International Labor Organization 389
        - 1. Complaints and Commissions of Inquiry 389
            - C.W. Jenks, Social Justice in the Law of Nations 390
            - *Report of the Commission Instituted Under Article 26 to Examine the Complaint on the Observance by Poland of the Freedom of Association and Right to Organize Conventions* 395
        - 2. Representations Against Members 408
            - *Report of the Committee Set up Under Article 24 to Consider the Representation Alleging Non–Observance of the Discrimination Convention by Czechoslovakia* 409
        - 3. Special Procedures on Freedom of Association 413
            - *Complaint Against the Government of China Presented by the International Confederation of Free Trade Unions* 415
            - *Complaint Against the Government of Canada Presented by the Canadian Labour Congress and the Postal, Telegraph and Telephone International* 421
        - 4. Interpretation of Conventions by the International Labor Office 426
            - International Labor Office, The International Labor Code, 1951 426
            - International Labor Office Notice and Memorandum Interpreting ILO Convention No. 111 427
    - B. The International Monetary Fund 431
        - *International Bank for Reconstruction and Development and International Monetary Fund v. All America Cables & Radio, Inc.* ... 432
        - Executive Board Decision on Unenforceability of Certain Exchange Contracts 438

Sec.		Page
2.	Dispute–Settlement and Interpretive Powers—Continued	

    C. The International Civil Aviation Organization 443
        T. Buergenthal, Law-Making in the International Civil Aviation Organization 443
        ICAO Council, Rules for the Settlement of Differences 445
        Application of Pakistan 448
        Memorial of Pakistan 449
        Preliminary Objections by the Government of India 452
        Decision of the ICAO Council 454
        Appeal Relating to the Jurisdiction of the ICAO Council 455
        ICAO Council Resolution on Korean Airliner Incident 470
        ICAO Council Resolution on Iran Airbus Incident 473
        Application of Iran in Aerial Incident Case 475
    D. The International Maritime Organization 479
    E. The United Nations 481
        1. Introduction 481
            United Nations Conference on International Organization 482
            Certain Expenses of the United Nations 483
            Competence of the General Assembly for the Admission of a State to the United Nations 483
        2. The ICJ Advisory Function: Namibia and Other Opinions 485
            Gross, The South West Africa Case: What Happened? 485
            Resolution on Termination of the Southwest Africa Mandate 489
            Resolution on Illegality of South African Presence in Namibia 490
            Legal Consequences for States of the Continued Presence of South Africa in Namibia (South West Africa) Notwithstanding Security Council Resolution 276 (1970) 492
            Ago, "Binding" Advisory Opinions of the International Court of Justice 516

Chapter 4. Enforcement Techniques 522

1. Introduction 522
    E. Luard, International Agencies: The Emerging Framework of Interdependence 522
2. Nonsanctions 524
    A. Informal Persuasion and Assistance 524
        1. The International Labor Organization 524
            Valticos, The International Labour Organization 524
            Report of the Committee of Experts on the Application of Conventions and Recommendations 528
        2. The International Monetary Fund 532
    B. The Mobilization of Shame 533
        1. The International Labor Organization 533
            Report of the Committee of Experts on the Application of Conventions and Recommendations 538
            Report of the Committee on the Application of Standards 539
        2. The International Monetary Fund 549

TABLE OF CONTENTS

Sec.		Page
2.	Nonsanctions—Continued	
	3. The International Atomic Energy Agency	549
	IAEA Board of Governors Resolution	549
	4. The World Health Organization	550
	WHO Resolution on Conditions of the Arab Population in the Occupied Territories	551
3.	Sanctions	554
	A. Authorized Retaliation in Kind	555
	General Agreement on Tariffs and Trade	555
	B. Sanctions Affecting Membership Rights	558
	1. Loss of Voting Rights	558
	a. The United Nations	558
	M. Whiteman, Digest of International Law	559
	b. Specialized Agencies	563
	2. Withholding Selected Benefits of Membership	564
	a. Financial Organizations	565
	Public Law 95–118, Section 701, as Amended	571
	b. Nonfinancial Organizations	575
	UNESCO Resolution on Israel	576
	Statement of the American Jewish Congress	578
	Statement on Israel by Amadou Mahtar M'Bow, Director-General of UNESCO	579
	Resolution of IAEA General Conference Regarding Technical Assistance to Israel	581
	3. Increasing the Burdens of Membership	583
	4. Suspension or Expulsion From Membership	585
	a. The United Nations	585
	(1) South Africa	585
	U.N. Secretariat Summary of U.N. Credentials Practice Through 1973	586
	General Assembly Debate	590
	U.N. Legal Counsel, Opinion on Rejection of Credentials	594
	(2) Israel in the General Assembly	598
	General Assembly Debate	598
	(3) Yugoslavia	600
	Security Council Resolution 777	602
	b. Other Organizations	603
	Convention of the World Meteorological Organization	604
	WMO Resolution Suspending South African Rights and Privileges	605
	Opinion of the ITU Legal Adviser	610
	Resolution Adopted by the ITU Plenipotentiary Conference Regarding Israel and Assistance to Lebanon	615
	OAS Resolution on the Exclusion of the Cuban Government	617

Sec.	Page
3. Sanctions—Continued	

C. U.N. Enforcement Action 620
   1. Rhodesia 621
      a. History 621
      b. The U.N. Response to UDI 623
         Security Council Resolution 232 624
         Security Council Resolution 253 625
         U.S. Department of State, Southern Rhodesia and the United Nations: The U.S. Position 626
         Statement of Dean Acheson 628
      c. Compliance and Noncompliance With Sanctions ... 629
         Diggs v. Shultz 631
      d. Independence for Zimbabwe and Ending the Sanctions 635
         M. Doxey, International Sanctions in Contemporary Perspective 635
   2. South Africa 638
      Security Council Resolution 418 639
   3. Iraq 642
      a. The Invasion of Kuwait and Initial U.N. Response 642
         Security Council Resolution 660 644
         Security Council Resolution 661 645
      b. History 647
         Agreed Minutes Between Kuwait and Iraq 649
      c. Enforcing the Economic Sanctions 650
         Security Council Resolution 665 652
         Security Council Resolution 670 653
      d. Assessing the Economic Sanctions 656
      e. Events Leading to War 659
         Security Council Resolution 674 659
         Security Council Resolution 678 662
      f. The War 664
      g. After the Fighting Stopped 669
         (1) Initial Post–War Demands on Iraq 669
            Security Council Resolution 686 669
         (2) Security Council Resolution 687 670
            Security Council Resolution 687 670
         (3) The Relationship Between Chapters VI and VII 685
         (4) The Compensation Fund 686
      h. Evaluation 688
   4. Yugoslavia 689
      Security Council Resolution 713 689
      Security Council Resolution 757 692
      Security Council Resolution 787 696
   5. Somalia 699
      Security Council Resolution 733 700

Sec.		Page
3. Sanctions—Continued		
6. Libya		701
Security Council Resolution 731		702
Security Council Resolution 748		704
Case Concerning Questions of Interpretation and Application of the 1971 Montreal Convention Arising From the Aerial Incident at Lockerbie		707
7. Coordinating U.N. and Regional Action		708
Security Council Resolution 788		712
8. "Quasi–Enforcement Action": The Khmer Rouge		714
9. Controlling Weapons of Mass Destruction		715

Chapter 5. The Evolving United Nations: Peacekeeping, Peacemaking and Humanitarian Intervention — 716

1. Peacekeeping and Peacemaking — 716
    - A. Introduction — 716
        - The Blue Helmets: A Review of United Nations Peacekeeping — 716
        - Model Status–of–Forces Agreement for Peace-keeping Operations — 723
    - B. Early Pathbreaking Efforts: UNEF and ONUC — 731
        1. Creation and Terms of Reference — 731
            - a. UNEF I — 732
                - The Blue Helmets: A Review of United Nations Peacekeeping — 732
                - Second and Final Report of the Secretary–General on the Plan for an Emergency United Nations Force — 735
                - General Assembly Resolution on Principles and Functions of UNEF — 737
                - Report of the Secretary–General on the Implementation of Security Council Resolution 340 — 739
                - Aide–Mémoire on the Presence and Functioning of UNEF I — 741
            - b. ONUC — 745
                - The Blue Helmets: A Review of United Nations Peacekeeping — 745
        2. Legitimacy — 756
            - *Certain Expenses of the United Nations* — 757
        3. Difficulties and Controversies — 764
            - a. UNEF I — 764
                - Special Report of the Secretary–General on Removal of UNEF From Egyptian Territory — 765
                - T. Franck, Nation Against Nation — 769
            - b. ONUC — 773
                - Message From the Secretary–General to the President of the Republic of the Congo — 775
                - Security Council Resolution 169 — 778
                - T. Boudreau, Sheathing the Sword: The U.N. Secretary–General and the Prevention of International Conflict — 783

Sec.		Page
1.	Peacekeeping and Peacemaking—Continued	
	C. Strife in Yugoslavia	785
	Security Council Resolution 743	789
	Security Council Resolution 781	797
	D. Civil Strife in Liberia and in Somalia	799
	1. Liberia	799
	2. Somalia	802
	E. Peacekeeping and the Democratic Process: Nicaragua	803
	1. ONUCA	804
	The Blue Helmets: A Review of United Nations Peacekeeping	804
	Report of the Secretary-General on Establishing ONUCA	805
	Report of the Secretary-General on the Need for Expansion of Onuca's Mandate	810
	Statement by the Secretary-General on the Need for Further Expansion of ONUCA's Mandate	811
	2. ONUVEN	814
	First Report of ONUVEN to the Secretary-General	814
	Letter Transmitting Final Report of Onuven	818
	F. The Principle of Periodic and Genuine Elections	819
	Resolution on Enhancing the Effectiveness of the Principle of Periodic and Genuine Elections	824
	Resolution on Respect for National Sovereignty and Non-Interference in Electoral Processes	827
	G. Peacemaking, Mainly by the Secretary-General	830
	1. Fact-Finding and Early Warning	830
	Declaration on Fact-Finding by the United Nations in the Field of the Maintenance of International Peace and Security	834
	2. Good Offices	840
	V. Pechota, The Quiet Approach: A Study of the Good Offices Exercised by the United Nations Secretary-General in the Cause of Peace	841
	Franck, The Good Offices Function of the UN Secretary-General	842
	V. Pechota, The Quiet Approach: A Study of the Good Offices Exercised by the United Nations Secretary-General in the Cause of Peace	850
2.	Humanitarian Intervention	852
	A. Iraq, The Kurds and the Shiites	852
	Security Council Resolution 688	853
	B. The Evolving U.N. Role	857
	Report of the Secretary-General on the Work of the Organization	858
	Resolution on Strengthening the Coordination of Humanitarian Emergency Assistance of the United Nations	862
	C. Bosnia-Herzegovina	867
	Security Council Resolution 780	871
	Report of the Secretary-General on the Establishment of the Commission of Experts	872

Sec.		Page
2.	Humanitarian Intervention—Continued	
	D. Somalia	875
	Security Council Resolution 794	877
3.	Beyond Peacekeeping	881
	A. Peace Enforcement	881
	B. New Forms of Trusteeship	882
	C. Preventive Deployment	883
	An Agenda for Peace	883
	Report of the UNPROFOR Exploratory Mission to Macedonia	885
4.	Nonstates, The U.N. and International Personality	889

Chapter 6. Protecting Basic Human Rights in the United Nations and in Regional Organizations 891

Sec.		Page
1.	Introduction	891
2.	The United Nations	892
	A. Making Human Rights Law Through the Universal Declaration and the Covenants	892
	After 30 Years, an International Bill of Human Rights	898
	B. The Covenants and the United States	902
	United States Reservations, Understandings, Declarations and Proviso to the Covenant on Civil and Political Rights	902
	C. The Enforcement Procedures of the Covenants	908
	1. The Covenant on Economic, Social and Cultural Rights	908
	ECOSOC Resolution Establishing the Committee on Economic, Social and Cultural Rights	909
	Letter From the Argentine Chargé D'Affaires in Geneva	912
	Reply From the Chair of the Committee on Economic, Social and Cultural Rights	914
	General Comment Number 3	917
	2. The Covenant on Civil and Political Rights	921
	a. Inter-state Communications	922
	b. Individual Communications	923
	Human Rights Committee Summary of Some Procedural Issues Decided in 1991	925
	Kelly v. Jamaica	930
	Zwaan-de Vries v. The Netherlands	940
	Delgado Páez v. Colombia	946
	Measures to Monitor Compliance With the Committee's Views Under the First Optional Protocol	953
	c. The Reporting System	955
	Revised Guidelines for the Preparation of State Party Reports	955
	Concluding Observations on Reports by Some States Parties Submitted Under Article 40 of the Covenant	959
	Consensus Statement on General Comments Under Article 40(4)	965
	General Comment Number 19, Concerning Article 23	966

Sec.		Page
2.	The United Nations—Continued	
	D. Enforcement Procedures of the Commission on Human Rights and its Sub-Commission on Prevention of Discrimination	969
3.	The Inter-American System	975
	A. Introduction	975
	B. The American Declaration of the Rights and Duties of Man	978
	C. The Inter-American Commission on Human Rights and its Communications Procedure	981
	Case No. 10,031 (United States)	983
	D. The Inter-American Court of Human Rights	993
	1. Advisory Opinions	993
	Restrictions to the Death Penalty	995
	2. Contentious Cases	1007
	Velásquez Rodríguez Case	1007
	E. Changing the Rules Unilaterally	1029
4.	The European System	1030
	A. Introduction	1030
	P. Van Dijk & G. Van Hoof, Theory and Practice of the European Convention on Human Rights	1030
	The Council of Europe and the Protection of Human Rights	1034
	B. Application of the Convention by the European Commission of Human Rights	1039
	Berberich v. Federal Republic of Germany	1041
	X, Y and Z v. Austria	1049
	Chrysostomos v. Turkey	1053
	An v. Cyprus	1062
	C. The Role of the Committee of Ministers	1065
	D. The European Court of Human Rights	1068
	Oberschlick v. Austria	1070
	Ringeisen v. Austria	1081
	E. Overlap With Global Human Rights Conventions	1085
	Effects of the Various Human Rights Instruments	1085
	A.M. v. Denmark	1090
	F. Reform of the European System	1095
	Ryssdal, Forty Years of the European Convention on Human Rights	1095
	Report of the Committee of Experts on the Improvement of Human Rights Procedures	1097
INDEX		1101

Table of Cases

The principal cases are in bold type. Cases cited or discussed in the text are roman type. References are to pages. Cases cited in principal cases and within other quoted materials are not included.

A.M. v. Denmark, 1090
An v. Cyprus, 1062
Applicability of Article VI, Section 22, of the Convention on the Privileges and Immunities of the United Nations (The Mazilu Case), 86
Application of (see name of party)
Arlington, County of, United States v., 67

Banco Frances e Brasileiro S. A. v. John Doe, 440
Banco Nacional de Cuba v. Sabbatino, 442
Barkanic v. General Administration of Civil Aviation of The People's Republic of China, 443
Berberich v. Federal Republic of Germany, 1041
Berizzi Bros. Co. v. S.S. Pesaro, 29
Boos v. Barry, 61
Broadbent v. Organization of American States, 36

Callejo v. Bancomer, S.A., 436
Case Concerning Questions of Interpretation and Application of the 1971 Montreal Convention Arising From the Aerial Incident at Lockerbie, 707
Case No. 10,031 (United States), 983
Catlin v. United States, 466
Certain Expenses of the United Nations, 248, 483, 710, 757
Chew Heong v. United States, 111
Chinese Translators Case, The, 123
Chrysostomos v. Turkey, 1053
Committee of United States v. Reagan, 633
Competence of the General Assembly for the Admission of a State to the United Nations, 483
Concerned Jewish Youth v. McGuire, 60
County of (see name of county)

Day & Zimmermann, Inc. v. Challoner, 441
Delgado Paez v. Colombia, 946
Dellums v. United States Nuclear Regulatory Com'n, 632
De Meyer v. Etat Belge, Belgian Conseil d'Etat, 349
Diggs v. Shultz, 631, 632, 634
Donald v. Orfila, 75
Donnelly v. United Kingdom, 1048, 1051

Filartiga v. Pena–Irala, 349, 895
Foxworth v. Permanent Mission of Uganda to United Nations, 68

Harris v. Polskie Linie Lotnicze, 443

International Finance Corp. v. GDK Systems, Inc., 25
International Refugee Organization v. Republic S.S. Corp., 21
Iran, United States v., 892
Iran in Aerial Incident Case, Application of, 475
Ireland v. United Kingdom, 1068

Keeney v. Tamayo-Reyes, 938
Kelly v. Jamaica, 930
Klaxon Co. v. Stentor Electric Mfg. Co., 439, 443
Kuwait v. AMINOIL, 359

Lauro Lines S.R.L. v. Chasser, 466
Legal Consequences for States of the Continued Presence of South Africa in Namibia (South West Africa) Notwithstanding Security Council Resolution 276 (1970), 492

LIAMCO v. Libyan Arab Republic, 359
Liu v. Republic of China, 443
Lutcher S. A. Celulose E Papel v. Inter-American Development Bank, 39

Marbury v. Madison, 708
McCleskey v. Kemp, 987
Melekh, United States v., 76
Membership in the United Nations, 140
Mendaro v. World Bank, 43
Miller v. California, 1080
Ministry of Home Affairs v. Kemali, Italian Court of Cassation, 349
Missouri v. Holland, 906

New Jersey, State of v. State of Delaware, 336
New York Times Co. v. Sullivan, 1078
Nicaragua v. United States, 651, 855

OAS Resolution on the Exclusion of the Cuban Government, 617
Oberschlick v. Austria, 1070
Opinion of the ITU Legal Advisor, 610
Osborn v. United States Bank, 22
Owners' Services Ltd. v. Italy, 1068

Palestine Liberation Organization, United States v., 106
People v. _____ (see opposing party)
Pink, United States v., 441
Pope v. Illinois, 1080

Reparation for Injuries Suffered in the Service of the United Nations, 7
Ringeisen v. Austria, 1081
Roy, People v., 76

767 Third Ave. Associates v. Permanent Mission of Zaire to United Nations, 61
Siderman de Blake v. Republic of Argentina, 897
State of (see name of state)
Strickland v. Washington, 938

Topco Calasiatic v. Libyan Arab Republic, 357

UNESCO Resolution on Israel, 576
United States v. _____ (see opposing party)
U.N. Legal Counsel, Opinion on Rejection of Credentials, 594
U.N. Secretariat Summary of U.N. Credentials Practice Through 1973, 586
U.S. Department of State, Southern Rhodesia and the United Nations: The U.S. Position, 626

Velasquez Rodriguez Case, 1007
Verlinden B.V. v. Central Bank of Nigeria, 24

Weiner, People v., 77
Westchester County on Complaint of Donnelly v. Ranollo, 76
Whitney v. Robertson, 442
Witherspoon v. Illinois, 987
WMD Resolution Suspending South African Rights and Privileges, 605

X, Y and Z v. Austria, 1049

Zschernig v. Miller, 441
Zwaan-de Vries v. The Netherlands, 940

INTERNATIONAL ORGANIZATIONS IN THEIR LEGAL SETTING

Second Edition

*

Chapter 1

LEGAL STATUS OF INTERNATIONAL ORGANIZATIONS AND OF ASSOCIATED PERSONS AND PREMISES

SECTION 1. INTRODUCTION
EL-ERIAN, FIRST REPORT ON RELATIONS BETWEEN STATES AND INTER-GOVERNMENTAL ORGANIZATIONS

Report to the International Law Commission by its Special Rapporteur, 1963.
[1963] 2 Y.B. Int'l L. Comm'n 159, 162–64.

Institutional co-operative plans and experiences between politically independent entities go far back in history, at least to ancient Greece. But the modern concept of international organization is the outcome of a century and a half of evolution in the co-operative practice of States in response to a rapidly changing world.

* * *

The evolution of co-operative forms of State practice took two parallel paths:

(1) An evolution from the stage of *ad hoc* temporary conferences which are convened for a specific purpose and which come to an end once the subject-matter is agreed upon and embodied in an international agreement, to the stage of permanent international organizations with organs that function permanently and meet periodically.

(2) An evolution from the level of purely administrative unions, each specializing in one kind of international activity of a basically technical character, to that of general international organizations whose scope of activities, though predominantly political, extends to all aspects of international co-operation, i.e., economic, social, technical, etc.

Two immediate tributary sources of present-day international organizations can be traced:

1. THE CONFERENCE SYSTEM

For several centuries, European States used to call an international conference in the aftermath of a war to reach an agreement on territorial changes and adjustments which resulted from it and to prepare a peace treaty sanctioning the new situation.

Some such peace conferences constitute landmarks in the history of international law, such as those of Westphalia (1648) and Utrecht (1713). But in the nineteenth century their importance acquired new dimensions and they extended their scope beyond that of peace settlements.

(a) *The Congress of Vienna and the Concert of Europe systems:* The Vienna settlement of 1815 is particularly relevant to international organization, and in many ways. The preceding conferences had aimed at establishing peace, but the Vienna Conference aimed, in addition, at the maintenance of peace within the new European system it had established.

> "It was considered by its leading participants as the forerunner of a series of regular consultations among the great powers which would serve as board meetings for the European community of nations." [6]

This scheme did not function except for the period from 1815 to 1822, during which four conferences took place. These revealed enough differences between the policies of the great powers to render such a system unworkable. But the technique of diplomacy by conference, outside the narrow case of peace settlements, whenever the European system was endangered, established itself as a basic feature of the century extending from 1815 to 1914. It is sufficient to mention a few examples such as the Paris Conference of 1856, the London Conferences of 1871 and 1912–13, the Berlin Congresses of 1878 and 1884–85, and the (Algeciras) Conference of 1906, to realize the great importance of this new technique.

The Congress of Vienna system was accompanied by what became known as the Concert of Europe. It first appeared in the Treaty of Chaumont of 1814, in which the parties undertook to act *"dans un parfait concert"*. Then it merged into the Vienna system and survived it after 1822. It was neither a formal nor an institutional arrangement. But it operated according to certain principles, the most important of which was the special status of the great powers who assumed the position of "self-appointed guardians of the European community and executive directors of its affairs". They legislated on behalf of this community, basically to the small Powers, and admitted nations to this "exclusive club". Thus they recognized the independence of Greece

---

6. Inis Claude, Jr., Swords into Plowshares, The Problems and Progress of International Organizations, p. 23 (2nd ed. rev.) (New York, 1959).

and Belgium in 1830 and declared in the Treaty of Paris 1856 that the Sublime Porte (of the Ottoman Empire) was admitted "à *participer aux avantages du droit public et du concert européen* ".

The political conference system which prevailed in nineteenth century European politics was a step forward towards the stage of international organization, but did not reach it. It did not develop "permanently functioning institutions". Conferences were sporadic rather than periodic. They were "the medicine of Europe rather than its daily bread". But they increased the awareness of States of the need for new means of international co-operation and of the possibilities of multilateral or quasi-parliamentary diplomacy.

(b) *Multilateral Treaties:* Another innovation of the Congress of Vienna was the technique of multilateral treaty. Up to that time, this technique was unknown. When a peace settlement included several States, the end result was a series of bilateral treaties between different pairs of parties. This was the case in the Peace of Westphalia. It was also the case of the Paris Treaty of 30 May 1814 which was composed of seven separate treaties, each between France and an allied Power, although they were identical in their content. Thus, even when the content was identical, these treaties were legally separate.

The Final Act of the Congress of Vienna was, for the first time, signed by all of the parties to the Congress, and bound all the other bilateral treaties issuing from it into "one common transaction". The evolution of the multilateral treaty culminated in the Paris Treaty of 1856 which took the initial form of a multilateral treaty without passing through the bilateral treaties stage.

The multilateral treaty was soon extended in scope beyond the collective settlement into the legislative field. Law-making treaties (*traités-lois*) soon made their appearance, also within the framework of international conferences. They included general rules of international law, thus asserting their role as an important source of that law (e.g. the appendix to the Final Act of the Congress of Vienna concerning the rank of diplomatic agents). They also extended beyond the strictly narrow traditional subjects of international law to regulate certain efforts at international co-operation in the humanitarian and social fields such as the suppression of the slave trade, which was dealt with in several multilateral conventions from the Final Act of the Congress of Vienna to the General Act of the Anti–Slavery Conference at Brussels in 1890.

The relevance of multilateral treaties to international organizations is so obvious as not to need to be mentioned. Suffice it to say that they provided the means for their creation.

(c) *The Hague Peace Conferences:* The 19th century witnessed an ascending trend in favour of arbitration. This trend began with the Jay Treaty of 1794 and continued throughout the 19th century to culminate in the two Hague International Peace Conferences of 1899 and 1907.

These two Conferences, though fitting in the conference patterns described above, deserve some attention because of their special contribution to the concept of international organization. The contribution lies in two of their features. The first is the scope of international activities envisaged by the regulations ensuing from them. They used the technique of multilateral conventions to introduce more adequate regulations of the basic problems of international relations, namely those of peace and war. They thus anticipated the major field of activity of the general international organizations which succeeded them. While they did not establish compulsory arbitration, they provided States with a standing arbitration machinery should they decide to use one; while they did not prohibit war, they tried to humanize it and limit its damage. The conventions which ensued exemplify international legislation as a principal source of international law better than most. They were "divorced from the immediate problems raised by particular wars or disputes" and were "concerned with international problems in abstract" and with institution building. * * *

The second element in the contribution of the Hague Conferences to the development of international organization is their orientation towards universality. While the first Conference was attended by only twenty-six States, mainly European, the second Conference was attended by forty-four States including most of the Latin–American republics, in addition to some Asian Powers.

A third potential contribution might be added. The Conferences of 1899 and 1907 showed the possibility of periodic meetings.

* * *

(d) *The Pan–American System:* The conference system was also resorted to on a regional level in the Pan–American system. In 1826, a conference of American Republics was held in Panama under the influence of Bolivar, but did not yield tangible results. The Pan-American system took shape, however, since the Washington Conference of 1889. Since then, several conferences have been held at somewhat regular intervals, usually of five years, culminating in the establishment of the Organization of American States in 1948. * * *

The periodic character of these conferences contributed in several ways to the techniques of international organization:

1. The conferences were not convened at the initiative of any one State, but the time and place of each were decided by the previous one.

2. The agenda of each conference was prepared by the governing body of the standing administrative organ, the Pan-American Union.

3. A greater possibility existed to undertake preparatory work before each conference than in the case of *ad hoc* conferences.

4. The periodic character made possible the development of more elaborate and formal procedural arrangements.

2. INTERNATIONAL ADMINISTRATIVE UNIONS

The second tributary source of present-day international organizations is the phenomenon of international administrative unions which appeared in the 19th century, especially in its second half. These were permanent agencies dealing with non-political technical international activities. They were called forth by the increasing complexity and interaction of technical, economic, social and cultural activities at the international level.

(a) *International river commissions:* The Final Act of the Congress of Vienna proclaimed in articles 108–117 the principle of freedom of navigation on international rivers (rivers separating or traversing several States) for all States. This proclamation which responded to a felt need arising from the intensification of commercial and economic activities led to the appearance of a new type of international machinery in the form of river commissions. Thus, the Convention of Mannheim of 1868 between the riparian States of the Rhine created the Central Commission for the Navigation of the Rhine, which was composed of one representative of each riparian State. The function of the Commission was to control the observance of the rules of the convention, its decisions were taken by unanimity and its powers were limited to recommending measures to riparian States for incorporation into their municipal law. Moreover, it had jurisdiction over certain categories of legal disputes concerning individuals. The European Danube Commission created by the Peace Treaty of Paris 1856 was given extended powers both as to the control and policing of navigation and as to the public works it could undertake to secure the navigability of the Danube estuaries.

(b) *Other administrative unions:* A host of other administrative unions in many fields appeared as need arose. Thus, the Universal Telegraphic Union was established in 1865, and the International Bureau of Telegraphic Administration was established and located at Berne as its central organ. The General Postal Union was established in 1874, also with its Bureau in Berne. (The International Bureau of Industrial Property in 1883 and of Literary Property in 1886; the International Convention on Railway Freight Traffic in 1890; the International Radio Telegraphic Convention in 1906; the Convention on the Creation of an International Office of Public Health in 1907; etc.)

Such unions had, in general, two organs:

1. Periodical conferences or meetings of the representatives of member States, whose decisions required usually the unanimity of votes;

2. A permanent secretariat, a Bureau, which assumed the administrative tasks.

These unions contributed to the concept of international organization a most important factor, namely the institutional element. Their permanent character which was secured through their standing organ, the Bureau, provided the threshold between the technique of the conference and that of the organization. Moreover, in some of them, the rules of unanimity and "no treaty obligation without ratification" were being pushed aside. Finally, they contributed to the awareness of States "of the potentialities of international organizations as a means of furthering an interest common to numerous States without detriment to that of any concerned".

POST–WORLD WAR I

The Versailles Treaty at the end of World War I is often regarded as the progenitor of the modern "universal" international organization. From it sprang the League of Nations and the International Labor Organization. The League, of course, was the forerunner of the United Nations. It faltered early in its history when the United States failed to join, and ultimately disintegrated with the onset of World War II. The ILO, on the other hand, became an effective instrument for the enhancement of labor conditions internationally, serving to demonstrate that organizations dealing with specialized areas of concern could develop considerable expertise and influence. The idea of specialized agencies thus became an integral part of the United Nations system and was written into the U.N. Charter, which was signed in 1945 at the United Nations Conference on International Organization in San Francisco. Specialized agencies are specifically contemplated in articles 57 to 59 of the Charter.

THE ISSUES REGARDING STATUS

The present chapter is concerned with the basic legal attributes of modern intergovernmental organizations as entities, and of persons who either represent political entities participating in such organizations or who represent the organizations directly. Broadly formulated, a number of issues arise: Do intergovernmental organizations occupy the same status in international law as individual nation-states? If not, what is their status, and what practical consequences flow from it? To what extent are such organizations recognized as having legal capacity in the domestic law of member states? What special privileges and immunities do they, or those persons associated with them enjoy in international and domestic law? How do any special privileges enjoyed by those persons differ from traditional privileges of diplomats accredited to a receiving state?

SECTION 2. INTERNATIONAL LEGAL CAPACITY

A. "INTERNATIONAL PERSONALITY"

Clearly, nation-states have "international personality" in the sense that they are recognized as subjects of international law, i.e. they have rights and duties directly supplied by international law. This is to be distinguished from rights and duties supplied by the domestic law of any given state, which may exist simultaneously (and sometimes in conflict) with rights and duties under international law. Thus, for example, a state may have an international duty supplied by a treaty to which it is a party, but the provisions of the treaty might have to be implemented by legislation enacted by the national legislature before they have the force of domestic law within the state. (In the United States, such treaty provisions are called non-self-executing; some treaty provisions do have the force of federal law and are called self-executing.) Our concern in this Section is strictly with the international dimension. We shall turn to some of the domestic law issues in the following two sections.

REPARATION FOR INJURIES SUFFERED IN THE SERVICE OF THE UNITED NATIONS
International Court of Justice, Advisory Opinion, 1949.
[1949] I.C.J. 174.

[Count Bernadotte, a Swedish national acting as a United Nations mediator in the Middle East, had been killed while performing his U.N. duties in Palestine. Traditionally, the state of a person's nationality has the right under international law to assert an international claim for damages when another state fails to live up to certain minimum standards for his or her safety. The right of an international organization to assert such a claim had never been tested. Consequently the General Assembly, acting under U.N. Charter *article 96*, requested an advisory opinion from the International Court of Justice on the following question (and one other, which is irrelevant here):

> In the event of an agent of the United Nations in the performance of his duties suffering injury in circumstances involving the responsibility of a State, has the United Nations, as an Organization, the capacity to bring an international claim against the responsible *de jure* or *de facto* government with a view to obtaining the reparation due in respect of the damage caused (a) to the United Nations, (b) to the victim or to persons entitled through him?

The Court said:]

It will be useful to make the following preliminary observations:

(*a*) The Organization of the United Nations will be referred to usually, but not invariably, as "the Organization".

* * *

(d) As this question assumes an injury suffered in such circumstances as to involve a State's responsibility, it must be supposed, for the purpose of this Opinion, that the damage results from a failure by the State to perform obligations of which the purpose is to protect the agents of the Organization in the performance of their duties.

(e) The position of a defendant State which is not a member of the Organization is dealt with later, and for the present the Court will assume that the defendant State is a Member of the Organization.

* * *

Competence to bring an international claim is, for those possessing it, the capacity to resort to the customary methods recognized by international law for the establishment, the presentation and the settlement of claims. Among these methods may be mentioned protest, request for an enquiry, negotiation, and request for submission to an arbitral tribunal or to the Court in so far as this may be authorized by the Statute.

* * *

But, in the international sphere, has the Organization such a nature as involves the capacity to bring an international claim? In order to answer this question, the Court must first enquire whether the Charter has given the Organization such a position that it possesses, in regard to its Members, rights which it is entitled to ask them to respect. In other words, does the Organization possess international personality? This is no doubt a doctrinal expression, which has sometimes given rise to controversy. But it will be used here to mean that if the Organization is recognized as having that personality, it is an entity capable of availing itself of obligations incumbent upon its Members.

To answer this question, which is not settled by the actual terms of the Charter, we must consider what characteristics it was intended thereby to give to the Organization.

The subjects of law in any legal system are not necessarily identical in their nature or in the extent of their rights, and their nature depends upon the needs of the community. Throughout its history, the development of international law has been influenced by the requirements of international life, and the progressive increase in the collective activities of States has already given rise to instances of action upon the international plane by certain entities which are not States. This development culminated in the establishment in June 1945 of an international organization whose purposes and principles are specified in the Charter of the United Nations. But to achieve these ends the attribution of international personality is indispensable.

The Charter has not been content to make the Organization created by it merely a centre "for harmonizing the actions of nations in the attainment of these common ends" (Article 1, para. 4). It has equipped that centre with organs, and has given it special tasks. It has defined the position of the Members in relation to the Organization by requiring them to give it every assistance in any action undertaken by it (Article 2, para. 5), and to accept and carry out the decisions of the Security Council; by authorizing the General Assembly to make recommendations to the Members; by giving the Organization legal capacity and privileges and immunities in the territory of each of its Members; and by providing for the conclusion of agreements between the Organization and its Members. Practice—in particular the conclusion of conventions to which the Organization is a party—has confirmed this character of the Organization, which occupies a position in certain respects in detachment from its Members, and which is under a duty to remind them, if need be, of certain obligations. It must be added that the Organization is a political body, charged with political tasks of an important character, and covering a wide field namely, the maintenance of international peace and security, the development of friendly relations among nations, and the achievement of international cooperation in the solution of problems of an economic, social, cultural or humanitarian character (Article 1); and in dealing with its Members it employs political means. The "Convention on the Privileges and Immunities of the United Nations" of 1946 creates rights and duties between each of the signatories and the Organization (see, in particular, Section 35). It is difficult to see how such a convention could operate except upon the international plane and as between parties possessing international personality.

In the opinion of the Court, the Organization was intended to exercise and enjoy, and is in fact exercising and enjoying, functions and rights which can only be explained on the basis of the possession of a large measure of international personality and the capacity to operate upon an international plane. It is at present the supreme type of international organization, and it could not carry out the intentions of its founders if it was devoid of international personality. It must be acknowledged that its Members, by entrusting certain functions to it, with the attendant duties and responsibilities, have clothed it with the competence required to enable those functions to be effectively discharged.

Accordingly, the Court has come to the conclusion that the Organization is an international person. That is not the same thing as saying that it is a State, which it certainly is not, or that its legal personality and rights and duties are the same as those of a State. Still less is it the same thing as saying that it is "a super-State", whatever that expression may mean. It does not even imply that all its rights and duties must be upon the international plane, any more than all the rights and duties of a State must be upon that plane. What it does mean is that it is a subject of international law and capable of possessing international rights and duties, and that it has capacity to maintain its rights by bringing international claims.

The next question is whether the sum of the international rights of the Organization comprises the right to bring the kind of international claim described in the Request for this Opinion. That is a claim against a State to obtain reparation in respect of the damage caused by the injury of an agent of the Organization in the course of the performance of his duties. Whereas a State possesses the totality of international rights and duties recognized by international law, the rights and duties of an entity such as the Organization must depend upon its purposes and functions as specified or implied in its constituent documents and developed in practice. The functions of the Organization are of such a character that they could not be effectively discharged if they involved the concurrent action, on the international plane, of fifty-eight or more Foreign Offices, and the Court concludes that the Members have endowed the Organization with capacity to bring international claims when necessitated by the discharge of its functions.

* * *

It cannot be doubted that the Organization has the capacity to bring an international claim against one of its Members which has caused injury to it by a breach of its international obligations towards it. The damage specified in Question I (a) means exclusively damage caused to the interests of the Organization itself, to its administrative machine, to its property and assets, and to the interests of which it is the guardian. It is clear that the Organization has the capacity to bring a claim for this damage. As the claim is based on the breach of an international obligation on the part of the Member held responsible by the Organization, the Member cannot contend that this obligation is governed by municipal law, and the Organization is justified in giving its claim the character of an international claim.

When the Organization has sustained damage resulting from a breach by a Member of its international obligations, it is impossible to see how it can obtain reparation unless it possesses capacity to bring an international claim. It cannot be supposed that in such an event all the Members of the Organization, save the defendant State, must combine to bring a claim against the defendant for the damage suffered by the Organization.

[The Court then turned to the question whether the Organization could bring a claim against a member state for the damage caused to the victim or to persons entitled through him. After some general discussion it continued:]

The Court is here faced with a new situation. The questions to which it gives rise can only be solved by realizing that the situation is dominated by the provisions of the Charter considered in the light of the principles of international law.

The question lies within the limits already established; that is to say it presupposes that the injury for which the reparation is demanded arises from a breach of an obligation designed to help an agent of the Organization in the performance of his duties. It is not a case in which the wrongful act or omission would merely constitute a breach of the general obligations of a State concerning the position of aliens; claims made under this head would be within the competence of the national State and not, as a general rule, within that of the Organization.

The Charter does not expressly confer upon the Organization the capacity to include, in its claim for reparation, damage caused to the victim or to persons entitled through him. The Court must therefore begin by enquiring whether the provisions of the Charter concerning the functions of the Organization, and the part played by its agents in the performance of those functions, imply for the Organization power to afford its agents the limited protection that would consist in the bringing of a claim on their behalf for reparation for damage suffered in such circumstances. Under international law, the Organization must be deemed to have those powers which, though not expressly provided in the Charter, are conferred upon it by necessary implication as being essential to the performance of its duties.

* * *

Having regard to its purposes and functions already referred to, the Organization may find it necessary, and has in fact found it necessary, to entrust its agents with important missions to be performed in disturbed parts of the world. Many missions, from their very nature, involve the agents in unusual dangers to which ordinary persons are not exposed. For the same reason, the injuries suffered by its agents in these circumstances will sometimes have occurred in such a manner that their national State would not be justified in bringing a claim for reparation on the ground of diplomatic protection, or, at any rate, would not feel disposed to do so. Both to ensure the efficient and independent performance of these missions and to afford effective support to its agents, the Organization must provide them with adequate protection.

* * *

For this purpose, the Members of the Organization have entered into certain undertakings, some of which are in the Charter and others in complementary agreements. The content of these undertakings need not be described here; but the Court must stress the importance of the duty to render to the Organization "every assistance" which is accepted by the Members in Article 2, paragraph 5, of the Charter. It must be noted that the effective working of the Organization—the accomplishment of its task, and the independence and effectiveness of the work of its agents—require that these undertakings should be strictly observed. For that purpose, it is necessary that, when an infringement occurs, the Organization should be able to call upon the responsible State to remedy its default, and, in particular, to obtain from the State reparation for the damage that the default may have caused to its agent.

In order that the agent may perform his duties satisfactorily, he must feel that this protection is assured to him by the Organization, and that he may count on it. To ensure the independence of the agent, and, consequently, the independent action of the Organization itself, it is essential that in performing his duties he need not have to rely on any other protection than that of the Organization (save of course for the more direct and immediate protection due from the State in whose territory he may be). In particular, he should not have to rely on the protection of his own State. If he had to rely on that State, his independence might well be compromised, contrary to the principle applied by Article 100 of the Charter. And lastly, it is essential that—whether the agent belongs to a powerful or to a weak State; to one more affected or less affected by the complications of international life; to one in sympathy or not in sympathy with the mission of the agent—he should know that in the performance of his duties he is under the protection of the Organization.

Upon examination of the character of the functions entrusted to the Organization and of the nature of the missions of its agents, it becomes clear that the capacity of the Organization to exercise a measure of functional protection of its agents arises by necessary intendment out of the Charter.

* * *

Having regard to the foregoing considerations, and to the undeniable right of the Organization to demand that its Members shall fulfil the obligations entered into by them in the interest of the good working of the Organization, the Court is of the opinion that, in the case of a breach of these obligations, the Organization has the capacity to claim adequate reparation, and that in assessing this reparation it is authorized to include the damage suffered by the victim or by persons entitled through him.

The question remains whether the Organization has "the capacity to bring an international claim against the responsible *de jure* or *de facto* government with a view to obtaining the reparation due in respect of the damage caused (a) to the United Nations, (b) to the victim or to persons entitled through him" when the defendant State is not a member of the Organization.

In considering this aspect of Question I (a) and (b), it is necessary to keep in mind the reasons which have led the Court to give an affirmative answer to it when the defendant State is a Member of the Organization. It has now been established that the Organization has capacity to bring claims on the international plane, and that it possesses a right of functional protection in respect of its agents. Here again the Court is authorized to assume that the damage suffered involves the responsibility of a State, and it is not called upon to express an opinion upon the various ways in which that responsibility might be engaged. Accordingly the question is whether the Organization has capacity to bring a claim against the defendant State to recover reparation in respect of that damage or whether, on the contrary, the defendant State, not being a member, is justified in raising the objection that the Organization lacks the capacity to bring an international claim. On this point, the Court's opinion is that fifty States, representing the vast majority of the members of the international community, had the power, in conformity with international law, to bring into being an entity possessing objective international personality, and not merely personality recognized by them alone, together with capacity to bring international claims.

Accordingly, the Court arrives at the conclusion that an affirmative answer should be given to Question I (a) and (b) whether or not the defendant State is a Member of the United Nations.

[The ruling on the capacity of the United Nations to bring a claim for its own damages against a member or nonmember state was unanimous. The ruling on the capacity to claim in respect of the agent's personal damages was by eleven votes to four.]

THE NATURE OF INTERNATIONAL PERSONALITY

What was the significance of deciding that the U.N. has international personality? Could an international organization assert an international claim without it?

What is the key to finding international personality? A provision in the constituent instrument saying the organization has it? The existence of organs with powers of their own? The extent to which the organization is political in nature?

Why didn't the Court in the Reparations Case simply hold that the claims could be asserted once it found that the U.N. has international personality? What else was required for a claim against (a) a member state; (b) a nonmember state?

Was the Court's reasoning convincing regarding the capacity to assert claims on behalf of agents of the Organization?

Can the reasoning in the Reparations Case be applied to any international organization other than the United Nations? In particular, could the doctrine of implied powers, based on functional necessity, apply to other organizations?

The International Law Commission is a U.N. body established by the General Assembly pursuant to *article 13(1)(a)* of the Charter. It is composed of 34 international lawyers charged with making proposals for the codification and progressive development of international law.[a] As of mid-1992, it was (slowly) proceeding with a project on defining the relations between states and international organizations. The Commission's Special Rapporteur, Leonardo Díaz-González, had pro-

a. See I. Sinclair, The International Law Commission (1987).

posed several draft articles of what would ultimately be either a declaration of rights and obligations or a multilateral treaty.

Draft article 5 said in part, "International organizations shall enjoy legal personality under international law * * *." It did not define what legal personality means under international law, but draft article 6 recognized that an international organization may have the capacity to conclude treaties, as determined "by the relevant rules of that organization and by international law."[b]

B. TREATY–MAKING CAPACITY

Treaty-making capacity is an important aspect of international personality. We will consider whether one global body—the International Atomic Energy Agency (IAEA)—and one regional body—the Organization of American States (OAS)—have it, and if so, what its scope is in those bodies.

One way in which the IAEA attempts to fulfill the broad objective of peaceful development of atomic energy is through a nuclear safeguard system designed, among other things, to try to ensure that plutonium produced by power-generating nuclear reactors is not extracted from spent reactor fuel rods and used for nuclear explosives. A state is required to accept IAEA safeguards for any project established with the Agency's assistance. Non-nuclear-weapon states that are parties to the Treaty on Non–Proliferation of Nuclear Weapons[a] are obligated to enter into safeguard agreements with the IAEA, and nuclear-material-exporting states that are parties to the Non–Proliferation Treaty have undertaken to require recipient states (including nonparties) to accept IAEA safeguards for the materials supplied.[b] All safeguards are administered pursuant to agreements between the IAEA and recipient states.

The safeguard system involves four steps. IAEA technicians review the design of a nuclear plant to be safeguarded, to ascertain that it permits effective control; the state is required to keep detailed records of plant operations and an inventory of nuclear material; the government makes periodic reports to IAEA; and the Agency makes on-site inspections.[c]

Assume that the IAEA is now considering whether to enter into a safeguard agreement with the Organization of American States, in which the IAEA would undertake to strengthen its usual safeguard procedures in Latin America in ways to be spelled out in the agreement, and would report regularly to the OAS on its inspections in Latin American countries. The IAEA Legal Adviser has been asked whether the Agency has the capacity under international law to enter into an

b. U.N. Doc. A/CN.4/424, at 9 (1989).
a. July 1, 1968, 21 U.S.T. 483, T.I.A.S. 6839, 729 U.N.T.S. 161.

b. See 14 Int'l Legal Materials 543 (1975).
c. See generally M. Shaker, The Nuclear Non-proliferation Treaty (3 vols. 1980).

agreement of that general type, and whether it and the OAS can, under their respective constituent instruments, enter into the specific agreement proposed. In addition, she has been asked what body of rules will govern possible excuses for nonperformance, if the agreement is concluded.

The International Law Commission has drafted two comprehensive multilateral codes on the law of treaties. One, the 1969 Vienna Convention on the Law of Treaties,[d] applies on its face only to treaties between states. The scope of the other is apparent from its title: the 1986 Vienna Convention on the Law of Treaties Between States and International Organizations or Between International Organizations.[e]

Article 6 of the 1986 Vienna Convention says, "The capacity of an international organization to conclude treaties is governed by the rules of that organization." Article 6 was a compromise between differing approaches espoused by blocs of states during the drafting process.[f] One side argued that the capacity of an international organization to conclude treaties exists as a matter of customary international law, though the authority to conclude any given treaties could be denied by the rules of the particular organization. The other side argued that an organization's capacity depended solely on its own rules.

Which side prevailed? See 1986 Vienna Convention *article 2, paragraphs 1(j) and 2*. Are the two approaches likely to lead to different results in many cases?

Some commentators, assessing the capacity of an international organization to conclude treaties, have stressed the international personality of the organization, the functional necessity for a given organization to conclude treaties if it is to perform its tasks, or the familiar constitutional doctrine of implied powers.[g] Are these considerations ruled out by the 1986 Vienna Convention?

Do the IAEA and the OAS have international personality under the tests of the U.N. Reparations Case?

If so, do they have authority to enter into the treaty we have contemplated—a binding agreement with each other on nuclear safeguards in Latin America?

Specifically, are the provisions of IAEA Statute *article III.A.5, III.B.1* and/or *III.D* grants of authority to the Agency to enter into

---

d. May 23, 1969, 1155 U.N.T.S. 331; entered into force January 27, 1980, when the 35th state deposited its ratification or accession. Not in force for the United States when this was written, but treated for most purposes as a reflection of customary international law.

e. March 21, 1986, U.N.Doc. A/CONF. 129/15 (1986), 25 Int'l Legal Materials 543 (1986); not in force when this was written.

f. See do Nascimento e Silva, The 1986 Vienna Convention and the Treaty-Making Power of International Organizations, 29 German Y.B.Int'l L. 68, 74–75 (1986).

g. See Hartmann, The Capacity of International Organizations to Conclude Treaties, in Agreements of International Organizations and the Vienna Convention on the Law of Treaties 127 (K. Zemanek ed. 1971).

agreements with other international organizations? Does the combination of *articles V.E.7* and *XVI.A* authorize a safeguard agreement with an organization such as the OAS? Does *article XII.A.6*?

On the OAS side, is the IAEA the type of organization contemplated by OAS Charter *articles 53(c), 53(d), 90(d)* or *117(h)*? Is an agreement on nuclear safeguards contemplated by any of those articles? What is the effect of *article 1, second paragraph*?

If these IAEA and OAS provisions leave room for doubt, does the doctrine of implied powers come to the rescue? Functional necessity?

How significant is it that the IAEA has in fact concluded general cooperation agreements with at least three regional organizations or organs thereof, one of which involves the OAS? The agreement involving the OAS provides for consultations on matters of common interest between the IAEA and the Inter-American Nuclear Energy Commission (an organ of the OAS). It was entered into directly with the Commission, which was treated as having legal personality of its own.[h]

A related question can arise concerning the means by which an organization is authorized to enter into an agreement. The question is whether someone in the secretariat can bind the organization simply by signing the agreement, or whether some form of ratification within the organization is required. Usually that question is resolved at the pre-signing stage, with an opinion from the organization's legal adviser if there is some doubt under the constituent instrument as to the proper method. It could arise later, however, if an organization asserts after an agreement has been concluded that the official who entered into it on its behalf had no authority to do so. That is not a frequent assertion, but neither is it an inconceivable one when an agreement on hindsight seems improvidently made and the organization would like to find a way out of it.

As the IAEA Legal Adviser, what would you tell the IAEA Director General regarding his authority to enter into the proposed safeguard agreement with the OAS? Consider IAEA Statute *articles V.E.7* and *XVI.A*, and the following excerpts—one from a book by a former IAEA Legal Adviser and the other from a memorandum by the U.N. Office of Legal Affairs.

[h] See P. Szasz, The Law and Practices of the International Atomic Energy Agency 307 (1970); C. Fenwick, The Organization of American States 538 (1963). The agreement appears in 396 U.N.T.S. 285.

P. SZASZ, THE LAW AND PRACTICES OF THE INTERNATIONAL ATOMIC ENERGY AGENCY
909 (1970).*

Most Agency agreements are concluded by authority of the Board, which derives its power from the general grant in Statute Article VI.F or under specific ones in Articles XIII and XV.C. The Board frequently delegates to the Director General the right to conclude certain agreements after it has approved them in principle, or even to enter into certain categories of agreements without specific approval.

All relationship agreements with international organizations require, pursuant to Statute Articles V.E.7 and XVI.A, the approval of the General Conference.

* * *

The Statute does not specifically grant to the Director General any function in connection with the conclusion of agreements, other than those relating to privileges and immunities. In practice, however, all agreements are concluded on behalf of the Agency by the Director General or his representative, except for those relationship agreements that come into force automatically on approval by the principal legislative organs of two organizations. The Director General's authority is derived by delegation from the Board, which is sometimes direct and explicit, sometimes implied (by the approval of a general course of action proposed by the Director General or by the tolerance of a known and established practice) and sometimes set forth in another agreement (e.g., the Director General's authority to conclude administrative arrangements for implementing relationship agreements is explicitly recited in these agreements).

MEMORANDUM, U.N. OFFICE OF LEGAL AFFAIRS
April 27, 1981.
1981 U.N. Juridical Y.B. 149.

* * *

The question whether a formal agreement on co-operation can be concluded between the United Nations Secretariat and intergovernmental organizations has been considered on several occasions and for legal and other considerations a negative reply was given in nearly every case. As a matter of general policy it was usually decided not to conclude such formal agreements without express authorization from the General Assembly or other competent deliberative organs. Hence, except in the case of an agreement on co-operation between the Secretariats of ECA and the OAU, there are no precedents where the United Nations formally concluded general agreements on co-operation with intergovernmental organizations such as OAU, OAS and the League of Arab States. In light of this policy and since there is no compelling legal reason to the contrary, we recommend that, unless the appropri-

---

* Reprinted by permission of the International Atomic Energy Agency.

ate authority specifically authorizes the formal conclusion of agreements on co-operation, these relationships be based on an informal memorandum of understanding and not on a formal agreement.

AUTHORITY WITHIN THE IAEA

Would the proposed agreement be a "relationship agreement"? Szasz refers to the agreements entered into by the IAEA with the U.N. and with seven of its specialized agencies as relationship agreements, and refers to the existing consultation agreement with the [OAS] Inter-American Nuclear Energy Commission as a "similar cooperation agreement."[i] The relationship agreements with the U.N. and with the specialized agencies provide for continuing coordination of activities on matters of mutual interest, including representation without vote by one organization at meetings of the other, cooperation between secretariats, exchange of pertinent information regarding proposed activities of interest to the other, and so forth.[j]

Suppose the Director General decides that he or his deputy could sign the agreement in such a way as to bind the IAEA without explicit approval from any other IAEA organ. A Deputy Director General does so, without any written delegation of authority. Could the IAEA General Conference later denounce the agreement on the ground that it was not bound by her signature? Consider 1986 Vienna Convention *articles 2(1)(c), 7(3), 8 and 46.*

Finally, note an important distinction between settling a treaty dispute involving international organizations and a similar dispute involving states. International organizations cannot turn to the International Court of Justice to adjudicate their differences in contentious proceedings. (We shall leave aside for the present the authority of the United Nations and its specialized agencies to obtain advisory opinions from the ICJ pursuant to U.N. Charter article 96.) Article 34(1) of the Court's Statute provides that "Only states may be parties in [contentious] cases before the Court." A leading authority on the work of the Court says the difficulty with broadening article 34(1) to include international organizations is that "the nature of the Organizations concerned and the relationships created by them are too different, and too unforeseeable, to be met by the simple formula which would place States and organizations of States on the same footing."[k] Is this a serious difficulty? Could it be overcome?

---

i. P. Szasz, supra, at 897.

j. See generally P. Szasz, supra, at 271–73, 290–91.

k. S. Rosenne, The Law and Practice of the International Court 290 (2d rev. ed. 1985).

Would it be worthwhile to try to amend the ICJ Statute to permit adjudication of disputes to which an international organization is a party?

SECTION 3. THE STATUS OF INTERNATIONAL ORGANIZATIONS IN THE DOMESTIC LAW OF THE UNITED STATES

A. LEGAL CAPACITY AND FEDERAL JURISDICTION

The presence or absence of "international personality" or treaty-making capacity under international law does not necessarily determine the legal capacity of an international organization under the domestic law of member or non-member states. Rather, one must look to the provisions of the domestic law of the state in question, including the domestic legislative effect of international agreements to which it is a party.

Since the constituent instruments of international organizations are normally in the form of international agreements (i.e. treaties in the international sense), those instruments may well have domestic legislative effect under the legal systems of the member states, as well as international significance. In the United States, this is so if the international agreement is of a form and type which can have legislative effect under the Constitution and which is intended to have that effect without further action by Congress. If such a self-executing international agreement serving as the constituent instrument sets forth the capacity of the international organization within its member states, or grants the organization certain privileges and immunities, that would establish the domestic (federal) law on the subject in the United States if it is a member. The result would be the same if the capacity, or privileges and immunities, were set forth in a self-executing agreement wholly apart from the constituent instrument of the organization, if the United States is a party to the agreement. In addition, Congress may legislate on the subject, supplementing the constituent instrument of an international organization, by specifying (for example) the privileges and immunities the organization is to enjoy in the United States. Congress may even override a constituent instrument—or any other international agreement—as a matter of federal law within the United States, if Congress explicitly says it is doing so or if the conflict between the agreement and a later Congressional enactment is direct and unavoidable. Similarly, a later self-executing treaty would supersede a prior inconsistent federal statute, as a matter of federal law in the United States.

At this point you should read U.N. Charter *articles 104* and *105*. Note that they deal with the legal capacity, privileges and immunities of the United Nations within the territories of its member states, but they are couched only in general terms relating to fulfillment of the organization's functions and purposes. A number of other international organizations have similarly general provisions in their constituent instruments. In such cases, there will normally be a separate agreement either among the member states or between the organization and the member state in which it has its headquarters, setting forth with greater particularity the organization's capacity, privileges and immunities in domestic law. In the case of the U.N., for example, there is the Convention on the Privileges and Immunities of the United Nations (the General Convention), discussed below.

Some other international organizations have constituent instruments spelling out capacity, privileges and immunities in detail. This is true especially of international financial organizations—the International Monetary Fund, the World Bank and similar development banks. Finally, there are some organizations with constituent instruments that are silent as to these matters; many organizations of this type have entered into separate agreements spelling out at least some of the capacities, privileges and immunities they are to enjoy in the territories of their member states.[a]

In 1945 the United States Congress enacted the International Organizations Immunities Act (IOIA), to provide specific capacities, privileges and immunities under United States law for certain organizations to be designated by the President. In 1946, the United Nations General Assembly adopted the General Convention, mentioned above, but the United States did not ratify it until 1970.[b]

We begin with capacities, and with a question of federal jurisdiction that has arisen in connection with international organizations' capacity to institute legal proceedings in American courts. The relevant statutory and treaty provisions are IOIA *sections 1* and *2* (22 U.S.C.A. *§§ 288* and *288a*), and General Convention *article 1, section 1*.

Through a series of Executive Orders, various U.S. Presidents have designated a long list of international organizations (including the U.N. and its specialized agencies, but also including many others) pursuant to section 1 of the IOIA. The list, however, does not include subsidiary organs of the U.N. that are created simply by General Assembly resolution, such as the U.N. Environmental Program (discussed later in this section).

If an international organization has been designated by the President under IOIA section 1, it clearly must be considered a legal entity for purposes of capacity to bring suit in federal and (by virtue of the Supremacy Clause) state courts in the United States. See *section 2(a)(iii)*. The same is true of the United Nations apart from the Act, since article 1 of the General Convention clearly would be self-executing.

a. On these matters generally, see 13 M. Whiteman, Digest of International Law 1–4, 32–45 (1968).

b. In 1947, the General Assembly adopted a counterpart Convention on the Privileges and Immunities of the Specialized Agencies, but the United States has not become a party to it.

Is that the same thing as saying that the federal courts have subject matter jurisdiction over suits brought by the United Nations or by other designated international organizations? Keep in mind that federal jurisdiction exists only pursuant to specific grants of power to federal courts to entertain admiralty proceedings and to hear cases in which there is diversity of citizenship among the parties or a "federal question" to be decided. The law of federal jurisdiction in cases involving international organizations is still largely undeveloped. The following case is one of the few reported so far.

INTERNATIONAL REFUGEE ORGANIZATION v. REPUBLIC S.S. CORP.

United States Court of Appeals, Fourth Circuit, 1951.
189 F.2d 858.

PARKER, CHIEF JUDGE.

These cases arise out of a controversy between the International Refugee Organization, an agency of the United Nations, and the Republic of Panama, and one Jose Jacintho de Medeiros, a citizen of Portugal. * * * No. 6202 involves a charge of fraud and deceit made by the I.R.O. against the corporation and Medeiros in a suit instituted against them to recover damages and establish a constructive trust.

* * *

The allegations of fraud in both cases are that the corporation and Medeiros obtained $840,000 from I.R.O. by means of false and fraudulent representations with respect to the ownership, title and speed of the S.S. San Francisco, a vessel chartered to the I.R.O. by the Republic Steamship Company represented by Medeiros as president.

In No. 6202, the action against Medeiros and the Republic Steamship Company was dismissed by the lower court for lack of jurisdiction.

* * *

The dismissal for lack of jurisdiction in No. 6202 is based upon the holding that a suit by the I.R.O. is not one of which the federal courts have been given jurisdiction. We think that this is error. The United Nations is an international organization of which the United States is a member, and article 104 of its charter provides that it shall enjoy in the territory of each of its members "such legal capacity as may be necessary for the exercise of its functions and the fulfillment of its purposes". 59 Stat. 1053. Article 13 of the Constitution of the I.R.O., which is an agency of the United Nations, contains a provision to like effect. In the International Organizations Immunities Act, 59 Stat. 669, 22 U.S.C.A. § 288a, Congress has undertaken to discharge the obligations assumed under these provisions by providing that international organizations such as I.R.O. shall "to the extent consistent with the instrument creating them, possess the capacity—

"(i) to contract;

"(ii) to acquire and dispose of real and personal property;

"(iii) *to institute legal proceedings*".

(Italics supplied.) This means, by necessary implication, that Congress has opened the doors of the federal courts to suits by such international organizations; for the right to institute legal proceedings means the right to go into court, and the federal courts are the only courts whose doors Congress can open.

* * *

Certainly an organization like the I.R.O., which is purchasing and chartering vessels and entering into all sorts of contracts in connection with the transportation of refugees, must have the right to go into court for the protection of its rights and interests; and in this country the logical courts for it to go into are the courts of the nation which has adhered to the international organization, not the local courts of the several states which have had no part therein. In determining its rights in this regard, we should give a liberal interpretation to the International Organizations Immunities Act. As was well said by Judge Goodman in Balfour, Guthrie & Co. v. United States, D.C., 90 F.Supp. 831, 833: "The broad purpose of the International Organizations Immunities Act was to vitalize the status of international organizations of which the United States is a member and to facilitate their activities. A liberal interpretation of the Act is in harmony with this purpose."

We think also that there is jurisdiction to entertain the suit by reason of 28 U.S.C.A. § 1331, which provides that the District Courts shall have jurisdiction of civil actions arising under the "Constitution, laws or treaties of the United States". Under the principles laid down in Osborn v. United States Bank, 9 Wheat. 738, 6 L.Ed. 204, this was certainly a civil action arising not only under the treaties creating the United Nations and the International Refugee Organization into both of which the United States had entered, but also under the act of Congress which gives the right to sue to public international organizations in which the United States participates. The right of federal corporations to invoke the jurisdiction of the federal courts has been curtailed by act of Congress but this involves no limitation of the doctrine of Osborn v. United States Bank, supra. On the contrary, it is an express recognition of that doctrine. * * * If a corporation may invoke the federal jurisdiction because created by a law of the United States, an international organization created by treaties to which the United States is a party may invoke the jurisdiction because created by a treaty of the United States. Especially is this true where the international organization is clothed by a law of the United States with the essential corporate functions of contracting, acquiring and disposing of property and suing in court.

* * *

FEDERAL JURISDICTION UNDER THE IRO CASE

Do you agree that section *2(a)(iii)* of the International Organizations Immunities Act is a statutory grant of federal jurisdiction?

What made this tort action "arise under" the U.N. Charter, the IRO Constitution and the International Organizations Immunities Act, for purposes of 28 U.S.C.A. § 1331?

In connection with these two questions, consider the Osborn and Verlinden cases, discussed below.

In the second part of its opinion in the IRO case, the court relied on Osborn v. Bank of the United States. An act of Congress had chartered the Bank of the United States, which sought an injunction to prevent the state of Ohio from taxing it. The defendants (appellants) argued that the federal court did not have subject matter jurisdiction. The U.S. Supreme Court said in part:

> The appellants contest the jurisdiction of the Court on two grounds:
>
> 1st. That the act of Congress has not given it.
>
> 2d. That, under the constitution, Congress cannot give it.
>
> 1. The first part of the objection depends entirely on the language of the act. The words are, that the Bank shall be "made able and capable in law," "to sue and be sued, plead and be impleaded, answer and be answered, defend and be defended, in all State Courts having competent jurisdiction, and in any Circuit Court of the United States."
>
> These words seem to the Court to admit of but one interpretation. They cannot be made plainer by explanation. They give, expressly, the right "to sue and be sued," "in every Circuit Court of the United States," and it would be difficult to substitute other terms which would be more direct and appropriate for the purpose. The argument of the appellants is founded on the opinion of this Court, in *The Bank of the United States v. Deveaux,* (5 *Cranch,* 85.) In that case it was decided, that the former Bank of the United States was not enabled, by the act which incorporated it, to sue in the federal Courts. The words of the 3d section of that act are, that the Bank may "sue and be sued," &c. "in Courts of record, or any other place whatsoever." The Court was of opinion, that these general words, which are usual in all acts of incorporation, gave only a general capacity to sue, not a particular privilege to sue in the Courts of the United States * * *.
>
> * * *
>
> The act of incorporation, then, confers jurisdiction on the Circuit Courts of the United States, if Congress can confer it.

2. We will now consider the constitutionality of the clause in the act of incorporation, which authorizes the Bank to sue in the federal Courts.

* * *

We think, then, that when a question to which the judicial power of the Union is extended by the constitution, forms an ingredient of the original cause, it is in the power of Congress to give the Circuit Courts jurisdiction of that cause, although other questions of fact or of law may be involved in it.

The case of the Bank is, we think, a very strong case of this description. The charter of incorporation not only creates it, but gives it every faculty which it possesses. The power to acquire rights of any description, to transact business of any description, to make contracts of any description, to sue on those contracts, is given and measured by its charter, and that charter is a law of the United States. This being can acquire no right, make no contract, bring no suit, which is not authorized by a law of the United States. It is not only itself the mere creature of a law, but all its actions and all its rights are dependent on the same law. Can a being, thus constituted, have a case which does not arise literally, as well as substantially, under the law?[c]

Does Osborn support the holding in the IRO case?

Verlinden B.V. v. Central Bank of Nigeria,[d] did not involve an international organization. It is nevertheless instructive. The plaintiff, a Dutch corporation, sued the Nigerian Central Bank, an instrumentality of the Nigerian government, for breach of a letter of credit. Jurisdiction was asserted under 28 U.S.C.A. § 1330, which gives federal district courts subject matter jurisdiction "of any nonjury civil action against a foreign state as to any claim for relief in personam in respect to which the foreign state is not entitled to immunity * * *." The Central Bank is a "foreign state" for purposes of this section.

The question was whether this statutory grant of jurisdiction was authorized by the "arising under" clause of Article III of the Constitution: "The judicial Power [of the United States] shall extend to all Cases * * * arising under this Constitution, the Laws of the United States, and Treaties made, or which shall be made, under their Authority."

The Second Circuit in Verlinden had held that section 1330 was not authorized by the "arising under" clause of Article III. The Supreme Court reversed, and had this to say:

c. 22 U.S. at 817–18, 823.

d. 461 U.S. 480, 103 S.Ct. 1962, 76 L.Ed.2d 81 (1983).

The controlling decision on the scope of Art. III "arising under" jurisdiction is Chief Justice Marshall's opinion for the Court in Osborn v. Bank of United States * * *. Osborn thus reflects a broad conception of "arising under" jurisdiction, according to which Congress may confer on the federal courts jurisdiction over any case or controversy that might call for the application of federal law.

[The Supreme Court then noted that every action against a foreign sovereign or its instrumentality calls for application of the federal Foreign Sovereign Immunities Act (which establishes the limits of a foreign state's immunity in a U.S. court). Thus the "arising under" test of Article III would be met.]

In reaching a contrary conclusion, the Court of Appeals relied heavily upon decisions construing 28 U.S.C. section 1331, the statute which grants district courts general federal-question jurisdiction over any case that "arises under" the laws of the United States. The [Court of Appeals] placed particular emphasis on the so-called "well-pleaded complaint" rule, which provides, for purposes of *statutory* "arising under" jurisdiction, that the federal question must appear on the face of a well-pleaded complaint and may not enter in anticipation of a defense.[e] * * *

Although the language of section 1331 parallels that of the "Arising Under" Clause of Art. III, this Court never has held that statutory "arising under" jurisdiction is identical to Art. III "arising under" jurisdiction. Quite the contrary is true. * * * Art. III "arising under" jurisdiction is broader than federal-question jurisdiction under section 1331, and the Court of Appeals' heavy reliance on decisions construing that statute was misplaced.[f]

Did the IRO case involve Article III or statutory "arising under" jurisdiction?

Verlinden was applied in International Finance Corp. v. GDK Systems, Inc.[g] The International Finance Corporation (IFC), an international organization designated under the IOIA and affiliated with the World Bank, had entered into contracts with GDK, a New York corporation that supplied computer expertise to international banking systems. The IFC sued GDK in a federal court for breach of contract, fraud and other common law claims for relief. GDK moved to dismiss the complaint for lack of federal subject matter jurisdiction.

The IFC relied on 22 U.S.C.A. § 282f, which provides that any action by or against the IFC in the United States "shall be deemed to arise under the laws of the United States, and the district courts of the United States shall have original jurisdiction of any such action."

e. [Emphasis in the original.]
f. 461 U.S. at 492–95, 103 S.Ct. at 1970–72, 76 L.Ed.2d at 91–93.
g. 711 F.Supp. 15 (D.D.C.1989).

GDK argued that this statute was unconstitutional because it went further than the "arising under" clause of Article III allowed. The District Court rejected that argument. It noted that the Supreme Court in Verlinden upheld the jurisdictional provision in the Foreign Sovereign Immunities Act against a similar constitutional challenge. The District Court went on to say:

> As in the Verlinden case, 22 U.S.C. § 282f is also part of a comprehensive statutory scheme related to foreign affairs and commerce.
>
> Furthermore, the IFC's legal status and rights and immunities arise from federal law and the obligations of the United States under an international agreement. * * * A federal question is thus implicit in every case to which the IFC is a party. For example, the very right of the IFC to enter into contracts, such as the ones in dispute in this case, arises under federal law. See Articles of Agreement of the IFC, Art. VI, § 2(i);[h] 22 U.S.C. § 282g (Art. VI, § 2 "shall have full force and effect in the United States.").[i]

The District Court also relied on the IRO case.

Did Verlinden dictate the result the District Court reached?

Was the IFC case stronger or weaker than the IRO case for federal subject matter jurisdiction?

B. PRIVILEGES AND IMMUNITIES OF ORGANIZATIONS

1. *The United Nations*

International organizations enjoy certain privileges and immunities under the laws of their member states, much as governments of foreign nation-states do. One such immunity is typically immunity from suit in the domestic courts of member states, although the extent of that immunity is not always clear. This is a distinct issue from that of capacity: An organization might have the capacity to sue or be sued, but be immune from suit; or it might not have the capacity to be sued as an entity, wholly apart from any immunity. The following problem deals with these points.

The United Nations General Assembly, by its Resolution 2997,[a] established the U.N. Environment Program. It has a Governing Council, with supervisory and policy-making powers; a Secretariat headed by an Executive Director who is in charge of the day-to-day activities of the Program; and an Environment Fund for financial support. There is no separate international agreement to serve as the constituent

---

h. [Art. VI, § 2 of the IFC Articles of Agreement is modeled on *Art. I, § 1* of the General Convention on the Privileges and Immunities of the United Nations. Subsection (i) gives the IFC the capacity to contract.]

i. 711 F.Supp. at 18.

a. 27 GAOR Supp. No. 30 (A/8730), at 43 (1973).

instrument; rather, the Program traces its existence solely to the General Assembly resolution.

Suppose that the Executive Director, acting pursuant to authorization from the Governing Council, enters into a contract with a private California research organization to pay the California organization a stipulated amount in return for a study to determine the most efficient means of coordinating all U.N. environmental programs. The contract is negotiated and signed at the headquarters of the Environment Program, in Nairobi, Kenya. The work for the study is to be performed in Los Angeles, New York, Geneva and Nairobi (the locations, respectively, of the contracting organization and of various U.N. bodies). In accordance with usual United Nations practice, the contract provides that all disputes under it are subject to arbitration. The contract says that arbitration, if needed, is to be in New York City.

Suppose a dispute then arises as to just what work is required under the contract. After fruitless negotiations between the Executive Director and the contractor, the Executive Director cancels the contract. The California organization then seeks to arbitrate the dispute, but the Executive Director refuses on the ground that the contract spelled out the required work so clearly that there is nothing to arbitrate. The California organization thereupon sues the United Nations and the Environment Program in the Federal District Court for the Southern District of New York, seeking to compel arbitration.

Would there be "federal question" jurisdiction under the International Refugee Organization case? (The order directing arbitration would be sought under the Federal Arbitration Act.[b] That Act, however, does not provide a grant of federal jurisdiction, either on its own or as a federal question under 28 U.S.C.A. § 1331.[c] Thus some other basis for jurisdiction would have to be found.)

If there is doubt about federal question jurisdiction, one would have to consider diversity jurisdiction. The amount in controversy would have to meet the requirements of 28 U.S.C.A. § 1332. Beyond that, there is very little authority, but such issues as these would arise: Is the United Nations a "citizen" of some state or foreign nation? If so, which one? Is it a foreign state? Or is it like an unincorporated association for diversity jurisdiction purposes, meaning that the "citizenship" of each member must be considered? If so, what is the "citizenship" of the member closest to home, the United States? And what about the U.N. Environment Program, if it is sued as a separate entity: If it is indeed subject to suit as a separate entity despite the fact that it is merely a creature of the General Assembly, of what state or nation is it a "citizen"? Would the question whether it is a separate entity be determined by state or federal law?

b. 9 U.S.C.A. § 4.

c. See 13B Wright, Miller & Cooper, Federal Practice and Procedure § 3569 (1984).

If those technical federal jurisdictional hurdles could be overcome, and if service of process can be made, it would be necessary to face the issue of immunity from suit on the part of the United Nations and the Environment Program. Assume that the Environment Program is not treated as a separate entity, and that the United Nations would be bound by the Environment Program contract under agency principles. Is the U.N. nevertheless immune from this action? Start with U.N. Charter *article 105,* and then consider the excerpt below from the report of the Rapporteur of Committee IV/2 of the 1945 San Francisco Conference that prepared the U.N. Charter. (The reference in it to the "proposed article" is to article 105.)

UNITED NATIONS CONFERENCE ON INTERNATIONAL ORGANIZATION
San Francisco, 1945.
Selected Documents 875–76 (1946), 13 Whiteman, Digest of Int'l L. 34–36 (1968).

Paragraph I(1) of this proposed article refers to the Organization considered as a distinct entity. In so doing it covers all the agencies of the Organization, that is, the agencies or authorities established by the Charter, as well as the other bodies and organisms which might subsequently be established by virtue of the powers conferred by the Charter. By way of examples of such bodies and organisms, we may point to those to be established by the General Assembly, the Security Council, and the Economic and Social Council, as contemplated by Chapters V, VI, and IX of the Dumbarton Oaks Proposals. Therefore there have been excluded from the provisions contemplated in the proposal of the Committee those agencies not belonging to the Organization, although they may have been brought into connection or relation with the Organization through application of the Charter. Paragraph I(2) refers to: (A) the representatives of the states members of the Organization; (B) the officials (functionaries, et cetera) of the Organization and of its organs, authorities, or agencies referred to in paragraph I(1).

* * *

The draft article proposed by the Committee does not specify the privileges and immunities respect for which it imposes on the member states. This has been thought superfluous. The terms "privileges" and "immunities" indicate in a general way all that could be considered necessary to the realization of the purposes of the Organization, to the free functioning of its organs, and to the independent exercise of the functions and duties of their officials: exemption from tax, immunity from jurisdiction, facilities for communication, inviolability of buildings, properties, and archives, et cetera. It would moreover have been impossible to establish a list valid for all the member states and taking account of the special situation in which some of them might find themselves by reason of the activities of the Organization or of its organs in their territory. But if there is one certain principle it is that no member state may hinder in any way the working of the Organization or take any measures the effect of which might be to increase its burdens, financial or other.

THE EFFECT OF ARTICLE 105

Does *article 105*, as embellished by the Rapporteur of Committee IV/2, answer the immunity question in the case presented?

Article 105 has been implemented in the United States, first in 1945 by *section 2(b)* of the International Organizations Immunities Act (IOIA), 22 U.S.C.A. § *288a(b)*, and then in 1970 by *article II, section 2* of the U.N. Convention on Privileges and Immunities (the General Convention). Read these provisions carefully.

SOVEREIGN IMMUNITY IN THE UNITED STATES

The doctrine of sovereign immunity grew up in suits against the governments of foreign states, not against international organizations. In Berizzi Brothers Co. v. S.S. Pesaro,[d] the Supreme Court applied the absolute theory of sovereign immunity to a foreign government-operated vessel. Under the absolute theory, virtually all acts and property of foreign governments are immune from the jurisdiction of domestic courts of another country, even if the acts or property are essentially commercial.

Although the Berizzi Brothers case was never overruled, the U.S. State Department in 1952 issued the Tate Letter,[e] in which it adopted the restrictive theory of sovereign immunity for cases against foreign governments. Under the restrictive theory, the immunity of a foreign government is recognized with respect to sovereign or public acts (*jure imperii*), but not with respect to acts of a private nature (*jure gestionis*). The courts quickly went along with the State Department, and accepted the restrictive theory.

Until January 1977, a defendant government could assert sovereign immunity either directly in the judicial proceedings or by requesting the State Department to issue a "suggestion of immunity" to the court. If the State Department received such a request and answered it (either by suggesting immunity or by saying that immunity was inappropriate), the courts followed the Department's determination. If the immunity defense was presented directly to the court, it would do its best to apply the public-private act distinction.

When the courts dealt with the public-private act distinction on their own, they had trouble deciding whether the test was to be applied

---

d. 271 U.S. 562, 46 S.Ct. 611, 70 L.Ed. 1088 (1926).   e. 26 Dep't State Bull. 984 (1952).

to the nature of the governmental act or to its purpose. The State Department came down on the side of looking to the nature of the act, though it was not always apparent how an act should be characterized in order to determine whether its nature was public or private. Some cases were fairly clear, but others were not. For example, it was clear that a foreign government would be immune from a suit in a U.S. court challenging its civil rights policies, and would not be immune from a suit for breach of a contract to buy office equipment. But it was far less clear whether it would be immune from a suit for breach of a contract to buy ammunition for its army.

Because of mounting dissatisfaction both within and outside the government as to the State Department's role in sovereign immunity cases, Congress enacted the Foreign Sovereign Immunities Act of 1976 (the FSIA).[f] The FSIA turns over to the courts all determinations of immunity in actions against foreign governments. It does not address immunities of international organizations in cases where actions are brought against them directly.

The FSIA codifies the restrictive theory of immunity for actions against foreign governments and their instrumentalities. In section 1603 it speaks in terms of "commercial activities" of foreign states, and says that the courts are to look at the nature rather than the purpose of the act to determine if it is commercial. Other key sections include:

FOREIGN SOVEREIGN IMMUNITIES ACT OF 1976
Oct. 21, 1976, as amended Nov. 19, 1988.
28 U.S.C.A. § 1602 et seq.

§ 1604. Immunity of a foreign state from jurisdiction

Subject to existing international agreements to which the United States is a party at the time of enactment of this Act a foreign state shall be immune from the jurisdiction of the courts of the United States and of the States except as provided in sections 1605 to 1607 of this chapter.

§ 1605. General exceptions to the jurisdictional immunity of a foreign state

(a) A foreign state shall not be immune from the jurisdiction of courts of the United States or of the States in any case—

(1) in which the foreign state has waived its immunity either explicitly or by implication, notwithstanding any withdrawal of the waiver which the foreign state may purport to effect except in accordance with the terms of the waiver;

(2) in which the action is based upon a commercial activity carried on in the United States by the foreign state; or upon an act performed in the United States in connection with a commercial

---

f. 28 U.S.C.A. § 1602 et seq.

activity of the foreign state elsewhere; or upon an act outside the territory of the United States in connection with a commercial activity of the foreign state elsewhere and that act causes a direct effect in the United States;

* * *

(6) in which the action is brought, either to enforce an agreement made by the foreign State with or for the benefit of a private party to submit to arbitration all or any differences which have arisen or which may arise between the parties with respect to a defined legal relationship, whether contractual or not, concerning a subject matter capable of settlement by arbitration under the laws of the United States, or to confirm an award made pursuant to such an agreement to arbitrate, if (A) the arbitration takes place or is intended to take place in the United States, (B) the agreement or award is or may be governed by a treaty or other international agreement in force for the United States calling for the recognition and enforcement of arbitral awards, (C) the underlying claim, save for the agreement to arbitrate, could have been brought in a United States court under this section or section 1607, or (D) paragraph (1) of this subsection is otherwise applicable.

* * *

§ 1609. Immunity from attachment and execution of property of a foreign state

Subject to existing international agreements to which the United States is a party at the time of enactment of this Act the property in the United States of a foreign state shall be immune from attachment, arrest and execution except as provided in sections 1610 and 1611 of this chapter.

§ 1610. Exceptions to the immunity from attachment or execution

(a) The property in the United States of a foreign state, * * * used for a commercial activity in the United States, shall not be immune from attachment in aid of execution, or from execution, upon a judgment entered by a court of the United States or of a State after the effective date of this Act, if—

(1) the foreign state has waived its immunity from attachment in aid of execution or from execution either explicitly or by implication, notwithstanding any withdrawal of the waiver the foreign state may purport to effect except in accordance with the terms of the waiver, or

(2) the property is or was used for the commercial activity upon which the claim is based, or

* * *

(6) the judgment is based on an order confirming an arbitral award rendered against the foreign State, provided that attachment in aid of execution, or execution, would not be inconsistent with any provision in the arbitral agreement.

APPLYING THE ACT TO THE UNITED NATIONS

Does the FSIA govern the issue of immunity in the hypothetical suit against the United Nations? Apart from any possible waiver of immunity, would the U.N. be immune from the suit? (Consider not only the FSIA, but the relevant provisions of the IOIA and of the General Convention on the Privileges and Immunities of the United Nations.)

Could it successfully be argued that the United Nations waived whatever immunity it had regarding this proceeding to compel arbitration, by reason of the arbitration clause in the contract? Assume, for purposes of this question, that such an arbitration clause in a contract with a foreign government would be considered a waiver of immunity. Note also the provision in the FSIA on actions to enforce arbitration agreements, 22 U.S.C.A. § 1605(a)(6), supra. But consider what the U.N. Office of Legal Affairs has to say about article II, section 2 of the General Convention:

MEMORANDUM, U.N. OFFICE OF LEGAL AFFAIRS
1948.
[1967] 2 Y.B. Int'l L.Comm'n 154, 225.

According to the reports of the Preparatory Commission of the United Nations, Article 2 of the General Convention was based on similar articles in the constitutions of international organizations. Some of these constitutional instruments * * * provide that the member government accord to the administration the facilities, privileges, exemptions and immunities which they accord to each other "including immunity from suit and legal process except with the consent of or so far as is provided for in any contract entered into by or on behalf of the Administration".

A similar provision is contained in Article IX, Section 3 of the Articles of the International Monetary Fund, providing for waiver of immunity for the purposes of any proceedings *or by the terms of any contract* thereby differentiating between the two forms of waiver. Apparently, it was not the intention of the Preparatory Commission or the General Assembly to extend waiver this far in so far as the United Nations was concerned, or such a provision would have been included, rather than just the words "legal process". In fact the words used in the original draft of this section were: "The Organization, its property and its assets wherever located and by whomsoever held shall enjoy immunity from every form of judicial process except to the extent that it expressly waives its immunity for the purpose of any proceedings or by the terms of any contract".

This wording was changed by the Legal Committee of the Preparatory Commission to read in the more restrictive fashion that it now stands. It must be concluded, therefore, that it was not the intention of the Preparatory Commission, or of the General Assembly, to extend the right of waiver to waiver in future by the terms of a contract.

ARGUABLY RELEVANT CASES

Consider whether the two cases summarized below help to answer the immunity issue in our hypothetical case.

The Food and Agriculture Organization (FAO), a specialized agency of the U.N., has its headquarters and some auxiliary facilities in Rome. According to the FAO, in 1982 the Italian Corte di Cassazione held that the FAO was not immune from two actions brought by landlords of premises the FAO had rented as auxiliary buildings for its operations. One action was for arrears of rent, and the other was an eviction proceeding.

Article VIII, section 16 of the FAO's Headquarters Agreement with Italy provides:

> FAO and its property, wherever located and by whomsoever held, shall enjoy immunity from every form of legal process except insofar as in any particular case FAO shall have expressly waived its immunity. It is, however, understood that no waiver of immunity shall extend to any measure of execution.

Note the similarity between this provision and *article II, section 2* of the U.N. General Convention. Unless there was something that does not meet the eye, how could the Italian court decide that the FAO was not immune? The FAO Council was not pleased with the decision.[g]

The second case is Standard Chartered Bank v. International Tin Council.[h] A bank sued the International Tin Council (ITC), an international organization headquartered in London, to recover on a defaulted loan. The loan agreement provided that it was to be governed by English law, and that the ITC irrevocably submitted to the jurisdiction of the High Court of Justice in England. The ITC argued that this express waiver of immunity was ineffective because its Headquarters Agreement with the United Kingdom (like the U.N. General Convention and the FAO Headquarters Agreement with Italy) required that any waiver be "in a particular case" and thus could not be anticipatory, by contract. The English judge swept that argument aside, saying:

---

[g] See Report of the Council of FAO, Doc. CL 82/REP, at 33–35 (1982); see also 1982 U.N. Juridical Y.B. 113.

[h] [1986] 3 All E.R. 257 (Queens Bench Div., Commercial Court).

The waiver must be in a particular case, but that in my view means no more than that it must relate to a specific transaction. I find no warrant in the language for reading the phrase "a particular case" as if it meant "a particular dispute" or "a particular legal proceeding." [i]

Is our hypothetical case distinguishable from the ITC case?

IMMUNITY FROM EXECUTION

Could the U.N. waive its immunity from execution, for purposes of proceedings in U.S. courts? See General Convention *article II, section 2*.

(The Foreign Sovereign Immunities Act, section 1611(a), provides that the property of international organizations entitled to the immunities of the International Organizations Immunities Act "shall not be subject to attachment or any other judicial process impeding the disbursement of funds to, or on the order of, a foreign state as the result of an action brought in the courts of the United States or of the States." This was apparently intended to apply only to actions against foreign states, in order to preclude plaintiffs from preventing payment of funds to defendant states by such U.S.-based international organizations as the International Monetary Fund and the World Bank. The House Judiciary Committee Report adds, "The reference to 'international organizations' in this subsection is not intended to restrict any immunity accorded to such international organizations under any other law or international agreement." [j])

TORT LIABILITY IN THE HEADQUARTERS DISTRICT

Another waiver issue may be raised by a 1986 U.N. General Assembly resolution. As is well known, the United Nations encountered a financial crisis in the 1980s, caused by the failure of some member states (notably the United States) to pay their assessed dues in full. At the same time, the U.N. was subject to steeply rising liability insurance premiums. (The U.N. maintains liability insurance coverage for accidents in the headquarters district in New York City, rather than simply using its immunity from suit as a shield. Indeed, the General Convention on the Privileges and Immunities of the United Nations, section 29, requires the U.N. to "make provisions for appropriate modes of settlement of * * * disputes arising out of contracts or other disputes of a private law character to which the United Nations is a party

---

i. [1986] 3 All E.R. at 262.

j. House Rep. No. 94–1487, 94th Cong., 2d Sess. 31 (1976). See also id. at 30. The section-by-section analysis in the House Report is based on the analysis prepared by the Department of State. See 15 Int'l Legal Materials 90, 102 (1976).

* * * .") k

To deal with the adverse synergism of reduced income and increased insurance costs, the General Assembly adopted Resolution 41/210 (1986), in the form of a regulation limiting the liability of the U.N. in "any tort action or in respect of any tort claim by any person against the United Nations * * * arising out of any act or omission, whether accidental or otherwise, in the Headquarters district * * *." The regulation limits the U.N.'s liability to out-of-pocket losses plus no more than $100,000 for pain and suffering, and prohibits punitive damages.

The regulation was adopted pursuant to *Article III, section 8* of the U.N. Headquarters Agreement. That section should be read in conjunction with *section 7* of the Agreement.

Has the United Nations waived its immunity from tort actions in U.S. courts arising out of accidents in the headquarters district?

If so (or if the U.N. were to waive its immunity explicitly when a tort action is brought against it), would the court be bound by the $100,000 limit on the U.N.'s liability for pain and suffering?

2. *Specialized Agencies*

Consider next whether the result would be the same if the contract with the California organization had been made, not by a subsidiary body of the U.N., but by the International Bank for Reconstruction and Development (IBRD, also known as the World Bank or just "the Bank") at its headquarters in Washington, D.C., to determine the economic effect of requiring pollution-control equipment for all Bank-financed industrial projects in developing countries. Assume that there is no arbitration clause in the contract, and that suit for breach of contract is brought against the IBRD in the District of Columbia. The Bank, a specialized agency of the U.N., is an "international organization" for purposes of the U.S. International Organizations Immunities Act. The U.N. Convention on Privileges and Immunities does not apply to the IBRD or to other specialized agencies, and the United States has not become a party to the separate convention that does deal with privileges and immunities of specialized agencies.

The World Bank's constituent instrument contains a provision that could be construed as a waiver of immunity. It could be argued, though, that the Bank would not be immune in our hypothetical case even in the absence of a waiver.

This argument stems from the link in *section 2(b)* of the International Organizations Immunities Act[a] to the immunities of foreign governments. When it was enacted, foreign governments had absolute

---

k. See Szasz, The United Nations Legislates to Limit its Liability, 81 Am.J.Int'l L. 739 (1987).

a. 22 U.S.C.A. § 288a(b).

immunity in American courts. But now that the Foreign Sovereign Immunities Act has codified the restrictive theory for them, arguably the IOIA incorporates by reference the restrictive theory for actions against international organizations.

This question arose in Broadbent v. Organization of American States,[b] but the court managed to duck it. Seven former OAS staff members sued the Organization for damages, claiming they had been improperly discharged. The court held that even if the restrictive theory applied, the employment of international civil servants would not be a commercial activity. Thus the OAS was immune, no matter which theory applied. Along the way the court said:

> Appellants—and the United States as *amicus curiae*—submit the following syllogism: the IOIA conferred on international organizations the same immunity enjoyed by foreign governments; the FSIA indicates that foreign governments now enjoy only restrictive immunity; therefore, international organizations enjoy only restrictive immunity.

* * *

The OAS and several other international organizations as *amici curiae* counter that Congress granted international organizations absolute immunity in the IOIA, and it has never modified that grant. They rely on three implications of a legislative intent *not* to apply to international organizations the post World War II evolutions in the doctrine of sovereign immunity.

First, the FSIA is generally silent about international organizations. No reference to such organizations is made in the elaborate definition of "state" in § 1603, and only § 1611 [15] even alludes to their existence. True, § 1611, dealing as it does with the attachment of property belonging to international organizations, presupposes a successful action against an international organization. However, that could follow a waiver of immunity. Alternatively, § 1611 would have application in case of an attempt to execute a judgment against a foreign state by attaching funds of that foreign state held by an international organization.

Second, by its own terms the IOIA provides for the modification, where appropriate, of the immunity enjoyed by one or more international organizations.

Under the statute, the President can withdraw or restrict the immunity and privileges thereby conferred. Specifically, it provides:

---

b. 628 F.2d 27 (D.C.Cir.1980).

15. 28 U.S.C. § 1611 (1979) provides in pertinent part:

* * * the property of those organizations designated by the President as being entitled to enjoy the privileges, exemptions, and immunities provided by the International Organizations Immunities Act shall not be subject to attachment or any other judicial process impeding the disbursement of funds to, or on the order of, a foreign state as the result of an action brought in the courts of the United States or of the states.

The president (is) authorized, in the light of the functions performed by any such international organization, by appropriate executive order to withhold or withdraw from any such organization or its officers or employees any of the privileges, exemptions, and immunities provided for in this title * * * or to condition or limit the enjoyment by any such organization or its officers or employees of any such privilege, exemption, or immunity.

The Senate Report on the IOIA stated: "This provision will permit the adjustment or limitation of the privileges in the event that any international organization should engage for example, in activities of a commercial nature." And, in floor debate on the legislation, its supporters pointed again to this provision as a limitation on commercial abuses by an international organization. Hence this provision may reveal that Congress intended to grant absolute immunity to international organizations giving to the President the authority to relax that immunity, including removal or restriction of immunity in cases involving the commercial activities of international organizations.

Finally, Congress may have concluded that the policies and considerations that led to the development of the restrictive immunity concept for foreign nations do not apply to international organizations like the OAS.[20]

We need not decide this difficult question of statutory construction. On either theory of immunity—absolute or restrictive—an immunity exists sufficient to shield the organization from lawsuit on the basis of acts involved here.[c] * * *

If the court in Broadbent had faced the issue regarding the incorporation by reference of the restrictive theory into the IOIA, how should it have come out? Consider the effect that should be given to these views:

20. Prior to its modification, the absolute immunity of states was justified by "the desirability of avoiding adjudication which might affront a foreign nation and thus embarrass the executive branch in its conduct of foreign relations." See Hearings on H.R. 11315 before the Subcommittee on Administrative Law and Governmental Relations, House Committee on the Judiciary, 94th Cong., 2d Sess. 29 (1976). As sovereign nations become more and more involved in the market place, as merchants rather than sovereigns, claims arising out of commercial transactions do not affront the sovereignty of the nations involved. Id. Recognition of this growing involvement in commercial activity was the basis of the movement to a restrictive concept. Moreover, most other commercial nations embrace restrictive immunity with regard to sovereigns. Thus, when our government and its instrumentalities are sued abroad in commercial litigation, the sovereign immunity defense is rarely available. H.R.Rep. No. 94–2487, 94th Cong., 2d Sess. 9 (1976). Congressional proponents of the restrictive immunity could thus indicate that use of the restrictive immunity concept would bring the United States into step with foreign nations. Id. at 54. But neither rationale for adopting the restrictive notion of immunity would seem to apply to international organizations. Such organizations do not regularly engage in commercial activities, nor do other nations apply the concept of restrictive immunity to them. Cf. Alfred Dunhill of London, Inc. v. Cuba, 425 U.S. 682, 699, 702, 96 S.Ct. 1854, 48 L.Ed.2d 301 (1975).

c. [628 F.2d at 31–33.]

(a) The U.S. State Department's Legal Adviser has said that, in the absence of specific provisions in their constituent instruments, "international organizations are now subject to the jurisdiction of our courts in respect of their commercial activities, while retaining immunity for their acts of a public character" by virtue of the Foreign Sovereign Immunities Act.[d]

(b) The U.N. Office of Legal Affairs, responding to a request for advice on the immunity of the U.N. Relief and Works Agency for Palestine Refugees in the Near East (UNRWA), has said:

> [T]he principal issue is whether the immunity of UNRWA is a matter to be judged under domestic law or some other system of law. For reasons of principle, as well as on sound practical grounds, we are strongly of the opinion that this matter should not be judged by domestic law except to the extent, of course, that it incorporates relevant international obligations. Domestic law may, therefore, be considered as a secondary but not a primary source of evidence of the law.
>
> Fortunately, there is another, well-established system of law by which this matter may be judged, namely, the public international law governing the status, privileges and immunities of international organizations. The formal sources of the system of law are to be found in the relevant constitutive instruments (of the United Nations and UNRWA), and multilateral and bilateral agreements to which the Member State in question is a party and by which it is, therefore, legally bound (*inter alia,* the Convention on the Privileges and Immunities of the United Nations). It can be pointed out in connection with the above-mentioned Convention that Member States obligate themselves to be in a position under their own laws to give effect to the Convention.
>
> A word about the nature of international organization immunity might also be useful in order to head off any arguments * * * based on restrictive immunity. The immunity accorded international organizations under this system of law is an absolute immunity and must be distinguished from sovereign immunity which in some contemporary manifestations, at least, is more restrictive.[e]

Was the U.N. Office of Legal Affairs saying that international organizations have absolute immunity under customary international law, or only as a matter of treaty law for parties to conventions such as the Convention on the Privileges and Immunities of the U.N., which spell out an absolute immunity requirement? Note that the United States is a party to that Convention, but not to the companion Convention on the Privileges and Immunities of the Specialized Agencies.

---

d. See Dep't of State File No. P80 0108–2131, quoted in 74 Am.J.Int'l L. 917, 918 (1980).

e. 1984 U.N. Juridical Y.B. 188.

WAIVER OF IMMUNITY

Whether or not the restrictive theory applies to international organizations, an organization could waive whatever immunity it has—at least if the waiver meets the requirements of federal law. Review IOIA *section 2(b)* (22 U.S.C.A. *§ 288a(b)*) and FSIA section 1605(a)(1). To apply these to the hypothetical case involving the World Bank and the private California research organization, consider also Article VII, section 3 of the World Bank Agreement, below. Then consider the Lutcher case, which construes an identical provision—Article XI—of the constituent instrument of the Inter-American Development Bank.

ARTICLES OF AGREEMENT OF THE INTERNATIONAL BANK FOR RECONSTRUCTION AND DEVELOPMENT

Opened for signature Dec. 27, 1945.
60 Stat. 1440, 3 Bevans 1390, 2 U.N.T.S. 134.

Art. VII, § 3. Position of the Bank with regard to judicial process

Actions may be brought against the Bank only in a court of competent jurisdiction in the territories of a member in which the Bank has an office, has appointed an agent for the purpose of accepting service or notice of process, or has issued or guaranteed securities. No actions shall, however, be brought by members or persons acting for or deriving claims from members. The property and assets of the Bank shall, wheresoever located and by whomsoever held, be immune from all forms of seizure, attachment or execution before the delivery of final judgment against the Bank.

LUTCHER S.A. v. INTER-AMERICAN DEVELOPMENT BANK

United States Court of Appeals, D.C.Circuit, 1967.
127 U.S.App.D.C. 238, 382 F.2d 454.

BURGER, CIRCUIT JUDGE. [Lutcher, a Brazilian company engaged in lumbering and the processing of paper pulp, sought damages and injunctive relief claiming that the Bank had violated loan agreements with it by participating in loans made to its competitors. The District Court granted the Bank's motion to dismiss, on the dual ground that the Bank was immune from suit and that the complaint failed to state a claim upon which relief could be granted. The Court of Appeals affirmed on the latter point, but had this to say about the Bank's claim that it was immune under the International Organizations Immunities Act:]

The answer in this case must be found in the Agreement establishing the Bank. The relevant provision is paragraph 1, Section 3 of Article XI; it provides:

Actions may be brought against the Bank only in a court of competent jurisdiction in the territories of a member in which the Bank has an office, has appointed an agent for the purpose of accepting service or notice of process, or has issued or guaranteed securities.

This provision is hardly a model of clarity; Appellants argue it constitutes a waiver of immunity. The Bank urges that such an interpretation "would wipe out Section 2(b) of the [International Organizations] Immunities Act," a result which it says can be avoided by interpreting the provision as only a partial waiver, allowing suit by bondholders, creditors, and beneficiaries of its guarantees, on the theory that in such cases vulnerability to suit contributes to the effectiveness of the Bank's operation.

Unless this provision is read as merely describing the available forum for such suits and actions as to which waiver had been otherwise made, it must itself be a waiver of immunity. We do not read it as a venue provision for actions resulting from individual waivers; rather it is a provision waiving immunity and laying venue for the suits permitted. The terms are clear that "actions may be brought against the Bank"; had the drafters intended this clause to be only a venue provision, the language would more likely have provided, in essence, that actions brought against the Bank pursuant to any waiver of immunity could be brought in certain named courts. We conclude the absence of such limitation was purposeful. The subscribing nations were certainly alert to the problem and it was entirely appropriate to resolve the immunity question in the organic law of the Bank rather than leave it to case-by-case decision. That this was a deliberate choice is indicated by the title of Article XI, "Status, Immunities and Privileges," and the fact that the second [sentence] of Section 3 expressly prohibits suits by members. The drafters thus manifested full awareness of the immunity problem and we conclude they must have been aware that they were waiving immunity in broad terms rather than treating narrowly a venue problem. Thus we cannot read it in a restrictive sense; we read it as permitting the assertion of a claim against the Bank by one having a cause of action for which relief is available.

Our conclusion on this score is not without support in the historical background of the Bank's creation. For example, in response to questions from the House Committee considering the bill providing for United States participation in the Bank, then Assistant Secretary of the Treasury Upton, who had headed the United States delegation on the drafting committee, submitted a memorandum. In it he assured the Committee that the bill conformed with the Agreement in waiving the right of the United States to sue the Bank. The section of the bill providing jurisdiction for courts in the United States, he said, was not inconsistent with the Agreement's prohibition against suits by members. It had a different function, for "under the agreement, the Bank may be sued by persons other than member countries."

The Special Report of the National Advisory Council on the Proposed Inter-American Development Bank contains a similar description of the Bank's status:

> To carry out its operations the Bank is to have full juridical personality, though actions may not be brought against the Bank by members or persons deriving claims from members. Other legal actions, however, may be brought against the Bank in courts of the countries in which the Bank has an office or has appointed an agent to act for it or has issued or guaranteed securities.

There is another strand to the question of the Bank's immunity that bears notice. In 1960 President Eisenhower issued, as we noted, his Executive Order qualifying the Bank for immunities available under the terms of the International Organizations Immunities Act. In 1962 President Kennedy amended President Eisenhower's Order by another Order, which is entitled as intended "to provide for an exception to the Inter-American Development Bank's immunity from suit specified in the International Organizations Immunities Act." This Order added the following clause to the Eisenhower Order:

> *Provided,* That such designation shall not be construed to affect in any way the applicability of the provisions of Section 3, Article XI, of the Articles of Agreement of the Bank.

As amended, the Order tracks the Orders qualifying the International Finance Corporation and the World Bank. Its effect could only have been to reinforce the waiver of immunity. The Eisenhower Order qualified the Bank "as a public international organization entitled to enjoy the privileges, exceptions, and immunities conferred by the International Organizations Immunities Act." By the terms of the Act, of course, the Bank enjoys immunity except to the extent that a waiver is shown. But the Kennedy Order removed the force of any argument that the Bank had had immunities conferred upon it by the Act regardless of its waiver. The Kennedy Order stated its purpose to be to provide for an *exception* to immunity, and it did so by decreeing that the designation of the Bank as an international organization entitled to enjoy the immunities conferred by the Act "shall not be construed to affect in any way the applicability of the provisions of Section 3, Article XI" of the Agreement. The only language in Section 3 concerned with exceptions to immunity is the language which we read as a waiver.

The Bank contends that, while Section 3 does waive immunity, it does so only with respect to suits brought by "bondholders, and other like creditors and the beneficiaries of its guarantees." The Bank seems to rest its argument on a broad assurance that it knows "the purpose and effect of the complex of statutory, international agreement and executive order provisions is this." The distinction made by the Bank is surely not necessary, as the Bank suggests it is, to preserve Section 2(b) of the Immunities Act, since that section expressly contemplates waiver.

There is an indication in Section 3 that bondholders have a special status under the agreement. The status conferred however is not that of the Bank's waiver of immunity, but rather the Bank's willingness to defend suits where it "has issued or guaranteed securities" even though venue might not otherwise lie in that jurisdiction. The status is conferred in the phrase which is disjunctively connected with other phrases laying venue—"in the territories of a member in which the Bank has an office, has appointed an agent for purpose of accepting service or notice of process, or has issued or guaranteed securities."

In fact, there are two features of Section 3 that militate against the Bank's argument. First, the drafters of the Agreement indicated that when they wanted to make an exception to waiver of immunity they knew how to do so. Prudently concerned with possible interference in bank operations by member countries, the drafters explicitly and expressly provided in [sentence] 2 of Section 3 that *members* could not sue the Bank. This insured that members would not, in the Bank's words, intrude into "essential policy decisions * * * entrusted to its officers and Board." Second, the drafters stated that the Bank could be sued "in the territories of a member in which the Bank has an office, has appointed an agent for the purpose of accepting service or notice of process, or has issued or guaranteed securities." They must have contemplated that the Bank would establish offices in the areas intended to be served. Provision for suit in *any* member country where the Bank has an office must have been designed to facilitate suit for some class other than creditors and bondholders, *i.e.,* borrowers; creditors suing to enforce bond obligations would more likely sue in United States Courts.

* * *

WAIVER BY THE BANK

The World Bank Agreement (the model for the Inter-American Development Bank Agreement) was drafted at the Bretton Woods Conference at the end of World War II, and entered into force two days before the U.S. International Organizations Immunities Act. Also drafted at the Bretton Woods Conference was the International Monetary Fund Agreement.[f] All three—the two Agreements and the Act—were drafted with each other in mind. Fund Agreement article IX, section 3, provides:

> The Fund, its property and its assets, wherever located and by whomsoever held, shall enjoy immunity from every form of judicial process except to the extent that it expressly waives its immunity for the purpose of any proceedings or by the terms of any contract.

Does this affect the court's position in the Lutcher case?

f. 60 Stat. 1401, 3 Bevans 1351, 2 U.N.T.S. 39.

What exactly was the significance to the waiver issue of President Kennedy's amendment to the Executive Orders designating the Inter-American Development Bank and the World Bank as eligible international organizations under the U.S. Act?

Was it sound policy for the court to construe a provision in an international organization's constituent instrument which "is hardly a model of clarity" as a waiver of immunity? (What policies, if any, underlie jurisdictional immunities for international organizations?[g] Would the policies differ for a Development Bank from those applicable to, say, the International Atomic Energy Agency?) Why do you suppose the IBRD Agreement was not more clearly drafted on the question of immunity?

The breadth of the waiver found in Lutcher was tested in the Mendaro case, below.

MENDARO v. WORLD BANK
United States Court of Appeals, D.C. Circuit, 1983.
717 F.2d 610.

WILKEY, CIRCUIT JUDGE:

This appeal requires us to decide whether the International Bank for Reconstruction and Development may be sued in United States courts by employees of the Bank seeking redress of employment related grievances. Appellant Susana Mendaro challenges the district court's dismissal of her action under Title VII of the Civil Rights Act of 1964, arguing that the Articles of Agreement of the International Bank for Reconstruction and Development ("Articles of Agreement") effectively waive the immunity from suit which the Bank would otherwise enjoy under the International Organizations Immunities Act. Because the facially broad waiver of immunity contained in the Bank's Articles of Agreement must be narrowly read in light of both national and international law governing the immunity of international organizations, we affirm the decision of the district court.

I. BACKGROUND

The International Bank for Reconstruction and Development, commonly referred to as the World Bank, is an international financial institution whose purposes include assisting the development of its member nations' territories, promoting and supplementing private foreign investment, and promoting long range balanced growth in international trade. To meet these objectives the Bank is empowered to make direct loans to its members or to businesses located in the territories of its members; participate in and guarantee loans placed through private investment channels; issue, guarantee, and acquire its own securities; and invest in and guarantee other securities.

* * *

---

g. See, e.g., Liang, The Legal Status of the United Nations in the United States, 2 Int'l L.Q. 577 (1948). See also the *Mendaro* case, infra.

The administrative staff of the World Bank is currently composed of nearly 6,000 employees, including citizens from 110 countries. Although the majority are employed at the Bank's headquarters in Washington, D.C., the Bank has offices and resident missions in thirty-six countries.

Susana Mendaro, an Argentine citizen, was hired as a researcher by the World Bank on 6 September 1977. She claims that during her term of employment she was the victim of a pattern of sexual harassment and discrimination by other Bank employees. Her supervisors allegedly refused to provide her with the same number of assignments as her male coworkers, and at times thwarted her efforts to complete those assignments she had been given. Mendaro alleges that one of her supervisors permitted other male employees to make unwanted verbal and physical advances toward her. In addition, Mendaro claims that the Bank refused to promote her to the position of consultant, although she allegedly performed some of the duties of consultants. Mendaro complained to the Bank about these problems, but felt that they had not been investigated or remedied effectively. Some time after these complaints she was informed that her appointment with the Bank would expire on 30 June 1979.

Subsequent to her termination Mendaro filed a complaint with the Equal Employment Opportunity Commission ("Commission") alleging discrimination and retaliatory termination on the basis of sex in violation of Title VII of the Civil Rights Act of 1964. The area office of the Commission dismissed the charges for lack of jurisdiction on 12 February 1980, concluding that the World Bank is an "international governmental agency * * * not subject to the laws of the United States or any other member nation * * *." On 22 July 1980 the full Commission ratified this decision, and refused to take jurisdiction over her complaint.

Mendaro then filed the present suit against the World Bank in the United States District Court for the District of Columbia. The World Bank responded by moving to dismiss the action, arguing that it is an international governmental organization not subject to its members' jurisdiction in suits arising out of the Bank's internal administrative affairs, such as the alleged violation of its employment contracts. Mendaro opposed the motion for dismissal. She conceded that the challenged activities of the Bank would ordinarily be immunized from judicial scrutiny, but claimed that the Articles of Agreement effectively waive the Bank's right to claim the immunities of an international organization. She cited as the primary basis of her argument Article VII section 3, which permits actions to be brought against the World Bank "in a court of competent jurisdiction in the territories of a member in which the Bank has an office, has appointed an agent for the purpose of accepting service or notice of process, or has issued or guaranteed securities." Reading the Articles of Agreement as a whole, and relying on our decision in *Broadbent v. Organization of American States,* the district court rejected Mendaro's interpretation of Article

VII section 3 and dismissed the action for lack of jurisdiction. Given the scope of the facially broad waiver of immunity under Article VII section 3 of the [Articles] of Agreement, the correctness of the district court's decision hinges on the extent of the World Bank's immunity from suit under the International Organizations Immunities Act.

II. Discussion

A. International Organizations Immunities Act

The primary source of national law on the immunity of international organizations is the International Organizations Immunities Act ("Act"), which confers judicial status and immunities upon those international organizations in which the United States participates pursuant to a treaty or congressional act, and which have been designated by the president as being entitled to enjoy the provisions of the Act. Section 2(b) of the Act defines the privileges accorded to qualified international organizations:

> International organizations, their property and their assets, wherever located, and by whomsoever held, shall enjoy the same immunity from suit and every form of judicial process as is enjoyed by foreign governments, except to the extent that such organizations may expressly waive their immunity for the purpose of any proceedings or by the terms of any contract.

The immunity conferred by section 2(b) is subject to two sources of limitation. First, the organization itself may expressly waive its immunity. Second, the President may specifically limit the organization's immunities when he selects the organization as one entitled to enjoy the Act's privileges and immunities. At any time thereafter, such as when the organization abuses its privileges, the immunity may be modified, conditioned, or revoked by executive order.

Although there has been no express waiver by the Bank of its immunity to this particular suit, the members of the World Bank effectively curtailed much of the Bank's immunity from judicial process in Article VII section 3 by stipulating the conditions under which actions may be brought against the Bank. When President Truman extended the Act's privileges and immunities to the World Bank, he limited the Bank's immunity by the terms of the functional waiver contained in the Bank's articles. Thus, even though the extensive immunity conferred by section 2(b) would normally insulate the Bank from jurisdiction over this type of action brought by its employees, this court must accept jurisdiction over Mendaro's claim unless the Articles of Agreement preserve the World Bank's immunity to suits by employees.

B. The Scope of Article VII, Section 3, of the Articles of Agreement

[Mendaro relied on Bank Agreement Article VII, section 3, and on the Lutcher case.]

However, we are unable to read the somewhat clumsy and inartfully drafted language of Article VII section 3—which the *Lutcher* court admitted was "hardly a model of clarity"—as evincing an intent by the members of the Bank to establish a blanket waiver of immunity from every type of suit not expressly prohibited by reservations in Article VII section 3. The interpretation urged by Mendaro is logical only if the waiver provisions are read in a vacuum, without reference to the interrelationship between the functions of the Bank set forth in the Articles of Agreement and the underlying purposes of international immunities. When the language of Article VII section 3 is approached from this viewpoint it is evident that the World Bank's members could only have intended to waive the Bank's immunity from suits by its debtors, creditors, bondholders, and those other potential plaintiffs to whom the Bank would have to subject itself to suit in order to achieve its chartered objectives. Since a waiver of immunity from employees' suits arising out of internal administrative grievances is not necessary for the Bank to perform its functions, and could severely hamper its worldwide operations, this immunity is preserved by the members' failure expressly to waive it. * * *

1. *Policies Underlying the Immunity of International Organizations*

The strong foundation in international law for the privileges and immunities accorded to international organizations denotes the fundamental importance of these immunities to the growing efforts to achieve coordinated international action through multinational organizations with specific missions. * * * One of the most important protections granted to international organizations is immunity from suits by employees of the organization in actions arising out of the employment relationship. Courts of several nationalities have traditionally recognized this immunity,[37] and it is now an accepted doctrine of customary international law.[38]

Like the other immunities accorded international organizations, the purpose of immunity from employee actions is rooted in the need to protect international organizations from unilateral control by a member nation over the activities of the international organization within its territory.[39] The sheer difficulty of administering multiple employment practices in each area in which an organization operates suggests that the purposes of an organization could be greatly hampered if it could be subjected to suit by its employees worldwide. But beyond

---

37. *See, e.g., International Inst. of Agriculture v. Profili,* 5 Ann.Dig. 413 (Italy, Court of Cassation 1931); *Chemidlin v. International Bureau of Weights & Measures,* 12 Ann.Dig. 281 (France, Tribunal Civil of Versailles 1945); *Dame Adrien & Others,* 6 Ann.Dig. 33 (France, Conseil d'Etat 1931).

38. *See* A. Plantey, The International Civil Service §§ 133–34 (1981); Seyersted, *Jurisdiction Over Organizations and Officials of States, The Holy See and Intergovernmental Organizations,* 14 Int'l & Comp. L.Q. 493, 526 (1965); Restatement of the Foreign Relations Law of the United States (Revised) § 464 Comment a & Reporters' Note 4 at 73 (Tentative Draft No. 4) (1983).

39. *See* A. Plantey, The International Civil Service § 1343 (1981); C.W. Jenks, International Immunities 17–18 (1961).

economies of administration, the very structure of an international organization, which ordinarily consists of an administrative body created by the joint action of several participating nations, requires that the organization remain independent from the intranational policies of its individual members. Consequently, the charters of many international financial institutions contain express provisions designed to guarantee the neutral operation of the organization despite the political policies of the member nations or the individual backgrounds of the organizations' officers, and most large international organizations have established administrative tribunals with exclusive authority to deal with employee grievances.

Decisions by United States courts have emphasized the importance of immunity from the jurisdiction of local courts in matters involving employment disputes.

[The court cited, inter alia, the Broadbent case, page 36 supra.]

2. *The Articles of Agreement*

Of course, like other immunities, the immunity from employee suits may be waived by the members of the international organization, or its administrative directors. However, under national and international law, waivers of immunity must generally be expressly stated. The Act confers immunity "except to the extent that such organizations *expressly* waive their immunity for the purpose of any proceedings or by the terms of any contract." * * * The requirement of an express waiver suggests that courts should be reluctant to find that an international organization has inadvertently waived immunity when the organization might be subjected to a class of suits which would interfere with its functions.

Article VII section 3 does expressly waive immunity, but the scope of its limitation on immunity is unclear. Since the purpose of the immunities accorded international organizations is to enable the organizations to fulfill their functions, applying the same rationale in reverse, it is likely that most organizations would be unwilling to relinquish their immunity without receiving a corresponding benefit which would further the organization's goals. Thus, most waivers are probably effected when an insistence on immunity would actually prevent or hinder the organization from conducting its activities. A nonspecific waiver such as that contained in Article VII section 3 should be more broadly construed when the waiver would arguably enable the organization to pursue more effectively its institutional goals. However, when the benefits accruing to the organization as a result of the waiver would be substantially outweighed by the burdens caused by judicial scrutiny of the organization's discretion to select and administer its programs, it is logically less probable that the organization actually intended to waive its immunity. Thus, limitations on immunity that subject the organization to suits which could significantly hamper the organization's functions are inherently less likely to have been intended, and a court's interpretation of the provision in dispute should start with that in mind.

Applying these principles to the World Bank's Articles of Agreement, we find no evidence that the members of the Bank intended to waive the Bank's immunity to employee suits. Other than the broad language of Article VII section 3, which does not affirmatively reserve the World Bank's immunity over employee actions, Mendaro has not pointed to any other articles which suggest the Bank's members were willing to subject the Bank to actions arising out of the Bank's dealings with its administrative staff. Her assertion that "there is nothing in the language of Article VII or in any other Article that limits the broad application of the waiver" is contradicted by Article VII section 1, which states that the purpose of the waiver of immunity is "*[t]o enable the Bank to fulfill the functions with which it is entrusted.*" Thus, we cannot construe the vague language of Article VII section 3 more broadly than necessary to enable the Bank to fulfill its functions.

The choice of terms adopted in Article VII section 3 also suggests that the Bank's immunity is limited only to the extent necessary to further its objectives. Article VII section 3 expressly subjects the Bank to suit in territories where the Bank has an office or an agent appointed to receive service of process, or has issued or guaranteed securities. These exceptions to its immunity were designed primarily to enhance the marketability of its securities and the credibility of its activities in the lending markets. The Bank is specifically empowered to guarantee securities in which it has invested, "for the purpose of facilitating their sale." This guarantee would mean little if beneficiaries of the guarantee could not sue to enforce the Bank's contracts. Potential investors would be much less likely to acquire the Bank's own securities if they could not sue the Bank to enforce its liabilities. Similarly, the commercial reliability of the Bank's direct loans and private loan guarantees would be significantly vitiated if its debtors and beneficiaries were required to accept the Bank's obligations without recourse to judicial process.

A waiver of immunity with respect to the World Bank's commercial transactions with the outside world is also evident under Article VII section 3. If this immunity were not waived the Bank would be unable to purchase office equipment or supplies on anything other than a cash basis. Even the normal use of telephone and utilities might be placed on other than usual commercial terms. Such a restriction would unreasonably hobble its ability to perform the ordinary activities of a financial institution operating in the commercial marketplace.[54]

It is thus clear that the Bank's articles waive the Bank's immunity from actions arising out of the Bank's external relations with its

---

54. Since we are construing the extent to which the Articles of Agreement waive the Bank's immunity, we express no opinion on whether the Bank would, in the absence of a waiver, enjoy absolute immunity under the Act, or only the restricted immunity for noncommercial activities contemplated by the Foreign Sovereign Immunities Act, 28 U.S.C. §§ 1602–1611 (1976).

debtors and creditors. However, a waiver of immunity to suits arising out of the Bank's internal operations, such as its relationship with its own employees, would contravene the express language of Article VII section 1. Rather than furthering the purposes and operations of the Bank, this waiver would lay the Bank open to disruptive interference with its employment policies in each of the thirty-six countries in which it has resident missions, and the more than 140 nations in which it could be involved in its lending and financing activities. Revising and administering consistent employment policies for a large administrative staff which includes citizens from more than 100 countries is difficult enough. If the Bank were required to adopt the local employment policies of each of its member countries this task would become nearly impossible. The employment laws of member nations rarely coincide precisely, and frequently conflict with those of other member nations. National policies governing mandatory retirement at a certain age often directly contradict each other. So, too, do national laws governing discrimination in hiring. Thus, for example, the Bank would be hard pressed to establish and administer effective employment practices regarding Jewish employees in offices located in Middle Eastern countries, absent immunity for its employment related policies. Since a waiver of immunity from suits arising out of the Bank's internal relations would create such devastating administrative consequences without materially advancing its chartered objectives, Article VII section 3 should not be construed as abrogating the Bank's immunity to actions arising out of its internal affairs.

It is true, as Mendaro argues, that many multinational corporations successfully operate worldwide, yet are often forced to conform their employment practices to the laws of each country in which they retain employees. While this argument suggests that it may be possible to devise and administer consistent and fair employment policies in multiple jurisdictions, it completely overlooks the distinctions between private corporations and international organizations. Unlike private corporations, which are organized under the laws of one or more individual countries, international organizations are created by the joint action of several states. By definition, activities of international organizations are designed to resolve problems spanning national boundaries, with a benefit to be reaped collectively by the organizations' member nations. International organizations thus owe their primary allegiance to the principles and policies established by their organic documents, and not to the evolving legislation of any one member.

* * *

3. *Decisions of the Courts and Executive Branch*

This interpretation of Article VII section 3 is consistent with our few prior decisions construing international charters containing a partial waiver of immunity from judicial process. * * * In *Lutcher* a debtor of the Inter–American Development Bank sued the Bank for breach of contract, alleging that the Bank had violated implied provisions of its loan agreement by making subsequent loans to the debtor's competitor. Although the court construed a waiver provision identical to Article VII section 3 broadly enough to uphold its jurisdiction, the action clearly arose out of the Bank's external lending activities. Additionally, the court noted that a waiver of immunity to suits by the Bank's borrowers would directly aid the Bank in attracting responsible borrowers. Thus, *Lutcher* does not require us to interpret Article VII section 3 in a manner that would expose the Bank to potentially crippling litigation but not appreciably advance the Bank's ability to perform its functions.

The result reached in these decisions has received the support of the Executive Branch. Considering whether the jurisdiction of the Equal Employment Opportunity Commission extends to the World Bank, the Department of State concluded that Article VII section 3

> was not designed (and should not now be construed) to subject the Bank to the full range of our domestic jurisdiction or to expose the Bank's internal personnel and administrative actions to review by our court and administrative agencies.

* * *

> Forcing the organizations to conform their personnel practices to the varying—and often conflicting—domestic laws in each country where they operate would create unmanageable administrative burdens and could well prevent them from carrying out the functions for which they were created.

Ordinarily the opinion of the Executive Branch interpreting a treaty to which the United States is a party is entitled to great weight. Given the consistency with which the conclusions of the Department of State have been followed by other agencies we find no reason to diverge from this interpretation of the Articles of Agreement.

III. Conclusion

We are persuaded that the members of the World Bank only intended to abrogate the Bank's immunity to actions relating to its external activities and contracts, and not the internal administration of its civil servants. Accordingly, the judgment of the district court is

Affirmed.

MENDARO AND LUTCHER

The court rejected Ms. Mendaro's assertion that nothing in Article VII of the Bank Agreement limited the broad application of the waiver, saying that it "is contradicted by Article VII section 1, which states that the purpose of the waiver of immunity is 'to enable the Bank to fulfill the functions with which it is entrusted.'" See page 48 supra. Article VII, section 1 actually says:

> To enable the Bank to fulfill the functions with which it is entrusted, the status, immunities and privileges set forth in this Article shall be accorded to the Bank in the territories of each member.

Did the court correctly apply Article VII, section 1? If not, can the court's result be justified?

Did the court in Mendaro successfully distinguish Lutcher?

How should a court finally resolve the immunity issue in the hypothetical suit for breach of contract against the World Bank?

EMPLOYMENT CONTRACTS

The plaintiffs in Broadbent, page 36 supra, sought damages from the OAS for breach of employment contracts. The plaintiffs were U.S. nationals or permanent residents, and were civil servants, not high policy-making officials. (The precise nature of their duties does not appear.) In Mendaro, the plaintiff was a researcher for the World Bank. She alleged violations of Title VII of the Civil Rights Act of 1964. The possible remedies under the Act include an injunction, reinstatement with or without back pay, "or any other equitable relief as the court deems appropriate." [h]

If the restrictive theory of immunity were to be applied to international organizations, how could the nature of the OAS activity in Broadbent be noncommercial? What about the nature of the World Bank activity in Mendaro? Consider the possible relevance of the materials below.

The [U.N.] International Law Commission has adopted draft Articles on Jurisdictional Immunities of States and Their Property. They do not purport to apply to international organizations, but they do deal with employment contracts entered into by states. Article 11 says:

> 1. Unless otherwise agreed between the States concerned, a State cannot invoke immunity from jurisdiction before a court of another State which is otherwise competent in a proceeding which relates to a contract of employment between the State and an individual for work performed or to be performed, in whole or in part, in the territory of that other State.
>
> 2. Paragraph 1 does not apply if:
>
> (a) the employee has been recruited to perform functions closely related to the exercise of governmental authority;
>
> (b) the subject of the proceeding is the recruitment, renewal of employment or reinstatement of an individual;

h. 42 U.S.C.A. § 2000e–5(g).

(c) the employee was neither a national nor a habitual resident of the State of the forum at the time when the contract of employment was concluded;

(d) the employee is a national of the employer State at the time when the proceeding is instituted; or

(e) the employer State and the employee have otherwise agreed in writing, subject to any considerations of public policy conferring on the courts of the State of the forum exclusive jurisdiction by reason of the subject-matter of the proceeding.[i]

The International Law Commission's commentary on article 11 contains these words of explanation:

> With the involvement of two sovereign States, two legal systems compete for application of their respective laws. The employer State has an interest in the application of its law in regard to the selection, recruitment and appointment of an employee by the State or one of its organs, agencies or instrumentalities acting in the exercise of governmental authority. It would also seem justifiable that for the exercise of disciplinary supervision over its own staff or government employees, the employer State has an overriding interest in ensuring compliance with its internal regulations and the prerogative of appointment or dismissal which results from unilateral decisions taken by the State.
>
> On the other hand, the State of the forum appears to retain exclusive jurisdiction if not, indeed, an overriding interest in matters of domestic public policy regarding the protection to be afforded to its local labour force. Questions relating to medical insurance, insurance against certain risks, minimum wages, entitlement to rest and recreation, vacation with pay, compensation to be paid on termination of the contract of employment, etc., are of primary concern to the State of the forum, especially if the employees were recruited for work to be performed in that State, or at the time of recruitment were its nationals or habitual or permanent residents there.
>
> * * *
>
> Paragraph 2(a) enunciates the rule of immunity for the engagement of government employees of rank whose functions are closely related to the exercise of governmental authority. Examples of such employees are private secretaries, code clerks, interpreters, translators and other persons entrusted with functions related to State security or basic interests of the State. Officials of established accreditation are, of course, covered by this subparagraph.
>
> * * *

---

i. Report of the International Law Commission on the Work of Its Forty-Third Session, 46 G.A.O.R.Supp. No. 10 (A/46/10), at 93 (1991).

Paragraph 2(b) is designed to confirm the existing practice of States in support of the rule of immunity in the exercise of the discretionary power of appointment or non-appointment by the State of an individual to any official post or employment position. * * * The rule of immunity applies to proceedings for recruitment, renewal of employment and reinstatement of an individual only. It is without prejudice to the possible recourse which may still be available in the State of the forum for compensation or damages for "wrongful dismissal" or for breaches of obligation to recruit or to renew employment. In other words, this subparagraph does not prevent an employee from bringing action against the employer State in the State of the forum to seek redress for damage arising from recruitment, renewal of employment or reinstatement of an individual.[j]

Should the International Law Commission's approach be applied to international organizations, such as the OAS or the World Bank? If so, would any employees other than those at the lowest end of the responsibility scale be covered? Consider what the court in Mendaro had to say about the uniqueness of international organizations.

IMMUNITY FROM EXECUTION

Consider, finally, whether execution could be levied against the World Bank's assets if judgment is obtained against it in our hypothetical suit brought by the private California research organization. Before 1976 the State Department maintained that a foreign *government's* assets in the United States were immune from execution in satisfaction of a judgment, even when the government itself was not immune from suit—unless, of course, there was a waiver of immunity from execution. But the State Department changed its tune in 1976, as reflected in sections 1609 and 1610 of the Foreign Sovereign Immunities Act.

Would the World Bank's assets be immune from execution in our case? Consider Bank Agreement Article VII, section 3, supra page 39; IOIA *section 2(b)* (22 U.S.C.A. *§ 288a(b)*); and FSIA sections 1609 and 1610, supra page 31.

j. Id. at 94–100.

SECTION 4. THE STATUS OF PERSONS AND PREMISES ASSOCIATED WITH INTERNATIONAL ORGANIZATIONS

A. INTRODUCTION

Customary international law has long accorded well defined privileges and immunities to diplomats representing their states in direct bilateral relations with other states, and to their diplomatic missions. These have included such things as inviolability of mission premises from entrance by agents of the receiving state except with the consent of the head of the mission, exemption from certain taxes of the receiving state, broad immunity from prosecution and from civil process for persons enjoying full diplomatic status and their families, and more restricted immunity (called "functional" immunity, meaning it is limited, in the case of civil process, to matters arising from the course of official duties) for members of the administrative and technical staff of the mission. These privileges and immunities were codified in the Vienna Convention on Diplomatic Relations,[a] which entered into force for the United States in 1972.

Although varying justifications have been offered over the years for diplomatic immunities, the prevailing one at present is that they are necessary "to ensure the efficient performance of the functions of diplomatic missions as representing states." Vienna Convention, supra, preamble.[b]

The Vienna Convention on Diplomatic Relations did not deal with the privileges and immunities of representatives of states to international organizations, nor did it deal with privileges and immunities of persons in the direct service of international organizations. Such representatives and secretariat personnel are not diplomats in the strict sense of the term, since they are not accredited to a receiving state. To some extent the traditional rules applicable to diplomats could be, and have been, applied to them by analogy, but their circumstances are not in all respects parallel with those of traditional state-to-state diplomats. For example, the resident representative of a foreign state to the United Nations would be authorized to carry out essentially diplomatic functions with the United States only insofar as those functions related to matters before the U.N. The ambassador of the same foreign state would have a much broader mandate in conducting diplomacy with the United States. A high official in the U.N. Secretariat, who has sworn not to take instructions from the state of his or her nationality, obviously would not be comparable to an ambassador whose duty is to carry out instructions from home.

A number of attempts, by statute and by international agreement, have been made to define the privileges and immunities of persons and

---

a. Apr. 18, 1961, 23 U.S.T. 3227, T.I.A.S. 7502, 500 U.N.T.S. 95, implemented in the United States by the Diplomatic Relations Act of 1978, 22 U.S.C.A. §§ 254a–254e, and 28 U.S.C.A. § 1364.

b. See also C. Wilson, Diplomatic Privileges and Immunities 17–25 (1967); Ling, A Comparative Study of the Privileges and Immunities of United Nations Member Representatives and Officials with the Traditional Privileges and Immunities of Diplomatic Agents, 33 Wash. & Lee L.Rev. 91, 93–95 (1976).

missions associated with international organizations. In fact, in order to find an answer to the questions that might arise in the United States concerning diplomatic immunities surrounding the U.N., one must consider—or at least be aware of—five international agreements and at least two federal statutes. In addition, it may be necessary to fill in possible lacunae with analogous provisions of the 1961 Vienna Convention on Diplomatic Relations, supra. The five agreements and two statutes are:

(a) U.N. Charter article 105(2) and (3);

(b) the bilateral Agreement Between the United States and the United Nations Regarding the Headquarters of the United Nations [c] (the Headquarters Agreement, which entered into force Nov. 21, 1947);

(c) Convention on the Privileges and Immunities of the United Nations (the General Convention) [d] (entered into force for the United States Apr. 29, 1970);

(d) Vienna Convention on the Representation of States in Their Relations with International Organizations of a Universal Character [e] (not in force at this writing);

(e) Convention on the Prevention and Punishment of Crimes Against Internationally Protected Persons, Including Diplomatic Agents [f] (entered into force Feb. 20, 1977);

(f) International Organizations Immunities Act (IOIA) [g] (effective Dec. 29, 1945);

(g) Act for the Prevention and Punishment of Crimes Against Internationally Protected Persons [h] (effective Oct. 8, 1976).

The latter Act ((g) above) implements the similarly-named Convention ((e) above), which obligates states parties to prosecute or extradite a person who commits, threatens or attempts a violent attack on the person, premises or means of transportation of an "internationally protected person." Under article 1(1)(b), that category includes "any representative or official of a State or any official or other agent of an international organization of an intergovernmental character who * * * is entitled pursuant to international law to special protection from any attack on his person, freedom or dignity, as well as members of his family forming part of his household * * *." The Act provides means by which to prosecute persons charged with these offenses.

No attempt will be made here to cover all the issues that could arise under these international agreements and statutes. Nor will we

[c.] June 26, 1947, 61 Stat. 3416, 12 Bevans 956, 11 U.N.T.S. 11, as implemented in the United States by the Joint Resolution of Aug. 4, 1947, 61 Stat. 756.

[d.] Feb. 13, 1946, 21 U.S.T. 1418, T.I.A.S. 6900, 1 U.N.T.S. 16.

[e.] Mar. 14, 1975, U.N. Doc. A/CONF.67/16, 69 Am.J.Int'l L. 730 (1975).

[f.] Dec. 14, 1973, 28 U.S.T. 1975, T.I.A.S. 8532, 1035 U.N.T.S. 167.

[g.] 22 U.S.C.A. §§ 288 et seq.

[h.] 18 U.S.C.A. § 112.

examine the issues that could arise regarding organizations other than the United Nations. Rather, the focus will be on a few significant problems concerning the U.N.

B. MISSION PREMISES

1. Protection From Demonstrations

U.N. member states maintain missions to the U.N. in New York City, from which they conduct their U.N. business. The missions normally are near the main U.N. headquarters district on the East River, but are not within it. Over the years, some of these missions have been targets for demonstrators who object to policies of the governments represented by the missions. During the cold war, the Soviet mission was a frequent target, but it has not been alone. Some of the demonstrations have been both noisy and blunt, causing the target missions to complain to U.S. authorities that their normal functions have been disrupted and their dignity impaired.

These demonstrations have caused real problems for U.S. officials, who have tried to balance the need (obligation?) to protect foreign missions and the U.S. constitutional requirement to allow free speech. In general, the U.S. response to foreign complaints has been sympathetic whenever actual or seriously threatened violence has been involved, but has been less so when only noise and insults have occurred. The following excerpt from the 1988 Report of the U.N. Committee on Relations with the Host Country illustrates the problem.

REPORT OF THE COMMITTEE ON RELATIONS WITH THE HOST COUNTRY
Nov. 25, 1988.
U.N. Doc. A/43/26.

* * *

8. At its 129th meeting, on 5 May 1988, the Committee resumed consideration of matters relating to the security of missions and the safety of their personnel. The representative of the Soviet Union indicated that the Soviet Mission to the United Nations in the last few months had faced serious problems in that regard. Although it had received co-operation from the United States authorities, which was appreciated, the Mission remained the target of negative political propaganda and acts of harassment against its personnel. Political demonstrations should not be aimed at missions. Such demonstrations produced direct insults and threats. It was necessary to discuss how missions were to be protected from such activities.

9. The representative of the United Kingdom expressed the view that a distinction must be made between the issues of the safety and protection of missions and the peaceful expression of opinion by the public in a democracy, which was a time-honoured right. However,

sometimes the distinction between what was acceptable and what was not was hard to draw. He further pointed out that peaceful expression of opinion by the public did not hamper the work of missions. As to the United Kingdom Mission, it had a daily "visitation" by a group of people who did not agree with one of his country's policies. Only when their demonstrations became unruly were the police called.

10. The representative of the United States referred to the United States Constitution, which provided precise guarantees for freedom of expression, assembly and speech. The United States protected the exercise of those rights and protected the safety and functions of diplomatic missions. The Soviet Mission was assigned the largest police detail of any mission in New York City. He requested to be informed of specific instances when Soviet mission functions were impeded by political demonstrations.

11. The representative of the Soviet Union wondered whether insults by demonstrators at passing diplomats could be regarded under the United States Constitution as freedom of expression. Demonstrations against missions obstructed the work of the United Nations and that was contrary to the provisions of the Headquarters Agreement. Therefore, when the United States Constitution was invoked against a foreign mission there was a conflict between the host country's national legislation and its obligations under the relevant provisions of international law.

THE DUTY TO PROTECT THE MISSION

If demonstrators have made the work of target missions more difficult, and if the police have made no special effort to contain noise or to break up demonstrations, has the United States breached any duty it owes to sending states under international law?

In 1964 the United Nations Legal Counsel said, "There is no specific reference to mission premises in the Headquarters Agreement and the diplomatic status of these premises therefore arises from the diplomatic status of a resident representative and his staff."[a] The Headquarters Agreement does provide in section 16(a) that "The appropriate American authorities shall exercise due diligence to ensure that the tranquility of the headquarters district is not disturbed by the unauthorized entry of groups of persons from outside or by disturbances in its immediate vicinity and shall cause to be provided on the boundaries of the headquarters district such police protection as is required for these purposes." The U.N. Secretary–General has relied on this provision in reminding the United States of the problems caused by hostile demonstrations outside mission premises.[b] But the headquarters district is a clearly defined area encompassing the buildings and

---

[a] [1967] 2 Y.B.Int'l L.Comm'n 187.   [b] Id.

office space used by the United Nations organization, not including the missions of individual states. Is section 16(a) relevant to our problem? Does U.N. Charter *article 105(2)* solve the problem?

Article 23(2)(a) of the 1975 Vienna Convention on the Representation of States in Their Relations with International Organizations of a Universal Character provides that "The host State is under a special duty to take all appropriate steps to protect the premises of the mission against any intrusion or damage and to prevent any disturbance of the peace of the mission or impairment of its dignity." This provision was taken almost verbatim from article 22(2) of the 1961 Vienna Convention on Diplomatic Relations, which is in force for the United States (and for most other nations).

Although the 1975 Convention is not in force, one must consider the argument that the adoption of a set of rules by an overwhelming majority at a broadly-based multilateral conference has at least some law-making effect—particularly as to a rule copied from a treaty in force for the relevant states in an analogous situation. Note that the process of assertion of rights or duties, and acquiescence by other states, is at the essence of the development of custom. Custom, of course, is a primary source of international law. International conferences (and plenary bodies within international organizations) provide convenient forums for assertion and acquiescence, or for the expression of consensus—which can be viewed as a step beyond assertion and acquiescence in the law-making process, since it represents a degree of affirmative agreement on the principles involved. The Vienna Convention on the Representation of States was adopted by a vote of 57 in favor to one against, with 15 abstentions.[c] But virtually all states, including the United States, that are hosts to major international organizations abstained and are unlikely to become parties to the Convention. In general, they objected to the expansion of traditional immunities given by the Convention to persons other than permanent diplomatic representatives to international organizations, and they questioned the need for the Convention in light of existing treaties such as the U.N. Headquarters Agreement and the General Convention.[d] It does not appear, however, that the host states objected specifically to the provisions of article 23. Does that article bear on the international law duty of the United States toward states with U.N. missions in New York City?

The General Assembly has been concerned about the disturbances directed against missions, and has urged the United States government to enforce the provisions of federal law dealing with protection of

c. U.N. Doc. A/CONF.67/SR.13 (1975).
d. See Fennessy, The 1975 Vienna Convention on the Representation of States in Their Relations With International Organizations of a Universal Character, 70 Am. J.Int'l L. 62 (1976).

foreign officials. The relevant federal statutory provisions appear below.

ACT FOR THE PREVENTION AND PUNISHMENT OF CRIMES AGAINST INTERNATIONALLY PROTECTED PERSONS
Oct. 8, 1976.
18 U.S.C.A. § 112.

(a) Whoever assaults, strikes, wounds, imprisons, or offers violence to a foreign official, official guest, or internationally protected person or makes any other violent attack upon the person or liberty of such person, or, if likely to endanger his person or liberty, makes a violent attack upon his official premises, private accommodation, or means of transport or attempts to commit any of the foregoing shall be fined not more than $5,000 or imprisoned not more than three years, or both. Whoever in the commission of any such act uses a deadly or dangerous weapon shall be fined not more than $10,000 or imprisoned not more than ten years, or both.

(b) Whoever willfully—

(1) intimidates, coerces, threatens, or harasses a foreign official or an official guest or obstructs a foreign official in the performance of his duties;

(2) attempts to intimidate, coerce, threaten, or harass a foreign official or an official guest or obstruct a foreign official in the performance of his duties; or

(3) within the United States and within one hundred feet of any building or premises in whole or in part owned, used, or occupied for official business or for diplomatic, consular, or residential purposes by—

(A) a foreign government, including such use as a mission to an international organization;

(B) an international organization;

(C) a foreign official; or

(D) an official guest;

congregates with two or more other persons with intent to violate any other provision of this section;

shall be fined not more than $500 or imprisoned not more than six months, or both.

(c) For the purpose of this section "foreign government", "foreign official", "internationally protected person", "international organization", and "official guest" shall have the same meanings as those provided in section 1116(b) of this title.

(d) Nothing contained in this section shall be construed or applied so as to abridge the exercise of rights guaranteed under the first amendment to the Constitution of the United States.

(e) If the victim of an offense under subsection (a) is an internationally protected person, the United States may exercise jurisdiction over the offense if the alleged offender is present within the United States, irrespective of the place where the offense was committed or the nationality of the victim or the alleged offender.

* * *

[Under section 1116(b), the persons protected include chiefs of state, presidents, vice presidents, ambassadors, foreign ministers and other cabinet officers of foreign governments, chief executive officers of international organizations, foreign persons notified to the United States government as officers or employees of foreign governments or international organizations, any other person who "is entitled pursuant to international law to special protection against attack upon his person, freedom or dignity," and certain members of the families of these persons.]

STATUTORY AND JUDICIAL PROTECTION

Note that the Act in subsection (d) expressly recognizes the tension between its subsection (b) and the First Amendment. Would subsection (b) apply if a demonstration, though within 100 feet of a mission, involved only the carrying of placards and the shouting of loud chants demanding better treatment for ethnic minorities, accompanied by loud insults directed at anyone coming or going to or from the mission?

If the United States does owe an international duty to a sending state to "prevent any disturbance of the peace of the mission or impairment of its dignity," would the First Amendment's restrictions on the federal government affect a determination of whether or not it had breached the duty? It is clear that provisions of domestic law cannot excuse what would otherwise be a breach of a duty under international law. But could it convincingly be argued that the First Amendment restrictions, rather than being offered as an excuse for failure to comply with an international duty to prevent disturbance of the peace of the mission, should simply be read into the duty so that the only "disturbances of the peace" or "impairments of dignity" encompassed by the international duty would be those perpetrated by individuals in a manner not protected by First Amendment rights?

In Concerned Jewish Youth v. McGuire,[e] the Second Circuit upheld a New York City police directive that restricted demonstrators seeking

---

e. 621 F.2d 471 (2d Cir.1980), cert. denied 450 U.S. 913, 101 S.Ct. 1352, 67 L.Ed.2d 337 (1981).

to publicize the Soviet Union's treatment of Jews. The Concerned Jewish Youth, a group espousing nonviolent principles, sought to demonstrate peacefully in front of the Soviet mission on East 67th Street in New York City, and to use sound amplification equipment at times of day when it would not disturb school, worship or sleep in the area. The captain in charge of the local police precinct restricted the demonstration on the mission block to twelve persons in a "bull pen" diagonally across the street from the mission, permitting any additional persons to demonstrate a block away. He also refused to allow any sound device to be used on the mission block, but said it could be used on the corner of the next block.

In its 2–1 decision, the court rejected the First Amendment claims of the Concerned Jewish Youth, saying that the police restrictions were necessary to further a strong governmental interest in protecting the Soviet mission and its personnel. To demonstrate the strong governmental interest, the court relied on article 22(2) of the 1961 Vienna Convention on Diplomatic Relations, section 16 of the Headquarters Agreement and 18 U.S.C.A. § 112. It also held that reasonable local police directives were not preempted by 18 U.S.C.A. § 112.

In Boos v. Barry,[f] the U.S. Supreme Court considered a provision of the District of Columbia Code that prohibited the display of any sign within 500 feet of a foreign embassy if the sign tended to bring the foreign government into "public odium" or "public disrepute." It also prohibited any congregation of three or more people within 500 feet of a foreign embassy. The Court struck down the first part (the "display" clause), as a content-based prohibition on speech not crafted with sufficient precision to withstand First Amendment scrutiny. The Court upheld the second part (the "congregation" clause) after it had been narrowly construed to permit dispersal by the police only when normal embassy activities have been or are about to be disrupted. The Court noted that the congregation clause was site-specific, applying only within 500 feet of an embassy.

Does Boos v. Barry cast doubt on Concerned Jewish Youth v. McGuire?

2. *Eviction*

Missions to the U.N. typically occupy rented office space near the U.N. Headquarters District. Not all missions have been consistently prompt with their payments of rent. If their lessors take action to collect the rent or to evict them, questions of immunity arise.

[f.] 485 U.S. 312, 108 S.Ct. 1157, 99 L.Ed.2d 333 (1988).

767 THIRD AVENUE ASSOCIATES v. PERMANENT MISSION OF ZAIRE
United States District Court, Southern District of New York, 1992.
787 F.Supp. 389.

SAND, DISTRICT JUDGE.

This action calls into question the rights of a private landlord who has leased premises to a foreign mission to the United Nations which has concededly defaulted on its rental obligations for over a year and a half. The premises at issue are the entire twenty-fifth floor of a commercial office building. The action presents the important question, apparently of first impression, whether such a landlord may regain possession of the premises from its tenant or whether such action is forever barred by the Foreign Sovereign Immunities Act * * * (the "FSIA"), or any treaty obligations.

[The plaintiffs were the owner, and its managing agent, of the office building. The defendant was the official delegation of the Republic of Zaire to the United Nations. In May 1982, plaintiff Sage Realty leased the premises to the Mission for ten years. In October 1987, after the Mission had failed to pay its rent for more than seven months, plaintiffs brought an action against it. The court entered a judgment in August 1989, terminating the lease and awarding damages to the plaintiffs. The Mission then paid plaintiffs the full amount of damages and remained in possession on a month-to-month basis.

[During the summer of 1990, the Mission again defaulted. After several demands for payment, the plaintiffs notified the Mission that they elected to terminate the tenancy. When the Mission did not move out, plaintiffs brought this action seeking unpaid rents and occupancy of the premises.

[Plaintiffs moved for summary judgment and the Mission moved to dismiss. The Mission did not contest its default on the rental payments, but claimed (inter alia) sovereign immunity. The court granted plaintiffs' motion, denied defendant's motion, awarded plaintiffs damages and directed the Mission to vacate the premises. The Mission filed a Notice of Appeal to the Second Circuit, and sought a stay of the judgment pending appeal. At that point the U.S. government appeared on Zaire's behalf, arguing that eviction would contravene U.S. treaty obligations. The District Court's opinion dealt with the motion for a stay.]

II. DISCUSSION

In deciding whether to grant a stay pending appeal, this Court must consider four factors: (1) whether Movants have made a strong showing of the likelihood of success on the merits; (2) whether Movants will be irreparably injured absent the stay; (3) whether granting the stay would substantially harm the other parties in the proceeding; and (4) where the public interest lies.

A. *Likelihood of Success on the Merits*

Of the four factors relevant to our decision to grant or deny a stay, the question of likelihood of success on the merits is the most hotly contested by the parties. Movants do not dispute the Mission's default on its rental obligations, but insist that the FSIA and other treaties relating to sovereign immunity preclude the remedy of eviction. Plaintiffs respond that those pronouncements do not apply to the situation at hand, and emphasize that if Movants' contentions were accepted, a private landlord could be forced to "host" its nonpaying diplomatic tenant *ad infinitum,* so that its property would in effect have been "taken."

1. Immunity Under the FSIA

The first basis for Movants' claim of immunity from eviction is section 1609 of the FSIA, which states:

> Subject to existing international agreements to which the United States is a party at the time of enactment of this Act, *the property in the United States of a foreign state shall be immune from attachment, arrest and execution.*

28 U.S.C. § 1609 (1991) (emphasis added). Sections 1610 and 1611 of the Act set forth certain exceptions to the general ban against execution or attachment, none of which are asserted by Plaintiff here. Movants cite this section for the proposition that although Plaintiffs may rightfully seek and obtain a monetary judgment against them, they may not regain possession of the Premises.

We have reviewed the language of the FSIA and the legislative history underlying it. Neither suggests immediately that Congress considered the precise situation at issue: whether an eviction constitutes an "attachment" or "execution" falling within the statutory prohibition. We have also reviewed a number of cases construing the statute in other factual contexts * * *.

* * *

After a careful review of the * * * authorities, we find that the sovereign immunity conferred by the FSIA does not include immunity from eviction for nonpayment of rent from privately owned premises. The statute by its very terms contemplates a situation in which a judgment creditor seeks to enforce its judgment against a sovereign by attaching or otherwise executing upon assets owned by the foreign state. Yet while that prohibition is crystal clear and efforts to evade it have understandably been rebuffed by other courts, * * * the circumstances of this case are sharply distinguishable. Here, instead of seeking to enforce the Judgment of this Court by attaching or executing upon the Mission's assets, Plaintiffs are merely attempting to regain possession of property which is rightfully theirs. That remedy is neither explicitly nor implicitly prohibited by the FSIA, and we decline Movants' invitation to expand the immunity conferred by that Act.

2. Immunity Under United States Treaty Obligations

Movants next claim that the Mission cannot be evicted in light of various treaties and charters to which the United States is a signatory.

Movants rely heavily on Article 22 of the Vienna Convention on Diplomatic Relations, which provides:

> (1) The premises of the mission shall be inviolable. The agents of the receiving State may not enter them, except with the consent of the head of the mission.
>
> (2) The receiving State is under a special duty to take all appropriate steps to protect the premises of the mission against any intrusion or damage and to prevent any disturbance of the peace of the mission or impairment of its dignity.

See Vienna Convention on Diplomatic Relations, April 18, 1961, art. 22(1) & 22(2), 23 U.S.T. 3227 (hereinafter the "Vienna Convention"). Although it is not cited in any of Movants' briefs, article 22(3) provides further that "The premises of the mission, their furnishings and other property thereon and the means of transport of the mission shall be immune from search, requisition, attachment or execution." *Id.,* art. 22(3).

In addition to those sections of the Vienna Convention, Movants find support for their position in the United Nations Charter and the 1946 Convention of the Privileges and Immunities of the United Nations (hereinafter the "U.N. Convention"). Those agreements confer upon representatives to the United Nations "such privileges and immunities, as are necessary for the independent exercise of their functions in connection with the Organization," U.N. Charter, August 8, 1945, art. 105(2), 59 Stat. 1031, 1053, and "inviolability for all papers and documents," U.N. Convention, February 13, 1946, art. IV, § 11(b), 21 U.S.T. 1418. Finally, Movants cite a number of cases that refer to the United States' legal obligation under these treaties to protect the premises of foreign missions. *See, e.g., Boos v. Barry,* 485 U.S. 312, 323, 108 S.Ct. 1157, 1165, 99 L.Ed.2d 333 (1988) (affirming the Nation's "need to protect diplomats"); *Concerned Jewish Youth v. McGuire,* 621 F.2d 471, 474 (2d Cir.1980), *cert. denied,* 450 U.S. 913, 101 S.Ct. 1352, 67 L.Ed.2d 337 (1981) (citing the United States' "substantial interest in protecting foreign officials and their property" to uphold restrictions on demonstrations outside the Soviet Permanent Mission).

We have scrutinized the language of these treaties, the background to their adoption, and the cases cited in Movants' briefs. Our review convinces us that the notion of protection from eviction from privately owned leased premises was not specifically addressed by any of the treaties. We conclude, however, that the treaties' grants of "inviolability" and "privileges and immunities" were prompted by concerns other than those present in this case.

The language of the above treaties demonstrates that they were driven by two principal concerns: first, a perceived need to protect the sovereign from mob violence and other harassment; and second, a recognition that the premises of the sovereign are entitled to protection from unannounced seizures or other invasions of privacy. The first of these concerns is reflected in the Vienna Convention's articulation of a "special duty" to protect the premises of the mission from any "intrusion," "damage," "disturbance of the peace," or "impairment of its dignity," and in a number of cases rejecting first amendment challenges in light of the government's obligation to protect foreign diplomats and their property. *See, e.g., Concerned Jewish Youth, supra; International Soc'y for Krishna Consciousness, Inc. v. City of New York*, 501 F.Supp. 684 (S.D.N.Y.1980); *Greenberg v. Murphy*, 329 F.Supp. 37 (S.D.N.Y. 1971). The second concern is reflected in the Vienna Convention's declaration of the "inviolability" of mission premises and immunity from search and seizure; in the U.N. Convention's assertion of "inviolability for all papers and documents"; and implicitly in the U.N. Charter's grant of privileges and immunities "necessary" for the independent exercise of United Nations functions.

* * *

[W]e remain unconvinced that permitting the eviction of the Mission would implicate either of the interests identified above. In the first place, we reject outright Movants' contention that the eviction would threaten the physical safety of Mission members. *See* Government's Supplemental Statement of Interest at 18 (noting that "should Zairian representatives * * * resist peaceful attempts by the United States Marshal to enter the mission, physical compulsion would be required"). Not only is it highly speculative that such resistance would occur, but it is doubtful that the treaties were intended to protect diplomats from injuries sustained resisting a party's lawful efforts to recover its own property.

Nor is the second concern applicable in this context, since although eviction would require entry of the Premises by a United States Marshal, such an entry would hardly be sudden or unexpected. Plaintiffs put the Mission on notice of their intent to evict them by letter dated April 26, 1991. Since that time, Plaintiffs not only commenced a court action but obtained a Judgment of eviction from this Court. Even the Government has informed the Mission over the course of pursuing "diplomatic alternatives" to eviction that the Mission could not expect to remain in the Premises indefinitely without paying rent. *See, e.g.,* Letter from Thomas R. Pickering, United States Representative to the United Nations, to Lukabu Khabouji N'Zaji, Zaire's Charge d'Affaires (February 11, 1992) (attached as Exh. A to Wolf Declaration) (warning that "Unlimited tenure in offices or residences without paying rent is unacceptable."). The Mission has not only had ample time to avoid a non-consensual entry by vacating voluntarily, therefore, but any entry at this point will have been preceded by so much notice that the privacy of Mission members or secrecy of Mission papers could not possibly be threatened.[5]

In sum, Movants have failed to demonstrate that either the FSIA or other treaties preclude Plaintiffs from evicting them from the

---

5. In an effort to bolster its contention that a mission cannot be entered for any purpose without consent, the Government describes how even in urgent situations such as a bomb scare, United States agents customarily refuse to enter a mission until they receive permission from its occupants. *See* Declaration of Robert C. Moller, Coun-

Premises. Because they have proffered no other defense to the Court's Judgment of eviction, Movants have not met their burden of demonstrating a likelihood of success on the merits.

B. *Irreparable Injury*

Another factor that we must consider is whether Movants will suffer irreparable injury unless a stay is granted. Movants first argue that the Mission will suffer irreparable harm if evicted because it will "no longer be able to carry out its functions" or "meet its agenda at the United Nations." * * * Movants also argue that our refusal to stay the eviction will inflict irreparable injury on the Government, both by "forcing" it to violate its international treaty obligations and by threatening the status of United States diplomatic personnel abroad.

Movants' first claim of irreparable harm is unconvincing. The Mission contends that eviction would interfere with its ability to function as a productive member of the United Nations. It has made no showing that the Premises at 767 Third Avenue are unique, however, or that it is restrained by anything other than its own financial condition from moving elsewhere. The Mission's failure to seek alternative housing arrangements during the pendency of this action undercuts the legitimacy of this claim of irreparable harm.

Movants' other claims of irreparable injury are more considerable. The Government alleges that our condonation of the eviction will force it to violate its international obligations, and expresses concern that our decision will compromise the protection afforded the United States mission in Zaire and other missions and personnel abroad.

Although the above discussion reflects our own view that the eviction does not contravene United States treaty obligations, we have no way of gauging whether the Government's predictions of international repercussions are realistic or overblown. Despite our willingness to acknowledge a national interest in blocking the eviction, however, we find unacceptable Movants' contention that the entire burden of these concerns should be borne by a single private landlord. The Government's obligation and ability to distribute that burden more broadly is discussed in greater detail in Part D, *infra*.

* * *

C. *Substantial Harm to Plaintiffs*

The third factor to consider in determining whether to grant Movants' application is whether the stay would "substantially harm" Plaintiffs. We find that this factor weighs heavily in Plaintiffs' favor.

* * *

sel for Host Country Affairs for the United States Mission to the United Nations, in Support of the Government's Supplemental Statement of Interest (Feb. 27, 1992), ¶¶ 3–6 (hereinafter "Moller Dec."). Those situations are distinguishable from the instant case, however, in that the sudden and unannounced entry by United States agents occasioned by a bomb scare could clearly compromise the confidentiality of mission affairs. In this case, by contrast, the Mission will have had more than ample time to ensure that its removal from the Premises is an orderly one.

D. *The Public Interest*

The final factor that we must consider is whether a stay pending appeal would serve the public interest. Movants raise essentially the same arguments with respect to this factor as they did with respect to their claim of irreparable injury—that the public interest is ill-served by forcing the Government to violate its obligations under international law and that we should exercise extreme care to prevent a landlord-tenant dispute from escalating into an "international incident."

In response to Movants' contentions, we return to an issue raised earlier in addressing their allegations of irreparable injury: that no matter how important the Executive Branch's asserted foreign policy objectives may be, Plaintiffs should not be forced to assume sole responsibility for them. If the interests are as significant as the Government insists, they can surely be promoted more equitably—possibly by designating United States or United Nations funds to insure collectibility of the Judgment—than by thrusting their entire burden on the shoulders of a single private landlord. As Plaintiffs have argued and as we suggested repeatedly at oral argument, any other conclusion would raise a serious issue as to whether Plaintiffs had been subjected to an unconstitutional "taking" under the Fifth Amendment.

THE REMEDY FOR NONPAYMENT OF RENT

Note the court's treatment of the FSIA. The relevant sections are set forth at pages 31–32 supra. Should the court have held the Mission of Zaire immune from the suit altogether?

If not, did it adequately get around section 1609? Consider the dictum from United States v. County of Arlington,[a] a case denying enforcement of a tax lien against an apartment house used by diplomatic representatives of what was then the German Democratic Republic:

> Undoubtedly, the purchase of this property was a commercial act regardless of its purpose. Consequently the GDR would be subject to suit under § 1605(a)(2) by the vendor if a dispute arose over the terms of sale. Referring to diplomatic and consular property, the House Report states: "[A] foreign state cannot deny to the local state the right to adjudicate questions of ownership, rent, servitudes, and similar matters, as long as the foreign state's possession of the premises is not disturbed."[b]

The Court in the Zaire case quoted and distinguished article 22 of the Vienna Convention on Diplomatic Relations, to which the United States is a party. Direct counterpart provisions are found in *article 23* of the 1975 Vienna Convention on the Representation of States in Their

---

a. 669 F.2d 925, 934 (4th Cir.1982), appeal dismissed 459 U.S. 801, 103 S.Ct. 23, 74 L.Ed.2d 39 (1982).

b. The court's quote is from H.R.Rep. No. 1487, 94th Cong., 2d Sess. 20, reprinted in [1976] U.S.Code Cong. & Ad.News 6604, 6619.

Relations with International Organizations of a Universal Character, which—as has already been noted above—is not in force, but was adopted by an overwhelming majority at an international conference. Did the court successfully distinguish the immunities provided by these articles? Is the inviolability of mission premises maintained if officials of the receiving state enter them in order to evict the mission?

What about the other treaties: U.N. Charter *article 105(2)* and General Convention *section 11(b)*?

Would the Italian Corte di Cassazione's decision in the FAO case, supra page ___, give support to the district court's decision in this case?

The district court mentioned that the U.S. Representative to the U.N. had become involved, in the course of pursuing diplomatic alternatives to court-ordered eviction. Does that tend to support the court's result or to undercut it?

Normally, courts in the United States accept the Executive Branch's interpretation of U.S. treaty obligations. Was the district court in this case too cavalier toward the Executive Branch's interpretation?

Did the district court's result in this case represent good policy?

As mentioned above, the Mission of Zaire filed a Notice of Appeal in this case. The appeal was later abandoned, and the case was settled without an eviction.

3. *Execution Against a Mission's Bank Account*

FOXWORTH v. PERMANENT MISSION OF UGANDA

United States District Court, Southern District of New York, 1992.
796 F.Supp. 761.

[The Permanent Mission of Uganda to the U.N. moved to vacate a writ of execution entered against its bank account. The writ stemmed from a default judgment obtained by Eva Foxworth, age 80, who had been struck by an automobile owned by the Mission. She suffered broken bones and was left unable to care for herself. When the Mission failed to satisfy the $250,000 personal injury judgment, a writ of execution was entered against its account with Chemical Bank in New York City. At that point the Mission entered its first appearance in the case, urging that the account was immune from execution since it was used for wages, allowances and travel expenses of Mission personnel. The U.S. State Department supported the Mission's motion to vacate, asserting that the writ violated U.S. obligations to Uganda and to the U.N.]

The United States is signatory to treaties which obligate it to give the missions and representatives of United Nations member states the facilities and legal protection necessary for performance of their diplomatic functions. Such treaties are "equal in stature and force" to the laws of the United States.

One of them, the United Nations Charter, ratified by the United States on August 8, 1945, provides:

> Representatives of the Members of the United Nations and officials of the Organization shall similarly enjoy such privileges and immunities as are necessary for the independent exercise of their functions in connection with the Organization.

U.N. Charter art. [105], para. 2. Following ratification, President Truman invited the United Nations to establish its permanent seat in the United States. On June 26, 1947, after the General Assembly decided on New York City as the site for its permanent headquarters, the United Nations Headquarters Agreement was entered by the United States and the United Nations. That agreement provides that representatives of the member states shall enjoy "the same privileges and immunities * * * as [the United States] accords to diplomatic envoys accredited to it." U.N. Headquarters Agreement art. V, sect. 15. This grant of immunity echoed that of the 1946 Convention on the Privileges and Immunities of the United Nations, February 13, 1946, which states that representatives of United Nations members shall enjoy "such * * * privileges, immunities and facilities * * * as diplomatic envoys enjoy." [Art. IV, sect. 11(g).]

The Vienna Convention on Diplomatic Relations, ratified by the United States in 1961, sets forth the privileges and immunities to which representatives of United Nations members are entitled. Article 25 of the Convention provides:

> The receiving State shall accord full facilities for the performance of the functions of the mission.

In addition, the preamble states that the purpose of the Vienna Convention is to "assure the efficient performance of the functions" of the missions.

* * *

Here, two of the parties to the relevant treaties, the United States, as represented by the Department of State, and the government of Uganda, as represented by its permanent mission to the United Nations, agree that attachment of the bank account constitutes a violation of both the United Nations Charter and the Vienna Convention. This is a reasonable interpretation consistent with the language of the treaties. In the case at hand, attachment of defendant's account by the United States Marshal will, according to defendant, force it to cease operations. This is contrary to the obligation of the United States to provide defendant the immunities necessary for operation under the United Nations Charter and its obligation to accord "full facilities" for the performance of the mission's functions under the Vienna Convention. *See Liberian Eastern Timber Corp. v. Government of the Republic of Liberia,* 659 F.Supp. 606, 608 (D.D.C.1987).

The treaties discussed above do not immunize defendant from being haled into court to answer for its tortious conduct. Although generally immune from suit under the Foreign Sovereign Immunities Act of 1976, foreign states are subject to the jurisdiction of state and federal courts in cases where damages are sought for personal injury or death caused by the tortious act of that foreign state or any official or employee of that foreign state. 28 U.S.C. § 1605(a). Thus, the default judgment entered in this case is valid and may be vacated only if the requirements of Fed.R.Civ.P. 60(b) are satisfied.

Because attachment of defendant's account will force defendant to cease operations, defendant's motion is granted. Defendant is reminded, however, that there remains an outstanding judgment pursuant to which it is liable to plaintiff in the amount of $250,120.

MISSION BANK ACCOUNTS AND U.S. OBLIGATIONS

The court did not mention FSIA section 1609 (quoted in the Zaire case at page 63 supra). As in that case, the exceptions in sections 1610 and 1611 would be inapplicable here. Should the court have granted defendant's motion on the basis of section 1609?

The court relied on several treaty obligations of the United States. One treaty provision it did not mention is *article 20(1)* of the 1975 Vienna Convention on the Representation of States in Their Relations with International Organizations of a Universal Character. It is the counterpart of article 25 of the 1961 Vienna Convention on Diplomatic Relations, quoted in the court's opinion. Was it relevant, even though the 1975 Convention was not in force?

Does the Foxworth case stand for the proposition that the 1961 Vienna Convention's provisions on privileges and immunities of diplomatic missions apply to U.N. missions?

A treaty obligation of the United States becomes domestic law without statutory implementation only if it is self-executing. U.S. courts have been reluctant to find provisions of the U.N. Charter to be self-executing, often noting the rather general language of the Charter. Is the Foxworth case authority for the proposition that U.N. Charter *article 105(2)* is self-executing? Leaving aside FSIA section 1609, could the result in Foxworth have been reached if the treaties involved were not self-executing?

The court quoted from *section 15* of the U.N. Headquarters Agreement and *section 11(g)* of the General Convention on the Privileges and Immunities of the U.N. Were those sections relevant? Note also *section 16* of the General Convention.

C. CIVIL SUIT AGAINST A DELEGATE TO THE U.N. OR A U.N. OFFICIAL: JURISDICTION AND IMMUNITY

Suppose that three French nationals depart from the French U.N. mission in an automobile, bound for a cocktail party and reception being given by the U.N. Secretary-General for persons associated with a three-week U.N. conference that has just begun. The three are a Deputy Permanent Representative of France to the U.N., a technical adviser to a French delegation temporarily in the United States for the conference, and a French member of the permanent staff of the U.N. Secretariat who is assigned as one of the principal organizers of the conference. (The Deputy Permanent Representative, though not a delegate to the conference, is in charge of liaison between the permanent French mission and its conference delegation.) Because of a temporary shortage of chauffeurs, the technical adviser (the lowest ranking of the three) is at the wheel.

(Note that U.N. receptions, though well supplied with food and drink, are not purely social occasions. As one experienced U.N. participant and observer has said, "Many deals are concluded over the dinner table or in a corner or a corridor during a reception. Many initiatives are prepared in this way and useful hints are given and taken, which are later developed during meetings of the different committees. * * * At times one is full of admiration for diplomats who apparently can work during and after big meals, and even settle world affairs over brandy and cigars." [a])

On the way to the reception, the automobile driven by the technical adviser collides with a car owned and driven by a private U.S. citizen. The U.S. citizen is injured, and now brings a civil suit in a federal district court against the French driver and the mission's insurer. The French driver is served with process in New York City. (The Diplomatic Relations Act, below, contemplates suits directly against insurers. In a case like this, though, the plaintiff might well want to join the driver as a defendant.)

In such a proceeding there would be two distinct preliminary issues. One would be whether the court has subject matter jurisdiction; the other would be whether the driver has immunity from suit. Although these are separate issues, they are interrelated. Because of cross-references in the Diplomatic Relations Act between the sections on subject matter jurisdiction and the sections on immunities, federal subject matter jurisdiction in actions against some U.N.-related defendants would be decided by reference to definitions designed primarily to delineate those persons entitled to immunity.

To be specific, the Diplomatic Relations Act amended 28 U.S.C.A. § 1351 to read:

> The district courts shall have original jurisdiction, exclusive of the courts of the States, of all civil actions and proceedings against—

* * *

---

a. Hambro, Permanent Representatives to International Organizations, 1976 Y.B. of World Affairs 30, 36–37.

(2) members of a mission or members of their families (as such terms are defined in section 2 of the Diplomatic Relations Act).

Is section 2 of the Diplomatic Relations Act, 22 U.S.C.A. § 254a (below), broad enough to encompass the technical adviser to the temporary French delegation, whose driving caused the accident in our hypothetical situation? If not, would there be some other basis for federal subject matter jurisdiction in the action against him? Would the answers be the same if either of the other two French nationals in the car had been driving and thus were the defendant?

Consider the Diplomatic Relations Act not only for its bearing on federal subject matter jurisdiction, but also as it relates to immunity from suit.

DIPLOMATIC RELATIONS ACT
Sept. 30, 1978, as amended.
22 U.S.C.A. § 254a et seq.

§ 245a. Definitions

As used in this Act—

(1) the term "members of a mission" means—

(A) the head of a mission and those members of a mission who are members of the diplomatic staff or who, pursuant to law, are granted equivalent privileges and immunities,

(B) members of the administrative and technical staff of a mission, and

(C) members of the service staff of a mission,

as such terms are defined in Article 1 of the Vienna Convention;

(2) the term "family" means—

(A) the members of the family of a member of a mission described in paragraph (1)(A) who form part of his or her household if they are not nationals of the United States, and

(B) the members of the family of a member of a mission described in paragraph (1)(B) who form part of his or her household if they are not nationals or permanent residents of the United States,

within the meaning of Article 37 of the Vienna Convention;

(3) the term "mission" includes missions within the meaning of the Vienna Convention and any missions representing foreign governments, individually or collectively, which are extended the same privileges and immunities, pursuant to law, as are enjoyed by missions under the Vienna Convention; and

(4) the term "Vienna Convention" means the Vienna Convention on Diplomatic Relations of April 18, 1961 * * *.

§ 254b. Privileges and immunities of mission of nonparty to Vienna Convention

With respect to a nonparty to the Vienna Convention, the mission, the members of the mission, their families, and diplomatic couriers shall enjoy the privileges and immunities specified in the Vienna Convention.

§ 254c. Extension of more favorable or less favorable treatment than provided under Vienna Convention; authority of President

The President may, on the basis of reciprocity and under such terms and conditions as he may determine, specify privileges and immunities for the mission, the members of the mission, their families, and the diplomatic couriers which result in more favorable treatment or less favorable treatment than is provided under the Vienna Convention.

* * *

§ 254d. Dismissal on motion of action against individual entitled to immunity

Any action or proceeding brought against an individual who is entitled to immunity with respect to such action or proceeding under the Vienna Convention on Diplomatic Relations, under section 254b or 254c of this title, or under any other laws extending diplomatic privileges and immunities, shall be dismissed. Such immunity may be established upon motion or suggestion by or on behalf of the individual, or as otherwise permitted by law or applicable rules of procedure.

[Section 254e instructs the Director of the State Department's Office of Foreign Missions to establish vehicle liability insurance requirements for missions, members of missions and their families, and high-ranking U.N. officials.[b] Another part of the Diplomatic Relations Act provides for direct actions against insurers in the federal courts in cases covered by the Act's insurance provisions.[c] Apart from the insurance regulations, there apparently has been no Executive Branch specification of privileges and immunities under section 254c.]

APPLYING THE DIPLOMATIC RELATIONS ACT AND INTERNATIONAL AGREEMENTS

The Senate Foreign Relations Committee report on the bill that became the Diplomatic Relations Act said, among other things:

> The term "mission" [is not] defined in the Vienna Convention, but the functions of a mission are described in article 3 of the

---

b. The requirements are in 22 C.F.R. Part 151.

c. 28 U.S.C.A. § 1364.

Convention. Paragraph 3 [of section 254a] expands the concept of mission to include missions such as the mission of the Commission of the European Communities and the Liaison Office of the People's Republic of China. Read in conjunction with the United Nations Headquarters Agreement, the Convention on Privileges and Immunities [of the United Nations] and [an Act concerning the OAS], the definition makes clear the intent that the United Nations and the OAS continue, as in the past, to be considered part of the diplomatic community for purposes of entitlement to privileges and immunities.

* * *

[Section 254b] specifically states that the provisions of the Convention shall apply to nonratifying nations. This expresses the intent that the provisions of the Vienna Convention be applied uniformly to the diplomatic community. Such application is also consistent with the customary practice of nations.[d]

Is the permanent French mission to the U.N. a "mission" within the meaning of section 254a? If so, is the technical adviser to the temporary French delegation a "member of a mission" under that section? Would either of the other two French nationals in our hypothetical situation be "members of a mission"?

Does the Diplomatic Relations Act resolve the question of the driver's immunity? If the driver was the technical adviser, as postulated, one should consider also *Article IV, sections 11* and *16,* of the General Convention on Privileges and Immunities of the United Nations. If the driver were the Deputy Permanent Representative, one should consider not only those provisions of the General Convention, but also *Article V, section 15* of the U.N. Headquarters Agreement.[e] If the driver were a French member of the U.N. Secretariat, one should consider *Article V, sections 17–19,* of the General Convention. In addition, to the extent that any of those provisions incorporate by reference the general law of diplomatic immunities, one would have to consider the relevant sections of the 1961 Vienna Convention on Diplomatic Relations. And that is not all. See also U.N. Charter *article 105(2).* Is it specific enough to provide any answers?

There is some doubt whether the references to "representatives" in article IV (sections 11 through 16) of the General Convention include resident ("permanent") representatives of foreign missions to the U.N., such as the French Deputy Permanent Representative. When the General Convention was drafted in 1945–1946, the practice had not yet developed of establishing permanent missions in New York City. Consequently the "representatives" contemplated by the Convention's drafters were members of essentially temporary delegations, like the

---

d. Senate Rep. No. 95–958, 95th Cong., 2d Sess. 4–5 (1978).

e. On the question whether Article IV of the General Convention would apply to the Deputy Permanent Representative, see the next paragraph in the text.

French technical adviser in New York for a three-week conference in our hypothetical problem. This has led the U.N. Secretariat to say that permanent representatives are "not contained in the General Convention * * *." f But John R. Stevenson, then the Legal Adviser to the U.S. Department of State, clearly indicated during the Senate Foreign Relations Committee's 1970 hearings on the General Convention that permanent as well as temporary representatives were covered by its article IV.g

Article IX, section 26 of the Headquarters Agreement says that "The provisions of this agreement shall be complementary to the provisions of the General Convention." It goes on to say that whenever provisions in the Agreement and Convention relate to the same subject matter, they shall be treated as complementary unless there is an "absolute conflict," in which case the Headquarters Agreement prevails.

Would the provisions of the General Convention and the Headquarters Agreement be self-executing? That is, would they constitute federal law in the United States, without any implementing act of Congress? How about U.N. Charter article 105(2)?

Of course, there is an act of Congress, in addition to the Diplomatic Relations Act, that deals with immunities in the context of international organizations. *Section 7* of the International Organizations Immunities Act, 22 U.S.C.A. § 288d, contains provisions allowing functional immunities for foreign representatives to international organizations and for employees of such organizations. Those provisions are of limited practical significance in cases involving representatives to the U.N. or personnel of the U.N., at least if the later provisions of the Headquarters Agreement and the General Convention are self-executing.h Probably the only instances involving the U.N. when the provisions in section 288d on immunities of persons from legal process would have independent significance are those when a representative does not fit within section 15 of the Headquarters Agreement or section 16 of the General Convention, or a U.N. official is not within a category designated by the Secretary–General under section 17 of the General

f. Study Prepared by the Secretariat, [1967] 2 Y.B.Int'l L.Comm'n 154, 164. See also Ling, A Comparative Study of the Privileges and Immunities of United Nations Member Representatives and Officials with the Traditional Privileges and Immunities of Diplomatic Agents, 33 Wash. & Lee L.Rev. 91, 95, 99–100 (1976).

g. See Sen.Exec.Rep. No. 91–17, 91st Cong., 2d Sess. 14, 29 (1970).

h. This does not mean that those provisions would necessarily be insignificant in cases involving representatives to, and employees of, other international organizations. For each organization, account would have to be taken of any privileges and immunities set forth in its constituent instrument (assuming the United States is a party), and of any other applicable treaty. Note, though, that the United States is not a party to the Convention on the Privileges and Immunities of the Specialized Agencies (the counterpart of the General Convention, which applies only to the U.N. itself).

For a case holding the Secretary–General of the Organization of American States immune under the International Organizations Immunities Act, see Donald v. Orfila, 788 F.2d 36 (D.C.Cir.1986).

Convention, and the person nevertheless claims immunity.[i] Such a claim could arguably be made if the person has been notified to and accepted by the U.S. Secretary of State as a representative, officer or employee, pursuant to *section 8* of the Act, 22 U.S.C.A. § 288e. But the category of person most likely to have to fall back on sections 288d and 288e is the employee of a mission or of the U.N. who does not qualify as an "official"—chauffeurs, interpreters, stenographers, workmen [j]—and these employees have been held, at least by lower courts, not to be entitled to immunity under the Act.[k]

For the present problem, assume that the Deputy Permanent Representative of France holds the rank of minister plenipotentiary, as contemplated by article V, section 15(1) of the Headquarters Agreement, and that the French member of the U.N. Secretariat staff has been designated by the Secretary–General as an official entitled to the immunities of article V, section 18 of the General Convention. The technical adviser to the temporary French delegation would be a "representative" within the meaning of article IV, section 16 of the General Convention. Consequently the International Organizations Immunities Act need be considered no further for purposes of the present problem.

As a matter of policy, why should there by any immunity in a civil action such as this, even if the French Deputy Permanent Representative were driving? The International Law Commission's Draft Articles on the Representation of States in Their Relations with International Organizations, which formed the basis for the 1975 Vienna Convention, provided in article 30(1)(d) that "[The head of mission and the members of the diplomatic staff of the mission shall] enjoy immunity from [the host state's] civil and administrative jurisdiction, except in the case of * * * an action for damages arising out of an accident caused by a vehicle used by the person in question outside the exercise of the functions of the mission where those damages are not recoverable from insurance."[l] The Committee of the Whole at the Vienna Conference went further and adopted an amendment permitting the action even for accidents within the mission's functions and even though there was insurance coverage. But then the entire vehicle accident exception was defeated in the plenary Conference session, apparently because some states feared that the diplomatic staff of a mission might deliberately be entrapped into a vehicle accident in order to exert political pressure against them.[m]

i. See, e.g., 1973 Digest of United States Practice in Int'l L. 25, 26.

j. The U.N. Secretary–General, relying on General Assembly Res. 76(1), has taken the position that all U.N. staff members are "officials" except those who are both recruited locally and paid hourly rates. See the U.N. Legal Counsel's opinions in 1975 U.N. Juridical Y.B. 183–84, and in 1981 id. 161–62. The latter is reproduced in part at page 80 infra.

k. See Westchester County v. Ranollo, 187 Misc. 777, 67 N.Y.S.2d 31 (New Rochelle City Ct.1946); cf. People v. Roy, 21 Misc.2d 303, 200 N.Y.S.2d 612 (Ct. of Special Sess.1959); United States v. Melekh, 190 F.Supp. 67 (S.D.N.Y.1960).

l. [1971] 2 Y.B. Int'l L.Comm'n 284, 303.

In those cases in which the determination of immunity turns on whether or not the person (a delegate or a U.N. Secretariat staff member) is performing an official function, is the court free to apply its own concepts of what is an official function and what is not? The Legal Counsel of the United Nations, responding to a dictum by a New York trial court to the effect that the court would make that decision,[n] has said:

> First and foremost, in the view of the United Nations Secretariat, it is exclusively for the Secretary-General to determine the extent of the authority, duties and functions of United Nations officials. These matters cannot be determined by, or be subject to scrutiny in national courts. It is clear that if such courts could over-rule the Secretary-General's determination that an act was "official", a mass of conflicting decisions would be inevitable, given the many countries in which the Organization operates. In many cases it would be tantamount to a total denial of immunity.[o]

Is that a strong argument? Is it relevant that section 30 of the General Convention says that if a difference arises under the Convention between the U.N. and a member state, "a request shall be made for an advisory opinion [of the ICJ, which] shall be accepted as decisive by the parties"?

The Secretary-General has not provided a great deal of guidance as to what acts he considers "official." On one occasion his Legal Counsel did have this to say:

> [T]ravel between home and office is not in itself considered to be an official act within the meaning of Section 18(a) of the Convention on the Privileges and Immunities of the United Nations which provides for immunity from legal process in respect of acts performed by officials "in their official capacity".

* * *

> There is no precise definition of the expressions "official capacity", "official duties", or "official business". These are functional expressions and must be related to a particular context. Indeed, it is doubtful whether a definition would be desirable since it would not be in the interest of the Organization to be bound by a definition which may fail to take into account the many and varied activities of United Nations officials.

---

m. See Fennessy, The 1975 Vienna Convention on the Representation of States in Their Relations with International Organizations of a Universal Character, 70 Am.J.Int'l L. 62, 70–71 (1976). At this writing, the 1975 Convention still had not received enough ratifications to be in force.

n. People v. Weiner, 85 Misc.2d 161, 169, 378 N.Y.S.2d 966, 975 (N.Y.C.Crim.Ct. 1976).

o. 70 Am.J.Int'l L. 581, 582–83 (1976).

Finally, there are certain pragmatic considerations which must be taken into account. While Headquarters practice does not exclude invoking immunity in certain traffic cases, a reverse practice in which immunity is automatically raised would give rise to considerable difficulties with the police and in the courts, not to mention the political consequences at a time when the general public and legislative bodies are opposed to privileges and immunities.

The practical handling of this question at Headquarters has not given rise to any difficulties, probably because of the firm position taken by the Secretary-General from the very beginning. Staff members are expected to obey local laws and regulations and as the Secretary-General stated in a 1949 press release: "If there is any infringement of any laws, traffic violations for example, a Secretariat member is in the same group—unless on official business—as the average citizen who may pass a red light.... He just pays his fine, and many already have".[p]

Does this help resolve the question whether the French driver in our hypothetical case (the technical adviser) was acting in his capacity as a representative? Would it resolve the question if the driver had been the French member of the U.N. Secretariat? If so, which way does it lead?

Consider, finally, whether France (in the case of the technical adviser) or the U.N. Secretary-General (if the French member of the U.N. Secretariat had been driving) would have a duty to waive any immunity the driver would otherwise have. See General Convention *Article IV, section 14,* and *Article V, sections 20 and 21.*

In the latter case (possible waiver of immunity of a U.N. Secretariat member), note that the great majority of U.N. officials—including the one in our hypothetical case—have functional rather than full diplomatic immunities. That is, they are immune only in respect of their official acts. As stated in General Convention article V, section 20, even then their immunities are in the interests of the U.N. and not for their personal benefit. Hence the authority of the Secretary-General to waive their immunities when that can be done without prejudice to the interests of the U.N.

The U.N. Legal Counsel has said, "Where a determination was made that no official act was involved, the Secretary-General had, by the terms of the [General Convention], both the right and the duty to waive the immunity of any official."[q] On another occasion the Legal Counsel said, without distinguishing between official and unofficial acts, that under General Convention section 20 "it would always be incumbent on the Secretary-General to waive the immunity from arrest or prosecution [i.e. in a criminal proceeding] in any case 'where

---

p. 1977 U.N. Juridical Y.B. 246, 247-48.

q. 1981 U.N. Juridical Y.B. 161.

in his opinion the immunity would impede the course of justice and can be waived without prejudice to the interest of the United Nations.'"[r]

Does General Convention Article V, section 20 rule out waiver when official acts are involved? If not, what yardstick is there to determine, in the case of an official act, whether immunity could be waived "without prejudice to the interests of the United Nations"?

Is there any reason to believe that a waiver would be more likely in a civil action than in a criminal proceeding (or vice versa)?

D. GOVERNMENTAL MEASURES RESTRICTING U.N.-RELATED PERSONS AND MISSIONS

U.N. member governments on several occasions have deemed it necessary or expedient to take measures—often in the name of national security—that restrict the activities of U.N.-related individuals or missions. A number of these restrictions have been imposed by the United States, as it attempts to balance its duties as host to the United Nations against its apprehensions about the possible use by foreign interests of their access to the U.N. as a springboard for activities that could affect U.S. security. But not all of these incidents have involved the United States.

1. Imprisonment of a Staff Member

In 1979–80, a Polish criminal proceeding caused great concern to the United Nations Staff Union and its members. Ms. Alicja Wesolowska, a Polish national employed as a stenographer by the U.N. Development Program (UNDP), was arrested in August 1979 while she was visiting her parents in Poland en route from her former UNDP assignment in New York to a new one in Mongolia. The Polish government held her without formal charges, and without allowing U.N. representatives to visit her, until March 1980. Then she was tried on a charge of "collecting and transmitting intelligence information on Polish citizens and on individuals from some other countries who were employed by the United Nations, as well as carrying out tasks assigned to her by said intelligence, i.e. of one of the NATO countries."[a]

The U.N. Secretary-General requested not only that his representative be permitted to visit her, but that a U.N. observer be allowed to attend her trial. These requests were denied and a secret trial was held. Ms. Wesolowska was sentenced to seven years in prison. Her sentence was upheld by the Supreme Court of Poland. After about 54 months she was released from prison, but was not immediately allowed to leave Poland.[b]

---

r. 1974 U.N. Juridical Y.B. 188.
a. Unofficial translation from Polish, in 21 UN Chronicle, No. 3, at 33 (1984).
b. Id.

Ms. Wesolowska had originally obtained her UNDP position without the approval of the Polish government. This ran counter to the usual East European practice at that time. East European nationals usually had been nominated by their own governments for U.N. positions, even those involving only hourly wages. Some observers suspected that Ms. Wesolowska's brashness in obtaining her U.N. job was her only offense.

A legal brief prepared (before the trial) on behalf of the Committee for the Release of Alicja Wesolowska took the position that, in the absence of specific charges publicly substantiated by evidence, it could not be determined whether Poland had violated Ms. Wesolowska's and the United Nations' immunities under General Convention section 18 and U.N. Charter articles 100(2) and 105(2); but, according to the brief, Poland had clearly violated a duty to permit U.N. officials access to her.

In light of the materials below, was Ms. Wesolowska an "official of the United Nations" within the meaning of General Convention *sections 17 and 18*? If so, did Poland breach a duty to the U.N. by deciding, on its own, that her acts were not within her "official capacity"? (Poland is a party to the Convention. The U.N. is not.)

Where does one find a duty to permit U.N. officials to have access to an arrested staff member?

Other questions could be asked, particularly concerning possible violations of Ms. Wesolowska's internationally-defined human rights. At this point, however, only the privileges and immunities questions are relevant. Consider the following materials, in addition to those already mentioned.

STATEMENT OF U.N. LEGAL COUNSEL ON THE MEANING OF "OFFICIALS" OF THE UNITED NATIONS

Dec. 1, 1981.
1981 U.N. Juridical Y.B. 161–62.

Section 17 of the Convention on the Privileges and Immunities of the United Nations stated that the Secretary–General would specify the categories of officials to which articles V and VII of the Convention should apply. The Convention on the Privileges and Immunities of the Specialized Agencies and the IAEA Agreement contained similar provisions. In 1946, the General Assembly had adopted resolution 76(I), in which it had approved the granting of the privileges and immunities referred to in articles V and VII of the Convention on the Privileges and Immunities of the United Nations to all members of the staff of the United Nations, with the exception of those who were recruited locally and were assigned to hourly rates. The specialized agencies and IAEA had taken similar actions. Consequently, all staff members regardless of rank, nationality or place of recruitment, whether Professional or General Service, were considered as officials of the organizations for the purposes of privileges and immunities except for those who were both locally recruited and employed at hourly rates. United Nations locally recruited staff such as clerks, secretaries and drivers were in nearly every case paid according to established salary or wage scales and not at hourly rates and they were, therefore, covered by the terms of General Assembly resolution 76(I).

MEMORANDUM OF U.N. LEGAL COUNSEL ON THE RIGHT TO VISIT STAFF MEMBERS IN CUSTODY

July 10, 1963.
1963 U.N. Juridical Y.B. 191-92.

1. In connexion with the recent arrest of a staff member, the question has arisen of the extent of the right of the United Nations to visit and converse with staff members held in custody or detention by the authorities of a State.

2. It is established by the advisory opinion of the International Court of Justice of 11 April 1949, on Reparation for injuries suffered in the service of the United Nations (I.C.J. Reports, 1949, p. 174), that in the event of an agent of the United Nations in the performance of his duties suffering injury in circumstances involving the responsibility of a State, the United Nations has the capacity to bring an international claim against the responsible State (whether it is or not a Member of the Organization), with a view to obtaining the reparation due in respect of the damage caused both to the United Nations and to the victim or to persons entitled through him. The United Nations therefore has, beyond any doubt, a right of diplomatic protection of its staff, at least within the limits of the questions put to the Court in the request for the advisory opinion.

3. The right to visit and converse with the person in respect of whom a State may possibly have violated its international obligations is a necessary consequence of a right of diplomatic protection. The State or organization having such a right of protection cannot exercise it unless there is an adequate opportunity to find out the facts of a case, and where the person concerned is in custody or detention, the only such opportunity is through access to that person. This is recognized, for example, in the Vienna Convention on Consular Relations of 24 April 1963.[c]

* * *

4. It is therefore clear that the United Nations has the right to visit and converse with one of its staff members in custody or detention whenever there is any possibility that the United Nations or the staff member in the performance of his duties may have been injured through the violation by a State of any of its obligations either toward

---

c. [This Convention applies to consular relations between states. It does not by its terms apply to international organizations. Ed.]

the United Nations or toward the person concerned. During such visits and conversations the United Nations representatives must have the right to pursue any line of discussion which would clarify the questions both whether an injury has occurred, and whether it was incurred in connexion with performance of the staff member's duties. The mere fact that there is no obvious connexion between the reason given for the detention by the State and the staff member's duties is insufficient to nullify the right of the United Nations to visit. If that were so, the right of protection of the United Nations would be made entirely dependent upon the reasons given by the detaining State, and that would make the right practically ineffective.

* * *

6. It follows from the foregoing that, when a United Nations staff member is arrested or detained by the authorities of a State, the Organization always has a right to send representatives to visit and converse with him with a view to ascertaining whether or not an injury has occurred to the United Nations or to him through non-observance by the State concerned of its international obligations, and whether or not such injury is connected with the performance of his duties. Furthermore, at least when the staff member is not a national of the detaining State, there are reasons for recognizing a broader interest of the United Nations in the matter, so that the staff member will not have to rely exclusively on the protection of his own State.

REPORT BY THE U.N. SECRETARY–GENERAL ON DETENTION OF STAFF MEMBERS
Aug. 19, 1988.
U.N. Doc. E/CN.4/Sub.2/1988/17, at 4.

* * *

18. When a staff member of the United Nations—whether internationally or locally recruited—is arrested or detained by government authorities, the Secretary–General has the right and the duty to find out the reasons for the arrest. Under the terms of the Charter of the United Nations (Article 105) and the Convention on the Privileges and Immunities of the United Nations (articles V and VI), all staff members are immune from legal process in respect of words spoken or written and all acts performed by them in their official capacity. As the Administrative Committee on Co-ordination pointed out in its report of 15 April 1980 (E/1980/34), * * * "International organizations, which are the instrument of international co-operation, cannot fully discharge their duties unless they can count on a completely independent international civil service".

19. It follows that the United Nations is entitled to functional protection of its staff members. It is for the Secretary–General alone, and not for Member States, to determine whether or not an act by a staff member has been performed in his official capacity. To that end,

he needs to learn the facts. He must be in a position to visit the staff member under arrest, to converse with him, to be apprised of the grounds for the arrest and the formal charges. He is entitled to assist the staff member in arranging legal counsel for his or her defence and to appear in legal proceedings to defend any United Nations interest affected by the arrest or detention. * * *

20. If it is established that the arrest or detention of a staff member is connected with his official duties, his right to immunity is invoked. If, on the other hand, it is found that the case is not connected with the person's official duties, the Secretary-General can and should waive immunity so that justice may take its course. In that case, the Secretary-General none the less ensures that the staff member under arrest and in detention is equitably treated and that due and proper procedures are followed.

THE U.N.'S RIGHTS

Did the U.N. Legal Counsel in 1963 and the Secretary-General in 1988 give the same reason for a right to visit an imprisoned staff member? If not, how did their arguments differ from each other? Was one more convincing than the other?

Both reached the same conclusion. If the conclusion is correct, does it follow that the U.N.'s visitation right exists when the staff member is imprisoned by her own government?

If Poland did violate the privileges or immunities of either Ms. Wesolowska or the United Nations, does it follow that the U.N. could assert an international claim against Poland under the U.N. Reparations Case, supra page 7?

As the above materials suggest, Ms. Wesolowska is far from the only U.N. staff member to have been detained by the governments of member states. For example, in 1990 the Secretary-General reported that over a period of about a year, 160 staff members of the United Nations Relief and Works Agency for Palestine Refugees in the Near East (UNRWA) had been arrested or detained, and staff members from eight other U.N. or U.N.-related bodies had been arrested, detained or abducted. UNRWA reported that in no case did it receive adequate and timely information on the reasons for the arrest and detention of its staff members. It had access to about 62 of those detained in the West Bank or Gaza Strip, but apparently not to those who had been removed from the occupied territories.[d]

d. See U.N. Doc. A/C.5/45/10, at 3 (1990). The U.N. General Assembly responded with Res. 45/240 (1990), calling on all member states to, inter alia, scrupulously respect the privileges and immunities of officials of the U.N. and the specialized agencies, and to enable the Secretary-General to exercise fully the right of functional protection—particularly with respect to immediate access to detained staff members.

2. *Experts on Missions*

In 1984 Dumitru Mazilu, a Romanian national, was nominated by his government (then headed by Nicolae Ceausescu) to serve a regular, three-year term as a member of the U.N. Sub-Commission on Prevention of Discrimination and Protection of Minorities. He was duly elected by the Commission on Human Rights, the Sub-Commission's parent body.

The Sub-Commission, in its 1985 session, requested Mr. Mazilu to prepare a report on human rights and youth, with particular focus on the right to life, education and work. When the 1987 session convened, neither Mr. Mazilu nor his report were at hand. The Romanian government informed the U.N. Office in Geneva that Mr. Mazilu had suffered a heart attack and was still in a hospital, so he could not attend the session. After the 1987 session, the U.N. Centre for Human Rights in Geneva made several unsuccessful attempts to contact Mr. Mazilu.

On December 31, 1987, the terms of all members of the Sub-Commission expired. In February 1988, the Commission on Human Rights elected new Sub-Commission members, including a replacement for Mr. Mazilu nominated by the Romanian government. In the meantime, Mr. Mazilu wrote a series of letters to the U.N. Information Centre in Bucharest, saying that he had been hospitalized twice, that he had been forced to retire from Romanian government service, and that strong governmental pressure was being exerted on him and his family.

When the Romanian government conveyed to the U.N. an offer by the new Romanian Sub-Commission member to complete the report on human rights and youth, the Under-Secretary-General for Human Rights replied that the Sub-Commission had entrusted the task to Mr. Mazilu. All of the Sub-Commission's special rapporteurs, including Mr. Mazilu, were invited to the Sub-Commission's 1988 session in Geneva, but Mr. Mazilu did not appear. Thereupon, the Sub-Commission asked the U.N. Secretary-General to request the Romanian government to facilitate a visit to Mr. Mazilu by a member of the Sub-Commission and the secretariat to help him complete his study on human rights and youth. The government replied that this would amount to interference in Romania's internal affairs.

Acting pursuant to a Sub-Commission resolution, the U.N. Secretary-General then addressed a Note Verbale to the Permanent Representative of Romania to the U.N., invoking the General Convention on Privileges and Immunities of the U.N. on behalf of Mr. Mazilu and requesting the Romanian government to accord him all the necessary facilities to complete his report. The government countered by saying that Mr. Mazilu was too ill to work, and had been retired on grounds of health.[a] The government asserted that the General Convention did not apply, since *Article VI, section 22* protects only "experts" on missions for the U.N., not special rapporteurs. The government added:

> Even if rapporteurs are to some extent seen as having the status of experts of the United Nations, * * * Section 22, of the Convention * * * make[s] it clearly apparent that an expert is not accorded such privileges and immunities anywhere and everywhere, but only in the country to which he is sent on mission and during the time spent on the mission, and also in the countries through which he must transit when travelling to meet the requirements of the mission. In the same way, the privileges and immunities only come into existence from the expert's time of departure, when he travels to accomplish the mission. In so far as the expert's journey to carry out the mission for the United Nations has not begun, for reasons entirely unconnected with his activity as an expert, there is no legal basis upon which to lay claim to privileges and immunities under the Convention, regardless of whether he is in his country of residence or in another country, in a capacity other than that of an expert.
>
> In the country of which he is a citizen, in the country where he has his permanent residence, or in other countries where he may be for reasons unconnected with the mission in question, the expert is only accorded privileges and immunities in relation to the content of the activity in which he engages during his mission (including his spoken and written communications).[b]

Over Romania's objection, the Economic and Social Council then requested the International Court of Justice to give an advisory opinion on the applicability of Article VI, section 22 in the case of Mr. Mazilu. The Secretary–General, in a written statement submitted to the Court, said that the request did not ask about the consequences if section 22 were found applicable; that is, it did not ask what privileges and immunities Mr. Mazilu enjoyed under section 22, nor whether they had been violated.

The Court first had to face a question raised by a reservation Romania had attached to its ratification of the General Convention, relating to the Court's jurisdiction to give the advisory opinion. That aspect of the case is examined in Chapter 3 of these materials, at pages 507–11 infra. For the present, it is enough to know that the Court found that it had jurisdiction and did give the opinion. Our focus at

---

[a] Mr. Mazilu eventually did submit an incomplete report, transmitted clandestinely to the U.N. Centre for Human Rights. He apparently had not received information sent to him by the Secretary–General.

[b] This excerpt from the government's statement is quoted in Judge Oda's separate opinion in the Mazilu Case, [1989] I.C.J. 200, 206–07, 29 Int'l Legal Materials 112, 115 (1990).

this point is on the Court's opinion concerning the applicability of section 22.

APPLICABILITY OF ARTICLE VI, SECTION 22, OF THE CONVENTION ON THE PRIVILEGES AND IMMUNITIES OF THE UNITED NATIONS (THE MAZILU CASE)

International Court of Justice, Advisory Opinion, 1989.
[1989] I.C.J. 177, 29 Int'l Legal Materials 100 (1990).

[After stating the facts concerning Mr. Mazilu and disposing of Romania's objections to the issuance of an advisory opinion on the matter, the Court focused on the General Convention.]

42. Acting in conformity with Article 105 of the Charter, the General Assembly approved the General Convention on 13 February 1946 and proposed it for accession by each Member of the United Nations. One hundred and twenty-four States, including Romania, are parties to the Convention.

43. As contemplated by Article 105 of the Charter, the General Convention determines the privileges and immunities enjoyed by the United Nations as such (Arts. II and III), lays down the privileges and immunities of the representatives of Members of the United Nations (Art. IV), and defines those of the officials of the Organization (Art. V). It contains in addition an Article VI entitled "Experts on Missions for the United Nations", divided into two Sections. [The Court quoted *sections 22 and 23.*] Finally, Article VII, Section 26, of the General Convention grants certain facilities to experts when travelling on the business of the Organization.

44. The Court will examine the applicability of Section 22 *ratione personae, ratione temporis* and *ratione loci,* that is to say it will consider first what is meant by "experts on missions" for the purposes of Section 22, and then the meaning to be attached to the expression "period of [the] missions", before considering the position of experts in their relations with the States of which they are nationals or on the territory of which they reside.

45. The General Convention gives no definition of "experts on missions". All it does is to clarify two points, one negative and the other positive. From Section 22 it is clear, first that the officials of the Organization, even if chosen in consideration of their technical expertise in a particular field, are not included in the category of experts within the meaning of that provision; and secondly that only experts performing missions for the United Nations are covered by Section 22. The Section does not, however, furnish any indication of the nature, duration or place of these missions.

46. Nor is there really any guidance in this respect to be found in the *travaux préparatoires* of the General Convention.

* * *

47. The purpose of Section 22 is nevertheless evident, namely, to enable the United Nations to entrust missions to persons who do not

have the status of an official of the Organization, and to guarantee them "such privileges and immunities as are necessary for the independent exercise of their functions". The experts thus appointed or elected may or may not be remunerated, may or may not have a contract, may be given a task requiring work over a lengthy period or a short time. The essence of the matter lies not in their administrative position but in the nature of their mission.

48. In practice, according to the information supplied by the Secretary-General, the United Nations has had occasion to entrust missions—increasingly varied in nature—to persons not having the status of United Nations officials. Such persons have been entrusted with mediation, with preparing reports, preparing studies, conducting investigations or finding and establishing facts. They have participated in certain peace-keeping forces, technical assistance work, and a multitude of other activities. In addition, many committees, commissions or similar bodies whose members serve, not as representatives of States, but in a personal capacity, have been set up within the Organization; for example the International Law Commission, the Advisory Committee on Administrative and Budgetary Questions, the International Civil Service Commission, the Human Rights Committee established for the implementation of the International Covenant on Civil and Political Rights, and various other committees of the same nature, such as the Committee on the Elimination of Racial Discrimination or the Committee on the Elimination of All Forms of Discrimination Against Women. In all these cases, the practice of the United Nations shows that the persons so appointed, and in particular the members of these committees and commissions, have been regarded as experts on missions within the meaning of Section 22.

49. According to that Section, experts enjoy the privileges and immunities therein provided for "during the period of their missions, including the time spent on journeys". The question thus arises whether experts are covered by Section 22 only during missions requiring travel or whether they are also covered when there is no such travel or apart from such travel. To answer this question, it is necessary to determine the meaning of the word *"mission"* in French and "mission" in English, the two languages in which the General Convention was adopted. Initially, in keeping with its Latin derivation, the word referred to a task entrusted to a person only if that person was sent somewhere to perform it. It implied a journey. The same connotation is apparent in the words, of the same derivation, "emissary", "missionary" and "missive". The French word *"mission"*, and the English word "mission", have however long since acquired a broader meaning and nowadays embrace in general the tasks entrusted to a person, whether or not those tasks involve travel.

50. The Court considers that Section 22, in its reference to experts performing missions for the United Nations, uses the word "mission" in a general sense. While some experts have necessarily to travel in order to perform their tasks, others can perform them without having to

travel. In either case, the intent of Section 22 is to ensure the independence of such experts in the interests of the Organization by according them the privileges and immunities necessary for the purpose. In some cases these privileges and immunities are designed to facilitate the travel of experts and their stay abroad, for instance those concerning seizure or searching of personal baggage. In other cases, however, they are of a far more general nature, particularly with respect to communications with the United Nations or the inviolability of papers and documents. Accordingly, Section 22 is applicable to every expert on mission, whether or not he travels.

51. The question whether experts on missions can invoke these privileges and immunities against the States of which they are nationals or on the territory of which they reside has also been raised. In this connection, the Court notes that Section 15 of the General Convention provides that the terms of Article IV, Sections 11, 12 and 13, relating to the representatives of Members "are not applicable as between a representative and the authorities of the State of which he is a national or of which he is or has been the representative". Article V, concerning officials of the Organization, and Article VI, concerning experts on missions for the United Nations, do not, however, contain any comparable rule. This difference of approach can readily be explained. The privileges and immunities of Articles V and VI are conferred with a view to ensuring the independence of international officials and experts in the interests of the Organization. This independence must be respected by all States including the State of nationality and the State of residence. Some States parties to the General Convention (Canada, the Lao People's Democratic Republic, Nepal, Thailand, Turkey and the United States of America) have indeed entered reservations to certain provisions of Article V, or of Article VI itself (Mexico and the United States of America), as regards their nationals or persons habitually resident on their territory. The very fact that it was felt necessary to make such reservations confirms the conclusion that, in the absence of such reservations, experts on missions enjoy the privileges and immunities provided for under the Convention in their relations with the States of which they are nationals or on the territory of which they reside.

52. To sum up, the Court takes the view that Section 22 of the General Convention is applicable to persons (other than United Nations officials) to whom a mission has been entrusted by the Organization and who are therefore entitled to enjoy the privileges and immunities provided for in this Section with a view to the independent exercise of their functions. During the whole period of such missions, experts enjoy these functional privileges and immunities whether or not they travel. They may be invoked as against the State of nationality or of residence unless a reservation to Section 22 of the General Convention has been validly made by that State.

53. In the light of the foregoing, the Court will now consider the situation of special rapporteurs of the Sub–Commission. This is a

question which touches on the legal position of rapporteurs in general, a category of persons whom the United Nations and the specialized agencies find it necessary to engage for the implementation of increasingly varied functions, and is thus one of importance for the whole of the United Nations system.

54. * * * The members of the Sub-Commission, since their status is neither that of a representative of a member State nor that of a United Nations official, and since they perform independently for the United Nations functions contemplated in the remit of the Sub-Commission, must be regarded as experts on missions within the meaning of Section 22.

55. In accordance with the practice followed by many United Nations bodies, the Sub-Commission has from time to time appointed rapporteurs or special rapporteurs with the task of studying specified subjects. These rapporteurs or special rapporteurs are normally selected from among members of the Sub-Commission. However, over the past ten years, special rapporteurs have, on at least three occasions, been appointed from outside the Sub-Commission. Furthermore, in numerous cases, special rapporteurs appointed from among members of the Sub-Commission have completed their reports only after their membership of the Sub-Commission had expired. In any event, rapporteurs or special rapporteurs are entrusted by the Sub-Commission with a research mission. Their functions are diverse, since they have to compile, analyse and check the existing documentation on the problem to be studied, prepare a report making appropriate recommendations, and present the report to the Sub-Commission. Since their status is neither that of a representative of a member State nor that of a United Nations official, and since they carry out such research independently for the United Nations, they must be regarded as experts on missions within the meaning of Section 22, even in the event that they are not, or are no longer, members of the Sub-Commission. Consequently they enjoy, in accordance with Section 22, the privileges and immunities necessary for the exercise of their functions, and in particular for the establishment of any contacts which may be useful for the preparation, the drafting and the presentation of their reports to the Sub-Commission.

56. * * * [T]he Court must now give its opinion on the question of the applicability of [Section 22] in the case of Mr. Dumitru Mazilu.

57. * * * [F]rom 13 March 1984 to 29 August 1985 Mr. Mazilu had the status of member of the Sub-Commission. From 29 August 1985 to 31 December 1987, he was both a member and a rapporteur of the Sub-Commission. Finally, although since the last-mentioned date he has no longer been a member of the Sub-Commission, he has remained one of its special rapporteurs. At no time during this period, therefore, has he ceased to have the status of an expert on mission within the meaning of Section 22, or ceased to be entitled to enjoy for

the exercise of his functions the privileges and immunities provided for therein.

58. Doubt was nevertheless expressed by Romania whether Mr. Mazilu was capable of performing his task as special rapporteur. Romania emphasized that he had been taken seriously ill in May 1987, and had therefore been placed on the retired list pursuant to decisions taken by the competent medical practitioners, in accordance with the applicable Romanian legislation; according to the Romanian written statement, he was at that time still unable to carry out his mandate as special rapporteur. Mr. Mazilu himself informed the United Nations that the state of his health did not prevent him from preparing the report entrusted to him or from going for this purpose to the Centre for Human Rights in Geneva. When a report by Mr. Mazilu was circulated as a document of the Sub-Commission, Romania expressed the view that it was obvious that "since becoming ill in 1987, Mr. Dumitru Mazilu does not possess the intellectual capacity necessary" for the preparation of "a report consistent with the requirements of the United Nations" * * *.

59. It is not for the Court to pronounce on the state of Mr. Mazilu's health, or on its consequences on the work he has done or is to do for the Sub-Commission. It is sufficient for it to note, first that it was for the United Nations to decide whether in the circumstances it wished to retain Mr. Mazilu as special rapporteur, and secondly to take note that decisions to that effect have been taken by the Sub-Commission.

60. In these circumstances Mr. Mazilu continues to have the status of special rapporteur, and as a consequence must be regarded as an expert on mission within the meaning of Section 22 of the General Convention. That Section is accordingly applicable in the case of Mr. Mazilu.

61. For these reasons,

The Court,

Unanimously,

Is of the opinion that Article VI, Section 22, of the Convention on the Privileges and Immunities of the United Nations is applicable in the case of Mr. Dumitru Mazilu as a special rapporteur of the Sub-Commission on Prevention of Discrimination and Protection of Minorities.

EXPERTS, OFFICIALS AND THE GENERAL CONVENTION

Did Romania take an unreasonable position regarding the applicability of General Convention *section 22* to experts in their own country? If not, why do you suppose it was unable to attract the vote of even a single judge?

As a result of this case, is everyone on assignment for the United Nations, other than a member of the secretariat, an "expert" for purposes of section 22?

Suppose Mr. Mazilu actually was too ill to do the thorough job expected of him. What purpose is served by giving him the protection of section 22?

Suppose that in 1988 Mr. Mazilu, back home in Bucharest, had committed a common crime unconnected with his duties as a special rapporteur. Could the Romanian police have arrested him? Is *section 23* of the General Convention an adequate safety valve for this situation?

Members of the International Law Commission spend about three months every year meeting together in Geneva. The rest of the time they hold positions in their home states as professors, government attorneys, etc. They normally do some Commission work in their home states. Suppose the British member, at home in London, does some research on a Commission project. Would his notes be immune from inspection or seizure by British authorities? Would his private correspondence?

U.N. officials and experts sometimes must venture into extremely hazardous areas where no central government may be in control. For example, Count Bernadotte was assassinated in Palestine while on a U.N. mission, leading to the Reparations Case, page 7 supra. That case established the standing of the U.N. to bring claims against member and nonmember states that have failed to meet obligations to protect agents of the organization. Such obligations could arise for governments under treaties, such as the General Convention, or custom. But what about resistance groups and other armed factions in a civil war situation? Are they under any international obligation to protect U.N. officials or experts?

These questions have arisen in some of the chaotic armed conflicts within states, or former states, in the 1990s. The U.N. Security Council has tried to deal with the situation. For example, on July 27, 1992, it adopted Resolution 767 regarding the situation in Somalia, where armed bands were fighting for power, causing massive civilian starvation in the process, and where no effective central government existed. Resolution 767 said, inter alia, that the Security Council:

> *Affirms* that all officials of the United Nations and all experts on mission for the United Nations in Somalia enjoy the privileges and immunities provided for in the Convention on the Privileges and Immunities of the United Nations of 1946 and in any other relevant instruments and that all parties, movements and factions in Somalia are required to allow them full freedom of movement and all necessary facilities * * *.

Did this establish, as a matter of law, that nongovernmental movements and factions have international obligations to afford U.N.

officials and experts the privileges and immunities of the General Convention?

If so, how could the obligation be enforced? Leaving aside the possibility of U.N. military intervention under Security Council authorization, presumably any such obligation could later be asserted in a claim for reparations against whichever faction wins the struggle and forms a government. Is that sufficient?

3. U.S. Security Measures

a. Abuse of Privileges of Residence

Unlike Ms. Wesolowska or Mr. Mazilu in the preceding cases, some high-ranking representatives to the U.N. and officials of the U.N. have what amounts to diplomatic immunity covering all their acts. See the Headquarters Agreement *Article V, section 15;* Convention on the Privileges and Immunities of the United Nations *Article V, section 19.* Occasionally they have become embroiled in espionage charges. Except in the case of a representative (not a U.N. official) charged by his own government, diplomatic immunities preclude normal criminal proceedings. The incident described below illustrates the issues that can arise in such cases.

In February 1978, the United States government formally requested Viet Nam's Permanent Representative to the U.N., Dinh Ba Thi, to leave the country. The United States alleged that he had engaged in espionage and had thus abused his privileges of residence. The Vietnamese mission to the U.N. denied the allegation, said that the U.S. action was "completely contrary to the Charter of the United Nations and the Headquarters Agreement between the United Nations and the United States," and announced that Dinh Ba Thi would not leave.[a] The U.N. Committee on Relations with the Host Country then took up the matter. The incident raised issues under U.N. Charter *article 105(2)* and under the Headquarters Agreement *Article IV, sections 11, 12* and *13.* As you read the excerpts below from the Committee's debate, consider which side had the best of the legal argument under those provisions.

DEBATE IN THE COMMITTEE ON RELATIONS WITH THE HOST COUNTRY

Feb. 9–14, 1978.

U.N. Docs. A/AC.154/SR. 69, at 3–7, 17–18; SR. 70, at 4–5; SR. 71, at 2–6; SR. 72, at 3–5.

MR. NGUYEN VAN LUU (*Observer for Viet Nam*) said that * * * Article 105, paragraph 2, of the Charter provided that representatives of the Members of the United Nations and officials of the Organization should enjoy such privileges and immunities as were necessary for the

---

[a.] U.N. Doc. A/AC154/161, Annex (1978).

independent exercise of their functions in connexion with the Organization. If the Charter was not to be accepted as supreme, the fate of the United Nations would be at the mercy of the current host country, which could at any time declare any representative of any country *persona non grata*. Section 12 of the Headquarters Agreement, although incomplete, was fully consistent with the Charter itself.

* * *

Mr. LEONARD (*United States of America*) said that the United States understood the concern of United Nations missions with regard to the departure of Ambassador Dinh Ba Thi of the Socialist Republic of Viet Nam. The events which had given rise to the situation had also been a matter of serious concern to his Government. * * * The United States Government had attempted to discuss the situation with the Permanent Mission of Viet Nam, but after an initial contact on 1 February the Mission had refused to discuss the issue further. Views had been exchanged with the Vietnamese Embassy in Paris, and it had been emphasized that the United States was requesting the departure of Ambassador Thi only because of his involvement in the case in question.

* * *

The case with which Ambassador Thi was connected was before the courts of the United States, and he was therefore not at liberty to discuss the relevant evidence. However, on 31 January a Federal grand jury sitting in Alexandria, Virginia, had returned an indictment against Ronald Louis Humphrey, an employee of the United States Information Agency, and Mr. Truong Dinh Hung, a national of Viet Nam resident in that area. The seven-count indictment charged that the defendants had conspired and acted to deliver material relating to the national defence of the United States to the Government of the Socialist Republic of Viet Nam. The indictment listed a series of overt acts charged to have taken place in Virginia, the District of Columbia and elsewhere, involving the delivery of classified documents and papers, and named five persons as unindicted co-conspirators, one of whom was Ambassador Dinh Ba Thi.

* * *

Mr. DINH BA THI (*Observer for Viet Nam*) * * * said that he had been indicted as a co-conspirator in a case of espionage against the United States merely on the ground that one of the two indicted persons had visited the Permanent Mission of Viet Nam. He wondered what law the United States had been following in accusing the head of a mission as a co-conspirator on the basis that a Vietnamese national had been received at the Mission. Accordingly, he categorically denied the allegations made. The representative of the United States had also said that his Government had tried to discuss the matter with the Vietnamese Mission on 1 February, but that the Mission had refused to discuss it. According to section 13 of the Headquarters Agreement, before taking the decision to expel a diplomat the United States Government was obliged to consult the Government concerned and the Secretary–General. According to the representative of the United States, his Government had undertaken such consultations in New York and in Paris on 1 February, before the decision was taken. That statement was false.

* * *

Mr. FALL (*Senegal*) suggested that the Legal Counsel should be asked to study the question to see whether the host country had followed the procedure outlined in the Headquarters Agreement. The Committee would never know the facts of the case; its role was to consider the questions of procedure. * * * Once the Committee had before it the opinion of the Legal Counsel and the texts of the United States and Viet Nam statements, it could decide what to do. If it was determined that the procedure set forth in the Headquarters Agreement had not been observed, that would mean that a dangerous precedent had been set and the Committee would have to alert the General Assembly with regard to the matter.

Mr. SUY (*Under–Secretary–General, Legal Counsel*) pointed out that the suggestion made by the representative of Senegal would entail action by the Secretary–General, through his Legal Counsel, that would exceed the mandate entrusted to him by the General Assembly. Although the study requested of the Legal Counsel would apparently concern a question of form, it would actually concern the substance of the matter being discussed by the Committee. He did not see how he could arbitrate on the substance of the question.

* * *

Mr. FALL (*Senegal*) explained that he was asking the Legal Counsel to determine in the light of the statements made by the representatives of the United States and the Socialist Republic of Viet Nam whether the consultation provided for in section 13(b) had taken place.

The CHAIRMAN pointed out that the representative of Senegal was in effect asking the Legal Counsel to take a decision on the facts. The Legal Counsel did not have a mandate to take such a decision.

* * *

Mr. NGUYEN VAN LUU (*Observer for Viet Nam*) said: * * * The present situation was not a matter of bilateral relations between two Governments, but of trilateral relations, since the United Nations was a signatory of the Headquarters Agreement. The United Nations should therefore give its opinion in a case where the host country was claiming that certain activities were covered by the Headquarters Agreement. As a party to that contract, the United Nations must examine the substance of the question; it must establish what activities were involved and whether or not they constituted an abuse of residence privileges. It was the United Nations itself which conferred international privileges and had the right to determine whether certain actions constituted an abuse of international privileges. Only where such abuse had occurred, would it allow the host country to use its right to declare a diplomatic representative *persona non grata*.

* * *

[At this point the Vietnamese government recalled Dinh Ba Thi, without admitting any wrongdoing on his part.]

Mr. FALL (*Senegal*) said that the departure of the Permanent Representative of Viet Nam had not resolved the problem. Very important questions of principle had been raised by the case and the Committee must take a position on it.

* * *

Mr. SUY (*Under-Secretary-General, Legal Counsel*), replying to the question raised by the representative of Senegal concerning the legal definition of "prior consultation" said that, according to the only existing dictionary on the terminology of international law, the expression was used to describe either joint consideration of a matter or the action of requesting the opinion of another Government. * * * Finally, according to a study prepared by the Secretariat some 15 years earlier on the expressions "in consultation with" and "after consultation with", a distinction must be made between "consultation" on the one hand and "agreement", "concurrence" or "consent" on the other unless it was clearly indicated in the text that the purpose of consultation was to secure agreement.

* * *

[A colloquy ensued between the U.S. representative and the Vietnamese observer as to what had actually happened when the U.S. emissaries contacted the Vietnamese mission in New York and the Vietnamese embassy in Paris. Neither side on those occasions had been willing to discuss the matter on the other side's terms. The United States concluded that there had been as much consultation as was possible under the circumstances. Viet Nam concluded that there had only been notification, not consultation.]

* * *

Mr. THIEMELE (*Ivory Coast*) observed that Ambassador Dinh Ba Thi was the first head of a permanent mission to be asked by the host country to leave United States territory since the United Nations had been set up in New York in 1946. The duty of the Committee was to determine whether the host country had acted in accordance with the appropriate procedures, and to make recommendations concerning the way in which any future such case should be handled. At the same time, the Committee should not go beyond its competence: it was not a tribunal and could not investigate the original causes of the problem. Section 13(b) of the Headquarters Agreement made it clear that it was for the United States alone to decide what constituted an abuse of a diplomat's right of residence in United States territory.

The two sides agreed that diplomatic contact had been made both in New York and in Paris, and that the United States had requested the departure of the Ambassador on 3 February. Whether those diplomatic contacts constituted consultations was not a matter which the Committee could decide. It must be content to note that meetings had taken place. However, there had already been mention of charges against Ambassador Dinh Ba Thi in the United States press before the diplomatic contacts had taken place; which implied that the United States Secretary of State had already decided to request that the Ambassador should leave the country. If that was true, the correct procedures had clearly not been followed.

* * *

Mr. PEDAUYÉ (*Spain*) said that the case involving Ambassador Dinh Ba Thi was extremely important not only because it concerned the host country's decision to expel the Permanent Representative of a Member State, but also because such a situation could recur and therefore had implications not only for the two Member States concerned but also for the entire United Nations membership. Furthermore, it had implications for any country which was host to an organization or specialized agency in the United Nations system.

* * *

Section 13(b)3 of the Headquarters Agreement stated that persons entitled to diplomatic privileges and immunities under section 15 should not be required to leave the United States otherwise than in accordance with the customary procedure applicable to diplomatic envoys accredited to the United States, and section 15 provided that permanent representatives to the United Nations were entitled to the same privileges and immunities as diplomatic envoys accredited to the United States. Accordingly, if permanent representatives to the United Nations were to enjoy the same privileges as diplomatic envoys accredited to the United States, they should also be subject to the same rules with regard to expulsion. In fact, the "customary procedure" referred to in section 13(b)3 was that reflected in article 9 of the 1961 Vienna Convention on Diplomatic Relations, which stated that "The receiving State may at any time and without having to explain its decision, notify the sending State that the head of the mission or any member of the diplomatic staff of the mission is *persona non grata*."

According to a certain logic, if mere notification of the declaration of *persona non grata* was the sole prerequisite for expulsion of diplomatic envoys governed by bilateral agreements, who were subject to far stricter control than diplomats accredited to the United Nations, then notification and nothing more should be required in the event of expulsion of diplomats accredited to the United Nations.

DECISION–MAKING AND "PERSONA NON GRATA"

The Committee discussed procedural and substantive issues, but reached no conclusions as to whether the United States properly consulted before declaring Dinh Ba Thi "persona non grata," or whether he had in fact abused his privileges of residence. Would it have been proper for the Committee to have decided those matters? If not, did the debate serve any useful purpose? (The Committee consists of 15 members representing their governments. Its mandate is to consider the security of member states' missions to the U.N., and to advise the United States on questions under the Headquarters Agreement.)

The U.N. Legal Counsel in this case declined to do any more than provide a rather abstract definition of "consultation." Should he have gone further, as suggested by Mr. Fall of Senegal?

Was there actually a duty to consult? If so, with whom? Consider not only section 13 of the Headquarters Agreement, supra, but article 9 of the 1961 Vienna Convention on Diplomatic Relations, quoted by Mr. Pedauyé of Spain. Consider also the positions taken by the speakers in the debate.

In 1975 the U.N. Secretariat tried to clarify the circumstances under which expulsion would or would not be proper under the Headquarters Agreement. In a telegram to the U.N. Conference on the Representation of States in Their Relations with International Organizations, the Secretariat said: [b]

> The Secretary–General's report to the General Assembly at its second session on the Headquarters Agreement states, with reference to Section 13(*b*):
>
>> "This procedure is in line with that followed in diplomatic relations in the case of a serious offence committed by a diplomatic representative in the country to which he is accredited but can only apply within very narrow limits since the United States is the host country and not the country to which beneficiaries of article IV are accredited.
>>
>> "The procedure laid down in section 13 cannot, for example, be applied in the case of a *persona non grata:* there must have been some activity outside his official capacity coming within the scope of specific laws or regulations." [17]
>
> In addition, the report of the Sub–Committee on Privileges and Immunities [18] approved by the Sixth Committee and incorporated in its report to the General Assembly states:

---

b. 1975 U.N. Juridical Y.B. 155, 156.

17. *Official Records of the Second Session of the General Assembly,* Sixth Committee, Annex 11, p. 331.

"The Sub–Committee considers that section 13(*b*) of the Agreement, providing for the application by the United States of America of the laws and regulations in force in its territory regarding the residence of aliens in the United States of America, should be construed to mean that before any person can be required to leave the country on charges of having abused his privileges, there must be really serious grounds which would preclude the possibility of unwarranted accusations against such a person.

"The Sub–Committee also emphasized the importance of section 13(*b*)(i), [relating to consultations]." [19]

Who would decide whether there were "really serious grounds"?

If the Committee on Relations with the Host Country had made a decision on the merits in the Dinh Ba Thi case, how should it have come out?

b. *Travel Restrictions*

In 1985 the United States announced that employees of the United Nations who were nationals of the U.S.S.R., Afghanistan, Cuba, Iran, Libya and Vietnam would be subject to travel restrictions in the United States. These were superimposed on existing travel restrictions applying to members of these countries' missions to the U.N. The reason given was concern about reports of espionage and other clandestine activities by some Secretariat personnel of these nationalities.

The restrictions included a requirement that these Secretariat personnel make any common carrier reservations for travel outside a 25–mile radius of Columbus Circle, New York City, through a bureau of the State Department; a requirement that these persons file a detailed itinerary with the U.S. mission to the U.N. two days in advance of any travel, official or personal, beyond the 25–mile radius; and a requirement of prior approval by the mission if the travel was personal. The U.S. government reserved the right to review whether the proposed travel was official or personal.[a]

The U.N. Secretary–General protested (politely):

---

18. Established by the Sixth Committee at its 36th meeting in 1947 (ibid., p. 3).

19. *Official Records of the Second Session of the General Assembly,* Plenary Meetings, vol. II, p. 1521.

a. Note Verbale to the Secretary–General by the Acting Permanent Representative of the United States, Aug. 29, 1985, 80 Am.J.Int'l L. 438 (1986). The restrictions on Libyan nationals were somewhat stricter than those outlined above.

NOTE VERBALE BY THE U.N. SECRETARY–GENERAL TO THE PERMANENT REPRESENTATIVE OF THE UNITED STATES
Sept. 9, 1985.
80 Am.J.Int'l L. 440–41 (1986).*

The Secretary–General of the United Nations presents his compliments to the Permanent Representative of the United States of America and has the honour to refer to the note of 29 August concerning certain measures that the United States Government wishes to apply to travel undertaken by members of the Secretariat of the United Nations.

I

The Secretary–General has noted with concern the suggestion in the communication that certain members of the United Nations Secretariat have engaged in espionage or other clandestine activities. At no time during his term of office has the United States Administration brought to the attention of the Secretary–General any evidence or charges against any member of the Secretariat. In the absence of any specific evidence or charges, he cannot accept any blanket unsubstantiated accusation against members of the staff of the United Nations. The Secretary–General wishes to emphasize that, in his capacity as chief administrative officer of the United Nations, he would fully investigate information brought to his attention and would proceed to take quick and effective action against any staff member shown to have engaged in any improper activities against the security of the Host State.

II

* * *

While [U.S.] legislation may contain certain directives addressed to organs of the United States Government, and the measures in question are evidently proposed in implementation of these directives, the Secretary–General is of the view that these measures are not compatible with the international obligations of the United States, vis-à-vis the Organization, under the latter's Charter, under the Headquarters Agreement and under the Convention on the Privileges and Immunities of the United Nations.

In particular:

(a) The proposed measures would seem to constitute discrimination among members of the Secretariat solely on the basis of their nationality, in violation of the principle that they are all international civil servants whose primary loyalty and responsibility are to the Organization. Any discrimination among them based on nationality runs counter to the essential character of the international civil service, as envisaged in the United Nations Charter.

---

*Reprinted with permission, c. The American Society of International Law. The note verbale also appears in 1985 U.N. Juridical Y.B. 150.

The unity of the international civil service is absolutely essential if the Organization is to carry out its world-wide obligations with staff members whose individual nationalities might otherwise not be acceptable to the governments with whom they have to deal or within whose jurisdiction they must operate. This principle of non-discrimination, indeed non-differentiation, is designed to protect both the Organization and its staff members, including American staff members serving in various countries.

(b) As applied to official travel, the proposed measures would improperly constrain the Secretary-General's choice of what staff members are to be assigned to carry out certain functions within the United States. The final provision of the note, whereby the United States Government reserves the right to review whether travel designated as official by the Secretary-General is "*bona fide* official travel of the United Nations", raises a particular problem with regard to the Secretary-General's independent exercise of his responsibilities under the Charter, free from national interference.

(c) As applied to private travel, in respect of which the proposed measures are even more restrictive, the question may be raised whether limiting staff members, who may spend years or even their entire working career assigned to Headquarters, to a distance of 25 miles from Columbus Circle, or just to the five boroughs of New York City, is, apart from being discriminatory, unduly onerous.

III

The note requests the Secretariat to ensure that the indicated measures are implemented. However, that would seem to be outside of both the legal and the practical capacity of the Organization. Furthermore, the Secretary-General does not see how he could instruct the Secretariat to implement measures that appear to him incompatible with the responsibilities entrusted to him by the Charter.

THE AFTERMATH

Discussions ensued between the U.N. Secretariat and the United States. They reached an uneasy accommodation in early 1986, to the effect that arrangements for official U.N. travel in the United States would continue to be made by the U.N. for all members of the Secretariat, but the U.N. would notify the U.S. government in advance of each trip.[b] Thus the U.N. avoided making any distinction for official travel based on the nationality of a staff member, and the U.S. government was assured that it would know the travel plans of the distrusted Secretariat personnel (along with the travel plans of many others with whom it had no quarrel). The U.N.-U.S. accommodation

---

b. U.N.Doc. ST/IC/86/4 (1986).

did not deal with U.S. travel restrictions on members of the distrusted missions to the U.N.

The matter was then discussed in the U.N. Committee on Relations with the Host Country. The East European representatives argued that the U.S. measures violated U.N. Charter *article 100(2)*. The U.S. representative rejected any implication that the United States was not fulfilling its obligations. He pointed out that there were no restrictions on official travel of any U.N. staff member.[c]

In later years, the United States extended its controls on private travel, to include U.N. Secretariat members and their dependents who were nationals of other countries then under Communist governments or—after Iraq's invasion of Kuwait in 1990—who were nationals of Iraq. In practice, these controls required prior notice to the U.S. mission for private travel beyond 25 miles from Columbus Circle and the making of common carrier and hotel reservations through the State Department bureau.[d] In all cases the U.N. Secretariat protested on the ground that the travel controls discriminated among Secretariat members.[e] The representative of China took the same position when controls were applied to Chinese nationals:

> This discriminatory treatment not only undermines the equality of the staff members of the United Nations as international civil servants but also infringes the responsibilities entrusted to the Secretariat by the Charter of the United Nations. Doubtless, these restrictions run counter to the international obligations that the United States has assumed under [the U.N. Charter, the Headquarters Agreement and the Convention on the Privileges and Immunities of the U.N.][f]

The matter came up again in the U.N. Committee in 1988 and 1989. The debate focused on the legal issues, particularly in the context of restrictions on travel by members of individual states' missions to the U.N.

REPORT OF THE U.N. COMMITTEE ON RELATIONS WITH THE HOST COUNTRY
Nov. 25, 1988.
43 GAOR Supp. No. 26 (A/43/26) at 7–8, 12.

25. The 130th meeting of the Committee, on 24 June 1988, was devoted exclusively to a discussion of the new travel regulations issued by the host country * * *.

26. The Permanent Representative of Bulgaria stated that the new restrictive measures by the host country were contrary to both the

---

c. 40 GAOR Supp. No. 26 (A/40/26), at 7–12 (1986).

d. In the case of China, the controls required only prior notice. Some of the controls were later removed.

e. See U.N.Docs. ST/IC/88/57 (1988); ST/IC/89/10 (1989); A/C.5/46/4, at 4–5 (1991).

f. U.N.Doc. A/AC.154/269, Annex II (1989).

letter and the spirit of the relevant provisions of a number of basic international legal instruments of a binding character. They constituted a clear violation of the fundamental principle on which the United Nations was based, namely the principle of the sovereign equality of all Members, as laid down in Article 2, paragraph 1, of the Charter of the United Nations. The restrictions were imposed in spite of the clear-cut provisions of section 15 of the 1947 Agreement regarding the Headquarters of the United Nations, which stipulated that members of the staff of permanent missions were entitled to the same privileges and immunities as accorded to diplomatic envoys accredited to the United States. Those measures also contravened article IV, section 11(g) of the 1946 Convention on the Privileges and Immunities of the United Nations, according to which representatives of Member States would enjoy such privileges, immunities and facilities as enjoyed by diplomatic agents. A generally recognized standard of those privileges, immunities and facilities was codified in the 1961 Vienna Convention on Diplomatic Relations. The host country's travel restrictions were in flagrant violation of articles 26 and 47 of the Vienna Convention concerning freedom of movement and travel and non-discrimination.[g] The restrictions imposed by the host country were completely unprovoked, unlawful, discriminatory and entirely unjustified. Their implementation would create serious and sometimes insurmountable obstacles to the exercise by the Mission of its official functions at the United Nations. * * *

27. [The observer of Czechoslovakia stated:] * * * Arbitrary travel restrictions by the host country constituted a clear violation by the United States of its obligations under international law. [He referred to the same instruments the Bulgarian representative had cited.] In addition, they were not consonant with the provisions of articles 26 and 83 of the Vienna Convention on the Representation of States in Their Relations with International Organizations of a Universal Character of 1975. While the Convention itself had not yet entered into effect, its provisions undoubtedly constituted a codification of the valid customary law in the matter. A decision by the host country to impose similar restrictive measures on United Nations Secretariat staff members from the four countries concerned represented a differentiation among staff members solely on the basis of their citizenship. Such actions were considered as discrimination among staff members of the United Nations Secretariat and interference with the authority of the Secretary-General under the Charter and the Headquarters Agreement. They were incompatible with the principle of independence of the international civil service.

* * *

40. In response, the representative of the United States stated that the measures taken by the host country pursuant to United States law were necessary to ensure national security. Official travel on

g. [These articles are the counterparts of *articles 26* and *83* of the 1975 Vienna Convention on the Representation of States. Ed.]

behalf of the United Nations remained wholly unaffected. United States Government fulfilment of host country obligations did not conflict with its inherent right to adopt legal measures safeguarding national security. Article 105, paragraph 2, of the Charter stipulated that "representatives of the Members of the United Nations and officials of the Organization shall similarly enjoy such privileges and immunities as are necessary for the independent exercise of their functions in connection with the Organization". While the United States Government might be prepared to balance national interests and run certain security risks with regard to bilateral missions, the United States Government was not obliged to engender the same risks *vis-à-vis* United Nations missions. The United States had not and would not hamper the legitimate functions of missions accredited to the United Nations. The United States Government had never failed to respect the privileges and immunities prescribed by the Charter, the Headquarters Agreement and the Convention on the Privileges and Immunities of the United Nations.

THE LEGAL ISSUES

How do you come out on the lawfulness of the U.S. travel restrictions as they applied to (a) members of the U.N. Secretariat (i) as originally imposed and (ii) as modified; and (b) foreign missions to the U.N.? (Could these questions come up again, in a post-cold war context?)

Note that the only parties to the U.N. Headquarters Agreement are the United Nations and the United States. Does it create rights that can properly be asserted by nonparties, such as Bulgaria and Czechoslovakia? Consider *articles 34–36* of the 1986 Vienna Convention on the Law of Treaties Between States and International Organizations or Between International Organizations.

c. *Size of a Mission*

In 1986 the United States set a limit on the size of the Soviet mission to the United Nations, forcing a reduction in its staff of almost 40% (from 275 to 170) over two years. At 275, the Soviet mission (actually the three missions representing the Soviet Union as it then existed, including the missions of Byelorussia and the Ukraine) was about twice as large as the next largest mission. According to the United States, staff members of the Soviet mission had been engaged in espionage. The large numbers of suspected staff members placed a substantial burden on the F.B.I., which had to keep track of them.

The U.S. *diktat* led to another inconclusive debate in the Committee on Relations with the Host Country.[a] During the debate, the U.N.

a. See 41 GAOR Supp. No. 26 (A/41/26) at 8–10 (1986).

Legal Counsel noted that *article 14* of the 1975 Convention on the Representation of States in Their Relations with International Organizations provides "that the size of the mission should not exceed what was reasonable and normal, having regard to the function of the Organization, the needs of the particular mission and the circumstances and conditions in the host State. While the Convention was not yet in force, that particular provision reflected a consensus on the matter. The determination of what, in any particular case * * * might be reasonable and normal did not depend on the considerations of the host State alone. If the host State had any reservations regarding the size of a mission, such reservations had to be resolved through consultations and, if they failed, dispute-settlement procedures." [b]

Does article 14 of the 1975 Convention preclude unilateral action by the host state, as the U.N. Legal Counsel apparently thought? If it doesn't preclude unilateral action, does it nevertheless imply a duty to consult before any action is taken?

Does *Article V, section 15* of the Headquarters Agreement (which was also cited during the debate) deal with entire missions, or only with those members of missions who are to be accorded full diplomatic privileges? (Article 13 of the 1975 Convention distinguishes diplomatic staff from administrative, technical and service staff. Article 13, like article 14 of that Convention, reflects a consensus.)

Does *Article IV, sections 11–13* of the Headquarters Agreement bear on the lawfulness of the U.S. action? If so, which way do these sections point?

The Soviet Union ultimately did reduce the size of its mission to 170 people, without admitting that it was under any duty to do so.

d. *The Attempt to Close an Observer Mission*

In December 1987 Congress enacted the Anti-Terrorism Act of 1987.[a] The Act declared the Palestine Liberation Organization a terrorist organization, but did not allege terrorist activities within the United States. It asserted that the PLO is "a threat to the interests of the United States, its allies, and to international law," [b] and forbade the establishment or maintenance of "an office, headquarters, premises, or other facilities or establishments within the jurisdiction of the United States at the behest or direction of, or with funds provided by" the PLO.[c]

The PLO has had observer status at the U.N. since General Assembly Resolution 3237 granted it in 1974.[d] In that connection the PLO maintains a small observer mission in New York City. Relying on

b. Id. at 9.
a. 101 Stat. 1406, 22 U.S.C.A. § 5201 et seq.
b. 22 U.S.C.A. § 5201(b).
c. 22 U.S.C.A. § 5202(3).
d. See pages 166–70 infra.

the Act, in March 1988 the Attorney General of the United States ordered the PLO observer mission to close.

The U.N. General Assembly took the position overwhelmingly that if the United States forced the PLO mission to close, it would violate the Headquarters Agreement.[e] The U.S. State Department conceded as much. The State Department did not invoke the "security reservation" attached by Congress to its original approval of the Headquarters Agreement. (That "reservation" is examined at pages 115-21 infra.)

Was the State Department's concession compelled by *Article IV, section 11* of the Headquarters Agreement? By *section 13?* Was the concession itself legally significant?

Despite the State Department's concession and the General Assembly support for the right of the PLO mission to remain, the U.S. Department of Justice brought an action in federal district court in New York to evict the PLO.

In the meantime, the U.N. Secretary–General had sought an assurance from the U.S. representative to the U.N. that despite the Anti-Terrorism Act, "the present arrangements for the PLO Observer Mission would not be curtailed or otherwise affected."[f] When no such assurance was forthcoming, the General Assembly requested the International Court of Justice to issue an advisory opinion as to whether the United States was under an obligation to enter into arbitration on this matter, in accordance with *Article VIII, section 21* of the Headquarters Agreement. The United States argued that arbitration would be futile, because the United States would follow the will of Congress even if that resulted in a violation of the Headquarters Agreement; it would also be premature, because the PLO mission would not be forced to close unless and until the federal court entered a final judgment against the PLO.

In April 1988, the ICJ issued a unanimous opinion that the United States "is under an obligation, in accordance with section 21 [of the Headquarters Agreement] to enter into arbitration for the settlement of the dispute between itself and the United Nations."[g] About two months later, the federal district court in New York issued its judgment in the PLO eviction proceedings.

UNITED STATES v. PALESTINE LIBERATION ORGANIZATION

United States District Court, Southern District of New York, 1988.
695 F.Supp. 1456.

PALMIERI, DISTRICT JUDGE.

The Anti-terrorism Act of 1987 (the "ATA"), is the focal point of this lawsuit. At the center of controversy is the right of the Palestine

---

e. G.A.Res. 42/229A, March 2, 1988, 27 Int'l Legal Materials 772 (1988), adopted by a vote of 143 to 1 (Israel).

f. Quoted in [1988] I.C.J. at 19.

g. Applicability of the Obligation to Arbitrate under Section 21 of the United Nations Headquarters Agreement of 26 June 1947, [1988] I.C.J. 12, 35.

Liberation Organization (the "PLO") to maintain its office in conjunction with its work as a Permanent Observer to the United Nations. The case comes before the court on the government's motion for an injunction closing this office and on the defendants' motions to dismiss.

I

BACKGROUND

* * *

In 1974, the United Nations invited the PLO to become an observer at the U.N., to "participate in the sessions and the work of the General Assembly in the capacity of observer." The right of its representatives to admission to the United States as well as access to the U.N. was immediately challenged under American law. Judge Costantino rejected that challenge in *Anti–Defamation League of B'nai B'rith v. Kissinger,* Civil Action No. 74 C 1545 (E.D.N.Y. November 1, 1974). The court upheld the presence of a PLO representative in New York with access to the United Nations, albeit under certain entrance visa restrictions which limited PLO personnel movements to a radius of 25 miles from Columbus Circle in Manhattan. It stated from the bench:

> This problem must be viewed in the context of the special responsibility which the United [States] has to provide access to the United Nations under the Headquarters Agreement. It is important to note for the purposes of this case that a primary goal of the United Nations is to provide a forum where peaceful discussions may displace violence as a means of resolving disputed issues. At times our responsibility to the United Nations may require us to issue visas to persons who are objectionable to certain segments of our society.

Id., transcript at 37, *partially excerpted in* Department of State, 1974 *Digest of United States Practice in International Law,* 27, 28.

Since 1974, the PLO has continued to function without interruption as a permanent observer and has maintained its Mission to the United Nations without trammel, largely because of the Headquarters Agreement, which we discuss below.

II

THE ANTI-TERRORISM ACT

In October 1986, members of Congress requested the United States Department of State to close the PLO offices located in the United States. That request proved unsuccessful, and proponents of the request introduced legislation with the explicit purpose of doing so.

The result was the ATA, 22 U.S.C. §§ 5201–5203. It is of a unique nature. We have been unable to find any comparable statute in the long history of Congressional enactments. The PLO is stated to be "a terrorist organization and a threat to the interests of the United States, its allies, and to international law and should not benefit from operating in the United States." 22 U.S.C. § 5201(b).

* * *

The ATA, which became effective on March 21, 1988, forbids the establishment or maintenance of "an office, headquarters, premises, or other facilities or establishments within the jurisdiction of the United States at the behest or direction of, or with funds provided by" the PLO, if the purpose is to further the PLO's interests. 22 U.S.C. § 5202(3). The ATA also forbids spending the PLO's funds or receiving anything of value except informational material from the PLO, with the same *mens rea* requirement. *Id.* §§ 5202(1) and (2).

* * *

The United States commenced this lawsuit the day the ATA took effect, seeking injunctive relief to accomplish the closure of the Mission. The United States Attorney for this District has personally represented that no action would be taken to enforce the ATA pending resolution of the litigation in this court.

* * *

IV

The Duty to Arbitrate

Counsel for the PLO and for the United Nations and the Association of the Bar of the City of New York, as *amici curiae*, have suggested that the court defer to an advisory opinion of the International Court of Justice. *Applicability of the Obligation to Arbitrate Under Section 21 of the United Nations Headquarters Agreement of 26 June 1947*, 1988 I.C.J. No. 77 (April 26, 1988) (U.N. v. U.S.). That decision holds that the United States is bound by Section 21 of the Headquarters Agreement to submit to binding arbitration of a dispute precipitated by the passage of the ATA. Indeed, it is the PLO's position that this alleged duty to arbitrate deprives the court of subject matter jurisdiction over this litigation.

* * *

Because these proceedings are not in any way directed to settling any dispute, ripe or not, between the United Nations and the United States, Section 21, is, by its terms, inapplicable.[18] The fact that the

---

18. The United Nations has explicitly refrained from becoming a party to this litigation. The International Court of Justice makes a persuasive statement that the proceedings before this court "cannot be an 'agreed mode of settlement' within the meaning of section 21 of the Headquarters Agreement. The purpose of these proceedings is to enforce the Anti-Terrorism Act of 1987; it is not directed to settling the

Headquarters Agreement was adopted by a majority of both Houses of Congress and approved by the President, see 61 Stat. at 768, might lead to the conclusion that it provides a rule of decision requiring arbitration any time the interpretation of the Headquarters Agreement is at issue in the United States Courts. That conclusion would be wrong for two reasons.

First, this court cannot direct the United States to submit to arbitration without exceeding the scope of its Article III powers. What sets this case apart from the usual situation in which two parties have agreed to binding arbitration for the settlement of any future disputes, requiring the court to stay its proceedings, cf. 9 U.S.C. § 3 (1982), is that we are here involved with matters of international policy. This is an area in which the courts are generally unable to participate.

* * *

The conduct of the foreign relations of our Government is committed by the Constitution to the executive and legislative—the "political"—departments of the government.

* * *

Resolution of the question whether the United States will arbitrate requires "an initial policy determination of a kind clearly for nonjudicial discretion;" deciding whether the United States will or ought to submit to arbitration, in the face of a determination not to do so by the executive, would be impossible without the court "expressing lack of the respect due coordinate branches of government;" and such a decision would raise not only the "potentiality" but the reality of "embarrassment from multifarious pronouncements by various departments on one question." It is for these reasons that the ultimate decision as to how the United States should honor its treaty obligations with the international community is one which has, for at least one hundred years, been left to the executive to decide.

* * *

Section 21 of the Headquarters Agreement cannot provide a rule of decision regarding the interpretation of that agreement for another reason: treating it as doing so would require the courts to refrain from undertaking their constitutionally mandated function. The task of the court in this case is to interpret the ATA in resolving this dispute between numerous parties and the United States. Interpretation of the ATA, as a matter of domestic law, falls to the United States courts. In interpreting the ATA, the effect of the United States' international obligations—the United Nations Charter and the Headquarters Agreement in particular—must be considered. As a matter of domestic law, the interpretation of these international obligations and their reconciliation, if possible, with the ATA is for the courts. It is, as Chief Justice

[alleged] dispute, concerning the application of the Headquarters Agreement."

U.N. v. U.S., supra, 1988 I.C.J. 12, ¶ 14, at 34.

Marshall said, "emphatically the province and duty of the judicial department to say what the law is." *Marbury v. Madison,* 5 U.S. (1 Cranch) 137, 177, 2 L.Ed. 60 (1803). That duty will not be resolved without independent adjudication of the effect of the ATA on the Headquarters Agreement. Awaiting the decision of an arbitral tribunal would be a repudiation of that duty.

* * *

In view of the foregoing, the court finds that it is not deprived of subject matter jurisdiction by Section 21 of the Headquarters Agreement and that any interpretation of the Headquarters Agreement incident to an interpretation of the ATA must be done by the court.

V

THE ANTI-TERRORISM ACT AND THE HEADQUARTERS AGREEMENT

If the ATA were construed as the government suggests, it would be tantamount to a direction to the PLO Observer Mission at the United Nations that it close its doors and cease its operations *instanter.* Such an interpretation would fly in the face of the Headquarters Agreement, a prior treaty between the United Nations and the United States, and would abruptly terminate the functions the Mission has performed for many years. This conflict requires the court to seek out a reconciliation between the two.

Under our constitutional system, statutes and treaties are both the supreme law of the land, and the Constitution sets forth no order of precedence to differentiate between them. U.S. Const. art. VI, cl. 2. Wherever possible, both are to be given effect.

* * *

The long standing and well-established position of the Mission at the United Nations, sustained by international agreement, when considered along with the text of the ATA and its legislative history, fails to disclose any clear legislative intent that Congress was directing the Attorney General, the State Department or this Court to act in contravention of the Headquarters Agreement. This court acknowledges the validity of the government's position that Congress has the power to enact statutes abrogating prior treaties or international obligations entered into by the United States. *Whitney v. Robertson,* * * * 124 U.S. at 193–95, 8 S.Ct. at 457–58; *The Head Money Cases,* * * * 112 U.S. at 597–99, 5 S.Ct. at 253–54. However, unless this power is clearly and unequivocally exercised, this court is under a duty to interpret statutes in a manner consonant with existing treaty obligations. This is a rule of statutory construction sustained by an unbroken line of authority for over a century and a half.

* * *

The American Law Institute's recently revised *Restatement (Third) Foreign Relations Law of the United States* (1988) reflects this unbroken line of authority:

> § 115. Inconsistency Between International Law or Agreement and Domestic Law: Law of the United States.
>
> (1)(a) An Act of Congress supersedes an earlier rule of international law or a provision of an international agreement as law of the United States *if the purpose of the act to supersede the earlier rule or provision is clear* and if the act and the earlier rule or provision cannot be fairly reconciled.

(emphasis supplied).

We believe the ATA and the Headquarters Agreement cannot be reconciled except by finding the ATA inapplicable to the PLO Observer Mission.

A. The Obligations of the United States under the Headquarters Agreement

The obligation of the United States to allow transit, entry and access stems not only from the language of the Headquarters Agreement but also from forty years of practice under it. Section 11 of the Headquarters Agreement reads, in part,

> The federal, state or local authorities of the United States shall not impose any impediments to transit to or from the headquarters district of: (1) representatives of Members * * *, (5) other persons invited to the headquarters district by the United Nations * * * on official business.

61 Stat. at 761 (22 U.S.C. § 287 note). These rights could not be effectively exercised without the use of offices. The ability to effectively organize and carry out one's work, especially as a liaison to an international organization, would not be possible otherwise. It is particularly significant that Section 13 limits the application of United States law not only with respect to the entry of aliens, but also their residence. The Headquarters Agreement thus contemplates a continuity limited to official United Nations functions and is entirely consistent with the maintenance of missions to the United Nations. The exemptions of Section 13 are not limited to members, but extend to invitees as well.

* * *

After the United Nations invited the PLO to participate as a permanent observer, the Department of State took the position that it was required to provide access to the U.N. for the PLO. 1974 *Digest of United States Practice in International Law,* 27–29; 1976 *Digest of United States Practice in International Law,* 74–75. The State Department at no time disputed the notion that the rights of entry, access and residence guaranteed to invitees include the right to maintain offices.

The view that under the Headquarters Agreement the United States must allow PLO representatives access to and presence in the vicinity of the United Nations was adopted by the court in *Anti-Defamation League of B'nai B'rith v. Kissinger, supra; see also Harvard Law School Forum v. Shultz,* 633 F.Supp. 525, 526–27 (D.Mass.1986). The United States has, for fourteen years, acted in a manner consistent with a recognition of the PLO's rights in the Headquarters Agreement. This course of conduct under the Headquarters Agreement is important evidence of its meaning.

Throughout 1987, when Congress was considering the ATA, the Department of State elaborated its view that the Headquarters Agreement contained such a requirement.

* * *

It seemed clear to those in the executive branch that closing the PLO mission would be a departure from the United States' practice in regard to observer missions, and they made their views known to members of Congress who were instrumental in the passage of the ATA. In addition, United States representatives to the United Nations made repeated efforts to allay the concerns of the U.N. Secretariat by reiterating and reaffirming the obligations of the United States under the Headquarters Agreement. * * * The United Nations' position that the Headquarters Agreement applies to the PLO Mission is not new. 1979 U.N.Jurid.Y.B. 169–70; *see* 1980 U.N.Jurid.Y.B. 188 ¶ 3.

"Although not conclusive, the meaning attributed to treaty provisions by the Government agencies charged with their negotiation and enforcement is entitled to great weight." *Sumitomo Shoji America, Inc. v. Avagliano,* 457 U.S. 176, 184–85, 102 S.Ct. 2374, 2379, 72 L.Ed.2d 765 (1982). The interpretive statements of the United Nations also carry some weight, especially because they are in harmony with the interpretation given to the Headquarters Agreement by the Department of State.

Thus the language, application and interpretation of the Headquarters Agreement lead us to the conclusion that it requires the United States to refrain from interference with the PLO Observer Mission in the discharge of its functions at the United Nations.

B. Reconciliation of the ATA and the Headquarters Agreement

[The court noted how American courts have strained to reconcile domestic statutes with international agreements.]

The principles enunciated and applied in [Chew Heong v. United States, 112 U.S. 536, 5 S.Ct. 255, 28 L.Ed. 770 (1884), and later cases,] require the clearest of expressions on the part of Congress. We are constrained by these decisions to stress the lack of clarity in Congress' action in this instance. Congress' failure to speak with one clear voice on this subject requires us to interpret the ATA as inapplicable to the

Headquarters Agreement. This is so, in short, for the reasons which follow.

First, neither the Mission nor the Headquarters Agreement is mentioned in the ATA itself. Such an inclusion would have left no doubt as to Congress' intent on a matter which had been raised repeatedly with respect to this act, and its absence here reflects equivocation and avoidance, leaving the court without clear interpretive guidance in the language of the act. Second, while the section of the ATA prohibiting the maintenance of an office applies "notwithstanding any provision of law to the contrary," 22 U.S.C. § 5202(3), it does not purport to apply notwithstanding any treaty. The absence of that interpretive instruction is especially relevant because elsewhere in the same legislation Congress expressly referred to "United States law (including any treaty)." 101 Stat. at 1343. Thus Congress failed, in the text of the ATA, to provide guidance for the interpretation of the act, where it became repeatedly apparent before its passage that the prospect of an interpretive problem was inevitable. Third, no member of Congress expressed a clear and unequivocal intent to supersede the Headquarters Agreement by passage of the ATA. In contrast, most who addressed the subject of conflict denied that there would be a conflict: in their view, the Headquarters Agreement did not provide the PLO with any right to maintain an office. Here again, Congress provided no guidance for the interpretation of the ATA in the event of a conflict which was clearly foreseeable. And Senator Claiborne Pell, Chairman of the Senate Foreign Relations Committee, who voted for the bill, raised the possibility that the Headquarters Agreement would take precedence over the ATA in the event of a conflict between the two. His suggestion was neither opposed nor debated, even though it came in the final minutes before passage of the ATA.

* * *

Congress failed to provide unequivocal interpretive guidance in the text of the ATA, leaving open the possibility that the ATA could be viewed as a law of general application and enforced as such, without encroaching on the position of the Mission at the United Nations.

That interpretation would present no inconsistency with what little legislative history exists. There were conflicting voices both in Congress and in the executive branch before the enactment of the ATA. Indeed, there is only one matter with respect to which there was unanimity—the condemnation of terrorism. This, however, is extraneous to the legal issues involved here. At oral argument, the United States Attorney conceded that there was no evidence before the court that the Mission had misused its position at the United Nations or engaged in any covert actions in furtherance of terrorism. If the PLO is benefiting from operating in the United States, as the ATA implies, the enforcement of its provisions outside the context of the United Nations can effectively curtail that benefit.

* * *

In sum, the language of the Headquarters Agreement, the longstanding practice under it, and the interpretation given it by the parties to it leave no doubt that it places an obligation upon the United States to refrain from impairing the function of the PLO Observer Mission to the United Nations. The ATA and its legislative history do not manifest Congress' intent to abrogate this obligation. We are therefore constrained to interpret the ATA as failing to supersede the Headquarters Agreement and inapplicable to the Mission.

INTERNATIONAL LAW, U.S. LAW AND THE PLO MISSION

Was the district court's reasoning convincing as to (a) the propriety of hearing the case despite *section 21* of the Headquarters Agreement and the ICJ's opinion regarding the U.S. duty to arbitrate; (b) the duty under the Headquarters Agreement to refrain from interfering with the PLO observer mission; and (c) Congressional intent?

After the district court dismissed the action, a conflict developed within the U.S. government over whether or not to appeal. The Justice Department wanted to appeal, but the State Department did not. President Reagan had to resolve the conflict. He decided that no appeal would be taken.[h] Thus the PLO observer mission remained open.

Did this case result in a victory for international law over domestic law, as applied by the U.S. legal system?

Was the U.S. position vindicated on the question of a duty to arbitrate?

e. *The Denial of a Visa to a U.N. Invitee*

In November 1988 the U.S. State Department denied a visa to Yasir Arafat, the Chairman of the PLO, when he applied for one in order to address the U.N. General Assembly. He had been invited to explain the action taken at the 1988 meeting of the Palestine National Council, which (inter alia) had declared a Palestinian Arab state, disavowed on behalf of that state the threat or use of force against the territorial integrity and political independence of any state, and indicated acceptance of key U.N. General Assembly and Security Council resolutions on the Middle East.[a]

The General Assembly adopted a resolution deploring the U.S. visa denial as a violation of the Headquarters Agreement.[b] The Assembly

---

[h] N.Y. Times, Aug. 30, 1988, p. A1, col. 6.

[a] Palestine National Council's Declaration of Independence, in U.N.Doc. A/43/827–S/20278, Annex III, 27 Int'l Legal Materials 1668 (1988).

[b] G.A.Res. 43/48 (1988), adopted by a vote of 151–2 (Israel, United States)–1 (United Kingdom).

then decided to convene temporarily at the U.N. complex in Geneva to hear Mr. Arafat.

The State Department issued a statement explaining its denial of a visa to Mr. Arafat:

U.S. STATE DEPARTMENT'S STATEMENT ON DENIAL OF A VISA TO YASIR ARAFAT
Nov. 26, 1988.
Dep't State Bull., Feb. 1989, at 53.

The 1947 UN headquarters agreement obligates the United States to provide certain rights of entry, transit, and residence to persons invited to the UN headquarters district in New York City.

The Congress of the United States conditioned the entry of the United States into the UN headquarters agreement on the retention by the U.S. Government of the authority to bar the entry of aliens associated with or invited by the United Nations "in order to safeguard its own security."

In this regard, U.S. law excludes members of the Palestine Liberation Organization (PLO) into the United States by virtue of their affiliation in an organization which engages in terrorism. The Secretary of State is vested by law with the discretion to recommend to the Attorney General that the prohibition against a particular PLO member be waived.

The UN General Assembly in 1974 invited the Palestine Liberation Organization to participate as an observer at the General Assembly. The United States acknowledged that this UN invitation obligates the United States to accord PLO observers entry, transit, and residence; therefore, visa waivers have been issued to such individuals as a routine practice. As a result, a PLO Observer Mission has been in operation at the United Nations since 1975. The PLO, therefore, has had, and continues to have, ample opportunity to make its positions known to the membership of the United Nations.

On November 24, 1988, we received an application from Mr. Yasir Arafat, Chairman of the PLO, for a visa to attend the UN General Assembly session in New York City as an invitee. The Secretary of State has decided not to recommend a waiver of ineligibility in this case; the visa application, therefore, is not approved.

The U.S. Government has convincing evidence that PLO elements have engaged in terrorism against Americans and others. This evidence includes a series of operations undertaken by the Force 17 and the Hawari organizations since the PLO claimed to foreswear the use of terrorism in the Cairo declaration of November 1985. As Chairman of the PLO, Mr. Arafat is responsible for actions of these organizations which are units of Fatah, an element of the PLO of which he also is chairman and which is under his control.

The most recent sign of Mr. Arafat's associations with terrorism was the presence at the Algiers session of the Palestine National Council this month of Abu Abbas, a member of the Executive Committee of the PLO who has been convicted by the Italian judicial system of the murder of an American citizen, Mr. Leon Klinghoffer.

In summary, we find that:

The PLO, through certain of its elements, has employed terrorism against Americans;

Mr. Arafat, as Chairman of the PLO, knows of, condones, and lends support to such acts; he, therefore, is an accessory to such terrorism;

Terrorism and those involved in it are a serious threat to our national security and to the lives of American citizens; and

The headquarters agreement, contained in Public Law 80–357, reserves to us the right to bar the entry of those who represent a threat to our security.

THE "SECURITY RESERVATION"

The 80th Congress, by a Joint Resolution, authorized the President to bring the Headquarters Agreement into force for the United States. In *section 6* of the Joint Resolution, Congress attached a reservation (if indeed it may properly be called that), quoted in part in the State Department's statement above. See its full text, in the Supplement to this book.

Section 6 originated in the Senate Foreign Relations Committee during its consideration of the then-unratified Headquarters Agreement. As drafted by that committee, it did not contain the language, "to safeguard its own security." The committee explained its position, after referring to sections 11 and 13 of the Headquarters Agreement:

It is the opinion of the committee that these provisions adequately protect the security of the United States and that the United Nations could not be expected to maintain its headquarters in this country if the United States were to impose restrictions upon access to the headquarters district which would interfere with the proper functioning of the Organization.

In order to remove any doubt as to the meaning of these provisions, the committee adopted an amendment to Senate Joint Resolution 144 making it clear that there is no amendment, or obligation to amend, the immigration laws in any way except to give effect to the rights referred to above.[c]

When the House Foreign Affairs Committee considered the Headquarters Agreement and the Joint Resolution, it added the language,

---

c. Sen.Rep. No. 559, 80th Cong., 1st Sess. 6 (1947).

"to safeguard its own security and" to section 6 of the Joint Resolution. It explained what it had done:

> An amendment added by the committee reserves the right of the United States to safeguard its own security along with the right to control entry of aliens into territory other than the headquarters area. This right of self-defense is given expression here as a premise underlying all American policy. This language was inserted in order to make explicit what is a premise of such an agreement in any case.[d]

To determine whether section 6 of the Joint Resolution is a reservation, consider the definition in Vienna Convention on the Law of Treaties Between States and International Organizations or Between International Organizations (the Vienna Convention on International Organizations' Treaties), *article 2(1)(d)*.

The definition in the Vienna Convention on International Organizations' Treaties was taken from the definition in the 1969 Vienna Convention on the Law of Treaties, with only those changes required by the focus on international organizations. It may be taken to represent customary international law.

Note that under the Vienna Convention on International Organizations' Treaties (again echoing the Vienna Convention on the Law of Treaties), a reservation may be accepted by silence for 12 months (*article 20(5)*). *Article 21* sets forth the effect of a reservation.

Is section 6 of the Joint Resolution actually a reservation?

In 1953 the United States created a stir at the U.N. when it denied visas to two representatives of nongovernmental organizations who were trying to attend meetings of U.N. bodies in New York. In both cases the nongovernmental organizations were allegedly communist-dominated, and in both cases the United States invoked section 6 of the Joint Resolution.

The U.S. action in 1953 engendered an exchange of legal memoranda between the Legal Department of the United Nations and the office of the U.S. State Department's Assistant Legal Adviser for United Nations Affairs.

The U.N. Legal Department asserted first, that section 6 of the Joint Resolution was never made known to the U.N. General Assembly as a reservation, and was never considered by the General Assembly nor accepted by it when it approved the Headquarters Agreement. The State Department rather easily rebutted this assertion.

The U.N. Legal Department's second argument was that section 6 of the Joint Resolution, even if it were in force, would not apply to the denial of visas to persons seeking to attend U.N. meetings in New York. Section 6, said the Legal Department, "refers to control by the United States of the entrance of aliens into any territory of the United States

---

d. H.R.Rep. No. 1093, 80th Cong., 1st Sess. 11 (1947).

other than the Headquarters District, its immediate vicinity, and the necessary area of transit." e

The office of the Assistant Legal Adviser replied that section 6 refers not only to controlling the entrance of aliens into any territory of the United States other than the headquarters district and vicinity, but also to safeguarding U.S. security. According to the State Department, this would allow the United States to safeguard its security even when persons considered security risks are on their way to and from the headquarters district.f

The U.S. Representative to the United Nations, Henry Cabot Lodge, found himself in the middle of the legal dispute. As the two documents below indicate, he did his best to work it out with Dag Hammarskjöld, the Secretary-General of the United Nations.

MEMORANDUM BY THE UNITED STATES REPRESENTATIVE AT THE UNITED NATIONS (LODGE)

May 19, 1953.
Foreign Relations of the United States 1952–1954 (III) at 278.

I discussed the problem with Secretary General Dag Hammarskjöld.

The Secretary General's position as stated to me is as follows:

"It is my understanding that the principle which should govern all classes of persons coming into the Headquarters on United Nations business is that no solution will ever be practical and lasting if it does not take into account both the necessity of the right of access being free from determination by any single government and the necessity that the security of the country where the Headquarters is established should not be endangered."

Mr. Hammarskjöld is prepared to agree with the essential point in our position, viz., that the United States has the right to take the steps necessary to safeguard its security. He has at the same time, however, made it perfectly clear that he cannot accept the interpretation of Section 6 of the Joint Resolution (PL 357—80th Congress) set forth in the position paper. He relies heavily on the 1947 Senate and House reports concerning that Resolution to support his contention (*a*) that the Congress never intended that Section 6 have the meaning we presently attribute to it, and (*b*) that such an interpretation was never made known to the 1947 General Assembly. My own reading of these reports and of the General Assembly records leads me to the conclusion that, if this matter goes to the General Assembly as it will if we force this issue, a persuasive case can be made in support of the Secretary-General's position. I, therefore, recommend that we not force the issue, particularly in view of the extent to which Mr. Hammarskjöld appears

e. U.N. Doc. E/2397 (1953) (emphasis in the original).

f. Foreign Relations of the United States 1952–1954 (III) at 262.

prepared to go along with us as a practical matter, apart from the legal interpretation of the Section 6 reservation.

ANNEX TO LETTER FROM HAMMARSKJÖLD TO LODGE
June 22, 1953.
Foreign Relations of the United States 1952–1954 (III) at 295.

I and my representatives have, during the past weeks, discussed with the Representative of the U.S. to the UN and members of his staff problems which have arisen in connection with the application for admission to the U.S. by persons desiring to come to the Headquarters District. Although the discussions commenced on the point of the legal interpretation of certain provisions of the Headquarters Agreement and of the U.S. authorizing legislation, it quickly became evident in the course of the discussions that there was agreement concerning the basic principles to be applied to the problems which had arisen, and that only matters of procedure required detailed attention. The procedural aspects have now been settled in a manner which in practice should assure the mutual satisfaction of the parties concerned.

The basic principles which have been recognized are the following: it is certain that the provisions of the Headquarters Agreement cannot be permitted to serve as a cover to enable persons in the U.S. to engage in activities, outside the scope of their official functions, directed against the host country. It is equally certain that in view of the nature of the obligations undertaken by the U.S. as host country when entering into the Headquarters Agreement, it must not arbitrarily and for reasons known only to itself make decisions to exclude persons falling within the categories set forth in Section 11 of the Headquarters Agreement, although it clearly has the right to deport such persons for abuse of privileges of residence under the Agreement.

Accordingly, procedures have been devised to make certain that, should there arise in the future any case involving a serious problem with respect to the admission to the U.S. of persons coming to the Headquarters District, the matter will receive the most prompt and careful consideration at the highest levels, and that the U.S. will consult with me and keep me as fully informed as possible to assure that the decision made is in accord with the rights of the U.S. Government to protect its own security under the Agreement. It is recognized that those rights may be exercised by granting a visa valid only for transit to and from the Headquarters District and for sojourn in its immediate vicinity. It is further recognized that to implement that right the U.S. has authority to define (a) "the immediate vicinity" of the Headquarters and the necessary routes of transit, (b) activities outside the scope of official functions which would constitute an abuse of the privileges of residence, and (c) the time and manner of expiration of the visa following the completion of the official functions.

BACK TO 1988

To return to the events of November 1988, the U.N. Legal Counsel responded to the U.S. State Department's justification for denying the visa to Mr. Arafat (page 114 supra), in a statement to the General Assembly's Sixth (Legal) Committee.

STATEMENT BY THE U.N. LEGAL COUNSEL ON THE U.S. DENIAL OF A VISA TO YASIR ARAFAT
Nov. 28, 1988.
U.N. Doc. A/C.6/43/7, at 1–4.

* * *

[The Legal Counsel pointed out that he had personally handed the visa request to Ambassador Okun of the United States mission to the U.N. The request was worded in the same way as are other PLO visa requests. He expressed the view to Ambassador Okun that the request fell under sections 11, 12 and 13 of the Headquarters Agreement, and that the necessary visa accordingly should be granted as soon as possible. His statement to the Sixth Committee continued:]

3. I note from the statement of the Department of State dated [26] November 1988 * * * that the United States recognizes that it is obligated to provide certain rights of entry, transit and residence to persons invited to the United Nations Headquarters district in New York. The statement of the Department of State goes on to say that "The Congress of the United States conditioned the entry of the United States into the Headquarters Agreement on the retention by the United States Government of the authority to bar the entry of aliens associated with or invited by the United Nations 'in order to safeguard its own security'." * * * This is the so-called security reservation * * *.

4. In this respect, I note that the Headquarters Agreement states in section 13(d) that "Except as provided above in this section and the General Convention, the United States retains full control and authority over the entry of persons * * * into the territory of the United States". Thus, the Headquarters Agreement makes it clear that there is an unrestricted right of the persons mentioned in section 11 to enter the United States for the purpose of proceeding to the Headquarters district.

5. The Agreement does not contain a reservation of the right *to bar* the entry of those who represent, in the view of the host country, a threat to its security. What is referred to in the statement of the Department of State is, apparently, section 6 of Public Law 80–357 which reads as follows:

> "Nothing in the Agreement shall be construed as in any way diminishing, abridging or weakening the right of the United States

to safeguard its own security and completely to control the entrance of aliens into any territory of the United States other than the Headquarters district and its immediate vicinity ... and such areas as it is reasonably necessary to traverse in transit between the same and foreign countries."

6. There is a difference of opinion between the United Nations and the United States on the legal character and validity in international law of that proviso. * * * In the present circumstances, it suffices to refer to the wording of section 6, whatever the international legal character of that proviso might be, which speaks of the need to "safeguard its own security and completely to control the entry of aliens into any territory of the United States *other than the Headquarters district and its immediate vicinity* (emphasis added) * * * and such areas as it is reasonably necessary to traverse in transit between the same and foreign countries".

7. Mr. Arafat's visa application is precisely to visit the Headquarters district and nothing else. The application thus situates itself precisely within the scope of section 11, precisely within the scope of the exception provided for in section 13(d) of the Headquarters Agreement and precisely within the area left open by section 6 of Public Law 80–357.

[The Legal Counsel referred to the 1953 exchange between Henry Cabot Lodge and Dag Hammarskjöld, supra pages 117–18. He said that, contrary to the understanding then reached, the United States on the current occasion had not consulted with the Secretary-General regarding Mr. Arafat's visa.]

9. In her statement this morning, the representative of the United States referred to, and I quote, "rare occasions" on which the United States had declined to issue visas to persons entering the United States for United Nations purposes in order to protect national security. The United States representative went on to assert that United Nations practice confirms that the United States had the right to decline the issuance of visas and the United Nations had, on a number of occasions since 1954, acquiesced in such a practice.

10. For the record, I wish to state that the United Nations has not acquiesced in such a practice. It is true that, on certain occasions, the United States has declined to issue visas to representatives of States or to persons invited to the United Nations, and the United Nations has not insisted where the requesting State itself, for reasons of its own, did not pursue the matter. The United Nations legal position regarding the obligation of the host country to grant visas has at all times been perfectly clear to the host country, as was the United Nations position with respect to the so-called security reservation.

11. As to the reasons given by the host country in the present case, I would like to indicate, finally, that the statement of the Department of State does not make the point that the presence of Mr. Arafat, Chairman of the Executive Committee of the PLO, at the United

Nations would *per se* in any way threaten the security of the United States. In other words, the host country did not allege that there was apprehension that Mr. Arafat, once in the United States, might engage in activities outside the scope of his official functions directed against the security of the host country. The reasoning given [by] the State Department * * * does not meet the standard laid down in the talks between Secretary–General Hammarskjöld and the United States authorities and reported back by Mr. Hammarskjöld in the report cited above.

12. To sum up, I am of the opinion that the host country was and is under an obligation to grant the visa request of the Chairman of the Executive Committee of the PLO, an organization which has been granted observer status by the General Assembly.

EVALUATING THE U.S. POSITION

How strong was the U.S. argument, based on the "security reservation"?

Note the reference to United States–United Nations practice, in paragraphs 9 and 10 of the Legal Counsel's statement. What is the legal significance, if any, of that practice?

In 1979 the U.N. Office of Legal Affairs gave an opinion that "it necessarily follows from the obligations imposed by Article 105 of the Charter of the United Nations that the Palestine Liberation Organization Observer enjoys immunity from legal process in respect of words spoken or written and all acts performed by members of the delegation in their official capacity before relevant United Nations organs."[g] Is this relevant to the legal argument over the U.S. denial of the visa to Mr. Arafat? If so, does it tend to support the U.S. or the U.N. position?

If the United States had a duty to allow Mr. Arafat to address the United Nations in New York, was it a duty owed just to the U.N., or was it owed also to either the PLO or Mr. Arafat? (Do *articles 34–36* of the 1986 Vienna Convention on International Organizations' Treaties answer this question?)

Does the United States have a separate duty to the U.N. to consult the Secretary–General before it decides whether or not to allow someone like Mr. Arafat to come to U.N. Headquarters?

E. THE U.N. ADMINISTRATIVE TRIBUNAL AND RIGHTS OF STAFF MEMBERS

There is a large body of international civil service law governing the rights and obligations of staff members within international organizations. The sources of international civil service law include the

[g.] 1979 U.N. Juridical Y.B. 169–70.

constituent instruments of the relevant organizations, staff rules and regulations promulgated by each organization, contracts of employment, general principles of law, and even common law established by international administrative tribunals.[a] Several international organizations have administrative tribunals, including the U.N., the ILO and the World Bank. Each of these three tribunals hears civil service cases not only from within its own organization, but also from other international organizations that have elected to use it. Thus, for example, the U.N. Administrative Tribunal hears cases arising not only within the U.N. (including its organs), but also those from the International Civil Aviation Organization, the International Maritime Organization and the U.N. Joint Staff Pension Fund.

Over the years, these Administrative Tribunals have developed a very substantial body of civil service law. Space does not permit anything approaching a full examination of this jurisprudence in these pages. We will be limited to examining the U.N. Administrative Tribunal, and even then in only one (albeit important) context.

The U.N. Administrative Tribunal consists of seven members from seven different states. It sits in panels of three. The U.N. General Assembly appoints its members for three-year terms. Members may be reappointed.[b]

Under the Statute of the U.N. Administrative Tribunal:

> The Tribunal shall be competent to hear and pass judgement upon applications alleging non-observance of contracts of employment of staff members of the Secretariat * * * or of the terms of appointment of such staff members. The words "contracts" and "terms of appointment" include all pertinent regulations and rules in force at the time of alleged non-observance, including the staff pension regulations.[c]

The Statute also provides that the Applicant must first submit the dispute to an appeals body established by the staff regulations, unless the Applicant and the Secretary–General have agreed to submit the application directly to the Administrative Tribunal.[d]

In May 1990 the Tribunal decided a particularly significant case involving the principle of U.N. Secretariat independence from member state influence or control. It arose out of the practice of "seconding" ("loaning" for designated periods) individuals from the service of their own governments to service in the U.N. Secretariat. Three Chinese nationals, seconded to the U.N. as translators on fixed-term contracts, brought the proceeding against the U.N. Secretary–General seeking to

---

a. For comprehensive treatment, see C. Amerasinghe, The Law of the International Civil Service (2 vols. 1988).

b. The Tribunal's judgments appear in a limited distribution series of U.N. documents under the symbol AT/DEC/, and are compiled from time to time in a set of volumes entitled Judgements of the United Nations Administrative Tribunal.

c. Statute of the U.N. Administrative Tribunal art. 2(1), in 2 Amerasinghe, supra note a, Appendix I.

d. Statute, supra, art. 7(1).

be retained as staff members beyond the end of their fixed terms. The Secretary–General agreed to direct submission, bypassing the intermediate appeals body.

THE CHINESE TRANSLATORS CASE
U.N. Administrative Tribunal Judgment No. 482, May 25, 1990.
U.N. Doc. AT/DEC/482.

* * *

The Applicants, Rong Qiu, Kefu Zhou and Jiping Yao, nationals of the People's Republic of China (China) and former students of the Beijing Institute of Foreign Languages, passed the 1984 United Nations Competitive Examination for Chinese Verbatim Reporters. * * * The three Applicants were offered five-year fixed-term appointments at the P–2, Step IV level, as Verbatim Reporters in the Department of Conference Services (DCS). Their letters of appointment stated, as a special condition, that they were "on secondment from the Government of China".

During the course of their employment with the United Nations, the Applicant Qiu's overall performance was rated as "very good" and "excellent" and the Applicant Yao's and the Applicant Zhou's overall performance was rated as "very good". The three Applicants were promoted to the P–3 level, effective 1 September 1986.

In a memorandum dated 1 May 1989, the Administrative Officer, DCS, requested the Personnel Officer in the Office of Human Resources Management (OHRM) that six Chinese Verbatim Reporters, including the Applicants Qiu and Yao, who were on secondment from the Government of the People's Republic of China (the Chinese Government) and whose appointments were due to expire on 15 September 1989 "be granted probationary appointments". She confirmed that they [occupied] * * * posts provided for in the budget and against which career appointments could be granted. * * * Nevertheless, the Administration did not submit the three recommendations for a probationary appointment to the appropriate appointment and promotion bodies. In a handwritten note inserted on the 1 May 1989 memorandum from DCS to OHRM, the Personnel Officer wrote: "DCS has informed me on [10 August 1989] to request from the Government of China an extension of appointment for two years."

In three notes verbales dated 11 August 1989, addressed to the Permanent Mission of the People's Republic of China (the Chinese Mission), the Secretary–General asked the Chinese Government to extend the Applicant Qiu's and the Applicant Yao's secondment until 15 September 1991 and the Applicant Zhou's secondment until 20 September 1991. In three separate replies dated 23 August 1989, the Chinese Mission informed the Secretariat that the Chinese Government had consented to the extension of the three Applicants' secondment until 31 December 1989 only. Each of the three letters stated: "[A] recommendation from the Chinese Government for his successor will be communicated to the Secretariat in a separate note".

In a letter dated 1 October 1989, the Applicant Qiu requested the Assistant Secretary–General, OHRM, to grant him a career appointment in accordance with paragraph 5 of Section IV of General Assembly resolution 37/126, which provides that "staff members on fixed-term appointments upon completion of five years of continuing good service shall be given every reasonable consideration for a career appointment", and with paragraph 5 of Section VI of General Assembly resolution 38/232, in which the Assembly "recommends that the organizations normally dispense with the requirement for a probationary appointment as a prerequisite for a career appointment following a period of five years' satisfactory service on fixed-term contracts". He stated that he would immediately resign from any post held in his home country, if this was a requirement for the United Nations to offer him a probationary appointment. Finally, he noted that he feared for his safety and that of his family if he were to return to China, because of his participation in protest activities against the manner in which the Chinese Government had dealt with the student demonstrations in Beijing.

In similar letters dated 2 October 1989, the Applicants Yao and Zhou requested the Assistant Secretary–General, OHRM, to grant them career appointments on the ground that they fulfilled the requirements set forth in General Assembly resolutions 37/126 and 38/232. The Applicant Yao stated that he had "never been associated with the Chinese Government". He also admitted his involvement in the protest against recent events in his home country and said that he would face serious consequences if his employment with the United Nations were terminated and he had to return to his country. The Applicant Zhou argued that as a staff member of the Secretariat, he should not "automatically be denied the right to equal treatment with other staff members because [he came] from a certain country". Furthermore, he asserted that recent events in his country gave him reason to fear for his safety and future if he were to return. He admitted to having been seconded from the Chinese Government but informed the Assistant Secretary–General, OHRM, that he had handed in his resignation to the Foreign Ministry of China in June 1989.

* * *

In a letter dated 12 December 1989, the Director, SATD, OHRM, informed the three Applicants that their request for a further appointment with the United Nations had "been carefully considered" by DCS and OHRM. He noted in this regard:

> "I appreciate your interest in remaining in the service of the United Nations, but I regret to inform you that the Organization is not in a position to offer you a new appointment at this time.

However, in consideration of the closeness of the date of expiration of your current fixed-term appointment, and in order to afford you more time to make new plans, your present appointment will be extended to 31 January 1990."

[The Applicants wrote letters to the Secretary–General on 14 and 20 December 1989 requesting review and reversal of the decision not to offer them new appointments.]

On 15 January 1990, the Acting Under–Secretary–General for Administration and Management informed each Applicant that:

* * *

I regret that you consider that Mr. Riesco's letter of 12 December 1989 did not show that you had received every reasonable consideration for a further appointment. Let me assure you that your case at that stage received such consideration. Following your request for review of the decision communicated to you in Mr. Riesco's letter of 12 December 1989, a further review was fully and completely conducted in the light of paragraph 5 of section IV of General Assembly resolution 37/126, which gives you the right to every reasonable consideration for a career appointment.

In considering your case, at all stages, your continuing good service as a verbatim reporter was taken into account, as well as the fact that your Department recommended you for a further appointment.

On the other hand, it was also necessary to take into account the interests of the Organization and in particular its functional needs. In this connection, it was important to ensure that the Chinese language services continued to function effectively and efficiently. Since the primary users of those services are representatives of the Government of the People's Republic of China, it is of critical importance for the effectiveness of the services that those representatives have confidence that their statements, both oral and written, will be objectively and fairly rendered, interpreted or reported. Furthermore, the efficient functioning of the Chinese language services would not be possible in a situation where staff members were antagonistic to each other because of expressly stated political animosities.

It would also not be in the interests of the Organization to disrupt the rotational system for the staffing of the Chinese language services, which has proven to be most effective. This system has enabled the establishment of a specialized language training programme at the Beijing Institute for Foreign Languages, the termination of which would make it immensely difficult to recruit language staff with the specific qualifications required to fill vacancies appropriately and expeditiously.

After weighing these factors again, the Secretary–General has confirmed his earlier conclusion as conveyed to you in Mr. Riesco's letter of 12 December 1989.

* * *

[On 28 February 1990 the Applicants filed their application with the Tribunal.]

Whereas the Applicants' principal arguments are that:

1. The Respondent failed to discharge his obligation under Article 100 and Article 101, paragraph 3, of the Charter and General Assembly resolutions 37/126 and 38/232, to give the Applicants every reasonable consideration for a career appointment.

2. Staff members do not serve Governments but, according to Article 100 of the Charter and Staff Regulation 1.1, serve the Organization. They do not have to agree with the policies of Governments in order to carry out their duties with impartiality.

3. The Respondent's decision not to extend the Applicants' appointments was based on illegal considerations, such as the wishes of the Chinese Government.

4. The establishment of a training institute in a Member State may not derogate from or replace Articles 100 and 101 of the Charter or the Staff Regulations and Rules.

Whereas the Respondent's principal arguments are that:

1. The Applicants did not have a legal expectancy of further employment upon expiry of their fixed-term appointments.

2. Appointments on secondment require the consent of all parties to the secondment arrangement. The Respondent properly sought the consent of the Chinese Government to an extension of the Applicants' appointments on secondment.

3. The Secretary–General is bound to give reasonable consideration to granting career appointments to staff on fixed-term appointments (including fixed-term appointments on secondment) with five years of continuing good service, but this requirement does not deprive the Secretary–General of his discretion in deciding whether the grant of career appointments is in the interests of the Organization.

4. The Secretary–General's assessment of the interests of the Organization in considering whether to offer career appointments to the Applicants cannot be challenged except on the basis of prejudice or improper motive.

5. The Respondent did not violate any applicable procedures through the manner in which he gave the Applicants every reasonable consideration for a career appointment.

* * *

Sec. 4   THE STATUS OF PERSONS AND PREMISES

The Tribunal * * * pronounces the following judgement:

* * *

VI. The Tribunal notes that the Applicant Yao's personnel file contains the contract accepted by students on entering the Institute. It is entitled "Agreement for Students" and includes the following provisions, which, in the opinion of the Tribunal, also apply to the two other Applicants:

1. * * * You are hereby invited by the United Nations to attend the United Nations Training Course for translators and interpreters at the Beijing Institute * * *. This offer is made to you subject to your acceptance of the following conditions:

* * *

2. Upon completion of the Course you will take the recruitment examination given at a date to be determined by the United Nations in consultation with the Institute.

3. If you successfully pass the recruitment examination and are selected for employment with the United Nations, the United Nations will offer you an appointment subject to a satisfactory medical examination. You will agree to accept such appointment, subject to the United Nations Staff Regulations and Rules, for a minimum period of five years, and to perform duties of an interpreter or a translator, at the Headquarters of United Nations or at any of its offices to which you may be assigned.

* * *

(Signature)
Head, Beijing Institute

[Each Applicant accepted these conditions, passed the recruitment examination, and was offered a five-year appointment.]

VII. * * * In the "Special Conditions" section of each contract it is noted: "On secondment from the Government of China". The Tribunal notes that no details concerning the nature and conditions of the employment with the Chinese Government from which the Applicants were seconded are given in the letters of appointment or in other documents submitted by the Administration.

VIII. Neither has the Administration produced any agreement concluded with the Chinese Government, such as envisaged in the Tribunal's case-law referred to below, concerning the secondment of the Applicants nor any document in which the competent authorities define the Applicants' situation in writing and specify the conditions of secondment. The Tribunal notes that no details are given concerning the Applicants' posts in their own country nor of the conditions governing their reintegration into those posts. It also notes that if such an agreement did exist, it was not brought to the Applicants, for their consent.

* * *

XIV. The three Applicants gave complete satisfaction in the performance of their functions in the United Nations, particularly during 1989 and until the date of their separation from service on 31 January 1990. There was no allegation of any sign of antagonism towards other colleagues, certainly not Chinese colleagues. There was no sign of political animosity.

* * *

XX. On the merits, the Applicants maintained, in their applications instituting these proceedings, that they had a legal expectancy of renewal of their fixed-term contracts or alternatively, a career appointment.

XXI. With regard to the renewal of the Applicants' fixed-term contracts, the Respondent maintains that, since they were on secondment, such renewal was subject to the agreement of the Chinese Government. As this agreement was not obtained, the Respondent concluded that the decision not to renew the contracts in question was in conformity with the applicable rules and with the case-law of the Tribunal (Judgement No. 192, *Levcik* (1974)).

* * *

XXIII. The Tribunal finds that the conditions laid down [in Judgement No. 192] for an official to be on secondment are not fulfilled in this case. The Applicants' status was not, in fact, "defined in writing by the competent authorities in documents specifying the conditions and particularly the duration of the secondment". Such documents, if they exist, have not been brought to the attention of the Applicants. The Applicants were not on genuine secondment within the meaning given to that term in Judgement No. 192, which reaffirms the definition established in Judgement No. 92, *Higgins* (1964): " * * * the term 'secondment' * * * implies that the staff member is posted away from his establishment of origin but has the right to revert to employment in that establishment at the end of the period of secondment and retains his right to promotion and to retirement benefits * * * " (Judgement No. 192, para. IV).

XXIV. As stated in Judgement No. 192, cited by the Respondent, it is only when these conditions are fulfilled that "the Secretary-General of the United Nations, as the administrative head of the Organization, is obliged to take into account the decision of the Government".

The Judgement adds, and the Tribunal can only reiterate and endorse this reasoning:

"Bearing in mind the provision in Article 100 of the Charter that 'in the performance of their duties the Secretary–General and the staff shall not seek or receive instructions from any Government or from any other authority external to the Organization', the Tribunal considers that in the absence of a secondment agreed to by all parties concerned in conformity with the above-mentioned principles, the Respondent cannot legally invoke a decision of a Government to justify his own action with regard to the employment of a staff member" (Judgement No. 192, para. V).

XXV. The Tribunal finds that the secondment of the Applicants was not effected in conformity with the principles applicable. Secondment is an objective situation. It is not for the United Nations Administration or the Government in question or staff members to invoke a secondment which does not exist. Accordingly, the Tribunal considers that it was not for the Respondent either to request authorization of, or to comply with the decision of a Government in order to renew the Applicants' contracts. This being so, the Tribunal finds that the decision not to renew the Applicants' fixed-term contracts was vitiated by extraneous reasons contrary to the interests of the United Nations, incompatible with Article 100 of the Charter.

The Applicants have also requested the Tribunal to recognize their right to a career appointment. Their pleas in this regard will now be examined by the Tribunal.

XXVI. Concerning their claim to career appointments, the Respondent acknowledges that the Applicants "upon completion of five years of continuing good service * * * had a right to every reasonable consideration to a career appointment".

XXVII. The Respondent recalls that the Secretary–General has discretionary powers when deciding whether granting a career appointment is in the interest of the Organization. At the same time, he acknowledges his discretion is not unlimited.

XXVIII. The Respondent cites, in this connection, an excerpt from Judgement No. 333, *Yakimetz,* para. XIX (1984), in which the Tribunal expresses itself in the following terms:

"In Judgement No. 54 (*Mauch*) [1954], the Tribunal stated that:

'While the measure of power here was intended to be left completely within the discretion of the Secretary–General, this would not authorize an arbitrary or capricious exercise of the power of termination, nor the assignment of specious or untruthful reasons for the action taken, such as would connote a lack of good faith or due consideration for the rights of the staff member involved' ".

The Applicants also invoke this precedent in support of their application.

XXIX. More generally, the Tribunal considers that the limits of the Secretary–General's discretionary powers are governed by the following principle established by the Tribunal's consistent case-law: the Secretary-General may not legally take a decision which is contrary to the Charter, in particular to Articles 100 and 101, or to the provisions of the Staff Rules and Regulations.

XXX. In this connection, the Tribunal agrees with the Respondent that the Secretary-General has the right to consult the Governments of Member States when he exercises his power of appointment, provided however that such consultation should not contravene the principles referred to in the preceding paragraph.

As the Tribunal states below, it holds that, in the present case, by accepting the position advocated by the Government consulted, the Secretary-General has not acted in conformity with the foregoing principles.

XXXI. Nevertheless, the Tribunal does not hold that the Secretary-General could not, in proper circumstances, take into consideration the requirements of the efficient functioning of the Beijing Institute of Foreign Languages. The Secretary-General stressed, in his letter of 15 January 1990, that the termination of the specialized language training programme "would make it immensely difficult to recruit language staff with the specific qualifications required to fill vacancies appropriately and expeditiously". As the Tribunal shows below, in this case, the alleged adverse effect on the efficient functioning of the Institute and on recruitment is pure speculation. It appears to the Tribunal also, that there might be other sources for the recruitment of qualified language staff.

XXXII. The Tribunal notes that there is no evidence in the files to support the existence of a threat to suppress the programme in question if the Applicants received career appointments.

* * *

XXXV. The Tribunal appreciates the Administration's concern that "it is of critical importance * * * that [the] representatives [of China] have confidence that their statements, both oral and written, will be objectively and fairly rendered, interpreted or reported".

XXXVI. But the Tribunal notes that during the period when the career appointments of the Applicants were considered, i.e. from 1 May 1989, to the termination of their services on 31 January 1990, no observation was made, and no complaint levelled against them concerning their performance. The reason invoked by the Administration for denying appointments to the Applicants is based on an inaccuracy, if not an error.

XXXVII. The Tribunal has also taken into account the terms of the letter addressed to the Applicants on 15 January 1990, on behalf of the Secretary-General, by the Acting Under-Secretary-General for Administration and Management:

"The efficient functioning of the Chinese language services would not be possible in a situation where staff members were antagonistic to each other because of expressly stated political animosities."

But the Tribunal notes that no act of this nature has been alleged against the Applicants. It notes moreover that the Applicants have never failed to maintain the discretion incumbent upon them as international civil servants. Even during 1989, no such complaint against them was made by their Government. Lastly, the Tribunal notes that nothing has been shown to indicate the possibility of such a problem arising in the future.

XXXVIII. In the opinion of the Tribunal, the Respondent's assumptions in this respect lack any factual basis. The Applicants' record as international civil servants, as recognized by the Administration itself, shows that they are devoid of any substance. They constitute arbitrary suspicions on the future conduct of the Applicants. The Applicants are being disciplined by the denial of appointments, for potential misconduct. The Tribunal considers that the Applicants are being tried for their imputed intentions. An attitude of irresponsibility is ascribed to international civil servants who, during many years of service, have not given the slightest justification for such a charge.

XXXIX. The Tribunal moreover recalls that the Secretary-General has the necessary powers to prevent any irresponsible conduct on the part of the staff under his authority.

XL. The Respondent acknowledges that discussions took place with representatives of the Chinese Mission throughout the period beginning on 1 May 1989. The Tribunal takes note that following those discussions, the Secretary-General denied the Applicants career appointments on 12 December 1989.

XLI. The Tribunal finds that the Secretary-General accepted the Chinese Mission's position that the Applicants should be denied an extension of their fixed-term contracts or be offered career appointments.

The Tribunal has shown that, in the absence of the necessary criteria for secondment consistent with case-law, it was not permissible for the Secretary-General to take into account the Chinese Mission's opposition to the renewal of the fixed-term contracts.

As regards career appointments, the Tribunal considers that these were withheld because of the Chinese Mission's position concerning the rotation system. The Tribunal notes that, in the opinion of the Chinese Mission, the rotation system categorically ruled out career appointments. The Tribunal considers that the Secretary-General could not defer to this opposition by the Chinese Mission without being in breach of his obligations under the Charter and the Staff Rules and Regulations, as well as under General Assembly resolutions 37/126 and 38/232 (see para. XXXIII).

XLII. Consequently, the Tribunal finds that the Secretary-General's decision to refuse the Applicants' request for career appointments exceeds the limits of his discretion. His decision is based on reasons which are contrary to the interests of the United Nations, erroneous or inaccurate as to fact, and specious. It ignores the basic principles of the international civil service, as enunciated in Articles 100 and 101 of the Charter.

XLIII. The Tribunal considers that the Secretary-General wrongly refused the Applicants career appointments, contrary to General Assembly resolutions 37/126 and 38/232. The decision of 12 December 1989, as confirmed on 15 January 1990, in respect of the three Applicants must therefore be rescinded, and career appointments granted to them with effect from 1 February 1990.

* * *

XLV. In accordance with article 9, paragraph 1, of its Statute, it is for the Tribunal to fix the amount of compensation to be paid to each Applicant for the injury sustained should the Secretary-General, within 30 days of the notification of the judgement, "decide, in the interest of the United Nations, that the applicant shall be compensated" [rather than granted a career appointment].

XLVI. With regard to the injury sustained, the Applicants estimate it, for each of them, as the net amount of their base salary for a period of three years. The compensation thus requested exceeds by one year's salary the maximum amount which the Tribunal would normally award.

The Tribunal considers that this is an "exceptional case" justifying the payment of higher compensation. The Tribunal notes that the Applicants have displayed outstanding professional ability and competence in the performance of their duties, that they had a reasonable expectancy of permanent employment and a career in the United Nations, that after offering them a career appointment the Administration proposed a two-year renewal of contract and then withdrew the offer, and that this vacillation constituted a particularly painful mental ordeal for the Applicants in the then prevailing circumstances, that the Administration has not acted in the Applicants' case with the prudence, care and attention to be expected of an international organization with regard to personnel questions, and lastly, that the rule that compensation may not exceed two years' net base salary would not, in this case, adequately compensate the Applicants for the injury they have sustained and will sustain if they are not granted career appointments.

* * *

THE TRIBUNAL AND STAFF INDEPENDENCE

Consider, first, the Administrative Tribunal's own status. Its governing Statute is a composite of General Assembly resolutions establishing the Tribunal and defining its competence. The question of its independence from the General Assembly arose in the 1950s, when the United States government successfully exerted pressure on the Secretary-General to dismiss certain U.S. nationals in the Secretariat who were considered to be sympathetic to communism. When the Administrative Tribunal overturned their dismissals, the U.S. government argued that the General Assembly, having created the Tribunal and defined its authority, could review and rescind the Tribunal's judgment.

The General Assembly requested an advisory opinion on this question from the International Court of Justice. The ICJ answered that "the General Assembly has not the right on any grounds to refuse to give effect to an award of compensation made by the Administrative Tribunal of the United Nations in favour of a staff member * * * whose contract of service has been terminated without his assent." [e] The ICJ considered the Tribunal's Statute, and said in part:

> This examination of the relevant provisions of the Statute shows that the Tribunal is established, not as an advisory organ or a mere subordinate committee of the General Assembly, but as an independent and truly judicial body pronouncing final judgments without appeal within the limited field of its functions.
>
> * * *
>
> It has been argued that an authority exercising a power to make regulations is inherently incapable of creating a subordinate body competent to make decisions binding its creator. There can be no doubt that the Administrative Tribunal is subordinate in the sense that the General Assembly can abolish the Tribunal by repealing the Statute, that it can amend the Statute and provide for review of the future decisions of the Tribunal and that it can amend the Staff Regulations and make new ones. There is no lack of power to deal effectively with any problem that may arise. But the contention that the General Assembly is inherently incapable of creating a tribunal competent to make decisions binding on itself cannot be accepted. It cannot be justified by analogy to national laws, for it is common practice in national legislatures to create courts with the capacity to render decisions legally binding on the legislatures which brought them into being.
>
> The question cannot be determined on the basis of the description of the relationship between the General Assembly and the Tribunal, that is, by considering whether the Tribunal is to be regarded as a subsidiary, a subordinate, or a secondary organ, or on the basis of the fact that it was established by the General Assembly. It depends on the intention of the General Assembly in establishing the Tribunal, and on the nature of the functions

---

e. Effect of Awards of Compensation Made by the United Nations Administrative Tribunal, [1954] I.C.J. 47, 62.

conferred upon it by its Statute. An examination of the language of the Statute of the Administrative Tribunal has shown that the General Assembly intended to establish a judicial body; moreover, it had the legal capacity under the Charter to do so.[f]

Shortly after this decision was rendered, the General Assembly added article 11 to the Tribunal's Statute, creating for the first time a mechanism for ICJ review of Administrative Tribunal judgments.[g] In light of this, is the ICJ's opinion on the effect of Administrative Tribunal awards of compensation still good law? Is it good policy?

We turn now to the Chinese Translators Case. Given the long-standing practice of secondment and the general understanding of what that means, why would the Tribunal be so particular about a written agreement in each case specifying the conditions and duration of the appointment?

If there had been such written agreements here, could the Secretary–General have taken into account the Chinese government's objections to renewal of the Applicants' contracts? If so, why would that be consistent with U.N. Charter *article 100*, while the same procedure is inconsistent with it in the absence of a written agreement?

Is the practice of secondment itself consistent with article 100? The U.N. General Assembly has said that it is.[h] Does that settle the matter?

On the question of a right to a career appointment, the Tribunal followed its existing precedent to the effect that the Secretary–General's discretion could not be exercised in an arbitrary or capricious manner, nor could specious or untruthful reasons be given, such as to connote a lack of good faith. See paragraph XXVIII. The Tribunal then proceeded to hold that the Secretary–General had not met the standard. See paragraph XLII. That is a serious charge against the top U.N. official. Did the Tribunal demonstrate bad faith on the Secretary–General's part? Consider, inter alia, the Acting Under-Secretary–General's letter of 15 January 1990, quoted in the judgment, and the Tribunal's response to it in paragraphs XXXVII–XXXIX.

It appears from the Applicants' submissions that they had participated in protest activities against the Chinese government's treatment of student demonstrations. Presumably, this was a reference to the 1989 Tienanmen Square demonstrations and the Chinese government's use of force against them. Was the Tribunal correct in saying that "the Applicants have never failed to maintain the discretion incumbent upon them as international civil servants" (paragraph XXXVII)?

f. Id. at 53, 61.
g. Article 11 is set forth at page 135 infra.
h. See G.A.Res. 45/239, Part II (1990).

In paragraph XLVI, the Tribunal awarded more than the normal amount of compensation. Was that tantamount to awarding punitive damages? Would that be appropriate? (International tribunals ordinarily do not award punitive damages, even in cases of gross human rights violations. Is there something about an international administrative tribunal that would set it apart?)

Is the crux of this case simply that the Secretary–General yielded to the wishes of a powerful member government, and the Tribunal felt that it had to take a strong stand against any such subservience? Is that a proper role for an administrative tribunal?

The Secretary–General lost this case. If you had been he, would you be altogether unhappy with the outcome? Is it an important case for the U.N. as an institution?

The Administrative Tribunal's Statute establishes a procedure for judicial review of the Tribunal's judgments, under certain circumstances. It involves the International Court of Justice, but a special procedure had to be devised in view of the fact that neither individuals, such as the parties in the Chinese Translators Case, nor the U.N. itself may be a party in a contentious case in the ICJ. See ICJ Statute *article 34(1)*. Here is how the Administrative Tribunal's Statute handles the matter:

Article 11

1. If a Member State, the Secretary–General or the person in respect of whom a judgement has been rendered by the Tribunal (including any one who has succeeded to that person's rights on his death) objects to the judgement on the ground that the Tribunal has exceeded its jurisdiction or competence or that the Tribunal has failed to exercise jurisdiction vested in it, or has erred on a question of law relating to the provisions of the Charter of the United Nations, or has committed a fundamental error in procedure which has occasioned a failure of justice, such Member State, the Secretary–General or the person concerned may, within thirty days from the date of the judgement, make a written application to the Committee established by paragraph 4 of this article asking the Committee to request an advisory opinion of the International Court of Justice on the matter.

2. Within thirty days from the receipt of an application under paragraph 1 of this article, the Committee shall decide whether or not there is a substantial basis for the application. If the Committee decides that such a basis exists, it shall request an advisory opinion of the Court, and the Secretary–General shall arrange to transmit to the Court the views of the person referred to in paragraph 1.

* * *

4. For the purpose of this article, a Committee is established and authorized under paragraph 2 of Article 96 of the Charter to request advisory opinions of the Court. The Committee shall be composed of the Member States the representatives of which have served on the General Committee of the most recent regular session of the General Assembly. The Committee shall meet at United Nations Headquarters and shall establish its own rules.

The Committee established by article 11(4) is a creature of the General Assembly, since—as noted above—the Administrative Tribunal's Statute is a composite of General Assembly resolutions. The Committee's only functions are to examine applications for review of U.N. Administrative Tribunal judgments, and to request an advisory opinion under article 11(2) if there is a sufficient basis for review in light of the grounds set forth in article 11(1).

In Application for Review of Judgment No. 158 of the United Nations Administrative Tribunal,[i] the ICJ held that the Committee was an organ of the United Nations, and had requested an advisory opinion on legal questions arising within the scope of its activities, within the meaning of U.N. Charter *article 96(2)*.[j] Is this a misuse of the advisory opinion mechanism to decide contentious cases between persons or entities not entitled to be parties before the Court?

Whatever the answer to the previous question may be, is the ICJ the appropriate body to review judgments of an Administrative Tribunal? If not, what body would be?

---

i. [1973] I.C.J. 166, 171–83.

j. See also Application for Review of Judgment No. 273 of the United Nations Administrative Tribunal, [1982] I.C.J. 325, 331–40.

Chapter 2

MEMBERSHIP AND PARTICIPATION IN INTERNATIONAL ORGANIZATIONS

SECTION 1. INTRODUCTION

The constituent instrument of an intergovernmental organization provides the "constitutional law" of the organization and thus speaks to the organization as such; but since many of the organization's decisions will be made by its organs consisting of representatives of member states, the constitutional law speaks indirectly as well to those states in the sense that it is designed to guide them as they participate in the decision-making process. See, e.g., the U.N. Admissions Case, at page 140 infra. In addition, many such instruments contain provisions that speak directly to member states, setting forth explicit rights and duties of individual states either in their relations with the organization or in their relations with each other. In this latter respect, constituent instruments operate just as other treaties do, creating rules to bind states under international law.

Our concern in this and the next three chapters will be primarily with constituent instruments as constitutional law. In any legal system—domestic as well as international—constitutional law has an obvious political dimension to go with its legal content. Often the political dimension seems predominant. But that is not to suggest that our primary concern, the legal content, is ignored. The secretariats of major international organizations maintain legal staffs to advise the organizations on legal questions arising from constituent instruments, and national delegations to major organizations similarly maintain legal staffs or call on lawyers from their governments' foreign offices for such purposes. An important question running through these chapters will be that of assessing the extent to which essentially legal criteria can and do influence (a) the positions taken by individual member states within international organizations, and (b) the ultimate decisions reached by the organizations themselves.

SECTION 2. ADMISSION TO MEMBERSHIP

A. THE UNITED NATIONS

1. "Statehood" and Conditions Attached to a Vote for Admission

In the early years of the United Nations, admission to membership was a significant and time-consuming issue for the organization. As indicated in the Introduction to this Chapter, the issue was partly legal and partly political, with the politics often seeming to overpower the legalities. At the height of the cold war, candidates favored by the Soviet Union could not get enough Western votes to be admitted, and candidates favored by the West were vetoed in the Security Council by the Soviet Union. It took a package deal in 1955 to admit several of these states at once—some from each bloc. After the cold war abated, and with the accession to statehood of many former colonies eager to participate on the world scene, admission became routine in most—but not all—cases.

Before we get to some of these cases, examine the legal conditions for membership. They are set forth in *article 4* of the U.N. Charter. Article 4 should be considered in light of the excerpt below from the report of the Rapporteur of Committee I/2 of the San Francisco Conference (at which the U.N. Charter was drafted).

UNITED NATIONS CONFERENCE ON INTERNATIONAL ORGANIZATION
San Francisco, 1945.
Selected Documents 505 (1946), 13 Whiteman,
Digest of International Law 192 (1968).

[T]he unanimous opinion of the Committee was that adherence to the principles of the Charter and complete acceptance of the obligations arising therefrom were essential conditions to participation by states in the Organization.

Nevertheless, two principal tendencies were manifested in the discussions. On the one hand, there were some who declared themselves in favor of inserting in the Charter specific conditions which new members should be required to fulfil especially in matters concerning the character and policies of governments. On the other hand, others maintained that the Charter should not needlessly limit the Organization in its decisions concerning requests for admission and asserted that the Organization itself would be in a better position to judge the character of candidates for admission.

The term "all peace-loving states", generally deemed insufficient, was retained, while the qualifications for membership were elaborated. To declare oneself "peace-loving" does not suffice to acquire membership in the Organization. What nation has ever professed any other sentiments? It is also necessary to prove two things: that a nation is ready to accept and fulfil the obligations of the Charter and that it is able to accept and fulfil them.

It was clearly stated that the admission of a new member would be subject to study, but the Committee did not feel it should recommend the enumeration of the elements which were to be taken into consideration. It considered the difficulties which would arise in evaluating the political institutions of states and feared that the mention in the Charter of a study of such a nature would be a breach of the principle of non-intervention or, if preferred, of non-interference. This does not imply, however, that in passing upon the admission of a new member, considerations of all kinds cannot be brought into account.

ARTICLE 4 AND EARLY U.N. PRACTICE

One of the basic conditions for membership in article 4 is statehood; that is, membership is open only to (certain kinds of) "states." According to the Restatement (Third) of Foreign Relations Law of the United States § 201 (1988):

> Under international law, a state is an entity that has a defined territory and a permanent population, under the control of its own government, and that engages in, or has the capacity to engage in, formal relations with other such entities.[a]

From the very outset, there has been a question whether the United Nations has strictly applied the statehood requirement. Among the original members were India, the Philippines, Lebanon, Syria, Byelorussia (now Belorus) and Ukraine. None of them was fully independent at the time (1945),[b] and the last two declared their independence only in 1991. Nevertheless, in the great majority of cases, an entity admitted to the U.N. has undeniably been a "state" under international law.

At the height of the cold war, the major question was not whether an applicant was a "state," but—in legal terms—whether it was able and willing to carry out the obligations of membership, and—in political terms—whether its allies could get it past the voting hurdles to admission without also having to admit states on the other side of the cold war. This led to the impasse already mentioned, which in turn led the General Assembly to request an advisory opinion from the International Court of Justice.

a. This is based on an older, widely recognized definition in the Montevideo Convention on Rights and Duties of States, Dec. 26, 1933, art. 1, 49 Stat. 3097, 3 Bevans 145, 165 L.N.T.S. 19.

b. See J. Dugard, Recognition and the United Nations 53–55 (1987).

CONDITIONS OF ADMISSION OF A STATE TO MEMBERSHIP IN THE UNITED NATIONS
International Court of Justice, Advisory Opinion, 1948.
[1948] I.C.J. 57.

* * *

On November 17th, 1947, the General Assembly of the United Nations adopted the following Resolution:

The General Assembly,

* * *

Requests the International Court of Justice to give an advisory opinion on the following question:

> Is a Member of the United Nations which is called upon, in virtue of Article 4 of the Charter, to pronounce itself by its vote either in the Security Council or in the General Assembly, on the admission of a State to membership in the United Nations, juridically entitled to make its consent to the admission dependent on conditions not expressly provided by paragraph 1 of the said Article? In particular, can such a Member, while it recognizes the conditions set forth in that provision to be fulfilled by the State concerned, subject its affirmative vote to the additional condition that other States be admitted to membership in the United Nations together with that State?

* * *

In framing this answer, it is necessary first to recall the "conditions" required, under paragraph 1 of Article 4, of an applicant for admission. This provision reads as follows:

> Membership in the United Nations is open to all other peace-loving States which accept the obligations contained in the present Charter and, in the judgment of the Organization, are able and willing to carry out these obligations.

The requisite conditions are five in number: to be admitted to membership in the United Nations, an applicant must (1) be a State; (2) be peace-loving; (3) accept the obligations of the Charter; (4) be able to carry out these obligations; and (5) be willing to do so.

* * *

Nor can it be argued that the conditions enumerated represent only an indispensable minimum, in the sense that political considerations could be superimposed upon them, and prevent the admission of an applicant which fulfils them. Such an interpretation would be inconsistent with the terms of paragraph 2 of Article 4, which provide for the admission of "*tout État* remplissant ces conditions"—"any *such* State". It would lead to conferring upon Members an indefinite and practically unlimited power of discretion in the imposition of new conditions. Such a power would be inconsistent with the very character of paragraph 1 of Article 4 which, by reason of the close connexion which it establishes between membership and the observance of the principles and obligations of the Charter, clearly constitutes a legal regulation of the question of the admission of new States. To warrant an interpretation other than that which ensues from the natural meaning of the words, a decisive reason would be required which has not been established.

Moreover, the spirit as well as the terms of the paragraph preclude the idea that considerations extraneous to these principles and obligations can prevent the admission of a State which complies with them. If the authors of the Charter had meant to leave Members free to import into the application of this provision considerations extraneous to the conditions laid down therein, they would undoubtedly have adopted a different wording.

* * *

It has been sought to deduce either from the second paragraph of Article 4, or from the political character of the organ recommending or deciding upon admission, arguments in favour of an interpretation of paragraph 1 of Article 4, to the effect that the fulfilment of the conditions provided for in that Article is necessary before the admission of a State can be recommended or decided upon, but that it does not preclude the Members of the Organization from advancing considerations of political expediency, extraneous to the conditions of Article 4.

But paragraph 2 is concerned only with the procedure for admission, while the preceding paragraph lays down the substantive law.

* * *

The political character of an organ cannot release it from the observance of the treaty provisions established by the Charter when they constitute limitations on its powers or criteria for its judgment. To ascertain whether an organ has freedom of choice for its decisions, reference must be made to the terms of its constitution. In this case, the limits of this freedom are fixed by Article 4 and allow for a wide liberty of appreciation. There is therefore no conflict between the functions of the political organs, on the one hand, and the exhaustive character of the prescribed conditions, on the other.

* * *

The second part of the question concerns a demand on the part of a Member making its consent to the admission of an applicant dependent on the admission of other applicants.

Judged on the basis of the rule which the Court adopts in its interpretation of Article 4, such a demand clearly constitutes a new condition, since it is entirely unconnected with those prescribed in Article 4. It is also in an entirely different category from those conditions, since it makes admission dependent, not on the conditions required of applicants, qualifications which are supposed to be fulfilled, but on an extraneous consideration concerning States other than the applicant State.

The provisions of Article 4 necessarily imply that every application for admission should be examined and voted on separately and on its own merits; otherwise it would be impossible to determine whether a particular applicant fulfils the necessary conditions. To subject an affirmative vote for the admission of an applicant State to the condition that other States be admitted with that State would prevent Members from exercising their judgment in each case with complete liberty, within the scope of the prescribed conditions. Such a demand is incompatible with the letter and spirit of Article 4 of the Charter.

For these reasons,

The Court,

by nine votes to six,

is of opinion that a Member of the United Nations which is called upon, in virtue of Article 4 of the Charter, to pronounce itself by its vote, either in the Security Council or in the General Assembly, on the admission of a State to membership in the United Nations, is not juridically entitled to make its consent to the admission dependent on conditions not expressly provided by paragraph 1 of the said Article; and that, in particular, a Member of the Organization cannot, while it recognizes the conditions set forth in that provision to be fulfilled by the State concerned, subject its affirmative vote to the additional condition that other States be admitted to membership in the United Nations together with that State.

[JUDGES BASDEVANT, WINIARSKI, SIR ARNOLD MCNAIR and READ dissented in a joint opinion which has been omitted here.]

THE SIGNIFICANCE OF THE ADMISSIONS CASE

Note particularly this passage from the opinion: "The political character of an organ cannot release it from the observance of the treaty provisions established by the Charter when they constitute limitations on its powers or criteria for its judgment. To ascertain whether an organ has freedom of choice for its decisions, reference must be made to the terms of its constitution." That passage could apply not only to the admission of new U.N. members, but also to virtually any act by a political organ that arguably runs counter to express conditions imposed by the relevant constituent instrument.

Where does this limitation come from? Is it a matter of treaty law? (Note that the organs of an international organization are not parties to the treaty that serves as the constituent instrument of the organization. Member states are the parties.)

Did the Court properly apply article 4? Is the Admissions Case significant today?

During the 1970s and 1980s, the contentious issues regarding admission to the U.N. arose from applications by divided states. The two Germanies were admitted as separate states in 1973, but became a single member in 1990 after reunification. When North and South Viet–Nam applied for separate memberships in 1975, the United States vetoed their applications. A single Vietnamese state applied in 1976, but the United States again exercised its veto. Viet–Nam was admitted, as a single state, in 1977.

In 1975 the Republic of Korea (South Korea) resubmitted an application it had originally put forward in 1949, but which had been vetoed then and three more times in the intervening years. The Security Council declined to put the resubmitted application on its agenda. The Democratic Republic of Korea (North Korea) had sought admission in 1949 and 1952, but no action had been taken on its applications. The impasse over the two Koreas lasted until 1991, when North Korea reluctantly reapplied as a separate state, in response to the virtual certainty that South Korea would finally be admitted in the absence of any Soviet or Chinese veto. The two Koreas were admitted in September 1991.

In recent years, the issues surrounding admission have not concerned divided states. Instead, the issues relate to new claims of independence outside the immediate post-colonial context of the 1960s. The new claimants have included Namibia, Palestine and the breakaway republics and other entities of Eastern Europe.

Eligibility issues regarding Namibia and Palestine have come up primarily in the specialized agencies rather than in the United Nations itself. Consequently they are examined in Subsection B, infra.[c] Issues regarding former republics of the Soviet Union, other than those republics admitted to the U.N. before 1992, concern ability and willingness to carry out Charter obligations as much as they do statehood. They are examined in that context below.

---

c. On at least one occasion, the statehood issue involving Palestine arose in a U.N. organ, rather than in a specialized agency. In 1977 the Palestine Liberation Organization applied for full membership in the Economic Commission for Western Asia (ECWA), one of the regional economic commissions established by the U.N. Economic and Social Council (ECOSOC). ECWA's terms of reference from ECOSOC contemplated that only states would be members. After receiving a legal opinion from the U.N. Legal Counsel, 1977 U.N. Juridical Y.B. 217, ECOSOC adopted its resolution 2089 (LXIII), in which it amended the ECWA terms of reference to mention the PLO as an eligible member.

2. Ability and Willingness to Carry Out Charter Obligations

Article 4(1) of the Charter requires not only that an applicant be a "state," but that, in the judgment of the Organization, it be "able and willing" to carry out the obligations contained in the Charter. From time to time this requirement has provided at least the ostensible reason for a veto when a newly-formed state has applied for admission. As you evaluate the instances summarized below, consider first, what are the Charter obligations that an applicant must be able and willing to carry out, and second, whether under the circumstances a convincing case was made that the applicant was not able and willing to carry them out.

(1) Bangladesh, formerly East Pakistan, became independent as a result of the India–Pakistan–Bangladesh war of December 1971. India participated heavily and decisively on Bangladesh's side, taking about 90,000 Pakistani prisoners of war. In addition, at the end of the war Bangladesh held 195 Pakistani prisoners whom it announced it would try for war crimes allegedly committed by them. The Security Council, in its Resolution 307 of Dec. 21, 1971, called upon "all those concerned to take all measures necessary to preserve human life and for the observance of the Geneva Conventions of 1949 and to apply in full their provisions as regards the protection of the wounded and sick, prisoners of war and civilian population * * *." The Geneva Convention Relative to the Treatment of Prisoners of War,[a] provides in article 118: "Prisoners of war shall be released and repatriated without delay after the cessation of active hostilities." India and Pakistan ratified the Convention shortly after it was drawn up, and Bangladesh announced on April 4, 1972, that it considered itself bound to it by succession to Pakistan.[b] Neither India nor Bangladesh acted immediately to repatriate or to bring to trial the prisoners of war.

At that point Bangladesh applied for admission to the United Nations. The Security Council debated the issue of its admission in August 1972, with the People's Republic of China casting a veto to block admission. The reason given was that Bangladesh (and India) had not complied earnestly with Security Council Resolution 307 and with a similar General Assembly resolution. The Chinese representative said: "The only conclusion to be drawn from the provisions of Article 4 of the Charter is that the implementation of the two relevant United Nations resolutions which gave expression to the will of the overwhelming majority of the countries of the world is an important indication of the applicant's ability and willingness to fulfil the obligations contained in the Charter. That is a most fundamental criterion in judging whether or not an applicant fulfils the requirements of Article 4 of the Charter."[c]

a. Aug. 12, 1949, 6 U.S.T. 3316, T.I.A.S. 3364, 75 U.N.T.S. 135.

b. See Levie, Legal Aspects of the Continued Detention of the Pakistani Prisoners of War by India, 67 Am.J.Int'l L. 512 (1973).

c. U.N. Doc. S/PV.1659, at 1–2 (1972).

In August 1973, India and Pakistan signed an agreement for the return of the Pakistani prisoners held by India. Pakistan agreed to recognize Bangladesh as a state. In April 1974, Bangladesh agreed to release the remaining 195 Pakistani prisoners of war. Bangladesh was then admitted to the United Nations, on September 17, 1974.

Presumably, China's veto of the Bangladesh application in 1972 was not motivated purely by a lawyerlike application of article 4 to the facts. Did China nevertheless make a reasonable argument that Bangladesh did not at that time meet the conditions of article 4?

(2) Upon the relinquishment in November 1975 by Portugal of its colonial control over Angola, there was an armed struggle for power among three Angolan political groups, each supported by foreign interests. Ultimately, in February 1976, the Popular Movement for the Liberation of Angola (MPLA), heavily supported by Soviet arms and Cuban troops, gained control of most Angolan territory and was recognized as the government by the great majority of other nations. When it announced in May 1976 that it would apply for United Nations membership, the United States asked it to delay its application until there were clear signs that the roughly 12,000 Cuban troops would leave the country. After a brief delay, the application was placed on the Security Council agenda for June 23, 1976, and was vetoed by the United States.

The United States representative explained the veto on the ground that Angola did not yet meet the requirements for membership set forth in article 4 because of the continuing presence and apparent influence of Cuban troops, massive in number in the Angolan context. The U.S. representative said that South Africa, which had at one time during the Angolan hostilities sent troops about 30 miles into Angola, had withdrawn them. Moreover, other neighboring African states had begun normalizing relations with Angola, so there was no apparent defensive need for the large Cuban force.[d]

The Cuban representative asserted that Cuban forces had gone to Angola at the request of the legitimate Angolan government, and Cuba had no intention of keeping them there indefinitely. He also noted that the Angolan government had been recognized by more than 100 countries, was a member of the Organization of African Unity, the World Health Organization and the International Labor Organization, and had recently attended a U.N. conference. Since Angola threatened no one, he continued, it met all the conditions in article 4 for admission.[e]

If Angola was indeed threatening no armed attack against any other state in June 1976, did the United States make a reasonable argument that Angola did not at that time meet the conditions of article 4?

d. See 75 Dep't St.Bull. 99 (1976).   e. See U.N. Doc. S/PV.1932, at 81–86 (1976).

When the Angolan application again came before the Security Council in November 1976, the United States abstained from voting, thus permitting the application to succeed. It did not appear that the magnitude of the Cuban presence in Angola had been reduced since June, but as many as half the troops apparently had been replaced by Cuban technical personnel. The U.S. representative questioned whether Angola was truly independent, but abstained "out of respect for the sentiments expressed by our African friends."[f] Would a U.S. veto in November 1976 have been legally justifiable?

(3) When the United States vetoed the application of reunified Viet–Nam in November 1976, it stressed the apparent unwillingness of Viet–Nam to give an accounting of the approximately 800 U.S. servicemen still considered missing in action from the Viet–Nam war. The veto was explained by William Scranton, the U.S. representative to the United Nations:

> The United States voted against the application for membership in the United Nations by the Socialist Republic of Viet Nam, not because we doubt that the Socialist Republic of Viet Nam is able to carry out the obligations of the United Nations Charter, but rather because the United States has serious doubts about the willingness of Viet Nam to do so. It is this lack of demonstrated will which leads the United States to conclude that the Socialist Republic of Viet Nam does not meet the standards established by Article 4 of the United Nations Charter.
>
> Let me be specific. The Socialist Republic of Viet Nam has failed so far to manifest satisfactory humanitarian or practical concern regarding American servicemen missing in action. It has failed, despite the information available to it, to account satisfactorily for Americans missing in action and to return the remains of those killed in the recent conflict in Indo–China, despite repeated efforts by the United States to persuade it to do so. * * *
>
> Through its record and policies, the Socialist Republic of Viet Nam has convinced my Government that it is not willing to carry out obligations of the Charter. As we all know, these obligations embrace not only the maintenance of international peace and security but observance of human rights.[g]

Did Mr. Scranton make a defensible legal argument?

In 1977 the United States refrained from vetoing a renewed Vietnamese application, and Viet–Nam was admitted.

(4) Consider the situation in Eastern Europe and the former Soviet Union, where established states began to disintegrate in the early 1990s. In December 1991, Russia, Belorus (formerly Byelorussia), Ukraine and seven other former Soviet republics formed the new Commonwealth of Independent States. Each had its own reasonably

---

f. 75 Dep't St.Bull. 742 (1976).   g. U.N. Doc. S/PV.1972, at 53 (1976).

well-established territory, population and government. When the United States and other Western states recognized them as independent states, their U.N. membership was assured. (Belorus and Ukraine were already members, having been admitted in 1945. Russia took over the Soviet Union's membership, without going through the admission process.[h] Estonia, Latvia and Lithuania—the three Baltic states that had been the first to break away from the Soviet Union—had been admitted in September 1991, three months before the Soviet Union ceased to exist.)

What about other small republics and ethnic enclaves? Within the former Soviet Union in mid-1992, at least 14 ethnic areas within the new states had separatist claims of their own. Yugoslavia had disintegrated, with the European Community and the United States having recognized Slovenia, Croatia and Bosnia–Herzegovina even as fighting raged in the latter two between Serbs and other ethnic groups. The division of the Czech and Slovak Republic was already on the horizon. Other separatist claims simmered in Europe and elsewhere.

In September 1992 the Security Council recommended, and the General Assembly decided, that the Federal Republic of Yugoslavia (Serbia and Montenegro)—which had formally declared itself the successor to the Socialist Federal Republic of Yugoslavia[i]—could not simply take over Yugoslav membership, and should instead apply anew for membership.[j] This was in response to Serbia's conduct in support of Bosnian Serbs in the ethnic warfare then raging in Bosnia–Herzegovina—a conflict that had heaped enormous suffering on civilians and caused the devastation of entire communities. In the General Assembly, the U.S. representative, Mr. Perkins, said that Serbia and Montenegro "must prove to the Members of the United Nations that the so-called Federal Republic of Yugoslavia is a peace-loving State."[k]

Did Mr. Perkins make a defensible legal point?

Was the treatment of Yugoslavia's membership consistent with the treatment of Russia as the successor to the Soviet Union? The other new states in the former Soviet Union acquiesced in Russia's claim to succession as a U.N. member. The other new states in the former Yugoslavia clearly would have objected to automatic U.N. succession by the Federal Republic of Yugoslavia. Is that a legally significant distinction?[l]

In these circumstances, can any neutral standards be found that could determine eligibility for U.N. membership under *article 4* of the Charter?

---

h. By far the most important issue raised by Russia's succession to Soviet membership concerned its permanent membership in the Security Council. Consequently these materials examine Russia's membership in that context. See pages 189–91 infra.

i. See U.N. Doc. S/23877 (1992).

j. S.C.Res. 777 (1992); G.A. Res. 47/1 (1992).

k. U.N. Doc. A/46/PV.86, at 22 (1992).

l. The Yugoslav membership question is considered in more detail in Chapter 4, in the context of sanctions.

If the United Nations admits secessionist entities as members while there are still questions about their economic viability or political stability, is it helping to establish a right of secession in international law?

If article 4 could be amended, should the standards still be tied in some way to statehood? (Note that amendments to the Charter must be ratified by all permanent members of the Security Council. See article 108.)

3. The Admission Procedure: Article 4(2)

General Assembly disenchantment with Soviet use of the veto to control admission of new members in the early years of the United Nations led to a request for a second ICJ advisory opinion on the subject. In November 1949, the General Assembly asked:

> Can the admission of a State to membership in the United Nations, pursuant to Article 4, paragraph 2, of the Charter, be effected by a decision of the General Assembly when the Security Council has made no recommendation for admission by reason of the candidate failing to obtain the requisite majority or of the negative vote of a permanent Member upon a resolution so to recommend?

The answer was given in the negative (by twelve votes to two), in Competence of the General Assembly for the Admission of a State to the United Nations.[a] The Court said:

> To hold that the General Assembly has power to admit a State to membership in the absence of a recommendation of the Security Council would be to deprive the Security Council of an important power which has been entrusted to it by the Charter. It would almost nullify the role of the Security Council in the exercise of one of the essential functions of the Organization. It would mean that the Security Council would have merely to study the case, present a report, give advice, and express an opinion. This is not what Article 4, paragraph 2, says.[b]

In recent years the veto has not been used to exclude applicants from membership. The issue, however, is not necessarily dead. One can envision applicants (e.g. Palestine, under circumstances prevailing when this was written) whose membership would be unpalatable to one or more permanent members of the Security Council. Does this mean that it is still too early to contemplate the abandonment (either voluntarily or by amending the Charter) of the veto over applications for membership?

A bit of history may help. Under the League of Nations Covenant (article I), new members were admitted by a two-thirds vote of the

---

a. [1950] I.C.J. 4.   b. Id. at 9.

Assembly, without requiring a recommendation from the Council. At the 1945 San Francisco Conference which formulated the U.N. Charter, several delegations supported continuation of that method.[c] Nevertheless, it was finally decided in committee to require a recommendation from the Security Council, and this was approved by the Conference. The reason was that "the purpose of the Charter is primarily to provide security against a repetition of [World War II] and that, therefore, the Security Council should assume the initial responsibility of suggesting new participating states."[d] Presumably the security against another world war would be provided by ensuring that a majority of members could not bring into the fold a state posing such a threat to one or more of the major powers that the Organization could not effectively keep the peace with that state's participation. Several delegations had Franco's Spain in mind (though it was eventually admitted in 1955).

Can the use of a Security Council veto over admissions be justified under the original rationale? Would the vital interests of the permanent members be affected by an abandonment of the veto in such cases? If not, should this be done by amending *article 4(2)*?

B. THE SPECIALIZED AGENCIES

INTRODUCTORY NOTE

Membership in the United Nations does not necessarily bring with it automatic membership in the specialized agencies. In many specialized agencies, though, it brings a right to membership under procedures that assure admission in the absence of some irregularity in the application. Usually, even for non-members of the U.N., applications for membership are not controversial. In a few instances, though, they have been.

The constituent instruments of the specialized agencies are not uniform in their descriptions of the entities that are eligible for full membership. Many of them limit the eligible category to "states." This is true, for example, of the International Labor Organization, the International Civil Aviation Organization and the World Health Organization. Some of them define the eligible group as "countries" or "sovereign countries." These include the International Monetary Fund, the World Bank (indirectly, because membership in it is linked to membership in the IMF), the International Telecommunication Union and the Universal Postal Union. Membership in the Food and Agriculture Organization is open to "nations" and, since November 1991, to certain "regional economic integration organizations."

The constituent instruments do not define "state," "country" or "nation." Would all three terms be synonymous with "statehood" as

---

[c]. See L. Goodrich, E. Hambro & A. Simons, Charter of the United Nations 93 (3d ed. 1969).

[d]. First Report of Rapporteur of Committee II/1 to Commission II, United Nations Conf. on International Organization 605 (Selected Docs., 1946).

that term is understood in customary international law? If not, how would one go about determining what is meant by these terms?

Approval for membership normally requires a two-thirds vote of the organization's plenary body. The exception is WHO, where only a simple majority is required. In some specialized agencies there are procedural preconditions to the vote, such as screening by a committee to determine the applicant's capacity to perform the obligations of membership.

We will examine four applications for membership in specialized agencies. One involves the former Soviet Union and the ILO; one Namibia and the ILO; another, "Palestine" and WHO; and finally, the European Economic Community and FAO.

1. *The Soviet Union's Application to the ILO*

The ILO's requirements for membership appear in *article 1* of the ILO Constitution. The ILO Director–General relied on article 1 in rejecting the original Soviet application in 1953:

REPORT OF THE SPECIAL STUDY MISSION ON INTERNATIONAL ORGANIZATIONS AND MOVEMENTS

House Comm. on Foreign Affairs, 1954.
House Rep. No. 1251, 83d Cong., 2d Sess. at 53,
13 Whiteman, Digest of Int'l L. 213 (1968).

The USSR applied for ILO membership by a note dated November 4, 1953 * * *. The application was not accepted. The reasons for nonacceptance are contained in the following press release issued by the Director–General of the ILO on November 16, 1953, which is quoted in part as follows:

> The Director–General has noted the statement contained in the communication from the legation of the USSR that "the Soviet Union will not consider itself bound by the provisions" of paragraphs 1 and 2 of Article 37 of the Constitution of the ILO and that "as regards the jurisdiction of the International Court of Justice, the Soviet Union will maintain the position that it has adopted hitherto, namely, that for the reference of any dispute to the International Court or any tribunal for decision the consent of all parties to the dispute is essential in each individual case."
>
> The only provision in the Constitution relating to admission to membership in the ILO of members of the United Nations is contained in Article 1, paragraph 3, which provides: "Any original member of the UN and any state admitted to membership of the UN by decision of the General Assembly in accordance with the provisions of the Charter may become a member of the ILO by communicating to the Director–General of the International Labor

Office its formal acceptance of the obligations of the Constitution of the ILO."

It will be observed that the Constitution makes no provision for membership on the basis of incomplete acceptance of obligations. The Director–General, therefore, draws the attention of the government of the USSR to these constitutional points concerning membership in the ILO.

ISSUES RAISED BY THE SOVIET APPLICATION

By a letter dated April 24, 1954, the Soviet Union informed the Director–General of its formal acceptance of the obligations of the ILO Constitution, without qualification. Consequently the Soviet Union was admitted.[a]

Paragraphs 1 and 2 of ILO Constitution *article 37,* to which the Soviet Union originally objected, concern dispute settlement. The Soviet objection was in the nature of a reservation to its acceptance of the treaty obligations in the ILO Constitution. A reservation is "a unilateral statement, however phrased or named, made by a state when signing, ratifying, accepting, approving or acceding to a treaty, whereby it purports to exclude or modify the legal effect of certain provisions of the treaty in their application to that state * * *." Vienna Convention on the Law of Treaties, art. 2(1)(d).

Article 20(3) of the Vienna Convention provides, "When a treaty is a constituent instrument of an international organization and unless it otherwise provides, a reservation requires the acceptance of the competent organ of that organization." Presumably the "competent organ" of the ILO would be either the Director–General or the General Conference, since they have the responsibilities concerning membership.[b] In 1948, before the Soviet membership question had arisen, the General Conference adopted article 27(1) of its Standing Orders (rules of procedure) requiring receipt by the Director–General of a "formal and unconditional acceptance" for adhesion to the Constitution by U.N. members.[c] If you were an attorney in the office of the Legal Adviser to the ILO, would you have advised the Director–General that article 27(1) of the Standing Orders settled his authority to reject the Soviet acceptance on the grounds stated by him?

[a]. 13 Whiteman, Digest of Int'l L. 213 (1968).

[b]. It might also be argued that the body within an organization having the authority to interpret its constituent instrument is the "competent organ." See Mendelson, Reservations to the Constitutions of International Organizations, 45 British Y.B. Int'l L. 137, 153 (1971). The ILO Constitution has no explicit provision for interpretation by an existing organ. A practice has developed by which the International Labor Office (under the Director–General) interprets labor conventions, but such conventions are distinct from the ILO Constitution.

[c]. See ILO, Constitution of the ILO and Standing Orders of the International Labour Conference 42 (1955), and G. Johnston, The International Labour Organisation 33 (1970).

Was article 27(1) of the Standing Orders consistent with article 1 of the ILO Constitution? Would that question have to be submitted either to the ICJ or to a special tribunal, under article 37 of the ILO Constitution?

If article 27(1) of the Standing Orders had not been in existence, what would you have advised the Director-General to do when the Soviet acceptance came in?

Suppose that, instead of deciding the question himself, the Director-General had submitted it to the General Conference, which decided by the requisite majority (but not unanimously) to allow the Soviet Union to accept membership on the terms initially set forth by the Soviets. Could a member state that voted against allowing the Soviet Union to accept with the reservation do anything to avoid having to treat the Soviet Union as a full-fledged member of the Organization? The Vienna Convention on the Law of Treaties probably reflects customary international law on the question of reservations, except as to specific time limitation provisions such as *article 20(5)*. It provides in *article 5* that it applies to constituent instruments of international organizations, even though it does not directly apply to treaties entered into by such organizations. The key provisions on reservations appear in *articles 19–21*.

Would acceptance of a reservation by the "competent organ" under Vienna Convention article 20(3) preclude any further claim by a dissident member state that the reservation is "incompatible with the object and purpose of the treaty" under article 19(c)? Would it preclude that state from treating the reserving state as a nonmember under article 20(4)(b), even though the former state has definitely expressed its intention not to have the instrument in force between them?

It is not always easy to tell whether a statement attached by an applicant state to its instrument of acceptance is a reservation or a mere declaration not intended to exclude or modify the legal effect of any provisions in the constituent instrument. Suppose the Soviet Union, instead of saying it would not be bound by ILO Constitution article 37, paragraphs 1 and 2, had said that it recognized the applicability of those paragraphs to questions relating to interpretation of the Constitution or other conventions; but many questions that might come up would (in its view) relate not to interpretation but to excuse for nonperformance, and as to the latter type of question it did not acknowledge the jurisdiction of the ICJ without the consent of all parties in the individual case. Should the Director-General have considered that statement a reservation requiring rejection of the Soviet application under ILO Constitution article 1, paragraph 3, and the Standing Order, or a mere declaration of the Soviet Union's interpretation of article 37? [d]

d. See generally Mendelson, Reservations to the Constitutions of International Organizations, 45 British Y.B. Int'l L. 137, 151–52, 159–60 (1971).

2. Namibia's Application to the ILO

The "statehood" requirement for admission to specialized agencies was tested by the U.N. Council for Namibia's applications for full membership before Namibia became independent. Namibia, formerly South West Africa, had been administered by South Africa under a Mandate issued by the League of Nations. In 1966 the U.N. General Assembly declared the Mandate terminated. In 1967 it established what became the Council for Namibia, to "administer South West Africa until independence," with law-making and law-enforcing authority and with instructions to "transfer all powers to the People of the Territory upon the declaration of independence * * *."

When South Africa declined to grant Namibia independence, the General Assembly began to adopt further measures to pry it from South African control. Among these was G.A. Resolution 32/9 (1977), which requested "all specialized agencies and other organizations and conferences within the United Nations system to grant full membership to the United Nations Council for Namibia so that it may participate in that capacity as the legal Administering Authority for Namibia * * *."

Subsequently, pre-independent Namibia (represented by the Council for Namibia) was admitted to the Food and Agriculture Organization, the International Labor Organization and some other specialized agencies. In each instance, Namibia was admitted under a procedure for granting full membership to states.

In the Food and Agriculture Organization, the United States voted against admission of Namibia as a full member. The U.S. representative said that the negative vote was cast "for reasons of a constitutional nature. We take the view that a state or nation in the sense meant by Article II of the FAO Constitution is a territory controlled by an internationally recognized government located in the territory that it controls or administers. We do not consider it wise for the future of this Organization or other Organizations in the United Nations System to take decisions that create confusion as to the meaning of the concept of state or nation as it relates to membership in the United Nations Organizations." [a]

In the ILO, Namibia was admitted despite some misgivings on the part of the ILO Legal Adviser.

OPINION OF THE ILO LEGAL ADVISER ON THE POSSIBLE ADMISSION OF NAMIBIA

June 12, 1978.
International Labor Conf., 64th Sess., Provisional
Record of Proceedings at 24/20–24/22.

[The Legal Adviser quoted ILO Constitution *article 1, paragraphs 2, 3 and 4,* dealing with admission to membership. He continued:]

---

[a]. FAO, Verbatim Records of Plenary Meetings of the Conference, FAO Doc. C 77/PV, at 61 (1977).

4. It is clear from these provisions that membership in the ILO is open to States, which may fall into one of three categories:

(a) Members of the ILO on 1 November 1945;

(b) Members of the United Nations; and

(c) other States.

Namibia does not fall into the first two categories. Accordingly, under paragraphs 2 and 4 of article 1 read together, it could become a Member only as "such other State as may" be admitted to the Organization by the General Conference by a vote concurred in by two-thirds of the delegates attending the session, including two-thirds of the Government delegates present and voting.

5. It is clear from the terms of paragraph 2 of article 1 that membership in the ILO is only open to "States". The first question to be considered is, accordingly, whether Namibia can be regarded as a State for that purpose.

6. The ILO Constitution does not contain a definition of the term "State". However, there are generally accepted criteria in international law for determining what constitutes a State. The best known formulation of the basic criteria for statehood is that laid down in article 1 of the Montevideo Convention 1933, which states that:

> "The State as a person of international law should possess the following qualifications: (a) a permanent population; (b) a defined territory; (c) government; and (d) capacity to enter into relations with other States."

* * * [W]hat is important is that an entity which calls itself a State should have plenary competence both to deal with its internal affairs and to perform international acts, enter into treaties, etc.

7. The ILO Constitution contains provisions regarding the rights and obligations of Members which appear to confirm the need to meet the basic criteria mentioned above. A few examples may be given:

(a) In accordance with the provisions of article 3, paragraph 1, of the Constitution, the meetings of the General Conference are composed of four representatives of each of the Members, of whom two shall be Government delegates and the other two shall be delegates representing respectively the employers and the workpeople of each of the Members. It seems clear that these provisions presuppose the existence of a Government.

(b) Under article 19 of the Constitution, any international labour Convention adopted by the Conference will be communicated to all Members for ratification, and each Member is under an obligation to bring the Convention, within the period specified in the article, before the authority or authorities within whose competence the matter lies, for the enactment of legislation or other action. If the Convention is ratified by the Member, it is also required to take action to make it effective. These various provisions of article 19 presuppose that Members of the ILO are capable of concluding treaties and international agreements, and are able to make them effective within their territory.

(c) According to article 29 of the Constitution, the government of a Member State which has been involved in a complaint under article 26 of the Constitution may, in certain specified circumstances, propose to refer the complaint to the International Court of Justice. Since, according to article 34 of the Statute of the International Court of Justice "only States may be parties in cases before the Court", the provisions of article 29 of the ILO Constitution presuppose that the Members of the ILO are "States" with standing to bring judicial action before the Court.

* * *

8. The practice of the International Labour Organisation has always been to require that Members should have full capacity to exercise the rights, and discharge the obligations, of membership in the Organisation, as laid down in the ILO Constitution. This practice is supported, in particular, by an Advisory Opinion of the Permanent Court of International Justice in the case concerning the application for membership of the ILO by the Free City of Danzig in 1930.[b] The facts of the case will be briefly recalled.

9. The Free City of Danzig was created in 1919 by the Treaty of Versailles. The City had a defined territory and population; it had its own flag, and issued passports to its nationals. It had independent legislative power, exercised through a parliament; it had a government and a Senate, as well as judicial courts made up of independent judges. However, in international relations the Free City of Danzig was subjected to certain restrictions. On the one hand, it was placed under the protection of the League of Nations; and on the other, the conduct of its foreign relations was entrusted to the Government of Poland.

10. When the Free City of Danzig applied to become a Member of the ILO in 1930, doubts were expressed by some Members as to whether its status was compatible with the rights and duties of membership in the Organisation. The question was referred to the Permanent Court of International Justice for an Advisory Opinion.

11. The Court said that it was impossible to avoid the conclusion that some of the steps which a Member of the ILO would take—some even which it might be bound to take—in pursuing the normal activities of membership would fall within the sphere of foreign relations. It

---

b. [P.C.I.J., Series B, No. 18. Ed.].

noted that the Free City of Danzig could not call upon Poland to take any step in connection with the foreign relations of the Free City which were opposed to the policy of Poland; and that there was no provision in the ILO Constitution which absolved a Member from complying with the obligations of membership or excused it from participating in the normal activities of the Organisation if it could not obtain the consent of some other Member of the Organisation. As a result, the Court held that the Free City of Danzig could not participate as a Member in the work of the International Labour Organisation.

* * *

13. [As of 1978,] Namibia has not yet attained independent statehood. Namibia is still under the administration of the United Nations, and the conduct of the foreign relations of Namibia is entrusted to the United Nations Council for Namibia. It seems to me to follow from the present terms of the ILO Constitution, from the meaning given to those terms in international law, from the practice of the ILO and particularly from the Advisory Opinion of the Permanent Court of International Justice in the Free City of Danzig case, that Namibia cannot be admitted as a Member of the ILO until it attains independence, and becomes able to exercise all the rights and discharge all the obligations of membership in the Organisation.

* * *

RESPONSE OF THE COUNCIL FOR NAMIBIA
June 21, 1978.
International Labor Conf., 64th Sess., Provisional
Record of Proceedings at 24/23–24/24.

[The Council noted that the ILO's Selection Committee had asked for the legal opinion set forth above. The Council continued:]

The delegation of the United Nations Council for Namibia maintains that it is a risky course of action to attempt to deny the quality of a State to Namibia, a country which nevertheless satisfies the criteria mentioned in the legal opinion: that is, a permanent population, possession of a well-defined territory; existence of a stable and internationally recognised legal structure; and the capacity to enter into relations with other States.

We also say that the United Nations Council for Namibia will be able, when required, to provide a delegation consisting of government representatives and workers' representatives, chosen in agreement with the organisation of Namibian workers, that it will find a solution to the question of representation of the employers and that the United Nations Council for Namibia is ready to sign the ILO Conventions.

* * *

In paragraph 6 the legal opinion admits that the ILO Constitution does not contain any definition of the expression "State". We believe that only the Conference itself can take a decision on this question. We see no other procedure. In the absence of any definition of the expression "State" in the ILO Constitution, the Legal Counsel could have stopped there, and reported to the Selection Committee the non-existence of a definition. However, the Legal Counsel has insisted on providing a definition of the expression "State", taken from the Montevideo Convention of 1933.

The definition deserves our attention. It comprises four elements. Firstly, a *permanent population.* In the case of Namibia there is no question about this. The population is stable, and has remained on its present territory since the nineteenth century and even longer. Secondly, a *well defined territory.* The territory was defined in the nineteenth century and its external frontiers remain the same. Thirdly, the *capacity to enter into relations with other States.* This condition is also satisfied. Namibia has already entered into relations with other States. At its 77th meeting, the Third United Nations Conference on the Law of the Sea decided "to invite the United Nations Council for Namibia to participate fully in its work". At the nineteenth FAO Conference, held in November last year, Namibia was admitted as a full Member. It is thus clear that Namibia has already entered into relations with almost the totality of States who are United Nations members. It should also be added that the United Nations Council for Namibia has signed with most member States of the United Nations agreements which allow the Council to issue to Namibian citizens travel documents which are almost universally recognised.

Fourthly, there is the element "government". We use the expression "legal administering authority". We believe that this legal structure for Namibia is adequate. There already exists a considerable body of legal opinion on the matter of occupation of one State by another. During the Second World War many States were occupied by other States. It was never said that the occupied States ceased to be States, even if their governments were non-existent or in exile outside the national territory. * * *

The following section of the opinion of the Legal Counsel is devoted to the realm of supposition or, as he says, presupposition. In paragraph 7 he lays out these presuppositions.

The first deals with the question of representation. As we have already stated, the Council is in a position to provide a satisfactory delegation. In any case, these questions should be dealt with at the level of the Credentials Committee. The degree of representativity of a delegation does not appear in the Constitution as a condition for admission.

The second presupposition deals with the international labour Conventions. In accordance with the dispositions of the Constitution, the delegation of the United Nations Council for Namibia is able to sign the international labour Conventions and to submit them for ratification to the United Nations Council for Namibia. * * * There is no mention in the Constitution of the need, cited by the Legal Counsel in his opinion, for a Member to be able to physically apply the conventions on its territory.

The third presupposition states that ILO Members can refer certain disputes to the International Court of Justice and that the Court in accordance with its own statutes can only hear States. It is therefore presupposed that all ILO Members must possess the quality of being able to bring their disputes before the Court, and that a country which does not possess this quality is not fit to be admitted to the ILO. It is understood that this is meant to mean Namibia. This is cart-before-the-horse type of argumentation and does not need to concern us.

* * *

The following section of the legal opinion, starting with paragraph 8, deals with the previous custom of the ILO. A custom can always be changed. However, the precedents cited in this section are not in contradiction with the position of Namibia. We read that the application of the Free City of Danzig was rejected. This is understandable, since it is stated that Poland was responsible for its international relations. If Poland had submitted the applications, things could have been different. It would appear that at this particular time Danzig was trying to escape from the influence of Poland.

* * *

THE STATEHOOD REQUIREMENT AND THE ILO

Who had the more convincing legal position—the ILO Legal Adviser or the Council for Namibia?

ILO Constitution article 37(1) provides, "Any question or dispute relating to the interpretation of this Constitution * * * shall be referred for decision to the International Court of Justice." Should the question of Namibia's statehood, as a prerequisite to admission, have been submitted to the Court?

Was Namibia's statehood a legal question at all?

3. *Palestine's Application to WHO*

In May 1989, the Palestine Liberation Organization, claiming to represent a new state of Palestine, applied for full membership in the World Health Organization. The PLO is an umbrella group consisting of the main organizations of the Palestine resistance movement. When it applied for Palestinian membership in the WHO, the PLO was headquartered in Tunisia. It announced that it would also apply for membership in other specialized agencies, including the International Labor Organization, the Food and Agriculture Organization, the International Telecommunication Union, and UNESCO.

This followed the November 1988 Declaration of Independence adopted by the Palestine National Council, the parliamentary body of the PLO. It declared "the establishment of the State of Palestine in the land of Palestine with its capital at Jerusalem." [a] The Declaration avowed the state of Palestine's commitment to the purposes and principles of the United Nations; it also said that, subject to the right of self defense, it rejects the threat or use of force against the territorial integrity and political independence of itself or of any other state.

The Declaration did not set forth the claimed territorial boundaries of the state of Palestine, but it did rely on U.N. General Assembly Resolution 181(II) of 1947, which partitioned Palestine (west of the Jordan River) into an Arab and a Jewish state. (The Jewish state—Israel—has not been confined to the lines drawn by that resolution since 1949, when armistice agreements with its neighboring Arab states ended its war of independence by drawing ostensibly-temporary demarcation lines outside the territory originally allocated to the Jewish state.)

A month after the Palestine National Council had proclaimed the "State of Palestine," the U.N. General Assembly adopted Resolution 43/177 (1988). In it, the General Assembly:

1. *Acknowledges* the proclamation of the State of Palestine by the Palestine National Council on 15 November 1988;

2. *Affirms* the need to enable the Palestinian people to exercise their sovereignty over their territory occupied since 1967;

3. *Decides* that, effective as of 15 December 1988, the designation "Palestine" should be used in place of the designation "Palestine Liberation Organization" in the United Nations system * * *.

The vote was 104–2(Israel, United States)–36, with 15 member states absent and one (Iran) not participating in the vote.

The PLO's application for membership in WHO was regarded as an important test case. For one thing, membership in any specialized agency means automatic admission to some of the others, such as the World Intellectual Property Organization, at least if the applicant is a "state." WHO seemed a likely organization for that foothold, and for a precedent in the case of organizations where admission would not be automatic, because WHO alone among specialized agencies requires a bare majority of votes in the plenary body—rather than two-thirds—for admission under non-automatic procedures. WHO Constitution article 3 provides, "Membership in the Organization is open to all States."

[a]. U.N. Doc. A/43/827–S/20278, Annex III, reprinted in 27 Int'l Legal Materials 1668, 1670 (1988).

The United States government opposed the PLO application, and undertook to persuade other governments to vote against it. The State Department threatened to make no further contributions to any international organization that made any change in the PLO's status as a mere observer.[b] The threat to withhold payments to WHO carried with it substantial leverage, inasmuch as the United States was being assessed 25 percent of the organization's regular budget.

These materials examine the legal issues surrounding withholding of assessments at pages 268–73 infra. The present focus is instead on the PLO's eligibility for membership.

In addition to using its financial leverage, the U.S. government put forward a legal argument:

CRITERIA FOR STATEHOOD UNDER INTERNATIONAL LAW: THE CASE OF THE PALESTINE LIBERATION ORGANIZATION

March 1989.
Enclosure with letter of Apr. 28, 1989, from U.S. Mission, Geneva, to Dr. Hiroshi Nakajima, Director–General of WHO.

[The U.S. argument began with the four requirements for statehood, as set forth in the Montevideo Convention on Rights and Duties of States, page 154 supra: (a) a permanent population; (b) a defined territory; (c) government; and (d) capacity to enter into relations with other states.]

This definition has received wide recognition among international law publicists and within the United Nations system.[2] Under this definition, the purported "State" of Palestine that was proclaimed in 1988 clearly fails to meet the requirement of government and, therefore, does not qualify as a State.

A State coming into existence must possess not merely a putative government, but actual and effective governmental control over the territory it claims to possess and over the population it claims to represent. As one noted commentator has stated, "modern states are territorial; their governments exercise control over persons and things within their frontiers."[3] Without actual control over such territory, a State could not serve the interests of the inhabitants of that territory, or regulate the affairs of its territory, or raise revenue from among its

---

b. See Dep't State Bull., July 1989, at 65–66.

2. See, e.g., I O'Connell, *International Law* 304–5 (1965) ("The traditional definition of 'state' was adopted in the Montevideo Convention"); Crawford, *The Creation of States in International Law* 36 (1979) (referring to the Montevideo formula as the "classical criteria for statehood"); Higgins, *The Development of International Law Through the Political Organs of the United Nations* 13–14 (1963) ("A study of United nations practice * * * will reveal a surprisingly close adherence to the traditional criteria of statehood" as articulated in the Montevideo Convention).

3. Brierly, *The Law of Nations* 126 (6th ed. 1963); see also Von Glahn, *Law Among Nations* 84 (5th ed. 1984) ("A state comes into existence when the community involved acquires (*inter alia*) an operating and effective government").

populace, or provide for their defense. In short, a purported State lacking effective governmental control over its territory would be nothing more than a "disembodied spirit,"[4] unable to perform the functions associated with modern statehood.[5]

International law scholars without exception have confirmed the necessity of effective governmental control among the criteria for statehood. As Dr. James Crawford states:

> The right to be a State is dependent at least in the first instance upon the exercise of full governmental powers with respect to some area of territory * * *. The requirement that a putative State have an effective government might be regarded as central to its claim to statehood.[6]

Professor Ian Brownlie would also require a State to have "a stable political community, supporting a legal order, in a certain area." In Brownlie's view, the best evidence of such a stable political community is "the existence of effective government, with centralized administrative and legislative organs."[7] To have centralized administrative and legislative organs is to have effective governmental control. Without such control, administrative and legislative organs can exist only in name, and can perform none of their assigned functions.

Conclusion

The Palestinian Liberation Organization ("PLO") is neither a State nor the government of a State. The purported "State" of Palestine that was proclaimed by the Palestinian National Congress in 1988 does not exercise governmental control over any territory, including the territory occupied by Israel since 1967. Accordingly, neither the PLO nor "Palestine" meets the criteria established for statehood in international law, and does not qualify for full membership status in international organizations where full membership is open solely to States.

THE RESPONSE

When the World Health Assembly (the WHO's plenary body) convened in May 1989, the government of Tonga introduced a draft

---

4. Cf. Statement of the United States in the United Nations Security Council concerning the admission of Israel, SCOR 383rd mtg., Dec. 2, 1948, 41, *reprinted in* I Whiteman, *Digest of International Law* 231 (1963) ("(O)ne cannot contemplate a State as a kind of disembodied spirit * * *. (T)here must be some portion of the earth's surface which its people inhabit and over which its Government exercises authority").

5. Once established as a State under international law, temporary loss of effective governmental control through belligerent occupation does not, however, result in the loss of statehood. *See, e.g.,* Crawford, *supra* note 2, at 57–58; Marek, *Identity and Continuity of States in Public International Law* 73–125 (1954).

6. Crawford, *supra* note 2, at 36–42 * * *.

7. Brownlie, Principles of Public International Law 75 (3rd ed. 1979). [So also in the fourth edition (1990), at 73. Ed.]

resolution that would take no action on the PLO application, instead requesting the Director-General "to pursue his studies on the application of Palestine" and to report back to the 1990 WHA session. During the debate, the representative of Algeria presented the Palestinian position. The representative of Libya chimed in with a constitutional argument.

WORLD HEALTH ASSEMBLY DEBATE
Verbatim Record, May 12, 1989.
WHO Doc. WHA42/1989/REC/2, at 227-36.

Mr. AIT CHALAL (*Algeria*) (*translation from the French*):

* * *

Last November a major and historic event took place in the structures of the Palestinian people, with the proclamation of the State of Palestine. That was a far-reaching event which has brought about a fundamental change in the situation. This State has already been recognized by some 100 countries. It has entered into diplomatic relations with a great many, large and small. Moreover, it has unofficial relations even with some that have always shown unmistakable hostility to the Palestinian cause. * * *

Certain persons are involving us in all kinds of legal arguments, arguments which I personally regard as, to say the least, specious, and which consist of raising problems of international law and arguing about the criteria for statehood.

If the point at issue is being a people, is there anyone amongst us who would presume to contest the existence of the Palestinian people? Without going back into the mists of time or into remote biblical history, we all know that the Philistines were not born yesterday. They are a people who have played a decisive role throughout the history of the region, both materially and spiritually. But without going back that far, I believe that the struggle currently being waged by the Palestinian people, that heroic struggle, the extraordinary efforts that they are making, and the incalculable sacrifices that they accept are the best proof of their existence as a people and of their desire for life, a real life as a people and a nation.

* * *

Now there is another argument, the territorial argument. Well, let us first respect our own decisions, and when I say our own decisions I mean the decisions of the United Nations: the State of Palestine was created in 1947 by United Nations resolution 181(II), it is not something newly created. The point at issue is merely that this territory is today very largely occupied, even wholly occupied by the Israeli army, following a policy of aggression and domination that continues down to this day. The Palestinian people are asking for nothing more than the recovery of their own territory. * * *

As regards State structures, as I said just now the most representative body of Palestine, I refer to the Palestine National Council, has decided to set up a State. Everyone is aware of the democratic and representative nature of this institution, which incorporates all the Palestinian forces whatever their political persuasion, and as you know these are extremely varied; but the essential point is that this body has decided, in the first place, to set up this State and, in the second place, to address a political issue of fundamental importance for the advent of an era of peace in the region.

It is on this basis and in terms of these new elements that we must consider all the problems relating to Palestine. I state very frankly that every humanitarian, social, economic or other aspect relating to Palestine has a fundamentally political connotation and must take account of the Palestinian people's struggle to regain their inalienable right to create their own State, and to establish the necessary structures so that they can live freely in an independent State like all the peoples of the world. * * *

Dr. AL-ZAIDI (*Libyan Arab Jamahiriya*) (*translation from the Arabic*):

* * *

The draft resolution before us now * * * is irrelevant to the issue. First, the second operative paragraph is not in compliance with the functions either of the Director-General or of the Organization as set out in Article 2 of the Constitution. The Organization does not have any mandate to undertake studies and research on the eligibility or legitimacy of States. Article 2 of the Constitution, Mr. President, is unequivocally clear on the functions and tasks of the Organization and its Director-General. How can we authorize the Director-General to undertake actions that are outside the competence of our Organization in the first place?

WHO AND PALESTINE

The draft resolution, effectively postponing the PLO's application for a year, was adopted by secret ballot.[c]

Did the United States or Algeria have the better argument on Palestinian eligibility for membership?

Does the WHO Constitution require that a political entity be a state under customary international law in order to be admitted? If not, what criteria would determine whether an entity is a "state" for purposes of WHO Constitution article 3?

What was the significance, if any, of U.N. General Assembly resolution 43/177, page 159 supra? Did it acknowledge that "Pales-

---

c. WHO Res. WHA42.1, May 12, 1989.

tine" is a state? If so, what effect do you suppose that would have? If not, what *did* resolution 43/177 do?

Note that the General Assembly does not have any formal power to bind the specialized agencies. Whatever formal power it does have would come from Chapter IV (articles 9–22) of the U.N. Charter, or from the relationship agreements the U.N. has entered into with the specialized agencies under U.N. Charter articles 57 and 63. Article IV of the relationship agreement between the U.N. and WHO, 19 U.N.T.S. 193, obligates WHO to consider "all formal recommendations which the United Nations may make to it" and affirms WHO's "intention of co-operating in whatever further measures may be necessary to make co-ordination of the activities of specialized agencies and those of the United Nations fully effective."

At this writing, the General Assembly had not taken a position on full membership of "Palestine" in the specialized agencies. In another context, in G.A. Res. 396 (1950), it recommended that whenever more than one authority claims to be the government representing an acknowledged member state and the General Assembly has chosen which one it will recognize, "the attitude adopted by the General Assembly * * * should be taken into account in other organs of the United Nations and in the specialized agencies * * *."

Does resolution 396 apply by analogy to the question of full membership of "Palestine" in the specialized agencies (such as WHO)?

Would the Namibia precedent in the ILO be relevant here?

If WHO had admitted Palestine to full membership, would that have been a conclusive (or persuasive) precedent in other specialized agencies that define eligible entities as "states"? What about those defining them as "countries" or "nations"?

The Libyan representative argued that the resolution called on the Director–General to do something beyond the functions of the Organization as set forth in *article 2* of the Constitution. That article sets out several functions, all related to achieving the objective of the Organization as pronounced in *article 1*. Did the Libyan representative have a good point?

Obviously, Palestinian membership was a highly charged political issue. Are the legal arguments irrelevant in a case like this?

When the World Health Assembly next met, in 1990, it requested the Director–General "to continue his studies on the application of Palestine." [d] At this writing, Palestine had not been admitted as a full member of WHO or of any other specialized agency.

4. *The European Economic Community and FAO*

In the autumn of 1991, the European Economic Community (EEC) applied for membership in the Food and Agriculture Organization.

---

[d] WHO Res. WHA43.1, May 10, 1990.

Under the FAO Constitution as it then existed, membership was limited to "nations." Since the EEC did not purport to be a "nation," an amendment to the FAO Constitution would be needed if it were to be admitted.

FAO committees began the process of drafting the amendment and consulting various parties, including the U.N. Office of Legal Affairs. Eventually the FAO Conference, meeting in November 1991, amended the FAO Constitution by adding, inter alia, *article II, paragraphs 3–10*, on admitting regional economic integration organizations to membership. The amendment also provided that a member organization "shall pay to the Organization a sum to be determined by the Conference, to cover administrative and other expenses arising out of its membership in the Organization." The FAO Committee on Constitutional and Legal Matters concluded that the amendment thus would not involve new obligations for existing members or associate members, so it took effect "forthwith." See *article XX, paragraph 2*. The EEC, having duly submitted an instrument accepting the relevant obligations of the FAO Constitution and a declaration specifying the competence transferred to it by its member states, was admitted to membership later in the same session of the Conference.[a]

Note that the only organizations eligible for membership are "regional economic integration organizations" that meet the conditions of article II, paragraph 4. The quoted language is not defined, except to the extent that paragraph 4 does so. Would any organization other than the EEC be eligible?

The FAO Conference attached a "commentary" to article II, paragraph 4:

> The term transfer of competence in respect of a given subject includes the transfer of treaty-making powers by Member States and means that complete power with respect to that subject is transferred and that no residual power remains with the Member States.[b]

Why would the transfer of competence have to include exclusive treaty-making powers? Is that attribute necessary for all members of an organization such as FAO? If a "nation" applying for membership under *article II, paragraph 2* appears not to have treaty-making power exclusive of autonomous areas within its claimed territory, could it be admitted?

Under article II, paragraphs 3–10, a "regional economic integration organization" shares its membership, in effect, with its member states. Depending on what competence its member states have delegated to it and what they have retained, it may participate and cast the number of votes of its members or they may participate and cast their own votes. Is this a workable scheme?

a. See FAO Doc. C 91/REP/18, at 2 (1991).

b. FAO Doc. C 91/REP/1, at 6 (1991).

If it is a workable scheme for FAO, would it be for the U.N. itself? The U.N. Office of Legal Affairs had its doubts. When it was consulted during the preparation of the FAO amendment, it said:

> With respect to Article [II.10] we are aware of course that it is the constituent instrument of the FAO that is being changed and understand that the proposal being discussed is the concept of alternative exercise of membership rights, a concept which may well be appropriate within the FAO context. These matters are clearly within the purview of the Member States of the FAO and we of course are not in any position to comment on any policy decisions which the FAO membership [chooses] to make on such matters. We would, however, express concern were such decisions to be taken out of the FAO context and used to justify attempts in the United Nations to encroach on the principle of "one state one vote" contained in Article 18 of the Charter of the United Nations. We are aware that the mandate of FAO is specialized and is one where a substantial transfer of competence from EEC states to the EEC may have occurred. Our concern therefore relates to the United Nations as a political organization, and [is] both legal and practical. The United Nations is bound by the principle "one state one vote" and could not depart from it without amending the charter. From a practical standpoint, this principle is reflected in our practice of not allowing one delegate to cast more than one vote. We have had occasions of one state being absent for a vote and delegating voting power to a delegate from another state, but we have always insisted, for reasons of orderly conduct of business, that each member state keep its nameplate and that its delegate (even if "borrowed" from another state) must sit and vote from behind that nameplate. A change in the United Nations charter on such [a] critical issue as "one state one vote" having no realistic probability of success at this juncture, it must be understood that whatever changes FAO makes to its constituent instrument cannot be invoked in the future as a precedent in the United Nations context.[c]

Why such concern?

At this writing, FAO was the only specialized agency in which the EEC was a full member. Would it make sense to amend the constituent instruments of any other specialized agencies, in order to admit the EEC or other regional organizations?

SECTION 3. OBSERVER STATUS AND NONVOTING PARTICIPATION

A. THE UNITED NATIONS

1. *The General Assembly*

On November 22, 1974, the U.N. General Assembly adopted Resolution 3237, noting the universality to which the United Nations aspires,

[c] FAO Doc. CL 100/9–Sup.1, at 2–3 (1991).

and inviting the Palestine Liberation Organization (PLO) to participate as an observer in the General Assembly and in its international conferences.[a] The vote was 95–17–19. The PLO representative then made a statement, arguing the case for return of territory formerly held by Palestinian Arabs.territory formerly held by Palestinian Arabs.

"Observer status" does not appear in the U.N. Charter, but the General Assembly had theretofore granted it to some nonmember states and to regional intergovernmental organizations. One of the arguments advanced by members opposed to observer status for the PLO was that it had never before been granted to an entity that was neither a state nor an intergovernmental organization.[b] In addition, it was argued that the General Assembly's action violated *article 35(2)* of the Charter.[c]

Was it a violation of article 35(2) to grant observer status to the PLO? There is no indication that the PLO accepted in advance the Charter's obligations regarding pacific settlement of its dispute with Israel. Does that affect your answer?

Do any other provisions of the Charter bear on observer status for the PLO in the General Assembly? How about article 11(2)? Or articles 1(2) and 55 on self-determination?

The General Assembly's grant of observer status to the PLO in 1974 established its right to be present and to make formal statements on agenda items relating to the situation in Palestine. The question soon arose whether the PLO could also participate in the general debate that takes up a few weeks at the beginning of each General Assembly session in the autumn. The usual speakers in the general debate (actually not much of a debate, but rather a succession of speeches) are heads of state, foreign ministers and other high governmental officials. The U.N. Office of Legal Affairs, faced in 1976 with a request from the PLO's observer to participate in the general debate, said that it would be inappropriate to invite an organization having observer status to participate.[d] Consequently, the PLO observer has not been allowed to make speeches in the general debate, but the

a. 29 GAOR Supp. 31 (A/9631), at 4 (1974).

b. For a summary of the debate, see 11 U.N. Monthly Chron., No. 11, at 36–44 (Dec. 1974). In 1990 the General Assembly conferred observer status on the International Committee of the Red Cross, a nongovernmental organization. At this writing, it is the only traditional NGO to have that status.

c. See Review of the 1974 General Assembly and the United States Position in the United Nations: Hearings Before the Subcomm. on Int'l Organizations of the House Comm. on Foreign Affairs, 94th Cong., 1st Sess. 83 (1975).

d. See R. Sybesma–Knol, The Status of Observers in the United Nations 285–86 (1981).

further question arose whether he could reply to statements about the Palestine situation made by other speakers.

GENERAL ASSEMBLY DEBATE
Oct. 11, 1977.
32 GAOR, 29th plen. mtg., at 571.

The PRESIDENT: The representative of the Palestine Liberation Organization has asked to be allowed to reply to the statement made by one of the speakers in the general debate. I intend to call on him to speak on the basis of General Assembly resolution 3237 (XXIX) of 22 November 1974, and particularly on the basis of the statement made by the President of the thirty-first session of the General Assembly * * * on 29 September 1976 * * *:

> "It is my duty to inform the Assembly that the question has been raised whether observers could participate in the general debate. I have held consultations with those concerned and, as a result of those consultations, the understanding has been reached that, in order to avoid creating a precedent that could give rise to certain problems and could prolong the general debate beyond the period allotted to it, the matter will not be pursued.
>
> * * *
>
> "I must make it quite clear, however, that if any speaker in the course of the general debate should make any remarks which call for a reply from an observer, I shall call on that observer in the plenary Assembly so that he may reply." e

The last sentence of this statement, which substantially was a ruling * * *, was not challenged by the Plenary Assembly and as such stands as a decision by the General Assembly. On the basis of that, I am intending to call on the representative of the Palestine Liberation Organization.

The representative of the United States would like to speak on a point of order.

Mr. LOWENSTEIN (*United States of America*): * * *

I wish simply to recall the consistent position of the United States that only representatives of Member States are qualified to participate in the general debate. We believe this is a sound practice which contributes to more effective and expeditious general debate.

The PRESIDENT: According to rule 71, the President of the General Assembly must immediately decide on a point of order raised by a representative. In what he has said the representative of the United States has not made an appeal against this decision, and accordingly I shall adhere to my intention to call on the representative of the PLO.

e. [U.N.Doc. A/31/PV.9, paras. 152–54 (1976).]

The representative of Israel wishes to speak. * * *

Mr. ELIAV (*Israel*): Israel wishes simply to place on record its objection to calling on the PLO in this general debate and to allowing it to make what is in effect a reply. Israel's objection is based on a cardinal point of principle which we believe should enjoy universal support—namely, that the Charter of this Organization and its rules of procedure be respected and upheld. Articles 3 and 4 of the Charter lay down that only States—I repeat States—can be Members of the Organization. Rule 73 of the rules of procedure of the General Assembly makes the right of reply in the plenary Assembly available to Members—I repeat to Members—and to no one else.

The PRESIDENT: We have the same situation. There is no appeal against the intention to call on the representative of the Palestine Liberation Organization, but only a reservation.

I now call on the representative of the Palestine Liberation Organization.

THE RIGHT TO REPLY

General Assembly Rule of Procedure 73, to which the representative of Israel alluded, says:

> During the course of a debate, the President may announce the list of speakers and, with the consent of the General Assembly, declare the list closed. He may, however, accord the right of reply to any member if a speech delivered after he has declared the list closed makes this desirable.

The European Communities and Canada sent written statements to the President of the General Assembly, opposing the grant to observers of the same right to speak in the general debate as is enjoyed by member states.[f] During the next General Assembly session, in 1978, the PLO representative again sought to exercise the right to reply. The President of that session granted it on the basis of General Assembly Resolution 3237 "and in accordance with the precedent established at the 29th plenary meeting of the thirty-second Session."[g] The United States objected to the principle involved, as well as to the interpretation of precedent, but the President adhered to his decision.[h] Written objections were then made by Israel, the European Communities and Canada.[i]

Was the Israeli legal argument, based on U.N. Charter articles 3 and 4 and on Rule 73, a strong one?

---

f. See U.N. Docs. A/32/280 and A/32/301 (1977).

g. 33 GAOR, 29th plen. mtg., at 572 (1978). The reference is to the General Assembly debate set forth in the text.

h. Id.

i. See U.N. Docs. A/33/307, 308 & 365 (1978).

Note how the precedent was established. It began with the statement by the President of the 31st session, quoted in the debate above. That statement of intention was never tested, because no observer at that session actually requested an opportunity to reply. When the request was finally made in the 32nd session, the President treated the matter as settled, despite the opposition of the United States, Israel, the European Communities and Canada. Would it have made any difference if they had objected to the statement in the 31st session? If you were the U.N. Legal Counsel and you were now asked whether an observer has a right to reply in the General Assembly, what would be your response?[j]

2. *The Security Council*

The question of PLO participation has also come up in the Security Council. On December 4, 1975, the Security Council met to consider a complaint by Lebanon concerning an Israeli air attack on Palestinian refugee camps in Lebanon. Egypt requested the participation of the PLO in the debate. As you read the excerpts below from the ensuing discussion, consider the strength of the arguments based on Rules 37 and 39 of the Security Council's provisional rules of procedure. Consider also whether *articles 30–32* of the Charter would have been relevant. Rule 37 provides:

> Any Member of the United Nations which is not a member of the Security Council may be invited, as the result of a decision of the Security Council, to participate, without vote, in the discussion of any question brought before the Security Council when the Security Council considers that the interests of that Member are specially affected, or when a Member brings a matter to the attention of the Security Council in accordance with Article 35(1) of the Charter.

Rule 39 provides:

> The Security Council may invite members of the Secretariat or other persons, whom it considers competent for the purpose, to supply it with information or to give other assistance in examining matters within its competence.

SECURITY COUNCIL DEBATE
Dec. 4, 1975.
30 SCOR, 1859th mtg., para. 6 et seq.

The PRESIDENT [Mr. Richard (*U.K.*)]:

The Security Council has before it in document S/11893 a letter dated 3 December 1975 from the Permanent Representative of Egypt to

---

[j]. The then-U.N. Legal Counsel has addressed the subject. See Suy, The Status of Observers in International Organizations, 160 Hague Academy, Recueil des Cours 75, 140–42 (1978). See also the Opinion of the U.N. Office of Legal Affairs, Status of the Palestine Liberation Organization in the United Nations, 1982 U.N. Juridical Y.B. 156.

the United Nations in which he requests the participation of the Palestine Liberation Organization in the debate during the discussion of the item in the Security Council.

* * * I have been asked to record that this proposal is not being put forward under rule 37 or rule 39 of the provisional rules of procedure of the Security Council, but, if it is adopted by the Council, the invitation to the Palestine Liberation Organization to participate in this debate will confer on it the same rights of participation as are conferred when a Member State is invited to participate under rule 37.

* * *

Mr. VINCI (*Italy*):

* * *

I want to make it very clear that we are indeed in favour of acceding to the request of the Permanent Representative of Egypt that we afford an opportunity to the representative of the Palestine Liberation Organization to express his views on this tragic occurrence. However, after very careful examination of the Charter, the rules of procedure of this Council and relevant precedents, and taking into account the principles on which this Organization is based, we have come to the conclusion that there is no other way that this can and should be done than under the clear provisions of rule 39 of the rules of procedure of the Security Council.

Unfortunately, in our view, some members of this Council feel differently and deem it inadvisable to meet the request of the representative of Egypt under rule 39, a course which is supported by well established practice. We are in fact faced with a motion requesting the participation of the Palestine Liberation Organization in the present debate on terms which are totally innovative with regard to such long practice. If that proposal were to be accepted, I fear it would create a precedent which might have unforeseeable consequences. In fact, to our mind this raises serious doubts and reservations as to its acceptability and its conformity with the provisions of the Charter, the rules of procedure and the spirit of this Organization.

I should like to elaborate on this issue so that the reasons for our doubts and reservations may be properly recorded. First of all, no one can fail to take for granted that so far this Organization is an organization of sovereign States. The rights, duties, privileges and responsibilities set and conceived within the United Nations are linked to the very essence of statehood. Whatever feelings, consideration or sympathy we may have for a given organization, whenever some form of relationship is being established between that organization and the United Nations we must accept the fact that there is an inherent difference between it and a sovereign State, to the extent that it lacks statehood.

* * *

Mr. ZAHAWI (*Iraq*):

* * *

It has been asked why this request for the participation of the Palestine Liberation Organization was not presented and is not being presented under rule 39 of the provisional rules of procedure. [Mr. Zahawi read rule 39 aloud.] That is rule 39 of the provisional rules of procedure—and I emphasize that: the provisional rules of procedure. Unfortunately, these provisional rules of procedure have not envisaged or taken into account the possibility of the participation of a party not a Member of the United Nations, nor yet a member of the Secretariat or "other person". We are faced with a situation in which the Palestine Liberation Organization happens to be the main target of this latest savage act of terrorism. This is a body that also happens to have been granted an official status within the United Nations—namely, the status of permanent observer, as the sole legitimate representative of the Palestinian people. Is that body to be invited to this Council to participate under a rule which considers only members of the Secretariat or individuals or other persons? We think not. Nor could it be invited under rule 37, obviously, because that applies only to the Members of this Organization.

It has all along been said that the Council, or any other body, for that matter, is the master of its own rules of procedure. In this case, it is the duty of the Council, then, to decide on these rules of procedure, especially since the matter is not provided for in the provisional rules we have before us.

* * *

The PRESIDENT:

* * *

I now, in accordance with the procedures agreed upon during our consultation, proceed to a vote on the proposal put forward by the permanent representative of Egypt * * * that there should be accorded an invitation to the Palestine Liberation Organization to participate in this debate, and that that invitation will confer upon it the same rights of participation as are conferred when a Member State is invited to participate under rule 37.

A vote was taken by show of hands.

In favour:	Byelorussian Soviet Socialist Republic, China, Guyana, Iraq, Mauritania, Sweden, Union of Soviet Socialist Republics, United Republic of Cameroon, United Republic of Tanzania
Against:	Costa Rica, United Kingdom of Great Britain and Northern Ireland, United States of America
Abstaining:	France, Italy, Japan

The PRESIDENT:

The result of the vote is as follows: 9 votes in favour, 3 against, with 3 abstentions. Accordingly, the proposal has been adopted.[a]

QUESTIONS ON THE PLO IN THE SECURITY COUNCIL

Why was it important for the Iraqi representative to show that rule 39 did not apply to the PLO? Why didn't it, in his view? Was his interpretation of rule 39 sound?

In the years after 1975, the United States continued to oppose PLO participation in Security Council debates under any procedure other than Rule 39. The United States was consistently voted down. In January 1989, after the Palestine National Council had declared a state of "Palestine," and after the U.N. General Assembly had acknowledged that declaration and decided that the designation "Palestine" should replace "PLO" in the U.N. system, the issue of PLO participation in the Security Council took a new twist.

From 1975 until January 1989, whenever the PLO wished to participate in a Security Council debate, its request was submitted by a member state. In January 1989, in connection with the Security Council's consideration of a draft resolution deploring the United States' downing of two Libyan jet aircraft over the Mediterranean Sea, the PLO submitted its own request. That this was regarded as more than a technicality is indicated by the ensuing colloquy in the Security Council.

SECURITY COUNCIL DEBATE
Jan. 11, 1989.
U.N.Doc. S/PV.2841, at 3–12, 36–37.

The PRESIDENT [Mr. Razali (*Malaysia*)]:

I should like to inform the Council that I have received a letter dated 9 January 1989 from the Alternate Permanent Observer of Palestine to the United Nations, which reads as follows:

> I have the honour to request that, in accordance with its previous practice, the Security Council invite the Alternate Permanent Observer of Palestine to the United Nations to participate in the debate on the [U.S.–Libya incident].

The request is not made pursuant to rule 37 or rule 39 of the provisional rules of procedure of the Security Council, but if it is approved the Council will invite the Alternate Permanent Observer of Palestine to participate, not under rule 37 or rule 39, but with the same rights of participation as under rule 37.

---

a. Even though two permanent members voted against the proposal, their votes did not amount to vetoes because the decision was on a procedural matter. See U.N. Charter article 27(2), and see the discussion at page 192 infra.

Does any member of the Security Council wish to speak on this request?

Mr. OKUN (*United States of America*): The United States will vote against the proposal before the Security Council on two grounds. First, we believe that the Council does not have before it a valid request to speak. Secondly, the United States maintains that the Observer of the Palestine Liberation Organization (PLO) should be granted permission to speak only if the request complies with rule 39 of the rules of procedure. In our view, it would be unwarranted and unwise for the Council to break with its own practice and its own rules.

Members of the Security Council, let us ask ourselves this question. Does a decision to break with our own rules and procedures enlarge or diminish the Council's ability to play a constructive role in the Middle East peace process? My delegation firmly believes such a decision diminishes the Council's ability to play such a role.

As all members of the Council are aware, it is a long-standing practice that Observers do not have the right to speak in the Security Council at their own request. Rather, a request must be made on the Observer's behalf by a Member State. My Government sees no justification for any departure from existing practice.

It is clear that General Assembly resolutions are not binding on the Security Council. In any event, there is nothing in resolutions recently adopted by the General Assembly that would warrant a change in Security Council practice. General Assembly resolution 43/177, which purported to change the designation of the PLO Mission, did so

> "without prejudice to the observer status and functions of the Palestine Liberation Organization within the United Nations system, in conformity with relevant United Nations resolutions and practice".

That resolution does not constitute recognition of any State of Palestine, and the United States and the majority of the Members of the United Nations do not recognize such a State.

* * *

[The vote on the PLO's request was 11 in favor, one opposed (U.S.) and 3 abstentions (Canada, France, U.K.). The request, being on a procedural matter, was thus approved. After the representatives of the U.K. and Canada explained their abstentions, noting among other things that their governments had not recognized a state of Palestine, the representative of Finland spoke.]

Mr. TORNUDD (*Finland*): My delegation's vote was based on the belief that the representative of the Palestine Liberation Organization (PLO) should be given the opportunity to participate in the Security Council debate in accordance with previous practice. I wish to make it clear, however, that we do not regard the outcome of the vote as a change in the observer status of the PLO at the United Nations. For good or ill, the practice of granting an invitation to participate in Council debates, without the right to vote, has been given very wide application in recent years. In our view it should follow from today's decision that States which are not Members of the United Nations must also be entitled to have their requests to participate submitted to the Council for a decision without intermediaries.

[The President announced that Algeria had requested that Mr. Maksoud, the Observer to the U.N. of the League of Arab States, be allowed to speak under Rule 39.]

Mr. MAKSOUD: * * * I should also like to take this opportunity to express my appreciation to the Council for extending an invitation to a member State of the League of Arab States, the State of Palestine. The enhanced legal and juridical position that it achieved when the General Assembly was discussing the question of Palestine in Geneva must be reflected in all the organs of the United Nations system.

* * *

Mr. AL-KIDWA (*Palestine*) (*interpretation from Arabic*): * * * We are proud to be seated for the first time behind the nameplate "Palestine". I should like to assure all members of the Council that the outcome—the victory—we have gained today will contribute in a considerable and positive way to the process of building peace in the Middle East and to the task of building a just and global peace.

[The draft resolution on the U.S.–Libya incident was eventually put to a vote. It was defeated because of the vetoes of three permanent members, France, the U.K. and the United States.]

THE SIGNIFICANCE OF IT ALL

If we were to limit our focus strictly to the right to be heard in the Security Council, was there any significant difference between what happened in 1975 and in 1989?

Clearly, the protagonists in 1989—the United States, the PLO and the League of Arab States—regarded the matter as much more significant than a mere argument over Security Council protocol. What was the broader issue? Was "the victory" (Mr. Al-Kidwa's words) legally significant on that issue?

Note the concern over precedent in Security Council practice. What was Finland's point in this regard? Does it appear that precedent has any real significance in the Security Council?

B. U.N.–RELATED ORGANIZATIONS

A number of specialized agencies have also adopted a practice of granting "observer" status to at least some entities that do not qualify for full membership. The International Labor Organization is one of these organizations. In 1954 it began inviting certain dependent territories that had not yet emerged as independent states to participate in its General Conferences as observers without vote. For example, in 1969 observer delegations from Bermuda and Grenada (both then non-self-governing territories) were present.[a] More recently, the ILO, like the U.N. General Assembly, has admitted a PLO observer delegation. This first occurred in 1975 at the 60th Session of the International Labor Conference (the annual plenary meeting of government, worker and employer representatives), which approved a report of its Standing Orders Committee amending the Standing Orders of the International Labor Conference to add a new subparagraph to article 2, paragraph 3, as follows:

> Apart from delegates and advisers the only persons permitted to enter the body of the hall shall be—
>
> * * *
>
> (k) representatives of liberation movements recognised by the Organisation of African Unity or the League of Arab States which have been invited by the Conference or the Governing Body to be represented at the Conference.

The Conference also permitted representatives of liberation movements which had been invited to attend the Conference (i.e. the PLO) to address the Conference and to participate without vote in the discussions of the Conference committees.[b] As a result of the decisions regarding the PLO, the U.S. labor delegation walked out of the Conference and the U.S. government delegation said that working relationships in the ILO would be damaged and subverted by the introduction of an entity that was neither a government nor a representative of employers or workers.[c]

The ILO Constitution says nothing about "observer status." It does, however, contain an article on the meetings of the General Conference. See *article 3.*

If the U.S. representatives wished to make a legal argument against PLO participation in the 1975 Conference, would they have found support in article 3?

SECTION 4. REPRESENTATION

A. THE GENERAL ASSEMBLY

1. *China*

The question of Chinese representation kept coming up in the United Nations, practically from the moment the People's Republic of

---

a. See G. Johnston, The International Labour Organisation 22 (1970).

b. See 58 ILO Official Bull., Series A, No. 1, at 106 (1975).

c. See Int'l Labor Conf., Record of Proceedings, 60th Sess., at 254–55 (1975).

China (Communist China) was proclaimed on the mainland in 1949 until October 1971. At the inception of the United Nations in 1945, the noncommunist Kuomintang (Chiang Kai-shek) government was in power and represented China as the Republic of China. See U.N. Charter *article 23(1)*. It was overthrown on the mainland in 1949 and fled to Taiwan.

In January 1950, the Soviet Union proposed a draft Security Council resolution that would have rejected the credentials of the Kuomintang representative. The draft resolution was defeated, receiving only three votes in favor. This led to the temporary Soviet boycott of the Security Council in the early 1950s.

The U.N. Secretary-General (Trygve Lie) stepped into the breach, and attempts were made in the General Assembly to adopt standards that could be applied to this and any other dispute over representation.

M. WHITEMAN, DIGEST OF INTERNATIONAL LAW
Vol. 13, at 252–255 (1968).

In March 1950 the Secretary-General of the United Nations (Lie) made public a memorandum, entitled "Legal Aspects of Problems of Representation in the United Nations". This memorandum read in part:

> The primary difficulty in the current question of the representation of Member States in the United Nations is that this question of representation has been linked up with the question of recognition by Member States.

> * * *

> [M]embership of a State in the United Nations and representation of a State in the organs is clearly determined by a collective act of the appropriate organs; in the case of membership, by vote of the General Assembly on recommendation of the Security Council, in the case of representation, by vote of each competent organ on the credentials of the purported representatives. Since, therefore, recognition of either State or government is an individual act, and either admission to membership or acceptance of representation in the Organization are collective acts, it would appear to be legally inadmissible to condition the latter acts by a requirement that they be preceded by individual recognition.

> * * *

> The Chinese case is unique in the history of the United Nations, not because it involves a revolutionary change of government, but because it is the first in which two rival governments exist. It is quite possible that such a situation will occur again in

the future and it is highly desirable to see what principle can be followed in choosing between the rivals. It has been demonstrated that the principle of numerical preponderance of recognition is inappropriate and legally incorrect. Is any other principle possible?

It is submitted that the proper principle can be derived by analogy from Article 4 of the Charter. This Article requires that an applicant for membership must be able and willing to carry out the obligations of membership. The obligations of membership can be carried out only by governments which in fact possess the power to do so. Where a revolutionary government presents itself as representing a State, in rivalry to an existing government, the question at issue should be which of these two governments in fact is in a position to employ the resources and direct the people of the State in fulfilment of the obligations of membership. In essence, this means an inquiry as to whether the new government exercises effective authority within the territory of the State and is habitually obeyed by the bulk of the population.

If so, it would seem to be appropriate for the United Nations organs, through their collective action, to accord it the right to represent the State in the Organization, even though individual Members of the Organization refuse, and may continue to refuse, to accord it recognition as the lawful government for reasons which are valid under their national policies.[a]

* * *

[In 1950, a subcommittee of the General Assembly's Ad Hoc Political Committee worked out a draft resolution that would have recommended, inter alia:]

(a) That whenever more than one authority claims to be the government entitled to represent a Member State in the United Nations, and this question becomes the subject of controversy in the United Nations, it should be considered in the light of the purposes and principles of the Charter and the circumstances of each case;

(b) That the following should be among the factors to be taken into consideration in determining any such question:

(i) The extent to which the new authority exercises effective control over the territory of the Member State concerned and is generally accepted by the population;

(ii) The willingness of that authority to accept responsibility for the carrying out by the Member State of its obligations under the Charter;

(iii) The extent to which that authority has been established through internal processes in the Member State.

---

a. U.N.Doc. S/1466 (1950).

Paragraph (b) above was deleted in the Ad Hoc Political Committee.

The resolution adopted by the General Assembly [b] included paragraph (a) above as its first operative paragraph [but did not contain any other standards by which to determine such questions].

MAKING THE CHANGE

Each year from 1950 through 1960, the Soviet Union attempted to include in the General Assembly agenda an item calling for the seating of representatives of the People's Republic of China in place of those from the Republic of China. These were years of Western dominance in the United Nations. Each year the General Assembly adopted a resolution postponing consideration of the matter.

Beginning in 1960, U.N. membership began to expand dramatically, with the admission of newly-independent states. With its new composition, the General Assembly became more willing to consider the Chinese representation question. In 1961 it was included in the General Assembly's agenda for the first time. Five member states, including the United States, proposed a resolution deciding "in accordance with article 18 of the [U.N. Charter] that any proposal to change the representation of China is an important question." The General Assembly adopted this resolution,[c] and rejected a Soviet draft resolution that would have removed the Republic of China (the Chiang Kai-shek government) as the representative of China. For the procedural significance of the U.S.-sponsored resolution, see *article 18(2)*.

Continued attempts to change the representation of China were unsuccessful until 1971. On several occasions during that period, the General Assembly reaffirmed that it was an important question under article 18. But in 1971 the General Assembly, by a narrow margin, refused to characterize the matter as an important question. Without any recommendation from the Security Council, the General Assembly adopted resolution 2758 (XXVI):

RESOLUTION ON REPRESENTATION OF CHINA
United Nations General Assembly, Oct. 25, 1971.
G.A.Res. 2758, 26 GAOR Supp. 29 (A/8429), at 2.

The General Assembly,

Recalling the principles of the Charter of the United Nations,

Considering that the restoration of the lawful rights of the People's Republic of China is essential both for the protection of the Charter of the United Nations and for the cause that the United Nations must serve under the Charter,

b. G.A.Res. 396 (V), Dec. 14, 1950. c. G.A.Res. 1668 (XVI), Dec. 15, 1961.

Recognizing that the representatives of the Government of the People's Republic of China are the only lawful representatives of China to the United Nations and that the People's Republic of China is one of the five permanent members of the Security Council,

Decides to restore all its rights to the People's Republic of China and to recognize the representatives of its Government as the only legitimate representatives of China to the United Nations, and to expel forthwith the representatives of Chiang Kai-shek from the place which they unlawfully occupy at the United Nations and in all the organizations related to it.

THE LEGAL ISSUES

In the debate preceding adoption of resolution 2758, Albania and others argued that neither U.N. Charter *article 4*, on admission of new members, nor *article 6*, on expulsion of members, governed the matter. The United States argued that it was a case of expulsion, which would be governed by article 6.

Should it have been treated as a membership matter under article 4? As an expulsion matter under article 6? What would have been the significance of treating it under either of those articles?

Since it was not treated as a matter within either of those articles, was there any nonpolitical standard that could or should have been applied? If the Trygve Lie test were used, how should the issue have been decided?

Resolution 2758 was adopted by more than a two-thirds majority, making the "important question" issue moot. Nevertheless, the General Assembly's about-face on that issue could be viewed as a significant precedent. Was the matter not an important question because it simply involved representation, rather than admission or expulsion of a member state? Or should it have been treated as an important question because it did "expel forthwith" the representatives of a permanent member of the Security Council?

The United States in 1971 had unsuccessfully proposed a compromise by which the People's Republic would have taken over China's seat in the Security Council, and both Chinas would have been represented in the General Assembly. Both Chinese regimes asserted that there was only one China, and that it included Taiwan as well as the mainland. If the General Assembly had adopted the U.S. proposal, would it have violated *article 2(7)* of the Charter? Did resolution 2758 violate article 2(7)?

A number of essentially legal arguments were made in the debate leading to the adoption of resolution 2758. If (as one might suspect) political considerations determined the outcome of the issues, why would the representatives waste their time with arguments about specific provisions of the Charter or about precedents? Do such arguments serve any useful purpose in these debates?

If the government of Taiwan were now to seek separate representation for Taiwan in the General Assembly, would it be proper to treat its request simply as a representation matter? Or would it have to apply for membership under article 4? If the latter, would it be eligible?

2. *Cambodia/Kampuchea*

In December 1978 a force of more than 100,000 Vietnamese troops invaded Cambodia (Kampuchea), driving the existing government of "Democratic Kampuchea," headed by Pol Pot, into a small area of countryside near the Thai border. From all accounts, the Pol Pot (Khmer Rouge) government had committed atrocious, massive human rights violations against its own people. The Vietnamese replaced it with a "People's Revolutionary Council of the People's Republic of Kampuchea," headed by Heng Samrin, which took control of the capital and most of the countryside.

At the 33rd session of the General Assembly, which ended just before the Vietnamese invasion of Cambodia, the representative of Democratic Kampuchea participated as the official Cambodian delegate, without challenge. In the 34th session, which began in September 1979, both Democratic Kampuchea and the People's Republic of Kampuchea claimed the right to represent Cambodia. The matter was first referred to the General Assembly's Credentials Committee, which recommended by a vote of 6 to 3 that the General Assembly accept the credentials of the delegation of Democratic Kampuchea.[d]

When the matter reached the floor of the General Assembly, two draft resolutions were introduced in addition to that of the Credentials Committee. One, put forward by Bulgaria and other Eastern European states, would have seated the delegation of the People's Republic of Kampuchea. The other, introduced by India and others, would have left the Cambodian seat vacant. The substance, but not all the rhetoric, of the ensuing six-hour debate is characterized by the excerpts below.

GENERAL ASSEMBLY DEBATE
Sept. 21, 1979.
34 GAOR, 3d plen. mtg., at 20–23.

Mr. YANKOV (*Bulgaria*): * * * The People's Revolutionary Council is sparing no efforts to bring the life of the people back to normal, to reunite the families of those who survived the massacre of 3 million human beings, and to restore national traditions and a decent way of life.

* * *

---

[d]. U.N. Doc. A/34/500, at 4 (1979).

As the sole legitimate and authentic representative of the Kampuchean people, the People's Revolutionary Council satisfies all the requirements for effective membership in our Organization. Why, then, and on what grounds, are that Government and its representatives being denied their rightful seat in the United Nations? Why, then, should the credentials of those who were overthrown by the Kampuchean people be recognized as valid when they are issued by a non-existent authority? Even if that authority claims to be a Government, it does not possess the elementary prerequisites of a Government that deserves a seat in this Organization.

I therefore submit that the question is not merely whether the Government is good or bad, as some allege; the question is which is the authentic Government exercising full control and effective power in Kampuchea according to the rules and customs of international law and practice.

* * *

Mr. MISHRA (*India*):

* * *

It is our conviction that the General Assembly should not take a definitive position at this moment. The best position for the General Assembly to take now is to wait and watch. If we were to accept the report of the Credentials Committee as it stands, I have no doubt that we would get involved in a very acrimonious debate which might spill over from this meeting to other meetings of the Assembly, and to the Main Committees of the Assembly. We should like to try to have a solution, a temporary one, which would give this Assembly the opportunity to take stock of the situation and, if necessary, to reopen the question even at this very session. This is the purpose and motive of our proposed amendment.

* * *

Mr. KOH (*Singapore*): * * * [W]e agree that the human rights record of the Government of Democratic Kampuchea is terrible; but we also argue, and we hope Members agree with us, that this gives no right under international law for any neighbouring State to take up armed force to invade its territory, to overthrow its Government, and to set up a puppet regime.

The next point that I would like to make is in response to an argument by my dear friend and colleague Ambassador Yankov of Bulgaria. He said that under international law we must recognize a Government which exercises effective control over its territory. He alleges that the People's Revolutionary Council of Kampuchea exercises effective control over the territory of Kampuchea, and must therefore be recognized by this Organization as its legal Government. My reply to Ambassador Yankov's argument is twofold. First, it is not true, as a matter of fact, that the Government of popular revolutionary Kampu-

chea exercises effective control over the entire territory of that country.
* * *

My second argument in response to Ambassador Yankov is that in international law it is true that one generally recognizes the Government which exercises effective control over a territory. But this is not an absolute rule without exceptions. We do not, for example, recognize a foreign power's control over territory that it has conquered by force.

REPRESENTATION: PRINCIPLE v. REALITY

The choice in this instance was between recognizing a brutal regime no longer in effective control of its territory, on one hand, or a regime propped up by an invading force, on the other (or, as India proposed, recognizing neither of them). At the end of the debate, the General Assembly voted to seat the representatives of Democratic Kampuchea (the Pol Pot government). The vote was 71 to 35, with 34 abstentions and 12 absences. From a purely legal standpoint, was that the proper result?

Could the Indian position be justified legally? [b]

If the approach recommended by Secretary–General Trygve Lie in 1950 were used, how would the Cambodian representation question have been resolved? Would the outcome of the Chinese representation experience provide a useful precedent?

From 1979 until 1989, large numbers of Vietnamese troops remained in Cambodia, maintaining order and supporting the government eventually led by Prime Minister Hun Sen. The General Assembly continued to recognize the opposition, which evolved into a coalition among the Khmer Rouge (still led by Pol Pot), a neutralist faction led by Prince Norodom Sihanouk, and a noncommunist faction led by Son Sann.

By 1989 the Vietnamese government no longer wished to continue its costly military presence in Cambodia, and announced that it would pull its troops out. A conference was held in Paris among Hun Sen and the leaders of the opposition groups, but it adjourned without reaching agreement on the future government or political structure of Cambodia. At the end of September 1989, Viet–Nam announced that its last troops had left Cambodia. The opposition groups asserted that many Viet-

---

b. See Warbrick, Kampuchea—Representation and Recognition, 30 Int'l & Comp.L.Q. 234 (1981).

namese soldiers, disguised as settlers, remained in Cambodia. Hun Sen remained in power in Phnom Penh, but opposition forces began making exploratory thrusts from their bases along the Thai border. Despite the announced Vietnamese withdrawal, the General Assembly again recognized the tripartite coalition in 1989 as Cambodia's representatives.

In 1990 the five permanent members of the Security Council agreed on a framework for a Cambodian political settlement, which the four main Cambodian parties—including the Hun Sen government and the Khmer Rouge—accepted. Pursuant to the settlement, the Cambodian parties agreed to form a Supreme National Council on which they would all be represented, to lead the country—with considerable help from the U.N.—to free elections for a democratically-elected government. The Supreme National Council could not immediately agree on the composition of a U.N. delegation. Consequently, Cambodia's General Assembly seat was left vacant ("temporarily unattended," according to diplomatic parlance) in 1990.

In 1991, the Supreme National Council did agree on Prince Norodom Sihanouk as the leader of its U.N. delegation. He was the leader of one of the parties represented in the Supreme National Council, and the head of the Cambodian state before Pol Pot and the Khmer Rouge took it over. The delegation's credentials were not challenged.

Was the General Assembly's refusal over the years to recognize the People's Republic of Kampuchea more a matter of law enforcement (to punish or deter international aggression) than of mere representation? If so, could it be effective?

Or was it simply a matter of trying to vindicate a basic principle of the U.N. Charter even if it would have no deterrent effect (and even if it involved recognizing a coalition dominated by the perpetrator of gross human rights violations)?

B. OTHER U.N. ORGANS AND RELATED ORGANIZATIONS

Once the General Assembly had recognized the People's Republic as the representative of China pursuant to General Assembly Resolution 2758, the same representation question arose in other organs of the U.N. (such as the Security Council and the Economic and Social Council) and in the related organizations (the specialized agencies, IAEA and GATT).

When the Chinese representation issue had first arisen in 1950, the General Assembly faced the question of possible conflicting decisions by the various organs and specialized agencies. It adopted the following resolution to try to deal with the problem.

RESOLUTION ON REPRESENTATION OF A MEMBER STATE
United Nations General Assembly, Dec. 14, 1950.
G.A.Res. 396, 5 GAOR Supp. 20 (A/1775), at 24.

* * *

The General Assembly,

Considering that difficulties may arise regarding the representation of a Member State in the United Nations and that there is a risk that conflicting decisions may be reached by its various organs,

Considering that it is in the interest of the proper functioning of the Organization that there should be uniformity in the procedure applicable whenever more than one authority claims to be the government entitled to represent a Member State in the United Nations, and this question becomes the subject of controversy in the United Nations,

Considering that, in virtue of its composition, the General Assembly is the organ of the United Nations in which consideration can best be given to the views of all Member States in matters affecting the functioning of the Organization as a whole,

1. *Recommends* that, whenever more than one authority claims to be the government entitled to represent a Member State in the United Nations and this question becomes the subject of controversy in the United Nations, the question should be considered in the light of the Purposes and Principles of the Charter and the circumstances of each case;

2. *Recommends* that, when any such question arises, it should be considered by the General Assembly, or by the Interim Committee if the General Assembly is not in session;

3. *Recommends* that the attitude adopted by the General Assembly or its Interim Committee concerning any such question should be taken into account in other organs of the United Nations and in the specialized agencies * * *.

THE GENERAL ASSEMBLY'S INFLUENCE

Resolution 396 implicitly acknowledged that General Assembly action on representation questions would not bind other U.N. organs, and merely "recommended" that the General Assembly's "attitude" be taken into account by them. In fact, the resolution had been watered down in committee to avoid any connotation that the General Assembly's action might be binding on other organs or on specialized agencies.[a] But compare the language of the 1971 resolution on Chinese representation (Resolution 2758, at page 179 supra). Does it assert the authority to make the decision for all U.N. organs, including the Security Council? Could any argument based on the Charter be made to support such authority?

[a] See Liang, Recognition by the United Nations of the Representation of a Member State: Criteria and Procedure, 45 Am. J.Int'l L. 689, 705 (1951).

Of course, the People's Republic did take over China's permanent seat in the Security Council. Can that be reconciled with the express mention in U.N. Charter article 23 of the Republic of China as a permanent member of the Security Council?

Clearly, the General Assembly's decision could not dictate Chinese representation in the related organizations, since they are separate entities and nothing in their constituent instruments or in their relationship agreements with the U.N. requires them to accept General Assembly representation decisions. In practice, virtually all the related organizations considered the Chinese representation question shortly after the General Assembly's decision. Most of them decided right away to recognize the People's Republic; a few waited.[b] The organizations made their own decisions, but they took into account General Assembly Resolutions 396 (on representation generally) and 2758 (on Chinese representation).

In the Food and Agriculture Organization (FAO), the Chinese representation question had a twist that tested the role of procedural regularity once the U.N. General Assembly had started the ball rolling.

FOOD AND AGRICULTURE ORGANIZATION DECISION ON REPRESENTATION OF CHINA
11 Int'l Legal Materials 562 (1972).*

At its fifty-seventh session, the Council of FAO was informed of the resolution of the General Assembly of the United Nations concerning the representation of China.

The relevant extract from the report of the Council is as follows:

1. The Director–General drew the attention of the Council to resolution 2758(XXVI) of the General Assembly of the United Nations on the restoration of the lawful rights of the People's Republic of China in the United Nations, and informed the Council that in view of the fact that the Government of the Republic of China had withdrawn from the Organization in 1951, the question presented itself in FAO in a different way than in the other Agencies in which China was at present a member. Recalling similar approaches to other governments recommended by the Council in the past * * *, the Director–General sought the Council's guidance as to the question whether an approach should be made to ascertain whether the Government of the People's Republic of China would wish to seek membership in FAO. * * *

2. The Council *authorized* the Director–General to invite the People's Republic of China to seek formal membership in the Organization and, if it so requests, to attend the Sixteenth Session of the Conference. * * *

b. See 11 Int'l Legal Materials 561–70 (1972); 12 id. 1526–27 (1973); 20 id. 774–81 (1981).

* Reprinted by permission of the American Society of International Law.

The Council adopted this decision unanimously on November 2, 1971. On the same date, the Director-General sent a cable to the Prime Minister of the Government of the People's Republic of China conveying an invitation for the People's Republic of China to seek formal membership in the Organization, and also, if it so requested, to attend the Sixteenth Session of the Conference.

* * *

At the Sixteenth Session of the Conference, the Director-General informed the Conference that he had received a reply from the Acting Foreign Minister of the People's Republic of China. He noted that while "no reference was made in this cable to formal membership in FAO, there is reason to believe that China will be interested in resuming its place in the Organization and it may well be that a positive move will be made after the close of the Conference session". The Director-General added that he had been advised that it would be legally possible for the People's Republic of China to resume, without being formally readmitted, the seat of China if it wished, since the notice of withdrawal given in 1951 by the Government of the Republic of China emanated from a government whose right to represent the State of China had already at that time been formally contested. This notice of withdrawal would not be held against the Government of the People's Republic of China which had no part in it and which had now been recognized as being the legitimate representative of China. This Government had indeed not been in a position to exercise, since the time of its establishment in 1949, its membership rights in FAO and had been prevented from making its contribution to the achievement of the aims of the Organization. Even if the People's Republic had wished in the past to take its place in FAO, it may be assumed that it would not have been recognized as the legitimate representative of China in view of the position taken by the General Assembly of the United Nations. The Director-General added that under the present circumstances the Government of the People's Republic of China should not, in his personal view, be deprived of the possibility of availing itself of the rights deriving from the original membership in the Organization. As a consequence, it would be permissible for the People's Republic to resume its place in FAO without any special formality. * * * The Conference then adopted on November 25, 1971, and by 68 votes in favor, none against, and 3 abstentions, Resolution 33/71 entitled "People's Republic of China", which reads as follows:

THE CONFERENCE

Recalling that China, after having participated in the Hot Springs Conference in 1943, became a founding Member of FAO in 1945 by accepting the Constitution of the Organization,

Recalling further that, after its establishment in 1949, the Government of the People's Republic of China in a telegram to the Director-General of FAO dated 12 May 1950 affirmed that it was the only legal Government representing the Chinese people,

Considering Resolution 2758 (XXVI) of 25 October 1971, by which the General Assembly of the United Nations decided to restore all its rights to the People's Republic of China and to recognize the representatives of its Government as the only legitimate representatives of China in the United Nations and "in all the Organizations related to it",

Considering further that the General Assembly of the United Nations, in its Resolution 396(V) of 15 December 1950, recommended that the attitude adopted by the General Assembly concerning the representation of a Member State should be taken into account by the Specialized Agencies,

* * *

Pursuant to Resolution 2758(XXVI) of the General Assembly of the United Nations,

1. *Authorizes* the Director–General, when the People's Republic of China manifests the wish to resume its place in the Organization, to take all appropriate measures to bring into effect the resumption by China of its place in the Organization; * * *.

THE FAO TURNABOUT

What manner of legal sleight-of-hand permitted the Director–General to turn what was to be an application for readmission into a simple representation and resumption of participation issue? The FAO Constitution, *article XIX*, expressly contemplates withdrawal from the Organization, and the only "China" recognized at the time by FAO and the U.N. withdrew in 1951 pursuant to that provision. There is also a formal admission procedure in *article II*, requiring an affirmative vote of two-thirds of the Conference and a formal declaration by the applicant that it will accept the obligations of the Constitution. The Director–General would have known before the 16th Session of the Conference that a two-thirds vote could be mustered, if the People's Republic would only make an application. He undoubtedly had legal advice before he addressed the Conference. If you had been the Director–General's legal adviser, would you have advised him to take the position he did? (Should the legal adviser to an international organization give advice on such questions without taking account of the objective sought by most or all of the organization's members—in this case, participation by the People's Republic of China?)

SECTION 5. DECISION–MAKING PROCEDURES

A. THE SECURITY COUNCIL

1. *Russia as Successor to the Soviet Union's Veto Power*

Article 23 of the U.N. Charter says that "the Republic of China, France, the Union of Soviet Socialist Republics, the United Kingdom of

Great Britain and Northern Ireland, and the United States of America shall be permanent members of the Security Council." This means, of course, that they have the veto power. But two of these named permanent members are no longer members of the United Nations. In October 1971 the People's Republic of China replaced the Republic of China in the U.N., and in December 1991 the Soviet Union ceased to exist.

In the case of China, succession of the People's Republic to permanent Security Council membership was inevitable once the representatives of the Republic of China had been unseated. The government of the People's Republic had long since solidified its control over all of mainland China, with the former representatives in control only of Taiwan. But in the case of the former Soviet Union, there were 15 newly-independent republics occupying its territory. The Russian Federation was by far the largest of them geographically and economically. On December 21, 1991, the heads of state of 11 of them, acting as the Council of the newly-created Commonwealth of Independent States, decided that:

> The States of the Commonwealth support Russia's continuance of the membership of the Union of Soviet Socialist Republics in the United Nations, including permanent membership of the Security Council, and other international organizations.[a]

On December 24, 1991, Boris Yeltsin, the President of the Russian Federation, wrote a letter to the U.N. Secretary–General informing him that "the membership of the [USSR] in the United Nations, including the Security Council and all other organs and organizations of the United Nations system, is being continued by the Russian Federation * * *. The Russian Federation maintains full responsibility for all the rights and obligations of the USSR under the Charter of the United Nations, including the financial obligations."[b] On December 27, 1991, the Russian flag replaced the Soviet flag in front of U.N. headquarters, without any formal action by the U.N. or its member states. From that point, Russia supplanted the Soviet Union as a permanent member of the Security Council.

Was this a proper procedure? In the absence of an amendment to the Charter, is a Russian negative vote on a substantive matter in the Security Council a veto? Consider the materials below.

The Vienna Convention on Succession of States in Respect of Treaties[c] was adopted in 1978. It still has not received the 15 ratifications needed for entry into force. One cannot say with confidence that

a. U.N. Doc. A/47/60 & S/23329, Annex V (1991).

b. Appendix to note verbale from the U.N. Secretariat to members' U.N. missions, Dec. 24, 1991.

c. U.N. Doc. A/CONF.80/31, 17 Int'l Legal Materials 1488 (1978).

its provisions reflect custom, but they do provide a starting point for analysis. Article 34(1)(a) says that when parts of a state separate to form one or more states, "any treaty in force at the date of the succession of States in respect of the entire territory of the predecessor State continues in force in respect of each successor State so formed * * *."

If this at first glance indicates that all of the new states within the former Soviet Union would automatically succeed to the Soviet Union's U.N. membership, including its permanent seat on the Security Council, it isn't so. Article 34(2)(b) contains a caveat if the application of the treaty to the successor state would be incompatible with the object and purpose of the treaty or would radically change the conditions for its operation. In addition, article 4(a) says that although the Vienna Convention applies to constituent instruments of international organizations, it is "without prejudice to the rules concerning acquisition of membership * * *." The International Law Commission's commentary on draft article 4 made clear the intent to leave membership issues to the rules of each organization, at least when the organization has a formal process of admission (as the U.N. does).[d]

There is some arguably-relevant U.N. practice, stemming from the separation of Pakistan from India in 1947.

WHITEMAN, DIGEST OF INTERNATIONAL LAW
Vol. 13, at 201–02 (1968).

The Indian Independence Act (10 & 11 Geo. 6, c. 30), which provided that the "Independent Dominions" of India and Pakistan should be "set up in India" on August 15, 1947, led to a memorandum by the United Nations Secretariat which stated, *inter alia:*

> "1. From the viewpoint of international law, the situation is one in which a part of an existing State breaks off and becomes a new State. On this analysis, there is no change in the international status of India; it continues as a State with all the treaty rights and obligations, and consequently, with all the rights and obligations of membership in the United Nations. The territory which breaks off, Pakistan, will be a new State; it will not have the treaty rights and obligations of the old State, and it will not, of course, have membership in the United Nations."[e]

* * *

When the Representative of Argentina (Arce) stated in the First Committee of the General Assembly on September 24, 1947, that "the Secretariat had made a decision which could only be taken by the General Assembly" and that the "decision" of the Secretariat "consti-

---

d. 3 U.N. Conference on Succession of States in Respect of Treaties, OR, U.N. Doc. A/CONF.80/16/Add. 2, at 8–9 (1979).

e. [U.N. Doc. A/CN.4/149 and Add. 1, 1962 [II] Y.B. Int'l L. Comm'n 101.]

tuted an unfounded discrimination, since both Dominions should have been regarded as original Members, or alternatively, both should have been considered new Members", the First Committee decided to refer to the Sixth (Legal) Committee the legal problem raised by Argentina and agreed "that any view of the Sixth Committee was for use in future cases and had no application in the present case".[f]

* * *

In the Sixth Committee, though there was objection to laying down "in advance rules for hypothetical cases", the Committee approved the following reply to the First Committee, October 7, 1947:

"1. As a general rule, it is in accordance with principle to assume that a State which is a Member of the United Nations does not cease to be a Member from the mere fact that its constitution or frontiers have been modified, and to consider the rights and obligations which that State possesses as a Member of the United Nations as ceasing to exist only with its extinction as a legal person internationally recognized as such.

"2. When a new State is created, whatever the territory and the population which compose it, and whether these have or have not been part of a State Member of the United Nations, this new State cannot, under the system provided for by the Charter, claim the status of Member of the United Nations unless it has been formally admitted as such in conformity with the provisions of the Charter.

"3. Each case must, however, be judged on its merits."[g]

INDIA/RUSSIA

Is the Indian case a precedent for Russia's continuation of Soviet U.N. membership? For Russia's succession to the Soviet permanent seat on the Security Council?

If the Sixth Committee's reply in 1947 is taken as authoritative, does it support or weaken the Russian claim to permanent Security Council membership in 1991?

Why do you suppose there was no fuss in the U.N. about the Russian claim?

2. *Procedural Issues*

Voting in the Security Council is governed by *article 27* of the Charter. Its most striking feature, of course, is the grant of veto power to the five permanent members. As one would expect, problems of

---

[f.] [2 GAOR 1st Comm., 59th mtg., at 5; *id.*, 6th Comm., at 304–05.]   [g.] [2 GAOR, 6th Comm., at 38, 40, 44.]

interpretation involving article 27 have centered on the authority of the permanent members. There have been three major issues:

(1) Under article 27(2), procedural matters are not subject to the veto. But what if there is a controversy over whether a particular matter is procedural or substantive? If a permanent member could veto a ruling or resolution stating that the matter is procedural, there would be a double veto—first a veto to prevent a matter from being treated as procedural, and then a veto on the merits.

The "San Francisco Statement" of four of the permanent members (the U.S., U.K., Soviet Union and Republic of China), which is part of the preparatory work for the Charter, tends to support the double veto except for a few enumerated matters that would unquestionably be procedural.[a] On three occasions in early Security Council practice, such a double veto was exercised. In 1949 the General Assembly intervened in G.A. Resolution 267 (III), setting forth a list of categories it regarded as procedural. On the few occasions thereafter when questions within those categories have arisen in the Security Council and a permanent member has attempted to prevent them from being considered procedural, the Security Council has disregarded the attempted veto.

(2) From time to time, some members have questioned whether Security Council decisions on substantive matters could be made if any permanent member abstained from voting. Note that article 27(3) calls for "the concurring votes of the permanent members," with a proviso that seems to distinguish abstention from a "concurring vote." The proviso might be thought to set forth a narrow, exclusive class of cases in which the abstention of a permanent member would not preclude a substantive decision. There is some preparatory work to support that interpretation.[b]

The Security Council has nevertheless consistently adopted substantive resolutions on a wide variety of matters (not limited to those mentioned in the article 27(3) proviso) despite permanent member abstention, and those resolutions have been accepted as valid within the Organization. Would you consider the Security Council's practice in this regard to have any legal significance?[c]

In November 1975, the Legal Adviser of the U.S. Department of State characterized this practice as "a positive contribution to the work of the Council, and hence to members of the United Nations in general, and as an excellent example of how the language of the charter permits important evolutionary changes without requiring textual changes."[d]

a. See United Nations Conference on International Organization 751–54 (Selected Documents, 1946).

b. See Report to the President on the Results of the San Francisco Conference 71–77 (Dep't State Conf. Series No. 71, 1945) (concerning the "Yalta formula" that became article 27(3)); see also [1945] 1 Foreign Relations of the United States 1258–60.

c. See the ICJ Advisory Opinion on Namibia, at page 492 infra.

d. 74 Dep't State Bull. 118, 119 (1976).

What criteria could be used to determine whether, or to what extent, evolutionary change of any given provision without Charter revision is permissible? Would the latitude for evolutionary change be different for provisions setting forth substantive standards (such as *article 4(1)*) than for purely procedural rules such as the "concurring vote" rule in article 27(3)?

(3) Article 27(3) says that in decisions under Chapter VI of the Charter, "a party to a dispute shall abstain from voting." The principle, of course, is that a state should not be both judge and party in its own cause.[e] Chapter VI, though, refers not only to "disputes," but to "any situation which might lead to international friction or give rise to a dispute." See *article 34*. Consequently it is arguable that there is a juridical distinction between a "dispute" and a "situation" under Chapter VI, and that an interested Security Council member must abstain from voting only if the case at hand is a "dispute" and that member is a party to it. Although the preparatory work for the Charter suggests that no such fine distinction was intended for article 27(3), the distinction has been observed in practice.[f]

The World Court has had some occasions to consider whether a matter is a "dispute" within the meaning of a compromissory or arbitration clause in an international agreement. In the Mavrommatis Palestine Concessions Case,[g] involving a compromissory clause in a League of Nations mandate, the Court said that a dispute is "a disagreement on a point of law or fact, a conflict of legal views or of interests between two persons."

In the Interpretation of Peace Treaties Case,[h] an advisory opinion interpreting arbitration clauses in World War II peace treaties with Bulgaria, Hungary and Romania, the Court said:

> Whether there exists an international dispute is a matter for objective determination. The mere denial of the existence of a dispute does not prove its non-existence. In the diplomatic correspondence submitted to the Court, the United Kingdom [and four other states] charged Bulgaria, Hungary and Romania with having violated, in various ways, the provisions of the articles dealing with human rights and fundamental freedoms in the Peace Treaties and called upon the three Governments to take remedial measures to carry out their obligations under the Treaties. The three Governments, on the other hand, denied the charges. There has thus arisen a situation in which the two sides hold clearly opposite views concerning the question of the performance or non-performance of certain treaty obligations. Confronted with such a situation, the Court must conclude that international disputes have arisen.

e. See U.N. Doc. A/AC.18/SC.3/4, at 2 (1948).

f. Se the ICJ Advisory Opinion on Namibia, at page 493 infra. On the negotiating history, see Liang, The Settlement of Disputes in the Security Council: The Yalta Voting Formula, 24 Brit.Y.B. Int'l L. 330, 349–50 (1947).

g. PCIJ, Ser. A, No. 2, at 11.

h. [1950] I.C.J. 65, 74.

Consider below whether these judicial definitions are, or should be, relevant in the context of article 27(3).

Attempts during the early years of Security Council practice to define just what was an article 27(3) "dispute" were inconclusive. As a result it is difficult to trace a consistent pattern of voting or abstention on matters in which Security Council members have been interested. On a number of occasions interested members have abstained.[i] But not always.

One instance of early Security Council practice does supply a possible test more closely tailored to article 27(3) than are the World Court definitions of "dispute." In 1951 the Security Council considered restrictions imposed by Egypt on the passage through the Suez Canal of ships bound for Israel.

REPERTOIRE OF THE PRACTICE OF THE SECURITY COUNCIL 1946–1951
U.N.Doc. ST/PSCA/1, at 170 (1954).

* * *

The representative of Egypt contended that the representatives of France, the Netherlands, Turkey, the United Kingdom and the United States, having submitted protests to the Egyptian Government on this matter, ought to abstain from voting in accordance with Article 27(3) on the joint draft resolution submitted by the representatives of France, the United Kingdom and the United States, to find the Egyptian restrictions "inconsistent with the objectives of a peaceful settlement".

The representative of Egypt recalled the definition of "dispute" and the interpretations of the proviso of Article 27(3) considered by the Interim Committee of the General Assembly, and stated:

"This fundamental and Charterwise principle—namely, that no State shall be judge and party—should apply and command our respect in all cases, whether there are two or more parties to a question. Furthermore, the Council cannot rightly subscribe to any attempt to defeat the *raison d'être* of this principle by claiming that it would at times impede the Council from discharging its duties * * *.

* * *

"We believe that an elementary principle of justice requires that a party to a dispute should not be a judge of it, and that it is this great principle which inspired the provision in Article 27 of the Charter that a party to a dispute should abstain from voting."

Speaking on behalf of the delegations of France, the Netherlands, Turkey, the United Kingdom and the United States, the representative

---

i. See L. Goodrich, E. Hambro & A. Simons, Charter of the United Nations: Commentary and Documents 229–30 (3d ed. 1969).

of the United Kingdom maintained that even under the definitions of "dispute" cited by the representative of Egypt, a dispute existed under the Charter only when a State brought a complaint to the Security Council against another State and the State against which the complaint had been made rejected it. Although more than two States could be involved in those circumstances, only Egypt and Israel were parties to the dispute before the Council. He further rejected the analogy between the Security Council and a court of law as implied in the reference to "judge and party". The representative of the United Kingdom added:

> "It is almost inevitable that in many, if not all, questions which come before the Council, a number of States members of the Council will be concerned to a greater or less degree, even though they may not be parties to the dispute with which the Council is dealing. In itself, this is certainly no reason why they should be debarred from voting."

* * *

At the 558th meeting on 1 September 1951, the representatives of France, the Netherlands, Turkey, the United Kingdom and the United States were among those who voted in favour of the joint draft resolution.

DISPUTES OR SITUATIONS?

Does the test suggested by the representative of the United Kingdom make sense? Was it properly applied in the case at hand?

Consider whether the test suggested by the U.K. representative (on behalf of France, among others) would resolve the question whether or not France should have abstained from voting in the Comoro Islands matter, below.

The Comoro Islands lie off the east coast of Africa, forming an archipelago at the northern entrance to the Mozambique Channel. There are four islands, one of which is Mayotte. The population of Mayotte is overwhelmingly Christian. On the other three islands, it is overwhelmingly Islamic. All four islands formerly comprised a single overseas territory of France. On December 22, 1974, a plebiscite was held in which about 94 percent of the population of the Comoros indicated their desire for independence, but about two-thirds of those on Mayotte voted to remain a French overseas territory. On July 5, 1975, the Comoros declared their independence from France. France did not attempt to use force to prevent Comorian independence. However, it did continue to maintain an official presence on Mayotte, including about 240 military personnel.

On October 17, 1975, the Security Council, with France not participating in the vote, recommended admission of a single Comorian state to the United Nations. It was admitted by the General Assembly on November 12. Nevertheless, the French Parliament continued to have reservations about the status of Mayotte. It scheduled a new referendum for that island to be held on February 8, 1976, to determine specifically whether the people there wished to remain with France or to be part of the new Comorian state. Under the French Constitution, this was a Parliamentary prerogative.

On January 28, 1976, the Head of the Comorian state sent a telegram to the President of the Security Council that began, "Flouting international law and morality, the French Government intends to organize a referendum in Mayotte on 8 February 1976." It went on to refer to the unity of the four Comoro Islands, characterized the proposed referendum as "flagrant aggression," and requested an urgent meeting of the Security Council.[j] The meeting was convened, and on February 5 the representatives of Benin, Guyana, Libya, Panama and Tanzania introduced a draft Security Council resolution that would have characterized the impending referendum as "an interference in the internal affairs of the Comoros," and would have called upon France "to desist from proceeding with the holding of the referendum in Mayotte * * *."[k] Much of the ensuing debate, in which the French representative found himself virtually alone, centered on the principle of self-determination. Representatives of African nations and others argued that the right of self-determination had been exercised and exhausted when the Comoros declared their independence from France, but the French representative countered by saying that "the primary question is implementing the will of the people and the right to self-determination of the inhabitants of the island [of Mayotte]. In other words, if the inhabitants are to be given the means to exercise self-determination, particular desires which they want no part of cannot be imposed on them. If we say that unity cannot be imposed, that is stating the answer of France to the problem of Mayotte."[l]

France vetoed the draft resolution on a vote of 11 in favor to 1 against (France), with 3 abstentions (Italy, U.K., U.S.). After the vote the following colloquy occurred.

SECURITY COUNCIL DEBATE
Feb. 6, 1976.
U.N.Doc. S/PV.1888, at 28–31.

Mr. PAQUI (*Benin*) (*interpretation from French*):

* * *

[M]y delegation wonders whether, in this particular case, France, as a party to the dispute, was entitled to participate in the vote. This is a situation which deserves to be carefully weighed because, in fact, on

j. See U.N. Doc. S/11953 (1976).
k. U.N. Doc. S/11967 (1976).
l. U.N. Doc. S/PV.1887, at 12 (1976).

the one hand we have here a State which is not a member of the Council and, on the other hand, we have a State which is a member of the Council and, furthermore, a permanent member enjoying the right of veto. This is a rather disquieting fact, which cannot but be stressed.

* * *

Mr. KIKHIA (*Libyan Arab Republic*):

* * *

My delegation would like to register its strong doubts as well as its most explicit reservations in connexion with the result of the voting of the Council on draft resolution S/11967. I do not want at this late hour to raise any problems or provoke any discussions of a juridical or procedural nature. However, my delegation would like to place on record, as our colleague from Benin has also done, that in our humble view, in accordance with Article 27, paragraph 3, of the Charter, if our understanding and interpretation of that Article is correct, France is not entitled to cast a positive or negative vote since France is a party to the dispute under discussion * * *.

* * *

Mr. de GUIRINGAUD (*France*) (*interpretation from French*):

I am surprised at the comment made by the representative of the Libyan Arab Republic, and equally I must say by what was said by the representative of Benin in somewhat vaguer terms. I am particularly surprised since the draft resolution we have just voted on has the delegation of Panama among its sponsors. Now, the representative of Panama, my good friend and colleague Mr. Boyd, yesterday drew a very eloquent comparison between the problem which at present subsists between France and the Comoros and the problem which on another occasion in the Council arose between Panama and another permanent member of the Council.

The representative of the Libyan Arab Republic was not with us in Panama in March 1973; the representative of Benin was not there either. But those who were with us there in Panama in March 1973 will recall that, in a matter which brought Panama into direct conflict with the United States, no one found it exceptional that Panama, which held the presidency, should have voted and that the United States also voted and exercised its right of veto.

* * *

And I think I should remind you that for 25 years now the Council has always felt that situations of the sort on which we had to take a decision today should not prevent States members of the Council or States directly or indirectly concerned in the matter from casting their vote as they would undoubtedly exercise their vote if this matter was considered in the context of Chapter VII of the Charter. To act in any other way would be tantamount to encouraging these States members of the Council to take measures of force as provided for in Article 39 to ensure that their right to vote was not challenged. I hardly need to stress the degree of absurdity we would reach if we were to apply that interpretation.

I shall not expatiate on this, but if the Council needed I could give a rather impressive list of precedents where delegations seated around this table, and others that were members of the Council at the time and are not today, in cases completely analogous and similar to the one with which we have had to deal with today, did not hesitate to use their right of veto, and cases where this right has never been challenged by anyone.

Mr. PAQUI (*Benin*) (*interpretation from French*):

I want to make one thing perfectly clear. When I put the question to the Council, I said that we were sorry; in other words, we had already noted this veto which had been cast. We are not challenging this veto. We simply raised a question so that members of the Council could give some thought to a particular category of cases in the future.

* * *

Mr. BOYD (*Panama*) (*interpretation from Spanish*):

* * *

I must make it clear that I am beginning to have some misgivings about what the representatives of Benin and the Libyan Arab Republic said just now. I am also wondering in my turn whether in this case the representative of France was in fact entitled to resort to his right of veto as a permanent member of the Security Council. Let us be quite clear. When the Council visited Panama, it did so to hold a series of special meetings in order to consider matters relating to the maintenance and the strengthening of peace in Latin America. In contrast to the particular case we are now considering, the Council did not visit Panama to consider a dispute. In Panama no representative claimed that the United States was not entitled to cast a veto. And so I do not think we can conclude from this that there is a precedent which can be resorted to by the representative of France under the pretext that this is a similar situation.

* * *

I believe that today we have been considering a matter relating to the peaceful settlement of disputes, and I really wonder whether the representative of France in this case was entitled to use his veto. In the case where the Security Council visited Panama, the Council essentially was dealing with a situation which affected the entire region and the Council, furthermore, adopted a number of resolutions. Hence, Panama was bringing no complaint before the Security Council; it did not level any accusations against the United States and the Council was not in fact dealing with a dispute between Panama and the United

States. The Security Council was dealing with matters relating to the strengthening of peace in Latin America.

* * *

Mr. de GUIRINGAUD (*France*) (*interpretation from French*):

Since my friend Ambassador Boyd of Panama is speaking for the record, so shall I. And I shall remind him that when on 21 March 1973 we voted in Panama we did not vote on the whole question of Latin America and the problems pertaining thereto. We voted on a very precise situation. I have the resolution before me. In one of the preambular paragraphs, the Council says explicitly:

> *Recalling* that it is a purpose of the United Nations to bring about, in conformity with the principles of justice and international law, adjustment or settlement of international disputes or situations which might lead to a breach of the peace.

In paragraph 3, the Council urged

> * * * the Governments of the United States of America and the Republic of Panama * * * to conclude without delay a new treaty aimed at the prompt elimination of the causes of conflict between them.

That was a very precise situation on which we took a vote.

* * *

Mr. BOYD (*Panama*) (*interpretation from Spanish*):

To conclude this debate, I should like to say to our friend the representative of France that at the meetings of the Security Council held in Panama in March 1973 at no time did any member of the Council request the President to take a stand on this point in Article 27.

* * *

Mr. de GUIRINGAUD (*France*) (*interpretation from French*):

I do not think it is necessary to pursue this debate endlessly. I simply wish to state in friendly terms, to my friend the Permanent Representative of Panama, that if no one raised this question in Panama, it was because there is an impressive list of precedents which entirely bears out the procedure that was followed today. It is not my intention now to go into those precedents, but if some day this discussion needs to be resumed, those precedents can be found. I think that those precedents will demonstrate that the representative of Panama was quite entitled to vote in Panama, as I was myself perfectly entitled to cast a vote today.

Mr. BOYD (*Panama*) (*interpretation from Spanish*):

I shall not reply at length to the representative of France since he was not able to refute my last argument regarding the occasion when the Council met in Panama, when no one complained or expressed any doubt as to the validity of the veto of the United States of America. He has now stated that he has a long list of precedents supporting his views. I shall tell him that this afternoon, one of the most distinguished and eminent jurists of the United Nations told me that there are also precedents to the contrary; and to mention a specific one, that of Argentina when it did not participate in the voting in the Eichmann case.

* * *

The PRESIDENT (*Mr. Moynihan, U.S.A.*):

In view of the fact that this issue has been raised, and obviously in no way establishing a precedent by this statement, I think the Council would wish to know that it had entered the mind of the President before the vote that there might indeed be a challenge to the right of France to vote. Accordingly, the Secretariat was consulted and a position was developed. The position of the Secretariat is contained in the *Repertoire of Practice of the Security Council* and was made available to the President; obviously, it is available to any member of the Council who might wish to see it, in view of the thoughtful remarks of the representative of Panama.

It is perhaps sufficient for me simply to say that, had the question of the right of France to vote been raised in a timely way, which is to say before the vote, the President of the Council believes that the right of France to participate in the voting would have been sustained.

Mr. KIKHIA (*Libyan Arab Republic*) (*interpretation from French*):

As I said, my colleagues from Benin and Panama and I myself registered our reservations, our doubts, on this question. We did not ask for a statement or a ruling by the President. In any case, it is not a question of discussing this problem here in the Council. We simply wished to register our reservations. This is a question of principle, and that is all. That is why we do not think that your last statement, Mr. President, is a ruling on the problem.

The PRESIDENT:

May I assure the representative of the Libyan Arab Republic that he is, of course, completely correct. It was not a ruling. It was a point of information that I felt the Council members might wish, if they wanted to know in what way the Secretariat advises the presidency in this matter as of this day. Presumably, there is some permanence in those views, but not necessarily, as those of us who have followed the law have learned.

THE FRENCH RIGHT TO VOTE

Although the statement of the President of the Security Council suggested that the U.N. Secretariat had prepared a legal opinion supporting the right of France to vote, all that the Secretariat had actually prepared was a compilation of previous Security Council practice involving the right to vote under article 27(3). As indicated earlier, it is difficult to find a consistent pattern from that practice. Did the very lack of consistent practice support Mr. Moynihan's "non-ruling" to the effect that France was entitled to vote?

Note that Messrs. Boyd and de Guiringaud did attach considerable importance to one precedent—that of the votes by Panama and the United States in 1973 on a resolution involving negotiation of a new Panama Canal treaty. Was the point being made by Mr. Boyd that (a) it was not a "dispute" under article 27(3) because that resolution was simply part of a broader examination of issues involving Latin America, or (b) a claim that a matter is a "dispute" may be waived by lack of any objection to voting by the parties, or (c) something else? How would you characterize the 1973 precedent? [m]

When the President of the Security Council responded to the telegram from the Head of the Comorian state requesting the urgent Security Council meeting, he said that such a meeting had been called and that "The Government of the Comoros, as a party to the dispute under consideration, may, in accordance with the usual practice, wish to send a representative to participate in the meeting without the right to vote." [n] That sounds as though he was referring to the right conferred by *article 32* of the Charter, though presumably the same invitation could have been issued under *article 31*. In any event, if the matter was a "dispute" when the President replied to the Comorian request for a meeting, how could it have been otherwise when France voted?

Was the French position in the Comoro Islands matter consistent with the French position in the 1951 Suez Canal matter? Was it consistent with the Egyptian position in the Suez Canal matter?

Is any test for resolving the dispute/situation dichotomy in the Security Council workable?

At one point in the Comoro Islands debate, Mr. de Guiringaud said that to prevent member states concerned in the matter from voting as they would if it had come up under Chapter VII of the Charter "would be tantamount to encouraging these States members of the Council to take measures of force as provided for in Article 39 to ensure that their right to vote was not challenged." Indeed, article 27(3) does not require abstention in matters arising under Chapter VII, and Security Council practice is consistent in cases involving the threat or use of armed

---

m. Members of the Security Council take precedent seriously. For example, in December 1989 China opposed any Security Council statement on the political upheaval in Romania, on the ground that it would violate U.N. Charter art. 2(7). The Chinese government apparently feared setting a precedent that could apply to its own treatment of political dissidents. See N.Y. Times, Dec. 27, 1989, p. A15, col. 6.

n. U.N. Doc. S/11964 (1976).

force. Directly involved states, including permanent members, have voted—even when challenged.[o] But in those cases a permanent Security Council member did not precipitate an armed conflict in order to preserve its veto. Should Mr. de Guiringaud's scenario be taken seriously?[p] Or was he just pointing out an anomaly in the Charter? If the latter, what, if anything, should be done about it?

3. A Short-Handed Security Council

Every year the General Assembly elects five states to serve two-year terms as non-permanent members of the Security Council. To be elected, a state must receive a majority of two-thirds of the General Assembly members present and voting.[a] Non-permanent members sit in the Security Council from January 1 of one year to December 31 of the next.

In the General Assembly election for Security Council seats to run from January 1, 1980, to December 31, 1981, Colombia and Cuba competed for the "Latin American seat." Repeated voting failed to produce a two-thirds majority for either of them by December 31, 1979, when the term of the previous holder ended. The issue thus arose whether the Security Council could validly conduct its business with only 14 members. Consider the U.N. Legal Counsel's opinion below, in light of U.N. Charter *articles 18, 23, 27 and 28*. The opinion is significant not only for resolution of the narrow issue presented, but as an illustration of pragmatic lawyering in the interpretation of international organizations' constituent instruments.

OPINION OF U.N. LEGAL COUNSEL ON THE INABILITY OF THE GENERAL ASSEMBLY TO ELECT A NON-PERMANENT MEMBER OF THE SECURITY COUNCIL

Dec. 31, 1979.

1979 U.N. Juridical Y.B. 164.

* * *

Article 23 of the Charter provides, *inter alia*, that:

---

o. Thus, when Argentina invaded the British-administered Falkland (Malvinas) Islands in 1982, the United Kingdom voted on its own draft Security Council resolution despite a challenge by the representative of Panama. The British representative said that the resolution arose under article 40 of the Charter, though the resolution did not explicitly identify the applicable article. See U.N. Doc. S/PV.2350, at 81–85 (1982); S.C.Res. 502 (1982).

p. As already noted, France did not use force in the Comoro Islands matter. The referendum was held as scheduled. Approximately 99.4 percent of the Mayotte voters elected to remain a part of France. 13 U.N.Chron., No. 3, at 5 (Mar. 1976). As of late 1991, the differences between the Comoros and France over Mayotte still had not been resolved. See G.A.Res. 46/9 (1991).

a. See U.N. Charter *art. 18(2)*.

"The General Assembly shall elect 10 other Members of the United Nations to be non-permanent members of the Security Council * * *".

* * *

In addition, rule 94 [of the rules of procedure of the General Assembly] contains detailed provisions on the conduct of the elections which leave no doubt as to the absolute nature of the obligation of the Assembly, since the balloting must continue until a result is achieved—that is, " * * * and so on until all the places have been filled."

* * *

The failure of the General Assembly to elect a non-permanent member would constitute a failure to comply with its constitutional functions and would violate the clear language of Article 23 of the Charter, the mandatory nature of which leads to the conclusion that a Security Council of less than 15 members would not be legally constituted in accordance with the Charter.

We now turn to the consideration of the consequences of such a failure of the General Assembly for the constitution and functioning of the Security Council. The question arises whether there are circumstances in which the Security Council may continue to function notwithstanding the fact that temporarily it may not be legally constituted in membership. The first such situation, which has never in fact occurred, is that foreseen in rule 140 of the rules of procedure of the General Assembly. It states:

"Should a member cease to belong to a Council before its term of office expires, a by-election shall be held separately at the next session of the General Assembly to elect a member for the unexpired term."

That rule applies also to the Security Council. However, the fact that that rule is part of the rules of procedure of the General Assembly indicates, first and foremost, the obligation of the General Assembly to hold a by-election. But the implication of that rule is that it may occur that between the cessation of membership in the Council and the time of the by-election in the General Assembly the Security Council does not consist of the number of members prescribed by Article 23 of the Charter. A membership short of the prescribed number would not, therefore, affect the functioning of the Security Council in this situation. * * *

A further situation in which the Security Council membership might no longer be in accordance with the constitutional requirements of the Charter would be during the period of time between the entry into force of a Charter amendment increasing the membership and the actual election of the new members. This very exceptional situation arose in connexion with the Charter amendments adopted by the General Assembly in 1963. The amendment increasing the membership of the Security Council was adopted by the General Assembly on 17 December 1963 and came into force on 31 August 1965. The Legal Counsel's opinion was sought on the legal position of the Security Council during the interim period between the entry into force of the amendment and the election of new members. The Legal Counsel was confronted with the alternatives presented by Articles 23 and 28 of the Charter respectively. In his opinion, he argued that, where the two alternatives are both possible, the

> "interpretation to be adopted is the one most consonant with the terms and purposes of the instruments as a whole. An interpretation tending to so extreme a consequence as a break in the functioning [of the Security Council] could not be accepted without clear support in the text itself * * *".

That legal opinion can be found in the *United Nations Juridical Yearbook, 1965,* on pages 224 and 225.

Therefore, notwithstanding the entry into force of the new Article 23 expanding the membership of the Council from 11 to 15, the Council continued to function under the previous regime until the election of the additional members.

A third situation in which the Security Council could be faced with a discrepancy between the prescribed membership and the actual membership could arise because of the inability of the General Assembly to reach agreement on an election. This situation, which we face today, may be distinguished from the two previous situations in which the temporary shortfall in membership was beyond the control of the Assembly although the Assembly has the ultimate obligation to fill the vacancy.

* * *

As indicated, Article 23 of the Charter provides that the Security Council "shall consist" of 15 Members of the United Nations. It is clear, therefore, that a legally constituted Security Council must have 15 members. However, Article 23 must be read in the context of the Charter as a whole, taking into particular consideration its object and purpose. The object and purpose of a treaty are of particular importance in the interpretation of treaties establishing international organizations because constitutions, such as the Charter, as distinct from mere contracts, are designed to give effect to certain purposes and principles in a moving political context.

In this broader perspective, it must be recognized that the Members of the United Nations have conferred on the Security Council "primary responsibility for the maintenance of international peace and security" (Article 24), which is one of the purposes of the Organization (Article 1, paragraph 1), and that the Security Council "shall be so organized as to be able to function continuously" (Article 28).

Thus, at the very least, the compositional requirement of Article 23 must be balanced against the requirements of other provisions of the

Charter concerning the functioning of the Council in so far as the non-compliance with the requirement of Article 23 does not run counter to the provisions of Article 27, which may be considered as an implied quorum provision.

Accordingly, an act of omission or the failure of the General Assembly to fulfil its constitutional obligations cannot be held to produce legal consequences so fundamental to the Organization as the paralysis of a principal organ. To argue otherwise would be to effect a constitutional amendment of the Charter through extra-constitutional means. Such a paralysis could have the gravest consequence for the whole system of the preservation of international peace and security, including a potential shift of well-established powers between the Security Council and the General Assembly.

The foregoing suggests that in theory and in practice the Security Council may continue to function notwithstanding the fact that it is not legally constituted.

In conclusion, while the failure of the General Assembly to elect a non-permanent member of the Security Council would be inconsistent with Article 23 of the Charter, such an act of omission could not produce legal consequences for the functioning of the Security Council, which is the organ primarily responsible for the maintenance of international peace and security. In such a situation, it would be the view of the Office of Legal Affairs that decisions of the Security Council taken in accordance with the relevant provisions of Article 27 of the Charter would constitute valid decisions.

AVOIDING SECURITY COUNCIL PARALYSIS

After 154 inconclusive General Assembly votes, and after the Soviet intervention in Afghanistan eroded Cuba's support, Cuba withdrew its candidacy. The Latin American states then endorsed a compromise candidate, Mexico, and on the 155th ballot (January 7, 1980) Mexico received the requisite two-thirds majority.[b]

Do you agree with the Legal Counsel's reasoning and conclusion?

What did he mean when he said that to conclude otherwise would produce a paralysis involving "a potential shift of well-established powers between the Security Council and the General Assembly"?

What if the impasse in the General Assembly had continued? Could the Security Council go on indefinitely with 14 members?

Should rule 140 of the General Assembly rules of procedure have been applied when the Soviet Union ceased to exist?

b. See N.Y. Times, Jan. 7, 1980, p. A2, col. 3; 17 U.N.Chron., No. 2, at 27 (1980).

4. *Future Composition and Structure*

With the end of the cold war, it became politically possible for the first time in many years to discuss openly, in the U.N., the possibility of changing the composition and structure of the Security Council. Some ideas were put forward at the General Assembly's 46th Session, in 1991.

GENERAL ASSEMBLY DEBATE ON SECURITY COUNCIL COMPOSITION AND STRUCTURE
Dec. 11, 1991.
U.N.Doc. A/46/PV.68, at 2–3, 6–8, 14–16, 22–23, 34–35, 38–40.

Mr. GHAREKHAN (*India*): Agenda item 38, entitled "Question of equitable representation on and increase in the membership of the Security Council", was first considered by the General Assembly at its thirty-fourth session—on 14 December 1979—at the initiative of [10 nonaligned states from Africa, Asia and Latin America]. Most of these countries, joined by [six others], submitted a draft resolution proposing an increase in the non-permanent membership of the Security Council from 10 to 14, along with some consequential changes. The proposal and the concept behind it were received with broad support across the Organization's membership. However, since an agreement on certain specifics could not be reached within the time available, and because the sponsors were keen to secure the widest possible support and avoid any sense of confrontation, they agreed to postpone the consideration of the item.

At the thirty-fifth session of the General Assembly, after further consultations the proposal was modified and submitted in the form of a new draft resolution calling for an increase in the Security Council membership to a total of 21 by adding six non-permanent seats. The draft resolution was sponsored by [20 states]. In addition, the draft resolution had the endorsement of the African Group as a whole. Again, for reasons similar to those in the past, the sponsors agreed to defer the consideration of their proposal.

The rationale behind the initiative, succinctly put in the explanatory memorandum accompanying the initial request for the inscription of the item on the agenda, was simple: the increase in the United Nations membership was not being reflected in the membership of the Security Council. Furthermore, in order to strengthen the Security Council's primary role in the maintenance of international peace and security, it was felt that the Council's composition should be reviewed with a view to providing for more balanced representation. The proposal as presented was a modest one, designed to strengthen the Council by making it more responsive and relevant to existing realities. This rationale and the reasons for the proposal as outlined 12 years ago are, I submit, all the more valid today.

* * *

In 1946 the United Nations had 51 Members, 11 of which were represented in the Security Council—a reasonably fair ratio. In 1963, the United Nations membership had grown to 113, and the feeling mounted that the Security Council did not retain the representative character it deserved. The result was the vote increasing the Council's membership to 15. The ratio of the Security Council membership to total United Nations membership at that time stood at 7.5, comparing * * * favourably with the figure of 4.6 in 1946. The comparison in fact suffered much more if one looked only at the ratio for the non-permanent category: it rose from 6.6 to 11.3. The position today is clearly even more unsatisfactory. With a membership of 166,[a] the Security Council has 11.1 United Nations Members represented in each of its seats. In such a context, can one argue that the Security Council, the principal organ for the maintenance of international peace and security, is representative enough to discharge its onerous responsibility in the expected transparent and democratic manner?

Rectification is possible in two ways. One of them is to readjust the present number of seats. This approach will, however, not address the main problem of overall under-representation of Members in the Security Council, besides generating its own difficulties. The only logical and politically acceptable method, therefore, is to expand the membership of the Security Council, keeping in mind the provisions of Article 23 of the Charter. My delegation does not intend to make a specific proposal at this stage. It would prefer to engage in urgent, wide-based and purposeful consultations in order to evolve an agreement on the figures and numbers involved, as well as on the exact methodology and its details. However, I would like to emphasize further here the urgency of this process. Momentous decisions affecting all of us are currently on the anvil of the major policy-making organs, and it is only appropriate that these are taken with a broader and more representative participation of the international community.

A main argument often advanced against an increase in the Security Council membership is that it would affect the Council's efficiency and effectiveness. My delegation is not convinced of this argument and cannot accept it. On the contrary, we believe that a more representative Council will prove more efficient and effective in that its decisions will have that much more weight behind them. Let us not be unmindful of the fact that during the long years of East–West confrontation the Security Council, despite its limited size, often remained paralysed. The Council has been capable or incapable of discharging its functions not because of its size but because of the imperatives of international life. Expansion of the Council is also discouraged on logistical or management grounds. But citing reasons of logistics and management in matters of international peace and security is difficult to accept, especially in the present era where more democratic and transparent conduct of international relations is being stressed. At any rate, we

a. [The membership has since increased even more. Ed.]

cannot allow management fears to block reforms that would go a long way to strengthen the Council.

* * *

Mr. ARRIA (*Venezuela*) (*interpretation from Spanish*): * * * I should like to address the subject of equitable representation in the membership of the Council together with the inseparable subject of the veto power of the permanent members of the Council. We believe that an increase in the membership of the Council, without the elimination of the anachronistic veto power, would not only be senseless but certainly would not be equitable.

* * *

I want to put into historical perspective the conflicting views that have been presented in connection with [the veto power]. From the very beginning—in San Francisco—the principle of the veto power was questioned. Its first severe critic was Mr. Herbert Evatt, the then representative of Australia, who called it an absurd imposition on the international community. Venezuela is on record as having made a similar statement. In San Francisco our then Minister of Foreign Affairs, Caracciolo Parra Perez presented our position by saying that it was his hope that this formula would, with the passage of time, evolve into a more democratic and representative system that could involve all nations.

In 1947 the then representative of Venezuela, Carlos Eduardo Stolk, said in the General Assembly:

> "The much debated question of revising the United Nations Charter in order to abolish or limit the veto power, is once again under discussion. Our country supports with unshakable determination the principle of the sovereign equality of all nations, which is not compatible with the privilege granted to the permanent members of the Security Council under Article 27 of the Charter. We recognize that the application of this Article has * * * impaired its authority and the prestige of the Organization". (*Official Records, second session, p. 73.*)

* * *

Mr. TRAXLER (*Italy*): * * *

As my Foreign Minister stated on 27 September, Italy feels that the time has come to adjust the structure of the Security Council. In fact, the new international reality underlines the need to involve in our collective responsibility countries that have hitherto played a role not commensurate with their importance and that are now acquiring new political and economic dimensions together with an awareness of their growing responsibilities.

Italy is in favour of an expansion of the Security Council with an increase in the number of both permanent and non-permanent members, which would not necessarily entail extending the right of veto to all the new permanent members. We feel that the selection of the latter should be made on the basis of such objective criteria as the size of the country's population, its gross national product and its contribution to the United Nations budget.

The Security Council was first expanded in 1963 to take account of the increase in the number of Member States. Since then, the United Nations membership has risen from 113 to 166, an increase of almost 50 per cent. This factor is in itself sufficient to warrant an expansion of this decision-making body of the Organization. Since it is required to make choices of major importance, the Security Council should fully reflect the evolution of the world community.

At the end of the Second World War it appeared logical that the preservation of what was then a new order should be primarily entrusted to the countries that were recognized as its major pillars. Subsequently, in an essentially bipolar situation, those same countries became the major proponents of the two conflicting ideologies that dominated the world. This situation has changed. Many countries and peoples are now painfully redefining their goals and aspirations, thereby often engendering conflicts with the goals and aspirations of their neighbours. Such hitherto unlimited commodities as air and water are now perceived as finite. Mankind's unchecked multiplication seems to lead to its own destruction.

In these circumstances the search for peace where it does not exist or its maintenance where it does requires even more intricate processes of crisis management. The same logic that identified a limited number of countries as founders and guardians of a certain order would now call for the attribution of a similar role to those few other countries that will be called upon to exercise the greater efforts and bear the major costs, social as well as economic, for the establishment and maintenance of a new order.

* * *

Mr. SARDENBERG (*Brazil*): * * * Arguments have been raised in the past to the effect that any increase in the Council's composition would endanger the efficiency of that principal organ of the United Nations. Nothing could be more foreign to our intent: we envisage a more balanced and representative composition for the Security Council, one that would further contribute to its effectiveness and responsiveness. Using simple reasoning, one could say that a one-member Council would be the most efficient, but it would certainly be the least democratic. One might also say that the most democratic Council would comprise the entire membership, but it would most probably be the least efficient. Somewhere between those two extremes, a sound and satisfactory solution should be found, by the usual diplomatic means.

Mr. GAMBARI (*Nigeria*): * * * It is true that the Council was expanded in 1963 from nine to 15 members, but its structure does not accord with present-day reality. The regional groups are not equitably represented. African and Asian countries have a total of three seats each; countries of the Latin American and Caribbean Group have two seats, as do those of Eastern Europe; while countries of the Group of Western European and Other States have a total of five seats. Furthermore, of the five permanent, veto-wielding members, three are from the Group of Western European and Other States, one each from Asia and the Eastern European Group, while Africa and Latin America do not have any. This arrangement can hardly be said to be democratic.

There is, therefore, the need to restructure the Security Council to make it more equitably representative and democratic. Many, ourselves included, have been wondering what effect the unification of Europe in 1992 will have on the makeup of the Security Council. For example, could a single European political entity continue to maintain two permanent seats and an additional one or two non-permanent seats on the Council? What of the developments in Eastern Europe, particularly the events unfolding in the Soviet Union? What impact will these have? There is also the question of those Member States that have now emerged as major contributors to the Organization. Are they, together with other countries that represent a great percentage of the world's population, not justified in seeking greater representation on the Security Council? There is also the issue of the continuing relevance of veto power, especially considering that not a single veto has been cast throughout 1990 and 1991, despite the Gulf crisis.

Questions like these should be examined objectively and discussed frankly. The legitimacy of the Council and the moral authority of the Organization can only be enhanced if the favourable wind of democratization that is sweeping across the world passes through the United Nations. This will go a long way towards promoting in the minds of many States the positive nature of the new world order which is emerging, a new world order in which the United Nations is expected to play a leading and crucial role.

AN ENLARGED, RESTRUCTURED SECURITY COUNCIL?

Note the several cross-currents in the debate about the future composition and structure of the Security Council. One simply has to do with size: it is argued that the Council should be enlarged to reflect the increasing membership of the U.N. Another has to do with equitable geographical distribution. Another has to do with the veto: some argue that it should be abolished; others say it might be retained, but those who hold it should not necessarily be those who had the political clout in 1945 to seize it. Yet another has to do with increasing the number of permanent members, without necessarily giving the veto power to the new ones.

Which, if any, of these proposals would enhance the ability of the Security Council to carry out its primary responsibility: the maintenance of international peace and security (see *article 24*)? Are the proposals based on "equity," such as those for increasing the size or changing the geographic distribution of Council membership, inconsistent with a goal of enhancing the Council's effectiveness?

Proposals to increase the number of permanent members, without giving the new ones the veto, have focused largely on Japan, India, Brazil and Nigeria. Why those four? Would an increase in permanent membership be sensible? If so, why not give the new permanent members the veto or, conversely, take it away from all permanent members?

Another suggestion, not discussed in the 1991 General Assembly debate, would transfer the British and French vetoes to the European Community. Presumably, as a matter of EC law, this could not be done until the EC has the authority, as an organization, to conduct foreign policy—extending beyond economic matters—on behalf of its members. If that hurdle is overcome, could the EC exercise a veto power in the Security Council without becoming a member of the U.N. in its own right?

Could EEC membership in the Food and Agriculture Organization (pages 164–66 supra) be a model for EC membership in the U.N.? If so, could it be a model for its membership in the Security Council?

Presumably, any of the proposals for altering the composition or structure of the Security Council would require Charter amendment. Is that a practical prospect? For the amendment procedures, see *articles 108 and 109*.

B. THE GENERAL ASSEMBLY AND OTHER BROADLY REPRESENTATIVE U.N. BODIES

1. Decision-Making Techniques

Decision-making in a plenary body composed of the representatives of more than 170 sovereign states is bound to be a process that is both highly political and inefficient. Each annual session of the U.N. General Assembly has an enormous agenda, reflecting the concerns not only of the membership as a whole, but also of various blocs within the membership. Most items on the agenda are considered by one of the Assembly's main committees before they reach the Assembly floor.[a]

a. The General Assembly has seven main committees: The First Committee (disarmament); Special Political Committee (political and security matters other than disarmament); Second Committee (economic and financial); Third Committee (social, humanitarian and cultural); Fourth Committee (trusteeship, including non-self-governing territories); Fifth Committee (administrative and budgetary); and Sixth Committee (legal). All members are represented on each main committee.

In addition, the General Assembly has a General Committee with 29 members (like an executive committee, meeting frequently during General Assembly sessions to keep things moving); a 9-member Credentials Committee to verify the credentials of

Much of the political bargaining process among individual nations or among blocs occurs in the committees, or in U.N. corridors while matters are before the committees. The committees then propose draft resolutions that are debated and (usually) adopted by the General Assembly itself.

The General Assembly's voting system is set forth in *article 18* of the Charter. The major legal issue presented by that article is whether, and if so by what criteria, a specific matter not enumerated in article 18(2) can be designated as an "important question" requiring the affirmative vote of two-thirds of the members present and voting. This issue arose, for example, when the General Assembly was debating whether to recognize the People's Republic of China as the representative of China. See pages __ supra. The issue has arisen in other contexts as well. These materials look at one of them, before the focus shifts to the ways in which decision-making in the General Assembly, and in the United Nations as a whole, may be made more effective than it has been.

In December 1981, Israel enacted legislation extending its laws, jurisdiction and administration to the Golan Heights—Syrian territory controlled by Israel since the 1967 war. The matter was brought before the U.N. Security Council, where the United States vetoed a draft resolution that would have condemned Israel. The matter was then submitted to an emergency special session of the General Assembly in early 1982, under the Uniting for Peace Resolution. The Under-Secretary-General for Political and General Assembly Affairs requested legal advice regarding the majority required for adoption of the draft resolution submitted to the General Assembly.

OPINION OF U.N. OFFICE OF LEGAL AFFAIRS ON MAJORITY REQUIRED FOR ADOPTION BY THE GENERAL ASSEMBLY OF A DRAFT RESOLUTION BEFORE IT

February 5, 1982.
1982 U.N. Juridical Y.B. 159.

* * *

4. The * * * emergency special session was convened at the request of the Security Council, which in its resolution 500 (1982) clearly indicated that the basis for its decision to call for an emergency session was the fact that the lack of unanimity of its permanent members prevented it from exercising its primary responsibility for the maintenance of international peace and security. The substantive item on the agenda of the ninth emergency special session of the General Assembly is identical with that on the agenda of the Security Council and it must therefore be considered as having the same character, i.e., a matter relating to the maintenance of international peace and security.

representatives; and several special or ad hoc committees dealing with specific topics ranging from relations with the host country to activities in outer space.

5. The draft resolution to which you refer is the only one before the Assembly on the substantive item for which the emergency special session was convened. By operative paragraph 2 of the draft resolution the General Assembly would determine the existence of "an act of aggression under the provisions of Article 39 of the Charter of the United Nations". Article 39 of the United Nations Charter is the first article in Chapter VII of the Charter which relates to action with respect to threats to the peace, breaches of the peace and acts of aggression. Paragraph 6 of the draft resolution determines the existence of "a continuing threat to international peace and security" and paragraph 12 contains provisions analogous to the measures which the Security Council may decide upon under Article 41 of the Charter, including interruption or severance of economic and diplomatic relations, both of which are measures enumerated in Article 41. The draft resolution thus falls clearly and unequivocally within the category of questions relating to the maintenance of international peace and security within the terms of Article 18, paragraph 2, of the Charter, and thus requires a two-thirds majority for adoption.

6. Article 18, paragraph 3, of the Charter provides that decisions on questions other than those enumerated in paragraph 2 of the same article including determinations of additional categories of important questions shall be made by a majority of the members present and voting. On occasion the General Assembly has used this procedure where a genuine doubt appeared to exist to determine whether a draft resolution was to be considered as coming within the ambit of paragraph 2 of Article 18. However, in a case as clear as the present one application of this procedure would not be proper.

"IMPORTANT QUESTIONS"

The General Assembly adopted the resolution (G.A. Resolution ES–9/1) by a vote of 86 in favor, 21 opposed and 34 abstaining. Since abstentions are not counted as votes, the resolution was adopted by more than two-thirds.

Would every question submitted to the General Assembly under the Uniting for Peace resolution be an "important question"?

At the end of the opinion, the Office of Legal Affairs indicated that the General Assembly has sometimes used the article 18(3) procedure to determine whether a draft resolution was to be considered as an important question. Under article 18(3), is this appropriate on a case-by-case basis, or must it be done by designating whole categories as important questions?

The Office of Legal Affairs said that this was such a clear case that the voting majority question should not be submitted to the General Assembly. What if the President of the General Assembly submitted it anyway? Would the legal opinion, above, or the General Assembly's decision control?

EFFECTIVE DECISION-MAKING

Bloc voting has been known to the General Assembly since the inception of the United Nations. In the early years, the Western capitalist nations formed the dominant bloc. But when U.N. membership began to swell in the 1960s with the accession of newly-independent states, the numerical voting majority shifted to the third-world, or non-aligned, bloc. In the 1970s, much of the concern about decision-making in the General Assembly and the Economic and Social Council focused (at least in Western eyes) on automatic majorities for resolutions favored by the third-world bloc. Effective implementation of the resolutions depended on support from the out-voted Western states. In some significant instances, that support was not forthcoming. For example, when the General Assembly in the mid-1970s adopted a series of resolutions establishing a "New International Economic Order" that seemed to reject traditional concepts of international law on the use and protection of foreign investment, many Western nations refused to recognize the basic principles of the new order or to participate fully in the shaping of new institutions to administer it.

The decision-making problem was clearly identified in 1965 by the person who later became the Director-General of the International Labor Office.

JENKS, UNANIMITY, THE VETO, WEIGHTED VOTING, SPECIAL AND SIMPLE MAJORITIES AND CONSENSUS AS MODES OF DECISION IN INTERNATIONAL ORGANISATIONS

Cambridge Essays in International Law 48 (Essays in Honour of Lord McNair, 1965).*

There is no more difficult problem confronting international organisations today than that of evolving modes of taking important decisions which will command general respect and give such decisions the weight necessary to make them effective in practice. The problem has been a continuing one throughout the history of international organisation and we are still far from having achieved any satisfactory solution of it. In the course of a generation it has completely changed its character. In the early days of the League of Nations the problem was primarily one of facilitating decisions which the inhibiting influence of the principle of unanimity frequently made it virtually impossible to secure; in the early days of the United Nations the veto replaced the

---

* Reprinted by permission of the executors of the estate of Clarence Wilfred Jenks.

principle of unanimity as the apparent crux of the problem. That phase has completely passed. The problem now is primarily one of devising procedures and safeguards to ensure that decisions are taken with a degree of deliberation and sense of responsibility commensurate with their importance. We appear to be entering upon a new phase in which the keynote is no longer either unanimity or majority decision but consensus. The wheel has not come, and will not come, full circle, but there has been a marked shift of emphasis from the desire to ensure that decisions are no longer blocked by a requirement of unanimity or a veto to the desire to ensure that they reflect a sufficiently wide consensus to make them effective in practice.

CONSENSUS–FORMATION

"Consensus," in the U.N. context, is usually defined as the making of decisions without a vote and without formal objection by any member state. U.N. Charter article 18 does not expressly contemplate a procedure to seek consensus without a General Assembly vote. Nor do the Charter articles dealing with voting in other organs. Until the practice began to shift toward consensus decision-making in the 1980s, formal votes were taken on most of the important resolutions considered by the General Assembly. Of course, the votes have been preceded not only by formal debates on the record, but—as indicated above—by informal consultations in committees and elsewhere.

From time to time, recommendations have been made from various quarters to institutionalize a consultation or conciliation procedure, in order to facilitate consensus-building. Only a few of these recommendations have been adopted. When they have been adopted, the resulting procedures have not always been effective. For example, in 1964 the General Assembly established the U.N. Conference on Trade and Development (UNCTAD) as an ongoing organ of the Assembly. To assuage the fears of the Western states that they would consistently be outvoted in UNCTAD, the Assembly established a conciliation procedure that would be triggered by requests from small groups of member states. The procedure involved a small conciliation committee that would try to hammer out a consensus on an issue, with formal voting suspended while the conciliation process continued.[b] The conciliation procedure became a dead letter.[c] A similar procedure, omitting the requirement that voting be suspended, was proposed a decade later for the Economic and Social Council.[d] It was never implemented.

Despite these apparent setbacks, the desire to promote decision-making by consensus remains strong. It is sometimes expressed in the

b. See G.A.Res. 1995, 19 GAOR Supp. 15 (A/5815), at 1 (1964).

c. See U.N.Doc. TD/283, at 9, n. 15 (1983).

d. See U.N.Doc. E/AC.62/9, at 5, 30–32 (1975).

context of proposals to streamline or sharpen the focus of the decision-making process. For example, in 1985 a group of past Presidents of the General Assembly made recommendations on the rationalization of the Assembly's procedures. The past Presidents said, among other things:

> A significant reduction in the number of resolutions would add considerable weight to the decisions of the General Assembly.
>
> * * *
>
> An increasing number of resolutions are being adopted by consensus. This trend must be encouraged as it promotes the process of negotiation.[e]

Johan Kaufmann, a former representative of the Netherlands to the United Nations, has made some pertinent suggestions for improving the decision-making process in the U.N. After noting the inevitable political resistance to implementing some of the recommendations of the past General Assembly Presidents (such as a recommendation that items that are "no longer relevant" should be dropped from the General Assembly's agenda), he suggested, inter alia, that negotiations in small contact groups without rigid mandates be used more often and earlier in the negotiating process than had occurred theretofore.[f]

Compare the position actually taken by the General Assembly, as set forth in an Annex to its Rules of Procedure:

> Without prejudice to Article 18 of the Charter of the United Nations and with a view to facilitating the work of the United Nations, including, whenever possible, the adoption by the General Assembly of agreed texts of resolutions and decisions, informal consultations should be carried out with the widest possible participation of Member States.[g]

There has been one relatively recent testing ground for procedures contemplating the use of small groups to achieve a goal of consensus in a large plenary body. This was the Third U.N. Conference on the Law of the Sea, which met about twice a year for eight or nine weeks at a time from 1973 through 1982. It ultimately produced the U.N. Convention on the Law of the Sea,[h] a comprehensive treaty on virtually all aspects of the law of the sea. The negotiations leading to adoption of the Convention were arduous, to say the least. Blocs quickly developed, including (for example) the Group of 77 (actually more than 100 developing countries), the Western industrialized states, coastal states, landlocked states, naval powers, states with mineral resources that might have to compete with deep seabed minerals, etc. Membership in some of these blocs shifted with the issue at hand. Thus, for example,

---

e. U.N.Doc. A/40/377, Appendix (1985). The Asian–African Legal Consultative Committee has made similar recommendations. See U.N.Doc. A/41/437, Annex (1986).

f. Kaufmann, Developments in Decision Making in the United Nations, in The UN Under Attack 17, 26 (J. Harrod & N. Schrijver eds. 1988).

g. General Assembly Rules of Procedure, Annex VIII, ¶ 1, U.N.Doc. A/520/Rev. 15/Amend. 1 (1991).

h. U.N.Doc. A/CONF. 62/122 (1982).

European landlocked states lined up with developing landlocked states on a number of issues.

The excerpt below describes and evaluates some of the formal and informal techniques that were tried in order to facilitate consensus decision-making at the Conference (sometimes called UNCLOS III). Consider whether those techniques might be effective in the U.N. General Assembly or other plenary bodies.

KOH & JAYAKUMAR, NEGOTIATING PROCESS OF UNCLOS III

1 United Nations Convention on the Law of the
Sea 1982: A Commentary 87, 95–101, 104.
(M. Nordquist ed. 1985) *

II. THE FORMAL NEGOTIATING STRUCTURE: SOME OBSERVATIONS

* * *

B. Why Was It Difficult for the Conference to Establish Groups of Limited Size?

25. It was difficult for the Conference to officially establish small negotiating groups for three main reasons.

26. *First,* few sovereign nations will allow other countries to represent their interests. All delegations were attending the Conference on the basis of sovereign equality and all were answerable to their Governments. Too many vital interests were at stake and delegations could not easily agree to allow others to represent their points of view. As late as the fifth session (1976), when it was proposed to establish three small negotiating groups on LL/GDS,[i] EEZ[j] and transit rights,[k] there was opposition for a variety of reasons, some of which were substantive. In any event, negotiating groups of the whole were established.

27. *Second,* the official establishment of small negotiating groups almost always led to two problems which caused delay and infighting. One was the problem of determining the allocation of the limited seats to the various interest groups or regional groups. The second problem was that each group invariably had problems within itself in determining which delegations should occupy the seats allotted to the group (this was more of a problem with the heterogeneous regional groups than with the homogeneous groups like LL/GDS or the coastal States).

28. *Third,* even if the Conference envisioned groups of limited size, there was the question as to whether they would be open-ended. In the official Conference structure, there was generally opposition to

---

* Reprinted by permission of Kluwer Academic Publishers and the University of Virginia Center for Oceans Law and Policy.

i. [Land-locked and geographically-disadvantaged states. Ed.]

j. [Exclusive Economic Zone. Ed.]

k. [Rights to pass through certain international straits with fewer restrictions than apply to the right of innocent passage. Ed.]

any move to make meetings of small groups closed. Delegations wanted meetings of the smaller negotiating groups to be open-ended so that other delegations could attend and observe. But this defeated the very objective of having small groups, which was to reduce the gallery atmosphere and to generate candor and frankness in the negotiations.

C. *Informal Private Negotiating Groups Had to Fill the Vacuum*

29. In view of all these problems, it is not surprising that the informal, private negotiating groups were created to fill a definite gap.

30. Why was it possible to create these informal private negotiating groups when similar attempts by the Conference to establish negotiating groups of limited size were unsuccessful? The explanation is largely that they were privately convened. Being private and unofficial, those delegations which were excluded were less resentful and had fewer reasons to object since these groups were not part of the official Conference structure. The conveners of the informal groups were acting in their personal capacity and, therefore, they could decide whom they wished to invite.

D. *Failure of the Conference's Only Attempt to Close Meetings of WG.21*

31. The difficulties of the official negotiating structure may be illustrated by referring to a decision taken by the Conference at the eighth session to establish a negotiating group on Committee I matters [relating to deep seabed exploration and exploitation] which would not only be of limited size but also would be closed to other delegations.

32. The decision originated from a proposal of the Group of 77 which had been agreed upon at an inter-sessional meeting of that Group, just before the eighth session (1979). After appropriate consultations, it was adopted by the General Committee. The negotiating group would have 21 members and its meetings would be closed to non-members. The rule was enforced and non-members were turned away. Very strong resentment was aroused and the Group of 77 had to meet in an emergency session and reverse its own proposal to bar non-members from attending meetings of WG.21. After only two days, the doors of WG.21 were again opened to all delegations.

33. Why was there such a strong reaction? *First,* delegations, while agreeable to the establishment of a small group, felt that there was no good reason to bar other delegations from observing. *Second,* there was also some bitterness among delegations over the procedure by which the decision had been taken. The General Committee, for the first time, had not submitted its recommendation to the plenary. The point was raised in the General Committee but the President replied that the General Committee was not changing procedure but only implementing it. This was not a good answer since every report of the General Committee had previously been submitted to the plenary for its approval. Had the recommendation of the General Committee been submitted to the plenary and had the Conference, as a whole, agreed to

this procedure, it is possible that there might not have been such a strong reaction. *Third,* at that time there were very few other meetings to keep delegations occupied. Often, having the right to attend meetings is more important than attending them.

E. *Establishment of Small, Official Negotiating Groups at the Seventh Session (1978)*

34. A breakthrough was, in a sense, achieved at the seventh session (1978) when the Conference decided to establish seven small negotiating groups [19] on the seven hard-core unresolved issues. The understanding was that each negotiating group would have "a nucleus of those countries principally concerned." Thus, Negotiating Group 1 had a nucleus of 50 States, Negotiating Group 4 had a nucleus of 39 States and Negotiating Group 5 had a nucleus of 36 States.

35. Even here, the Conference could not avoid that open-ended element. It was stressed that, while each negotiating group had a nucleus, it was on the "clear understanding that they would be open-ended in the sense that any participant not included in the original nucleus would be free to join the groups with the same status as the original members" (A/CONF.62/62, para. 3).

F. *Examples of How the Negotiations Were Actually Conducted*

36. Initially, all the meetings of Negotiating Group 2 on financial arrangements [regarding deep seabed exploration and exploitation] were meetings of the whole. This stage helped to inform interested delegations on complex issues relating to financial arrangements, the different positions held by delegations on these issues, the merits and demerits of the various proposals and the concepts and terminologies contained in the technical papers relating to the subject. This stage was also necessary in order to give all delegations a sense of participation in the negotiating process. Once the objectives of stage one were achieved the Chairman started to call meetings of "financial experts." The meetings were deliberately held in small rooms which could accommodate not more than 30 persons. Although these meetings were open to all, by saying that these meetings were meetings of experts, and by holding them in small conference rooms, the Chairman succeeded in reducing the size of his negotiating group from 140 to 30. The group of financial experts was thus able to go into the issues in much greater depth and to sharpen the focus of the issues in contention. By regular reporting to the group in plenary, those delegations which were not attending meetings of the smaller group were kept informed of the group's progress.

37. At a certain point, the Chairman came to the conclusion that stage two had been completed and it was time to move into the third and final stage of the negotiations. At this point, he further reduced the size of the negotiating group. He invited the representatives of

---

19. The decisions concerning these negotiating groups are set out in A/CONF.62/62 (1978), Off.Rec. X. See also A/CONF.62/63 (1978), Off.Rec. IX.

Argentina, Mauritius and Pakistan to represent the Group of 77. He invited the representative of the United States to represent the Western industrialized countries. He chaired the negotiation between the three representatives of the Group of 77 and the representative of the United States for two consecutive days and succeeded in arriving at an agreement. Similarly, the Chairman himself negotiated an agreement with the representative of the Soviet Union.

* * *

III. THE UNIQUE NATURE OF THE RULES OF PROCEDURE AND THEIR EFFECT ON THE NEGOTIATIONS

A. *The Unique Nature of the Rules of Procedure*

39. * * * The UNCLOS Rules of Procedure were unique, *first*, in having built-in devices for avoiding or delaying the taking of decisions by voting and, *second*, in providing for special rules concerning the majority of votes required for the taking of decisions.

Special Rules on Avoiding or Delaying the Taking of Decisions on Substantive Matters by Vote

40. The following features of the Rules of Procedure of the Conference (A/CONF.62/30/Rev.3) sought to avoid or delay the taking of decisions on substantive matters by vote:

(a) Before any substantive matter could be put to a vote, the Conference should have decided that all efforts at reaching agreement had been exhausted. This determination should be by a two-thirds majority of representatives present and voting, providing that such majority also included a majority of the States participating in that session of the Conference [Rules 37(1) and 39(1)].

(b) Before making such a determination, several other procedures could be invoked:

(i) When the substantive matter comes up for voting for the first time, the President may, and shall if requested by at least 15 representatives, defer the taking of a vote by a period not exceeding 10 days. Such procedure can be applied only once on any matter [Rule 37(2)(a)].

(ii) At any time the Conference, on the President's proposal or on a motion by one representative, may decide to defer the taking of a decision on any substantive matter for a specified period of time [Rule 37(2)(b)].

(iii) During the period of deferment, the President shall make every effort, with the assistance as appropriate of the General Committee, "to facilitate the achievement of general agreement, having regard to the overall progress made on all matters of substance which are closely related," and the President will make a report to the Conference prior to the end of the deferment period [Rule 37(2)(c)].

(iv) If, at the end of the deferment period, agreement is still not reached, then the Conference shall make the determination that all efforts at reaching agreement have been exhausted [Rule 37(2)(d)].

(v) If the Conference does not make such a determination, the President or any representative may propose, after a period of no less than five days from the last vote on such determination, that such a determination be made. The five days' delay is not applicable in the last two weeks of the session [Rule 37(2)(e)].

(vi) No vote is to be taken on any substantive matter less than two working days after an announcement is made that the Conference is going to vote on the matter [Rule 37(3)].

(vii) All these special procedures and Rule 37 do not apply to the adoption of the text of the Convention as a whole. But the Convention, as a whole, shall not be put to vote less than four working days after the adoption of its last article [Rule 39(2)].

Special Rules Concerning the Majority of Votes Required for the Taking of Decisions (Rule 39)

41. The Rules of Procedure (A/CONF.62/30/Rev.3) provided that:

(a) On all matters of substance, including the adoption of the text of the Convention as a whole, decisions are to be taken by a two-thirds majority of the representatives present and voting, provided that such a majority shall include a majority of States participating in that session (such a proviso is not found in the UN General Assembly's Rules of Procedure).

(b) The same majority is required for any determination that all efforts at reaching agreement have been exhausted.

(c) On all matters of procedure, decisions shall be taken by a majority of representatives present and voting. (This is similar to UN General Assembly practice.)

(d) If a dispute arises as to whether a matter is procedural or substantive, the President shall rule on the question. Any appeal against the ruling shall be immediately put to the vote and the President's ruling shall stand unless the appeal is approved by a majority of representatives present and voting. This, again, is similar to normal UN practice.

B. Background to These Special Rules of Procedure

42. What is the explanation for the decision to incorporate these unusual features in the Rules of Procedure? The underlying philosophy appears to have been the achievement of a Convention commanding the widest possible support. Hence, it was felt that it was necessary to work into the Rules safeguards against hasty voting, for cooling-off periods and to provide for special majorities. Another underlying rationale was that important interest groups, e.g., the major powers, who were numerically in the minority, did not want to be railroaded into voting where they might not have the votes to win.

* * *

D. How Did the Rules of Procedure Affect the Negotiations?

50. The Rules of Procedure on decision-making were scrupulously observed until the very end of the Conference. The resort to voting was rare, in accordance with the letter and spirit of the Gentlemen's Agreement.

51. While the Rules and their observance may be remarkable, there is no doubt that the observance of the letter and spirit of the Rules inevitably (insofar as they discouraged the taking of votes) meant a longer conference. The delegates had to keep the discussions and negotiations going, session after session, in the hope that a compromise would eventually emerge.

52. The Rules, in other words, partly accounted for the very long duration of the Conference. If not for the unique features of the Rules, voting on numerous issues could easily have been taken. However, to have done so would have put in jeopardy the collective goal of the Conference, which was to adopt a Convention which would enjoy the widest possible support. * * *

FORMAL AND INFORMAL PROCEDURES

If consensus is important, is it better to try to institutionalize procedures (such as referrals of contested issues to small negotiating groups) that could lead to it, or to leave the process unstructured in order to allow negotiating groups to form on their own?

If institutionalized procedures are any part of the answer, how should they be structured in the U.N. General Assembly? Is the Law of the Sea Conference a useful model for the General Assembly or the Economic and Social Council?

Consensus decision-making in the U.N. may have some drawbacks to go with the advantages many have seen in it. For example, is it an unalloyed benefit to have much of the discussion/negotiation leading to adoption of a resolution held beyond the public eye? Could the absence of a vote mask substantial disagreement or a lack of political will to carry out the resolution? Could the give-and-take necessary to achieve consensus result in resolutions having little meaningful content?

Is consensus decision-making simply an evolutionary stage on the way to a more mature form of majority decision-making? If the latter, are special procedures needed in order to ensure that the majority's decisions will be effective?

2. Restructuring Proposals

Most close observers of the U.N. have felt that more needs to be done than simply to improve the procedures for decision-making. Thus, suggestions have been made for structural changes as well.

Much of the debate has concerned the U.N.'s efforts in the economic and social fields. These fields are increasingly regarded not only as important in themselves, but also as inextricably tied to the U.N.'s attempts to deal with political issues. Secretary-General Boutros Boutros-Ghali has said:

> [I]t is futile, if not counterproductive, to separate out the political and the economic and social missions of the Organization. The concept of an integrated approach to cooperation in these areas lies at the heart of the Charter of the United Nations. * * * [The linkage of these missions] stems from the basic premise that the Organization's actions, if they are to contribute to lasting peace, must be directed to addressing at the same time not only the immediate but also the underlying causes of conflict: political oppression, social injustice and blatant economic disparities.[a]

According to *article 60* of the Charter, responsibility in the economic and social fields lies in the General Assembly and, under its authority, in the Economic and Social Council (ECOSOC). For years, ECOSOC has been much criticized. It has been thought to be too large (54 members) to be an effective, action-oriented body, and too small to be truly representative of the U.N. membership. Until recently it met twice a year, in addition to a brief organizational meeting, with a broad agenda that seemed to lack focus. Member states sent relatively junior government ministers as their representatives and did not give them authority to make significant decisions.

Structural problems have also arisen from the broadening of the U.N.'s functions in the economic and social fields. As originally conceived, the General Assembly and ECOSOC would be policy-making bodies, leaving the actual operation of economic and social programs to others. To a substantial extent, they still are. But over the years the General Assembly has also created operational bodies. These include UNICEF, established to provide a range of services for children; the U.N. Development Program (UNDP), with its primary focus on technical assistance for developing countries; the World Food Program (WFP), designed to use food as an aid to economic and social development; the U.N. Population Fund (UNFPA, after its former name), to promote and support population and family planning activities; and the U.N. Drug Control Program (UNDCP), which funds efforts to control trafficking in illicit drugs.

ECOSOC and its related organs have been slow to adapt their structures and agendas to deal efficiently with these operational activities. They have not always been well coordinated with each other. Each operational entity has its own governing body, but some member

---

a. U.N. Doc. E/1992/82/Add.1, at 3.

states have argued that these bodies "are too large, too unwieldy and meet too infrequently to provide the guidance and support needed by the executive heads." [b]

The General Assembly so far has not dealt directly with these issues. In May 1991, however, it did adopt a plan to restructure and revitalize ECOSOC.[c] The General Assembly's measures focused on how ECOSOC's sessions are organized. It was decided to hold a four-day organizational session each February to decide on the agenda of a single substantive session, to be held for four to five weeks each summer. The substantive session is organized in segments, in this order:

(a) A high-level segment of four days, with member states' participation at ministerial level, devoted to one or more major economic and/or social policy themes to be determined at the organizational session. This is followed by a one-day discussion of important developments in international economic cooperation, with the ministers joined by the heads of multilateral financial and trade institutions in the U.N. system.

(b) A four-or-five-day coordination segment, devoted to the coordination of the policies and activities of the specialized agencies and other U.N. bodies dealing with economic and social matters. Discussion is organized around one or more themes selected at the organizational session. The heads of the relevant agencies and other bodies are invited to participate. Any recommendations are submitted to the General Assembly and forwarded, as appropriate, to the governing bodies of the specialized agencies and other bodies. The Secretary–General is to report to following sessions of ECOSOC on the steps taken by the U.N. system to give effect to the recommendations.

(c) A two-or-three-day operational segment focusing on the implementation of policy recommendations and decisions of the General Assembly and coordination of activities in the U.N. system.

(d) A committee segment, with meetings of the Social Committee beginning after completion of the coordination segment, and meetings of the Economic Committee beginning after the operational segment. The committees submit reports, with specific recommendations on issues, to the plenary session of ECOSOC, and monitor the implementation of General Assembly decisions in the social and economic fields.

(e) Adoption of the report of the overall session by ECOSOC.

In addition, Resolution 45/264 called for a review of the composition of ECOSOC and of its subsidiary bodies, as well as a review of the Secretariat structure in the economic and social fields.

b. U.N.Doc. E/1992/64, at 11.   c. G.A.Res. 45/264, Annex (1991).

When this was written, it was too early to assess the performance of ECOSOC under its new meeting structure. Many observers would say, however, that considerably more is needed if the U.N.'s economic and social functions are to be effectively carried out. Several studies have been conducted, resulting in a variety of proposals.

In December 1985 the General Assembly authorized the appointment of a group of 18 experts from around the world to review the efficiency of the U.N.'s administrative and financial functions. The group issued its report in 1986. It noted, among other things, the sustained growth in the agenda of the United Nations, leading to new organs, committees, commissions and expert groups. These often have overlapping agendas that lead to duplicated work. Moreover, the group noted the significant growth in the number of conferences and meetings held annually under U.N. auspices; these present difficulties particularly for smaller states with limited personnel resources, and too often result in the inefficient use of those resources. The group criticized the efficiency and organization of the Secretariat, and stressed the compelling need for widespread agreement among member states on budgetary matters.[d]

The group made 71 recommendations for improvement. Leaving aside budgetary matters, noteworthy for our purposes were Recommendation 2, calling for a significant reduction in the number and duration of conferences and meetings, including those of the subsidiary bodies of the General Assembly and the Economic and Social Council; Recommendation 3, calling for streamlining the methods of work of the General Assembly and its subsidiary organs by (inter alia) merging agenda items and reducing the number of resolutions adopted; and Recommendation 8 calling for a small, high-level body to conduct a careful study of the intergovernmental structure in the economic and social fields, in order to identify ways to avoid duplication and improve coordination among U.N. bodies dealing with such subjects as trade, development, population, children, environment, human settlements, refugees and food.[e]

In 1987, a distinguished panel convened by the United Nations Association (a nongovernmental body) issued a report recommending structural reforms in the U.N.'s economic and social spheres.[f] A summary of some of the panel's recommendations appears below.

d. Report of the Group of High-Level Intergovernmental Experts To Review the Efficiency of the Administrative and Financial Functioning of the United Nations, 41 GAOR Supp. No. 49 (A/41/49), at 1–2 (1986).

e. Id. at 5, 7.

f. United Nations Association of the U.S.A., A Successor Vision: The United Nations of Tomorrow (1987). For somewhat different proposals by a seasoned U.N. observer, see M. Bertrand, The Third Generation World Organization (1989). A useful summary of U.N. reform efforts through the mid-1980s appears in Donini, Resilience and Reform: Some Thoughts on the Processes of Change in the United Nations, in Revitalizing the Study of International Organizations: Report of a Conference on Teaching About International Organizations from a Legal and Policy Perspective 81 (P. Alston & R. Pangalangan eds. 1987).

EXECUTIVE SUMMARY OF "A SUCCESSOR VISION: THE UNITED NATIONS OF TOMORROW"

U.N.Doc. A/42/620, at 6–10 (1987).

* * *

I. Relating Functions to Structure

* * *

A. Global Watch

9. In order to identify the issues on which convergence of interests exists, the United Nations needs: (a) a setting where emerging issues of urgent global significance can be spotlighted and their implications for national and international policy choices and human welfare given prominent international attention by a small senior body; (b) a capacity at the staff level to monitor, and put into usable form, data on "global watch issues", to examine systematically implications for national and international security and welfare, and to identify overlapping interests and the margins for potential agreement.

* * *

II. Strengthening Structure

12. The panel has given considerable attention to the deficiencies of the present United Nations structure in the economic and social area, and these include: a generally low level of representation; overlapping between the General Assembly, the Economic and Social Council, and the United Nations Conference on Trade and Development (UNCTAD); a lack of intellectual authority; the absence of a system for identifying emerging global issues; and the weakness of co-ordination and joint planning in the United Nations system. While institutional changes are clearly needed, a balance has to be struck between what may be desirable ultimately, and the kinds of constructive practical steps that Member States could undertake immediately. Consequently, the panel has made the following recommendations:

A. Ministerial Board

13. To provide a high-level centre for the conduct of global watch consultations described above, a small Ministerial Board of not more than 25 Governments should be established in affiliation with the Economic and Social Council. The Board would be composed of delegates with the seniority and expertise to consult effectively, issue communiqués and initiate or propose *ad hoc* actions with regard to matters on which there is agreement that enhanced international management is essential.

(a) *Functions:* (i) Global watch—high-level consultations and exchange of views on any urgent international problems not within the jurisdiction of the Security Council; (ii) Consensus-building—through *ad hoc* working groups of the most affected countries, the Board will forge communities of interest on matters before it; (iii) Converting agreements into action—when appropriate the Board shall propose actions by or under the aegis of the United Nations proper (General Assembly would have to authorize), by other international agencies, [or] by individual member countries of the United Nations;

(b) *Agenda:* the Board could address any issues of imminent or clearly foreseeable consequence for human security and welfare not within the jurisdiction of the Security Council, for example, matters associated with natural disasters, the global biosphere, the special problems of the least developed countries, international debt, disease control, illegal capital flight, international narcotics trafficking, cross-border population movements, urban overpopulation, etc.;

(c) *Composition and procedures:* the 25 members would consist of a core of permanent members made up of the largest developing and developed countries, and a larger number of rotating members (criteria for determining "permanent" and "rotating" might be population and economic size); it is expected that Governments would be represented at a high level by ministers or other officials from the ministries which are most directly relevant to the agenda subject; meetings would be held on an as-needed basis, normally one to three days in duration; all decisions would be taken by consensus;

* * *

(e) *Organizational status:* while ultimately the Board should be given an explicit basis in the Charter of the United Nations, for the present it should be attached to the Economic and Social Council, but report to the General Assembly directly once a year at the same time as the Council makes its report;

(f) *Why a new body?:* existing United Nations machinery is inadequate to address, authoritatively and effectively, urgent issues of human security and welfare. The Second and Third Committees and the Economic and Social Council are too large, too comprehensive in their agendas, and their delegations often too junior to have the authority for so important a task.

B. A Two-step Approach Towards a More Integrated United Nations System

14. Why is a more integrated system necessary?: It is essential to create an apparatus for identifying, analysing and proposing responses to the kinds of issues described above that is integrated intellectually and employs the sectoral expertise of the economic and social agencies of the United Nations in a co-ordinated manner. Most problems requiring international management overlap the spheres of several agencies and United Nations programmes. YET THERE IS NO CENTRE AT THE CENTRE OF THE UNITED NATIONS SYSTEM and therefore no means for putting to work the system's rich potential for interdisciplinary analysis to identify the global issues on which nation-

al interests converge and where high levels of co-operation are necessary and feasible.

15. The two-step approach: the panel recommends the creation of a single commission, composed of the Directors–General of all the main agencies in the economic and social fields, mandated to develop integrated responses to global issues through joint programming, and development of a consolidated United Nations system budget. Such a commission, however, is not feasible for immediate implementation owing to the scale of the constitutional, structural and budgetary changes involved. The panel therefore adopted the commission as a medium-term goal towards which the United Nations system should evolve. As an immediate step in the direction of the United Nations commission, it calls for a commission with advisory powers only.

1. Step 1—the United Nations Advisory Commission

(a) Composition: The Advisory Commission would consist of five persons, selected by the Secretary–General, with outstanding international reputations in the economic and social field;

(b) Function: It would identify emerging issues of a global or regional scale that cross over several [agencies' fields or concerns.] Following consultations with agency heads, it would propose joint approaches to these problems. It would also present proposals to the new Ministerial Board, suggesting actions by Member States or international institutions regarding these "cross-over" issues. It would conduct regular reviews of the major programme emphases in the economic and social area in the light of global trends. Finally, it would prepare the agendas and follow-up on the decisions of the annual United Nations system summits (a proposal of the Group of 18 adopted last December), and participate in the summits on a co-equal basis with the specialized agency heads;

(c) Support: The Advisory Commission would be served by a small inter-agency staff seconded from the main economic and social agencies of the United Nations.

2. Step 2—The United Nations Commission

(a) Composition: The Commission would be composed of 15 to 18 commissioners, including Directors–General of the principal specialized agencies and the Bretton Woods organizations. The Commission would be nominated by the Ministerial Board and confirmed by the General Assembly, except for the heads of the International Monetary Fund (IMF), World Bank and the General Agreement on Tariffs and Trade (GATT) whose appointment procedures would not change;

(b) Function: The Commission would have the same functions as the Advisory Commission, except that it would also prepare a consolidated United Nations system programme budget from the submissions of every participating agency (except for the IMF, World Bank and GATT) for submission to the General Assembly for its approval;

(c) Support: The Commission would have its own budget and, like the Ministerial Board, would draw upon the Department of International Economic and Social Affairs for substantive support.

III. Development Assistance Board

16. In order to improve the quality and coherence of United Nations development assistance and to reduce overlap and duplication, the separate executive boards of the United Nations Development Programme, the United Nations Fund for Population Activities, the World Food Programme and the United Nations Children's Fund should be replaced by a single Development Assistance Board. The Board would exercise oversight of all programme proposals, conducting reviews before the start of the fund-raising efforts in order to ensure influence upon the overall scope and content of work programmes. The Board would also be responsible for development of a conceptual framework for United Nations development assistance which leads gradually to appropriate specialization.

IV. Elimination of Second and Third Committees; Expansion of the Economic and Social Council to Plenary Size

17. To eliminate the nearly complete duplication of agendas and debates between the Economic and Social Council and the General Assembly's committees dealing with economic and social matters (Second and Third), and to end the waste of scarce human resources that results from this duplication, the Second and Third Committees of the General Assembly should be discontinued and their duties assumed by the Economic and Social Council, which would be enlarged to plenary size and strengthened by structural and procedural reforms, including the addition of a Reports and Agenda Committee.

THE NORDIC PROPOSAL

Another reform proposal has come from the Nordic countries. They focused on the problem of international development:

> Overlapping and duplication of work, limited responsiveness as well as lack of transparency and accountability have prevented the system from acquiring sufficient financing or the "critical mass" necessary to play a leading role in international development issues * * *.[g]

They have elaborated their view of the need for reform and summarized their proposal:

g. U.N. Doc. E/1992/91, Annex, at 3.

NORDIC MEMORANDUM ON REFORM OF UNITED NATIONS GOVERNANCE AND FINANCE
U.N. Doc. E/1992/91, Annex, at 3–6 (1992).

* * *

2. IMPROVED GOVERNANCE STRUCTURES

2.1 Weaknesses in the Present System of Governance

Basically, the system of governance, leadership and funding needed for the political "meeting place" function is distinctly different from that needed for the operative or "executive" function. This has important implications for the design of United Nations activities. It is considered important that the respective roles and tasks of different organizations and bodies within the system be better defined to complement each other and to form a coherent whole.

The governance of United Nations development activities at the highest level is fragmented. At present governance functions are delegated to an array of councils and boards that deal separately with each organization. There is need for a body to give effective high-level guidance and cohesion to the executive organs of the United Nations operational activities.

At the same time there is need for a body for each programme and fund to provide operational guidance to the Organization.

The sessions of many governing bodies have become huge gatherings simultaneously dealing with a wide spectrum of matters at different levels of governance, from overall political issues to micro-management. New, small, governing bodies that would meet more frequently, are needed to improve the effectiveness and efficiency of the system.

2.2 An Improved Governance Structure

Governance Reform Objectives

The governance reform proposal of the Nordic United Nations project advocates *inter alia* a division of responsibility under the General Assembly at two different levels.

Key objectives and considerations in the design of a new governance structure should be the following:

(a) To increase the importance and impact of United Nations intergovernmental bodies in the international policy-dialogue on development issues;

(b) To improve the impact of United Nations development cooperation through effective policy-making and priority-setting regarding operational activities for development;

(c) To increase the responsiveness of United Nations funds and programmes to governing body decisions, through greater transparency and accountability in the interface between governance and management;

(d) To ensure that principles of universality and representation are combined with good and effective governance.

Policy Guidance and Priority–Setting: The Functions of an International Development Council

In order to fulfil the above objectives and considerations there is a need to assign to a single body the task of high level discussion on development issues and the provision of policy guidance to the United Nations system in its development activities. These functions regarding operational development activities are distinct from other issues tackled in the economic and social sectors of the United Nations.

For the sake of illustration the Nordic countries have defined these functions as functions of an International Development Council (IDC). The intention is not to propose establishment of a new body, but to underline that these are a set of functions that belong together and should be designated as a responsibility to some existing body.

The concrete IDC functions could be broken down as follows:

(a) To establish overall objectives and operational strategies for key areas in international development cooperation;

(b) To discuss the mandates, powers, structures and the division of labour of United Nations intergovernmental and executive bodies in order to avoid any gaps or duplications;

(c) To give policy guidance to the United Nations operational activities including the distribution of tasks among the various actors and coordination within the system;

(d) To review and discuss the reports on the work of funds and programmes.

While several options for integrating the IDC functions into present United Nations structure exist, they should preferably be delegated to one of the existing bodies, as the creation of new bodies should be avoided.

The options for integrating the IDC functions into the present structure include the following:

(a) The Economic and Social Council as at present (it should, however, be noted that the Council has a limited membership);

(b) Merging of the Second and Third Committees of the General Assembly;

(c) The Council to be strengthened and enlarged to become a universal body being in session in parallel with the General Assembly; the Second and Third Committees of the General Assembly to be abolished.

The guiding principle in any option should be to establish a clear division of roles and mandates between the General Assembly and the Council in order to avoid the present overlapping and duplication of work between these two governance layers.

Operational Governance: Small Executive Bodies

The establishment of a small executive body for each of the United Nations funds and programmes would be an integral element in the new governance structure, with the key function of providing a link between the member States and the management of each organization. These bodies would primarily exercise operational governance, which includes:

(a) Monitoring the performance of the funds and programmes;

(b) Assuming that the mandates, policies, priorities and strategies set by higher-level governing bodies are carried out, and in a transparent manner;

(c) Deciding on plans and budgets;

(d) Encouraging and examining new programme initiatives.

The mode of work and the composition of the small executive bodies should reflect the United Nations basic character of a joint and shared undertaking between the economically more developed countries and the developing countries. The principles of composition should strike a balance between representation and efficiency, with the following considerations:

(a) The size would be limited to 15–20 members;

(b) Members would represent groups of member States in the form of constituencies, taking into account i.e. regional balance between developed and developing countries, with the possibility of a representation of 50 per cent from recipient countries and 50 per cent from donor countries;

(c) Members would be chosen within each constituency;

(d) Size of contributions to United Nations operational activities for development would be taken into account in the composition of constituencies among donor countries;

(e) Continuity in membership would be secured through a three-year period of service of the executive body members.

The executive bodies would work on the basis of the principle of consensus. In cases of disagreement, decisions could e.g. be taken by "double majority" i.e. majority among the recipient constituency and majority among the donor constituency.

THE SECRETARY–GENERAL'S PROPOSAL

Secretary–General Boutros Boutros–Ghali has supplied his own views about making ECOSOC more responsive to current needs, and about connecting its functions with those of the Security Council:

> [ECOSOC's functions] could be furthered by the introduction of a flexible, high-level inter-sessional mechanism, which would enable the Economic and Social Council and its Bureau to respond in

a continuing and timely way to rapidly changing developments in the economic and social sphere, maintain a continuing dialogue with organizations of the system in their respective areas of activity, build and expand agreement on common ends and objectives, and adapt the policy agenda in the economic and social field in response to changing requirements. Such a role should be rooted in sound analysis and a sound understanding of developments and global trends—relying on the fact-finding capabilities of the United Nations and the United Nations system. It should encompass an "early warning" function, covering developments and trends that may lead to threats to security and well-being, in areas ranging from energy to debt, from the risk of famine to the spread of disease. This role would need to be supported by high-level expert advice.

In the same broad context, in the report prepared pursuant to the Security Council's request, I have recommended that the Security Council invite a reinvigorated and restructured Economic and Social Council to provide reports, in accordance of Article 65 of the Charter, on those economic and social developments that may, unless mitigated, threaten international peace and security.[h]

The United States government has supported the Nordic proposal, adding that ECOSOC should serve as the International Development Council and that the General Assembly's Second and Third Committees (on economic and financial matters and on social, humanitarian and cultural matters, respectively) should be abolished. Developing countries have tended to view this as undermining the importance of the General Assembly, reducing it to a mere debating body.[i] Do they have a point? Is it a significant issue?

Can all of the proposals be synthesized into a single, workable plan that would be acceptable to the U.N. membership as a whole? If so, what would it look like? Would it require a Charter amendment?

3. The U.N. Budget Process

In the late 1980s the United Nations encountered a financial crisis, when the United States withheld part of its assessed dues as a result of dissatisfaction with the decision-making process by which U.N. budgets are adopted and with the resulting level of U.N. expenditures. As will appear below, the financial crisis continued into the 1990s. For the U.N. Charter provisions on the budget, see *articles 17, 18(2) and 19*.

Since the United States is assessed 25% of the total U.N. budget, U.S. concern with these matters is substantial. The leverage the United States attains from withholding part of its assessed dues is substantial as well.

h. U.N. Doc. E/1992/82/Add. 1, at 6.   **i.** See U.N. Observer & Int'l Rep., Aug. 1992, at 10.

U.S. withholdings occurred under several statutory commands, notably the Kassebaum amendment,[a] which in its original form required that U.S. payments be cut back from the assessed 25% to 20% of the budget unless the U.N. and its specialized agencies adopted weighted voting on budgetary matters. The Kassebaum amendment resulted in a $42 million shortfall in the U.S. assessment of $210 million for the 1986 U.N. budget. Other U.S. withholdings added to the shortfall until the net amount withheld from the U.N. exceeded $500 million.

Our focus at this point is not on the lawfulness of the withholding, but on the issue of fair and effective U.N. decision-making in the budget context. A formal change to weighted voting would require a Charter amendment, an uncertain prospect and not a practical solution during the 1980s. Thus, the General Assembly in 1985 turned to less dramatic means of bringing the United States back into the fold. Its 18–member Group of High–Level Intergovernmental Experts to Review the Efficiency of the Administrative and Financial Functioning of the United Nations issued a report near the end of 1986.[b] The report focused not only on budgetary procedures, but also on several purely administrative matters within the U.N.

The Group was unable to agree on specific budgetary procedures. It did, however, criticize the operation of then-current procedures. Those procedures involved the preparation of a medium-term plan every six years (with amendments possible during the six years) and a program budget every two years. The Committee for Programme and Coordination examined the program content, while the Advisory Committee on Administrative and Budgetary Questions examined the administrative and financial aspects. Then, as now, the draft budget is submitted to the General Assembly's Fifth Committee and then to the General Assembly itself.

The Group of Intergovernmental Experts criticized the U.N. Secretariat for presenting virtually final budgets to this committee process, and stressed that "A procedure must therefore be developed which makes it possible for Member States to exercise—at the very beginning of the planning and budget process, as well as throughout the whole process—the necessary intergovernmental leadership, particularly regarding the setting of priorities within the resources likely to be available."[c] The General Assembly responded with Resolution 41/213 (1987), which said in part that it:

> 5. *Reaffirms* that the decision-making process is governed by the provisions of the Charter of the United Nations and the rules of procedure of the General Assembly;
>
> 6. *Agrees* that, without prejudice to paragraph 5 above, the Committee for Programme and Co-ordination should continue its

---

a. 22 U.S.C.A. § 287e, note.

b. See 41 GAOR Supp. No. 49 (A/41/49) (1986).

c. U.N. Doc. A/41/49, at 28 (1986).

existing practice of reaching decisions by consensus; explanatory views, if any, shall be presented to the General Assembly;

7. *Considers it desirable* that the Fifth Committee, before submitting its recommendations on the outline of the programme budget to the General Assembly in accordance with the provisions of the Charter and the rules of procedure of the Assembly, should continue to make all possible efforts with a view to establishing the broadest possible agreement; * * *.

In Annex I to the resolution, the General Assembly established a budget process that includes, inter alia, creation of a contingency fund expressed as a percentage of the overall budget to accommodate unforeseen expenditures. If expenditures are later proposed that would exceed the balance in the contingency fund, they could be funded only by eliminating other costs or by being included in a later biennial budget.

In Annex II to the resolution, the President of the General Assembly quoted a legal opinion of the U.N. Legal Counsel on paragraphs 5, 6 and 7 of the resolution, set forth above. The opinion concluded:

It is our opinion that these * * * paragraphs read separately or together do not in any way prejudice the provisions of Article 18 of the Charter of the United Nations * * *.

What does this mean? Do paragraphs 5, 6 and 7 of the resolution have any legal effect?

After a shaky start, the process contemplated by Resolution 41/213, with its view to budgetary decision-making by consensus, has worked reasonably well from the U.S. point of view. It has seemed also to be acceptable to third-world and other member states. By 1990, the U.S. Congress had begun appropriating the full assessments and had begun a gradual process of paying arrearages, including those for peacekeeping. Even so, substantial arrearages remained unpaid, and the Congressional budgetary process continued to result in a long lag time for payment of current assessments.

From the point of view of major contributors, like the United States, is consensus decision-making on the budget likely to be an adequate long-term substitute for votes weighted according to each state's assessed share of the budget?

Short of amending the U.N. Charter, could some other means be devised that would (a) control the budget, (b) adequately fund the organization's essential functions, and (c) satisfy third-world members as well as the major contributors?

Would an amendment to the Charter be feasible on the budgetary issue?

C. U.N.–RELATED ORGANIZATIONS

In international organizations other than the U.N. itself, a combination of simple majority and qualified majority (e.g. two-thirds) voting is often mandated by the constituent instrument. Thus, for example, article V.C of the IAEA Statute calls for decisions by the General Conference (the plenary body of all members) to be made by a simple majority, except that a two-thirds majority is required for financial questions, amendments to the Statute, suspensions of members and those (unspecified) questions that the Conference by a simple majority vote determines should be decided by a two-thirds majority.[a] The Board of Governors, with fewer members, decides all matters by simple majority except the budget and any other questions the Board determines should be decided by a two-thirds majority. As a practical matter, the Board usually operates by consensus.[b]

JENKS, UNANIMITY, THE VETO, WEIGHTED VOTING, SPECIAL AND SIMPLE MAJORITIES AND CONSENSUS AS MODES OF DECISION IN INTERNATIONAL ORGANISATIONS

Cambridge Essays in International Law 48 (Essays in Honour of Lord McNair, 1965).[*]

[In constituent instruments of international organisations, to] make the majority principle more palatable and give greater weight and responsibility to decisions, provision is often made for a special majority.

The special majority most commonly required is two-thirds of the votes cast, or in some cases of the total number of possible votes, but provision is sometimes made for other types of special majority. A higher proportion of affirmative votes, such as three-fourths or four-fifths, may be required. There may be a provision that the required majority must include certain votes or a certain proportion of certain votes. In the International Labour Conference, in which government, employer and worker delegates have separate votes, decisions on the admission, expulsion or suspension of Members require a two-thirds majority of the possible number of votes including a two-thirds majority of the government votes cast. In Commodity Councils "distributed" majorities, that is to say concurring majorities of conflicting interests separately counted, are required for certain votes. Other formulae are no doubt conceivable.

The circumstances in which a special majority is required vary somewhat from one organisation to another, but they tend to include questions of membership, finance, the adoption of constitutional amendments, the exercise of pre-legislative and quasi-legislative powers, and certain elections; there is sometimes, as in the Charter of the United Nations, provision that further classes of cases on which a special majority shall be required may be specified by a simple majority, or, as

---

a. Cf. U.N. Charter article 18.

b. See Szasz, The Law and Practices of the International Atomic Energy Agency 168, 177 (1970).

[*] Reprinted by permission of the executors of the estate of Clarence Wilfred Jenks.

in the Constitution of the Labour Organisation, a provision that a special majority may be provided for in any instrument conferring new powers on the Conference.

[Another device sometimes used to avoid simple majority voting involves the assignment of different weights to the votes of different members. Jenks suggested that weighted voting is adopted primarily by organizations with rather circumscribed and well defined functions, where an obvious and straightforward method of weighting the votes can be agreed to. As he put it:]

It is therefore not surprising that there are only three important groups of international organisations in which weighted voting is today an accepted and important principle.

The first consists of the financial specialised agencies of the United Nations system, the International Monetary Fund and the International Bank for Reconstruction and Development and its affiliates (the International Finance Corporation and the International Development Association), in which the quota or subscription contributed to the resources of the agency determines the voting power of each Member.

The second consists of a number of international commodity councils in which the voting power of each Member is determined by the value or volume of its exports or imports.

The third consists of the European Communities and the Consultative Assembly (but not the Committee of Ministers) of the Council of Europe.[c]

Weighted voting may be, and probably should be, adopted in further international organisations for specific purposes as they are created, but it seems unlikely to afford a solution in any foreseeable future for the problems of existing or projected world organisations with general responsibilities.

WEIGHTED VOTING AND CONSENSUS DECISION–MAKING

If weighted voting is both appropriate and politically acceptable in the International Monetary Fund and other financial institutions, and if—as Jenks suggested—it would make sense in other international organizations, why isn't it more widely used? If the answer is that the smaller states would not stand for it, why does their influence prevail on this point?

Aside from the organizations Jenks mentioned, what types of organization would be most appropriate for weighted voting?

In several specialized agencies, consensus decision-making is the norm, even though the constituent instruments spell out voting require-

---

c. [A fourth type of organization utilizing weighted voting is the international space satellite operating agency. Such agencies have been developed after Jenks made the above observations. Ed.]

ments. Is the argument for consensus decision-making the same in specialized agencies as it is in the United Nations itself? Is consensus decision-making equally desirable for all specialized agencies?

To the extent that consensus decision-making is desirable, should provisions requiring serious efforts at reaching consensus be written into the constituent instruments of international organizations?

In the ILO General Conference, the voting delegation from each member state consists of four persons: two government representatives and one each representing employers and workers. Employers and workers are also represented in the Governing Body. The purpose is to achieve direct, independent representation of those whose interests are especially affected. Would non-governmental voting delegates be useful in other international organizations? If so, in which types of organization? What problems might there be?

Developed-country concerns about decision-making in international organizations have focused on the formal means by which the organizations' representative bodies resolve the differences among their members. The day-to-day affairs of organizations, however, are not conducted by those bodies. They are conducted by the organizations' secretariats. For reasons having to do with history, politics and expertise, nationals of developed countries hold more key positions in many secretariats than would be allocated to them under a system of proportional representation.[d] These secretariat officials, like other such officials, are sworn to allegiance to the organizations rather than to their own governments, but of course they bring with them whatever values their own upbringing and cultures have instilled. Secretariat officials, regardless of nationality, do affect what goes on in international organizations:

> The significance of what the Third World sees as the "colonisation of secretariats" lies in the capacity of bureaucracies to define problems and shape policy options by influencing flows of information, as well as their ability to promote or obstruct implementation of policy decisions.[e]

Would this be a significant counterbalance to whatever voting disadvantage the financially powerful states have in international organizations? Should it be?

SECTION 6. VOLUNTARY WITHDRAWAL AND WITHHOLDING OF SUPPORT

INTRODUCTORY NOTE

From time to time, member states have become sufficiently disenchanted with the United Nations or some of the specialized agencies to

---

[d]. The formal model for selection of secretariat personnel is U.N. Charter article 101(3), referring primarily to standards of efficiency, competence and integrity, but with due regard paid to geographic diversity.

[e]. C. Wells, The UN, UNESCO and the Politics of Knowledge 16 (1987).

give notice of withdrawal from them, or to withhold financial support from them without actually attempting to withdraw. The materials below examine some of these instances.

The constituent instruments of the United Nations and the World Health Organization say nothing about voluntary withdrawal of member states. The constituent instruments of the other specialized agencies contain withdrawal clauses. (The UNESCO Constitution originally did not, but was amended in 1954 to provide for withdrawal.)

The U.N. Charter and the constituent instruments of all the specialized agencies require member states to contribute to the finances of the organization, in most cases through payment of annual dues. None of them contains any provision expressly authorizing the withholding of dues.

A. THE UNITED NATIONS

Since the U.N. Charter says nothing about voluntary withdrawal, one must look to such sources as the general law of treaties and the preparatory work of the Charter to find relevant rules or principles. Note, first, that the Vienna Convention on the Law of Treaties says in *article 5* that it applies to constituent instruments of international organizations.[a] Vienna Convention *article 56* covers withdrawal from a treaty containing no provision on the subject. *Article 57* deals with suspension of the operation of a treaty.

After you have read those articles, consider the following account of the Charter's preparatory work and of Indonesia's purported withdrawal from the U.N. in 1965.

M. WHITEMAN, DIGEST OF INTERNATIONAL LAW
Vol. 13, at 220–28 (1968).

When the question of withdrawal from the United Nations was first considered at the United Nations Conference on International Organization, the Drafting Subcommittee of Committee I/2 was "strongly of the opinion that withdrawal should be impossible".

* * *

Various delegates favored a statement on withdrawal, and a Special Subcommittee was appointed to draft a report on the question of withdrawal.

* * *

---

a. *Article 4* says that the Convention applies only to treaties concluded by states after it entered into force with regard to those states, but it also says that this is without prejudice to the application of any rules in the Convention that would apply anyway. Most of the substantive provisions in the Convention have been thought to reflect customary international law. The Convention entered into force in January 1980.

The Subcommittee transmitted to Committee I/2 a draft declaration on withdrawal which the full Committee discussed on June 17, 1945. A proposal that a provision on withdrawal should be included in the Charter was rejected by Committee I/2 by a vote of 19 to 24. The Committee then adopted the following commentary, frequently referred to as a declaration, on withdrawal:

> The Committee adopts the view that the Charter should not make express provision either to permit or to prohibit withdrawal from the Organization. The Committee deems that the highest duty of the nations which will become Members is to continue their cooperation within the Organization, for the preservation of international peace and security. If, however, a Member because of exceptional circumstances feels constrained to withdraw, and leave the burden of maintaining international peace and security on the other Members, it is not the purpose of the Organization to compel that member to continue its cooperation in the Organization.
>
> It is obvious, however, that withdrawals or some other form of dissolution of the Organization would become inevitable if, deceiving the hopes of humanity, the Organization was revealed to be unable to maintain peace or could do so only at the expense of law and justice.
>
> Nor would it be the purpose of the Organization to compel a Member to remain in the Organization if its rights and obligations as such were changed by Charter amendment in which it has not concurred and which it finds itself unable to accept, or if an amendment duly accepted by the necessary majority in the Assembly or in a general conference fails to secure the ratification necessary to bring such amendment into effect.
>
> It is for these considerations that the Committee has decided to abstain from recommending insertion in the Charter of a formal clause specifically forbidding or permitting withdrawal.
>
> [See The United Nations Conference on International Organization 507 (Selected Documents, 1946).]

This commentary was approved by Commission I on June 19, 1945, and by the Conference on June 25, 1945.

[The President of Commission I, in the third meeting of the Commission, June 19, 1945, said: "Nothing about withdrawal was provided in the Dumbarton Oaks Proposals.[b] For some states, it appeared to be essential that some possibility for withdrawal should be provided for, while on the other hand, the fear was expressed that such a clause might lead to abuses and gravely weaken the Organization. In the end, we decided that no mention would be made, but with a very clear understanding that we did not consider that withdrawal ought to be a normal faculty of any member to be exercised at any time without any

---

[b] The Dumbarton Oaks Proposals preceded the San Francisco Conference and formed the working drafts for the Conference. [Ed.]

motives at all. But, on the other hand, we accepted in the report * * * the decision that in some exceptional circumstances, examples of which are given in the report, withdrawal would be inevitable and ought not to be prevented by the Organization." c

* * *

On January 20, 1965, the First Deputy Prime Minister and Minister for Foreign Affairs of Indonesia (Subandrio) addressed a letter to the Secretary–General stating in part:

> On 31 December 1964, the Head of the Permanent Mission of Indonesia to the United Nations in New York conveyed to Your Excellency the content of President Sukarno's statement on that date, to the effect that Indonesia would withdraw from the Organization if neo-colonialist 'Malaysia' were seated in the Security Council. Pursuant to that statement I have to inform you that on 7 January 1965, after the seating of 'Malaysia' as member of the Security Council, our Government, after very careful consideration, has taken the decision to withdraw from the United Nations.

The letter described the election of Malaysia to the Security Council as "a mockery of the sense of the Council itself" since, "according to Article 23 of the Charter, the election of a non-permanent member of the Council should be guided by the importance and contribution of the candidate-country in the maintenance of peace and security in the world". The letter stated further:

> As to your personal appeal, Mr. Secretary–General, that Indonesia should not withdraw from its co-operation with the United Nations, I want to assure you that Indonesia still upholds the lofty principles of international co-operation as enshrined in the United Nations Charter. This, however, can be implemented outside as well as inside the United Nations body.

[U.N. Doc. S/6157 (1965).]

* * *

The Secretary–General replied to the First Deputy Prime Minister and Minister for Foreign Affairs of Indonesia on February 26, 1965, in part as follows:

> I have the honour to acknowledge the receipt of your letter dated 20 January 1965 [S/6157]. The position of your Government recorded therein has given rise to a situation in regard to which no express provision is made in the Charter. It is to be recalled, however, that the San Francisco Conference adopted a declaration relating to the matter.

* * *

c. The United Nations Conf. on Int'l Organization 563 (Selected Docs., 1946).

Your statement that "Indonesia has decided at this stage and under the present circumstances to withdraw from the United Nations" and your assurance that "Indonesia still upholds the lofty principles of international co-operation as enshrined in the United Nations Charter" have been noted.

* * *

In conclusion, I wish to express both the profound regret which is widely felt in the United Nations that Indonesia has found it necessary to adopt the course of action outlined in your letter and the earnest hope that in due time it will resume full co-operation with the United Nations.

[U.N. Doc. S/6202 (1965).]

In a letter to the Secretary-General, March 8, 1965, the Deputy Permanent Representative of the United Kingdom (Jackling) referred to the Indonesian notice of withdrawal and stated:

Without prejudice to their views as to the circumstances which might legally justify a Member State in withdrawing from the United Nations, Her Majesty's Government wish to place formally on record their conviction that the reason for withdrawal advanced in the letter of 20 January from the First Deputy Prime Minister and Minister for Foreign Affairs of Indonesia—namely the election of a non-permanent member of the Security Council which the Government of Indonesia unilaterally considers as not fulfilling the requirements of Article 23 of the Charter—is not a circumstance so exceptional in nature as to justify the Government of Indonesia in withdrawing from the Organization.

[U.N. Doc. S/6229 (1965).]

* * *

[As a result of the Indonesian notice of withdrawal:]

On 1 March 1965, pursuant to the Secretary-General's instructions, the necessary administrative actions were taken by the Secretariat, *inter alia,* to remove the Indonesian name-plate and flag. Thereafter, Indonesia ceased to be listed as a Member of the Organization, or of United Nations principal and subsidiary organs of which it had been a member solely by virtue of its membership in the United Nations itself. Furthermore, the name of Indonesia does not appear in resolution 2118(XX) of 21 December 1965, whereby the Assembly fixed the scale of assessments of Member States for the financial years 1965, 1966 and 1967—nor is it assessed in the same resolution as a non-member for the expenses of certain organs in which non-members participate.

[U.N. Doc. A/PV.1420, at 1–2 (1966).]

In a telegram of September 19, 1966, from the Ambassador of Indonesia to the United States to the Secretary–General of the United Nations, the Ambassador stated:

> * * * I hereby have the honour upon instruction of my Government to inform you that my Government has decided to resume full cooperation with the United Nations and to resume participation in its activities starting with the Twenty–First Session of the General Assembly.

[U.N. Docs. A/6419 and S/7498 (1966).]

The President of the Twenty-first Session of the General Assembly (Pazhwak, Afghanistan), in Plenary Session on September 28, 1966, read the telegram from the Indonesian Ambassador and stated:

> * * * It would therefore appear that the Government of Indonesia considers that its recent absence from the Organization was based not upon a withdrawal from the United Nations but upon a cessation of co-operation. The action so far taken by the United Nations on this matter would not appear to preclude this view. If this is also the general view of the membership, the Secretary–General would give instructions for the necessary administrative actions to be taken for Indonesia to participate again in the proceedings of the Organization. It may be assumed that, from the time that Indonesia resumes participation, it will meet in full its budgetary obligations. If it is the general view that the bond of membership has continued throughout the period of non-participation, it would be the intention of the Secretary–General to negotiate an appropriate payment with the representatives of Indonesia for that period and to report the outcome of his negotiations to the Fifth Committee for its consideration.
>
> Unless I hear any objection, I would assume that it is the will of the membership that Indonesia should resume full participation in the activities of the United Nations and that the Secretary–General may proceed in the manner I have outlined.
>
> There being no objection, I invite the representatives of Indonesia to take their seats in the General Assembly.

[U.N. Doc. A/PV.1420, at 2 (1966).]

A report by the Secretary–General to the Fifth Committee of the General Assembly dealing with Indonesia's contributions for 1965 and 1966, dated December 6, 1966, stated:

> * * * As a result of [negotiations with the Secretary–General,] Indonesia has offered to pay 10 per cent of the amount which it would have been assessed for the regular budget and for the Special Account for the United Nations Emergency Force (UNEF) for the period of its non-participation on the basis of the rate (0.39 per cent) proposed for Indonesia in the scale of assessments for the financial years 1965–1966 and 1967 recommended by the Committee on Contributions in its report to the nineteenth session of the

General Assembly. It has also offered to pay 25 per cent of the amounts which it would have been assessed for 1966 at the 0.39 per cent rate for the regular budget and the Special Account of UNEF, this percentage corresponding approximately to the proportion of the year 1966 during which it will have resumed co-operation with the Organization.

The Secretary-General believes, in the light of the considerations outlined above and of the fact that Indonesia derived no benefits during the period of non-participation, that the above proposals may be regarded as appropriate by the Fifth Committee.

[21 GAOR, Agenda item 77, Annexes, at 2 (U.N. Doc. A/C.5/ 1097 (1966).)]

The Fifth Committee and the General Assembly approved the contributions proposed for Indonesia for 1965 and 1966, as described above.

SCHWELB, WITHDRAWAL FROM THE UNITED NATIONS: THE INDONESIAN INTERMEZZO
61 Am.J.Int'l L. 661, 671–72 (1967).*

It is submitted that the Indonesian intermezzo leaves the law concerning withdrawal from the United Nations in the following state:

Members of the United Nations have the right to withdraw from the Organization, but only in the exceptional circumstances set forth in the interpretative commentary. A withdrawal for other than exceptional circumstances is not permissible and constitutes a breach of that Member's international obligations. The term "exceptional circumstances" is undoubtedly not very precise; nor is the explanation of this term contained in the interpretative Declaration. However, every legal system operates with general concepts which leave a wide margin of appreciation to those who are called upon to interpret and to apply them. Public international law, including the law of the Charter, is no exception. Under all these general concepts there exists a hard core of situations which undoubtedly come within it. There is a penumbra of twilight situations in regard to which it is contested or contestable whether they are covered by the term. And, finally, there are situations which are manifestly outside the scope of the provision. The division into these three types of factual situations can be discovered also in the case of the rule that only "exceptional circumstances" justify withdrawal from the Organization. The Indonesian case of 1965 came within the third type: the facts adduced by Indonesia clearly did not qualify as "exceptional circumstances."

It must be added that in the present state of the organization of the international community it is, generally speaking, not possible to pre-

---

* Reprinted with permission, c. The American Society of International Law.

vent a Member State from committing this breach of its obligation and to force it to remain within the Organization. Unless the circumstances are such that the purported withdrawal constitutes a threat to the peace or a breach of the peace—and a situation is hardly conceivable where the withdrawal in itself and without any additional act can be so classified—the United Nations has no legal remedy to enforce its claim for continued membership of the state purporting to withdraw. The rule that a Member must not withdraw for reasons other than those coming within the terms of the interpretative commentary remains therefore a *lex imperfecta,* a legal norm for the breach of which no effective legal sanction is provided. The obligation of the Member state concerned not to withdraw, which derives from the rule, is nevertheless a genuine legal obligation, subsisting even if disregarded by that state and capable of being implemented by it. In returning to the United Nations in 1966 Indonesia fulfilled an obligation which it had "accepted" in 1950 (Article 4 of the Charter), which it has been bound to "fulfill in good faith" (Article 2(2)) and which its previous government had violated in 1965.

QUESTIONS ON WITHDRAWAL FROM THE U.N.

Assume, as is probably the case, that Vienna Convention *articles 56(1)* and *57* reflect pre-existing customary international law. Under article 56(1), did Indonesia have the right to withdraw from the United Nations in January 1965, as it purported to do? Would the argument in Indonesia's favor be stronger under article 56(1)(a) or 56(1)(b)?

What if it is established that the parties intended to admit the possibility of withdrawal (Vienna Convention article 56(1)(a)), but only on certain conditions? Is that the case regarding the U.N.? If so, did Indonesia satisfy the conditions?

If there is doubt about Indonesia's right to withdraw under the circumstances, the doubt could be resolved in Indonesia's favor if the other members of the U.N., or presumably the Secretary–General acting on behalf of the U.N., acquiesced in the withdrawal. Did the Secretary–General acquiesce, in his reply to Indonesia (S/6202, at pages 241–42 supra)? Did the Secretary–General and the General Assembly acquiesce later on?

If you had been the United Nations Legal Counsel, would you have advised at the time of Indonesia's decision to "resume participation" in 1966 that the admission procedure of *article 4* should be followed? In fact, the U.N. Office of Legal Affairs did give an opinion on that occasion.[d] The statement of the President of the General Assembly referring to the Indonesian absence as not a withdrawal but a "cessation of co-operation," contemplating resumption of participation, was taken almost verbatim from that legal opinion. The U.N. Charter does

---

d. See 1966 U.N. Juridical Y.B. 222.

not say anything about "cessation of co-operation." Was this instead a case of suspension of the operation of a treaty (the Charter) for Indonesia, as contemplated by Vienna Convention article 57? Did the case fit within the conditions for suspension set forth in that article? (If so, does that mean that all the duties of the Charter—even those in *article 2(3)* and *(4)*—were suspended for Indonesia?)

If there was in fact no withdrawal and no suspension, was the Secretary–General justified in recommending acceptance of less than the full amount of Indonesia's financial assessment for the period in which it was not cooperating? On the other hand, if there was a suspension of the operation of the Charter as to Indonesia, how could assessment of any financial obligation be justified for that period?

Would it be lawful for a member state to withdraw when Security Council enforcement action has been taken against it? For example, would it have been lawful for Iraq to assert "exceptional circumstances" and thus to withdraw from the U.N. after the Persian Gulf war of 1991, when Iraq's invasion of Kuwait had brought on Security Council-authorized military action that destroyed substantial parts of Iraq's infrastructure, and when Security Council economic sanctions against it were still in force?

(The Persian Gulf situation and its aftermath are examined in detail in Chapter 4, infra. For the present it is enough to know that comprehensive economic sanctions were maintained against Iraq after the war, and that the Security Council in Resolution 687, adopted under *Chapter VII* of the Charter, had imposed several other conditions that Iraq asserted were beyond the competence of the Council, or were interventions in Iraq's domestic affairs, or both. These included (inter alia) orders to accept the destruction or removal of all chemical, biological and nuclear weapons, and all ballistic missiles with a range of more than 150 kilometers, as well as a determination of Iraq's liability under international law for any direct loss, damage or injury to foreign governments and nationals resulting from Iraq's invasion and occupation of Kuwait.)

If Iraq had withdrawn under those circumstances, could the U.N. lawfully have done anything about it? Would Iraq, or any other withdrawing state in these circumstances, still be subject to Security Council monitoring or regulation? See U.N. Charter *article 2(6)*.

The declaration adopted at San Francisco seemed to contemplate withdrawal if a member's rights and obligations were changed by a Charter amendment it could not accept, or if an amendment accepted by the General Assembly failed to secure the necessary ratifications. See page 240 supra. In the 1990s, for the first time in decades, it has become plausible to think about meaningful Charter revision. Does the San Francisco declaration open the door to debilitating withdrawals from the organization if significant revisions are adopted?

WITHHOLDING OF SUPPORT

As noted at page 233, in the late 1980s the United States withheld significant portions of its assessed U.N. dues. These withholdings, aggregating hundreds of millions of dollars, brought the U.N. to the brink of insolvency. The funds were withheld largely because of dissatisfaction with the decision-making process in the General Assembly and in other U.N. bodies where the United States does not have a veto. In particular, the U.S. Congress objected to large-scale U.N. spending on salaries and expenses of Secretariat staff members and on projects not regarded as being cost-effective. The remedy initially sought was weighted voting on budgetary matters, with the weights based on assessed U.N. budgetary shares.

The United States has also threatened to withhold payment of dues over the Palestine issue. In November 1988 the Palestine National Council—the parliamentary body of the Palestine Liberation Organization (PLO)—declared "the establishment of the State of Palestine." [e] In December 1988, the U.N. General Assembly acknowledged the Palestine National Council's declaration and changed the PLO's designation to "Palestine" in the U.N. system.[f] When Arab states in the fall of 1989 proposed draft General Assembly resolutions referring explicitly to "the State of Palestine," the U.S. State Department warned that a cutoff in U.S. funding would be the result if any such resolution were adopted.[g] The Arab states then decided not to press for a vote.[h]

The United States has not been the only major contributor that has withheld assessed U.N. contributions. In the 1960s, a major financial crisis for the U.N. grew out of the refusal of the Soviet Union and France to pay expenses the General Assembly had apportioned to them for peacekeeping operations by the United Nations Emergency Force (UNEF) in the Middle East and the United Nations Operation in the Congo (ONUC).

The General Assembly created UNEF in 1956, after vetoes by the United Kingdom and France had blocked Security Council attempts to call for a cease fire and withdrawal of forces at the height of hostilities following Egyptian nationalization of the Suez Canal. In December 1956, the General Assembly adopted resolution 1089(XI), in which it decided that UNEF expenses would be borne by the United Nations "and shall be apportioned among the Member States, to the extent of $10 million, in accordance with the scale of assessments adopted by the General Assembly for contributions to the annual budget of the Organi-

---

e. Palestine National Council's Declaration of Independence, in U.N.Doc. A/43/827–S/20278, Annex III, at 15 (1988).

f. G.A.Res. 43/177 (1988), adopted by a vote of 104–2 (Israel, United States)–36, with 15 member states absent and one (Iran) not participating in the vote.

g. N.Y.Times, Nov. 28, 1989, p. A3, col. 1.

h. N.Y.Times, Dec. 7, 1989, p. A8, col. 3.

zation for the financial year 1957 * * *." Similar assessments were made in subsequent General Assembly resolutions.

The Security Council created ONUC in 1960, in response to widespread violence and fears of foreign intervention in the former Belgian Congo (now Zaïre) after its independence. The Security Council soon reached an impasse concerning the scope of ONUC's operations. After a Soviet veto of a draft resolution approving ONUC's activities, the General Assembly entered the fray under the Uniting for Peace Resolution. The General Assembly adopted resolutions treating ONUC expenses as "expenses of the Organization" within the meaning of Charter *article 17(2)*, and apportioned them according to the regular scale.

Bulgaria, Czechoslovakia, France, Poland, Romania and the Soviet Union announced that they would not contribute to ONUC expenses. The Soviet Union explained its position:

> The Charter specifically provides that where action is involved, then questions relating to that action—i.e., questions concerning the scale and contingents of armed forces to be employed in such action—are to be decided by the Security Council alone. Article 48, paragraph 1, of the Charter provides that: "The action required to carry out the decisions of the Security Council for the maintenance of international peace and security shall be taken by all the Members of the United Nations or by some of them, as the Security Council shall determine."
>
> Thus it rests with the Security Council itself to determine which Members of the United Nations shall take action to carry out the decisions of the Security Council.
>
> The Charter further provides that the contributions of Members of the United Nations to the maintenance of international peace and security are to be determined by the Security Council in accordance with a special agreement or agreements (Article 43) * * *.[i]

To try to deal with the Charter interpretation question, the General Assembly requested an advisory opinion from the ICJ on whether the expenses the Assembly had authorized for UNEF and ONUC constituted "expenses of the Organization" within the meaning of article 17(2). A portion of the Court's opinion appears below.

CERTAIN EXPENSES OF THE UNITED NATIONS
International Court of Justice, Advisory Opinion, 1962.
[1962] I.C.J. 151, 164, 167–68.

[The Court noted that it had been asked to interpret only the phrase "expenses of the Organization." It rejected arguments that only administrative or other limited "expenses" were contemplated by article 17. It also rejected arguments that only the Security Council could

---

i. 15 GAOR, pt. II, 5th Comm., 825th meeting, at 2 (1961).

authorize any peacekeeping activities, and that financing for peacekeeping could only be arranged by agreements under *article 43*. The Court continued:]

By Article 17, paragraph 1, the General Assembly is given the power not only to "consider" the budget of the Organization, but also to "approve" it. The decision to "approve" the budget has a close connection with paragraph 2 of Article 17, since thereunder the General Assembly is also given the power to apportion the expenses among the Members and the exercise of the power of apportionment creates the obligation, specifically stated in Article 17, paragraph 2, of each Member to bear that part of the expenses which is apportioned to it by the General Assembly. When those expenses include expenditures for the maintenance of peace and security, which are not otherwise provided for, it is the General Assembly which has the authority to apportion the latter amounts among the Members. The provisions of the Charter which distribute functions and powers to the Security Council and to the General Assembly give no support to the view that such distribution excludes from the powers of the General Assembly the power to provide for the financing of measures designed to maintain peace and security.

* * *

[The Court turned from considering the general structure of the Charter to an examination of the specific expenditures enumerated in the request for an advisory opinion.] In determining whether the actual expenditures authorized constitute "expenses of the Organization within the meaning of Article 17, paragraph 2, of the Charter", the Court agrees that such expenditures must be tested by their relationship to the purposes of the United Nations in the sense that if an expenditure were made for a purpose which is not one of the purposes of the United Nations, it could not be considered an "expense of the Organization".

The purposes of the United Nations are set forth in Article 1 of the Charter. The first two purposes as stated in paragraphs 1 and 2, may be summarily described as pointing to the goal of international peace and security and friendly relations. The third purpose is the achievement of economic, social, cultural and humanitarian goals and respect for human rights. The fourth and last purpose is: "To be a center for harmonizing the actions of nations in the attainment of these common ends."

The primary place ascribed to international peace and security is natural, since the fulfilment of the other purposes will be dependent upon the attainment of that basic condition. These purposes are broad indeed, but neither they nor the powers conferred to effectuate them are unlimited. Save as they have entrusted the Organization with the attainment of these common ends, the Member States retain their freedom of action. But when the Organization takes action which warrants the assertion that it was appropriate for the fulfilment of one of the stated purposes of the United Nations, the presumption is that such action is not *ultra vires* the Organization.

If it is agreed that the action in question is within the scope of the functions of the Organization but it is alleged that it has been initiated or carried out in a manner not in conformity with the division of functions among the several organs which the Charter prescribes, one moves to the internal plane, to the internal structure of the Organization. If the action was taken by the wrong organ, it was irregular as a matter of that internal structure, but this would not necessarily mean that the expense incurred was not an expense of the Organization. Both national and international law contemplate cases in which the body corporate or politic may be bound, as to third parties, by an *ultra vires* act of an agent.

In the legal systems of States, there is often some procedure for determining the validity of even a legislative or governmental act, but no analogous procedure is to be found in the structure of the United Nations. Proposals made during the drafting of the Charter to place the ultimate authority to interpret the Charter in the International Court of Justice were not accepted; the opinion which the Court is in course of rendering is an *advisory* opinion. As anticipated in 1945, therefore, each organ must, in the first place at least, determine its own jurisdiction. If the Security Council, for example, adopts a resolution purportedly for the maintenance of international peace and security and if, in accordance with a mandate or authorization in such resolution, the Secretary–General incurs financial obligations, these amounts must be presumed to constitute "expenses of the Organization".

[The Court went on to examine in detail the several resolutions relating to assessment of UNEF and ONUC expenses, concluding that the expenses were "expenses of the Organization" within the meaning of article 17(2).]

THE SEQUEL

The Soviet Union and France did not consider the Court's advisory opinion authoritative. They proceeded to withhold their shares of the peacekeeping assessments until they had exceeded the equivalent of all dues they owed for two full years. The United States then argued that their right to vote in the General Assembly was automatically suspended, under U.N. Charter *article 19*. Most other member states were unwilling to suspend the Soviet and French voting rights, and an impasse resulted.

The United States ultimately relented. The then-U.S. representative to the U.N., Arthur Goldberg, after noting the "intransigence of a few Member States and their unwillingness to abide by the rule of law," bowed to the consensus in the General Assembly that it should proceed with the full participation of the Soviet Union and France. He added, in what has since become known as the Goldberg reservation, "[I]f any Member State could make an exception to the principle of collective financial responsibility with respect to certain United Nations activities, the United States reserved the same option to make exceptions if, in its view, there were strong and compelling reasons to do so. There could be no double standard among the Members of the Organization."[j]

Several years later, France softened its position and repaid the amount it had withheld. In the late 1980s, the Soviet Union began making substantial repayments. The United States took their place as the largest withholder of assessments.

Meanwhile, in 1978 the Legal Adviser of the U.S. Department of State had written a legal memorandum on the obligation to pay U.N. assessments. His memorandum said in part:

> Although the nature and extent of the obligation to pay assessments has not been analyzed by the International Court of Justice, most of the developed States which submitted written and oral statements to the Court in its advisory proceedings on *Certain Expenses of the United Nations* made it clear that they interpreted Article 17 as imposing a legal obligation on members to pay the amount assessed to them by the General Assembly. The written statement of the United States contended,
>
>> Article 17(2) provides: 'The expenses of the Organization shall be borne by the Members as apportioned by the General Assembly.' The language of the provision is mandatory: expenses '*shall* be borne.' (Emphasis added.) Accordingly, the General Assembly's adoption and apportionment of the Organization's expenses create a binding international legal obligation on the part of States Members to pay their assessed shares.
>>
>> The history of the drafting of Article 17(2) demonstrates that it was the design of the authors of the Organization's constitution that the membership be legally bound to pay apportioned expenses.
>
> * * *
>
> G.A.Res. 1583(XV), which established an ad hoc fund for UN operations in the Congo, recognized that "the assessment * * * [of expenses] against Member States creates binding legal obligations on such States to pay their assessed shares." With the exception of France and Belgium, which abstained because they questioned the constitutionality of the resolution, all concerned developed States voted in favor of the resolution in committee.
>
> Thus, while some members have challenged the classification of certain expenditures as "expenses of the Organization" within Article 17, no Member State has directly challenged the thesis that

---

[j]. 19 GAOR, Annex 21, U.N.Doc. A/5916/Add.1, at 86 (1965).

Article 17 empowers the General Assembly to create binding legal obligations to pay assessments for proper "expenses of the Organization." This conclusion is strongly supported by the preparatory work of the San Francisco Conference which drafted the charter.[k]

Consider whether the following arguments would justify withholding (by the United States or others) in light of the U.N. Charter, the practice in the U.N. described above, and the Vienna Convention on the Law of Treaties:

(a) The Charter obligation to pay dues has fallen into disuse ("desuetude") whenever a member state refuses, as a matter of principle, to pay amounts assessed to it. The evidence would be the General Assembly's refusal to apply the article 19 loss-of-vote sanction against the Soviet Union, France and several other withholding states.

Several writers have said that a treaty may be modified or terminated by desuetude. It has been said that "this can happen only with the full consent of all the parties to such a treaty. If parties to a treaty accept a subsequent practice as law, this amounts to a tacit modification or abrogation of the treaty."[l] The same writer has added that desuetude "differs from a *waiver* of particular breaches of a treaty by the implied admission that the other party is legally entitled to disregard the treaty. Mere *non-use* of a right conferred by a treaty suffices even less to establish desuetude."[m]

Desuetude does not appear in the Vienna Convention as a ground for suspending or terminating a treaty obligation. When the International Law Commission was drafting the Vienna Convention on the Law of Treaties, it considered including a provision on desuetude. In the end it concluded that, although desuetude may be a factual cause for termination (or presumably for suspension) of treaty obligations, the legal basis would be the consent of the parties.[n]

(b) There is an inherent right to withhold dues assessed improperly by an international organization.

This argument stems from the separate opinion of Judge Fitzmaurice in the Expenses Case. He said that "Member States cannot, in my opinion, be bound to contribute to expenditures incurred outside the scope and framework of the Charter (even if these are not illegal *in se*), except by their specific consent given *ad hoc* in relation to the particular case."[o] He recognized the risk of abuse if every member state could unilaterally determine that a particular expense is ultra vires, so he concluded that there is at least a strong prima facie presumption that

---

k. Hansell, The Legal Character of U.N. Budget Assessments, Aug. 7, 1978, in 1979 Digest of United States Practice in Int'l Law 226.

l. 1 G. Schwarzenberger, International Law as Applied by International Courts and Tribunals 535 (3d ed. 1957). See also Simma, Termination and Suspension of Treaties: Two Recent Austrian Cases, 21 German Y.B.Int'l L. 74, 93 (1978).

m. G. Schwarzenberger & E. Brown, A Manual of International Law 137 (6th ed. 1976) (emphasis in the original).

n. [1966] 2 Y.B.Int'l L.Comm'n 237, U.N. Doc. A/CN.4/SER.A/1966/Add.1.

o. [1962] I.C.J. at 205.

duly voted expenditures are proper. In addition, he suggested that there might be "no positive obligation to contribute to the expenses of carrying out social and economic activities of a permissive character (except for Member States supporting or not opposing the activity concerned) * * *." p

(c) The Goldberg reservation represents the current law of the U.N. Charter, since member states did not object to it. (For widely accepted rules of treaty interpretation, see Vienna Convention *articles 31 and 32*.)

(d) The breach of article 17(2) by the Soviet Union, France and others excuses nonbreaching parties from performing their duties under that article. Vienna Convention *article 60* deals with material breach, and the permissible responses to it. *Article 45* deals with possible problems from the passage of time after a breach.

The International Law Commission's commentary on the draft that became article 60 contains this passage:

> [The Commission] preferred the term "material" to "fundamental" to express the kind of breach which is required. The word "fundamental" might be understood as meaning that only the violation of a provision directly touching the *central* purposes of the treaty can ever justify the other party in terminating the treaty. But other provisions considered by a party to be essential to the effective execution of a treaty may have been very material in inducing it to enter into the treaty at all, even [though] these provisions may be of an ancillary character.q

(e) A fundamental change of circumstances has occurred since the Charter was adopted, excusing at least some members from their article 17(2) obligations. The relevant Vienna Convention provision is *article 62*. See also *article 44*.

In the late 1980s, for example, U.S. influence over voting outcomes in the General Assembly had eroded significantly since the Charter entered into force, and the dollar amount of U.S. assessments had grown substantially. The growth in real dollars (adjusted for inflation), however, was much smaller than the growth in terms of enumerated dollars; in addition, the percentage of the U.N. budget assessed to the United States had decreased over the years, and the amount of the U.S. assessment as a percentage of U.S. gross national product had not increased.r

---

p. [1962] I.C.J. at 215.

q. [1966] 2 Y.B.Int'l Law Comm'n 172, 255, U.N. Doc. A/CN.4/SER.A/1966/Add.1 (emphasis in the original).

r. Compare United States Contributions to International Organizations (annual reports) with Statistical Abstract of the United States 462 (1989) (table showing changes in purchasing power of U.S. dollar).

Would any of these arguments justify the threatened U.S. withholding if the General Assembly were to adopt a resolution treating Palestine as a state? For the attributes of a state under international law, see page 154 supra. As of 1990, at least 90 national governments had recognized Palestine as a state, after the Palestine National Council declared the establishment of the "State of Palestine" in 1988. Most Western governments had not recognized Palestine as a state.

Nothing in the U.N. Charter expressly regulates the General Assembly's discretion on treating an entity as a state, except in the context of admission to membership (article 4). Under customary international law, there apparently is no duty to refrain from recognizing as a state an entity that does not have all the attributes of statehood.[s]

B. U.N.–RELATED ORGANIZATIONS

M. WHITEMAN, DIGEST OF INTERNATIONAL LAW

Vol. 13, at 229–33 (1968).

The Constitution of the World Health Organization contains no provision for withdrawal. The International Health Conference which drew up the Constitution in 1946 adopted the following "declaratory statement":

> A Member is not bound to remain in the Organization if its rights and obligations as such are changed by an amendment of the Constitution in which it has not concurred and which it finds itself unable to accept.

In the joint resolution providing for membership and participation by the United States in the World Health Organization, Congress included the following:

> Sec. 4. In adopting this joint resolution the Congress does so with the understanding that, in the absence of any provision in the World Health Organization Constitution for withdrawal from the Organization, the United States reserves its right to withdraw from the Organization on a one-year notice: *Provided, however,* That the financial obligations of the United States to the Organization shall be met in full for the Organization's current fiscal year.

On June 14, 1948, President Truman accepted the Constitution of the World Health Organization on behalf of the United States subject to the provisions of the joint resolution (Public Law 643, 80th Cong., 62 Stat. 441, 442). The Secretary–General of the United Nations "informed all the States parties to the Constitution that he was not in a position to determine whether the United States had become a party to the Constitution, but he was, however, prepared to be guided by the

---

[s.] See J. Crawford, The Creation of States in International Law 35 (1979).

action of the Health Assembly in regard to this matter, since under article 75 of the Constitution it is a competent body to settle any question concerning the interpretation or application of the Constitution." The First World Health Assembly, on July 2, 1948, adopted a resolution recognizing "the validity of the ratification [of the Constitution of WHO] by the United States of America".

* * *

[Feinberg, Unilateral Withdrawal from an International Organization, 39 British Y.B.Int'l L. 189, 204 (1963), points out, "On 12 February 1949 the Union of Soviet Socialist Republics informed W.H.O. that, since it was dissatisfied with certain aspects of the Organization's work, it no longer considered itself a member. Similar communications were sent by the Ukrainian Soviet S.R. and the Byelorussian Soviet S.R. on 14 and 17 February. In his reply to the Soviet Union's cable of notification, the Director-General stressed, *inter alia*, that 'because [the] Constitution of W.H.O. makes no * * * provision [for withdrawal], * * * [he] cannot accept * * * [the] communication as a withdrawal from the Organization'. The Executive Board approved the action taken by the Director-General, and decided to place the question on the agenda of the Second Assembly. On the recommendation of the Committee on Constitutional Matters, the Assembly on 25 June 1949 fully endorsed the steps taken by the Executive Board and the Director-General; expressed its deep regret at the absence of the representatives of the three members in question; and invited them to reconsider their intention and resume active participation." *]

[Whiteman continues:]

The Third World Health Assembly in 1950, noting that the Union of Soviet Socialist Republics, the Ukrainian Soviet Socialist Republic, the Byelorussian Soviet Socialist Republic, and Albania, Bulgaria, Czechoslovakia, Hungary, and Romania had notified the World Health Organization that they no longer considered themselves members of the Organization, adopted resolutions stating "that while the World Health Organization will always welcome the resumption by these Members of full cooperation in the work of the Organization, it is not considered that any further action at this stage is desirable".

The Third World Health Assembly also adopted a resolution noting the announcement of the withdrawal of the Government of China and declaring "that the resumption by China of full participation in the work of the Organization will be welcomed".

In 1953 the Sixth World Health Assembly adopted a resolution welcoming the return of China to active participation in the World Health Organization and declaring "that, until China's financial situation has improved, a payment of an annual sum of not less than $10,000 shall be considered adequate to avoid the application of Article 7 of the Constitution [relating to the suspension of voting privileges of Members

---

* Reprinted by permission of The Royal Institute of International Affairs.

in arrears in their payments]". The resolution also included a decision "that the payment of the equivalent of US $125,000, to be applied to the arrears due to the Organization for 1953 and prior years, shall be accepted" and "that the balance of the arrears of China for the years prior to 1954 together with the amount remaining unpaid for 1954 shall be subject to future arrangements, when the financial condition of this country improves".

* * *

The Ninth World Health Assembly (1956) adopted a resolution which stated in part:

> Considering that, during the period in which [the Eastern European] Members were not actively participating in the work of the Organization, the Members who were actively participating carried the financial burden of the Organization, bore the cost of acquiring assets which now belong to the Organization, and of providing to Members not actively participating certain services of the Organization,
>
> 1. DECIDES that contributions must be paid in full for the years during which the Members participated actively in the work of the Organization (including the year during which the intention of the Member concerned no longer to participate in the work of the Organization was communicated to the Organization);
>
> 2. DECIDES that, for those years during which the Members did not actively participate in the work of the Organization, a token payment of five per cent of the amount assessed each year shall be required which shall, upon payment, be considered as discharging in full the financial obligations of those Members for the years concerned;
>
> 3. DECIDES that the payments required under paragraphs 1 and 2 above must be paid in US dollars or Swiss francs; and may be paid in equal annual instalments over a period not exceeding ten years * * *.

* * *

In 1957 the Executive Board of the World Health Organization noted with satisfaction communications from Albania, Bulgaria, Poland, and the Union of Soviet Socialist Republics notifying the Director–General of the World Health Organization of their resumption of active participation in the Organization.

The original Constitution of the United Nations Educational, Scientific and Cultural Organization, November 16, 1945, contained no clause concerning withdrawal from membership.

* * *

In December 1952 and January 1953, Poland, Hungary, and Czechoslovakia announced that they were withdrawing from UNESCO, alleging that the Organization was becoming an instrument in the cold war "against the peace-loving nations". The UNESCO General Conference adopted resolutions denying the allegations and inviting the three States to reconsider their decisions to withdraw.

[The three states returned to UNESCO in the second half of 1954. They were permitted to pay their arrearages over periods of several years. At the insistence of the UNESCO Contributions Committee, all three eventually paid in full although Poland and Czechoslovakia initially balked at paying anything for 1953.[a]]

AD HOC WITHDRAWAL

Taking into account the negotiating history of the respective constituent instruments, and applying Vienna Convention on the Law of Treaties *article 56*, would you say that the parties' original intentions regarding withdrawal were the same under the U.N. Charter, the WHO Constitution and the original UNESCO Constitution—none of which has (or had, in the case of UNESCO) any provision on withdrawal? Why would the United States attach an "understanding" on withdrawal when it accepted the WHO Constitution, but not when it joined UNESCO?

What was the legal significance of the UNESCO insistence that Hungary, Poland and Czechoslovakia pay their assessments for the period of their nonparticipation in the organization? Note that under the UNESCO Constitution, U.N. members are automatically entitled to UNESCO membership. Poland and Czechoslovakia (but not Hungary) were U.N. members when they resumed participation in UNESCO, so the absence of any formalities of readmission in their cases would not necessarily be inconsistent with a right of withdrawal.

Based on the materials so far in this Section, would the following be a correct statement of the law regarding suspension of participation in a "universal" international organization? In the absence of a provision in the constituent instrument on withdrawal or suspension of participation, a member state may suspend its participation at any time and without cause, subject to a duty to pay at least a portion of its budgetary assessment for the time it was away. It cannot, however, withdraw except as indicated in Vienna Convention on the Law of Treaties article 56(1), and a right of withdrawal is not to be implied from the nature of a treaty creating a global organization related to the United Nations.

Is that a sensible solution, when one considers both the desire for very broad participation in these organizations and the difficulty of enforcing a rule against voluntary suspension of participation? Is it consistent with Vienna Convention *article 57*?

a. See Feinberg, supra, at 209–10; 1985 U.N.Juridical Y.B. 156, 178.

EXPRESS PROVISIONS FOR WITHDRAWAL

The other specialized agencies do have provisions on withdrawal in their constituent instruments. In fact, the UNESCO incident described above prompted the amendment of the UNESCO Constitution setting forth a right of withdrawal.

M. WHITEMAN, DIGEST OF INTERNATIONAL LAW
Vol. 13, at 233–36 (1968).

At the second extraordinary session of the UNESCO General Conference in 1953, the United States proposed that the Director-General and the Executive Board of the Organization formulate "the necessary amendments to the Constitution to provide for withdrawal from membership in the Organization". The United States representative (Perkins) stressed "practical considerations", stating:

> The Organization cannot be in the very anomalous position for all time to come of continuing assessments against Member States that have declared they are not Members. It would be really futile to make assessments against such States when they have declared a year or more in advance that they were no longer Members, the implication being that they had no further intention of contributing to the work of the Organization. * * *

* * *

In accordance with the resolution regarding procedure for the withdrawal from membership, adopted at the second extraordinary session of the General Conference, July 4, 1953, the Director-General submitted to the eighth session of the General Conference two draft Constitutional amendments relating to withdrawal from membership.

> The first of those resolutions [of amendment] envisaged unilateral withdrawal, i.e. that the Member State concerned should simply give notice of its withdrawal, [sic] The second resolution stipulated that a withdrawal must be accepted by a two-thirds majority of the General Conference.

The Administrative Commission of the General Conference decided that the draft providing for unilateral withdrawal "should serve as a basis for a Constitutional amendment".

* * *

The resolution for the adoption of an amendment to article II (Membership) of the Constitution was adopted by the General Conference in Plenary Session on December 8, 1954. The amendment provides for the insertion in article II of a new paragraph 6 reading:

Any Member State or Associate Member of the Organization may withdraw from the Organization by notice addressed to the Director-General. Such notice shall take effect on 31 December of the year following that during which the notice was given. No such withdrawal shall effect [sic] the financial obligations owed to the Organization on the date the withdrawal takes effect. Notice of withdrawal by an Associate Member shall be given on its behalf by the Member State or other authority having responsibility for its international relations.

PRACTICE UNDER WITHDRAWAL PROVISIONS

After the UNESCO Constitution had been amended to provide a right of withdrawal, South Africa exercised that right because of criticism of its domestic policies by the organization. The UNESCO Executive Board denied that the organization had acted improperly, and "urgently appealed" to South Africa to reconsider before its decision took effect.[b] South Africa did not reconsider, and remained outside the organization.

The Food and Agriculture Organization Constitution, article XIX, gives members an express right of withdrawal on one year's notice, at any time after the expiration of four years from the date the member joined the organization. The Republic of China exercised this right in 1951. After the U.N. General Assembly recognized the People's Republic as the Chinese representative, it was allowed to participate as a member of FAO without any formal readmission.[c] South Africa withdrew from FAO in 1963,[d] and had not rejoined as of mid-1992.

The Convention on International Civil Aviation (the constituent instrument of the International Civil Aviation Organization (ICAO)—a specialized agency examined in Chapters 3 and 4, infra) contains an express right of denunciation (withdrawal) in article 95, on one year's notice. The Republic of China exercised its right in 1950, but formally rejoined the organization on January 1, 1954.[e] In 1971, ICAO recognized the People's Republic as the Chinese representative.[f]

In the first twenty-five years following World War II, five member states gave notice of withdrawal from the International Labor Organization pursuant to *article 1, paragraph 5* of its Constitution, which permits withdrawal on two years' notice. Two of the five (Venezuela in 1955 and Indonesia in 1965) rescinded their notices of withdrawal before they took effect, one (Yugoslavia) was readmitted four years

b. See Report of the Director General [of UNESCO] on the Activities of the Organization in 1965, at 19.

c. 11 Int'l Legal Materials 562–64 (1972).

d. 13 Whiteman, Digest of Int'l Law 242 (1968).

e. T. Buergenthal, Law-Making in the International Civil Aviation Organization 35–36 (1969).

f. 11 Int'l Legal Materials 567 (1972).

after it had withdrawn, and one (Albania) was readmitted in 1991. South Africa remained outside the organization.[g]

In 1975 the United States submitted a notice of intent to withdraw from the ILO. In the late 1960s and early 1970s the United States became increasingly disturbed at what seemed to it to be the increasing politicization of the ILO. The matter came to a head in 1975 when the ILO permitted the Palestine Liberation Organization to participate in its General Conference, but, as the document below demonstrates, that was not the only irritant.

LETTER FROM THE U.S. SECRETARY OF STATE TO THE DIRECTOR GENERAL OF THE INTERNATIONAL LABOR ORGANIZATION
Nov. 5, 1975.
U.N. Doc. A/C.5/1704, Annex, at 1–3; 14 Int'l Legal Materials 1582 (1975).

This letter constitutes notice of the intention of the United States to withdraw from the International Labour Organisation. It is transmitted pursuant to article 1, paragraph 5, of the Constitution of the organization, which provides that a member may withdraw provided that a notice of intention to withdraw has been given two years earlier to the Director General and subject to the member having at that time fulfilled all financial obligations arising out of its membership.

Rather than express regret at this action, I would prefer to express confidence in what will be its ultimate outcome. The United States does not desire to leave the ILO. The United States does not expect to do so. But we do intend to make every possible effort to promote the conditions which will facilitate our continued participation. If this should prove impossible, we are in fact prepared to depart.

* * *

1. The Erosion of Tripartite Representation

The ILO exists as an organization in which representatives of workers, employers, and Governments may come together to further mutual interests. The Constitution of the ILO is predicated on the existence within member States of relatively independent and reasonably self-defined and self-directed worker and employer groups. * * * In particular, we cannot accept the workers and employers groups in the ILO falling under the domination of Governments.

---

g. South Africa originally attempted to withdraw without giving two years' notice, on the ground that the ILO's hostility toward its apartheid system amounted to a breach of the Organization's obligations to it under the ILO Constitution and thus justified its immediate termination of its duties under the Constitution. Cf. Vienna Convention on the Law of Treaties art. 60. South Africa's assertion was not accepted by the ILO, and it remained a member for the two-year notice period. See C. Jenks, Social Justice in the Law of Nations 64–66 (1970): 49 ILO Official Bull., No. 2, at 199–202 (1966).

2. SELECTIVE CONCERN FOR HUMAN RIGHTS

The ILO Conference for some years now has shown an appallingly selective concern in the application of the ILO's basic conventions on Freedom of Association and Forced Labour. It pursues the violation of human rights in some member States. It grants immunity from such citations to others. * * *

3. DISREGARD OF DUE PROCESS

The ILO once had an enviable record of objectivity and concern for due process in its examination of alleged violations of basic human rights by its member States. The Constitution of the ILO provides for procedures to handle representations and complaints that a member State is not observing a convention which it has ratified. Further, it was the ILO which first established fact-finding and conciliation machinery to respond to allegations of violations of trade union rights. In [the early 1970s,] however, sessions of the ILO conference increasingly have adopted resolutions condemning particular member States which happen to be the political target of the moment, in utter disregard of the established procedures and machinery. * * *

4. THE INCREASING POLITICIZATION OF THE ORGANIZATION

In [the early 1970s] the ILO has become increasingly and excessively involved in political issues which are quite beyond the competence and mandate of the organization. The ILO does have a legitimate and necessary interest in certain issues with political ramifications. It has major responsibility, for example, for international action to promote and protect fundamental human rights, particularly in respect of freedom of association, trade union rights and the abolition of forced labour. But international politics is not the main business of the ILO. Questions involving relations between States and proclamations of economic principles should be left to the United Nations and other international agencies where their consideration is more relevant to those organizations' responsibilities. Irrelevant political issues divert the attention of the ILO from improving the conditions of workers— that is, from questions on which the tripartite structure of the ILO gives the organization a unique advantage over the other, purely governmental, organizations of the United Nations family.

* * *

I hope that this letter will contribute to a fuller appreciation of the current attitude of the United States toward the ILO. In due course the United States will be obliged to consider whether or not it wishes to carry out the intention stated in this letter and to withdraw from the ILO. During the next two years the United States for its part will work constructively within the ILO to help the organization return to its basic principles and to a fuller achievement of its fundamental objectives.

U.S. WITHDRAWAL PRACTICE

To the surprise of many, the United States allowed its notice of withdrawal from the ILO to take effect as scheduled, and thus ceased to be a member as of November 4, 1977. The reason given was that the ILO had continued to follow those practices the U.S. had deemed objectionable in its letter of November 5, 1975. This deprived the ILO of about $20 million a year in U.S. dues until the United States rejoined on February 18, 1980.

Was there anything legally improper about the U.S. withdrawal?

When the United States rejoined, President Carter and the U.S. State Department announced that the ILO had made progress in all four areas cited in the 1975 U.S. notice of withdrawal. It had adopted several resolutions strengthening its tripartite decisionmaking system; it had applied its human rights machinery to Eastern Europe; it had improved its regard for due process; and its meetings had become less politicized, particularly on Middle East issues.[h] The extent to which the changes were attributable to the U.S. withdrawal was not clear; many observers thought there was some cause and effect relationship, but few thought that the U.S. withdrawal alone was responsible.[i] A particularly significant due process change actually was adopted several years after the United States rejoined.[j]

To return to 1977, the question arose as the United States' two-year notice-of-withdrawal period was about to expire, whether the period could be extended without having to give another two years' notice. If so, it was thought that the United States might extend the deadline somewhat and continue to participate. (As noted above, the United States did not do so.) The ILO Legal Adviser considered the matter and concluded that the extension would be permissible, with all rights and obligations of membership (including financial obligations) remaining in force. The Legal Adviser found that ILO Constitution article 1, paragraph 5 (the withdrawal provision) was ambiguous on this point. Thus he examined its context, and made these two points in particular:

> (a) The essence of paragraph 5 of Article 1 of the Constitution is that no State may withdraw without having given two years' notice of its intention so to do. The purpose of the notice period is

---

h. See 80 Dep't State Bull., April 1980, at 65.

i. See L. McHugh, U.S. Withdrawal from the International Labor Organization: Successful Precedent for UNESCO? vii (Congressional Research Service Rep. No. 84–202, 1984); R. Coate, Unilateralism, Ideology, & U.S. Foreign Policy: The United States In and Out of UNESCO 55–56 (1988).

j. See amended Article 17 of the Standing Orders of the Conference, Int'l Labor Conf., 72d Sess., Provisional Record of Proceedings, Draft Amendments to the ILO Constitution and Conf. Standing Orders 11 (1986) (dealing with procedure when a resolution condemning a member state is proposed).

to give the Organisation time to adjust to the consequences of withdrawal, particularly the financial consequences. This is adequately confirmed in the "preparatory work" (which expressly rejects a possible one year notice period). The considerations which make impossible withdrawal after less than two years do not apply to a longer notice period. A State which, say, gave three years' notice from the beginning, would give the Organisation greater time to adjust, while an extension of notice would permit relaxation of any conservatory measures already taken or planned to the extent consistent with the extension.

(b) The aim of the membership provisions of the Constitution in their entirety is to achieve universality; this is made amply clear by the records of the 1945 session of the Conference, as well as various provisions in the Preamble to the Constitution and the Declaration of Philadelphia annexed thereto. In that light, it would not make sense to require that membership cease at a time when the State concerned is prepared to continue membership at least for a specified further period.[k]

Are these strong arguments? Are they consistent with Vienna Convention on the Law of Treaties *articles 31 and 32*, on treaty interpretation?

If the ILO Legal Adviser's opinion was correct, could a state such as the United States exert its leverage by giving the two-year notice, and then extend it a month at a time indefinitely? Could it instead simply say at the end of the original two-year period that it is extending its notice without any new effective date, and then withdraw whenever it decides it has had enough?

What policies underlie an explicit withdrawal provision in an international organization's constituent instrument?

In addition to its withdrawal from the ILO, the United States has withdrawn from UNESCO. As noted at page 259 supra, the UNESCO Constitution was amended in 1954 to permit withdrawal upon notice effective on December 31 of the year following that during which the notice is given. The United States gave its notice to UNESCO on December 28, 1983. Although several factors appear to have influenced the U.S. decision, one in particular was in the public eye at the time. Many member states in UNESCO had been pressing the organization to adopt a "New World Information and Communications Order," which the U.S. government and Western media regarded as a move toward greater governmental control worldwide over the press. In addition, the United States was concerned about growth in the UNESCO budget, extension of UNESCO's activities beyond those originally contemplated, and the growing authority exercised by the Director General. Consider the reasons given in the letter from U.S.

k. 1977 U.N. Juridical Y.B. 248, 250.

Secretary of State George P. Schultz, and consider also the reply from Amadou–Mahtar M'Bow, then the Director General of UNESCO.

LETTER FROM THE U.S. SECRETARY OF STATE TO THE DIRECTOR GENERAL OF UNESCO
Dec. 28, 1983.
84 Dep't State Bull., Feb. 1984, at 41.

Dear Mr. Director General:

The purpose of this letter is to notify you within the terms of Article Two Paragraph Six of the Constitution that my Government will withdraw from the United Nations Educational, Scientific and Cultural Organization effective December 31, 1984.

You may be assured that the United States will, within the terms of the Constitution, seek to meet fully all of its legitimate financial obligations.

* * *

For a number of years, as you know from statements we have made at the Executive Board and elsewhere, we have been concerned that trends in the management, policy and budget of UNESCO were detracting from the organization's effectiveness. We believed these trends to be leading UNESCO away from the original principles of its Constitution. We felt that they tended to serve—willingly or unwillingly, but improperly—the political purposes of a few member states. During this period we worked energetically to encourage the organization to reverse these trends; to redirect itself to its founding purposes; to rigorously avoid becoming a servant of one or another national policy; and to manage itself in a way that rewarded efficiency, promoted fearless program evaluation and followed priorities based on program value rather than on past habit, political expediency or some other extraneous consideration.

* * *

At the same time, we also recognized, and expressed our strong concern about, those pressures to divert UNESCO to politically motivated ends which emanated from member states, rather than from within the organization itself. We consistently worked in the Executive Board and General Conference to minimize or eliminate the resulting political content—tendentious and partisan—from UNESCO resolutions and programs.

* * *

REPLY FROM THE DIRECTOR GENERAL OF UNESCO

Jan. 18, 1984.
Staff of House Foreign Affairs Comm., 98th Cong., 2d Sess., Report on U.S. Withdrawal from UNESCO, Appendix 3 (Comm. Print 1984); 23 Int'l Legal Materials 224 (1984).

Dear Mr. Secretary,

* * *

While it is not for me to voice an opinion on a sovereign decision by your Government, I cannot but say how deeply I regret the withdrawal from the Organization of one of its founder members, whose authorities, educators, scientists and intellectuals of all kinds have hitherto made an outstanding and constant contribution to the work of Unesco and have undoubtedly themselves benefited from that co-operation.

I have always emphasized the need to maintain the universality of the Organization * * *. Your Government's decision to withdraw, if it were to come into effect, would affect the very principle of that universality.

* * *

It is true that, in the thirty-seven years since its foundation, there may have been some changes in the subjects of immediate concern to Unesco and in the weight of emphasis placed by the General Conference on particular aspects of the programmes which it has adopted. The fact is that immense changes have taken place in international society as a result of decolonization and the accession of the peoples of the former colonies to independence and their entry into international life. The number of Unesco's Member States has increased from 28, mainly Western countries, at the time of its establishment, to 161 today. The peoples represented by these new Member States belong to the most widely varying cultures and spiritual traditions, and their economic and social situations differ very greatly. These peoples have enriched the Organization with their diversity but have also brought with them their own subjects of concern. It is in keeping with Unesco's mission to help them solve their problems in order to attain its "objectives of international peace and of the common welfare of mankind", a mankind which has at long last found its true dimensions.

NOTICE OF WITHDRAWAL FROM UNESCO

Did the Secretary of State's letter give the UNESCO Director General and other member states notice of what needed to be done to forestall U.S. withdrawal on December 31, 1984? Was it as explicit as the 1975 letter of intent to withdraw from the ILO?

Was there any legal requirement that either letter give reasons for withdrawal? (If not, why wouldn't there be such a requirement?)

The UNESCO Director General referred to the principle of universality in his response to the U.S. notice of intent to withdraw. Is that a legal principle? If so, what is its significance?

In July 1984, midway through the year while U.S. withdrawal from UNESCO was pending, Gregory Newell, the Assistant Secretary of State for International Organization Affairs, wrote the UNESCO Director General regarding the steps the United States wished UNESCO to take.

LETTER FROM THE ASSISTANT SECRETARY OF STATE FOR INTERNATIONAL ORGANIZATION AFFAIRS TO THE DIRECTOR GENERAL OF UNESCO
July 13, 1984.
Staff of House Foreign Affairs Comm., 99th Cong., 1st Sess.,
Report on Assessment of U.S.–UNESCO Relations,
Appendix 4 (Comm. Print 1984).

* * *

[In order to put U.S. views on UNESCO's program in context,] I wish in this letter to delineate those basic changes we regard as most necessary if UNESCO is to regain the confidence and support of all segments of its membership.

Among the reforms advocated by the United States and the other members of the Western Information Group, three are of fundamental importance. They involve, first, creation of a mechanism to ensure that, in major matters, UNESCO decisions and programs enjoy the support of all geographic groups, including the support of the group that contributes the major part of UNESCO's budget; second, a return to concentration on UNESCO's original purposes, with which we can all agree; third, the assumption by member states of their rightful authority in the organization, through the strengthening of the General Conference and, in particular, its Executive Board. * * *

The representational principle of one-nation, one-vote, is not inappropriate in UNESCO. But it should be understood that the UNESCO decision-making system can be unrealistic, when it encourages the facile consensus adoption of programs which establish cumulative trends antithetical to the position of the geographic group that contributes an overwhelmingly large part of the budget.

* * *

We have, for years, participated in UNESCO's consensus process, and have tried to protect our interests to the degree possible. But we now find ourselves in deep disagreement with the direction that UNESCO programs have taken in areas such as human rights, disarmament, budget, press freedom, and the role of the state vis-à-vis that of the individual. * * *

We would hope that the Executive Board would consider the following at its [next] session:

A strengthened drafting and negotiating group at the General Conference, directed to consider contentious issues, which issues would be decided only upon the basis of full agreement among all the geographic groups represented.

The introduction of a similar mechanism for the Executive Board.

A procedure for voting on the budget that would ensure that no budget would pass without the affirmative support of members who together contribute at least 51% of the organization's funds.

* * *

Examples of divisive activities are found in certain uncritical and simplistic approaches to disarmament, economic theorizing, and global standard-setting (except where consensus is possible and the need for universal norms is widely felt in the international community, e.g., in the area of copyright). It is in areas such as these that UNESCO, instead of acting as a unifier of member states, becomes, rather, a partisan participant in existing quarrels, or even, in several cases, the initiator of new quarrels. It is, for example, in such areas as the promotion of "collective" rights and the creation of a "New World Information and Communication Order" that UNESCO has most visibly taken sides in the struggle between libertarians and statists, between those whose primary concern is for the individual and those who are willing to subordinate the individual's well-being to that of society or the state. This is not an appropriate role for a United Nations specialized agency.

THE WITHDRAWAL

On December 19, 1984, Secretary of State Shultz notified the Director General that "the evidence that could have persuaded us to rescind or modify our original withdrawal notice is not present."[1] Thus the United States ceased to be a member of UNESCO on December 31, 1984.[m]

In both the ILO and UNESCO, the United States had a great deal of leverage when it gave notice of its intent to withdraw, since the United States provided 25% of the budgeted funds of each organization. In both cases, the organizations moved toward the U.S. position during the notice period, though not far enough to forestall U.S. withdrawal. Is there anything wrong with using the withdrawal mechanism in this way?

l. Appendix 8 to the House Foreign Affairs Committee Print quoted above.

m. For a detailed discussion of the legal issues raised by the U.S. withdrawal, see 1985 U.N. Juridical Y.B. 156.

If you represented a small member state resentful of the withdrawal tactics of the United States, would you favor a change in the withdrawal provisions in specialized agencies' constituent instruments? (Why is there a waiting period in these instruments? The Articles of Agreement of the International Monetary Fund and World Bank provide that withdrawal is effective immediately upon notice. Would that be a workable provision for the ILO and UNESCO?)

Disaffected member states have sometimes taken steps short of invoking a withdrawal provision, to express their dissatisfaction with an international organization. Occasionally this has amounted to suspension of all participation in the organization; on other occasions it has taken the form of withheld dues, or at least a threat to withhold them.

If there is an express provision for withdrawal in an organization's constituent instrument, does that negate any implied right to suspend all participation?

For example, after UNESCO in November 1974 decided to suspend its assistance to Israel and took action leaving Israel as the only member not belonging to a UNESCO regional group, Israel announced that it would suspend cooperation with UNESCO until those measures were revoked. (Israel later was admitted to the appropriate regional group.) If we assume that the UNESCO measures were not such a material breach of the organization's duties to Israel as to justify Israel's response under the law of treaties,[n] would Israel be entitled to "suspend cooperation" without withdrawing, despite the express UNESCO withdrawal procedure?

There is at least one other precedent for temporary nonparticipation short of withdrawal in an organization having an express withdrawal procedure. When ICAO in 1947 took action under pressure from the U.N. General Assembly that would have eventually resulted in the expulsion of Franco Spain, the latter suspended its participation. When the General Assembly relented in its attitude toward Franco in 1950, Spain resumed its participation in ICAO without much fuss by the organization.[o]

The United States has been the primary party involved in the actual or threatened withholding of dues from specialized agencies. These materials examine this practice in two contexts, both of which arose in 1989: "Palestine's" application for membership in the World Health Organization, and the Food and Agriculture Organization's

---

n. The UNESCO measures involving Israel are examined in Chapter 4, infra.

o. See 13 M. Whiteman, Digest of Int'l L. 210–11 (1968); T. Buergenthal, Law-Making in the International Civil Aviation Organization 39–42 (1969).

resolution on the provision of technical assistance to the Palestinian people.

(1) *"Palestine's" application to WHO:* For background regarding "Palestine's" eligibility for membership in WHO, see the materials on "statehood" in the U.N. and the specialized agencies, at pages 138–39 and 153–58 supra; see also the materials relating specifically to Palestine and WHO at pages 158–64 supra.

If "Palestine" fit within the international law definition of a "state" in 1989, its admission to WHO or to any other organization with similar conditions for membership would not violate the constituent instrument, assuming that all procedural requirements were met. In that case, other members clearly would not be entitled to withhold dues in response if the constituent instrument makes fulfillment of members' financial obligations a duty.

Does the WHO Constitution make payment of dues obligatory? See *articles* 7 and 56. Note also the following excerpt from the legal memorandum of the Legal Adviser of the U.S. Department of State in 1978. After he had argued that U.N. Charter article 17(2) makes payment of U.N. assessments obligatory, he said:

> As the Constitutions of the Specialized Agencies use parallel language, it can be assumed that the intent of the drafters was the same as that of the drafters of the Charter itself. Without contrary evidence, consistent interpretation necessitates the conclusion that assessments thereunder also create a binding legal obligation.[p]

If "Palestine" was not a state under customary international law in 1989, would it follow that it was ineligible for membership in WHO? Note that the WHO Constitution does not contain its own definition of "state."

If WHO, or another specialized agency, were to admit a nonstate in disregard of the requirements for membership in its constituent instrument, would the United States be entitled to withhold its dues under Vienna Convention on the Law of Treaties, *article 60?*

If there are problems with article 60, could the United States make a strong argument under the customary international law of reprisal? In general, the law of reprisal authorizes a state injured by a violation of international law (usually by another state) to apply limited measures—short of the use of armed force—against the violator even though those measures themselves normally would be prohibited under international law. The law of reprisal requires that the aggrieved state try to settle the matter short of reprisal, if that is feasible, and applies a rough test of proportionality to the measures taken in reprisal.[q] A

---

[p]. Hansell, The Legal Character of U.N. Budget Assessments, Aug. 7, 1978, in 1979 Digest of United States Practice in Int'l Law 226, 227.

[q]. See Willem Riphagen's Sixth Report on State Responsibility, [1985] 2 Y.B.Int'l L.Comm'n, pt. 1, at 3, 11, U.N. Doc. A/CN.4/SER.A/1985/Add.1; Naulilaa In-

measure is not necessarily disproportionate just because it exceeds the breaching act in intensity by enough to provide some degree of deterrence against repeated or similar breaches.[r]

(2) *FAO's resolution on the provision of technical assistance to the Palestinian people:* On November 29, 1989, after a heated debate, the FAO Conference (the plenary body of FAO) adopted the following resolution by a vote of 96 in favor, two opposed (Israel, United States), and 14 abstaining. Another 45 member states declined to participate in the vote.

FAO CONFERENCE RESOLUTION ON PROVISION OF TECHNICAL ASSISTANCE TO THE PALESTINIAN PEOPLE
Nov. 29, 1989.
FAO Doc. C 89/REP/2, at 8.

THE CONFERENCE,

* * *

Recognizing that the policies and practices of the Israeli occupation authorities impede the basic requirements for the development of the economy of the occupied Palestinian territory, including the agricultural sector.

Affirming the importance of supporting the agricultural sector in the occupied Palestinian territory,

Expressing its opposition to the Israeli confiscation of Palestinian land and expropriation of Palestinian water resources:

* * *

2. *Requests* the Director–General to send a mission to study and evaluate the situation of the agricultural sector in the occupied Palestinian territory, taking into consideration the conditions of the farmers under the existing occupation policies and practices, and to prepare a report comprising possible technical interventions to be executed by FAO;

3. *Requests* the Director–General to organize a symposium on the Palestinian agricultural sector;

4. *Requests* the Director–General to include the occupied Palestinian territory in future FAO programmes and activities, and in line with the present cooperation and coordination between the Palestine Liberation Organisation and other UN Agencies;

---

cident Arbitration, 2 UNRIAA 1012 (1928), summarized in 6 G. Hackworth, Digest of Int'l L. 154–55 (1943).

r. U.S.–France Air Services Arbitral Award, 18 UNRIAA 417, 443–44, 54 Int'l L.Reports 304, 338 (1979); Schachter, International Law in Theory and Practice 193–94 (1991).

5. *Calls* for free access of FAO staff and experts to the occupied Palestinian territory * * *.

THE RESPECTIVE POSITIONS

The day before the FAO Conference was scheduled to vote on the resolution, the U.S. Secretary of Agriculture sent a telegram to Eduoard Saouma, the Director General of FAO:

DEAR EDUOARD:

I have carefully reviewed the language of the resolution adopted by Commission I regarding the provision of technical assistance to the Palestinian People. While I have no objection to FAO becoming involved in projects in the occupied territories, I think it would be ill-advised for the organization to do so in such a way as to involve itself in the geopolitical process.

There is considerable concern about this issue both in the administration and in the Congress. It would be regrettable if key officials in the U.S. Government came to feel about FAO as they were forced to about UNESCO. I reiterate that I have no difficulty with the substantive issue of FAO involvement in agricultural development assistance in the occupied territories.[s]

On December 1, 1989, the FAO Director General replied by letter:

Dear Clayton,

Mr. Monroe has brought me your personal message regarding the eventual consequences that the adoption, by the FAO Conference, of the Resolution on technical assistance to the Palestinian People could have on your Government's perception of FAO. I have also been very much concerned by the various press articles published recently by influential US newspapers on this subject.

I must first put on record that this Resolution was an issue that I did not seek or welcome, and that I did everything possible to deflect/defuse the problem. * * *

[Several meetings with interested parties] and my own personal interventions had the effect of considerably moderating the language of the Resolution. But you should be aware that in my efforts the financial position of your country vis-à-vis the Organization did not help. Moreover, I must put on record that to depict the Resolution adopted in FAO as a text going beyond what has been done on this subject throughout the United Nations System would be a gross misrepresentation.

* * *

---

s. Transmitted by the Department of State, No. 378982, Nov. 28, 1989.

The FAO Resolution was introduced on the initiative of Egypt, the privileged partner of the US in the Region. It does not employ the strong terms used in other UN fora, such as WHO, and avoids highly controversial points. This is probably why France, as the country holding the Presidency of the EEC Council, and in the name of all EEC members, spoke in favour of the Resolution. Indeed all the traditional allies of the US voted in favour of the Resolution, including the United Kingdom and all Scandinavian countries attending the Conference. In fact, the US and Israel were the only two countries to cast dissenting votes out of 112 Member Nations present and voting.

No one in all good faith could find in this FAO Resolution a credible pretext for cutting off dues to FAO, unless your Government were first to stop paying its dues to all UN bodies which have adopted more controversial and far-reaching texts on the matter, sometimes on a yearly basis and over the past ten years.[t]

On the Conference floor, after the resolution had been adopted, the United States and Saudi Arabian representatives explained their positions:

Gerald Monroe (*United States*): * * * The US regrets that the sponsors of this Resolution have rejected several means by which they could have achieved their purported purpose, in favour of a Resolution which contains an unbalanced attack upon a member of FAO, and which will decrease rather than increase, the chances for successfully implementing an FAO program.

* * *

Atif Bukhari (*Saudi Arabia*) (original in Arabic): On behalf of the Arab group, which sponsored this draft resolution, we * * * would like to stress that we did not intend to introduce this resolution as a politicization of the work of the Organization, and we call upon the Organization not to enter into such a politicization, but to concentrate its efforts towards introducing appropriate assistance in the Palestinian Arab Territories.[u]

In January 1990, the U.S. State Department notified Dr. Saouma that the United States would pay only $18 million of its 1989 FAO budget assessment (of $61.4 million). The U.S. letter cited four areas of concern: the size of FAO's 1990–91 budget ($569 million), adopted without a consensus; the need to reform FAO's organizational structure, management processes and decision-making; politicization, as exemplified by the resolution on technical assistance to the Palestinian people; and insufficient efforts to recruit Americans for secretariat positions.[v]

---

t. FAO File No. DG/89/1689.

u. FAO Doc. C 89/PV/21, at 19 (1989).

v. Letter from John R. Bolton, Assistant Secretary for International Organization Affairs, to Dr. Eduoard Saouma, Jan. 3, 1990.

The $18 million payment was just enough to prevent the United States from losing its vote in the Conference under FAO Constitution article III(4), which removes the vote of a member in arrears by the amount of its two preceding years' assessments. (The United States was already substantially in arrears before January 1990.)

Does the United States have an obligation to pay the dues the FAO Conference assesses to it? See FAO Constitution *articles XVIII(2)* and *III(4)*.

If there is an obligation, would it be excused on the grounds asserted by the various U.S. representatives in their opposition to the resolution on the provision of technical assistance to the Palestinian people? Consider, in this regard, whether FAO was acting in accordance with its own purposes as set forth in its Constitution.

The FAO Director General, in his letter to the U.S. Secretary of Agriculture, asserted that other U.N. bodies had adopted more controversial and far-reaching texts on the Palestine matter. Was that relevant to any legal issue relating either to adoption of the FAO resolution or to the U.S. reaction?

If there is doubt about the lawfulness of the U.S. withholding, what lawful way was there for the United States to express its displeasure?

Is there an ethical problem here? [w]

---

[w]. The United States is not the only member to withhold dues because of dissatisfaction with the proceedings at a plenary meeting of a specialized agency. In 1990 the United Kingdom cut in half its subscription to the International Telecommunication Union in protest at the debate in the 1989 ITU Plenipotentiary Conference. Financial Times, Feb. 15, 1990, p. 4, col. 8.

Chapter 3

RULE MAKING AND DISPUTE SETTLEMENT

SECTION 1. RULE–MAKING POWERS

INTRODUCTORY NOTE

Since the decline in the 18th Century of natural law as the acknowledged basis for international order, the orthodox view has been that the only legitimate source for an international right or obligation is the express or tacit consent of each state to which it applies. This positivist doctrine finds expression in the sources of international law enumerated in *article 38(1)* of the Statute of the International Court of Justice, particularly the first two sources—international conventions (treaties) and custom. But treaty-formulation and custom-building can be slow and cumbersome processes; moreover, once a rule is embodied in a treaty or in custom, it may be difficult to adapt it to keep pace with changing circumstances. As the face of the world changes at an accelerating rate, international law has had to try to find ways to keep up. One way is to nudge away from strict positivism; that is, away from the notion that any new or amended rule of international law can be applied to a given state only if that state has expressly consented to it. Norms of general application can then come into existence as norms do in domestic law for individuals and corporate entities through legislation and administrative rule-making.

To the extent that states are willing to divest themselves of their sovereignty for this purpose, they have the means by which to do it over a wide variety of matters, in the United Nations and its related agencies on a global scale, and in various regional groupings such as the European Communities on a narrower geographic scale. As we have seen, these organizations have organs—typically a large plenary body, a smaller chamber that can meet relatively frequently, and a secretariat—capable of acting as rule-makers and/or rule-administrators, if empowered to do so by the member states. The principal inquiry of this Section will be into the extent to which, and ways in which, this can come about in the global organizations. Five organizations with differing "rule-making" practices have been selected for study.

Before we get to that, some definitions are needed. The term "rule-making" has been chosen for this section in order to avoid limiting the inquiry to those normative acts that would be done in a domestic legal system only by a legislature (as distinguished from a regulatory agency or other body with norm-creating functions). Nevertheless, the inquiry is essentially into matters that are "legislative" in the sense summarized in E. Yemin, Legislative Powers in the United Nations and Specialized Agencies 6 (1969): "[L]egislative acts have three essential characteristics: they are unilateral in form, they create or modify some element of a legal norm, and the legal norm in question is general in nature, that is, directed to indeterminate addressees and capable of repeated application in time." By "unilateral in form," he meant that the norm is promulgated by a designated person or body, and not by agreement among all those to be governed by it. The second element—creation or modification of a legal norm—is more elusive. Although Yemin did not put it quite this way, it may be thought of as the creation or modification of a standard intended, and reasonably likely in practice, to carry more weight than a suggestion or an exhortation. The clearest case, of course, would be the rule designed to govern conduct through use of mandatory language, with express, meaningful sanctions enforceable by a duly constituted enforcement agency. That is a relatively rare phenomenon in international organizations, and in international law generally. Yet international organizations do often create or modify norms that are considered by member states as more than mere suggestions or exhortations; it will be the business of this section to identify, compare and evaluate instances in which that clearly or arguably happens.

There is one type of legal norm created by international organizations—in fact the type falling most clearly within the definition—that will not be examined in any detail: the internal body of rules of any given organization. In most organizations of any size, some organ or organs will have the power to make certain rules for the internal functioning of the organization. Examples would include the Rules of Procedure of the U.N. General Assembly and Security Council. Another typical example is the authority to approve the budget of the organization and to assess member states for their shares. See, e.g., U.N. Charter *article 17*. Under *article 18(2)*, these matters do not require the consent of all member states for enactment, and *article 19* provides a sanction for failure to meet the resulting financial obligations. (The sanction is not always meaningful and enforceable.) In any event, our primary focus will not be on internal rules, but on those with broader standard-setting significance.

The purposes and structure of each organization discussed below are set forth in the Introductions to Selected International Organizations in the Supplement to this book.

A. THE INTERNATIONAL LABOR ORGANIZATION

Much of the legal work of the ILO consists of the promulgation and supervision of labor conventions (treaties) and recommendations. As of August 1, 1992, the International Labor Conference had approved 173 labor conventions and 180 recommendations. A few of the conventions were not yet in force and some had been superseded by later conventions. Each was adopted under the ILO's unique tripartite representation system in which labor and employers' groups, as well as governments, participate. In the annual General Conference, each member state is represented by two government representatives and one each from labor and employers' groups.

Draft conventions and recommendations are submitted to the Conference, often under the "double discussion" procedure. This calls for discussion during the first annual session at which the proposal is made, with further discussion, and possible adoption, at the next annual session. When a convention is adopted, it is not signed by government representatives (as most multilateral non-ILO conventions would be), but is simply approved by the requisite majority of votes at the Conference.

The collection of ILO conventions and recommendations is sometimes referred to as "international labor legislation" or the "International Labor Code."[a] It is acknowledged, though, that there are significant differences between ILO "legislation" and legislation enacted by a duly empowered domestic body such as the United States Congress. As you read the materials below, consider the extent to which ILO rule-making resembles a true legislative process as defined in the Introductory Note to this section.

VALTICOS, THE INTERNATIONAL LABOUR ORGANIZATION
The Effectiveness of International Decisions 134–35.
(S. Schwebel ed. 1971).*

Since its establishment in 1919, the International Labour Organization has regarded it essential that one of its main courses of action should be the formulation of standards on labour policies which would be embodied in legal instruments of an international character.

The following main reasons can be given for this approach. The first was the problem of international competition: as proposals for the introduction of national legislation on labour matters were often objected to on the ground that such legislation would increase the production

---

a. See, e.g., G. Johnston, The International Labour Organisation 90–91 (1970); N. Valticos, International Labour Law 46 (1979); V.-Y. Ghebali, The International Labour Organisation: A Case Study on the Evolution of U.N. Specialised Agencies 210–12 (1989); cf. V. Leary, International Labour Conventions and National Law 11–14 (1982).

* Reprinted by permission of A.W. Sijthoff International Publishing Co.

cost and would jeopardize the relative position of the country concerned vis-à-vis its competitors in the world markets, it was hoped that the adoption of international labour standards would minimize the kind of unfair competition described as "social dumping". A more general objective for the adoption of international labour standards was to establish universal and lasting peace upon a firm internationally defined basis of social justice. Still more widely, it is felt that social progress should be promoted through concerned international action for reasons of justice and humanity, and that this could best be done on the basis of clearly defined standards of policy.

International labour standards are contained in two different kinds of instruments: Conventions, which, following ratification, become binding on ratifying States, and Recommendations which are not designed for the creation of obligations but are essentially guides for national action.

* * *

The relative appropriateness of Conventions and Recommendations respectively to deal with a given question depends in each case on the subject-matter and the degree of maturity of the question. Recommendations may be adopted, in particular, when the complexity of the subject and wide differences in the circumstances of different countries make it impossible to provide for a universal and uniform mode of application of international standards, or where this is an exploratory measure, with a view to the subsequent embodiment of the standards in a Convention, or where a more detailed Recommendation aims at supplementing a Convention drafted in more general terms.

* * *

These instruments relate to the most varied fields of labour policy. They can be grouped into three main categories. The first group in which Conventions and Recommendations were adopted, in particular during the first part of the activity of the Organization, related to the traditional and most urgent fields of labour protection, especially at that time, such as conditions of work and living (hours of work, weekly rest, holidays with pay), work of women and children, social security, industrial hygiene and safety, etc. The second group of instruments dealt with basic machinery and institutions without which the labour protection cannot be made really effective: labour inspection, employment service, labour statistics and minimum wage-fixing machinery. Finally, after a beginning in this field in the Thirties, the Conference has since the Second World War adopted a series of instruments aimed at promoting and ensuring the human rights and fundamental freedoms of workers, that is freedom of association, freedom from forced labour and freedom from discrimination in employment and occupation. In framing these standards an increasing effort is made to develop devices so as to allow the necessary flexibility for Conventions designed to be ratified by countries which have very different economic and social conditions and legal traditions, while maintaining the necessary firmness in regard to basic standards.

THE ILO RULE–MAKING PROCESS

ILO conventions and recommendations may also be grouped into two functional categories: promotional and duty-specific. Promotional instruments are worded in general terms, and are intended to push domestic legal systems toward goals—particularly in the human rights field. The more specific instruments are legislative in tone, and often could create direct rights and duties without further legislation, in domestic legal systems that recognize self-executing treaty provisions. These materials consider an example in each of these categories at pages 281–90 infra.

The procedure by which the General Conference adopts conventions and recommendations, and the obligations of member states once these instruments are adopted, appear in ILO Constitution *articles 4(1); 19(1), (2), (3), (5) & (6); 20; and 22.*

As indicated in Chapter 2, many non-ILO conventions may be ratified subject to reservations that purport to exclude or modify the legal effect of provisions to which the reserving state objects in whole or in part. The International Labor Office has consistently taken the position, accepted by member states, that labor conventions adopted by the General Conference may not be ratified subject to any reservation. The reasons are summarized in the excerpt below from a statement given by the International Labor Office in response to a request from the International Court of Justice when the Court was considering, at the request of the U.N. General Assembly, whether reservations could be made to a non-labor convention (the U.N.-sponsored Genocide Convention of 1948).

MEMORANDUM BY THE INTERNATIONAL LABOR OFFICE
Jan. 12, 1951.
Reservations to the Convention on the Prevention and Punishment of the Crime of Genocide, I.C.J. Pleadings 216, 235–36, 34 ILO Official Bull. 274, 287–88 (1951).

* * *

(c) The special considerations applicable to international labour conventions may be summarized as follows:

(i) they are adopted by a conference with a unique tripartite composition by a special procedure provided for in an international instrument of a constituent character, the Constitution of the International Labour Organization; and in this respect they are in a position entirely different from all other international instruments;

(ii) the governing constituent instrument [in article 19(5)(b) and (d)] contemplates the submission of conventions to national competent authorities, normally legislatures, in the form in which they were adopted by the Conference, and provides for ratification when the consent of the competent authority is obtained;

(iii) the governing constituent instrument [in articles 3 and 24] grants to employers' and workers' organizations rights to invoke, and to initiate procedures in connexion with the application of, the provisions of conventions, and gives their representatives an important place in the international organs entrusted with the supervision of such application, and the individual conventions provide for consultation with such organizations in connexion with the application of a wide range of provisions leaving certain matters to national discretion; the purpose of all these provisions would be completely frustrated by the acceptance of reservations in regard to which governments alone had been consulted * * *;

* * *

(v) the governing constituent instrument [in article 19(3)] provides a procedure for the modification of the provisions of conventions to meet special circumstances, and a wide range of further procedures, adapted to the circumstances of individual cases, are provided for by the terms of the various conventions; provision has therefore been made for the necessary flexibility by other procedures expressly sanctioned by the Constitution and the Conference * * *.

MORE ON THE ILO RULE–MAKING PROCESS

Many labor conventions contain a "flexibility clause" of the sort contemplated by article 19(3) and paragraph (v) above. These clauses take various forms, as indicated by an ILO Working Party:

The Working Party considers it useful to recall * * * that existing flexibility devices include, in particular, the possibility of accepting only some parts of a Convention; the possibility of excluding certain sectors of activity, categories of workers or areas of the country from its scope: "escalator" clauses allowing for implementation by stages; the adoption of Conventions laying down only basic principles; and the possibility of accepting alternative obligations.[b]

Flexibility clauses have not been thought appropriate for all labor conventions. In 1984, the Director–General of the ILO, referring to

---

b. Report of the Working Party on International Labour Standards, 70 ILO Official Bull., Ser. A, Special Issue, at 4 (1987).

speakers at the 1984 session of the International Labor Conference, said:

> A great many speakers stressed the fact that there could be absolutely no question of flexibility in the case of standards concerning basic rights such as freedom of association, the abolition of forced labour and the elimination of discrimination.[c]

The humanitarian motives behind this view are apparent. Are there any disadvantages in excluding flexibility clauses from ILO human rights conventions?

Is the flexibility clause a complete substitute for the ability to attach reservations in conventions for which a flexibility clause is appropriate?[d] Are the other reasons for rejecting reservations convincing?

Compare the ILO process for adopting conventions with the usual process at international "law-making" conferences not convened by the ILO. Typically at such conferences only governments will be represented, and each government will instruct its representative as to how to vote on major issues. Conventions are signed at these conferences, and often require ratification before they become binding.

There is normally no obligation on governments participating in such a conference to submit signed conventions to any domestic approval or ratification process. (Thus, in the case of the United States, there would normally be no international obligation to submit such a non-labor convention to the Senate for its advice and consent or to Congress for legislative approval.) Moreover, even if such a convention is approved by the domestic process, the state is not normally under any international obligation to ratify it. That is, it does not have to take the final step of signifying to the other signatories or parties its intention to be bound. If it does not ratify such a convention, it is not bound by it. As noted above, if a state does become a party to such a convention it could do so subject to a reservation, unless precluded by the treaty itself or unless the reservation is incompatible with the object and purpose of the treaty.

In the case of a resolution (not a convention) adopted by a non-ILO conference, normally the maximum obligation would be to consider it in good faith before acting on a matter to which it relates.

Obviously, on the matter of reservations, ILO conventions differ from many others. In what other respects does ILO rule-making differ from the usual international rule-making by way of conventions (or resolutions) adopted at non-ILO conferences? Do the differences, including those concerning reservations, bear on the "legislative" nature of the respective processes?

c. International Labor Conf., 70th Sess., Record of Proceedings 44/11 (1984).

d. Flexible standards are not unique to the ILO among U.N. specialized agencies. For discussion of their occasional use in the International Telecommunication Union, see J. Savage, The Politics of International Telecommunications Regulation 182–83 (1989).

Could the ILO process be used for conventions adopted at U.N.-sponsored conferences?

A significant example of a coordinated ILO convention and recommendation of the promotional type is found in the 1951 Equal Remuneration Convention and Equal Remuneration Recommendation. The Convention came into force in May 1953 for the original parties to it. More than 110 states have ratified it. The United States is not a party.

CONVENTION CONCERNING EQUAL REMUNERATION FOR MEN AND WOMEN WORKERS FOR WORK OF EQUAL VALUE

ILO Convention No. 100, adopted June 29, 1951.
165 U.N.T.S. 303, 1 International Labour Conventions and Recommendations 1919–1991, at 529 (1992).

* * *

ART. 2

1. Each Member shall, by means appropriate to the methods in operation for determining rates of remuneration, promote and, in so far as is consistent with such methods, ensure the application to all workers of the principle of equal remuneration for men and women workers for work of equal value.

2. This principle may be applied by means of—

(a) national laws or regulations;

(b) legally established or recognised machinery for wage determination;

(c) collective agreements between employers and workers; or

(d) a combination of these various means.

ART. 3

1. Where such action will assist in giving effect to the provisions of this Convention measures shall be taken to promote objective appraisal of jobs on the basis of the work to be performed.

2. The methods to be followed in this appraisal may be decided upon by the authorities responsible for the determination of rates of remuneration, or, where such rates are determined by collective agreements, by the parties thereto.

3. Differential rates between workers which correspond, without regard to sex, to differences, as determined by such objective appraisal, in the work to be performed shall not be considered as being contrary to the principle of equal remuneration for men and women workers for work of equal value.

* * *

ART. 6

1. This Convention shall be binding only upon those Members of the International Labour Organisation whose ratifications have been registered with the Director-General.

2. It shall come into force twelve months after the date on which the ratifications of two Members have been registered with the Director-General.

3. Thereafter, this Convention shall come into force for any Member twelve months after the date on which its ratification has been registered.

* * *

ART. 9

1. A Member which has ratified this Convention may denounce it after the expiration of ten years from the date on which the Convention first comes into force, by an act communicated to the Director-General of the International Labour Office for registration. Such denunciation shall not take effect until one year after the date on which it is registered.

RECOMMENDATION CONCERNING EQUAL REMUNERATION FOR MEN AND WOMEN WORKERS FOR WORK OF EQUAL VALUE

ILO Recommendation No. 90, adopted June 29, 1951.
1 International Labour Conventions and Recommendations
1919–1991, at 531 (1992).

* * *

Whereas the Equal Remuneration Convention, 1951, lays down certain general principles concerning equal remuneration for men and women workers for work of equal value;

* * *

Whereas it is desirable to indicate certain procedures for the progressive application of the principles laid down in the Convention;

Whereas, it is at the same time desirable that all Members should, in applying these principles, have regard to methods of application which have been found satisfactory in certain countries;

The Conference recommends that each Member should, subject to the provisions of Article 2 of the Convention, apply the following provisions and report to the International Labour Office as requested by the Governing Body concerning the measures taken to give effect thereto:

1. Appropriate action should be taken, after consultation with the workers' organisations concerned or, where such organisations do not exist, with the workers concerned—

(a) to ensure the application of the principle of equal remuneration for men and women workers for work of equal value to all employees of central Government departments or agencies; and

(b) to encourage the application of the principle to employees of State, provincial or local Government departments or agencies, where these have jurisdiction over rates of remuneration.

2. Appropriate action should be taken, after consultation with the employers' and workers' organisations concerned, to ensure, as rapidly as practicable, the application of the principle of equal remuneration for men and women workers for work of equal value in all occupations, other than those mentioned in Paragraph 1, in which rates of remuneration are subject to statutory regulation or public control, particularly as regards—

(a) the establishment of minimum or other wage rates in industries and services where such rates are determined under public authority;

(b) industries and undertakings operated under public ownership or control; and

(c) where appropriate, work executed under the terms of public contracts.

3. (1) Where appropriate in the light of the methods in operation for the determination of rates of remuneration, provision should be made by legal enactment for the general application of the principle of equal remuneration for men and women workers for work of equal value.

* * *

4. When, after consultation with the organisations of workers and employers concerned, where such exist, it is not deemed feasible to implement immediately the principle of equal remuneration for men and women workers for work of equal value, in respect of employment covered by Paragraph 1, 2 or 3, appropriate provision should be made or caused to be made as soon as possible, for its progressive application, by such measures as—

(a) decreasing the differentials between rates of remuneration for men and rates of remuneration for women for work of equal value;

(b) where a system of increments is in force, providing equal increments for men and women workers performing work of equal value.

* * *

6. In order to facilitate the application of the principle of equal remuneration for men and women workers for work of equal value,

appropriate action should be taken, where necessary, to raise the productive efficiency of women workers by such measures as—

(a) ensuring that workers of both sexes have equal or equivalent facilities for vocational guidance or employment counselling, for vocational training and for placement;

(b) taking appropriate measures to encourage women to use facilities for vocational guidance or employment counselling, for vocational training and for placement;

(c) providing welfare and social services which meet the needs of women workers, particularly those with family responsibilities, and financing such services from general public funds or from social security or industrial welfare funds financed by payments made in respect of workers without regard to sex; and

(d) promoting equality of men and women workers as regards access to occupations and posts without prejudice to the provisions of international regulations and of national laws and regulations concerning the protection of the health and welfare of women.

THE CONVENTION AND RECOMMENDATION

What exactly does the Convention require parties to do?

Could a member state, acting in good faith, ratify the Equal Remuneration Convention and then simply bring the companion Recommendation before its legislative authorities, without pressing them to enact legislation giving effect to it? See ILO Constitution *article 19(6)(b) and (d)*. If so, what good is the Convention? Is the Recommendation something more than a recommendation?

Article 22 of the ILO Constitution requires member governments to report periodically on the effect they have given to labor conventions they have ratified. When the International Labor Office sends the text of a convention to governments with the request that they report on how they have applied it, the text of any companion recommendation goes along with it for a report under ILO Constitution *article 19(6)(d)*.[e] The Equal Remuneration Convention and Recommendation would be handled in this way. Does this make the Recommendation a virtual protocol to the Convention?

Is the Equal Remuneration Recommendation directed only to states that become parties to the Convention?

Why weren't the provisions of the Recommendation simply put into the Convention in mandatory language?

e. See Valticos, The Sources of International Labour Law: Recent Trends, in International Law and Its Sources 179, 182–83 (W. Heere ed., 1989).

Compare the Equal Remuneration Convention and Recommendation with the 1988 Convention and Recommendation on Safety and Health in Construction. Only a few representative provisions in the 1988 Convention and Recommendation are set forth here.[f]

CONVENTION CONCERNING SAFETY AND HEALTH IN CONSTRUCTION

ILO Convention No. 167, adopted June 20, 1988.
2 International Labour Conventions and Recommendations 1919–1991, at 1398 (1992).

* * *

PART I. SCOPE AND DEFINITIONS

Article 1

1. This Convention applies to all construction activities, namely building, civil engineering, and erection and dismantling work, including any process, operation or transport on a construction site, from the preparation of the site to the completion of the project.

2. A Member ratifying this Convention may, after consultation with the most representative organisations of employers and workers concerned, where they exist, exclude from the application of the Convention, or certain provisions thereof, particular branches of economic activity or particular undertakings in respect of which special problems of a substantial nature arise, on condition that a safe and healthy working environment is maintained.

3. This Convention also applies to such self-employed persons as may be specified by national laws or regulations.

Article 2

For the purpose of this Convention:

(*a*) The term "construction" covers:

   (i) building, including excavation and the construction, structural alteration, renovation, repair, maintenance (including cleaning and painting) and demolition of all types of buildings or structures;

   (ii) civil engineering, including excavation and the construction, structural alteration, repair, maintenance and demolition of, for example, [such things as airports, docks, dams, roads, bridges, etc.];

   (iii) the erection and dismantling of prefabricated buildings and structures, as well as the manufacturing of prefabricated elements on the construction site; * * *

(*d*) the term "worker" means any person engaged in construction;

(*e*) the term "employer" means:

---

f. The Convention has 44 articles. The Recommendation has 53 paragraphs.

(i) any physical or legal person who employs one or more workers on a construction site; and

(ii) as the context requires, the principal contractor, the contractor or the subcontractor; * * *.

Part II. General Provisions
Article 3

The most representative organisations of employers and workers concerned shall be consulted on the measures to be taken to give effect to the provisions of this Convention.

Article 4

Each Member which ratifies this Convention undertakes that it will, on the basis of an assessment of the safety and health hazards involved, adopt and maintain in force laws or regulations which ensure the application of the provisions of the Convention.

Article 5

1. The laws and regulations adopted in pursuance of Article 4 above may provide for their practical application through technical standards or codes of practice, or by other appropriate methods consistent with national conditions and practice.

2. In giving effect to Article 4 above and to paragraph 1 of this Article, each Member shall have due regard to the relevant standards adopted by recognised international organisations in the field of standardisation.

* * *

Part III. Preventive and Protective Measures
Article 13
Safety of Workplaces

1. All appropriate precautions shall be taken to ensure that all workplaces are safe and without risk of injury to the safety and health of workers.

2. Safe means of access to and egress from all workplaces shall be provided and maintained, and indicated where appropriate.

3. All appropriate precautions shall be taken to protect persons present at or in the vicinity of a construction site from all risks which may arise from such site.

Article 14
Scaffolds and Ladders

1. Where work cannot safely be done on or from the ground or from part of a building or other permanent structure, a safe and suitable scaffold shall be provided and maintained, or other equally safe and suitable provision shall be made.

2. In the absence of alternative safe means of access to elevated working places, suitable and sound ladders shall be provided. They shall be properly secured against inadvertent movement.

3. All scaffolds and ladders shall be constructed and used in accordance with national laws and regulations.

4. Scaffolds shall be inspected by a competent person in such cases and at such times as shall be prescribed by national laws or regulations.

* * *

Article 28
Health Hazards

1. Where a worker is liable to be exposed to any chemical, physical or biological hazard to such an extent as is liable to be dangerous to health, appropriate preventive measures shall be taken against such exposure.

2. The preventive measures referred to in paragraph 1 above shall comprise—

(a) the replacement of hazardous substances by harmless or less hazardous substances wherever possible; or

(b) technical measures applied to the plant, machinery, equipment or process; or

(c) where it is not possible to comply with subparagraphs *(a)* or *(b)* above, other effective measures, including the use of personal protective equipment and protective clothing.

3. Where workers are required to enter any area in which a toxic or harmful substance may be present, or in which there may be an oxygen deficiency, or a flammable atmosphere, adequate measures shall be taken to guard against danger.

4. Waste shall not be destroyed or otherwise disposed of on a construction site in a manner which is liable to be injurious to health.

* * *

PART IV. IMPLEMENTATION

Article 35

Each Member shall—

(a) take all necessary measures, including the provision of appropriate penalties and corrective measures, to ensure the effective enforcement of the provisions of the Convention;

(b) provide appropriate inspection services to supervise the application of the measures to be taken in pursuance of the Convention and provide these services with the resources necessary for the accomplishment of their task, or satisfy itself that appropriate inspection is carried out.

Part V. Final Provisions

* * *

Article 39

1. A Member which has ratified this Convention may denounce it after the expiration of ten years from the date on which the Convention first comes into force, by an act communicated to the Director–General of the International Labour Office for registration. Such denunciation shall not take effect until one year after the date on which it is registered.

2. Each Member which has ratified this Convention and which does not, within the year following the expiration of the period of ten years mentioned in the preceding paragraph, exercise the right of denunciation provided for in this Article, will be bound for another period of ten years and, thereafter, may denounce this Convention at the expiration of each period of ten years under the terms provided for in this Article.

RECOMMENDATION CONCERNING SAFETY AND HEALTH IN CONSTRUCTION

ILO Recommendation No. 175, adopted June 20, 1988.
2 International Labour Conventions and Recommendations 1919–1991, at 1410 (1992).

* * *

I. Scope and Definitions

1. The provisions of the Safety and Health in Construction Convention, 1988 (hereinafter referred to as "the Convention") and of this Recommendation should be applied in particular to:

(a) building, civil engineering and the erection and dismantling of prefabricated buildings and structures, as defined in Article 2*(a)* of the Convention;

(b) the fabrication and erection of oil rigs, and of offshore installations while under construction on shore.

[The Recommendation sets forth detailed definitions of terms, corresponding with the definitions in the Convention.]

* * *

II. General Provisions

4. National laws or regulations should require that employers and self-employed persons have a general duty to provide a safe and healthy workplace and to comply with the prescribed safety and health measures.

* * *

III. Preventive and Protective Measures

* * *

Safety of Workplaces

12. Housekeeping programmes should be established and implemented on construction sites which should include provision for—

(a) the proper storage of materials and equipment;

(b) the removal of waste and debris at appropriate intervals.

13. Where workers cannot be protected against falls from heights by any other means—

(a) adequate safety nets or safety sheets should be erected and maintained; or

(b) adequate safety harnesses should be provided and used.

14. The employer should provide the workers with the appropriate means to enable them to use individual protective equipment and should ensure its proper use. Protective equipment and protective clothing should comply with standards set by the competent authority, taking into account as far as possible ergonomic principles.

15. (1) The safety of construction machinery and equipment should be examined and tested by type or individually, as appropriate, by a competent person.

(2) National laws and regulations should take into consideration the fact that occupational diseases may be caused by machinery, apparatus and systems which do not take account of ergonomic principles in their design.

Scaffolds

16. Every scaffold and part thereof should be of suitable and sound material and of adequate size and strength for the purpose for which it is used and be maintained in a proper condition.

17. Every scaffold should be properly designed, erected and maintained so as to prevent collapse or accidental displacement when properly used.

18. The working platforms, gangways and stairways of scaffolds should be of such dimensions and so constructed and guarded as to protect persons against falling or being endangered by falling objects.

19. No scaffold should be overloaded or otherwise misused.

20. A scaffold should not be erected, substantially altered or dismantled except by or under the supervision of a competent person.

* * *

Health Hazards

41. (1) An information system should be set up by the competent authority, using the results of international scientific research, to

provide information for architects, contractors, employers and workers' representatives on the health risks associated with hazardous substances used in the construction industry.

(2) Manufacturers and dealers in products used in the construction industry should provide with the products information on any health risks associated with them and on the precautions to be taken.

(3) In the use of materials that contain hazardous substances and in the removal and disposal of waste, the health of workers and of the public and the preservation of the environment should be safeguarded as prescribed by national laws and regulations.

(4) Dangerous substances should be clearly marked and provided with a label giving their relevant characteristics and instructions on their use. They should be handled under conditions prescribed by national laws and regulations or by the competent authority.

(5) The competent authority should determine which hazardous substances should be prohibited from use in the construction industry.

* * *

44. Whenever new products, equipment and working methods are introduced, special attention should be paid to informing and training workers with respect to their implications for safety and health.

SAFETY AND HEALTH REQUIREMENTS

Is the 1988 Convention Concerning Safety and Health in Construction a "promotional" convention? Why would it be so much more detailed than the Equal Remuneration Convention?

Article 1(2) of the 1988 Convention is one type of flexibility clause mentioned at page 279 supra. Does it eviscerate the Convention's protections?

In an ILO member state such as the United States, where treaty provisions may have direct effect as domestic law (without any implementing statute) if they are intended to be self-executing, would any of the provisions set out above from the 1988 Convention have that effect? Do the corresponding provisions in the Recommendation help to answer this question?

If the provisions of the 1988 Convention would not be self-executing, what good are they?

What does the 1988 Recommendation add to the Convention?

Note article 39 of the 1988 Convention. Suppose a member state ratifies the Convention three years after it first came into force for several other states. When could that member state denounce it?

Why do you suppose article 39 permits denunciation at all? Why only at ten-year intervals?

Does article 39 bear on the legislative nature of the Convention?

Some insights into the use of recommendations and their relationship to conventions appear in the excerpt below.

INTERNATIONAL LABOR OFFICE, THE INTERNATIONAL LABOUR CODE, 1951
Vol. 1, Preface, at LXXII–LXXIII (1952).

* * *

On general principles it would seem inappropriate to have recourse to the form of a Convention in cases in which the object of the Conference is not to secure the acceptance by Governments of binding obligations but primarily or solely to influence the development of legislation and practice by defining an international standard; the appropriate instrument for this purpose is the Recommendation. * * * Any attempt to enhance the authority of what is in substance a Recommendation by expressing it in Convention form in the hope of securing for it such additional prestige as may attach to Conventions would seem to be calculated to undermine the authority of Conventions and Recommendations alike. It obscures the true character of Conventions as instruments one of the essential purposes of which is the creation of obligations, and tends to discredit the Convention technique by resulting in widespread failure to ratify, and it equally tends to discredit the Recommendation by gratuitously implying that because a Recommendation is not an instrument for the creation of obligations it is therefore ineffective as an instrument designed to influence policy and legislation by the definition of an international standard.

* * *

In order that Recommendations may be of real weight in the development of social policy, they must strike an appropriate balance between the ideal and the immediately practicable and between precision and flexibility. Good judgment is the only reliable scale for this purpose and no sufficient substitute for it can be found in any fixed rules or principles, but it is both possible and desirable to formulate certain general principles which afford useful guidance. If the standard laid down by a Recommendation is an obviously impracticable one, or can be attained only by a very limited number of countries, it will not serve as an immediate target for national action, though it may come to be regarded as a distant or ultimate objective. On the other hand, a standard which represents no substantial advance upon average existing practice is also of very limited utility. The standards laid down by Recommendations should therefore represent a compromise between the ideal and average existing practice. What compromise is appropriate in a given case must depend upon the facts and circumstances of the case, and more particularly upon the extent to which an improvement of existing practice is regarded as attainable within a reasonable period. On this point there will frequently be wide divergences of view, based on different assessments of the social needs and temper of the times, the order of priority of different social claims, and the probable development of productivity, and on differences of view in regard to the equitability of the distribution of national income. In general, however, since a Recommendation is not intended to create obligations having the same binding character as the provisions of Conventions, it could reasonably aim at a higher standard than it would be appropriate to provide for in a Convention.

"NON–BINDING" RULES

Implicit in the Labor Office's analysis of recommendations is the proposition that they may be used to break the trail for subsequent conventions transforming the recommended norms into binding rules. Some other international organizations follow a similar process.[g] Is that likely to be an effective means of international rule-making?

If a particular standard would be appropriate for a convention in the sense that it is not so rigorous as to dissuade member states from ratifying it, would there ever be an advantage in adopting it instead as a recommendation?

The former Assistant Director–General of the ILO has said: [h]

> [ILO] Conventions can and do serve as a guide and a source of inspiration even to governments which have not found it possible to ratify them. This results from the authority which attaches to instruments adopted by an assembly composed of representatives of governments, employers and workers of practically all countries of the world.

It has been noted, for example, that the Equal Remuneration Convention "was very widely quoted in Britain to indicate that there was an obligation on the British government to introduce equal pay, when Britain had not ratified the Convention."[i] The ILO Committee on Freedom of Association (examined in Section 2, infra) has applied the standards of ILO conventions on trade union rights even against member states that are not parties to those conventions.

Are we dealing with true international legislation?

---

g. See 2 D. Leive, International Regulatory Regimes 563 (1976) (WHO, FAO and WMO); Review of the Multilateral Treaty-Making Process, U.N. Doc. ST/LEG/SER.B/21, at 26 (1985) (U.N. General Assembly declarations).

h. Valticos, The Sources of International Labour Law: Recent Trends, in International Law and Its Sources 179, 185 (W. Heere ed. 1989).

i. E. Luard, International Agencies: The Emerging Framework of Interdependence 142 (1977).

A noteworthy assessment of the effectiveness of ILO labor standards concluded in part as follows.

E. LUARD, INTERNATIONAL AGENCIES: THE EMERGING FRAMEWORK OF INTERDEPENDENCE
147–48 (1977).*

The ILO has acquired authority because it has established standards that are widely respected. But it now faces a number of new problems. First, so far as standards are concerned, there is a real risk that if the ILO goes on passing more and more Conventions, on ever more detailed subjects, each receiving little attention, and often only a handful of ratifications, the Conventions as a whole may lose their force as widely endorsed world standards. This will be particularly so if, as in some recent cases, the wording is vague and generalized, rather than concrete and specific. A general feeling will be encouraged that it is of little importance whether Conventions are ratified or not. And they will lose the authority they once had as part of a universal international code. Recommendations and resolutions proliferate ever more lavishly at every conference. Usually these are demanded by the worker delegates. Some are needed, because of changes in technology or to bring up-to-date older instruments. But the growing numbers tend to weaken the force of all: it is doubtful if the Ten Commandments would have had much influence if multiplied to a thousand. The Organisation might do well to select a certain number of Conventions and to make these a basic minimum standard, all of which, or a set proportion of which, should be ratified within a certain period by all members. Much of its efforts and the examinations of its supervisory bodies could then be devoted to ensuring ratification of this basic minimum, rather than devoting the same level of activity to a whole range of Conventions of varying importance.

There is a second major dilemma which the ILO faces in this connection, one faced by a number of agencies. The labour standards appropriate to a very wealthy and high advanced industrial country are not those appropriate to developing countries. That is true even of the basic standards, such as hours of work, health and safety regulations, holidays, social security, and other provisions. If the ILO sets standards suitable for advanced countries, they may be unattainable by the majority; whereas, if it sets them for the majority, they may be far too low for the advanced countries. This problem is recognized, but not solved. Here, too, it might be best to pick out the basic, minimum provisions that all countries can be expected to reach, whatever their stage of development, and concentrate on seeing that these at least are achieved. Without this, there will always exist a ready-made excuse at hand for some countries to justify failing to adopt even the minimum

* Reprinted by permission of Oceana Publications, Inc.

standards. For the more developed countries, perhaps an additional set of standards, or even a different minimum, including for example more advanced levels of social security, holiday provisions and so on, could be established. Without distinctions of this kind, a basis of comparison becomes impossible: conventions will either be well beyond what developing countries can reasonably be expected to achieve, or they will be far below what developed countries ought to demand.

PROLIFERATION AND FLEXIBILITY

Twice in recent years the ILO has addressed Luard's concerns, first in 1979 and again in 1987. On each occasion a Working Party identified a group of instruments that should be emphasized. In 1979 these totaled 78 conventions and 76 recommendations.[j] By 1987 the totals had increased to 89 conventions and 81 recommendations.[k] The priority list in 1987 included eight conventions on human rights (freedom of association, abolition of forced labor, and nondiscrimination), and many instruments in such other fields as employment policy, conditions of employment and occupational safety, health and welfare. The Governing Body dealt with out-of-date conventions in 1985 by deciding no longer to request detailed reports on them.[l]

Would these measures meet Luard's first concern?

On the second point, regarding standards that are set at too high a level for some countries and too low for others, note that for many years the ILO has used flexibility clauses in its conventions. See page 279 supra, as well as article 1(2) of the Convention Concerning Safety and Health in Construction, page 285 supra.

Do flexibility clauses meet Luard's second concern?

Consider also whether the process of amending the ILO Constitution involves "international legislation." See ILO Constitution *article 36*. In 1986 the International Labor Conference, acting under article 36, adopted amendments to the ILO Constitution. One of them amends article 36 itself, as set forth in bracketed article 36 in the Documents Supplement. (As of January 1992, the amendments had not been ratified or accepted by enough member states to enter into force.)

What was the amendment to article 36 designed to accomplish?

Would a nonratifying member state whose government representatives voted against an amendment in the ILO General Conference be

---

j. Final Report of the Working Party on International Labour Standards, Mar. 2, 1979, 62 ILO Official Bull., Ser. A, Special Issue, at 14–22 (1979).

k. Report of the Working Party on International Labour Standards, Feb. 23, 1987, 70 ILO Official Bull., Ser. A, Special Issue, at 29–37 (1987).

l. See 70 ILO Official Bull., Ser. A, Special Issue, at 55 (1987).

bound by it if it is adopted by the requisite number of votes cast at the Conference and it is ratified by the requisite members? Is the answer the same if amended article 36 is in force?

Does article 36, in its pre–1986 or amended form, involve legislative authority in any sense different from that involved in the promulgation of ILO conventions and recommendations? [m]

B. THE INTERNATIONAL MONETARY FUND

The International Monetary Fund's Articles of Agreement (the Fund Agreement) contain both a code of conduct for member states in international monetary matters, and the charter for the institution designed to administer that code and to participate actively in economic stabilization by providing monetary resources to tide members over bad balance-of-payments times. One of the pillars of the original code of conduct, from the inception of the Fund at Bretton Woods in 1944 until the 1971 monetary crisis leading to the comprehensive revision of the Agreement that became effective in 1978, was the concept of exchange rate stability. This involved the power of the Fund to approve or object to proposed changes in the par values of members' currencies—a power the Fund was unable to exercise effectively in the post-1971 years of exchange rate instability. Another mainstay of the original code of conduct, retained in the 1978 amendment, is the principle of currency convertibility through elimination of national restrictions on the use of foreign exchange in international trade and in other "current international transactions."

The Fund provides international reserves in two principal ways: by permitting its member states to draw foreign currencies under defined circumstances from a pool of currencies paid in by all members according to the quotas assigned to each of them, and by distributing designated amounts of "special drawing rights" (reserve assets created pursuant to the 1969 amendment of the Fund Agreement) accepted by member states as supplementary reserves.

From the Introduction to the Fund in the Supplement to these materials, note particularly that the Fund's Board of Governors and its Executive Board operate under a weighted voting system. The weights are tied to members' quotas, so the heaviest contributors have the most votes. Unless otherwise specified in the Fund Agreement, decisions are made by a majority of the weighted votes cast.

---

m. See generally E. Yemin, Legislative Powers in the United Nations and Specialized Agencies 50, 53–54, 57 (1969); R. Zacklin, The Amendment of the Constitutive Instruments of the United Nations and Specialized Agencies 161–62 (1968). The ILO Constitution dates back to the Paris Peace Conference in 1919. For the interesting story of the progression from recognition at that early date of the need to get away from the unanimity principle for amendment, through the adoption of an amendment provision that took first steps away from the unanimity requirement, to the revision of the amendment provision after World War II, see R. Zacklin, supra, at 60–67, 87–92.

Unlike the ILO, the Fund does not prepare or adopt conventions for ratification by its member states. From time to time, however, it asserts authority in ways that bear some legislative characteristics. In this subsection, we shall consider primarily its authority over the exchange rate policies of its members following the 1971 collapse of the post-World War II system of fixed exchange rates among currencies.

To understand the Fund's role, it is necessary to have at least a rudimentary grasp of the workings of exchange rates. As we have seen, the Fund Agreement was originally constructed around the concept of exchange rate stability—the concept that under normal circumstances the values of national currencies in relation to each other should remain constant (plus or minus a very small margin) in order to facilitate certainty in international trade and thereby to enhance international economic welfare. For example, from November 1967 until June 1972, one (British) pound sterling equalled $2.40. Stability was achieved by intervention in the foreign exchange markets by national central banks. The central bank would buy the nation's own currency (with gold or with some strong currency—usually U.S. dollars—other than its own) when demand for it was weak, thus preventing a fall in its value. Conversely, it would sell its own currency when demand for it was strong.

It was recognized that there could be occasional pressures on the value of any given national currency which might require a change in its official par value (exchange rate), but it was thought that these would be exceptional cases. Such pressures could occur, for example, when the rate of inflation in Country A exceeds that in its major trading partners for some time, so that its goods gradually are priced out of the international market. When that happens under a system of fixed exchange rates, Country A's exports decline, its balance of payments goes into the red as it continues to import, and it dips into its reserves in order to pay for the excess of imports over exports. It borrows (e.g., from the Fund, as above) in order to maintain an adequate level of reserves, but unless it is able to halt inflation or increase productivity at home, eventually it needs to do something further to correct its balance of payments. The "something" is often devaluation, making its currency cheaper in terms of foreign currencies. Thus, for example, Britain reduced the value of the pound from $2.80 to $2.40 in 1967. This meant that British exporters who needed to earn a pound in their own currency in order to make a profit on the sale of a widget could now do so by charging only $2.40 to a United States importer, instead of $2.80. Because of devaluation of the pound, they could again become price competitive in the United States and elsewhere.

The trouble with this system was that devaluations were taken as indications of the failure of a government's economic policies and therefore were postponed until the nation's financial situation became grim indeed. When devaluation of a major currency was in the wind, speculation in that currency would begin and would make the nation's reserve situation even worse. The system cracked, and was finally broken open in August 1971 when the United States not only imposed a temporary import surcharge, but also announced that it would suspend the redemption of dollars with gold. This meant that the dollar, the central reserve asset held by most foreign countries, was no longer convertible into the only reserve asset considered more secure.

The world monetary system was thrown into crisis, and a number of important trading nations eventually decided no longer to maintain fixed par values for their currencies in terms either of gold or of other currencies. In other words, they allowed their currencies to float, with the foreign exchange markets determining the day-to-day currency values. (In practice, no country allows a completely free float of its currency; central banks still intervene to make sure that the float does not go too far up or down.) Floating rates have a certain attraction, since they automatically allow the kind of adjustment described above in connection with the British devaluation—when Country A's rate of inflation goes up, the volume of its exports goes down, demand for its currency to pay for its exports goes down, the value of its currency goes down, the foreign price of its exports consequently can go down (as in the devaluation example above), and the volume of its exports can again rise.

By mid–1973 it was apparent that, for several key IMF member states, floating exchange rates were more than a brief transitional arrangement between fixed parity regimes. Some governments were floating their currencies independently of any other currency; some in Europe were maintaining relatively fixed rates against other designated European currencies, but those currencies in the aggregate were floating against other currencies; very few of the major industrialized members were abiding by the basic obligation of the Fund Agreement to maintain fixed exchange rates against a single standard. The Fund was moving to reform itself in order to take account of these realities, and had created an ad hoc committee of the Board of Governors, which was attempting to restore some order to the chaos. From this process came the 1978 revision of the Fund Agreement, including *article IV,* which no longer requires each member to maintain a fixed par value for its currency.

Even before the revision entered into force, the Fund's Executive Board adopted a decision on surveillance over exchange rate policies. The decision implements revised *article IV.*

IMF EXECUTIVE BOARD DECISION ON SURVEILLANCE OVER EXCHANGE RATE POLICIES

Decision No. 5392–(77/63), April 29, 1977, as amended by Decision No. 6026–(79/13), Jan. 22, 1979. Selected Decisions and Selected Documents of the International Monetary Fund 9 (17th issue, 1992).

GENERAL PRINCIPLES

* * *

The principles and procedures set out below, which apply to all members whatever their exchange arrangements and whatever their balance of payments position, are adopted by the Fund in order to perform its functions under Section 3*(b)*. They are not necessarily comprehensive and are subject to reconsideration in the light of experience. They do not deal directly with the Fund's responsibilities referred to in Section 3*(a)*, although it is recognized that there is a close relationship between domestic and international economic policies. This relationship is emphasized in Article IV which includes the following provision: "Recognizing * * * that a principal objective [of the international monetary system] is the continuing development of the orderly underlying conditions that are necessary for financial and economic stability, each member undertakes to collaborate with the Fund and other members to assure orderly exchange arrangements and to promote a stable system of exchange rates."

PRINCIPLES FOR THE GUIDANCE OF MEMBER'S EXCHANGE RATE POLICIES

A. A member shall avoid manipulating exchange rates or the international monetary system in order to prevent effective balance of payments adjustment or to gain an unfair competitive advantage over other members.

B. A member should intervene in the exchange market if necessary to counter disorderly conditions which may be characterized inter alia by disruptive short-term movements in the exchange value of its currency.

C. Members should take into account in their intervention policies the interests of other members, including those of the countries in whose currencies they intervene.

PRINCIPLES OF FUND SURVEILLANCE OVER EXCHANGE RATE POLICIES

1. The surveillance of exchange rate policies shall be adapted to the needs of international adjustment as they develop. The functioning of the international adjustment process shall be kept under review by the Executive Board and Interim Committee and the assessment of its operation shall be taken into account in the implementation of the principles set forth below.

2. In its surveillance of the observance by members of the principles set forth above, the Fund shall consider the following developments as among those which might indicate the need for discussion with a member:

(i) protracted large-scale intervention in one direction in the exchange market;

(ii) an unsustainable level of official or quasi-official borrowing, or excessive and prolonged short-term official or quasi-official lending, for balance of payments purposes;

(iii) (a) the introduction, substantial intensification, or prolonged maintenance, for balance of payments purposes, of restrictions on, or incentives for, current transactions or payments, or

(b) the introduction or substantial modification for balance of payments purposes of restrictions on, or incentives for, the inflow or outflow of capital;

(iv) the pursuit, for balance of payments purposes, of monetary and other domestic financial policies that provide abnormal encouragement or discouragement to capital flows; and

(v) behavior of the exchange rate that appears to be unrelated to underlying economic and financial conditions including factors affecting competitiveness and long-term capital movements.

3. The Fund's appraisal of a member's exchange rate policies shall be based on an evaluation of the developments in the member's balance of payments against the background of its reserve position and its external indebtedness. This appraisal shall be made within the framework of a comprehensive analysis of the general economic situation and economic policy strategy of the member, and shall recognize that domestic as well as external policies can contribute to timely adjustment of the balance of payments. The appraisal shall take into account the extent to which the policies of the member, including its exchange rate policies, serve the objectives of the continuing development of the orderly underlying conditions that are necessary for financial stability, the promotion of sustained sound economic growth, and reasonable levels of employment.

PROCEDURES FOR SURVEILLANCE

I. Each member shall notify the Fund in appropriate detail within thirty days after the Second Amendment becomes effective of the exchange arrangements it intends to apply in fulfillment of its obligations under Article IV, Section 1. Each member shall also notify the Fund promptly of any changes in its exchange arrangements.

II. Members shall consult with the Fund regularly under Article IV. In principle, the consultations under Article IV shall comprehend the regular consultations under Articles VIII and XIV, and shall take place annually. They shall include consideration of the observance by members of the principles set forth above as well as of a member's obligations under Article IV, Section 1. Not later than three months after the termination of discussions between the member and the staff, the Executive Board shall reach conclusions and thereby complete the consultation under Article IV.

* * *

IV. The Managing Director shall maintain close contact with members in connection with their exchange arrangements and exchange policies, and will be prepared to discuss on the initiative of a member important changes that it contemplates in its exchange arrangements or its exchange rate policies.

V. If, in the interval between Article IV consultations, the Managing Director, taking into account any views that may have been expressed by other members, considers that a member's exchange rate policies may not be in accord with the exchange rate principles, he shall raise the matter informally and confidentially with the member, and shall conclude promptly whether there is a question of the observance of the principles. If he concludes that there is such a question, he shall initiate and conduct on a confidential basis a discussion with the member under Article IV, Section 3(b). As soon as possible after the completion of such a discussion, and in any event not later than four months after its initiation, the Managing Director shall report to the Executive Board on the results of the discussion. If, however, the Managing Director is satisfied that the principles are being observed, he shall informally advise all Executive Directors, and the staff shall report on the discussion in the context of the next Article IV consultation; but the Managing Director shall not place the matter on the agenda of the Executive Board unless the member requests that this procedure be followed.

[The 1979 amendment added the following supplemental surveillance procedure:]

Whenever the Managing Director considers that a modification in a member's exchange arrangements or exchange rate policies or the behavior of the exchange rate of its currency may be important or may have important effects on other members, whatever the member's exchange arrangement may be, he shall initiate informally and confidentially a discussion with the member before the next regular discussion under Article IV. If he considers after this prior discussion that the matter is of importance, he shall initiate and conduct an ad hoc consultation with the member and shall report to the Executive Board, or informally advise the Executive Directors, on the consultation as promptly as the circumstances permit after conclusion of the consultation.

IMF SURVEILLANCE

Does Fund Agreement article IV impose any meaningful obligations on member states? If so, what are they?

Does article IV authorize the Fund to issue rules binding on member states? Did the Fund purport to do so?

Does the Executive Board Decision add anything to article IV? If so, what?

Does anything in the Decision encroach on the domestic affairs of member states?

Refer to Fund Agreement *article XXVII, section 1.* Are the powers in that section to suspend Fund provisions and to adopt interim rules truly legislative? Could a weighted simple majority vote of the Executive Board temporarily amend the Fund Agreement once a provision has been suspended?

Who is to determine if the prerequisites ("an emergency or the development of unforeseen circumstances threatening the activities of the Fund") are met? If they ever could be met, it would seem that they were in August 1971, when the United States' closing of its "gold window" caused widespread exchange rate floating and threw the international monetary system into chaos. Yet the Executive Board, which could have acted under the Fund Agreement's then-extant equivalent to article XXVII, section 1, did not suspend the provision establishing margins within which exchange rates could fluctuate. The former Fund General Counsel offered this explanation:

> At that time, it was necessary to have a unanimous vote in the Executive Board for such a decision. Some Executive Directors were unwilling to appear to approve the general floating of currencies and the circumstances that had produced the situation. A suspension of the operation of the margins for exchange transactions would have given more formal recognition to the situation and would have made it more difficult to argue that it continued to be invalid. The preference for a continued state of unambiguous invalidity was intended to spur the membership toward agreement on a legal regime of stable but adjustable par values.[a]

Of course, the membership was not spurred into a legal regime of stable but adjustable par values, as the 1978 amendment to the Fund Agreement attests. In retrospect, did the Executive Board make a wise

---

[a.] J. Gold, The Rule of Law in the International Monetary Fund 35 (I.M.F. Pamphlet Series, No. 32, 1980).

legislative decision when it refrained from bringing the law closer to the conduct of the member states supposedly governed by it?

Compare the procedure for amending the Fund Agreement with the ILO amendment procedure. See Fund Agreement *article XXVIII*. The United States, alone, and the European Communities, as a bloc, would have more than 15 percent of the total voting power. Thus neither of them could be bound by an amendment against its will. Do they have the same privileged position with respect to amendments to the ILO Constitution? What accounts for any difference?

C. THE INTERNATIONAL CIVIL AVIATION ORGANIZATION

T. BUERGENTHAL, LAW–MAKING IN THE INTERNATIONAL CIVIL AVIATION ORGANIZATION

3–5 (1969).*

The International Civil Aviation Organization came into being on April 4, 1947, when the Convention on International Civil Aviation—its constitutive instrument—entered into force. The Convention emerged from the International Civil Aviation Conference which met in Chicago, Illinois, from November 1 to December 7, 1944. The Chicago Conference was attended by representatives of more than fifty states who had been invited by the U.S. Government to join with it in establishing a legal framework for the development of international civil aviation after the Second World War.

In addition to being the constitution of the International Civil Aviation Organization, the Convention is a multilateral agreement that seeks to promote the orderly, safe, and efficient development of international aviation. With a view to achieving these objectives, the Convention defines the rights and obligations of the Contracting States in international civil aviation matters, and contains undertakings by them to cooperate in programs for the facilitation of international air transport and the improvement of air navigation services and installations.

Probably the most important substantive clause to be found in the Convention is Article 5. It provides that any civil aircraft which is registered in a Contracting State has the right, when it is not engaged in scheduled international air services, to fly over or to land for non-traffic purposes in the territory of any other Contracting State without prior authorization. Aircraft of scheduled international air services do not enjoy similar rights because the states participating in the Chicago Conference were unable to agree upon a generally acceptable formula

---

* Reprinted by permission of the Procedural Aspects of International Law Institute, Inc.

for the commercial exploitation of international air transport. Under a compromise worked out at Chicago, provisions for the exchange of transit and commercial rights for scheduled international air services, while not included in the Convention, were embodied in two separate instruments—the International Air Services Transit Agreement and the International Air Transport Agreement.

ICAO RULE–MAKING

ICAO participates in its most traditional form of international lawmaking—the preparation and promulgation of treaties—through its Legal Committee. The Committee, which is open to all member states, considers aviation issues that might appropriately be resolved by multilateral conventions. It assigns the preparatory and drafting work to a rapporteur or subcommittee, and ultimately decides whether to adopt a draft convention and recommend that it be referred to an international conference for further discussion and possible adoption by states.[a] Several significant air law conventions have been concluded in this fashion, including the Tokyo Convention on Offenses and Certain Other Acts Committed on Board Aircraft,[b] the Hague Convention for the Suppression of Unlawful Seizure of Aircraft,[c] the Montreal Convention for the Suppression of Unlawful Acts Against the Safety of Civil Aviation[d] and its Protocol for the Suppression of Unlawful Acts at Airports Serving International Civil Aviation.[e] The procedure is not "legislative," since norms are created only for those states that consent to them by becoming parties to the conventions. There is no requirement comparable to that in the ILO Constitution regarding submission of a convention to the appropriate domestic authorities for possible acceptance.

The Convention on International Civil Aviation (the Chicago Convention), however, does give the ICAO Council—the representative organ with 33 (eventually to be 36) member states—the authority to set aviation standards without going through the treaty process. The Council does this by adopting Annexes to the Chicago Convention consisting of "International Standards and Recommended Practices" on matters related to international air navigation, safety and efficiency. See Chicago Convention *articles 12, 28, 37, 38, 54(1) and 90.* Note that under article 90(a), the Council adopts Annexes by "the vote of two-thirds of the Council," subject to being overridden by a majority of the

a. See Guldimann, International Air Law in the Making, 27 Current Legal Probs. 233, 242–44 (1974).

b. Sept. 14, 1963, 20 U.S.T. 2941, T.I.A.S. 6768, 704 U.N.T.S. 219.

c. Dec. 16, 1970, 22 U.S.T. 1641, T.I.A.S. 7192, 860 U.N.T.S. 105.

d. Sept. 23, 1971, 24 U.S.T. 564, T.I.A.S. 7570, 1971 U.N. Jurid. Y.B. 143.

e. Feb. 24, 1988, ICAO Doc. 9518, 27 Int'l Legal Materials 627 (1988).

member states when the Annex or amendment of an Annex is submitted to them.

The ICAO Assembly has said that a Standard is "any specification * * * the uniform application of which is recognized as necessary for the safety or regularity of international air navigation and to which Contracting States will conform in accordance with the Convention; in the event of impossibility of compliance, notification to the Council is compulsory under Article 38 of the Convention." [f]

The Assembly has said that a Recommended Practice is "any specification * * * the uniform application of which is recognized as desirable in the interest of safety, regularity or efficiency of international air navigation and to which Contracting States will endeavour to conform in accordance with the Convention." [g] (The Assembly, though it is the plenary body of the organization, is not given express power in the Chicago Convention to interpret it.)

Over the years, the Council has adopted 18 Annexes, and has amended them as circumstances have changed. The Annexes are:

Annex 1—Personnel Licensing: Licensing of flight crews, air traffic controllers and aircraft maintenance personnel;

Annex 2—Rules of the Air: Rules relating to the conduct of visual and instrument flights;

Annex 3—Meteorological Service for International Air Navigation: Provision of meteorological services and reporting of meteorological observations from aircraft;

Annex 4—Aeronautical Charts: Specifications for the charts used in international aviation;

Annex 5—Units of Measurement to be Used in Air and Ground Operations;

Annex 6—Operation of Aircraft: Specifications for aircraft operations around the world at a safety level above a prescribed minimum;

Annex 7—Aircraft Nationality and Registration Marks;

Annex 8—Airworthiness of Aircraft: Certification and inspection of aircraft according to uniform procedures;

Annex 9—Facilitation: Streamlining of such things as customs, immigration and health formalities for passengers, crews and cargo at airports;

Annex 10—Aeronautical Telecommunications: Standardization of communications equipment and procedures;

---

f. Assembly Res. A27–10, Appendix A, in Resolutions Adopted by the Assembly and Index to Documentation, 27th Sess., ICAO Doc. 9551, A27–RES, at 52 (1989).

g. Id.

Annex 11—Air Traffic Services: Establishment and operation of air traffic control, flight information and alerting services;

Annex 12—Search and Rescue: Organization and operation of facilities for search and rescue;

Annex 13—Aircraft Accident Investigation: Uniformity in the notification, investigation and reporting of accidents;

Annex 14—Aerodromes: Specifications for the design and equipment of airports;

Annex 15—Aeronautical Information Services: Methods for collecting and disseminating information required for flight operations;

Annex 16—Environmental Protection: Specifications relating to aircraft noise and engine emissions;

Annex 17—Safeguarding International Civil Aviation Against Acts of Unlawful Interference: Specifications for aircraft security;

Annex 18—The Safe Transport of Dangerous Goods by Air: Specifications for the labeling, packing and shipping of dangerous cargo.

Annex 2, Rules of the Air, contains only International Standards and no Recommended Practices. All the other Annexes contain both.

There appears never to have been an occasion on which a majority of member states has disapproved an Annex or an amendment to an Annex under article 90, once it has been adopted by the two-thirds majority vote of the Council. The reason is explained in part by the nonpolitical nature of most Standards and Practices, and in part by a careful preparation and prior consultation procedure.

For all Annexes except Annex 9 on Facilitation, the preparatory body is the ICAO Air Navigation Commission. It currently consists of 15 persons, appointed by the Council, who have aeronautical expertise.[h] Its procedure involves preparatory meetings by bodies such as air navigation conferences (open to all member states) or technical panels to recommend new Standards and/or Recommendations; studies by the ICAO Secretariat and technical representatives of member states; consultations with member governments; and a full review by the Commission itself before the final Standards and/or Practices are submitted to the Council for adoption. The Council then adopts them and submits them to the member states pursuant to Chicago Convention article 90.[i]

What are the advantages and disadvantages of this procedure compared with one that would involve the same preliminary steps, but

---

h. In 1989 the Assembly approved a protocol that will increase the size of the Air Navigation Commission to 19 members when two-thirds of the ICAO members have ratified the protocol.

i. See ICAO Public Information Office, Memorandum on ICAO 17–18 (14th ed. 1990); Fitzgerald, The International Civil Aviation Organization—A Case Study in the Implementation of Decisions of a Functional International Organization, in The Effectiveness of International Decisions 156, 170–71 (S. Schwebel ed. 1971).

with adoption by a majority vote in the Assembly and no subsequent submission to member states for possible disapproval?

The degree of conformity of member states' legislation and regulations with International Standards and Recommended Practices varies from state to state and from situation to situation, with some member states being technologically or financially hard pressed to comply with all of them. Not all discrepancies have been notified to ICAO, and the Organization no longer presumes compliance from lack of notification. ICAO tries to help members when they have difficulties, by supplying technical manuals, personnel training, etc., but these have not solved all the problems of implementation and reporting.

Consider the legal consequences for member states from (a) International Standards and (b) Recommended Practices. For example, take Annex 11 to the Chicago Convention, on Air Traffic Services. It "pertains to the establishment of airspace, units [control towers, etc.] and services necessary to promote a safe, orderly and expeditious flow of air traffic. * * * Its purpose, together with Annex 2, is to ensure that flying on international air routes is carried out under uniform conditions designed to improve the safety and efficiency of air operation. The Standards and Recommended Practices in Annex 11 apply in those parts of the airspace under the jurisdiction of a Contracting State wherein air traffic services are provided and also wherever a Contracting State accepts the responsibility of providing air traffic services over the high seas or in airspace of undetermined sovereignty."[j]

Annex 11, paragraph 3.7.1 deals with air traffic control clearances (authorizations for aircraft to proceed under conditions specified by a control tower or other air traffic control unit). It provides:

3.7.1.1 An air traffic control clearance shall indicate:

(a) aircraft identification as shown in the flight plan;

(b) clearance limit [the point to which an aircraft is granted the clearance];

(c) route of flight;

(d) level(s) of flight for the entire route or part thereof and changes of levels if required;

(e) any necessary instructions or information on other matters such as approach or departure manoeuvres, communications and the time of expiry of the clearance.

3.7.1.2 Recommendation. Standard departure and arrival routes and associated procedures should be established when necessary to facilitate:

(a) the safe, orderly and expeditious flow of air traffic;

---

j. Annex 11, Foreword, at v (9th ed. 1990).

(b) the description of the route and procedure in air traffic control clearances.[k]

Subparagraph 3.7.1.1 is an International Standard; subparagraph 3.7.1.2 is a Recommended Practice. What is the legal effect of each upon member states? Consider the ICAO Assembly's definition of Standards and Recommended Practices, supra. Consider also:

At the 1944 Chicago Conference, where the Chicago Convention was negotiated, a report of one of the main committees said:

> The committee believes that in certain branches of regulatory action some subjects should be fully standardized, while upon others the internationally agreed documents should represent only recommendations implying no obligation, but expressive of a hope that the several nations will follow the recommendations as closely as may be practicable under their particular circumstances. It is believed that in the future development of their technical documents considerable freedom should be exercised in the introduction of such recommendations, some of which may thereafter become international standards if they gain a sufficient degree of acceptance during the probationary period of mere recommendations.[l]

On the other hand, Edward Warner, the reporting delegate of the same committee and a future President of the ICAO Council, said:

> [I]t may be well that I say something of the legal status which the text of the permanent Convention establishes for the Annexes. In consideration of the recognized need for the utmost flexibility in the adoption and amendment of Annexes, in order that they may be kept abreast of the development of the aeronautical arts, the Convention leaves the Council with a free hand for future action. No Annex is specifically identified in the Convention; and there is no limit to the adoption by the Council of any Annexes which may in future appear to be desirable. On the other hand, and in fact as a necessary consequence of that flexibility, the Annexes are given no compulsory force. It remains open to any State to adopt its own regulations in accordance with its own necessities; but I believe that I represent the general views of those who have been most active in the work of Committee II in expressing full confidence that in fact the practical result will be the maintenance of absolute world uniformity in many respects, and of a very high degree of uniformity in the other matters upon which the Annexes may touch.[m]

The commentators are divided. Some interpret the Convention and its preparatory work to mean that International Standards are legally binding except to the extent that a state has properly opted out

---

k. Annex 11 at 18 (9th ed. 1990).

l. Report of Committee II, 1 Proceedings of the International Civil Aviation Conference 708 (1948).

m. Id. at 92.

of a Standard under article 38." Others take the position that Standards were never intended to be binding, or that states' failure consistently to notify ICAO of differences under article 38 shows a lack of obligation, even though Standards have greater normative significance than do Recommended Practices.°

How do you come out?

Does it really matter whether ICAO International Standards are legally binding or not? (Why or why not?)

Suppose a member state has found it impracticable to comply with an International Standard on air navigation in the landing pattern at its airports, and has instead promulgated its own regulation which it has notified to all airlines using its international airport. It has not notified ICAO of the discrepancy. If a civil aircraft of another member state crashes at the international airport because of an inadequacy in the landing pattern regulation that would not have been present under the ICAO standard, could the state of the aircraft's registration successfully assert an international claim for the loss against the noncomplying state? (Such a claim could arguably be asserted if the loss was caused by the respondent state's failure to comply with a duty under international law designed for the protection of foreign nationals. The claim would not be adjudicated in the courts of either member state, but would be settled by negotiations between the foreign ministries of the two states, or if that failed, it might be submitted to the ICAO Council under a procedure to be examined in the next section.)

Suppose the Federal Aviation Administration of the United States promulgates a rule, applicable to U.S. air carriers in their Transatlantic flights, that differs from an ICAO International Standard in Annex 2 for flight over the high seas. (See *article 12* of the Convention.) The United States immediately notifies ICAO of the differences between its rule and the International Standard, giving the reasons why it has been found impracticable to apply the ICAO Standard. Would the United States be in violation of its international obligations under the Convention if its carriers then comply with the U.S. rule? ᵖ

Under the 1982 U.N. Convention on the Law of the Sea, coastal states are entitled to claim 200–mile exclusive economic zones, for purposes of controlling the living and nonliving resources in those offshore areas. Although the 1982 Convention expressly recognizes all states' freedom of navigation and overflight in exclusive economic zones

n. See D. Bowett, The Law of International Institutions 145 (4th ed. 1982); B. Cheng, The Law of International Air Transport 68–70 (1962); J. Naveau, International Air Transport in a Changing World 54 (1989); Skubiszewski, Enactment of Law by International Organizations, 41 Brit.Y.B.Int'l L. 198, 211 (1965–66).

o. See C. Alexandrowicz, The Law-Making Functions of the Specialised Agencies of the United Nations 45–46; T. Buergenthal, supra, at 98–101; E. Yemin, Legislative Powers in the United Nations and Specialized Agencies 138–44, 149–50 (1969); Erler, Regulatory Procedures of ICAO as a Model for IMCO, 10 McGill L.J. 262, 263–65 (1964).

p. See Milde, Interception of Civil Aircraft vs. Misuse of Civil Aviation, 11 Annals of Air & Space L. 105, 106 (1986).

(article 58), it does not say that they are part of the high seas. As of mid–1992, the 1982 Convention still had not received enough ratifications to enter into force, but most of its provisions, other than those relating to the deep seabed, were regarded as having become part of customary international law. Under article 12 of the Chicago Convention, what is the legal effect of the International Standards in Annex 2 over exclusive economic zones?

A case study in ICAO rule-making arose out of the incident in 1983 when the Soviet Union shot down Korean Airlines flight 007 in Soviet airspace. The case study illustrates how the Council operates legislatively in a politically-sensitive situation; the role of the ICAO Legal Bureau; and the difficulties posed when important member states disagree with the approach being taken.

In the pre-dawn hours of August 31, 1983, Korean Airlines flight 007, from Anchorage, Alaska, to Seoul, South Korea, strayed about 500 kilometers off course to the north, over Soviet territory. A subsequent ICAO investigation was not able to determine conclusively the reason for the deviation, but air crew error appeared to be the most likely explanation. In any event, Soviet authorities, perhaps thinking that the airliner was an intelligence aircraft, ordered Soviet fighters to shoot it down. Everyone on board was killed in the crash.

The matter was taken up by both the ICAO Council and the Assembly. The latter adopted an amendment to the Chicago Convention, which will be examined at the end of this subsection. Our focus here is on the Council, assisted by the Air Navigation Commission. The sequence of events in the Commission and Council is described below by the former Director of the ICAO Legal Bureau, speaking in his personal capacity.

MILDE, INTERCEPTION OF CIVIL AIRCRAFT vs. MISUSE OF CIVIL AVIATION
11 Annals of Air & Space L. 105, 108 et seq. (1986).*

After initial work directly related to the destruction of the Korean Airlines aircraft, the Air Navigation Commission made a detailed review of the current ICAO provisions on the subject of identification and interception of civil aircraft with a view to identifying potential improvements. During the year 1984, the Air Navigation Commission, through its Ad Hoc Working Group on Interception, prepared draft amendments to Annexes 2, 6 (Parts I and II), 10 (Volume I) and 11, [and other ICAO instruments.] The Commission identified a number of items on which it was considered necessary to seek specific comments of States and international organizations. The most important question was the acceptability of upgrading the Special Recommendations in

* Reprinted by permission of the Institute and Centre of Air and Space Law, McGill University.

Attachment A to Annex 2 to the status of Standards and Recommended Practices.

One of the problems faced by the Working Group of the Air Navigation Commission at the very outset of its deliberations was the interpretation of Articles 3 and 54(*l*) of the Convention on International Civil Aviation. Article 3(a) states peremptorily that the Convention shall be applicable only to civil aircraft and shall not be applicable to state aircraft; paragraph (b) of that Article similarly states in a peremptory way that aircraft used in military service shall be deemed to be state aircraft. Doubts were expressed in the Working Group whether the drafting of Standards relating to interception carried out by military aircraft was in fact within the constitutional purview of the Organization. Since the Air Navigation Commission is composed of technical experts, it sought legal advice on this point from the ICAO Secretariat. The view given to the Commission's Working Group by the ICAO Legal Bureau was that the purpose of drafting new provisions on interception of civil aircraft did not necessarily mean drafting provisions relating to military aircraft; the real legislative purpose would be to draft provisions pertaining to the safety of international civil aviation which was a legitimate constitutional purpose of the Organization. In the past, the Organization never refrained from adopting decisions and regulations dealing with the safety of international civil aviation even if that meant interfacing or coordination with the operation of state aircraft. Under Article 3(d) of the Convention, the States have accepted a legal undertaking to have due regard for the safety of navigation of civil aircraft when issuing regulations for their state aircraft. While Article 3(d) of the Convention was not a source of legislative authority of the ICAO Council, it did not constitute an obstacle to adoption of Standards relating to safety of civil aviation in the situations of interception.

The Working Group of the Air Navigation Commission accepted this legal interpretation and proceeded to the drafting of detailed Standards in a proposed amendment of Annex 2 relating to interception. Among the rules so drafted were clear-cut provisions that contracting States shall take steps to ensure that interception of civil aircraft will be undertaken only as a last resort and, if undertaken, the interception will be limited to determining the identity of the aircraft, unless it is necessary to guide the aircraft away from a prohibited, restricted or danger area or instruct it to effect a landing at a designated aerodrome.

* * *

Three months later, on 24 and 26 September 1985, the discussion continued and addressed the basic legal issues raised in the proposed amendment to Annex 2. The Representative of the United States stated that he was well aware that the position he would take on this matter was not a popular one; his Government strongly objected to the proposed amendment to paragraph 3.8.1 and Appendix B, sections 1 and 2 of Annex 2 which would repeat in the form of Standards certain principles already covered under special recommendations contained in Attachment A. His Government felt strongly that adoption of these Standards would clearly violate the Chicago Convention by going beyond the legal parameters it provided. Article 3(a) of the Convention clearly stated that the Convention was applicable only to civil aircraft and not to State aircraft. Since the proposed Standards were contrary to the fundamental provisions of ICAO's charter embodied in Article 3 of the Convention, their adoption by the Council would be *ultra vires* and therefore of no legal effect.

At the same meeting the Representative of the Union of Soviet Socialist Republics said that his Government had no difficulty of substance with adoption of the amendments presented by the Commission. He did not believe that adoption of procedures for interception of civil aircraft involving State aircraft would necessarily lead to a review of the Chicago Convention and expressly stated that he would support the majority view of the Council. However, at a later stage of the discussions the position of the USSR changed and identified with that of the USA.

The position of the USA was fully supported in the Council by Egypt and Pakistan; Norway, speaking on behalf of the Nordic States, shared the USA position based on Article 3 of the Chicago Convention but felt that, if the Council considered it necessary to upgrade existing material or include new material in Annex 2, the status of such material should not be higher than a Recommended Practice. The Representatives of Czechoslovakia and of the USSR joined those preferring the status of guidance material for the provisions on interception of civil aircraft, basing themselves on the legal controversy related to Article 3 of the Convention.

* * *

Requested to clarify the legal issue, the Director of the Legal Bureau said first that no international civil servant would purport to give an authoritative interpretation of an international instrument. Only sovereign States could give an interpretation of an authoritative nature. In the context of Chapter XVIII of the Convention the Council was invested with the adjudicatory power of giving a binding interpretation of the Convention and its Annexes. In late 1983 the Legal Bureau of ICAO was asked to give a general legal opinion to the Working Group of the Air Navigation Commission, which opinion was repeated in the Council and twice elaborated upon at meetings of the Commission itself. The opinion was modest in its impact and said that while Article 3(d) of the Chicago Convention was not a source of the legislative authority of the Council, it was believed that it presented no obstacle to the development of uniform international rules to be observed in the interception of civil aircraft. It was clear that Article 3 was not to be disregarded. The Commission very cautiously tried not to regulate the conduct of military or State aircraft, but to regulate if possible the conduct of States with respect to preserving the safety of international civil aviation, a very different matter. It was strongly believed that this was fully within the authority and jurisdiction of ICAO as specifically spelled out among its objectives under Article 44 of the Convention. The legal opinion also stated that the Commission would not be breaking new ground and establishing a precedent. There was a firm precedent in that respect in existing legislation, as in February 1974 the Council had adopted without difficulty in Appendix A to Annex 2 very specific regulations on signals to be initiated by intercepting aircraft, i.e. State aircraft. Until today no State had filed any difference.

* * *

In view of the clear cut division of views in the Council concerning the legal acceptability of paragraph 3.8.1 of the draft amendment to Annex 2 considerable diplomatic effort had been made to reach some degree of consensus, particularly bearing in mind that the doubts about the legality of adopting Standards relating to interception of civil aircraft were expressed by only a minority of the Council. At that stage of the discussion the Representative of the United Kingdom proposed new wording as a replacement for the existing paragraph 3.8.1 * * * in the interest of reaching a compromise solution which might be generally acceptable to the Council as a whole. He noted that under Article 3(d) of the Chicago Convention, contracting States have undertaken to "have due regard for the safety of navigation of civil aircraft" when issuing regulations for their State aircraft. It accordingly appeared possible that the use of this wording in paragraph 3.8.1 might meet the concerns expressed about the legal ability of the Council to take the action proposed. The text proposed by the Representative of the United Kingdom read as follows:

"3.8.1 Interception of civil aircraft shall be governed by appropriate regulations and administrative directives issued by contracting States in compliance with the Convention on International Civil Aviation, and in particular Article 3(d) under which contracting States undertake, when issuing regulations for their State aircraft, to have due regard for the safety of navigation of civil aircraft. Accordingly, in drafting appropriate regulations and administrative directives due regard shall be had to the provisions of Appendix A, Section 2 and Appendix B, Section 1."

[These Sections deal with signals to be used by intercepting and intercepted aircraft (such as rocking the wings), and principles to be observed regarding interception (such as the principle that interception of civil aircraft will be undertaken only as a last resort). Ed.]

* * *

The Representative of the United States stated he could not support the United Kingdom proposal which he considered contrary to Article 3(a) of the Convention which limited application of its operative provisions to civil aircraft. According to him, Article 3(a) and (d) made it clear that ICAO had no authority to issue Standards and Recommended Practices dealing with the operation of State aircraft and ICAO could not therefore revise, expand or paraphrase in the form of Standards the content of Articles 3(d) or 3 *bis* and he confirmed again that his administration would agree only to strengthening provisions of the guidance material in Attachment A to Annex 2. This view was echoed by the Representative of the USSR and by the Representative of Egypt. On the other hand the proposal of the United Kingdom was supported by the Representatives of France, Lebanon, Jamaica, Japan, Belgium, Federal Republic of Germany and by Australia.

At this point the President of the Council put the proposal of the United Kingdom to a vote and it carried by 13 votes to 5 with 10 abstentions. The result of the vote did in fact not represent even a statutory majority of the Council, but under Rule 63 of the Rules of Procedure for the Council the majority of the votes cast is considered to be sufficient in the absence of any request for "statutory majority". However, for the adoption of the entire text of the proposed Standards a two-thirds majority (22 votes) would be required.

This vote represented a turning point in the discussions and thereafter the Council proceeded with consideration of the proposed amendment paragraph by paragraph and, finally, on 10 March 1986 a vote on the entirety of the proposed amendment to Annex 2 resulted in 22 votes in favour, 4 opposed and 6 abstentions.

Immediately after the vote the Representative of the United States said that his Government continued to hold the view that adoption of the rules on interception as Standards was *ultra vires* and would treat them accordingly. The Representative of the USSR expressed regret over the result and also stated that his Government considered the amendment *ultra vires*.

The vote of 22 Members of the Council in favour represents just a bare two-thirds majority required for the adoption of Standards under Article 90 of the Chicago Convention. After the vote it appeared that the Representatives on the Council were surprised by this result and in fact did not expect that the required majority would be reached. In the history of the quasi-legislative function of the Council it has been a well established tradition that important amendments to Standards and Recommended Practices were usually adopted by unanimous consensus or at least by very convincing majority without opposing votes.

It is difficult to analyze what led to the change in mood of the Council and why on 7 February 1986 the crucial proposal of the United Kingdom carried by only 13 votes in favour with 5 opposing votes and 10 abstentions and why one month later the entire package of the amendment received the requisite two-thirds majority. It is worth noting that during the 117th Session of the Council, just prior to the continuation of substantive discussions on Annex 2, the Council of ICAO considered a particular complaint against the interception of a civil aircraft and after a politically charged and divisive discussion adopted a resolution condemning that particular act of interception. The political polarization which occurred during that discussion may well have influenced the decision of States with respect to Amendment 27 to Annex 2.

It could have been expected that some of the States objecting to the adoption of Amendment 27 to Annex 2 on constitutional grounds would have registered their disapproval in conformity with Article 90(a) of the Chicago Convention. However, by the date prescribed by the Council—27 July 1986—no State has registered a disapproval with the amendment. Consequently, on 27 July 1986 the amendment has become effective * * *.

The Acting Representative of the United States of America informed the Secretary General in a letter dated 21 July 1986 as follows:

"This is to inform you that the United States of America does not wish to register disapproval of Amendment 27 * * * of Annex 2 * * *, provided that, however, the United States of America does not accept any provision of Annex 2 or any other Annex, as constituting a Standard or Recommended Practice applicable to State aircraft. In accordance with Article 3(a) of the Convention on International Civil Aviation, the Convention and its Annexes are not applicable to State aircraft. Insofar as any provision of Annex 2 addresses the operation or control of State aircraft, the United States of America considers such provision to be in the nature of a Special Recommendation of the Council, advisory only, and not requiring the filing of differences under Article 38 of the Convention".

This statement has to be accepted as a declaration of principle and does not amount to a disapproval of the amendment.

LEGAL ADVICE AND LEGAL EFFECT

Do you agree with the Legal Bureau's advice that the International Standard in Annex 2, section 3.8.1 was not *ultra vires* under Chicago Convention *article 3?*

The Director of the Legal Bureau said that no international civil servant (presumably including himself) would purport to give an authoritative interpretation of an international instrument. Why not? What *did* he give?

If we assume that an International Standard is binding on any member state that has not properly registered its disapproval, what does section 3.8.1. require nonobjecting members to do?

Note the U.S. position, as expressed in the letter of July 21, 1986, quoted above. Is it open to a member state to decide for itself that a provision adopted by the proper Council majority as an International

Standard is merely a "Special Recommendation of the Council"? If not, or if there is doubt about it, what is the legal effect of section 3.8.1 on the United States?

Leaving aside the unique questions raised by Annex 2, section 3.8.1, to what extent do ICAO's rule-making powers encroach on the domestic affairs of the member states? In this connection consider whether, from the standpoint of the constitutional law of the United States, any of ICAO's rule-making powers would amount to an unconstitutional delegation of Congress' legislative power. Could there be a delegation-of-legislative-power problem if ICAO Standards and Recommended Practices do not have direct effect as domestic law in the United States? Would any of them have that effect?

Why would the constituent instrument of ICAO (the Chicago Convention) bestow rule-making authority that comes closer in some instances to true legislation than that of the ILO?

Compare the standard-setting authority of the World Health Organization (WHO), another specialized agency of the United Nations. Articles 21 and 22 of the WHO Constitution authorize the Health Assembly (the plenary body of the WHO) to adopt by simple majority regulations binding on all members except those that notify the Director-General of their rejection or reservations within a designated time. The Health Assembly has used this authority to produce only two sets of regulations. Only one of those, the International Health Regulations, is of major importance. The Health Regulations are designed to prevent the international spread of such diseases as cholera, the plague and yellow fever.

WHO, like the ILO, struggled with the problem of reservations. Because article 22 of the WHO Constitution expressly allows reservations to WHO regulations, the organization could not do as the ILO did and refuse to allow them. Nevertheless, the Health Assembly tried to preserve as much uniformity as possible in the application of its Health Regulations, by deciding that a reservation is not valid unless the Health Assembly accepts it.[q] In effect, the Assembly has the power to determine that a reservation is "incompatible with the object and purpose" of the Regulations, and thus to prevent them from entering into force for a state that maintains the objectionable reservation.[r] The Assembly has rejected several reservations.

The Health Assembly's position on reservations reduces the number of states bound by the Health Regulations, while promoting uniformity of obligation among states bound by them. Is this sensible?

q. See Vignes, Le Réglement Sanitaire International, 11 Ann. Français de Droit Int'l 649, 659–64 (1965); International Health Regulations, July 25, 1969, WHO Doc. WHA22.46 (1969), in 21 U.S.T. 3003, T.I.A.S. 7026, 764 U.N.T.S. 3.

r. See Vienna Convention on the Law of Treaties, art. 19(c), 1155 U.N.T.S. 331.

The Health Assembly usually acts by adopting nonbinding recommendations, rather than binding regulations. For example, in 1981 it adopted the International Code of Marketing of Breast-milk Substitutes,[s] a nonbinding code designed to contribute to the safe nutrition of infants, after considering whether to adopt it as a set of binding regulations. More than 130 states have given effect to its principles.[t]

Why would the Health Assembly lean toward recommendations rather than regulations? Is this sensible? If so, should the Health Regulations be downgraded to recommendations?

Finally, consider the process of amending the Chicago (ICAO) Convention. It provides in article 94(a), "Any proposed amendment to this Convention must be approved by a two-thirds vote of the Assembly and shall then come into force in respect of States which have ratified such amendment when ratified by the number of contracting States specified by the Assembly. The number so specified shall not be less than two-thirds of the total number of contracting States." Under article 94(b), the Assembly may specify that any state that has not ratified an approved amendment within a specified period ceases to be a member of ICAO and a party to the Convention. The article 94(b) power has never been used.

The Assembly has adopted several amendments under article 94(a), most of them having to do with the structure and internal functioning of the Organization. For example, a series of amendments to article 50(a) has gradually increased the size of the Council from 21 to 27, then to 30, then to 33, with a further amendment increasing it to 36 in the process of being ratified by member states when this was written. None of these amendments has been ratified by all the member states, but each of them has been implemented when the requisite two-thirds of the member states had ratified it. No member state has protested when the amendments have been implemented, and all members have been allowed to vote for the larger Council.[u]

What is the status of the amendments, after they have received the requisite number of ratifications, for member states that have not ratified them? Is it the same as for nonratifying member states of the ILO when amendments to its Constitution have received enough acceptances to be in force?

Not all amendments to the Chicago Convention have been concerned strictly with internal organizational matters. For example, at the behest of the U.N. General Assembly, the ICAO Assembly in 1947

s. WHO Res. WHA34.22, Annex, in WHO Doc. WHA34/1981/REC/1, at 64 (1981).

t. Vignes, Role of WHO in International Health Legislation 5 (unpublished).

u. See Milde, Chicago Convention—45 Years Later: A Note on Amendments, 14 Annals of Air & Space L. 203, 208 (1989).

approved a new article 93 *bis*. It came into force in 1961, when the requisite number of members had ratified it. It provides that a state expelled from the U.N. or whose government has been recommended by the U.N. General Assembly to be expelled from specialized agencies shall automatically cease to be a member of ICAO, and a state suspended from the U.N. shall be suspended from ICAO at the request of the U.N.

In 1947 the intent was to exclude Spain, under General Franco, from ICAO, but the provision was never invoked because Spain voluntarily withdrew (and then rejoined ICAO after the General Assembly had changed its attitude). What would be the position of a state that had not ratified the amendment adding article 93 *bis* if the U.N. General Assembly recommended that it be expelled from the specialized agencies?

The ICAO Assembly, at an extraordinary session in 1984, shortly after the Soviet Union had shot down Korean Airlines flight 007, approved a new article 3 *bis* to the Chicago Convention. It provides in part:

(a) The contracting States recognize that every State must refrain from resorting to the use of weapons against civil aircraft in flight and that, in case of interception, the lives of persons on board and the safety of aircraft must not be endangered. This provision shall not be interpreted as modifying in any way the rights and obligations of States set forth in the Charter of the United Nations.

(b) The contracting States recognize that every State, in the exercise of its sovereignty, is entitled to require the landing at some designated airport of a civil aircraft flying above its territory without authority or if there are reasonable grounds to conclude that it is being used for any purpose inconsistent with the aims of this Convention; it may also give such aircraft any other instructions to put an end to such violations. For this purpose, the contracting States may resort to any appropriate means consistent with relevant rules of international law, including the relevant provisions of this Convention, specifically paragraph (a) of this Article. Each contracting State agrees to publish its regulations in force regarding the interception of civil aircraft.[v]

Arguably, article 3 *bis*, paragraph (a), above, reflects pre-existing customary international law.[w] Suppose an ICAO member state de-

---

[v]. Assembly Resolutions in Force (as of 6 October 1989), ICAO Doc. 9558, at I–5. At this writing, fewer than 102 states (the number required for entry into force) had ratified article 3 *bis*.

[w]. See Lowenfeld, Looking Back and Looking Ahead, 83 Am.J.Int'l L. 336, 341 (1989); Milde, Interception of Civil Aircraft vs. Misuse of Civil Aviation, 11 Annals of Air & Space L. 105, 113 (1986). But see Cheng, The Destruction of KAL Flight KE007, and Article 3 *bis* of the Chicago Convention, in Air Worthy: Liber Amicorum Honouring Professor Dr. I.H. Ph.

clines to ratify article 3 *bis* on the ground that its airspace is sacrosanct, and it cannot agree to tie its hands regarding the use of weapons when unauthorized aircraft intrude. Would that state be prohibited from shooting down foreign civil aircraft in its airspace (a) before article 3 *bis* enters into force; (b) after it enters into force? (Assume that it has no legitimate claim of self-defense.)

Suppose that article 3 *bis* has entered into force. A national of a state that has ratified it consummates a major drug deal in the capital of that state and tries to escape by private aircraft registered there. Could the government shoot down his plane over its own territory without violating article 3 *bis*?[x]

Is Chicago Convention article 94(a), as written, a workable amendment clause for the constituent instrument of an international organization with wide membership?

D. THE INTERNATIONAL MARITIME ORGANIZATION

The International Maritime Organization (IMO) concerns itself with the safety, efficiency and pollution-control aspects of shipping at sea. It does not deal directly with such ocean issues as basic navigation rights, fishing, mineral exploitation on the continental shelves or deep seabed, or marine scientific research. Nevertheless, as we shall see, several basic ocean issues regulated under the 1982 U.N. Convention on the Law of the Sea have implications for IMO and are affected by IMO normative practices.

Unlike ICAO, where the Council is the primary quasi-legislative body, in IMO the rule-making work is carried out in the Assembly and in committees. Particularly important are the Maritime Safety Committee (MSC) and the Marine Environmental Protection Committee (MEPC), both of which are open to all IMO member states. Both of them are authorized, among other things, to perform functions conferred by conventions other than the IMO's constituent instrument, the IMO Convention. That authorization has significant rule-making implications, as will appear below.

IMO committees have prepared several important conventions regulating the efficiency of maritime services, maritime safety and marine environmental protection. Among them are:

> Convention on Facilitation of International Maritime Traffic (the Facilitation Convention),[a] which promotes uniformity in the formalities, documentary requirements and procedures concerning customs, immigration and health matters for ships calling at foreign ports;

Diederiks–Verschoor 47, 59–61 (J. Storm van's Gravesande & A. van der Veen Vonk eds. (1985).

a. Apr. 9, 1965, 18 U.S.T. 411, T.I.A.S. 6251, 591 U.N.T.S. 265.

x. See Cheng, supra note w, at 65–67.

International Convention for the Prevention of Pollution by Ships (MARPOL 73/78),[b] which regulates the discharge from ships of wastes and other harmful substances, including oil, other than the deliberate dumping of wastes not generated on board the ship (covered by the London Ocean Dumping Convention [c]);

International Convention for the Safety of Life at Sea (SOLAS),[d] covering a wide range of safety concerns (ship construction, life-saving equipment, radio operations, safety of navigation, carriage of dangerous goods, etc.);

Convention on the International Regulations for Preventing Collisions at Sea (COLREG),[e] regulating such things as lights, lookouts, safe speeds, action to avoid collisions, traffic separation schemes, and standards for ships in overtaking, head-on and crossing situations.

As will appear below, much of the actual regulating under these conventions stems not directly from the negotiated and ratified terms of the conventions themselves (which tend to supply only the framework for regulation), but from annexes to them and from recommendations adopted by IMO organs pursuant to them. The excerpt below discusses two of the conventions—SOLAS and COLREG—plus various IMO recommendations including the comprehensive International Maritime Dangerous Goods Code (IMDG Code) adopted under SOLAS.

C. HENRY, THE CARRIAGE OF DANGEROUS GOODS BY SEA
73–75, 80–84 (1985).*

The recommendation is the single most important instrument of action available to the Organization. The power to adopt recommendations and the categories of recommendations which can be adopted are specified in the Convention. A first category consists of the recommendations of a general nature permitted in respect of Article 1(a)(b) and (c) of the Convention (Article 2(a)). These provisions of Article 1 deal with the purposes of the Organization. A second category of recommendations are those issued under Article 2(b), by virtue of which suitable instruments adopted by the Organization are recommended to States. Recommendations dealing with the settlement of disputes in matters

---

b. Nov. 2, 1973, 12 Int'l Legal Materials 1319 (1973), with Protocol, Feb. 17, 1978, 17 id. 546 (1978).

c. Convention on the Prevention of Marine Pollution by Dumping of Wastes and Other Matter, Dec. 29, 1972, 26 U.S.T. 2403, T.I.A.S. 8165, 1046 U.N.T.S. 120.

d. Nov. 1, 1974, 32 U.S.T. 47, T.I.A.S. 9700, 1184 U.N.T.S. 2, with Protocol, Feb. 17, 1978, 32 U.S.T. 5577, T.I.A.S. 10009, and amendments of Nov. 20, 1981, and June 17, 1983, in IMO, International Convention for the Safety of Life at Sea (Consol. text 1986). A Protocol of Nov. 11, 1988, IMO Doc. HSSC/CONF/11 (1988), was not yet in force at this writing.

e. Oct. 20, 1972, 28 U.S.T. 3459, T.I.A.S. 8587.

* Copyright © 1985 from The Carriage of Dangerous Goods by Sea, by C. Henry. Reprinted with permission of St. Martin's Press, Incorporated.

concerning unfair restrictive business practices by shipping concerns form the third category (Article 3). Finally, there is the specific stipulation of Article 15(j) of the Convention which empowers the Assembly to recommend for adoption by members regulations and guidelines concerning maritime safety and the prevention and control of marine pollution from ships or amendments to such regulations and guidelines. In 1977, for the first time in the IMO Convention, a distinction was made between "regulations" and "guidelines", although no definitions were offered. * * *

In keeping with its mandate, IMO has issued a wide range of recommendations under a variety of names: codes, guidelines, regulations, procedures and recommendations.

* * *

The question which evidently arises from this plethora of instruments is the determination of criteria for labelling them as codes, procedures, regulations, or guidelines. Are there any reasons for the use of a particular term? How are these instruments to be distinguished? It appears, however, that no particular significance has been attached to the use of different expressions, though a distinction has been drawn between resolutions of a merely advisory character and so-called "codes" which rank somewhere in between binding conventions and non-binding resolutions.

The IMO Convention itself does not really make any distinctions in that regard, nor does the practice of the Organization. The instruments concerned all embody technical standards which States are requested to implement. The "Guidelines for Inert Gas Systems", for instance, were adopted by the MSC at its 42nd session and were thereafter published by the Organization. Paragraph 1(2)(1) specifies that the " * * * status of these Guidelines is advisory". Starting from this instrument, one may probably make a generalization to the effect that guidelines are essentially advisory. But this does not tell us much since recommendations are generally of an advisory nature; this characteristic is not peculiar to guidelines. While no distinction can be drawn on the basis of the legal effect of these instruments, it might be possible to do so by considering their scope. Codes are generally wider in scope and more voluminous than recommendations or guidelines. IMO Codes are actually held in high esteem by experts in the field they cover. It has been said that they have become indispensable tools for the conduct of maritime shipping. The language of the codes is not limited by the formal restrictions governing the drafting of conventions. The texts are usually more descriptive than regulatory in the strict sense of the word, and they often present alternative solutions to a given problem. It is for this reason that the codes are increasingly used as a testing ground for regulatory concepts later to be incorporated into conventions.

A closer look at the recommendatory instruments of IMO reveals that, as a rule, two technical methods are used in their elaboration.

One method consists in identifying the aim to be achieved without specifying the means. The other method is to specify the aim pursued as well as the means to be used. The latter technique is employed in urgent situations where there is a pressing need for harmonization, as was the case for the Resolution embodying a "Recommendation on the Use of Pilotage Services in the Sound". The purpose of the Recommendation was expressly stated. It was adopted in view of the " * * * urgent need to protect the vulnerable Baltic Sea area, which has been designated as a special area, against pollution". Due to the risk of grounding or collision, the navigation of large oil tankers, chemical tankers and gas carriers through the Sound, as an entrance to the Baltic Sea area, was seen to constitute a potential danger for pollution of the entire Baltic Sea area. The Resolution identified the means to be used by recommending that:

> * * * oil tankers in loaded conditions with a draught of seven meters or more, and all loaded chemical tankers and gas carriers, irrespective of size, when navigating in the part of the Sound which is delimited by a line connecting Svinbaden Lighthouse and Hornbaek Harbour and Aflandohage (the southernmost point of the Amager Island), should use the pilotage services established by the Governments of Danemark and Sweden.

Functions of IMO Recommendations

In order to assess the status of IMO recommendations and their actual value, it is necessary to analyse the functions of these instruments. The latter form, in many instances, an essential component of a regulatory regime embodied in a treaty. Examples of such instruments abound. The IMDG Code supplements Chapter VII of SOLAS 1960 and 1974. Recommendations of IMO adopting traffic separation schemes supplement Regulation 10 of the COLREG Convention. The latter, however, fall into a separate category since Regulation 10 of the Convention clothes these additional "recommendations" with binding force for States Parties to COLREG. IMO is recognized as the only international body responsible for establishing and recommending measures on an international level concerning the routeing of ships. Many of the conventions for which IMO acts as the depositary and under which it performs operational and administrative duties empower the Organization to adopt supplementary standards or more detailed provisions. The "Recommendation Concerning Fire Safety Requirements for Passenger Ships Carrying more than 36 Passengers", for example, was adopted by IMO in accordance with Resolution 1, Item 3, of the International Conference on the Safety of Life at Sea, 1974. The Recommendation supplements Chapter II–2 of SOLAS, 1974, entitled "Construction, Fire Protection, Fire Detection and Fire Extinction".

* * *

Another type of recommendatory instruments are those facilitating the implementation of conventions. This is the case of two instruments respectively entitled "Procedures for the Control of Ships" and "Substandard Ships: Guidelines on Control Procedures". These recommendations were adopted to assist flag States in securing compliance with the SOLAS and Load Lines Conventions.

* * *

Sometimes IMO recommendations deal with issues not yet covered by treaty. They fill a void pending the development, adoption and implementation of more formal binding instruments. In that sense, IMO recommendatory instruments act as a precursor to conferences which the Organization will subsequently call to adopt conventions drafted by it. Consequently, a certain amount of State practice develops in respect of standards included in such recommendations, fostering uniformity and harmonization even before the standards are embodied in conventions.

* * *

The Legal Effect of IMO Recommendations

The legal effect of a resolution of an international organization is conditioned by three main factors: the circumstances surrounding the adoption of the resolution, its content and the modalities prescribed for the control of its application. Recommendations are generally considered as non-binding. This is true, in particular, for recommendations of IMO, with the exception of those relating to traffic separation schemes in respect of States Parties to the COLREG Convention, where one of their vessels uses such a scheme.

* * *

The recommendations have basically reflected a concern for human life, for goods at sea and for the marine environment.

The reflection of these concerns has clothed these instruments with a high practical value. It is this practical value which dominates over any desire to enforce legal obligations and thus reflects the notion of mutual interest. In many instances, it is hard to imagine that a State could refuse to apply certain standards to ships flying its flag without compromising the safety of navigation. This was the case, for instance, in respect of the COLREG before they were made formally mandatory.

* * *

IMO recommendations play an equally important role for the formation of customary international law in the area of maritime transport. According to Thommen, custom as a source of maritime law can be proved by:

> examining the practice of maritime nations * * *. The public and private laws, a series of bilateral treaties or diplomatic declarations, instructions to naval officers and decisions of courts in several maritime nations are some of the important ingredients of international maritime custom.

A large body of maritime law has its origin in uniform standards, criteria and specifications which, although they are of a non-treaty character and result from an international legislative process different from national law-making procedures, give rise to the same kind of formulated legal norms as those created nationally. The non-treaty instruments of IMO may be equally or even more effective in assisting the peaceful conduct of international activities than conventions. A recommendation or code which is widely accepted and voluntarily put into effect may lead to more positive and significant results than a treaty which is not ratified and applied or is ratified and applied by only a few States.

The use of non-treaty instruments by the Organization has engendered a process which, without disregarding the treaty approach, supplements and replaces it by procedures which may be equally effective or more suitable. This is because recommendations take account of what States are willing to accept at a given stage. They allow for compromise solutions which guarantee a much wider application of standards. They embody conciliatory approaches and discard radical solutions which would be doomed to failure on the practical level.

It thus seems well settled that IMO recommendations have no binding character by themselves. This deficiency, if it can be so termed, has not adversely affected the ability of the Organization to contribute to the creation of international norms. Since IMO recommendations are in fact widely accepted and implemented, they have achieved a high degree of unification of laws in force. Many of them have become mandatory after their incorporation into international conventions or national legislation. For instance, some twelve countries have fully implemented the Code for the Construction and Equipment of Ships Carrying Dangerous Chemicals in Bulk (BCH), while nine apply it on a voluntary basis. The Code for the Construction and Equipment of Ships Carrying Liquefied Gases in Bulk (GC) is being implemented in whole or in part by fifteen countries, whereas nine countries are conforming to the Gas Carrier Code for Existing Ships. Finally, the IMDG Code is applied by thirty-seven countries to date. While the numbers of States might appear small as compared to the actual membership of the Organization, this is not at all significant. What matters most is that the standards are adopted and implemented by countries which have an actual stake in shipping activities, namely, the traditional maritime nations and the States with a special interest in shipping, either because they are the largest ship-owning nations or because they have the largest interest in providing shipping services. Without the collaboration of these States in the implementation and enforcement of standards, IMO standard-setting activities would be doomed to failure since most of the regulations' impact would be lost. If these States adopt and implement IMO regulations, by contrast, 90 per cent of the world's total shipping tonnage is caught.

What, in fact, accounts for the wide implementation of IMO recommendations, apart from the mutual interest and practical value of these instruments? Firstly, the recommendations contain very precise elements which can be directly used in the formulation of national legislation. They can be said to perform the role of model laws in that regard. Secondly, the procedure of elaboration of the recommendations guarantees their effectiveness. As we have seen, the procedure used for recommendations is that resorted to in the elaboration and adoption of conventions. Thirdly, the experts in charge, pooled from government departments and private industry to draft provisions in IMO organs, are in many cases the very individuals responsible for their implementation at the national level. These experts represent a wide variety of interests, and their recommendations are the result of long and exhaustive research. Fourthly, as is the case for the ICAO, the implicit sanction of reciprocity is particularly effective in the field of shipping. While that sanction is nowhere mentioned in the IMO Convention, it is clear that States which accept higher standards for their ships will be reluctant to admit to their ports ships of States subscribing to lower standards. Shipping is a highly competitive free-enterprise industry and provides fertile ground for the application of reciprocity. States with substantial shipping interests will not lightly ignore IMO recommendations if in so doing they reduce their competitiveness, run safety risks, or are denied access to the ports of other States.

* * *

Finally, despite the express provisions of the rules of procedure for IMO organs which call for decisions to be adopted by majority, most IMO organs operate under the consensus procedure which implies the absence of objection to standards thereby adopted, or their general acceptance.

In conclusion, it can be said that IMO recommendations embody standards and norms which are the result of long and detailed research carried out by experts who are drawn from the major maritime States, from specialized non-governmental institutions and from private industry, who feed their own perspectives, varied backgrounds and interests into the procedure, and who will be called upon to implement the standards produced in another capacity. In addition, the method of elaboration of these recommendations, their high practical value, the level of flexibility which they embody and the principle of reciprocity have elevated them to a status transcending that of simple recommendatory instruments and permit IMO recommendations which contain technical standards to be considered as international legislation.

IMO "LEGISLATION"

The author mentions, as a reason for the effectiveness of IMO recommendations, the fact that the procedure for their adoption is the same as the procedure for adopting conventions. At pages 59–61 she outlines the procedure: first, a proposal from a member state, group of states, or interested international organization to study a particular subject, indicating the proposed action; then approval of the proposal by the Assembly or Council; assignment of the subject to the appropriate IMO subcommittee; preparation of drafts and their submission to states and international organizations for comments; consideration and adoption of the relevant document (draft treaty or recommendation); and any necessary implementation to put it into force (ratification in the case of a treaty, but not in the case of a recommendation).

What exactly does the author mean when she says that "IMO recommendations which contain technical standards [may] be considered as international legislation"? Are they binding, as a matter of international law? If not, does it matter?

In what respects are IMO recommendations comparable to, or different from, recommendations of the ILO and ICAO?

In 1973 the IMO (then called the Intergovernmental Maritime Consultative Organization) convened a conference to deal with the growing problem of pollution from spills of harmful substances carried at sea. A multilateral convention already existed for the prevention of pollution of the sea by oil, but it was thought to be inadequate—in part because oil was not the only potentially harmful substance transported at sea.

The 1973 conference produced the International Convention for the Prevention of Pollution from Ships. It was later amended by a 1978 Protocol. Together the Convention and Protocol, often called MARPOL 73/78, with their Annexes and Appendices to Annexes, provide a detailed system for curtailing discharges from ships of designated pollutants. These are oil (Annex I), noxious liquid substances in bulk (Annex II), harmful substances carried in containers (Annex III), sewage (Annex IV), and garbage (Annex V). Each Annex contains a series of regulations that apply to ships at sea, port reception facilities, etc. Each Annex has Appendices listing the substances covered by the Annex and setting forth forms for certificates of compliance and record books.

The Annexes and Appendices are the important instruments for international rulemaking purposes. Their usefulness would diminish fairly rapidly, however, if they could not be amended from time to time to deal with changing technologies and new discoveries regarding the properties of the substances covered. It would be far too cumbersome to limit the amendment process to the traditional convening of formal conferences of all contracting parties at which protocols of amendment would be signed subject to ratification by the parties. Instead, MARPOL 73/78 uses the committees of IMO and somewhat streamlined means of "ratification." [f] The amendment process appears in article 16 of MARPOL 73/78, reproduced below along with article 14(1). How well would it work in practice?

INTERNATIONAL CONVENTION FOR THE PREVENTION OF POLLUTION BY SHIPS

Nov. 2, 1973, with Protocol of Feb. 17, 1978.
12 Int'l Legal Materials 1319 (1973) & 17 id. 546 (1978).

ARTICLE 14
Optional Annexes

(1) A State may at the time of signing, ratifying, accepting, approving or acceding to the present Convention declare that it does not accept any one or all of Annexes III, IV and V (hereinafter referred to as "Optional Annexes") of the present Convention. Subject to the above, Parties to the Convention shall be bound by any Annex in its entirety.

* * *

ARTICLE 16
Amendments

(1) The present Convention may be amended by any of the procedures specified in the following paragraphs.

(2) Amendments after consideration by the Organization:

(a) any amendment proposed by a Party to the Convention shall be submitted to the Organization and circulated by its Secretary-General to all Members of the Organization and all Parties at least six months prior to its consideration;

(b) any amendment proposed and circulated as above shall be submitted to an appropriate body by the Organization for consideration;

(c) Parties to the Convention, whether or not Members of the Organization, shall be entitled to participate in the proceedings of the appropriate body;

(d) amendments shall be adopted by a two-thirds majority of only the Parties to the Convention present voting;

(e) if adopted in accordance with sub-paragraph (d) above, amendments shall be communicated by the Secretary-General of the Organization to all the Parties to the Convention for acceptance;

---

f. A more recent IMO-related convention, the International Convention on Oil Pollution Preparedness, Response and Co-operation, Nov. 30, 1990, art. 14, IMO Doc. OPPR/CONF/25 (1990), also uses an IMO committee for an amendment process based on that in MARPOL 73/78.

(f) an amendment shall be deemed to have been accepted in the following circumstances:

  (i) an amendment to an Article of the Convention shall be deemed to have been accepted on the date on which it is accepted by two-thirds of the Parties, the combined merchant fleets of which constitute not less than fifty per cent of the gross tonnage of the world's merchant fleet;

  (ii) an amendment to an Annex to the Convention shall be deemed to have been accepted in accordance with the procedure specified in sub-paragraph (f)(iii) unless the appropriate body, at the time of its adoption, determines that the amendment shall be deemed to have been accepted on the date on which it is accepted by two-thirds of the Parties, the combined merchant fleets of which constitute not less than fifty per cent of the gross tonnage of the world's merchant fleet. Nevertheless, at any time before the entry into force of an amendment to an Annex to the Convention, a Party may notify the Secretary–General of the Organization that its express approval will be necessary before the amendment enters into force for it. The latter shall bring such notification and the date of its receipt to the notice of Parties;

  (iii) an amendment to an Appendix to an Annex to the Convention shall be deemed to have been accepted at the end of a period to be determined by the appropriate body at the time of its adoption, which period shall be not less than ten months, unless within that period an objection is communicated to the Organization by not less than one-third of the Parties or by the Parties the combined merchant fleets of which constitute not less than fifty per cent of the gross tonnage of the world's merchant fleet whichever condition is fulfilled;

  (iv) an amendment to Protocol I to the Convention shall be subject to the same procedures as for the amendments to the Annexes to the Convention, as provided for in sub-paragraphs (f)(ii) or (f)(iii) above;

  (v) an amendment to Protocol II to the Convention shall be subject to the same procedures as for the amendments to an Article of the Convention, as provided for in sub-paragraph (f)(i) above:

(g) the amendment shall enter into force under the following conditions:

  (i) in the case of an amendment to an Article of the Convention, to Protocol II, or to Protocol I or to an Annex to the Convention not under the procedure specified in sub-paragraph (f)(iii), the amendment accepted in conformity with the foregoing provisions shall enter into force six months after the date of its acceptance with respect to the Parties which have declared that they have accepted it;

(ii) in the case of an amendment to Protocol I, to an Appendix to an Annex or an Annex to the Convention under the procedure specified in sub-paragraph (f)(iii), the amendment deemed to have been accepted in accordance with the foregoing conditions shall enter into force six months after its acceptance for all the Parties with the exception of those which, before that date, have made a declaration that they do not accept it or a declaration under sub-paragraph (f)(ii), that their express approval is necessary.

(3) Amendment by a Conference:
  (a) Upon the request of a Party, concurred in by at least one-third of the Parties, the Organization shall convene a Conference of Parties to the Convention to consider amendments to the present Convention.
  (b) Every amendment adopted by such a Conference by a two-thirds majority of those present and voting of the Parties shall be communicated by the Secretary-General of the Organization to all Contracting Parties for their acceptance.
  (c) Unless the Conference decides otherwise, the amendment shall be deemed to have been accepted and to have entered into force in accordance with the procedures specified for that purpose in paragraph (2)(f) and (g) above.

(4) (a) In the case of an Amendment to an Optional Annex, a reference in the present Article to a "Party to the Convention" shall be deemed to mean a reference to a Party bound by that Annex.
  (b) Any Party which has declined to accept an amendment to an Annex shall be treated as a non-Party only for the purpose of application of that Amendment.

THE AMENDMENT PROCESS

Suppose an amendment to an Annex is submitted to the appropriate IMO body and is adopted by a two-thirds majority of the parties to the Convention present and voting. Peru, a party to the Convention, is present but abstains from voting. If the IMO body decides to use the acceptance procedure in article 16(2)(f)(ii), and the amendment is then accepted by two-thirds of the parties having more than 50% of the gross tonnage of the world's merchant fleet, would Peru be bound by the amendment if it remains silent during the acceptance process?

Suppose the IMO body decides instead not to use the acceptance procedure in article 16(2)(f)(ii) and sets ten months as the period for objections under article 16(2)(f)(iii). Suppose only one-tenth of the parties, having 5% of the gross tonnage of the world's merchant fleet, object within that time. What would be the position of Peru if it declares in the eleventh month that its express approval is necessary?

Under article 16(2)(f)(ii), could the appropriate body decide that acceptance will be required by two-thirds of the Parties, the combined merchant fleets of which constitute 75% of the gross tonnage of the world's merchant fleet?

Are the amendment procedures in article 16 streamlined enough? Are the time limits too long?

Note the composition of IMO "bodies" (committees), and voting rights in the committees, for the purpose of considering proposed amendments to MARPOL. See article 16(2)(c) and (d). Although allowing nonmembers of IMO to participate with voting rights in IMO committees was once legally controversial, it is now settled not only by provisions such as MARPOL article 16(2)(c) and (d), but also by an amendment to the IMO Convention.[g] But does it make sense? Why not just eliminate the complicated amendment procedure of article 16(2) and have all proposed amendments considered by conferences of MARPOL parties under the procedure in article 16(3)?

The IMO's rule making authority got a boost from the 1982 United Nations Convention on the Law of the Sea. The Convention represents an attempt to provide a comprehensive regime for the oceans. It reflects years of detailed negotiations, and many delicate compromises, among nations with sometimes-conflicting, sometimes-complementary interests. As of 1992, ten years after it was adopted, it was not yet in force. The slow pace of submitting ratifications was attributable primarily to doubts many states had about the Convention's provisions on deep seabed mining. The United States, in particular, objected to that part of the Convention. Other parts, however, have received widespread approval and have been thought to represent customary international law.

We will focus only on Part XII, concerning protection and preservation of the marine environment. A few articles in Part XII deal, directly or indirectly, with pollution from ships—the same subject covered by MARPOL 73/78, above. Assume that the Convention enters into force, with these articles intact, for a significant number of maritime and coastal states.

CONVENTION ON THE LAW OF THE SEA
Dec. 10, 1982.
U.N. Doc. A/CONF.62/122.

ARTICLE 194

Measures to Prevent, Reduce and Control Pollution of the Marine Environment

1. States shall take, individually or jointly as appropriate, all measures consistent with this Convention that are necessary to pre-

g. See IMO Convention *arts. 31, 41.*

vent, reduce and control pollution of the marine environment from any source, using for this purpose the best practicable means at their disposal and in accordance with their capabilities, and they shall endeavour to harmonize their policies in this connection.

2. States shall take all measures necessary to ensure that activities under their jurisdiction or control are so conducted as not to cause damage by pollution to other States and their environment, and that pollution arising from incidents or activities under their jurisdiction or control does not spread beyond the areas where they exercise sovereign rights in accordance with this Convention.

* * *

Article 197
Co-operation on a global or regional basis

States shall co-operate on a global basis and, as appropriate, on a regional basis, directly or through competent international organizations, in formulating and elaborating international rules, standards and recommended practices and procedures consistent with this Convention, for the protection and preservation of the marine environment, taking into account characteristic regional features.

* * *

Article 211
Pollution from vessels

1. States, acting through the competent international organization or general diplomatic conference, shall establish international rules and standards to prevent, reduce and control pollution of the marine environment from vessels and promote the adoption, in the same manner, wherever appropriate, of routeing systems designed to minimize the threat of accidents which might cause pollution of the marine environment, including the coastline, and pollution damage to the related interests of coastal States. Such rules and standards shall, in the same manner, be re-examined from time to time as necessary.

2. States shall adopt laws and regulations for the prevention, reduction and control of pollution of the marine environment from vessels flying their flag or of their registry. Such laws and regulations shall at least have the same effect as that of generally accepted international rules and standards established through the competent international organization or general diplomatic conference.

3. States which establish particular requirements for the prevention, reduction and control of pollution of the marine environment as a condition for the entry of foreign vessels into their ports or internal waters or for a call at their off-shore terminals shall give due publicity to such requirements and shall communicate them to the competent international organization.

* * *

4. Coastal States may, in the exercise of their sovereignty within their territorial sea, adopt laws and regulations for the prevention, reduction and control of marine pollution from foreign vessels, including vessels exercising the right of innocent passage. Such laws and regulations shall, in accordance with Part II, section 3, not hamper innocent passage of foreign vessels.

5. Coastal States, for the purpose of enforcement as provided for in section 6, may in respect of their exclusive economic zones adopt laws and regulations for the prevention, reduction and control of pollution from vessels conforming to and giving effect to generally accepted international rules and standards established through the competent international organization or general diplomatic conference.

6. (a) Where the international rules and standards referred to in paragraph 1 are inadequate to meet special circumstances and coastal States have reasonable grounds for believing that a particular, clearly defined area of their respective exclusive economic zones is an area where the adoption of special mandatory measures for the prevention of pollution from vessels is required for recognized technical reasons in relation to its oceanographical and ecological conditions, as well as its utilization or the protection of its resources and the particular character of its traffic, the coastal States, after appropriate consultations through the competent international organization with any other States concerned, may, for that area, direct a communication to that organization, submitting scientific and technical evidence in support and information on necessary reception facilities. Within 12 months after receiving such a communication, the organization shall determine whether the conditions in that area correspond to the requirements set out above. If the organization so determines, the coastal States may, for that area, adopt laws and regulations for the prevention, reduction and control of pollution from vessels implementing such international rules and standards or navigational practices as are made applicable, through the organization, for special areas. These laws and regulations shall not become applicable to foreign vessels until 15 months after the submission of the communication to the organization.

(b) The coastal States shall publish the limits of any such particular, clearly defined area.

(c) If the coastal States intend to adopt additional laws and regulations for the same area for the prevention, reduction and control of pollution from vessels, they shall, when submitting the aforesaid communication, at the same time notify the organization thereof. Such additional laws and regulations may relate to discharges or navigational practices but shall not require foreign vessels to observe design, construction, manning or equipment standards other than generally accepted international rules and standards; they shall become applicable to foreign vessels 15 months after the submission of the communication to the organization, provided that the organization agrees within 12 months after the submission of the communication.

IMO AND THE CONVENTION ON THE LAW OF THE SEA

There is general agreement that the "competent international organization," for purposes of article 211, is IMO.

Do articles 194, 197 and 211 give IMO binding rule-making authority? If so, exactly what could IMO bind states to do?

If these articles do give the IMO binding rule-making authority, would its MARPOL regulations bind states that are parties to (a) both MARPOL and the Convention on the Law of the Sea; (b) MARPOL but not to the Convention; (c) the Convention but not to MARPOL; (d) neither MARPOL nor the Convention? In this connection, note article 311(2) and (3) of the Convention on the Law of the Sea:

> 2. This Convention shall not alter the rights and obligations of States Parties which arise from other agreements compatible with this Convention and which do not affect the enjoyment by other States Parties of their rights or the performance of their obligations under this Convention.
>
> 3. Two or more States Parties may conclude agreements modifying or suspending the operation of provisions of this Convention, applicable solely to the relations between them, provided that such agreements do not relate to a provision derogation from which is incompatible with the effective execution of the object and purpose of this Convention, and provided further that such agreements shall not affect the application of the basic principles embodied herein, and that the provisions of such agreements do not affect the enjoyment by other States Parties of their rights or the performance of their obligations under this Convention.

Suppose a particular port state and a particular flag state are parties to both MARPOL and the Convention on the Law of the Sea. Could the port state adopt pollution-control standards more stringent than those established under MARPOL for the flag state's vessels entering its ports or passing through its territorial sea? See Convention on the Law of the Sea article 211(3) and (4).

Could a coastal state ever adopt pollution-control standards for its exclusive economic zone more stringent than those established under MARPOL? See article 211(6).

Is there anything undemocratic about giving organizations like IMO and ICAO the rule-making power they have?

E. THE UNITED NATIONS

INTRODUCTORY NOTE

The International Law Commission, created by the General Assembly pursuant to article 13(1) of the Charter and consisting of 34 eminent international lawyers from as many nations, is the U.N. body expressly charged with the duty of formulating rules of international law. Its charge covers both the progressive development and codification of international law; that is, it may develop new formulations, or it may simply codify existing law. But it does not have any express legislative power of its own; it simply reports the fruits of its labor to the General Assembly, sometimes in the form of a draft resolution to be adopted by the Assembly, sometimes in the form of a draft treaty to be approved by the Assembly and then submitted to an international conference for eventual adoption by interested states. It is thus possible (and traditional) to view the International Law Commission simply as a body that consolidates and proposes rules, rather than as a body that creates them.

If a "rule" is defined as a specific, incontestably binding legal norm, the traditional view is clearly correct. If, on the other hand, we think in terms of legal norms in a broader sense, the traditional view may not fully describe the situation. A leading British scholar has defined a norm as "an authoritative provision of law that continues to command significant community expectation as to its contemporary validity and which may be appropriately invoked and applied in the particular factual context."[a] The formulations of the International Law Commission have had at least some normative effect, even before the General Assembly or an international conference has acted upon them.[b] For example, the Commission's draft articles on the law of treaties—a combination of codified pre-existing customary rules and progressively-developed new ones—established the prevailing standards for the law of treaties even before the Vienna Convention on the Law of Treaties, to which they gave birth, had been signed.

The Security Council has the power under the U.N. Charter to make binding legislative decisions concerning international peace and security. The most significant of these have come in the context of attempts to induce compliance by all U.N. members with organizational norms stemming either from the Charter itself or from resolutions adopted under the Charter. Consequently they raise problems more closely related to the concerns of the next Chapter (on enforcement mechanisms) than to the general rule-making focus of this one.

a. Higgins, The Role of Resolutions of International Organizations in the Process of Creating Norms in the International System, in International Law and the International System 21 (W. Butler ed. 1987).

b. See, e.g., Jennings, Recent Developments in the International Law Commission: Its Relation to the Sources of International Law, 13 Int'l & Comp.L.Q. 385 (1964).

The General Assembly is the most representative organ within the United Nations itself. Each member state is represented, with one vote apiece. We shall examine its influence on the development of international norms.

---

1. The General Assembly as a Participant in the Shaping of International Law

a. Theory and Practice

The General Assembly has on several occasions acted as a facilitator for the creation of international legislative rules through the traditional process of treaty-making. It has done this primarily by convening conferences open to all U.N. members and sometimes to others, on specific subjects considered ready for regulation by one or more broad, multilateral treaties. As suggested above, the conferences have often worked from a draft treaty prepared by the International Law Commission, which typically is revised somewhat at the conference and then adopted in its revised form. It does not formally become law until ratified by the number of states specified in the treaty. Products of this traditional "legislative" process include the four 1958 Geneva Conventions on the Law of the Sea, the 1961 and 1963 Vienna Conventions on Diplomatic and Consular Relations, respectively, and the 1969 Vienna Convention on the Law of Treaties.

Sometimes the format changes. For example, in 1973 the General Assembly convened the Third United Nations Conference on the Law of the Sea on the basis of preparatory work done in its Seabed Committee (which had not produced an agreed draft convention), rather than on the basis of any preparatory work by the International Law Commission. On a few occasions the General Assembly has simply adopted a draft convention prepared by the Commission, as in the case of General Assembly Resolution 3166 (XXVIII), of December 14, 1973, adopting the Convention on the Prevention and Punishment of Crimes Against Internationally Protected Persons, including Diplomatic Agents.

In all of these instances, however, the conventions are not formally binding until ratified by the designated number of states, and even then are formally binding only on those states that do ratify or accede. There is no express obligation comparable to that in the ILO Constitution to submit U.N.-endorsed conventions to the appropriate domestic authorities for their consideration or approval.

More interesting from a legislative perspective is the question of the possible normative effect of General Assembly resolutions that are not tied to the preparation of treaties. Aside from budgetary, procedural and trusteeship matters, these resolutions are adopted pursuant to Charter *articles 10–14*. Do these articles give the General Assembly the power to legislate in the sense of adopting rules binding upon member states?

A vast amount has been written about the normative effects of General Assembly resolutions. The excerpts below give a sampling of the views expressed by scholars and jurists.

J. CASTAÑEDA, LEGAL EFFECTS OF UNITED NATIONS RESOLUTIONS
12, 170–71 (1969).*

Malintoppi has formulated a suggestive thesis to provide sanction for recommendations with a juridical framework. He reasons thus:

In every international organization there is a general rule according to which member states are bound to cooperate in achieving its purposes. The basic obligation of the members is to act in such a way that the charter's goals may be fulfilled. There is a strict correlation between this obligation and the purposes of the organization. The organ's adoption of a recommendation represents an expression of a general social feeling. It is a manifestation of the manner in which the purposes of the treaty must be fulfilled in the eyes of the organization. The member who does not observe it is opposing not only a social consensus but also the juridical system that is the normative superstructure of that social environment. The pressure that a recommendation brings to bear on its addressees means this: faced with conduct contrary to the recommendation, and to the extent to which it is contrary, the social group can act, in its turn, against the asocial conduct of whomsoever does not carry out the recommendation, directing its reprobation against the author of the conduct. This is the *social sanction* of recommendations.[23]

* * *

Perhaps the most serious consequence of the absence of an international legislator is the difficulty faced by the organs that apply international law of knowing when a practice has become a true rule of law and when it is still a potential, embryonic rule, and of knowing whether a principle recognized by some but not all states is a general principle of law in the sense of Article 38 of the Statute of the Court, that is, a true source of law. Regarding nonconventional rules, there is no sign or criterion, formal and external, that indicates accurately when, under what conditions, and to what extent, the transition from a prejuridical stage to the sphere of true law occurs. The determination of this dividing line, indispensable for the application of law, and implicitly

---

* Reprinted from J. Castañeda, Legal Effects of United Nations Resolutions (New York: Columbia University Press, 1969), by permission of the publisher. (Emphasis in the original.)

23. Malintoppi, Le Raccomandazioni internazionali 49 et seq. (Milan, 1958).

made each day by governments and international organs and tribunals, may be subject to a markedly subjective appreciation. In a particularly dynamic environment of accelerated changes, such as modern international society's, it is natural that marginal zones should be very extensive and their demarcation most controversial. Thus, it is often necessary to rely on an authoritative determination, with full probative value, to attest to the character of the rules applied by the international community. The eminent author and judge Benjamin Cardozo stated this problem admirably in one of his judgments: "International law, or the law that governs between States," he said, "has at times, like the common law within states, a twilight existence during which it is hardly distinguishable from morality or justice, till at length the imprimatur of a court attests its jural quality." [New Jersey v. Delaware, 291 U.S. 361, 383 (1934).]

This function has been traditionally performed by international tribunals and, in a secondary, ancillary, and occasional way, even by national tribunals; Cardozo's phrase refers to the imprimatur of a court. But it cannot be concluded that this function belongs only to tribunals as a matter of principle. There is no essential reason preventing other broadly representative international organs from validly expressing on behalf of the international community what, in the community's opinion, *is* international law at a given moment. Moreover, the function considered here is not jurisdictional from the point of view of substance. It is not a question of *stating* the law with reference to a specific case that has assumed the character of a contention, but of expressing previously, in a general manner, whether a certain practice or principle has acquired the "jural quality" that allows it to be considered a part of the body of positive international law. In this sense, it is not a jurisdictional function, but a function that may be characterized as "quasi-legislative."

The juridical character of a practice or a principle derives ultimately from activities carried out, or attitudes assumed, by the states, and depends on the evaluation made and the meaning attributed by the international community to the activities or attitudes of its members. Therefore, a broadly representative organ, such as the General Assembly, is especially well qualified to examine and evaluate those activities and attitudes and to express, through declarative resolutions, the scope and meaning that the international community ascribes to them. These Assembly resolutions do not *create* law, but they *may authoritatively prove its existence.*

Inversely, an Assembly resolution can be proof that a customary rule is no longer one. If the majority of members of the international community express, through a resolution, their rejection of a customary rule, it is evident that that rule lacks the element of *opinio juris.*

SCHWEBEL, THE EFFECT OF RESOLUTIONS OF THE U.N. GENERAL ASSEMBLY ON CUSTOMARY INTERNATIONAL LAW
73 Proc.Am.Soc'y Int'l L. 301–05 (1979).*

It is trite but no less true that the General Assembly of the United Nations lacks legislative powers. Its resolutions are not, generally speaking, binding on the States Members of the United Nations or binding in international law at large. It could hardly be otherwise. We do not have a world legislature. If we had one, hopefully it would not be composed as is the General Assembly on the basis of the unrepresentative principle of the sovereign equality of states, states which in turn are represented by governments so many of which are themselves not representative of their peoples. As the Secretary of State recently put it:

> In considering the decisionmaking process in the United Nations, it is important to bear in mind that, while the one-state, one-vote procedure for expressing the sense of the General Assembly is from many points of view unsatisfactory, the incorporation of this principle in the Charter was balanced by giving the Assembly only recommendatory powers.[1]

Thus, at the San Francisco Conference on International Organization, only one state voted for a proposal that would have permitted the General Assembly to enact rules of international law that would become binding for the members of the Organization once they had been approved by a majority vote in the Security Council. A review of the authority of the General Assembly as set forth in the Charter of the United Nations demonstrates that it has the broadest powers to discuss and to recommend; not a phrase of the Charter suggests that it is empowered to enact or alter international law.

The General Assembly does, of course, have certain internal and financial powers which are binding. But, putting resolutions on such subjects aside, and despite the General Assembly's lack of legislative authority, can other resolutions of the General Assembly have effect in international law; in particular, may other resolutions—some of which are termed "Declarations"—create or change international law?

On this, opinion is sharply divided. At one pole are those who maintain that the distinctions between recommendations and binding decisions are fundamental. The General Assembly has recommendatory powers. Its recommendations may and do embrace aspects of international law, but they remain recommendations, which states are

---

* Reprinted with permission, c. The American Society of International Law. When the above remarks were made, Schwebel was Deputy Legal Adviser in the U.S. State Department. Later he became a Judge of the International Court of Justice. The views reproduced here were expressed in his personal capacity.

1. The Secretary's Report to the President on Reform and Restructuring of the U.N. System, Dept.St.Publ. 8940 (June, 1978).

legally free to accept and implement or oppose and disregard. Those who deny that the General Assembly enacts or alters international law point out that, in fact, States Members of the United Nations often vote for much with which they actually disagree. They often go along with a consensus when their reservations are not secondary but primary. They often vote casually: their delegates may be * * * loosely instructed; they may vote because the members of their group have decided or are disposed so to vote rather than because the immediate interests or considered views of their government so suggest. The members of the General Assembly typically vote in response to political not legal considerations. They do not conceive of themselves as creating or changing international law. It normally is not their intention to affect international law but to make the point which the resolution makes. The issue often is one of image rather than international law: states will vote a given way repeatedly not because they consider that their reiterated votes are evidence of a practice accepted as law but because it is politically unpopular to vote otherwise. The U.N. General Assembly is a forum in which states can express their views; the expressed views of states undeniably may be elements of that state practice which can give rise to customary international law; but what states *do* is more important than what they say. It is especially more important than what they may say in a General Assembly context. General Assembly resolutions, however often repeated, are insufficient elements of state practice of themselves to establish international legal obligations. Thus General Assembly resolutions are neither legislative nor sufficient to create custom, not only because the General Assembly is not authorized to legislate but also because its members, as Professor Arangio–Ruiz tellingly sums it up, don't "mean it."[2] That is to say, in fact, states often don't meaningfully support what a resolution says and they almost always do not mean that the resolution is law. This may be as true or truer in the case of unanimously adopted resolutions as in the case of majority-adopted resolutions. It may be truer still of resolutions adopted by "consensus."

* * *

[Later in his remarks, Schwebel noted that "the United Nations has in recent years witnessed the adoption of resolutions by fake consensus," i.e. without formal objection at the time of adoption, but with the expression of serious opposition by several members before or immediately after adoption.]

Yet the other pole of this problem also has much to be said for it. It readily acknowledges that the U.N. Charter gives the General Assembly no legislative powers. But it maintains that, in practice, many of its resolutions have had effects in and on international law; and that

2. Arangio–Ruiz, *The Normative Role of the General Assembly of the United Nations and the Declaration of Principles of Friendly Relations,* 3 Recueil des cours 431, at 457 (1972).

this practice, this broad construction of the General Assembly's powers, is now accepted and established.

This school of thought, of which Oliver Lissitzyn is an acute exponent, does not accept the contention that, in the development of customary international law, what states do necessarily is more important than what they say. According to the traditional view, it notes, customary international law is created by uniformities in the actual conduct of states if such conduct is accompanied by the conviction that it is required by international law. But it questions whether the emergence of customary international law is confined to this process of reciprocal claims and mutual tolerances. Uniformity of conduct creates expectations of continuation of the same sort of conduct. States and other international actors develop their policies and plan their actions on the basis of such expectations. There is therefore a common interest in the fulfillment of these expectations and in the stability of conduct, an interest which is translated into the doctrine that "custom" or "general practice" creates legally binding rules. But, Professor Lissitzyn maintains, "expectations may rest not only on actual conduct, but also on other forms of communication, including the verbal." He points out that this is clear in the case of treaties. He concludes that:

> Statements or declarations not binding as treaties may also give rise to reasonable expectations. If such statements or declarations emanate from a large number of States and purport to deal with a legal matter, they may be regarded in some circumstances as indications of a general consensus amounting to a norm of international law.[3]

And accordingly, he assigns legal value to some verbal expressions of consensus by the General Assembly.

* * *

It has also been maintained that repeated resolutions of the General Assembly may evidence a practice accepted as law. Judge Tanaka has pointed out that international organizations today afford states a medium for the concentrated and accelerated expression of their views which did not exist when customary international law only grew disparately and unevenly through the bilateral interactions of states. And scholars as perceptive as Castaneda and Higgins have pointed out that, apart from the impact which the practice of the General Assembly may have on the development of customary international law, declarations of the General Assembly which authoritatively find what the law is—which are declaratory of international law—can have an important effect in codifying and even progressively developing international law.

The Office of Legal Affairs of the Secretary–General of the United Nations has written that " * * * there is probably no difference between a 'recommendation' or a 'declaration' in United Nations practice as far as strict legal principle is concerned." This memorandum,

---

3. See Lissitzyn, International Law Today and Tomorrow, at 34–36 (1965).

written in 1962, transmitted to the General Assembly and apparently accepted by the membership, states that:

> A "declaration" or a "recommendation" is adopted by resolution of a United Nations organ. As such it cannot be made binding upon Member States, in the sense that a treaty or convention is binding upon the parties to it, purely by the device of terming it a "declaration" rather than a "recommendation" * * *. However, in view of the greater solemnity and significance of "declaration," it may be considered to import, on behalf of the organ adopting it, a strong expectation that Members of the international community will abide by it. Consequently, insofar as the expectation is gradually justified by State practice, a declaration may by custom become recognized as laying down rules binding upon states.[5]

This important statement makes two key points: first, that declarations are recommendations, that is to say, that they are not inherently binding; second, that a declaration may "by custom become recognized as laying down rules binding upon States" insofar as—and only insofar as—that is "gradually justified by State practice." The statement imports that such state practice cannot simply consist of further declarations or resolutions of the General Assembly; the actual behavior of states must manifest itself so clearly and consistently as to evidence a practice. But then the question arises, is the source of international law the General Assembly's resolution or state practice? The answer may be that the General Assembly's declaration may, depending on its terms and content, be taken as a valid element and articulation of state practice provided that it finds sufficient other support in the actual conduct of states. This interpretation appears to be consistent with the advisory opinions of the International Court of Justice which afford weight in the development of international law to General Assembly declarations respecting nonselfgoverning territories [General Assembly Resolutions 1514(XV) and 2625 (XXV)].

Erik Suy, [then] the Legal Counsel of the United Nations, has more recently concluded:

> The General Assembly's authority is limited to the adoption of resolutions. These are mere recommendations having no legally binding force for member states. Solemn declarations adopted either unanimously or by consensus have no different status, although their moral and political impact will be an important factor in guiding national policies. Declarations frequently contain references to existing rules of international law. They do not create, but merely restate and endorse them. Other principles contained in such declarations may appear to be new statements of legal rules. But the mere fact that they are adopted does not confer on them any specific and automatic authority. The most one could say is that overwhelming (or even unanimous) approval is an indication of *opinio juris sive necessitatis;* but this does not create

---

5. U.N. Doc., E/CN.4/L.610 (Apr. 2, 1962).

law without any concomitant practice, and that practice will not be brought about until states modify their national policies and legislation. It may also arise, however, through the mere repetition of principles in subsequent resolutions to which states give their approval. The General Assembly, through its solemn declarations, can therefore give an important impetus to the emergence of new rules, despite the fact that the adoption of declarations per se does not give them the quality of binding norms.[6]

Suy's analysis quite rightly emphasizes the importance of state practice. However, it also gives weight to "the mere repetition of principles in subsequent resolutions to which states give their approval" which, for the reasons indicated above, is open to question.

HIGGINS, THE ROLE OF RESOLUTIONS OF INTERNATIONAL ORGANIZATIONS IN THE PROCESS OF CREATING NORMS IN THE INTERNATIONAL SYSTEM
International Law and the International System 21–23, 25–30.
(W. Butler ed. 1987).*

* * *

In 1963 the present writer wrote the following about the role of the United Nations in lawmaking:

> The UN is a very appropriate body to look to for indications of developments in international law, for international custom is to be deduced from the practices of states, which includes their international dealings as manifested by their diplomatic actions and public pronouncements. With the development of international organizations, the votes and views of states have come to have legal significance as evidence of customary international law * * * Collective acts by states, repeated by and acquiesced in by sufficient numbers with sufficient frequency, eventually attain the status of law. The existence of the United Nations—and especially its accelerated trend towards universality of membership since 1955—now provides a very clear, very concentrated focal point for state practice. Here, then, is the reason for looking to United Nations practice in a search for the direction of the development of international law.[1]

Looking back at this from a distance of some twenty-four years, two points are striking. The first is how moderate and indeed cautious those views seem today, though in 1963 they were regarded as very radical. There is nothing in this approach that suggests a belief in

---

6. Suy, *Innovations in International Law–Making Processes*, The International Law and Policy of Human Welfare (Macdonald, Johnston and Morris eds. 1978).

* Reprinted by permission of Kluwer Academic Publishers.

1. R. Higgins, *The Development of International Law Through the Political Organs of the United Nations* (1963), p. 2.

"instant custom," or that the distinction between decisions and recommendations is to be ignored. * * *

[I]t is clear that clarity of intent, *opinio juris*, repetition, and agreement or acquiescence of sufficient and relevant states, are all required for custom; and that these conditions remain pertinent for United Nations practice as evidence of custom.

* * *

The second point is this: my views were directed to the place of United Nations practice in the development of international law. There was in the theoretical analysis virtually no reference to *resolutions* as such. Resolutions are but one manifestation of State practice. But in recent years there has been an obsessive interest with *resolutions* as an isolated phenomenon. Intellectually, this is hard to understand or justify. We can only suppose that it is easier—that is, it requires less effort, less rigour, less by way of meticulous analysis—to comment on the legal effect of a resolution than to look at a collective practice on a certain issue in all its complex manifestations. The political bodies of international organizations engage in debate; in the public exchange of views and positions taken; in expressing reservations upon views being taken by others; in preparing drafts intended for treaties, or declarations, or binding resolutions, or codes; and in decision-making that may or may not imply a legal view upon a particular issue. Some of these activities may result in resolutions of one sort or another. But the fashion in recent years has been to examine the resolution to the exclusion of all else. We are examining only a part of the picture.

One important element in the phenomenon of the examination of resolutions is the question of their binding quality. For certain commentators, that is enough: a negative answer indicates the irrelevance of resolutions in the law-making process.

* * *

In 1970 I wrote:

The passing of binding decisions is not the only way in which law development occurs. Legal consequences can also flow from acts which are not, in the formal sense, "binding". And, further, law is developed by a variety of non-legislative acts which do not seek to secure, in any direct sense, "compliance" from Assembly members: I refer here to the "law declaring" activities of the Assembly.[7]

* * *

We turn to those activities where the international organization is unambiguously facing outwards, i.e. concerned with general international law rather than its own procedural powers or even the direct interpretation of its own constituent instrument. Prominent among

---

7. Higgins, ["The United Nations and Lawmaking," *Proc. ASIL* (1970), p. 42].

such activities is the passing of resolutions that purport to be declaratory of contemporary international law. Can we reject their legal relevance *simply* on the ground that they are recommendatory, or incapable of directly binding the membership at large? What status is therefore to be accorded to them?

There is a vast literature on this question, and it is possible to group authors into certain "schools of thought" on this issue. There is no monolithic view, either in the East or West. * * *

Looking along a spectrum [of authors' views], we can perhaps see at one end those who are deeply sceptical, in the generalized fashion, about the relevance of General Assembly resolutions—such writers as Judge Sir Gerald Fitzmaurice, Judge Stephen Schwebel and Professors Francis Vallat, David Johnson, Arangio–Ruiz.[16] The Englishmen in this group all arrive at their position primarily by an emphasis in their writings, or judicial decisions, on the recommendatory nature of Assembly resolutions and their inability to bind. The difficulties with that approach already have been indicated. Judge Schwebel and Professor Arangio–Ruiz[17] arrive at their position through a different route. They fully accept that resolutions can contribute to the formation of customary international law, but express deep scepticism as to whether this really happens.

* * *

Somewhere towards the middle of the spectrum there are other Western international lawyers who downplay the significance of Assembly resolutions as non-binding, but accept that it would be wholly exceptional for any single resolution to have normative results. They argue rather that the decentralized method of international law-making can cause the metamorphosis of "General Assembly recommendations from non-binding resolutions to inchoate normative principles."[20] Certain resolutions may be a first step[21] in the process of law creation; and looked at as a whole they may in certain circumstances (depending on subject matter, size and nature of majorities, *opinio juris*) be evidence of developing trends of customary law. Among this group

16. G. Arangio–Ruiz, "The Normative Role of the General Assembly of the United Nations and the [Declaration] of Principles of Friendly Relations," *Recueil des cours,* CXXXVII (1972), 431; S. Schwebel, "The Effect of Resolutions of the UN General Assembly on Customary International Law," *Proc. ASIL* (1979), p. 380; F. Vallat, "The General Assembly and the Security Council of the United Nations," *BYIL,* XXIX (1952), 96; G. Fitzmaurice, "The Future of Public International Law and of the International Legal System in the Circumstances of Today," in Institut de droit international, *Livre du Centenaire* (1973), pp. 270–274; D.H.N. Johnson, "The Effect of Resolutions of the General Assembly of the UN," *BYIL,* XXXII (1955–56), 97.

17. Arangio–Ruiz, note 16 above, p. 457.

20. Joyner, ["UN Resolutions and International Law," *California Western International Law Journal,* XI (1981),] p. 464. This fine article is an important contribution to the debate.

21. M. Lachs, "The Threshold in Law Making," in *Völkerrecht als Rechtsordnung Internationale Gerichtsbarkeit Menschenrechte: Festschrift für Hermann Mosler* (1983), p. 497.

would be Oscar Schachter, Manfred Lachs, Christopher Joyner, Julius Stone, and this writer.

At what could be termed the radical end of the spectrum are those who invest Assembly resolutions with considerably greater legal significance. In this context [should] be mentioned Richard Falk, who has written of the "quasi legislative" competence of the General Assembly,[22] and Jorge Castaneda, who has argued that through its repeated efforts to declare principles of international law, the General Assembly has secured powers beyond the recommendatory powers listed in the UN Charter.[23]

Underlying these positions are many complicated and interesting issues, one or two of which may briefly be mentioned. When we look at resolutions as a first step in the formation of custom, or as part of the evidence of the existence of general practice, is it enough that we look at the resolutions alone?

* * *

[T]he present writer does not think United Nations resolutions should be excluded from an analysis of what may constitute custom at a given moment. But resolutions cannot be a *substitute* for ascertaining custom: this task will continue to require that other evidences of State practice be examined alongside those collective acts evidenced in General Assembly resolutions.

The next question is whether the fact that Assembly resolutions are deliberately "law-declaring" imparts to them a special status. [Professor Higgins quoted from the 1962 memorandum of the U.N. Office of Legal Affairs, set out in the excerpt from Schwebel, at page 340 supra.]

Some writers have suggested that Declarations, especially when unanimous or near unanimous, are a species of treaty law indicating a willingness to enter into obligations on the international plane. This was the view of Kozhevnikov when writing in 1957[30] and has also been attributed to Tunkin, but whether correctly is doubtful. It has certainly been embraced by some Western scholars.[31] Others have taken a more cautious view, but have nonetheless emphasised that deliberative efforts to state the law, carefully drawn up after study and a full exchange of legal views, do merit particular consideration.

* * *

22. See R. Falk, "On the Quasi–Legislative Competence of the General Assembly," *AJIL*, LX (1966), 782; Castaneda, [*Legal Effects of United Nations Resolutions* (1970)].

23. G.J. Kerwin, "The Role of UN General Assembly Resolutions in Determining Principles of International Law in United States Courts," *Duke Law Journal* (1983), p. 879.

30. F.I. Kozhevnikov, "Obshchepriznannye printsipy i normy mezhdunarodnogo prava," *SGiP*, no. 12 (1957), p. 17.

31. See Arangio–Ruiz, note 16 above.

As with much of international law, there is no easy answer to the question "What is the role of resolutions of international organizations in the process of creating norms in the international system?" To answer the question we need to look at the subject matter of the resolutions in question, at whether they are binding or recommendatory, at the majorities supporting their adoption, at repeated practice in relation to them, at evidence of *opinio juris*. When we shake the kaleidoscope and the pattern falls in certain ways, they undoubtedly play a significant role in creating norms.

SCHREUER, RECOMMENDATIONS AND THE TRADITIONAL SOURCES OF INTERNATIONAL LAW
20 German Y.B.Int'l L. 103, 116–18 (1977).*

* * *

In examining the legal significance of recommendations it will, however, be appropriate to make careful distinctions concerning their authority and the legal consequences flowing from them. Not every formally adopted resolution has the same significance. Its value as a basis for decision will depend on a number of circumstances all influencing the extent of its authority.

Part of these circumstances are the objectives of its sponsors and the sentiments underlying its adoption, which can often be ascertained from preparatory work, the wording of the text, especially the preamble, and attendant statements.[64] The motives of any individual delegation, which may be less influenced by the spirit of the recommendation than by political considerations of self-interest,[65] are only of secondary importance.

The degree of consensus underlying a recommendation cannot be ascertained by a simple counting of votes, although a unanimous or near-unanimous vote will certainly endow a resolution with considerable added authority. The support by the politically most important Members is, no doubt, of special relevance.[66] A recommendation showing a broad consensus between Members of the different "blocs" or of groupings with divergent interests in its subject-matter, will carry a

---

* Reprinted by permission of Duncker & Humblot GmbH, Berlin.

64. *Asamoah,* [The Legal Significance of the Declarations of the General Assembly of the United Nations 63 (1966), at] 68; *Bleicher,* [The Legal Significance of Re-Citation of General Assembly Resolutions, 63 Am J.Int'l L. 444 (1969), at] 453.

65. Cf. *Arangio–Ruiz,* [The Normative Role of the General Assembly of the United Nations and the Declaration of Principles of Friendly Relations, 1972 (III) Recueil des cours 419,] 457; *Asamoah,* [supra, at 53 et seq.]; *Bailey,* [Making International Law in the United Nations, 1967 Proc. Am.Soc'y Int'l L. 233,] 237; *Rauschning,* [in Berichte der DGV 1969,] 225; *Fitzmaurice,* [The Future of Public International Law and of the International Legal System in the Circumstances of Today, Institut de Droit International, Livre du centenaire 1873–1973, 196,] 271.

66. See however to the contrary: *D'Amato,* [On Consensus, 1970 Can.Y.B.Int'l L. 104,] 117, who seems to base his concept of big powers on somewhat narrow, purely military considerations.

high degree of authority. Recommendations involving questions of highly developed technology, like outer space or the use of nuclear energy, will not carry much weight unless endorsed also by the Members who have that technology at their disposal. A recommendation involving strongly controversial subjects, such as certain economic questions, will not enjoy much authority if it does not represent the interests of both or all sides but has been forced through by a purely numerical majority. The division of votes will often also give important clues as to the degree of realism shown by a resolution. A recommendation carried by a majority of Members, with corresponding interests against the will of a determined sizeable minority may be no more than the assertion of a claim by that group of States.

Extreme and intransigent language is often a sign of impotence rather than of determination. An indeterminate and vague wording may be just the expression of an agreement to disagree between the States voting for a recommendation.

Sometimes the weight to be attributed to a recommendation may be gathered from the attitude of the adopting organs towards questions of its implementation. A frequent invocation and citation in later resolutions [67] or the institution of formal procedures for the supervision of its implementation, can be taken as a sign of determination to pursue the recommendation's objectives.

A recommendation's significance will not least depend on the moral authority of the adopting organ. Only the maintenance of high and impartial standards of decision-making in the international organ will endow its recommendations with persuasive force for all sectors of the international community. The application of politically motivated double standards or the use of general resolutions to champion positions in political quarrels are liable to undermine the credibility of the international organ even in areas of relative agreement.

Of course, the long term impact of a recommendation is ultimately dependent on the actual conduct of its addressees. If a decision-maker confronted with a recommendation has knowledge of subsequent practice, he will, no doubt, have to take it into consideration. Individual cases of non-observance, which are not expressive of a general rejection of its principles, should not, however, be credited with too much importance and should not be taken to override a Member's otherwise positive attitude. There can be no doubt that the provisions of the Universal Declaration of Human Rights have repeatedly been violated since its adoption in 1948. These violations, as far as they have become known, have generally been regarded as unlawful and have prompted a

---

67. Cf. especially *Bleicher*, [supra]; see also *Schwelb*, [Neue Etappen der Fortentwicklung des Völkerrechts durch die Vereinten Nationen, Archiv des Völkerrechts, 1966, 1,] 16 et seq.; *Sohn*, [Protection of Human Rights Through International Legislation, René Cassin Amicorum Discipulorumque Liber, 1969, vol. 1, 325,] 329; see also Judge *Tanaka*, [dissenting opinion in South–West Africa, Second Phase, Judgment, 1966 I.C.J. 291,] 292.

variety of reactions.[68] The States responsible have usually not maintained that these violations were legal but have either denied them or justified them by reference to special circumstances.

* * *

The limited and qualified authority of recommendations also requires a view of their legal consequences which is different from those of mandatory rules. By virtue of their non-binding character, they do not absolutely require a decision in conformity with their provisions. On the other hand, this does not mean that it is open to decision-makers to ignore them arbitrarily. There is at least a duty to consider them in good faith.[69]

A recommendation can, moreover, usually serve as a presumption of legality in favour of conduct which is in accordance with its tenets. A State acting in accordance with the recommendations of the United Nations General Assembly will enjoy the benefit of the doubt should the legality of its conduct be called into question.[70] On the other hand, action contrary to the provisions of a recommendation can result in a shifting of the burden of proof against the person violating it.[71] A State or an individual charged with war crimes may well be put into the position of having to try to prove the legality of conduct which is contrary to the Universal Declaration of Human Rights.

Recommendations are of particular importance where other legal considerations do not yield a clear and satisfactory answer. Especially in the interpretation of applicable legal prescriptions like treaty provisions and also domestic statutes, recommendations can be an important help. In such a situation a decision which is in accordance with the policies expressed by an authoritative recommendation is to be preferred.[72]

---

68. Cf. *Buergenthal,* [The United Nations and the Development of Rules Relating to Human Rights, 1965 Proc.Am.Soc'y Int'l L. 132].

69. Cf. Judge *Lauterpacht,* [separate opinion in South–West Africa—Voting Procedure, Advisory Opinion of June 7, 1955, 1955 I.C.J.] 118 et seq.; also Judge *Klaestad,* [id. at 88]; *Asamoah,* [supra,] 59, 227; *Bindschedler,* [La délimitation des compétences des Nations Unies, 1963 (I) Recueil des cours 307,] 346; *John Dugard,* The Legal Effect of United Nations Resolutions on Apartheid, South African Law Journal, 1966, 44 at 50 et seq.; *Sorensen,* Principes de Droit international public, 1960 (III) Recueil des cours 1,] 98.

70. Cf. *Francis Vallat,* The Competence of the United Nations General Assembly, [1959 (II) Recueil des cours 203, at 231]; see also *Henry G. Schermers,* International Institutional Law, 1972, vol. 2, 497 on the "legitimizing effect" of recommendations, with further references.

71. *Sir Gerald Fitzmaurice,* Hersch Lauterpacht—the Scholar as Judge, Part II, [1962 Brit.Y.B.Int'l L. 1, at 8 et seq.].

72. *Sir Gerald Fitzmaurice,* The Law and Procedure of the International Court of Justice 1951–1954, [1958 Brit.Y.B.Int'l L. 1, at 5].

NORMATIVE EFFECT?

The excerpt from Castañeda deals in two quite distinct senses with the normative effects of resolutions that are formally recommendations. How does the effect of an international organization's recommendation as described at the beginning of the Castañeda excerpt (relying on Malintoppi) differ from the effects he described toward the end?

None of the commentators quoted above says that General Assembly resolutions in and of themselves create binding rules for member states, or—at the other end of the spectrum—that such resolutions are totally irrelevant to the shaping of international law. Do any of these commentators ascribe independent legal significance, apart from what governments actually do outside the U.N., to General Assembly normative resolutions? If so, and if that legal significance is short of "true law" (fully binding law), just what *is* the legal significance in the eyes of each of them? Is there a bright line between nonlaw and true law?

Do General Assembly resolutions fit into any of the sources of international law designated in the Statute of the International Court of Justice, article 38(1)?

Without specifying which subparagraph of article 38 it had in mind—or whether it had article 38 in mind at all—the General Assembly, in a resolution adopted by consensus calling on states to consider making better use of the International Court of Justice, said that it "[recognized] that the development of international law may be reflected inter alia, by declarations and resolutions of the General Assembly which may to that extent be taken into consideration by the International Court of Justice * * *."[a] Does this "recognition" have any legal significance?

The excerpt above from Schwebel displays his skepticism regarding the significance of consensus (the absence of formal objection) in the adoption of General Assembly resolutions. Some scholars have stressed consensus as a demonstration of widespread acceptance of norms set forth in General Assembly resolutions adopted without formal objection.[b] Under this view, failure to object amounts to acquiescence in the asserted norms, and thus may go a long way toward establishing the *opinio juris* required for the creation or crystallization of custom. But others either note, along with Schwebel, that apparent consensus may not be genuine consensus, or that consensus texts tend to be so watered down as to be of little use in applying norms to real situations.[c] Can these views be reconciled?

Schwebel and Higgins both emphasize the need not only to look at General Assembly resolutions themselves, but also to examine other

---

a. G.A.Res. 3232 (XXIX), Nov. 22, 1974.

b. See Jiménez de Aréchaga's discussion in Change and Stability in International Law-Making 48–49 (A. Cassese & J. Weiler eds. 1988); Sloan, General Assembly Resolutions Revisited (Forty Years After), 58 Brit.Y.B.Int'l L. 39, 140 (1987).

c. See Condorelli, The Role of General Assembly Resolutions, in Change and Stability, supra, at 37, 42–47; Delupis, The Legal Value of Recommendations of International Organisations, in International Law and the International System 47, 54–55 (W. Butler ed. 1987).

indicators of state practice in order to determine whether there is a rule of international law corresponding with the norms put forward in the resolutions. To put it in traditional terms relating to custom, there must be state practice plus *opinio juris*. Resolutions might supply the *opinio juris*, but can they supply the state practice as well? Sometimes courts seem to have said they can (and do).

In the human rights field, for example, the U.S. Second Circuit Court of Appeals has relied in part on the Universal Declaration of Human Rights,[d] a 1948 General Assembly resolution, to find that customary international law prohibits torture under color of state authority.[e] The Universal Declaration was adopted not as a "statement of law or of legal obligation [but rather] as a common standard of achievement for all peoples of all nations."[f] Article 5 of the Universal Declaration says, "No one shall be subjected to torture or to cruel, inhuman or degrading treatment or punishment." Consistently with the position taken by Schreuer at page 346 supra, the Court gave little or no weight to the many well-known instances around the world of torture sponsored or conducted by states.[g]

Similarly, the International Court of Justice has relied primarily on resolutions of the U.N. and O.A.S. General Assemblies to find a rule of customary international law coinciding with U.N. Charter article 2(4)'s prohibition of the threat or use of force against the territorial integrity or political independence of any state.[h] In particular, the Court relied on the U.N. Declaration on Principles of International Law Concerning Friendly Relations and Co-operation Among States in Accordance with the Charter of the United Nations,[i] a General Assembly resolution adopted by consensus. The Declaration enunciates a host of principles dealing with nonuse of force against the territorial integrity or political independence of any state, the peaceful settlement of disputes, nonintervention in the affairs of other states, equal rights of states and self-determination. The Court said it had to find an *opinio juris* as to the nonuse of force and added, "This *opinio juris* may, though with all due caution, be deduced from, *inter alia*, the attitude of

d. G.A.Res. 217A, Dec. 10, 1948.

e. Filartiga v. Pena–Irala, 630 F.2d 876, 883–85 (2d Cir.1980). Italian courts have given other proscriptions in the Universal Declaration the force of law, though they speak in terms of general principles of law rather than in terms of custom. See Ministry of Home Affairs v. Kemali, Italian Court of Cassation, Feb. 1, 1962, 40 Int'l L.Rep. 191, 195; Decision No. 1566/64, Court of Appeal of Milan, Sept. 8, 1964, 7 Y.B.Eur.Conv. on Human Rights 536 (1964). In Belgium, the Universal Declaration apparently is treated only as a statement of principle, and is not given legal effect. See De Meyer v. État Belge, Belgian Conseil d'État, Feb. 9, 1966, 47 Int'l L.Rep. 196, 197.

f. Statement by Eleanor Roosevelt, just before the General Assembly adopted the Universal Declaration, 19 Dep't State Bull. 751 (1948). Mrs. Roosevelt was the primary motivating force behind the Universal Declaration.

g. Filartiga, supra, at 884, n. 15. See also Humphrey, The Universal Declaration of Human Rights: Its History, Impact and Juridical Character, in Human Rights: Thirty Years After the Universal Declaration 21 (B. Ramcharan ed. 1979).

h. Military and Paramilitary Activities in and Against Nicaragua (Nicar. v. U.S.), Merits, [1986] I.C.J. 14, 101–02.

i. G.A.Res. 2625, Oct. 24, 1970.

the Parties and the attitude of States towards certain General Assembly resolutions, and particularly [the Declaration on Principles of International Law, above]."[j] The Court did not ask whether governments actually refrain consistently from using force against the territorial integrity or independence of other states. As in the case of torture, one might expect upon examination to find a great deal of inconsistent state practice.

How can these cases be explained without raising General Assembly resolutions, or at least certain key ones, to the level of legislation?[k]

How significant is it that the key General Assembly resolutions on which the courts relied, above, were both "Declarations"? Recall what the U.N. Office of Legal Affairs and Eric Suy, the former U.N. Legal Counsel, said about declarations at pages 340–41 supra. A Commission of the Institute of International Law—a body of eminent (primarily European) international law scholars—has said:

> The legal status of resolutions designated as declarations is not different from that of other resolutions. Yet this particular form may emphasize the importance of the norms enunciated. Declarations are suitable for a comprehensive treatment of a subject or for expressing principles the purpose of which is to influence the progressive development of international law.[l]

The same Commission identified several types of resolution, including "law-declaring resolutions" (which may, among other things, "constitute evidence of international custom") and "law-developing resolutions" (which may, among other things, "[contribute] to the creation of international custom"). In either case, according to the Commission, "The authority of a resolution is enhanced when it is adopted by consensus."[m] A law-declaring resolution "may constitute evidence of customary law or of one of its ingredients (custom-creating practice, *opinio juris*), in particular when that has been the intention of States in adopting the resolution or when the procedures applied have led to the elaboration of a statement of law."[n] A law-developing resolution "may influence state practice, or initiate a new practice that constitutes an ingredient of new customary law [and] may contribute to the consolidation of State practice, or to the formation of the *opinio juris communis*."[o] The full Institute did not adopt the Commission's conclusions, but did express the wish that its work should be studied by all concerned.

Under the Commission's taxonomy, was the Universal Declaration of Human Rights a law-declaring or law-developing resolution (or

---

j. [1986] I.C.J. at 99–100.

k. See O. Schachter, International Law in Theory and Practice 90 (1991); Kirgis, Custom on a Sliding Scale, 81 Am.J.Int'l L. 146 (1987).

l. Conclusion 12 of the Institute of International Law's 13th Commission, in 62 (II) Yearbook of the Institute of International Law 274, 282 (1987).

m. Conclusion 16, in id. at 284.

n. Conclusion 20, in id. at 286.

o. Conclusion 22, in id.

neither)? How about the Declaration on Principles of International Law?

Oscar Schachter, in an important recent study, has argued that it is appropriate to treat "law-declaring resolutions as evidence for the asserted proposition of law." This, he says, avoids the dilemma of placing formally non-binding resolutions in the same category as formally binding instruments, while recognizing that they are official expressions of the governments concerned.[p] Under this approach, if a law-declaring General Assembly resolution is adopted by an overwhelming majority, but not unanimously, what would its effect be upon the dissenting state(s)? What weight should be given to the extent of state practice outside the resolution itself, and any expressed attitude of the currently-dissenting state(s) toward that practice?[q]

Schreuer pointed out that a recommendation can supply a presumption that conduct consistent with it is lawful. See page 347 supra. In other words, according to this argument, a General Assembly resolution could establish that there is no rule *prohibiting* the conduct (whether or not there is a rule of positive custom authorizing it). Do you agree?

We turn now to two case studies of the effect of formally nonbinding U.N. resolutions. The first concerns the law of expropriation; the second, a rather circumscribed aspect of international environmental law.

b. *The Law of Expropriation*

The United States and other capital-exporting states have traditionally argued that customary international law provides certain minimum standards for the protection of a foreign investor whose property is expropriated by a host government. According to these states, an expropriation must be for a public purpose, nondiscriminatory, and accompanied by prompt, adequate and effective compensation. "Adequate" compensation is usually defined as fair market value of the expropriated property. "Promptness" is said to be a soon as is reasonable under the circumstances, and "effectiveness" means that the compensation must be in a currency the investor can convert into other currencies if he wishes.[a]

A corollary is the proposition that any alleged failure to meet the minimum standard may be made the subject of a diplomatic claim on behalf of the investor by the investor's government, and may be

---

p. O. Schachter, International Law in Theory and Practice 89 (1991).

q. See id. at 90–92.

a. See Restatement 2d, Foreign Relations Law of the United States §§ 187–190 (1965); Restatement 3d, Foreign Relations Law of the United States § 712 (1987).

submitted to international adjudication or arbitration if the respondent state has consented to do so (even if the consent was given before the expropriation).

Before World War II, the development of custom in this field was dominated by the European states plus Canada and the United States. Since most of them were both capital exporters and capital importers, it was to their mutual advantage to recognize the traditional rights and duties. About the only consistent objectors were several Latin American states, who particularly resisted the proposition that disputes involving foreign private investors could be made the subject of diplomatic claims or of any other form of dispute settlement beyond what was provided by the legal system of the host state. Their position was generally supported after World War II by the new Communist governments of Eastern Europe. With the decolonization of the early 1960s and the resulting emergence of new states—all of which would for the foreseeable future be capital importers—the Latin American and East European nations found a host of new allies. "Sovereignty over natural resources" was a rallying cry as new nations became resentful over what they perceived to be unfair exploitation of their natural resources by foreign-owned companies making large profits, which seemed to be remitted back home rather than reinvested in the host country.

Much of this battle has been fought in the General Assembly and in related U.N. bodies. As early as 1952 the General Assembly adopted a resolution stressing "the sovereignty of any State over its natural resources." [b] In 1958 it established a Commission on Permanent Sovereignty over Natural Resources, "to conduct a full survey of the status of this basic constituent of the right to self-determination, with recommendations, where necessary, for its strengthening * * *." [c] The United States opposed both these resolutions, but participated actively in the work of the Commission once it had been established. Eventually the Commission produced a draft resolution which, after amendment, was adopted by the General Assembly in the form below (quoted only in part).

DECLARATION ON PERMANENT SOVEREIGNTY OVER NATURAL RESOURCES

United Nations General Assembly, Dec. 14, 1962.
G.A.Res.1803, 17 GAOR Supp. 17 (A/5217), at 15.

The General Assembly,

* * *

Attaching particular importance to the question of promoting the economic development of developing countries and securing their economic independence,

b. G.A.Res. 626 (VII).   c. G.A.Res. 1314 (XIII).

Noting that the creation and strengthening of the inalienable sovereignty of States over their natural wealth and resources reinforces their economic independence,

* * *

Declares that:

1. The right of peoples and nations to permanent sovereignty over their natural wealth and resources must be exercised in the interest of their national development and of the well-being of the people of the State concerned.

2. The exploration, development and disposition of such resources, as well as the import of the foreign capital required for these purposes, should be in conformity with the rules and conditions which the peoples and nations freely consider to be necessary or desirable with regard to the authorization, restriction or prohibition of such activities.

3. In cases where authorization is granted, the capital imported and the earnings on that capital shall be governed by the terms thereof, by the national legislation in force, and by international law. The profits derived must be shared in the proportions freely agreed upon, in each case, between the investors and the recipient State, due care being taken to ensure that there is no impairment, for any reason, of that State's sovereignty over its natural wealth and resources.

4. Nationalization, expropriation or requisitioning shall be based on grounds or reasons of public utility, security or the national interest which are recognized as overriding purely individual or private interests, both domestic and foreign. In such cases the owner shall be paid appropriate compensation, in accordance with the rules in force in the State taking such measures in the exercise of its sovereignty and in accordance with international law. In any case where the question of compensation gives rise to a controversy, the national jurisdiction of the State taking such measures shall be exhausted. However, upon agreement by sovereign States and other parties concerned, settlement of the dispute should be made through arbitration or international adjudication.

* * *

8. Foreign investment agreements freely entered into by or between sovereign States shall be observed in good faith; States and international organizations shall strictly and conscientiously respect the sovereignty of peoples and nations over their natural wealth and resources in accordance with the Charter and the principles set forth in the present resolution.

THE DECLARATION AND ITS AFTERMATH

Resolution 1803, above, was the product of intensive negotiations in the General Assembly's Second Committee among the various blocs represented in the United Nations in 1962: the Western (capitalist) bloc, the Communist bloc, and the third world. During the negotiations, doctrinaire positions of both the Western and Communist blocs were either abandoned or voted down.[d] Eventually the Declaration was adopted by a vote of 82 states in favor, 2 opposed (France and South Africa), and 12 abstaining (Burma, Cuba, Mongolia and almost all Eastern European states).

In the early 1970s the burgeoning third-world majority in the United Nations began to push for new recognition of sovereign rights over natural resources. In December 1973, the General Assembly adopted a resolution "[affirming] that the application of the principle of nationalization carried out by States, as an expression of their sovereignty in order to safeguard their natural resources, implies that each State is entitled to determine the amount of possible compensation and the mode of payment * * *."[e]

In May 1974, in a special session, the General Assembly adopted a "Declaration on the Establishment of a New International Economic Order."[f] The Declaration said, inter alia, that the new international economic order should be founded on the principle of "Full permanent sovereignty of every State over its natural resources and all economic activities. In order to safeguard these resources, each State is entitled to exercise effective control over them and their exploitation with means suitable to its own situation, including the right to nationalization or transfer of ownership to its nationals, this right being an expression of the full permanent sovereignty of the State." The U.S. representative objected on the ground that "the present Declaration does not couple the assertion of the right to nationalize with the duty to pay compensation in accordance with international law. * * * The governing international law cannot be, and is not, prejudiced by the passage of this resolution."[g]

At its regular session in 1974, the General Assembly approved a resolution entitled "Charter of Economic Rights and Duties of States." This represented the culmination of a long and sometimes acrimonious negotiating/drafting process initiated by the Mexican government. A Working Group produced the first draft, which in its preamble declared that "it is a fundamental purpose of this Charter to codify and develop rules for the establishment of the new international economic order * * *."[h] During the debate in the General Assembly's Second Committee, this preambular language was modified as appears below.[i] The

d. For a summary of the negotiations, see Schwebel, The Story of the U.N.'s Declaration on Permanent Sovereignty Over Natural Resources, 49 A.B.A.J. 463 (1963).

e. G.A.Res. 3171 (XXVIII). The vote was 108 in favor to one opposed (U.K.), with 16 abstentions (most of the industrialized countries, including the U.S.).

f. G.A.Res. 3201 (S–VI). The resolution was adopted without a vote, but the United States, West Germany, Japan, France and the United Kingdom entered reservations.

g. U.N. GAOR, 6th Special Sess., 2229th mtg., at 8 (1974).

h. U.N. Doc. A/9946 (1974).

i. For further discussion, see Brower & Tepe, The Charter of Economic Rights and

General Assembly then adopted the Charter by a vote of 120 in favor, six opposed (Belgium, Denmark, Federal Republic of Germany, Luxembourg, U.K. and U.S.), with ten abstentions.

CHARTER OF ECONOMIC RIGHTS AND DUTIES OF STATES
United Nations General Assembly, Dec. 12, 1974.
G.A.Res. 3281, 29 GAOR Supp. 31 (A/9631), at
50, 14 Int'l Legal Materials 251 (1975).

The General Assembly,

* * *

Declaring that it is a fundamental purpose of this Charter to promote the establishment of the new international economic order, based on equity, sovereign equality, interdependence, common interest and co-operation among all States, irrespective of their economic and social systems,

* * *

Solemnly adopts the present Charter of Economic Rights and Duties of States.

* * *

Art. 2

1. Every State has and shall freely exercise full permanent sovereignty, including possession, use and disposal, over all its wealth, natural resources and economic activities.

2. Each State has the right:

(a) To regulate and exercise authority over foreign investment within its national jurisdiction in accordance with its laws and regulations and in conformity with its national objectives and priorities. No State shall be compelled to grant preferential treatment to foreign investment;

(b) To regulate and supervise the activities of transnational corporations within its national jurisdiction and take measures to ensure that such activities comply with its laws, rules and regulations and conform with its economic and social policies. Transnational corporations shall not intervene in the internal affairs of a host State. Every State should, with full regard for its sovereign rights, co-operate with other States in the exercise of the right set forth in this subparagraph;

(c) To nationalize, expropriate or transfer ownership of foreign property, in which case appropriate compensation should be paid by the

Duties of States: A Reflection or Rejection of International Law?, 9 Int'l Lawyer 295 (1975); Rozental, The Charter of Economic Rights and Duties of States and the New International Economic Order, 16 Va. J.Int'l L. 309 (1976); White, A New International Economic Order?, id. 323.

State adopting such measures, taking into account its relevant laws and regulations and all circumstances that the State considers pertinent. In any case where the question of compensation gives rise to a controversy, it shall be settled under the domestic law of the nationalizing State and by its tribunals, unless it is freely and mutually agreed by all States concerned that other peaceful means be sought on the basis of the sovereign equality of States and in accordance with the principle of free choice of means.

[Other provisions of the Charter deal with such things as exploitation of shared natural resources, the right to associate in organizations of primary commodity producers, economic and social cooperation, and so forth, with particular emphasis on rights of developing countries.]

THE ECONOMIC CHARTER AND RESOLUTION 1803

While the draft was still in the Second Committee, 14 of the industrialized nations, including the United States, introduced a proposed amendment to article 2, which would have tied the right to expropriate foreign property to the achievement of a public purpose and to the payment of "just compensation in the light of all relevant circumstances." It also would have said that expropriating states "shall fulfil in good faith their international obligations." [j] The proposed amendment was voted down by a large margin.

Chapter I of the Charter of Economic Rights and Duties, as adopted, contains a list of principles identified as "fundamentals of international economic relations" among states. One of them is: "Fulfilment in good faith of international obligations." Does this cast a different light on article 2 than one would discern from reading it alone? [k] If so, how can we explain the overwhelming rejection of the Western amendment to article 2?

In recent years, the General Assembly has not paid much further attention to the issues surrounding sovereignty over resources or expropriation. In fact, those issues have receded somewhat in day-to-day international practice as world communism has receded and as the expropriations of the 1960s and 1970s have become *faits accomplis*. Nevertheless, it would be naïve to think either that expropriation of foreign-held property will no longer be a live issue, or that there is nothing to be learned about the General Assembly's role in the development of international law from examining its role in the expropriation area.

Is anything left of Resolution 1803 after the General Assembly's adoption of the Charter of Economic Rights and Duties? Arbitrators

---

j. U.N.Doc. A/9946, at 16 (1974).

k. See Schachter, International Law in Theory and Practice 304–05 (1991).

have thought so. In this connection, the arbitral decision most frequently cited is the TOPCO/CALASIATIC case, below.

TOPCO/CALASIATIC v. LIBYAN ARAB REPUBLIC
International Arbitral Tribunal, Merits, 1977.
17 Int'l Legal Materials 1 (1978).

[Texaco Overseas Petroleum Co. (TOPCO) and California Asiatic Oil Co. (CALASIATIC) had oil concession rights to a producing field in Libya. The Libyan government nationalized their rights in a two-stage process during 1973 and 1974. The government offered no compensation, and negotiations between the companies and the Libyan government proved fruitless.

[The concession agreements provided for arbitration of such disputes. The companies requested arbitration, but the Libyan government refused to arbitrate. In accordance with the arbitration clause in the agreements, the companies then requested the President of the International Court of Justice to appoint a sole arbitrator. He appointed René-Jean Dupuy, Secretary General of The Hague Academy of International Law and Professor of Law at the University of Nice. The Libyan government made no appearance in the proceedings.

[In the course of a long award on the merits in favor of the companies, the arbitrator considered the effect of the General Assembly resolutions on expropriation, particularly Resolution 1803 and the Charter of Economic Rights and Duties. He said:]

[W]hile it is now possible to recognize that resolutions of the United Nations have a certain legal value, this legal value differs considerably, depending on the type of resolution and the conditions attached to its adoption and its provisions. Even under the assumption that they are resolutions of a declaratory nature, which is the case of the Charter of Economic Rights and Duties of States, the legal value is variable. Ambassador Castañeda, who was Chairman of the Working Group entrusted with the task of preparing this Charter, admitted that "it is extremely difficult to determine with certainty the legal force of declaratory resolutions", that it is "impossible to lay down a general rule in this respect", and that "the legal value of the declaratory resolutions therefore includes an immense gamut of nuances" ("La Valeur Juridique des Résolutions des Nations Unies", 129 R.C.A.D.I. 204 (1970), at 319–320).

* * *

[T]he absence of any binding force of the resolutions of the General Assembly of the United Nations implies that such resolutions must be accepted by the members of the United Nations in order to be legally binding. In this respect, the Tribunal notes that only Resolution 1803 (XVII) of 14 December 1962 was supported by a majority of Member States representing all of the various groups. By contrast, the other Resolutions mentioned above, and in particular those referred to in the

Libyan Memorandum, were supported by a majority of States but not by any of the developed countries with market economies which carry on the largest part of international trade.

[I]t appears essential to this Tribunal to distinguish between those provisions stating the existence of a right on which the generality of the States has expressed agreement and those provisions introducing new principles which were rejected by certain representative groups of States and having nothing more than a *de lege ferenda* value only in the eyes of the States which have adopted them; as far as the others are concerned, the rejection of these same principles implies that they consider them as being *contra legem*. With respect to the former, which proclaim rules recognized by the community of nations, they do not create a custom but confirm one by formulating it and specifying its scope, thereby making it possible to determine whether or not one is confronted with a legal rule. As has been noted by Ambassador Castañeda, "[such resolutions] do not create the law; they have a declaratory nature of noting what does exist" (129 R.C.A.D.I. 204 (1970), at 315).

On the basis of the circumstances of adoption mentioned above and by expressing an *opinio juris communis*, Resolution 1803 (XVII) seems to this Tribunal to reflect the state of customary law existing in this field. Indeed, on the occasion of the vote on a resolution finding the existence of a customary rule, the States concerned clearly express their views. The consensus by a majority of States belonging to the various representative groups indicates without the slightest doubt universal recognition of the rules therein incorporated, *i.e.*, with respect to nationalization and compensation the use of the rules in force in the nationalizing State, but all this in conformity with international law.

While Resolution 1803 (XVII) appears to a large extent as the expression of a real general will, this is not at all the case with respect to the other Resolutions mentioned above, which has been demonstrated previously by analysis of the circumstances of adoption. In particular, as regards the Charter of Economic Rights and Duties of States, several factors contribute to denying legal value to those provisions of the document which are of interest in the instant case.

—In the first place, Article 2 of this Charter must be analyzed as a political rather than as a legal declaration concerned with the ideological strategy of development and, as such, supported only by non-industrialized States.

—In the second place, this Tribunal notes that in the draft submitted by the Group of 77 to the Second Commission (U.N.Doc A/C.2/L. 1386 (1974), at 2), the General Assembly was invited to adopt the Charter "as a first measure of codification and progressive development" within the field of the international law of development. However, because of the opposition of several States, this description was deleted from the text submitted to the vote of the Assembly.

* * *

The absence of any connection between the procedure of compensation and international law and the subjection of this procedure solely to municipal law cannot be regarded by this Tribunal except as a *de lege ferenda* formulation, which even appears *contra legem* in the eyes of many developed countries. Similarly, several developing countries, although having voted favorably on the Charter of Economic Rights and Duties of States as a whole, in explaining their votes regretted the absence of any reference to international law.

EVALUATION

The arbitrator in TOPCO/CALASIATIC went on to decide that restitution in kind was the appropriate remedy.[l]

Other arbitrators have considered Resolution 1803 relevant to the asserted duty to pay compensation. In LIAMCO v. Libyan Arab Republic,[m] the sole arbitrator, an attorney practicing in Beirut, noted that Resolution 1803 provides that a property owner is entitled to "adequate compensation" and that the Charter of Economic Rights and Duties says "appropriate compensation" is due. (Is this a correct reading of the two resolutions?) The arbitrator awarded the market value of the nationalized physical assets, and—applying an "equitable compensation" standard—approximately one-third of the lost profits the company had claimed.

In Kuwait v. AMINOIL,[n] a three-member arbitral tribunal said that Resolution 1803 "codifies positive principles" regarding compensation. The tribunal noted that Kuwait was a capital-exporting as well as a capital-importing state, and awarded the company the depreciated replacement cost of its fixed assets, plus expected future profits over the remaining 30 years of its oil concession.

There are several other arbitral awards in recent years, consistently holding—or at least saying—that full compensation is due for expropriation of foreign-owned property. Included among these are several from the Iran–U.S. Claims Tribunal and some from arbitrations under the auspices of the International Centre for Settlement of Investment Disputes. Some of these discuss the General Assembly resolutions, but for the most part they rely on the terms of individual concession agreements and on previous arbitral awards as precedents.[o]

The Western view received another boost in 1986 when the International Law Association (a private, multinational body of international lawyers, not to be confused with the U.N.'s International Law

---

l. For this, he relied on the Chorzow Factory Case (Germany v. Poland), P.C.I.J. Ser. A, No. 17, at 47 (1928).

m. 20 Int'l Legal Materials 1, 67 (1981).

n. 21 Int'l Legal Materials 976, 1032 (1982).

o. See Norton, A Law of the Future or a Law of the Past? Modern Tribunals and the International Law of Expropriation, 85 Am.J.Int'l L. 474 (1991).

Commission) adopted a Declaration on the Progressive Development of Principles of Public International Law Relating to a New International Economic Order. The I.L.A. Declaration said, inter alia, that a state may expropriate property "subject to the principle of international law requiring a public purpose and non-discrimination, to appropriate compensation as required by international law, and to any applicable treaty * * *."p

What exactly has been the role of Resolution 1803 in the development of customary international law on compensation for expropriation?

What exactly is the standard required by Resolution 1803? Can the arbitral awards, centering on a "full compensation" standard, be considered collectively as an authoritative interpretation of Resolution 1803? To the extent that they can be, do they support a quasi-legislative role for the General Assembly?

c. Use of Shared Natural Resources

Like expropriation of foreign-owned property, the unilateral use of internationally-shared natural resources has engendered substantial controversy. Thus, when state A, upstream on an international river, wishes to build a dam or to allow a potentially-polluting industry to build a plant next to the river, one issue is whether—absent a treaty obligation—it owes a duty to consult or otherwise take into account the interests of downstream states. Similar questions arise in connection with the use of boundary rivers, groundwaters, lakes spanning national borders, transnational air basins, mineral deposits, and so forth.

As in the case of expropriation, the rules in this field have largely been left to be made by "soft law" techniques rather than by treaties. In this field, however, a wider variety of U.N. and nongovernmental bodies has had a hand in making soft law.

The General Assembly convened the U.N. Conference on the Human Environment in June 1972. The Conference produced the U.N. Declaration on the Human Environment, and adopted recommendations as well as an Action Plan for the environment. The Declaration was based on draft principles prepared by the Intergovernmental Working Group on the Declaration on the Human Environment. The draft principles proposed that states would have a duty to ensure that activities within their control do not damage the environment of other states or of areas beyond the limits of national jurisdiction, and a duty to consult other interested parties before undertaking any activity that might damage the environment outside the acting state. The former of these duties made it into the final Declaration, but the latter (the duty to consult) did not. The reason why it did not, and the ensuing effort to resurrect it, make an illustrative story of soft law-making in the General Assembly and other bodies.

p. Rep. of 62d Conf. of the I.L.A., 1986, at 1, 7. See also id. at 433–34.

The problem stemmed primarily from a dispute between Brazil and Argentina. In the early 1970s, Brazil was planning the large Itaipu Dam on the Parana River just upstream from the Argentine border. Argentine officials were afraid that the dam could cause climate modification, disappearance of some fish species, impairment of navigability downstream, a change in the river's course, and pollution of the drinking water for six large cities. Argentina asserted a right to be consulted before the plans for the dam were set. Brazil retorted that any duty to consult applied only to boundary rivers and other resources shared simultaneously, rather than to river systems flowing from one country into another. This dispute reached such proportions that it became a major factor blocking inclusion of the duty to consult in the Declaration.

Meanwhile, the International Law Association had been working for several years on rules for the use of international rivers. In 1966 the I.L.A. adopted the Helsinki Rules on the Uses of the Waters of International Rivers.[a] Article 29 said that a state "should" notify interested river basin states of any proposed construction or installation that would alter the basin's regime in such a way that a dispute might arise, and should allow a reasonable time for the other states to submit their views.

In 1974, the I.L.A. added a new article to the Helsinki Rules, providing in part:

> 1. A riparian State intending to undertake works to improve the navigability of that portion of a river or lake within its jurisdiction is under a duty to give notice to the co-riparian States;
>
> 2. If these works are likely to affect adversely the navigational uses of one or more co-riparian States, any such co-riparian State may, within a reasonable time, request consultation. The concerned co-riparian States are then under a duty to negotiate * * *.[b]

The story is continued in the excerpt below.

F. KIRGIS, PRIOR CONSULTATION IN INTERNATIONAL LAW
80–82 (1983).*

The I.L.A.'s tortuous path toward prior consultation as an agreed norm has been mirrored in the United Nations. As we have seen, the U.N. Conference on the Human Environment omitted a provision on prior consultation from its 1972 Declaration on the Human Environment, even though such a provision had been prepared by the Conference's Intergovernmental Working Group. The General Assembly took up the matter and in 1973 adopted its Resolution 3129, which recited

---

a. Rep. of 52d Conf. of the I.L.A., 1966, at 484, 518.

b. Rep. of 56th Conf. of the I.L.A., 1974, at xiii.

* Reprinted by permission of The Procedural Aspects of International Law Institute.

the need to pursue the elaboration of international environmental norms, and then "considered" that "co-operation between countries sharing [natural resources common to two or more states] and interested in their exploitation must be developed on the basis of a system of information and prior consultation within the framework of the normal relations existing between them." [192] The debate in the Second Committee clearly indicated a general understanding that a normative principle, not just a desired goal, was being proposed.[193] It was clear, of course, that among the principal "common" or "shared" resources would be international watercourse systems. Most representatives seemed to assume, though it was never made explicit, that this would include successive as well as contiguous watercourses.

A year later, the General Assembly adopted the Charter of Economic Rights and Duties of States. It provides in article 3: "In the exploitation of natural resources shared by two or more countries, each State must co-operate on the basis of a system of information and prior consultations in order to achieve optimum use of such resources without causing damage to the legitimate interest of others." [194] The sponsors of the Charter amended it in the Second Committee to delete preambular language declaring that a fundamental purpose of the Charter was to codify and develop rules, but the language of article 3 remained mandatory. It seems clearly to reflect the normative expectations of the great majority of U.N. member states.

In early 1974, the U.N. Environment Programme [c] began a struggle to refine further these prior notification and consultation norms. The Governing Council entrusted a working group with the task, but it took the group until 1978 to produce an agreed text. Although the working group's explanatory note sounds as though the principles were drafted without intent to codify or develop international law, the Governing Council approved the text, "Desiring to promote and develop international law regarding the conservation and harmonious exploitation of natural resources shared by two or more States." [195] The principles obviously take account of trends in state practice, including practice embodied in resolutions and recommendations of international organizations.

---

192. G.A.Res. 3129, para. 2, 28 U.N. GAOR, Supp. (No. 30) at 48, U.N. Doc. A/9030 (1973). The vote was 77–5–43.

193. *See, e.g.,* U.N. Docs. A/C.2/SR.1564, at 23 (1973) (Yugoslavia, which introduced the draft resolution on behalf of the 53 sponsors); A/C.2/SR.1565, at 19–20 (Argentina); A/C.2/SR.1566, at 5 (the Netherlands); *id.* at 18 (Mexico); A/C.2/SR.1567, at 27–28 (Paraguay, in opposition); A/C.2/SR.1568, at 10–11 (Algeria); A/C.2/SR.1569, at 16 (Uruguay, in opposition); *id.* at 17 (Canada); *id.* at 20 (Brazil, in opposition); A/C.2/SR.1570, at 3 (Ethiopia, in opposition); *id.* at 5 (Chile).

194. G.A.Res. 3281, art. 3, 29 U.N. GAOR, Supp. (No. 31) at 50, U.N. Doc. A/9631 (1974). The vote was 120–6–10. Although the United States voted against the Charter as a whole, it voted in favor of this article, which was adopted by separate votes of 97–7–25 in the Second Committee and 99–8–29 in the General Assembly.

c. [An organ of the U.N. General Assembly. Ed.]

195. 33 U.N. GAOR, Supp. (No. 25) at 154, U.N. Doc. A/33/25 (1978). The text was approved by consensus, with four delegations declining to join in it.

Principle 6 of the agreed text provides in part:

1. It is necessary for every State sharing a natural resource with one or more other States:

(a) to notify in advance the other State or States of the pertinent details of plans to initiate, or make a change in, the conservation or utilization of the resource which can reasonably be expected to affect significantly the environment in the territory of the other State or States; and

(b) upon request of the other State or States, to enter into consultations concerning the above-mentioned plans; and

(c) to provide, upon request to that effect by the other State or States, specific additional pertinent information concerning such plans; and

(d) if there has been no advance notification as envisaged in sub-paragraph (a) above, to enter into consultations about such plans upon request of the other State or States.[196]

Although the agreed text contains no definition of shared natural resources, one definition seems to have had substantial support: "The term 'shared natural resource' means an element of the natural environment used by man which constitutes a biogeophysical unity and is located in the territory of two or more States."[197] This seems broad enough to include successive as well as contiguous waterways—a position that comports with the International Law Commission's view that, at least for non-navigational purposes, waters of an international watercourse are shared natural resources to the extent that their use in the territory of one state affects their use in the territory of another state within the same watercourse system.[198]

In deference to continuing resistance from Brazil and a few others, and out of a sense of caution, the U.N. General Assembly in its thirty-fourth session simply took note of the principles in the agreed text, rather than approving them. It did so, however, "without prejudice to the binding nature of those rules already recognized as such in international law."[199]

---

196. Draft Principles of Conduct in the Field of the Environment for the Guidance of States in the Conservation and Harmonious Utilization of Natural Resources Shared by Two or More States, U.N.Doc. UNEP/IG.12/2, at 9, 12 (1978), in 17 Int'l Legal Materials 1097, 1098 (1978). Principle 7 says that exchange of information, notification, and consultations are carried out in "good faith and in the spirit of good neighbourliness and in such a way as to avoid any unreasonable delays."

197. Report of the Intergovernmental Working Group of Experts on Natural Resources Shared by Two or More States, 5th sess., U.N.Doc. UNEP/IG.12/2, at 7 (1978), in 17 Int'l Legal Materials 1094, 1097 (1978). * * *

198. Draft article 5(1) on the law of the non-navigational uses of international watercourses, [1980] 2 Y.B.Int'l L.Comm'n, pt. 2, at 120, U.N.Doc. A/CN.4/SER.A/1980/Add.1 (Part 2).

199. G.A.Res. 34/186, 34 U.N. GAOR Supp. (No. 46) at 128, U.N. Doc. A/34/46 (1979). See also [1980] 2 Y.B.Int'l L.Comm'n, pt. 2 at 125, U.N. Doc. A/CN.4/SER.A/1980/Add.1 (Part 2).

The [then] U.N. Legal Counsel, referring to the resolutions on shared resources adopted by the various U.N. organs, has suggested that:

> [T]hose resolutions and the discussions regarding them will, in case of a dispute, be used largely as expressing the legal principles according to which prior consultations and exchange of technical information are necessary prerequisites for any potentially damaging use of international rivers. Past practice has already affirmed these principles, and the adopted resolutions have certainly given them more weight, and may even have consecrated them as legal principles.[200]

LATER DEVELOPMENTS

The impact of the U.N. Environment Program's principles on shared resources is suggested by a 1983 episode:

> When the Government of Uganda, under gentle World Bank pressure, had to consult other Nile Basin countries on a proposed water use project for Lake Victoria in December 1983, it did so by way of reference to, among other documents, [the U.N. Environment Program's principles]. Three months later, the governments of Egypt and Sudan in their replies in turn referred to the guidelines as "jointly honored principles of cooperation," thereby quietly promoting them to the status of common regional standards.[d]

In 1982 the I.L.A. got back in the act with its Montreal Rules of International Law Applicable to Transfrontier Pollution. They set forth a duty to give notice to states likely to be affected by planned activities that might entail a significant risk of transfrontier pollution. Article 6 then provides:

> Upon request of a potentially affected State, the State furnishing the information shall enter into consultations on transfrontier pollution problems connected with the planned activities and pursue such consultations in good faith and over a reasonable period of time.[e]

In 1986 the I.L.A. adopted Rules on International Groundwaters, which set forth, inter alia, a duty to consult and exchange relevant information for the purposes of preserving groundwaters from degradation and of considering joint or parallel quality standards and environmental protection measures.[f]

---

200. Suy, *Innovations in International Law–Making Process,* in The International Law and Policy of Human Welfare 187, 193 (R. MacDonald, D. Johnston, & G. Morris eds. 1978).

d. P. Sand, Lessons Learned in Global Environmental Governance 16 (World Resources Inst.Rep., 1990).

e. Rep. of 60th Conf. of the I.L.A., 1982, at 1, 2.

f. Rep. of 62d Conf. of the I.L.A., 1986, at 21, 268.

During the 1980s and early 1990s the International Law Commission of the United Nations worked to codify the law of non-navigational uses of international watercourses. At the Commission's 1987 session, it considered, inter alia, draft articles proposed by Professor Stephen McCaffrey, its special rapporteur, that would impose a duty of prior notification and consultation when potentially injurious uses of international watercourses are contemplated. The special rapporteur relied on rather extensive state practice for the notification/consultation duties.[g] The Commission provisionally adopted the draft articles on prior notification and consultation at its 1988 session.[h] It approved the full set of articles on watercourses at its 1991 session, subject to final adoption in a later year.

The International Law Commission, as an arm of the U.N. General Assembly, has as its mandate "the progressive development of international law and its codification."[i] Would its final adoption of the articles on prior notification and consultation establish customary international law regarding potentially injurious non-navigational uses of international watercourses?

In June 1992 the General Assembly convened the U.N. Conference on Environment and Development, marking the twentieth anniversary of the Stockholm Conference on the Human Environment. More than 170 states participated in the 1992 Conference, held in Rio de Janeiro. The Conference produced the Rio Declaration on Environment and Development.[j] Principle 19 says:

> States shall provide prior and timely notification and relevant information to potentially affected States on activities that may have a significant adverse transboundary environmental effect and shall consult with those States at an early stage and in good faith.

The General Assembly endorsed the Rio Declaration at its 47th Session.

What does Principle 19 add, if anything, to the international law of prior notification and consultation regarding the use of shared natural resources?

In the end, has the General Assembly made law on this subject?

2. The General Assembly in a Quasi-Constitutive Role

INTRODUCTORY NOTE

The inquiry now shifts to the role of the General Assembly in the process by which new states or other entities with some attributes of

g. See Third Report on the Law of the Non-Navigational Uses of International Watercourses, U.N.Doc. A/CN.4/406, at 35–67 (1987).

h. See Report of the Int'l Law Comm'n on the Work of its 40th Sess., U.N.Doc. A/43/10, at 114–39 (1988); McCaffrey, The Fortieth Session of the International Law Commission, 83 Am.J.Int'l L. 153, 160–66 (1989).

i. U.N.Charter art. 13(1)(a).

j. U.N. Doc. A/CONF.151/5/Rev.1, 31 Int'l Legal Materials 876 (1992).

international personality (other than international organizations) are constituted. The present focus is thus on its capacity to influence or control changes in the international legal status of organized groups or of territories, as distinguished from the preceding subsection's focus on the development and revision of international norms that affect behavior among states.

The General Assembly does not have express power to create or recognize new states. It does have trusteeship powers under Chapter XII of the U.N. Charter, and has the power to admit new states to U.N. membership on the Security Council's recommendation. Trusteeships, however, concern territories that are not yet states, and admission to U.N. membership is supposed to follow accession to statehood rather than being a constitutive part of it.[a] Nevertheless, the General Assembly has participated significantly in the formation and international recognition of actual states and of entities claiming nascent statehood. This subsection examines its role in the statehood claims made by Israel in the 1940s and later by Palestine and Namibia.

Traditionally, a valid claim to statehood requires the satisfaction of four criteria: a permanent population; a defined territory; self-government; and capacity to enter into formal relations with other states.[b]

a. Israel

The modern claim for a national home for the Jewish people in Palestine stems from the late 19th century, but the movement's first real success at an official level came on November 2, 1917, when the British Foreign Secretary issued the Balfour Declaration in the form of a letter to Lord Rothschild, a Zionist supporter. The operative part of the letter said, "His Majesty's Government view with favour the establishment in Palestine of a national home for the Jewish people, and will use their best endeavours to facilitate the achievement of this object, it being clearly understood that nothing shall be done which may prejudice the civil and religious rights of existing non-Jewish communities in Palestine, or the rights and political status enjoyed by Jews in any other country."[a] At that time, during the First World War, the British army had recently occupied Palestine, which was still formally part of the Ottoman (Turkish) Empire. In 1923, Turkey renounced its sovereignty in the Treaty of Lausanne.

Article 22 of the League of Nations Covenant, drawn up at the end of World War I, set up a system of mandates by which certain "advanced nations" were entrusted with the tutelage of "those colonies and territories which as a consequence of the late war have ceased to be

---

a. But see J. Dugard, Recognition and the United Nations 79 (1987).

b. Cf. Restatement 3d, Foreign Relations Law of the United States § 201 (1987); Montevideo Convention on Rights and Duties of States, Dec. 26, 1933, art. 1, 49 Stat. 3097, 3 Bevans 145, 165 L.N.T.S. 19.

a. See 3 The Arab–Israeli Conflict 31 (J. Moore ed. 1974) (photographic reproduction of the original letter).

under the sovereignty of the States which formerly governed them and which are inhabited by peoples not yet able to stand by themselves under the strenuous conditions of the modern world * * *." The British government was given the Mandate for Palestine. The Mandate (a formal document issued by the Council of the League of Nations) stated in its preamble that the Principal Allied Powers had agreed that the Mandatory should be responsible for putting into effect the Balfour Declaration, and provided in article 2, "The Mandatory shall be responsible for placing the country under such political, administrative and economic conditions as will secure the establishment of the Jewish national home * * *." In article 7 it called for the enactment of a Palestine nationality law, which would contain provisions "to facilitate the acquisition of Palestinian citizenship by Jews who take up their permanent residence in Palestine." [b]

At the time of the Mandate there were about 84,000 Jews and 650,000 Arabs in Palestine. The Arabs never acknowledged the validity of the Mandate, and there were Arab riots during the 1920's and 1930's. Meanwhile, the British government vacillated, at times seeming to favor partition between an Arab and a Jewish state, and at other times leaning toward a unified Palestinian state.

After the dissolution of the League of Nations, it was contemplated (but not legally required) that mandated territories would be placed under the trusteeship system established in the U.N. Charter.[c] But the British government had had enough of the problems of Palestine. On April 2, 1947, it asked the U.N. General Assembly in effect to take over the matter and to make recommendations, under article 10 of the Charter, concerning the future government of Palestine. By that time Jewish immigration had increased the Jewish population of Palestine to about 650,000, but the Arab population had grown substantially also, to about 1,200,000.

Faced with the problem of a Mandatory that wanted to pull out, the General Assembly appointed a special committee to investigate the Palestine situation and to make recommendations.[d] In its Report,[e] the Special Committee on Palestine reviewed the Jewish and Arab arguments and made the recommendations outlined below. In essence, the Jewish case relied on the Balfour Declaration and the Mandate for Palestine, as well as Biblical sources, for a right to return to Palestine and to establish a Jewish state there. The Arab case sought the creation of a unified state under Arab control west of the Jordan River, based on the Arab numerical majority there, the possession of the land for centuries by a predominately Arab population, and certain pledges made by some of the Allied Powers during World War I. By a vote of seven to three, the majority of the Special Committee recommended

b. 3 The Arab–Israeli Conflict, supra note a, at 75–77.

c. See particularly U.N. Charter art. 80.

d. G.A.Res. 106 (SI), May 15, 1947.

e. 2 GAOR Supp. 11, Vol. I, U.N. Doc. A/364 (Sept. 3, 1947).

partition between an Arab and a Jewish state, as the least of all evils. "Every other proposed solution would tend to induce the two parties to seek modification in their favour by means of persistent pressure. The grant of independence to both States, however, would remove the basis for such efforts." [f] The majority also recommended that a treaty be concluded between the two states creating an economic union with a common external customs system, a common currency and a unified transportation and communications system. The minority of three recommended creation of a single federal state, on the theory that such a state would be a more viable solution for the peoples of Palestine as a whole and that, given the proper conditions, there was a reasonable chance to achieve the necessary cooperation between Palestinian Jews and Arabs.

A commentator sympathetic to the Arab cause has noted the Arab opposition to the partition proposal, on grounds that it ran counter to the desires of the majority of the inhabitants of Palestine and that it was beyond the legal competence of the United Nations. He has pointed out that several attempts were made, before the General Assembly acted, to obtain an advisory opinion from the International Court of Justice on the legal issues. These attempts were voted down by "political forces" that were in favor of partition.[g] Another commentator, less sympathetic, found "obstructionist motives" behind the Arab proposals for an advisory opinion.[h]

The General Assembly adopted the partition recommendation in Resolution 181 (II), below. The vote was 33 in favor, 13 opposed, and 10 abstaining.

RESOLUTION ON PALESTINE
United Nations General Assembly, Nov. 29, 1947.
G.A.Res. 181, 2 GAOR, Resolutions (A/519), at 131.

The General Assembly,

* * *

Having received and examined the report of the Special Committee (document A/364) including a number of unanimous recommendations and a plan of partition with economic union approved by the majority of the Special Committee,

Considers that the present situation in Palestine is one which is likely to impair the general welfare and friendly relations among nations;

Takes note of the declaration by the mandatory Power that it plans to complete its evacuation of Palestine by 1 August 1948;

---

f. Report, supra, at 47.

g. Cattan, Recollections on the United Nations Resolution to Partition Palestine, 4 Palestine Y.B.Int'l L. 260, 262 (1987/88).

h. Potter, The Palestine Problem Before the United Nations, 42 Am.J.Int'l L. 859, 860 (1948).

Recommends to the United Kingdom, as the mandatory Power for Palestine, and to all other Members of the United Nations the adoption and implementation, with regard to the future government of Palestine, of the Plan of Partition with Economic Union set out below;

* * *

Calls upon the inhabitants of Palestine to take such steps as may be necessary on their part to put this plan into effect;

Appeals to all Governments and all peoples to refrain from taking any action which might hamper or delay the carrying out of these recommendations * * *.

* * *

Part I

Future Constitution and Government of Palestine

A. *Termination of Mandate, Partition and Independence*

1. The Mandate for Palestine shall terminate as soon as possible but in any case not later than 1 August 1948.

2. The armed forces of the mandatory Power shall be progressively withdrawn from Palestine, the withdrawal to be completed as soon as possible but in any case not later than 1 August 1948.

* * *

3. Independent Arab and Jewish States and the Special International Regime for the City of Jerusalem, set forth in part III of this plan, shall come into existence in Palestine two months after the evacuation of the armed forces of the mandatory Power has been completed but in any case not later than 1 October 1948. The boundaries of the Arab State, the Jewish State, and the City of Jerusalem shall be as described in parts II and III below.

4. The period between the adoption by the General Assembly of its recommendation on the question of Palestine and the establishment of the independence of the Arab and Jewish States shall be a transitional period.

B. *Steps Preparatory to Independence*

1. A Commission shall be set up consisting of one representative of each of five Member States. The Members represented on the Commission shall be elected by the General Assembly on as broad a basis, geographically and otherwise, as possible.

2. The administration of Palestine shall, as the mandatory Power withdraws its armed forces, be progressively turned over to the Commission; which shall act in conformity with the recommendations of the General Assembly, under the guidance of the Security Council.

[The resolution then set out the duties and authority of the Commission and of Provisional Councils of Government for each state, during the transitional period. This segment of the resolution was never implemented.

[Part II of the resolution set forth, in detail, boundary lines for the Arab state and the Jewish state. Part III set forth the boundaries of the City of Jerusalem, and formulated specific provisions for a Statute of the City.]

THE RESPONSE

Whatever may have been the technical legal effect of Resolution 181, there could be no doubt about the expectations it created among the Jewish people of Palestine. "In the small hours of Sunday, 30 November 1947, tumultuous rejoicings broke forth from every Jewish city, town, village, and hamlet in Palestine. The night before, the General Assembly of the United Nations—in a resolution drily known in the official records as Resolution 181 (II) on the Future Government of Palestine—had recommended the establishment of a Jewish state. Thus one chapter of Jewish history was being brought to an end and another was opening. * * * Only those conscious of the Jews' timeless yearning for their national redemption could grasp the depths of the fervour with which they greeted that decision of the United Nations. For the Jews of Palestine—and, indeed, for many Jews the world over—that historic resolution of the General Assembly marks a turning point in their lives."[i]

Armed violence between Arab and Jewish groups in Palestine began almost immediately. Despite Security Council calls for order, the situation remained extremely unstable when the British Mandate was terminated on May 14, 1948. On that same day the Provisional Jewish Government proclaimed the state of Israel. As put by the Provisional Government in its communication to the United States, "I have the honor to notify you that the state of Israel has been proclaimed as an independent republic within frontiers approved by the General Assembly of the United Nations in its Resolution of November 29, 1947, and that a provisional government has been charged to assume the rights and duties of government for preserving law and order within the boundaries of Israel, for defending the state against external aggression, and for discharging the obligations of Israel to the other nations of the world in accordance with international law."[j] The United States immediately recognized the state of Israel.[k] So did several other states, but the Arab states declared that a direct threat to peace in Palestine had occurred and said that they were compelled to intervene for the purpose of restoring peace and security, and "in order

i. Report of a Study Group set up by the Hebrew University of Jerusalem: Israel and the United Nations 17–18 (1956). Reprinted by permission of the Carnegie Endowment for International Peace.

j. 2 Whiteman, Digest of International Law 167–68 (1963).

k. Id. at 168.

to fill the vacuum created by the termination of the Mandate and the failure to replace it by any legally constituted authority * * *."¹

In the ensuing hostilities, Israeli forces advanced beyond the boundaries set by Resolution 181, and large numbers of Arabs living within Israel's proclaimed borders fled. Armistice agreements were signed in 1949 drawing armistice demarcation lines outside the frontiers originally proclaimed by Israel. The armistice lines, however, were not to be considered territorial boundaries.[m] Israel was admitted to the United Nations on May 11, 1949.

Where did the General Assembly get its authority to issue Resolution 181? From *article 10* of the Charter? If so, was Resolution 181 a mere recommendation? On these points, consider the position taken by Ian Brownlie, a leading British authority on international law:

> It is doubtful if the United Nations has a "capacity to convey title", in part because the Organization cannot assume the role of territorial sovereign: in spite of the principle of implied powers the Organization is not a state and the General Assembly only has a power of recommendation. Thus the resolution of 1947 containing a partition plan for Palestine was probably *ultra vires,* and, if it was not, was not binding on member states in any case.[n]

Consider whether the General Assembly's authority—including authority to do more than recommend—could be based on its status as successor to the League of Nations Council in respect of mandates. Under article XXII of the League of Nations Covenant, the Council was to receive an annual report from the Mandatory and could, under some circumstances, define the degree of control to be exercised by the Mandatory. In the Advisory Opinion on the International Status of South West Africa,[o] the World Court held that League of Nations Mandates continued in existence despite the demise of the League, until other arrangements were agreed upon between the U.N. and mandatory states.[p] The Court also held that the General Assembly succeeded to League of Nations supervisory functions under article 10 of the Charter, so South Africa (in the case of the South West Africa Mandate, which was before the Court) was under an international obligation to submit to the supervision of the General Assembly and to render annual reports to it.[q] The Charter, however, did not require a mandatory state such as South Africa to enter into a trusteeship agreement with the General Assembly.[r]

In a later case, the Advisory Opinion on Legal Consequences for States of the Continued Presence of South Africa in Namibia (South

---

l. U.N. Doc. S/745, at 5 (1948).

m. See, e.g., the Israeli–Egyptian Armistice Agreement, Feb. 24, 1949, art. V(2), 42 U.N.T.S. 251.

n. I. Brownlie, Principles of Public International Law 172–73 (4th ed. 1990). Reprinted by permission of Oxford University Press.

o. [1950] I.C.J. 128.

p. Id. at 134.

q. Id. at 136–37.

r. Id. at 138–40.

West Africa) Notwithstanding Security Council Resolution 276,[s] the Court again referred to the United Nations as the supervisory institution over the South West Africa Mandate, in its capacity as successor to the League. It held that the General Assembly had the power to declare the South West Africa Mandate terminated and to conclude that South Africa has no other right to administer the Territory. The Court said, "This is not a finding on facts, but the formulation of a legal situation. For it would not be correct to assume that, because the General Assembly is in principle vested with recommendatory powers, it is debarred from adopting, in specific cases within the framework of its competence, resolutions which make determinations or have operative design."[t]

Can it be said that because the General Assembly has supervisory powers over a League of Nations mandate and may even terminate the authority of a mandatory state, it has the power to create new states within the mandated territory? How else can the existence, and the original territorial boundaries, of the state of Israel be explained? Note, incidentally, that the General Assembly was a much smaller body in 1947 than it is now. To the extent that its Resolution 181 did have constitutive effect for the establishment of the state of Israel, was it true international legislation under the definition given at page 275 supra?

b. Palestine

In the late 1940s, after the initial hostilities between Arabs and the new state of Israel had ebbed, Jordan occupied the West Bank and Egypt occupied the Gaza Strip. In 1950, Jordan purported to annex the West Bank. The Arab League denounced the Jordanian claim, and only the United Kingdom and Pakistan ever recognized the annexation. During the six-day war of June 1967, Israel occupied the West Bank, the Gaza Strip, the portion of Jerusalem it did not already control, and other Arab-held territories.[a] Israel moved its capital to Jerusalem, and Israeli settlements proliferated in the West Bank. Some Israeli leaders gave justifications for the settlements that sounded increasingly like full territorial claims.

Despite all this, Jordan continued to provide administrative services to the West Bank after 1967. On July 31, 1988, however, Jordan decided to sever its remaining administrative ties.[b] In October 1988, King Hussein of Jordan reaffirmed that he accepted the Palestine Liberation Organization (PLO) as the "sole, legitimate representative of

---

s. [1971] I.C.J. 16.
t. Id. at 50.
a. See Arsanjani, United Nations Competence in the West Bank and Gaza Strip, 31 Int'l & Comp.L.Q. 426 (1982).

b. See 27 Int'l Legal Materials 1037 (1988).

the Palestinian people." [c] The PLO's origin and early status are summarized in the excerpt below.

COMMENT, FOLLOWING IN ANOTHER'S FOOTSTEPS: THE ACQUISITION OF INTERNATIONAL LEGAL STANDING BY THE PALESTINE LIBERATION ORGANIZATION
3 Syracuse J. of Int'l L. & Commerce 221, 232–33 (1975).*

[I]n January 1964, creation of the Palestine Liberation Organization was authorized at an Arab summit conference pursuant to an Arab League Council decision of the previous September to "affirm a Palestinian entity and place the cause of liberation in the hands of the Palestinians themselves." [63] The following May, a Palestine National Congress met in Jerusalem and adopted a charter stating that the PLO:

> shall be responsible for the direction of the Palestinian people in its struggle for the liberation of its homeland, in all liberational, political, and financial fields and also for whatever measures may be required by the Palestine case on the inter-Arab and international levels.[64]

The Congress immediately notified U.N. Secretary General U Thant that the PLO would be "the only legitimate spokesman for all matters concerning the Palestine people." [65]

Today, after prevailing in challenges for Palestinian leadership and having undergone major changes of composition, the PLO retains the support of the Arab League and has increasingly been allowed to act on the international plane as the exclusive agent of the Palestinian people. It has been accepted as an observer-member of the organization of non-aligned countries, and has been invited to participate in numerous international conferences. Its chairman, Yasser Arafat, attended the Second Islamic Summit Conference in February 1974, has negotiated with government officials in the Soviet Union, East Germany, Poland and France and was invited to and did address the United Nations General Assembly.

THE GENERAL ASSEMBLY AND THE PLO

In 1974 the General Assembly accorded the PLO observer status in its sessions and in international conferences convened by it. Many specialized agencies have followed suit. In 1974 the General Assembly

---

c. N.Y. Times, Oct. 24, 1988, p. A8, col. 4.

* Reprinted by permission of the Syracuse Journal of International Law & Commerce.

63. J. Cooley, Green March, Black September: The Story of the Palestinian Arabs 95 (1973).

64. [L. Kadi, Arab Summit Conferences and the Palestine Problem 108 (1966).]

65. Id. at 106.

also adopted Resolution 3236 (XXIX)[d] by a vote of 89 in favor, eight opposed and 37 abstaining. Among other things, Resolution 3236 identified the PLO as "the representative of the Palestinian people," reaffirmed "the inalienable rights of the Palestinian people in Palestine, including: (a) The right to self-determination without external interference; (b) The right to national independence and sovereignty," and recognized "the right of the Palestinian people to regain its rights by all means in accordance with the purposes and principles of the Charter of the United Nations * * *."

The right to self-determination of peoples, mentioned in U.N. Charter article 55 and repeatedly stressed in General Assembly resolutions beginning with the Declaration on the Granting of Independence to Colonial Countries and Peoples,[e] has been applied in the U.N. primarily as a basis for the right to independence of peoples and territories under colonial control (including Namibia) or under U.N. trusteeships. Note the prominent place given to the right of self-determination of "the Palestinian people" in Resolution 3236 (and repeated in other General Assembly resolutions on Palestine). Does this represent a significant extension of that right?

Does the quoted language, above, from Resolution 3236 say that the right to self-determination is something other than a right to national independence and sovereignty? If so, what do you suppose it is?

In 1975 the General Assembly established a Committee on the Exercise of the Inalienable Rights of the Palestinian People, initially composed of 20 member states and later increased to 23. No Western states are members of the Committee. In 1976 the Committee recommended that the Security Council establish a timetable for Israeli evacuation of the occupied territories, and that "The evacuated territories, with all property and services intact, should be taken over by the United Nations, which with the co-operation of the League of Arab States, will subsequently hand over these evacuated areas to the Palestine Liberation Organization as the representative of the Palestinian people * * *."[f] The General Assembly adopted a resolution that took note of the Committee's report and "endorses the recommendations contained therein, as a basis for the solution of the question of Palestine * * *."[g]

The International Conference on the Question of Palestine, convened by the General Assembly, was held in 1983. It was attended by 117 states. It adopted the Geneva Declaration on Palestine, which said among other things that settlement of the Palestine problem "must be based on the implementation of the relevant United Nations resolutions concerning the question of Palestine and the attainment of the

d. Nov. 22, 1974, 29 GAOR Supp. No. 31, at 4.

e. G.A.Res. 1514 (XV), 15 GAOR Supp. No. 16, at 66 (1960).

f. 31 GAOR Supp. No. 35, at 15 (1976).

g. G.A.Res. 31/20, Nov. 24, 1976. The vote was 90–16–30, with the United States, Israel and most Western European states opposed.

legitimate, inalienable rights of the Palestinian people, including the right to self-determination and the right to the establishment of its own independent state in Palestine and should also be based on the provision by the Security Council of guarantees for peace and security among all States in the region, including the independent Palestinian State, within secure and internationally recognized boundaries." [h]

In December 1987, the *intifadeh,* or uprising, began in the West Bank and Gaza Strip. It involved persistent rock-throwing at Israeli patrols, boycotts of Israeli products, commercial strikes, refusals to cooperate with Israeli military authorities, and other forms of resistance (sometimes more lethal than rock-throwing). The *intifadeh* was instigated, enforced and largely carried out by young Palestinian Arab men. Israeli forces reacted in a variety of ways, using rubber bullets against demonstrators, detaining suspects for long periods in camps, sometimes destroying houses of the families of prime suspects, and deporting some suspected leaders of the uprising. It did not appear that the PLO had a major hand in organizing the *intifadeh.*

In November 1988, while the *intifadeh* was in full swing, the Palestine National Council (PNC) met in Algiers. The PNC, acting as the parliamentary body of the PLO, declared "the establishment of the State of Palestine." A month later, the U.N. General Assembly acknowledged "the proclamation of the State of Palestine." The PNC proclamation, one commentator's analysis of it, and the General Assembly resolution appear below.

PALESTINIAN PROCLAMATION OF INDEPENDENCE

Palestine National Council, Nov. 15, 1988.
U.N. Doc. A/43/827–S/20278, Annex III, reprinted
in 27 Int'l Legal Materials 1668, 1670 (1988).

On the same terrain as God's apostolic missions to mankind and in the land of Palestine was the Palestinian Arab people brought forth. There it grew and developed, and there it created its unique human and national mode of existence in an organic, indissoluble and unbroken relationship among people, land and history. * * * [T]he international community, in article 22 of the Covenant of the League of Nations of 1919 and in the Lausanne Treaty of 1923, recognized that the Palestinian Arab people was no different from the other Arab peoples detached from the Ottoman State and was a free and independent people.

Despite the historical injustice done to the Palestinian Arab people in its displacement and in being deprived of the right to self-determina-

h. U.N. Doc. A/38/497–S/16038, para. 2 (1983). Security Council Res. 242, Nov. 22, 1967, which has long been recognized as the definitive word from the Security Council so far on the Middle East, calls for "acknowledgement of the sovereignty, territorial integrity and political independence of every State in the area and their right to live in peace within secure and recognized boundaries free from threats or acts of force * * *."

tion following the adoption of General Assembly resolution 181 (II) of 1947, which partitioned Palestine into an Arab and a Jewish State, that resolution nevertheless continues to attach conditions to international legitimacy that guarantee the Palestinian Arab people the right to sovereignty and national independence.

* * *

By virtue of the natural, historical and legal right of the Palestinian Arab people to its homeland, Palestine, and of the sacrifices of its succeeding generations in defence of the freedom and independence of that homeland.

Pursuant to the resolutions of the Arab Summit Conferences and on the basis of the international legitimacy embodied in the resolutions of the United Nations since 1947, and

Through the exercise by the Palestinian Arab people of its right to self-determination, political independence and sovereignty over its territory:

The Palestine National Council hereby declares, in the Name of God and on behalf of the Palestinian Arab people, the establishment of the State of Palestine in the land of Palestine with its capital at Jerusalem.

The State of Palestine shall be for Palestinians, wherever they may be, therein to develop their national and cultural identity and therein to enjoy full equality of rights. Their religious and political beliefs and human dignity shall therein be safeguarded under a democratic parliamentary system based on freedom of opinion and the freedom to form parties, on the heed of the majority for minority rights and the respect of minorities for majority decisions, on social justice and equality, and on non-discrimination in civil rights on grounds of race, religion or colour or as between men and women, under a Constitution ensuring the rule of law and an independent judiciary and on the basis of true fidelity to the age-old spiritual and cultural heritage of Palestine with respect to mutual tolerance, coexistence and magnanimity among religions.

The State of Palestine shall be an Arab State and shall be an integral part of the Arab nation, of its heritage and civilization and of its present endeavour for the achievement of the goals of liberation, development, democracy and unity. * * *

The State of Palestine declares its commitment to the purposes and principles of the United Nations, to the Universal Declaration of Human Rights and to the policy and principles of non-alignment.

* * *

The State of Palestine further declares * * * that it believes in the solution of international and regional problems by peaceful means in accordance with the Charter of the United Nations and the resolutions adopted by it, and that, without prejudice to its natural right to defend itself, it rejects the threat or use of force, violence and intimidation against its territorial integrity and political independence or those of any other State.

* * *

KHALIDI, THE RESOLUTIONS OF THE 19TH PALESTINE NATIONAL COUNCIL
19 J. Palestine Studies Issues 74, at 29, 34–35 (1990).*

* * *

The most important section of the declaration grounds the Palestinian people's right to independence not only in their natural and historic rights in the land of Palestine and in the general principle of self-determination of peoples, as might be expected, but also on two specific elements of international legality. The first is Article 22 of the Covenant of the League of Nations of 1919, which recognized that the peoples formerly part of the Ottoman Empire, including the Palestinian people, "have reached the stage of development where their existence as independent nations can be provisionally recognized, subject to the rendering of administrative advice and assistance by a Mandatory until such time as they are able to stand alone." Although the Palestinians (unlike the peoples of Syria, Lebanon, Iraq, and Jordan to which the same article applied) were never allowed to exercise this independent existence, the PNC could claim with some justification that the League of Nations had provided a basis in international law dating back to 1919 for the independence of Palestine.

The second element of legality cited as a basis for Palestinian independence is the United Nations General Assembly's partition resolution 181 of 29 November 1947. In a carefully-worded section, the declaration states: "Despite the historical injustice done to the Palestinian people by their dispersion and their being deprived of the right of self-determination after UN General Assembly Resolution 181 of 1947, which partitioned Palestine into two states, one Arab and one Jewish, that resolution still provides the legal basis for the right of the Palestinian Arab people to national sovereignty and independence."

This brief passage has revolutionary import in terms of modern Palestinian political discourse. Earlier PNC resolutions, going back to 1974, have implicitly accepted the principle of two states in Palestine, one Arab and one Jewish. But never before has this principle, or the UN resolution that embodies it, explicitly been accepted by the PNC, or for that matter, by any other representative Palestinian body. Indeed, rejection of partition in letter and spirit is at the heart of the Palestinian National Charter adopted at the first PNC in Jerusalem in 1964 (the so-called Covenant), its updated version of 1968, and most authoritative statements of the Palestinian position ever since the first partition plan

---

* Reprinted by permission of the Institute for Palestine Studies.

put forward in the Peel Commission report of 1937. The 1964 Charter states categorically that "Palestine is an Arab homeland," implying exclusivity, and that partition of the country along the lines of resolution 181 or on any other basis, and the creation of a Jewish state there, are fundamentally illegitimate.

Twenty-four years after the adoption of the Palestine National Charter embodying these ideas—which largely reflected the thinking of the pre–1948 generation of Palestinian political leaders who were members of the first PNC—the 19th PNC resolved in the Declaration of Independence to base the international legitimacy of Palestinian independence partly on the 1947 partition resolution that mandated the establishment of a sovereign Jewish state in part of Palestine.

The PNC was therefore recognizing that for all the injustices inherent in partition, new realities had been created, notably the Jewish state explicitly mentioned in the declaration; just as the international legitimacy of this Jewish state was partly grounded in the partition resolution, so too, was that of a Palestinian state. It is worth noting that this declaration, and the profound transformation in Palestinian thinking that is exemplifies, was unanimously approved by the 19th PNC. This means that even those groups, such as the PFLP,[i] which dissented in 1974 from the PLO's new two-state approach in its earliest phases, have now accepted it.

RESOLUTION ON PROCLAMATION OF THE STATE OF PALESTINE
United Nations General Assembly, Dec. 15, 1988.
G.A. Res. 43/177, 43 GAOR Supp. No. 49 (A/43/49), at 62.

The General Assembly,

* * *

Recalling its resolution 181 (II) of 29 November 1947, in which, *inter alia,* it called for the establishment of an Arab State and a Jewish State in Palestine,

* * *

Aware of the proclamation of the State of Palestine by the Palestine National Council in line with General Assembly resolution 181 (II) and in exercise of the inalienable rights of the Palestinian people,

Affirming the urgent need to achieve a just and comprehensive settlement in the Middle East which, *inter alia,* provides for peaceful coexistence for all States in the region,

Recalling its resolution 3237 (XXIX) of 22 November 1974 on the observer status for the Palestine Liberation Organization and subsequent relevant resolutions,

i. [Popular Front for the Liberation of Palestine. Ed.]

1. *Acknowledges* the proclamation of the State of Palestine by the Palestine National Council on 15 November 1988;

2. *Affirms* the need to enable the Palestinian people to exercise their sovereignty over their territory occupied since 1967;

3. *Decides* that, effective as of 15 December 1988, the designation "Palestine" should be used in place of the designation "Palestine Liberation Organization" in the United Nations system, without prejudice to the observer status and functions of the Palestine Liberation Organization within the United Nations system, in conformity with relevant United Nations resolutions and practice * * *.

A STATE OF PALESTINE?

The vote on General Assembly Resolution 43/177, above, was 104 in favor, two opposed (Israel and the United States) and 36 abstaining, with 15 member states absent and one (Iran) not participating in the vote.

Did the General Assembly recognize a new state of Palestine in Resolution 43/177? Did it do so if one considers together Resolution 43/177, Resolution 181 (the original partition resolution, page 368 supra) and the Palestinian Proclamation of Independence? In this respect, note the seemingly slight difference in translation of the key section in the Proclamation referring to Resolution 181, when one compares the Proclamation as set out at pages 375–76 supra and as quoted by Khalidi at page 377 supra.

In December 1990, the General Assembly adopted Resolution 45/68,[j] by a vote of 144 to 2 (Israel and U.S.), with no abstentions. Among other things, it called for a Middle East peace conference, "with the participation of all parties to the conflict, including the Palestine Liberation Organization, on an equal footing;" it reaffirmed the "principles [of] (a) The withdrawal of Israel from the Palestinian territory occupied since 1967, including Jerusalem, and from the other occupied Arab territories; (b) Guaranteeing arrangements for security of all States in the region, including those named in Resolution 181 (II) of 29 November 1947, within secure and internationally recognized boundaries * * *."

Did Resolution 45/68 recognize a state of Palestine?[k]

Did it recognize Israel's borders as the 1949 armistice lines?

Was Resolution 45/68 any more or any less authoritative than Resolution 181? Why?

[j]. 45 GAOR Supp. No. 49 (A/45/49), at 31.

[k]. For one view, see Gowlland–Debbas, Collective Responses to the Unilateral Declarations of Independence of Southern Rhodesia and Palestine: An Application of the Legitimizing Function of the United Nations, 1990 Brit. Y.B. Int'l L. 135, 148–53.

If the General Assembly has recognized a new state of Palestine, would that be a conclusive determination of statehood simply on the basis of the Assembly's own powers?

Recall the four traditional criteria for statehood, page 154 supra. Does Palestine meet all four? Some commentators have argued that it does. Taking the criteria one by one, it has been said that (a) the territory does not have to be determinate, as shown by the fact that Israel is recognized as a state despite its lack of fixed territorial boundaries (except with Egypt); (b) the Palestinian people constitute the population, and have for centuries; (c) the PLO serves as the provisional government of Palestine, effectively controlling substantial sections of the territory and providing public services to Palestinians in Palestine and abroad; and (d) Palestine's capacity to enter into international relations is shown by the fact that more than 100 states had recognized it as a state within two years of the Proclamation of Independence, and by the General Assembly resolutions discussed above.[l]

A contrary argument stresses the notion of independence: "the existence of an organized community on a particular territory, exclusively or substantially exercising self-governing power, and secondly, the absence of the exercise of another state, and of the right of another state to exercise, self-governing powers over the whole of that territory."[m]

On the question of the PLO as the government of Palestine, note that the PLO has an institutional structure that includes several departments with governmental functions, such as health, education, finance and military affairs. It has been said that "the PLO provides comprehensive medical and health services, an economic infrastructure, the cultural focus, the educational basis, social welfare services, and so forth, in a manner comparable to that of any sovereign territorial state."[n] As of the early 1990s, however, most of these services were supplied outside of the West Bank and Gaza Strip.

c. Namibia

Consider, finally, the General Assembly's role in Namibia's transition from a mandated territory to statehood. After World War I, South Africa was given a League of Nations Mandate over South West Africa. When the United Nations succeeded the League, South Africa refused to enter into a trusteeship agreement with respect to South West Africa, and quickly refused even to submit the reports to the General Assembly that the World Court had said were required. South Africa

---

l. See Boyle, Create the State of Palestine!, American–Arab Affairs, No. 25, at 86 (1988); Boyle, The Creation of the State of Palestine, 1 European J. Int'l L. 301, 302–03 (1990).

m. Crawford, The Creation of the State of Palestine: Too Much Too Soon?, 1 European J.Int'l L. 307, 309 (1990).

n. C. Rubenberg, The Palestine Liberation Organization: Its Institutional Infrastructure 58 (1983).

had imposed its apartheid system on South West Africa, an imposition that other members of the U.N. came to regard as inconsistent with South Africa's duty, expressly set forth in its Mandate for South West Africa, to "promote to the utmost the material and moral well-being and the social progress of the inhabitants of the territory * * *." After a series of skirmishes in the World Court proved inconclusive, the General Assembly in 1966 adopted its Resolution 2145 (by a vote of 114–2 (South Africa, Portugal) with 3 abstentions), which declared that South Africa had failed to fulfill its obligations under the Mandate and had, in fact, disavowed the Mandate. It went on to decide that the Mandate was terminated, that South Africa had no other right to administer the territory, "and that henceforth South West Africa comes under the direct responsibility of the United Nations * * *."[a]

The Security Council reaffirmed General Assembly Resolution 2145, declared that the continued presence of South Africa in what had by then come to be known as Namibia was illegal, and called upon all states to refrain from certain dealings with South Africa in regard to Namibia.[b] The World Court in its 1971 advisory opinion upheld the General Assembly's termination of the Mandate.[c] It also said, inter alia, that Security Council Resolution 276 imposed an obligation on South Africa to withdraw its administration from Namibia.[d]

After the General Assembly adopted Resolution 2145, it established a United Nations Council for South West Africa, later called the Council for Namibia. It initially had 11 members, but was enlarged in stages to 31. In 1990, after Namibia had emerged as a state and had been admitted to the United Nations, the Council for Namibia was dissolved. It is worth examining as the primary mechanism by which the General Assembly sought to wrest control over Namibia from South Africa in the years leading to Namibian statehood.

RESOLUTION ESTABLISHING THE COUNCIL FOR SOUTH WEST AFRICA (NAMIBIA)

United Nations General Assembly, May 19, 1967.
G.A. Res. 2248, GAOR 5th Special Sess., Supp. 1 (A/6657), at 1.

The General Assembly,

* * *

II

1. *Decides* to establish a United Nations Council for South West Africa * * * and to entrust to it the following powers and functions, to be discharged in the Territory [of South West Africa]:

---

a. 21 GAOR Supp. No. 16, at 2 (1966).

b. Security Council Res. 276 (1970). General Assembly Resolution 2145 and Security Council Resolution 276 are set out at pages 489 and 490 infra, in connection with an examination of the Charter interpretation and dispute settlement aspects of the situation.

c. [1971] I.C.J. 16.

d. The opinion is set forth at page 492 infra.

(a) To administer South West Africa until independence, with the maximum possible participation of the people of the Territory;

(b) To promulgate such laws, decrees and administrative regulations as are necessary for the administration of the Territory until a legislative assembly is established following elections conducted on the basis of universal adult suffrage;

(c) To take as an immediate task all the necessary measures, in consultation with the people of the Territory, for the establishment of a constituent assembly to draw up a constitution on the basis of which elections will be held for the establishment of a legislative assembly and a responsible government;

(d) To take all the necessary measures for the maintenance of law and order in the Territory;

(e) To transfer all powers to the people of the Territory upon the declaration of independence;

* * *

IV

1. *Decides* that the Council shall be based in South West Africa;

* * *

3. *Further requests* the Council to proceed to South West Africa with a view to:

(a) Taking over the administration of the Territory;

(b) Ensuring the withdrawal of South African police and military forces;

(c) Ensuring the withdrawal of South African personnel and their replacement by personnel operating under the authority of the Council;

* * *

VI

Decides that South West Africa shall become independent on a date to be fixed in accordance with the wishes of the people and that the Council shall do all in its power to enable independence to be attained by June 1968.

THE COUNCIL FOR NAMIBIA

Resolution 2248, above, was adopted by a vote of 85 in favor, two opposed, and 30 abstaining.

The Council for Namibia was never able to establish an effective presence in the territory of Namibia. Operating outside the territory, it concentrated on advocating Namibian independence; representing it internationally, particularly by becoming a member or associate member of several U.N. agencies (including, for example, full membership in the ILO); promoting conservation of its natural resources; and training Namibians to administer the country upon independence.

In connection with its effort to conserve Namibian natural resources, the Council in September 1974 adopted its Decree No. 1, below.

DECREE FOR THE PROTECTION OF THE NATURAL RESOURCES OF NAMIBIA
United Nations Council for Namibia, Sept. 27, 1974.
Decree No. 1, U.N.Doc. A/AC.131/33.

The United Nations Council for Namibia,

Recognizing that, in the terms of General Assembly resolution 2145 (XXI) of 27 October 1966 the Territory of Namibia (formerly South West Africa) is the direct responsibility of the United Nations,

* * *

Acting in terms of the powers conferred on it by General Assembly resolution 2248 (S–V) of 19 May 1967 and all other relevant resolutions and decisions regarding Namibia,

Decrees that

1. No person or entity, whether a body corporate or unincorporated, may search for, prospect for, explore for, take, extract, mine, process, refine, use, sell, export, or distribute any natural resource, whether animal or mineral, situated or found to be situated within the territorial limits of Namibia without the consent and permission of the United Nations Council for Namibia or any person authorized to act on its behalf for the purpose of giving such permission or such consent;

2. Any permission, concession or licence for all or any of the purposes specified in paragraph 1 above whensoever granted by any person or entity, including any body purporting to act under the authority of the Government of the Republic of South Africa or the "Administration of South West Africa" or their predecessors, is null, void and of no force or effect;

* * *

4. Any animal, mineral or other natural resource produced in or emanating from the Territory of Namibia which shall be taken from the said Territory without the consent and written authority of the United Nations Council for Namibia or of any person authorized to act on behalf of the said Council may be seized and shall be forfeited to the benefit of the said Council and held in trust by them for the benefit of the people of Namibia;

* * *

6. Any person, entity or corporation which contravenes the present decree in respect of Namibia may be held liable in damages by the future Government of an independent Namibia * * *.

THE EFFECT OF THE COUNCIL'S DECREE

General Assembly Resolution 3295, in December 1974, requested all U.N. member states "to take all appropriate measures to ensure the full application of, and compliance with," Council Decree No. 1.

In 1975 the representative of the Netherlands to the U.N. said, in the Fourth Committee of the General Assembly:

> [A]ccording to article 81 of the Charter, the administration of a trust territory can be exercised not only by one or more States but also by the United Nations itself as administering authority. Further, article 85 provides that the functions of the United Nations with regard to trusteeship agreements for all areas not designated as strategic shall be exercised by the General Assembly.
>
> Consequently, in those cases where the UN itself functions as the administering authority of a trust territory, it is the General Assembly which possesses the legal powers necessary for the exercise of the administration. Such administrative powers with regard to a specific territory are of an entirely different character than the general powers of the Assembly concerning questions dealt with by the UN. They are, therefore, by no means limited to the making of recommendations as provided for in article 10 of the Charter.
>
> In respect of Namibia, the General Assembly has delegated the exercise of those executive powers to the UN Council for Namibia. In its resolution 2248 (S–V) the General Assembly has entrusted to the Council the powers and functions to administer the territory and, among other things, to promulgate such laws, decrees and administrative regulations as are necessary for the administration of the territory. My government holds the opinion that the General Assembly was legally fully competent to do so.[e]

Contrast the British position. In 1988 the British Minister of State for Defence Procurement said:

> I am afraid that decree number one of the United Nations Council for Namibia was made outside the competence of the General Assembly which set up that particular Council. Therefore we regard it as null and void.[f]

---

e. Press release issued by the Netherlands Mission to the U.N., summarized in U.N. Doc. A/C.4/SR.2151, at 15–16 (1975).

f. 493 House of Lords Debates, col. 1044, Feb. 23, 1988, reprinted in 59 British Y.B.Int'l L. 451 (1988).

The Council for Namibia made one attempt to enforce its Decree No. 1 in the courts of a U.N. member state. In 1987 it began proceedings in the District Court of The Hague against a Dutch company (Urenco), its government-controlled business partner (UCN) and the government of the Netherlands, alleging that Urenco and UCN had used uranium products from Namibia without the consent of the Council. The complaint sought an injunction plus liquidated damages for any violation of the injunction. Urenco and UCN defended on the ground, in part, that the Council could not be considered to be the government of a state of Namibia, which they said did not then exist. The government of the Netherlands did not challenge the Council's authority, but argued that the companies' activities did not violate Decree No. 1.[g]

If the case had gone to judgment, should the court have treated Decree No. 1 as the law of Namibia? Should it have done so if the Dutch government had not taken a position on the General Assembly's competence in the matter? (Assume that the court would apply international law as the controlling source of law.) Consider not only the General Assembly's powers in *articles 10-14* and the articles mentioned in the Dutch statement, but also *articles 75-77* and *79*.

If the answer to the preceding question is yes, does it follow that the General Assembly could endow the PLO with authority to legislate for the West Bank while it is under Israeli occupation, and that U.N. members would be under an international duty to recognize any such legislation as emanating from the legitimate authority in that territory? Or could the General Assembly accomplish the same thing by creating a Council for Palestine, along the lines of the Council for Namibia?

Could the General Assembly endow indigenous groups in other disputed territories (for example, in Europe or in East Timor) with legislative authority over the territories they occupy? Would it matter whether or not the territories are within the recognized boundaries of an existing state?

Over the years, the Security Council as well as the General Assembly adopted resolutions designed to prod South Africa to relinquish its control over Namibia. In particular, in 1978 the Security Council adopted its Resolution 435, in which it decided "to establish under [the Security Council's] authority a United Nations Transition Assistance Group [UNTAG] * * * to assist [the Secretary-General's] Special Representative to carry out the mandate * * * to ensure the early independence of Namibia through free elections under the supervision and control of the United Nations."

g. The summary of the case is based on U.N.Doc. A/AC.131/322 (1990), which does not indicate any outcome. See also 19 Neth.Y.B.Int'l L. 316-17 (1988).

This resolution had little effect until December 1988, when the governments of Angola, Cuba and South Africa entered into an agreement accepting its implementation. South Africa agreed to withdraw all its military forces from Namibia in accordance with Resolution 435; Cuba and Angola agreed to a staged, total withdrawal from Angola of the Cuban troops that had been supporting the government there; and all three states agreed to refrain from the threat or use of force against the territorial integrity, inviolability of borders or independence of any state of southwestern Africa.[h]

The agreement held. Under the supervision of UNTAG, South African military forces were withdrawn from Namibia, and in November 1989 a Constituent Assembly was elected to draft a constitution for an independent Namibia. In the election, about 57 percent of the vote went to the Southwest African People's Organization (SWAPO), which had long been recognized by the U.N. General Assembly as the legitimate indigenous representative of the Namibian people. The Democratic Turnhalle Alliance, a multiracial group favored by the South African government, received about 29 percent of the vote. These two groups set out to draft a constitution, again with U.N. assistance.

Since adoption of a constitution required a two-thirds vote, neither body could impose its will entirely on the other. The negotiations produced a remarkable document, summarized below.

REPORT ON HUMAN RIGHTS PROVISIONS IN THE CONSTITUTION OF NAMIBIA
Ad Hoc Working Group on Southern Africa, Feb. 20, 1990.
U.N.Doc. E/CN.4/1990/7/Add.1, at 6–7.

* * *

39. On 9 February 1990, the Constituent Assembly unanimously adopted the Constitution for an independent Namibia. It [became] operative on 21 March 1990, the day of independence. The *Ad Hoc* Working Group has studied the main elements of the Constitution, which proclaims the Republic of Namibia as a sovereign, secular, democratic and unitary State based on the principles of democracy, the rule of law and justice for all. The multi-party democratic State has the characteristics of a presidential system. Chapter 3 (articles 5 to 25) incorporates most of the fundamental rights and freedoms laid down in the Universal Declaration of Human Rights, subject only to the declaration of a state of emergency (article 26), which must first be approved by a resolution of the National Assembly. In article 4, the Constitution deals with the acquisition and loss of citizenship. Article 26 elaborates circumstances in which a state of emergency may be declared.

40. Articles 79, 80 and 81 refer to the administration of justice. The Constitution provides for an independent judicial machinery capa-

h. U.N. Doc. A/43/989–S/20346, Annex (1988), reprinted in 28 Int'l Legal Materials 957 (1989).

ble of protecting basic human rights. It contains provisions for legal safeguards through the judicial power vested in the courts, and through the establishment of an ombudsman who is competent to provide individuals with legal assistance or advice as required.

* * *

42. All rights provided for in the International Covenant on Civil and Political Rights are taken into account. The Constitution further contains provisions on the rights of the child under article 15, the right to private property in article 16 and the right to education in article 20. The Constitution provides for primary education that is compulsory and free of charge and the right of individuals to create their own educational establishments.

INDEPENDENCE

The U.N. Secretary-General, Javier Pérez de Cuéllar, went to Namibia to administer the oath of office to the first President of the independent state.

REPORT ON THE IMPLEMENTATION OF SECURITY COUNCIL RESOLUTION 435

Secretary-General of the United Nations, March 28, 1990.
U.N.Doc. S/21215, at 1.

1. It is with great satisfaction that I have the honour to report to the Security Council that, shortly after midnight on 20/21 March 1990, at the National Stadium in Windhoek, the flag of the Republic of South Africa was lowered and the flag of the Republic of Namibia was raised, thus marking the accession of Namibia to independence in accordance with Security Council resolution 435 (1978). Immediately thereafter, in accordance with schedule 7 of the Constitution approved by the Namibian Constituent Assembly on 9 February 1990 (S/20967/Add.2), I administered the oath of office to Mr. Sam Nujoma, who had been elected to the office of President of the Republic of Namibia by the Constituent Assembly on 16 February 1990, in accordance with article 134 of the Constitution. On 22 March 1990 the South African Administrator General, Advocate Louis Pienaar, left Namibia and was seen off by President Nujoma.

2. Thus was achieved, in dignity and with great rejoicing, the goal of independence for Namibia for which the United Nations and its Member States have striven for so long.

INDEPENDENT NAMIBIA

On April 23, 1990, Namibia became a member of the United Nations.

It took more than 23 years from the time the General Assembly determined that South Africa had no right to administer Namibia until independence was declared. Clearly, U.N. pressure was not the only factor—perhaps not the major factor—in persuading South Africa to relinquish its control over Namibia. Economic and political pressures from politically powerful states had a great deal to do with it, as did pressures at home in South Africa. Could it nevertheless be said that the U.N., and particularly the General Assembly, played a constitutive role in the drama of Namibian statehood?

Is it significant that the U.N. Secretary–General administered the oath of office to Namibia's first President?

SECTION 2. DISPUTE–SETTLEMENT AND INTERPRETIVE POWERS

INTRODUCTORY NOTE

It is useful for analytical purposes to separate international organizations' quasi-judicial functions from their quasi-legislative functions (the subject of the previous section) and their enforcement functions (the subject of the next chapter). In practice, however, the lines separating these functions are not always bright. Sometimes dispute-settlement or interpretive organs perform an essentially law-making function, as is done in domestic common-law systems, in order to fill in gaps in existing norms. And sometimes dispute-settlement or interpretive organs are invoked more for enforcement purposes than for the pure purpose of finding out which party is right in a dispute or of clarifying an existing norm. One taxonomy has called these the creative (quasi-legislative), review (quasi-judicial) and correction (enforcement) functions, and has noted that systems of international supervision may combine elements of all three.[a] This section emphasizes the review function, but the correction function is also quite apparent in some of the materials.

International organizations have devised a variety of ways to try to settle disputes among members, or to provide them with interpretations of their obligations under constituent instruments or related conventions.[b] Some of these mechanisms are spelled out in constituent instruments; some of them have simply been developed by the organizations in response to needs that may not have been fully perceived at

---

a. See van Hoof & de Vey Mestdagh, Mechanisms of International Supervision, in Supervisory Mechanisms in International Economic Organisations 1, 11–14 (P. van Dijk ed. 1984).

b. For a summary of the dispute-settlement and interpretation procedures of the specialized agencies, see D. Bowett, The Law of International Institutions 147–51 (4th ed. 1982).

the outset.^c

The materials raise several questions: What leeway does the particular constituent instrument give for development of new mechanisms? How broad is the jurisdiction of the dispute-settlement or interpretive body? Is the particular method essentially adjudicative—involving relatively formal proceedings by which facts are found and legal principles are applied, with an outcome binding on the parties? Or is it conciliatory, with the thrust being to help the parties settle any dispute themselves, without much attention to following or establishing precedent? Or is it advisory, to be used even if—or only if—there is no active dispute between parties? Why would the particular mechanism be where it is on this spectrum?

What safeguards are there to ensure that impartial decisions will be made? What provisions for appeals are there, and are they useful? What is the effect of a decision on member states not directly involved in the case? Would a particular decision have any binding or persuasive effect outside the body that issues it? To what extent is a particular dispute-settlement mechanism also an enforcement mechanism?

A. THE INTERNATIONAL LABOR ORGANIZATION

The ILO has a number of procedures—some expressly contemplated in its Constitution and some having evolved separately—that play a part in dispute settlement and interpretation of the ILO Constitution or labor conventions. One of these—the system of ILO review of reports by member states on measures they have taken to give effect to labor conventions they have ratified—is more a compliance mechanism than a dispute-settlement or interpretive one, and thus will be studied in the next chapter. The others, to be examined in this subsection, include (1) the procedure for Commissions of Inquiry to investigate complaints of governments' noncompliance with ratified conventions; (2) the procedure for representations from employers' or workers' associations about governments' noncompliance; (3) the related procedure for the Governing Body's Committee on Freedom of Association; and (4) interpretation of labor conventions outside these procedures.

1. *Complaints and Commissions of Inquiry*

ILO Constitution *articles 26–33* establish a procedure for investigating complaints that a member is not "securing the effective observance" of any labor convention it has ratified. Such complaints may be filed by any member state that has ratified the same convention or by

---

c. One of the more sophisticated of these has been developed in the General Agreement on Tariffs and Trade (GATT), which is not a specialized agency of the U.N. though it serves much the same function a specialized trade agency would. Space does not permit examination of the GATT dispute-settlement system, which involves panels of trade specialists appointed by, and reporting to, the GATT Council.

any delegate to the International Labor Conference. In addition, the ILO Governing Body, itself, may initiate the procedure. See article 26. The Governing Body may appoint a Commission of Inquiry, whose functions are set out in article 28. In theory, at least, there is a right of appeal from Commission of Inquiry reports to the International Court of Justice. See articles 29, 31 and 32.

C.W. JENKS, SOCIAL JUSTICE IN THE LAW OF NATIONS
48–54 (Royal Institute of International Affairs, 1970).*

For many years this procedure appeared to be a dead letter. A complaint concerning the application of the Hours of Work (Industry) Convention, 1919, to Indian railways was submitted by the Indian Workers' delegate to the Conference in 1934, but the Governing Body did not consider it necessary to appoint a Commission of Inquiry. The procedure was not invoked again until 1961.

Why the procedure remained unused for so long is largely a speculative matter. The answer is perhaps primarily that the availability of less formal procedures, and in particular the regular discussion of annual reports at the International Labour Conference, reduced the number of occasions for recourse to it, but partly that the special advantages which it might present were not fully appreciated; until the procedure had been successfully applied it remained a somewhat feared unknown; no doubt many governments hesitated, and still hesitate, to set precedents which might be followed by invoking the procedure against themselves.

In 1961 Ghana submitted a complaint alleging failure by Portugal to fulfil her obligations under the Abolition of Forced Labour Convention 1957. The Governing Body appointed a Commission of Inquiry to consider the complaint and it fell to that Commission to put the flesh upon the bare bones of constitutional provisions which, prior to its appointment, had come to be widely regarded as obsolete and inoperative.[68]

The Commission was conscious, it states in its report, "not only of the absence of specific precedents for the procedural decisions which it was called upon to make, but also of the significance for the future of the manner in which it discharged its duties". On taking up their duties the members of the Commission had made a solemn declaration which was in effect an oath of office based on that made by judges of the International Court of Justice. The Commission emphasized

---

* Reprinted by permission of The Royal Institute of International Affairs.

68. The Chairman of the Commission was Ambassador Paul Ruegger of Switzerland who had previously been Chairman of the International Committee of the Red Cross and had served as Chairman of the ILO Forced Labour Committee; his colleagues were a former judge of the International Court of Justice (Enrique Armand-Ugon) who had previously been Chief Justice of Uruguay and the Chief Justice of Senegal (Isaac Forster), subsequently elected a judge of the International Court of Justice.

throughout the judicial nature of its task, but considered "that its functions were not confined to examining only such information as might be submitted by or in support of the parties", but that it should itself take all necessary steps to ensure, in accordance with the general directive given to it by the Governing Body, that it had at its disposal "thorough and objective information concerning the questions at issue". This directive provided that the Commission should begin its work by examining the particulars furnished by the Government of Ghana and the observations of the Government of Portugal with a view to determining on which matters it needed fuller information, and should then, through the Director–General, consult the Governments of Ghana and Portugal, but without being bound by the views of either of them, with a view to ensuring that it had at its disposal such thorough and objective information. The procedure adopted included written statements by the parties and an opportunity to submit information from a number of governments and non-governmental organizations selected by the Commission. The Commission requested the Government of Portugal to arrange for the presence of witnesses whom it wished to hear; all of the witnesses so requested attended and gave evidence. Each party was also given, and Ghana availed herself of, the opportunity to call witnesses. All witnesses were heard in Geneva in private but in the presence of both parties who had full opportunity of cross-examination; the Commission itself questioned the witnesses extensively. There were opening and closing addresses by counsel for each side.

At various successive stages of its procedure the Commission had to consider whether it had before it allegations or evidence sufficiently precise to justify its proceeding further in the matter; at each of these stages it took the view that the public importance of the issues raised by the complaint justified it in pursuing the matter further, but that it should not be assumed in any future case that so full an inquiry was called for as a matter of course in the absence of the submission by the complainant of substantial evidence or a strong *prima facie* case.

On completing the hearing of witnesses, the Commission decided that, without prejudging the question of whether or not it had any satisfactory evidence of failure to give effect to the provisions of the Convention, it was desirable for it to visit Angola and Mozambique for the purpose of completing the information at its disposal; it received the full co-operation of the Portuguese authorities in arranging such visits.

The visits were carried out in accordance with a programme drawn up by the Commission and accepted by the Portuguese authorities; they did not include formal hearings or any other arrangements which "would have involved the exercise of special powers of inspection and judicial investigation" but were designed primarily for the purpose of enabling the Commission

> to gain a direct impression of the situation in the territories mentioned in the complaint and to know the practical conditions in

which the main economic activities mentioned in the allegations were carried out, while also providing an opportunity to check the exactitude of these allegations.

With this general purpose the Commission sought information from various representatives of the administrative authorities, from representatives of the management of every private or public undertaking visited, and from manpower and personnel managers. One of the main objects of the visit was to afford the Commission an opportunity to speak directly to African workers; by deciding itself where it wanted to go and choosing the workers whom it wished to question without prior warning and at the last moment it was able to talk freely and spontaneously with a large number of workers without the presence of any representative of management or of the authorities; adequate interpretation facilities for this purpose were available throughout.

* * *

On the conclusion of the visits to Angola and Mozambique the Commission decided that it had the information necessary to complete its report. The report, which was unanimous, contains its findings of law and fact and far-reaching recommendations for further remedial action; these included a recommendation that the Committee of Experts on the Application of Conventions and Recommendations should be kept regularly informed of progress. The Commission summarized briefly as follows the essence of its substantive findings. Forced labour was for many years a major factor in the economies of many African countries. Recourse to forced labour has been increasingly condemned. The decisive steps in this evolution were the adoption by the ILO of the Forced Labour Convention, 1930, and the Abolition of Forced Labour Convention, 1957. Although Portugal enacted the abolition of slavery in 1858 with effect from 1878 (thus taking legislative action in the matter prior to the United States and fully abolishing slavery prior to Brazil), her action lagged substantially behind that of the majority of states with responsibilities in Africa in the abolition of forced labour. For this reason, forced labour had come to be widely associated with Portuguese Africa. There was, however, no question of any failure to discharge an international obligation in the matter during the period preceding 1956, as no international obligation had been assumed. Far-reaching changes had occurred in Portuguese policy, legislation, and practice in connection with the ratification of the Forced Labour Convention, 1930, on 26 June 1956, and the ratification of the Abolition of Forced Labour Convention, 1957, on 23 November 1959. While fully satisfied of the *bona fides* of the changes made in Portuguese policy, the Commission was not satisfied that all of the obligations of the Abolition of Forced Labour Convention, 1957, were implemented in full as from the date of the coming into force of the Convention for Portugal, namely 23 November 1960. It noted a number of cases in which important changes for the purpose of bringing the law and practice into full conformity with the requirements of the Convention had been made since the complaint was lodged, but in which the provisions of the Convention were not fully applied immediately after its coming into force for Portugal. It also formulated important findings and recommendations concerning further steps necessary to give full effect to the provisions of the Convention, including: a substantial reinforcement of the labour inspection service; a comprehensive manpower policy, including provision for periodical manpower surveys, a public employment service at major employment centres in replacement of earlier methods of recruitment of labour, a broadly-based programme of intensive vocational training, and measures to correct endemic underemployment; further measures to make conditions of employment sufficiently attractive to secure the necessary labour without compulsion; and grievance procedures adequate to enable the worker to secure redress for violation of the law without victimization. There has continued to be political controversy concerning the matter but the report was accepted by both parties and substantial progress appears to have been made in implementing the recommendations of the Commission * * *.

While the proceedings in the Ghana-Portugal case were pending, Portugal initiated what were in effect counter-proceedings by charging Liberia with failure to fulfil her obligations under the Forced Labour Convention, 1930, and a second Commission was appointed by the Governing Body to consider this new complaint.

The Portugal-Liberia Commission modelled its procedure on that of the Ghana-Portugal Commission, of which its Chairman had been a member, but was called upon to consider some new situations and problems.

The Liberian Government claimed, before the Governing Body and again at the opening of the oral proceedings, that the complaint should be summarily dismissed on the grounds that it was politically motivated, that it was in the nature of a reprisal, and that the substance of the complaint had been met: the Commission rejected the first two of these submissions and considered it necessary to examine the substance of the complaint in order to pass upon the third.

Apart from this claim for the summary dismissal of the complaint and its rejection, the procedure followed, until the completion of the hearing of witnesses, much the same course as that of the earlier Commission.

* * *

The Commission gave a number of interesting rulings on matters of evidence. It declined to hold extracts from publications and affidavits inadmissible as evidence but treated them as of little value; it held that the technical rules of evidence applied to the conduct of trials in municipal courts were inapplicable to its proceedings and that it could not disregard an allegation because it had not been fully proved if the facts were peculiarly within the knowledge of the respondent government and that government had not thought fit to make a full and frank disclosure of them; it indicated that while it would naturally treat with great respect a view expressed by the Attorney–General of Liberia on a matter of Liberian law, it must also have regard to his admission that the Supreme Court had never had occasion to decide the matter and to the fact that his view, which was in the nature of an *ex parte* statement before the Commission, would not be binding upon the Supreme Court.

The central issues in the case were the inconsistency of Liberian legislation with the requirements of the Convention and the failure of Liberia to furnish the reports on its application required by the [ILO] Constitution; in the course of the proceedings the major discrepancies between the laws of Liberia and the requirements of the Convention were eliminated by the amendment of the legislation, though some anomalies remained to be rectified, a report was furnished and undertakings for the future were given.

LATER CASES

Since 1970, when Jenks wrote the summary above, the complaints procedure has picked up steam. As of March 1992, at least 15 complaints had been filed, and nine of those had been referred to Commissions of Inquiry. The respondent states in referred cases, in addition to Portugal and Liberia, have been Greece, Chile, Haiti and the Dominican Republic (co-respondents), Poland, the Federal Republic of Germany, Romania and Nicaragua.

We will focus on the complaint against Poland. It was a particularly sensitive case, involving important freedom of association issues stemming from attempts by the then-government of Poland to curb Solidarity, the independent trade union whose activities ultimately led to the demise of the communist government and the rise to the Polish Presidency of Lech Walesa, the Solidarity leader.

The complainants were two workers' delegates to the International Labor Conference, one from France and the other from Norway. The Governing Body appointed a Commission of Inquiry consisting of Nicolas Valticos (Greece; former Assistant Director–General of the ILO), Chair; Andrés Aguilar (Venezuela; former President of the International Labor Conference) and Jean François Aubert (Switzerland; Professor of Constitutional Law), members. Despite the Commission's efforts to obtain Poland's cooperation, the government of Poland refused to participate in the proceedings on the ground that they constituted an interference in its domestic affairs. The Commission went ahead anyway.

Set forth below are excerpts from the Commission's report, showing the procedure it established (very much like the procedure other recent Commissions of Inquiry have used), and giving samples from the Commission's conclusions.

REPORT OF THE COMMISSION INSTITUTED UNDER ARTICLE 26 TO EXAMINE THE COMPLAINT ON THE OBSERVANCE BY POLAND OF THE FREEDOM OF ASSOCIATION AND RIGHT TO ORGANIZE CONVENTIONS

67 ILO Official Bulletin, Series B, Special Supp., at 2–3, 21–23, 125–27, 130–31, 133–37, 148–49 (1984).

1. * * * The complaint is worded as follows:

Mr. Secretary–General of the Conference,

The undersigned Workers' delegates at the 68th Session (1982) of the International Labour Conference hereby lodge with the International Labour Office, under article 26 of the Constitution of the International Labour Organisation, a complaint concerning failure by the Government of Poland to observe Conventions Nos. 87 and 98.

The complaint is based on the following facts.

I. According to indications officially furnished by the Polish authorities following the proclamation of martial law in Poland on 13 December 1981, the activities of trade union organisations have been suspended and many members and leaders of the Solidarity trade union, including those who represented the Polish workers at the 67th Session of the International Labour Conference (1981), have been arrested and have remained interned to this day. Moreover, pursuant to the proclamation of martial law, the right to strike has been suspended, and workers and trade unionists have been prosecuted and sentenced for going on strike. These decisions and these measures constitute in themselves a violation of Article 4 of Convention No. 87, which states that "workers' and employers' organisations shall not be liable to be dissolved or suspended by administrative authority", and of Article 3, which provides that:

"1. Workers' and employers' organisations shall have the right to draw up their constitutions and rules, to elect their representatives in full freedom, to organise their administration and activities and to formulate their programmes.

2. The public authorities shall refrain from any interference which would restrict this right or impede the lawful exercise thereof."

II. It appears also, in the light of the information available, that trade unionists have been dismissed from their jobs by reason of their trade union affiliation and activity; moreover, loyalty oaths entailing renunciation of affiliation to the Solidarity trade union have been required under penalty of dismissal, in particular from certain categories of public servants * * *. This practice constitutes a clear-cut violation of Article 1 of Convention No. 98, which provides that "workers shall enjoy adequate protection against acts of anti-union discrimination".

* * *

IV. It appears that among the various measures of internment decided by the Polish authorities * * * courts have sentenced many workers to several years of imprisonment and to loss of their civic rights on the grounds of trade union activities and strike action. Finally, further arrests seem to have taken place, as shown by the lists attached.[1]

* * *

Geneva, 16 June 1982.

(*Signed*) Marc Blondel, (*Signed*) Liv Buck,
Delegate of the workers of France   Delegate of the workers of Norway

2. Poland ratified Conventions Nos. 87 and 98 on 25 February 1957. These Conventions came into force for the country on 25 February 1958. The complainants, Mr. Blondel and Mrs. Buck, were, at the time when they filed their complaint, Workers' delegates of their countries to the 68th Session of the Conference and, as such, empowered, under article 26, paragraph 4, of the Constitution of the ILO, to file a complaint.

* * *

64. The Commission invited the Government of Poland to nominate a person empowered to represent it before the Commission with any substitutes it might wish. The Commission asked the complainants to state whether they intended to attend the session personally and, if not, to supply the names of their representatives and any substitutes.

65. The Commission drew up a list of witnesses it wished to hear. It informed the Government of Poland that it wished to hear as witnesses the Ministers of Labour, the Interior, Justice and Trade Union Affairs or their representatives. It also informed the Government that, wishing to have a general view of the different trends in the Polish trade union movement, it considered that the evidence of the following persons, or of persons empowered to represent them, should be heard: the Polish Workers' delegate and substitute delegates to the 67th Session of the International Labour Conference in June 1981, the Polish Employers' delegate who took part in the same session of the Conference and the leaders of the trade unions set up under the Trade Union Act of 8 October 1982. The Commission informed the complainants of this step.

66. The Commission addressed letters to the Polish Workers' and Employers' delegates to the 67th Session of the International Labour

---

1. Lists of 182 persons sentenced to imprisonment and 113 persons under arrest were appended to the complaint.

Conference in June 1981, informing them that they were invited to come and give evidence before it in that capacity or to appoint a person empowered to represent them.

67. The Commission invited the Government of Poland and the complainants to communicate, before 10 December 1983, the names and descriptions of the witnesses they wished to designate, with a brief indication of the points on which these persons wished to give evidence. It informed them that it would itself decide, on the basis of the information obtained in this way, whether it would hear each of the witnesses in question.

68. The Commission also decided to invite those workers' and employers' organisations having consultative status with the ILO and universal in scope to designate representatives to explain their views during the session and informed the Government and the complainants accordingly.

69. The Commission asked the Government of Poland to ensure that the persons whom the Commission thought should be heard as witnesses and the persons designated by the Government and also any witnesses proposed by the complainants could, if they lived in Poland, come to give evidence in Geneva and enjoy full protection against any kind of measure that might be taken against them by reason of their statements before the Commission and, in particular, that no obstacle should be placed in the way of their return to Poland.

70. The Commission adopted the [following] rules of procedure:

* * *

Rules for the Hearing of Witnesses

1. The Commission will hear all witnesses in private sittings. The information and evidence presented to the Commission therein are to be treated as absolutely confidential by all persons whom the Commission permits to be present.

2. The Government of Poland and the complainants will each be requested to designate a representative to act on their behalf before the Commission. The representatives will be expected to be present throughout the hearing of witnesses and will be responsible for the general presentation of their witnesses and evidence.

3. Witnesses may not be present except when giving evidence.

* * *

5. The function of the Commission is to ascertain facts. The opportunity to furnish evidence and to make statements is given only for the purpose of obtaining factual information bearing on the matters that the Commission has been set up to examine. The Commission will give witnesses all reasonable latitude to furnish such information but will not accept any communication or statement of a political character or in any other way irrelevant to the issues referred to it.

6. The Commission will require each witness to make a solemn declaration identical to that provided for in the Rules of Court of the International Court of Justice. This declaration reads: "I solemnly declare upon my honour and conscience that I will speak the truth, the whole truth and nothing but the truth."

7. Each witness will be given an opportunity to make a statement before questions are put to him. * * *

8. The Commission or any member of the Commission may put questions to witnesses at any stage.

9. The representatives or their substitutes present in accordance with the rules laid down in paragraph 2 above will be permitted to put questions to the witnesses, in an order to be determined by the Commission.

10. All questioning of witnesses will be subject to control by the Commission.

11. Any failure on the part of a witness to reply satisfactorily to a question put will be noted by the Commission.

12. The Commission reserves the right to recall witnesses, if necessary.

* * *

Conclusions on the Substance of the Case

477. The allegations made by the complainants had their origin in the measures taken by the authorities against the trade union movement—principally against Solidarity—following the proclamation of martial law in Poland on 13 December 1981. In the information and observations furnished [to other ILO bodies,] the Government of Poland insisted on the necessity of taking account of the political, economic and social situation in Poland before martial law, which would have led the country to the brink of civil war, led to a growing crisis in the economy and endangered the fundamental interests of the Polish nation and State. The complainants and various international trade union organisations, in the documents that they supplied to the Commission, also referred to the period preceding martial law to indicate that in their opinion none of the activities of Solidarity justified the repressive measures taken by the Government.

* * *

478. The * * * Commission received a considerable quantity of information, both in the written documents submitted to it and during the session devoted to the hearing of evidence.

* * *

International Obligations Under Conventions Nos. 87 and 98 and Martial Law

479. Before dealing with these various points, the Commission considers it useful to examine the question raised by the fact that the

measures alleged by the complainants were initially taken under martial law. This problem was already considered by an earlier Commission of Inquiry appointed under article 26 of the Constitution of the ILO to examine complaints relating to the violation of Conventions Nos. 87 and 98.[16] As that Commission pointed out, neither of these Conventions contains a provision allowing the possibility of basing a plea of emergency, as an exception to the obligations arising under the Conventions, on the terms of the Conventions themselves. Furthermore, the plea of emergency to justify restrictions on the civil liberties that are essential to the proper exercise of trade union rights can be advanced before an international authority only in circumstances of extreme gravity constituting a case of *force majeure* and provided that any measures affecting the application of the Convention are limited in scope and in duration to what is strictly necessary to deal with the situation in question.

480. In the present case, the information in the possession of the Commission on the circumstances prevailing before the proclamation of martial law do not enable it to conclude that a situation existed in Poland such as to justify the temporary non-observance of the Conventions in question. * * * Even if it were admitted that a situation of emergency existed in December 1981, the measures which this might have justified could be taken only "to the extent strictly required by the exigencies of the situation", and the complete suppression of the entire trade union movement would have gone beyond these exigencies, as appearing from the information available.

* * *

Suspension and Dissolution of Trade Union Organisations

482. The measures taken by the authorities after the proclamation of martial law led to the complete liquidation of the trade union structures which had existed during the preceding period. * * *

483. To justify the proclamation of martial law and the measures suspending trade union activity that resulted from it and the subsequent dissolution of the trade unions, the Government of Poland insisted on the necessity of averting the imminent danger of civil war, restoring law and order, ensuring the normal operation of the state administration and saving the national economy from collapse. The Government maintained that * * * extremist elements among the leaders of Solidarity had directed the organisation towards political action and called for the seizure of power and the overthrow of the political system. According to the leaders of the branch unions, certain

---

16. Report of the Commission appointed under article 26 of the Constitution of the International Labour Organisation to examine the complaints concerning the observance by Greece of the Freedom of Association and Protection of the Right to Organise Convention, 1948 (No. 87), and of the Right to Organise and Collective Bargaining Convention, 1949 (No. 98), ILO: *Official Bulletin*, Vol. LIV, No. 2, Special supplement, 1971, paras. 102–112, pp. 24–26.

groups within Solidarity even had arms and the country was thus heading for open confrontation.

* * *

493. Having examined the reasons underlying the measures taken by the authorities, the Commission must deal with the conformity—or non-conformity—with Convention No. 87 of the procedure followed in suspending and then dissolving the trade unions. The suspension of trade union activities was decreed on 13 December 1981 by the President of the Council of Ministers on the basis of the Decree of 12 December 1981 respecting martial law. It was thus a measure taken by administrative authority constituting an evident violation of Article 4 of Convention No. 87, which provides that "workers' and employers' organisations shall not be liable to be dissolved or suspended by administrative authority".

* * *

496. As to the cancellation of the registration of the existing trade unions by virtue of the Trade Union Act, the Government has stated that it was unable to resort to a judicial procedure since this would have revived profound divisions in society. It emphasised that this measure did not constitute dissolution by administrative authority but a decision of the supreme legislative body and that there was therefore no breach of the guarantees provided for by Article 4 of the Convention, which covered only administrative decisions.

* * *

498. * * * [I]n the opinion of the Commission, the essential aspect of the problem is not so much that of the compatibility or incompatibility of dissolution by legislative authority with Article 4 of Convention No. 87. The essential point is that the principal consequence of the cancellation of the registration of the trade unions and of the absence of all possibility of re-establishing similar ones was to deprive the workers of the right to join the existing unions which had been freely and lawfully set up since 1980, and thus of joining organisations of their own choosing. It has to be concluded that the Act of 8 October 1982, by pronouncing the dissolution of the trade unions, infringed the guarantees provided for by Article 2 of Convention No. 87 respecting the free choice of organisations and at the same time violated Article 8, paragraph 2, of the Convention, under which the law of the land shall not be such as to impair, nor be applied so as to impair, the guarantees provided for by the Convention.

* * *

Internment and Conviction of Leaders and Members of Solidarity

506. The documents submitted to the Commission devote much space to the mass measures of arrest and detention taken against the leaders and members of Solidarity. The trade unionists who have been,

or are, in detention can be divided into two main groups: those—the greater number—who were interned under martial law, because "their previous behavior suggested that they would not respect law and order or that they would carry on activities contrary to security or the defence of the State", and those who have been prosecuted in the courts and sentenced or whose trial is still going on, most of whom have been prosecuted for infringing the provisions of martial law or for attempting to overthrow the political system in force.

* * *

508. Another important element in the information furnished to the Commission relates to the conditions of internment prevailing in the camps. It was affirmed, by eye witnesses among others, that physical coercion and brutality—sometimes with lasting effects—had been used against the internees and that, in general, the conditions imposed on detainees were often very severe, particularly during the early days of internment.

* * *

512. It is appropriate to evaluate the facts concerning the internment and detention of leaders and members of trade unions in the light of the provisions of Article 3 of Convention No. 87. This article, after stating that workers' and employers' organisations shall have the right to draw up their constitutions and rules, to elect their representatives in full freedom, to organise their administration and activities and to formulate their programmes, provides that "the public authorities shall refrain from any interference which would restrict this right or impede the lawful exercise thereof". Furthermore, the guarantees thus granted to trade union organisations can be effectively ensured only if a number of basic civil liberties are respected. The Commission must once more refer to the resolution, adopted without opposition by the International Labour Conference in 1970, concerning trade union rights and their relation to civil liberties. In this resolution, which thus reflects the views of the parties to the Convention on the implications of the Convention, the International Labour Conference put particular emphasis on certain civil liberties defined in the Universal Declaration of Human Rights and in the Covenant on Civil and Political Rights, ratified by Poland, which it stressed as essential for the normal exercise of trade union rights. These include the right to freedom and security of persons and freedom from arbitrary arrest and detention; freedom of opinion and expression and in particular freedom to hold opinions without interference and to seek, receive and impart information and ideas through any media and regardless of frontiers; freedom of assembly and the right to a fair trial by an independent and impartial tribunal.

513. It follows from all these elements that Convention No. 87 has neither the aim nor the effect of prohibiting a government from using its legitimate powers in respect of law and order when trade unionists

commit crimes or offences covered by national law. * * * On the other hand, these rules do imply both that the public authorities cannot deprive trade unionists of their freedom for reasons related to their membership or their legitimate trade union activity or in order to put an end to such membership or activity and that, when trade unionists are accused of political or criminal offences that the government considers to be unrelated to their trade union activities, the persons in question shall have the benefit of normal judicial proceedings initiated at the earliest possible moment.

514. Since the arrest or conviction of trade unionists does not in itself constitute a violation of the Convention, the real grounds on which these measures were based must be sought and it is only if these measures were actually directed against trade union activities as such that there has been an infringement of the guarantees provided for by Convention No. 87. Furthermore, since the persons concerned are entitled to a presumption of innocence, it is incumbent on the government to show that the measures taken by it were not occasioned by the trade union activities of these persons.

515. If the statements of the Government on the grounds for the internments are considered, it will be seen that the Government confined itself to a general assertion that the measures were taken because of political activities and not because of trade union activities. No concrete evidence has been produced in support of this assertion. The Commission, however, is bound to note that the persons interned included the great majority of the national leaders and a large number of regional leaders of the organisation Solidarity. In the opinion of the Commission, it is difficult to conceive that so great a number of trade union leaders had undertaken activities likely to endanger the security or the defence of the State, whereas, as the Commission has already observed, shortly before the proclamation of martial law, the Congress of the organisation had adopted a programme that was essentially of a trade union nature. It will further be observed that the immense majority of the trade unionists interned were not subjected to any subsequent judicial investigation. These various elements may justify the belief that one of the aims of the Government, in depriving the majority of the leaders of Solidarity of their freedom, was to suppress or prevent the activities and development of the trade union movement embodied by this organisation and that it therefore acted in violation of Article 3 of Convention No. 87.

516. As the Commission has already stated, the grounds for the sentences pronounced by the courts were the organisation of strikes and participation in the strikes or the distribution of publications of the dissolved organisation Solidarity. The question that arises in these cases is thus to determine whether such activities can be considered to be of a trade union nature.

517. Convention No. 87 provides no specific guarantee concerning strikes. The supervisory bodies of the ILO, however, have always taken

the view—which is shared by the Commission—that the right to strike constitutes one of the essential means that should be available to trade union organisations for, in accordance with Article 10 of the Convention, furthering and defending the interests of their members. An absolute prohibition of strikes thus constitutes, in the view of the Commission, a serious restriction on the right of trade unions to organise their activities (Article 3 of the Convention) and, moreover, is in conflict with Article 8, paragraph 2, under which "the law of the land shall not be such as to impair, nor shall it be so applied as to impair, the guarantees provided for [by the Convention]".

518. As to the printing and the distribution of publications, the Commission must point out that the right to the free expression of thought is of special importance as an integral part of the freedom to which trade union organisations are entitled. As the Committee on Freedom of Association has often stressed,[27] the right to express opinions through the press or otherwise is one of the essential elements of trade union rights. The prohibition of trade union publications and the conviction of trade unionists for infringing this prohibition cannot therefore be anything but a violation of the right of trade unions to organise their activities, as recognised in Article 3 of Convention No. 87.

519. With regard to the nature of the legal proceedings instituted, the Commission is bound to observe that it has little information on the way in which the trials of the trade unionists were conducted. Although certain evidence given during the hearings alleged the failure to respect certain fundamental rights in the judicial field such as the right of defence, the Commission cannot, in view of the small number of concrete cases brought to its attention, conclude that, generally speaking, the guarantees of normal judicial procedure were systematically disregarded.

520. Another question concerning the detentions which the Commission must examine is that of the conditions imposed on the detainees and, in particular, the most serious allegation of all, the ill-treatment said to have been inflicted on them. The information from the Government available to the Commission on this point was extremely limited. However, from the many statements made during the hearings and the substantial documentation submitted to it on this point, the Commission is led to believe that the standard minimum rules for the treatment of prisoners[28] were not always observed in Poland during the period of martial law. This was true, in particular, of certain internment camps, where the rules regarding detention premises, food, physical exercise, contact with the outside world and the

---

27. See ILO: *Freedom of Association—Digest of decisions of the Freedom of Association Committee of the Governing Body of the ILO* (Geneva, 2nd edition, 1976), para. 399.

28. Adopted by First United Nations Congress on the Prevention of Crime and the Treatment of Offenders in 1955 and approved by the Economic and Social Council by resolutions of 1957 and 1977.

imposition of forced labour on persons detained and placed in the military camps seem to have been largely disregarded.

* * *

587. If Conventions Nos. 87 and 98 are to be fully observed in Poland, it is obviously indispensable that the legislation be amended to bring it into conformity with these texts. The fulfilment of this condition, though necessary, is not enough. The effective application of the Conventions on freedom of association is not merely a matter of texts. It also depends to a large extent on the general context, on the relations established between workers, employers and the public authorities and on the climate of freedom, dialogue and mutual respect in which these relations can be established.

* * *

590. * * * Such a climate presupposes and requires a general effort of understanding and agreement on the part of all concerned. The first measures taken by the Government, in suspending martial law and releasing most of the persons in detention, could be a move in this direction if they were followed by broad and generous measures for the release and amnesty of all workers still in prison or already sentenced on account of the recent events, by the abolition of all exceptional measures and by the full restoration of freedom of expression and of assembly. It would be of the greatest importance for the full observance of the Conventions on freedom of association if, as provided by the Final Act of the Conference on Security and Cooperation in Europe, adopted at Helsinki in 1975, the Government of Poland, which subscribed to that Act, were to "promote and encourage the effective exercise of civil, political, economic, social, cultural and other rights and freedoms all of which derive from the inherent dignity of the human person and are essential for his free and full development".

THE ROLE AND PRACTICE OF COMMISSIONS OF INQUIRY

Did the complainants in the proceedings described by Jenks, or in the case against Poland, have any direct stake in the outcome? Why would ILO Constitution *article 26(1)* and *(4)* have been drafted in such a way as to give them standing?

What do you think of the procedures for taking evidence adopted by the Commissions of Inquiry? How did the procedures in the proceedings described by Jenks differ from those in the case against Poland? Were any differences significant?

Note particularly the procedure in the case against Poland, in paragraphs 64–70 of the Report, and in the Commission's rules for the hearing of witnesses. Was the procedure well designed for fairness and thoroughness?

In the more recent case against the Federal Republic of Germany, another Commission of Inquiry adopted virtually identical rules for the hearing of witnesses, except that the introductory sentence of paragraph 5 ("The function of the Commission is to ascertain facts") was omitted.[a] Why do you suppose that sentence was omitted?

In connection with the previous question, compare the mandate for Commission of Inquiry reports, in ILO Constitution *article 28*, with the scope of the report in the case against Poland. Did the Commission go beyond the mandate of article 28?

Would you characterize the proceedings of Commissions of Inquiry as primarily adjudicative? As primarily conciliatory?

The case against Poland is interesting on several levels. We have already considered it on a procedural level. Politically, it put pressure on the government of Poland to ease up on Solidarity and it may in some degree have contributed to the communist government's eventual demise. Of course, it is not a purpose of the ILO Commission of Inquiry process to bring about the demise of governments, and there is no indication that the Commission in the case against Poland set out to do so. Nevertheless, it is legitimate to ask whether any pro-union, anti-government bias may have slipped in. Do you think so?

On a more jurisprudential level, the case is interesting as a contribution to the development of international labor law. In particular:

In paragraphs 479–80, the Commission dealt with the argument that an emergency was at hand in Poland, possibly justifying some departures from the freedom of association conventions (numbers 87 and 98) through the imposition of martial law. The Commission found no such exception written into the conventions, yet it indicated that *force majeure* might justify limited departures. It then found that conditions in Poland did not qualify for the *force majeure* exception, and even if they did, the government's measures went too far. Where did the Commission get all this? From customary international law? Was it just applying the basic treaty rule of *rebus sic stantibus* (fundamental change of circumstances), without saying so?

Do you have any problems with the Commission's conclusions on the suspension and dissolution of trade union organizations (paragraphs 482–498)?

Regarding the internment of Solidarity leaders, the Commission concluded in paragraph 515 that the "various elements [identified in that paragraph] may justify the belief that one of the aims of the Government, in depriving the majority of the leaders of Solidarity of their freedom, was to suppress or prevent the activities and development of the trade union movement embodied by this organisation and that it therefore acted in violation of Article 3 of Convention No. 87." For Article 3, see paragraph I of the complaint in this case, at page 395

a. 70 ILO Official Bulletin, Series B, Supp. 1, at 21–22 (1987).

supra. Was this a holding that Poland had violated Article 3? Does Article 3 clearly prohibit internment of labor leaders for their trade union activities? If not, how did the Commission arrive at its conclusion?

Note the Commission's allocation of the burden of proof on this point, in paragraph 514. Was that important to the outcome? Was it proper?

The Commission found other violations of Article 3 of Convention No. 87. See paragraphs 517 (right to strike) and 518 (freedom of expression). Can these conclusions be justified, in terms of what Article 3 actually says?

In paragraph 520, the Commission said it believed that Poland did not always observe the Standard Minimum Rules for the Treatment of Prisoners in connection with the detentions of Solidarity members. As footnote 28 indicates, the Standard Minimum Rules have the force of recommendations by the U.N. Economic and Social Council for the humane treatment of prisoners. Is it the business of an ILO Commission of Inquiry to make determinations regarding violations of those Rules?

Among the Standard Minimum Rules the Commission said "seem[ed] to have been largely disregarded" are the rule that every prisoner is to be provided with nutritious, wholesome food at the usual hours, the rule that every prisoner is to have at least an hour of daily exercise outside if weather permits, and the rule that prisoners are to be allowed to communicate with family and friends at regular intervals.[b] Is this case authority for the proposition that those rules are part of customary international law? If so, or if even arguably so, note the relevance of ILO Commission of Inquiry reports for lawyers engaged in international human rights work, even when the victims of abuses are not trade union members.

In paragraphs 587 and 590, page 404 supra, the Commission made recommendations. Were they within the mandate of ILO Constitution article 28? Did they amount to interference in Poland's domestic affairs?

Note that ILO Constitution *articles 29, 31* and *32* permit appeal of a Commission of Inquiry report to the International Court of Justice. No such appeals have been taken. Could appeals be taken in all cases? For example, if Poland had wished to appeal from the report above, could it have done so in light of ICJ Statute *article 34(1)?*

If an appeal is properly before the ICJ, it could presumably hold a hearing de novo, under the procedure set forth in ICJ Statute *articles*

---

b. Standard Minimum Rules for the Treatment of Prisoners, paras. 20(1), 21(1), 37, in U.N. Centre for Human Rights, Human Rights: A Compilation of International Instruments 190, 193–94, 197, U.N. Doc. ST/HR/1/Rev. 3 (1988).

42–52. Thus it would be in a position to review a Commission of Inquiry's findings of fact.[c] Would you have as much confidence in its findings as you would in those of a Commission of Inquiry?

Could the ICJ review a Commission of Inquiry's conclusions of law? If so, would it be better equipped than a Commission to determine what the law is?

How could the ICJ review a Commission's recommendations, such as those in the cases involving Portugal and Poland, as contemplated in ILO Constitution article 32?

Could a better appellate procedure be devised?

Consider whether a respondent state would be bound by a Commission of Inquiry's report if no appeal is taken. The then-Chief of the International Labor Standards Department of the ILO has said that "The Commissions of Inquiry which may be appointed to investigate complaints are called upon to decide, as a question of law, whether a Convention is being observed; their decisions are binding unless one of the parties appeals to the International Court of Justice."[d] Presumably, if they are binding it is because the ILO Constitution makes them so. The only provisions that could do so are in *articles 28–33*. Do they make decisions of Commissions of Inquiry binding? Would all aspects of the decisions—findings of fact, conclusions of law, and recommendations—be binding?

Isn't it an oxymoron to say that "recommendations" could be binding? Does ILO Constitution article 33 nevertheless have that effect?

If two ILO member states have a dispute over the effective observance of a labor convention they have both ratified, including a dispute over the relevant facts, could they agree to submit their dispute to a mechanism for dispute settlement outside the ILO?

This question could arise under the proposed United Nations Rules for the Conciliation of Disputes Between States. The U.N. Rules would establish a nonmandatory form of third-party conciliation of disputes between states, other than "disputes of a purely legal nature in which

---

c. Article 87(1) of the ICJ Rules of Court provides that when a case is brought "concerning a matter which has been the subject of proceedings before some other international body, the provisions of the Statute and of the Rules governing contentious cases shall apply." 17 Int'l Legal Materials 1286, 1300 (1978). The Rules include detailed provisions for written and oral proceedings. There is nothing to suggest that an appeal could not raise questions of fact as well as questions of law.

d. Valticos, The International Labour Organisation: Its Contribution to the Rule of Law and the International Protection of Human Rights, 9 J. of the Int'l Comm'n of Jurists, No. 2, at 3, 24 (1968). See also Osieke, The Exercise of the Judicial Function with Respect to the International Labour Organisation, 47 Brit.Y.B.Int'l L. 315, 336–39 (1974–75).

no questions of responsibility or reparation arise and in which there is no disagreement as regards the facts." [e] The proposed Rules define the roles of the conciliator or conciliation commission and of the disputing states. An explanatory comment says that if the disputing states are parties to a multilateral convention containing conciliation provisions, they may agree to use the U.N. Rules rather than the multilateral convention provisions, taking into account that article 41 of the Vienna Convention on the Law of Treaties "requires them to inform States parties to the convention in question of the amendments that they have made in light of their decision to apply the [U.N. Rules]." [f] Presumably the ILO Constitution, with its article 26, would be such a "convention in question."

The International Labor Office, commenting on the proposed U.N. Rules, considered whether two disputing ILO member states could thus opt out of the article 26 procedure. The Labor Office said:

> There would seem to be no formal obstacle to the two States seeking conciliation under the draft [U.N. Rules] before a complaint is filed in accordance with the ILO Constitution, but this is perhaps unlikely. On the other hand, once a complaint has been filed, the further proceedings are in the hand of ILO organs and it is difficult to see how recourse to the United Nations conciliation procedure could then be envisaged (quite apart from the question whether a bilateral departure from the constitutional provisions, as envisaged in [the explanatory comment above], is permissible).[g]

Is the ILO analysis correct? Consider not only the ILO Constitution, but also Vienna Convention *article 41*.

2. *Representations Against Members*

ILO Constitution articles 24 and 25 allow associations of employers or of workers to make "representations" to the ILO that a member has failed to secure the effective observance within its jurisdiction of any labor convention to which it is a party. The procedure under these articles does not involve appointing a Commission of Inquiry, but rather a committee of three members of the ILO Governing Body. The committee consists of a government member, an employer member and a worker member. Under the Governing Body's Standing Orders (rules of procedure), the committee considers the allegations and reports back to the Governing Body. As in the case of "complaints" leading to Commissions of Inquiry, there is no requirement that the initiating party be directly affected by the member's infraction.

The "representation" procedure has been used more often than the "complaint" procedure. Since World War II, at least 24 representa-

---

e. Article 1(1), in U.N. Doc. A/C.6/45/L.2, Annex I (1990).

f. Id., Annex II, para. 4.

g. U.N. Doc. A/46/383, at 12 (1991).

tions under article 24 have been filed.[a] We will consider one such case which, like the Polish case above, came up in a politically charged context involving efforts by a then-communist Eastern European state to control internal dissent.

On January 1, 1977, some 257 Czechoslovak nationals issued the Charter 77 Manifesto, publicizing human rights violations allegedly committed by the Czechoslovak government. The allegations related primarily to freedom of expression and association. Shortly after the Manifesto was published, several of its authors and signatories were demoted or dismissed from their state-controlled jobs. This prompted the International Confederation of Free Trade Unions to file a representation under article 24.

REPORT OF THE COMMITTEE SET UP UNDER ARTICLE 24 TO CONSIDER THE REPRESENTATION ALLEGING NON–OBSERVANCE OF THE DISCRIMINATION CONVENTION BY CZECHOSLOVAKIA

May 29, 1978.
61 ILO Official Bulletin, Series A, No. 3, at 1.

1. By letter of 28 January 1977, the International Confederation of Free Trade Unions (ICFTU) presented a representation under article 24 of the Constitution of the International Labour Organisation, alleging non-observance of the Discrimination (Employment and Occupation) Convention, 1958 (No. 111), by the Government of Czechoslovakia.

2. The Discrimination (Employment and Occupation) Convention, 1958 (No. 111), was ratified by Czechoslovakia on 21 January 1964. It came into force for Czechoslovakia one year later, on 21 January 1965, under the normal procedure.

* * *

6. The Committee provided for under article 2, paragraph 3, of the Standing Orders was appointed by the Governing Body at its 203rd Session * * *.

[The Committee first decided that the representation was in the form prescribed by the Standing Orders. It then invited the ICFTU to supply further information, and invited the Czech government to submit its observations on the representation. Deadlines were set for these responses. Within its deadline, the ICFTU submitted further information, including copies of dismissal and demotion notices issued by the Czech government to some of the individuals involved. The government said it needed more time to reply, and ultimately submitted two sets of observations. The Committee then examined the merits:]

---

a. See V.–Y. Ghebali, The International Labour Organisation: A Case Study on the Evolution of U.N. Specialised Agencies 233 (1989).

13. The representation alleges that the Government has taken repressive measures affecting the employment of authors or signatories of documents which brought to public attention criticism of the Government's policy in the field of human rights. According to the individual notifications and judicial decisions * * *, dismissals with or without notice and other measures affected the employment of workers because they had signed or supported the Manifesto * * *, and court decisions held, in particular, that these dismissals had been validly carried out under sections 46(1)(e) or 53(1)(c) of the Labour Code.

14. Sections 46 and 53 of the Labour Code of Czechoslovakia [as of 1977] * * * enumerate a limited number of cases in which the employment relationship may be terminated with notice (s. 46), or, exceptionally, without notice (s. 53). Section 46(1)(e) authorises dismissal with notice "if the worker does not meet the criteria laid down by law for the performance of the agreed job or, through no fault of the organisation, does not fulfil requirements that are an essential condition for the proper performance of his work; * * *". Section 53(1)(c) permits dismissal without notice "if the worker has endangered the safety of the State and his retention in the organisation until the expiry of the period of notice is impossible without danger to the due performance of the organisation's tasks." * * *

16. Under Article 1 of Convention No. 111, the term "discrimination" includes in particular "any distinction, exclusion or preference made on the basis of * * * political opinion * * * which has the effect of nullifying or impairing equality of opportunity or treatment in employment or occupation" (paragraph 1(a)). "Any distinction, exclusion or preference in respect of a particular job based on the inherent requirements thereof shall not be deemed to be discrimination" (paragraph 2). Under Article 4 of the Convention, "Any measures affecting an individual who is justifiably suspected of, or engaged in, activities prejudicial to the security of the State shall not be deemed to be discrimination, provided that the individual concerned shall have the right to appeal to a competent body established in accordance with national practice."

* * *

19. [T]he question raised does not concern the formal compliance of the terms of sections 46 and 53 of the Labour Code with the Convention's provisions, nor those of court or other procedures existing under national legislation. On the other hand, it is important to determine whether the cases in which, under these provisions, a worker is considered as having endangered the security of the State or as having failed to meet the requirements or the discipline required for a job, are themselves consistent with the basic protection provided for by the Convention.

20. In its additional observations * * * the Government states that the allegations referred to in the representation, on the subject of the situation subsequent to the beginning of 1977, concern persons who,

after holding important posts in state administration, were engaged in activities aimed at the violation of the public order, at the hampering of the international position of the Czechoslovak Socialist Republic and at the achievement of a change of the socialist social order through unconstitutional methods. It refers to the tendentious character of the arguments of this group of persons on points such as the existence of hidden unemployment, the employment of women, the standard of living, admission to education. It states that the Czechoslovak constitutional system is, as in other States, protected by law against activities and attacks endangering it, and that the termination of employment was only carried out in a small number of cases, as a function of the concrete activity of the person and the incompatibility of such activity with his working assignment. The Government adds that freedom of expression is guaranteed by the Constitution; that citizens are at the same time obliged to uphold the Constitution and other laws and to pay heed to the interest of the socialist State and the society of working people; that persons are not subjected to sanctions for the expression of different political opinions, but that the permission to express opinions does not mean that to engage in activity prohibited by law or to violate the rules of employment.

21. The Committee notes that, according to the notifications and decisions submitted in support of the representation, these notifications and decisions were motivated by the workers signing or adhering to a document such as the Manifesto * * *. This Manifesto contains various criticisms concerning the policy of the Government, and it is not for the Committee to assess whether these criticisms are well founded or inaccurate. Nevertheless, whatever the nature of the assertions in this document, the Committee does not consider the general statements of the Government as constituting an adequate response to the specific allegations concerning dismissals and other measures referred to in the representation. It does not emerge from the information available that the signing or adhering to such a document could in itself be considered, in relation to the principal protection envisaged by the Convention on matters of political opinion * * *, as an activity against the security of the State or incompatible with the requirements of their forms of employment. Finally, the Committee notes that it does not emerge from the information available that the alleged decisions and measures were not in fact taken for the reasons referred to earlier in this paragraph, or that they have been reviewed.

22. [The Committee said that even though the Government had indicated its continuing willingness to cooperate, the Committee could not recommend that the Governing Body consider the Government's reply satisfactory for purposes of ILO Constitution articles 24 and 25.]

CONCLUSION

23. In light of the considerations set forth above, the Committee recommends to the Governing Body * * *:

(a) that it decide to open the discussion on the application of article 25 of the Constitution, under which, if the statement received is not deemed to be satisfactory by the Governing Body, the latter shall have the right to publish the representation and the statement made in reply to it;

(b) that at the present session it fix a date during its 208th Session (November 1978) on which the deliberations concerning this affair shall take place;

(c) that, in conformity with paragraph 5 of article 26 of the Constitution, it invite the Government in question to send a representative to take part in its discussions.

THE ARTICLE 24 PROCESS

What exactly did the committee find wrong with the Czech government's reply to the ICFTU representation? Was the committee sensitive to the sociopolitical system then in force in socialist states such as Czechoslovakia? Should it be sensitive to such things?

Did the committee make findings of fact or reach conclusions of law? If so, what were they? If not, what function did the committee serve?

The Governing Body decided, under ILO Constitution *article 25,* to publish the committee's report along with the representation and reply. Was it appropriate to publish the committee's report, under the terms of article 25? Was the decision to publish it primarily one relating to dispute settlement or to enforcement?

Sometimes the article 24 process leads to appointment of a Commission of Inquiry under article 26. This occurred, for example, when the World Federation of Trade Unions made a representation that the Federal Republic of Germany had violated the Discrimination Convention. The case concerned the eligibility for employment in certain public service positions of persons whose political attitudes or activities the government considered questionable. The committee submitted a report containing conclusions with which the German government disagreed. The Governing Body, acting under article 26(4), then appointed a Commission of Inquiry. It issued a lengthy report, judicious in tone, but nevertheless critical of the German government's policies.[b]

Is there a need for both the article 24 "representation" procedure and the article 26 "complaint" procedure? Does each serve a different purpose?

---

b. 70 ILO Official Bulletin, Series B, Supp. 1 (1987).

3. *Special Procedures on Freedom of Association*

At the heart of the labor movement is the right freely to form, join and participate in trade unions that are independent of employer control and that have the right to assert the economic interests of their members. The case against Poland showed that the ILO considers this to be so even in socialist societies. The principle is reflected in the preamble of the ILO Constitution, which expressly recognizes "the principle of freedom of association."

Several labor conventions have been drawn up to protect workers' right to organize. These include the Convention Concerning Freedom of Association and Protection of the Right to Organize, 1948 (ILO Convention No. 87), the Convention Concerning the Application of the Principles of the Right to Organize and to Bargain Collectively, 1949 (Convention No. 98), and the Convention Concerning the Promotion of Collective Bargaining, 1981 (Convention No. 154). The first two are particularly important, and have been widely ratified (though not by the United States). Convention No. 87 grants the basic right to form and join trade unions that are free from governmental interference. Convention No. 98 protects workers from anti-union discrimination by employers and from employer domination of trade unions.

It was feared at first that the two basic Conventions—particularly No. 87—would not be widely ratified for some time. If that happened, the article 26 Commission of Inquiry procedure would not be effective as to these basic trade union rights, because it depends on ratification by the states involved in the proceedings. Since the Governing Body placed considerable importance on the principles of freedom of association, it decided to establish special machinery in that field, modeled on the Commission of Inquiry, but not depending on ratification of the freedom of association conventions.[a]

As a result, in 1950 the Governing Body, in coordination with the U.N. Economic and Social Council, established a procedure for a nine-member Fact-Finding and Conciliation Commission. Members are to be persons of high standing, competence and impartiality. The nine members would not normally sit *en banc;* rather, the Commission sits in panels of three or five members. Complaints may be filed with the Governing Body, for referral to the Commission, by organizations of workers or employers, by governments, and by the U.N. General Assembly or Economic and Social Council.

This gave the Governing Body two commissions to which it could refer freedom of association disputes deserving of commission investigation and resolution. Complaints against a member state that has ratified the freedom of association conventions could be referred to a Commission of Inquiry under article 26, on the Governing Body's own motion if need be. Complaints against a state not party to at least one

---

[a]. See Nafziger, The International Labor Organization and Social Change: The Fact-Finding and Conciliation Commission on Freedom of Association, 2 N.Y.U.J. of Int'l L. & Politics 1, 11 (1969).

of the relevant conventions could be submitted to the Fact–Finding and Conciliation Commission. In the latter situation—involving a complaint against a state not party to a relevant convention—it was thought essential that consent of the government be obtained before the complaint could be referred to such a Commission. This requirement has meant that very few cases actually go to a Fact–Finding and Conciliation Commission. As of 1989, only five cases had been referred to one.[b]

When the Fact–Finding and Conciliation procedure was first established, complaints alleging violations of freedom of association rights were examined initially by the Officers of the Governing Body, in order to determine whether the consent of the respondent state should be sought for the referral of the complaint to the Commission. Shortly thereafter, in 1951, the Governing Body decided that the preliminary examination should be carried out by a broader group of its members. Accordingly, it established the Governing Body Committee on Freedom of Association, consisting of three government, three employer and three worker members, with an equal number of substitutes. The Committee meets in Geneva three times a year, and reports to the full Governing Body.

Although the Committee on Freedom of Association was originally conceived as a screening body, it began to expand its functions when it became evident that governments would not readily consent to referrals to the Fact–Finding and Conciliation Commission. Over time, it became a quasi-judicial body, considering freedom of association complaints on their merits, reaching conclusions, and making recommendations to the Governing Body as to what should be done in each case. It has now considered over 1500 cases, and has developed procedures by which it hears them.

When a complaint is received, the ILO Director–General informs the complainant that supporting information should be supplied within a month. If the complaint is sufficiently substantiated, it and the supporting materials are forwarded to the respondent government, which is requested to respond by a given date. The Committee may request further information from both parties. If the government fails to respond at all, the Committee may go forward with the case on the basis of whatever information is available to it. When governments do cooperate, a "direct contact" procedure is often used, by which an ILO representative is sent to the country concerned (with the government's express consent) to ascertain the facts and to seek solutions. In some cases, the Committee holds oral hearings. Once it has as much evidence as it needs or is likely to get, it prepares its report.[c]

b. See V.–Y. Ghebali, The International Labour Organisation: A Case Study on the Evolution of U.N. Specialised Agencies 236–37 (1989).

c. The foregoing summary is based primarily on ILO, Freedom of Association: Digest of Decisions and Principles of the Freedom of Association Committee of the Governing Body of the ILO 12–18 (3d ed. 1985).

The Committee publishes its reports in the ILO Official Bulletin. In each case it considers on the merits, it notes whether or not the respondent state has ratified the relevant freedom of association conventions, and then sets forth the complainant's allegations and the government's response, followed by its own conclusions and recommendations.

These materials consider two of the Committee's reported cases—one, like the Commission of Inquiry case involving Poland, a case arising from a highly volatile and well-publicized political situation; the other a more mundane, and more typical, freedom of association dispute.

The first case, below, arose out of the events leading up to, and including, the attack by Chinese troops on demonstrators in Tienanmen Square, Beijing, in June 1989. The complaint was filed by the International Confederation of Free Trade Unions (ICFTU) against the Chinese government. The Committee report excerpted below was the second report in the case, the first having been an interim one that concluded with requests to the Chinese government to reply to the complaint with specifics instead of generalities.[d]

COMPLAINT AGAINST THE GOVERNMENT OF CHINA PRESENTED BY THE INTERNATIONAL CONFEDERATION OF FREE TRADE UNIONS

ILO Committee on Freedom of Association Case No. 1500 (1990).
73 ILO Official Bulletin, Series B, No. 1, at 99.

* * *

289. China has ratified neither the Freedom of Association and Protection of the Right to Organise Convention, 1948 (No. 87), nor the Right to Organise and Collective Bargaining Convention, 1949 (No. 98).

A. Previous Examination of the Case

290. In the complaint submitted in June 1989 the ICFTU referred to the mass arrest of activists of the Workers' Autonomous Federation (WAF), an independent trade union movement created in May 1989 in several parts of China. Among the main grievances voiced by the WAF were the wide discrepancy in working and living conditions between the workers and the plant managers, the lack of workplace democracy, the lack of genuine workers' representation, the poor working conditions and the deterioration of the workers' living standards. On 28 May 1989 the WAF issued its statutes, the main thrust of which was that the organisation should be autonomous, independent and democratic and that it should serve the principles of representing and defending the workers' interests. The WAF was seeking ways to legalise its

---

d. The numbered paragraphs in the report represent paragraph numbering in the entire issue of the Official Bulletin, not the number of paragraphs in the individual report on China.

organisation within the Constitutional Order of the People's Republic of China.

291. According to the ICFTU, many and probably most of the WAF's representatives were killed during the army's attack on the crowd in Tiananmen Square during the night of 3–4 June 1989. However, the arrest of independent trade union activists began before the attack. Bai Dong Ping, a WAF leader, was allegedly arrested at the end of May 1989, released on 1 June and rearrested on 20 June and was believed to be held in Szechuan Province. Some detainees showing signs of violent beatings were shown on the television. Twenty-six workers were allegedly publicly tried at Changchun and condemned for blocking traffic and advocating a strike. On 21 June three workers from Shanghai were allegedly executed, after the initial Higher People's Court had upheld the death sentences passed three days earlier. The workers, Xu Guoming, Xie Hanwu and Yan Xuerong, were allegedly found guilty of setting alight a train which had crashed into a peaceful demonstration at a Shanghai railway station and of obstructing the fire-fighters' work.

* * *

294. In its reply, the Government stated that the ICFTU's complaint alleging the violation of Convention No. 87 was completely unfounded and was a case of blatant intervention in the internal affairs of China, which the Government could not accept. According to the Government, the events that took place in Beijing at the end of spring and the beginning of summer 1989 were politically motivated disturbances fomented by a group of individuals in collusion with certain anti-Chinese foreign forces, and organised according to a premeditated plan. The aim of the rebellion was to overthrow the Government and the socialist regime established by the Constitution.

295. The Government added that the Workers' Autonomous Federation was one of two groups that had organised and participated in the disturbances. The WAF did not represent the working masses and was merely an illegal organisation hastily improvised by a few individuals on behalf of the workers. It had incited the population to cease work by going on strike, barricaded roads against troops sent to apply martial law and engaged in frenzied beating, wrecking, looting, burning and massacring, thereby endangering the safety of the State and the interests of the people. The Government had been obliged to take drastic action to put a stop to the rebellion and to dissolve the WAF in order to defend law and order and preserve the life and property of the population. According to the Government, no foreign country, international organisation or foreigner whatsoever had the right to interfere in this matter. The Government had dissolved the WAF quite simply because it was violating the Constitution and the laws of the country, and this, in the Government's view, had nothing to do with Convention No. 87.

* * *

D. The Committee's Conclusions

319. Before examining the merits of the present case, the Committee recalls that China, upon joining the ILO, undertook like all member States to respect the fundamental rights set out in the ILO's Constitution and the Declaration of Philadelphia, including freedom of association.

* * *

321. The Committee notes first of all that the statements of the complainant, on the one hand, and of the Government, on the other, differ considerably with regard to the nature and objectives of the WAF. * * *

322. In this respect, the Committee recalls that the meaning given to the term "organisation" by the ILO covers all organisations of workers or employers created to promote and defend the interests of the workers or employers. In this particular case the Committee notes that, according to the ICFTU, the main thrust of the statutes of the Beijing WAF was that the organisation should be autonomous, independent and democratic and that it should serve the principles of representing and defending the workers' interests. Furthermore, according to the complainant, the grievances voiced by the WAFs concerned the lack of workplace democracy, the lack of genuine workers' representation, the poor working conditions and the deterioration of the workers' living standards. These claims have not been denied by the Government which itself recognises that the Provisional Memorandum of the Beijing WAF accepted the Constitution and the law of the country, although it states that this subsequently proved not to be true. In the Committee's opinion, the WAFs' grievances referred to by the ICFTU are part of the normal activities of workers' organisations seeking to promote and defend the interests of their members. The WAF organisations would therefore appear to have been workers' organisations in the sense given to them by the ILO.

323. As to the argument that the WAF organisations did not apply for registration, the Committee is of the opinion that the absence of any such request does not necessarily mean that the workers did not wish to create organisations, especially as the legislation appears to provide for a trade union monopoly that does not leave any room for organisations outside the existing trade union structure. The 1987 Provisional Regulations on the Handling of Labour Disputes in state enterprises, for example, refer only to "the trade union committee", which would seem to exclude the existence of several trade union committees. In the present case, the Committee must note that the Government has relied on the fact that the WAFs were not registered as an excuse for declaring them illegal. In this respect the Committee recalls that if the conditions for granting registration are tantamount to obtaining prior permission from the public authorities for the establishing or functioning of a trade union, this would undeniably constitute an infringement of the principles of freedom of association * * *.

324. In addition, the Committee expresses its deep concern that the information supplied by the Government shows that the legislative provisions currently in force in China are in clear contradiction with the right of workers to set up and join organisations of their own choosing, and with the right of trade unions to organise their administration and activities and to formulate their programmes of action. In particular, the Committee would point out that the Government cites the suspected opposition of the WAFs to the constitutional provisions concerning the leading role of the Communist Party and to the establishment of a socialist regime as justification for the measures taken; it explains that all reactionary organisations which threaten the security of the State are banned. The Government also states that one of the Beijing WAF's leaders is accused of having incited the population to oppose the Government and of having created a trade union of his own choosing. The Committee must recall that unity within the trade union movement should not be imposed by the State through legislation because this would be contrary to the principles of freedom of association. The Committee must also point out that the right of workers to establish organisations of their own choosing implies, in particular, the effective possibility of forming, in a climate of full security, organisations independent both of those which exist already and of any political party * * *. It can only note that these basic principles have not been respected in this particular case. Consequently, the Committee urges the Government to take the measures necessary to guarantee, both in law and in practice, the right of workers to set up organisations of their own choosing and the right of these organisations to function freely.

325. As regards the violence said to have been engaged in by the WAFs and their leaders, the Committee notes the information supplied by the Government. It must however draw attention to the fact that all the examples of violence cited in its reply (setting fire to military vehicles, blocking roads and preventing access to public buildings) concern events that occurred when the WAFs were reduced to operating illegally.

326. In this respect, the Committee considers that for a trade union contribution to be properly useful and credible, it must be able to engage in its activities in a climate of freedom and security. This implies that, in so far as they may consider that they do not have the essential freedom to fulfil their mission directly, trade unions would be justified in demanding that these freedoms and the right to exercise them be recognised and that these demands be considered as coming within the scope of legitimate trade union activities.

327. As regards the deaths and detentions of and ill-treatment inflicted on the WAFs' leaders and activists, the Committee expresses its grave concern at the seriousness of these allegations concerning which the Government has not yet supplied sufficiently detailed replies.

328. In this respect, the Committee recalls that, as stated in the resolution concerning trade union rights and their relation to civil

liberties adopted by the International Labour Conference in 1970, the absence of civil liberties removes all meaning from the concept of trade union rights, and the rights conferred upon workers' and employers' organisations must be based on respect for those civil liberties.

329. The complaint referred to the death of WAF leaders in the course of the assault on Tiananmen Square by the armed forces during the night of 3-4 June 1989. The Government has not responded to these allegations. The Committee therefore requests it to send its observations on this point and, inter alia, to indicate the exact circumstances surrounding the death of these WAF leaders.

330. The Government confirms that three workers from Shanghai were sentenced to death and executed for setting fire to railway carriages and police vehicles and preventing the fire-fighters from doing their work in the course of events that occurred in the night of 6-7 June 1989. The Committee deplores the extreme rapidity in which the judgements were handed down and the sentences carried out since the executions took place two weeks after the incidents concerned, during which the case was judged on two occasions—once by a court of first instance and again on appeal. This rapidity implies that the accused were not able to enjoy the usual judicial guarantees. The Committee expresses the firm hope that such summary proceedings will not be resorted to again.

331. The Government also confirms that nine workers from Changchun were arrested and seven of them were sent to labour education camps. To justify these measures the Government indicates that the persons concerned were guilty of murder, theft and rape. The Committee requests the Government to supply precise information on the events on which these accusations are based, and in particular to supply the judgements involved.

332. The Government mentions however that some workers had organised strikes, blocked roads and engaged in activities against the Government, without any further details. The Committee must therefore remind the Government that strikes are one of the essential means that workers and their organisations should have to further and defend their economic and social interests * * *. Furthermore, the Committee considers that the arrest of strikers involves serious risks of abuse and serious threats to freedom of association. The competent authorities should receive appropriate instructions in order to avoid the risks that such arrests may carry for freedom of association * * *.

333. As regards the arrest of WAF leaders and activists, the Committee notes that those found guilty were sent to labour education camps and that a re-education policy was adopted for those WAF leaders who had not violated the law. The Committee requests the Government to supply information on the reasons for and the nature and objectives of this education through labour which is imposed on these trade unionists.

* * *

The Committee's Recommendations

334. In the light of its foregoing interim conclusions, the Committee invites the Governing Body to approve the following recommendations:

[The Committee set forth eight paragraphs of recommendations, for the most part reiterating the comments it made in its conclusions, above. For example, one of its recommendatory paragraphs was:]

(b) The Committee recalls that the right of workers to establish organisations of their own choosing implies, in particular, the effective possibility of forming, in a climate of full security, organisations independent both of those which exist already and of any political party. The Committee deplores that this basic principle has not been respected in this particular case. The Committee expresses its deep concern that the constitutional and legislative provisions currently in force in China are in clear contradiction with the right of workers to set up organisations of their own choosing and with the right of these organisations to function freely. It urges the Government to take the measures necessary to guarantee these rights, both in law and in practice.

THE COMMITTEE'S ROLE

As the Committee noted, China had ratified neither of the basic freedom of association conventions. Does this substantiate China's claim that the complaint was an intervention in China's internal affairs?

Since China hadn't ratified the relevant conventions, what source of law did the Committee use in reaching conclusions critical of China? Is it appropriate to judge ILO member states by standards to which they have not expressly agreed?

In paragraph 323, the Committee said that conditions tantamount to requiring permission from the public authorities for establishing a union would infringe the principles of freedom of association. This principle is drawn from article 2 of Convention No. 87, which says that workers have the right to establish and join organizations of their own choosing "without previous authorization." As of January 1, 1990, there were 99 states parties to Convention No. 87. Since China was not one of them, was the Committee saying, in effect, that article 2 reflects customary international law for (at least) states members of the ILO? Would it be general custom or special custom?

In paragraphs 325 and 326, the Committee addressed the violent acts allegedly committed by the WAFs and their leaders. Did the Committee condone violence as a means of obtaining trade union rights on the part of unions that have been denied recognition by their governments? Would that be an appropriate stance for an international dispute-settlement body to take?

Note the Committee's concern with civil liberties and due process, in paragraphs 327–31, and its reaffirmation of the right to strike, in paragraph 332. Its approach was consistent with that of the Commission of Inquiry in the case involving Poland, page 395 supra: it stressed these rights even though they do not appear explicitly in the relevant labor conventions. (They do appear in other treaties widely ratified by ILO member states. The International Covenant on Civil and Political Rights, in force for 89 states as of January 1, 1990, contains provisions on the right to life, conditions of detention, and due process in criminal proceedings; the International Covenant on Economic, Social and Cultural Rights, in force for 94 states as of the same date, recognizes not only the right to form trade unions, but also the right to strike, "provided that it is exercised in conformity with the laws of the particular country." e) Why do you suppose member states have not objected seriously to the Committee's approach, except in some cases when it is aimed at them as respondent states?

Note also that the Committee was not willing to let the Chinese government off the hook when information was lacking about questionable acts—such as commitment of activists to labor education camps (paragraph 333). This technique, of keeping pressure on, is similar to that used by the ILO Committee of Experts, a body designed to oversee members' compliance with conventions they have ratified. The Committee of Experts is examined in the next chapter of these materials.

Is it appropriate for the Committee on Freedom of Association to wade into a highly-charged political situation, such as that stemming from the Tienanmen Square incident? Can it be objective in such cases? (There were no Committee members from any communist state.)

We turn now to a more mundane case, involving a Western respondent state. The complaint was filed by two umbrella labor organizations, one Canadian and the other international, on behalf of the Canadian Union of Postal Workers (CUPW).

COMPLAINT AGAINST THE GOVERNMENT OF CANADA PRESENTED BY THE CANADIAN LABOUR CONGRESS AND THE POSTAL, TELEGRAPH AND TELEPHONE INTERNATIONAL

ILO Committee on Freedom of Association Case No. 1451 (1989).
72 ILO Official Bulletin, Series B, No. 3, at 17.

* * *

47. Canada has ratified [both Convention No. 87 and Convention No. 98].

e. International Covenant on Economic, Social and Cultural Rights, Dec. 16, 1966, art. 8(1)(d), 993 U.N.T.S. 3.

A. THE COMPLAINANTS' ALLEGATIONS

[The complainants alleged that the Canadian government breached basic ILO principles, particularly those in Convention No. 98, by enacting Bill C-86, the Postal Services Continuation Act, 1987, to end a lawful strike by Canadian postal workers. In June 1986, a large majority of CUPW members ratified a set of demands prepared by their union, focusing on such issues as job security. Under pre-existing provisions of the Canada Labor Code, these demands were put to a collective bargaining process. After 15 months, no agreement had been reached. A conciliation commissioner was appointed, but he too failed to bring the parties to an agreement. At that point, a postal strike was lawful. The union initiated rotating strikes. The Canada Post Office employed replacement workers for strikers, and apparently most of the mail got through.

[On the seventh day of the strike, the Labor Minister announced that the government was ready to introduce a Bill in the legislature to end the dispute. The next day, it introduced Bill C-86 in the House of Commons. Sections 3 and 7 had the effect of ordering the postal workers back to work and appointing a mediator/arbitrator to deal with the dispute. Section 11 disqualified union officers or representatives from holding any union position for five years if they were convicted of an offense under the Bill. The Bill was enacted, terminating the strike.

[The government submitted an extensive reply to the complaint.]

* * *

C. THE COMMITTEE'S CONCLUSIONS

93. The complainants allege that the Government breached the principles of freedom of association by enacting the Postal Services Continuation Act, 1987, which ordered the postal workers back to work. For its part, the Government submits it had extended every possible means of mediation and conciliation to the parties without any result, and that it acted in the public interest since a protracted and disruptive work stoppage could not be tolerated.

94. The Committee takes note of the elaborate and extensive reply submitted by the Government, and in particular of the fact that the parties had negotiated for more than a year, that this was the second major postal strike within four months; it also notes the considerations relating to the financial losses incurred by business and to the potentially severe hardships experienced by recipients of family and social welfare payments who depend on the mail for their income.

95. The Committee feels however compelled to state that the issue is basically this: the postal workers were legally on strike and the Government, through special legislation, ordered them back to work after seven days of work stoppage.

96. The Government points out, rightly so, that the Committee has recognized in the past that there are circumstances where restrictions and even prohibitions of strikes are justifiable. However, the Committee hastens to say that these are exceptions to the general rule and that the right to strike is one of the legitimate and essential means through which workers and their organizations may defend their economic and social interests * * *.

97. It follows that restrictions or even prohibitions of the right to strike can only be justified in a limited number of situations: civil servants and workers in essential services in the strict sense of the term, i.e. those services whose interruptions would endanger the life, personal safety or health of the whole or part of the population * * *, provided however these workers have access to adequate procedures, such as conciliation and arbitration, where the parties concerned can participate at all stages and in which the awards are binding on both parties and are fully and promptly implemented.

98. The Committee * * * fails to see how postal services could be said genuinely to constitute essential services in the strict sense of the term. It is true that businesses will experience problems and losses during a postal strike, and may even have to lay off employees; companies relying heavily or exclusively on the mail—such as direct mail undertakings—will be particularly affected by such a strike. It is equally true that some individuals, who depend on mail delivery to obtain their unemployment benefits, old-age pension, family or social allowance cheques, will be inconvenienced. Nevertheless, unfortunate as these consequences are, they cannot justify an abridgement of the fundamental rights guaranteed by Conventions Nos. 87 and 98, unless they reach the point where they affect the life, personal safety or health of the whole or part of the population. In the opinion of the Committee, such was not the case here, especially in view of the uncontradicted allegation that most of the mail was getting through, according to the employer's own figures.

* * *

100. * * * [I]n this instance, the strike was allowed to last only seven days before the Government decided to introduce back-to-work legislation. That Act restricted, with an immediate application to a work stoppage called in conformity with the law, the right to strike granted to postal workers by the federal legislation. In all the circumstances, and despite the protracted negotiations which did not enable the parties to settle their differences, the Postal Services Continuation Act, 1987 does not appear to be conducive to sound industrial relations, which should be founded on a predictable and stable legislative framework respecting the principles of freedom of association.

101. Although the Government submits that back-to-work legislation is relatively uncommon and is adopted only when the continuation of a particular dispute would have severe consequences for the national interest, the Committee cannot fail to stress that the Postal Services Continuation Act, 1987 was the second almost identical legislation enacted in less than two months affecting large numbers of workers.

102. Needless to say, provisions like section 11(1) of the Postal Services Continuation Act, which disqualifies union officers or representatives from holding any union position during five years if they are convicted of an offence under the Act (which itself violates the principles of freedom of association) also constituted a breach of the right freely to elect representatives, guaranteed to workers by Article 3 of Convention No. 87, and an interference in the free functioning of union organizations.

103. Finally, the Committee notes that the Supreme Court of Canada held in 1987 that the Constitution Act does not guarantee the right to strike, and that the freedom of association guaranteed by the Canadian Charter of Rights, which is enshrined in the Constitution, does not embody the right to strike. The Committee certainly respects the judgement of the highest court of Canada, but points out that this is a different forum and that the Committee's mandate is to evaluate, with a view to making a recommendation to the Governing Body, whether certain situations of fact and/or legislation are in conformity with the principles of freedom of association, as established in international Conventions.

The Committee's Recommendations

104. In the light of its foregoing conclusions, the Committee invites the Governing Body to approve the following recommendations:

(a) The Committee considers that the provisions of the Postal Services Continuation Act, 1987, which ordered the postal workers back to work seven days after the beginning of a legal strike and instituted compulsory arbitration in circumstances that were not endangering the life, personal safety or health of the whole or part of the Canadian population, are not in conformity with the principles of freedom of association.

(b) The Committee draws to the Government's attention that section 11(1) of the Postal Services Continuation Act, 1987, constituted an interference in the free functioning of union organizations, and violated the right freely to elect representatives, guaranteed to workers by Article 3 of Convention No. 87.

THE COMMITTEE AND THE "NORMAL" CASE

In neither the case against China nor the one against Canada did the Committee say anything about the complainants exhausting domestic remedies before they turned to the international remedy provided by the ILO. Certainly in the China case, and perhaps in the Canada case, it could have been argued that the usual international law exhaustion-of-remedies requirement should be excused, on the ground that any attempt to pursue domestic remedies after the government had acted, under the circumstances of those cases, would have been futile. But the Committee didn't even address that point, and the complainants saw no need to argue it. In fact, the Committee has never had an exhaustion-of-domestic-remedies requirement. Is there a good reason for that?

The right to strike was at the heart of the case against Canada. The Committee acknowledged that there could be some circumstances in which a restriction on, or even a prohibition of, strikes would be justifiable (paragraph 96). But it was very strict about the circumstances. Should it have given more deference to the political process in a democracy, like Canada, to determine the exigencies that justify curtailment of a strike by public employees?

In paragraph 103, the Committee paid its respects to the Supreme Court of Canada's determination that Canadian basic law does not guarantee a right to strike, but then pointed out that a proceeding before the ILO Committee on Freedom of Association is another matter. Did the Committee, in effect, reverse the Supreme Court of Canada? If so, where does an ILO committee get such authority? If not, what did the Committee do?

Article 3 of Convention No. 87 gives workers' organizations the right "to elect their representatives in full freedom." In paragraph 102, the Committee summarily concluded that section 11(1) of the Canadian act violated that provision. It was rather less diplomatic in saying so than it often is in dealing with member states' legislation. Why so? Can a quasi-adjudicative body in an international organization afford to be that decisive?

As the two cases in this Section have indicated, the Committee on Freedom of Association has had to consider disputes arising in a wide variety of social, political and economic systems. It has taken strong positions in favor of such things as a right to strike and a right to basic civil liberties. It is sometimes accused of reflecting only Western, or at least nonsocialist, values. Can an international human rights dispute-settlement and enforcement mechanism operate evenhandedly in applying standards to countries with domestic systems as different from each other as those of China and Canada?

4. *Interpretation of Conventions by the International Labor Office*

INTERNATIONAL LABOR OFFICE, THE INTERNATIONAL LABOR CODE, 1951

Vol. 1, Preface, at CVIII–CIX (1952).

The Constitution of the Organisation provides that "Any question or dispute relating to the interpretation * * * of any Convention * * * shall be referred for decision to the International Court of Justice", and this provision has always been regarded as implying that the Court alone is competent to formulate an interpretation of the provisions of an international labour Convention which will be of binding authority. The Constitution as amended in 1946 permits the Governing Body to make and submit to the Conference for approval rules providing for the appointment of a tribunal for the expeditious determination of any dispute or question relating to the interpretation of a Convention which may be referred thereto by the Governing Body or in accordance with the terms of a Convention, but * * * the Governing Body has taken no action on the basis of the provision; it does not substantially affect the exclusive jurisdiction of the Court. In practice, however, only one case relating to the interpretation of a Convention, that relating to the interpretation of the Convention concerning employment of women during the night, 1919, has been submitted to the Court, and it has been not uncommon for Governments in doubt as to the meaning of an international labour Convention to ask the International Labour Office for its opinion on the subject. The Office has always considered it to be its duty to assist Governments in this manner, though it has invariably pointed out that it has no special authority to interpret the texts of Conventions; the opinions given by the Office have, when of sufficient general interest, been submitted to the Governing Body and published. Though not authoritative in the same final sense as an interpretation by the Court, these interpretations therefore enjoy such authority as derives from their having been formulated by the International Labour Office in its official capacity at the request of Governments of Members of the Organisation.

INTERPRETATION BY THE ICJ

Five cases involving interpretation of the ILO Constitution, in addition to the one case involving interpretation of a labor convention, have been referred to the World Court. All of the cases, however, were referred to it before 1933. In view of the availability of legal opinions from the International Labor Office, does *article 37(1)* of the ILO Constitution—the provision for referring disputes over interpretation to the Court—serve any useful purpose?

More than 100 opinions have been issued by the International Labor Office. An example appears below.

INTERNATIONAL LABOR OFFICE NOTICE AND MEMORANDUM INTERPRETING ILO CONVENTION NO. 111
March 10, 1959.
42 ILO Official Bulletin, No. 7, at 395.

By letter dated 24 January 1959 the Secretary of State for Public Health and Social Affairs of the Tunisian Republic requested from the International Labour Office certain information concerning the interpretation of the Discrimination (Employment and Occupation) Convention, 1958 (No. 111) (Article 1, paragraph 1(*a*)).

With the usual reservation that the Constitution does not give him any special authority to interpret Conventions adopted by the International Labour Conference, the Director–General of the International Labour Office, by letter dated 10 March 1959, transmitted to the Secretary of State for Public Health and Social Affairs of the Tunisian Republic a memorandum prepared by the International Labour Office on this question.

The text of this document is as follows:

(TRANSLATION)

The Secretary of State for Public Health and Social Affairs of the Tunisian Republic has requested the Director–General of the International Labour Office for an opinion as to the scope of the Discrimination (Employment and Occupation) Convention, 1958, Article 1 of which provides that—

1. For the purpose of this Convention the term "discrimination" includes—

    (*a*) any distinction, exclusion or preference made on the basis of race, colour, sex, religion, political opinion, national extraction or social origin, which has the effect of nullifying or impairing equality of opportunity or treatment in employment or occupation * * *.

The Tunisian Government's request is drafted in the following terms:

* * * the Convention specifically prohibits discrimination based on "national extraction".

Thus the question arises as to whether the prohibition of all forms of discrimination applies to all the inhabitants of a country whether nationals or foreigners, or whether its purpose is to lay down a standard of complete equality as between nationals; it being understood that a country may, within the framework of a policy designed to combat unemployment, order certain restrictions to be imposed on the use of foreign labour.

The preparatory work which preceded the adoption of the Convention shows quite clearly that the phrase "any distinction, exclusion or preference on the basis of * * * national extraction" only covers discrimination which might exist in a State with respect to its own nationals on account of their foreign extraction; and does not cover discrimination between nationals of that State on the one hand and persons of foreign nationality on the other.

When the Governing Body decided to place the question of discrimination in employment and occupation on the agenda of the 40th Session of the International Labour Conference (1957) it expressed the opinion that the documents laid before the Conference should deal with discrimination based on all the motives enumerated in Article 2(1) of the Universal Declaration of Human Rights.

This instrument enunciates the principle of equality of rights "without distinction of any kind, such as race, colour, sex, language, religion, political or other opinion, national or social origin, property, birth or other status".

Consequently the questionnaire contained in the report which was forwarded by the International Labour Office to the governments referred to "national origin" among the motives for discrimination which might be prohibited by the Convention. The report itself actually stressed that the concept of "national origin" was composed of two distinct elements: one based on the natural distinction of foreign ancestry, the other on the judicial distinction of nationality.

Following the replies submitted by the governments to the above-mentioned questionnaire, it appeared that a more restrictive concept should be adopted. In fact a certain number of governments raised objections concerning the granting of equal rights in employment to nationals and foreigners alike, particularly on account of the necessity for these governments to ensure priority of employment to their own nationals.

So as to take these objections into consideration the Office deemed it necessary to state that distinctions based on nationality would not be covered by the proposed Convention, and suggested that the expression "national extraction" should be substituted for "national origin".

* * *

This view was accepted by the Committee on Discrimination at the 40th Session of the Conference (June 1957) when this matter was first discussed. An amendment designed to give a wider scope to the definition of discrimination, by taking up once more the term "national origin", was rejected by the Committee. Finally the term "national extraction" used in the Committee's proposed conclusions was adopted by the Conference at its 40th Session.

* * *

It was for the Conference to take a final decision on the matter. At its 42nd Session (June 1958) a lengthy debate took place in the Committee on Discrimination regarding this point. As a result of this debate the Committee expressly emphasized in its report, which was adopted by the Conference, that "distinctions, exclusions or preferences made on the basis of national extraction meant distinctions between nationals of the ratifying country made on the ground of foreign ancestry or foreign birth".

Thus it was agreed that the definition of the term "discrimination" covered distinctions made in a State as between its own nationals and not distinctions made with respect to foreign nationals.

METHOD AND EFFECT OF LABOR OFFICE INTERPRETATIONS

Is there an analogy in domestic legal systems to the International Labor Office's practice of issuing opinions such as this one?

Note the heavy reliance on the preparatory work in the Labor Office's interpretation of the Discrimination Convention. This is typical of the Office's interpretations. But on the one occasion when the World Court was asked to interpret a labor convention, it reiterated the rule it had previously espoused in non-labor cases that "there is no occasion to have regard to preparatory work if the text of a convention is sufficiently clear in itself." [a] In that case and in others not involving labor conventions, however, the Court did consider preparatory work in order, as it said, to confirm the interpretation it had reached by examining the text of the convention. The Vienna Convention on the Law of Treaties, articles 31 and 32, sets forth rules of interpretation based on the World Court's established approach: First, one looks to the ordinary meaning of the words of the treaty, considered in their context and in light of the treaty's object and purpose; resort is then had to the preparatory work only to confirm the meaning already ascertained, or to determine the meaning if the text is ambiguous or obscure or if the text leads to a manifestly absurd or unreasonable result. In light of this, and in light of the express primacy given to interpretation by the ICJ in article 37(1) of the ILO Constitution, can International Labor Office interpretations relying primarily on preparatory work without first finding the text of a convention ambiguous or obscure be regarded as authoritative in any sense?

Since the International Labor Office has no express authority in the ILO Constitution to issue such opinions, what legal effect do they

[a]. Interpretation of the Convention of 1919 Concerning Employment of Women During the Night, PCIJ Ser. A/B, No. 50, at 378 (1932).

have even if the Office's use of preparatory work is proper? Consider the following excerpt from a memorandum prepared by the Office:[b] "[I]t has happened that the same point of interpretation has been raised by more than one member of the Organisation. In these cases the Office has been able to point out that when the point was previously raised and it was consulted thereon, the information supplied by it and the conclusion to which it appeared to lead had been accepted by the member in question and had given rise to no objection after publication in the Official Bulletin. The process of the development of international law is in fact an exactly similar process and the tacit acceptance of an interpretation acted on by a Member and communicated through the Official Bulletin constitutes important authority which can always be invoked for that interpretation." Is that tantamount to saying that such interpretations have become customary international law for member states? On the other hand, could an argument for binding effect be made under ILO Constitution *article 19(5)(d)*?[c]

If the International Court of Justice were asked to interpret article 1 of the Discrimination Convention, would it simply follow the Office's interpretation (to which no objections were made by member states)?

Another aspect of the possible legal significance of such opinions has been asserted by the International Labor Office:[d] "[I]t would seem that, when an opinion given by the Office has been submitted to the Governing Body and published in the Official Bulletin and has met with no adverse comment, the Conference must, in the event of its subsequently including in another convention a provision identical with or equivalent to the provision which has been interpreted by the Office, be presumed, in the absence of any evidence to the contrary, to have intended that provision to be understood in the manner in which the Office has interpreted it."[e] The domestic law analogy would be to the re-enactment by Congress of a statute after it had been interpreted in a certain way by a federal court, in which case the argument is frequently made that Congress intended the statute to mean what the court had said it meant, or it would have changed the language. Is the argument stronger or weaker in the ILO context outlined in the quotation above?

On a few occasions the International Labor Office has been approached for an interpretation when the meaning of a provision was actively disputed between two member states. In such instances it has refrained from giving an interpretation.[f] Is there any good reason for such reticence?

b. Minutes of the Ninth Sess. of the Governing Body 365–66 (1921).

c. See Osieke, The Exercise of the Judicial Function with respect to the International Labour Organisation, 47 Brit. Y.B.Int'l L. 315, 323 n. 4 (1974–75).

d. 23 ILO Official Bulletin, No. 1, at 32 (1938).

e. See also Jenks, The Interpretation of International Labor Conventions by the International Labour Office, 20 British Y.B.Int'l L. 132, 133 (1939).

f. See McMahon, The Legislative Techniques of the International Labor Organization, 41 British Y.B.Int'l L. 1, 90–91 (1965–66).

The World Health Organization (WHO) has a procedure for interpreting its Health Regulations comparable in some respects to that of the ILO. (The Health Regulations (a) require member states to have facilities and personnel at ports, airports and other entry-exit places in order to prevent the spread of certain communicable diseases, (b) prohibit some overzealous health measures that could impose unnecessary barriers to trade, and (c) establish a notification system for certain epidemiological information.[g]) When doubt about the meaning of a Health Regulation arises—often as a result of an informal allegation by one member state that another is not complying with a Regulation—the WHO Director–General's office interprets it. Usually these interpretations are then included in the Director–General's report to the WHO Committee on the International Surveillance of Communicable Diseases (consisting of 6 to 12 health experts from WHO advisory panels). If approved by the Committee, they are included in its report to the plenary body, the Health Assembly. If the Health Assembly approves the Committee's report, as it normally does, and if a particular interpretation is deemed important enough, it will appear as a footnote to the next edition of the Health Regulations. All of this is done without formal authorization in the WHO Constitution, although the Health Regulations, themselves, contemplate an interpretive role for the Director–General.[h] There appear to have been no objections to this procedure by member states.[i]

Would it be useful to include in the constituent instruments of all specialized agencies and similar organizations a provision expressly empowering the secretariat to issue formal interpretations of the constituent instruments and of conventions related to the purposes of the organizations? If it ever would be, should the United States propose that such interpretations expressly be made binding on all member states? Should provisions for review of the secretariat's interpretation be included? If so, to what sort of body?

B. THE INTERNATIONAL MONETARY FUND

The Fund Agreement, unlike the ILO Constitution, contains a number of significant provisions directly regulating the conduct of member states. Some of the provisions impose rather technical obligations regarding such matters as the convertibility of currencies and recognition by member states of some controls imposed by other member states on the availability or use of foreign exchange. Consequently it was thought important at the Bretton Woods Conference of 1944, when the Fund and World Bank Agreements were drafted, to include a provision for authoritative interpretation of each Agreement by in-

---

g. See 1 D. Leive, International Regulatory Regimes xxxviii (1976).

h. International Health Regs. art. 106(1), 21 U.S.T. 3003, T.I.A.S. 7026, 764 U.N.T.S. 3.

i. D. Leive, supra, at 49–53.

house organs able to bring technical expertise and expeditious decision-making to the task. The Fund Agreement's provision on interpretation is *article XXIX*.

The Fund's weighted voting system (based on each member's capital contribution to the Fund) applies to decisions by the Executive Board and the full Board of Governors under article XXIX. (Formal votes are rarely taken on such matters as these, with decisions normally being made by consensus.) Note that any appeal to the Board of Governors is first referred to a Board Committee on Interpretation. Each member of the Committee is to have one vote, thus circumventing the weighted voting system for that intermediate appellate stage. The decision of the Committee can be overturned by the full Board only by an 85 percent majority of the total voting power in the Board.[a]

For some of the regulatory provisions of the Fund Agreement to be fully effective, it is important that they be uniformly interpreted and applied in the domestic law of member states as well as in intergovernmental relations among states.[b] Consequently the focus in this subsection will be primarily on the effect in domestic law of interpretation by the Fund. In a significant decision by the Federal Communications Commission in 1953, an interpretation by the Executive Directors of the Fund and Bank was central to the outcome.

INTERNATIONAL BANK FOR RECONSTRUCTION AND DEVELOPMENT AND INTERNATIONAL MONETARY FUND v. ALL AMERICA CABLES & RADIO, INC.

Federal Communications Commission, 1953.
17 F.C.C. 450.

[The World Bank and the Fund alleged that the respondent telegraph companies were improperly charging them higher rates for telegraph messages than were being charged the United States government. Fund Agreement article IX, section 7, and Bank Agreement article VII, section 7, provide in substance that official communications of the Bank and Fund are to be accorded the same "treatment" by members as official communications of other members. Section 10 of the same articles requires each member to take such action as is necessary in its own territory to make effective, in terms of its own law, the principles set forth in those articles. One of the questions in the case was whether the two sections 7 apply to rates. After the proceeding had been commenced, the F.C.C. asked the Executive Directors of the Bank and Fund to interpret the two sections 7. The Executive

---

a. See Gold, Weighted Voting Power: Some Limits and Some Problems, 68 Am. J.Int'l L. 687, 696–99 (1974).

b. The same is true with respect to regulatory provisions of ILO conventions, but the ILO Constitution, as noted earlier, contains no express authorization for in-house interpretation of labor conventions that could be used to incorporate International Labor Office interpretations automatically into domestic law.

Directors decided, under the powers of interpretation in their respective Articles of Agreement (article XXIX in the case of the Fund), that the two sections 7 did apply and required that the rates be no higher than those charged the U.S. government in its communications with foreign governments. No attempt was made to refer the question to the Board of Governors.

[The F.C.C., after stating the facts, turned to the effect of article IX, section 7, and article VII, section 7, of the respective Agreements in U.S. (federal) law. The United States had joined the Bank and Fund pursuant to Congressional authorization in the Bretton Woods Agreements Act,[c] which contained the relevant statutory provisions. The F.C.C. said:]

Section 11 of the Bretton Woods Agreements Act provides as follows:

> The provisions of article IX, sections 2 to 9 both inclusive, and the first sentence of article VIII, section 2(b), of the Articles of Agreement of the Fund, and the provisions of article VI, section 5(i), and article VII, sections 2 to 9, both inclusive of the Articles of Agreement of the Bank, shall have full force and effect in the United States and its Territories and possessions upon acceptance of membership by the United States in, and the establishment of, the Fund and the Bank, respectively.

Section 12 of the Bretton Woods Agreements Act directs the Governor and Executive Director of the Bank appointed by the United States to obtain an official interpretation by the Bank as to its authority to make or guarantee loans for certain purposes, and if the Bank does not interpret its powers to include the making or guaranteeing of such loans, then to propose and support an amendment to the Articles of Agreement for the purpose of explicitly authorizing such loans.

Section 13 of the Bretton Woods Agreements Act directs the Governor and Executive Director of the Fund appointed by the United States to obtain an official interpretation by the Fund as to its authority to use its resources for certain purposes and, if the Fund interprets its authority to extend to any of these purposes, then to propose and support an amendment to the Articles of Agreement for the purpose of expressly negativing such interpretation.

* * *

The record in this proceeding includes a letter from the Department of State dated June 2, 1950, and signed by Jack B. Tate, Deputy Legal Adviser, containing the following paragraph:

> By virtue of its membership in the Fund and Bank, the United States is obliged to conform to the provisions of the respective Articles of Agreement, including the provisions of the respective Articles relating to interpretation of the Articles. As a conse-

---

c. 22 U.S.C.A. § 286 et seq.

quence, the United States is obliged to carry out the Articles of Agreement as interpreted in accordance with the provisions of the Articles. Since the United States does not intend to require that the interpretations under reference be referred to the respective Boards of Governors, the United States is under an international obligation to act in conformity with the interpretations issued by the respective Executive Directors of the Fund and Bank.

* * *

The basic question, therefore, which we must determine in this proceeding is whether the term "treatment," as used in the Articles of the Bank and Fund, relates to rate matters as contended by the complainants or is confined to other matters such as priorities and freedom from censorship as contended by the defendants. In making this determination it should be clear that the issue presented to us is not whether, as a matter of communications policy, the Bank or Fund should be authorized to secure lower government rates, where such rates are in existence, but rather whether as a matter of fact the Bank and the Fund have already been authorized to receive such rates by binding international agreements as confirmed by the Bretton Woods Agreements Act. And while we would not necessarily have reached the conclusion that the Bank or Fund should, as a matter of communications policy, be authorized to receive government rates were this presented to us as a matter of first impression we believe, on the basis of the record before us, that it must be determined that the term "treatment" does include rates for communications service and that the United States is accordingly obligated to provide the official communications of the Bank and the Fund the same treatment with respect to rates as is afforded to similar official communications of member foreign governments.

We believe that the question as to the application of the term "treatment" in the Bank and Fund Articles to rates has been conclusively determined by the Bank and Fund Executive Directors' interpretation, by unanimous vote, that the language in question applies to rates charged for official communications of the Bank and the Fund. Under the terms of the Bank and Fund Articles of Agreement, this interpretation, in effect, is final. This procedure for issuing interpretations binding member governments does indeed appear novel; but it also appears to point the way toward speedy, uniform and final interpretations. This procedure is not only an integral part of the Bank and Fund Articles, which have been accepted by the United States, but its use was specifically invoked with respect to questions of interpretation by Sections 12 and 13 of the Bretton Woods Agreements Act; and the United States Congress, by directing that an amendment of the Articles be sought if the requested interpretations were not satisfactory, appears to have recognized in these two Sections that the United States is bound by the results of the interpretations. The United States Government is therefore bound by the Executive Director's interpretation of the term "treatment" and is under an international obligation to act in conformity therewith.

* * *

Our conclusion as to the obligation of the United States Government to act in conformity with the Executive Directors' interpretations was reached independently of the communications from the Department of State. However, the view of the State Department that the United States is under an international obligation to act in conformity with the Executive Directors' interpretations is entitled to great weight and constitutes an additional basis for our conclusion.

* * *

The Bank and Fund privilege for communications is enforceable without further legislative action. We do not have here the question which has been the subject of many court decisions and legal [treatises], namely, whether an executive agreement or treaty is self-executing or requires domestic legislative implementation, since by the terms of the Bretton Woods Agreements Act the privilege for communications is specifically given full force and effect in the United States and its territories and possessions.

[The Commission concluded "that the interpretation of the Executive Directors that the communications privileges granted the Bank and Fund include rate treatment is binding on the United States, and thus on this Commission * * *." It therefore ordered the respondent telegraph companies to charge the same rates for Bank and Fund official messages as were charged the United States government.]

QUESTIONS ON INTERPRETATION BY THE EXECUTIVE BOARD

Article XXIX(b) of the Fund Agreement says that the decision of the Board of Governors shall be "final." The F.C.C. decision gives the same effect to an unappealed decision of the Executive Board. Is there any reasonable meaning that could be given to "finality" in article XXIX(b) other than that given by the State Department and the F.C.C.? Compare article XXIX(b) with the language of the Chicago Convention on International Civil Aviation *article 86,* and with ICJ Statute *articles 59* and *60.*

If the text of article XXIX is unclear as to the binding character of Executive Board interpretations, resort could be had to the preparatory work even under the restrictive approach to interpretation taken by the ICJ and the Vienna Convention on the Law of Treaties. At the Bretton Woods Conference, three alternatives were proposed for what became article XXIX. The first simply said that questions of interpretation between two or more members "shall be resolved by the Fund." The second introduced the two-step process within the Fund, stating that questions of interpretation would be submitted to the Executive Directors "for their opinion" and that once an opinion had been given, "a member may require that the question be submitted to the Board [of Governors] and the opinion of the Board is final." The third alternative was worded essentially as article XXIX now is.[d] Compare the text of article XXIX with the quoted language above from the first two (rejected) alternatives. Does this shed any light on the binding or nonbinding nature of Executive Directors' interpretations?

In Callejo v. Bancomer, S.A.,[e] the U.S. Court of Appeals for the Fifth Circuit said:

> According to some commentators, since Art. XXIX of the Fund Agreement makes interpretations by the Fund binding on signatory nations, they are subsidiarily binding on the courts of signatory nations, including those of the United States. See J. Gold, *Interpretation by the Fund* 31–42 (IMF Pamphlet Series No. 11, 1968) * * *. We express no view on this question here, and employ the Fund's interpretation merely as persuasive rather than as binding authority.

The court in Callejo was dealing with a letter from the Director of the IMF Legal Department in response to an inquiry from counsel for one of the parties in the case, saying that provisions of Mexico's exchange control regulations requiring certain repayments to be made in Mexican pesos were consistent with the Fund Agreement. The letter apparently had been authorized by the Fund's Executive Board, which had previously approved the Mexican regulations under Fund Agreement article VIII, section 2(a). It does not appear that the Executive Board had issued a formal interpretation under article XXIX. Does Callejo cast doubt on what the F.C.C. said about the authority in domestic legal proceedings of Executive Board interpretations under article XXIX?

Is there any reason why a federal court might treat an article XXIX interpretation differently from the treatment given it by an administrative agency such as the F.C.C.?

Consider the types of issue appropriate for submission to the Fund's Executive Board under article XXIX. For example, in the situation that came before the F.C.C., suppose there had been a dispute whether the telegraph companies actually were charging the Bank and Fund higher rates than the U.S. government. Could the Executive Board resolve that question under its article XXIX authority?

There was an ongoing dispute over the meaning of the "treatment of official communications" provision when the Executive Directors issued their interpretation. Moreover, it was a dispute directly involving pecuniary interests of the Bank and Fund. The International Labor Office would decline to give an interpretation of a provision in a

---

d. See 1 Proceedings and Documents of the United Nations Monetary and Financial Conf., 1944, at 58–59, 236–37, 291, 969 (U.S. Dept. of State, 1948).

e. 764 F.2d 1101, 1119 n. 26 (5th Cir. 1985).

labor convention when there is an active dispute over its meaning, even if the dispute did not directly involve the ILO's pecuniary interests. Should the Bank and Fund, as a matter of policy, follow the ILO practice? [f]

On the facts of the case before the F.C.C., could a due process argument be raised concerning the F.C.C.'s treatment of the Executive Directors' interpretation?

ARTICLE VIII, SECTION 2(b)

The Executive Board has issued several formal interpretations over the years, involving various provisions of the Fund Agreement. The one that has generated the most discussion, and that is most likely to affect private parties, involves article VIII, section 2(b). This section recognizes that certain national regulations ("exchange control regulations," intended to conserve foreign exchange by restricting its availability to private persons and entities) might be appropriate for balance-of-payments purposes. Under some circumstances, such regulations might be maintained consistently with the Fund Agreement, even though the thrust of the Agreement is to reduce and ultimately eliminate restrictions on the availability of foreign exchange for such current transactions as payments for imports.

Private parties have been known to enter into contracts circumventing exchange control regulations, and then attempt to enforce those contracts in the courts of a member state other than the state whose exchange controls are involved. In such a case there is a risk that the court might fail to enforce the exchange control regulations of the other nation, on any of at least three grounds: straightforward choice of forum law, refusal to enforce a "revenue law" of another nation, or a determination that the foreign regulations violate the forum's public policy. Article VIII, section 2(b) was inserted in the Fund Agreement to try to deal with this risk, whenever the regulation is consistent with the Fund Agreement.

Article VIII, section 2(b) has been called "an unparalleled phenomenon in international law. The history of international law reveals no other provision that has had such an impact." [g] That is saying a lot for a very cryptic provision. In fact, its cryptic nature led the Executive Board to issue an interpretation of it shortly after the Fund came into existence. As you read the interpretation, consider the effect it would have on the application of article VIII, section 2(b), in a case arising in a federal court in the United States.

[f.] Compare the General Regulations of the Universal Postal Union, art. 113(2), authorizing the UPU International Bureau (the UPU secretariat) to give opinions even on questions in dispute, at the request of the parties involved.

[g.] Ebke, Article VIII, Section 2(b), International Monetary Cooperation, and the Courts, 23 Int'l Lawyer 677 (1989).

EXECUTIVE BOARD DECISION ON UN-ENFORCEABILITY OF CERTAIN EXCHANGE CONTRACTS

Decision No. 446-4 (1949).
Selected Decisions and Selected Documents of the International Monetary Fund 350 (17th issue 1992).

The Board of Executive Directors of the International Monetary Fund has interpreted, under Article XVIII of the Articles of Agreement [Article XXIX of the revised Agreement], the first sentence of Article VIII, Section 2(b), which provision reads as follows:

> "Exchange contracts which involve the currency of any member and which are contrary to the exchange control regulations of that member maintained or imposed consistently with this Agreement shall be unenforceable in the territories of any member."

The meaning and effect of this provision are as follows:

1. Parties entering into exchange contracts involving the currency of any member of the Fund and contrary to exchange control regulations of that member which are maintained or imposed consistently with the Fund Agreement will not receive the assistance of the judicial or administrative authorities of other members in obtaining the performance of such contracts. That is to say, the obligations of such contracts will not be implemented by the judicial or administrative authorities of member countries, for example by decreeing performance of the contracts or by awarding damages for their non-performance.

2. By accepting the Fund Agreement members have undertaken to make the principle mentioned above effectively part of their national law.

* * *

An obvious result of the foregoing undertaking is that if a party to an exchange contract of the kind referred to in Article VIII, Section 2(*b*) seeks to enforce such a contract, the tribunal of the member country before which the proceedings are brought will not, on the ground that they are contrary to the public policy (*ordre public*) of the forum, refuse recognition of the exchange control regulations of the other member which are maintained or imposed consistently with the Fund Agreement. It also follows that such contracts will be treated as unenforceable notwithstanding that under the private international law of the forum, the law under which the foreign exchange control regulations are maintained or imposed is not the law which governs the exchange contract or its performance.

CHOICE OF LAW

A number of definitional problems are posed by article VIII, section 2(b). For example, what is meant by "exchange contracts which involve the currency of any member"? The Fund Agreement does not say, nor does the Executive Board interpretation. Clearly that language would encompass a contract in which the only object is to exchange one member state's currency for another's, but it probably goes further and includes any contract the performance of which would affect the foreign exchange resources of the member involved.[h] Our concern, happily, will not be with such technical questions.

Suppose an American bank and a Peruvian resident enter into a contract in the United States by which the Peruvian borrows Peruvian currency (the inti) and agrees to repay U.S. dollars on a given date in the future—clearly an exchange contract involving the currency of Peru (a member of the IMF), within the meaning of article VIII, section 2(b). Assume that it is contrary to Peru's Fund-approved exchange control regulations limiting the purposes for which dollars can be used by Peruvian residents. It would therefore be unenforceable under Peruvian law, but it does not contravene any state or federal law in the United States. The American bank refuses to disburse the loan, and is sued for damages by the Peruvian in a federal district court in the United States. The bank's defense is that Peruvian law applies, and that the contract is unenforceable under that law. Under the law of the American state where the contract was entered into and where the federal district court sits, the law of the place of contracting would apply. On the choice of law issue, is the court bound to apply Peruvian law by Executive Directors' Decision No. 446–4, above? Consider the following materials and questions relating to enforceability of the contract.

Do the F.C.C. decision and the State Department position quoted in it stand for the proposition that the federal district court would be bound by the choice of law rules contained in the Executive Board's interpretation of article VIII, section 2(b)? Is the issue resolved by the lack of any objection by member states to the interpretation since its issuance in 1949?

On the relationship between state and federal choice of law, Klaxon Co. v. Stentor Electric Mfg. Co.,[i] held that federal courts in diversity cases must apply the choice of law rules of the states in which they sit. Klaxon, however, was not a case with international implications, nor was it a case in which a federal statute might preclude the application

---

h. See Gold, The Cuban Insurance Cases and the Articles of the Fund 33 (1966). American courts have tended, however, to interpret "exchange contract" narrowly. See Ebke, supra note g.

i. 313 U.S. 487, 61 S.Ct. 1020, 85 L.Ed. 1477 (1941).

of an otherwise available state remedy. Section 11 of the Bretton Woods Agreements Act, quoted in the F.C.C. decision, enacts the first sentence of article VIII, section 2(b), of the Fund Agreement into federal statutory law in the United States. On the other hand, it does not enact article XXIX (the article giving the Executive Board the authority to interpret the Fund Agreement) into statutory law. Does that mean that although a federal court in the United States would be obliged to apply the first sentence of article VIII, section 2(b), as written (since it has the effect of an Act of Congress), it would not be bound to apply the specific choice of law rule embodied in the Executive Board's interpretation (since such interpretations do not have the effect of Acts of Congress)? In this connection the General Counsel of the Fund has written, "The suggestion that an Article [XXIX] interpretation may not be binding * * * would seem to be answered by the reflection that the provision which has been given the force of law is a provision of the Articles and therefore should carry with it any interpretation of the provision that is adopted under the Articles. If a court were to reject an Article [XXIX] interpretation in favor of a different interpretation of its own, this would not carry out the legislative intent to give the force of law to the provision of the Articles [such as article VIII, section 2(b)]."[j] But if a court, on its own, reasonably interprets and applies article VIII, section 2(b), isn't it giving it the force of law?"[k]

If the federal district court would not be bound as a matter of federal statutory law to apply the Executive Board's choice of law interpretation, is it free (or required) to (a) apply the state's "place of contracting" choice of law rule, leading to forum law, under Klaxon; (b) apply the "revenue law" or "public policy" escape device under state law, and thus decline to recognize the Bank's defense based on the Peruvian exchange control regulation; or (c) fashion its own federal choice of law rule which might or might not choose Peruvian law? As to these questions, consider the following cases:

Banco Frances e Brasileiro, S.A. v. John Doe:[l] A private Brazilian bank brought suit in a New York court for fraud and deceit against several private individuals, claiming that they had fraudulently obtained travelers checks in U.S. dollars from it in violation of Brazilian exchange control regulations. Rejecting the "revenue law" and "public policy" defenses, the New York Court of Appeals said that "United States membership in the IMF makes it impossible to conclude that the currency control laws of other member States are offensive to this State's public policy so as to preclude suit in tort by a private party.

---

j. Gold, Certain Aspects of the Law and Practice of the International Monetary Fund, in The Effectiveness of International Decisions 71, 87–88 (S. Schwebel ed. 1971).

k. On the effect of the interpretation provisions of the Fund Agreement in domestic law, compare Mann, International Corporations and National Law, 42 Brit. Y.B.Int'l L. 145, 167–68 (1967), and Nussbaum, Exchange Control and the International Monetary Fund, 59 Yale L.J. 421, 426 (1950), with the article by Gold, supra note j, and Gold, Interpretation by the Fund 31–42 (1968).

l. 36 N.Y.2d 592, 370 N.Y.S.2d 534, 331 N.E.2d 502 (1975), cert. denied 423 U.S. 867, 96 S.Ct. 129, 46 L.Ed.2d 96 (1975).

* * * Moreover, where a true governmental interest of a friendly nation is involved—and foreign currency reserves are of vital importance to a country plagued by balance of payments difficulties—the national policy of co-operation with Bretton Woods signatories is furthered by providing a State forum for suit." m Presumably, the court meant to limit its rather broad statement to currency control laws imposed consistently with the Fund Agreement. (The court cited article VIII, section 2(b), but did not analyze it or mention the Fund's interpretation of it. Does the court's reasoning turn on the specific requirements of either that provision or the Fund's interpretation? Does its reasoning apply equally to defenses based on a foreign currency control law, as in our hypothetical case?)

Day and Zimmermann, Inc. v. Challoner: n In a federal diversity case arising in Texas, involving a complaint seeking damages for wrongful death and personal injury resulting from the premature explosion of a howitzer round in Cambodia during the Viet Nam war, the Supreme Court vacated a Court of Appeals decision that had fashioned a federal choice-of-law rule to avoid choice of Cambodian law under the Texas choice-of-law rule. The Court of Appeals had chosen Texas' strict liability law on the merits, in order not to "frustrate well established American policies" if it had applied Cambodia's less liberal recovery rules. The Supreme Court's per curiam opinion followed Klaxon and said, "A federal court in a diversity case is not free to engraft onto * * * state [choice of law] rules exceptions or modifications which may commend themselves to the federal court, but which have not commended themselves to the State in which the federal court sits. The Court of Appeals in this case should identify and follow the Texas conflicts rule." o (Would our case be distinguishable?)

United States v. Pink: p An executive agreement entered into by the President under his Constitutional authority to appoint and receive ambassadors was held to override inconsistent state law that would have denied effect to a foreign nationalization recognized as effective by the executive agreement.

Zschernig v. Miller: q An Oregon probate law, making the inheritance rights of aliens conditional on the aliens' rights to enjoy the property in their own countries and on reciprocal inheritance rights of Americans, was held an unconstitutional interference with the federal foreign affairs power. It appeared that state courts were questioning whether laws in some Communist countries granting such rights were actually followed and whether statements of diplomats from those countries affirming the inheritance rights were made in good faith.

m. 36 N.Y.2d at 598, 370 N.Y.S.2d at 539, 331 N.E.2d at 506.

n. 423 U.S. 3, 96 S.Ct. 167, 46 L.Ed.2d 3 (1975).

o. 423 U.S. at 4–5, 96 S.Ct. at 168.

p. 315 U.S. 203, 62 S.Ct. 552, 86 L.Ed. 796 (1942).

q. 389 U.S. 429, 88 S.Ct. 664, 19 L.Ed.2d 683 (1968).

Banco Nacional de Cuba v. Sabbatino:[r] The act of state doctrine—precluding courts in the United States from reviewing the validity of certain acts by a foreign government within its own territory—was held to be an aspect of federal law in a diversity case, since it is "concerned with a basic choice regarding the competence and function of the Judiciary and the National Executive in ordering our relationships with other members of the international community * * *." The result was to compel choice of the foreign law despite the forum's contrary public policy, and to allow recovery in favor of a foreign governmental instrumentality that had sued an American defendant for conversion of the documents of title to a shipload of sugar.[s] The foreign instrumentality's title to the sugar was based on an expropriation while the sugar was in the foreign territory. The conversion occurred when the defendant obtained the documents of title from the instrumentality without paying for them.

Whitney v. Robertson:[t] "When [a treaty and an Act of Congress] relate to the same subject, the courts will always endeavor to construe them so as to give effect to both, if that can be done without violating the language of either * * *." (Does this suggest what courts should do when an obligation under an international agreement and an asserted nonstatutory federal choice of law rule relate to the same subject?)

Suppose a foreign government-owned bank (an instrumentality of the foreign government) enters into an exchange contract in the United States with an American private party, involving the foreign currency. If a dispute then arises and the foreign bank invokes its own government's Fund-approved exchange control regulations to excuse its performance, the American party might well bring suit against it in a federal court in the United States. Since the bank is a government instrumentality, it would be immune from suit—and the federal court would lack subject matter jurisdiction—unless one of the exceptions from immunity in the Foreign Sovereign Immunities Act of 1976 applies.[u] One exception is for actions based on commercial activities in the United States. Assume that this exception does apply, so the bank is not immune and the case reaches the merits.

One issue on the merits would be whether the U.S. court should (must?) apply the foreign country's exchange control regulation. The Foreign Sovereign Immunities Act says that if the instrumentality is not immune, it "shall be liable in the same manner and to the same

---

r. 376 U.S. 398, 84 S.Ct. 923, 11 L.Ed.2d 804 (1964).

s. The result on the specific facts was later overturned by Congress in the second Hickenlooper Amendment, 22 U.S.C.A. § 2370(e)(2).

t. 124 U.S. 190, 194, 8 S.Ct. 456, 458, 31 L.Ed. 386, 388 (1888).

u. Public Law 94–583 (1976), as amended by Public Law 100–669 (1988), 28 U.S.C.A. §§ 1330, 1602 et seq.

extent as a private individual under like circumstances." [v] Does this answer the question?

In cases under the Act not involving exchange contracts, the federal circuits have split over whether to look to federal common law for the applicable choice-of-law rules, or to apply the forum state's choice of law by analogy to the *Klaxon* rule for diversity cases, supra.[w] Are these cases relevant?

Would a federal district court's adoption of the Executive Board's choice-of-law interpretation raise constitutional problems relating to delegation of legislative or judicial authority? Article I, section 1 of the Constitution vests all legislative powers in the Congress, and Article III, section 1 vests the judicial power of the United States in the Supreme Court and in such inferior courts as Congress may from time to time establish.[x]

C. THE INTERNATIONAL CIVIL AVIATION ORGANIZATION

The ICAO Council has the authority to perform a dispute-settlement role, in addition to its rule-making and administrative functions. As you read the materials, keep in mind the question of the Council's efficacy as a dispute-settlement body. Start with Chicago Convention Chapter XVIII ("Disputes and Default"), *articles 84–88*.

INDIA–PAKISTAN

An early instance of dispute settlement under article 84 involved India and Pakistan, as described below.

T. BUERGENTHAL, LAW–MAKING IN THE INTERNATIONAL CIVIL AVIATION ORGANIZATION
137–39 (1969).*

The complaint by India against Pakistan was formally submitted to the Council by India in April of 1952. The complaint charged Pakistan with acts violating Articles 5, 6, and 9 of the Convention, and with

---

v. 28 U.S.C.A. § 1606.

w. Compare Harris v. Polskie Linie Lotnicze, 820 F.2d 1000 (9th Cir.1987), and Liu v. Republic of China, 892 F.2d 1419 (9th Cir.1989), cert. dismissed 497 U.S. 1058, 111 S.Ct. 27, 111 L.Ed.2d 840 (1990) (both looking to federal common law, and finding it in the Restatement (Second) of Conflict of Laws), with Barkanic v. General Administration of Civil Aviation of The People's Republic of China, 923 F.2d 957 (2d Cir.1991) (favoring application of the forum state's choice of law).

x. See generally L. Henkin, Foreign Affairs and the Constitution 196–201 (1972).

* Reprinted by permission of the Procedural Aspects of International Law Institute, Inc.

violations of the International Air Services Transit Agreement. India alleged, in particular, that Pakistan refused to permit Indian aircraft engaged in commercial air service between India and Afghanistan to fly over West Pakistan.

When the Indian complaint was submitted to the Council, no rules of procedure had as yet been enacted for the settlement of disputes under Article 84 of the Convention. Recognizing that it would initially have to decide what rules of procedure were to be applied, the Council invited India and Pakistan "to designate representatives to consult with the Council on the future course of action to be followed." This invitation was designed to produce an acceptable procedure for the disposition of this case. The Council recognized that more time would be needed before any generally applicable rules could be drafted.

In the meantime, the Council granted Pakistan's request for a 30-day period within which to file an answer to the Indian complaint. When Pakistan's reply had been received, the Council appointed a Working Group of three Council Representatives to consider and recommend to the Council "what steps could properly be taken by the Council during the remainder of the * * * session."

After consulting with the parties, the Working Group presented a report containing two basic recommendations. The first suggested that the parties provide the Council with certain additional information relating to the dispute. The second proposed that the parties be urged "to enter into further direct negotiations as soon as possible with a view to limiting to the greatest possible extent the outstanding issues." This proposal was prompted by the consideration that the Working Group had concluded, after consulting with the parties, that Pakistan and India were receptive to the possibility of reaching a negotiated settlement. The Council accepted these recommendations, and shortly thereafter appointed another Working Group to study the case with a view to ascertaining what further action should be taken.

The new Working Group informed the Council that Pakistan was prepared to discuss with India the possibility of opening two air routes over West Pakistan in exchange for certain concessions by India, and suggested that "no possibility of settlement by direct negotiations should be missed." The Council accepted this suggestion and set a time limit within which the parties were requested to submit a progress report on their negotiations. Before this deadline had expired, the parties informed the Council that they had reached an amicable settlement of their dispute.

THE RULES OF PROCEDURE

Drawing on its experience in this dispute, the Council in 1957 adopted procedural rules. One of its concerns was that it would be an unwieldly trier of facts. Consequently it provided for a committee "of five individuals who shall be Representatives on the Council of Member States not concerned in the disagreement" to undertake a preliminary examination of disagreements submitted to the Council under article 84, if requested to do so by the Council in a particular case.[a] Before this provision was adopted, a question was raised whether the Council could properly delegate any of its functions under article 84 to such a committee.[b] Chicago Convention articles 54(d), 54(e) and 55(a) authorize the Council to establish the Air Transport Committee (chosen from among members of the Council), the Air Navigation Commission and subordinate air transport commissions, but there is no express provision for a committee to undertake preliminary examinations of disagreements. If you had been an ICAO Legal Officer at the time and had only this information, the text of article 84 and the context and purpose of the Chicago Convention to go on, would you have advised that the delegation of authority to such a committee was permissible?

Among the other procedural rules adopted by the Council were those below on promoting negotiations between the parties and on Council decisions in article 84 proceedings.

ICAO COUNCIL, RULES FOR THE SETTLEMENT OF DIFFERENCES
ICAO Doc. 7782/2, at 1–3, 6–7 (1975).

* * *

Art. 2

Any Contracting State submitting a disagreement to the Council for settlement (hereinafter referred to as "the applicant") shall file an application to which shall be attached a memorial containing:

(*a*) The name of the applicant and the name of any Contracting State with which the disagreement exists (the latter hereinafter referred to as "the respondent");

(*b*) The name of an agent authorized to act for the applicant in the proceedings, together with his address, at the seat of the Organization, to which all communications relating to the case, including notice of the date of any meeting, should be sent;

(*c*) A statement of relevant facts;

(*d*) Supporting data related to the facts;

(*e*) A statement of law;

(*f*) The relief desired by action of Council on the specific points submitted;

---

a. See Rules for the Settlement of Differences art. 6(2), ICAO Doc. 7782/2, at 4 (1975).

b. See Fitzgerald, The Judgment of the International Court of Justice in the Appeal Relating to the Jurisdiction of the ICAO Council, 12 Canadian Y.B.Int'l L. 153, 157–58 (1974).

(g) A statement that negotiations to settle the disagreement had taken place between the parties but were not successful.

* * *

ART. 5
Preliminary Objection and Action Thereon

(1) If the respondent questions the jurisdiction of the Council to handle the matter presented by the applicant, he shall file a preliminary objection setting out the basis of the objection.

(2) Such preliminary objection shall be filed in a special pleading at the latest before the expiry of the time-limit set for delivery of the counter-memorial.

(3) Upon a preliminary objection being filed, the proceedings on the merits shall be suspended and, with respect to the time-limit fixed under Article 3(1)(c), time shall cease to run from the moment the preliminary objection is filed until the objection is decided by the Council.

(4) If a preliminary objection has been filed, the Council, after hearing the parties, shall decide the question as a preliminary issue before any further steps are taken under these Rules.

* * *

ART. 14
Negotiations During Proceedings

(1) The Council may, at any time during the proceedings and prior to the meeting at which the decision is rendered as provided in Article 15(4), invite the parties to the dispute to engage in direct negotiations, if the Council deems that the possibilities of settling the dispute or narrowing the issues through negotiations have not been exhausted.

(2) If the parties accept the invitation to negotiate, the Council may set a time-limit for the completion of such negotiations, during which other proceedings on the merits shall be suspended.

(3) Subject to the consent of the parties concerned, the Council may render any assistance likely to further the negotiations, including the designation of an individual or a group of individuals to act as conciliator during the negotiations.

(4) Any solution agreed through negotiations shall be recorded by Council. If no solution is found the parties shall so report to Council and the suspended proceedings shall be resumed.

ART. 15
Decision

(1) After hearing arguments, or after consideration of the report of the Committee, as the case may be, the Council shall render its decision.

(2) The decision of the Council shall be in writing and shall contain:

- (*i*) the date on which it is delivered;
- (*ii*) a list of the Members of the Council participating;
- (*iii*) the names of the parties and of their agents;
- (*iv*) a summary of the proceedings;
- (*v*) the conclusions of the Council together with its reasons for reaching them;
- (*vi*) its decision, if any, in regard to costs;
- (*vii*) a statement of the voting in Council showing whether the conclusions were unanimous or by a majority vote, and if by a majority, giving the number of Members of the Council who voted in favour of the conclusions and the number of those who voted against or abstained.

(3) Any Member of the Council who voted against the majority opinion may have its views recorded in the form of a dissenting opinion which shall be attached to the decision of Council.

(4) The decision of the Council shall be rendered at a meeting of the Council called for that purpose which shall be held as soon as practicable after the close of the proceedings.

(5) No Member of the Council shall vote in the consideration by the Council of any dispute to which it is a party.

NONADJUDICATIVE PROCEDURES

Note the emphasis in article 14 on negotiation and conciliation. A number of other international organizations also stress informal, nonadjudicative means of dispute-settlement, sometimes to the exclusion of formal procedures. For example, as a practical matter the dispute-settlement process in the WHO relies almost entirely on the mediation efforts of the Director–General.[c] Such a process has obvious advantages over formal adjudication in an organization lacking effective enforcement powers. But that is essentially a negative reason for adopting nonadjudicative procedures. Are there affirmative reasons as well?

The composition of the ICAO Council is better suited to a conciliation-mediation function than to dispassionate adjudication of disputes. It has acted as a conciliator-mediator on occasions in addition to the first India–Pakistan dispute, participating, for example, in the negotiated settlement of a 1958 dispute between Jordan and the United Arab Republic. As you read the materials below, consider whether the Council can effectively perform any dispute-settlement role beyond

---

c. See 1 D. Leive, International Regulatory Regimes 54–58 (1976).

conciliation and mediation.ᵈ

INDIA AND PAKISTAN AGAIN

In 1971 India and Pakistan became involved in another dispute concerning the right of overflight. In January of that year an Indian airliner was hijacked and diverted to Lahore, Pakistan. Ultimately the hijackers blew up the aircraft on the ground at the Lahore airport. India claimed that Pakistan had failed to take appropriate steps to restore control over the aircraft to its commander and to save the aircraft. India then presented a claim to Pakistan for damages for the destroyed aircraft and its cargo, and a day later withdrew its permission for Pakistani aircraft to overfly Indian territory between West and (what was then) East Pakistan.

Pakistan asserted that this violated the Chicago Convention, the International Air Services Transit Agreement of 1944 and the India-Pakistan Bilateral Air Services Agreement of 1948. Accordingly, Pakistan filed with the ICAO Council an "Application" under article 84 of the Convention and under the related article II, section 2, of the International Air Services Transit Agreement.ᵉ The Council invited the parties to negotiate, and offered its assistance. India, however, asserted that the Council had no jurisdiction, for reasons that appear below. The Council decided that it did have jurisdiction, and India then appealed to the International Court of Justice on the jurisdictional issue. Set forth below are Pakistan's Application addressed to the President of the ICAO Council, excerpts from its attached Memorial and India's Preliminary Objections before the Council, the Council decision as communicated to the parties, and excerpts from the ICJ opinion deciding India's appeal.

APPLICATION OF PAKISTAN

Before the ICAO Council, Mar. 3, 1971.

Appeal Relating to the Jurisdiction of the ICAO Council, I.C.J. Pleadings 65.

Sir,

* * *

The illegal and unjust action by the Government of India of suspending Pakistan aircraft flights over its territory from the 4th February, 1971, in breach of its international obligations, has caused and is causing great injustice, hardship, loss and injury to Pakistan which requires immediate attention and action of the Council.

---

d. On the role of the ICAO Council as a conciliator-mediator, with particular reference to the Jordan–U.A.R. dispute, see T. Buergenthal, Law-Making in the International Civil Aviation Organization 162–64 (1969); Gariepy & Botsford, The Effectiveness of the International Civil Aviation Organization's Adjudicatory Machinery, 42 J.Air L. & Commerce 351, 358–59 (1976).

e. Pakistan also filed a "Complaint" under article II, section 1, of the Transit Agreement. Issues arising from the "complaint" procedure are examined later in this subsection.

In view of the disagreement between the two contracting States of Pakistan and India relating to the application of the Convention on International Civil Aviation, 1944, the International Air Services Transit Agreement, 1944 and the Bilateral Air Services Agreement, 1948 between the two countries which could not be settled by negotiation, it is requested that the application may be taken up urgently and the matter be decided by the Council and reliefs may be granted as stated in the attached Memorial.

* * *

Accept, Sir, the assurances of our highest consideration.

(*Signed*) A. Qadir,
Air Vice Marshal,
Joint Secretary to the Government of Pakistan.

MEMORIAL OF PAKISTAN
Before the ICAO Council, Mar. 3, 1971.
Appeal Relating to the Jurisdiction of the ICAO Council, I.C.J. Pleadings 66.

* * *

Statement of relevant facts—

In a note dated 4th February 1971 handed over to the Government of Pakistan, the Government of India conveyed its decision "to suspend, with immediate effect, the overflight of all Pakistani aircraft, civil or military, over the territory of India".

In a Note dated 5th February 1971, the Government of Pakistan protested to the Government of India that its decision to suspend flights of Pakistan aircraft over India was arbitrary and unilateral and a serious breach of multilateral and bilateral agreements.

* * *

Pakistan comprises of two wings which are situated more than 1,000 miles apart with Indian Territory in between. Air services between the two wings are thus a vital link between the two wings of Pakistan. As a result of the decision of the Government of India to suspend overflights of Pakistan aircraft over its territory, Pakistan International Airlines, the national airline of Pakistan, has been compelled to re-route its flights between the two wings of Pakistan and other international scheduled flights by circumventing the Indian territory. This has more than doubled the flight time between the two wings, considerably increased the flight time of other international flights and reduced frequency of flights on all sectors. These factors have resulted in considerable increase in the cost of operation of services of Pakistan International Airlines, loss of business and other losses to the airline, inconvenience to passengers, immense loss and injury to Pakistan and have adversely affected the economic situation of the country.

* * *

The Government of Pakistan conveyed to the Government of India that the flights of Pakistan International Airlines which connected two wings of Pakistan carry, apart from passengers, essential supplies to East Pakistan. The suspension of these flights has also adversely affected the relief operations in East Pakistan currently going on in view of the recent devastations caused by the cyclone and tidal bore. In the same note the Government of India was called upon to rescind its decision to suspend overflights of Pakistan aircraft.

The Government of India sought to link the recent hijacking incident in which two nationals of the State of Jammu and Kashmir hijacked an Indian aircraft from Indian-occupied Kashmir to Lahore in Pakistan, with the arbitrary suspension of flights of Pakistan aircraft over Indian territory. * * * It is submitted that reference by India to the hijacking incident is irrelevant and has no relation whatsoever with the suspension of flights of Pakistan aircraft over Indian territory. Such flights are governed by multilateral and bilateral agreements and there is no legal basis or justification whatsoever for their suspension.

* * *

Statement of Law—

Pakistan and India are parties to the Convention on International Civil Aviation, 1944, the International Air Services Transit Agreement, 1944 and the Bilateral Air Services Agreement, 1948.

By virtue of Article 5 of the Convention on International Civil Aviation, 1944, each Contracting State agreed that all aircraft of the other contracting States not engaged in scheduled international air services shall have the right to make flights into or in transit nonstop across its territory and to make stops for non-traffic purposes without the necessity of obtaining prior permission subject to the right of that State to require landing. By denying this right to Pakistan aircraft engaged in other than scheduled international air services to overfly its territory or make a technical stop, India has unilaterally and arbitrarily violated the provisions of the Convention without any valid reason and is in breach of its obligations thereunder.

Under Article 1 of the International Air Services Transit Agreement, India has granted to Pakistan the following freedoms of the air in respect of scheduled international air services:

(1) the privilege to fly across its territory without landing;

(2) the privilege to land for non-traffic purposes.

* * *

By virtue of the Bilateral Air Services Agreement with India of 1948, Pakistan International Airlines, the designated airline of Pakistan, has the right, *inter alia,* to transit across the territory of India without landing on its scheduled international air services. The decision of the Government of India to stop such overflights of Pakistan's designated airline contravenes the provisions of the Agreement and is in breach of its obligations thereunder.

* * *

The decision of the Government of India is arbitrary, unilateral and illegal and is in violation of the Conventions and Agreements aforesaid and is contrary and repugnant to International Law.

Reliefs Desired—

The Government of Pakistan seeks among others, the following reliefs by action of the ICAO Council:

(1) To decide and declare that the decision of the Government of India suspending the overflights of Pakistan aircraft over the territory of India, is illegal and in violation of India's international obligations under the Convention and Agreements aforesaid.

(2) To find and declare that Pakistan has the following freedoms of the air in respect of scheduled international air services:

  (a) the privilege to fly its aircraft across the Indian territory without landing;

  (b) the privilege to land its aircraft in Indian territory for non-traffic purposes.

(3) To find and declare that Pakistan aircraft have the right, subject to observance of the terms of the Convention on International Civil Aviation, 1944 to make flights into or in transit non-stop across Indian territory and to make stops for non-traffic purposes in that territory without the necessity of obtaining prior permission, and subject to the right of India to require landing of non-scheduled flights.

(4) To find and declare that Pakistan aircraft are entitled to operate flights between the two wings of Pakistan and beyond by direct route over its territory.

(5) To direct the Government of India to immediately rescind their illegal decision aforesaid and not to impede in any manner the overflights of Pakistan aircraft over the territory of India.

(6) To decide and declare that the decision of the Government of India of suspending flights of Pakistan aircraft over the Indian territory is causing injustice, hardship, loss and injury to Pakistan.

(7) To direct that the Government of India should adequately compensate and indemnify Pakistan for the losses and injury suffered by it as a result of the arbitrary, unilateral and illegal decision of the Government of India in breach of its international obligations.

* * *

Efforts were made by Pakistan to negotiate with India but were not successful.

PRELIMINARY OBJECTIONS BY THE GOVERNMENT OF INDIA

Before the ICAO Council, May 28, 1971.
Appeal Relating to the Jurisdiction of the ICAO Council, I.C.J. Pleadings 98.

* * *

The Government of India find on a perusal of Pakistan's Application and Complaint, and the Memorials and Attachments, that Pakistan's Application and Complaint are not competent and not maintainable, and that the Council has no jurisdiction to handle the matters presented by Pakistan. The Government of India, therefore, file these Preliminary Objections under Article 5 of the Rules to both the Application and the Complaint.

* * *

The Government of India would like to clarify that this is not a Counter-Memorial and that they are not here dealing with the merits of the Application and the Complaint made by Pakistan but are strictly confining themselves to the Preliminary Objections to the competence and maintainability of Pakistan's Application and Complaint and the jurisdiction of the Council.

* * *

Under Article 84 of the Convention and under Article 1(1) of the Rules, two of the conditions which are required to be fulfilled in order to make the Application competent and maintainable and in order that the Council may have jurisdiction to deal with it and handle the matter presented by the Applicant, are the following:

(a) There should be a disagreement between the two contracting States, and

(b) the disagreement should relate to the interpretation or application of the Convention.

* * *

Both the aforesaid conditions postulate and presuppose the continued existence and operation of the Convention as between two States. If the Convention has been terminated, by repudiation, abrogation or otherwise, or has been suspended, as between two States, any dispute relating to such termination or suspension cannot possibly be referred to the Council under the aforesaid Articles of the Convention and the Rules, since in such a case no question of "interpretation" or "application" of the Convention can possibly arise (there being no Convention in operation as between the two States). Further, there cannot possibly be a disagreement on a point of interpretation or application of a treaty which is not in operation as between two States. In other words, so long as two contracting States accept the existence, operation and efficacy of the Convention as between them, all points of disagreement as to the interpretation or application of the Convention would be within the jurisdiction of the Council. But any question of termination or suspension of the Convention as between two States cannot be referred to the Council under the aforesaid Articles.

What is stated above regarding the Convention also represents accurately the position under the Transit Agreement which confers limited jurisdiction on the Council in identical words.

* * *

The composition of the Council and its powers and functions are, again, in keeping with the limited jurisdiction which has been conferred upon it by Article 84 of the Convention, Article II of the Transit Agreement, and Article 1 of the Rules, to hear international disputes. The sovereign power of a State to suspend, or to abrogate or otherwise terminate an international treaty—not seldom involving vastly complicated questions of fact and international law—are outside the scope of the Council's jurisdiction under the aforesaid Articles.

To sum up, the scheme of the aforesaid Articles is simple and clear. So long as the Convention or the Transit Agreement continues to be in operation as between two States, any disagreement as to the *construction* of its Articles or the *application* of the Articles to the existing state of facts, can be referred to the Council; and likewise, *any action taken under* the Transit Agreement can be referred to the Council. But if a State has terminated or suspended the Convention or the Transit Agreement vis-à-vis another State, there cannot possibly be any question of interpretation or application of the treaty, or of action under the treaty, and the Council is not the forum for deciding such disputes. These disputes are usually in the realm of political confrontation between two States, often involving military hostilities not amounting to war, and these matters of political confrontation or military hostilities are outside the ambit of the Council's competence. The question of overflying raised by Pakistan, is directly connected with military hostilities in the past and continues to be inextricably tied up with the posture of political confrontation bordering on hostility adopted by Pakistan.

[India then argued that Pakistan had repudiated the Convention with respect to India, since Pakistan's conduct was allegedly inimical to the principle of safety in civil aviation, and that India had acquiesced in that repudiation. In the alternative, India argued that it had suspended or terminated the agreements with respect to Pakistan because Pakistan's conduct made it unsafe for Indian aircraft to overfly Pakistan; it was enough, India argued, that it had done so, and the question whether it was justified in doing so was irrelevant since the issue of justification for suspension or termination was not within the Council's jurisdiction.

[India argued further that overflights between India and Pakistan had been governed before the 1965 India–Pakistan war solely by a special regime stemming from the 1948 India–Pakistan Bilateral Air Services Agreement, which India apparently regarded as superseding the multilateral agreements from 1948 until 1965, insofar as those agreements dealt with overflight. The 1948 regime had not been revived after the 1965 war, India argued, but had been replaced by a new bilateral regime which granted overflight rights only when permission was granted. Since the Council had no jurisdiction to resolve disputes arising under these bilateral agreements, India concluded that it had no jurisdiction to hear the case.]

DECISION OF THE ICAO COUNCIL
Identical letters to the Representatives of India and Pakistan, July 30, 1971.
Appeal Relating to the Jurisdiction of the ICAO
Council, I.C.J. Pleadings 350, 398.

The Secretary General of the International Civil Aviation Organization presents his compliments and has the honour to refer to the Preliminary Objections, dated 28 May 1971, filed by the Government of India and relating respectively to the Application of the Government of Pakistan, dated 3 March 1971, filed under Article 2 of the Rules for the Settlement of Differences and the Complaint of the Government of Pakistan dated 3 March 1971, filed under Article 21 of the said Rules.

On 29 July 1971, the Council decided not to accept the Preliminary Objections aforesaid.

* * *

The Secretary General desires, on this occasion, once more to draw your attention to the Council's resolution of 8 April 1971 in which the parties were invited to negotiate.

The Secretary General takes the opportunity of conveying to your Excellency, the assurances of his highest consideration.

(*Signed*) Assad Kotaite,
Secretary General.

THE COUNCIL'S PROCEDURE

A number of significant questions about the Council's procedure in this case have been raised by a former Principal Legal Officer of the ICAO. He has pointed out, for example, that the members of the ICAO Council hearing cases like this are representatives of their states, not persons following their own consciences. In fact, some of them wished to defer a decision on India's preliminary objections until they could receive instructions from their respective governments, and others apparently had actually received instructions.[f] The member of the

---

[f] See Fitzgerald, The Judgment of the International Court of Justice in the Appeal Relating to the Jurisdiction of the ICAO Council, 12 Canadian Y.B. Int'l L. 153, 168–69 (1974).

Council representing India, however, could not vote. See Chicago Convention art. 84. (Pakistan did not have a representative on the Council.) For the most part, Council members have no legal training or experience; one of the reasons given by representatives seeking to delay the decision in the India–Pakistan case until they could receive instructions was their desire to obtain opinions from their governments' legal advisers.[g] Query, though, whether it was necessary to obtain instructions from home if legal advice was all that was needed. Article 8(1) of the Council's Rules for the Settlement of Differences provides that the Council may obtain an "expert opinion" from virtually any individual or body it may select; presumably that would include an expert legal opinion.

Is the dispute-settlement procedure under article 84 appropriate for its task?

Is the ICAO Council as an adjudicator any less well suited to its task than the ILO Governing Body Committee on Freedom of Association, which consists of nonlawyer representatives of member states and of employers' and workers' organizations?

During the Council's deliberations on India's preliminary objections (after oral arguments had been made), the Indian representative to the Council and Pakistani observers were present. Both sides participated in the discussion.[h] Is this sound practice for third-party dispute-settlement?

Article 5(4) of the Council's Rules for the Settlement of Differences provides, "If a preliminary objection has been filed, the Council, after hearing the parties, shall decide the question as a preliminary issue before any further steps are taken under these Rules." The Council did that, but it gave no reasons for its decision. Contrast the practice of the ICJ, which has often decided preliminary objections before turning to the merits, with an opinion giving its reasons. Could there be any good reason for the ICAO Council not to have given reasons for its decision on India's preliminary objections?

APPEAL RELATING TO THE JURISDICTION OF THE ICAO COUNCIL
International Court of Justice, 1972.
[1972] I.C.J. 46.

* * *

10. The substance of the dispute between the Parties, as placed before the Council of ICAO ("the Council") by Pakistan on 3 March

---

g. See Appeal Relating to the Jurisdiction of the ICAO Council, I.C.J. Pleadings 55–56.

h. See Fitzgerald, supra note f, at 170. In addition, some Council members appear to have participated in the actual decision without having been present for all the oral hearings or having read a transcript of them. See Gariepy & Botsford, supra note d, at 359.

1971, relates to the suspension by India of overflights of Indian territory by Pakistan civil aircraft, on and from 4 February 1971, arising out of a "hijacking" incident involving the diversion of an Indian aircraft to Pakistan. It should be mentioned here that hostilities interrupting overflights had broken out between the two countries in August 1965, ceasing in the following month, and that after this cessation the Parties adopted what is known as the Tashkent Declaration of 10 January 1966, by which, and more especially by a consequential Exchange of Letters between them dated 3/7 February 1966, it was agreed, *inter alia*, that there should be "an immediate resumption of overflights across each other's territory *on the same basis as that prior to 1 August 1965* * * *", i.e., prior to the hostilities—(emphasis added). Pakistan has interpreted this undertaking as meaning that overflights would be resumed on the basis of the Convention and Transit Agreement ("the Treaties"); but India has maintained that these Treaties having (as she alleges) been suspended during the hostilities, were never as such revived, and that overflights were to be resumed on the basis of a "special regime" according to which such flights could take place in principle, but only after permission had been granted by India—whereas under the Treaties they could take place as of right, without any necessity for prior permission. This special regime, India contends, replaced the Treaties as between the Parties; but Pakistan denies that any such regime ever came into existence, and also claims that, not having been registered as an international agreement under Article 102 of the United Nations Charter, it cannot now be invoked by India. Consequently Pakistan maintains that, at least since January/February 1966, the Treaties have never ceased to be applicable, and that, in accordance with them (Article 5 of the Convention and Article I, Section 1, of the Transit Agreement), her civil aircraft have "the right * * * to make flights into or in transit non-stop across [Indian] territory and to make stops for non-traffic purposes *without the necessity of obtaining prior permission*" * * *.

[Pakistan first argued that the Court had no jurisdiction to hear India's appeal, since the Court's jurisdiction rested on article 84 of the Chicago Convention, and India was precluded from relying on that article in view of its argument that the Convention had been suspended or terminated between itself and Pakistan. The Court brushed Pakistan's argument aside, holding that a mere allegation by one party that a treaty was no longer operative could not be used to defeat the jurisdictional clauses or preclude it from relying on them. To hold otherwise would make them essentially dead letters.]

17. Greater weight is to be attached to Pakistan's contention that in the case of these Treaties, the jurisdictional clauses themselves do not allow of India's appeal in the present case because, on their correct interpretation, they only provide for an appeal to the Court against a final decision of the Council on the merits of any dispute referred to it, and not against decisions of an interim or preliminary nature such as are here involved. These clauses read as follows:

Article 84 of the Convention
Settlement of Disputes

If any disagreement between two or more contracting States relating to the interpretation or application of this Convention and its Annexes cannot be settled by negotiation, it shall, on the application of any State concerned in the disagreement, be decided by the Council. No member of the Council shall vote in the consideration by the Council of any dispute to which it is a party. Any contracting State may, subject to Article 85, appeal from the decision of the Council to an ad hoc arbitral tribunal agreed upon with the other parties to the dispute or to the Permanent Court of International Justice. Any such appeal shall be notified to the Council within sixty days of receipt of notification of the decision of the Council.

Section 2 of Article II of the Transit Agreement

If any disagreement between two or more contracting States relating to the interpretation or application of this Agreement cannot be settled by negotiation, the provisions of Chapter XVIII of the above-mentioned Convention—[*nota:* this Chapter contains Article 84 above quoted]—shall be applicable in the same manner as provided therein with reference to any disagreement relating to the interpretation or application of the above-mentioned Convention.

On the wording of these provisions the case in favour of Pakistan's interpretation of them is as follows. The disagreement on interpretation or application which is to be decided by the Council under Article 84 is a disagreement on a substantive issue of merits, and it is this which is to "be decided by the Council". Consequently, the words giving a right of "appeal from the decision of the Council" ("the" decision, not "a" decision) must be confined to such a decision. Also, the disagreement that is referable to the Council under Article 84, and hence ultimately appealable, has to be one that could not "be settled by negotiation". Such a disagreement would normally be confined to the substantive merits of the issue involved, since disagreements about jurisdiction are (so the argument runs) not usually in the negotiable category. This consideration reinforces the view that only those decisions of the Council that consist of final decisions on the merits are appealable under Article 84. It is also pointed out that the Council's "Rules for the Settlement of Differences" (in Articles 5 and 15) provide for different procedures for dealing with the two types of decision, and that in the case of jurisdictional decisions, the rules do not include any obligation to give reasons for the decision, as should normally be the case for an appealable decision.

18. This view would certainly have to be regarded as correct in respect of any procedural or otherwise genuinely interlocutory decisions of the Council, such as decisions about the manner in which a case was to be presented to it; as to the time-limits within which written pleadings were to be deposited; or as to the production or admissibility

of documents or other evidence, etc. The Court however thinks that a decision of the Council relative to its jurisdiction to entertain a dispute does not come within the same category as the matters just mentioned, even though, like them, it necessarily has a preliminary character;—for although, in the purely temporal sense, a preliminary question is involved, that question is, in its essence, a substantial question crucially affecting the position of the parties relative to the case, notwithstanding that it does not decide the ultimate merits. In consequence, the Court considers that for the purposes of the jurisdictional clauses of the Treaties, final decisions of the Council as to its competence should not be distinguished from final decisions on the merits. In support of this view the following further points may be noted:

(a) Although a jurisdictional decision does not determine the "ultimate merits" of the case, it is a decision of a substantive character, inasmuch as it may decide the whole affair by bringing it to an end, if the finding is against the assumption of jurisdiction. A decision which can have that effect is of scarcely less importance than a decision on the merits, which it either rules out entirely or, alternatively, permits by endorsing the existence of the jurisdictional basis which must form the indispensable foundation of any decision on the merits. A jurisdictional decision is therefore unquestionably a constituent part of the case, viewed as a whole, and should, in principle, be regarded as being on a par with decisions on the merits as regards any right of appeal that may be given.

(b) Nor should it be overlooked that for the party raising a jurisdictional objection, its significance will also lie in the possibility it may offer of avoiding, not only a decision, but even a hearing, on the merits,—a factor which is of prime importance in many cases. An essential point of legal principle is involved here, namely that a party should not have to give an account of itself on issues of merits before a tribunal which lacks jurisdiction in the matter, or whose jurisdiction has not yet been established.

(c) At the same time, many cases before the Court have shown that although a decision on jurisdiction can never directly decide any question of merits, the issues involved may be by no means divorced from the merits. A jurisdictional decision may often have to touch upon the latter or at least involve some consideration of them. This illustrates the importance of the jurisdictional stage of a case, and the influence it may have on the eventual decision on the merits, if these are reached—a factor well known to parties in litigation.

(d) Not only do issues of jurisdiction involve questions of law, but these questions may well be as important and complicated as any that arise on the merits—sometimes more so. They may, in the context of such an entity as ICAO, create precedents affecting the position and interests of a large number of States, in a way which no ordinary procedural, interlocutory or other preliminary issue could do. It would indeed be hard to accept the view that even the most routine decisions of the Council on points of the interpretation or application of the Treaties should be automatically appealable, while decisions on jurisdiction, which must *ex hypothesi* involve important general considerations of principle, should not be, despite the drastic effects which, as already noticed (*supra*, sub-paragraph *(a)*), they are capable of having.

(e) A concluding consideration is that supposing an appeal were made to the Court from the final decision of the Council on the merits of a dispute;—it would hardly be possible for the Court either to affirm or reject that decision, if it found that the Council had all along lacked jurisdiction to go into the case. This shows that questions relating to the Council's jurisdiction cannot in the last resort be excluded from the Court's purview: it is merely a question of what is the stage at which the Court's supervision in this respect is to be exercised. Clearly, not only do obvious reasons of convenience call for such exercise as early as possible—in the present case, here and now—but also substantial considerations of principle do so—for it would be contrary to accepted standards of the good administration of justice to allow an international organ to examine and discuss the merits of a dispute when its competence to do so was not only undetermined but actively challenged. Yet this is precisely what the Court would be allowing if it now held itself not to have jurisdiction to deal with the matter because it could only hear appeals from final decisions of the Council on the merits.

* * *

26. Before leaving this part of the case, and since this is the first time any matter has come to it on appeal, the Court thinks it useful to make a few observations of a general character on the subject. The case is presented to the Court in the guise of an ordinary dispute between States (and such a dispute underlies it). Yet in the proceedings before the Court, it is the act of a third entity—the Council of ICAO—which one of the Parties is impugning and the other defending. In that aspect of the matter, the appeal to the Court contemplated by the Chicago Convention and the Transit Agreement must be regarded as an element of the general regime established in respect of ICAO. In thus providing for judicial recourse by way of appeal to the Court against decisions of the Council concerning interpretation and application—a type of recourse already figuring in earlier conventions in the sphere of communications—the Chicago Treaties gave member States, and through them the Council, the possibility of ensuring a certain measure of supervision by the Court over those decisions. To this

extent, these Treaties enlist the support of the Court for the good functioning of the Organization, and therefore the first reassurance for the Council lies in the knowledge that means exist for determining whether a decision as to its own competence is in conformity or not with the provisions of the treaties governing its action. If nothing in the text requires a different conclusion, an appeal against a decision of the Council as to its own jurisdiction must therefore be receivable since, from the standpoint of the supervision by the Court of the validity of the Council's acts, there is no ground for distinguishing between supervision as to jurisdiction, and supervision as to merits.

27. The Court now turns to the substantive issue of the correctness of the decisions of the Council dated 29 July 1971. The question is whether the Council is competent to go into and give a final decision on the merits of the dispute in respect of which, at the instance of Pakistan, and subject to the present appeal, it has assumed jurisdiction. The answer to this question clearly depends on whether Pakistan's case, considered in the light of India's objections to it, discloses the existence of a dispute of such a character as to amount to a "disagreement * * * relating to the interpretation or application" of the Chicago Convention or of the related Transit Agreement * * *. If so, then prima facie the Council is competent. Nor could the Council be deprived of jurisdiction merely because considerations that are claimed to lie outside the Treaties may be involved if, irrespective of this, issues concerning the interpretation or application of these instruments are nevertheless in question. The fact that a defence on the merits is cast in a particular form, cannot affect the competence of the tribunal or other organ concerned—otherwise parties would be in a position themselves to control that competence, which would be inadmissible. * * *

28. Before proceeding further, it will be convenient to re-state Pakistan's claim in its simplest form, and without going into any details or side issues. It is to the effect that India, by suspending—or rather, strictly, refusing to allow overflight of her territory by Pakistan civil aircraft—was in breach of the Treaties, which Pakistan claims have never ceased to be applicable, and both of which conferred overflight rights, and certain landing rights, on Pakistan—and that this suspension, or rather prohibition, did not take place, or was no longer taking place, in the particular circumstances—viz. "war" or declared "state of national emergency"—in which, according to Article 89 of the Convention * * * it could alone (so Pakistan contends) be justified. Consequently the legal issue that has to be determined by the Court really amounts to this, namely whether the dispute, in the form in which the Parties placed it before the Council, and have presented it to the Court in their final submissions * * * is one that can be resolved without any interpretation or application of the relevant Treaties at all. If it cannot, then the Council must be competent.

29. In effect, India has sought to maintain that the dispute could be resolved without any reference to the Treaties, and hence that, this being so, it is a dispute with which the Council can have no concern,

and which lies entirely outside its competence. The claim that the Treaties are irrelevant to the present situation regarding Pakistan overflights is based on and involves the following main contentions:—

(1) The Treaties are not in force, or they are suspended, because

(a) they were or became terminated or suspended as between the Parties upon the outbreak of hostilities in 1965 and have never been revived, but were replaced by a "special regime" in respect of which the Council could have no jurisdiction, and according to which Pakistan aircraft could only overfly India with prior permission (see as to this, paragraph 10, supra);

(b) India in any case became entitled under general international law to terminate or suspend the Treaties as from January 1971, by reason of a material breach of them, for which Pakistan was responsible, arising out of the hijacking incident that then occurred.

(2) The issue involved by the case presented to the Council by Pakistan is one of the termination or suspension of the Treaties, not of their interpretation or application which alone the Council is competent to deal with under the relevant jurisdictional clauses. This contention postulates that the notion of interpretation or application does not comprise that of termination or suspension.

30. The first of these main contentions, under both its heads, clearly belongs to the merits of the dispute into which the Court cannot go; but certain preliminary points are relevant to the jurisdictional aspects of the case and to a correct appreciation of the Indian position in that respect.

(a) As regards the contention that the Treaties were terminated or suspended, such notices or communications as there were on the part of India appear to have related to overflights rather than to the Treaties as such; although, admittedly, overflight rights constitute a major item of the Treaties, and a termination or suspension may well relate to part only of a treaty.
* * *

(b) India does not appear at the time of the hijacking incident to have indicated which particular provisions of the Treaties—more especially of the Chicago Convention—were alleged to have been breached by Pakistan. She was not of course in any way obliged to do so at that stage, but the point is a material one on the jurisdictional issue for reasons to be stated later (see *infra*, paragraph 38). * * *

(c) As mentioned, the justification given by India for the suspension of the Treaties in February 1971 (if in fact anything other than a quasi-permanent prohibition of overflights was involved) was not said to lie in the provisions of the Treaties themselves, but in a principle of general international law, or of international treaty law, allowing of suspension or termination on this ground—and the 1969 Vienna Convention on the Law of Treaties was in particular invoked. In consequence, so it was said, the Chicago Convention and Transit Agreement were irrelevant and had no bearing on the matter, because the Indian action had been taken wholly outside them, on the basis of general international law.

31. In considering further the Indian contentions * * * a convenient point of departure will be the question mentioned in subparagraph *(c)* [above] because, in the proceedings before the Court, this question assumed almost more prominence in the Indian arguments than any other. Furthermore, it involves a point of principle of great general importance for the jurisdictional aspects of this—or of any—case. This contention is to the effect that since India, in suspending overflights in February 1971, was not invoking any right that might be afforded by the Treaties, but was acting outside them on the basis of a general principle of international law, "therefore" the Council, whose jurisdiction was derived from the Treaties, and which was entitled to deal only with matters arising under them, must be incompetent. Exactly the same attitude has been evinced in regard to the contention that the Treaties were suspended in 1965 and never revived, or were replaced by a special régime. The Court considers however, that for precisely the same order of reason as has already been noticed in the case of its own jurisdiction in the present case, a mere unilateral affirmation of these contentions—contested by the other party—cannot be utilized so as to negative the Council's jurisdiction. The point is not that these contentions are necessarily wrong but that their validity has not yet been determined. Since therefore the Parties are in disagreement as to whether the Treaties ever were (validly) suspended or replaced by something else; as to whether they are in force between the Parties or not; and as to whether India's action in relation to Pakistan overflights was such as not to involve the Treaties, but to be justifiable *aliter et aliunde;*—these very questions are in issue before the Council, and no conclusions as to jurisdiction can be drawn from them, at least at this stage, so as to exclude *ipso facto* and *a priori* the competence of the Council.

* * *

33. The Court now proceeds to the last main category of Indian contention which, though more nearly relevant to the purely jurisdictional issue than those so far discussed, is nonetheless, like them, closely bound up with the merits. This contention is to the effect that Article 84 of the Chicago Convention, and hence by reference Section 2 of Article II of the Transit Agreement, only allows the Council to entertain disagreements relating to the "interpretation or application" of these instruments,—whereas (according to India) what is involved in this case is not any question of the interpretation or application of the

Treaties, but of their termination or suspension—and since (so India contends) the notion of interpretation or application does not extend to that of termination or suspension, the Council's competence is automatically excluded. Alternatively expressed, the Indian contention is that, since the Treaties have been terminated or suspended, it follows *ex hypothesi* that no question of their interpretation or application can arise, such as alone the Council would be competent to consider: non-existent treaties cannot be interpreted or applied.

34. It is evident that this contention, although getting much nearer to the real issue of what the Council can properly take cognizance of under the jurisdictional clauses of the Treaties, having regard to their actual wording, involves the same underlying assumption that the Treaties have in fact been (validly) terminated or suspended, and also that a unilateral act or allegation of India's in that sense suffices. In consequence three strands to this Indian contention can be seen to be interwoven: (i) the Treaties are terminated or suspended, so they cannot be interpreted or applied at all; (ii) the question whether they have been (validly) terminated or suspended, is not one of interpretation or application; (iii) in any event the answer to that question depends on considerations lying outside the Treaties altogether. On each of these grounds India contends that the issues involved are not within the Council's terms of reference which are limited to interpreting and applying the Treaties. Once more it is evident that, with respect to all three strands of this Indian contention, with the possible exception of certain aspects of the second one, the argument involves and depends upon questions of merits. In relation to it, the Parties debated at considerable length whether the notion of the interpretation and application of a treaty can, at least in some circumstances, embrace that of a termination or suspension of it; and also as to whether any inherent limitations on the powers of the Council to deal with certain types of legal questions must be presumed. But until it has been determined by the proper means that what is involved is indeed an issue solely of termination or suspension of the Treaties, and further that no question of their interpretation or application arises or can arise (and this is the only real issue involved here), the problem of whether the one notion is comprised by the other can, for present purposes, be regarded as hypothetical.

35. Thus far, only the negative aspects of the case have been examined; that is, the reasons why the various contentions so far considered do not have any real bearing on the question of the competence of the Council. It is now time to turn to the positive aspects, from which it will appear not only that Pakistan's claim discloses the existence of a "disagreement * * * relating to the interpretation or application" of the Treaties, but also that India's defences equally involve questions of their interpretation or application.

36. * * * Specific provisions of the Treaties—in particular Article 5 of the Convention and Section 1 of Article I of the Transit Agreement—were cited by Pakistan as having been infringed by India's

denial of overflight rights. The existence of a "disagreement" relating to the application of the Treaties was affirmed. There can therefore be no doubt about the character of the case presented by Pakistan to the Council. It was essentially a charge of breaches of the Treaties—and in order to determine these, the Council would inevitably be obliged to interpret and apply the Treaties, and thus to deal with matters unquestionably within its jurisdiction.

* * *

37. India also * * * has made charges of a material breach of the Convention by Pakistan, as justifying India in purporting to put an end to it, or suspend its operation and that of the Transit Agreement. Thus the case is one of mutual charges and countercharges of breach of treaty which cannot, by reason of the very fact that they are what they are, fail to involve questions of the interpretation and application of the treaty instruments in respect of which the breaches are alleged. It is however possible to be more specific than this, for not only do Pakistan's claims cite particular articles of the Treaties, but both India's counter-charges and her defences to those of Pakistan, can be seen to involve various treaty provisions. These will now be considered in turn.

38. In the first place, India's allegation of a material breach of the Treaties by Pakistan, as justifying India in treating them as terminated or suspended, is inherently and by its very nature, one that must involve the examination of the Treaties in order to see whether, according to the definition of a material breach of treaty contained in Article 60 of the 1969 Vienna Convention on the Law of Treaties, there has been (paragraph 3*(b)*) a violation by Pakistan of "a provision essential to the accomplishment of the object or purpose of the Treaty". The fact that * * * India has in very comprehensive language alleged a material breach of the Treaties, can only increase the need for considering what particular provisions are involved by this allegation. Even if the allegation, because of its generality, is to be regarded as one of conduct on the part of Pakistan amounting to a complete "repudiation of the treaty" (see paragraph 3*(a)* of Article 60 of the Vienna Convention), it would still be necessary to examine the Treaties in order to see whether, in relation to their provisions as a whole, and in particular those relating to the "safety of air travel" which India herself invoked * * *, Pakistan's conduct must be held to constitute such a repudiation.

* * *

[The Court also discussed articles 89 and 95 of the Convention and comparable articles in the Transit Agreement. Article 89 provides in substance that the Convention does not restrict freedom of action in time of war. Article 95 permits any party to denounce the Convention on a year's notice. India and Pakistan disagreed as to whether these provisions established the sole means by which the Treaties could be suspended or terminated.]

43. The Court must obviously refrain from pronouncing on the validity or otherwise of the opposing views of the Parties as to the object and correct interpretation of Articles 89 and 95, since this touches directly upon the merits of the case. But this opposition cannot but be indicative of a direct conflict of views as to the meaning of the Articles, or in other words of a "disagreement * * * relating to the interpretation or application of [the] Convention";—and if there is even one provision—and especially a provision of the importance of Article 89—as to which this is so, then the Council is invested with jurisdiction, were it but the only such provision to be found, which is clearly not the case.

* * *

46. For these reasons,

THE COURT,

by thirteen votes to three,

(1) rejects the Government of Pakistan's objections on the question of its competence, and finds that it has jurisdiction to entertain India's appeal;

by fourteen votes to two,

(2) holds the Council of the International Civil Aviation Organization to be competent to entertain the Application and Complaint laid before it by the Government of Pakistan on 3 March 1971; and in consequence, rejects the appeal made to the Court by the Government of India against the decision of the Council assuming jurisdiction in those respects.

THE COURT'S DECISION

Were the Court's reasons persuasive for holding the Council's preliminary decision appealable? Did it adequately dispose of Pakistan's argument based on the language of Chicago Convention article 84? In this connection, did the Court adequately consider articles 14 and 15 of the Council's Rules for the Settlement of Differences, pages 446–47 supra, and the fact that the Council gave no reasons for its denial of India's preliminary objections?

In domestic courts in the United States, the usual rule is that a lower court order is not appealable unless it is "final." This is the rule in the federal court system, subject to limited statutory exceptions.[i] One of the exceptions permits appeal from an interlocutory district court order, at the discretion of the Court of Appeals, if the district court has certified that there is substantial ground for a difference of opinion as to the question of law involved and that immediate appeal

---

i. See 28 U.S.C.A. §§ 1291, 1292.

may materially advance the ultimate termination of the litigation.[j]

In Catlin v. United States,[k] the landowner-respondent in condemnation proceedings had moved to dismiss on the ground that the federal district court lacked subject matter jurisdiction. The Supreme Court held that the order denying the motion was not a "final decision" and thus was not appealable. The Court explained the doctrine of nonappealability of interlocutory orders as follows: "The foundation of this policy is not in merely technical conceptions of 'finality.' It is one against piecemeal litigation. 'The case is not to be sent up in fragments * * *.' [Citation omitted.] Reasons other than conservation of judicial energy sustain the limitation. One is elimination of delays caused by interlocutory appeals."[l] Is there any reason for a different rule when the issue is the appealability of a preliminary decision by the ICAO Council upholding its subject matter jurisdiction?

If India had a right under international law to suspend or terminate the Treaties as between itself and Pakistan, and had done so, would the Council have had jurisdiction to consider the merits of the case?

Did the Court in paragraph 30 deal with this point by finding that India had not purported to suspend or terminate the Treaties? If so, why did it write paragraph 31?

Does the following fairly state the essence of paragraphs 18 and 31? Although the Council made a final (and therefore appealable) decision as to its competence (jurisdiction), it did not decide whether the Treaties ever were validly suspended or replaced by something else. If that is a fair representation of what the Court said, can any sense be made of it? Wouldn't it be the case that either (a) the Council's decision on its jurisdiction was not final (and therefore not appealable) because it postponed for ultimate determination on the merits the essential jurisdictional question whether the Treaties were still in force between the parties; or (b) the Council actually did decide that jurisdictional question, as indicated in the terse statement in its decision that it "decided not to accept the Preliminary Objections" of India, in which case it was the Court's duty—once it decided to hear the appeal—to review that holding and to decide as a matter of law whether the Treaties were still in force between India and Pakistan?

India's second argument, asserted before the Council and summarized by the Court in paragraph 29(2), appears to have been that even if it had not already validly suspended or terminated the Treaties with

j. 28 U.S.C.A. § 1292(b).

k. 324 U.S. 229, 65 S.Ct. 631, 89 L.Ed. 911 (1945).

l. 324 U.S. at 233–34, 65 S.Ct. at 634. In Lauro Lines v. Chasser, 490 U.S. 495, 109 S.Ct. 1976, 104 L.Ed.2d 548 (1989), defendant was not allowed to appeal before trial from an order denying its motion to dismiss based on a forum-selection clause in a steamship ticket. The Supreme Court said that for a pretrial order to be immediately appealable, "[W]e have insisted that the right asserted be one that is essentially destroyed if its vindication must be postponed until trial is completed." 490 U.S. at 499, 109 S.Ct. at 1978.

respect to Pakistan, it was now asserting the right to do so; that right could be decided by an appropriate third-party adjudicator, but the Council was not the one because its jurisdiction was limited to the interpretation or application of the Treaties. Did the Court adequately answer that argument?

Suppose that after the Court's decision the ICAO Council had held the Chicago Convention and the Transit Agreement still in force between India and Pakistan, and had made detailed findings of fact regarding the events surrounding the hijackers' demolition of the Indian airliner at the Lahore airport. If the ultimate finding was that Pakistan had done all it could under the circumstances to save the aircraft, and that India had violated the Convention and Agreement, would it have been appropriate for the Council to grant Pakistan all the forms of relief requested in its memorial? (See page 451 supra.)

If the Council had held that India had violated the Convention and Agreement, would the Council's decision be binding on India, in the sense that India could no longer argue that it had not violated international law? Assume that no appeal was taken from the Council's decision on the merits.

In fact, after the appeal as to the Council's jurisdiction had been decided, the parties did not pursue the matter before the Council. Instead, they attempted to negotiate their differences. In 1976 they finally reached a settlement, which seems to have been satisfactory to both sides. Did the ICJ play a significant role in (a) settling the dispute, (b) strengthening the ICAO dispute-settlement process, or (c) establishing principles of international law?

Under the Transit Agreement, the ICAO Council has another dispute-settlement function related to the adjudicative function we have been considering, but distinct from it. This too was involved in the Appeal Relating to the Jurisdiction of the ICAO Council, in a portion of the opinion (omitted above) relating to Pakistan's "Complaint" against India under article II, section 1, of the Transit Agreement. On the question of the appealability of the Council's determination that it had jurisdiction to consider the "Complaint" (as distinguished from the "Application," which we have been considering up to now), the Court said: [m]

> A special jurisdictional issue exists * * *, not on Pakistan's "Application" to the Council, but on her "Complaint" * * * ostensibly made under and by virtue of Section 1 of Article II of the Transit Agreement, which reads as follows:
>
>> A contracting State which deems that action by another contracting State under this Agreement is causing injustice or

---

m. [1972] I.C.J. at 57–59.

hardship to it, may request the Council to examine the situation. The Council shall thereupon inquire into the matter, and shall call the States concerned into consultation. Should such consultation fail to resolve the difficulty, the Council may make appropriate findings and recommendations to the contracting States concerned. If thereafter a contracting State concerned shall in the opinion of the Council unreasonably fail to take suitable corrective action, the Council may recommend to the Assembly of the above mentioned Organization that such contracting State be suspended from its rights and privileges under this Agreement until such action has been taken. The Assembly by a two-thirds vote may so suspend such contracting State for such period of time as it may deem proper or until the Council shall find that corrective action has been taken by such State.

* * *

The Court has no doubt that the situation contemplated by Section 1 of Article II of the Transit Agreement is quite a different one from that of Article 84 of the Convention (and hence of Section 2 of Article II of the Transit Agreement)—so that whatever may be the exact legitimate range of a "complaint" made under Section 1, its primary purpose must be to permit redress against legally permissible action that nevertheless causes injustice or hardship. In other words, the basic situation contemplated by Section 1 is where a party to the Agreement, although acting within its legal rights under the Treaties, has nevertheless caused injustice or hardship to another party—a case not of illegal action—not of alleged breaches of the Treaties—but of action lawful, yet prejudicial. In such a case it is to be expected that no right of appeal to the Court would lie—for the findings and recommendations to be made by the Council under this Section would not be about legal rights or obligations: they would turn on considerations of equity and expediency such as would not constitute suitable material for appeal to a court of law.

Is the Council better equipped to perform its function under this provision of the Transit Agreement than in the context we have been considering to this point? (Its Rules for the Settlement of Differences require that any "Complaint" under article II, section 1, be referred to its committee of five; "Applications" go to the committee of five only if the Council decides to refer them in specific cases. Why the difference?)

If the Council's determination that it had jurisdiction to hear the other aspects of the India–Pakistan case was appealable, why shouldn't its jurisdictional determination on article II, section 1, be appealable? Was the Court's reasoning on this point convincing?

No member state has invoked the Council's formal dispute-settlement authority since the India–Pakistan case. Nevertheless, the ICAO has occasionally performed an investigative/dispute-settlement function since then.

On September 1, 1983, Korean Air Lines flight 007, bound from Anchorage, Alaska, to Seoul, South Korea, strayed over Soviet airspace and was intercepted by Soviet military aircraft. The Soviets said that after they tried unsuccessfully to get the airliner to land, they "terminated its flight" with two air-to-air missiles. Flight 007 crashed into the Sea of Japan, killing everyone on board.

In September 1983, the ICAO Council directed the Secretary General "to institute an investigation to determine the facts and technical aspects relating to the flight and destruction of the aircraft and to provide * * * a complete report [to the Council] * * *."[n]

The investigation was conducted by a team of technical experts from the Secretariat. They made field visits to Japan, South Korea and the United States. The Secretary–General and the leader of the investigative team also visited the Soviet Union, but the Soviet government did not allow a full investigation in its territory and gave the team limited assistance. Members of the team observed search and salvage efforts in the Sea of Japan, and observed Boeing flight simulation studies in Seattle. The aircraft's "black box" was not made available.

The investigative team found that the KAL flight crew and aircraft were properly certificated. The flight began straying to the right of its assigned course soon after its departure. It intruded into Soviet airspace, where it was twice subjected to interception attempts by Soviet military aircraft. Soviet authorities assumed that the airliner was an intelligence aircraft. When shot down at 6:24 a.m. local time, it was about 300 nautical miles north of its assigned route, and was still over Soviet territory. The team postulated that the flight crew probably had incorrectly set the aircraft's navigation systems and through inattentiveness had allowed it to stray off course for five and a half hours.[o]

The report consisted almost entirely of descriptions and findings of fact. It noted, among other things, that the preliminary report of the Soviet Accident Investigation Commission stated that the aircraft was flying with its navigation and strobe lights off and its cabin lights extinguished. The report added that the Defense Agency of Japan had monitored air-to-ground communications from the Soviet interceptor

---

n. ICAO Council Res. of Sept. 16, 1983, ICAO Doc. 9428–C/1079, at 21 (1984), 22 Int'l Legal Materials 1150 (1983).

o. See Report of ICAO Fact–Finding Investigation, Dec. 1983, 23 Int'l Legal Materials 865 (1984). A later study, conducted outside ICAO, has cast doubt on the ICAO team's conclusion. See N.Y. Times, Feb. 20, 1992, p. A12, col. 1.

aircraft, and those communications contradicted the Soviet report that the lights were off. Nevertheless, the report came to no clear conclusion on this point. It did say:

> There was no evidence that complete visual identification procedures were employed. Such visual identification should have resulted in a recognition of the type of aircraft involved as well as the civilian airline markings.[p]

Was this a finding of fact or a conclusion of law? How about the following passage from the report?

> In accordance with the ICAO Council's special recommendations * * * interception of civil aircraft should be avoided and should be undertaken only as a last resort. Furthermore, an interception should be limited to determining the identity of the aircraft and providing any navigational guidance necessary for the safe conduct of the flight. To eliminate or reduce the need for interception of civil aircraft, all possible efforts should be made by intercept control units to secure identification of any aircraft which may be a civil aircraft, and to issue any necessary instructions or advice to such aircraft * * *.[q]

The ICAO Council met again in March 1984 and adopted the following resolution:

ICAO COUNCIL RESOLUTION ON KOREAN AIRLINER INCIDENT

March 6, 1984.
ICAO Doc. 9442–C/1082, at 10 (1984), 23 Int'l Legal Materials 937 (1984).

THE COUNCIL, * * *

2) HAVING CONSIDERED the report of the investigation by the Secretary General and the subsequent technical review by the Air Navigation Commission;

3) RECOGNIZING that, although this investigation was unable, because of lack of necessary data, to determine conclusively the precise cause for the serious deviation of some 500 kilometers from its flight plan route by the Korean aircraft into the airspace above the territory under the sovereignty of the Soviet Union, no evidence was found to indicate that the deviation was premeditated or that the crew was at any time aware of the flight's deviation;

4) REAFFIRMING that, whatever the circumstances which, according to the Secretary General's report, may have caused the aircraft to stray off its flight plan route, such use of armed force constitutes a violation of international law, and invokes generally recognized legal consequences;

p. Report, supra, at 899.   q. Id. at 897–98.

5) RECOGNIZING that such use of armed force is a grave threat to the safety of international civil aviation, and is incompatible with the norms governing international behavior and with the rules, Standards and Recommended Practices enshrined in the Chicago Convention and its Annexes and with elementary considerations of humanity;

* * *

1) CONDEMNS the use of armed force which resulted in the destruction of the Korean airliner and the tragic loss of 269 lives;

2) DEEPLY DEPLORES the Soviet failure to cooperate in the search and rescue efforts of other involved States and the Soviet failure to cooperate with the ICAO investigation of the incident by refusing to accept the visit of the investigation team appointed by the Secretary General and by failing so far to provide the Secretary General with information relevant to the investigation;

3) URGES all Contracting States to cooperate fully in the work of examining and adopting an amendment to the Chicago Convention at the 25th Session (Extraordinary) of the ICAO Assembly and in the improvement of measures for preventing a recurrence of this type of tragedy.

THE AMENDMENT AND THE NEXT INCIDENT

The ICAO Assembly did adopt an amendment to the Chicago Convention at its extraordinary session in May 1984. The amendment would add a new article 3 *bis*. It says, *inter alia*, that "every State must refrain from resorting to the use of weapons against civil aircraft in flight * * *." See page 317 supra. This reflects existing customary international law, binding even on nonmembers of ICAO, subject to the right of necessary and proportional self-defense.[r]

On July 3, 1988, a U.S. Navy ship, the U.S.S. Vincennes, on duty in the Persian Gulf during the Iran–Iraq war, shot down Iran Air Flight 655. The crew of the Vincennes had mistakenly identified it through electronic means as a threatening military aircraft. Instead, the Iranian airbus was on a scheduled commercial flight from Bandar Abbas, Iran, to Dubai. All 290 passengers and crew on board were killed. At the time of the incident, the airbus was over Iranian 12–mile territorial waters, and the Vincennes apparently was within those waters.[s]

The United States immediately conducted an investigation. The U.S. investigation concluded that the incident occurred because of a

---

[r]. See Fitzgerald, The Use of Force Against Civil Aircraft: The Aftermath of the KAL Flight 007 Incident, 22 Can. Y.B.Int'l L. 291, 304–05 (1984).

[s]. See Newsweek, July 13, 1992, at 29 et seq.

series of human errors by Vincennes crew members, who were under stress from an engagement with Iranian gunboats.[t]

On July 14 the ICAO Council, meeting at the request of Iran, directed the Secretary General also to begin an immediate investigation. The ICAO investigation report contained detailed findings of fact.[u] Among them were findings that flight 655 was 20 minutes late leaving Bandar Abbas, but climbed in a normal flight path and carried out normal communications with air traffic control. United States naval ships were not equipped to monitor civil air traffic control frequencies for flight identification purposes. The USS Vincennes had information on civil flight schedules, but did not have information on the flight plans or flight progress of individual civil aircraft. When the Vincennes and a companion naval ship suspected that flight 655 was hostile, they made a total of eleven radio challenges: seven on a military distress frequency and four on the international air distress frequency. Civil aircraft did not carry equipment capable of tuning into the military distress frequency, and flight 655 apparently was not monitoring the international air distress frequency despite instructions from Iran Air to do so. Thus flight 655 did not respond to any of the radio challenges. There was no co-ordination between U.S. warships and the civil air traffic control units responsible for the Gulf area.

The ICAO investigation found that the Vincennes' mistake about the flight's intent was based on a number of factors, including the fact that Bandar Abbas was a joint civil/military airfield; U.S. intelligence had warned that Iranian F–14 aircraft had been deployed at Bandar Abbas; it was anticipated that Iran would provide air support for surface engagements with U.S. warships; and the radar contact with the flight that turned out to be 655 could not be correlated with a scheduled time of departure of a civil flight.

As was the case with the ICAO report on the Korean Air Lines incident, the report consisted almost entirely of statements of fact. Included was a discussion of U.S. issuance of a NOTAM for the Persian Gulf area, warning that aircraft in the area should monitor the two distress frequencies mentioned above and that unidentified aircraft whose intentions were unclear would be contacted on those frequencies. (A NOTAM is a Notice to Airmen, issued pursuant to ICAO international standards and recommended practices contained in Annex 15 to the Chicago Convention.) The NOTAM was distributed to states throughout the Persian Gulf area. The ICAO report continued:

> 2.2.4 *Aeronautical information service authority.* In accordance with the provisions of ICAO Annex 15, ICAO Contracting States provided an aeronautical information service and published aeronautical information concerning the territory of the State as well as areas outside its territory in which the State was responsi-

---

t. N.Y. Times, Aug. 3, 1988, p. A1, col. 6.

u. Report of ICAO Fact–Finding Investigation, Nov. 1988, 28 Int'l Legal Materials 900 (1989).

ble for air traffic services. International NOTAM Offices were designated by States for the international exchange of NOTAMs in accordance with the ICAO regional air navigation plans. The United States NOTAM concerning the Gulf, Strait of Hormuz, Gulf of Oman and Arabian Sea covered an area within the responsibility of International Notam Offices Abu Dhabi, Baghdad, Bahrain, Bombay, Karachi, Kuwait, Muscat and Tehran. Therefore, the promulgation of the NOTAM was not in conformity with the provisions of ICAO Annex 15.

2.2.5 *Safety implications.* The full implications of the rules of engagement of the United States warships were not sufficiently reflected in the notice promulgated by the United States. It was not specified what was considered to be "operating in a threatening manner", what distance was considered "well clear of United States warships", and what was meant with "could place the aircraft at risk by United States defensive measures". The safety risks imposed by the presence of naval forces in the Gulf area to civil aviation may have been underestimated, in particular as civil aircraft operated on promulgated tracks including standard approach and departure routes from airports in the area.[v]

Did these two paragraphs contain findings of fact or conclusions of law?

When the ICAO Council first considered the group of experts' report, it decided to refer it to the ICAO Air Navigation Commission. The Commission was directed to report back to the Council with safety recommendations, which it did. The Council then adopted the following resolution:

ICAO COUNCIL RESOLUTION ON IRAN AIRBUS INCIDENT
March 17, 1989.
28 Int'l Legal Materials 898 (1989).

THE COUNCIL * * *

Having considered the report of the fact-finding investigation instituted by the Secretary General pursuant to the decision of the Council of 14 July 1988 and the subsequent study by the Air Navigation Commission of the safety recommendations presented in that report;

Expressing appreciation for the full co-operation extended to the fact-finding mission by the authorities of all States concerned;

Recalling that the 25th Session (Extraordinary) of the Assembly in 1984 unanimously recognized the duty of States to refrain from the use of weapons against civil aircraft in flight;

---

v. 28 Int'l Legal Materials at 910–11 (1989).

Reaffirming its policy to condemn the use of weapons against civil aircraft in flight without prejudice to the provisions of the Charter of the United Nations;

Deeply deplores the tragic incident which occurred as a consequence of events and errors in identification of the aircraft which resulted in the accidental destruction of an Iran Air airliner and the loss of 290 lives;

* * *

Notes the report of the fact-finding investigation instituted by the Secretary General and endorses the conclusions of the Air Navigation Commission on the safety recommendations contained therein;

Urges States to take all necessary measures to safeguard the safety of air navigation, particularly by assuring effective co-ordination of civil and military activities and the proper identification of civil aircraft.

INFORMAL DISPUTE SETTLEMENT

Is there any legal objection to the ICAO fact-finding and blame-allocating efforts in the Korean Airlines and Iran Air cases, conducted outside the formal dispute-settlement procedure expressly established by the Chicago Convention? Consider whether Chicago Convention *articles 54(i), (j), (k)* or *(n)* and *55(c)* or *(e)* answer the question.

If any of these provisions gave the Council adequate authority to act in the Korean and Iranian airliner incidents, is there any legal problem with delegating the investigations to the Secretariat? (Note that in both cases the Council referred the investigative teams' reports to the ICAO Air Navigation Commission—composed of representatives of 15 member states [w]—for review before taking any action. The Air Navigation Commission's review, however, was limited to the safety recommendations.)

Was it proper for either the investigative teams or the Council to make judgments about the conduct of member states, without holding hearings and allowing each side to present evidence and argument in an orderly fashion?

Would it be advisable to have written rules for such investigations? If so, should they be in (a) the organization's constituent instrument; (b) the Council's rules of procedure; or (c) somewhere else?

Within a few days after the Iran airbus was shot down, the United States announced that it would offer *ex gratia* compensation to the families of the victims. The offers were $250,000 for a full-time wage-earning victim, and $100,000 for all others.

w. A 1989 protocol will increase the size of the Commission to 19 when two-thirds of the ICAO membership has ratified it.

On May 17, 1989, Iran filed an Application with the International Court of Justice, seeking review of the ICAO Council's disposition of the Iran airbus incident in the Council's resolution of March 17, 1989. In its Application, Iran claimed that the United States had violated several provisions of the Chicago Convention, as will appear below. Iran invoked the Court's jurisdiction under article 84 of the Chicago Convention.

Iran also claimed that the United States had violated the 1971 Montreal Convention for the Suppression of Unlawful Acts Against the Safety of Civil Aviation, and separately invoked the Court's jurisdiction under the compromissory clause in that Convention. The materials below focus on the claims under the Chicago Convention.

APPLICATION OF IRAN IN AERIAL INCIDENT CASE

Before the ICJ, May 17, 1989.
28 Int'l Legal Materials 843 (1989).

* * *

I. STATEMENT OF FACTS

This dispute arises from the destruction of an Iranian aircraft, Iran Air Airbus A-300B, flight 655, and the killing of its 290 passengers and crew by two surface-to-air missiles launched from the USS *Vincennes,* a guided-missile cruiser on duty with the United States Persian Gulf/Middle East Force in the Iranian airspace over the Islamic Republic's territorial waters in the Persian Gulf on 3 July 1988. The civil passenger aircraft, while in the course of a regularly-scheduled international commercial flight, and while operating within its previously prescribed and published time and course patterns, was intercepted and destroyed, within its own national airspace over its own national territorial waters, by two missiles fired by the United States warship that had positioned itself in the Iranian territorial waters.

II. JURISDICTION OF THE COURT

As Members of the United Nations, the United States and the Islamic Republic are parties to the Statute of the Court, Article 36(1) of which provides that "The jurisdiction of the Court comprises * * * all matters specifically provided for * * * in treaties and conventions in force." The two countries are parties to both the Chicago Convention of 1944 (15 *UNTS* 295) as amended and the Montreal Convention of 1971.

* * *

Immediately after this flagrant violation of the principles enshrined in the Chicago Convention took place, the Islamic Republic referred to the ICAO Council and in its final submission before the Council it sought:

"1. Condemnation of the shooting down of IR 655 by the United States military forces in the Persian Gulf.

2. Explicit recognition of a crime of international character relating to the breach of international law and legal duties of [the United States as] a Contracting State of ICAO.

3. Explicit recognition of the responsibilities of the United States Government, and calling for effecting compensation for moral and financial damages.

4. Demand for the immediate termination of present obstacles, restrictions, threats, and the use of force against civilian aircraft in the region, including Council's appeal to relevant international bodies to demand the withdrawal of all foreign forces from the Persian Gulf."

The ICAO Council, however, pursuant to its decision of 17 March 1989, in effect dismissed all Iranian requests and limited itself to the following and a number of general observations not relevant to those requests:

"*Deeply deplores* the tragic incident which occurred as a consequence of events and errors in identification of the aircraft which resulted in the accidental destruction of an Iran Air airliner and the loss of 290 lives."

* * *

In the circumstances which are described above and which the Government of the Islamic Republic will set out more fully in its Memorial and subsequent written and oral pleadings, there exists a dispute between the Government of the United States and the Government of the Islamic Republic concerning the interpretation and application of the Chicago Convention and the Montreal Convention. The Islamic Republic contends that the action of the United States with respect to Iran Air flight 655 has violated certain provisions of the Chicago and Montreal Conventions. The Government of the United States has denied this contention. Since 3 July 1988, the date the aircraft was destroyed and thereby 290 lives were taken, efforts to resolve the dispute have been unsuccessful.

III. THE CONTENTIONS OF THE ISLAMIC REPUBLIC

The Government of the Islamic Republic contends that, by its destruction of Iran Air flight 655 and taking 290 lives, its refusal to compensate the Islamic Republic for damages arising from the loss of the aircraft and individuals on board and the continuous interference with the Persian Gulf aviation, the Government of the United States has violated the Chicago and Montreal Conventions and that the ICAO Council has erred in its decision of 17 March 1989. In particular, the Islamic Republic contends that:

(a) the ICAO Council decision was erroneous in that the Government of the United States' destruction of IR 655 and taking of 290 lives has

indeed violated the Preamble and Articles 1, 2, 3 *bis* and 44*(a)* and *(h)* of the Chicago Convention;

(b) the ICAO Council decision was in error also because the continuation of the United States interferences with the Persian Gulf aviation violated Annex 15 of the Chicago Convention and Recommendation 2.6/1 of the Third Middle East Regional Air Navigation (MID RAN) Meeting of ICAO;

* * *

IV. JUDGMENT REQUESTED

Accordingly, while reserving the right to supplement and amend this submission as appropriate in the course of further proceedings, the Islamic Republic requests the Court to adjudge and declare as follows:

(a) that the ICAO Council decision is erroneous in that the Government of the United States has violated the Chicago Convention, including the Preamble, Articles 1, 2, 3 *bis* and 44*(a)* and *(h)* and Annex 15 of the Chicago Convention as well as Recommendation 2.6/1 of the Third Middle East Regional Air Navigation Meeting of ICAO;

(b) that the Government of the United States has violated Articles 1, 3 and 10(1) of the Montreal Convention; and

(c) that the Government of the United States is responsible to pay compensation to the Islamic Republic, in the amount to be determined by the Court, as measured by the injuries suffered by the Islamic Republic and the bereaved families as a result of these violations, including additional financial losses which Iran Air and the bereaved families have suffered for the disruption of their activities.

THE ICJ AND ICAO AGAIN

As of January 1, 1993, the ICJ had not yet decided the jurisdictional issues.

Is this the type of case contemplated by Chicago Convention *article 84* for appeal to the ICJ?

If so, would it matter for purposes of ICJ jurisdiction that Iran apparently made little or no effort to negotiate its differences with the United States? [x]

Is Chicago Convention *article 89* relevant to the ICJ jurisdictional question? If so, how? [y]

---

[x]. See Scheffer, Non–Judicial State Remedies and the Jurisdiction of the International Court of Justice, 27 Stanford J.Int'l L. 83, 131–37 (1990).

[y]. On this and many other questions raised by the Aerial Incident Case, see Linnan, Iran Air Flight 655 and Beyond: Free Passage, Mistaken Self-Defense, and State Responsibility, 16 Yale J.Int'l L. 245 (1991).

Should the ICJ have jurisdiction over an appeal such as this?

Leaving aside jurisdictional questions, how strong were Iran's assertions that the United States violated Chicago Convention *articles 1, 2, 3 bis* and *44(a)* and *(h)?* Article 3 *bis* had not yet been ratified by enough member states to enter into force, but its prohibition of the use of weapons against civil aircraft in flight is generally regarded as reflecting customary international law.

Note that Iran also claimed that the United States violated Annex 15 of the Chicago Convention. See also the excerpt from the ICAO report, pages 472–73 supra. As summarized in an ICAO booklet, Annex 15 has this to say (inter alia):

> NOTAM are classified into two classes, i.e., I and II, and distributed on global, national and regional bases: by direct means of telecommunications in a Class I NOTAM, and mail, or other distribution, for the less urgent Class II NOTAM. Both classes contain information concerning the establishment, condition or change in any aeronautical facility, service, procedure or hazard— the timely knowledge of which is essential to personnel concerned with flight operations.
>
> * * *
>
> Responsibilities and functions of all ICAO Member States in providing this type of information are set out in Annex 15, which provides directions on how the information should be gathered, what steps are to be taken to ensure the adequacy and authenticity of the information, exchange of information procedures, and distribution techniques to predetermined locations.
>
> Pre-flight information service is provided to pilots by means of plain-language information bulletins drawn from NOTAM which, in turn, are coded for brevity. NOTAM information might include advice that a certain airspace will be temporarily closed because, for example, of rocket research, or that a non-directional radio navigation beacon at a particular location would be inoperative. Other information which could be contained in NOTAM can include cosmic radiation forecasts, or significant changes in the level of protection normally available at an airport to serve rescue and fire fighting needs.[z]

If the ICJ reaches the merits on Iran's claims, what weight, if any, should it give to the views contained in the ICAO report, pages 472–73 supra, regarding the U.S. NOTAM and Annex 15? Would those views constitute a source of law for the Court under ICJ Statute *article 38?* Would it make a difference if the relevant provisions in Annex 15 were recommended practices, rather than international standards?

---

[z]. ICAO, The Convention on International Civil Aviation: The First 40 Years 35–36 (1984).

Consider whether the Council under the present Chicago Convention could issue interpretations of the Convention or of the Transit Agreement, on the order of the interpretations issued by the International Labor Office or the IMF Executive Directors. If so, would its interpretation be binding on member states in their relations with each other (i.e. in international law)?[a]

ICAO is not the only specialized agency engaging in informal dispute settlement. For example, the World Health Organization's Secretariat extends its good offices to help settle some disputes under the International Health Regulations.[b] UNESCO is authorized to extend its good offices to resolve disputes over the implementation of the Convention on the Means of Prohibiting and Preventing the Illicit Import, Export and Transfer of Ownership of Cultural Property.[c] Other examples could be given.

D. THE INTERNATIONAL MARITIME ORGANIZATION

IMO Convention *article 69* gives the IMO Assembly a role in settling questions or disputes concerning the interpretation or application of the Convention. *Article 70* requires referral to the ICJ, for an advisory opinion, of any legal question regarding the Convention that cannot be settled under article 69.

The Convention does not specify the procedure to be followed if a question or dispute is referred to the Assembly, nor do the Assembly's Rules of Procedure. Rule 24, however, does authorize the Assembly to establish such temporary or, upon recommendation of the Council, permanent subsidiary bodies as it considers necessary. Moreover, any of the standing committees—the Maritime Safety Committee, the Marine Environment Protection Committee, the Legal Committee or the Technical Co-operation Committee—could make recommendations to the Assembly on matters, including matters of interpretation, falling within its mandate.

On a few occasions the Assembly has been asked to exercise its article 69 power of interpretation. For example, it has wrestled with the question whether a state party to a convention administered by an IMO body (such as the Maritime Safety Committee) could vote in that body even if it is not a member of the IMO. When this question first

---

[a] See Chicago Convention *art. 54.* See also Professor Sohn's comments in The Effectiveness of International Decisions 392–93 (S. Schwebel ed. 1971).

[b] See 1 D. Leive, International Regulatory Regimes: Case Studies in Health, Meteorology and Food 44–45 (1976).

[c] Nov. 14, 1970, art. 17(5), 823 U.N.T.S. 231, 10 Int'l Legal Materials 289 (1971).

came up in 1972–73, it was referred initially to the Legal Committee. The Legal Committee promptly passed the buck to the Council and the Assembly. The Council then asked the Organization's Legal Adviser for an opinion. The ensuing opinion was crafted in such a manner as to allow the Council and Assembly to come out either way on the issue.[a] The Council concluded that the Assembly could interpret the Convention to allow non-members to vote under these circumstances.[b] The Assembly did so.[c]

Although the article 69 power has seldom been used, the IMO does participate actively in the interpretation of maritime conventions through its Maritime Safety and Marine Environment Protection Committees. When they are faced with interpretive questions regarding conventions they administer, they proceed cautiously by circulating drafts during two or three committee sessions and then deciding by consensus. If a contracting party does not like a committee interpretation, it will propose a modification rather than flouting the interpretation. Several interpretations have been modified as a result of this process.[d]

When the issues are likely to be more sensitive politically than those raised by maritime safety and environmental conventions, the states parties and the IMO Secretariat have been reluctant to give the Organization interpretive authority. For example, during the negotiations leading to the adoption of the Convention for the Suppression of Unlawful Acts Against the Safety of Maritime Navigation,[e] Iran proposed an article that would have authorized parties to submit matters concerning interpretation or application of the convention to the IMO, which would "make appropriate recommendations."[f] This was not adopted. Several delegations did not want to put the IMO Secretariat in the position of taking sides in a dispute among member states, and some were concerned about making the IMO a "super national body" with the last word on the convention's meaning.[g]

Why such timidity? Could IMO emulate the U.N. Environment Program (UNEP), which has no formal dispute-settlement powers, but which has nevertheless begun to play a role in settling environmental disputes? The UNEP Executive Director has reported:

> [T]here have been several instances where UNEP has acted, upon request, as mediator or facilitator in environmental disputes.

a. The legal opinion is quoted in Mensah, The Practice of International Law in International Organisations, in International Law: Teaching and Practice 146, 159–61 (B. Cheng ed. 1982).

b. Id. at 161.

c. Resolution A.294(VIII), in IMCO Assembly, Resolutions and Other Decisions, 8th Sess. 231 (1974); see also Resolution A.361(IX), in IMCO Assembly, Resolutions and Other Decisions, 5th Extraordinary Sess. and 9th Sess. 263 (1976).

d. Interview with Dr. T.A. Mensah, Assistant Secretary–General, IMO, July 22, 1988.

e. 27 Int'l Legal Materials 672 (1988).

f. IMO Doc. SUA/CONF/CW/WP.3, at 3 (1988).

g. Interview with C.M. Young, of the IMO Legal Division, July 18, 1988; Young, unpublished manuscript on the negotiating history of the convention, at 62 (1988).

Just recently, at the request of the two Governments concerned, UNEP sent an expert team to examine the conflicting claims of two European States concerning transboundary air pollution. The UNEP team studied the situation, ascertained the facts and formulated a co-operative scheme between the two Governments to solve the problem and enhance the environment—for the benefit of all concerned.[h]

What lessons are to be learned here about the potential role of an international organization in interpreting, and settling disputes regarding, the norms of the organization?

E. THE UNITED NATIONS

1. Introduction

An entire course could be built around dispute settlement and Charter interpretation in the United Nations. Chapter 2 has considered several issues that fall into this category, such as the question of participation by the PLO in Security Council dispute settlement, and the right of a permanent member of the Security Council to vote on a disputed matter in which it is interested. Chapters 4, 5 and 6 will examine U.N. dispute settlement in such contexts as threats to the peace, breaches of the peace, and alleged human rights violations. This subsection will consider some other areas, particularly involving Charter interpretation by the major U.N. organs (including the International Court of Justice) in the context of a dispute between South Africa and the organization over self-determination for Namibia, that lasted about 40 years.[a]

As will appear below, the ICJ is by no means the only authoritative interpreter of the U.N. Charter. Nevertheless, as the principal judicial organ of the United Nations (see Charter *article 92*), it has Charter interpretation as one of its primary tasks. It has had several opportunities to interpret the Charter under its jurisdiction to give advisory opinions when requested by the General Assembly, Security Council or other authorized U.N. organs and specialized agencies. See Charter *article 96* and ICJ Statute *articles 65–68*. It has also interpreted the Charter in some contentious cases brought under ICJ Statute *article 36*. Both types of jurisdiction—advisory and contentious—have been involved in the Namibia situation, with a 1971 advisory proceeding raising an unusual number of significant Charter interpretation questions.

The excerpts below provide an introduction to some of the issues surrounding interpretation of the Charter by U.N. organs, and lead into some of the issues raised in the 1971 ICJ opinion on Namibia. We begin with a report from the San Francisco Conference that produced the U.N. Charter in 1945.

h. U.N.Doc. UNEP/GC.16/4/Add.2, at 5 (1991).

a. Namibia became an independent state on March 21, 1990.

UNITED NATIONS CONFERENCE ON INTERNATIONAL ORGANIZATION
Report of Rapporteur of Committee IV/2, San Francisco, 1945.
Selected Documents 879–80 (1946).

Committee II/2 referred to this Committee the following question:

How and by what organ or organs of the Organization should the Charter be interpreted?

Discussion of the question brought out the following conclusions:

In the course of the operations from day to day of the various organs of the Organization, it is inevitable that each organ will interpret such parts of the Charter as are applicable to its particular functions. This process is inherent in the functioning of any body which operates under an instrument defining its functions and powers. It will be manifested in the functioning of such a body as the General Assembly, the Security Council, or the International Court of Justice. Accordingly, it is not necessary to include in the Charter a provision either authorizing or approving the normal operation of this principle.

Difficulties may conceivably arise in the event that there should be a difference of opinion among the organs of the Organization concerning the correct interpretation of a provision of the Charter. Thus, two organs may conceivably hold and may express or even act upon different views. Under unitary forms of national government the final determination of such a question may be vested in the highest court or in some other national authority. However, the nature of the Organization and of its operation would not seem to be such as to invite the inclusion in the Charter of any provision of this nature. If two member states are at variance concerning the correct interpretation of the Charter, they are of course free to submit the dispute to the International Court of Justice as in the case of any other treaty. Similarly, it would always be open to the General Assembly or to the Security Council, in appropriate circumstances, to ask the International Court of Justice for an advisory opinion concerning the meaning of a provision of the Charter. Should the General Assembly or the Security Council prefer another course, an *ad hoc* committee of jurists might be set up to examine the question and report its views, or recourse might be had to a joint conference. In brief, the members or the organs of the Organization might have recourse to various expedients in order to obtain an appropriate interpretation. It would appear neither necessary nor desirable to list or to describe in the Charter the various possible expedients.

It is to be understood, of course, that if an interpretation made by any organ of the Organization or by a committee of jurists is not generally acceptable it will be without binding force. In such circumstances, or in cases where it is desired to establish an authoritative interpretation as a precedent for the future, it may be necessary to embody the interpretation in an amendment to the Charter. This may always be accomplished by recourse to the procedure provided for amendment.

CERTAIN EXPENSES OF THE UNITED NATIONS
International Court of Justice, Advisory Opinion, 1962.
[1962] I.C.J. 151, 157.

[The question posed was whether certain expenses authorized by the General Assembly for peacekeeping operations in the Middle East and in what was then the Congo constituted "expenses of the Organization" within the meaning of *article 17(2)* of the Charter. The Court ultimately answered in the affirmative. Part of its analysis relied on the practice of the General Assembly and the Security Council, as an aid to interpreting the extent of their powers under the Charter. Before examining specific instances in which those bodies had acted, it made the following remarks.]

Turning to the question which has been posed, the Court observes that it involves an interpretation of Article 17, paragraph 2, of the Charter. On the previous occasions when the Court has had to interpret the Charter of the United Nations, it has followed the principles and rules applicable in general to the interpretation of treaties, since it has recognized that the Charter is a multilateral treaty, albeit a treaty having certain special characteristics. In interpreting Article 4 of the Charter, the Court was led to consider "the structure of the Charter" and "the relations established by it between the General Assembly and the Security Council"; a comparable problem confronts the Court in the instant matter. The Court sustained its interpretation of Article 4 by considering the manner in which the organs concerned "have consistently interpreted the text" in their practice (*Competence of the General Assembly for the Admission of a State to the United Nations,* [below]).

COMPETENCE OF THE GENERAL ASSEMBLY FOR THE ADMISSION OF A STATE TO THE UNITED NATIONS
International Court of Justice, Advisory Opinion, 1950.
[1950] I.C.J. 4, 8–9.

[The question was whether admission to the U.N. under *article 4(2)* could be accomplished by a decision of the General Assembly when the Security Council had made no recommendation for admission. The Court first examined the text of article 4(2) and concluded that its plain meaning required a recommendation of the Security Council. It continued:]

The Court considers it necessary to say that the first duty of a tribunal which is called upon to interpret and apply the provisions of a treaty, is to endeavour to give effect to them in their natural and ordinary meaning in the context in which they occur. If the relevant words in their natural and ordinary meaning make sense in their context, that is an end of the matter. If, on the other hand, the words in their natural and ordinary meaning are ambiguous or lead to an unreasonable result, then, and then only, must the Court, by resort to other methods of interpretation, seek to ascertain what the parties really did mean when they used these words.

* * *

When the Court can give effect to a provision of a treaty by giving to the words used in it their natural and ordinary meaning, it may not interpret the words by seeking to give them some other meaning. In the present case the Court finds no difficulty in ascertaining the natural and ordinary meaning of the words in question and no difficulty in giving effect to them. Some of the written statements submitted to the Court have invited it to investigate the *travaux préparatoires* of the Charter. Having regard, however, to the considerations above stated, the Court is of the opinion that it is not permissible, in this case, to resort to *travaux préparatoires*.

* * *

The organs to which Article 4 entrusts the judgment of the Organization in matters of admission have consistently interpreted the text in the sense that the General Assembly can decide to admit only on the basis of a recommendation of the Security Council. In particular, the Rules of Procedure of the General Assembly provide for consideration of the merits of an application and of the decision to be made upon it only "if the Security Council recommends the applicant State for membership" (Article 125). The Rules merely state that if the Security Council has not recommended the admission, the General Assembly may send back the application to the Security Council for further consideration (Article 126). This last step has been taken several times: it was taken in Resolution 296(IV), the very one that embodies this Request for an Opinion.

MECHANICS OF CHARTER INTERPRETATION

The Charter contains no express provision setting forth how or by what organs it should be interpreted. Consequently, even under the World Court's restrictive "plain meaning" rule (applied in the 1950 Admission Case, above, to the Charter as it had been to other treaties), it would seem permissible to consider the preparatory work at the San Francisco Conference in determining what interpretation procedure was intended. What do you think of the procedure (non-procedure?) for interpretation of the Charter put forward at the San Francisco Conference? Why would states have been reluctant to give the power of authoritative interpretation or judicial review to the ICJ?

2. The ICJ Advisory Function: Namibia and Other Opinions

The Namibia question in the U.N. was intimately connected with South Africa's practice of apartheid and the extension of that practice to Namibia, which (as South West Africa) had been mandated to South Africa under the League of Nations Mandates system. A brief legal history up to 1966 appears in the excerpt below, written by the chief counsel to Liberia and Ethiopia in their unsuccessful contentious proceedings against South Africa in the 1960s.

GROSS, THE SOUTH WEST AFRICA CASE: WHAT HAPPENED?
45 Foreign Affairs 36 (1966).*

* * *

The Territory of South West Africa, a German colony prior to the First World War, was entrusted to South Africa in 1920 as a Mandate under the League of Nations Covenant. The Mandate System * * * comprised certain colonies and territories which, as a consequence of the war, had ceased to be under the sovereignty of the defeated states.

These colonies and territories, in the words of Article 22 of the League Covenant, were "inhabited by peoples not yet able to stand by themselves under the strenuous conditions of the modern world."

* * *

The heart and essence of the system is embodied in Article 22 of the Covenant: "the principle that the well-being and development of such peoples form a sacred trust of civilization and that securities for the performance of this trust should be embodied in this Covenant." The same Article provides that "the tutelage of such peoples should be entrusted to advanced nations who by reason of their resources, their experience or their geographical position can best undertake this responsibility, and who are willing to accept it, and that this tutelage should be exercised by them as Mandatories on behalf of the League."

A Mandate for German South West Africa, accordingly, was "conferred upon his Britannic Majesty to be exercised on his behalf by the Union of South Africa" (then a member of the British Empire). His Britannic Majesty, in turn, agreed to accept the Mandate on behalf of the Union of South Africa and undertook "to exercise it on behalf of the League of Nations." As in the case of all Mandates, a Mandate agreement was confirmed by the Council of the League of Nations. This instrument, together with Article 22 of the Covenant itself, com-

---

* Excerpted by permission from Foreign Affairs, October 1966. Copyright 1966 by Council on Foreign Relations, Inc.

prises the principles and defines the terms for the governance of the Territory.

As early as 1922, South Africa adopted the view that "C Mandates" (in which category South West Africa was placed) were—in the words of the South African leader, General Jan Christiaan Smuts—"in effect not far removed from annexation." The Permanent Mandates Commission, until it ceased to function in 1939, frequently recorded its disagreement with South African assertions of sovereignty over the Territory, as well as of the right to incorporate it as a fifth province. South Africa, nevertheless, submitted reports to the Commission and recognized the legal existence of the Mandate.

Soon after the dissolution of the League and the commencement of United Nations operations, and certainly by 1949, it became obvious that South Africa's conception of its legal obligations under the Mandate was essentially at variance with those of other members of the United Nations. In 1947, South Africa submitted its first and last report to the United Nations. By the end of 1948, it openly referred to "the previous Mandate, since expired."

The United Nations General Assembly, on December 6, 1949, requested the Court for an Advisory Opinion on certain questions concerning the Mandate. These centered upon the international status of the Territory and the international obligations of South Africa arising therefrom. The Government of South Africa, which appeared before the Court, contended that the Mandate had expired with the dissolution of the League. The Court unanimously held to the contrary, stating:

> The Mandate was created in the interest of the inhabitants of the territory, and of humanity in general, as an international institution with an international object—a sacred trust of civilization. * * * If the Mandate lapsed, as the Union Government contends, the latter's authority would equally have lapsed. To retain the rights derived from the Mandate and to deny the obligations thereunder could not be justified.

The Court ruled that the necessity for international supervision over the Mandate continues to exist despite the disappearance of the League of Nations Council, in as much as such supervision is an essential element of the Mandate System and the United Nations has an international organ performing supervisory functions similar to those performed by the League. Hence, the Court held, " * * * South Africa is under an obligation to submit to supervision and control of the General Assembly and to render annual reports to it." [1]

In response to another question posed by the General Assembly, the Court unanimously held that South Africa has no competence to

---

1. The Court also held, five Judges dissenting, that the Charter did not require South Africa to place the Territory under the Trusteeship System, even though this was the "normal course," which the framers of the Charter had "expected." The Territory, indeed, is the anomalous exception.

modify unilaterally the international status of the Territory or any of the "international rules respecting the rights, powers and obligations relating to the administration of the Territory and the supervision of that administration."

* * *

The 1950 Advisory Opinion, which was promptly accepted by the General Assembly, remained a dead letter. Year after year, unsuccessful efforts were made by successive agencies of the Assembly, and on its behalf, to negotiate with South Africa on the basis of the Advisory Opinion of 1950. South Africa, however, repudiated the Opinion, explicitly repeating its contention that the Mandate had lapsed.

All the while, the South African Government was extending, with increasing severity, the racially discriminatory laws and regulations which comprise the apartheid policy, and which were rigidly applied in the Territory—as in South Africa itself. These official policies and practices were universally condemned in regularly repeated United Nations resolutions. The response was a steady tightening of repressive administrative action. By 1960, it had become crystal clear that the process of resolution-passing by the General Assembly was no more than a perennial autumn rite.

* * *

Early in 1960, the Asian–African group at the United Nations discussed the feasibility of judicial recourse and explored availability of legal counsel. Subsequently, the Liberian Government requested the author [Mr. Gross] to prepare a Memorandum of Law for circulation to governments in advance of the Second Conference of Independent African States, scheduled to convene at Addis Ababa in June 1960. After full discussion, * * * the conference concluded "that the international obligations of the Union of South Africa concerning the Territory of South West Africa should be submitted to the International Court of Justice for adjudication in a contentious proceeding."

* * *

The new ingredient which would be introduced by a favorable judgment in a contentious proceeding—and this was the heart of the matter—would be the potential application of Article 94 of the United Nations Charter. The explicit grant of power to the Security Council to compel compliance with a Court Judgment (as distinguished from an Advisory Opinion) expressly vests in the Council what may be called an "executive" function, analogous to that in normal municipal systems. There was never any secret about the significance of Article 94 in the decision to seek judicial recourse.

* * *

In November 1960, Ethiopia and Liberia instituted proceedings against South Africa, by applications requesting the Court to adjudicate upon the issues in dispute between them and to grant suitable relief. The subject of the dispute was defined in the Applicants' Memorials: Whether the Mandate was still in force, whether the United Nations had supervisory authority, and whether South Africa was violating its obligations under the Mandate by, among other things, imposing an extreme form of racial discrimination upon the "non-White" inhabitants of the Territory.

The South African Government, as was its right under the rules of the Court, entered "preliminary objections," challenging the Applicants' standing to bring the suit and contending that the Court had no jurisdiction "to hear or adjudicate upon the questions of law and fact raised by the Applicants." After consideration of the briefs and arguments of the Parties, the Court rendered its Judgment of December 21, 1962, dismissing the objections and upholding its competence to proceed with the merits of the dispute which the Applicants had referred to it. The vote was 8 to 7.

The 1962 Judgment examined the origin and nature of the Mandate System, the character of South Africa's obligations as Mandatory, the legal interest of the applicants in the performance of the Mandate and the functions of the United Nations and of the Court under the Mandate scheme. On all points the Court found that the Applicants had the required standing to bring the issue before it, and that it had jurisdiction to adjudicate upon the merits of the dispute.

* * *

The Judgment of July 18, 1966 [in a second phase of the same case] rejected the Applicants' claims. It did so on the ground that " * * * the Applicants cannot be considered to have established any legal right or interest appertaining to them in the subject-matter of the present claims, and that, accordingly, the Court must decline to give effect to them." Again the vote was 8 to 7.

* * *

Little purpose would be served by an analysis here of the judicial alchemy by which the dissenting opinions of 1962 were transmuted into the Judgment of 1966. As Judge Padilla Nervo (Mexico) pointed out in his dissenting opinion, the 1966 majority merely was "reproducing on the present occasion the arguments adduced in dissenting opinions against the Judgment of 1962." The 1966 Judgment, indeed, is essentially a paraphrase of the 1962 joint dissenting opinion of Sir Gerald Fitzmaurice (U.K.) and the President of the Court, Sir Percy Spender (Australia), who broke a deadlock by casting a second vote, as permitted by the Court's Statute. On the basis of the same reasons which they advanced in the 1962 Judgment and which were rejected, the majority in 1966 found that the right of the Applicants to an adjudication on the merits of the dispute was an "antecedent" question, which "appertained to the merits of the case," and held that although the Applicants had sufficient standing to "activate" the Court, they were not entitled to a judgment on the validity of their claim. Hence the Court did not even pass upon the issue whether the Mandate is in existence or whether South Africa [had] a right unilaterally to modify the terms of the Mandate.

THE AFTERMATH

Frustration resulting from the Court's reversal of its 1962 decision led the General Assembly to adopt its Resolution 2145(XXI), below.[a]

RESOLUTION ON TERMINATION OF THE SOUTHWEST AFRICA MANDATE
United Nations General Assembly, Oct. 27, 1966.
G.A.Res. 2145, 21 GAOR Supp. 16 (A/6316), at 2.

The General Assembly,

Reaffirming the inalienable right of the people of South West Africa to freedom and independence in accordance with the Charter of the United Nations, General Assembly resolution 1514(XV) of 14 December 1960 [the Declaration on the Granting of Independence to Colonial Countries and Peoples] and earlier Assembly resolutions * * *,

* * *

Convinced that the administration of the Mandated Territory by South Africa has been conducted in a manner contrary to the Mandate, the Charter of the United Nations and the Universal Declaration of Human Rights,

* * *

Considering that all the efforts of the United Nations to induce the Government of South Africa to fulfil its obligations in respect of the administration of the Mandated Territory and to ensure the well-being and security of the indigenous inhabitants have been of no avail,

* * *

Affirming its right to take appropriate action in the matter, including the right to revert to itself the administration of the Mandated Territory,

1. *Reaffirms* that the provisions of General Assembly resolution 1514(XV) are fully applicable to the people of the Mandated Territory of South West Africa and that, therefore, the people of South West Africa have the inalienable right to self-determination, freedom and independence in accordance with the Charter of the United Nations;

---

a. Resolution 2145 was adopted by a vote of 114 in favor, two opposed (South Africa and Portugal) and three abstentions.

2. *Reaffirms further* that South West Africa is a territory having international status and that it shall maintain this status until it achieves independence;

3. *Declares* that South Africa has failed to fulfil its obligations in respect of the administration of the Mandated Territory and to ensure the moral and material well-being and security of the indigenous inhabitants of South West Africa and has, in fact, disavowed the Mandate;

4. *Decides* that the Mandate conferred upon His Britannic Majesty to be exercised on his behalf by the Government of the Union of South Africa is therefore terminated, that South Africa has no other right to administer the Territory and that henceforth South West Africa comes under the direct responsibility of the United Nations * * *.

THE SECURITY COUNCIL STEPS IN

The South African government objected to Resolution 2145 on the ground that the General Assembly had no power, under the U.N. Charter or as successor to the supervisory authority of the League of Nations, to terminate the Mandate.[b]

The General Assembly followed with resolutions calling on South Africa to comply with Resolution 2145, and creating and supervising the United Nations Council for South West Africa (later the Council for Namibia) which was directed to administer the territory until its independence. The Security Council also began to adopt resolutions dealing with the Namibian issue, leading to its adoption in 1970 of S.C. Resolution 276 (adopted 13–0–2, with France and the United Kingdom the abstainers):

RESOLUTION ON ILLEGALITY OF SOUTH AFRICAN PRESENCE IN NAMIBIA
United Nations Security Council, Jan. 30, 1970.
S.C.Res. 276, 25 SCOR, Resolutions & Decisions 1–2.

The Security Council,

Reaffirming the inalienable right of the people of Namibia to freedom and independence recognized in General Assembly resolution 1514 (XV) of 14 December 1960,

Reaffirming General Assembly resolution 2145 (XXI) of 27 October 1966, by which the United Nations decided that the Mandate for South West Africa was terminated and assumed direct responsibility for the Territory until its independence,

b. U.N.Docs. A/7045/Add.9 and S/8357/Add.9, at 2–4 (1968); 13 Whiteman, Digest of Int'l Law 761–62 (1968).

Reaffirming Security Council resolution 264 (1969) of 20 March 1969 in which the Council recognized the termination of the Mandate and called upon the Government of South Africa to withdraw immediately its administration from the Territory,

Reaffirming that the extension and enforcement of South African laws in the Territory together with the continued detentions, trials and subsequent sentencing of Namibians by the Government of South Africa constitute illegal acts and flagrant violations of the rights of the Namibians concerned, the Universal Declaration of Human Rights and the international status of the Territory, now under direct United Nations responsibility,

Recalling Security Council resolution 269 (1969) of 12 August 1969,

1. *Strongly condemns* the refusal of the Government of South Africa to comply with the resolutions of the General Assembly and Security Council pertaining to Namibia;

2. *Declares* that the continued presence of the South African authorities in Namibia is illegal and that consequently all acts taken by the Government of South Africa on behalf of or concerning Namibia after the termination of the Mandate are illegal and invalid;

* * *

5. *Calls upon* all States, particularly those which have economic and other interests in Namibia, to refrain from any dealings with the Government of South Africa which are inconsistent with paragraph 2 of the present resolution * * *.

THE NAMIBIA ADVISORY OPINION

In S.C. Resolution 284 (1970), the Security Council asked the ICJ for an advisory opinion on the following question: "What are the legal consequences for States of the continued presence of South Africa in Namibia, notwithstanding Security Council resolution 276 (1970)?" In the opinion below, the Court answered this question, and in doing so dealt with several issues important to the dispute-settlement and Charter interpretation process of the United Nations in matters of direct concern to the organization. As you read the excerpts from the opinion, keep in mind the general question of defining, comparing and evaluating the roles of the General Assembly and Security Council as interpreters of their own powers under the Charter, and of the ICJ as the adjudicative body of the Organization.

LEGAL CONSEQUENCES FOR STATES OF THE CONTINUED PRESENCE OF SOUTH AFRICA IN NAMIBIA (SOUTH WEST AFRICA) NOTWITHSTANDING SECURITY COUNCIL RESOLUTION 276 (1970)

International Court of Justice, Advisory Opinion, 1971.
[1971] I.C.J. 16.

[The Court first rejected an objection by South Africa to the participation of three Judges who had formerly been representatives of their governments in other United Nations organs dealing with matters concerning South West Africa.]

10. By a letter from the Secretary of Foreign Affairs dated 13 November 1970, the Government of South Africa made an application for the appointment of a judge *ad hoc* to sit in the proceedings, in terms of Article 31, paragraph 2, of the Statute of the Court. The Court decided, in accordance with the terms of Article 46 of the Statute of the Court, to hear the contentions of South Africa on this point in camera, and a closed hearing, at which representatives of India, the Netherlands, Nigeria and the United States of America were also present, was held for the purpose on 27 January 1971.

11. By an Order dated 29 January 1971, the Court decided to reject the application of the Government of South Africa. The Court thereafter decided that the record of the closed hearing should be made accessible to the public.

* * *

20. The Government of South Africa has contended that for several reasons resolution 284 (1970) of the Security Council, which requested the advisory opinion of the Court, is invalid, and that, therefore, the Court is not competent to deliver the opinion. A resolution of a properly constituted organ of the United Nations which is passed in accordance with that organ's rules of procedure, and is declared by its President to have been so passed, must be presumed to have been validly adopted. However, since in this instance the objections made concern the competence of the Court, the Court will proceed to examine them.

21. The first objection is that in the voting on the resolution two permanent members of the Security Council abstained. It is contended that the resolution was consequently not adopted by an affirmative vote of nine members including the concurring votes of the permanent members, as required by Article 27, paragraph 3, of the Charter of the United Nations.

22. However, the proceedings of the Security Council extending over a long period supply abundant evidence that presidential rulings and the positions taken by members of the Council, in particular its

permanent members, have consistently and uniformly interpreted the practice of voluntary abstention by a permanent member as not constituting a bar to the adoption of resolutions. By abstaining, a member does not signify its objection to the approval of what is being proposed; in order to prevent the adoption of a resolution requiring unanimity of the permanent members, a permanent member has only to cast a negative vote. This procedure followed by the Security Council, which has continued unchanged after the amendment in 1965 of Article 27 of the Charter, has been generally accepted by Members of the United Nations and evidences a general practice of that Organization.

23. The Government of South Africa has also argued that as the question relates to a dispute between South Africa and other Members of the United Nations, South Africa, as a Member of the United Nations, not a member of the Security Council and a party to a dispute, should have been invited under Article 32 of the Charter to participate, without vote, in the discussion relating to it. It further contended that the proviso at the end of Article 27, paragraph 3, of the Charter, requiring members of the Security Council which are parties to a dispute to abstain from voting, should have been complied with.[c]

24. The language of Article 32 of the Charter is mandatory, but the question whether the Security Council must extend an invitation in accordance with that provision depends on whether it has made a determination that the matter under its consideration is in the nature of a dispute. In the absence of such a determination Article 32 of the Charter does not apply.

25. The question of Namibia was placed on the agenda of the Security Council as a "situation" and not as a "dispute". No member State made any suggestion or proposal that the matter should be examined as a dispute, although due notice was given of the placing of the question on the Security Council's agenda under the title "Situation in Namibia". Had the Government of South Africa considered that the question should have been treated in the Security Council as a dispute, it should have drawn the Council's attention to that aspect of the matter. Having failed to raise the question at the appropriate time in the proper forum, it is not open to it to raise it before the Court at this stage.

26. A similar answer must be given to the related objection based on the proviso to paragraph 3 of Article 27 of the Charter. This proviso also requires for its application the prior determination by the Security Council that a dispute exists and that certain members of the Council are involved as parties to such a dispute.

27. In the alternative the Government of South Africa has contended that even if the Court had competence to give the opinion

---

c. [The members of the Security Council in 1970 were Burundi, China, Columbia, Finland, France, Nepal, Nicaragua, Poland, Sierra Leone, Spain, Syria, U.S.S.R., U.K., U.S.A. and Zambia. Ed.]

requested, it should nevertheless, as a matter of judicial propriety, refuse to exercise its competence.

28. The first reason invoked in support of this contention is the supposed disability of the Court to give the opinion requested by the Security Council, because of political pressure to which the Court, according to the Government of South Africa, has been or might be subjected.

29. It would not be proper for the Court to entertain these observations, bearing as they do on the very nature of the Court as the principal judicial organ of the United Nations, an organ which, in that capacity, acts only on the basis of the law, independently of all outside influence or interventions whatsoever, in the exercise of the judicial function entrusted to it alone by the Charter and its Statute. A court functioning as a court of law can act in no other way.

30. The second reason advanced on behalf of the Government of South Africa in support of its contention that the Court should refuse to accede to the request of the Security Council is that the relevant legal question relates to an existing dispute between South Africa and other States. In this context it relies on the case of *Eastern Carelia* and argues that the Permanent Court of International Justice declined to rule upon the question referred to it because it was directly related to the main point of a dispute actually pending between two States.

31. However, that case is not relevant, as it differs from the present one. For instance one of the States concerned in that case was not at the time a Member of the League of Nations and did not appear before the Permanent Court. South Africa, as a Member of the United Nations, is bound by Article 96 of the Charter, which empowers the Security Council to request advisory opinions on any legal question. It has appeared before the Court, participated in both the written and oral proceedings and, while raising specific objections against the competence of the Court, has addressed itself to the merits of the question.

32. Nor does the Court find that in this case the Security Council's request relates to a legal dispute actually pending between two or more States. It is not the purpose of the request to obtain the assistance of the Court in the exercise of the Security Council's functions relating to the pacific settlement of a dispute pending before it between two or more States. The request is put forward by a United Nations organ with reference to its own decisions and it seeks legal advice from the Court on the consequences and implications of these decisions. This objective is stressed by the preamble to the resolution requesting the opinion, in which the Security Council has stated "that an advisory opinion from the International Court of Justice would be useful for the Security Council in its further consideration of the question of Namibia and in furtherance of the objectives the Council is seeking". It is worth recalling that in its Advisory Opinion on *Reservations to the Convention on the Prevention and Punishment of the Crime of Genocide,* the Court stated: "The object of this request for an

Opinion is to guide the United Nations in respect of its own action" (*I.C.J.Reports 1951,* p. 19).

33. The Court does not find either that in this case the advisory opinion concerns a dispute between South Africa and the United Nations. In the course of the oral proceedings Counsel for the Government of South Africa stated:

> * * * our submission is not that the question is a dispute, but that in order to answer the question the Court will have to decide legal and factual issues which are actually in dispute between South Africa and other States.

34. The fact that, in the course of its reasoning, and in order to answer the question submitted to it, the Court may have to pronounce on legal issues upon which radically divergent views exist between South Africa and the United Nations, does not convert the present case into a dispute nor bring it within the compass of Articles 82 and 83 of the Rules of Court.[d] A similar position existed in the three previous advisory proceedings concerning South West Africa: in none of them did South Africa claim that there was a dispute, nor did the Court feel it necessary to apply the Rules of Court concerning "a legal question actually pending between two or more States". Differences of views among States on legal issues have existed in practically every advisory proceeding; if all were agreed, the need to resort to the Court for advice would not arise.

35. In accordance with Article 83 of the Rules of Court, the question whether the advisory opinion had been requested "upon a legal question actually pending between two or more States" was also of decisive importance in the Court's consideration of the request made by the Government of South Africa for the appointment of a judge *ad hoc.* As already indicated, the Court heard argument in support of that request and, after due deliberation, decided, by an Order of 29 January 1971, not to accede to it. This decision was based on the conclusion that the terms of the request for advisory opinion, the circumstances in which it had been submitted (which are described in para. 32 above), as well as the considerations set forth in paragraphs 33 and 34 above, were such as to preclude the interpretation that an opinion had been "requested upon a legal question actually pending between two or more States". Thus, in the opinion of the Court, South Africa was not entitled under Article 83 of the Rules of Court to the appointment of a judge *ad hoc.*

* * *

---

d. [Article 82 provided that the Court in advisory proceedings is to be guided by the rules for contentious cases "to the extent to which it recognizes them to be applicable; for this purpose it shall above all consider whether the request for the advisory opinion relates to a legal question actually pending between two or more States." Article 83 extended the right to appoint an ad hoc judge, in ICJ Statute *art. 31,* to advisory proceedings when an opinion has been requested "upon a legal question actually pending between two or more States." In the revised Rules of Court, these provisions are in Article 102(2) & (3). See 17 Int'l Legal Materials 1286, 1303 (1978). Ed.]

39. The view has also been expressed that even if South Africa is not entitled to a judge *ad hoc* as a matter of right, the Court should, in the exercise of the discretion granted by Article 68 of the Statute, have allowed such an appointment, in recognition of the fact that South Africa's interests are specially affected in the present case. In this connection the Court wishes to recall a decision taken by the Permanent Court at a time when the Statute did not include any provision concerning advisory opinions, the entire regulation of the procedure in the matter being thus left to the Court (*P.C.I.J., Series E, No. 4*, p. 76). Confronted with a request for the appointment of a judge *ad hoc* in a case in which it found there was no dispute, the Court, in rejecting the request, stated that "the decision of the Court must be in accordance with its Statute and with the Rules duly framed by it in pursuance of Article 30 of the Statute" (Order of 31 October 1935, *P.C.I.J., Series A/B, No. 65*, Annex 1, p. 69 at p. 70). It found further that the "exception cannot be given a wider application than is provided for by the Rules" (*ibid.*, p. 71). In the present case the Court, having regard to the Rules of Court adopted under Article 30 of the Statute, came to the conclusion that it was unable to exercise discretion in this respect.

40. The Government of South Africa has also expressed doubts as to whether the Court is competent to, or should, give an opinion, if, in order to do so, it should have to make findings as to extensive factual issues. In the view of the Court, the contingency that there may be factual issues underlying the question posed does not alter its character as a "legal question" as envisaged in Article 96 of the Charter. The reference in this provision to legal questions cannot be interpreted as opposing legal to factual issues. Normally, to enable a court to pronounce on legal questions, it must also be acquainted with, take into account, and, if necessary, make findings as to the relevant factual issues. The limitation of the powers of the Court contended for by the Government of South Africa has no basis in the Charter or the Statute.

41. The Court could, of course, acting on its own, exercise the discretion vested in it by Article 65, paragraph 1, of the Statute and decline to accede to the request for an advisory opinion. In considering this possibility the Court must bear in mind that: "A reply to a request for an Opinion should not, in principle, be refused." (*I.C.J. Reports 1951*, p. 19.) The Court has considered whether there are any "compelling reasons", as referred to in the past practice of the Court, which would justify such a refusal. It has found no such reasons. Moreover, it feels that by replying to the request it would not only "remain faithful to the requirements of its judicial character" (*I.C.J.Reports 1960*, p. 153), but also discharge its functions as "the principal judicial organ of the United Nations" (Art. 92 of the Charter).

[At this point the Court entered into a lengthy discussion of the League of Nations Mandate system and of the Mandate for South West Africa. As we have seen, League of Nations Covenant article 22(1) provided in part that there should be applied to mandated territories "the principle that the well-being and development of such peoples form a sacred trust of civilisation." Article 22(7) provided that the Mandatory (i.e. South Africa) was required to render to the League of Nations Council an annual report in reference to the mandated territory. The Court continued:]

87. The Government of France in its written statement and the Government of South Africa throughout the present proceedings have raised the objection that the General Assembly, in adopting resolution 2145(XXI), acted *ultra vires*.

88. Before considering this objection, it is necessary for the Court to examine the observations made and the contentions advanced as to whether the Court should go into this question. * * * It was argued that the Court should not assume powers of judicial review of the action taken by the other principal organs of the United Nations without specific request to that effect, nor act as a court of appeal from their decisions.

89. Undoubtedly, the Court does not possess powers of judicial review or appeal in respect of the decisions taken by the United Nations organs concerned. The question of the validity or conformity with the Charter of General Assembly resolution 2145(XXI) or of related Security Council resolutions does not form the subject of the request for [an] advisory opinion. However, in the exercise of its judicial function and since objections have been advanced, the Court, in the course of its reasoning, will consider these objections before determining any legal consequences arising from those resolutions.

* * *

92. The terms of the preamble and operative part of resolution 2145(XXI) leave no doubt as to the character of the resolution. In the preamble the General Assembly declares itself "*Convinced* that the administration of the Mandated Territory by South Africa has been conducted in a manner contrary" to the two basic international instruments directly imposing obligations upon South Africa, the Mandate and the Charter of the United Nations, as well as to the Universal Declaration of Human Rights. In another paragraph of the preamble the conclusion is reached that, after having insisted with no avail upon performance for more than twenty years, the moment has arrived for the General Assembly to exercise the right to treat such violation as a ground for termination.

93. In paragraph 3 of the operative part of the resolution the General Assembly "*Declares* that South Africa has failed to fulfil its obligations in respect of the administration of the Mandated Territory and to ensure the moral and material well-being and security of the indigenous inhabitants of South West Africa and has, in fact, disavowed the Mandate". In paragraph 4 the decision is reached, as a consequence of the previous declaration "that the Mandate conferred upon His Britannic Majesty to be exercised on his behalf by the Government of the Union of South Africa is *therefore* terminated * * * ". (Empha-

sis added.) It is this part of the resolution which is relevant in the present proceedings.

94. In examining this action of the General Assembly it is appropriate to have regard to the general principles of international law regulating termination of a treaty relationship on account of breach. For even if the mandate is viewed as having the character of an institution, as is maintained, it depends on those international agreements which created the system and regulated its application. As the Court indicated in 1962 "this Mandate, like practically all other similar Mandates" was "a special type of instrument composite in nature and instituting a novel international regime. It incorporates a definite agreement * * * " (*I.C.J. Reports 1962*, p. 331). The Court stated conclusively in that Judgment that the Mandate " * * * in fact and in law, is an international agreement, having the character of a treaty or convention" (*I.C.J. Reports 1962*, p. 330). The rules laid down by the Vienna Convention on the Law of Treaties concerning termination of a treaty relationship on account of breach (adopted without a dissenting vote) may in many respects be considered as a codification of existing customary law on the subject. In the light of these rules, only a material breach of a treaty justifies termination, such breach being defined as:

(*a*) a repudiation of the treaty not sanctioned by the present Convention; or

(*b*) the violation of a provision essential to the accomplishment of the object or purpose of the treaty (Art. 60, para. 3).

95. General Assembly resolution 2145(XXI) determines that both forms of material breach had occurred in this case. By stressing that South Africa "has, in fact, disavowed the Mandate", the General Assembly declared in fact that it had repudiated it. The resolution in question is therefore to be viewed as the exercise of the right to terminate a relationship in case of a deliberate and persistent violation of obligations which destroys the very object and purpose of that relationship.

96. It has been contended that the Covenant of the League of Nations did not confer on the Council of the League power to terminate a mandate for misconduct of the mandatory and that no such power could therefore be exercised by the United Nations, since it could not derive from the League greater powers than the latter itself had. For this objection to prevail it would be necessary to show that the mandates system, as established under the League, excluded the application of the general principle of law that a right of termination on account of breach must be presumed to exist in respect of all treaties, except as regards provisions relating to the protection of the human person contained in treaties of a humanitarian character (as indicated in Art. 60, para. 5, of the Vienna Convention). The silence of a treaty as to the existence of such a right cannot be interpreted as implying the exclusion of a right which has its source outside of the treaty, in general

international law, and is dependent on the occurrence of circumstances which are not normally envisaged when a treaty is concluded.

* * *

102. In a further objection to General Assembly resolution 2145(XXI) it is contended that it made pronouncements which the Assembly, not being a judicial organ, and not having previously referred the matter to any such organ, was not competent to make. Without dwelling on the conclusions reached in the 1966 Judgment in the *South West Africa* contentious cases, it is worth recalling that in those cases the applicant States, which complained of material breaches of substantive provisions of the Mandate, were held not to "possess any separate self-contained right which they could assert * * * to require the due performance of the Mandate in discharge of the 'sacred trust'" (*I.C.J. Reports 1966,* pp. 29 and 51). On the other hand, the Court declared that: "* * * any divergences of view concerning the conduct of a mandate were regarded as being matters that had their place in the political field, the settlement of which lay between the mandatory and the competent organs of the League" (*ibid.,* p. 45). To deny to a political organ of the United Nations which is a successor of the League in this respect the right to act, on the argument that it lacks competence to render what is described as a judicial decision, would not only be inconsistent but would amount to a complete denial of the remedies available against fundamental breaches of an international undertaking.

103. The Court is unable to appreciate the view that the General Assembly acted unilaterally as party and judge in its own cause. In the 1966 Judgment in the *South West Africa* cases, referred to above, it was found that the function to call for the due execution of the relevant provisions of the mandate instruments appertained to the League acting as an entity through its appropriate organs. The right of the League "in the pursuit of its collective, institutional activity, to require the due performance of the Mandate in discharge of the 'sacred trust'", was specifically recognized (*ibid.,* p. 29). Having regard to this finding, the United Nations as a successor to the League, acting through its competent organs, must be seen above all as the supervisory institution, competent to pronounce, in that capacity, on the conduct of the mandatory with respect to its international obligations, and competent to act accordingly.

104. It is argued on behalf of South Africa that the consideration set forth in paragraph 3 of resolution 2145(XXI) of the General Assembly, relating to the failure of South Africa to fulfil its obligations in respect of the administration of the mandated territory, called for a detailed factual investigation before the General Assembly could adopt resolution 2145(XXI) or the Court pronounce upon its validity. The failure of South Africa to comply with the obligation to submit to supervision and to render reports, an essential part of the Mandate, cannot be disputed in the light of determinations made by this Court on

more occasions than one. In relying on these, as on other findings of the Court in previous proceedings concerning South West Africa, the Court adheres to its own jurisprudence.

105. General Assembly resolution 2145(XXI), after declaring the termination of the Mandate, added in operative paragraph 4 "that South Africa has no other right to administer the Territory". This part of the resolution has been objected to as deciding a transfer of territory. That in fact is not so. The pronouncement made by the General Assembly is based on a conclusion, referred to earlier, reached by the Court in 1950:

> The authority which the Union Government exercises over the Territory is based on the Mandate. If the Mandate lapsed, as the Union Government contends, the latter's authority would equally have lapsed. (*I.C.J. Reports 1950*, p. 133.)

This was confirmed by the Court in its Judgment of 21 December 1962 in the *South West Africa* cases (Ethiopia v. South Africa; Liberia v. South Africa) (*I.C.J. Reports 1962*, p. 333). Relying on these decisions of the Court, the General Assembly declared that the Mandate having been terminated "South Africa has no other right to administer the Territory". This is not a finding on facts, but the formulation of a legal situation. For it would not be correct to assume that, because the General Assembly is in principle vested with recommendatory powers, it is debarred from adopting, in specific cases within the framework of its competence, resolutions which make determinations or have operative design.

106. By resolution 2145(XXI) the General Assembly terminated the Mandate. However, lacking the necessary powers to ensure the withdrawal of South Africa from the Territory, it enlisted the co-operation of the Security Council by calling the latter's attention to the resolution, thus acting in accordance with Article 11, paragraph 2, of the Charter.

* * *

108. Resolution 276 (1970) of the Security Council, specifically mentioned in the text of the request, is the one essential for the purposes of the present advisory opinion. Before analysing it, however, it is necessary to refer briefly to resolutions 264 (1969) and 269 (1969), since these two resolutions have, together with resolution 276 (1970), a combined and a cumulative effect. Resolution 264 (1969), in paragraph 3 of its operative part, calls upon South Africa to withdraw its administration from Namibia immediately. Resolution 269 (1969), in view of South Africa's lack of compliance, after recalling the obligations of Members under Article 25 of the Charter, calls upon the Government of South Africa, in paragraph 5 of its operative part, "to withdraw its administration from the territory immediately and in any case before 4 October 1969". The preamble of resolution 276 (1970) reaffirms General Assembly resolution 2145(XXI) and espouses it, by referring to the

decision, not merely of the General Assembly, but of the United Nations "that the Mandate of South West Africa was terminated". In the operative part, after condemning the non-compliance by South Africa with General Assembly and Security Council resolutions pertaining to Namibia, the Security Council declares, in paragraph 2, that "the continued presence of the South African authorities in Namibia is illegal" and that consequently all acts taken by the Government of South Africa "on behalf of or concerning Namibia after the termination of the Mandate are illegal and invalid". In paragraph 5 the Security Council "*Calls upon* all States, particularly those which have economic and other interests in Namibia, to refrain from any dealings with the Government of South Africa which are inconsistent with operative paragraph 2 of this resolution".

109. It emerges from the communications bringing the matter to the Security Council's attention, from the discussions held and particularly from the text of the resolutions themselves, that the Security Council, when it adopted these resolutions, was acting in the exercise of what it deemed to be its primary responsibility, the maintenance of peace and security, which, under the Charter, embraces situations which might lead to a breach of the peace. (Art. 1, para. 1.) In the preamble of resolution 264 (1969) the Security Council was "*Mindful* of the grave consequences of South Africa's continued occupation of Namibia" and in paragraph 4 of that resolution it declared "that the actions of the Government of South Africa designed to destroy the national unity and territorial integrity of Namibia through the establishment of Bantustans are contrary to the provisions of the United Nations Charter". In operative paragraph 3 of resolution 269 (1969) the Security Council decided "that the continued occupation of the territory of Namibia by the South African authorities constitutes an aggressive encroachment on the authority of the United Nations * * * ". In operative paragraph 3 of resolution 276 (1970) the Security Council declared further "that the defiant attitude of the Government of South Africa towards the Council's decisions undermines the authority of the United Nations".

110. As to the legal basis of the resolution, Article 24 of the Charter vests in the Security Council the necessary authority to take action such as that taken in the present case. The reference in paragraph 2 of this Article to specific powers of the Security Council under certain chapters of the Charter does not exclude the existence of general powers to discharge the responsibilities conferred in paragraph 1. Reference may be made in this respect to the Secretary-General's Statement, presented to the Security Council on 10 January 1947, to the effect that "the powers of the Council under Article 24 are not restricted to the specific grants of authority contained in Chapters VI, VII, VIII and XII. * * * [T]he Members of the United Nations have conferred upon the Security Council powers commensurate with its responsibility for the maintenance of peace and security. The only

limitations are the fundamental principles and purposes found in Chapter I of the Charter." e

111. As to the effect to be attributed to the declaration contained in paragraph 2 of resolution 276 (1970), the Court considers that the qualification of a situation as illegal does not by itself put an end to it. It can only be the first, necessary step in an endeavour to bring the illegal situation to an end.

112. It would be an untenable interpretation to maintain that, once such a declaration had been made by the Security Council under Article 24 of the Charter, on behalf of all member States, those Members would be free to act in disregard of such illegality or even to recognize violations of law resulting from it. When confronted with such an internationally unlawful situation, Members of the United Nations would be expected to act in consequence of the declaration made on their behalf. The question therefore arises as to the effect of this decision of the Security Council for States Members of the United Nations in accordance with Article 25 of the Charter.

113. It has been contended that Article 25 of the Charter applies only to enforcement measures adopted under Chapter VII of the Charter. It is not possible to find in the Charter any support for this view. Article 25 is not confined to decisions in regard to enforcement action but applies to "the decisions of the Security Council" adopted in accordance with the Charter. Moreover, that Article is placed, not in Chapter VII, but immediately after Article 24 in that part of the Charter which deals with the functions and powers of the Security Council. If Article 25 had reference solely to decisions of the Security Council concerning enforcement action under Articles 41 and 42 of the Charter, that is to say, if it were only such decisions which had binding effect, then Article 25 would be superfluous, since this effect is secured by Articles 48 and 49 of the Charter.

114. It has also been contended that the relevant Security Council resolutions are couched in exhortatory rather than mandatory language and that, therefore, they do not purport to impose any legal duty on any State nor to affect legally any right of any State. The language of a resolution of the Security Council should be carefully analysed before a conclusion can be made as to its binding effect. In view of the nature of the powers under Article 25, the question whether they have been in fact exercised is to be determined in each case, having regard to the terms of the resolution to be interpreted, the discussions leading to it, the Charter provisions invoked and, in general, all circumstances that might assist in determining the legal consequences of the resolution of the Security Council.

115. Applying these tests, the Court recalls that in the preamble of resolution 269 (1969), the Security Council was "*Mindful* of its

e. [The three asterisks in this paragraph signify the Court's own editing of the Secretary General's statement. Ed.]

responsibility to take necessary action to secure strict compliance with the obligations entered into by States Members of the United Nations under the provisions of Article 25 of the Charter of the United Nations". The Court has therefore reached the conclusion that the decisions made by the Security Council in paragraphs 2 and 5 of resolution 276 (1970), as related to paragraph 3 of resolution 264 (1969) and paragraph 5 of resolution 269 (1969), were adopted in conformity with the purposes and principles of the Charter and in accordance with its Articles 24 and 25. The decisions are consequently binding on all States Members of the United Nations, which are thus under obligation to accept and carry them out.

[The Court went on to decide that South Africa was under an obligation to withdraw its administration from Namibia. In addition, it said that U.N. member states were under an obligation to abstain from entering into treaty relations with South Africa when it purported to act on behalf of Namibia, and to abstain from invoking or applying existing bilateral treaties concluded on behalf of Namibia insofar as those treaties involved active intergovernmental cooperation. An exception was made for multilateral treaties of a humanitarian character. Member states were also found to be under an obligation to abstain from maintaining diplomatic or consular missions to South Africa which would include Namibia in their jurisdiction. Although South African official acts on behalf of Namibia were held illegal and invalid, that invalidity was said not to extend to those acts, such as registration of births, deaths and marriages, which could be ignored only to the detriment of the inhabitants of Namibia.

[States not members of the U.N. were said to be under more general duties, and could not expect the U.N. or its members to recognize the validity or effect of any relationship with South Africa concerning Namibia. The Court concluded:]

by 13 votes to 2,

(1) that, the continued presence of South Africa in Namibia being illegal, South Africa is under obligation to withdraw its administration from Namibia immediately and thus put an end to its occupation of the Territory;

by 11 votes to 4,

(2) that States Members of the United Nations are under obligation to recognize the illegality of South Africa's presence in Namibia and the invalidity of its acts on behalf of or concerning Namibia, and to refrain from any acts and in particular any dealings with the Government of South Africa implying recognition of the legality of, or lending support or assistance to, such presence and administration;

(3) that it is incumbent upon States which are not Members of the United Nations to give assistance, within the scope of subpara-

graph (2) above, in the action which has been taken by the United Nations with regard to Namibia.

PROCEDURAL NICETIES IN THE NAMIBIA OPINION

In analyzing the Namibia opinion, consider, first, the use of a characterization process as an interpretive tool for defining procedural rights within the U.N. system. If the Namibian situation had been characterized by either the Security Council or the ICJ as a "dispute" regarding a legal question pending between two or more states, or between a state and the United Nations, what procedural consequences could arise? See paragraphs 10–11, 23–26, 30–35, 39–41 of the opinion. See also U.N. Charter *articles 27(3)* and *32;* ICJ Rules of Court article 83 (now article 102(3)) (when an advisory opinion is requested upon a legal question actually pending between two or more States, Article 31 of the Statute [of the ICJ, providing for appointment of ad hoc judges of the nationality of the parties before the Court in contentious cases] shall apply"); ICJ Statute article 68 ("In the exercise of its advisory functions the Court shall further be guided by the provisions of the present Statute which apply in contentious cases to the extent to which it recognizes them to be applicable").

Did South Africa's argument based on U.N. Charter article 32 fail because the Security Council, having absolute discretion, chose not to characterize the matter as a "dispute," or because South Africa had waived its article 32 rights, or for some other reason? See paragraphs 24 and 25 of the opinion. (Would the doctrine of waiver be appropriate under article 32?) If the Court had concluded that South Africa had wrongfully been excluded from the Security Council debate leading to the request for an advisory opinion, would it have declined to issue the opinion?

Suppose that you had been an adviser to one of the Security Council members at the time S.C. Res. 284 was being considered, and that your government wanted to make a good faith determination whether South Africa should be invited to participate under article 32. Would you advise that article 32 appears to contemplate this sort of "dispute"? See the separate opinion of Judge Dillard (U.S.A.) in the Namibia case.[f]

Why did the Court reject South Africa's argument based on the failure of parties to a dispute to refrain from voting, under article 27(3) of the Charter? See paragraph 26, and note the similar issue involving France and the Comoros, in Chapter 2 at pages 196–200. If South Africa's position regarding article 27(3) were upheld, could the Security Council have adopted any resolution regarding South Africa's relationship with Namibia?

f. [1971] I.C.J. at 155.

Note South Africa's argument in paragraphs 21 and 22 that the Security Council resolution requesting an advisory opinion was not adopted by the affirmative vote required by article 27(3) of the Charter. In light of the text of article 27(3), is there a convincing answer to the South African argument? See the discussion of this point in Chapter 2 at pages 192–93. Consider also the treatment of the South African contention by Judge Dillard in his separate opinion in the Namibia case:

> The contention reveals the weakness of an indiscriminate application of the textual approach when coupled with the plain and ordinary meaning canon of interpretation. Had the critical clause read: "*all five* permanent members, *who must be present and voting* * * * ", the contention might have been justified. In the absence of such a precise prescription the subsequent conduct of the parties is clearly a legitimate method of giving meaning to the Article in accordance with the expectations of the parties, including, in particular, the permanent members.[g]

Which of the following explains the significance given to the practice of U.N. organs in interpreting specific Charter provisions that relate to them: (a) the process of development of international norms through assertion of a right or an authority, and acquiescence by nonasserting states; (b) the principle that the organ exercising specific powers is the organ best equipped to interpret them, at least in the absence of disapproval by a substantial proportion of the membership; or (c) something else? Would it ever make any difference?

ADVISORY OPINIONS IN ONGOING DISPUTES

Apart from article 32 of the Charter, should the Court have declined to issue an advisory opinion on the ground that advisory opinions are inappropriate in cases involving ongoing disputes between the U.N. and a member state? See paragraphs 30–34, 40–41. The Eastern Carelia case, P.C.I.J., Series B, No. 5, in which the Permanent Court of International Justice declined to give an advisory opinion on a matter in dispute between two states, is distinguishable on the grounds given by the Court in paragraph 31. But does that settle the question? How could the Court possibly find that the request for an advisory opinion in the Namibia case did not relate to a legal dispute between two or more states, or between South Africa and the U.N. (paragraphs 32–34)? In the contentious proceeding brought earlier against South Africa by Ethiopia and Liberia, the Court had decided in 1962 that there was a dispute between the parties within the meaning of article 7(2) of the South African Mandate, which provided, "The Mandatory agrees that, if any dispute whatever should arise between the Mandatory and another Member of the League of Nations relating to the interpretation or the application of the provisions of the Mandate, such dispute, if it cannot be settled by negotiation, shall be submitted to the Permanent Court of International Justice * * *." Although the Court

---

g. Id. at 153–54.

ultimately held in 1966 that Ethiopia and Liberia lacked "any legal right or interest" sufficient to bring the proceeding, the earlier finding of a "dispute" was not overturned. Was there no longer a "dispute" in 1971, or was it just that the 1971 request for an advisory opinion didn't relate to the dispute?

Is there any reason why actively disputed issues between states should not be the subjects of advisory opinions that could interpret the powers of U.N. organs or assist them in properly exercising their powers? The issue was squarely presented in the ICJ's Advisory Opinion on the Western Sahara.[h] The Western Sahara had been under Spain's control for nearly 100 years under a Spanish claim that it was terra nullius (belonged to no one) at the time Spain took control and thus could be annexed by effective occupation and assertion of governmental authority. Morocco, on the other hand, claimed historic rights to the Western Sahara, antedating the original Spanish occupation. In 1974 Morocco proposed to Spain that they submit this issue to the ICJ in a contentious proceeding (which would have required Spain's consent, under ICJ Statute article 36(1)). Spain did not consent, but proposed a referendum among the nomadic people of the Western Sahara. Meanwhile, the General Assembly on several occasions had considered the Saharan question in the context of decolonization and self-determination for the Saharan peoples. In December 1974 it decided that it should seek an advisory opinion on the legal aspects of the problem. Accordingly, it asked the Court whether the Western Sahara was terra nullius when Spain took control, and if not, what were the legal ties between that territory, Morocco and Mauritania.

Spain argued that the Court should not respond, on the ground that the request for an opinion was simply a way around Spain's refusal to give its consent to the contentious proceeding proposed by Morocco, and thus would obliterate the distinction between contentious and advisory proceedings. Spain also argued that important questions of fact were involved that could not adequately be resolved in advisory proceedings, since there are no parties to such cases whom the Court can order to produce necessary evidence. The Court gave the opinion, noting that Spain, Morocco and Mauritania had produced extensive documentary evidence, whether or not they had been required to do so, and that the General Assembly had deemed the Court's opinion "of assistance to it for the proper exercise of its functions concerning the decolonization of the territory."[i] The Court distinguished the Eastern Carelia case on the ground that it there lacked sufficient materials to enable it to find the necessary facts, and had no prospect of obtaining the evidence because one of the interested parties had refused to take part.

On the expansion of the Court's advisory role into contentious matters, consider not only the Namibia and Western Sahara cases, but

h. [1975] I.C.J. 12.   i. [1975] I.C.J. at 27.

also the advisory opinion in the Privileges and Immunities case, otherwise known as the Mazilu case.[j]

In 1985 Dumitru Mazilu, a Romanian national, was a member of the U.N. Sub–Commission on Prevention of Discrimination and Protection of Minorities, a subsidiary body of the U.N. Commission on Human Rights. The Sub–Commission requested him to prepare a report on human rights and youth. His term on the Sub–Commission expired before he could submit his report. The Romanian government reported that Mr. Mazilu was too ill to continue his work, and nominated a new Romanian national to take his place. Mr. Mazilu wrote a series of letters to the U.N. Information Centre in Bucharest, saying that he had been forced to retire from Romanian government service and that strong governmental pressure was being exerted on him and his family.

When the Romanian government conveyed to the U.N. an offer by the new Romanian Sub–Commission member to complete the report on human rights and youth, the Under–Secretary–General for Human Rights replied that the Sub–Commission had entrusted the task to Mr. Mazilu. The U.N. Secretary–General then invoked the General Convention on Privileges and Immunities of the United Nations, *section 22,* on behalf of Mr. Mazilu and requested the Romanian government to accord him all the necessary facilities to complete his report. The government reiterated that he was too ill to work, and asserted that the General Convention did not apply, since section 22 protects only "experts" on missions for the U.N., not special rapporteurs. Moreover, said the government, even an expert is protected by section 22 only while traveling on a mission, not before any journey for the U.N. has begun.

Over Romania's objection, the U.N. Economic and Social Council (the parent body of the Commission on Human Rights) then adopted a resolution reciting that "a difference has arisen between the United Nations and the Government of Romania as to the applicability of the Convention" to Mr. Mazilu, and requesting, on a priority basis, an advisory opinion "on the legal question of the applicability of [section 22] in the case of Mr. Dumitru Mazilu as Special Rapporteur of the Sub–Commission."[k]

The Secretary–General, in a written statement submitted to the Court, said that the request did not ask about the consequences if section 22 were found applicable; that is, it did not ask what privileges and immunities Mr. Mazilu enjoyed under section 22, nor whether they had been violated.

The Court found that the Economic and Social Council was a proper body to make the request under U.N. Charter *article 96(2).* The Court continued:

j. [1989] I.C.J. 177.

k. [1989] I.C.J. at 178.

29. The Court has next to consider the contention of Romania, on the basis of the reservation made by it to Section 30 of the General Convention, that the Court "cannot find that it has jurisdiction to give an advisory opinion" in the present case. Section 30 of the General Convention provides:

> "All differences arising out of the interpretation or application of the present convention shall be referred to the International Court of Justice, unless in any case it is agreed by the parties to have recourse to another mode of settlement. If a difference arises between the United Nations on the one hand and a Member on the other hand, a request shall be made for an advisory opinion on any legal question involved in accordance with Article 96 of the Charter and Article 65 of the Statute of the Court. The opinion given by the Court shall be accepted as decisive by the parties."

Romania acceded to the General Convention, and its instrument of accession was deposited with the Secretary–General on 5 July 1956. The instrument of accession contained the following reservation:

> "The Romanian People's Republic does not consider itself bound by the terms of section 30 of the Convention which provide for the compulsory jurisdiction of the International Court in differences arising out of the interpretation or application of the Convention; with respect to the competence of the International Court in such differences, the Romanian People's Republic takes the view that, for the purpose of the submission of any dispute whatsoever to the Court for a ruling, the consent of all the parties to the dispute is required in every individual case. This reservation is equally applicable to the provisions contained in the said section which stipulate that the advisory opinion of the International Court is to be accepted as decisive."

30. It is claimed by Romania that, because of the reservation made by it to Section 30, the United Nations cannot, without Romania's consent, submit a request for advisory opinion in respect of its difference with Romania. The reservation, it is said, subordinates the competence of the Court to "deal with any dispute that may have arisen between the United Nations and Romania, including a dispute within the framework of the advisory procedure," to the consent of the parties to the dispute. Romania points out that it did not agree that an opinion should be requested of the Court in the present case and concludes that the Court is without jurisdiction.

31. The jurisdiction of the Court under Article 96 of the Charter and Article 65 of the Statute, to give advisory opinions on legal questions, enables United Nations entities to seek guidance from the Court in order to conduct their activities in accordance with law. These opinions are advisory, not binding. As the

opinions are intended for the guidance of the United Nations, the consent of States is not a condition precedent to the competence of the Court to give them.

* * *

32. Romania however relies on its reservation to Section 30 of the General Convention; but that Section operates on a different plane and in a different context from that of Article 96 of the Charter. When the provisions of the Section are read in their totality, it is clear that their object is to provide a dispute settlement mechanism. The first sentence of the Section provides for the case where a difference arises out of the interpretation or application of the General Convention between States parties to it, and contains two elements. The first is the treaty obligation to refer the difference to the Court, unless another mode of settlement is decided upon by the parties; the second is the object of the reference to the Court, namely to settle the difference.

* * *

34. In case of a request for an advisory opinion made under Section 30, the Court would of course have to consider any reservation which a party to the dispute had made to that Section. In the particular case of Romania, the Court would have to consider whether the effect of its reservation could be to act as a bar to the operation of the procedure of request for advisory opinion, or merely to deprive any opinion given of the decisive effect attributed to such opinions by Section 30. But in the present case, the resolution requesting the advisory opinion made no reference to Section 30, and it is evident from the dossier that, in view of the existence of the Romanian reservation, it was not the intention of the Council to invoke Section 30. The request is not made under that Section, and the Court does not therefore need to determine the effect of the Romanian reservation to that provision.

35. Romania however contends that although the Council resolution 1989/75 dated 24 May 1989 does not allude to Section 30 of the General Convention as the basis of its request for advisory opinion, the question which it raises nevertheless relates to the applicability of a substantive provision of the General Convention "to a concrete case considered to be a dispute between a State party to the Convention and the United Nations". It argues that

> "If it were accepted that a State party to the Convention, or the United Nations, might ask for disputes concerning the application or interpretation of the Convention to be brought before the Court on a basis other than the provisions of Section 30 of the Convention, that would disrupt the unity of the Convention, by separating the substantive provisions from those relating to dispute settlement, which would be tantamount to a modification of the content and extent of the

obligations entered into by States when they consented to be bound by the Convention."

However, the nature and purpose of the present proceedings are, as explained above, that of a request for advice on the applicability of a part of the General Convention, and not the bringing of a dispute before the Court for determination. Furthermore, the "content and extent of the obligations entered into by States"—and, in particular, by Romania—"when they consented to be bound by the Convention" are not modified by the request and by the present advisory opinion.

36. The Court thus finds that the reservation made by Romania to Section 30 of the General Convention does not affect the Court's jurisdiction to entertain the present request.

37. While, however, the absence of the consent of Romania to the present proceedings can have no effect on the jurisdiction of the Court, it is a matter to be considered when examining the propriety of the Court giving an opinion. It is well settled in the Court's jurisprudence that when a request is made under Article 96 of the Charter by an organ of the United Nations or a specialized agency for an advisory opinion by way of guidance or enlightenment on a question of law, the Court should entertain the request and give its opinion unless there are "compelling reasons" to the contrary.

* * *

38. In view of the emphasis placed by Romania on its reservation to Article 30 of the General Convention and the absence of its consent to the present request for advisory opinion, the Court must consider whether in this case "to give a reply would have the effect of circumventing the principle that a State is not obliged to allow its disputes to be submitted to judicial settlement without its consent". The Court considers that in the present case to give a reply would have no such effect. Certainly the Council, in its resolution requesting the opinion, did conclude that a difference had arisen between the United Nations and the Government of Romania as to the *applicability* of the Convention to Mr. Dumitru Mazilu. But this difference, and the question put to the Court in the light of it, are not to be confused with the dispute between the United Nations and Romania with respect to the *application* of the General Convention in the case of Mr. Mazilu.

39. In the present case, the Court thus does not find any compelling reason to refuse an advisory opinion.

On the merits, the Court concluded that section 22 applies to special rapporteurs, whether or not they have to travel to perform their tasks. It also concluded that at no time during the relevant period had

Mr. Mazilu ceased to be a special rapporteur of the Sub–Commission. See pages 86–90 supra.

Didn't Romania foresee this very situation when it made its reservation to General Convention section 30? If so, can the Court's jurisdictional decision be justified?

Could *any* Romanian reservation to the General Convention have prevented the Court from issuing an advisory opinion in this case?

Suppose the Economic and Social Council had asked the Court not only whether section 22 was applicable to Mr. Mazilu, but also whether it required the Romanian government to allow him to attend Sub–Commission meetings held in Geneva. Would the Court have had jurisdiction to give an advisory opinion? If so, should it have used its discretion to decline to give the opinion? Do you think it *would* have?

Has the Court gone too far in issuing advisory opinions without the consent of states parties to disputes?

The former U.N. Secretary–General, Javier Pérez de Cuéllar, argued for even wider authority to request advisory opinions to help resolve disputes. He said:

> Another deficiency in the working of the system of collective security is the insufficient use of the principal judicial organ of the United Nations, the International Court of Justice. Many international disputes are justiciable; even those which seem entirely political (as the Iraq–Kuwait dispute prior to invasion) have a clearly legal component. If, for any reason, the parties fail to refer the matter to the Court, the process of achieving a fair and objectively commendable settlement and thus defusing an international crisis situation would be facilitated by obtaining the Court's advisory opinion. Article 96 of the Charter authorizes the General Assembly and the Security Council to request such an opinion from the Court. I, therefore, repeat the suggestion I have made before that the extension by the General Assembly of the authority to the Secretary–General would be wholly in accord with the complementary relationship between the three concerned organs of the United Nations, which has grown fruitfully over the years. Such a development would also strengthen the role of the Secretary–General, which is a frequently stated objective of the membership as indicated by statements made at the highest level. This would be an important way of developing international law and legal norms as the basis of the activity of the United Nations and of international relations.[1]

Could the General Assembly authorize the Secretary–General to request advisory opinions under U.N. Charter *article 96(2),* or are such

---

1. Report of the Secretary–General on the Work of the Organization, 46 GAOR Supp. No. 1 (A/46/1), at 4 (1991). Boutros Boutros–Ghali has expressed a similar view. See U.N. Doc. A/47/277–S/24111, at 11 (1992).

authorizations limited to inter-governmental organs? [m]

If it could, would it be a good idea? (Why might the General Assembly be reluctant to do so?)

If the General Assembly were to give the authorization, should any limitations be placed on the questions the Secretary–General could ask the Court? [n]

AD HOC JUDGES

To return to the specific points raised by the Namibia opinion, note that article 31 of the ICJ Statute allows any party in a contentious case to appoint an ad hoc judge if no judge of its nationality is on the Bench. Article 102(3) (at the time of the Namibia case, article 83) of the Court's Rules extends that right to advisory proceedings when an opinion has been requested "upon a legal question actually pending between two or more States." See paragraph 35 of the Namibia opinion. Could the Court have granted South Africa's request for appointment of an ad hoc judge without undermining what it had said on other procedural issues?

Why are there provisions in the ICJ Statute and Rules of Court for appointment of such partisan judges?

THE COURT AND THE GENERAL ASSEMBLY

In paragraph 89 of the Namibia opinion the Court said, "Undoubtedly, the Court does not possess powers of judicial review or appeal in respect of the decisions taken by the United Nations organs concerned." (In this connection, recall the negotiating history of the Charter, at page 482 above.) But if the Court wasn't exercising the power of judicial review, what was it doing in the ensuing paragraphs? If those paragraphs fell short of judicial review, what purpose did they serve? (Consider the Court's relationship with the General Assembly and with the Security Council, as well as its status as an organ of the United Nations. Would it have been proper for the Court to take into account its possible effect on the U.N. efforts then being made to free Namibia from South African control, in determining whether, and if so, how deeply, to delve into judicial review of General Assembly Resolution 2145?)

Concerning G.A. Resolution 2145, the Court was "unable to appreciate the view that the General Assembly acted unilaterally as party and judge in its own cause." See paragraph 103. But did the General Assembly simply act as a detached supervisory institution, as the Court seemed to suggest? If not, one might call it a party to the cause. Was it also the judge, in the sense that the Court deferred to its determination that there had been a material breach?

What constituted the material breach on the part of South Africa?

---

m. See S. Rosenne, The Law and Practice of the International Court 673 (2d rev. ed. 1985).

n. See Szasz, The Role of the Secretary–General: Some Legal Aspects, 24 N.Y.U.J.Int'l L. & Pol. 161, 194 (1991).

In addition to the question whether the General Assembly could and did make an unreviewable material breach determination, there is the question of the legal effect of its decision that the Mandate was terminated. As viewed by the Court, was that simply a recommendation under *articles 10–14* of the Charter? If not, what made it more than a recommendation? (Judge Dillard's separate opinion concluded that the General Assembly's supervisory power over the Mandate "included the power ultimately to terminate for material breach." [1971] I.C.J. at 168.)

South Africa responded to this part of the opinion by saying:

> The 1971 advisory opinion of the International Court of Justice on which many States take their stand, is not only entirely untenable but is clearly and demonstrably the result of political manoeuvring instead of objective jurisprudence. An advisory opinion is, as its name indicates, advisory only. The weight to be attached to it depends ultimately on the cogency of its reasoning. Every State which accepts the 1971 advisory opinion of the International Court of Justice should indicate clearly whether it accepts the reasoning of the Court on which that opinion was based. And how many States would unequivocally declare that they accept the Court's conclusion concerning the powers of the General Assembly which necessarily implied that the General Assembly had the power to make findings of fact and of law which would bind even non-consenting States? How many States would agree that the General Assembly could ordain a given political and economic system for all countries of the world; or prescribe political independence for Northern Ireland; or for Scotland; or prohibit State religions. If States do not accept that the General Assembly can lay down legally binding rules in these matters, then they cannot accept and do not truly accept the Court's 1971 opinion.º

Was South Africa's specter real?

If the Court had simply taken the validity and conclusive effect of Resolution 2145 for granted, would there have been anything left for it to decide under the terms of the Security Council's request for an advisory opinion in its Resolution 284?

THE COURT AND THE SECURITY COUNCIL

Was the judicial review issue any different regarding S.C. Resolution 276 from that concerning G.A. Resolution 2145?

Did the Court adequately substantiate its holding that *article 24* of the Charter authorized S.C. Resolution 276? See paragraph 110. Interestingly, the Secretary–General's 1947 statement, which the Court quoted only in part in that paragraph, relied both on the text of article 24(1) and on the preparatory work at the San Francisco Conference; the portion quoted by the Court as the primary support for its article 24

---

o. U.N. Doc. S/11948, at 1–2 (1976).

holding was from the part of the statement relying on the preparatory work. The Court omitted all references to the San Francisco Conference. The portion of the Secretary–General's 1947 statement from which the Court's excerpts were taken reads as follows:

> Furthermore, the records of the San Francisco Conference demonstrate that the powers of the Council under Article 24 are not restricted to the specific grants of authority contained in Chapters VI, VII, VIII and XII. In particular, the Secretary–General wishes to invite attention to the discussion at the fourteenth meeting of Committee III/1 at San Francisco, wherein it was clearly recognized by all the representatives that the Security Council was not restricted to the specific powers set forth in Chapters VI, VII, VIII and XII. (I have in mind document 597, Committee III/1/30.) It will be noted that this discussion concerned a proposed amendment to limit the obligation of Members to accept decisions of the Council solely to those decisions made under the specific powers. In the discussion, all the delegations which spoke, including both proponents and opponents of this amendment, recognized that the authority of the Council was not restricted to such specific powers. It was recognized in this discussion that the responsibility to maintain peace and security carried with it a power to discharge this responsibility. This power, it was noted, was not unlimited, but subject to the purposes and principles of the United Nations.
>
> It is apparent that this discussion reflects a basic conception of the Charter, namely, that the Members of the United Nations have conferred upon the Security Council powers commensurate with its responsibility for the maintenance of peace and security. The only limitations are the fundamental principles and purposes found in Chapter I of the Charter.[p]

Wouldn't reliance on this full passage have strengthened the Court's article 24 holding? Did the Court follow its avowed "plain meaning" approach to interpretation of the Charter? If not, why not?

Would you want to know how the Secretary–General's statement was received by the members of the Security Council?[q] Did the Court ask this question?

What are the requirements for valid Security Council action under article 24? Were they met with respect to Resolution 276? Are they meaningful?

Could a resolution adopted under article 24 be binding on all members under article 25? If so, was paragraph 5 of Resolution 276

---

p. 2 SCOR (91st meeting, 1947), 13 Whiteman, Digest of Int'l Law 466–67 (1968).

q. See L. Goodrich, E. Hambro & A. Simons, Charter of the United Nations

binding on them?[r] See paragraphs 113–115 of the opinion.

Was the Court's use of articles 24 and 25 simply an evasion of the strictures of Chapter VII of the Charter? Note that paragraph 5 of Resolution 276 called for a partial interruption of economic relations with South Africa in matters affecting its control over Namibia. That is one of the sanctions available under article 41, if there has been a finding (not made in Resolution 276) of a threat to the peace, breach of the peace or act of aggression, under article 39.[s]

In paragraph 114, the Court outlined the factors to be considered in determining whether a Security Council resolution is binding. Was the Court's approach to this issue consistent with its "plain meaning" approach to treaty interpretation? Should there be a different approach?

REGIONAL ORGANIZATIONS AND ADVISORY OPINIONS

Suppose a regional organization, such as the Organization of American States, wishes to ask the ICJ for an advisory opinion on a legal question bearing on the activities of the regional body. Such a question might arise, for example, under *Chapter VIII* of the U.N. Charter, which gives a rather bare outline of the relationship between the U.N. and regional organizations. Or it might arise directly under the constituent instrument of the regional organization.

Could the OAS request an ICJ advisory opinion in either of those cases? See U.N. Charter *article 96*. Alternatively, could the U.N. General Assembly or Security Council request such an advisory opinion on behalf of the OAS?[t]

BINDING ADVISORY OPINIONS

The Mazilu case, supra pages 507–10, arose out of a dispute between the United Nations and a member state, involving the applicability of the General Convention on the Privileges and Immunities of the United Nations. The compromissory clause in that convention covers not only disputes between states parties, but also disputes between the U.N. and a state party. Since the U.N. is not a state and thus cannot be a party to a contentious case in the ICJ,[u] the dispute

204–05 (3d ed. 1969), noting the members' general approval.

r. For the U.S. government's misgivings about the Court's reasoning in this part of the opinion, see 1975 Digest of United States Practice in Int'l Law 88–90.

s. See Judge Petrén's separate opinion, [1971] I.C.J. at 136.

t. See Remarks by Stephen Schwebel, in Contemporary International Law Issues: Sharing Pan–European and American Perspectives 242, 244–45 (1991), discussing (inter alia) the experience under the League of Nations.

u. See I.C.J. Statute *art. 34(1)*.

between the U.N. and Romania could only have been submitted by means of a request for an advisory opinion.

To try to achieve as much parity as possible between the result in such a case and the result in a contentious case between states parties to the General Convention, the compromissory clause says that the advisory opinion "shall be accepted as decisive by the parties." [v] Romania's reservation to the clause was designed to avoid submission to the Court's binding (or "decisive") adjudication. But not all states parties to the General Convention have established such reservations. Thus it would appear that under some circumstances, an "advisory" opinion interpreting the Convention in a dispute between the U.N. and a party could be binding—not by reason of anything in the U.N. Charter or the ICJ Statute, but by reason of the Convention itself.

The General Convention is not the only treaty that contemplates "binding advisory opinions" in disputes between the U.N. or a U.N.-related organization, on one side, and a state party, on the other. Some other conventions on privileges and immunities of international organizations, and several headquarters agreements with host states, have similar compromissory clauses.[w] A few other conventions involving international organizations have comparable clauses.[x]

A judge of the International Court of Justice, writing shortly after the Mazilu case, has expressed concern about the use of "binding advisory opinions" in disputes involving international organizations. Consider the questions he raised:

AGO, "BINDING" ADVISORY OPINIONS OF THE INTERNATIONAL COURT OF JUSTICE
85 Am.J.Int'l L. 439, 450–51 (1991).*

(1) Should the system conceived in 1946 for the purpose of settling disputes between states and international organizations, and applied since then with increasing frequency, be considered satisfactory and accordingly not undergo any change? Should it not be regarded as somewhat complicated and logically inconsistent?

(2) What reason can there be to continue to subject the settlement of disputes concerning the interpretation or application of an international instrument to different procedures depending on whether the parties to the dispute are two states or a state and the United Nations itself or one of the organizations belonging to its system? This disparity of treatment might have had a raison d'être when those international organizations had not yet become active participants in international

---

v. See General Convention section 30, supra page 508.

w. See Ago, "Binding" Advisory Opinions of the International Court of Justice, 85 Am.J.Int'l L. 439 notes 2 & 3, and 449 note 44.

x. Id. at 439, note 5.

* Reprinted with permission, c. The American Society of International Law.

life as distinct legal persons with their own interests and rights, different from those of the states that constitute them. At that phase of their development, they could be regarded as entities that had not matured to the point that they could be subjected to *decisions* of the International Court of Justice. But can this differentiation be justified now that it has become commonplace for international organizations and states to be parties, on an equal footing, to disputes concerning the interpretation and application of bilateral agreements, as well as general conventions? Furthermore, does the need to retain such a distinction not seem doubtful, since the general conventions adopted immediately after the creation of the United Nations and the main specialized agencies that define their privileges and immunities provided that "advisory opinions" adopted through proceedings to which they would be parties would have conclusive effect for these organizations?

(3) Would it not be simpler and more satisfactory to amend the Statute of the Court to permit the United Nations and the organizations in the UN system to be parties to cases before the Court? Has the time not come to allow international organizations prosecuting claims against states or resisting claims by them to take the main road, rather than the byway of an "advisory" procedure artificially given decisive value and binding effect, which so ill become its intrinsic nature? Moreover, does natural justice not require that, whenever a dispute arises between a state and an international organization, the two parties should possess the same power to institute proceedings before the Court?—a feature of the present system being that only the organization may, in its discretion, request an advisory opinion, whether binding or not. At this point, I should like to observe that it would not be difficult to ensure that the proposed modification would not expose international organizations to the danger—more theoretical than real—of the reckless institution of proceedings against them.

(4) Finally, if the proposal I have just made were accepted, would the result not be, first, to restore all the necessary clarity to the distinction between the two procedures that the International Court of Justice is institutionally called upon to apply; and second, to enable the international organizations concerned to enjoy the benefits that can be derived only from a contentious procedure, such as the capacity to intervene in a case to which other entities are parties or to request the adoption of interim measures, and, in the final analysis, the attribution to a "decision" involving such an organization the full measure of authority inherent in a genuine judgment, particularly that of *res judicata?*

INTERNATIONAL ORGANIZATIONS AND CONTENTIOUS CASES

Judge Ago said that it would not be difficult to ensure that international organizations would not be exposed to the reckless institution of contentious proceedings against them. How could that be done? Could ICJ Statute *article 50* be used here?

At the end of the excerpt above, Judge Ago said that his proposed amendment could enable international organizations to derive the benefits available only in a contentious procedure, such as capacity to intervene or to request interim measures, and the benefit of res judicata once a judgment has been rendered. Could some of those benefits be realized under the existing advisory opinion procedure, pursuant to *article 68*? If so, which ones could be? Intervention is covered by I.C.J. Statute *articles 62–63;* see also the Land, Island and Maritime Frontier Dispute Case (El Salvador v. Honduras),[y] in which a chamber of the Court said that an intervening state does not thereby become a party to the case, though it could become a party if the original parties consent. Interim measures ("provisional measures") are covered by I.C.J. Statute *article 41*. The effect of judgments in contentious cases appears in I.C.J. Statute *articles 59–60*.

Would the benefits of U.N. Charter *article 94* be available to an international organization absent a Charter amendment?

Is an I.C.J. Statute amendment of the sort suggested by Judge Ago feasible?

ARMED FORCE, THE ICJ AND THE SECURITY COUNCIL

In the Case Concerning Military and Paramilitary Activities in and Against Nicaragua (Nicaragua v. United States),[z] arising during the period of U.S. support for the Nicaraguan contras in their attempt to overthrow the Sandinista government, the United States argued that even if the Court had jurisdiction, it should decline to hear the merits on admissibility grounds. The United States argued that in an ongoing armed conflict situation, *article 24* of the Charter gives the Security Council, not the ICJ, primary responsibility for the maintenance of international peace and security. Moreover, *article 39* says that the Security Council is the organ to determine the existence of any threat to the peace, breach of the peace or act of aggression. In addition, *article 51* expressly contemplates that the Security Council will be the U.N. body involved when one of the parties claims the right of self-defense (in this case, collective self-defense, claimed by the United States). Finally, the United States argued that if the ICJ were to hear the case and render a judgment on the merits, there could be conflicting decisions of the Court and the Security Council on the same matter, and both decisions would be binding on the parties.

The Court rejected these arguments and proceeded to hear the merits.[a] From the standpoint of the proper allocation of functions

---

y. [1990] I.C.J. 92, 134–35.

z. [1984] I.C.J. 392 (jurisdiction and admissibility).

a. Id. at 431–36.

between the ICJ and the Security Council, was that a justifiable result? Consider each of the Charter provisions raised by the United States. Consider also *article 12(1)*. Is it relevant that there is no counterpart in the Charter to article 12(1) concerning the Court and the Council? Is it relevant that a few days before Nicaragua brought the proceedings in the ICJ, the United States had vetoed a draft Security Council resolution that would have condemned the U.S. mining of Nicaraguan harbors as a violation of international law?

If we accept the Court's approach in this case, could the Court ever decline, on inadmissibility grounds, to decide a question raised during wartime by one state about the lawfulness of another's use of force? *Should* it ever decline to do so?

THE SECRETARIAT

Note, finally, the Charter interpretation and dispute-settlement functions of the U.N. Secretariat. The Office of Legal Affairs issues formal and informal legal opinions interpreting the Charter, at the request of such persons as the Secretary–General, the Presidents of the General Assembly and Security Council, and others. An example is the Secretary–General's statement (actually prepared by the Office of Legal Affairs) on the Security Council's powers under article 24, discussed above. Many of the opinions are on rather technical issues. Legal opinions considered particularly significant are published in the United Nations Juridical Yearbook. The net effect is much like that concerning opinions issued by the International Labor Office: the opinions do not have the formal sanction of the organization's constituent instrument, but the practice has evolved of issuing them, publishing them and relying on them as precedents.

Occasionally the Secretariat makes legal determinations that directly affect the legal positions of member states. A striking example, raising questions about the process to be used when a legal assessment of a member state's conduct is to be made, occurred in December 1991. Javier Pérez de Cuéllar, the outgoing Secretary–General, issued a report in response to paragraph 6 of Security Council Resolution 598 (1987), which asked him to explore the question of entrusting an impartial body with inquiring into responsibility for the war in the 1980s between Iraq and Iran. The Secretary–General's report said in part:

> 4. For the purpose of paragraph 6, although elements of the positions of the two parties on that paragraph were known to me, I requested the Governments of Iran and Iraq, in identical letters dated 14 August 1991, to provide me in the most comprehensive manner possible with their detailed views on the subject-matter of that paragraph. At the same time, in order to obtain the fullest

understanding of the subject-matter, I decided to consult separately some independent experts. * * *

5. It is evident that the war between Iran and Iraq, which was going to be waged for so many years, was started in contravention of international law, and violations of international law give rise to responsibility for the conflict, which question is at the centre of paragraph 6 [of Resolution 598]. The area of violation of international law that should be of specific concern to the international community in the context of paragraph 6 is the illegal use of force and the disregard for the territorial integrity of a Member State.

There were of course in the course of the conflict massive violations of various rules of international humanitarian law.

6. The Iraqi reply to my letter of 14 August 1991 is not a substantial one; therefore I am bound to rely on explanations given by Iraq earlier. That these explanations do not appear sufficient or acceptable to the international community is a fact. Accordingly, the outstanding event under the violations referred to in paragraph 5 above is the attack of 22 September 1980 against Iran, which cannot be justified under the Charter of the United Nations, any recognized rules and principles of international law or any principles of international morality and entails the responsibility for the conflict.

7. Even if before the outbreak of the conflict there had been some encroachment by Iran on Iraqi territory, such encroachment did not justify Iraq's aggression against Iran—which was followed by Iraq's continuous occupation of Iranian territory during the conflict—in violation of the prohibition of the use of force, which is regarded as one of the rules of *jus cogens*.

* * *

9. The events of the Iran–Iraq war, which for many years provided the news headlines in the world media, are well known to the international community. The position of the parties, expressed on many occasions in official documents, are also public knowledge. In my opinion it would not seem to serve any useful purpose to pursue paragraph 6 of resolution 598 (1987).[b]

Was it appropriate for the Secretary–General to respond in this way, without entrusting the matter to a separate body? Did he afford Iraq due process before concluding that it had violated a rule of *jus cogens*?

What legal effect, if any, would the Secretary–General's findings and conclusions have if, as appears to have been the case, no government except Iraq objected to them?

b. U.N. Doc. S/23273 (1991).

The Secretary–General has several other tools that can be used to help settle or avoid disputes between states. For example, he may (and often does) provide his "good offices" to help governments reach negotiated settlements, acting essentially as a mediator without power to bind the parties. He may also send fact-finding missions to troubled areas, with the consent of the receiving states, seeking not only to gather information, but also to help defuse situations involving threats to the peace. These techniques relate particularly to the U.N.'s peacemaking and peacekeeping roles. They are examined in Chapter 5, infra.

Chapter 4

ENFORCEMENT TECHNIQUES

SECTION 1. INTRODUCTION

E. LUARD, INTERNATIONAL AGENCIES: THE EMERGING FRAMEWORK OF INTERDEPENDENCE
1-3 (1977).*

Clearly international government is something different in kind from government within nations. Though there exists in the international community a relatively elaborate administrative structure, a wide variety of political institutions, and many public services, international bodies do not possess the ultimate sanction of authority, the power to impose decisions, which, in the final resort, national governments can exert, and which many would regard as the hallmark of government. Instead decisions are reached, programmes initiated, expenditure approved, mainly through the *voluntary* acceptance of sovereign national states.

This difference is not so great as may at first appear. The role that compulsion plays even in national societies is a limited one. The citizen in a national state does not obey his government mainly because he is afraid of the buffets of the policeman's truncheon or the threat of imprisonment. He obeys because he is usually aware, if only unconsciously, that the effective functioning of his society would be impossible without some co-operation among its citizens; because he wishes, through such co-operation, to share the benefits society provides; above all because he is *conditioned* to conform with those behaviour patterns widely expected within his community.

National governments for the most part co-operate with international organizations for precisely similar reasons. They too usually pay their dues, because they recognize that the system could not work at all otherwise. They too usually remain members of international bodies because they do not wish to forgo some of the benefits of the association. They too normally co-operate in the programmes decided on,

---

* Reprinted by permission of Oceana Publications, Inc.

because governments also are to some extent conditioned by the international system to act as others expect them to act. The desire for good name, to play the role demanded, to conform is today almost as powerful a motive among states in international society as among individuals in national states.

Obedience is not universal in either case. Individuals in national societies do sometimes rebel. They do break the speed limit, do violate the planning laws, do refuse to be conscripted, occasionally even decline to pay their taxes altogether. Similarly in the international community, nations do sometimes refuse to take part in a particular programme, do refuse to contribute to a particular expenditure, occasionally even withdraw from an international organization altogether. But such situations are rare. Very few nations have ever defaulted altogether on the contributions for which they are assessed in any of the various UN Agencies, and then only for short periods. Only one nation (Indonesia) has ever withdrawn from the UN altogether, and she returned within two years.

For the most part a sufficient majority comply most of the time with the programmes and decisions of international organizations to make it possible to organize on an international level the services which the majority decide on. To the extent that nations effectively cooperate with the proposals and decisions made, there is at least a skeleton of government. Government consists perhaps essentially in the capacity to secure compliance. To a limited degree and in limited fields this does exist today at the international level.

COMMENTS ON COMPLIANCE

Nations do normally comply with the norms of the organizations they have joined. For the most part, they have considered the long term benefits of compliance to outweigh any short term gain they might realize from noncompliance with a particular norm on a particular occasion. But not invariably. Consequently international organizations with relatively well-defined regulatory functions have devised means of inducing members to channel their conduct in the directions indicated by the organizations' norms.

Some of these means involve an element of coercion or punishment. As the materials in Section 3, infra, will suggest, international organizations have had considerable difficulty in devising and applying fair and effective sanctions in that sense.

Before we turn to coercive sanctions, we shall focus on means by which organizations attempt to persuade their members to comply with norms absent any element of overt coercion or punishment. The norms may be established by constituent instruments, by conventions adopted within the organizations' structures, or simply by decision-making bodies within the organizations. In the latter case, noncompliance with a norm would not necessarily involve a breach of an obligation under international law if, for example, the norm is a recommendation or guideline issued by the organization.

SECTION 2. NONSANCTIONS

INTRODUCTORY NOTE

In general, noncoercive compliance mechanisms fall within two interrelated categories: (a) informal persuasion, usually through consultations between the organization and the wayward member, and sometimes supplemented by technical assistance to boost the member's ability to comply; and (b) what has aptly been called "the mobilization of shame,"[a] involving an exposure of the member's shortcomings so that all who are interested can see and criticize. Often these two methods are connected, with the mobilization of shame either looming ahead if informal persuasion should fail, or being used in a mild way while informal persuasion is tried. Nevertheless, they are analytically distinct methods, so they will be considered in separate subsections below.

A. INFORMAL PERSUASION AND ASSISTANCE

1. *The International Labor Organization*

The Constitution of the International Labor Organization contains specific reporting obligations owed by member states to the Organization. *Article 19* requires reports on unratified conventions and on ILO recommendations when requested by the Governing Body. *Article 22* requires reports on ratified conventions. As ILO practice has evolved, detailed reports on the application of ratified conventions are now due only every four years, except for reports on ratified ILO human rights conventions (due every two years).

VALTICOS, THE INTERNATIONAL LABOUR ORGANIZATION
The Effectiveness of International Decisions 134, 144–48.
(S. Schwebel ed. 1971).*

REPORTS ON RATIFIED CONVENTIONS

The general procedure of supervision of the application of ratified Conventions is based on the obligation of governments, under article 22 of the Constitution of the ILO, to supply * * * reports on the measures taken by them to give effect to Conventions which they have ratified. By virtue of the same article, these reports must be made in such form and contain such particulars as the Governing Body requests in the report forms adopted to this effect.

* * *

---

a. See A. Zimmern, The League of Nations and the Rule of Law 460 (1936).

* Reprinted by permission of A.W. Sijthoff International Publishing Co.

States are required to communicate copies of their reports to the representative organizations of employers and workers in their country (article 23(2) of the Constitution). These organizations may make observations on the application of the provisions of a Convention, and States are requested to supply information in their reports on any such observations received and to add any comments that they may consider useful.

Reports on Unratified Conventions and on Recommendations

The Constitution of the ILO has also provided, in article 19, paragraphs 5, 6 and 7, that States Members must at the request of the Governing Body submit reports indicating the position of their law and practice in regard to the matters dealt with in Conventions which they have not ratified or in Recommendations, showing the extent to which effect has been given or is proposed to be given to their provisions. In the case of a Convention, States Members must also indicate the difficulties which prevent or delay ratification. In the case of a Recommendation, they must indicate the modifications which have been found necessary in applying the instrument. Copies of these reports also must be communicated to representative organizations of employers and workers. In application of the provisions of article 19, the Governing Body chooses each year a limited number of Conventions and Recommendations of current interest and requests States to supply reports on them.

Examination of Reports

(a) *Summary of reports*

The Director–General is required by the Constitution (article 23, paragraph 1) to lay before each annual session of the International Labor Conference a summary of the information and reports which have been communicated to him by member States.

(b) *The Committee of Experts on the Application of Conventions and Recommendations*

The reports supplied by governments have been subject, since 1927, to technical examination by the Committee of Experts on the Application of Conventions and Recommendations. This Committee is composed of [20] independent members who are appointed in their personal capacity and not as representatives of governments by the Governing Body of the ILO, on the proposal of the Director–General. The requirements of impartiality and independence, and of eminent qualifications in the legal or social fields, have remained the basic criteria in the appointment of members of the Committee. Accordingly, the experts are at present drawn mainly from the judiciary, from academic circles (professors of international or labour law) and from amongst persons with considerable experience in public administration.

* * *

In order to comply with its terms of reference, the Committee of Experts examines the situation of the States by consulting, in the first place, the reports supplied by governments, official journals, compilations of legislation, etc., and also any available information on practical application and data contained in any comments made by employers' or workers' organizations.

The comments made by the Committee of Experts on the basis of this examination take various forms. In the case of ratified Conventions, the comments are normally made in the form of observations drawing attention to a divergency existing between the national legislation and practice, on the one hand, and the provisions of the Convention, on the other hand. The aim of these observations is not to condemn, but to try to persuade governments to ensure fuller compliance. The observations are incorporated in the printed report of the Committee and communicated both to governments and for discussion to the Conference (see below). However, since 1957, in order that the Committee's report and the discussion at the Conference may be centered on the more important points, the comments adopted by the Committee of Experts have, in a large number of cases, taken the form of requests; this is done when the point at issue is technical or involves a discrepancy of relatively minor importance, or when the object is to obtain more detailed information. These requests are communicated directly to governments on behalf of the Committee, without being reproduced *in extenso* in its report.

Apart from the cases of discrepancies, the Committee of Experts also reports and lists, each year, the cases of progress made as a result of its previous comments * * *.

In 1967, the Committee of Experts put forward a proposal concerning the possibilities of *direct contacts* with governments in certain cases where, in addition to its customary procedure based on the examination of reports and legislative texts, a fuller assessment of all aspects of a particular situation might prove useful.

* * *

The Committee follows the same procedure in matters relating to the obligation on States to submit Conventions and Recommendations to the competent authorities.

* * *

(c) [*The Committee on the Application of Standards*]

The International Labor Conference, at each session, appoints a special committee comprising government, employers' and workers' representatives, which is called on to examine the question of the application of Conventions and Recommendations. This committee bases its work on the observations made by the Committee of Experts. It invites the governments concerned to participate in its work with a view to providing additional information with regard to the discrepancies noted and to the measures which they have taken or contemplate taking to eliminate these discrepancies. During the Committee's discussions, employers' and workers' representatives can express their views on the manner in which Conventions are applied, whether in their own country, or in other countries. The Conference Committee summarizes its discussions and any conclusions which it may reach in a report which it submits to the Conference and which is discussed by the latter in plenary session. In recent years, the Conference Committee has in its report drawn the special attention of the Conference to cases in which governments appear to have encountered serious difficulties in fulfilling certain of their obligations under the Constitution of the International Labor Organization or ratified Conventions.

THE COMMITTEE OF EXPERTS

Unlike Commissions of Inquiry, discussed in the last chapter, the Committee of Experts is not mentioned in the ILO Constitution. *Article 23(1)* merely provides that "The Director-General shall lay before the next meeting of the Conference a summary of the information and reports communicated to him by Members in pursuance of articles 19 and 22." Yet the Committee of Experts has been in existence since 1927, surviving the comprehensive amendments to the ILO Constitution in 1946. It was established by the ILO Governing Body in response to a 1926 resolution of the General Conference. The reason was that the General Conference had found itself unable adequately to consider the reports member states were required to submit. Despite some pointed queries by Eastern bloc states during the cold war years concerning the constitutionality of the Committee and its practices, its legitimacy and role now seem to be firmly established.

What explains its legitimacy? Is it the implied powers doctrine, stemming from the U.N. Reparations Case, supra pages 7–13? If so, why should the power to create such a supervisory body be implied in the case of the ILO? Would a similar power properly be implied in the case of any other specialized agencies with which you are familiar?

On the other hand, would it be proper to say that *any* international regulatory agency has the inherent power to create its own supervisory body, in the absence of an express prohibition in its constituent instrument? [b]

If there is doubt about the explanations above, is the matter settled by longstanding practice in the ILO, despite the demurrers by the former socialist bloc as recently as the late 1980s?

b. Compare Seyersted, International Personality of Intergovernmental Organizations: Do Their Capacities Really Depend upon Their Constitutions?, 4 Indian J.Int'l L. 1, 66–67 (1964), with I. Brownlie, Principles of Public International Law 689–91 (4th ed. 1990). A doctrinal discussion appears in Qureshi, The Mechanism of Economic "Surveillance" in the Framework of International Organisations, University of Manchester Faculty of Law Working Paper No. 5, at 10–15 (1991).

Note the two procedures used by the Committee of Experts that do not involve public disclosure of the failure on the part of a member state to meet its obligations: the informal direct request and the use of direct contacts. Note also that only one of the uses of the informal direct request involves a request for more information; in other cases, the "request" is used to explain to the government the respect (usually relatively minor) in which it has fallen short of full compliance and to suggest ways in which the situation might be corrected. If that does not work, the Committee of Experts at a later meeting would make the discrepancy public by issuing its "observations." [c]

The direct contact procedure was devised particularly to deal with cases of persistent noncompliance, when requests, observations and discussions have been unavailing. In practice, direct contacts sometimes take place with respect to serious discrepancies before any public observations are made, and usually occur at the instance of the governments concerned rather than the Committee of Experts or the Conference Committee. The principles and procedure have been set forth by the Committee of Experts as follows.

REPORT OF THE COMMITTEE OF EXPERTS ON THE APPLICATION OF CONVENTIONS AND RECOMMENDATIONS
International Labor Conf., 58th Sess., Rep. III,
Part 4A, at 16–17 (1973).

In view of the purpose of direct contacts, which is simply to continue and to amplify orally the dialogue which the supervisory bodies have already begun with governments by means mainly of written comments, it does not seem appropriate to subject the establishment of these contacts to rules which are excessively rigid and formal. Moreover, experience appears to show that the success of such contacts has been due in large part to the absence of strict formalism in the procedure. However, taking account of that experience, the principles which should be followed in establishing such contacts are restated below:

> (i) the discrepancies noted and the practical or legal difficulties encountered in the application of a ratified Convention, as well as the difficulties met with in matters connected with international standards, including more particularly difficulties in fulfilling various constitutional obligations (articles 19 and 22 of the Constitution) and possible obstacles to the ratification of a given Convention, should be sufficiently important to warrant such contacts;

---

[c] See the comments by Nicolas Valticos in The Effectiveness of International Decisions 448 (S. Schwebel ed. 1971).

(ii) the Committee of Experts may suggest the possibility of having recourse to direct contacts, whereupon the Director-General will explore the matter with the government concerned; the Conference Committee may also make such a suggestion, following its discussion of a case; the government concerned may itself take the initiative;

(iii) the contacts should in all cases take place with the full consent of the government concerned;

(iv) the points to be dealt with should be clearly specified in advance;

(v) while these contacts are taking place, the supervisory bodies will suspend their examination of cases for a period which will normally not exceed one year, so as to be able to take account of the outcome of these contacts;

(vi) the form which the contacts will take should be determined in the light of their purpose, which is to enable the government to explain all the elements of the case, so as to permit the Committee to assess fully all the facts involved;

(vii) the contacts should bring together persons thoroughly acquainted with all aspects of the case, including government representatives with sufficient responsibility and experience to speak with authority about the position in their country and about their own government's attitudes and intentions in the matter;

(viii) it will be for the Director–General to designate the representative on behalf of the International Labour Organisation, who will be either an independent person or an ILO official fully conversant with the case; normally, it would not appear appropriate that this representative be a member of the Committee of Experts, but this possibility might be left open in certain special cases;

(ix) the representative of the Director–General may, in agreement with the government concerned, visit the country to hold discussions on the matter with government representatives, in order to explain the point of view of the supervisory bodies, acquaint himself in detail with the government's position and the exact nature of the difficulties in question, and make available to the Committee of Experts any relevant information supplied to him by the government;

(x) the representative of the Director–General should, in the course of his assignment, make contact with the organisations of employers and workers so as to keep them informed of the topics discussed and elicit their points of view.

THE USE OF NONPUBLIC REMEDIES

In 1979 the Committee of Experts reviewed the first ten years of the direct contact procedure, expressing qualified satisfaction with the results. One of the benefits was the acquainting of workers' organizations within the country of the ILO's efforts and views, so those organizations could better influence their governments' adoption of needed legislative or other measures.

The Committee of Experts noted that of the 222 cases of nonapplication of conventions examined in direct contacts between 1969 and 1978, there were 115 cases of progress relating to 56 conventions. In the usual case, however, fruitful resort to direct contacts had come at least ten years after the Committee had first taken up the matter.[d]

By mid–1988, the direct contacts procedure had been applied in more than 300 cases in about 40 countries, most of them in the third world.[e] Not all of these cases emanated from the Committee of Experts; some stemmed from the work of the ILO Committee on Freedom of Association.

In the 1980s, the line between direct contacts and technical assistance began to blur. In 1988 the Committee of Experts said:

> The Committee welcomed the recent administrative measures taken by the International Labour Office to strengthen the links between international labour standards and the technical co-operation activities of the ILO. These measures are based on the principle that the development and application of international labour standards and technical co-operation are the two principal channels of action available to the ILO in order to promote the objectives of social justice that were set for it by its constituent bodies. The complementary nature of these two activities derives from the text of article 10 of the ILO Constitution and the more detailed provisions set out in this connection in the Declaration of Philadelphia. These guide-lines have been unceasingly recalled by the Conference and the Governing Body over the past 25 years which have been marked by a constant extension of programmes of practical activities. Even if, in general, the primary objective of technical co-operation is not directly to promote the standard-setting provisions adopted by the International Labour Conference, these practical ILO activities cannot in any circumstances be in contradiction with the basic principles governing these standards.[f]

In 1989 the Conference Committee reviewed direct contacts and technical assistance in the previous year, considering them to be opposite sides of the same coin:

> During 1988, direct contacts missions concerning freedom of association took place in Colombia, Côte d'Ivoire, Haiti and Nicara-

---

d. See Report of the Committee of Experts on the Application of Conventions and Recommendations, Int'l Labor Conf., 65th Sess., Rep. III, Part 4A, at 13, 16–25 (1979).

e. See V.-Y. Ghebali, The International Labour Organisation 228 (1989); Valticos, International Labour Law, in Comparative Labour Law and Industrial Relations 77, 92–93 (R. Blanpain ed. 1987).

f. Report of the Committee of Experts on the Application of Conventions and Recommendations, Int'l Labor Conf., 75th Sess., Rep. III, Part 4A, at 23 (1988).

gua. Direct contacts took place in Bangladesh concerning the Indigenous and Tribal Populations Convention, 1957 (No. 107) and Guatemala concerning the Abolition of Forced Labour Convention, 1957 (No. 105). Another direct contacts mission was undertaken in the Dominican Republic and Haiti with a view to the implementation of the recommendations made in 1983 by the Commission of Inquiry concerning Haitian workers in the sugar plantations of the Dominican Republic. The Regional Advisers on Standards, whose task consisted essentially in assisting governments to fulfil their obligations under the ILO Constitution and ratified Conventions, visited 20 countries in Africa, America, and Asia and the Pacific. Nineteen officials, two employers and four observers from 23 countries undertook training in the International Labour Standards Department. This Department organised two regional seminars on international labour standards designed for government officials directly responsible for questions relating to international labour standards and, in particular, on the fulfilment by States of the obligations deriving from the ILO Constitution and ratified Conventions. In addition, the Regional Advisers on Standards participated in the work of a number of seminars organised by other ILO departments in various regions of the world.[g]

Technical assistance is used in other organizations, as well, to try to alleviate the burden of complying with norms. This happens, for example, in the International Civil Aviation Organization, where the assistance takes the form not only of expert advice, but even (on occasion) the actual operation of some functions in national departments of civil aviation.[h] It happens also in the World Meteorological Organization, where the assistance takes the form of personnel training and help in establishing national meteorological services.[i]

Is the blurring of the line between direct contacts, as an enforcement measure, and technical assistance, as a training or operational device, a positive development in the effort to induce greater compliance with international standards?

Is the direct contacts procedure, or something like it, a useful enforcement mechanism in the hands of international organizations generally, or is its usefulness limited to the ILO? Note that the procedure in the ILO is linked closely with the requirement that member states report regularly on their application of conventions and recommendations. Not all organizations have such a requirement. Moreover, they do not always have an information network comparable to that provided by the ILO's tripartite structure, which includes worker and employer representatives as well as government officials.

g. Report of the Committee on the Application of Standards, Int'l Labor Conf., 76th Sess., Record of Proc., at 26/11 (1989).

h. For a brief summary, see the ICAO booklet, Memorandum on ICAO 48–50 (14th ed. 1990).

i. See 1 D. Leive, International Regulatory Regimes 298 (1976).

If a report submitted by an ILO member government does not provide the full information needed by the Committee of Experts (or if a government does not submit its report at all), the Committee of Experts and Conference Committee can and do rely on trade unions and employer organizations to supply further information and, sometimes, to apply some direct pressure from within the country.[j] They have an incentive to do so, since correction of any deficiencies in the practical application of ILO Conventions will normally benefit workers or employers, or both.

Several possible keys to the success of a direct contact enforcement mechanism could be envisaged. One, just mentioned, might be the assurance of prompt and accurate reports on the situation in member states. This is not easily achieved, even in the ILO, where nearly 90 percent of the reports had not been submitted on time in 1990.[k] Another key might be the express or implied threat of public exposure if a government refuses to cooperate or responds unsatisfactorily to the informal pressure. (The International Labor Office plays down this threat, but governments know it exists.) Another might be the independence of the initiating body (in the ILO, the Committee of Experts). Finally, the key might be the use of specialists from the organization to discuss the issues with similar specialists from the "respondent" government, making it likely that they will understand each other and share the same values. Which of these would be the most important key to success? Which would be the least important?

2. *The International Monetary Fund*

The International Monetary Fund Agreement contains express provisions for consultations with members in circumstances calling for the application of pressure to induce them to act consistently with the goals of the Fund. This may be done even if a member is not violating any provision in the Agreement. For example, *article XII, section 8* provides in part, "The Fund shall at all times have the right to communicate its views informally to any member on any matter arising under this Agreement." It also says that the Fund, acting by special majority vote, may decide to publish a report to a member regarding certain matters within its control that are particularly damaging to the balance of payments of other members.

---

j. See Valticos, Les Méthodes de la Protection Internationale de la Liberté Syndicale, 144 Hague Academy, Recueil des Cours 77, 101 (1975). ILO Convention No. 144, 1089 UNTS 354, requires parties to it to engage in consultations among representatives of the government, employers and workers at least once a year regarding, inter alia, the reports to be made under ILO Constitution article 22. The related ILO Recommendation 152 calls on all ILO members (not just those ratifying Convention No. 144) to do the same thing.

k. See Report of the Committee on the Application of Standards, Int'l Labor Conf., 77th Sess., Provisional Record of Proceedings at 27/14 (1990).

More significant is *article IV, section 3*, which requires the Fund to "exercise firm surveillance over the exchange rate policies of members." It also requires members to provide the Fund with the information necessary for surveillance, and to consult with it, on request, regarding the member's exchange rate policies. Acting under this authority, the Fund's Executive Board has adopted a Decision on Surveillance over Exchange Rate Policies, set forth at pages 298–300 supra. Note that the Decision contemplates regular, annual consultations, but it also provides for ad hoc consultations in two situations. See Paragraph V of the 1977 Decision and the 1979 supplemental surveillance procedure, at page 300 supra.

What is the difference between these two situations? Why do you suppose the Executive Board decided to add the 1979 procedure?

In many cases, the IMF Managing Director could choose which of the two procedures to invoke, if he wishes to discuss exchange rate policies with a member between regular article IV consultations. What would dictate the choice?

Why would these consultations be shrouded in secrecy? Should that be the case in other specialized agencies?

B. THE MOBILIZATION OF SHAME

1. *The International Labor Organization*

We have already seen one relatively moderate form of mobilization of shame used by the ILO: the Committee of Experts' published "observations." As indicated in Subsection A, these observations are considered by the Conference Committee on the Application of Standards (formerly the Committee on the Application of Conventions and Recommendations). It selects the most significant ones and discusses them with the governments concerned. The Conference Committee is tripartite, consisting of representatives of employers and workers as well as governments. Its size varies from year to year, but it always has well over 100 members. Thus the mere examination and discussion of the observations involves some mobilization of shame: the "respondent" government must either explain itself or remain embarrassingly silent in front of private as well as public persons from a variety of nations. These may include representatives from within its own territory of the workers or employers who were intended to receive the benefit of the norm in question.

Since 1957 the ILO Conference Committee has not only discussed the more significant "observations," but has mentioned in its report to the full Conference the most serious deficiencies, naming the countries involved. Until 1980 this was in the form of a "special list" containing seven categories of default, including such things as failure to file reports on Conventions, failure to respond to the observations and direct requests of the Committee of Experts, repeated failure to take part in the Conference Committee discussions concerning the country, and—in category 7—"continued failure to implement fully the Conventions concerned." Category 7 was regarded as the most serious. It was expressed in the Conference Committee's reports as follows:

> The Committee examined the application of certain Conventions in various countries and noted with grave concern that in some of them there was continued failure to implement fully the Conventions concerned and that full information should therefore be supplied on the measures taken to ensure such compliance. The Committee draws particular attention, in this connection, to the following cases: [Names of states and of the Conventions each had failed to implement].

The special list was usually accompanied by "special paragraphs" pointing out, diplomatically, relatively serious failures by named member states to comply with specific conventions they had ratified. A country's appearance in a special paragraph was a signal that it might appear in category 7 of the special list in the following year if it did not mend its ways.

Each year, including the years since 1980, the Conference Committee's report is presented to the full Conference for adoption and is published as part of the Conference proceedings. The Committee's inclusion of a state in the special list, or even in a special paragraph, put it very much in the spotlight, but the ultimate stage in the mobilization of shame was, and still is, the adoption of the report by the full Conference.

Occasionally the use of category 7 of the special list touched off a serious controversy in the organization. Such a case was the inclusion of the Soviet Union in category 7 in 1974. The Committee of Experts had concluded that the Soviet Union was not fully complying with the Convention Concerning Forced or Compulsory Labor, 1930,[a] to which it was a party. In general, the Convention requires each party "to suppress the use of forced or compulsory labor in all its forms within the shortest possible period." There are some exceptions, including one for "any work or service which forms part of the normal civic obligations of the citizens." The Committee of Experts criticized a decree of the Russian Republic that authorized an official body to direct to specific employment any person "evading socially useful work and leading an anti-social, parasitic way of life." It also criticized Soviet regulations that effectively prevented farmworkers from leaving a collective farm without the consent of a management committee and the general meeting of the collective farm.

In the Conference Committee, the Soviet representative argued strenuously against the Committee of Experts' conclusions. Nevertheless, the Conference Committee included the Soviet Union in category 7 of the special list. When the full Conference considered the Conference Committee's report, the Soviet Union and its allies alleged that the

---

a. ILO Convention No. 29, 39 U.N.T.S. 56.

Committee of Experts had distorted the relevant Soviet legislation, had discredited the ILO supervisory system, and had violated the established procedure by which—according to the Soviet representative—a member could be placed in category 7 only after its deficiencies had been discussed in previous years by the full Conference. These points were disputed, with some vigor, by Western representatives. When it came time to vote on adoption of the Conference Committee's report, nobody voted against it, but there were so many abstentions that the necessary quorum for adopting it was not obtained.[b]

For purposes of mobilizing shame regarding the Soviet Union's performance under the Forced Labor Convention, did it make any difference whether a quorum was obtained?

The matter did not end there. For several years, a sparring match ensued between the Committee of Experts and the Soviet Union. Gradually the Russian Republic and the Soviet Union loosened their rules on parasitic lifestyles and on collective farms. Each time the Committee of Experts expressed some satisfaction, but asked for more information. Each time the Soviet Union reported back, without fully satisfying the Committee. This went on until the dissolution of the Soviet Union and political/economic reforms in the Republics rendered the issues moot.

The machinery for mobilizing shame within the ILO changed somewhat in 1980. As the Soviet case illustrated, the former procedure touched sensitive nerves in some governments, particularly those representing socialist states. It was argued that the special list and special paragraphs constituted a form of judgment inappropriate in a nonjudicial body. Condemnations of governments were said to be counterproductive, and could dissuade them from ratifying labor conventions. Moreover, it was said that the procedure was not equitable because it allowed representatives of countries that had not ratified conventions to criticize countries that had.[c]

Responding to these criticisms, the Conference Committee abandoned its special list, and instead began including in its annual report a section entitled "Application of Ratified Conventions." Under this heading are subsections formulated in these terms:

b. For the key points in the debate and the result of the vote, see International Labor Conf., 59th Sess., Record of Proceedings at 733–36, 738–40, 750–52, 758–60 (1974), set forth in the first edition of this book at pages 449–457. Under the Conference's Standing Orders, or rules of procedure, in force in 1974, for a quorum the total number of votes cast for and against had to equal half the number of delegates attending. Thus a large number of abstentions could prevent a quorum from being achieved. Under 1986 amendments to the Standing Orders, abstentions would be counted toward a quorum.

c. See Report of the Committee on the Application of Conventions and Recommendations, Int'l Labor Conf., 65th Sess., Provisional Record of Proceedings at 36/15 (1979).

Cases of progress

The Committee noted with satisfaction that in the following cases governments have introduced changes in their law and practice in order to eliminate divergencies previously discussed by the Committee: [Identification of states and the relevant conventions].

Special cases

The Committee considered it appropriate to draw the attention of the Conference to the discussions it had regarding certain cases mentioned in the following paragraphs. [Several paragraphs appear at this point, discussing specific cases and naming the states involved.]

Continued failure to implement

During its examination of the application of certain Conventions the Committee noted with grave concern that there has been continued failure over several years to eliminate serious deficiencies in the application [by named states, of specific] ratified Conventions which it had previously discussed.[d]

Is there any difference between the use (in the former procedure) of special paragraphs and category 7 of the special list, on one hand, and (in the new procedure) "Special cases" and "Continued failure to implement," on the other?

To give one year's experience under the new procedure as an example, in 1987 the Conference Committee singled out three member states as "Cases of progress": Guatemala (one convention), Panama (one convention) and Uruguay (three conventions). It designated four member states as "Special cases": Bangladesh (one convention), the Dominican Republic (two conventions), Ecuador (three conventions) and Pakistan (five conventions), devoting a paragraph to the problems it found with each of these states' application of the conventions. Under "Continued failure to implement," the Committee named only Iran, regarding the Discrimination (Employment and Occupation) Convention, 1958.[e]

Third world states have not been the only ones to feel pressure under the current procedure. A case involving the United Kingdom illustrates some of the system's strengths and weaknesses, in the context of freedom of association—one of the principles stressed by the ILO.

In 1984 the British Trades Union Congress complained to the ILO Committee on Freedom of Association that the British government had adopted a policy depriving the 7,000 employees at the Cheltenham

---

d. Report of the Committee on the Application of Conventions and Recommendations, Int'l Labor Conf., 66th Sess., Provisional Record of Proceedings at 37/19, 20–21 (1980).

e. Report of the Committee on the Application of Conventions and Recommendations, Int'l Labor Conf., 73d Sess., Provisional Record of Proceedings at 24/15–16 (1987).

Government Communications Headquarters (GCHQ) the right to belong to a trade union. They were offered the option of resigning from their union in return for a cash payment, or applying for a transfer to another civil service job. Employees at GCHQ who took neither option would be dismissed.

The British government did not dispute the facts. It said that GCHQ's functions are to ensure the security of the U.K.'s military and official communications, and to provide intelligence services. No interruption of these national security functions could be allowed, yet there had been seven strikes over pay disputes at GCHQ between 1979 and 1981. The only solution, it said, was to limit GCHQ employees to membership in a public employees' staff association, rather than a trade union.

The U.K. is a party to the basic ILO freedom of association conventions, including numbers 87, 98 and 151. Convention No. 87 says, in article 2: "Workers and employers, without distinction whatsoever, shall have the right to establish and, subject only to the rules of the organisation concerned, to join organisations of their own choosing without previous authorization." Article 9(1) says, "The extent to which the guarantees provided for in this Convention shall apply to the armed forces and the police shall be determined by national laws or regulations."

Convention No. 98 protects workers from anti-union discrimination in respect of their employment. Its article 5(1) is identical with article 9(1) of Convention No. 87, above.

Convention No. 151 deals specifically with the right to organize, and conditions of employment, in the public service. It, too, repeats article 9(1) of Convention No. 87, in article 1(3). The remainder of its article 1 provides:

> 1. This Convention applies to all persons employed by public authorities, to the extent that more favourable provisions in other international labour Conventions are not applicable to them.
>
> 2. The extent to which the guarantees provided for in this Convention shall apply to high-level employees whose functions are normally considered as policy-making or managerial, or to employees whose duties are of a highly confidential nature, shall be determined by national laws or regulations.

The British government argued, in essence, that Conventions No. 87 and No. 151 should be read together; Convention No. 151 was the more specific of the two in relation to public services, and the exception for employees with highly confidential duties in its article 1(2) would make little sense if it were subject to article 2 of Convention No. 87.[f]

---

[f] 67 ILO Official Bull., Series B, No. 2, at 112, 116–17 (1984). The British argument is set forth more fully in the excerpt from the 1989 Conference Committee's report, infra.

The Committee on Freedom of Association rejected the argument, and said that the British action contravened article 2 of Convention No. 87. It recommended that the government negotiate with the civil service unions to try to reach an agreement that would ensure freedom of association without disrupting essential national security services. When the government stuck to its legal position, that Committee decided to call the matter to the attention of the Committee of Experts.

In 1985 the Committee of Experts agreed with the conclusions of the Committee on Freedom of Association. It noted, though, that the British government had raised important legal questions about the relationship between the freedom of association conventions, and suggested that the International Court of Justice might be requested to provide an opinion under the relevant provisions of the ILO Constitution.[g] That was not done, and the matter remained on the agendas of the Committee on Freedom of Association, the Committee of Experts and the Conference Committee.

We pick up the story with the Committee of Experts in 1989:

REPORT OF THE COMMITTEE OF EXPERTS ON THE APPLICATION OF CONVENTIONS AND RECOMMENDATIONS
Convention No. 87.
International Labor Conf., 76th Sess., Rep. III, Part 4A, at 234 (1989).

The Committee notes with regret that 13 employees at GCHQ have now been dismissed because of their refusal to give up membership of the union of their choice. The Committee notes that the Government remains of the view that Convention No. 87 cannot be examined in isolation from Conventions Nos. 98 and 151, and that Article 1(2) of the latter takes precedence over Convention No. 87. The Committee must again remind the Government that the supervisory bodies of the ILO have consistently taken the view that this is not the case, and that Article 2 of Convention No. 87 guarantees to all workers without distinction whatsoever, including public servants, the right freely to establish and to join organisations of their own choosing.

The Committee also notes that the Government considers that the functions carried out by the staff of GCHQ are in many cases identical with those carried out by members of the armed forces working in the same field. In support of this proposition the Government refers to the decision of the European Commission of Human Rights in Case No. 11603/85. The Government seems to suggest that this means that the civilian workforce at GCHQ should be regarded as falling within the scope of the "armed forces" exemption in Article 9 of the Convention. In this connection the Committee must point out that it has always taken the view that the armed forces and the police are the only

---

g. Report of the Committee of Experts on the Application of Conventions and Recommendations, International Labor Conf., 71st Sess., Rep. III, Part 4A, at 193, 194 (1985). The relevant provision of the ILO Constitution is *article 37(1)*.

categories of workers which, in accordance with the Convention, may be excluded from the guarantees provided therein. For these purposes, only workers who are recognised under national law or regulations as forming part of the army or the police can be regarded as coming within the scope of the exemption. This does not appear to be the case in relation to civilian employees at GCHQ.

The Committee notes with regret that the Government still feels that no useful purpose would be served by renewed negotiations with the relevant trade unions. The Committee remains of the view that such negotiations offer the most appropriate means of providing a resolution to this issue which is consistent with the requirements of the Convention. In the light of the foregoing, the Committee can only: (1) urge the Government to reconsider its position on the usefulness of further negotiations; and (2) reiterate that workers at GCHQ are entitled to join the organisation of their own choosing in accordance with Article 2 of the Convention.

THE CONFERENCE COMMITTEE

A spirited debate took place when the Conference Committee considered this part of the Committee of Experts' report. The flavor of the debate, and its result, are indicated in the excerpts below from the 1989 report of the Conference Committee.

REPORT OF THE COMMITTEE ON THE APPLICATION OF STANDARDS
Convention No. 87.
International Labor Conf., 76th Sess., Record of Proceedings, at 26/54–59 (1989).

[As summarized by the ILO, one of the British Government representatives said, in part:]

The Government appreciated the work done by the Committee of Experts, which had a difficult and complex task in looking at the application of conventions and interpreting them in the light of national laws and in the context of the diverse socio-economic factors and institutional structures in each country. The Committee of Experts was a distinguished authority in law whose opinions were respected. But in complex areas there were often divergent views, even among experts and within rational and democratic organisations—of which the ILO must surely rank as a leading example—it should be possible to say: yes, we understand why you came to these conclusions, but we think it is possible to make a different interpretation.

The Government's actions in respect of the General Communications Headquarters of Cheltenham (GCHQ) were taken solely in the interests of protecting national security. Although the GCHQ was not part of the Foreign and Commonwealth Office, it was in fact one of the security and intelligence services and formed [an] integral part of the United Kingdom's organisation for defence and national security. It provided vital indispensable operational support to the armed forces of the United Kingdom and its allies, including a continuing watch for any form of armed hostile activity. The speaker conveyed his Government's disappointment with the Committee of Experts' rejection of the argument that the workforce at GCHQ might fall within the scope of the "armed forces exemption" in Article 9 of the Convention. The functions of GCHQ were very closely connected with those of the armed forces and the Government found it hard to believe that GCHQ would not fall within the spirit of the exemption. Consequently, this was very much the kind of borderline case which Convention No. 151 was designed to clarify. GCHQ should operate continuously if national security needs were to be met and there had been severe disruption there through industrial action, with 10,000 work-days lost between 1979 and 1981. The Government's actions had been taken in the firm belief that it was unacceptable to have a top secret intelligence establishment vulnerable to national strike action.

In framing its Conventions, the ILO had taken account of the special issues * * * in matters of national defence and security; Convention No. 151 contained a specific exclusion clause for those involved in work of a highly secret or confidential nature. In formulating its action on GCHQ the Government took the view that it remained within the letter and spirit of these instruments. Convention No. 87 could and should be examined in conjunction with Conventions Nos. 98 and 151. It appeared to the Government that because of earlier disputes about the application of Convention No. 87 to the public service, an instrument dealing specifically with this area—Convention No. 151—had been adopted and this new Convention took precedence over the generality of Convention No. 87. The Government's interpretation of the preamble of Convention No. 151 was that it had been adopted with the two earlier Conventions in mind. Conventions Nos. 87 and 151 were interwoven with each other to such an extent that the power in Article 1(2) of the latter Convention to disapply the guarantees provided by that Convention would be of no utility or practical effect unless it was intended to have the effect of disapplying also the associated provisions of the earlier Convention. This meant it was for governments to determine—by means of national law and regulations—the extent to which the protections provided for in the Convention applied to public service workers engaged in highly confidential work: this was precisely what the Government had done.

* * *

The Committee of Experts was on record as recognising the difficulties inherent in interpreting the interrelation of these Conventions. In addition, the Court of Appeal in the United Kingdom specifically considered this issue, concluding that the Conventions should be read together and that Article 1(2) of Convention No. 151 took precedence over Convention No. 87. Therefore, the Government did not believe that its actions at GCHQ represented a breach of Convention No. 87.

* * *

The Government noted the Committee of Experts' view that it should undertake renewed negotiations with the relevant national trade unions. In fact, discussions were held with the national trade unions following the Government's announcement of 25 January 1984, and in those discussions the unions urged that a "no disruption agreement" would provide adequate safeguards. These proposals, which were of a limited nature, leaving the determination of the areas to be covered by the agreement for later negotiation, were very carefully considered by the government but had to be rejected, as they did not provide sufficient guarantee that conflicting pressures would not produce difficulties in the future.

* * *

The Employer member of Sweden, commenting on the report of the Committee of Experts, emphasised that he did not suggest that the Experts were not impartial or independent, but he questioned their expertise. The Committee of Experts had forgotten the basic principles governing the interpretation of treaties between States, as could be seen in the increasing number of overinterpretations in the reports of the past few years; he cautioned against that trend. He referred in particular to the present case and expressed the hope that the Experts would reconsider their position in that respect. The GCHQ establishment should be classified in the category of armed forces or police, and only the International Court of Justice could give an authoritative interpretation of the Convention. There were two ways to accomplish this: either the Conference or a majority of the Governing Body could ask for an opinion, or a government other than the United Kingdom or a worker delegate could make a constitutional complaint. The Governing Body could then establish a Commission of Inquiry whose conclusions could be appealed to the International Court of Justice by the Government. This course has now been open for five years and has not been used. Therefore, this Committee should not deal with this case any more, and the workers, if they so wish, could go to the Court by presenting a constitutional complaint.

* * *

The Worker member of the Netherlands stated that he was really concerned about the possible consequences of this case for the ILO supervisory system, especially in view of the final comments of the Employers' members. The key sentence in the Government's declaration was, "we understand how the Committee of Experts came to its conclusions but we came to different conclusions and we should be allowed to do it". Back in 1978 there was a debate in this Committee between the Government representatives of the United Kingdom and of the USSR on this very point. The USSR representative had then been defending the point the British Government is now making, and the British representative had then submitted that that position would undermine the whole ILO supervisory machinery if this Committee would accept it. In cases where there were differences of opinion for 20 years, this Committee always showed its concern by expressing its views in a special paragraph. The key question here was: should the present Committee accept the Committee of Experts' views on this case, which included their views expressed in several reports in previous years. In the past two years the present Committee by and large always accepted the views of the Committee of Experts.

* * *

The Chairman of the Committee proposed the following conclusions:

The Committee took note of the information submitted by the Government representative and of the detailed discussions which took place in the Committee. The Committee expressed its concern at the situation discussed by the Committee of Experts, which noted in its report that the GCHQ workers still did not enjoy union rights, contrary to the Convention. It recalled in that respect the conclusions of the Committee on Freedom of Association as regards the GCHQ case. The Committee noted with regret that the Government had dismissed some GCHQ workers during the proceedings pending before the Committee on Freedom of Association, and that the Government does not consider that it would be useful to hold negotiations with the workers' associations on the right to organise of workers. The Committee expressed the firm hope that the Government will reconsider its position, through dialogue with the trade unions, with a view to finding solutions to the factual and legal situation, that would be in full conformity with the Convention. The Committee expressed the firm hope that the next report of the Government requested by the Committee of Experts will contain information on definite developments in this situation, in conformity with the Convention. * * *

The Workers' members proposed that these conclusions be mentioned in a special paragraph of the present Committee's general report since, although this was an important case which had been discussed on many occasions, the Government had not initiated negotiations with the trade unions concerned and the situation had not progressed.

* * *

The Workers' members requested that a nominal vote be held to decide whether this case should be mentioned in a special paragraph.

* * *

The Government member of the United States wondered whether this case should be pushed so far. She considered that * * * if there had been an egregious violation of freedom of association there would be no question that a special paragraph was merited. Indeed, this was a very special case. She was concerned that a vote on this matter would damage the good will and consensus which were so important to the work of the Committee.

* * *

The Committee adopted the conclusions proposed by the Chairman with regard to the GCHQ issue and decided that, in a later sitting, a nominal vote would be held to decide on the appropriateness of mentioning this case in a special paragraph unless, in the meantime, the Workers' and Employers' members could conclude an agreement on this issue.

At a later sitting the Committee proceeded to a record vote at the request of the Workers' members for the registration of this case in a special paragraph of the report of the Committee.

The results of the vote were as follows: 56,845 votes in favour; 60,398 votes against; 9,555 abstentions. Consequently, the Committee decided not to register this case in a special paragraph of its report.

After the results of the vote had been announced, various Government members went on [to] explain the reasons for their vote.

* * *

The Workers' members * * * explained the reasons why they had proposed the use of a special paragraph: firstly, because they thought all the possibilities of dialogue and conciliation had not been exhausted within the country; secondly, because of the dismissal of 13 workers for faithfulness to their trade union during the course of the procedure before the Committee on Freedom of Association; and thirdly, in order to urge and encourage the British Government not to close the door but rather to reopen negotiations. * * *

A Government member of Ecuador explained that he had, with much regret, voted in favour of mentioning this case in a special paragraph in the hope that this would spur other countries to reflect on the tendency towards singling out situations in small countries which were sometimes the result of pressure from political interests outside the country. He expressed satisfaction that a democratic vote in connection with the present case had shown that principles of equity were not always violated.

* * *

A Government member of France stated that he had voted "No", essentially because of the jurisprudence of the Committee. The long-standing work practices of the present Committee allowed stable and objective positions to be taken, whether the country was large or small, industrialised or developing. According to tradition, a special paragraph could be used when the country in question met two criteria; firstly, that it had been under examination for a long time without any progress being made and, secondly, that it was a very serious case of violation of human rights. Each case of a special paragraph had to be put into perspective, that is, related to and compared with others. It had not seemed to him that the present case met the two criteria mentioned above.

* * *

A Government member of the United Kingdom noted that his Government had voted "No" because it felt that registration of this case as a special paragraph would be disproportionate and that it would undermine the force of ILO sanctions.

THE PLENARY PROCEEDINGS

When the Conference Committee's report was considered by the International Labor Conference, the U.K. case was discussed again. The Workers' adviser of the United States made a long statement amplifying the workers' viewpoint. He said, among other things:

> In short, it is our conviction that the effort by the Workers for a special paragraph in this case was lost because of a failure on the part of the Employers and certain Governments—for reasons extraneous to what was really involved—to perceive its real purpose, and that was to urge and encourage the British Government not to slam the door shut on further negotiations with the trade unions. If this does not represent a violation of freedom of association, then we Workers don't know what does.
>
> Now, I give you this case as a background because the Workers in this Committee believe it illustrates—and in fact triggered—a perceptible trend towards inequality of treatment in cases involving large and powerful industrial countries—as contrasted with developing countries—when it comes to applying the observations of the Experts in an impartial manner * * *.

* * *

> As our Workers' Vice-Chairman has already informed you, a special paragraph is not a condemnation of a court. In this Committee where dialogue is pre-eminent, its fundamental purpose is to highlight the case as one of importance and to encourage and to stimulate compliance with obligations freely assumed.[h]

EVALUATING THE PROCEDURE

The dispute over the British government's treatment of the GCHQ workers was essentially a legal one. Were the Committee of Experts and the Conference Committee the appropriate bodies to resolve it?

---

h. International Labor Conf., 76th (1989). Sess., Record of Proceedings at 31/32

Consider ILO Constitution *article 37,* as well as the material below on the role of the Committee of Experts.

There has been controversy among members of the Conference Committee about the Committee of Experts' role as quasi-authoritative interpreter of labor conventions. Employers' members, relying on article 37, have questioned the Committee of Experts' competence to do so, particularly with respect to the right to strike—a right that does not appear explicitly in any of the conventions. Workers' members, understandably, have supported the Committee of Experts on the right to strike.

The Committee of Experts has given this justification for its quasi-judicial role over the whole range of labor conventions:

> The [Committee's] terms of reference do not require it to give definitive interpretations of Conventions, competence to do so being vested in the International Court of Justice by article 37 of the Constitution of the ILO. Nevertheless, in order to carry out its function of determining whether the requirements of Conventions are being respected, the Committee has to consider and express its views on the content and meaning of the provisions of Conventions and to determine their legal scope, where appropriate. It therefore appears to the Committee that, in so far as its views are not contradicted by the International Court of Justice, they are to be considered as valid and generally recognised. * * * The Committee considers that acceptance of the above considerations is indispensable to maintenance of the principle of legality and, consequently, for the certainty of law required for the proper functioning of the [ILO].[i]

One of the objections voiced by the employers' members has been the alleged failure of the Committee of Experts to follow the rules of treaty interpretation in Vienna Convention on the Law of Treaties *articles 31–32*. Those articles adopt the "plain meaning rule" of treaty interpretation articulated in several ICJ decisions. The workers' members have responded:

> The Workers' members questioned the arguments made by the Employers' members concerning the use by the Committee of Experts of the method of interpretation provided for at Article 31 of the Vienna Convention. They believed that ILO Conventions were not comparable to traditional treaties between States as the parties concerned were not only States but also organisations of employers and workers, who participated in their elaboration. In addition, Article 31(3)*(b)* of the Vienna Convention provides that practice may be used to identify the intention of the parties in a given interpretation. The Workers' members considered that the fact that the parties are not States alone, meant that nonconforming practice by one or several States should not reflect upon the

---

i. Report of the Committee of Experts on the Application of Conventions and Recommendations, International Labor Conf., 77th Sess., Rep. III, Part 4A, at 8 (1990).

intention of the parties. Moreover, the tripartite preparatory work for the Freedom of Association and Protection of the Right to Organise Convention, 1948 (No. 87), proved that this Convention had to be interpreted very broadly, particularly as concerns the right to join organisations of one's choice, which was recognised for all workers without distinction of any kind.[j]

Did the workers' members make a sound legal argument with respect to (a) labor conventions generally, and (b) the right to strike, in particular?

The ILO Secretary–General has tried to defuse the issue:

> The mandate of the Committee of Experts is to carry out a preliminary technical and legal examination of reports periodically submitted by member States on measures taken by them to implement Conventions they have ratified. The opinions of the Committee of Experts merit careful attention and great respect; * * * these opinions are accepted by member States in the vast majority of cases. But these opinions are not authoritative as concerns interpretations to which they may give rise. This authority attaches exclusively to the International Court of Justice * * *.[k]

The U.S. government has chimed in with a statement attached to its ratification of the Abolition of Forced Labor Convention: the "conclusions and practice" of the Committee of Experts, it said, "are not legally binding on the United States and have no force and effect on courts in the United States."[l]

In light of all this, what interpretive authority *does* the Committee of Experts have?

To return to the case at hand, consider also the Conference Committee procedure. Why should the British government representatives in the Conference Committee have been allowed to vote?

Note the two possible avenues, mentioned in the debate, by which the matter could have been submitted to the International Court of Justice. Why do you suppose neither avenue was used? Would the ICJ be an appropriate arbiter in a case like this?

Did the British government argue, in essence, that in a close case a government ought to get the benefit of the legal doubt?

Could there be any justification for such a result? Would it matter, for purposes of this question, whether the forum is an ILO committee or the ICJ?

Did the Committee of Experts and the Conference Committee take the position that in a close case a government ought not to stand firm

---

j. International Labor Conf., 78th Sess., Provisional Record of Proceedings at 24/7 (1991).

k. International Labor Conf., 77th Sess., Record of Proceedings at 27/9 (1990).

l. 74 ILO Official Bull., Ser. A, No. 3, at 133 (1991).

on its legal argument? Is that a sound position for an international organization, such as the ILO, to take?

Note the workers' representatives' view of the purpose of special paragraphs in the Conference Committee's reports. Can it fairly be said that the special paragraphs do not represent judgments about governments' conduct? If so, why was there such a fuss about mentioning the British government in a special paragraph in this case?

Can there be effective mobilization of shame without getting judgmental?

In this case, the U.K. escaped mention in a special paragraph. Did it escape the mobilization of shame?

Note the concerns expressed by several speakers about the even-handedness, or lack thereof, of the process. As we have seen, not only did the U.K. duck a special paragraph in this case, but in 1974, when the Soviet Union did not escape mention in category 7 of the special list, it managed to forestall adoption of the report by the full Conference. Several third-world governments have not had such success. But as we have also seen, plenty of disapprobation fell upon the U.K. in 1989 and the Soviet Union in 1974. Is the even-handedness issue just a matter of form, or is there substance to it?

The Committee of Experts again considered the British GCHQ case in 1991. It stuck to its position, as did the British government. The Committee said, in part:

> [R]ecalling that workers whose functions relate to security matters would fall into the category of those in respect of whom it is permissible to curtail the right to strike, the Committee considers that these workers should not be denied the right to belong to the organisations of their own choosing as guaranteed by Article 2 of [Convention No. 87].
>
> Recalling that it is now more than six years since the Government last held formal discussions with the unions on this matter, and noting the stated preparedness of the [Trades Union Congress] to adopt a positive approach to renewed negotiations, the Committee considers that the time is right for a resumption of dialogue; accordingly, it again urges the Government to reconsider its position in relation to the reopening of discussions * * *.[m]

The Conference Committee again discussed the matter in 1991, and again asked the government to resume dialog with the unions.[n]

The British government's 1992 report essentially reiterated its position. The Committee of Experts' tone became a bit testier:

---

m. Report of the Committee of Experts on the Application of Conventions and Recommendations, International Labor Conf., 78th Sess., Rep. III, Part 4A, at 218 (1991).

n. Report of the Committee on the Application of Standards, International Labor Conf., 78th Sess., Provisional Record of Proceedings at 24/63 (1991).

The Committee deplores that it has been unable to note any tangible progress on this question or even a resumption of discussions, despite the very broad consensus that has emerged in the supervisory bodies.°

The question arises whether the ILO's mobilization-of-shame technique is fair and effective. The British case, and the Soviet case discussed earlier, are somewhat atypical because they involved two of the most powerful members. But an enforcement mechanism has to be judged, at least in part, on its effectiveness across the board—even against those most capable of defying it.

One knowledgeable observer—the former General Counsel of the International Monetary Fund—has said this about the mobilization of shame as an enforcement technique:

> Experience in the Fund and in other international organizations shows that decisions of a critical character are a powerful international judgment. The mobilization of shame by the judgment of peers is not shrugged off by the member against which the verdict is delivered.ᵖ

Does the ILO's experience with its more powerful members bear out his assessment? If not, what other enforcement technique would you suggest?

Would the ILO process be transferable to other organizations? In this connection, note its dependence on self-reporting by member governments so that the supervisory bodies will have the necessary facts. As we have seen, the ILO has had difficulty in obtaining useful reports from some member governments. UNESCO has had even more difficulty in connection with its own reporting system. Reasons given in the ILO have included the lack of qualified personnel in developing countries to prepare detailed and complex reports; lack of appreciation in some countries of the extent of the reporting obligation when conventions are ratified; and (even in industrialized countries) the burden of preparing an ever-increasing number of reports to several international organizations on a wide variety of topics. What can be done about the problem of assuring the submission of prompt and accurate reports?

NONGOVERNMENTAL ORGANIZATIONS

Nongovernmental organizations (labor unions) play an important role in engaging the ILO mobilization-of-shame machinery, as the

---

o. Report of the Committee of Experts on the Application of Conventions and Recommendations, International Labor Conf., 79th Sess., Rep. III, Part 4A, at 243 (1992).

p. Gold, The Rule of Law in the International Monetary Fund 31 (IMF Pamphlet Series, No. 32, 1980).

British Trades Union Congress did in the case we have examined. More generally, NGOs often publicize apparent violations of international norms within the sphere of their interests, or bring the apparent violations to the attention of relevant international organizations with the aim of having them mobilize shame. Some of these NGOs are focused entirely within an individual country; some are much more internationally-oriented. They have played very important roles in several fields, notably human rights and environmental protection.

Are NGOs part of the answer to the reporting problem?

2. *The International Monetary Fund*

One organization to which the ILO's process would not be directly transferable is the International Monetary Fund. Although the IMF Agreement gives it the authority to publish a report regarding a member's practices that seriously affect the balance of payments of others, the authority is not used. Nor does the IMF have a supervisory body comparable to the ILO Committee of Experts. Nevertheless, its expert staff does conduct frequent consultations with members, and the results of the consultations are reported to the Executive Board if the Managing Director of the Fund is not satisfied with members' policies. This operates as a form of the mobilization of shame, as noted above by the former IMF General Counsel.

Why would the Fund shy away from the public use of this enforcement technique?

3. *The International Atomic Energy Agency*

It was discovered in the aftermath of the Persian Gulf war in 1991 that Iraq was well on the way to producing nuclear weapons. This, despite Iraq's undertaking not to do so as a non-nuclear state party to the Nuclear Nonproliferation Treaty, and despite its undertaking to accept International Atomic Energy Agency safeguards under its safeguards agreement with the IAEA. The IAEA Board of Governors reacted by adopting the resolution below.

IAEA BOARD OF GOVERNORS RESOLUTION
July 18, 1991.
IAEA Press Release IAEA/1176, IK/35.

The Board of Governors,

* * *

1. *Finds,* on the basis of the report of the Director–General in GOV/2530, that the Government of Iraq has not complied with its obligations under its safeguards agreement with the Agency [872 U.N.T.S. 219];

2. *Condemns* this non-compliance by the Government of Iraq with its safeguards agreement;

3. *Calls upon* the Government of Iraq to remedy this non-compliance forthwith, including placing any and all additional source and special fissionable material within Iraq's territory, under its jurisdiction or its control, regardless of quantity or location under Agency safeguards in accordance with the relevant provisions of [the safeguards agreement] and in accordance with relevant technical determinations of the Agency;

4. *Decides,* in accordance with Article XII.C of the Statute, to report this non-compliance to all members of the Agency and to the Security Council and General Assembly of the United Nations; * * *.

AN EFFECTIVE TECHNIQUE?

This was the first time the IAEA had condemned a state party to the Nuclear Nonproliferation Treaty for concealing a nuclear program. Iraq objected to the resolution, essentially on the ground that it had been cooperating with the nuclear inspection teams that had been on its territory since the end of the Gulf war.[a] Shortly thereafter, further evidence was uncovered showing that Iraq had, indeed, been conducting a sophisticated, clandestine program to develop nuclear weapons.[b] At the next regularly-scheduled IAEA General Conference in the autumn of 1991, the plenary body adopted a resolution condemning Iraq, much as the Board of Governors' resolution, above, had done.[c] The U.N. General Assembly then "noted with appreciation" these statements by the IAEA.[d]

Is the mobilization-of-shame enforcement technique of any use in a situation like this?

4. *The World Health Organization*

Sometimes, public condemnations by plenary bodies of specialized agencies have raised issues about the legitimate limits of the mobilization of shame. This has occurred particularly when the government or state being shamed is in disfavor with a majority of members for reasons not universally regarded as being within the agency's ambit of concern. This has happened occasionally in the ILO, but for the sake of variety we will examine it in another agency, the World Health Organization.

In 1978, a three-member WHO Special Committee of Experts examined health conditions of the Arab population in the territories occupied by Israel. The Committee examined such things as the health care infrastructure (hospitals, blood banks, maternal and child care services, etc.), the availability of pharmaceutical drugs and technical

a. U.N.Doc. S/22826, at 3 (1991).
b. See U.N.Doc. S/23165 (1991).
c. IAEA Res. GC(XXXV)568 (1991).
d. G.A.Res. 46/16 (1991).

equipment, the staffing of health services, including mental health services, and the physical and mental condition of prisoners. It made several recommendations concerning better health-care facilities, including facilities for mental disorders; improved training for health workers; establishing a health education program for the local population; more responsibilities and opportunities for the Arab health staff; establishing a social welfare service; and an improved health insurance plan. It went on to say:

> [T]he Committee wishes to reaffirm the reality recognized by all concerned with public health that, whatever improvements are made in health services in a particular area, and whatever technical measures are taken, a complete state of physical, mental and social well-being cannot be achieved when the population is obliged to live under the authority of an occupying power. The Committee considers that the health problems of the occupied territories can be solved only to the extent that the political problem can be solved.[a]

The World Health Assembly (WHO's plenary body) considered the report. A heated debate ensued, in which the representatives of Israel and the United States asserted that the draft resolution based on the report was a political statement going beyond WHO's legitimate concerns. After the debate, the resolution was adopted by a vote of 63 in favor, 21 opposed and 12 abstaining:

WHO RESOLUTION ON CONDITIONS OF THE ARAB POPULATION IN THE OCCUPIED TERRITORIES

World Health Assembly, May 1978.
Res. WHA 31.38, in 2 Handbook of Resolutions and Decisions of the World Health Assembly and the Executive Board 1973–1984, at 370 (1985).

The Thirty-first World Health Assembly,

* * *

Taking note of the principles set forth in the Constitution of the World Health Organization, particularly the principle that the health of all peoples is fundamental to the attainment of peace and security, and aware of its responsibility for ensuring proper health conditions for all peoples, particularly those peoples suffering from exceptional situations, especially foreign occupation and settler colonialism;

Having considered the Report of the Special Committee of Experts * * *;

* * *

Convinced that the occupation of territories by force gravely affects the health, social, psychological, mental and physical conditions of the

---

a. WHO Doc. A31/37, at 7 (1978).

population under occupation and that this can be only rectified by the complete and immediate termination of the occupation;

* * *

III

1. EXPRESSES its deep concern at the poor health and psychological conditions suffered by the inhabitants of the occupied Arab territories;

2. CONDEMNS the inhuman practices to which Arab prisoners and detainees are subjected in Israeli prisons, resulting in the deterioration of their health, psychological and mental conditions;

3. CONDEMNS Israel for its refusal to implement World Health Assembly resolutions calling upon it to allow refugees and displaced persons to return to their homes;

4. CONDEMNS Israel for its refusal to apply the Fourth Geneva Convention Relative to the Protection of Civilian Persons in Time of War of 12 August 1949;

5. CALLS UPON Israel to desist forthwith from the establishment of settlements in the occupied Arab territories and from requisitioning and confiscating Arab lands for the establishment of these settlements, as the establishment of these settlements deprives the inhabitants of the occupied territories of their rights to their land and property and the enjoyment of their natural resources, thereby affecting the health, psychological and social conditions of those inhabitants; * * *.

HEALTH CONCERNS OR POLITICS?

Part III of the WHO resolution clearly was intended to mobilize shame against Israel. Did it go beyond a concern for health conditions? Did the WHO Special Committee of Experts go beyond that concern?

Was the resolution ultra vires, i.e. beyond WHO's authority as set forth in its Constitution? See especially the *Preamble* and *articles 1, 2, 18 and 23*.

The resolution condemned Israel for its refusal to apply the Fourth Geneva Convention Relative to the Protection of Civilian Persons in Time of War.[b] The U.N. Security Council, with the United States concurring, has said that the Fourth Geneva Convention applies to the territories occupied by Israel as a result of the 1967 war. The Security Council has had the situation in the Middle East, including the occupied territories, on its agenda since the 1967 war.

Articles 27 and 49 of the Fourth Geneva Convention apply for the duration of any occupation, even if military operations have ended. Article 27 deals with humane treatment of the population, and article

---

b. Aug. 2, 1949, 6 U.S.T. 3516, 75 U.N.T.S. 287.

49 calls upon the occupying state not to transfer parts of its own civilian population to the occupied territory. The Security Council has characterized the Israeli settlements in the occupied territories as illegal under article 49,[c] but it has not expressly accused Israel of violating article 27 or any other article dealing with health matters.

The Relationship Agreement between the U.N. and WHO contains two provisions on cooperation between the two organizations:

> Article IV(3). The [WHO] affirms its intention of co-operating in whatever further measures may be necessary to make co-ordination of the activities of the specialized agencies and those of the United Nations fully effective.
>
> Article VII. The [WHO] agrees to co-operate with the [Security] Council in furnishing such information and rendering such assistance for the maintenance or restoration of international peace and security as the Security Council may request.[d]

Was Part III of the Health Assembly resolution, particularly the paragraph relating to the Fourth Geneva Convention, in furtherance of a duty to cooperate with the U.N.; in violation of such a duty; or unrelated to any such duty? (Is U.N. Charter *article 12* relevant?)

The Health Assembly has continued to adopt resolutions on conditions in the occupied territories. For example, in 1985 it adopted a resolution that, among other things:

> *Condemns* Israel for its continuing occupation, its arbitrary practices against the Arab population, and its continuing establishment of Israeli settlements in the Arab occupied territories, including Palestine and the Golan; and for its illegal exploitation of the natural wealth and resources of the Arab inhabitants in those territories, especially the appropriation of water resources and their diversion for the purpose of occupation and settlement, all of which have devastating and long-term effects on the mental and physical health conditions of the population under occupation;
>
> *Condemns* Israel for its policy aiming at making the population of the occupied Arab territories, including Palestine and the Golan, dependent on the Israeli health system, by hindering the normal development of the Arab health institutions, as part of Israel's overall plan of annexation of those territories;
>
> *Condemns* Israel for continuously raising obstacles to the implementation of resolution WHA 36.27, sub-paragraph 8(2), which requests the establishment of three health centers in the occupied Arab territories, including Palestine, under the direct supervision of WHO;

---

c. See, e.g., Security Council Res. 452 (1979), in 34 SCOR, Resolutions and Decisions of the Security Council 1979, at 8 (1980).

d. U.N.–WHO Relationship Agreement, July 10, 1948, 19 U.N.T.S. 193.

Demands an immediate end to occupation, violence and repression, and to the establishment of new settlements; also demands that those settlements already established be dismantled, in order to enable the Palestinian people to exercise its inalienable national rights, as a prerequisite to the establishment of a social and health system that would be able to ensure health for all by the year 2000
* * * .[e]

Was it within the Health Assembly's authority to determine that Israel's appropriation of water resources for purposes of occupation and settlement is illegal?

If so, was there anything wrong with the way in which the Health Assembly went about it?

Leaving that aside, was the 1985 resolution ultra vires?[f]

Should the constituent instrument of an international organization expressly constrain the authority of the plenary organ (or of other organs) to condemn member states?

SECTION 3. SANCTIONS

INTRODUCTORY NOTE

At the international level, punitive sanctions have three possible purposes: compulsion, deterrence and retribution.[a] In any given case, only one or two of the purposes might be sought or be attainable.

Compulsion may be distinguished from deterrence by thinking of it as an attempt to coerce a change in the ways of an actor (in the case of intergovernmental organizations, usually a national government) that is engaged in a continuing course of norm-encroaching conduct. Deterrence may be seen as an attempt to preclude, or at least reduce the likelihood of, repeat performances of particular norm-encroaching acts by the offending government or similar performances by others. Retribution involves harm for the offender in order to demonstrate that the community or body imposing the harm does not condone the offensive act.

As you read the materials on sanctions, try to determine which of these purposes is being sought. Ask also whether the purpose is being met. If so, what explains it? If not, why not?

e. Resolution WHA 38.15 (1985), in 3 Handbook of Resolutions and Decisions of the World Health Assembly and the Executive Board 132 (2d ed. 1985–1989).

f. UNESCO has also adopted resolutions attempting to mobilize shame in respect of Israeli conduct in the occupied territories, raising legal issues similar to those raised by the WHO resolutions. See, e.g., UNESCO Executive Board Res. 130/EX/PX/DR.1 (1988), reprinted in 4 Palestine Y.B. Int'l L. 124 (1987/88).

a. See Nossal, International Sanctions as International Punishment, 43 International Organization 301, 316–22 (1989).

A. AUTHORIZED RETALIATION IN KIND

Various forms of retaliation (sometimes under the rubric of retorsion or reprisal) have long been recognized, de facto if not always de jure, as sanctions for breaches of international law. There have been attempts to regulate these sanctions, and it is now widely held that armed reprisals by individual states acting on their own authority, not in self defense, violate international law.

On the other hand, with the proliferation of international organizations after World War II, states have accepted the legitimacy of certain forms of retaliation in kind, authorized by international organizations as sanctions against conduct by members (and occasionally by nonmembers) running counter to the organizations' norms. One prominent example is Chapter VII of the U.N. Charter, on enforcement action, which is considered later in these materials. For the present, we will concentrate on actual and proposed retaliation sanctions relating to the General Agreement on Tariffs and Trade (GATT) and the ICAO.

GATT is a multilateral trade agreement and an organization. It seeks to reduce tariffs and other barriers to international trade, and to eliminate discriminatory treatment in international commerce. It has convened several rounds of negotiations to accomplish these goals, resulting in binding obligations among members. In addition, GATT as an agreement contains a rather detailed set of rules for the conduct of trade. These include rules prohibiting such things as customs duties at rates higher than those bound under GATT tariff negotiations, protective domestic taxes applied to imports, laws and regulations discriminating against imports, import quotas and certain export subsidies. There are several exceptions, and there is a provision for waiver by the GATT in individual cases.

Retaliation is the ultimate sanction under the GATT for conduct of member states inconsistent with the organization's norms. It is even a potential sanction for trade-damaging conduct that does not violate any organizational norm.

GENERAL AGREEMENT ON TARIFFS AND TRADE
Signed, Oct. 30, 1947.
IV GATT, Basic Instruments and Selected Documents 1 (1969).

Art. XXIII. Nullification or Impairment

1. If any contracting party should consider that any benefit accruing to it directly or indirectly under this Agreement is being nullified or impaired or that the attainment of any objective of the Agreement is being impeded as the result of

   (a) the failure of another contracting party to carry out its obligations under this Agreement, or

   (b) the application by another contracting party of any measure, whether or not it conflicts with the provisions of this Agreement, or

(c) the existence of any other situation,

the contracting party may, with a view to the satisfactory adjustment of the matter, make written representations or proposals to the other contracting party or parties which it considers to be concerned. Any contracting party thus approached shall give sympathetic consideration to the representations or proposals made to it.

2. If no satisfactory adjustment is effected between the contracting parties concerned within a reasonable time, or if the difficulty is of the type described in paragraph 1(c) of this Article, the matter may be referred to the CONTRACTING PARTIES. The CONTRACTING PARTIES shall promptly investigate any matter so referred to them and shall make appropriate recommendations to the contracting parties which they consider to be concerned, or give a ruling on the matter, as appropriate. The CONTRACTING PARTIES may consult with contracting parties, with the Economic and Social Council of the United Nations and with any appropriate intergovernmental organization in cases where they consider such consultation necessary. If the CONTRACTING PARTIES consider that the circumstances are serious enough to justify such action, they may authorize a contracting party or parties to suspend the application to any other contracting party or parties of such concessions or other obligations under this Agreement as they determine to be appropriate in the circumstances. If the application to any contracting party of any concession or other obligation is in fact suspended, that contracting party shall then be free, not later than sixty days after such action is taken, to give written notice to the Executive Secretary to the CONTRACTING PARTIES of its intention to withdraw from this Agreement and such withdrawal shall take effect upon the sixtieth day following the day on which such notice is received by him.

GATT NONUSE OF RETALIATION

At this writing there had been only one instance in which the Contracting Parties [a] had authorized retaliation under article XXIII. They authorized the Netherlands to suspend GATT concessions made to the United States, in retaliation for U.S. import restrictions on dairy products.[b] The authority to retaliate was not actually exercised by the Netherlands, and the U.S. import restrictions were not removed.

There have been a few recent indications that the article XXIII retaliation sanction may be resuscitated, and there have been some instances of article XXIII-style retaliation without the benefit of autho-

---

a. In GATT parlance, the Contracting Parties are all states parties to GATT, acting collectively as the plenary body of the organization. References to contracting parties (without capital letters) are to parties in their individual capacities.

b. See GATT, Basic Instruments and Selected Documents, 1st Supp. 32 (1953).

rization from the Contracting Parties.ᶜ If it ever does come back into use, one question would concern the magnitude of retaliation permitted by article XXIII. Note that it says the Contracting Parties may authorize the suspension of such obligations "as they determine to be appropriate in the circumstances." Although that seems quite open-ended, there is some negotiating history to the effect that it was not intended to be used punitively; instead, the idea was to provide for "a compensatory adjustment in the obligations which a Member has assumed." ᵈ

If a contracting state erects barriers to the trade of other contracting parties that violate the GATT—for example, by imposing unauthorized import quotas on products that compete with domestically-produced products—why shouldn't it be contemplated that the Contracting Parties would collectively authorize punitive retaliation? Is it because punitive retaliation would be counterproductive?

If retaliation is limited to "compensatory adjustment," i.e. a balanced withdrawal of trade concessions (which would presumably be in the form of a balanced increase of import duties or imposition of quotas on specific products exported from the offending party), could it nevertheless have a deterrent effect?

If the Contracting Parties were inclined to do so, could they authorize all contracting parties, and not just those directly injured by the import quotas, to retaliate under the provisions of article XXIII? Would that ever be a good idea?

Very few specialized agencies even contemplate the use of authorized retaliation in kind by member states as a sanction. One that does contemplate it, but apparently does not use it, is the Universal Postal Union. Article 2 of the Universal Postal Convention says, in part, "When a member country fails to observe [provisions in the Convention and in the UPU Constitution regarding freedom of transit of mail passed along by the postal administration of another member], postal administrations of other member countries may discontinue their postal service with that country." ᵉ

Would this be an effective sanction in the UPU? If so, why do you suppose it isn't used? Is the UPU's basic function—seeing that the mail gets through—relevant here?

Would authorized retaliation in kind be an effective sanction in any other organization with which you are familiar?

c. See J. Jackson, The World Trading System: Law and Policy of International Economic Relations 96 (1989).

d. See GATT Analytical Index, Article XXIII-77, 78, Doc. GATT/LEG/2 (1989).

e. 2 Annotated Code of the Universal Postal Union 11 (1991).

B. SANCTIONS AFFECTING MEMBERSHIP RIGHTS

1. *Loss of Voting Rights*

a. *The United Nations*

U.N. Charter *article 19* addresses the important problem of ensuring that member states pay their dues with reasonable promptness. A member that is more than two years in arrears "shall have no vote in the General Assembly." As the U.N. has become increasingly active in peacekeeping, humanitarian assistance and other endeavors after the end of the cold war, the problem of inducing members to pay their assessed dues on time has become acute. Annual dues are payable on January 1 of each year, yet few member states pay in full by then. Many, of course, are in arrears from prior years as of each new year; when they make payments, the amounts are first credited to their arrears and only after those are eliminated are any further payments credited to current obligations.

The magnitude of the problem is illustrated by figures from a recent year. As of April 1, 1992, current and accumulated unpaid dues, including peacekeeping assessments, amounted to about $1.8 billion. Only 39 states had paid their 1992 dues by then. Eighteen states were more than two years in arrears, and thus had lost their right to vote in the General Assembly under a literal reading of article 19—absent a General Assembly decision under the last sentence of that article, permitting a member to vote "if [the Assembly] is satisfied that the failure to pay is due to conditions beyond the control of the Member." (The United States was not among them, even though its arrears were far larger than those of any other member.)[a]

The principal legal issue relating to the loss-of-vote sanction is whether or not it is automatic in the absence of a decision by the General Assembly to permit a member to vote. At pages 247–53 supra, these materials outline the incident in the 1960s, when the Soviet Union and France refused to pay expenses the U.N. General Assembly had apportioned to them for peacekeeping operations by the United Nations Emergency Force (UNEF) in the Middle East and the United Nations Operation in the Congo (ONUC), and the situation in the 1980s, when the United States withheld substantial portions of dues apportioned to it. The Soviet Union and France argued that the General Assembly's apportionment of expenses was ultra vires, since peacekeeping was a matter for the Security Council, but the International Court of Justice in an advisory opinion[b] said that the expenses were "expenses of the Organization" within the meaning of U.N. Charter *article 17(2)*. The United States, in the 1980s, withheld dues out of dissatisfac-

---

[a] See U.N. Doc. A/46/600/Add.2 (1992).

[b] Certain Expenses of the United Nations, [1962] I.C.J. 151.

tion with the budget-setting process, in which the United States had only one vote, but which resulted in an apportionment to the United States of 25% of the budgeted expenses.

By the autumn of 1990, the accumulated U.S. arrearages to the entire U.N. system (including specialized agencies) exceeded $600 million. Congress then appropriated funds to cover current assessments plus approximately 20 percent of the arrearages, with the expectation that further appropriations for arrearages would be forthcoming in later years.

At this point we shall assume that none of the Soviet, French or U.S. withholdings was proper under the Charter. The question then becomes one of applying U.N. Charter article 19. We pick up the story of the Soviet Union and France in 1963, after the I.C.J. had given its opinion that the peacekeeping expenses were "expenses of the Organization," and after the General Assembly had accepted the Advisory Opinion.[c]

M. WHITEMAN, DIGEST OF INTERNATIONAL LAW
Vol. 13, at 323–27, 330–32 (1968).

When the Fourth Special Session of the General Assembly opened on May 14, 1963, the Secretary–General notified the President of the General Assembly (Zafrulla Khan) that "one Member State, Haiti, is in arrears in the payment of its financial contribution to the United Nations within the terms of Article 19 of the Charter". In acknowledging the Secretary–General's letter, the President of the General Assembly wrote in part:

> I would have made an announcement drawing the attention of the Assembly to the loss of voting rights in the Assembly of the Member State just mentioned, under the first sentence of Article 19, had a formal count of vote taken place in the presence of a representative of that State at the opening plenary meeting. As no such vote took place, and as the representative of Haiti was not present, this announcement became unnecessary.

Haiti paid a portion of its arrears before its representatives appeared in Plenary Session or in the Fifth Committee, the only main committee which sat during the Special Session of the General Assembly. [See 58 Am.J.Int'l L. 753, 759–60 (1964).]

On June 10, 1963, the Soviet Representative addressed a letter to the Secretary–General in which he stated his Government's position with respect to article 19 of the United Nations Charter. He declared:

> It is self-evident that the above provision [the first sentence] of Article 19 must be applied in strict conformity with those provi-

---

c. See G.A.Res. 1854 (XVII), Dec. 19, 1962. The vote was 76 to 17, with 8 abstentions. See 17 GAOR, Plenary, 1199th meeting, at 1199.

sions of the Charter which lay down the procedure for taking decisions regarding the suspension of the rights of Member States. Such provisions are contained in Article 18, paragraph 2, of the Charter, which reads: "Decisions of the General Assembly on important questions shall be made by a two-thirds majority of the Members present and voting. These questions shall include * * * the suspension of the rights and privileges of membership * * *."

Thus, it is clear from Article 18 that the question whether or not a particular State Member of the United Nations shall retain its right to vote in the General Assembly can be decided only by the General Assembly itself and a decision on the suspension of that right requires a two-thirds majority of the Members present and voting.

He stated further in the same letter:

In the light of the whole of Article 19 there is no basis whatever for any automatic deprivation of a Member State's right to vote in the General Assembly. The Charter does not permit it. Therefore, it is impossible to recognize as having legal force an approach to this question which in violation of the United Nations Charter would consist of the President of the General Assembly declaring, without the Assembly itself having considered and decided the question in accordance with Article 18, that a particular Member of the Organization had lost its right to vote in the General Assembly. Such an approach would be arbitrary and unlawful, contrary to the Charter of the United Nations.

In this letter I am not taking up the special question whether the provisions of Article 19 concerning a Member State's loss of the right to vote in the General Assembly can be applied at all if the arrears of that Member State exceed its two-year contribution to the United Nations budget because those arrears include payments due for "United Nations Operations in the Congo" or for covering other expenses which cannot be imposed on States Members of the United Nations as obligations. The position of the Soviet Government on these matters is well known. [U.N. Doc. A/5431 (1963).]

During the calendar year 1964, the arrears of several members of the United Nations exceeded their assessed contributions for 1962 and 1963. In February 1964 the Office of the Legal Adviser, Department of State, prepared a memorandum entitled "Article 19 of the Charter of the United Nations, Memorandum of Law". Its conclusions were summarized as follows:

(A) The first sentence of Article 19, which provides that a Member in arrears to a specified extent "shall have no vote in the General Assembly," entails no decision of the General Assembly to suspend a Member's vote; it is mandatory and automatic in effect. The second sentence, which provides that the General Assembly "may, nevertheless, permit such a Member to vote if it is satisfied that the failure to pay is due to conditions beyond the control of the Member", is permissive in effect * * *.

(B) The records of the San Francisco Conference demonstrate the intention of the drafters of the Charter that the application of the first sentence of Article 19 entail [sic] no decision of the General Assembly to suspend a Member's vote * * *.

(C) The practice of the United Nations confirms the plain meaning of Article 19 and the intention of the Charter's drafters * * *.

(D) The fact that a Member is in arrears within the terms of Article 19 is, by established practice, computed and reported by the Secretary–General, or reported by the Committee on Contributions on the basis of the computations of the Secretary–General * * *.

(E) Assessments for peacekeeping operations, including those for UNEF and ONUC, are included in the computation of arrears within the terms of Article 19 * * *.

* * *

(H) The analogous constitutional provisions and practice of the Specialized Agencies similarly show that (i) a provision that a Member in arrears "shall have no vote" is mandatory and automatic in effect, and (ii) the finding of the fact of arrears is a ministerial, mathematical calculation performed by the Secretariat and accepted by the Assembly without challenge * * *. [58 Am.J.Int'l L. 753–54 (1964).] *

* * *

[On December 1, 1964, an understanding was reached that issues other than those that could be disposed of without objection would not be raised during that session of the General Assembly.]

* * *

At a meeting of the Special Committee on August 16, 1965, the United States Representative (Goldberg) stated (in summary):

With regard to the specific question being dealt with by the Committee, he pointed out that the United States continued to believe that the concept of collective financial responsibility adopted by the United Nations in 1945 was a sound principle, that Article 17 of the Charter clearly empowered the General Assembly to assess and apportion among Member States "the expenses of the Organization", that the costs of peace-keeping operations, once assessed and apportioned by the Assembly, were expenses of the Organization within the meaning of Article 17—a proposition which had been upheld by the International Court of Justice and accepted by the General Assembly by an overwhelming vote * * *

* Reprinted with permission, c. The American Society of International Law.

and, finally, that Article 19 was clear beyond question about the sanction to be applied to Member States two years in arrears in the payment of their contributions.

* * *

On the other hand, on the basis of the entire history of the problem of the financing of peace-keeping operations, the United States had regretfully concluded that, at the present stage in the development of the United Nations, the General Assembly was not prepared to carry out the relevant provisions of the Charter, that is, to apply the loss-of-vote sanction provided in Article 19. The intransigence of a few Member States and their unwillingness to abide by the rule of law had created that state of affairs, and while the United States continued to maintain that Article 19 was applicable in present circumstances, it recognized that the consensus of opinion in the Assembly was against application of the Article and in favour of having the Assembly proceed normally. The United States would not seek to frustrate that consensus, since it was not in the interest of the world to have the Assembly's work immobilized, particularly in view of present world tensions. It agreed that the Assembly must proceed with its work. At the same time, if any Member State could make an exception to the principle of collective financial responsibility with respect to certain United Nations activities, the United States reserved the same option to make exceptions if, in its view, there were strong and compelling reasons to do so. There could be no double standard among the Members of the Organization. * * * [19 GAOR, Annex 21, U.N. Doc. A/5916/Add.1, at 86–87 (1965).]

APPLYING ARTICLE 19

With the change of position by the United States, no further attempts were made to apply the article 19 loss-of-vote sanction against the parties in default on UNEF and ONUC assessments. The twentieth session of the General Assembly (in 1965) then proceeded normally.

In 1968 the Legal Counsel of the U.N. Secretariat issued an opinion taking the same position as the United States on the automatic application of article 19, justifying the omission of two financially delinquent states (Haiti and the Dominican Republic) from a roll call vote in the General Assembly.[d] Can there be any serious doubt about the automatic loss of voting rights under article 19?

What exactly was the Soviet counter-argument? In assessing the Soviet position, consider, inter alia, the relationship between *article 5* and *article 18(2)*.

[d]. See 1968 U.N. Juridical Y.B. 186; U.N. Doc. A/7146 & Annex, 7 Int'l Legal Materials 1187, 1189 (1968).

If the U.S. legal argument on article 19 was strong, was it sound strategy to use it as the United States did? Could the same argument be used against the United States in the 1990s, if its arrearages equal the amount of its assessments for the previous two years?

When the plenary body of an international organization is faced with a constitutional question and disposes of it somehow, it arguably creates a precedent for future cases. Is the precedent stemming from the Soviet/French case simply that there is a double normative standard regarding the automatic application of article 19 to delinquent "expenses of the Organization," depending on the power of the delinquent member? Or is the precedent that each member state may opt out of an extraordinary assessment under article 17(2), at least if it makes a reasonable argument against the propriety of the assessment, and can thus legitimately avoid the article 19 sanction? Or was there no precedent after all, since no votes were taken until the United States and others had waived their right to object to voting by the Soviets or the French?

If you represented the United States government in the 1990s, would you make any of the arguments suggested by the questions above, if U.S. arrearages reach the point at which article 19 could be applied?

Is the problem of applying article 19 against powerful members different in kind from problems of applying sanctions in domestic law impartially among persons?

b. *Specialized Agencies*

The constituent instruments of a number of specialized agencies contain loss-of-vote sanctions. Some are similar to U.N. Charter article 19, in that they are automatic, at least on their face, if arrearages accumulate beyond a determined amount. These include the constituent instruments of the ILO, IMO and UNESCO. Others give the plenary body discretion to suspend voting rights or not, when arrearages occur. These include the constituent instruments of ICAO, WHO and WMO.

In this connection, compare ILO Constitution *article 13(4)* with ICAO Convention *article 62*. Do they differ in any material respect other than as to the automatic application of the sanction? Which is preferable?

Does the ILO provision differ in any significant respect from U.N. Charter article 19?

Consider also IMO Convention *article 56*. It is thought to be a particularly stringent example of the loss-of-vote sanction—too stringent, on its face, to be effective. What makes it more stringent than the comparable provisions in the other agencies' constituent instruments?

As this was written, an IMO working group was considering whether to propose amendments to article 56. Proposals being discussed included lengthening the period of arrearages before the sanction would apply; suspending any sanction if the member is making installment payments under an approved plan; and/or authorizing a more drastic sanction than loss of vote.[a] Would any or all of these be a good idea?

The World Health Organization's loss-of-vote sanction is in WHO Constitution *article 7*. Is its application limited to cases of financial delinquency? Is the sanction limited to loss of vote?

On at least one occasion, Arab states in WHO proposed that Israel's voting privileges be suspended under article 7. When the United States threatened to withdraw from WHO, the effort was abandoned for the time being.[b] Would it have been an ultra vires act if the Health Assembly had suspended Israel's voting privileges for the reasons given in its resolutions on the occupied territories, pages 551–54 supra?

When financially strapped member states have been in arrears to WHO, the Health Assembly typically has adopted resolutions expressing "serious concern," naming the delinquent states, but has decided not to suspend their voting privileges.[c] Is this another example of mobilization of shame? Is it appropriate?

Issues arise relating to equal application of the loss-of-vote sanction to powerful members in the specialized agencies as well as in the U.N. itself. By the autumn of 1990, the United States' arrearages to the Food and Agriculture Organization exceeded its assessments for the previous two years. As a result, it stood to lose its vote in the November 1991 FAO Conference unless it paid enough to reduce the arrearages below the two-year level.[d] The U.S. government took this quite seriously, and paid just enough to prevent the sanction from taking effect, even though it continued to disapprove of FAO's budget-setting practices.[e]

2. *Withholding Selected Benefits of Membership*

INTRODUCTORY NOTE

In a sense, the loss of voting rights amounts to the withholding of a benefit of membership, and thus could be considered under this heading. Instead, we will consider here the withholding of funds or services that an organization might supply to its members were it not for their failure, or alleged failure, to comply with some relevant norm. Sometimes a withholding-of-benefits sanction, in this sense, is expressly set forth in the organization's constituent instrument; sometimes not.

a. See IMO Docs. WGFM 9/5 (1990); WGFM 13/7 (1991); WGFM 14/6 (1991).

b. See 26 Keesing's Contemp. Archives 30252 (1980).

c. See, e.g., Res. WHA 40.5 (1987), naming 12 member states.

d. See FAO Constitution *art. III(4)*.

e. See Washington Weekly Rep., Jan. 11, 1991, p. 2.

Even in the absence of express authorization in the constituent instrument, organizations have found ways on occasion to apply selective loss-of-benefit sanctions.

a. Financial Organizations

An express withholding-of-benefits sanction is set forth in the International Monetary Fund Agreement, which authorizes the Fund to declare a member ineligible to use the Fund's general financial resources if the member fails to fulfill any of its obligations under the Agreement.[a] (Other provisions of the Fund Agreement set forth specific instances of failure to comply with the letter or purposes of the Agreement that can also lead to a declaration of ineligibility.) If the ineligibility does not induce the appropriate corrective measures by the member within "a reasonable period," the Fund may suspend the member's voting rights, and could ultimately expel the member.[b]

Since its inception in 1945, the International Monetary Fund has had currencies to make available to member governments in balance-of-payments difficulties. Each member pays into the Fund monetary assets equivalent to its designated quota. The quotas reflect roughly the financial strengths of members, and are adjusted from time to time. Each member pays 75 percent of its quota in its own currency, and the remaining 25 percent in currencies acceptable to the Fund or in the Fund's own special drawing rights. The credit created by the 25 percent payment is known as the member's "reserve tranche."

A member state in balance-of-payments difficulties may request that the Fund allow it to draw stronger currencies than its own, from the Fund's holdings of other members' currencies. When it does draw on the Fund, it actually buys other currencies in exchange for its own, with an obligation to repurchase its own currency in the future. Unless other members have been drawing out its currency, this would increase the Fund's holdings of its currency above 75 percent of its quota. When the drawing brings the Fund's holdings to no more than 100 percent of its quota, the drawing is said to be in the reserve tranche. Beyond the reserve tranche, a member may draw against four additional "credit tranches," each generally equal to 25 percent of the member's quota, until the Fund's holdings of its currency equal 200 percent of its quota. A member may draw additional amounts if the Fund grants a waiver of the 200 percent limitation. The Fund has done so in certain well-defined circumstances.

During the first twenty years of the Fund's existence, only one member was declared ineligible to use these resources, although another became ineligible without any declaration, under a provision no longer in the Fund Agreement. A third withdrew from the Fund after

---

a. See Fund Agreement *art. XXVI, section 2(a)*. A declaration of ineligibility may be adopted by a simple majority of the weighted votes in the Fund.

b. See Fund Agreement art. XXVI, section 2(b) & 2(c).

ineligibility proceedings against it were begun.[c] The Fund's General Counsel referred to the early experience as "a deliberate policy of restraint."[d]

In recent years, however, the restraint has faded. By September 1991 the Fund had declared twelve member states ineligible to use its general resources. Almost all of these declarations came after 1984. This reflects both the increased seriousness of debt-servicing problems in many third-world countries, and the Fund's increasing frustration with members that do not appear to make an adequate effort to meet their repurchase obligations.

Presumably, the advantages of this tougher enforcement policy are that it brings home to members the need to take decisive action to correct budget-deficit and balance-of-payments problems, rather than allowing them to assume that the Fund's resources would always be available to bail them out; and it conserves scarce Fund resources by denying them to governments that appear to be making inefficient use of them. Are there disadvantages, as well?

On a more informal level, the Fund also makes use of a withholding-of-benefits sanction. It involves graduated severity of terms and conditions for the normal use of the Fund's resources. For a member state to have access to funds in the first credit tranche, the Fund requires only that the member demonstrate that it is making reasonable efforts to overcome its balance-of-payments difficulties. But things get tougher in the credit tranches beyond the first (the "upper credit tranches"). In these tranches the Fund almost always requires a stand-by or extended arrangement under which the funds are released over a period of one to three years, rather than all at once. The process is described in the excerpt below:

> The length of stand-by arrangements has typically been between 12 and 18 months in recent years, but may extend up to 3 years. [Extended arrangements typically run for 3 years, but they may be lengthened to 4 years].
>
> Purchases of the amounts available under a stand-by arrangement in the upper credit tranches or under an extended arrangement are "phased"—that is, they are made available in installments at specified intervals during the period of the arrangement. The member's right to draw is subject to its observance of the performance criteria and other specified conditions. These criteria typically cover credit policy, government or public sector borrowing requirements, and policies on trade and payments restrictions. Performance criteria also frequently cover the contracting or net use of short-, medium-, and long-term foreign debt, as well as changes in the level of external reserves.

[c.] See Gold, The "Sanctions" of the International Monetary Fund, 66 Am.J.Int'l L. 737, 756 (1972).

[d.] Id. at 755.

Performance criteria allow the member and the IMF to assess the member's progress in carrying out policies during the stand-by (or an extended) arrangement, and they signal the need for possible corrective policies. When performance criteria have not been observed, further purchases are permitted only after the IMF and the member reach understandings—following consultations and Executive Board action—for the resumption of purchases.[e]

This process is known as conditionality: access to the Fund's resources beyond a basic level is conditioned on observance of the performance criteria. It gives the Fund leverage in a much less abrasive way than would occur if the Fund formally threatened to declare members ineligible to use the Fund's resources whenever they failed to remedy their balance-of-payments problems.

Conditionality has caused some difficulties for members, especially the developing countries. Many of them have regarded the conditions as excessively stringent, and in some cases domestic political unrest has followed adoption by the government of unpopular economic decisions suggested or imposed by the Fund. Sometimes there have been riots after the Fund and foreign private banks have made their funds conditional on closer adherence by governments to stabilization programs that have included large reductions in government subsidies, or removal of price controls, for such staples as basic food items and gasoline.

In 1979 the Fund's Executive Board adopted guidelines on conditionality.[f] Despite continuing discontent from the representatives of some developing countries, the Executive Board reaffirmed the guidelines in 1988.

The guidelines contain a number of standards and procedures, including some designed to alleviate developing countries' concerns. For example, paragraph 4 of the guidelines says:

> In helping members to devise adjustment programs, the Fund will pay due regard to the domestic social and political objectives, the economic priorities, and the circumstances of members, including the causes of their balance of payments problems.

The key provision in the guidelines, though, is paragraph 9:

> The number and content of performance criteria may vary because of the diversity of problems and institutional arrangements of members. Performance criteria will be limited to those that are necessary to evaluate implementation of the program with a view to ensuring the achievement of its objectives. Performance criteria will normally be confined to (i) macroeconomic variables, and (ii) those necessary to implement specific provisions of the Articles or

e. IMF Survey, Supplement on the IMF, at 15–16 (1992).

f. Executive Board Decision No. 6056–(79/38), March 2, 1979, in Selected Decisions and Selected Documents of the International Monetary Fund 60 (17th Issue 1992).

policies adopted under them. Performance criteria may relate to other variables only in exceptional cases when they are essential for the effectiveness of the member's program because of their macroeconomic impact.

The Fund's former General Counsel, Sir Joseph Gold, has provided a commentary on the guidelines. Regarding paragraph 9, he said in part:

> Specific prices of commodities or services, specific taxes, or other detailed measures to increase revenues or to reduce expenditures would not be considered macroeconomic variables. The Fund may wish to know, however, what a member's intentions are on matters of this kind in order to have a view on whether there is a reasonable prospect that the member will be able to meet performance criteria.
>
> The restraint that the Fund observes by confining itself to macroeconomic variables is not absolute if other economic variables meet the restrictive test spelled out in the last sentence of Paragraph 9. Sometimes, a member may wish to have certain variables treated as performance criteria even though the Fund would not consider them macroeconomic, in order to strengthen the government's control of domestic economic developments.
>
> Paragraph 9 recognizes that there can be no fixed list of performance criteria. In view of the effect of excessive demand in the economy on the balance of payments, however, a performance criterion that is always employed is a ceiling on the expansion of credit by the central bank or the banking system. Another performance criterion in constant use is directed against the introduction of multiple currency practices, the introduction or intensification of restrictions on payments and transfers for current international transactions, or the introduction or intensification, for balance of payments reasons, of restrictions on trade.[g]

Would it be permissible, under these guidelines, for the Fund to make it a performance criterion that a government eliminate its subsidies for milk, bread and gasoline? Is the Fund well equipped to consider any noneconomic implications of such a criterion?

The Fund has said, "While questions of income distribution do not form part of IMF conditionality, the IMF attaches considerable importance to improving program design to protect the poor from the possible short-run adverse effects of policy adjustments."[h] How could this be done without interfering in the domestic policies of members, if the short-run effect is a substantial increase in the price of staples? Should the Fund ignore questions of income distribution?

[g] Gold, Conditionality 33 (IMF Pamphlet Series, No. 31, 1979). Reprinted by permission of the International Monetary Fund.

[h] IMF Survey, Supplement on the IMF 13 (1992).

Why might members sometimes wish to have certain variables treated as performance criteria even though the Fund would not ordinarily treat them as such?

THE WORLD BANK

The World Bank, of course, also has money to lend—or to withhold. With its affiliated institutions, the International Development Association and the International Finance Corporation, it invests in development projects in low-income member states. Loans by the Bank have typically gone heavily into agriculture and infrastructure (power, transportation, telecommunications), and into industrial projects, although in recent years the Bank has branched out into other fields as well, such as education, health and environmental preservation. By 1990, the Bank was making loan commitments of about $15 billion annually.[i]

Because the Bank raises most of its funds in the capital markets of its industrialized members, it must protect its credit standing.[j] Thus it must be able to withhold loans when repayment prospects are poor, or when economic conditions in the borrowing country are such that the loans are unlikely to be productive.[k] The Bank Agreement requires the Bank in making a loan to "pay due regard to the prospects that the borrower * * * will be in a position to meet its obligations under the loan. * * *."[l]

The power to withhold loans on creditworthiness grounds would amount to nothing more than normal banking practice, and would have little to do with sanctions, were it not for the additional factors to which we now turn. First, before the Bank makes a loan it normally evaluates the economic policies and performance of the applicant member, and may extract an informal commitment from the member that it will change certain general economic policies as a condition to receiving the loan. Moreover, in the loan agreement itself, more detailed promises may be made by the member to follow designated practices deemed by the Bank to promote the efficient completion and operation of the financed project, or designed to foster economic efficiency in the country. These might have to do with the rates to be charged by a financed public utility to assure profitable operation, or appointment of competent management personnel, or other controls.[m]

If a promise in a loan agreement were violated, there might be a double-barreled sanction (wholly apart from any judicial remedy): with-

---

i. See 1990 World Bank Ann.Rep. 13.

j. Its affiliate, the International Development Association, gets its capital by appropriations from the governments of its industrialized members, and thus does not have the same credit rating constraint.

k. See generally B. de Vries, Remaking the World Bank 55–77 (1987).

l. Bank Agreement art. III, section 4(v).

m. See Nurick, Certain Aspects of the Law and Practice of the International Bank for Reconstruction and Development, in The Effectiveness of International Decisions 100, 103–14 (S. Schwebel ed. 1971).

holding of any disbursements not yet made on the loan, and refusal to make additional loans. Consequently the Bank has considerable power to establish and enforce specific policies regarding economic development in borrowing member states. It has no such power regarding economic growth policies in its industrialized member states, since they do not borrow from it. In this respect, the Bank's financial leverage is less widely felt than the IMF's, since even the industrialized states sometimes need to draw on the Fund's resources for balance-of-payments purposes.

The World Bank and the IMF do not always hold all the cards in their dealings with members, or—if they do—they do not always play them. Consider the following two incidents.

In 1980 the government of Jamaica decided to forego further drawings under its IMF stand-by arrangement, rather than try to meet the Fund's conditions calling for substantial restrictions on government spending. Jamaica had already accumulated drawings equal to about 360 percent of its quota—more, in relation to quota, than any other member state. It was not clear how Jamaica would be able to meet its obligation to repurchase its own currency under the circumstances.

In 1986 the World Bank approved a loan to Argentina, to be disbursed in two tranches. Disbursement of the second tranche was conditioned upon Argentina's meeting a condition attached by the Bank. When Argentina failed to meet the condition, the Bank's Executive Board, "after a heated debate," approved disbursement anyway.[n]

The World Bank Agreement contains provisions designed to preclude non-banking considerations from creeping into loan decisions. Thus, Bank Agreement article IV, section 10, says that the Bank and its officers "[shall not] be influenced in their decisions by the political character of the member or members concerned. Only economic considerations shall be relevant to their decisions, and these considerations shall be weighed impartially in order to achieve [the Bank's purposes, including the supplementing of private capital by providing financing for productive uses]." In addition, Bank Agreement article V, section 5(c), says that the President, officers and staff of the Bank owe their duty entirely to the Bank, and obligates member states to "refrain from all attempts to influence any of them in the discharge of their duties."

Charges have sometimes been made that the Bank, despite these admonitions, has withheld loans as a sanction against politically-motivated conduct of some member states deviating from the norms favored by the Bank's more influential members. Until the mid–1970s, the charges focused largely on the Bank's policy not to lend to a member state that had expropriated foreign property without compensation, or

[n] Bandow, What's Still Wrong With the World Bank, 33 Orbis 73, 85–86 (1989).

that had defaulted in payment of an external debt. For example, Peru expropriated the properties of the American-owned International Petroleum Company in 1968, claiming that no compensation was owed because IPC did not have title to the minerals it had been exploiting and thus owed the Peruvian government the profits from their sale. The amount allegedly owed to Peru would have provided more than a complete setoff to IPC's compensation claim. Other Peruvian expropriations of American-owned properties followed. From 1968 until 1973 (when the U.S. government began to engage in fruitful negotiations with Peru regarding compensation for expropriated properties), the Bank authorized no new development loans for Peru.

In the mid-1970s, questions about possible politicization of the Bank's lending policies shifted from expropriation to human rights. In 1977 the U.S. Congress enacted legislation authorizing continued participation by the United States in the World Bank and in other international financial institutions, raising the human rights issue. It provides in part, as later amended:

PUBLIC LAW 95–118, SECTION 701, AS AMENDED
Originally enacted, Oct. 3, 1977.
22 U.S.C.A. § 262d.

(a) The United States Government, in connection with its voice and vote in the International Bank for Reconstruction and Development, [its affiliates and other development banks] shall advance the cause of human rights, including by seeking to channel assistance toward countries other than those whose governments engage in—

> (1) a pattern of gross violations of internationally recognized human rights, such as torture or cruel, inhumane, or degrading treatment or punishment, prolonged detention without charges, or other flagrant denial to life, liberty, and the security of person; or

> (2) provide refuge to individuals committing acts of international terrorism by hijacking aircraft.

* * *

(d) The United States Government, in connection with its voice and vote in the institutions listed in subsection (a) of this section, shall seek to channel assistance to projects which address basic human needs of the people of the recipient country.

* * *

(f) The United States Executive Directors of the institutions listed in subsection (a) of this section are authorized and instructed to oppose any loan, any extension of financial assistance, or any technical assistance to any country described in subsection (a)(1) or (2) of this section, unless such assistance is directed specifically to programs which serve the basic human needs of the citizens of such country.

THE LEGISLATION IN PRACTICE

While the bill that became 22 U.S.C.A. section 262d was being considered by the Senate, its floor manager (Senator Sparkman) said this about the provision that became section 262d(f):

> Before the Senate votes * * *, it is important to be clear about the meaning of the word "oppose" as it is used in subsection [262d(f)].
>
> Subsection [262d(f)] requires U.S. Executive Directors of specified international financial institutions to oppose assistance to any country described in subsection (a)(1) or (2) of the bill. Subsection [262d(f)] does not require the U.S. Executive Director to vote "no" on any assistance. * * * The Executive Director could, for example, engage in informal efforts to persuade his counterparts representing other governments that a loan should not be extended because of the human rights record of the recipient government. Such persuasive representations could stop a loan before it is presented to the Board. It was the clear intention of the [House-Senate] conference that "oppose" meant voting against, abstaining, or voting "present." º

Since 1977, U.S. representatives to multilateral development banks have on several occasions voted against, or abstained on, proposed loans on human rights grounds. For example, after the June 1989 Tiananmen Square incident in China, in which the Chinese authorities used armed force to quash student demonstrators urging democratic reforms, the United States government decided to withhold support for World Bank loans to China. Since the United States has more than 17 percent of the weighted votes among the Bank's Executive Directors, and since the U.S. position inevitably influences others, this resulted in a substantial reduction in World Bank loans to China. The United States softened its position somewhat on China about a year later, and then lifted its opposition to new loans in the autumn of 1990, after China had supported U.S.-sponsored U.N. Security Council resolutions on the Persian Gulf crisis.

When the U.S. Executive Director of the World Bank withheld support for loans to China because of the Tiananmen Square incident, did the United States violate Bank Agreement article IV, section 10, or article V, section 5(c), page 570 supra? Would it matter whether he actually voted "no" or simply tried to persuade others to withhold their support?

In answering these questions, consider the opinion of the World Bank's General Counsel, given in the context of a debate over a

---

o. 123 Cong.Rec. 30166 (1977).

proposed loan to a member whose human rights record had been raised by some of the Bank's Executive Directors:

1. The Board of Executive Directors, as an organ of the Bank, is subject to the provision of Article IV, Section 10 of the Bank's Articles of Agreement and is therefore prohibited from interfering in the political affairs of any member or from being influenced in its decisions by the political character of the member concerned. Only economic considerations, which are weighed impartially, are relevant to the Board's decisions. However, political events which have a bearing on the economic conditions of a member or on the member's ability to implement a project or the Bank's ability to supervise the project may be taken into consideration by the Board.

2. An Executive Director is an official of the Bank who is appointed or elected by a member or members of the Bank and whose votes depend on the voting strength of the member or members who appointed or elected him, owes his duty both to the Bank and his "constituency." He may express the views of such a "constituency" and vote on its instructions, but he may not split his votes. However, he is not to act simply as an ambassador of the government or governments which appointed or elected him and is expected to exercise his individual judgment in the interest of the Bank and its members as a whole. Members of the Bank are under an obligation not to influence the Bank's President and staff in the discharge of their duties, and Executive Directors are under the duty not to act as the instrumentality of members to exert such prohibited influence.[p]

If an Executive Director of the Bank is an "official of the Bank," does that mean he or she is an "officer" within the meaning of article IV, section 10? The World Bank's Annual Report lists Executive Directors and officers separately, with the officers being such people as the President, Vice Presidents, and heads of departments.[q] The Bank Agreement refers to "officers and staff" as persons appointed by the President,[r] while the Executive Directors are appointed by members or elected by members' representatives on the Board of Governors.[s]

If the Bank's Executive Directors are not "officers," would article IV, section 10 apply to them or to their governments? If they are "officials of the Bank," but not "officers," would article V, section 5(c) apply to them?

If the World Bank rejects a proposed loan because of the borrowing government's gross violations of internationally-recognized human

---

[p.] Shihata, Prohibition of Political Activities Under the IBRD Articles of Agreement and Its Relevance to the Work of the Executive Directors (1987) (unpublished World Bank document, quoted in Shihata, The World Bank and Human Rights: An Analysis of the Legal Issues and the Record of Achievements, 17 Denver J. Int'l L. & Pol'y 39, 46 (1988); also in I. Shihata, The World Bank in a Changing World 106–07 (1991)).

[q.] See, e.g., 1990 World Bank Ann. Rep. 225–29.

[r.] Bank Agreement art. V, section 5(d).

[s.] Id. art. V, section 4(b).

rights, would the Bank, itself, be acting inconsistently with Bank Agreement article IV, section 10?

In May 1992 the Bank announced, in as delicate a manner as possible, that the fourth Consultative Group Meeting for Malawi (consisting of representatives from the Bank, other interested international bodies and the major donor countries) had decided not to make new loans to Malawi, except for humanitarian assistance, until progress had been made toward "good governance" in Malawi. Malawi at the time was a one-party state under the control of its "life president," Hastings Kamuzu Banda. According to the World Bank's press release:

> Delegates underlined * * * that good governance is a critical element for equitable economic development. * * * [D]onors continued to express deep concern about the lack of progress in the area of basic freedoms and human rights, and accordingly stressed the need for early implementation of appropriate reforms. Donors are seeking tangible and irreversible evidence of a basic transformation in the way Malawi approaches these matters, so that there is [a] fundamental shift in the way human rights in Malawi are viewed. Donors reiterated that governance issues are central not only to progress in poverty alleviation and human rights, but also to the sustainability of Malawi's economic reform program.[t]

Because the World Bank co-finances with donor countries, any decision by those countries to suspend loans affects what the Bank does. Does this excuse the Bank from complying with Bank Agreement article IV, section 10 in a case like this? Did it in fact comply, given the link asserted in its press release between governance issues and sustained economic reform?

Compare the World Bank Agreement with the approach taken in the Agreement Establishing the European Bank for Reconstruction and Development.[u] The European Bank was created in 1990 to help revive the economies of Central and East European countries after the demise of communism there. Article 1 sets forth the European Bank's purpose:

> [T]he purpose of the Bank shall be to foster the transition towards open market oriented economies and to promote private and entrepreneurial initiative in the Central and Eastern European countries committed to and applying the principles of multiparty democracy, pluralism and market economics.

Article 32(2) of the European Bank Agreement is the counterpart to World Bank Agreement article IV, section 10. Article 32(2) says:

> The Bank, its President, Vice–President(s), officers and staff shall in their decisions take into account only considerations relevant to the Bank's purpose, functions and operations, as set out in this Agreement. Such considerations shall be weighed impartially

---

t. World Bank Press Release, Paris, May 13, 1992.

u. May 29, 1990, 29 Int'l Legal Materials 1077 (1990).

in order to achieve and carry out the purpose and functions of the Bank.

If an Eastern European government uses armed force to put down a pro-democracy demonstration in its capital, would the issues relating to withholding of loans by the European Bank be the same as they were in the World Bank after the Tiananmen Square incident?

Is there any good reason why the World Bank Agreement should differ from the European Bank Agreement in this respect?

b. *Nonfinancial Organizations*

The World Health Organization and the International Atomic Energy Agency are two nonfinancial organizations with express authority to withhold services and other selected benefits from members. WHO Constitution *article 7* permits the Health Assembly (WHO's plenary body) to suspend WHO's health-related services to a member in arrears in its financial obligations "or in other exceptional circumstances." IAEA Statute *article XII.A.7*, concerning safeguard agreements for nuclear projects, provides that if a recipient state fails to take requested steps to correct a deficiency within a reasonable time, the IAEA may "suspend or terminate assistance and withdraw any materials and equipment made available by the Agency or a member in furtherance of the project." The decision would be made by the 35-member Board of Governors.

Are the WHO and IAEA sanctions likely to be equally effective?

Occasionally, international organizations have withheld selected benefits, or have threatened to do so, without express authority in their constituent instruments. For example, in 1971 the ICAO Assembly decided not to invite South Africa to any ICAO meetings other than those the ICAO (Chicago) Convention expressly held open to all members, and denied it access to ICAO documents or communications except insofar as the Convention specifically required that they be provided or insofar as the documents were for meetings South Africa could attend.[a] It was clear that the action was taken because of South Africa's human rights policies, rather than because of its policies relating to civil aviation. Since the Chicago Convention deals only with civil aviation, and in any event does not contemplate the sanction adopted, there was doubt about the propriety of the ICAO Assembly's action.[b]

Israel, too, has been the focus of withholding-of-benefits sanctions not expressly contemplated by the sanctioning organizations' constituent instruments.

Beginning shortly after the end of the Six-Day War in 1967, Israel has carried out projects involving selective archaeological excavations

---

a. ICAO Assembly Res. A18-4, Resolutions Adopted by the Assembly and Index to Documentation, 18th Sess., ICAO Doc. 8958, A18-RES, at 28 (1971).

b. For further materials on this, see the first edition of this book, at pages 543-47.

at historic sites in the city of Jerusalem. This has aroused opposition in the U.N. and in UNESCO, the specialized agency directly concerned with the cultural heritage of mankind.

It has been argued that Israel has violated the Hague Convention for the Protection of Cultural Property in the Event of Armed Conflict,[c] to which Israel and the surrounding Arab states are parties. That Convention defines "cultural property" as, inter alia, archaeological sites, and provides in article 5 that any party occupying any part of the territory of another party "shall as far as possible support the competent national authorities of the occupied country in safeguarding and preserving its cultural property."

Although article 5 does not expressly set forth a duty not to excavate, the U.N. Special Committee to Investigate Israeli Practices Affecting the Human Rights of the Population of the Occupied Territories has construed it in tandem with a 1956 UNESCO General Conference resolution that stated, "In the event of armed conflict, any Member State occupying the territory of another State should refrain from carrying out archaeological excavations in the occupied territory." Noting also that the occupying power is placed in a secondary position to the occupied country under article 5 of the Hague Convention, the U.N. Special Committee concluded that the Convention should be interpreted as precluding archaeological excavations by an occupying state, and has considered Israel an occupying state.[d]

On a number of occasions before 1974, the UNESCO General Conference called on Israel to refrain from carrying out archaeological excavations. In 1974, it adopted the resolution below, by a vote of 54–21–25.

UNESCO RESOLUTION ON ISRAEL
UNESCO General Conference, Nov. 20, 1974.
Resolution 3.427, 1 Records of the General Conference,
18th Sess., Resolutions, at 59.

The General Conference,

Taking into account the importance attached by Unesco, in accordance with its Constitution, to the protection and preservation of the world heritage of monuments of historic or scientific value,

* * *

Aware of the exceptional importance of the cultural property in the Old City of Jerusalem, not only to the countries directly concerned but to all humanity, on account of their unique cultural, historical and religious value,

---

c. May 14, 1954, 249 U.N.T.S. 240.
d. See U.N. Doc. A/9148, at 12–15 (1973). See also Nafziger, UNESCO–Centered Management of International Conflict Over Cultural Property, 27 Hastings L.J. 1051, 1055–60 (1976).

Recalling that since the fifteenth session of the General Conference (1968) the Organization has urgently called on Israel to desist from any archaeological excavations in the City of Jerusalem and from any alteration of its features or its cultural and historical character, particularly with regard to Christian and Islamic religious sites [citing General Conference resolutions],

Bearing in mind that, at its seventeenth session, the General Conference, in resolution 3.422:

(a) *Noted* "that Israel persists in not complying with the relevant resolutions and that its attitude prevents this Organization from undertaking the mission which is incumbent upon it under the terms of the Constitution";

(b) *Invited* "the Director-General to continue his efforts to establish the effective presence of Unesco in the City of Jerusalem and thus make possible the actual implementation of the resolutions adopted by the General Assembly and the Executive Board for that purpose";

Recalling that the Executive Board, at its 94th session (decision 4.4.1):

(a) was convinced by the purport of the Director-General's report on the mission of his representative to the City of Jerusalem that "Israel persists in not complying with the relevant resolutions and that its attitude prevents this Organization from undertaking the mission which is incumbent upon it under the terms of its Constitution",

(b) condemned Israel's persistent violation of the resolutions adopted by the General Conference and the Executive Board in this regard,

(c) has submitted the matter to the General Conference to take such appropriate measures as are within its competence,

Whereas Israel, in persistently violating the resolutions adopted by the General Conference and the Executive Board with a view to preserving the cultural heritage of the City of Jerusalem, defies wilfully the world conscience and the international community,

Whereas the General Conference cannot remain passive before Israel's continuous persistence in violating its resolutions,

Guided by precedents adopted by the General Conference since its fourteenth session upon the persistent violation of its resolutions and the violation of the aims stipulated in the Constitution [citing resolutions],

1. *Reaffirms* all the resolutions mentioned above and insists on their implementation;

2. *Condemns* Israel for its attitude which is contradictory to the aims of the Organization as stated in its Constitution by its persistence in altering the historical features of the City of Jerusalem and by

undertaking excavations which constitute a danger to its monuments, subsequent to its illegal occupation of this city;

3. *Invites* the Director–General to withhold assistance from Israel in the fields of education, science and culture until such time as it scrupulously respects the aforementioned resolutions and decisions.

THE AFTERMATH

On the next day the General Conference rejected, by a vote of 48–38–31, an Israeli resolution seeking inclusion of Israel in UNESCO's European regional group. That left Israel as the only UNESCO member not belonging to one of its regional groups. Since regional activities were becoming increasingly important in UNESCO, this left Israel largely isolated from the work of the organization.

The United States representative, explaining why he had voted against resolution 3.427, above, said that "the essential objective of this resolution is not, and I repeat, not, the preservation or protection of historical sites and monuments. Whatever the claimed intentions of those who sponsored it might be, the resolution in fact imposes a completely unjustified sanction upon a Member State of this Organization for reasons that seem to us to be largely motivated by political considerations." [e]

The Israeli rebuttal to the charge contained in resolution 3.427 is reflected in the following excerpt.

STATEMENT OF THE AMERICAN JEWISH CONGRESS
February 1975.
Hearings on Review of the 1974 General Assembly and the United States Position in the United Nations, before a Subcomm. of the House Comm. on Foreign Affairs, 94th Cong., 1st Sess., at 82.

These actions were accompanied by factual allegations which contradict the reports of UNESCO's own Director–General, whose representatives visited Jerusalem many times in the past several years. For example, the Director–General's latest report, based on visits to Jerusalem in December, 1973 and April, 1974 by Professor Raymond Lemaire of the Roman Catholic University of Louvain, reaffirmed the conclusion of prior studies that Israeli authorities have consistently and painstakingly cared for all religious and historical sites there. Referring to the archaeological excavations at the foot of the Temple Mount, the report [f] stated:

> The excavations are being carried out by a perfectly well-qualified team of experts of various kinds, who are extremely attentive to all aspects and to all the periods of which remains have been found on the site. The same care is expended on the preser-

---

e. 1974 Digest of United States Practice in International Law 45.

f. [UNESCO Doc. 94 Ex/14, Annex (1974). Ed.]

vation of remains of the Omayyad palaces as on those of the Herodian period.

The report further stated that the excavations in the Old City's Jewish Quarter were being

> carried out with the utmost care and employing the most expert methods. These excavations have already led to discoveries of the utmost importance in relation to the history of Jerusalem.

CONGRESS AND THE UNESCO RESPONSE

The action by the General Conference sparked an angry reaction in many Western political, educational and scientific circles. One manifestation of that anger was the decision by the United States Congress in December 1974 to withhold the U.S. contribution to the UNESCO budget.[g] The Western reaction prompted the Director General of UNESCO to respond in part as follows.

STATEMENT ON ISRAEL BY AMADOU MAHTAR M'BOW, DIRECTOR–GENERAL OF UNESCO
UNESCO Courier, Jan. 1975, at 34.

* * *

Israel has neither been ousted from Unesco nor from any regional group within the Organization. Israel continues to be a member of Unesco, as one of the 135 Member States, which make up the Organization.

* * *

During the eighteenth session of the General Conference, Israel, like Canada and the United States of America, introduced a draft resolution with a view to being included "in the list of countries entitled to participate in the European regional activities in which the representative character of States is an important factor." While the resolutions referring to Canada and the United States were adopted, the one tabled by Israel was rejected by the General Conference, that is, by the duly accredited representatives of the governments of the Member States of Unesco.

Thus, Israel is in exactly the same situation it was in prior to the eighteenth session of the General Conference.

* * *

The second resolution "invites the Director–General to withhold assistance from Israel in the fields of education, science and culture

---

g. These withholdings were temporary. By October 1978 the United States had paid all its arrears and current dues to UNESCO.

until such time as it scrupulously respects the resolutions and decisions" of the Executive Board and the General Conference.

This resolution is based essentially on [several U.N. resolutions], as well as on the decisions of the Unesco General Conference at its fifteenth and seventeenth sessions and of the Unesco Executive Board at its 82nd, 83rd, 88th, 89th and 90th sessions. When it adopted a new resolution, the General Conference considered that the Israeli Government had not heeded the urgent appeals made to it since 1968 calling on it to "desist from any archaeological excavations in the city of Jerusalem and from any modifications of its features or its cultural and historical character, particularly with regard to Christian and Islamic religious sites." Noting that the excavations and works were continuing which it considered susceptible of endangering the Christian and Islamic sites, the General Conference decided six years after issuing its first notification, to condemn the attitude of Israel, which it considered "contradictory to the aims of the Organization as stated in its Constitution * * *."

LEGITIMATE SANCTIONS?

UNESCO Constitution *article I, sections 1 and 2(c)* set forth the Organization's purposes and its functions as they might relate to the Israeli excavations. Express sanctions appear only in *article II, sections 4 and 5* (suspension and expulsion from UNESCO, tied to suspension and expulsion from the U.N.), and in *article IV, section 8(b)* (loss of vote for financial arrearages).

Does UNESCO have the authority to impose a withholding-of-benefit sanction on a member state, as it purported to do in Resolution 3.427?

Was the essence of the UNESCO position that (a) Israel was violating the 1954 Hague Convention; (b) Israel was endangering historical monuments, thus interfering with UNESCO's effort to accomplish its purposes; or (c) Israel was ignoring UNESCO resolutions addressed to it? Does the answer bear on the legitimacy of the sanction?

If Israel's excavations actually were damaging monuments in Jerusalem, the UNESCO resolution could be said to be an attempt to protect monuments of history, in accordance with UNESCO Constitution article I, section 2(c). But if Israel was simply researching the history of Jerusalem and making its findings available to others, without damaging existing monuments, UNESCO presumably should have been supporting the work rather than taking punitive action on account of it—unless *any* excavations by Israel would violate the 1954 Hague Convention, as alleged by the U.N. Special Committee. If we assume that the majority of UNESCO member states were truly concerned about possible damage to existing monuments and upholding international norms, and if mere diplomacy would not have deterred Israel from going ahead with the excavations, do you suppose there was anything else UNESCO could have done to deal even-handedly with the problem?

Israel was not dependent on UNESCO for assistance in education, science or culture, and in fact was contributing more financially to the Organization in 1974 than it received in return. Was the essence of Resolution 3.427 the withholding of benefits or something else?

The 1976 UNESCO General Conference admitted Israel to the European regional group. At that session, and at each session since 1974, the General Conference has adopted a resolution expressing disapproval of Israel's activities regarding the heritage and historical sites of Jerusalem, and has reaffirmed its previous resolutions on the subject. It has not, however, repeated its attempt to impose a withholding-of-benefit sanction, even though Israel has continued to excavate in and around Jerusalem. Does that amount to tacit acknowledgment that the sanction is ineffective?

Israel has also had problems with the International Atomic Energy Agency, stemming from Israel's air attack on an Iraqi nuclear reactor in June 1981. Israel asserted that the attack, which destroyed the reactor, was in self-defense as a result of a continuing threat of nuclear attack by Iraq. In September 1981, the IAEA General Conference (the plenary body of IAEA) adopted a resolution by a vote of 51 in favor, 8 opposed, with 27 abstentions, suspending technical assistance to Israel:

RESOLUTION OF IAEA GENERAL CONFERENCE REGARDING TECHNICAL ASSISTANCE TO ISRAEL
Sept. 26, 1981.
23 IAEA Bull., No. 4, at 45 (1981).

The General Conference,

Having considered the agenda item *Military attack on Iraqi nuclear research centre and its implications for the Agency,*

Recalling the resolution adopted by the Board of Governors on 12 June 1981 on the same subject, which *inter alia* strongly condemned Israel for this premeditated and unjustified attack on the Iraqi nuclear research centre and recommended to the General Conference that it consider all the implications of the attack, including suspending the exercise by Israel of the privileges and rights of membership,

Taking note of resolution 487 (1981) adopted by the Security Council of the United Nations on 19 June 1981, which strongly condemned the military attack by Israel as a clear violation of the Charter of the United Nations and the norms of international conduct and which called upon Israel urgently to place its nuclear facilities under Agency safeguards,

* * *

Considering that Iraq has fully subscribed to the Agency's safeguards regime and is a party to the Treaty on the Non-Proliferation of Nuclear Weapons and has fulfilled its obligations thereunder,

* * *

Gravely concerned that Israel's military aggression against a safeguarded nuclear research facility has caused considerable damage to the safeguards regime and could seriously jeopardize the development of nuclear energy for peaceful purposes,

Expressing indignation at the loss of life and damage to nuclear facilities caused by this wilful act,

Deploring the rejection by Israel of the repeated calls, including that of the Security Council on 19 June 1981, to place its nuclear facilities under Agency safeguards, and

Recalling the provisions of Article XIX.B of the Statute of the Agency,

> 1. Considers that the Israeli act of aggression against the safeguarded Iraqi nuclear installations constitutes an attack against the Agency and its safeguards regime, which is the foundation of the Treaty on the Non-Proliferation of Nuclear Weapons;
>
> 2. Decides to suspend immediately the provision of any assistance to Israel under the Agency's technical assistance programme;
>
> 3. Also decides to consider at its twenty-sixth regular session the suspension of Israel from the exercise of the privileges and rights of membership if by that time it has not complied with the provisions of Security Council resolution 487 of 19 June 1981;
> * * *.

EVALUATING THE SANCTION

IAEA Statute *article XIX.B,* invoked in the resolution, authorizes the General Conference to suspend from the privileges and rights of membership any member that has persistently violated the Statute or any agreement entered into by it pursuant to the Statute.

The Agency's objectives, set forth in *article II,* are essentially to foster the peaceful development and use of atomic energy, and to ensure that its assistance is not used for military purposes.

The Statute contains detailed provisions for IAEA inspection of nuclear facilities that have been subjected to Agency safeguards. (Iraq's facility had been subjected to these safeguards, and the IAEA had not found any violation.) The Statute, in article XII.B, sets out a procedure if an inspection reveals noncompliance. Under the procedure, the IAEA Board of Governors is to call upon the respondent state to remedy its noncompliance; if it does not do so, the Board may suspend any assistance the Agency is giving the respondent, call for the return of any materials and equipment that had been provided to it, and suspend it from the exercise of the privileges and rights of membership under article XIX.B, above. Since Iraq had not been found to be in violation of any IAEA standards, the noncompliance procedure had not been invoked against it.

The relationship agreement between the United Nations and the IAEA provides:

> Article V. The Agency shall consider any resolution relating to the Agency adopted by the General Assembly or by a Council of the United Nations. Any such resolution shall be referred to the Agency together with the appropriate records. Upon request the Agency shall submit a report on any action taken, in accordance with the statute of the Agency, by it or by its members as a result of its consideration of any resolution referred to it under the present article.
>
> * * *
>
> Article IX. The Agency shall co-operate with the Security Council by furnishing it at its request with such information and assistance as may be required in the exercise of its responsibility for the maintenance or restoration of international peace and security.[h]

Did the IAEA General Conference have the authority to impose the withholding-of-benefit sanction on Israel, as it purported to do in operative paragraph 2 of its September 1981 resolution?

Hindsight, based on Iraq's war with Iran throughout most of the 1980s, its invasion of Kuwait in 1990 and the ensuing revelations of Iraq's clandestine efforts to produce materials useable for nuclear weapons, might suggest that Israel did the international community a favor in 1981. Did the IAEA sanction the wrong party in 1981? Should the IAEA simply have turned a blind eye to the Israeli raid?

3. *Increasing the Burdens of Membership*

Closely related to benefit-withholding sanctions, but less commonly found, are burden-increasing sanctions. The International Monetary Fund, for example, is authorized to increase the normal charges it imposes for use of the Fund's resources if a member state makes unduly protracted use of them. In effect, a penalty charge may be levied.[a] The safeguard against abuse is that a weighted majority (70 percent of the total voting power) is required for the penalty charge to be imposed.

h. 281 U.N.T.S. 369.

a. See Fund Agreement, art. V, §§ 8(c) & (d).

At one time during discussions on the reform of the international monetary system, the IMF Board of Governors' ad hoc Committee of 20 suggested that charges be imposed on member states' accumulations of excessive monetary reserves resulting from a large balance-of-payments surplus, and on deficiencies of reserves by member states unwilling to correct significant deficits in their balance of payments.[b] This proposal was not adopted. If such a system of Fund-imposed charges on reserve surpluses and deficiencies were triggered automatically by a formula, could it be a fair and effective means of inducing member states to adopt policies that would keep their balances of payments roughly in equilibrium?

In an effort to respond effectively to the chronic U.N. financial crisis, Javier Pérez de Cuéllar, the outgoing Secretary–General, proposed in the autumn of 1991 that interest be charged on assessed contributions that are not paid on time.[c] Since many member states typically pay their contributions months after the due date, and some have been more delinquent than that, the interest charges could, in the aggregate, help to alleviate the financial crisis and presumably could nudge some members toward prompt payment. The United States (one of the late remitters even in the best of times) strenuously objected to the proposal. It pointed out that some states' legislative and appropriation procedures (including its own) would not mesh with the U.N.'s payment schedule, and that interest charges would add to the financial burden of developing countries.[d]

Is the U.S. position convincing? Why shouldn't delinquent payments to the U.N. be treated as delinquent payments to a private bank are?

What about pecuniary sanctions for violations of nonfinancial obligations? Would it be feasible to give the U.N. or other international organizations the authority to fine governments that violate the organizations' nonfinancial norms? If so, what safeguards should there be?

Constituent instruments sometimes contain nonpecuniary burden-increasing provisions to be applied when a member deviates from organizational norms. Typical of that sort of provision are consultation requirements in the Fund Agreement and in GATT. For example, a Fund member retaining exchange restrictions as a "transitional arrangement" upon joining the Fund must consult the Fund annually about retaining or removing them. Under GATT article XII:4(b), a contracting party that takes advantage of a provision in the GATT

---

b. See the proposed Outline of Reform of the Fund, 3 IMF Survey 193, 200–01 (1974), and see generally Gold, "Pressures" and Reform of the International Monetary System, 7 N.Y.U.J. Int'l L. & Pol. 423 (1974).

c. See U.N.Doc. A/46/600/Add.1 (1991).

d. See Int'l Docs.Rev., 2 Dec. 1991, at 3.

permitting certain import quotas for balance-of-payments purposes must consult annually with the Contracting Parties (acting together as a plenary body). In like fashion, when the Contracting Parties grant a waiver from GATT obligations, they normally require periodic consultations for the duration of the waiver.

In none of these cases is the consultation requirement thought of as a punitive sanction. Nevertheless, when a government is considering whether to invoke an escape clause that contains an obligation to consult the relevant organization periodically until the member returns to conformity, presumably the burdens of complying with that obligation will enter into the decision. Under what circumstances, if any, might those burdens be effective deterrents?

4. Suspension or Expulsion From Membership

a. The United Nations

(1) South Africa

U.N. Charter *article 5* authorizes the General Assembly, upon the recommendation of the Security Council, to suspend the membership privileges of a member against which preventive or enforcement action has been taken under Chapter VII of the Charter. *Article 6* permits the General Assembly, again on the recommendation of the Security Council, to expel a member that has persistently violated the principles of the Charter.

If the benefits of membership in the United Nations or any other organization are substantial, presumably the threat of suspension or expulsion could be a significant deterrent to conduct running counter to the organization's norms. But the threat would have to be real; that is, the organization would have to be prepared actually to suspend or expel if the circumstances warranted it. In this connection, expulsion poses particular problems since it means the organization loses whatever influence it may have had over the recalcitrant state. Consequently the threat of expulsion appears to be credible in only two situations: (a) the case in which a member ceases to contribute anything to the organization but continues to obtain substantial benefits from it; and (b) the case in which most member governments wish to express a fundamental moral condemnation of highly visible policies followed by another member government.[a]

In the early 1970s there was serious talk in the United Nations about expelling South Africa under the second rationale suggested above. The effort resulted in 1974 in action having at least some of the trappings of suspension (rather than expulsion). To understand the

---

a. See Constas, The Capacity of International Organizations to Exercise Political "Pressure," 26–27 Revue Hellenique de Droit International 338, 356–57 (1973–74). Cf. Jenks, Some Constitutional Problems of International Organizations, 22 Brit.Y.B. Int'l L. 11, 25–26 (1945), expressing skepticism about expulsion as a useful sanction.

legal framework of that effort, begin by reading carefully U.N. Charter *articles 5, 6 and 18(2)*.

Because of the Security Council's role under articles 5 and 6, the effort in the General Assembly did not concentrate solely on formal suspension or expulsion of South Africa. Beginning with the twenty-fifth session (1970), the General Assembly focused also on the acceptability of the credentials issued by the government in Pretoria to the South African U.N. representatives.

Rule 27 of the General Assembly's Rules of Procedure provides:

> The credentials of representatives and the names of members of a delegation shall be submitted to the Secretary General if possible not less than one week before the opening of the session. The credentials shall be issued either by the Head of the State or Government or by the Minister for Foreign Affairs.[b]

At the beginning of each General Assembly session, a nine-member Credentials Committee is appointed. It examines the credentials of representatives, usually simply approving a memorandum from the Secretary–General, which in turn is based on a routine examination of the face of each set of credentials to see if they appear in order. The results of this process with respect to South African credentials from 1970 through 1973 appear in the excerpt below.

U.N. SECRETARIAT SUMMARY OF U.N. CREDENTIALS PRACTICE THROUGH 1973

Nov. 23, 1973.
1973 U.N. Juridical Y.B. 139, 140–41.

* * *

At its twenty-fifth, twenty-sixth and twenty-seventh sessions, after considering the reports of the Credentials Committee concluding that all credentials should be accepted, the General Assembly on each occasion adopted a resolution approving the report "except with regard to the credentials of the representatives of South Africa". At the twenty-fifth session, when that formulation was used for the first time, the President of the General Assembly [Mr. Hambro], after consulting the Legal Counsel * * *, provided in the meeting the following interpretation, which was not contested: a vote in favour of the aforementioned formulation would mean "on the part of this Assembly, a very strong condemnation of the policies pursued by the Government of South Africa. It would also constitute a warning to that Government as solemn as any such warning could be. But, apart from that, [the formulation] would not seem to me to mean that the South African delegation is unseated or cannot continue to sit in this Assembly; if adopted, it will not affect the rights and privileges of membership of South Africa."

---

b. U.N.Doc. A/520/Rev. 15 (1985). See also 1985 U.N. Juridical Y.B. 128.

At its twenty-eighth session [1973], the General Assembly, on a point of order adopted when the Minister for Foreign Affairs of South Africa was about to take the floor in the general debate, decided to suspend its 2140th meeting until the Credentials Committee had reported to it on the credentials of the representatives of South Africa. The Committee having concluded in its report that the credentials were in order, the General Assembly, on the basis of an amendment proposed by Syria, decided to add to that report a paragraph reading: "The General Assembly rejects the credentials of the representatives of South Africa". The President of the General Assembly was led to give his interpretation of the vote in an open meeting; he adopted the same interpretation as his predecessors, and concluded: "Since it is not held that the credentials of South Africa are not in keeping with the terms of rule 27 of the rules of procedure, the vote that has just taken place * * * does not affect the rights and privileges of South Africa as a Member of the Organization." The Chairman of the African Group, speaking on behalf of 41 States, then stated that the group did not intend to challenge "the ruling or the personal interpretation" of the President, but intended to study the implications of the ruling and to take any appropriate steps at a future stage.

REJECTION OF SOUTH AFRICA'S CREDENTIALS IN 1974

At the 29th session of the General Assembly, in 1974, the Credentials Committee concluded that all credentials should be accepted "with the exception of the credentials of the representative of South Africa." The General Assembly debate on approval of the Credentials Committee's report focused on the purpose of the Committee's review of credentials. The representative of Australia said, for example, that the verification of credentials "is limited to the verification of the identity of the official Government signatory of a delegation's credentials, and does not extend to questioning the right of a particular Government to issue credentials."[c] The representative of Uganda, on the other hand, supported the Credentials Committee, saying that the delegation occupying the South African seat represented a minority of less than 20 percent of the population; moreover, the Pretoria regime consistently violated Charter principles by its atrocities against the non-white majority and by its occupation of Namibia.[d]

The Australian statement reflected the belief, shared by most Western governments at the time, that there is a significant difference between verifying credentials and determining which government should represent a member state. On the other hand, there was some precedent in the General Assembly for using the credentials process to question the legitimacy of the government issuing the credentials. The

c. U.N.Doc. A/PV.2281, at 97 (1974). d. 11 U.N. Monthly Chron., No. 9, at 8 (1974).

precedent involved not only South Africa, but also Hungary from 1956 to 1963 (after the Soviet Union had crushed the Hungarian revolt of 1956). Note also the post–1974 case of Cambodian representation, pages 181–84 supra.

The General Assembly adopted a resolution approving the Credentials Committee's report in 1974, without saying what effect the rejection of the South African representative's credentials would have. Solely on the question of deciding whether to accept or reject the South African credentials in 1974 (leaving aside the practical effect of rejection), which side had the stronger position?

Would the winning side have strengthened its position by characterizing the issue strictly as one of representation, rather than as approval of credentials? Note that there was no rival South African delegation attempting to present its credentials, nor was there any serious doubt about the white minority regime's control of government in South Africa.

What exactly is the scope of the precedent for rejection of credentials that appear on their face to be in order?

The General Assembly also adopted a resolution in 1974, calling on the Security Council to "review the relationship between the United Nations and South Africa in the light of the constant violation by South Africa of the principles of the Charter and the Universal Declaration of Human Rights." [e] The Security Council took up the matter, and on October 30, 1974, voted on a resolution that would have recommended to the General Assembly the immediate expulsion of South Africa under U.N. Charter article 6. France, the United Kingdom and the United States vetoed the resolution.

The debate leading to the veto consumed eleven meetings of the Council.[f] Those arguing for expulsion emphasized the manifestations of apartheid as it then existed in South Africa, involving such things as the highly unequal distribution of land including the creation of Bantustans ("national homelands"), the classification of the population by race, the barriers to free movement, the denial of the right to assemble freely, unequal educational opportunities, the prohibition of inter-racial marriages, the denial of voting rights to most of the population, and the use of torture, cruel and degrading treatment by the authorities. It was argued that these practices violated the basic human rights provisions in the U.N. Charter (*articles 1, 13 and 55*), as well as articles 1 and 2 of the Universal Declaration of Human Rights (the basic provisions on nondiscrimination).

It was also said that South Africa was violating *article 2* of the Charter by illegally occupying Namibia despite the 1966 General Assembly termination of its League of Nations Mandate over that territo-

e. G.A.Res. 3207 (XXIX).

f. The summary of the debate, in the text, is based on U.N.Docs. S/PV.1796, at 7–11, 13–16, 18, 21–26; S/PV.1800, at 27, 29–38, 42–43, 56; S/PV.1807, at 26–30; S/PV.1808, at 21–22, 26–30 (1974).

ry. Moreover, South Africa had refused to apply the Security Council sanctions against Rhodesia, in violation of *article 25* of the Charter.

The South African Foreign Minister, speaking pursuant to U.N. Charter *article 31,* noted the longstanding South African position that Charter *article 2(7)* prohibited U.N. involvement in South Africa's relationship with its own citizens. He nevertheless presented the South African government's case, stressing historical developments that resulted in separate white and black settlements, and suggesting that conditions for black citizens in South Africa were better than in many other African countries despite admittedly discriminatory practices in South Africa. He said that his government would do everything in its power to move away from discrimination based on race, though it would not happen overnight. Regarding Namibia, he said that South Africa had no designs on it and would grant it self-determination as soon as its people were ready to exercise that right. He finished by asking what would be achieved if his country were expelled from the United Nations.

The United States representative stressed U.S. abhorrence of apartheid and rejection of South Africa's failure to comply with international law by withdrawing from Namibia. But he argued against expulsion, since that would reduce or eliminate any influence the U.N. might have over South Africa. History, he said, holds no example of a pariah state that reformed itself in exile.

Several speakers, including some favoring expulsion, expressed concern about the precedent that might be set. For example, the representative of Somalia said that it would be unthinkable for article 6 to be invoked except for violations of the Charter's principles that are universal in their implications, stubbornly maintained despite repeated warnings, and that constitute a major assault on the authority and integrity of the United Nations. The representative of Australia stressed that this was a well-documented case established over many years. The representative of the United States said that expulsion would bring into question the concept of a forum in which ideas and ideals are voiced, along with conflicting views, until reason prevails.

As already indicated, the expulsion resolution failed because of the negative votes of France, the United Kingdom and the United States. As a legal matter, *could* South Africa have been expelled under the terms of article 6?

If expulsion had not been vetoed, what exactly would have been the precedent?

After the expulsion resolution had failed, the President of the Security Council wrote to the President of the General Assembly, notifying him that the Security Council had taken no action and that it "remained seized" of the matter.[g] The General Assembly then turned

g. U.N.Doc. A/9847, at 2 (1974).

to the effect to be given to its rejection of the South African delegation's credentials.

GENERAL ASSEMBLY DEBATE
Nov. 12, 1974.
29 U.N. GAOR (2281st plen. mtg.) at 840–41, 854–55.

Mr. SALIM (*United Republic of Tanzania*): [Addressing the President of the General Assembly for its 29th session, Abdelaziz Bouteflika, of Algeria] * * *

We recognize that the Security Council is still seized with the matter and we express our firm hope that soon that organ will again be convened to consider this problem.

On the other hand, we are still faced in this Assembly with the problem of the status of the South African delegation to the twenty-ninth session of the United Nations General Assembly. It is to this matter that I now wish to address myself.

We adopted a decision in this Assembly regarding the rejection of the credentials of South Africa. For the first time, the Credentials Committee itself rejected the credentials of the *apartheid* régime. We believe that this decision has certain logical consequences. Previously, the Assembly gave the South African régime a chance to mend its ways. This year, the Assembly was not prepared to go on issuing warnings regarding the South African régime. The matter was referred to the Security Council, which failed to act. So we are still seized with the matter of the effect of our decision regarding the credentials of that régime.

As I have indicated before, that decision has certain logical consequences. I would like, for the sake of clarity, to emphasize that in pursuing the logical consequences of this decision we shall not be infringing the provisions of Article 12 of the Charter, for the matter of which the Security Council is seized is the question of allowing the *apartheid* régime to remain in the Organization, and not the question of the credentials of the South African delegation in the current General Assembly.

So, to conclude, I should like to ask your guidance, Sir, on the effect of the decision of the General Assembly to reject the credentials of the *apartheid* régime. I make this request in the name of the African group, over which I have the honour to preside. And I do so because we find it to be a serious anomaly to have the delegation of South Africa taking part in the proceedings of our Organization when the credentials of that delegation have been so decisively rejected, first by the Credentials Committee and later by this Assembly. I do so especially in view of the fact that by referring this matter to the Security Council, the Assembly rejected the notion of indefinitely continuing with serious warnings to the *apartheid* régime of South Africa.

* * *

The PRESIDENT (*interpretation from French*):

Today, for the first time, I am asked to state here my interpretation of the General Assembly's decision to reject the credentials of the delegation of South Africa. In that connexion, I must say that the General Assembly, at its 2248th meeting on 30 September 1974, took two decisions. First, it approved the report of the Credentials Committee rejecting the credentials of the delegation of South Africa. Second, it adopted resolution 3207 (XXIX), in which it called upon the Security Council to review the relationship between the United Nations and South Africa in the light of the constant violation by South Africa of the principles of the Charter and the Universal Declaration of Human Rights.

In his letter of 31 October 1974, the President of the Security Council informed the General Assembly that the Council had not been able to adopt a resolution on this item and accordingly remained seized of the matter.

However, the absence of a decision by the Security Council in no way affects the General Assembly's rejection of the credentials of the delegation of South Africa. Since its twenty-fifth session the General Assembly has been regularly rejecting, each year, the credentials of that delegation. It did so until last year by adopting an amendment to the report of the Credentials Committee. In 1970, Mr. Hambro, who was then President of the Assembly, stated the following after the adoption of the amendment rejecting the credentials of the delegation of South Africa: " * * * the amendment as it is worded at present"—and I emphasize "as it is worded at present"—"would not seem to me to mean that the South African delegation is unseated or cannot continue to sit in this Assembly."

It is clear that the opinion of Mr. Hambro, a legal authority to whom I wish to pay a tribute, was based above all on the exact words of the decision adopted by the General Assembly in the form of an amendment. That opinion did not mean that if the amendment had been worded in some other way it might not have had different consequences for the legal position of the South African delegation in this Assembly.

The question is all the more worthy of consideration because rule 29 of our rules of procedure states:

> Any representative to whose admission a Member has made objection shall be seated provisionally with the same rights as other representatives until the Credentials Committee has reported and the General Assembly has given its decision.

That text perhaps does not indicate with sufficient clarity what should happen once the General Assembly has taken a decision confirming the objection to the admission of a representative or a delegation. Now, year after year the General Assembly has decided, by ever-larger majorities, not to recognize the credentials of the South African delegation, and during this session the Credentials Committee itself took the initiative of rejecting those credentials. * * *

It would therefore be a betrayal of the clearly and repeatedly expressed will of the General Assembly to understand this to mean that it was merely a procedural method of expressing its rejection of the policy of *apartheid*. On the basis of the consistency with which the General Assembly has regularly refused to accept the credentials of the South African delegation, one may legitimately infer that the General Assembly would in the same way reject the credentials of any other delegation authorized by the Government of the Republic of South Africa to represent it, which is tantamount to saying in explicit terms that the General Assembly refuses to allow the South African delegation to participate in its work.

Thus it is, as President of the twenty-ninth session of the General Assembly, that I interpret the decision of the General Assembly, leaving open the question of the status of the Republic of South Africa as a Member of the United Nations which, as we all know, is a matter requiring a recommendation from the Security Council. My interpretation refers exclusively to the position of the delegation of South Africa within the strict framework of the rules of procedure of the General Assembly. That is my belief.

Mr. SCALI (*United States of America*):

Mr. President, my delegation regrets that we have no choice but to challenge your ruling. We did not come to this decision lightly, and we do so only because of the overriding importance of the issue, the fundamental rights of a Member State under the Charter of the United Nations.

There is also an obvious conflict, Mr. President, between your ruling and the legal opinion given to this Assembly on 11 November 1970 at the twenty-fifth session. Further, there is a conflict between your ruling and the practice that the General Assembly has consistently followed in the four years since then, at the twenty-fifth, the twenty-sixth, the twenty-seventh and twenty-eighth sessions and at the sixth special session held in spring this year. In addition, as we all know, during this twenty-ninth session, South Africa was allowed to vote without objection after the Assembly's decision on its credentials was made.

The legal opinion given at the twenty-fifth session remains as valid today, in our view, as it was then. It affirms that under the Charter the Assembly may not deprive a Member of any of the rights of membership. The Assembly may be master of its rules of procedure, but no majority, no matter how large, can ignore or change the clear provisions of the Charter in this way. We consider it to be a violation of the rules of procedure and of Articles 5 and 6 of the Charter for the Assembly to attempt to deny a Member State of the United Nations its right to participate in the Assembly, through this type of unprecedented action. Article 5 of the Charter expressly lays down rules by which a Member may be suspended. Article 6 of the Charter specifically provides the process by which a Member may be expelled. The Assembly is not empowered to deprive a Member of the rights and privileges of membership other than in accordance with Articles 5, 6 and 19 of the Charter. In our view, none of these circumstances applies in this case.

* * *

Mr. President, your action is taken in the context of the Assembly's action on the credentials item. The policy of a Government is not a legitimate consideration in this context. Those policies may rightly be examined at other times and in other contexts, but not here. In the present case no one can reasonably argue with the technical propriety of the credentials of the South African delegation. South Africa is not the only Member State whose Government is not chosen by free elections where all adults are entitled to vote.

In our view, we must not seek to change the membership regulations to convert this into an organization of like-minded Governments. Were we to apply that criterion we should cease to be a universal institution and would become very different indeed.

Those facts and a respect for the Charter have led past Presidents of the General Assembly to rule that decisions involving the non-acceptance or rejection of South African credentials constitute an expression of international outrage at the heinous policy of *apartheid*. But each of those Presidents has also ruled that such decisions do not serve to deprive South Africa of its fundamental rights of membership—rights which include the right to take its seat in the General Assembly, to speak, to raise questions and make proposals, and to vote.

Mr. President, we consider that your ruling fails to take into account that law of the Charter, the existing legal opinion and the consistent series of applicable precedents. For those reasons and pursuant to rule 71, we must respectfully challenge your ruling. We request that, in accordance with rule 71, you put this challenge immediately to a vote.

* * *

The PRESIDENT (*interpretation from French*):

The General Assembly has before it a challenge by the representative of the United States of America to the President's ruling. He has specifically invoked rule 71. I shall start by reading out rule 71:

> During the discussion of any matter, a representative may rise to a point of order, and the point of order shall be immediately decided by the President in accordance with the rules of procedure. A representative may appeal against the ruling of the President. The appeal shall be immediately put to the vote, and the President's ruling shall stand unless overruled by a majority of the members present and voting. A representative rising to a point of

order may not speak on the substance of the matter under discussion.

[The vote upheld the President's ruling, by a margin of 91 to 22, with 19 abstentions. The effect was to suspend South Africa from participation in the General Assembly's 29th session. Although the ruling applied only to that session, South Africa did not seek to participate again until the reconvened 33rd session, as will appear below.]

QUESTIONS ON THE GENERAL ASSEMBLY'S ACTION

Was the General Assembly entitled to act at all, in light of U.N. Charter *article 12(1)?*

What, if anything, distinguishes the General Assembly's action from the suspension of rights and privileges of membership under *article 5?* In 1970 the Legal Counsel of the U.N. Secretariat gave the following opinion (referred to by the United States representative, above), at the request of the General Assembly.

U.N. LEGAL COUNSEL, OPINION ON REJECTION OF CREDENTIALS
Nov. 11, 1970.
1970 U.N. Juridical Y.B. 169–70.

[The opinion quoted General Assembly rule 27, page 586 supra.]

* * *

While normally the examination of credentials, both in the Credentials Committee and in the General Assembly, is a procedural matter limited to ascertaining that the requirements of rule 27 have been satisfied, there have nevertheless been a few instances involving rival claimants where the question of which claimant represents the true government of the State has arisen as a substantive issue. This issue of representation may, as in the case of the Republic of the Congo (Leopoldville) at the fifteenth session and Yemen at the sixteenth session, be considered in connexion with the examination of credentials, or it may, as in the case of China, be dealt with both in connexion with credentials and as a separate agenda item.

Questions have also been raised in the Credentials Committee with respect to the representatives of certain Members, notably South Africa and Hungary, where there was no rival claimant. There has, however, been no case where the representatives were precluded from participation in the meetings of the General Assembly. The General Assembly, in the case of Hungary from the eleventh to the seventeenth session and in the case of South Africa at the twentieth session, decided to take no action on the credentials submitted on behalf of the representatives of Hungary and South Africa. Under rule 29 any representative to whose admission a Member has made objection is seated provisionally with the same rights as other representatives until the Credentials Committee has reported and the General Assembly has given its decision.

Should the General Assembly, where there is no question of rival claimants, reject credentials satisfying the requirements of rule 27 for the purpose of excluding a Member State from participation in its meetings, this would have the effect of suspending a Member State from the exercise of rights and privileges of membership in a manner not foreseen by the Charter. Article 5 of the Charter lays down the following requirements for the suspension of a Member State from the rights and privileges of membership:

(a) Preventive or enforcement action has to be taken by the Security Council against the Member State concerned;

(b) The Security Council has to recommend to the General Assembly that the Member State concerned be suspended from the exercise of the rights and privileges of membership;

(c) The General Assembly has to act affirmatively on the foregoing recommendation by a two-third vote, in accordance with Article 18, paragraph 2, of the Charter, which lists "the suspension of the rights and privileges of membership" as an "important question".

The participation in meetings of the General Assembly is quite clearly one of the important rights and privileges of membership. Suspension of this right through the rejection of credentials would not satisfy the foregoing requirements and would therefore be contrary to the Charter.

SUSPENSION OF SOME OR ALL RIGHTS

In the context of an advisory opinion on the conditions for admission of new members to the U.N., a procedure involving both the Security Council and the General Assembly, the I.C.J. has affirmed that Charter provisions apply even to these political bodies:

> The political character of an organ cannot release it from the observance of the treaty provisions established by the Charter when they constitute limitations on its powers or criteria for its judgment. To ascertain whether an organ has freedom of choice for its decisions, reference must be made to the terms of its constitution.[h]

The right to participate in the General Assembly would be one of the "rights and privileges of membership" that could be suspended

---

[h.] Conditions of Admission of a State to Membership in the United Nations, [1947– 48] I.C.J. 57, 64.

under article 5. But would there be others? Consider whether a suspension might affect rights and privileges under *articles 23, 27, 31, 32, 35, 51, 61, 67, 86 and/or 105(2)*. If only one of the suspendable rights or privileges is suspended, must the procedure under articles 5 and 18(2) be followed?[i]

If the rejection of the South African credentials did not have the effect given it by the President of the General Assembly, would it have any effect at all? Recall the conclusion drawn by an earlier President of the Assembly, Mr. Hambro, when the General Assembly declined to accept South Africa's credentials at the 25th session. See page 586 supra. Was that tantamount to saying it had no effect?

Did the President for the 29th session, Mr. Bouteflika, successfully distinguish Mr. Hambro's decision?

The majority in favor of Mr. Bouteflika's ruling exceeded two-thirds. If it had been only 51 percent, would the ruling have been properly upheld?

The U.N. Legal Counsel's opinion noted that the Hungarian delegation's credentials had been questioned after the Soviet Union had forcibly ended the 1956 Hungarian uprising, but this had not led the U.N. General Assembly to refuse to seat the Soviet-supported Hungarian representatives. On the other hand, the ILO General Conference did refuse to admit delegates and advisers appointed by the Hungarian delegation to its sessions in 1958 and 1959. The stated reason was that the government had been installed by the armed intervention of another state and thus was not representative of the Hungarian people.[j] Was that a relevant precedent for the U.N. General Assembly's refusal to seat the South African delegation?

In May 1979 the General Assembly reconvened its 33rd session, to discuss Namibia. At the beginning of the debate a South African government representative took the South African seat for the first time since the General Assembly's refusal in 1974 to permit that government to participate. The U.N. Secretariat said that South Africa would not be entitled to vote (because it had not paid its dues since the 1974 incident), but that it did have a right to be present. Nevertheless, the General Assembly voted, 96 to 19, with 9 abstentions, to reject the South African credentials. The South African delegation left the room. After another unsuccessful attempt to participate in 1981, the South African government did not try again to take the South African seat in the General Assembly in the 1980s.

Was the General Assembly's 1974 action a direct precedent for the 1979 rejection of the South African government's credentials? Note

i. For an argument counter to that of the U.N. Legal Counsel, see Suttner, Has South Africa Been Illegally Excluded from the United Nations General Assembly?, 17 Comp. & Int'l L.J. of Southern Africa 279 (1984).

j. See Osieke, Ultra Vires Acts in International Organizations—The Experience of the International Labour Organization, 1976–77 British Y.B. Int'l L. 259, 270–73.

that the General Assembly has frequently permitted nonmember states to participate as observers, without vote. Is that relevant here?

In 1989, South Africa relinquished its control of Namibia. In February 1990, Sam Nujoma, the leader of SWAPO, was elected the first President of Namibia, which formally became independent on March 21, 1990. In February 1990, recently-elected President F.W. de Klerk of South Africa legalized the African National Congress and about 30 other banned opposition groups. He also freed Nelson Mandela, a leader of the black resistance movement, from 25 years in prison. The South African parliament then began a series of repeals of most of the laws that had formalized apartheid, including those having to do with registration by race, segregated housing and education, internal passports, etc. At this writing, however, black South Africans still did not have the right to vote for elected representatives. Nor had the white South African government attempted again to take a seat in the U.N. General Assembly.

In 1974, were the substantive conditions met for suspension of South Africa under U.N. Charter *article 5?* That article refers to "preventive or enforcement action * * * taken by the Security Council * * *." The reference is to action with respect to threats to the peace, breaches of the peace, and acts of aggression, under Chapter VII of the Charter. The Security Council had several times called upon all states to observe an arms embargo against South Africa.[k] These resolutions conceivably could have fallen within the concept of preventive or enforcement action under article 41, except that in none of them did the Security Council actually determine the existence of a threat to the peace, breach of the peace or act of aggression under article 39. Instead, it found that the situation in South Africa "is seriously disturbing international peace and security * * *."[l] That may sound like a finding of a threat to the peace or breach of the peace, but the highly technical practice of the Security Council in this area shows that it is not the same thing.[m] Thus it is evident that by 1974, no "preventive or enforcement action" had been taken against South Africa within the meaning of article 5.[n]

Are we to conclude that, given the appropriate Security Council recommendation under article 6, South Africa could have been expelled in 1974, but that it could not have been subjected to the lesser sanction of suspension of its rights and privileges under article 5? If so, does that make any sense?

k. See, e.g., S.C. Res. 181 (1963), 18 SCOR Resolutions and Decisions 7 (1966); S.C. Res. 191 (1964), 19 id. at 13 (1966); S.C. Res. 311 (1972), 27 id. at 10 (1973).

l. S.C. Res. 181 (1963).

m. See, e.g., the debate leading to the adoption of S.C. Res. 191, summarized in 1964 U.N. Yearbook 113–15.

n. The Security Council took limited enforcement action against South Africa in 1977, under Chapter VII. S.C. Res. 418, 32 SCOR Resolutions and Decisions 5 (1977).

(2) Israel in the General Assembly

From 1982 through 1989, the Arab states and a few others tried to persuade the U.N. General Assembly to reject the Israeli delegation's credentials. When the Arab effort began in 1982, the U.S. Secretary of State, with the backing of the Congress, warned that if Israel were excluded from the General Assembly the United States would withdraw from participation in the Assembly and would withhold payments to the United Nations. Nevertheless, during the General Assembly session that fall, Iran challenged the Israeli delegation's credentials by proposing an amendment to the Credentials Committee's report. The next day, Finland raised a point of order and moved to adjourn debate on Iran's proposed amendment. The point of order was upheld, in effect ending the matter for that session.

Essentially the same scenario was replayed in each subsequent General Assembly session until declining support led the Arab states to abandon the effort in 1990. In 1988, for example, the representative of Democratic Yemen presented the Arab challenge:

GENERAL ASSEMBLY DEBATE
Oct. 18, 1988.
U.N. Doc. A/43/PV.33, at 42–48.

Mr. AL–ASHTAL (*Democratic Yemen*) (*interpretation from Arabic*): * * *

The General Assembly, in resolution ES–9/1, of 5 February 1982, noted the following:

"that Israel's record and actions established conclusively that it is not a peace-loving Member State and that it has not carried out its obligation under the Charter".

On this basis we challenge the credentials of the delegation of Israel to the forty-third session of the General Assembly for the following reasons.

First, Israel has not complied with Security Council resolutions concerning the Palestinian question and the situation in the Middle East, thereby violating Article 25 of the Charter.

Second, Israel has not implemented General Assembly resolutions on the question of Palestine and the situation in the Middle East calling for the restoration to the Palestinian people of their inalienable rights, including the right to return and the right to self-determination and to establish their independent State, Palestine, and stressing the need for the ending of the Israeli occupation of Arab territories, in keeping with the principle of the non-admissibility of the acquisition of territories by force, and for Israeli withdrawal from all the territories occupied since 1967, including Jerusalem and the Syrian Golan Heights.

Third, Israel has not implemented General Assembly resolutions concerning other matters in connection with the question of Palestine and the situation in the Middle East.

Fourth, Israel is violating human rights in the occupied Palestinian territories and the other occupied Arab territories, including Jerusalem, and, in particular, it is violating the provisions of the Fourth Geneva Convention of 12 August 1949. Here we refer specifically to the escalation of Israeli repression against the Arab Palestinian people in the occupied Palestinian territories and against the inhabitants of the other occupied Arab territories, including the deportation of Arab citizens from these lands, since the beginning of the Palestinian uprising against the Israeli occupation.

Fifth, Israel persists in the annexation of Arab and Palestinian territories, including Jerusalem and the Golan, thereby violating the provisions of the United Nations Charter and international laws.

Sixth, Israel is continuing its acts of aggression against Arab countries and extending them to Lebanon, Iraq and Tunisia.

Seventh, Israel's co-operation with the racist South African régime, especially in the nuclear and economic fields, continues.

Eighth, and finally, the credentials of the delegation of Israel at the forty-third session of the General Assembly are issued from the occupied city of Jerusalem, in violation of Security Council resolutions, especially resolution 478 (1980), and relevant General Assembly resolutions, especially resolution 35/169E, dated 15 December 1980.

The PRESIDENT (*interpretation from Spanish*): I call on the representative of Norway, on a point of order.

Mr. TELLMANN (*Norway*): * * *

On behalf of the Nordic countries, I formally move that no action be taken on the [challenge to the Israeli credentials] and ask the President to be good enough to put this motion immediately to a vote. The motion is made within the terms of rule 74 of the rules of procedure of the General Assembly. It should be emphasized that our motion is motivated by our dedication to upholding the capacity and authority of the United Nations to act in fulfilment of its primary purpose, the maintenance of international peace and security.

[The Norwegian motion was adopted.]

THE ISRAELI CREDENTIALS

Security Council Resolution 478 and General Assembly Resolution 35/169E (1980), cited by Mr. Al-Ashtal, are each to the same effect. In Resolution 478, the Security Council:

Censures in the strongest terms the enactment by Israel of the "basic law" on Jerusalem * * *;

Affirms that the enactment of the "basic law" by Israel constitutes a violation of international law * * *;

Determines that all legislative and administrative measures and actions taken by Israel, the occupying Power, which have altered or purport to alter the character and status of the Holy City of Jerusalem, and in particular the "basic law" on Jerusalem, are null and void and must be rescinded forthwith; * * *

Decides not to recognize the "basic law" and such other actions by Israel that, as a result of this law, seek to alter the character and status of Jerusalem * * *.

Did Mr. Al–Ashtal make a persuasive legal argument for rejecting the Israeli delegation's credentials?

Did Mr. Tellmann, of Norway, make a counter-argument? If so, what was it?

Did Mr. Al–Ashtal frame an argument for the expulsion of Israel, in the guise of an argument about credentials? (As in the case of South Africa, expulsion would require a recommendation by the Security Council—a most unlikely event.)

(3) Yugoslavia

The suspension/expulsion question came up again in 1992, when the United States and others mounted an effort to remove what was left of Yugoslavia from the United Nations because of its conduct toward Croatia and Bosnia–Herzegovina. This came in the wake of the disintegration of post-World War II Yugoslavia into separate states of Slovenia, Croatia, Bosnia–Herzegovina and a rump Yugoslavia, with Macedonia waiting also to be recognized. The rump Yugoslavia (the Federal Republic of Yugoslavia) was a federation of Serbia and Montenegro. The government in Belgrade was actively supporting—some said directing—Serbian armed resistance to the recognized governments of Croatia and Bosnia. Bosnia had been turned into a disaster area, particularly in Sarajevo and some other cities with high concentrations of Muslim Slavs. There were large numbers of refugees (at least 360,000 of whom had crossed into neighboring republics [a]), attacks on civilians and civilian property, and widespread hunger and devastation that appeared to be primarily attributable to the Belgrade-supported Serbian resistance.

In a letter to the President of the Security Council, the U.S. representative to the U.N. said:

> This is to apprise you that serious questions have arisen regarding whether the Federal Republic of Yugoslavia is the continuation of the Socialist Federal Republic of Yugoslavia for purposes of membership in the United Nations. Until such time as these questions are resolved, the participation of the representa-

---

[a.] See U.N.Doc. S/23900, at 3 (1992).

tives of the Federal Republic of Yugoslavia in the activities of the Security Council or the General Assembly should be viewed as without prejudice to the disposition of these questions.[b]

Several other governments issued similar statements.

A joint session of the parliaments of Serbia and Montenegro issued a Declaration on April 27, 1992:

>   1. The Federal Republic of Yugoslavia, continuing the state, international legal and political personality of the Socialist Federal Republic of Yugoslavia, shall strictly abide by all the commitments that the SFR of Yugoslavia assumed internationally,
>
>   At the same time, it is ready to fully respect the rights and interests of the Yugoslav Republics which declared independence. The recognition of the newly formed states will follow after all the outstanding questions negotiated on within the Conference on Yugoslavia have been settled,
>
>   Remaining bound by all obligations to international organizations and institutions whose member it is, the Federal Republic of Yugoslavia shall not obstruct the newly formed states to join these organizations and institutions, particularly the United Nations and its specialized agencies.
>
> * * *
>
>   4. The Federal Republic of Yugoslavia has no territorial aspirations towards any of its neighbours. Respecting the objectives and principles of the United Nations Charter and CSCE [Conference on Security and Cooperation in Europe] documents, it remains strictly committed to the principle of non-use of force in settling any outstanding issues.[c]

The President of the Security Council responded by saying that the members of the Council had held consultations and had agreed that the April 27 Declaration "does not prejudge decisions that may be taken by appropriate United Nations bodies or their national positions on this matter." [d]

As will appear in more detail later in this chapter, during the fighting in Croatia in September 1991 the Security Council imposed a mandatory arms embargo on Yugoslavia under Chapter VII of the Charter.[e] Then, in May 1992 at the height of the crisis in Bosnia–Herzegovina, the Security Council imposed further Chapter VII sanctions against the Federal Republic of Yugoslavia (Serbia and Montenegro). This involved an embargo on trade; restrictions on the supply of financial resources; suspension of air transportation and officially-sponsored cultural, scientific and sporting activities.[f] Nevertheless, the

b. U.N.Doc. S/23879 (1992).
c. U.N.Doc. S/23877, at 2, 3 (1992).
d. U.N.Doc. S/23878 (1992).
e. S.C.Res. 713 (1991).
f. S.C.Res. 757 (1992).

fighting continued in Bosnia, even after the United Nations managed to establish a humanitarian presence to bring food to starving residents.

The representative of the Socialist Federal Republic of Yugoslavia continued to occupy the Yugoslav seat in the U.N. after Slovenia, Croatia and Bosnia-Herzegovina had been admitted. Nevertheless, he reportedly was not allowed officially to circulate a letter describing himself as the representative of the new Federal Republic of Yugoslavia.[g] Note also the statements by the U.S. and other representatives, and by the President of the Security Council, designed to preclude acquiescence in the claim of the new Federal Republic to be the automatic successor to the Yugoslav seat. Were these tactics legally effective to avoid acquiescence?

In September 1992, the Security Council—at the initiative of the U.K., France and Belgium—adopted the resolution below.

SECURITY COUNCIL RESOLUTION 777
Sept. 19, 1992.
U.N. Doc. S/RES/777 (1992).

The Security Council,

* * *

Considering that the state formerly known as the Socialist Federal Republic of Yugoslavia has ceased to exist,

* * *

Considers that the Federal Republic of Yugoslavia (Serbia and Montenegro) cannot continue automatically the membership of the former Socialist Federal Republic of Yugoslavia in the United Nations; and therefore *recommends* to the General Assembly that it decide that the Federal Republic of Yugoslavia (Serbia and Montenegro) should apply for membership in the United Nations and that it shall not participate in the work of the General Assembly * * *.

SUSPENSION OR EXPULSION IN DISGUISE?

In Resolution 47/1 (1992), the General Assembly implemented the Security Council's recommendation, deciding that the Federal Republic of Yugoslavia should apply for membership and that it "shall not participate in the work of the General Assembly."

Was this preferable, from a legal point of view, to a suspension or expulsion of the Federal Republic of Yugoslavia, as the successor to the Socialist Federal Republic, from the United Nations? Under the circumstances prevailing in the autumn of 1992, *could* "Yugoslavia"

g. See Weller, The International Response to the Dissolution of the Socialist Federal Republic of Yugoslavia, 86 Am. J.Int'l L. 569, 596 (1992).

(Serbia and Montenegro) lawfully have been suspended from U.N. membership upon a vote of the Security Council and General Assembly under article 5? Could it lawfully have been expelled under article 6?

Would it have been proper instead simply to reject the credentials of the representatives of the Federal Republic of Yugoslavia in the General Assembly, relying on the South African precedent? Was the practical effect the same?[h]

What about the precedent by which Russia was treated as the successor to the Soviet Union without any formal process whatever, after the U.S.S.R. had disintegrated into separate states? See pages 146–47 and 189–91 supra.

b. Other Organizations

The constituent instruments of several U.N.-related organizations are silent on suspension or expulsion of members. On the other hand, some do contain suspension and/or expulsion provisions.

The Statute of the International Atomic Energy Agency provides in *article XIX.B* that a member which "has persistently violated the provisions" of the Statute or of any related agreement may be suspended by a two-thirds vote of the General Conference upon recommendation by the Board of Governors. Shortly after the U.N. had taken the action described above regarding the Federal Republic of Yugoslavia, the IAEA General Conference did likewise. It decided that the Federal Republic could not automatically continue the membership of the former Socialist Federal Republic of Yugoslavia. The Federal Republic would have to apply for membership, and in the meantime it could not take part in the General Conference or the Board of Governors. It did not appear that Yugoslavia had persistently violated the provisions of the IAEA Statute or of any related agreement. Did the General Conference simply circumvent article XIX.B?

In the case of the International Monetary Fund, expulsion is the ultimate sanction if lesser measures fail to bring a noncooperating member around. As these materials have indicated, the Fund may declare a member ineligible to use the general resources of the Fund, if informal pressures toward compliance have not worked. Under a Fund Agreement amendment that entered into force in November 1992, the next step would be suspension of voting rights if the member persists in its violation. Only if that does not work could the Fund require the member to withdraw from membership by a vote of 85 percent of the total voting power in the Board of Governors.[a]

Under the UNESCO Constitution, members whose privileges of U.N. membership have been suspended are suspended from the rights

---

[h] See the letter from the U.N. Legal Counsel to the representatives of Bosnia–Herzegovina and Croatia, Sept. 29, 1992, in 3 Int'l Docs. Rev., No. 34, at 5 (1992).

[a] Fund Agreement *art. XXVI, section 2.*

and privileges of UNESCO if the U.N. requests it, and members expelled from the U.N. are automatically expelled from UNESCO.[b]

The International Maritime Organization Convention goes further, and says that no state may "remain a Member of the Organization contrary to a resolution of the General Assembly of the United Nations."[c] Apparently, the General Assembly could recommend that the IMO expel a member for whatever reason commends itself to a majority of the General Assembly, and the IMO Convention would require that the member be expelled. Would an IMO organ have to make a decision, or would expulsion be automatic under the provision quoted above?

We now turn to suspension and expulsion practice in three other U.N.-related organizations—the World Meteorological Organization, the Universal Postal Union and the International Telecommunication Union. We will then take a brief look at practice in a regional organization—the Organization of American States.

The constituent instrument of the World Meteorological Organization contains a provision on suspension, which has been used against South Africa. WMO tied its use against South Africa to fulfillment of the Organization's purposes, as set forth in article 2 of the constituent instrument, below. The reference in article 31 to "Congress" is to the plenary body of WMO.

CONVENTION OF THE WORLD METEOROLOGICAL ORGANIZATION
Signed Oct. 11, 1947.
1 U.S.T. 281, T.I.A.S. 2052, 77 U.N.T.S. 143, as amended, T.I.A.S. 8175.

With a view to co-ordinating, standardizing and improving world meteorological and related activities, and to encouraging an efficient exchange of meteorological and related information between countries in the aid of human activities, the contracting States agree to the present Convention, as follows:

* * *

Art. 2. Purposes

The purposes of the Organization shall be:

(a) To facilitate world-wide co-operation in the establishment of networks of stations for the making of meteorological observations as well as hydrological and other geophysical observations related to meteorology, and to promote the establishment and maintenance of centres charged with the provision of meteorological and related services;

(b) To promote the establishment and maintenance of systems for the rapid exchange of meteorological and related information;

b. UNESCO Constitution art. II(4) & (5).

c. IMO Convention art. 10.

(c) To promote standardization of meteorological and related observations and to ensure the uniform publication of observations and statistics;

(d) To further the application of meteorology to aviation, shipping, water problems, agriculture and other human activities;

(e) To promote activities in operational hydrology and to further close co-operation between Meteorological and Hydrological Services; and

(f) To encourage research and training in meteorology and, as appropriate, in related fields and to assist in co-ordinating the international aspects of such research and training.

* * *

ART. 31. SUSPENSION

If any Member fails to meet its financial obligations to the Organization or otherwise fails in its obligations under the present Convention, Congress may by resolution suspend it from exercising its rights and enjoying privileges as a Member of the Organization until it has met such financial or other obligations.

WMO RESOLUTION SUSPENDING SOUTH AFRICAN RIGHTS AND PRIVILEGES

WMO Congress, May 1975.
Resolution 38 (Cg–VII), Seventh World Meteorological Congress, Abridged Report with Resolutions 136.

The Congress,

Noting:

(1) The Charter of the United Nations and the Universal Declaration of Human Rights,

* * *

(4) That [U.N. General Assembly resolutions] request, in particular, all specialized agencies to take the necessary steps to cease all financial, economic, technical and other assistance to the Government of the Republic of South Africa and to discontinue all kinds of support to it until it renounces its policy of racial discrimination and colonial oppression,

(5) That [other General Assembly resolutions] request, in particular, all specialized agencies to deny Membership or privileges of Membership to the South African régime, which should be totally excluded from participation in all international organizations as long as it continues to practise apartheid and fails to abide by the United Nations resolutions concerning Namibia,

(6) That the Government of the Republic of South Africa has in no way changed the policies and practices which were categorically condemned by the United Nations,

(7) That the United Nations and the specialized agencies including ILO, FAO, UNESCO, WHO, ICAO, UPU, ITU and IMCO have already taken measures to deny Membership to South Africa or certain privileges of Membership such as participation in meetings and voting,

Noting further:

(1) That, by virtue of Article 2 of the WMO Convention, each Member of WMO has undertaken to meet the *purposes* listed under this article,

(2) That Sixth Congress placed on record that "the discriminatory and colonial policies practised by the Government of the Republic of South Africa were not conducive to promoting the technical and scientific collaboration necessary to the fulfilment of the *objectives* of WMO",

(3) That, by virtue of Article VI of the UN/WMO Agreement established in accordance with Article 25 of the WMO Convention, WMO has undertaken "to co-operate with and render all possible assistance to the United Nations",[d]

(4) That the undertakings referred to under paragraphs (1) and (3) above place upon each Member of WMO an obligation to meet the provisions of Article 2 of the WMO Convention and the provisions of appropriate UN resolutions,

Considers:

(1) That the *objectives* of WMO express the obligations placed upon Members to fulfil the *purposes* of the Organization defined in Article 2 of the Convention; any deliberate failure to meet such obligations which lie within the means of a Member is in fact a failure on the part of that Member to fulfil the purposes of the Organization;

(2) That the Government of the Republic of South Africa has thereby failed and continues to fail to meet the obligations placed upon all Members as referred to in *Noting further* (4) above;

(3) That the provisions of Article 31 of the WMO Convention regarding suspension of Membership are therefore applicable;

Decides that the Government of the Republic of South Africa shall be immediately suspended from exercising its rights and enjoying privileges as a Member of WMO until it renounces its policy of racial discrimination, and abides by the United Nations resolutions concerning Namibia * * *.

---

d. [Article VI of the U.N.–WMO Relationship Agreement reads in full: "The [WMO] agrees to co-operate with and to render all possible assistance to the United Nations, its principal and subsidiary organs, in accordance with the United Nations Charter and the World Meteorological Convention, taking fully into account the particular position of the individual Members of the Organization which are not members of the United Nations." Ed.]

USE OF THE SUSPENSION POWER

The WMO resolution attempted to bring the case against South Africa within the terms of WMO Convention article 31, on suspension. Did it succeed?

In the 1960s several other specialized agencies, lacking express suspension or expulsion powers, considered amending their constituent instruments to be able to suspend or expel South Africa. The agencies included FAO, ILO and ICAO. The amendments either failed of adoption in the plenary organs, or if adopted, failed to receive enough ratifications to enter into force.[e]

These blunted efforts did not end South Africa's difficulties in U.N.–related organizations. For example, the Universal Postal Union (UPU), by its Resolution C 2 in 1974, excluded South Africa from its Congress (the UPU's plenary body) and from all other UPU meetings. In 1979 the International Atomic Energy Agency excluded South Africa from its General Conference, and later considered suspending all of the government's rights and privileges of membership.

In 1979 the UPU went further than it had in 1974. The UPU Congress adopted Resolution C 6, expelling South Africa from the organization.[f] The resolution relied in part on the 1974 resolution, which declared that South Africa was deliberately violating the U.N. Charter, the Universal Declaration of Human Rights and the fundamental principles of the UPU, and that by so doing South Africa had by its own accord excluded itself from the international community.

The preamble to the UPU Constitution sets forth two broad goals: "developing communications between peoples by the efficient operation of the postal services, and * * * contributing to the attainment of the noble aims of international collaboration in the cultural, social and economic fields." [g] The organization's specific objectives are to organize and improve postal services and to promote international collaboration in maintaining a single postal territory among the member countries.

Under article 2 of the UPU Constitution, "Member countries of the Union are: (a) Countries which have membership status at the date on which this Constitution comes into force. (b) Countries admitted to membership in accordance with article 11." Article 11 says, among other things, "Any member of the United Nations may accede to the Union." Article 12 says, in part, "Each member country may withdraw from the Union by [one year's] notice of denunciation of the Constitution given through diplomatic channels to [the Swiss government]."

e. See 13 M. Whiteman, Digest of Int'l Law 241–45 (1968).

f. UPU, Compendium of Congress Decisions (Paris 1947—Hamburg 1984), at 20 (1985).

g. Constitution of the Universal Postal Union, as amended, in 1 Annotated Code of the Universal Postal Union (issued after each UPU Congress session).

The Constitution says nothing about suspension or expulsion of members.

There was a lengthy debate in the UPU Congress before Resolution C 6, the expulsion resolution, was adopted. The tenor of the debate leading to its adoption is indicated in the following summary.[h]

The representative of Malaysia said one of the fundamental principles of the international postal service was the unrestricted flow of mail between countries. The key word, he said, was "freedom." He said that "it would be contrary to that principle to grant freedom to governments which themselves did not respect the freedom of others."

The representative of Ireland, speaking on behalf of the members of the European Community, said that "the expulsion of a member of the UPU in the form proposed * * * would be contrary to the Constitution of the UPU, which did not provide for expulsion of members."

The representative of Tanzania responded that South Africa had cast aside the principles of human rights that were the foundation of the U.N. and its specialized agencies, including the UPU. "Why allow a country that did not ensure the equality of its citizens to remain a member? The Constitution should be made for people, and not the other way around. There was nothing to prevent Congress, the highest body of the UPU, from taking appropriate steps to enable the resolution to be adopted."

The representative of Botswana noted his country's common border with South Africa and its condemnation of South Africa's discriminatory practices. But he added, "There would appear to be no article [in the UPU Constitution] which empowers this Congress to expel a Member State. If ever any action is taken in that direction, it would be illegal."

The representative of Kuwait said, "Some speakers had argued that the Acts of the UPU did not provide for the expulsion of a member country. However, those Acts provided that the Union could accept a country as a member. If therefore the Union had the right to grant membership, it had also the right to withdraw it."[i]

The representative of Algeria mentioned the humanitarian concerns of the UPU and added, "If no text existed in the Acts which permitted the broaching of an exclusion procedure, none existed either which prohibited the exclusion of a country whose policy constituted a challenge to the international community."

The representative of the Yemen Arab Republic said, "According to article 12 of the Constitution, any country might withdraw from the

---

h. Summarized from records of the UPU 18th Congress, 6th, 7th and 8th plenary meetings (1979).

i. [UPU Constitution article 11(1) says that any member of the United Nations may accede to the Union. The only discretion regarding admission concerns non-members of the U.N. Under article 11(4), their applications require approval of two-thirds of all UPU members. Ed.]

Union if it did not apply the Constitution. Therefore, his delegation considered that South Africa had chosen to expel itself."

The representative of Japan concluded that, "According to well-established practice, it would first be necessary to alter the Constitution [since it provided only for voluntary withdrawal]. At present, [the proposal] was unconstitutional and inadmissible. No other specialized agency had made a decision to expel a country. An awkward and dangerous precedent would be set."

The representative of Mali "was amazed to note that [some] speakers made mention [of] legal scruples in the face of such a distressing situation, which consisted of South Africa holding in contempt both the law and human beings whose only crime was to be born black."

The representative of Madagascar said that his delegation "thought that the present august assembly, which was sovereign, could, for once, arrogate to itself the right to ignore the restrictive framework of its regulatory texts in order to cope with a system which constantly violated the most basic laws and which denied the smallest rights to the black South African population."

EVALUATING THE UPU ACTION

Were the arguments on either side legal arguments?

Which were the strongest arguments on either side? Could they be used against any member other than South Africa?

Before the vote was taken, the representatives debated whether UPU Constitution article 30(1) ("Amendment of the Constitution") applied to the situation. It says, "To be adopted, proposals submitted to Congress and relating to this Constitution must be approved by at least two-thirds of the member countries of the Union." There were 160 member countries, not all of which participated in the meeting. The vote on the expulsion resolution was 77 in favor, 44 against and 13 abstaining. Should it have been considered adopted?

In 1981 South Africa rejoined the UPU, taking advantage of UPU Constitution article 11, supra, which allows any member of the U.N. to accede to the UPU. When the UPU Congress next met, in 1984, another heated debate ensued. At the end of the debate, the Congress voted to exclude South Africa from the Union "until a future Congress of the UPU decides otherwise."[j] The vote was 77 in favor, 46 opposed and 10 abstaining.

Were the issues raised by the 1984 exclusion resolution the same as in 1979?

In the 1980s, Israel joined South Africa as the focus of attempts not only in the U.N. itself, but also in its related agencies, to apply the

[j] UPU, 3 Documents of the 1984 Hamburg Congress, at 932, 933 (1985).

sanction of suspension, expulsion or exclusion. For example, after the Israeli air attack on a nuclear reactor near Baghdad, Iraq, on June 7, 1981, an attempt was made in the International Atomic Energy Agency to suspend Israel from the rights and privileges of membership. (Israel asserted that the attack, which destroyed the reactor, was in self-defense as a result of a continuing threat of nuclear attack by Iraq.) On the morning of the last day of the 1982 IAEA General Conference session, a resolution that would have suspended Israel's membership was rejected because it did not receive the two-thirds majority required for adoption. The vote was 43 in favor, 27 opposed, and 17 abstaining.

That afternoon, Iraq proposed an amendment to the report of the Credentials Committee, adding "except Israel" to the approval of the participating representatives' credentials. After a procedural skirmish, the amendment was adopted by a vote of 41 to 39. It was a symbolic victory, since it came on the afternoon of the last day of the session, but it nevertheless caused a protest by the United States and some other member states. The United States suspended its participation in some IAEA activities, and temporarily withheld payment of its contributions to the IAEA.

In 1982, after Israel's invasion of Lebanon, a resolution was introduced in the Plenipotentiary Conference of the International Telecommunication Union (ITU) to exclude Israel from the Conference and from all other meetings of the ITU. At the urging of the delegates from the Netherlands and Norway, the Chair of the Conference asked the Union's Legal Adviser for an opinion. His response appears below. References in it to document 120 are to the proposed resolution. References to Nos. 2, 97 and 156 are to paragraphs in the ITU Convention, the Union's constituent instrument at that time. The Convention has been reformulated and re-adopted several times.[k] Each version has been identified by the site and date of the ITU Plenipotentiary Conference that adopted it. In 1982, the operative version was the Malaga–Torremolinos Convention of 1973.

OPINION OF THE ITU LEGAL ADVISER
Oct. 18, 1982.
1982 U.N. Juridical Y.B. 214.

* * *

I do not intend to go through the whole document 120 (Rev. 2). I shall only present you my legal opinion thereon with regard to two legal issues involved therein. The first one concerns the second preambular paragraph of the draft resolution, which reads:

"*Considering* that the fundamental principles of the International Telecommunication Convention are designed to strengthen

---

k. At the ITU's Plenipotentiary Conference in Nice, 1989, a formal Constitution for the organization was finally adopted. See Final Acts of the Plenipotentiary Conf., Nice, 1989 at 1 (1990). The Constitution is intended to be more stable than the periodically-revised versions of the ITU Convention have been. The new Constitution did not wholly supersede the Convention, which was again revised in 1989.

peace and security in the world by developing international cooperation and better understanding among peoples".

In this respect, I submit to this august Conference that "the fundamental principles", in the wording referred to in the above preambular paragraph, can be found neither in any of the provisions nor in the preamble [127] to the Convention. This is in particular true for the part stating that those principles "are designed to strengthen peace and security in the world".

Having given this clarification, I shall now take up the second and, in my opinion, fundamental legal issue involved in the draft resolution under consideration. It concerns the third and last operative paragraph "resolves" thereof. I note that it has been pointed out during the preceding debate that this operative paragraph indeed does not provide for the exclusion of the Member State in question from the Union. I submit, however, that its contents aim at suspension from the exercise of the rights and privileges of membership in the Union and thus touch the fundamental rights of a member in respect of its participation in the conferences, meetings and consultations of the Union, as they are stipulated in paragraph 2 (Nos. 8 to 10) of article 2 of the Convention.[129]

[The Legal Adviser quoted the passage set out at page 141 supra, from the first Admissions Case, 1947–48 I.C.J. 57, 64.]

* * *

[During the debate on the proposed resolution,] some delegates stated rather frequently that they consider this Conference as sovereign to the extent that it can go beyond what the Contracting States in the basic instrument of the Union, namely the Convention, have agreed upon and provided for. I submit to this Conference, with my utmost respect, that this is simply not the case. The Contracting States, by ratifying, or acceding to, the Convention and depositing the respective instrument with the Secretary–General of the Union, have agreed upon, and stipulated, the complete framework within which and under

---

127. The text of the preamble to the Convention reads as follows:

"While fully recognizing the sovereign right of each country to regulate its telecommunication, the plenipotentiaries of the Contracting Governments, with the object of facilitating relations and cooperation between the peoples by means of efficient telecommunication services, have agreed to establish this Convention which is the basic instrument of the International Telecommunication Union."

129. Paragraph 2 of article 2 of the Convention reads as follows:

"8   2. Rights of Members in respect of their participation in the conferences, meetings and consultations of the Union are:

"(a) all Members shall be entitled to participate in conferences of the Union, shall be eligible for election to the Administrative Council and shall have the right to nominate candidates for election to any of the permanent organs of the Union;

"9 (b) each Member shall have one vote at all conferences of the Union, at all meetings of the International Consultative Committees and, if it is a Member of the Administrative Council, at all sessions of that Council;

"10 (c) each Member shall also have one vote in all consultations carried out by correspondence."

which alone even a plenipotentiary conference of the Union, as the latter's supreme organ, is allowed to act.

* * *

It is clearly the intention of the draft resolution to sanction one member of the Union. The legal question thus arises: does the Convention provide for sanctions against members of the Union, and, if so, for what types of sanction?

Looking at the Convention, everyone in this august Conference realizes that there are sanctions provided for in the Convention, namely, in its Nos. 97 and 156.

I shall deal first with No. 156.[132] This is an automatic sanction, without any action needed by any of the organs of the Union, imposed upon any "signatory Government", which, "from the end of a period of two years from the date of entry into force of the Convention", has not "deposited an instrument of ratification" of the Convention. Such member of the Union will automatically lose its right to vote at any of the conferences and meetings of the Union in which it participates.

* * *

The second, equally automatic sanction is the loss of the right to vote, as provided for in No. 97 of the Convention.[138] [The previous Plenipotentiary Conference (Malaga–Torremolinos, 1973)] rejected the idea of temporary suspension of any member's eligibility to the permanent organs of the Union.[140] I submit to the Conference the conclusion that its predecessor, the Malaga–Torremolinos Conference of 1973, thus

---

132. The text of No. 156 (i.e., subpara. (2) of para. 2 of art. 45) of the Convention reads as follows:

"156 (2) From the end of a period of two years from the date of entry into force of this Convention, a signatory Government which has not deposited an instrument of ratification in accordance with 154 shall not be entitled to vote at any conference of the Union, or at any session of the Administrative Council, or at any meeting of any of the permanent organs of the Union, or during consultation by correspondence conducted in accordance with the provisions of the Convention until it has so deposited such an instrument. *Its rights, other than voting rights, shall not be affected.*" (Emphasis added.)

138. The text of No. 97 (i.e., para. 7 of art. 15) of the Convention reads as follows:

"97. 7. A Member which is in arrears in its payments to the Union shall lose its right to vote as defined in 9 and 10 for so long as the amount of its arrears equals or exceeds the amount of the contribution due from it for the preceding two years."

* * *

140. * * *

"At the *Chairman's* request, the *Legal Adviser*, in responding to the question put by the delegate of Mexico, referred to document No. 236 of the Malaga–Torremolinos Conference. From paragraph 3.24 of that document it was clear that in Committee 4 (Budgetary Questions) several administrative measures of a 'sanction' character had been considered and that the Committee, after extensive debate, had come to the following conclusion: Members in arrears in the payments of their contributions due to the Union should temporarily lose their voting rights; temporary suspension of their eligibility to the permanent organs of the Union was, however, regarded as inadvisable. In the light of those conclusions and in the absence of any provision in the Convention to the contrary, the Legal Adviser was of the opinion that members, though deprived of their right to vote, in accordance with Nos. 97 and 156 of the Convention remained eligible for posts within the Union's organs."

considered indeed the possibility of introducing sanctions other than only the loss of the right to vote, but that it rejected this idea when it adopted the text of the Convention at present in force, which, consequently, provides only for one sanction against a member of the Union, i.e., the loss of the right to vote, as stipulated in Nos. 97 and 156 of the Convention.

* * *

What does it mean, in legal terms, that the Convention does not contain any other provisions foreseeing any other sanction against a member? Does it mean that the Convention—or in other, perhaps better, words, the predecessor Plenipotentiary Conferences and, after them and even more important, the Contracting States—remained deliberately silent, because it was intended to leave free way for the imposition upon a member of the Union of any other, further sanctions? Or does it mean that it was not intended to provide a possibility for the imposition of any such other sanctions, e.g., like the one now envisaged in the last operative paragraph of the draft resolution in document 120 (Rev. 2)?

The last sentence I quoted from No. 156 of the Convention, i.e., that all other rights shall not be affected, is in my opinion already a clear indication and a convincing argument in favour of the second interpretation. In addition, I also submit for consideration by the present Conference the argument that the Malaga–Torremolinos Conference of 1973, which adopted the Convention at present in force, was very well aware of other possible sanctions against members of the Union, such as suspension from the exercise of certain rights and privileges of membership or expulsion. Both types of sanction have existed since 1946 in Articles 5 and 6 respectively of the Charter of the United Nations, with very specified and strict conditions, requiring even a two-thirds majority for any adoption of such measures, because of their being considered as "important questions". * * * During the debates on the "exclusion" or "temporary exclusion" of two other members "from the Plenipotentiary Conference and from all other conferences and meetings" of the Union, which led to the adoption by that Conference of its resolutions Nos. 30 [143] and 31,[144] articles 5 and 6 of the United Nations Charter have been expressly referred to. Nevertheless, that Conference did not change the Convention at all in this respect, as it could have done by inserting therein provisions similar to those contained in Articles 5 and 6 of the United Nations Charter. Therefore,

---

143. See resolution No. 30 of the Union's Plenipotentiary Conference, Malaga–Torremolinos, 1973, entitled "Exclusion of the Government of Portugal from the Plenipotentiary Conference and from all other conferences and meetings of the Union".

144. See resolution No. 31 of the Union's Plenipotentiary Conference, Malaga–Torremolinos, 1973, entitled "Exclusion of the Government of the Republic of South Africa from the Plenipotentiary Conference and from all other conferences and meetings of the Union".

the absence of other sanctions in the provisions of the Convention in force can, in legal analysis and according to my opinion, only mean that the Contracting States, first through their Plenipotentiaries in 1973, and thereafter through the deposit of their instruments of ratification of, or accession to, the Convention, did not intend to give the power to any of the organs of the Union, including the latter's supreme organ itself, i.e., the Plenipotentiary Conference, to impose upon a member of the Union any other additional sanction not expressly provided for in the Convention.

The preceding arguments [are] strengthened by the fact that for the first time the Malaga–Torremolinos Conference of 1973 included "the principle of universality" * * * in paragraph 1 of article 1 of the Convention, dealing with the composition of the Union. This principle has always, during the Union's long history, been a fundamental and guiding principle, without ever having been spelt out in precise words in any Conventions prior to 1973. It is now explicitly contained in No. 2 of the Convention in the following terms: "The International Telecommunication Union shall comprise members which, having regard to the principle of universality and the desirability of universal participation in the Union, shall be: * * * ". Consequently, the adoption by this Conference of the last operative paragraph "resolves" of the draft resolution contained in document 120 (Rev. 2) would, in my legal opinion, also run counter to this principle now enshrined in the Convention.

* * *

The adoption of [the paragraph in question] would, in my considered opinion, not be in conformity with the Convention and could, with good justification, be considered as illegal by any Contracting State Party to the Convention.

THE FATE OF THE DRAFT RESOLUTION

After further debate on the draft resolution in document 120, including debate on the legal issues,[1] document 120 was amended by secret ballot. The amendment, among other things, deleted the language that would have excluded Israel from the Conference and other meetings. The amended resolution was adopted by secret ballot as Resolution No. 74, below.

1. See Minutes of the 16th Plenary (1983). Meeting, Oct. 19, 1982, ITU Doc. No. 457–E

RESOLUTION ADOPTED BY THE ITU PLENIPOTENTIARY CONFERENCE REGARDING ISRAEL AND ASSISTANCE TO LEBANON

Resolution No. 74, 1982.
International Telecommunication Convention—Final Protocol, * * * Resolutions, Recommendations and Opinions, Nairobi, 1982, at 338, 339.

The Plenipotentiary Conference of the International Telecommunication Union (Nairobi, 1982),

recalling the Charter of the United Nations and the Universal Declaration of Human Rights;

considering that the fundamental principles of the International Telecommunication Convention are designed to strengthen peace and security in the world by developing international cooperation and better understanding among peoples;

* * *

noting that Israel has refused to accept and carry out the numerous relevant resolutions of the Security Council and the United Nations General Assembly;

alarmed by the grave situation in the Middle East resulting from Israel's invasion of Lebanon;

concerned at the destruction of telecommunications in Lebanon;

condemns without appeal the continuing violation by Israel of international law;

further condemns the massacres of Palestinian and Lebanese civilians; * * *.

THE LEGAL ADVICE AND ITS EFFECT

Does the ITU Legal Adviser's opinion stand for any (or all) of the following constitutional law principles for international organizations?

(a) It is improper for the plenary body of an organization to redefine the organization's fundamental principles beyond those expressly set forth in its constituent instrument.

(b) The plenary body of an organization is not at liberty to exceed the powers expressly or impliedly to be found in the constituent instrument.

(c) When an organization's constituent instrument contains a sanction for specified conduct of a member state, the organization may impose neither any other sanction for that conduct, nor any sanction at all for any other conduct.

(d) When an organization aspires to universality and its constituent instrument says nothing about suspension, exclusion or expulsion of members, the universality principle precludes the imposition of those sanctions.

Did the Plenipotentiary Conference, by adopting Resolution No. 74, acquiesce in any of these principles? Did it reject any of them?

Shortly before the vote was taken, the United States Secretary of State issued a statement threatening to withdraw the U.S. delegation from the ITU plenipotentiary conference, and to suspend payments to the ITU, if Israel were excluded.[m] Nevertheless, the exclusion of Israel was defeated by a margin of only four votes.[n] Do these facts affect your answers to the previous questions? If so, is the ITU Legal Adviser's opinion significant, of itself?

In footnotes 143 and 144, the ITU Legal Adviser referred to two resolutions that had been adopted at the 1973 Plenipotentiary Conference, excluding Portugal and South Africa from the Conference and from all other conferences and meetings of the Union. The next two Conferences (1982 and 1989) adopted resolutions continuing the exclusion of South Africa.[o] Like the 1973 resolution, the later resolutions relied in large part on U.N. General Assembly resolutions denouncing South Africa's policies on apartheid and on Namibia. In particular, they relied on General Assembly Resolution 2426 (1968), in which the General Assembly appealed to the specialized agencies to withhold from the government of South Africa "financial, economic, technical and other assistance." The ITU has entered into a typical relationship agreement with the U.N., as contemplated by U.N. Charter *articles 57 and 63*. It calls on the ITU to co-operate with the U.N. to make coordination of the activities of specialized agencies and of the U.N. fully effective, and to "render all possible assistance" to the U.N. in accordance with the U.N. Charter and the ITU Convention.[p]

Is the South African case in the ITU distinguishable from the Israeli case?

What precedent, if any, can be extracted from all the attempts in the United Nations and its related agencies to exclude, suspend or expel disfavored member states?

If there is a precedent, does it depend on the presence or absence of an express provision in the constituent instrument on suspension or expulsion?

Do the materials contain any lessons on how, or if, provisions on suspension or expulsion should be drafted for constituent instruments of "universal" organizations?

m. Secretary of State's statement of Oct. 16, 1982, in 82 Dep't State Bull., Dec. 1982, at 63.

n. See J. Savage, The Politics of International Telecommunications Regulation 53 (1989).

o. Resolution No. 14, Nairobi, 1982; Resolution No. 12, Nice, 1989.

p. Articles IV(3) and VI, in Agreements Between the United Nations and the Specialized Agencies, U.N. Doc. ST/SG/1, at 105, 107, 108 (1952).

REGIONAL ORGANIZATIONS

In 1962 the Organization of American States (OAS) excluded the Cuban government from participation in the organization. The resolution excluding the Cuban government, below, was adopted by a vote of 14 to 1 (Cuba), with 6 abstentions.

OAS RESOLUTION ON THE EXCLUSION OF THE CUBAN GOVERNMENT

Resolution VI, 8th Meeting of Consultation of OAS
Ministers of Foreign Affairs, Jan. 31, 1962.
OAS Doc. OEA/Ser.F/11.8, 46 Dept. State Bull. 281 (1962),
13 Whiteman, Digest of International Law 247 (1968).

WHEREAS—

The inter-American system is based on consistent adherence by its constituent states to certain objectives and principles of solidarity, set forth in the instruments that govern it;

Among these objectives and principles are those of respect for the freedom of man and preservation of his rights, the full exercise of representative democracy, nonintervention of one state in the internal or external affairs of another, and rejection of alliances and agreements that may lead to intervention in America by extracontinental powers;

* * *

The present Government of Cuba has identified itself with the principles of Marxist–Leninist ideology, has established a political, economic, and social system based on that doctrine, and accepts military assistance from extracontinental communist powers, including even the threat of military intervention in America on the part of the Soviet Union;

* * *

Such a situation in an American state violates the obligations inherent in membership in the regional system and is incompatible with that system;

The attitude adopted by the present Government of Cuba and its acceptance of military assistance offered by extracontinental communist powers breaks down the effective defense of the inter-American system; and

No member state of the inter-American system can claim the rights and privileges pertaining thereto if it denies or fails to recognize the corresponding obligations,

The Eighth Meeting of Consultation of Ministers of Foreign Affairs, Serving as Organ of Consultation in Application of the Inter–American Treaty of Reciprocal Assistance

DECLARES:

1. That, as a consequence of repeated acts, the present government of Cuba has voluntarily placed itself outside the inter-American system.

* * *

3. That the American states have a collective interest in strengthening the inter-American system and reuniting it on the basis of respect for human rights and the principles and objectives relative to the exercise of democracy set forth in the Charter of the Organization; and, therefore,

RESOLVES—

1. That adherence by any member of the Organization of American States to Marxism–Leninism is incompatible with the inter-American system and the alignment of such a government with the communist bloc breaks the unity and solidarity of the hemisphere.

2. That the present Government of Cuba, which has officially identified itself as a Marxist–Leninist government, is incompatible with the principles and objectives of the inter-American system.

3. That this incompatibility excludes the present Government of Cuba from participation in the inter-American system.

THE EXCLUSION OF THE CUBAN GOVERNMENT

The OAS Charter contains a provision (article 148) permitting member states to withdraw, effective two years from the date of formal notice of denunciation. It contains no provision for suspension or expulsion. Membership in the OAS is limited to American states; the organization serves in part as a mechanism for consultation and occasional confrontation on economic, political and social matters of common interest to the members, including emergency consultations in the event of an armed attack or other act of aggression against a member state; and the organization, through subsidiary councils, performs a number of largely recommendatory and promotional functions concerning economic, social, educational, scientific, cultural and juridical matters. In addition, the OAS Charter contains an expression of "fundamental rights and duties of states" based largely on the principle of nonintervention in the internal affairs of other member states. Complementing the OAS Charter is the Inter-American Treaty of Reciprocal Assistance (the Rio Treaty),[q] which sets forth duties to respond collectively in the event of armed attack or other aggression directed against a member state from outside the Americas, and also provides for certain peacekeeping functions in connection with disputes among American states.

q. Sept. 2, 1947, 62 Stat. 1681, 4 Bevans 559, 21 U.N.T.S. 77.

As a justification for "excluding" the Castro government of Cuba, it could be argued that there is an implied power of suspension or expulsion, absent anything in the constituent instrument to the contrary, when the organization is regional (rather than "universal") and consists of member states who share—or purport to share—common values and goals which they seek to effectuate through the organization.[r]

Did the Ministers of Foreign Affairs rely on this justification to get rid of the Castro government? If not, what justification could there be?

For purposes of an implied power of suspension or expulsion, is a distinction between "universal" and regional organizations convincing?

A 1986 amendment to the OAS Charter inserted this paragraph into *article 1:*

> The Organization of American States has no powers other than those expressly conferred upon it by this Charter, none of whose provisions authorizes it to intervene in matters that are within the internal jurisdiction of the Member States.

If the question of excluding the Cuban government had arisen after this amendment entered into force, could the OAS have lawfully done what it did?

What did the OAS accomplish in terms of its organizational goals by placing the Cuban government outside its ambit?

The Conference on Security and Cooperation in Europe (CSCE) has only recently begun to develop the organs needed to transform it from a periodic meeting of governments (mostly European, but also including Canada, the United States and the former Soviet republics) into a continuously functioning international organization. It originally set out to develop confidence-building and arms control mechanisms for Europe during the cold war, and to foster human rights—particularly in Eastern Europe. With the end of the cold war and the renewal of old ethnic conflicts in Europe, CSCE began to focus on peacekeeping and peacemaking.

In particular, the Yugoslav conflicts of 1991 and 1992 caught the attention of CSCE. After the United Nations had adopted the second of its Chapter VII enforcement resolutions against Yugoslavia (examined later in this chapter), and while the armed conflict in Bosnia-Herzegovina was still intense, a July 1992 summit meeting of CSCE governments decided to suspend Yugoslavia (Serbia and Montenegro) from participation for three months, blaming it for aggression in Bosnia and Croatia.[s]

---

[r] Cf. H. Schermers, International Institutional Law 81–82 (1980).

[s] See N.Y. Times, July 9, 1992, p. A13, col. 1.

Given the still-rudimentary structure and operational capability of CSCE, suspension for three months meant little more than non-invitation to one or two meetings of CSCE parties that might be held during that time. In these circumstances, is suspension from participation merely symbolic?

Is the power of suspension or expulsion, assuming it exists, likely to be an effective sanction in a regional organization? Is it likely to be effective in the U.N.? In any of the specialized agencies?

C. U.N. ENFORCEMENT ACTION

INTRODUCTORY NOTE

U.N. Charter *Chapter VII* empowers the Security Council to take enforcement action in case of a threat to the peace, breach of the peace or act of aggression. Enforcement action, in this context, means measures directed against a putative or actual state that is causing the trouble. It does not include U.N. peacekeeping, which is not directed against any state, but rather is an attempt to maintain relative tranquility in a volatile area until the parties are able to work out their differences. The next chapter of this book examines some aspects of U.N. peacekeeping.

At this writing, Chapter VII sanctions had been imposed against six states and one territory. The first involved broad economic sanctions against a nonmember territory, Rhodesia, after the 1965 unilateral declaration of independence from the United Kingdom by the white minority government of Ian Smith. (Rhodesia later became the independent state of Zimbabwe, free of sanctions.) The second occasion involved an arms embargo against South Africa in 1977.

The remaining Chapter VII sanctions have all been adopted since mid-1990. The Security Council imposed economic and military sanctions against Iraq after its invasion of Kuwait in August 1990. An arms embargo against Yugoslavia during the fighting in Croatia in the autumn of 1991 was extended in May 1992, after the conflict had spread to Bosnia–Herzegovina, to include a trade embargo, restrictions on financial resources, suspension of air transportation and other measures against what was left of Yugoslavia (Serbia and Montenegro). The trade embargo was tightened in November 1992. In January 1992 an arms embargo was imposed on Somalia during the devastating civil war there. In March 1992, the Security Council imposed a variety of sanctions against Libya arising out of its noncooperation in delivering named suspects in the bombing of a Pan Am flight over Lockerbie, Scotland; the sanctions included an arms embargo and suspension of air service to and from Libya. An arms embargo was applied against Liberia in November 1992.

1. Rhodesia

a. History

Explorers and missionaries in the 19th century preceded the surge of gold mining and other economic activities spearheaded by Cecil Rhodes.[a] In 1888 Rhodes obtained a concession for mineral rights from local tribal chiefs. In the same year all of the area that became Rhodesia and Zambia was proclaimed a British sphere of influence. The British South Africa Company was chartered in 1889 and the settlement of Salisbury, eventually the capital of Rhodesia, was established in 1890. In 1895 the territory, under the British South Africa Company's administration, was formally named Rhodesia (also known as Southern Rhodesia), after Cecil Rhodes. A landlocked territory in south-central Africa, it eventually occupied about 150,820 square miles.

In 1923, a constitution was adopted conferring self government upon Rhodesia, subject to supervision of the United Kingdom. An elected legislature was established, as was an independent judiciary. The right to vote was limited to persons of European descent. The United Kingdom retained several controls, including the power to legislate for Rhodesian affairs, to revoke or suspend the constitution, to appoint a Governor acting as the British crown's representative, and to disallow certain legislation passed by the Rhodesian legislature. The power in the United Kingdom to legislate for internal Rhodesian affairs and to disallow legislation adopted by the Rhodesian legislature remained dormant, and the United Kingdom eventually acknowledged that a custom had developed which precluded the exercise of these powers.

After 1923, there was a gradual increase in the exercise by Rhodesia of the power to participate in its own capacity in international affairs. It negotiated and concluded trade agreements with some foreign governments, and eventually became a contracting party to the General Agreement on Tariffs and Trade. At first, the United Kingdom generally conducted international negotiations on behalf of Rhodesia, but beginning in 1949 Rhodesia did so on its own behalf. Beginning in 1923, Rhodesia provided for its own defense. In World War II, its forces operating outside Rhodesia were integrated into the British Imperial Defense forces.

The United Kingdom, in concluding international agreements on its own behalf, followed the practice of permitting Rhodesia to choose whether or not it wished to accede to the conventions, with one notable exception. No such choice was afforded Rhodesia by the United King-

---

[a]. This historical outline is based in part on C. Palley, The Constitutional History and Law of Southern Rhodesia 1888–1965 (1966), where much greater detail than appears here can be found. For discussion from an international law perspective, see R. Zacklin, The United Nations and Rhodesia: A Study in International Law (1974).

dom when it entered into the Bretton Woods Agreements, establishing the International Monetary Fund and the World Bank. Despite its inclusion without consent, Rhodesia later acknowledged that it was bound by the Agreements.

Until 1949, Rhodesia did not confer its own nationality, but thereafter either it, or the Federation of which it became a part, did so.

In 1953, the Federation of Rhodesia and Nyasaland was created and a constitution was adopted along lines similar to the Rhodesian constitution of 1923. In April 1957, the United Kingdom formally announced that the Federation was to be entrusted with "responsibility for External Affairs to the fullest extent possible consistent with the responsibility which Her Majesty's Government must continue to have in International Law, so long as the Federation is not a separate international entity." The United Kingdom, in general, treated the Federation as a full member of the British Commonwealth vis-à-vis the other members, and let it settle its own disputes with other members.

In 1961 the British Government brought together African nationalist leaders and representatives of the European-led Salisbury government to draft a constitution for Rhodesia. In December a constitution was granted by the United Kingdom and approved by the predominantly European electorate in Rhodesia. It removed most of the remaining legal controls held by the British Government. The Rhodesian Government was headed by a Governor, appointed by the British Crown on the recommendation of officials in Salisbury. The Governor had essentially the same limited powers exercised by the British monarch. A Prime Minister, elected by the majority party in the Rhodesian Parliament, governed the territory. Except in the field of day-to-day diplomatic representation abroad, Rhodesia enjoyed a high degree of autonomy.

The significant features added by the 1961 constitution were a Bill of Rights and a second electoral roll with lower economic and educational franchise qualifications, thus permitting a number of Africans to qualify to vote. Both rolls were technically non-racial. The second roll in fact consisted almost exclusively of Africans and elected 15 representatives (13 of them black) out of a total of 65 seats in the Legislative Assembly in the elections of April 1965. The first roll, overwhelmingly European because of the higher educational and economic criteria, elected the other 50 representatives. Europeans constituted slightly less than five percent of the population.

In 1963, the Federation of Rhodesia and Nyasaland was dissolved. The British Secretary of State for Commonwealth Relations stated that Rhodesia now enjoyed "complete internal self-government." However, the British Crown was still represented in Rhodesia by the Governor. Rhodesia continued to exercise the same powers over its foreign affairs as had been exercised by the Federation. It succeeded to most Federation memberships in international organizations. As had been the case before the Federation, Rhodesian diplomatic representatives served on the staffs of British ambassadors abroad until the Rhodesian unilateral declaration of independence (UDI), except in South Africa and, in July 1965, in Portugal. In those countries Rhodesia established independent representation before UDI. The United Kingdom did not acquiesce in independent diplomatic representation abroad, and asserted that the British government was responsible for Rhodesian representation.

Until November 1965, the U.K. consistently argued in the United Nations that Rhodesia was self-governing and that the United Kingdom consequently was not an "administering state" within the meaning of the U.N. Charter. However, a special committee of the U.N. in 1962 stated that Rhodesia had "not yet attained a full measure of self-government" under *article 73* of the Charter, and that the United Kingdom therefore had certain responsibilities as an administering state.

Despite its insistence that Rhodesia was self-governing, the U.K. did not acknowledge formal independence, demanding that the Rhodesian authorities first demonstrate their intention to move toward majority rule. This produced an impasse, resulting in Rhodesia's unilateral declaration of independence from the United Kingdom on November 11, 1965. A new constitution was promulgated by the Rhodesian minority government under Ian Smith.

The United Kingdom formally asserted that Rhodesia remained a part of the U.K. dominions and that the U.K. had "responsibility and jurisdiction as heretofore." The United Kingdom declared that any action in promulgation of the new Rhodesian constitution was void, and prohibited enactment of laws or transaction of business by the Rhodesian legislature. At the same time, the U.K. made clear its intention not to use armed force to end the rebellion.

b. *The U.N. Response to UDI*

An urgent meeting of the U.N. Security Council was held on November 12, 1965, at the request of the British representative. The Security Council adopted Resolution 216, condemning "the unilateral declaration of independence made by the racist minority in Southern Rhodesia" and calling upon "all States not to recognize this illegal racist minority regime in Southern Rhodesia and to refrain from rendering any assistance to this illegal regime." Eight days later, the Security Council adopted Resolution 217, which determined that the situation was "extremely grave * * * and that its continuance in time constitutes a threat to international peace and security." Resolution 217 also called upon all states "to do their utmost in order to break all economic relations with Southern Rhodesia, including an embargo on oil and petroleum products."

In April 1966, the Greek oil tanker Joanna V was headed for Beira, a major port in Mozambique (then under the control of Portugal), with the apparent intention of discharging its oil for transhipment to Rhodesia.[a] Vessels of the British navy were on patrol in the area. When the British government suggested to its Greek counterpart that force be used, if necessary, to prevent the Joanna V from reaching Beira, the Greek government replied that it would not give its permission unless the U.N. authorized the British action. Although a British frigate stopped and boarded the Joanna V, it did not try to prevent the tanker from reaching Beira. Before the tanker could discharge its oil, and while another tanker, the Manuela, was on its way to Beira, the U.K. requested a meeting of the Security Council to obtain authorization to use force if necessary. The United States took the position in the Security Council debate that the Council's authorization would legitimize what would otherwise be an unlawful use of force on the high seas.[b] On April 9, the Security Council adopted Resolution 221, which formally determined that the situation in Rhodesia constituted a threat to the peace; called upon the Portuguese government not to receive at Beira any oil destined for Rhodesia; called upon the U.K. "to prevent by the use of force if necessary the arrival at Beira of vessels reasonably believed to be carrying oil destined for Rhodesia;" and empowered the U.K. to arrest and detain the Joanna V if it departed after discharging its oil cargo there. Two days later, a British naval vessel diverted the Manuela from its intended destination at Beira. In August 1966, the Joanna V left Beira without having discharged its oil.

As a matter of international law, would Resolution 221 have justified the U.K. in using force to arrest and detain the Joanna V if her oil cargo had been discharged at Beira? (What article of the Charter authorized Resolution 221? Did *article 25* apply to it?)

Later in 1966, the Security Council began to act explicitly under Chapter VII of the Charter:

SECURITY COUNCIL RESOLUTION 232
Dec. 16, 1966.
21 SCOR, Resolutions and Decisions 1966, at 7 (1968).

The Security Council, * * *

Deeply concerned that the Council's efforts so far and the measures taken by the administering Power [the U.K.] have failed to bring the rebellion in Southern Rhodesia to an end,

* * *

Acting in accordance with Articles 39 and 41 of the United Nations Charter,

1. *Determines* that the present situation in Southern Rhodesia constitutes a threat to international peace and security;

---

a. The facts outlined in this paragraph are based primarily on the account in J. Nkala, The United Nations, International Law, and the Rhodesian Independence Crisis 91–98 (1985). See also 13 M. Whiteman, Digest of Int'l Law 741 (1968); U.N. Docs. S/7256 & S/7501 (1966).

b. 21 SCOR, 1276th mtg., at 15 (1966).

2. *Decides* that all States Members of the United Nations shall prevent:

(a) The import into their territories of [selected Rhodesian exports, including chrome, tobacco and copper];

(b) Any activities by their nationals or in their territories [in aid of the export of these commodities from Rhodesia];

(c) Shipment in vessels or aircraft of their registration of any of these commodities [from Rhodesia];

(d) [Arms shipments to Rhodesia];

(e) Any activities by their nationals or in their territories [leading to the supply of any aircraft or motor vehicles to Rhodesia or their manufacture in Rhodesia];

(f) [Oil shipments to Rhodesia];

notwithstanding any contracts entered into or licenses granted before the date of the present resolution;

3. *Reminds* Member States that the failure or refusal by any of them to implement the present resolution shall constitute a violation of Article 25 of the United Nations Charter; * * *.

SECURITY COUNCIL RESOLUTION 253
May 29, 1968.
23 SCOR, Resolutions and Decisions 1968, at 5 (1970).

The Security Council, * * *

Noting with great concern that the measures taken so far have failed to bring the rebellion in Southern Rhodesia to an end,

* * *

Affirming the primary responsibility of the Government of the United Kingdom to enable the people of Southern Rhodesia to achieve self-determination and independence, and particularly their responsibility for dealing with the prevailing situation,

* * *

Reaffirming its determination that the present situation in Southern Rhodesia constitutes a threat to international peace and security,

Acting under Chapter VII of the Charter of the United Nations,

* * *

2. *Calls upon* the United Kingdom as the administering Power in the discharge of its responsibility to take urgently all effective measures to bring to an end the rebellion in Southern Rhodesia * * *;

3. *Decides* that, in furtherance of the objective of ending the rebellion, all States Members of the United Nations shall prevent:

[Here follows a list of measures amounting to a comprehensive trade embargo, except for medical supplies, educational equipment and material, publications, news material and, "in special humanitarian circumstances, foodstuffs"];

4. *Decides* [that Member States shall impose an embargo on investments in Rhodesia];

5. *Decides* that all States Members of the United Nations shall [prevent the entry into their territories of persons traveling on Rhodesian passports and persons ordinarily resident in Rhodesia who may have supported the illegal regime there];

6. *Decides* that all States Members of the United Nations shall prevent [their aircraft from operating to or from Rhodesia, and from connecting with any Rhodesian aircraft];

* * *

11. *Calls upon* all States Members of the United Nations to carry out these decisions of the Security Council in accordance with Article 25 of the Charter of the United Nations and reminds them that failure or refusal by any one of them to do so would constitute a violation of that Article; * * *.

LEGALITY OF THE SANCTIONS

The Security Council's adoption of economic sanctions against Rhodesia in S.C.Res. 232 was the first explicit resort to article 41 sanctions in the U.N.'s history. The U.S. Department of State prepared a background paper arguing the legal justification.

U.S. DEPARTMENT OF STATE, SOUTHERN RHODESIA AND THE UNITED NATIONS: THE U.S. POSITION
March 1967.
56 Dep't State Bull. 366, 375–76.

In ordering mandatory economic sanctions against Southern Rhodesia, the Security Council acted on solid legal grounds. Because a number of attacks have been launched against the action, however, its legal foundations are reviewed here.

1. It is argued that the situation in Southern Rhodesia poses no threat to international peace, as is required before mandatory sanctions can be applied, or that if there is a threat it is posed not by the actions of the Smith regime but by the possibility of action against that regime by African states.

Under the U.N. Charter, the members have entrusted to the Security Council the power to "determine the existence of any threat to the peace" and to "decide what measures shall be taken * * * to maintain or restore international peace and security." This is what the Council has done in the Rhodesian case, and under article 25 of the Charter all U.N. members are obligated to accept and carry out the Council's decisions.

The Council had ample basis on which to make a finding of a threat to the peace. The illegal rebellion of the Smith regime in Rhodesia has obstructed political development in that territory toward independence on the basis of majority rule, in defiance of the principles and obligations of the U.N. Charter. In the political context of the African Continent, such action could lead to civil strife that might involve other parties on one or both sides of the conflict. This does not necessarily presuppose deliberate forcible action by other African states against Rhodesia, although some states might very well become involved in such conflict eventually whether they wished to or not.

The Council thus concluded that the Smith regime's rebellion posed a threat to stability, security, and peace in the area, with which it must seek to deal effectively.

2. It is argued that the Security Council's action violates article 2, paragraph 7, of the Charter, which prohibits U.N. intervention in "matters which are essentially within the domestic jurisdiction of any state."

There is no basis for this contention. First of all, Southern Rhodesia is not a "state" and has not been recognized as such by a single government or international organization.

Secondly, the Security Council's move cannot be considered "intervention" since the Council acted at the specific request of the legitimate sovereign, the United Kingdom.

Third, the situation in Southern Rhodesia can in no way be considered a matter of "domestic jurisdiction." The U.N. has consistently recognized that Southern Rhodesia falls under the provisions of article 73. This article calls on members administering a territory "whose peoples have not yet attained a full measure of self-government * * * to develop self-government, to take due account of the political aspirations of the peoples, and to assist them in the progressive development of their free political institutions. * * *" Therefore, Rhodesia is the subject of international responsibilities owed by Great Britain on behalf of the peoples of Rhodesia to the international community. It is the discharge of these responsibilities which the Smith regime is trying to frustrate and obstruct.

Fourth, article 2, paragraph 7, specifically provides that the principle of nonintervention shall not prejudice enforcement measures under chapter VII. Economic sanctions are such measures.

THE COUNTERARGUMENT

Consider also the argument made by Dean Acheson, a former U.S. Secretary of State and an international lawyer.

STATEMENT OF DEAN ACHESON
July 7, 1971.
Hearings on U.N. Sanctions Against Rhodesia—Chrome, before the Senate Comm. on Foreign Relations, 92d Cong., 1st Sess. 37–38.

As stated by Mr. John A. Armitage on June 17, 1971, on behalf of the State Department before a subcommittee of the House Foreign Affairs Committee * * *:

> Our policy with regard to Southern Rhodesia is based primarily on that regime's action to deny an effective voice to its African majority in the determination of Rhodesia's future * * *. This is abhorrent to this country.

* * *

Mr. Armitage further told the House subcommittee that the United States is committed to continue sanctions by article 25 of the Charter requiring members to "accept and carry out the decisions of the Security Council in accordance with the present Charter." To be sure, in quoting the article, Mr. Armitage conveniently omitted the concluding phrase, * * * and this makes quite a difference.

The decisions of the Security Council which members agree in the Charter to carry out are to relate to threats to the peace, breaches of the peace, or acts of aggression. None have occurred. The threats have all been made and aggressions originated by others. Rhodesia has merely declared its independence, though without the acquiescence that Britain has granted to her other once connected territories. Rhodesia has threatened no one.

The complaint is over Rhodesia's internal matters in which the United Nations may not intervene by article 2, section 7 of the Charter. The answer to this, says the State Department is that Great Britain has invited intervention and that Rhodesia is not a state because no other state has recognized it as such.

The essence of sovereignty is the will and ability to exercise it. Britain has neither in regard to Rhodesia; and has had neither for 5 years. I venture to say that nothing could induce the British Government to take over responsibility of conducting the internal affairs of Rhodesia, which it has not had for 50 years, if ever. A state comes into being not by form—external recognition (else how did the first state come into being?)—but by taking over, exercising, and maintaining the powers of sovereignty.

The sanctions resolution is a nullity. Furthermore, it is a failure; to continue to comply with it will injure our national interests; and the only way to get rid of it is to disregard it.

QUESTIONS ON THE USE OF CHAPTER VII SANCTIONS

Was the Security Council action justifiable in terms of the Charter?

If the United States government had concluded that the action was not justifiable, would this have permitted it under the law of the Charter to resume imports from Rhodesia? [c]

What precisely was Mr. Acheson's article 25 argument? How strong was it? In this connection, consider some of the preparatory work for the U.N. Charter. The Dumbarton Oaks proposal for the eventual article 25 was worded slightly differently from the final version. It said, "All members of the Organization should obligate themselves to accept the decisions of the Security Council and to carry them out in accordance with the provisions of the Charter." According to the leading scholar on the history of the Charter, a committee at the San Francisco Conference "questioned whether [the phrase, 'in accordance with the provisions of the Charter'] was intended to modify the decisions of the Council or the compliance of the members. The Coordination Committee * * * changed the order of the wording so as to make clear that the members would be obligated to carry out only those Charter decisions that were legally mandatory. Its 'recommendations,' under the Charter would be precisely that, and therefore not obligatory." [d]

c. Compliance and Noncompliance With Sanctions

In its Resolution 253 (1968), the Security Council established a Sanctions Committee, to deal with the question of Rhodesia. The states represented on the Committee were the same as those represented on the Security Council. The Committee examined reports from the Secretary–General on implementation of the sanctions and received, from a variety of sources, reports of alleged sanctions violations. In addition, it considered ways in which sanctions could be made more effective.

When the Committee received reasonably reliable information concerning possible violations of sanctions, it requested the Secretary–General to communicate the allegations to the governments concerned. They were requested to investigate, to take appropriate action against any violators, and to provide the Committee with any further information available to them. If the Committee deemed the information inadequate, it requested additional information, including copies of commercial documents for the suspect transactions.

The Committee issued annual reports, in which it set forth the alleged sanctions violations brought to its attention and quoted relevant

---

[c]. The United States did resume imports of chrome from Rhodesia for about six years, pursuant to a mandate from Congress. See pages 631–34 infra.

[d]. See R. Russell, A History of the United Nations Charter 665; 1022 (1958).

portions of any replies to its requests. If a government's reply did not adequately settle the matter, the case was kept open while further information was sought, and appeared again in the next annual report. If no reply was received, the Committee named the nonresponding state on a quarterly list which it issued as a press release. If the Committee exhausted its inquiries without being able to resolve an alleged sanctions violation, it sent a standard note to the governments from which no further replies were pending. The note included the following paragraph:

> The Committee is not satisfied on the basis of the information in its possession that there has not been a breach of sanctions. The Committee hopes that the Government of _____ will pursue the matter further and inform it immediately of any further information that may come to light. Meanwhile, the Committee has decided to place in its permanent records the fact that insufficient information has been received to date to enable it to dispose of the case in a conclusive manner.[a]

Note that this procedure combined direct pressures and mobilization of shame—"nonsanctions" examined in Section 2, supra. It brought to light some violations and apparently engendered some tightening of controls by governments. But it was not very successful at getting behind the documents of suspect transactions to discover whether goods invoiced to or from South Africa (or Mozambique, before its independence) really were going to, or coming from, Rhodesia. Nor did the Sanctions Committee always enjoy the full cooperation of governments purporting to comply with the sanctions. In the words of one close observer of international sanctions, "Apart from a few important cases which were initially brought to light through the detective-work of investigative journalists, the cases dealt with by the Committee represented no more than the tip of the iceberg of sanctions evasion."[b]

Can you devise a more effective, yet politically attainable, system of information gathering, direct pressures and mobilization of shame to induce member governments to enforce economic sanctions imposed by the Security Council?

Could *article 5* or *6* of the Charter be used against a member state that either does not enforce article 41 sanctions or enforces them only selectively?

THE UNITED STATES AND RHODESIAN SANCTIONS

The Rhodesian sanctions were implemented in the United States by Executive Orders issued pursuant to the United Nations Partic-

a. Eighth Report of the [Committee], U.N. Doc. S/11927/Add.1, at 3 (1976).

b. M. Doxey, International Sanctions in Contemporary Perspective 108 (1987). See also Anglin, United Nations Economic Sanctions Against South Africa and Rhodesia, in The Utility of Economic Sanctions 23, 41 (D. Leyton–Brown ed. 1987).

ipation Act.[c] For the most part, the United States complied with the Rhodesian sanctions. In 1971, however, Congress enacted legislation designed to compel the President to resume importing chrome from Rhodesia. The opinion below considered it.

DIGGS v. SHULTZ
U.S. Court of Appeals, D.C.Circuit, 1972.
152 U.S.App.D.C. 313, 470 F.2d 461, cert. denied 411
U.S. 931, 93 S.Ct. 1897, 36 L.Ed.2d 390 (1973).

McGowan, Circuit Judge:

This is an appeal from the dismissal by the District Court of a complaint seeking declaratory and injunctive relief in respect of the importation of metallurgical chromite from Southern Rhodesia. The gravamen of this action was an asserted conflict between (1) the official authorization of such importation by the United States, and (2) the treaty obligations of the United States under the United Nations Charter. Plaintiff-appellants sought summary judgment, as did defendant-appellees alternatively to a motion to dismiss for failure to state a claim upon which relief could be given.

The District Court's ruling for appellees was grounded primarily upon lack of standing, but it encompassed as well a concept of the nonjusticiability of the issues raised. Although we believe there was standing upon the part of at least some of the appellants to pursue their cause of action judicially, we think that cause is not one in respect of which relief can be granted. Accordingly, we affirm the judgment of dismissal.

I

In 1966 the Security Council of the United Nations, with the affirmative vote of the United States, adopted Resolution 232 directing that all member states impose an embargo on trade with Southern Rhodesia—a step which was reaffirmed and enlarged in 1968. In compliance with this resolution, the President of the United States issued Executive Orders 11322 and 11419, 22 U.S.C. § 287c, establishing criminal sanctions for violation of the embargo. In 1971, however, Congress adopted the so-called Byrd Amendment to the Strategic and Critical Materials Stock Piling Act, 50 U.S.C. § 98–98h, which provides in part:

> Sec. 10. Notwithstanding any other provision of law * * * the President may not prohibit or regulate the importation into the United States of any material determined to be strategic and critical pursuant to the provisions of this Act, if such material is the product of any foreign country or area not listed as a Communist-dominated country or area * * * for so long as the importation into the United States of material of that kind which is the product

---
c. Dec. 20, 1945, 22 U.S.C.A. § 287c.

of such Communist-dominated countries or areas is not prohibited by any provision of law.

Since Southern Rhodesia is not a Communist-controlled country, and inasmuch as the United States imports from Communist countries substantial quantities of metallurgical chromite and other materials available from Rhodesia, the Byrd Amendment contemplated the resumption of trade by this country with Southern Rhodesia. By direction of the President, the Office of Foreign Assets Control issued to the corporate appellees in this case a General License authorizing the importation of various materials from Southern Rhodesia, and they began importation.

Alleging that the Byrd Amendment did not and could not authorize issuance of such a license contrary to this country's treaty obligations, appellants sought to enjoin further importation, to require official seizure, and to restrain use, of materials already imported under the General License, and to declare the General License null and void.

II

[The court found that several plaintiffs had standing. They included persons refused entry into Rhodesia or deported from it, and an author whose book was banned in Rhodesia.^d]

III

The District Court, in its comments to the effect that non-justiciability would necessitate dismissal of the complaint even if standing be found, reasoned as follows: It is settled constitutional doctrine that Congress may nullify, in whole or in part, a treaty commitment. Congress, by the Byrd Amendment in 1971, acted to abrogate one aspect of our treaty obligations under the U.N. Charter, that is to say, our continued participation in the economic sanctions taken against Southern Rhodesia. The considerations underlying that step by Congress present issues of political policy which courts do not inquire into. Thus, appellants' quarrel is with Congress, and it is a cause which can be pursued only at the polls and not in the courts.

In this court appellants do not seriously contest the first of these propositions, namely, the constitutional power of Congress to set treaty obligations at naught.[4] They seek, rather, to show that, in the Byrd Amendment, Congress did not really intend to compel the Executive to end United States observance of the Security Council's sanctions, and

---

d. [Sixteen years later, the D.C. Circuit held that Diggs v. Shultz was no longer good law on the standing issue. See Dellums v. Nuclear Regulatory Comm'n, 863 F.2d 968, 976 (D.C.Cir.1988). Ed.]

4. * * * Although appellants concede that Congress has the power to override treaty obligations, they contend that our commitment to the U.N. has more force than an ordinary treaty. Appellants argue on the basis of their interpretation of the U.N. Charter that Congress could override Resolution 232 only by withdrawing from the U.N. entirely. There is, however, no evidence that this country's membership in that organization was intended to be on the all-or-nothing basis suggested by appellants.

that, therefore, it is the Executive which is, without the essential shield of Congressional dispensation, violating a treaty engagement of this country. Appellants point out in this regard that the Byrd Amendment does not in terms require importation from Southern Rhodesia, but leaves open two alternative courses of action. The statute says the President may not ban importation from Rhodesia of materials classified as critical and strategic unless importation from Communist countries is also prohibited. Instead of permitting resumption of trade with Rhodesia, the President, so it is said, could (1) have banned importation of these materials from Communist nations as well as from Rhodesia, or (2) have taken steps to have these materials declassified, thereby taking them in either case out of the scope of the Byrd Amendment.

* * *

We think that there can be no blinking the purpose and effect of the Byrd Amendment. It was to detach this country from the U.N. boycott of Southern Rhodesia in blatant disregard of our treaty undertakings. The legislative record shows that no member of Congress voting on the measure was under any doubt about what was involved then; and no amount of statutory interpretation now can make the Byrd Amendment other than what it was as presented to the Congress, namely, a measure which would make—and was intended to make—the United States a certain treaty violator. The so-called options given to the President are, in reality, not options at all. In any event, they are in neither case alternatives which are appropriately to be forced upon him by a court.

Under our constitutional scheme, Congress can denounce treaties if it sees fit to do so, and there is nothing the other branches of government can do about it. We consider that this is precisely what Congress has done in this case; and therefore the District Court was correct to the extent that it found the complaint to state no tenable claim in law.

Affirmed.

WILBUR K. MILLER, SENIOR CIRCUIT JUDGE, concurs in the result.

CONGRESS, THE PRESIDENT, THE COURTS AND THE U.N.

The court gave short shrift to the appellants' argument that the U.N. Charter should not be considered an ordinary treaty under the well-established rule that, as a matter of domestic law within the United States, Congress may override a treaty obligation simply by enacting inconsistent legislation. See footnote 4 of the opinion; see also Committee of United States Citizens v. Reagan.[e] Should the U.N. Charter be treated just as any other treaty for this purpose? Is *article 103* relevant here?

e. 859 F.2d 929, 937 (D.C.Cir.1988).

If a U.S. court were to treat the Charter as superior to other treaties and thus at least potentially able to prevail over subsequent federal legislation, there would still be a question whether the particular Charter provision is self-executing. If not, it would not have the effect of federal law in the United States and thus could not, standing alone, prevail over federal legislation. According to the Restatement Third, Foreign Relations Law of the United States section 111(4), an international agreement of the United States is non-self-executing:

> (a) if the agreement manifests an intention that it shall not become effective as domestic law without the enactment of implementing legislation,
>
> (b) if the Senate in giving consent to a treaty, or Congress by resolution, requires implementing legislation [not applicable here], or
>
> (c) if implementing legislation is constitutionally required.

In practice, some provisions of an agreement could be self-executing while others are not. All provisions of the U.N. Charter that have come before U.S. courts have been held non-self-executing. But *article 25* has never been considered in a reported case. Should it be held self-executing?

In Diggs v. Shultz, if the court had decided that Congress did not require the President to resume imports of chrome from Rhodesia, should the court have enjoined him from doing so?

Could the U.N. Sanctions Committee have done anything about the U.S. violation?

In March 1977 the Byrd Amendment was repealed.

When economic sanctions are imposed, it is likely that the burdens of compliance will fall unequally on member states. The Rhodesian sanctions fell particularly heavily on Zambia, Mozambique and Botswana, all of which were dependent on Rhodesia for supplies and markets; in addition, Zambia and Botswana depended on Rhodesian transportation routes.

The U.N. Co-ordinator of Assistance to Zambia estimated the cost to Zambia of implementing the Rhodesian sanctions over the first decade at about $650 million, not counting unquantifiable costs such as the opportunity cost of diverting government officials' attention to sanctions-related matters rather than to pressing domestic concerns. Zambia turned to the Security Council for assistance. The Security Council appealed to member states to provide immediate technical, financial and material assistance to Zambia,[f] but the response through

---

f. See Security Council Res. 329 (1973).

the first decade of sanctions totaled only about $100 million.[g]

When Mozambique remained under Portuguese control, it did not apply the sanctions against Rhodesia. In March 1976, however, the independent government of Mozambique announced that it would apply them.[h] Like Zambia, it incurred costs in excess of assistance from other U.N. member states.

Consider the effect of U.N. Charter *articles 49–50*. Do they obligate member states to assist heavily-burdened states like Zambia and Mozambique in the Rhodesian sanction situation? Do they give such states any rights they wouldn't otherwise have?[i]

Is there anything in the Charter authorizing the Security Council to impose a binding obligation to assist states like Zambia and Mozambique? Consider particularly *articles 2(5), 2(7), 24, 25, 39–41, 49 and 50*.

Could compliance by a member state with sanctions be treated as a contribution to a peacekeeping operation, with its cost mandatorily apportioned among member states by the General Assembly under *article 17(2)*? Consider *articles 43 and 50*.[j]

Alternatively, could the Security Council excuse states like Zambia and Mozambique (or Jordan in the more recent case of sanctions against Iraq) from applying the sanctions? See *article 48*. Would it be advisable to do so?

d. Independence for Zimbabwe and Ending the Sanctions

In the mid–1970s the U.N. sanctions began to wear down the Ian Smith government in Rhodesia, but as the excerpt below points out, they were not the only—probably not even the major—factor leading to the transformation of Rhodesia into an independent Zimbabwe.

M. DOXEY, INTERNATIONAL SANCTIONS IN CONTEMPORARY PERSPECTIVE
45–46 (1987).*

In seeking to make an overall assessment of the effects of sanctions on the Rhodesian situation, it is hard to disentangle cause and effect. From 1965 first British and then UN sanctions obviously had a direct and generally adverse effect on the economy, particularly by hitting Rhodesia's export trade which brought a serious shortage of foreign exchange. But there was much adaptability and resilience and to the extent that economic sanctions stimulated agriculture and diversifica-

---

g. See U.N. Doc. E/5867, at 5–9 (1976).

h. See U.N. Doc. S/12005, at 8 (1976).

i. See L. Goodrich, E. Hambro & A. Simons, Charter of the United Nations: Commentary and Documents 337–42 (3d & rev. ed. 1969).

j. See the U.N. Legal Counsel's memorandum of June 15, 1976, in 1976 U.N. Juridical Y.B. 203; see also the Expenses Case, [1962] I.C.J. 151, 166, 167.

* Reprinted by permission of St. Martin's Press, Inc.

tion they might possibly have been viewed as useful and certainly not fulfilling the hopes of their backers. Similarly, Rhodesia's greatly enhanced dependence on South Africa which brought close economic integration was not a preferred outcome, and the disposition to negotiate an acceptable settlement may have been lessened by the mood of defiance and by the development of vested interests in the continuation of sanctions which marked the white Rhodesian scene.

But from the mid–1970s the situation in Rhodesia clearly deteriorated steadily. It was not that sanctions per se were more effective, although some of the predicted long-term effects of inability to maintain employment opportunities for increasing numbers of black school-leavers were beginning to be felt in both economic and political terms. Rather, external developments posed new and serious problems.

The first oil shock was followed by an international recession, while changes in the political configuration of the Southern African region were much to the disadvantage of the Smith regime. And all commentators agree that the steadily escalating level of guerrilla warfare inside Rhodesia had a devastating effect on the economy and on white morale. Statistics covering economic performance during the sanctions years are now available from the Zimbabwe Statistical Office. Perhaps the most telling are figures of white migration which still showed a small net gain in 1975 but showed a net loss of 41,246 for the years 1976–9. For a total white population of some 260,000 this was very serious indeed.

Taking the full range of economic restrictions in conjunction with the isolation of Rhodesia from the international community, and the universal non-recognition of its independent status, one must ascribe a cumulatively damaging effect to the overall UN programme. In the early years, the Smith regime hoped for a "withering away" of isolation; not only would economic sanctions break down (and here the Byrd amendment gave undue grounds for optimism) but international political acceptance would gradually come about. This proved a serious miscalculation of the calibre and tenacity of the forces ranged against Rhodesia, which were to grow stronger, not weaker, in terms both of moral credibility and of the economic strength of many of the third world countries whose goodwill Britain and other western powers could not afford to forfeit. Over fifteen years, the UN norms of non-discrimination and majority rule progressively delegitimised the Rhodesian and South African concepts of white minority rule and apartheid. Sanctions against Rhodesia, while not bringing an immediate result, contributed to the process of undermining white rule there (and in Southern Africa as a whole) but the guerrilla war, the independence of Angola and Mozambique, and pressure from South Africa for a settlement were probably of greater direct significance.

INDEPENDENCE

In 1977 these pressures led to negotiations between the Ian Smith government and the internal Rhodesian nationalist groups led by Bishop Abel Muzorewa. In March 1978 Smith signed the Salisbury Agreement with Muzorewa and two other black leaders, providing for qualified majority rule and eventual elections with universal suffrage. The civil service, the military and the judiciary were to remain under white control. Joshua Nkomo's Zimbabwe African People's Union (ZAPU) and Robert Mugabe's Zimbabwe African National Union (ZANU), both based outside Rhodesia, rejected the Salisbury Agreement.

The U.N. Security Council, in Resolution 423 (1978), declared the internal settlement illegal and unacceptable. Elections were held under the Salisbury Agreement, and Muzorewa was named Prime Minister. The Security Council, in Resolution 448 (1979), declared the results null and void.

In the fall of 1979 the British government convened the Lancaster House Conference in London, bringing together the three contending groups: the Muzorewa government, Nkomo's ZAPU contingent, and Mugabe's ZANU group. In a stunning diplomatic development, the negotiations led to agreement on a cease-fire, a new constitution and elections for full majority rule.

On December 11, 1979, Zimbabwe–Rhodesia reverted to a British possession when its parliament repealed the 1965 unilateral declaration of independence and voted to dissolve itself. A British governor was sent to preside over the transition and the elections leading to independence. Elections were held in February 1980. Robert Mugabe's party won the majority of seats, and Mugabe was named the first Prime Minister of Zimbabwe.

As soon as Zimbabwe–Rhodesia reverted to a British possession in December 1979, the British government unilaterally terminated its participation in the U.N. sanctions against Rhodesia. So did Canada, New Zealand and the United States, before the Security Council lifted its sanctions. The U.K. explained its decision:

> The situation which was determined by the Security Council in its resolution 232 (1966) * * * to constitute a threat to international peace and security, as reaffirmed by subsequent resolutions of the Council, has * * * been remedied and the purpose of the measures which were decided upon by the Council on the basis of that determination has been achieved. In these circumstances, the obligations of Member States under Article 25 of the Charter in relation to those measures are, in the view of the Government of the United Kingdom, to be regarded as having been discharged. This being so, the United Kingdom is terminating the measures

which were taken by it pursuant to the decisions adopted by the Council in regard to the then situation of illegality.[a]

Was it lawful for the United Kingdom and others to stop participating in the U.N. sanctions before the Security Council had terminated them? Consider Security Council Resolutions 232 and 253, at pages 624–26 supra; U.N. Charter *article 25*; Vienna Convention on the Law of Treaties articles *56, 57 and 62*. Consider also General Assembly Resolution 34/192 (1979)[b] (adopted by a vote of 107–16–21), which reaffirmed the U.K.'s authority in support of the right of self-determination in Southern Rhodesia, expressed concern about "the threats South Africa poses to the independence, unity and peace of Zimbabwe" and about "the threat posed by mercenaries to the establishment of genuine independence in Zimbabwe," and deplored "the moves by certain States to lift sanctions unilaterally, in violation of the measures imposed by the Security Council * * *." The resolution went on to declare that Security Council Resolution 253 "can be revoked only by a decision of the Council and that any unilateral action in this regard would be in violation of the obligation assumed by Member States under Article 25 of the Charter * * *."

On December 21, 1979, after ZAPU and ZANU had accepted the Lancaster House accords, the Security Council decided "to call upon States Members of the United Nations to terminate the measures taken against Southern Rhodesia under Chapter VII of the Charter * * *."[c]

Did this obligate member states to terminate sanctions?

Suppose the elections had not been held, and the situation had degenerated back into guerrilla warfare. Would the sanctions have been automatically reinstated, without further Security Council action? If not, would a resolution to reinstate them have been subject to the veto of the five permanent members?

2. South Africa

On November 4, 1977, for the first time in its history, the Security Council imposed mandatory Chapter VII sanctions against a member state: it ordered an arms embargo against South Africa. The impetus was provided by the South African government's measures two weeks earlier, when it banned 18 domestic civil rights organizations, closed two major black newspapers and arrested or banned at least 50 leaders of black or multiracial groups.

Under South African law then in force, a banned organization was suspended from all activities, usually for a specific, renewable period.

---

a. U.N. Doc. S/13688 (1979).

b. 34 GAOR, Resolutions and Decisions (A/34/46), at 2 (1979).

c. Security Council Resolution 460, 34 SCOR, Resolutions and Decisions 1979, at 15 (1980).

A banned individual was restricted to a designated area, sometimes his or her home; in addition, a banning order restricted the number and identity of persons with whom he or she could communicate, and prevented the banned person's views from being disseminated. A banning order against an individual normally was of five years' duration, but was renewable.

South Africa's crackdown came at a time of mounting anger and persistent questioning regarding the mysterious September 1977 death of Steven Biko in a South African jail. He had been the leader of the black consciousness movement in South Africa.

SECURITY COUNCIL RESOLUTION 418
Nov. 4, 1977.
32 SCOR, Resolutions and Decisions 1977, at 5 (1978).

The Security Council,

Recalling its resolution 392 (1976) strongly condemning the South African Government for its resort to massive violence against and killings of the African people, including schoolchildren and students and others opposing racial discrimination, and calling upon that Government urgently to end violence against the African people and take urgent steps to eliminate *apartheid* and racial discrimination,

Recognizing that the military build-up and persistent acts of aggression by South Africa against the neighbouring States seriously disturb the security of those States,

* * *

Gravely concerned that South Africa is at the threshold of producing nuclear weapons,

Strongly condemning the South African Government for its acts of repression, its defiant continuance of the system of *apartheid* and its attacks against neighbouring independent States,

Considering that the policies and acts of the South African Government are fraught with danger to international peace and security,

* * *

Convinced that a mandatory arms embargo needs to be universally applied against South Africa in the first instance,

Acting therefore under Chapter VII of the Charter of the United Nations,

1. *Determines,* having regard to the policies and acts of the South African Government, that the acquisition by South Africa of arms and related matériel constitutes a threat to the maintenance of international peace and security;

2. *Decides* that all States shall cease forthwith any provision to South Africa of arms and related matériel of all types, including the

sale or transfer of weapons and ammunition, military vehicles and equipment, paramilitary police equipment, and spare parts for the aforementioned, and shall cease as well the provision of all types of equipment and supplies, and grants of licensing arrangements, for the manufacture or maintenance of the aforementioned;

* * *

4. *Further decides* that all States shall refrain from any cooperation with South Africa in the manufacture and development of nuclear weapons;

5. *Calls upon* all States, including States non-members of the United Nations, to act strictly in accordance with the provisions of this resolution;

* * *

7. *Decides* to keep this item on its agenda for further action, as appropriate, in the light of developments.

SOUTH AFRICA'S THREAT TO THE PEACE AND THE U.N. RESPONSE

The "persistent acts of aggression by South Africa against the neighbouring States" were South Africa's incursions into Angola in pursuit of the paramilitary forces of the Southwest Africa People's Organization (SWAPO). Those incursions had been going on for some time.

Several members of the Security Council explained their positions regarding Resolution 418.[a] For example, the representative of the United States said, "We have just sent a very clear message to the Government of South Africa that the measures which were announced on 19 October have created a new situation in South Africa's relationship with the rest of the world."

The representative of Mauritius said, "[W]ere it not for the inclusion of preambular paragraph 2, which recognizes that 'the military build-up and persistent acts of aggression by South Africa against the neighbouring States seriously disturb the security of those States,' it would have been difficult for African members, especially for my delegation, to accept the first operative paragraph."

The representative of India said that the resolution was a warning to South Africa and an encouragement to those struggling against apartheid. "In the last analysis, it is an expression of the determination of the Security Council to make South Africa conform to the general will of mankind for the abolition of apartheid."

[a]. See U.N. Doc. S/PV. 2046, at 9–10, 28–30, 31 (1977).

In 1986 the Security Council reaffirmed Resolution 418.[b]

Consider exactly what precedent was set by Resolution 418. Does it stand for the proposition that a mandatory arms embargo is appropriate under Chapter VII of the Charter against a member state that (a) practices apartheid; (b) enforces apartheid by harsh measures; (c) persistently defies the U.N.; (d) conducts military incursions into other states' territories; (e) does all of these things; or (f) not only does all of these things, but is at the threshold of producing nuclear weapons?

Would Resolution 418 be juridically appropriate, under the terms of Chapter VII, if the answer is (a), (b) or (c)?

In each of the two years before Resolution 418 was adopted—i.e. in 1975 and 1976—the United States, France and the United Kingdom vetoed draft resolutions that would have applied mandatory sanctions against South Africa. In both cases the draft resolutions were directed against South Africa's then-extant policy of retaining control over Namibia.

The U.S. delegate explained his vote in 1975 by saying, "[M]y government believes that the situation in Namibia, however illegal, however unacceptable to the international community, does not constitute a threat to international peace and security. * * * [W]e cannot accept the view that there exists a threat to the peace in Namibia in a situation where the wrongdoer, South Africa, has offered, even if on terms not entirely to our liking, to enter into discussions with the organized international community on the objective of self-determination for Namibia."[c] At that time, SWAPO, a militant body with guerrilla warfare capabilities, was operating in Namibia. There was not yet an indigenous government in control of neighboring Angola and thus no immediate threat to South African control from across that border.

When the Security Council again considered the matter in 1976, a government hostile to continuing South African control over Namibia had come to power in Angola. South Africa had set a target date for Namibian independence under conditions unacceptable to most U.N. members. South Africa had also been accused of mounting aggression from Namibia against Angola during the Angolan civil war following its independence, and of conducting a military buildup in Namibia.

Why did South Africa pose a threat to the peace in 1977, but not in 1975 or 1976? Or did it pose a threat to the peace in all three years, leaving adoption of Chapter VII sanctions to the politics of the day—particularly on the part of the five permanent Security Council members?

Do international lawyers have anything useful to say about such questions?

b. Security Council Res. 591 (1986), 41 SCOR, Resolutions and Decisions 1986, at 17–18 (1987).

c. 73 Dep't. State Bull. 42, 44 (1975).

Namibia became independent in March 1990, on terms acceptable to the United Nations. This did not affect Resolution 418, which continued in force.

As in the case of the Rhodesian sanctions, it is difficult to measure the effect of the limited sanctions against South Africa. A report prepared by the U.N. Secretariat [d] has noted the cost to South Africa of developing its own arms industry to replace imported arms, and the high cost of illicit imports when those could be obtained. It went on to mention disinvestment in South Africa by several transnational corporations, and stressed the impact of measures taken in 1985 by transnational banks to cease all new lending to South Africa. Neither disinvestment nor bank lending moratoria were required by any U.N. sanctions.

3. Iraq

a. The Invasion of Kuwait and Initial U.N. Response

On August 2, 1990, Iraq invaded Kuwait and quickly overran the country. This followed Iraqi dissatisfaction over Kuwait's breaches of oil production quotas set by the Organization of Petroleum Exporting Countries (OPEC), and unsuccessful negotiations in which Iraq claimed that Kuwait was drilling for, and selling, oil belonging to Iraq. In addition, Iraq had unsuccessfully urged Kuwait to forgive all or a substantial part of the debt Iraq had incurred to it during the Iran–Iraq war of the 1980s. As will appear below, Iraq also asserted a territorial claim to Kuwait. Some observers thought, though, that the major Iraqi objective was control over Kuwait's Bubiyan and Warbah islands at the head of the Persian Gulf. Those islands dominate the approach to Iraq's only functional port and naval base, at Umm Qasr. See the map below.

d. U.N. Doc. E/C.10/1990/8 (1990).

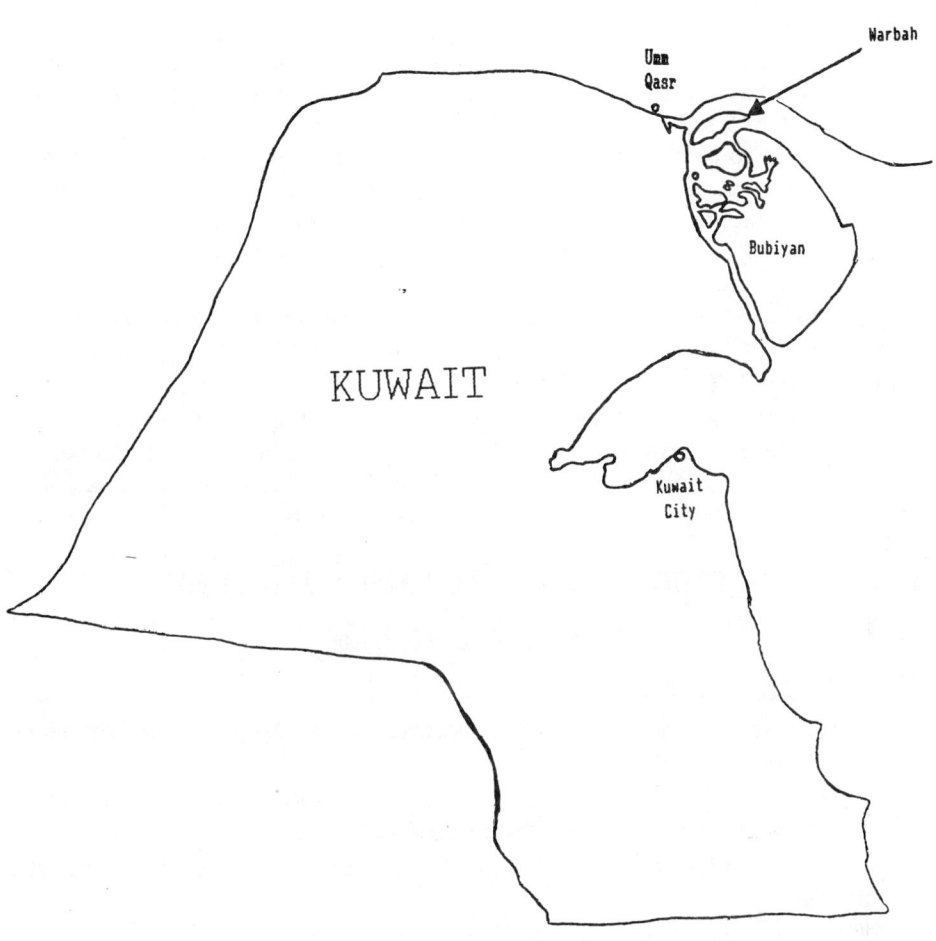

President Bush immediately condemned the Iraqi move as naked aggression, began moving warships in the direction of the Persian Gulf and the Red Sea, and froze $30 billion in Iraqi and Kuwaiti assets in the United States. The Arab League met in emergency session and issued a statement condemning Iraqi aggression against Kuwait, but a third of the members did not vote for it. The 12-member European Community immediately imposed an embargo on oil imports from Iraq and Kuwait, and announced that its members would no longer sell arms to Iraq. The United States began airlifting supplies and military forces to Saudi Arabia and eventually to other sheikdoms in the

Persian Gulf area, with their consent and apparently at their request. Within days, a substantial multinational military and naval force, including some Arab contingents, was arrayed around Iraq and Kuwait.

Iraq, after announcing at first that it would pull back from Kuwait, reinforced its military forces there. It also restricted the movement of foreigners in Iraq and Kuwait. It eventually allowed many nationals of third-world countries, and some women, children and ill or elderly men from Western countries, to leave. According to news reports, other Western civilians were restricted to quarters in or near possible military and industrial targets as human shields against attack. In Kuwait, Iraq ordered foreign embassies to close, and when some—including the U.S. embassy—defied the order, Iraq cut off water and electricity to the embassies. Large-scale plunder of Kuwaiti property and mistreatment of persons were reported.[a]

As soon as the United States government learned of the Iraqi invasion, it began efforts to persuade other members of the Security Council to take action. On August 2, less than a day after the invasion, the Security Council adopted its first resolution on the crisis.

SECURITY COUNCIL RESOLUTION 660
Aug. 2, 1990.
U.N.Doc. S/RES/660 (1990).

The Security Council,

Alarmed by the invasion of Kuwait on 2 August 1990 by the military forces of Iraq,

Determining that there exists a breach of international peace and security as regards the Iraqi invasion of Kuwait,

Acting under Articles 39 and 40 of the Charter of the United Nations,

1. *Condemns* the Iraqi invasion of Kuwait;

2. *Demands* that Iraq withdraw immediately and unconditionally all its forces to the positions in which they were located on 1 August 1990;

3. *Calls upon* Iraq and Kuwait to begin immediately intensive negotiations for the resolution of their differences and supports all efforts in this regard, and especially those of the League of Arab States;
* * *

ECONOMIC SANCTIONS

When it became apparent that Iraq would not respond to the Security Council's mere condemnation and demands, the United States

---

a. An assessment of the damage to property appears in U.N. Doc. S/22535, Annex (1991). An interim report on mistreatment of persons appears in U.N. Doc. S/22536, Annex (1991).

began to push for more forceful Security Council action. On August 6, the Security Council adopted Resolution 661 by a vote of 13 in favor, none opposed and two abstaining (Cuba and Yemen), imposing economic sanctions against Iraq. It was the first time in U.N. history that the Security Council had imposed comprehensive economic sanctions on a member state under Chapter VII of the U.N. Charter.

SECURITY COUNCIL RESOLUTION 661
Aug. 6, 1990.
U.N.Doc. S/RES/661 (1990).

The Security Council,

Reaffirming its resolution 660 (1990) of 2 August 1990,

Deeply concerned that that resolution has not been implemented and that the invasion by Iraq of Kuwait continues with further loss of human life and material destruction,

Determined to bring the invasion and occupation of Kuwait by Iraq to an end and to restore the sovereignty, independence and territorial integrity of Kuwait,

* * *

Affirming the inherent right of individual or collective self-defence, in response to the armed attack by Iraq against Kuwait, in accordance with Article 51 of the Charter,

Acting under Chapter VII of the Charter of the United Nations,

1. *Determines* that Iraq so far has failed to comply with paragraph 2 of resolution 660 (1990) and has usurped the authority of the legitimate Government of Kuwait;

2. *Decides,* as a consequence, to take the following measures to secure compliance of Iraq with paragraph 2 of resolution 660 (1990) and to restore the authority of the legitimate Government of Kuwait;

3. *Decides* that all States shall prevent:

(a) The import into their territories of all commodities and products originating in Iraq or Kuwait exported therefrom after the date of the present resolution;

(b) Any activities by their nationals or in their territories which would promote or are calculated to promote the export or transshipment of any commodities or products from Iraq or Kuwait; and any dealings by their nationals or their flag vessels or in their territories in any commodities or products originating in Iraq or Kuwait and exported therefrom after the date of the present resolution, including in particular any transfer of funds to Iraq or Kuwait for the purposes of such activities or dealings;

(c) The sale or supply by their nationals or from their territories or using their flag vessels of any commodities or products, including weapons or any other military equipment, whether or not originating in their territories but not including supplies intended strictly for medical purposes, and, in humanitarian circumstances, foodstuffs, to any person or body in Iraq or Kuwait or to any person or body for the purposes of any business carried on in or operated from Iraq or Kuwait, and any activities by their nationals or in their territories which promote or are calculated to promote such sale or supply of such commodities or products;

4. *Decides* that all States shall not make available to the Government of Iraq or to any commercial, industrial or public utility undertaking in Iraq or Kuwait, any funds or any other financial or economic resources and shall prevent their nationals and any persons within their territories from removing from their territories or otherwise making available to that Government or to any such undertaking any such funds or resources and from remitting any other funds to persons or bodies within Iraq or Kuwait, except payments exclusively for strictly medical or humanitarian purposes and, in humanitarian circumstances, foodstuffs;

5. *Calls upon* all States, including States non-members of the United Nations, to act strictly in accordance with the provisions of the present resolution notwithstanding any contract entered into or licence granted before the date of the present resolution;

6. *Decides* to establish, in accordance with rule 28 of the provisional rules of procedure of the Security Council, a Committee of the Security Council consisting of all the members of the Council, to undertake the following tasks and to report on its work to the Council with its observations and recommendations:

(a) To examine the reports on the progress of the implementation of the present resolution which will be submitted by the Secretary-General;

(b) To seek from all States further information regarding the action taken by them concerning the effective implementation of the provisions laid down in the present resolution; * * *.

THE LEGAL AND HUMANITARIAN ISSUES

Which article in Chapter VII authorized Resolution 661?

Were all provisions of the resolution binding? For example, did paragraph 5 obligate all states (or at least all member states) to apply the economic sanctions despite any pre-existing contracts?

The resolution spoke to all states, including non-members. See the introduction to paragraph 3, and paragraph 5. What gives the U.N. authority to speak to non-members? Would they be bound by the resolution? See U.N. Charter *article 2(6);* Vienna Convention on the Law of Treaties *articles 35 and 38.*

Did the resolution adequately provide for humanitarian concerns?

b. History

To fill in the Iraqi claims regarding Kuwait, some history is in order.[a] Before World War I, the Ottoman Empire encompassed all of what are now Syria, Lebanon, Israel, Jordan and Kuwait, but only parts of what are now Iraq and Saudi Arabia. Kuwait was at the very edge of the Empire, and the Ottoman governors allowed its sheiks considerable autonomy. By the late 19th Century, the British had important political and commercial interests in the Middle East, and became concerned that other European powers might get a foothold in Kuwait. Thus, in 1899, when the sheik of Kuwait (Mubarak) approached the British in an effort to enhance his autonomy from Ottoman rule, he found the British receptive. An agreement was entered into between the sheik of Kuwait and the British government, in which the sheik pledged himself and his successors not to deal with any foreign power within his territory unless the British government had consented, in return for money and what amounted to a British promise of protection.

The first attempt to define the border between Kuwait and Basrah Province (southern Iraq) came in the British–Ottoman draft convention of July 29, 1913. It said that the sheik of Kuwait exercised autonomy in a semi-circle with Kuwait City at the center, including several Persian Gulf islands—among them, Warbah and Bubiyan, which were to become important in the modern Iraq–Kuwait dispute. The draft convention was signed, subject to ratification. World War I intervened, and it was never ratified.

During World War I, Britain declared war on the Ottoman Empire, and British forces gained control of the Persian Gulf area. With the end of the war in 1918, the Ottoman Empire was reduced to its home base, modern Turkey. British dominance in the Middle East, outside of Syria and Lebanon, continued. The League of Nations granted Great Britain mandates to administer Palestine, Transjordan and Iraq, but not Kuwait—which remained a British protectorate outside the League of Nations system. Territorial boundaries were not clearly defined in the Gulf area.

After World War I, a boundary dispute arose between the sheiks of Kuwait and what is now Saudi Arabia. The British High Commissioner in Iraq, Sir Percy Cox, convened the Uqair conference in November 1922, to try to settle the dispute. When the conference reached an impasse, Sir Percy called in the parties and, in effect, dictated the borders not only between Kuwait and Saudi Arabia, but also between Kuwait and Iraq. This left Iraq with no coastline on the Persian Gulf.

---

[a] The historical account is based primarily on Khadduri, Iraq's Claim to the Sovereignty of Kuwayt, 23 N.Y.U.J. Int'l L. & Pol. 5 (1990); Wash. Post, Aug. 31, 1990, p. A1, col. 2; N.Y. Times, Sept. 3, 1990, p. 7 col. 1. For the Iraqi perspective, see U.N. Doc. S/24044 (1992).

On behalf of the British government, in 1923 he also recognized the sheik of Kuwait's claim to Warbah and Bubiyan islands in an exchange of letters with the British Political Agent in Kuwait. His position apparently reflected British concerns that Iraq would be the most powerful state in the region, and would potentially be too powerful for British tastes if it had a convenient port on the Gulf.

Iraq became an independent state in 1932, when the British mandate was terminated. On July 21, 1932, the Prime Minister of Iraq sent a note to the British High Commissioner requesting the agreement of the Kuwaiti authorities to a boundary described in general terms that reflected the 1922–1923 boundary, including the islands. The note was forwarded to the sheik of Kuwait, who accepted the boundary in a letter dated August 10, 1932. It appears that under the then-existing Iraqi constitution, however, any international agreement had to be approved by the parliament and then ratified by the king. This was not done. In October 1932 the Prime Minister resigned, and nothing further was done about the boundary at that point.

> The arbitrary borders that divided Iraq and the other Arab lands of the old Ottoman Empire caused severe economic dislocations, frequent border disputes, and a debilitating ideological conflict. * * * In the south, the British-created border (drawn through the desert on the understanding that the region was largely uninhabited) impeded migration patterns and led to great tribal unrest. Also in the south, uncertainty surrounding Iraq's new borders with Kuwait, with Saudi Arabia, and especially with Iran led to frequent border skirmishes.[b]

In 1951 another attempt was made to settle the Iraq–Kuwait boundary, but it failed. In 1958 the Iraqi monarchy was overthrown. In April 1961, the Iraqi Prime Minister asserted that there was no frontier between Iraq and the Kuwaiti people. On June 19, 1961, the British government formally terminated the protectorate over Kuwait. Iraq did not recognize Kuwait's independence, and massed troops on the existing border. The troops pulled back when Britain rushed to Kuwait's assistance, but Iraq still did not recognize Kuwait as an independent state.

The Iraqi regime that had taken power in 1958 was overthrown in 1963. The new ruling Baath party—the predecessor to Saddam Hussein's regime—recognized Kuwait's independence in "Agreed Minutes" signed at a meeting between Kuwaiti and Iraqi representatives in Baghdad. A considerable sum of money may have passed from Kuwait to Iraq as part of the deal, though it is not mentioned in the Agreed Minutes. The government of Kuwait registered the Agreed Minutes with the U.N. Secretariat under U.N. Charter *article 102(1)*. Apparent-

---

b. Library of Congress (Federal Research Division), Iraq: A Country Study 40 (4th ed. 1990).

ly, neither Kuwait nor Iraq ever submitted them to any domestic ratification process.

AGREED MINUTES BETWEEN KUWAIT AND IRAQ
Oct. 4, 1963.
Document 7063, 485 U.N.T.S. 326.

* * *

Believing in the need to rectify all that blemished the Iraqi-Kuwaiti relations as a result of the attitude of the past Kassim regime towards Kuwait before the dawn of the blessed revolution of the 14th of Ramadhan;

Convinced with the national duty dictating the inauguration of a new page consistent with the bonds and relations between the two Arab countries which are free from the artificial gap created by the past regime in Iraq;

* * *

The two delegations have agreed to the following:

1. The Republic of Iraq recognized the independence and complete sovereignty of the State of Kuwait with its boundaries as specified in the letter of the Prime Minister of Iraq dated 21.7.1932 and which was accepted by the ruler of Kuwait in his letter dated 10.8.1932;

2. The two Governments shall work towards reinforcing the fraternal relations subsisting between the two sister countries, inspired by their national duty, common interest and aspiration to a complete Arab Unity;

3. The two Governments shall work towards establishing cultural, commercial and economical co-operation between the two countries and the exchange of technical information.

In order to realize all the foregoing objectives, they shall immediately establish diplomatic relations between them at the level of ambassadors.

MORE HISTORY

The letters mentioned in paragraph 1 of the Agreed Minutes are the Iraqi note of July 21, 1932, and the Kuwaiti letter of August 10, 1932, described above.

When Saddam Hussein seized power in Iraq in 1969, he reasserted Iraq's territorial claims to Kuwait. Meanwhile, tensions arose between Iraq and Iran. Ostensibly to protect against a possible Iranian attack, Iraq requested Kuwait to allow Iraqi troops to be stationed in a position extending a short distance into Kuwait's claimed territory. Kuwait reluctantly agreed. The troops remained until 1977. They did not return when war broke out between Iraq and Iran in 1980.

The 50–mile–long Rumaila oil field straddles the border between Iraq and Kuwait, near Basrah. Most of it is in recognized Iraqi territory. Before the Iraq–Iran war, Iraq operated 225 oil wells in the Rumaila field. Kuwait also had wells in the field. During the Iraq–Iran war, Iraq mined its wells to prevent them from falling into Iranian hands, while Kuwait continued to pump oil from its wells. Iraq resumed pumping from its wells only after its war with Iran ended in 1988. Saddam Hussein later claimed that Kuwait owed Iraq $2.4 billion for oil taken from the Rumaila field. He charged also that Kuwait greatly exceeded its OPEC oil production quota in 1989, driving down world oil prices and depriving Iraq of billions of dollars in potential oil revenue.

Shortly after the invasion of Kuwait in 1990, Iraq announced that it had annexed Kuwait as part of Iraq. The Security Council promptly adopted Resolution 662 (1990), unanimously declaring that the annexation "has no legal validity and is * * * null and void."

Did this leave Iraq with any plausible claim to sovereignty over Kuwait?

c. *Enforcing the Economic Sanctions*

On August 12, 1990, the United States government announced an "interdiction" policy to use force, if necessary, to prevent any ships from contravening the international trade sanctions embodied in Security Council Resolution 661, supra. The government refrained from calling it a blockade, but the effect was the same. At that time the Security Council had not yet explicitly authorized the use of force to support its trade sanctions. The United States reported its action to the Security Council, and gave this justification:

> In accordance with Article 51 of the Charter of the United Nations, I wish * * * to report that the United States, at the request of the Government of Kuwait, [has] joined the Government of Kuwait in taking actions to intercept vessels seeking to engage in trade with Iraq or Kuwait in violation of the mandatory sanctions imposed in Security Council resolution 661 (1990). These actions are being taken by the United States in the exercise of the inherent right of individual and collective self-defense, recognized in Article 51 of the Charter. The application of this inherent right in response to the Iraqi armed attack on Kuwait has been affirmed in resolution 661 (1990).
>
> The United States has joined the Government of Kuwait and other Governments in taking these actions to ensure that the trade sanctions designed to secure the compliance of Iraq with resolution 660 (1990) and to restore the legitimate Government of Kuwait, are effective. The military forces of the United States will use force

only if necessary and then only in a manner proportionate to prevent vessels from violating such trade sanctions contained in resolution 661 (1990).[a]

The exiled government of Kuwait confirmed that, acting under U.N. Charter article 51, it had "requested some nations to take such military and other steps as are necessary to ensure the effective and prompt implementation of Security Council resolution 661 (1990)."[b]

Did the United States give one legal justification or two for its actions? (Were there two plausible justifications?) In answering these questions, consider the following paragraphs.

In the Case Concerning Military and Paramilitary Activities in and Against Nicaragua,[c] the International Court of Justice said that for a right of collective self-defense to arise, an armed attack must have occurred and the victim state must have declared itself to have been attacked. In addition, "in customary international law * * * there is no rule permitting the exercise of collective self-defence in the absence of a request by the State which regards itself as the victim of an armed attack." This explains why the U.S. government made sure that it had a request from the Kuwaiti government-in-exile before it announced the "interdiction." Does it provide a convincing legal justification under the circumstances in August 1990? See U.N. Charter *article 51*, and note the reference to it in the preamble to Security Council resolution 661.

Consider also whether the incident involving oil tankers at the port of Beira in April 1966, after the Rhodesian unilateral declaration of independence in 1965, provides a precedent. After the Security Council had adopted resolutions condemning the declaration of independence and calling upon all states not to recognize the "illegal racist minority regime in Southern Rhodesia," but before the Council had adopted mandatory economic sanctions, an oil tanker docked at the Mozambique port of Beira (then under Portuguese control) with the apparent intention of delivering oil for Rhodesia, and another was heading for the port. The United Kingdom requested and obtained Security Council Resolution 221, specifically calling upon it to use force if necessary to prevent the arrival of oil tankers at Beira believed to be carrying oil for Rhodesia. The British navy then diverted the second oil tanker, and the first left without discharging its oil. See pages 623–24 supra, for further details.

The unilateral U.S. "interdiction" did not sit well with most other members of the Security Council. They took the position that another Security Council resolution was needed in order to authorize any threat or use of armed force, and that it was premature to adopt such a resolution while there was no indication of any significant breaches of the sanctions against Iraq. In addition, the Soviet Union took the

a. U.N. Doc. S/21537 (1990).
b. U.N. Doc. S/21498 (1990).
c. (Nicaragua v. United States), [1986] I.C.J. 14, 105.

position that any use of armed force should be under U.N. supervision pursuant to U.N. Charter *articles 42–49*, rather than by naval or military forces of individual nations acting under a general authorization from the Security Council.

Note especially articles 43 and 47. No agreements under article 43 have ever been concluded, largely because immediately after War II—when the United States led an effort to negotiate them—the Soviet Union feared that they would be used to establish threatening Western military bases. The Military Staff Committee (article 47) met perfunctorily for many years, finally getting down to substantive business only in 1990 with the advent of the Persian Gulf crisis. Even then, it was not able to influence policy decisions in any significant way.

Under pressure from the other governments, and to avoid difficulties if ships from countries sympathetic to the sanctions were boarded by U.S. naval ships, the United States began a concentrated effort to win the support of the other Security Council members for a new resolution authorizing the use of force to police the trade sanctions. The United States, however, did not want to place its naval ships or military forces under U.N. command or under the command of anyone not subject to President Bush's authority. Since that was inconsistent with the Soviet position, which stressed use of the Military Staff Committee, the negotiations over the appropriate resolution were intense. Eventually a compromise was reached, and at 4:10 a.m. on Saturday, August 27, the Security Council adopted the resolution below. The vote was 13 to none, with Cuba and Yemen abstaining.

SECURITY COUNCIL RESOLUTION 665
August 27, 1990.
U.N.Doc. S/RES/665 (1990).

The Security Council,

* * *

Having decided in resolution 661 (1990) to impose economic sanctions under Chapter VII of the Charter of the United Nations,

* * *

1. *Calls upon* those Member States co-operating with the Government of Kuwait which are deploying maritime forces to the area to use such measures commensurate to the specific circumstances as may be necessary under the authority of the Security Council to halt all inward and outward maritime shipping in order to inspect and verify their cargoes and destinations and to ensure strict implementation of the provisions related to such shipping laid down in resolution 661 (1990);

2. *Invites* Member States accordingly to co-operate as may be necessary to ensure compliance with the provisions of resolution 661 (1990) with maximum use of political and diplomatic measures, in accordance with paragraph 1 above;

3. *Requests* all States to provide in accordance with the Charter such assistance as may be required by the States referred to in paragraph 1 of this resolution;

4. *Further requests* the States concerned to co-ordinate their actions in pursuit of the above paragraphs of this resolution using as appropriate mechanisms of the Military Staff Committee and after consultation with the Secretary-General to submit reports to the Security Council and its Committee established under resolution 661 (1990) to facilitate the monitoring of the implementation of this resolution;
* * *.

SOURCE AND EFFECT OF RESOLUTION 665

Was Resolution 665 adopted pursuant to U.N. Charter article 42? If not, what article in the Charter authorized it?

Did operative paragraph 1 of the resolution, as adopted, authorize the U.S. Navy to use force to stop, board and seize merchant vessels bound for, or departing from, Iraq and Kuwait? If so, would "political and diplomatic measures," under operative paragraph 2, have to be tried first? (What "political and diplomatic measures" would these be?)

Would any use of force under operative paragraph 1 be subject to the control of the Military Staff Committee?

The embargo on maritime shipping to and from Iraq, supported by Resolution 665, was effective. The question arose, however, whether it could be circumvented by aircraft flying in and out of Iraq over the territories of neighboring states.

Enforcement of an air embargo was a problem. It is one thing to stop and search vessels at sea; it is quite another to "stop" (shoot down) aircraft in flight. When the Soviet Union shot down Korean Air Lines flight 007 in 1983, a broad consensus emerged that the use of weapons against civil aviation is a violation of customary international law. An amendment to the Chicago Convention on International Civil Aviation (*article 3 bis*), codifying this custom, has been adopted. At the time of the Persian Gulf crisis, it was in the process of being ratified by the members of the International Civil Aviation Organization. None of the Security Council members wanted to authorize destructive unilateral action otherwise prohibited by customary international law. They settled on Resolution 670, below.

SECURITY COUNCIL RESOLUTION 670
Sept. 25, 1990.
U.N.Doc. S/RES/670 (1990).

The Security Council,

* * *

Determined to ensure by all necessary means the strict and complete application of the measures laid down in resolution 661 (1990),

Determined to ensure respect for its decisions and the provisions of Articles 25 and 48 of the Charter of the United Nations,

* * *

Recalling the provisions of Article 103 of the Charter of the United Nations,

Acting under Chapter VII of the Charter of the United Nations,

1. *Calls upon* all States to carry out their obligations to ensure strict and complete compliance with resolution 661 (1990) and in particular paragraphs 3, 4 and 5 thereof;

2. *Confirms* that resolution 661 (1990) applies to all means of transport, including aircraft;

3. *Decides* that all States, notwithstanding the existence of any rights or obligations conferred or imposed by any international agreement or any contract entered into or any licence or permit granted before the date of the present resolution, shall deny permission to any aircraft to take off from their territory if the aircraft would carry any cargo to or from Iraq or Kuwait other than food in humanitarian circumstances, subject to authorization by the Council or the Committee established by resolution 661 (1990) and in accordance with resolution 666 (1990), or supplies intended strictly for medical purposes or solely for UNIIMOG;[d]

4. *Decides further* that all States shall deny permission to any aircraft destined to land in Iraq or Kuwait, whatever its State of registration, to overfly its territory unless:

(a) The aircraft lands at an airfield designated by that State outside Iraq or Kuwait in order to permit its inspection to ensure that there is no cargo on board in violation of resolution 661 (1990) or the present resolution, and for this purpose the aircraft may be detained for as long as necessary; or

(b) The particular flight has been approved by the Committee established by resolution 661 (1990); or

(c) The flight is certified by the United Nations as solely for the purposes of UNIIMOG;

5. *Decides* that each State shall take all necessary measures to ensure that any aircraft registered in its territory or operated by an operator who has his principal place of business or permanent residence in its territory complies with the provisions of resolution 661 (1990) and the present resolution;

---

d. [UNIIMOG was the U.N. Iran–Iraq Military Observer Group, set up to monitor the cease-fire between Iran and Iraq. Ed.]

6. *Decides further* that all States shall notify in a timely fashion the Committee established by resolution 661 (1990) of any flight between its territory and Iraq or Kuwait to which the requirement to land in paragraph 4 above does not apply, and the purpose for such a flight;

7. *Calls upon* all States to co-operate in taking such measures as may be necessary, consistent with international law, including the Chicago Convention, to ensure the effective implementation of the provisions of resolution 661 (1990) or the present resolution;

8. *Calls upon* all States to detain any ships of Iraqi registry which enter their ports and which are being or have been used in violation of resolution 661 (1990), or to deny such ships entrance to their ports except in circumstances recognized under international law as necessary to safeguard human life;

* * *

12. *Decides* to consider, in the event of evasion of the provisions of resolution 661 (1990) or of the present resolution by a State or its nationals or through its territory, measures directed at the State in question to prevent such evasion; * * *.

THE EFFECT OF RESOLUTION 670

Suppose that a U.N. member state had previously entered into a bilateral air services agreement with Iraq, authorizing use of its airfields and airspace by aircraft with cargo destined for Iraq. Would Resolution 670 supersede that agreement, and (a) excuse it from its duties to Iraq under the agreement, if it denied use of its airfields and airspace by those aircraft; and/or (b) require it to deny such use of its airfields and airspace, whether it wanted to or not? Would the answers be the same if the state were not a member of the United Nations?

If an aircraft overflying a member state's territory did not comply with paragraph 4, could that state use weapons against it? The President of the ICAO Council, in a statement to the Security Council in October 1990, said:

> Under [paragraph] 7, the resolution calls upon all States to co-operate in taking the necessary measures to ensure the effective implementation of the resolution—consistent with international law, including the Chicago [ICAO] Convention. The practical meaning of this provision is that any enforcement or other "necessary measures" have to refrain from the use of weapons against civil aircraft in flight; this rule is a part of general customary international law and has been only expressly recognized in a codified form in Article 3 *bis* of the Chicago Convention * * *.[e]

e. U.N. Doc. S/21862, at 5 (1990).

Does that settle the issue? If so, how could an air embargo be enforced?

Although the thrust of Resolution 670 related to an air embargo, paragraph 8 dealt also with the sea embargo. Questions similar to those asked just above could arise here, as well. Suppose that a U.N. member state had a bilateral treaty with Iraq requiring it to permit entry to, and exit from, its ports for all ships registered in Iraq. If it detained an Iraqi ship under paragraph 8, would it be in violation of its obligation to Iraq under that treaty?

d. Assessing the Economic Sanctions

As the Rhodesian case demonstrated, economic sanctions can impose hardships far beyond those intended to be imposed on the offending government. Those subjected to hardships include persons in other states who depend on trade or other contacts with the sanctioned state. Often, neighboring states—like those bordering on Rhodesia at the time of its unilateral declaration of independence—are the hardest hit.

In the case of the Iraq sanctions, the external effects fell heavily on Jordan. Iraq was Jordan's largest export market and was a major source of its imports. Most importantly, in the year before the sanctions were imposed, Iraq supplied Jordan with 80 percent of its crude petroleum and fuel oil, at highly favorable prices. In addition, Jordan's only seaport, Aqaba, was highly dependent on shipments to and from Iraq as a source of income. The Secretary-General's representative, assigned to assess Jordan's problems, estimated that it would lose almost $1 billion in 1990 alone, if it complied fully with the sanctions.[a]

Jordan had essentially two options: to appeal for help to the Security Council, under U.N. Charter *article 50,* or to defy the sanctions at least insofar as its basic energy needs dictated. In essence, it exercised both options. It appealed to the Security Council Committee established by Resolution 661, which in turn appealed to all states to provide assistance.[b] Jordan also continued to import oil from Iraq. The Security Council looked the other way until the air war commenced against Iraq.

The appeals under article 50 provided very little relief. Could the Security Council or the General Assembly effectively implement it? See pages 634–35 supra.

Is it satisfactory to alleviate some of the hardships of economic sanctions by looking the other way while hard-hit states violate them? Would it be possible to tailor sanctions in such a way that these states are given partial or full exemptions?

The Secretary–General has said, in the context of the Iraq sanctions, that article 50 should "be supplemented by appropriate agree-

a. See U.N. Doc. S/21938, at 4 (1990). also U.N. Doc. S/21938 (1990).
b. See U.N. Doc. S/21786 (1990); see

ments creating obligations to assist concretely the disadvantaged third State or States."[c] What obligations could feasibly be created? To whom would they run: The United Nations? Individual states? If to the United Nations, could individual states enforce them? See Vienna Convention on the Law of Treaties Between States and International Organizations or Between International Organizations *article 36*.[d]

Should the Charter be amended to deal with these problems?

Those subject to hardships also include the people of the sanctioned state who may not have substitutes for the foreign-supplied goods or services, or for the foreign markets, made unavailable by the sanctions. If the sanctioned state were a democracy, and if the people were convinced that their hardships were the doing of their own government, presumably they would impose pressure upon the government to change its ways or they would vote the government out of office. But in Iraq in 1990, the government was immune from these internal pressures.

In the case of an authoritarian or totalitarian state with effective control over its population, are economic sanctions subject to the objection that their primary effect on the sanctioned state is to impose hardship on innocent persons, without any real likelihood of forcing the government to yield?

A U.S. scholar who had studied the effectiveness of economic sanctions in a wide variety of cases argued that the economic sanctions against Iraq did have a reasonably good chance of succeeding. Referring to a comprehensive study of economic sanctions in the 20th century he and two co-authors had recently published,[e] he argued in part:

> Overall, by our measures, sanctions have contributed to a successful outcome in about 34 percent of the cases, beginning with the First World War. However, the odds are far higher today in the Middle East for three reasons.
>
> First, on no previous occasion have sanctions attracted the degree of support than they have in the Iraq case.
>
> Second, never have they been so comprehensive in their coverage.
>
> Third, never have they imposed such enormous costs on the target country.
>
> If steps are taken to sustain and strengthen these sanctions, they can succeed in forcing Saddam Hussein to withdraw from Kuwait. However, patience will be required.

c. U.N. Doc. A/46/1, at 6 (1991).

d. This article is based on article 36 of the Vienna Convention on the Law of Treaties, which is based in part on a dictum in Free Zones of Upper Savoy and the District of Gex, P.C.I.J., Ser. A/B, No. 46, at 147–48 (1932).

e. G. Hufbauer, J. Schott & K. Elliott, Economic Sanctions Reconsidered: History and Current Policy (2d ed. 1990).

History suggests that 1 or 2 years will pass before the sanctions prevail.

There are costs to waiting, and, of course, there can be no guarantee of success. But the two key questions are whether the costs of waiting would be higher than the economic and the human costs of going to war and whether a better guarantee can be given on the stability of this region, following the destruction of Saddam Hussein and his regime.

Now, as I said, the sanctions against Iraq are unique in the history of these weapons in the 20th century. We think, my coauthors and I think, that the unique features argue for their success.

First, the embargo covers virtually 100 percent of Iraq's trade. In the average successful sanctions case, the sender country, the country imposing the sanctions or the country group, accounted for only 28 percent of the target's trade. So, the trade coverage in this case is about four times what has typically been necessary to achieve success.

Second, the impact of the embargo on the Iraqi economy will be enormous—over 40 percent of Iraq's gross national product.

Prior to this case, the costs imposed on the target by sanctions never exceeded 16 percent of GNP, and the average cost in successful sanctions cases was under 3 percent of GNP, or one-twentieth or so of the impact on Iraq.

The cost to the target country reached double digits on only three previous occasions of sanctions in this century, and in all three of those cases, sanctions contributed to a positive outcome.

* * *

By contrast [to the case of sanctions against Rhodesia,] Saddam Hussein has no champions, and the international commitment to sanctions against Iraq is far stronger than against Rhodesia.

The complete economic embargo of Iraq was agreed to by the U.N. Security Council less than a week after its invasion of Kuwait, and that is unprecedented.

Since the sanctions against Iraq were imposed so swiftly, so decisively, and so comprehensively, there is a high probability that, combined with a credible military threat, they can contribute to the withdrawal of Iraqi forces from Kuwait, the restoration of an independent government in Kuwait, and the release of the hostages.[f]

With the benefit of hindsight, would you concur with Professor Hufbauer's judgment?

[f]. U.S. Policy in the Persian Gulf: Hearings Before the Senate Comm. on Foreign Relations, 101st Cong., 2d Sess., pt. 1, at 60–61 (1990).

Is it feasible to maintain comprehensive economic sanctions at a high level of effectiveness for one or two years?

Did Professor Hufbauer accurately identify the objective of the sanctions?

e. Events Leading to War

In the autumn of 1990, as military and naval forces hostile to Iraq gathered in Saudi Arabia, the Persian Gulf and elsewhere, reports emanating from Iraq and Kuwait raised serious questions about Iraq's treatment of civilians and civilian property. Iraq announced that some foreign civilians would be scattered among Iraqi military bases, oil sites and industrial complexes as virtual human shields against attack. Within Kuwait, there were reports of torture and summary execution of Kuwaitis suspected of being associated with the resistance movement. Hospitals and schools were reportedly stripped of equipment; drugs and medicines were removed to Iraq. Private homes were looted. Thousands of automobiles were stolen. The Kuwaiti central bank reportedly had $500 million in gold removed and a similar amount taken in banknotes and other securities. As Kuwaiti and other civilians fled, they were apparently replaced by Iraqi families who were ordered to occupy vacated apartments and houses. Iraq shut off water and electricity to Western embassies in Kuwait. The border area with Iraq was incorporated into Basrah province of Iraq. Kuwait City and its environs were made a new Iraqi province.

Many of the actions mentioned above are violations of the Fourth Geneva Convention, on civilians and civilian property,[a] or the Vienna Convention on Diplomatic Relations.[b] The Security Council expressed its interest in these matters by adopting Resolutions 664 and 674. The latter resolution provided in part:

SECURITY COUNCIL RESOLUTION 674
Oct. 29, 1990.
U.N.Doc. S/RES/674 (1990).

The Security Council, * * *

Condemning the actions by the Iraqi authorities and occupying forces to take third-State nationals hostage and to mistreat and oppress Kuwaiti and third-State nationals, and the other actions reported to the Security Council, such as the destruction of Kuwaiti demographic records, the forced departure of Kuwaitis, the relocation of population in Kuwait and the unlawful destruction and seizure of public and private property in Kuwait, including hospital supplies and equipment,

[a] Relevant provisions of the Fourth Geneva Convention include articles 1, 2, 4 through 6, 18, 27, 28, 31 through 35, 42, 47 through 50, 53 and 56.

[b] See particularly article 25.

in violation of the decisions of the Council, the Charter of the United Nations, the Fourth Geneva Convention, the Vienna Conventions on Diplomatic and Consular Relations and international law,

Expressing grave alarm over the situation of nationals of third States in Kuwait and Iraq, including the personnel of the diplomatic and consular missions of such States,

Reaffirming that the Fourth Geneva Convention applies to Kuwait and that as a High Contracting Party to the Convention Iraq is bound to comply fully with all its terms and in particular is liable under the Convention in respect of the grave breaches committed by it, as are individuals who commit or order the commission of grave breaches,

* * *

Acting under Chapter VII of the Charter of the United Nations,

* * *

1. *Demands* that the Iraqi authorities and occupying forces immediately cease and desist from taking third-State nationals hostage, mistreating and oppressing Kuwaiti and third-State nationals and any other actions, such as those reported to the Security Council and described above, that violate the decisions of this Council, the Charter of the United Nations, the Fourth Geneva Convention, the Vienna Conventions on Diplomatic and Consular Relations and international law;

* * *

6. *Reaffirms* its demand that Iraq immediately protect the safety and well-being of diplomatic and consular personnel and premises in Kuwait and in Iraq, take no action to hinder these diplomatic and consular missions in the performance of their functions, including access to their nationals and the protection of their person and interests and rescind its orders for the closure of diplomatic and consular missions in Kuwait and the withdrawal of the immunity of their personnel;

* * *

8. *Reminds* Iraq that under international law it is liable for any loss, damage or injury arising in regard to Kuwait and third States, and their nationals and corporations, as a result of the invasion and illegal occupation of Kuwait by Iraq;

* * *

10. *Requires* that Iraq comply with the provisions of the present resolution and its previous resolutions, failing which the Security Council will need to take further measures under the Charter; * * *

THE EFFECT OF RESOLUTION 674

Is Resolution 674 a final, binding determination that Iraq's actions outlined in the "Condemning" paragraph were in violation of international law?

Is it a final, binding determination that Iraq is liable under international law for any loss, damage or injury arising from the invasion and occupation of Kuwait (paragraph 8)?

Is the Security Council a judicial body? Does it provide procedural due process for the parties whose interests it affects? (These questions come up again, in even sharper focus, in connection with Resolution 687, page 670 infra.)

During the autumn of 1990, before the Security Council adopted Resolution 678, below, the United States took the position that it could (if it wished) lawfully use armed force not just to interdict sanctions violations, but also directly against Iraqi military targets in order to liberate Kuwait, without any further authorization from the Security Council. Eventually it sought and obtained that authorization. But what about its pre-authorization claim? See pages 650–52 supra, and note the two basic requirements for the lawful exercise of the right of individual or collective self-defense under customary international law: necessity and proportionality.

In November 1990, the rotating presidency of the Security Council fell to the United States. (The presidency rotates each month among the 15 Security Council members. It is more than a ceremonial position. The President has a great deal of influence over the Council's agenda for the month, and makes rulings on procedural points that sometimes influence debates, or even determine their outcome.) The U.S. government decided to use the Council presidency as an opportunity to press for Security Council authorization for eventual military action against Iraq if the Iraqi occupation of Kuwait did not end promptly.

After extensive lobbying, the United States secured the adoption of Resolution 678, below.[c]

---

[c] The lobbying apparently included a threat to cut off aid to at least one Security Council member (Yemen) if it voted against the U.S. proposal. See N.Y. Times, Dec. 5, 1990, p. A22, col. 1. Yemen voted against Resolution 678, which was adopted by a vote of 12–2 (Cuba, Yemen) –1 (China). In late January 1991, the State Department reduced its aid to Yemen from a planned $22 million to less than $3 million. Reuters dispatch, Jan. 28, 1991.

SECURITY COUNCIL RESOLUTION 678
Nov. 29, 1990.
U.N.Doc. S/RES/678 (1990).

The Security Council, * * *

Acting under Chapter VII of the Charter,

1. *Demands* that Iraq comply fully with resolution 660 (1990) and all subsequent relevant resolutions, and decides, while maintaining all its decisions, to allow Iraq one final opportunity, as a pause of goodwill, to do so;

2. *Authorizes* Member States co-operating with the Government of Kuwait, unless Iraq on or before 15 January 1991 fully implements, as set forth in paragraph 1 above, the foregoing resolutions, to use all necessary means to uphold and implement resolution 660 (1990) and all subsequent relevant resolutions and to restore international peace and security in the area;

3. *Requests* all States to provide appropriate support for the actions undertaken in pursuance of paragraph 2 of the present resolution; * * *.

PRECEDENT FOR RESOLUTION 678?

The only arguable precedent for Resolution 678 was the Security Council's response to North Korea's invasion of South Korea in June 1950. After determining that the attack constituted a breach of the peace, the Security Council "*Recommend[ed]* that the Members of the United Nations furnish such assistance to the Republic of Korea as may be necessary to repel the armed attack and to restore international peace and security in the area." [d]

The Security Council recommended in the Korean situation that members providing military forces make them available to a unified command under the United States, and requested the United States to designate the commander of the forces.[e] Although the U.N. Secretary-General informally suggested establishment of a U.N. committee to supervise U.N. participation, the United States rejected the idea and did little more than report periodically to the Council on the military operations it commanded.[f]

In 1990 the United States also resisted U.N. supervision, when the Soviet Union tried to revitalize the Military Staff Committee. The coalition forces assembled against Iraq under Resolution 678 were

---

d. Security Council Res. 83, U.N. Doc. S/1511 (1950).
e. Security Council Res. 84, U.N. Doc. S/1588 (1950).
f. See R. Russell, The United Nations and United States Security Policy 124–25 (1968); cf. D. Bowett, United Nations Forces 42–43 (1964); L. Goodrich & A. Simons, The United Nations and the Maintenance of International Peace and Security 454–80 (1955).

commanded by a U.S. General, Norman Schwarzkopf, who reported directly to Washington.

Were the Security Council resolutions in the Korean situation direct precedents for Security Council Resolution 678?

What article of the U.N. Charter authorized the Korean resolutions? Resolution 678? Consider *articles 24, 25, 36, 37, 38, 40, 42, 43, 48, 49, 51 and 106.*

Was Resolution 678 ultra vires? Note that no agreements under article 43 had been concluded. The original intent of the drafters of the Charter apparently was that article 43 agreements were to be *the* means by which the Security Council would implement its authority to engage in Chapter VII enforcement action through the use of armed force.[g] But in the Expenses Case, the ICJ said:

> [A]n argument which insists that all measures taken for the maintenance of international peace and security must be financed through agreements concluded under Article 43, would seem to exclude the possibility that the Security Council might act under some other Article of the Charter. The Court cannot accept so limited a view of the powers of the Security Council under the Charter. It cannot be said that the Charter has left the Security Council impotent in the face of an emergency situation when agreements under Article 43 have not been concluded.[h]

The Expenses Case involved U.N. peacekeeping operations, which are designed to reduce tensions, and to keep hostile parties from resorting to armed force or from resuming hostilities after a cease-fire has been declared. Consequently they are not directed against any state and are not considered enforcement action under Chapter VII. Would the above excerpt from that case apply equally to Chapter VII enforcement action?

Could the Security Council *require* member states to use armed force against an aggressor, in the absence of article 43 agreements?[i]

In 1992, Secretary-General Boutros Boutros-Ghali recommended that article 43 be resuscitated, with member states making armed forces and facilities available to the Security Council on a permanent basis. He thought that post-cold war political circumstances would allow this to be done. He added:

> The ready availability of armed forces on call could serve, in itself, as a means of deterring breaches of the peace since a potential aggressor would know that the Council had at its disposal a means of response. Forces under Article 43 may perhaps never

---

g. See J.-P. Cot & A. Pellet, La Charte des Nations Unies 717–18 (1985); L. Goodrich, E. Hambro & A. Simons, Charter of the United Nations 316 (3d rev. ed. 1969).

h. Certain Expenses of the United Nations, [1962] I.C.J. 151, 167.

i. On this and several other points raised by the Security Council resolutions relating to the Persian Gulf crisis, see Schachter, United Nations Law in the Gulf Conflict, 85 Am.J.Int'l L. 452 (1991).

be sufficiently large or well enough equipped to deal with a threat from a major army equipped with sophisticated weapons. They would be useful, however, in meeting any threat posed by a military force of a lesser order.ʲ

Would Saddam Hussein have been deterred from invading Kuwait if article 43 had been implemented before 1990? If not, should article 43 agreements nevertheless be pursued, as envisaged by Mr. Boutros–Ghali?

Could the Military Staff Committee have been given a significant role in the Persian Gulf situation, short of responsibility for the actual direction of the armed forces acting under Resolution 678? See U.N. Charter *articles 45, 46 and 47*. One commentator argued, before Resolution 678 had been adopted, that it could:

> [The requirement in article 47(3) that the Military Staff Committee be responsible to the Security Council for the "strategic direction of any armed forces placed at the disposal of the Security Council"] has never been tested and could be narrowly tailored for the military operations authorized by the Security Council.
>
> For example, the Military Staff Committee could be [asked] to mediate disputes among various national contingents of the multinational force, to coordinate (without necessarily having full access to) the flow of intelligence and military information within the multinational force, and to participate in long-range planning exercises. But all of this could be done with express limitations on the scope of the Military Staff Committee's duties and how it might relate to a unified or coordinated command structure approved or acknowledged by the Security Council.ᵏ

Do you agree that this would be consistent with article 47?

f. The War

On January 16, 1991, the day after the Security Council's deadline expired, the United States and coalition forces launched massive air attacks on Iraq. Iraq's resistance was largely ineffective, as most of the Iraqi air force flew to sanctuary in Iran. Nevertheless, a few coalition aircraft were shot down. Iraq displayed the captured pilots to crowds in Baghdad, and broadcast interviews with them on television. Iraq then announced that it would disperse them among potential air raid targets as human shields, but backed down when the United States protested to the Iraqi embassy in Washington. Iraq launched indiscriminate Scud missile attacks on Israel and Saudi Arabia, hitting civilian areas with the few missiles that penetrated anti-missile defenses. The missiles were armed with conventional warheads.

j. U.N. Doc. A/47/277–S/24111, at 13 (1992).

k. D. Scheffer, The United Nations in the Gulf Crisis and Options for U.S. Policy 15–16 (UNA–USA Occasional Paper No. 1, rev. ed. 1991).

In late January, Iraq released millions of barrels of crude oil from Kuwaiti offshore wells in the Persian Gulf. The objective was unclear. Three possibilities were suggested: to create a defensive barrier against an amphibious assault; to foul Saudi Arabian desalinization plants on the Gulf; or simply to cause allied consternation.

At the end of the fighting, after the outcome had become clear, retreating Iraqi forces set fire to many oil wells in Kuwait. This caused massive atmospheric pollution and released toxic chemicals that spread over populated areas. It took a large multinational team of firefighters nine months to extinguish all of the fires.

On the coalition side, bombing attacks were carried out against targets with military significance, even in populated areas. Aircraft used high-technology "smart bombs" to minimize collateral damage from attacks on military targets in civilian areas, but some collateral damage occurred anyway. Questions were raised about whether all of the targets, such as some bridges, were truly military. Attacks on power supplies had a military purpose, but also inflicted serious harm on civilians by depriving water pumping stations and sewage treatment plants of electricity. Mistakes may have been made in identifying some targets that were truly military if identified properly. The prime example was an attack on a target in Baghdad identified by the United States as a military command center, which killed hundreds of civilians who were sheltered there. Iraq claimed that the building had long been a civilian air raid shelter.

Much of the infrastructure of Baghdad was destroyed or severely damaged. Military communications were disrupted, and military facilities and equipment, including several Scud missile sites, were destroyed. The air strikes, however, did not induce Saddam Hussein to pull out of Kuwait. On February 23, 1991, coalition forces launched ground attacks against Iraqi forces in Kuwait and southern Iraq. One hundred hours later, the battle was over.

Many of the actions described above raised issues under the laws of war. These materials do not examine those issues in any detail. The arguably-relevant treaties and instruments are the four 1949 Geneva Conventions (particularly the third, on prisoners of war,[a] and the fourth, on civilians [b]), Protocol I to the Geneva Conventions,[c] the Regulations Annexed to 1907 Hague Convention IV,[d] the Judgment of the International Military Tribunal at Nuremberg,[e] and the 1977 Convention on the Prohibition of Military or any Other Hostile Use of Environmental Modification Techniques.[f]

a. Aug. 12, 1949, 6 U.S.T. 3316, 75 U.N.T.S. 135.

b. Aug. 12, 1949, 6 U.S.T. 3516, 75 U.N.T.S. 287.

c. Dec. 12, 1977, 1125 U.N.T.S. 3.

d. Oct. 18, 1907, 36 Stat. 2277, 1 Bevans 631.

e. Sept. 30–Oct. 1, 1946, 22 Trial of the Major War Criminals Before the International Military Tribunal, Nuremberg 497 (1948).

f. May 18, 1977, 31 U.S.T. 333, 1108 U.N.T.S. 151. In early 1991, when the fighting was going on, Iraq and Israel were parties to the four Geneva Conventions,

After the war, the Secretary–General suggested the need for collective reflection on such questions as "the mechanisms required for the Council to satisfy itself that the rule of proportionality in the employment of armed force is observed and the rules of humanitarian law applicable in armed conflicts are complied with." [g] What mechanisms would be feasible? For the U.N. response to this question in the former Yugoslavia in 1992, see pages 870–75 infra.

The Security Council did not meet during the first four weeks of the 1991 air war. With the United States effectively controlling military operations, assisted by some other U.N. members, pressure began to build for the Security Council to meet and at least to exercise some influence over the operations. On February 13, 1991, before the ground war had begun, the United Kingdom proposed that the Council meet in private session to discuss the war. This provoked a debate over whether the meeting should be public or private.

The Security Council's Rules of Procedure (which are still technically "provisional") provide, "Unless it decides otherwise, the Security Council shall meet in public." [h] Yemen and Cuba, in particular, argued against meeting in private after all previous meetings on the Persian Gulf situation had been in public. The Yemeni representative said that there had been only three exceptions to the tradition of holding public meetings. In each case the private meeting had been brief, held for the purpose of hearing sensitive information. [i]

The Indian representative also favored an open meeting:

> My delegation is deeply concerned that it has not been possible for the Council to meet formally even once on this matter since the expiry of the deadline, on 15 January, set by resolution 678 (1990). This has not reflected well on the prestige of the Council and the United Nations. * * * The perception in which the Council is held by the international community ought to be of concern to the Council; at least, it is of concern to my delegation. [j]

The United States supported the British proposal for a private meeting, "because it will encourage genuine and effective give and take." The U.S. representative continued:

but not to Protocol I, the 1907 Hague Regulations or the 1977 Environmental Convention. The United States was a party to all of these instruments except Protocol I. Kuwait and Saudi Arabia were parties to the Geneva Conventions and Protocol I, but not to the 1907 Hague Regulations. Kuwait was a party to the 1977 Environmental Convention, subject to a reservation that says it is bound only toward states parties to the Convention, and the obligation terminates "with respect to any hostile state which does not abide by the prohibition contained therein." Saudi Arabia was not a party to the 1977 Environmental Convention.

g. Report of the Secretary–General on the Work of the Organization, 46 G.A.O.R. Supp. No. 1 (A/46/1), at 3 (1991).

h. Provisional Rules of Procedure of the Security Council, Rule 48, U.N. Doc. S/96/Rev. 7 (1982).

i. U.N. Doc. S/PV.2977 (Part I) at 6–7 (1991).

j. Id. at 51.

At the present juncture, when Iraq remains intransigent and it is not clear what additional steps the Council might take to ensure compliance with its resolutions, our concern is that a meeting will be subject either to misinterpretation or to exploitation. Above all else, we must not do anything which will prolong the conflict, and that, most particularly, includes sending signals, which Iraq will misuse or misperceive, that the Council is not firm in its decisions and is not intent on seeing them implemented.[k]

A vote was taken. By a margin of 9–2–4, the members decided to hold the meeting in private. This did not mean that no record of the proceedings would be kept; under Rules 49 and 51, a verbatim record of a private meeting is made available to participating representatives, unless the Council decides to make only a single copy to be kept by the Secretary–General. The Council did not make that decision in this case. The debate in the private meeting was inconclusive.

Was a private meeting appropriate in this case? Is a private meeting of the Security Council ever appropriate?

Did the United States and other coalition forces exceed their mandate under Security Council Resolution 678, by carrying the air and ground war beyond what may have been strictly necessary to drive Iraq out of Kuwait? Of course, this is partly a factual question: How much force was necessary to drive Iraq out of Kuwait? That is difficult for persons who are not military experts to answer. But it is also a legal question: Did the Security Council authorize the United States and others to do more than drive Iraq out of Kuwait?

In connection with this question, compare Resolution 678 with the excerpt from Security Council Resolution 83 (relating to the Korean War), page 662 supra. Resolution 83 was adopted in the absence of the Soviet Union, which was boycotting the Security Council at the time. When it returned to the Council, it effectively blocked any further action by that body. The General Assembly then took up the matter, acting under the Uniting for Peace Resolution, G.A. Resolution 377A (V).

In the General Assembly, the question arose whether Security Council Resolution 83 authorized the U.S.-led unified command to pursue North Korean forces across the 38th Parallel (i.e. into North Korea). There were two views: one was that the Resolution should be construed simply to allow the system of collective security to be vindicated, as it would be if the North Korean forces were pushed out of South Korea; the other was that the Resolution should be construed to allow such force as was needed to end the aggression by removing the threat of a new attack. Under pressure from the United States, the latter view prevailed in the General Assembly, which recommended in

---

k. Id. at 47.

G.A. Resolution 376 (V) that "All appropriate steps be taken to ensure conditions of stability throughout Korea * * *." This recommendation was interpreted as justifying unified force operations beyond the 38th Parallel.[l]

Do you suppose the lawyers in the U.S. Department of State were aware of all this when they drafted the instrument that became Security Council Resolution 678? Did they do their job well?

Could it convincingly be said that although Resolution 678 did not limit the fighting to the territory of Kuwait, it nevertheless authorized no greater force than that necessary to drive Iraq out of Kuwait—thus casting doubt on the legitimacy of any use of additional force to neutralize Iraq as a military threat to other states in the region? The British representative said in the closed Security Council meeting, while the fighting was going on:

> We are not seeking to bring about the destruction, occupation or dismemberment of Iraq or to decide who governs that country. We are seeking the liberation of Kuwait, no more and no less. The military action will end as soon as the objectives laid down by the Council have been achieved.[m]

Compare the formulation by the U.S. representative at a resumption of the same meeting:

> When all else failed, the coalition against Iraqi aggression acted, as it continues to act, under the authority given it by the Security Council to implement fully the Council's resolutions. Our goals are not grandiose; they are simple and straightforward: to get Iraq out of Kuwait, to restore the legitimate authority of its Government and to restore peace and security in the area—period, full stop.[n]

Were the British and American statements of goals the same? If not, were any differences significant?

Are there lessons to be learned here, about how broadly the Security Council should authorize the use of armed force when future breaches of the peace or acts of aggression occur?

What about the future of article 43, with its call for agreements between member states and the Security Council to make available armed forces, assistance and facilities for article 42 enforcement action? In November 1991, the then-U.S. Ambassador to the U.N., Thomas R. Pickering, had this to say:

> A vital question about Article 43 is whether and what kind of command arrangements it implies. In my view, Article 43 agree-

---

l. See J. Castañeda, Legal Effects of United Nations Resolutions 91 (1969); R. Russell, The United Nations and United States Security Policy 126–27 (1968); L. Goodrich & A. Simons, The United Nations and the Maintenance of International Peace and Security 469–70 (1955).

m. U.N. Doc. S/PV.2977 (Part II), at 74–75 (1991).

n. Id. at 267.

ments are not incompatible with their signatories' exercise of wide military latitude when those agreements are invoked. In this sense, the agreement might be less a format for direct control than an expression of the general capacity of the world community to enforce decisions and, hence, act as a means of deterrence. Delegated enforcement is explicitly anticipated in the Charter, most relevantly in articles 48 and 53.[o]

Do you agree that the articles cited by Mr. Pickering would authorize the loose structure he had in mind? Is that the only feasible article 43 format?

g. After the Fighting Stopped

(1) Initial Post–War Demands on Iraq

At midnight on February 27, 1991, the coalition forces suspended their combat operations. On March 2, the Security Council adopted the first of its significant post-war resolutions.

SECURITY COUNCIL RESOLUTION 686
March 2, 1991.
U.N. Doc. S/RES/686 (1991).

The Security Council, * * *

Acting under Chapter VII of the Charter,

* * *

2. *Demands* that Iraq implement its acceptance of all twelve [previous] resolutions and in particular that Iraq:

(a) Rescind immediately its actions purporting to annex Kuwait;

(b) Accept in principle its liability under international law for any loss, damage, or injury arising in regard to Kuwait and third States, and their nationals and corporations, as a result of the invasion and illegal occupation of Kuwait by Iraq;

(c) Immediately release under the auspices of the International Committee of the Red Cross, Red Cross Societies, or Red Crescent Societies, all Kuwaiti and third country nationals detained by Iraq and return the remains of any deceased Kuwaiti and third country nationals so detained; and

(d) Immediately begin to return all Kuwaiti property seized by Iraq, to be completed in the shortest possible period;

3. *Further demands* that Iraq:

(a) Cease hostile or provocative actions by its forces against all Member States, including missile attacks and flights of combat aircraft;

* * *

---

[o]. Hearings on Relations in a Multipolar World, Before the Senate Comm. on Foreign Relations, 102d Cong., 1st Sess., at 62 (1991).

(c) Arrange for immediate access to and release of all prisoners of war under the auspices of the International Committee of the Red Cross and return the remains of any deceased personnel of the forces of Kuwait and the Member States cooperating with Kuwait pursuant to resolution 678 (1990); * * *.

THE EFFECT OF RESOLUTION 686

Did Resolution 686 obligate Iraq, as a matter of international law, to comply with paragraphs 2 and 3? Did it have teeth? (The day after Resolution 686 was adopted, Iraq informed the President of the Security Council that "it has agreed to fulfill its obligations under the said resolution." [a])

Was paragraph 2(b) essentially adjudicative? Essentially legislative? What precedent, if any, did it set?

(2) Security Council Resolution 687

On April 3, 1991, the Security Council adopted Resolution 687, the most comprehensive resolution in its history. The vote was 12–1(Cuba)–2(Ecuador, Yemen).

SECURITY COUNCIL RESOLUTION 687
April 3, 1991.
U.N. Doc. S/RES/687 (1991).

The Security Council, * * *

Noting that Iraq and Kuwait, as independent sovereign States, signed at Baghdad on 4 October 1963 "Agreed Minutes Between the State of Kuwait and the Republic of Iraq Regarding the Restoration of Friendly Relations, Recognition and Related Matters", thereby recognizing formally the boundary between Iraq and Kuwait and the allocation of islands, which were registered with the United Nations in accordance with Article 102 of the Charter of the United Nations and in which Iraq recognized the independence and complete sovereignty of the State of Kuwait within its borders as specified and accepted in the letter of the Prime Minister of Iraq dated 21 July 1932, and as accepted by the Ruler of Kuwait in his letter dated 10 August 1932,

Conscious of the need for demarcation of the said boundary,

Conscious also of the statements by Iraq threatening to use weapons in violation of its obligations under the Geneva Protocol for the Prohibition of the Use in War of Asphyxiating, Poisonous or Other Gases, and of Bacteriological Methods of Warfare, signed at Geneva on 17 June 1925, and of its prior use of chemical weapons and affirming

---

a. U.N. Doc. S/22320, Annex (1991).

that grave consequences would follow any further use by Iraq of such weapons,

Recalling that Iraq has subscribed to the Declaration adopted by all States participating in the Conference of States Parties to the 1925 Geneva Protocol and Other Interested States, held in Paris from 7 to 11 January 1989, establishing the objective of universal elimination of chemical and biological weapons,

Recalling also that Iraq has signed the Convention on the Prohibition of the Development, Production and Stockpiling of Bacteriological (Biological) and Toxin Weapons and on Their Destruction, of 10 April 1972,

* * *

Aware of the use by Iraq of ballistic missiles in unprovoked attacks and therefore of the need to take specific measures in regard to such missiles located in Iraq,

Concerned by the reports in the hands of Member States that Iraq has attempted to acquire materials for a nuclear-weapons programme contrary to its obligations under the Treaty on the Non–Proliferation of Nuclear Weapons of 1 July 1968,

Recalling the objective of the establishment of a nuclear-weapons-free zone in the region of the Middle East,

Conscious of the threat that all weapons of mass destruction pose to peace and security in the area and of the need to work towards the establishment in the Middle East of a zone free of such weapons,

Conscious also of the objective of achieving balanced and comprehensive control of armaments in the region,

* * *

Bearing in mind its objective of restoring international peace and security in the area as set out in recent resolutions of the Security Council,

Conscious of the need to take the following measures acting under Chapter VII of the Charter,

1. *Affirms* all [Security Council resolutions on Iraq since its invasion of Kuwait], except as expressly changed below to achieve the goals of this resolution, including a formal cease-fire;

A

2. *Demands* that Iraq and Kuwait respect the inviolability of the international boundary and the allocation of islands set out in the "Agreed Minutes Between the State of Kuwait and the Republic of Iraq Regarding the Restoration of Friendly Relations, Recognition and Related Matters", signed by them in the exercise of their sovereignty at Baghdad on 4 October 1963 and registered with the United Nations * * *;

3. *Calls upon* the Secretary–General to lend his assistance to make arrangements with Iraq and Kuwait to demarcate the boundary between Iraq and Kuwait * * *;

4. *Decides* to guarantee the inviolability of the above-mentioned international boundary and to take as appropriate all necessary measures to that end in accordance with the Charter of the United Nations;

B

5. *Requests* the Secretary–General, after consulting with Iraq and Kuwait, to submit within three days to the Security Council for its approval a plan for the immediate deployment of a United Nations observer unit to monitor the Khor Abdullah and a demilitarized zone, which is hereby established, extending ten kilometres into Iraq and five kilometres into Kuwait from the boundary referred to in the "Agreed Minutes Between the State of Kuwait and the Republic of Iraq Regarding the Restoration of Friendly Relations, Recognition and Related Matters" of 4 October 1963;

* * *

C

* * *

8. *Decides* that Iraq shall unconditionally accept the destruction, removal, or rendering harmless, under international supervision, of:

(a) All chemical and biological weapons and all stocks of agents and all related subsystems and components and all research, development, support and manufacturing facilities;

(b) All ballistic missiles with a range greater than 150 kilometres and related major parts, and repair and production facilities;

9. *Decides,* for the implementation of paragraph 8 above, the following:

(a) Iraq shall submit to the Secretary–General, within fifteen days of the adoption of the present resolution, a declaration of the locations, amounts and types of all items specified in paragraph 8 and agree to urgent, on-site inspection as specified below;

(b) The Secretary–General * * * shall develop, and submit to the Council for approval, a plan calling for the completion of the following acts within forty-five days of such approval:

> (i) The forming of a Special Commission, which shall carry out immediate on-site inspection of Iraq's biological, chemical and missile capabilities, based on Iraq's declarations and the designation of any additional locations by the Special Commission itself;
>
> (ii) The yielding by Iraq of possession to the Special Commission for destruction, removal or rendering harmless, taking into account the requirements of public safety, of all items speci-

fied under paragraph 8(a) above, including items at the additional locations designated by the Special Commission under paragraph 9(b)(i) above and the destruction by Iraq, under the supervision of the Special Commission, of all its missile capabilities, including launchers, as specified under paragraph 8(b) above;

(iii) The provision by the Special Commission of the assistance and cooperation to the Director–General of the International Atomic Energy Agency required in paragraphs 12 and 13 below;

10. *Decides* that Iraq shall unconditionally undertake not to use, develop, construct or acquire any of the items specified in paragraphs 8 and 9 above and requests the Secretary–General, in consultation with the Special Commission, to develop a plan for the future ongoing monitoring and verification of Iraq's compliance with this paragraph, to be submitted to the Security Council for approval within one hundred and twenty days of the passage of this resolution;

11. *Invites* Iraq to reaffirm unconditionally its obligations under the Treaty on the Non–Proliferation of Nuclear Weapons of 1 July 1968;

12. *Decides* that Iraq shall unconditionally agree not to acquire or develop nuclear weapons or nuclear-weapons-usable material or any subsystems or components or any research, development, support or manufacturing facilities related to the above; to submit to the Secretary–General and the Director–General of the International Atomic Energy Agency within fifteen days of the adoption of the present resolution a declaration of the locations, amounts, and types of all items specified above; to place all of its nuclear-weapons-usable materials under the exclusive control, for custody and removal, of the International Atomic Energy Agency, with the assistance and cooperation of the Special Commission as provided for in the plan of the Secretary–General discussed in paragraph 9(b) above; to accept, in accordance with the arrangements provided for in paragraph 13 below, urgent on-site inspection and the destruction, removal or rendering harmless as appropriate of all items specified above; and to accept the plan discussed in paragraph 13 below for the future ongoing monitoring and verification of its compliance with these undertakings;

13. *Requests* the Director–General of the International Atomic Energy Agency, through the Secretary–General, with the assistance and cooperation of the Special Commission as provided for in the plan of the Secretary–General in paragraph 9(b) above, to carry out immediate on-site inspection of Iraq's nuclear capabilities based on Iraq's declarations and the designation of any additional locations by the Special Commission; to develop a plan for submission to the Security Council within forty-five days calling for the destruction, removal, or rendering harmless as appropriate of all items listed in paragraph 12 above; to carry out the plan within forty-five days following approval

by the Security Council; and to develop a plan, taking into account the rights and obligations of Iraq under the Treaty on the Non–Proliferation of Nuclear Weapons of 1 July 1968, for the future ongoing monitoring and verification of Iraq's compliance with paragraph 12 above, including an inventory of all nuclear material in Iraq subject to the Agency's verification and inspections to confirm that Agency safeguards cover all relevant nuclear activities in Iraq, to be submitted to the Security Council for approval within one hundred and twenty days of the passage of the present resolution;

14. *Takes note* that the actions to be taken by Iraq in paragraphs 8, 9, 10, 11, 12 and 13 of the present resolution represent steps towards the goal of establishing in the Middle East a zone free from weapons of mass destruction and all missiles for their delivery and the objective of a global ban on chemical weapons;

* * *

E

16. *Reaffirms* that Iraq, without prejudice to the debts and obligations of Iraq arising prior to 2 August 1990, which will be addressed through the normal mechanisms, is liable under international law for any direct loss, damage, including environmental damage and the depletion of natural resources, or injury to foreign Governments, nationals and corporations, as a result of Iraq's unlawful invasion and occupation of Kuwait;

17. *Decides* that all Iraqi statements made since 2 August 1990 repudiating its foreign debt are null and void, and demands that Iraq adhere scrupulously to all of its obligations concerning servicing and repayment of its foreign debt;

18. *Decides also* to create a fund to pay compensation for claims that fall within paragraph 16 above and to establish a Commission that will administer the fund;

19. *Directs* the Secretary–General to develop and present to the Security Council for decision, no later than thirty days following the adoption of the present resolution, recommendations for the fund to meet the requirement for the payment of claims established in accordance with paragraph 18 above and for a programme to implement the decisions in paragraphs 16, 17 and 18 above, including: administration of the fund; mechanisms for determining the appropriate level of Iraq's contribution to the fund based on a percentage of the value of the exports of petroleum and petroleum products from Iraq not to exceed a figure to be suggested to the Council by the Secretary–General, taking into account the requirements of the people of Iraq, Iraq's payment capacity as assessed in conjunction with the international financial institutions taking into consideration external debt service, and the needs of the Iraqi economy; arrangements for ensuring that payments are made to the fund; the process by which funds will be allocated and claims paid; appropriate procedures for evaluating losses, listing claims

and verifying their validity and resolving disputed claims in respect of Iraq's liability as specified in paragraph 16 above; and the composition of the Commission designated above;

F

20. *Decides*, effective immediately, that the prohibitions against the sale or supply to Iraq of commodities or products, other than medicine and health supplies, and prohibitions against financial transactions related thereto contained in resolution 661 (1990) shall not apply to foodstuffs notified to the Security Council Committee established by resolution 661 (1990) concerning the situation between Iraq and Kuwait or, with the approval of that Committee, under the simplified and accelerated "no-objection" procedure, to materials and supplies for essential civilian needs as identified in the report of the Secretary-General dated 20 March 1991, and in any further findings of humanitarian need by the Committee;

21. *Decides* that the Security Council shall review the provisions of paragraph 20 above every sixty days in the light of the policies and practices of the Government of Iraq, including the implementation of all relevant resolutions of the Security Council, for the purpose of determining whether to reduce or lift the prohibitions referred to therein;

22. *Decides* that upon the approval by the Security Council of the programme called for in paragraph 19 above and upon Council agreement that Iraq has completed all actions contemplated in paragraphs 8, 9, 10, 11, 12 and 13 above, the prohibitions against the import of commodities and products originating in Iraq and the prohibitions against financial transactions related thereto contained in resolution 661 (1990) shall have no further force or effect;

23. *Decides* that, pending action by the Security Council under paragraph 22 above, the Security Council Committee established by resolution 661 (1990) shall be empowered to approve, when required to assure adequate financial resources on the part of Iraq to carry out the activities under paragraph 20 above, exceptions to the prohibition against the import of commodities and products originating in Iraq;

* * *

29. *Decides* that all States, including Iraq, shall take the necessary measures to ensure that no claim shall lie at the instance of the Government of Iraq, or of any person or body in Iraq, or of any person claiming through or for the benefit of any such person or body, in connection with any contract or other transaction where its performance was affected by reason of the measures taken by the Security Council in resolution 661 (1990) and related resolutions;

* * *

H

32. *Requires* Iraq to inform the Security Council that it will not commit or support any act of international terrorism or allow any organization directed towards commission of such acts to operate within its territory and to condemn unequivocally and renounce all acts, methods and practices of terrorism;

I

33. *Declares* that, upon official notification by Iraq to the Secretary-General and to the Security Council of its acceptance of the provisions above, a formal cease-fire is effective between Iraq and Kuwait and the Member States cooperating with Kuwait in accordance with resolution 678 (1990);

34. *Decides* to remain seized of the matter and to take such further steps as may be required for the implementation of the present resolution and to secure peace and security in the area.

AN EXTRAORDINARY RESOLUTION

Before Resolution 687 was adopted, the six nonaligned members of the Security Council proposed several amendments that would have toned it down considerably. With one minor exception, these were rejected by the permanent members. One of the rejected amendments would have added a paragraph saying that the circumstances were unique, requiring unprecedented actions "which do not set undue precedents."[a] Since that disclaimer was rejected, it is arguable that some provisions in the resolution do set precedents. It thus becomes important not only in connection with Iraq, but possibly also for future cases, to examine the resolution with some care.

The Security Council said in Resolution 687 that it was acting under Chapter VII of the Charter. Which article in Chapter VII authorized the resolution?

In identical letters to the U.N. Secretary-General and the President of the Security Council on April 6, 1991, the Foreign Minister of Iraq said that Iraq had "no choice but to accept" Resolution 687.[b] He nevertheless made several vehement complaints about the resolution. Among other things, he said that it "constitutes an unprecedented assault on [Iraq's] sovereignty, and the rights that stem therefrom, embodied in the Charter and in international law and practice." This raised an issue under U.N. Charter *article 2(7)*. Was Resolution 687 consistent with article 2(7)?

Did operative paragraphs 2 through 4 of Resolution 687 determine that Iraq's boundary with Kuwait is as set out in the 1963 "Agreed

---

a. See Int'l Docs.Rev., 8 April 1991, p. 4.

b. U.N. Doc. S/22456, Annex (1991).

Minutes" (supra page 649), subject only to detailed demarcation? If so, was that determination binding upon Iraq?

In connection with these questions, note the letters of July 21 and August 10, 1932, mentioned at page 648 supra, as well as the terms of the 1963 "Agreed Minutes." Iraq has argued that these instruments are not binding upon it, because they were not ratified by the competent legislative body as (according to Iraq) "is internationally recognized and stated by the constitutions of all countries" in the case of border treaties, and because the British government forced the Iraqi Prime Minister into the 1932 correspondence.[c] The United States pointed out, though, that Iraq had not protested the 1963 agreement's registration with the United Nations.[d]

Did the Iraqi arguments have any substance? See Vienna Convention on the Law of Treaties *articles 45, 46, 51, 52.* Was the Security Council the proper body to deal with them?

Among its several objections to Resolution 687, Iraq asserted that, "[T]he Security Council has imposed a specific position with regard to the Iraqi–Kuwaiti boundary, whereas the custom in law and in practice in international relations is that boundary questions are left to an agreement between the States, because this is the sole basis that can guarantee the principle of the stability of boundaries."[e] Two somewhat different responses seem to have been given to this. The United States, the moving force behind Resolution 687, conceded that border disputes are to be negotiated directly between states, except in this unique situation where one state attempted to destroy another's very existence by force. "Certainly, the United States does not seek, nor will it support, a new role for the Security Council as the body that determines international boundaries."[f] The Secretary–General instead stressed Iraq's agreement to the Security Council's plan, by its acceptance of Resolution 687 in its letters of April 6, 1991.[g]

Was either response convincing? If so, which was the more sound legally? (Was Vienna Convention on the Law of Treaties *article 52* relevant? It has an exact counterpart in article 52 of the Vienna Convention on the Law of Treaties Between States and International Organizations or Between International Organizations.)

The Secretary–General appointed a five-member Iraq–Kuwait Boundary Demarcation Commission, which completed a major part of its work in the summer of 1992. A section of the boundary was set about 580 feet into an area Iraq had controlled before the war. Iraq said this was unacceptable, but the Security Council approved the demarcation and warned that it was prepared to maintain it by "all

c. See Iraqi documents reprinted in 13 Houston J. Int'l L. 282, 284 & 286, 288 (1991).

d. U.N. Doc. S/PV.2981, at 86 (1991).

e. U.N. Doc. S/22558, at 5 (1991).

f. U.N. Doc. S/PV.2981, at 86 (1991).

g. U.N. Doc. S/22558, at 8 (1991).

necessary measures." [h]

A U.N. observer force, UNIKOM, was deployed along the Iraq-Kuwait border, in accordance with paragraph 5. Previous U.N. observer forces in other areas were established with the voluntary consent of the governments on whose territories they were stationed. Was Resolution 687 a significant departure from that precedent? If so, is it a salutary development?

Did Iraq have a legitimate objection to paragraphs 8 through 10 of Resolution 687, when it argued that they would "deprive it of its lawful right to acquire weapons and military matériel for defence * * *, thus endangering the country's internal and external security"?[i]

Security Council Resolution 707, adopted in August 1991, "demanded" that Iraq allow the Special Commission, formed under paragraph 9 of Resolution 687, to have unrestricted access to "any and all areas, facilities, equipment, records and means of transportation" which it wished to inspect for purposes of ensuring compliance with paragraphs 8 through 10 of Resolution 687. Resolution 715, adopted in October 1991, approved a detailed monitoring plan submitted by the Secretary-General,[j] ordering Iraq to accept the inspection of any site, facility or other item designated by the Special Commission, to accept overflight of any area designated by the Commission, and to refrain from interfering with the Commission's exercise of its functions under Resolutions 687, 707 and the plan. The Commission later demanded that Iraq destroy 36 categories of equipment and nine buildings associated with past development of ballistic missiles.[k] Iraq's position was that Resolutions 707 and 715 were "impossible to implement" because they imposed what amounted to a "super-government" on Iraq.[l] Is that a legal argument? Did Iraq have a point?

After Resolution 687 was adopted, Iraq on several occasions prevented or hindered U.N. inspectors' efforts to gain access to facilities in Iraq suspected of storing, or being capable of producing, materials for nuclear weapons or documents related to them. The United States suggested that it was ready to use military force against suspected nuclear facilities in Iraq, unless full inspection could be conducted promptly. After one such suggestion, Iraq submitted to the U.N. a new list of previously-undeclared nuclear research and development laboratories, storage sites and nuclear manufacturing plants that apparently had been operating in violation of Iraq's obligations under the Nuclear Nonproliferation Treaty. U.N. inspectors visited these sites. Despite Iraqi efforts to remove incriminating evidence, the inspectors obtained documents sufficient to establish that Iraq had an ambitious nuclear

---

h. U.N. Doc. S/24044 (1992); S.C. Res. 773 (1992).

i. U.N. Doc. S/22456, at 4 (1991).

j. See U.N. Doc. S/22871/Rev.1 (1991).

k. See Wash. Post, Mar. 16, 1992, p. A14, col. 2.

l. See Wash. Post, Feb. 19, 1992, p. A22, cols. 3–4.

weapons program.ᵐ

Paragraphs 12 and 13 of Resolution 687 raise significant questions about the relationship between the Nuclear Nonproliferation Treaty (NPT)ⁿ and the U.N. Charter. Under the NPT, non-nuclear-weapon states parties (such as Iraq) undertake, among other things, not to manufacture or otherwise acquire nuclear weapons or other nuclear explosive devices. They also undertake to accept safeguards, as set forth in an agreement with and administered by the International Atomic Energy Agency (IAEA), to prevent any fissionable material from being diverted to nuclear weapons or other nuclear explosive devices. The NPT says that it is not to be interpreted as affecting the "inalienable right of all the Parties to the treaty to develop research, production and use of nuclear energy for peaceful purposes * * *." ᵒ

In Resolution 707 (1991), the Security Council condemned "noncompliance by the Government of Iraq with its obligations under its safeguards agreement with the [IAEA], as established by the resolution of the Board of Governors * * *, which constitutes a violation of its commitments as a party to the [NPT]." Does this recognize the IAEA Board of Governors as the authoritative judge of violations of safeguards agreements, and therefore of the NPT?

Note also what the International Court of Justice said in the Namibia Advisory Opinion about the U.N. General Assembly's authority to determine that South Africa had materially breached its obligations under the old League of Nations Mandate for Southwest Africa, pages 497–500 supra. Is a norm of international institutional law developing, to the effect that the relevant supervisory body of an organization may authoritatively determine whether or not member states have breached regulatory agreements within the organization's ambit?

To return to Resolution 687: Responding to paragraph 13, the Director–General of the IAEA submitted to the Security Council a plan for the future monitoring of Iraq's compliance with paragraph 12. The Security Council, acting under Chapter VII of the Charter, approved the plan in Resolution 715 (1991). Under the plan, the IAEA was given unprecedented rights within the territory of a member state:

> (a) to carry out inspections, at any time and without hindrance, of any site, facility, area, location, activity, material or other item in Iraq upon designation by the Special Commission or its successor, or upon its own initiative. Iraq shall provide imme-

---

m. Originally it was thought that a nuclear device could have been developed within 12 to 18 months. U.N. Doc. S/23165, at 5 (1991). Later indications were that it would have taken considerably longer.

n. July 1, 1968, 21 U.S.T. 483, T.I.A.S. 6839, 729 U.N.T.S. 161.

o. Id. art. IV(1).

diate and unimpeded access to, and shall take the measures necessary to enable inspectors to arrive at, the location where inspection activities are to be carried out by the time notified by the Agency;

(b) to inspect any number of sites, facilities, areas, locations, activities, materials or items simultaneously or sequentially;

(c) to conduct unannounced inspections and inspections upon short notice;

(d) to secure any site, facility, area, location, activity, material or item to be inspected and prevent any material or other item from being taken to or from the site until the inspection is concluded;

(e) to stop and inspect vehicles, ships, aircraft or any other means of transportation within Iraq. This also includes the right of the Agency to restrict and/or stop movement of suspected material, equipment or other items;

(f) to inspect imports or exports of material and other items upon arrival or departure;

(g) to establish special modes of monitoring and inspection, including prolonged or continuous presence of inspectors, use of instruments and other arrangements to facilitate monitoring and verification;

(h) to secure full and free access at any time to all sites, facilities, areas, locations, activities, material and other items, including documentation, all persons and all information which, in the Agency's judgement, may be necessary for its monitoring and verification activities. This includes unimpeded access to all nuclear material, facilities and installations, as well as equipment and non-nuclear material relevant to Iraq's undertakings, and all documentation related thereto;

(i) to request, receive, examine, retain, copy and remove any record, data and information, including documentation; to examine and photograph, including by videotaping, any activity or item; and to retain and move any item;

(j) to conduct interviews with any personnel at any site, facility, area or location under inspection, and with any Iraqi official;

(k) to install containment and surveillance equipment and other equipment and devices and to construct facilities for observation, testing, verification, monitoring and inspection activities;

(*l*) to verify inventories, and to take and analyze with its own instrumentation, or to request Iraq under the observation of Agency Inspectors to take and/or analyze, samples, and to remove and export samples for off-site analysis;

(m) to mark, tag, or otherwise identify any material or other item;

(n) to use its own instrumentation to collect data during inspections and aerial overflights, including photographic, video, infrared and radar data.[p]

The IAEA was also given the right of unrestricted freedom of entry into, exit from, and movement within Iraq, using its own means of transportation (including aircraft), and the right to remove from Iraq any material, including documentation.

As approved by Resolution 715, the IAEA's inspection rights within Iraqi territory are much more intrusive than its rights under the NPT, and therefore much more intrusive than its rights with respect to any other state. To the extent that its rights stem from Security Council resolutions, rather than from an undertaking by Iraq, is there a problem under U.N. Charter *article 2(7)*? How about *article 2(1)*?

In an attempt to avoid future undetected violations of the NPT by states other than Iraq, the Director–General of the IAEA has offered these suggestions:

> [T]he ability of the regular IAEA inspections under the NPT * * * to uncover possible undeclared nuclear installations and material would increase drastically if the IAEA were to be routinely provided with relevant information available to Member States, e.g. through satellites. The right which exists under IAEA NPT-type safeguards agreements to perform so-called "special inspections"—and which has so far been used only with regard to declared installations—might then be used to request inspection of undeclared installations and material which, it is reasonably believed, should have been declared. If such a request were to be rejected, the Board of Governors of the IAEA might submit the matter to the Security Council. In this manner a procedure would be in place to uphold obligations under non-proliferation treaties and safeguards agreements.[q]

Could the Security Council require a government to allow IAEA inspection of undeclared installations and material, if the government has not threatened to use force against any other state?

If a government materially breaches the NPT or any other multilateral arms control convention, could the Security Council legitimately treat that as a threat to the peace under Chapter VII?

The monitoring efforts of the Special Commission and IAEA appear to have been reasonably successful. By mid–1992 a pattern had developed, involving demands by inspectors (e.g. to see additional sites), followed by Iraqi rejections, followed by statements by or on behalf of the Security Council (or by the U.S. government) warning of further forceful action, culminating in Iraqi acquiescence in at least the mini-

---

p. U.N. Doc. S/22872/Rev.1, at 15–16 (1991).

q. Statement of Hans Blix to the 46th Sess. of the U.N. General Assembly, Oct. 21, 1991, reprinted in IAEA Pamphlet C18, at 25, 28 (1991). See also Blix, Verification of Nuclear Non-proliferation: Securing the Future, 34 IAEA Bull., No. 1, at 2, 4–5 (1992).

mum demands. Would outright Iraqi refusal to permit inspection of a key site have justified a United States air attack against the site, without further authorization from the Security Council? Note that all of the Security Council resolutions on Iraq, including Resolution 678, remained in force after the initial fighting stopped. Consider also paragraphs 33 and 34 of Resolution 687.

Would it ever be appropriate for the Security Council to authorize, in advance, unilateral action to enforce obligations it has imposed on an aggressor state under Chapter VII?

What is the significance, if any, of the monitoring experience in Iraq for future U.N. efforts to control means of mass destruction outside the IAEA safeguards framework?

Did paragraph 16 of Resolution 687 make a conclusive determination that Iraq is liable under international law for any environmental damage resulting from its invasion and occupation of Kuwait? Iraq asserted that this paragraph was evidence of the resolution's "biased and iniquitous nature," because Iraq's liability for environmental damage has not been established.[r]

Iraq has said that the International Court of Justice is the U.N. organ authorized to render judgments and determine levels of reparations, and that the Security Council has, "under great pressure from the United States of America, Britain and France, been converted from a political into a judicial authority."[s] Was the Security Council acting as a judicial body when it adopted paragraph 16? Note the established principle that a state's consent is required before it may be subjected to an international adjudication of its rights or duties.[t] This is the case in the ICJ and in other international tribunals.

The Security Council held no hearings and heard no arguments from legal counsel before it acted. Nor did those who voted for paragraph 16 (and the other paragraphs of Resolution 687) purport to be acting independently from their governments. Is there anything wrong with this?

Are these questions rendered moot by Iraq's grudging acceptance of Resolution 678?

Is there any legally significant difference between the judgment made by the Security Council in paragraph 16 of Resolution 687 and its

---

r. U.N. Doc. S/22456, at 5 (1991). International environmental law, as it applies to war, is not well developed. Space limitations preclude examining it in detail here. Suffice it to say that Iraq was not a party to the most pertinent multilateral treaties in 1990–91, and the customary law on damage to the environment in wartime is hazy at best. See generally The Gulf War: Environment as a Weapon, 1991 ASIL Proc. 214.

s. U.N. Doc. S/22643, at 2–3 (1991).

t. For discussion of this point in the context of the Security Council, see E. Lauterpacht, Aspects of the Administration of International Justice 37–48 (1991).

determination in Resolution 662 (1990) that Iraq's purported annexation of Kuwait "has no legal validity and is * * * null and void"?

Could the questions regarding paragraph 16 of Resolution 687 legitimately be raised as well regarding paragraph 17?

The Security Council's mandate under the Charter is to maintain (or restore) international peace and security. See *article 24*. What did paragraph 17 have to do with that? Was it ultra vires?

In paragraphs 18 and 19, did the Security Council impose a tax on Iraqi oil exports? If so, is that a proper Security Council function? (The Secretary–General proposed 30% of the value of Iraq's oil exports as the maximum assessment; this was accepted by the Security Council.[u])

Paragraphs 20 through 23 were an attempt to provide a mechanism for humanitarian relief for the people of Iraq. Within a short time after the fighting stopped, serious shortages of food, medicines and other necessities were reported. The problem was that Iraq apparently did not have sufficient finances to import adequate quantities of these items under the terms of paragraph 20, unless it could earn foreign exchange by exporting oil. The United States was reluctant to let it export oil, unless the proceeds could be strictly monitored and channeled to the basic needs of the Iraqi public. This would require a further U.N. intrusion into what would normally be the domestic affairs of a member state.

Ultimately, the Security Council, acting under Chapter VII of the Charter, adopted Resolutions 706 and 712 (1991). These resolutions approved the export of a limited quantity of oil, subject to several conditions. Among them were the requirement that every contract provide that it enter into force only after approval of the Security Council committee established under Resolution 661; proceeds from oil sales were to be deposited in an escrow account administered by the Secretary–General; the oil while under Iraqi title was to be immune from attachment, garnishment or execution; and the U.N. was to monitor the importation and distribution of food and medicines in Iraq.[v]

In the Security Council debate on these measures, the representatives of Iraq, Yemen, Cuba and Ecuador raised questions about the wisdom or propriety of acting under Chapter VII of the Charter.[w] Was it appropriate to adopt humanitarian measures under Chapter VII? Why would the sponsors of Resolutions 706 and 712 want to invoke Chapter VII?

The paragraph of Security Council Resolution 712 that dealt with immunity of Iraqi oil from domestic legal proceedings said that the Security Council, acting under Chapter VII:

u. S.C. Res. 705 (1991).

v. The plan, as approved by the Security Council, appears in U.N. Doc. S/23006 (1991).

w. See U.N. Doc. S/PV.3004, at 42, 56, 68–70, 101–02 (1991).

> *Decides* that petroleum and petroleum products subject to resolution 706 (1991) shall while under Iraqi title be immune from legal proceedings and not be subject to any form of attachment, garnishment or execution, and that all States shall take any steps that may be necessary under their respective domestic legal systems to assure this protection, and to ensure that the proceeds of sale are not diverted from the purposes laid down in resolution 706
> * * *.

Iraq objected to the oil export plan on the ground that it violated Iraq's sovereignty. No oil was exported under Resolutions 706 and 712. If Iraqi oil had been exported to the United States under these resolutions, would it have been immune from attachment in U.S. courts at the hands of Iraq's creditors, without any action by Congress? See U.N. Charter *articles 24, 25* and *48*. Would the key paragraph of Resolution 712, above, be self-executing in the United States? If not, would it matter?

Frustrated by Iraq's refusal to implement the oil export plan, the Security Council in October 1992 adopted Resolution 778. Acting under Chapter VII of the Charter, it decided that all states in which there were funds of the Iraqi government representing the proceeds of the sale of Iraqi oil for which payment was made after August 6, 1990, would be transferred to the escrow account contemplated by Resolutions 706 and 712, up to $200 million per transferring state; funds required to satisfy existing Iraqi debts to third parties could be excluded. The Council also directed all states in which petroleum products owned by the Iraqi government were found to convert them to cash and transfer the proceeds to the escrow account. The Secretary–General was directed to transfer 30% of these funds to the compensation fund for payment of claims arising from Iraq's invasion of Kuwait, and to use the remainder for the U.N. costs of eliminating Iraq's weapons of mass destruction, humanitarian relief in Iraq, and certain other U.N. costs arising from the war. The funds transferred under Resolution 778 would be replenished from future Iraqi oil exports under the system provided in Resolutions 706 and 712.

It was clear that the funds generated by Resolution 778 would fall far short of the amount needed for the contemplated purposes. Leaving that aside, was Resolution 778 proper under Chapter VII? Could such a resolution have been adopted under any other U.N. Charter provisions?

To return once again to Resolution 687, what was the legal effect of paragraph 29? Was it within the Security Council's proper functions under the Charter? (It appears to have caught on. A similar provision appeared in Security Council Resolution 757 (1992), imposing a trade embargo on Serbia and Montenegro.)

Paragraph 32 required Iraq to inform the Security Council that it renounces terrorism. The Iraqi Foreign Minister did so.[x] Is it appropriate for the Security Council to single out a government—not the one most often accused of state-sponsored terrorism—for a declaration renouncing terrorism? Is it consistent with U.N. Charter *article 2(1)*? Note also *article 24(2)*.

Does Resolution 687 supply a precedent for possible Security Council action under Chapter VII to impose mandatory arms control measures on countries in the Middle East other than Iraq? Note particularly the preamble and paragraph 14.

(3) The Relationship Between Chapters VI and VII

In Resolution 687, the Security Council said that it was acting under Chapter VII of the U.N. Charter. That was not the only option available to it. Several of the measures in Resolution 687 might have been adopted, in somewhat different form, under Chapter VI. See particularly *articles 36* and *37*. But note that article 37 contemplates that the parties to the dispute will refer it to the Security Council. (Does article 36 contemplate the same thing?) What if they don't? Could the Security Council consider itself empowered to act under article 37 if only one of the parties—in this case, presumably Kuwait—referred the dispute to it?

If the Security Council were properly seized of the matter under Chapter VI, would measures of the sort it adopted in Resolution 687 have had the same legal effect as they had under Chapter VII? Note that in the Namibia case, the ICJ said that *article 25* of the Charter is not limited to enforcement action under Chapter VII. See page 502 supra.

The representative of Ecuador raised a legal issue concerning paragraphs 2 and 3 of Resolution 687 and the relationship between Chapters VI and VII. He said:

> Article 36 of the Charter did not give the Security Council the authority under Chapter VII to pronounce on the territorial limits between Iraq and Kuwait or to stipulate arrangements demarcating the boundary in question.[a]

When the Security Council acts under Chapter VII, is *article 36* relevant? On the other hand, if the Security Council undertakes to perform the function contemplated by Chapter VI—pacific settlement of disputes, in this case regarding the demarcation of the Iraq–Kuwait boundary after the ceasefire—is it proper to invoke Chapter VII at all?

Suppose the Security Council had chosen to act under Chapter VI in the Iraq–Kuwait boundary matter, and had recommended that the two states establish an impartial commission to determine the precise

---

x. U.N. Doc. S/22687, at 3 (1991).   a. U.N. Doc. S/24117 (1992).

boundary. Could the Security Council, in the same resolution, lawfully provide that if either Iraq or Kuwait failed to cooperate in establishing the commission or in carrying out its decision, new sanctions under Chapter VII would be imposed?[b]

(4) The Compensation Fund

Yet another major set of issues in the aftermath of the Persian Gulf war had to do with the adjudication and payment of claims against Iraq. In accordance with paragraph 19 of Resolution 687, the Secretary–General submitted a report to the Security Council,[a] proposing a U.N. Compensation Fund to be administered by a U.N. Compensation Commission. As approved by the Security Council, the Commission would have a Governing Council composed of all states members of the Security Council at any given time, with no member having veto power. Decisions are to be by majority vote for most purposes. The Governing Council is to be assisted by a Secretariat and by Commissioners who are experts in relevant fields including international law. The Commissioners are to act in their personal capacities. Payments into the Fund were contemplated from the levy on Iraqi oil exports, as directed by paragraph 19 of Resolution 687. The Governing Council is to administer the Fund and decide on procedures for settling claims against Iraq.

The Secretary–General appears to have drawn on the experience of the Iran–U.S. Claims Tribunal, making modifications to accommodate the enormous volume and monetary amounts of the anticipated claims. Claims would normally be submitted only by governments on behalf of their individual nationals and corporations. This is designed to relieve the Commission of the burden of sorting through tens of thousands of individual claims.

When a claim is submitted, the Secretariat is to make a preliminary assessment to determine whether it is admissible on its face. If so, it is to be submitted to a Panel of three Commissioners. The Panel may request additional evidence and, in large or complex cases, may hold hearings at which governments and private parties may present their views and expert testimony may be presented. The Panel's decision is subject only to the approval of the Governing Council, which is to make the final determination. The Governing Council could remand the claim to the Panel for further proceedings, if it deemed that to be appropriate.

The Secretary–General characterized the Commission's functions this way:

> The Commission is not a court or an arbitral tribunal before which the parties appear; it is a political organ that performs an essentially fact-finding function of examining claims, verifying

---

b. On the relationship between Chapters VI and VII in other contexts, see N. White, The United Nations and the Maintenance of International Peace and Security 71–73 (1990).

a. U.N. Doc. S/22559 (1991).

their validity, evaluating losses, assessing payments and resolving disputed claims. It is only in this last respect that a quasi-judicial function may be involved.[b]

Security Council Resolution 692 (1991) established the Fund and Compensation Commission, in accordance with the Secretary–General's report. It directed the Governing Council to establish the procedure for processing claims.[c] It also decided that if the Governing Council notifies the Security Council that Iraq has failed to carry out Governing Council decisions regarding payments into the Fund, the Security Council intends to reimpose the embargo on Iraqi oil exports.

Was this within the Security Council's authority under the U.N. Charter? The government of Iraq thought not. It charged that the Security Council had usurped the functions of the International Court of Justice, by establishing a political body (the Governing Council) to make essentially judicial decisions. Such a body, Iraq said, lacks the independence and high qualifications of the judges of the ICJ, and will "make the criterion for consideration of compensation based on the interests and policies of the States members of the Council, not on the principles of international law, without according Iraq the right to defend itself or consult its current and future economic interests."[d] Did Iraq have a point?

The process of adjudicating the claims against Iraq was bound to be enormously complicated, in light of the many thousands of individual claims by persons of several nationalities, the difficulty of establishing what property was lost and its value, problems of evaluating personal injury and death claims, imponderables about the extent of environmental damage, and so forth. Would the ICJ be an appropriate forum to decide all of this? If not, could a more appropriate forum have been devised than the one the Secretary–General and Security Council settled on?

The Secretary–General foresaw thorny legal questions arising from the availability to claimants of domestic legal systems. He said:

> [T]here is another matter that requires consideration by the Commission and regarding which the Governing Council should establish guidelines, namely the question of the exclusivity or non-exclusivity of the claims procedure foreseen in paragraph 19 of the resolution. It is clear from paragraph 16 of the resolution that the debts and obligations of Iraq arising prior to 2 August 1990 are an entirely separate issue and will be addressed "through the normal mechanisms". It is also clear from paragraph 16 that the resolution and the procedure foreseen in paragraph 19 relate to liability under international law. Resolution 687 (1991) could not, and does not, establish the Commission as an organ with exclusive compe-

---

b. Id. at 7.

c. The Governing Council's Provisional Rules for Claims Procedures appear in U.N. Doc. S/24363, Annex 1, 31 Int'l Legal Materials 1053 (1992).

d. U.N. Doc. S/22643, at 3 (1991).

tence to consider claims arising from Iraq's unlawful invasion and occupation of Kuwait. In other words, it is entirely possible, indeed probable, that individual claimants will proceed with claims against Iraq in their domestic legal systems. The likelihood of parallel actions taking place on the international level in the Commission and on the domestic level in national courts cannot be ignored. It is, therefore, recommended that the Governing Council establish guidelines regarding the non-exclusivity of claims and the appropriate mechanisms for coordination of actions at the international and domestic levels in order to ensure that the aggregate of compensation awarded by the Commission and a national court or commission does not exceed the amount of the loss. A particular problem might arise in this regard concerning default judgements obtained in national courts.[e]

Note the Secretary–General's assertion that Resolution 687 not only does not, but could not, give the Commission competence to the exclusion of domestic legal systems in considering claims arising from Iraq's invasion and occupation of Kuwait. Why couldn't Resolution 687 (or a new Security Council resolution) do so?

The Secretary–General said that the Governing Council should establish guidelines regarding the non-exclusivity of claims. The Governing Council did so.[f] Space does not permit an examination of them, but assume that they prove to be workable. Should the Security Council take on the responsibility of establishing claims commissions at the end of all armed conflicts that involve significant civilian losses?

h. Evaluation

How do you evaluate the role of the Security Council in the Persian Gulf situation, from August 1990 on? Did it do what it was supposed to do under the U.N. Charter? Consider these observations by a former U.N. Under Secretary–General, who was for many years the leading U.N. official for peacekeeping:

> The truth is that in the Iraq–Kuwait case, collective security, for all its ultimate success, turned out to mean war on a large scale. * * * Although the outcome was widely acclaimed, the procedure has inevitably raised questions among the broader membership of the United Nations about the control and direction of future actions. These questions will have to be addressed if the world organization is to continue to have universal character and support, which is its main characteristic and strength.[a]

Are the tools available to the Security Council adequate in cases like this? If there is doubt, should the Charter be amended? How?

---

e. U.N. Doc. S/22559, at 7–8 (1991).

f. See U.N. Doc. S/24611, Annex II, 31 Int'l Legal Materials 1069 (1992).

a. Urquhart, United Nations Diplomacy in 1990, The Diplomatic Record 1990–1991 at 21, 25, 27 (D. Newsom ed. 1992).

What do you foresee as the future role of the Security Council when there is a clear threat to, or breach of, international peace and security?

4. *Yugoslavia*

In the autumn of 1991, Slovenia and Croatia, two provinces of Yugoslavia, declared their independence. In March 1992, Bosnia–Herzegovina followed suit. The federal government at first resisted Slovenia's independence, and sent armed forces to quash it. After a brief period of fighting, the federal forces withdrew.

The asserted independence of Croatia and Bosnia–Herzegovina was a much more sensitive matter, primarily because of the substantial Serbian minority living within those territories. Longstanding distrust between Serbs and Croats flared into violence first, as Serbs resisted absorption in an independent Croat state. When the Serbian-controlled federal armed forces intervened on the side of the Serbs, large-scale fighting ensued. Eventually, after much bloodshed within Croatia, the Serbs and federal armed forces gained control over those areas of Croatia heavily populated by Serbs. The aim apparently was to establish a greater Serbia, which would include those areas.

The European Community made repeated, unsuccessful efforts to mediate the dispute and end the fighting. Proclaimed cease-fires were quickly ignored. All the while, the fighting remained confined to Yugoslavia, and largely to Croatia. Later, when Bosnia–Herzegovina declared its independence, even more destructive fighting occurred there.

With encouragement from the Yugoslav central government, the Security Council met in September 1991 to consider the situation in Croatia. The meeting produced the resolution below.

SECURITY COUNCIL RESOLUTION 713
Sept. 25, 1991.
U.N. Doc. S/RES/713 (1991).

The Security Council,

Conscious of the fact that Yugoslavia has welcomed the convening of a Security Council meeting * * *,

Having heard the statement by the Foreign Minister of Yugoslavia,

Deeply concerned by the fighting in Yugoslavia which is causing a heavy loss of human life and material damage, and by the consequences for the countries of the region, in particular in the border areas of neighbouring countries,

Concerned that the continuation of this situation constitutes a threat to international peace and security,

Recalling its primary responsibility under the Charter of the United Nations for the maintenance of international peace and security,

Recalling also the provisions of Chapter VIII of the Charter of the United Nations,

* * *

Recalling the relevant principles enshrined in the Charter of the United Nations and, in this context, noting the Declaration of 3 September 1991 of the States participating in the Conference on Security and Cooperation in Europe that no territorial gains or changes within Yugoslavia brought about by violence are acceptable,

* * *

5. *Appeals urgently to and encourages* all parties to settle their disputes peacefully and through negotiation at the Conference on Yugoslavia, including through the mechanisms set forth within it;

6. *Decides,* under Chapter VII of the Charter of the United Nations, that all States shall, for the purposes of establishing peace and stability in Yugoslavia, immediately implement a general and complete embargo on all deliveries of weapons and military equipment to Yugoslavia until the Security Council decides otherwise following consultation between the Secretary-General and the Government of Yugoslavia;

* * *

8. *Decides* to remain seized of the matter until a peaceful solution is achieved.

SANCTIONS DURING A WAR OF SECESSION

Resolution 713 was adopted before Croatia had been recognized as an independent state. In the debate leading to Resolution 713, several participants sought to justify the Security Council's Chapter VII involvement in what still seemed to be a civil war. The representative of Zimbabwe said, "We are told that there are arms flowing in from different countries, * * * for different agendas and different purposes. I think it would be a great help if those arms were not allowed to enter Yugoslavia. * * * We support that initiative and the use of the powers under Chapter VII of the Charter specifically for that purpose."[a]

The representative of Yemen characterized the situation as "an example of the new type of problems that will face the United Nations in the last decade of the twentieth century and thereafter. * * * Those new problems will no doubt make it necessary for the United Nations, and particularly for the Security Council, to deal with them creatively, in order to avoid their aggravation and escalation to the point where they would threaten regional and international security."[b]

The representatives of India and the Soviet Union stressed Yugoslavia's consent. The Indian representative went on to say that "the

[a] U.N. Doc. S/PV.3009, at 32 (1991). [b] Id. at 33.

Council's consideration of the matter relates not to Yugoslavia's internal situation as such, but specifically to its implication for peace and security in the region. * * * The Council's intervention becomes legitimate and acceptable only when any conflict it faces has serious implications for international peace and security." [c]

The British representative said that "this conflict * * * has a strong international dimension. The patchwork of nationalities and minorities throughout Central and Eastern Europe means that full-scale war might not be confined easily to a single territory." [d]

Did all of these justifications satisfy the conditions set forth in U.N. Charter *article 39* for Chapter VII action?

The situation did have some potentially serious, observable spillover effects on neighboring countries, particularly Bulgaria and Hungary. For example, by November 1991, more than 40,000 Yugoslav refugees had reached Hungary. Aircraft from the federal forces in Yugoslavia had repeatedly entered Hungarian air space. Serbia had accused Bulgaria and Hungary of trying to annex parts of Yugoslavia.[e]

Would the apparent acquiescence of the central Yugoslav government eliminate any *article 2(7)* objection, even if there was no threat to international peace and security?

When Bosnia–Herzegovina's independence was recognized by the European Community and the United States in April 1992, an ethnic conflict that had begun about a month earlier escalated into an even more intense and intractable war than had occurred in Croatia. The major ethnic groups in Bosnia–Herzegovina were Slavic Muslims (about 44% of the population), Serbs (about 31%) and Croats (about 17%). They were intermingled throughout Bosnia–Herzegovina. Bosnian Serbs, supported by the remaining Yugoslav government in Serbia, sought to establish their own independent areas, "cleansed" of Muslims and Croats. Mistrust among extremists ran in all three directions.

Heavy fighting killed and injured scores of civilians, reduced much of Sarajevo and other Bosnian towns to rubble, and engendered a massive refugee flow into Croatia and neighboring states. The fighting continued unabated despite several announced ceasefires. At first, the resident Serbian irregulars were supported in the field by the Yugoslav People's Army (JNA), which consisted largely of Serbs from Serbia, Bosnia and Croatia. JNA itself conducted some attacks within Bosnia. Eventually the Serbian citizens serving in JNA withdrew, but that left about 80% of the JNA forces in Bosnia intact, effectively controlled by Bosnian Serbs. It was apparent that much of the weaponry that

c. Id. at 46.
d. Id. at 57.

e. See Financial Times, Nov. 28, 1991, p. 3, col. 1.

remained—including heavy mortars used for shelling cities—had been supplied by Serbia.

The withdrawal of regular Serbian forces did little to stem the fighting. Ceasefire violations occurred on all sides. United States and European Community leaders became convinced that a lasting peace could be secured only if Serbia withdrew its support for the Serbian nationalists in Bosnia.

In the spring of 1992, the Security Council lost its patience with the situation in general, and with the Serbian authorities in particular. First it demanded in Resolution 752 that the fighting cease. When that had no effect, it adopted its second Chapter VII resolution on Yugoslavia.

SECURITY COUNCIL RESOLUTION 757
May 30, 1992.
U.N. Doc. S/RES/757 (1992).

The Security Council,

* * *

Deploring the fact that the demands in resolution 752 (1992) have not been complied with * * *,

Deploring further that its call for the immediate cessation of forcible expulsions and attempts to change the ethnic composition of the population has not been heeded, and *reaffirming* in this context the need for the effective protection of human rights and fundamental freedoms, including those of ethnic minorities,

* * *

Noting that the claim by the Federal Republic of Yugoslavia (Serbia and Montenegro) to continue automatically the membership of the former Socialist Federal Republic of Yugoslavia in the United Nations has not been generally accepted,

* * *

Recalling its primary responsibility under the Charter of the United Nations for the maintenance of international peace and security,

Recalling also the provisions of Chapter VIII of the Charter of the United Nations, and the continuing role that the European Community is playing in working for a peaceful solution in Bosnia and Herzegovina, as well as in other republics of the former Socialist Federal Republic of Yugoslavia,

* * *

Determining that the situation in Bosnia and Herzegovina and in other parts of the former Socialist Federal Republic of Yugoslavia constitutes a threat to international peace and security,

Acting under Chapter VII of the Charter of the United Nations,

1. *Condemns* the failure of the authorities in the Federal Republic of Yugoslavia (Serbia and Montenegro), including the Yugoslav People's Army (JNA), to take effective measures to fulfil the requirements of resolution 752 (1992);

2. *Demands* that any elements of the Croatian Army still present in Bosnia and Herzegovina act in accordance with paragraph 4 of resolution 752 (1992) without further delay;

3. *Decides* that all States shall adopt the measures set out below, which shall apply until the Security Council decides that the authorities in the Federal Republic of Yugoslavia (Serbia and Montenegro), including the Yugoslav People's Army (JNA), have taken effective measures to fulfil the requirements of resolution 752 (1992);

4. *Decides* that all States shall prevent:

(a) The import into their territories of all commodities and products originating in the Federal Republic of Yugoslavia (Serbia and Montenegro) exported therefrom after the date of the present resolution;

(b) Any activities by their nationals or in their territories which would promote or are calculated to promote the export or trans-shipment of any commodities or products originating in the Federal Republic of Yugoslavia (Serbia and Montenegro); * * *

(c) The sale or supply by their nationals or from their territories or using their flag vessels or aircraft of any commodities or products, whether or not originating in their territories, but not including supplies intended strictly for medical purposes and foodstuffs notified to the Committee established pursuant to resolution 724 (1991), to any person or body in the Federal Republic of Yugoslavia (Serbia and Montenegro) or to any person or body for the purposes of any business carried on in or operated from the Federal Republic of Yugoslavia (Serbia and Montenegro), * * *;

5. *Decides* that all States shall not make available to the authorities in the Federal Republic of Yugoslavia (Serbia and Montenegro) or to any commercial, industrial or public utility undertaking in the Federal Republic of Yugoslavia (Serbia and Montenegro), any funds or any other financial or economic resources and shall prevent their nationals and any persons within their territories from removing from their territories or otherwise making available to those authorities or to any such undertaking any such funds or resources and from remitting any other funds to persons or bodies within the Federal Republic of Yugoslavia (Serbia and Montenegro), except payments exclusively for strictly medical or humanitarian purposes and foodstuffs;

6. [Paragraphs 4 and 5 do not apply to trans-shipment of goods through the Federal Republic of Yugoslavia;]

7. *Decides* that all States shall:

(a) Deny permission to any aircraft to take off from, land in or overfly their territory if it is destined to land in or has taken off from the territory of the Federal Republic of Yugoslavia (Serbia and Montenegro), unless the particular flight has been approved, for humanitarian or other purposes consistent with the relevant resolutions of the Council, by the Committee established by resolution 724 (1991);

(b) Prohibit, by their nationals or from their territory, the provision of engineering and maintenance servicing of aircraft registered in the Federal Republic of Yugoslavia (Serbia and Montenegro) or operated by or on behalf of entities in the Federal Republic of Yugoslavia (Serbia and Montenegro) or components for such aircraft, the certification of airworthiness for such aircraft, and the payment of new claims against existing insurance contracts and the provision of new direct insurance for such aircraft;

8. *Decides* that all States shall:

(a) Reduce the level of the staff at diplomatic missions and consular posts of the Federal Republic of Yugoslavia (Serbia and Montenegro);

(b) Take the necessary steps to prevent the participation in sporting events on their territory of persons or groups representing the Federal Republic of Yugoslavia (Serbia and Montenegro);

(c) Suspend scientific and technical cooperation and cultural exchanges and visits involving persons or groups officially sponsored by or representing the Federal Republic of Yugoslavia (Serbia and Montenegro);

9. *Decides* that all States, and the authorities in the Federal Republic of Yugoslavia (Serbia and Montenegro), shall take the necessary measures to ensure that no claim shall lie at the instance of the authorities in the Federal Republic of Yugoslavia (Serbia and Montenegro), or of any person or body in the Federal Republic of Yugoslavia (Serbia and Montenegro), or of any person claiming through or for the benefit of any such person or body, in connection with any contract or other transaction where its performance was affected by reason of the measures imposed by this resolution and related resolutions;

* * *

11. *Calls upon* all States, including States not members of the United Nations, and all international organizations, to act strictly in accordance with the provisions of the present resolution, notwithstanding the existence of any rights or obligations conferred or imposed by any international agreement or any contract entered into or any licence or permit granted prior to the date of the present resolution;

* * *

16. *Decides* to keep under continuous review the measures imposed by paragraphs 4 to 9 above with a view to considering whether

such measures might be suspended or terminated following compliance with the requirements of resolution 752 (1992); * * *.

SANCTIONS IN A CONFUSED SITUATION

In a report received by the Security Council an hour after it adopted Resolution 757, the Secretary–General expressed uncertainty about whether the Serbian government continued to exercise control over the Serb forces in Bosnia–Herzegovina. He noted, for example, that Serb irregulars had attacked a convoy of the Yugoslav People's Army that was withdrawing from Bosnia.[f]

In a confused situation like this, should the Security Council establish some sort of fact-finding mechanism to report to it before it imposes Chapter VII sanctions? What sort of mechanism would work?

One might argue that the purpose of sanctions—at least in this case—is not only compulsion in an ongoing situation, but also deterrence and/or retribution. Are deterrence and retribution legitimate purposes for Chapter VII sanctions like those in Resolution 757—sanctions that will fall most heavily on the civilian population of the sanctioned state?

Just eight days before Resolution 757 was adopted, the General Assembly admitted Slovenia, Croatia and Bosnia–Herzegovina to U.N. membership. Was Resolution 757 any stronger because of their admission to membership than it would have been otherwise?

Note the warning in Resolution 757 to the Federal Republic of Yugoslavia (Serbia and Montenegro) about its own membership status. The message was that it might have to reapply, and might not be admitted. Should the issue have been put that way, rather than as one of suspension or expulsion under *article 5* or *6*? See pages 600–03 supra. Could suspension or expulsion be justified under article 41, without having to go through article 5 or 6?

While Resolution 757 was in force, and while the Security Council remained seized of the situation in Bosnia–Herzegovina, the General Assembly adopted Resolution 46/242 (1992). In it, the General Assembly expressed its grave concern regarding the situation in Bosnia–Herzegovina, which, it said, "constitutes a threat to international peace and security." The General Assembly went on to demand, inter alia, that the parties to the conflict stop fighting, that interference from outside Bosnia–Herzegovina cease immediately, and that units of the Yugoslav People's Army and elements of the Croatian army be withdrawn, disarmed or subjected to the authority of the government of Bosnia–Herzegovina.

Did the General Assembly contravene U.N. Charter *article 12(1)?* Does the answer depend on whether the thrust of the General Assem-

---

f. See U.N. Doc. S/24049 (1992); Wash. Post, June 4, 1992, p. A21, col. 1.

bly's action was consistent with the measures taken by the Security Council?

Would it make any difference, in terms of the Resolution's effect, whether or not the General Assembly contravened article 12(1)?

The trade sanctions under Resolution 757 were porous. Substantial quantities of oil, for example, continued to find their way to Serbia. Much of this appeared to be facilitated by the exemption in paragraph 6 of Resolution 757 for trans-shipped goods. Barges and other ships on the Danube carrying goods marked "transit" managed to unload in Serbia and leave without accounting for the goods. A lesser quantity of goods appeared to be arriving by sea.

The Security Council tried to deal with the situation by adopting Resolution 787, below. The vote was 13 in favor, none opposed, and two (China and Zimbabwe) abstaining.

SECURITY COUNCIL RESOLUTION 787
Nov. 16, 1992.
U.N. Doc. S/RES/787 (1992).

The Security Council,

Reaffirming its resolution 713 (1991) of 25 September 1991 and all subsequent relevant resolutions,

Reaffirming its determination that the situation in the Republic of Bosnia and Herzegovina constitutes a threat to the peace, and reaffirming that the provision of humanitarian assistance in the Republic of Bosnia and Herzegovina is an important element in the Security Council's effort to restore peace and security in the region,

Deeply concerned at the threats to the territorial integrity of the Republic of Bosnia and Herzegovina, which, as a State Member of the United Nations, enjoys the rights provided for in the Charter of the United Nations,

* * *

Noting with grave concern the report of the Special Rapporteur appointed following a special session of the Commission on Human Rights to investigate the human rights situation in the former Yugoslavia, which makes clear that massive and systematic violations of human rights and grave violations of international humanitarian law continue in the Republic of Bosnia and Herzegovina,

* * *

Deeply concerned about reports of continuing violations of the embargo imposed by its resolutions 713 (1991) and 724 (1991) of 15 December 1991,

Deeply concerned also about reports of violations of the measures imposed by its resolution 757 (1992) of 30 May 1992,

* * *

2. *Reaffirms* that any taking of territory by force or any practice of "ethnic cleansing" is unlawful and unacceptable, and will not be permitted to affect the outcome of the negotiations on constitutional arrangements for the Republic of Bosnia and Herzegovina, and insists that all displaced persons be enabled to return in peace to their former homes;

3. *Strongly reaffirms* its call on all parties and others concerned to respect strictly the territorial integrity of the Republic of Bosnia and Herzegovina, and affirms that any entities unilaterally declared or arrangements imposed in contravention thereof will not be accepted;

4. *Condemns* the refusal of all parties in the Republic of Bosnia and Herzegovina, in particular the Bosnian Serb paramilitary forces, to comply with its previous resolutions, and demands that they and all other concerned parties in the former Yugoslavia fulfil immediately their obligations under those resolutions;

5. *Demands* that all forms of interference from outside the Republic of Bosnia and Herzegovina, including infiltration into the country of irregular units and personnel, cease immediately * * *;

* * *

7. *Condemns* all violations of international humanitarian law, including in particular the practice of "ethnic cleansing" and the deliberate impeding of the delivery of food and medical supplies to the civilian population of the Republic of Bosnia and Herzegovina, and reaffirms that those that commit or order the commission of such acts will be held individually responsible in respect of such acts;

* * *

9. *Decides,* acting under Chapter VII of the Charter of the United Nations, in order to ensure that commodities and products transshipped through the Federal Republic of Yugoslavia (Serbia and Montenegro) are not diverted in violation of resolution 757 (1992), to prohibit the transshipment of crude oil, petroleum products, coal, energy-related equipment, iron, steel, other metals, chemicals, rubber, tyres, vehicles, aircraft and motors of all types unless such transshipment is specifically authorized on a case-by-case basis by the Committee established by resolution 724 (1991) under its no-objection procedure;

10. *Further decides,* acting under Chapter VII of the Charter of the United Nations, that any vessel in which a majority or controlling interest is held by a person or undertaking in or operating from the Federal Republic of Yugoslavia (Serbia and Montenegro) shall be considered, for the purpose of implementation of the relevant resolutions of the Security Council, a vessel of the Federal Republic of Yugoslavia (Serbia and Montenegro) regardless of the flag under which the vessel sails;

11. *Calls upon* all States to take all necessary steps to ensure that none of their exports are diverted to the Federal Republic of Yugoslavia (Serbia and Montenegro) in violation of resolution 757 (1992);

12. Acting under Chapters VII and VIII of the Charter of the United Nations, *calls upon* States, acting nationally or through regional agencies or arrangements, to use such measures commensurate with the specific circumstances as may be necessary under the authority of the Security Council to halt all inward and outward maritime shipping in order to inspect and verify their cargoes and destinations and to ensure strict implementation of the provisions of resolutions 713 (1991) and 757 (1992);

13. *Commends* the efforts of those riparian States which are acting to ensure compliance with resolutions 713 (1991) and 757 (1992) with respect to shipments on the Danube, and reaffirms the responsibility of riparian States to take necessary measures to ensure that shipping on the Danube is in accordance with resolutions 713 (1991) and 757 (1992), including such measures commensurate with the specific circumstances as may be necessary to halt such shipping in order to inspect and verify their cargoes and destinations and to ensure strict implementation of the provisions of resolutions 713 (1991) and 757 (1992);

* * *

16. *Considers* that, in order to facilitate the implementation of the relevant Security Council resolutions, observers should be deployed on the borders of the Republic of Bosnia and Herzegovina, and requests the Secretary-General to present to the Council as soon as possible his recommendations on this matter; * * *.

TAKING THE NEXT STEPS

Note the link in Resolution 787 between the provision of humanitarian aid and the restoration of peace and security. Is that potentially an important connection for future Security Council action in other volatile situations?

"Ethnic cleansing" referred to the efforts—largely successful at that point—of Bosnian Serbs to force other ethnic groups, especially Muslims, from areas in Bosnia the Serbs wished to claim for themselves. Is Resolution 787 an authoritative determination that "ethnic cleansing" by one ethnic group directed against another is a violation of international law, even if done by an ethnic group not recognized as a state? If so, is it a violation of custom? Of the U.N. Charter?

Does paragraph 7 of Resolution 787 establish that those individuals responsible for "ethnic cleansing" are guilty of war crimes?

Does paragraph 3 establish, as a matter of international law, that any proclaimed Serbian political entity in Bosnia-Herzegovina is not entitled to be recognized as a state?

Is it the proper business of the Security Council to determine that vessels bear the nationality of a state other than the flag state? See paragraph 10.

Paragraph 12 tracked the language of Security Council Resolution 665 (1990), paragraph 1, page 652 supra, regarding enforcement of the trade embargo against Iraq. Like Resolution 665, it presumably trumped any inconsistent treaty rights of maritime states relating to freedom of navigation or innocent passage whenever a naval vessel, acting under the Security Council authorization, stopped and inspected a vessel at sea. NATO and the Western European Union dispatched naval vessels to do just that. Were U.N. member states who were in a position to do that *obliged* to do so?

Did paragraph 12 of Resolution 787 and paragraph 1 of Resolution 665 authorize naval vessels to seize merchant vessels found to be carrying contraband?

It appears that Danube River riparian states have a right of free navigation on the river, vis-à-vis each other.[g] Did paragraph 13 of Resolution 787 override that right?

Are resolutions such as 787 likely to be effective to restore peace and security?

The Security Council's attempts to restore order in the former Yugoslavia have also included peacekeeping, peacemaking and humanitarian assistance. As in Somalia and some other troubled areas in the 1990s, the line separating these measures from enforcement action has been blurred. Nevertheless, for analytical purposes, this book treats them separately before it examines how they mesh with enforcement measures. Chapter 5 examines the Security Council's expanded role in the former Yugoslavia (and elsewhere).

5. Somalia

In January 1991, revolutionary forces in Somalia ended President Mohammed Siad Barre's 21 years of dictatorial rule, and he fled from the capital, Mogadishu. An internecine struggle for power ensued between two clans of the same political party, the United Somali Congress, rooted in personal animosity between the leaders of the two clans. The result was anarchy in the capital, producing some 500,000 refugees and an undetermined, but substantial, number of civilian casualties. The warring clans cut off food supplies to civilians, causing famine in the capital and elsewhere.

With the approval of the Somali mission to the U.N., the Security Council met in January 1992 and adopted Resolution 733 (1992). The

---

[g] See R. Baxter, The Law of International Waterways 136–37 (1964); B. Vitányi, The International Regime of River Navigation 110–11 (1979).

resolution was as much an effort to provide humanitarian assistance as it was an enforcement measure, but it did include action under Chapter VII.

SECURITY COUNCIL RESOLUTION 733
Jan. 23, 1992.
U.N. Doc. S/RES/733 (1992).

The Security Council,

* * *

Gravely alarmed at the rapid deterioration of the situation in Somalia and the heavy loss of human life and widespread material damage resulting from the conflict in the country and aware of its consequences on the stability and peace in the region,

Concerned that the continuation of this situation constitutes, as stated in the report of the Secretary–General, a threat to international peace and security,

Recalling its primary responsibility under the Charter of the United Nations for the maintenance of international peace and security,

Recalling also the provisions of Chapter VIII of the Charter of the United Nations,

* * *

4. *Strongly urges* all parties to the conflict immediately to cease hostilities and agree to a cease-fire and to promote the process of reconciliation and of political settlement in Somalia;

5. *Decides,* under Chapter VII of the Charter of the United Nations, that all States shall, for the purposes of establishing peace and stability in Somalia immediately implement a general and complete embargo on all deliveries of weapons and military equipment to Somalia until the Security Council decides otherwise;

6. *Calls on* all States to refrain from any action which might contribute to increasing tension and to impeding or delaying a peaceful and negotiated outcome to the conflict in Somalia, which would permit all Somalis to decide upon and to construct their future in peace; * * *.

CIVIL WAR AND TOKEN ENFORCEMENT ACTION

The fighting in Somalia appears to have been entirely an internecine struggle between two clans, without significant assistance to either clan from outside the country. In the post-cold war world, no superpower had a vested interest in victory by either clan. Where was the threat to international peace and security?

If the answer to the previous question is "Nowhere," what precedent did Resolution 733 set? The Security Council actually met at the request of the permanent mission of Somalia. The Somali chargé d'affaires said:

> [L]et me assure the Council that any measures—even if coercive—to resolve the current crisis in Somalia cannot and will not be interpreted as interference in our internal affairs since their effect will be the saving of human lives and the restoration of human dignity. The situation cries out for the help of the United Nations and particularly the Security Council.[a]

Does this significantly limit the precedent? Note that because of the absence of a functioning central government in Somalia, there could be a question about the authority of the chargé d'affaires to speak for her country. She was appointed by the interim prime minister, whose own authority was not recognized by all the clans vying for control in Somalia.[b]

Did the question about the chargé d'affaires' authority make it legally imperative that the Security Council find a continuing threat to international peace and security?

Paragraph 5 of the resolution could not have made much difference, since there were very few arms being transferred to Somalia anyway. Is this an effective use of Chapter VII?

Resolution 733, in paragraphs omitted from the excerpt set forth above, requested the U.N. Secretary-General and others to undertake humanitarian assistance to the people of Somalia. Chapter VII resolutions directed at other countries, such as Iraq, have sometimes contained narrow humanitarian exceptions from economic sanctions, and Resolution 757 on Yugoslavia contained some provisions aimed at supplying humanitarian relief in Bosnia, but never before had a Security Council sanctions resolution given such prominence to humanitarian goals. If the Security Council becomes increasingly involved in internal conflicts, one might expect to see more resolutions combining elements of coercion with humanitarian efforts.

This in fact occurred in the context of Somalia in December 1992, when the Security Council adopted Resolution 794 to deal with the interference by Somali armed gangs with the delivery of food for starving civilians. Resolution 794 included a paragraph adopted under Chapter VII, authorizing the Secretary-General and member states "to use all necessary means to establish as soon as possible a secure environment for humanitarian relief operations in Somalia." It is examined further in Chapter 5 of this book.

6. Libya

On December 21, 1988, a bomb exploded on Pan American flight 103, destroying the aircraft over Lockerbie, Scotland. Everyone on

---

a. U.N. Doc. S/23507, at 5 (1992).
b. See interview with Ms. Fatun Mohammed Hasan, Somali chargé d'affaires, 14 U.N. Observer & Int'l Rep., No. 6, at 3 (June 1992).

board was killed. A lengthy United States–United Kingdom investigation initially focused on a Palestinian group and Syria, but—according to published reports—the evidence eventually pointed instead toward two Libyan officials. The United States then charged the two Libyan officials with responsibility for the bombing. They were indicted in November 1991 for trial in a U.S. court. The United Kingdom filed parallel charges against them.

The British and American governments jointly declared that Libya must surrender for trial those charged with the offense; accept responsibility for the acts of Libyan officials; disclose whatever it knew about the incident, including access to witnesses and other evidence; and pay appropriate compensation. The U.K., U.S. and France (in a related case) made "requests" to Libya in all these respects.[a] When Libya did not comply, the Security Council—at the urging of the U.K., U.S. and France—adopted Resolution 731, below, in January 1992.

SECURITY COUNCIL RESOLUTION 731
Jan. 21, 1992.
U.N. Doc. S/RES/731 (1992).

The Security Council,

Deeply disturbed by the world-wide persistence of acts of international terrorism in all its forms, including those in which States are directly or indirectly involved, which endanger or take innocent lives, have a deleterious effect on international relations and jeopardize the security of States,

Deeply concerned by all illegal activities directed against international civil aviation, and affirming the right of all States, in accordance with the Charter of the United Nations and relevant principles of international law, to protect their nationals from acts of international terrorism that constitute threats to international peace and security,

* * *

Deeply concerned over the results of investigations, which implicate officials of the Libyan Government and which are contained in Security Council documents that include the requests addressed to the Libyan authorities by France, the United Kingdom of Great Britain and Northern Ireland and the United States of America in connection with the legal procedures related to the attacks carried out against Pan American flight 103 and Union de transports aérens flight 772;

Determined to eliminate international terrorism,

1. *Condemns* the destruction of Pan American flight 103 and Union de transports aérens flight 772 and the resultant loss of hundreds of lives;

---

a. See U.N. Docs. S/23306, S/23308 and S/23309 (1991).

2. *Strongly deplores* the fact that the Libyan Government has not yet responded effectively to the above requests to cooperate fully in establishing responsibility for the terrorist acts referred to above against Pan American flight 103 and Union de transports aérens flight 772;

3. *Urges* the Libyan Government immediately to provide a full and effective response to those requests so as to contribute to the elimination of international terrorism;

4. *Requests* the Secretary–General to seek the cooperation of the Libyan Government to provide a full and effective response to those requests; * * *.

JOCKEYING FOR POSITION

The Secretary–General sent a representative to discuss the matter with the Libyan government, pursuant to paragraph 4 of the resolution. The Arab League also interceded. At one point it appeared that Libya would release the two officials to the Arab League, which would then deliver them for trial in a Western court. But that fell through, and it became apparent that Libya did not intend to surrender them for trial in the United States or the United Kingdom.

On January 18, 1992, Libya proposed arbitration with the United States and United Kingdom, under the 1971 Montreal Convention for the Suppression of Unlawful Acts Against the Safety of Civil Aviation,[b] which is described below. The U.S. and U.K. showed no inclination to arbitrate. On March 3, 1992, the Libyan government brought proceedings in the International Court of Justice against the United States and United Kingdom, asking the Court to declare that the respondents had breached their obligations to Libya under several articles of the Montreal Convention. Libya also asked the Court to declare that the respondents are obligated to desist from such breaches and "from the use of any and all force or threats against Libya, including the threat of force against Libya, and from all violations of the sovereignty, territorial integrity, and political independence of Libya."

The Montreal Convention makes it an offense to commit enumerated terrorist acts against civil aircraft, including destroying an aircraft in service. The articles cited by Libya obligate the state where the alleged offender is present to "establish its jurisdiction" over the offense and submit the case to its authorities for prosecution, if it does not extradite him. Extradition is made subject to the law of the requested state. (According to the Libyan government, Libyan law does not permit the extradition of Libyan nationals.[c] Many other states

---

b. 24 U.S.T. 565, 10 Int'l Legal Materials 1151 (1971).

c. See U.N. Doc. S/23672, Annex II (1992), reproduced in 31 Int'l Legal Materials 739, 740 (1992). For other documents

refuse to extradite their own nationals.) Under article 11(1) of the Montreal Convention, all contracting states are to "afford one another the greatest measure of assistance in connection with criminal proceedings brought in respect of the offences. The law of the State requested shall apply in all cases."

For the Court's jurisdiction, Libya relied on article 14 of the Montreal Convention:

> Any dispute between two or more Contracting States concerning the interpretation or application of this Convention which cannot be settled through negotiation, shall, at the request of one of them, be submitted to arbitration. If within six months from the date of the request for arbitration the Parties are unable to agree on the organization of the arbitration, any one of those Parties may refer the dispute to the International Court of Justice * * *.

Libya asked the Court to indicate these provisional measures:

> (a) to enjoin the [respondents] from taking any action against Libya calculated to coerce or to compel Libya to surrender the accused individuals to any jurisdiction outside of Libya; and
>
> (b) to ensure that no steps are taken that would prejudice in any way the rights of Libya with respect to the legal proceedings that are the subject of Libya's Application.

On March 31, 1992, before the Court could respond to Libya's request for provisional measures, the Security Council adopted Resolution 748:

SECURITY COUNCIL RESOLUTION 748
March 31, 1992.
U.N. Doc. S/RES/748 (1992).

The Security Council,

* * *

Deeply concerned that the Libyan Government has still not provided a full and effective response to the requests in [Security Council] Resolution 731 (1992),

Convinced that the suppression of acts of international terrorism, including those in which states are directly or indirectly involved, is essential for the maintenance of international peace and security,

* * *

Reaffirming that, in accordance with the principle in Article 2, paragraph 4 of the Charter of the United Nations, every state has the duty to refrain from organizing, instigating, assisting or participating in terrorist acts in another state or acquiescing in organized activities

on the Libyan standoff with the U.N., see id. 717–57.

within its territory directed toward the commission of such acts, when such acts involve a threat or use of force,

Determining in this context that the failure by the Libyan Government to demonstrate, by concrete actions, its renunciation of terrorism, and in particular its continued failure to respond fully and effectively to the requests in Resolution 731 (1992), constitute a threat to international peace and security,

Determined to eliminate international terrorism,

* * *

Acting under Chapter VII of the Charter of the United Nations,

1. *Decides* that the Libyan Government must now comply without any further delay with paragraph 3 of Resolution 731 (1992) * * *;

2. *Decides also* that the Libyan Government must commit itself definitively to cease all forms of terrorist action and all assistance to terrorist groups and that it must promptly, by concrete actions, demonstrate its renunciation of terrorism;

3. *Decides* that, on 15 April 1992 all States shall adopt the measures set out below, which shall apply until the Security Council decides that the Libyan Government has complied with paragraphs 1 and 2 above;

[Here follow sanctions requiring all states to deny any aircraft permission to take off from, land in or overfly their territory if it is bound for or from Libya (except in case of humanitarian need, as approved by a committee established by the resolution); to prohibit the supply of aircraft or aircraft components to Libya or the provision of maintenance for Libyan aircraft; to prohibit arms transfers to Libya as well as training related to Libyan arms; to withdraw any of their military advisors from Libya; to reduce Libyan diplomatic and consular staffs in their territories, prevent the operation of Libyan Arab Airlines offices, and deny entry to, or expel, accused Libyan terrorists;]

7. *Calls upon* all States, including States not members of the United Nations, and all international organizations, to act strictly in accordance with the provisions of the present resolution, notwithstanding the existence of any rights or obligations conferred or imposed by any international agreement or any contract entered into or any licence or permit granted before 15 April 1992;

* * *

13. *Decides* that the Security Council shall every 120 days, or sooner should the situation so require, review the [sanctions] in the light of the compliance by the Libyan Government with paragraphs 1 and 2 above, taking into account, as appropriate, any reports provided by the Secretary–General on his role as set out in paragraph 4 of Resolution 731 (1992); * * *.

CHAPTER VII AND TERRORISM

Resolution 748 marked the first time the Security Council had taken Chapter VII enforcement action on the basis of state-supported terrorism. According to the representative of the United States, "The evidence revealing Libya's involvement in these acts of terrorism indicates a serious breach of international peace and security." [d] Are isolated or occasional terrorist acts, if sponsored or encouraged by governments, the kind of breach of the peace contemplated by Chapter VII? The Charter contains no definition of "breach of the peace" or the other key terms in *article 39,* nor is the preparatory work any help.[e]

Is the application of Chapter VII to state-sponsored terrorism a salutary development? What are the limits to Security Council action under Chapter VII?

The Security Council made no findings of fact adopting the conclusions of the U.S. or U.K. investigations, though in Resolution 731 it did express its concern "over the results of the investigations, which implicate officials of the Libyan Government and which are contained in Security Council documents." One of those documents sets forth the U.S. grand jury indictment against the two Libyans, with detailed assertions of facts based on the U.S.–U.K. investigation.[f] Was there an adequate basis for the imposition of Chapter VII sanctions?

If there are significant factual questions that bear on the propriety of taking enforcement action, is the Security Council equipped to resolve them?

Does it matter that Libya was being asked to surrender its own nationals, in light of the general practice of governments in non-common law systems to refuse to extradite their nationals?

The sanctions, summarized above, were tailored to the circumstances of the case in the sense that they dealt with aviation, arms, diplomatic and consular relations, and terrorists. Does Chapter VII, or Security Council practice, require such fine tuning?

Note paragraph 13 of Resolution 748. Should all Chapter VII resolutions contain periodic review provisions of that sort? What would be accomplished by it?

On April 14, 1992, the day before the sanctions in Resolution 748 entered into effect, the ICJ issued its Order in response to the Libyan request for provisional measures.

---

d. U.N. Doc. S/PV.3063, at 66 (1992).

e. See J.-P. Cot & A. Pellet, La Charte des Nations Unies 654–59 (1985); L. Goodrich, E. Hambro & A. Simons, Charter of the United Nations 293–98 (3d rev. ed. 1969).

f. U.N. Doc. S/23317, Annex (1991).

CASE CONCERNING QUESTIONS OF INTERPRETATION AND APPLICATION OF THE 1971 MONTREAL CONVENTION ARISING FROM THE AERIAL INCIDENT AT LOCKERBIE

(Libya v. United States and United Kingdom), Request
for Indication of Provisional Measures.
International Court of Justice, 1992.
[1992] I.C.J. 114, 31 Int'l Legal Materials 665 (1992).

* * *

41. Whereas the Court, in the context of the present proceedings on a request for provisional measures, has in accordance with Article 41 of the Statute, to consider the circumstances drawn to its attention as requiring the indication of such measures, but cannot make definitive findings either of fact or of law on the issues relating to the merits, and the right of the Parties to contest such issues at the stage of the merits must remain unaffected by the Court's decision;

42. Whereas both Libya and the United States, as Members of the United Nations, are obliged to accept and carry out the decisions of the Security Council in accordance with Article 25 of the Charter; whereas the Court, which is at the stage of proceedings on provisional measures, considers that prima facie this obligation extends to the decision contained in resolution 748 (1992); and whereas, in accordance with Article 103 of the Charter, the obligations of the Parties in that respect prevail over their obligations under any other international agreement, including the Montreal Convention;

43. Whereas the Court, while thus not at this stage called upon to determine definitively the legal effect of Security Council resolution 748 (1992), considers that, whatever the situation previous to the adoption of that resolution, the rights claimed by Libya under the Montreal Convention cannot now be regarded as appropriate for protection by the indication of provisional measures;

44. Whereas, furthermore, an indication of the measures requested by Libya would be likely to impair the rights which appear prima facie to be enjoyed by the United States by virtue of Security Council resolution 748 (1992);

45. Whereas, in order to pronounce on the present request for provisional measures, the Court is not called upon to determine any of the other questions which have been raised before it in the present proceedings, including the question of its jurisdiction to entertain the merits of the case; and whereas the decision given in these proceedings in no way prejudges any such question, and leaves unaffected the rights of the Government of Libya and the Government of the United States to submit arguments in respect of any of these questions;

46. For these reasons,

THE COURT,

By eleven votes to five,

Finds that the circumstances of the case are not such as to require the exercise of its power under Article 41 of the Statute to indicate provisional measures.

THE RELATIONSHIP BETWEEN THE SECURITY COUNCIL AND THE COURT

Libya had argued to the Court that the Security Council infringed the rights conferred upon it by the Montreal Convention, and had characterized the situation under Chapter VII as a pretext to avoid applying the Montreal Convention; thus, said Libya, the Court need not refrain from indicating provisional measures.[g] Did the Court answer these arguments in paragraph 42? Did it leave the door open for itself, later in these proceedings or in other proceedings, to determine for itself whether or not the Security Council has exceeded its authority under the Charter?[h] On the absence from the Charter and ICJ Statute of any power of judicial review, see Chapter 3 of these materials, at pages 482 and 497.

Why would the measures Libya requested "be likely to impair the rights which appear prima facie to be enjoyed by the United States by virtue of" Resolution 748?

When this was written, the Court had not yet decided whether it had jurisdiction to hear the merits—a matter contested by the United States and United Kingdom. If the Security Council's enforcement action against Libya were still in effect when the Court decided the jurisdictional question, should that have any bearing on the Court's determination?

In a case like this, is there a conflict between *article 24(1)* and *article 92* of the Charter? Between article 24(1) of the Charter and *article 36* of the ICJ Statute?

7. *Coordinating U.N. and Regional Action*

Chapter VIII of the U.N. Charter contemplates peacekeeping activities by regional organizations. In fact, *article 52(2)* requires U.N. members entering into such organizations to make every effort to resolve local disputes through them before referring them to the Security Council. *Article 52(4)* adds the arguably-contradictory caveat that the article "in no way impairs the application of Articles 34 and

---

g. As summarized by the Court in paragraphs 38 and 39 of the Opinion.

h. For a suggestion that this case might be the ICJ's *Marbury v. Madison*, see Franck, The "Powers of Appreciation": Who Is the Ultimate Guardian of UN Legality?, 86 Am.J.Int'l L. 519 (1992).

35." *Article 35* allows any member to bring any dispute to the attention of the Security Council or General Assembly. Organization of American States Charter *article 23,* as amended in 1985, requires that disputes between member states be submitted to the procedures in that Charter, but adds that it is not to be interpreted as impairing the rights and obligations of member states under U.N. Charter articles 34 and 35. Presumably, then, a U.N. member that is also a member of a regional organization—even the OAS—could bring a dispute directly to the Security Council, bypassing any dispute-settlement mechanisms in the regional organization.[a]

Several regional bodies exist with at least the potential to resolve local or regional conflicts, including not only the Organization of American States, but also the Organization of African Unity, the Arab League, and the Conference on Security and Cooperation in Europe. These bodies, however, have not been particularly effective at dispute settlement when there is a threat to the peace or breach of the peace. Moreover, they either do not have the power to apply sanctions against member states or, if they have the power, they have not been able to use it consistently and effectively.

When Iraq invaded Kuwait, the Arab League was split and unable to act. In the case of Yugoslavia in 1991, the Conference on Security and Cooperation in Europe, which at that time could act only by consensus among its members, took a back seat to the European Community—an organization not currently designed to deal with armed conflict situations, especially in a nonmember state.[b] In Somalia, neither the Organization of African Unity nor the Arab League acted. In the Libyan case, the Arab League did become involved and at one point thought it had a commitment from Libya to turn over the two suspects to it; when pressed, however, Libya did not follow through. In all these cases, the United Nations had to act if any international organization was to do so.

Article 53(1) of the Charter authorizes the Security Council to use regional organizations for enforcement action under its authority. Article 53(1) also says that no enforcement action shall be taken by regional organizations without the authorization of the Security Council. Regional organizations—especially the Organization of American States—on several occasions have taken action intended to prod or even coerce a member state into compliance with the particular organization's norms. On none of these occasions has the Security Council

a. See Acevedo, The Right of Members of the Organization of American States to Refer Their "Local" Disputes Directly to the United Nations Security Council, 4 Am.U.J.Int'l L. & Pol'y 25 (1989). See also U.N. Charter *article 103.*

b. The CSCE's inability to respond to the Yugoslavian situation spurred its members to change the rule requiring consensus. The CSCE Council decided in 1992 that "appropriate action may be taken by the [CSCE] Council or the Committee of Senior Officials, if necessary in the absence of the consent of the State concerned, in cases of clear, gross and uncorrected violations of relevant CSCE commitments." Prague Document on Further Development of CSCE Institutions and Structures, Jan. 30, 1992, para. 16.

expressly authorized the action in advance. The legal questions thus raised relate to the definition of "enforcement action" and the possibility of tacit authorization by the Security Council.

The ICJ, in the Expenses Case,[c] considered the meaning of "enforcement action" in a context different from that which concerns us here. The Court held that the expenses of the United Nations Emergency Force in the Middle East (UNEF) and the U.N. armed operations in what was then the Congo (ONUC) were proper expenses of the organization, even though UNEF was authorized by the General Assembly (rather than by the Security Council) and ONUC, though authorized initially by the Security Council, came to be directed by the Secretary–General who, among other things, did not proceed under *article 48* in determining which member states would participate. Both UNEF and ONUC were designed to help restore order in volatile situations—the Middle East after the 1956 hostilities and the Congo during the civil conflict that erupted when it became an independent state.

The Expenses Case is examined more fully in Chapter 5, below. The important points for present purposes are that the Court treated "enforcement action" as action of the type contemplated by Chapter VII of the U.N. Charter; the Court held that UNEF did not involve enforcement action because the U.N. forces were deployed with the consent of the governments concerned; and the military operations of ONUC did not involve enforcement action because they were not directed against any state that was determined to have committed an act of aggression or breach of the peace.

Enforcement action became an issue in the article 53(1) context during the Cuban missile crisis in 1962. During the summer and early autumn of 1962, more than 100 shiploads of arms, including missiles and jet aircraft, were sent to Cuba from the Soviet Union.[d] U.S. aerial reconnaissance showed four missile launching sites being constructed in Cuba. Key members of the Kennedy administration met in emergency sessions to come up with a response. They decided on a blockade, euphemistically called a quarantine, of Cuba. They also decided to put the matter before the OAS Council, which voted unanimously to authorize the quarantine. The U.N. Security Council was not asked for its authorization. The Soviet Union proposed a draft Security Council resolution that would have condemned the quarantine, but no vote was taken on it.

The U.S. Department of State argued that the OAS action was not "enforcement action" and thus did not require Security Council authorization under article 53(1), because it was not obligatory on OAS members. In other words, since the OAS merely authorized its mem-

c. [1962] I.C.J. 151.

d. See generally A. Chayes, The Cuban Missile Crisis (1974), on which the above statement of facts is based.

bers to impose a quarantine but did not require them to do so, there was no enforcement action.[e]

Is this convincing? When the U.N. Security Council has acted under Chapter VII, has it always required U.N. member states to participate?

Another argument was that even if the OAS action was "enforcement action," the Security Council could, and did, authorize it tacitly, by considering the matter and refraining from acting on the draft resolution that would have condemned the OAS action.[f] Is that convincing?

Similar "enforcement action" questions arose when the OAS reacted to the ouster of elected Haitian President Jean–Bertrand Aristide in the autumn of 1991. The OAS Ministers of Foreign Affairs condemned the events in Haiti as a denial of the right of self-determination. In October 1991, after recommending in a resolution that all states suspend their economic, financial and commercial ties with Haiti and urging them to provide no military, policy or security assistance of any kind,[g] the Ministers of Foreign Affairs adopted another resolution directed specifically at OAS member states. In the second resolution, the Ministers "urged" member states "immediately to freeze the assets of the Haitian State and to impose a trade embargo on Haiti, except for humanitarian aid."[h] This was communicated to the Security Council, which took no action. The U.N. General Assembly adopted a resolution "welcoming" the two OAS resolutions and requesting the Secretary-General to consider providing support sought by his OAS counterpart in implementing the resolutions.[i]

When these measures failed to bring about a return to democracy in Haiti by mid-May 1992, the OAS Ministers of Foreign Affairs adopted another resolution that, inter alia, "urged" member states to deny port facilities to any vessel not abiding by the trade embargo, to deny entry visas to the perpetrators and supporters of the coup d'état, and to freeze their assets.[j] Again the Security Council took no action.

Were the OAS measures against Haiti consistent with U.N. Charter article 53(1)? Consider also *article 103*.

A civil war broke out in Liberia in 1989. Although an accord was reached in October 1991 among the Liberian parties (called the Yamoussoukro IV Accord), the situation continued to be unstable. The principal effort to keep the peace was undertaken not by the U.N. or the Organization of African Unity, but by the Economic Community of West African States (ECOWAS), which established a multinational

e. See Department of State Memorandum: Legal Basis for the Quarantine of Cuba, Oct. 23, 1962, in id., Appendix III; Meeker, Defensive Quarantine and the Law, 57 Am.J.Int'l L. 515 (1963).

f. See Meeker, supra note e, at 522.

g. OAS Res. MRE/RES.1/91, reprinted in U.N. Doc. A/46/231, Appendix (1991).

h. OAS Res. MRE/RES.2/91, reprinted in U.N. Doc. A/46/550–S/23127 (1991).

i. G.A. Res. 46/7 (1991).

j. OAS Res. MRE/RES.3/92 (1992).

force led by Nigeria, called ECOMOG. See Chapter 5, Section 1.D.1 of these materials. ECOMOG established control over the capital, Monrovia, but had little influence elsewhere in Liberia in late 1992 when the main rebel group, the National Patriotic Front of Liberia, resumed fighting after a lull.

At this point the U.N. Security Council stepped in.

SECURITY COUNCIL RESOLUTION 788
Nov. 19, 1992.
U.N. Doc. S/RES/788 (1992).

The Security Council,

* * *

Determining that the deterioration of the situation in Liberia constitutes a threat to international peace and security, particularly in West Africa as a whole,

Recalling the provisions of Chapter VIII of the Charter of the United Nations,

* * *

Welcoming the continued commitment of the Economic Community of West African States (ECOWAS) to and the efforts towards a peaceful resolution of the Liberian conflict,

* * *

1. *Commends* ECOWAS for its efforts to restore peace, security and stability in Liberia,

* * *

4. *Condemns* the continuing armed attacks against the peace-keeping forces of ECOWAS in Liberia by one of the parties to the conflict;

* * *

6. *Calls upon* all parties to the conflict to respect and implement the cease-fire and the various accords of the peace process, including the Yamoussoukro IV Accord of 30 October 1991 * * *;

* * *

8. *Decides,* under Chapter VII of the Charter of the United Nations, that all States shall, for the purposes of establishing peace and stability in Liberia, immediately implement a general and complete embargo on all deliveries of weapons and military equipment to Liberia until the Security Council decides otherwise;

9. *Decides* within the same framework that the embargo imposed by paragraph 8 shall not apply to weapons and military equipment destined for the sole use of the peace-keeping forces of ECOWAS in

Liberia, subject to any review that may be required in conformity with [a contemplated] report of the Secretary–General;

10. *Requests* all States to respect the measures established by ECOWAS to bring about a peaceful solution to the conflict in Liberia;

* * *.

ENFORCEMENT ACTION AND REGIONAL FORCES

Did the presence of regional peacekeeping forces in what was otherwise a civil war situation create the threat to international peace and security? Note that the Security Council made no finding that the rebels in Liberia threatened the peace of other states in the area.

Did Resolution 788 amount to an enforcement action authorization for ECOWAS under U.N. Charter *article 53(1)?*

If so, what consequences would flow from it? For example, could the U.N. General Assembly treat the expenses of ECOMOG as "expenses of the [U.N.] Organization" under Charter *article 17(2)* and charge them to the U.N. budget? Outside the budget context, would the General Assembly be barred by *article 11(2)* of the Charter from adopting any resolution on the Liberian situation while Resolution 788 was in force?

If Resolution 788 did not authorize ECOWAS enforcement action, did it have any legal effect beyond the arms embargo in paragraph 8?

Why should the U.N. Charter require Security Council authorization for regional enforcement action?

8. *"Quasi–Enforcement Action": The Khmer Rouge*

As has been noted earlier in these materials, the brutal Khmer Rouge regime in Cambodia was driven from power by invading Vietnamese forces in 1978. Although the Vietnamese installed and supported a new government in Phnom Penh, the Khmer Rouge maintained control over a small area near the Thai border. Other political factions also remained in the picture. In October 1991, the rival factions signed the Paris Agreements calling for a cease-fire, the creation of a U.N. Transitional Authority in Cambodia (UNTAC) with civilian and military components, and a Supreme National Council representing the Cambodian people. UNTAC was given broad powers to establish the conditions needed for free elections to be held in 1993, including supervision and control of key Cambodian administrative agencies, bodies and government offices. UNTAC military functions included the demobilization and disarming of the forces vying for control of Cambodia, including the Khmer Rouge.[a]

When the Khmer Rouge resisted demobilization and refused full UNTAC access to the territory under its control, the Security Council adopted Resolution 766 (1992), deploring the action of "the Party that has failed so far" to cooperate and reaffirming UNTAC's mission. When that produced no results, the Security Council adopted Resolution 792 (1992). In it, without mentioning Chapter VII of the Charter, the Security Council:

* * *

7. *Condemns* the failure by the PDK [Khmer Rouge] to comply with its obligations;

8. *Demands* that the PDK fulfil immediately its obligations under the Paris Agreements; * * *

10. *Calls on* those concerned to ensure that measures are taken, consistent with [provisions of the Paris Agreements designed to preclude outside military assistance to any Cambodian parties] to prevent the supply of petroleum products to the areas occupied by any Cambodian party not complying with the military provisions of those Agreements and *requests* the Secretary–General to examine the modalities of such measures;

11. *Undertakes* to consider appropriate measures to be implemented should the PDK obstruct the implementation of the peace plan, such as the freezing of the assets held by the PDK outside Cambodia;

* * *

13. *Supports* the decision of the Supreme National Council * * * to set a moratorium on the export of logs from Cambodia in order to protect Cambodia's natural resources; *requests* States, especially neighbouring States, to respect this moratorium by not importing such logs; and *requests* UNTAC to take appropriate measures to secure the implementation of such moratorium; * * *.

In the Security Council debate leading to the adoption of Resolution 792, the Chinese representative said that the resolution "contains elements relating to sanctions" and added, "we are not in favour of any form of sanction measures against any Cambodian party." Consequently, he said, China would abstain from voting on the resolution.[b]

Did Resolution 792 amount to Chapter VII enforcement action against the Khmer Rouge? For the ICJ's definition of enforcement action, see the Expenses Case at pages 759 and 762–63 infra. Is there anything in Chapter VII that would preclude enforcement action against a body such as the Khmer Rouge?

If Resolution 792 did not amount to enforcement action, did paragraph 10 nevertheless impose a binding oil embargo on the areas

a. See U.N. Doc. A/46/608–S/23177 (1991), reprinted in 31 Int'l Legal Materials 174 (1992).

b. See U.N. Doc. S/PV.3143, at 4 (1992).

occupied by the Khmer Rouge? Could that legitimately be done without acting under Chapter VII?

Did paragraph 13 impose a binding moratorium on the export of logs from Cambodia? If not, why the request to UNTAC "to take appropriate measures to secure the implementation of such moratorium"? What could a lightly-armed force such as UNTAC do? (It was later reported that Thailand, through which exported logs would pass, stationed troops to enforce the moratorium at checkpoints on the border with Khmer Rouge-controlled areas.[c])

A bright line has traditionally separated Chapter VII enforcement action from other Security Council efforts to maintain or restore peace. Is it disappearing? (This question is explored further in Chapter 5.)

9. Controlling Weapons of Mass Destruction

On January 31, 1992, a summit-level meeting of the U.N. Security Council was held. It was the first time the Security Council had ever met at the level of heads of state and government. At the end of the meeting, the President of the Security Council made a statement on behalf of the members of the Council. Among other things, he said:

> The proliferation of all weapons of mass destruction constitutes a threat to international peace and security. The members of the Council commit themselves to working to prevent the spread of technology related to the research for or production of such weapons and to take appropriate action to that end.[a]

Does this amount to a finding under U.N. Charter *article 39?*

Whether it does or not, does it mean that the Security Council, acting under Chapter VII, could prohibit all new sales or purchases of any weapons of mass destruction it might specify?

Could it order all existing weapons of mass destruction to be dismantled, either globally or in designated states deemed untrustworthy, without waiting for an act of aggression of the sort that occurred against Kuwait?

Could the Security Council threaten or take enforcement action against a state that offers another state new technology for the production of a weapon of mass destruction, without any new finding that the weapon, if produced by the recipient state, is likely to be used offensively?

Whether or not the Security Council could legitimately do any of these things, has it made a conclusive determination that state-sponsored or -condoned international sales of weapons of mass destruction violate international law? Has it determined that such sales are international crimes?

c. Wash.Post, Jan. 2, 1993, p. A16, col. 5.

a. U.N. Doc. S/23500 (1992), reprinted in 31 Int'l Legal Materials 759, 762 (1992).

Chapter 5

THE EVOLVING UNITED NATIONS: PEACEKEEPING, PEACEMAKING AND HUMANITARIAN INTERVENTION

SECTION 1. PEACEKEEPING AND PEACEMAKING

A. INTRODUCTION

Chapter 4 examined U.N. enforcement action designed to maintain or restore peace, under U.N. Charter Chapter VII. Enforcement action is directed against a state or other political entity, and has a coercive design. U.N. peacekeeping, on the other hand, is not directed "against" a particular wrongdoer and traditionally has involved coercion only in a minimal sense, if at all. Its nature and characteristics as of 1990 are described below in a publication issued by the U.N. As will appear later, there has been some evolution since 1990.

THE BLUE HELMETS: A REVIEW OF UNITED NATIONS PEACEKEEPING
4–9 (2d ed. 1990).
U.N. Sales No. E.90.I.18.*

The evolution of international relations after the Second World War quickly brought to the fore differences which existed among the Member States, and in particular the five permanent members of the Security Council, and these inevitably affected the functioning of the Organization. New conflicts arose, particularly during the process of decolonization, and many could not be resolved by peaceful means. A way had to be found to stop hostilities and to control conflicts so that they would not develop into broader conflagrations. Out of that need, United Nations peace-keeping operations evolved as, essentially, hold-

---

* Copyright 1990 United Nations. Reprinted by permission of the United Nations Department of Public Information.

ing actions. There was not, and still is not, any particular theory or doctrine behind them. They were born of necessity, largely improvised, a practical response to a problem requiring action. The term "peace-keeping operation" did not gain currency until much later.

[The leading U.N. civilian authority on peacekeeping has said: "The technique of peacekeeping is a distinctive innovation by the United Nations. The Charter does not mention it. It was discovered, like penicillin. We came across it, while looking for something else, during an investigation of the guerrilla fighting in northern Greece in 1947." [a]]

As the United Nations practice has evolved over the years, a peace-keeping operation has come to be defined as an operation involving military personnel, but without enforcement powers, undertaken by the United Nations to help maintain or restore international peace and security in areas of conflict. These operations are voluntary and are based on consent and co-operation. While they involve the use of military personnel, they achieve their objectives not by force of arms, thus contrasting them with the "enforcement action" of the United Nations under Article 42.

[A former Legal Counsel of the United Nations has defined peace-keeping operations as "actions involving the use of military personnel in international conflict situations on the basis of the consent of all parties concerned and without resorting to armed force except in cases of self-defence." [b]]

Peace-keeping operations have been most commonly employed to supervise and help maintain cease-fires, to assist in troop withdrawals, and to provide a buffer between opposing forces. However, peace-keeping operations are flexible instruments of policy and have been adapted to a variety of uses, including helping to implement the final settlement of a conflict.

Peace-keeping operations are never purely military. They have always included civilian personnel to carry out essential political or administrative functions, sometimes on a very large scale, as, for instance, in the Congo operation or in the independence process in Namibia. In both those operations, and in several others, civilian police have also played an important role. During the resurgence of peace-keeping that has taken place in the later 1980s, * * * the expectation has developed that the peace-keeping operations of the future, like that in Namibia, may well be closely integrated civilian/military undertakings with overall responsibility in the field being entrusted to a civilian rather than a military officer.

a. [Brian Urquhart, The United Nations, Collective Security, and International Peacekeeping, in Negotiating World Order: The Artisanship and Architecture of Global Diplomacy 59, 62 (A. Henrikson ed. 1986). Ed.]

b. [Suy, Peace-keeping Operations, in A Handbook on International Organizations 379 (R.-J. Dupuy ed. 1988). Ed.]

It is difficult to subsume all these various operations under any one clause of the Charter. It is clear that they fall short of the provisions of Chapter VII * * *, which deal with enforcement. At the same time they go beyond purely diplomatic means or those described in Chapter VI of the Charter. As former Secretary-General Dag Hammarskjöld put it, peace-keeping might be put in a new Chapter "Six and a Half". Initially, questions were raised about the legality of the United Nations' use of military personnel in a manner not specifically provided for in the Charter. In recent years, however, something close to consensus has developed that these operations can be considered as having a basis, apart from the principle of consent, in the broad powers conferred by the Charter upon the United Nations and especially the Security Council.

Characteristics

In practice, there has evolved a broad degree of consensus on the essential characteristics of peace-keeping operations and on the conditions that must be met if they are to succeed.

The first of these essential characteristics is that peace-keeping operations are set up only with the consent of the parties to the conflict in question. Their consent is required not only for the operation's establishment but also, in broad terms, for the way in which it will carry out its mandate. The parties are also consulted about the countries which will contribute troops to the operation. It is a key principle that the operation must not interfere in the internal affairs of the host countries and must not in any way favour one party against another. This requirement of impartiality is fundamental, not only on grounds of principle but also to ensure that the operation is effective. A United Nations operation cannot take sides without becoming a part of the conflict which it has been set up to control or resolve. For their part, the parties to the conflict are expected to provide continuing support to the operation by allowing it the freedom of movement and other facilities which it needs to carry out its task. This co-operation is essential. The peace-keepers have no rights of enforcement and their use of force is limited to self-defence, as a last resort. This means that if a party chooses not to co-operate, it can effectively defy a peace-keeping operation.

In line with the Security Council's primary responsibility for the maintenance of international peace and security, peace-keeping operations have mainly been established by the Council (though two were, exceptionally, authorized by the General Assembly). This means that no operation can be established without a broad consensus within the international community that it is the right thing to do. It is the Security Council's responsibility to ensure that the operation is given a mandate which is clear, accepted by the parties concerned and practicable in the situation existing on the ground. Also essential is the continuing support of the Security Council, which may be asked by the Secretary-General to intervene if one or other of the parties fails to provide the necessary support and co-operation. If the mandate is unclear or ambiguous, the operation is likely to face recurrent difficulties and its activities may become controversial, with the consequent risk that it may lose the necessary support of the Security Council or the necessary agreement of one of the parties concerned. Nevertheless, there have been times when the mandate of a peace-keeping operation has not been as clear as could have been wished, e.g., when the Security Council has decided that the primary requirement of international peace and security requires the creation of an operation even if it is clear from the outset that the operation will not easily achieve the objectives given to it.

The military personnel who serve in peace-keeping operations are provided by Member States on a voluntary basis.[c] Once so provided, they pass under the command of the Secretary–General in all operational matters, as the Secretary–General is responsible for the direction of the operation and is required to report thereon at regular intervals to the Security Council. Those who serve in military observer missions are almost invariably unarmed. Those who serve in peace-keeping forces are equipped with light defensive weapons but are not authorized to use force except in self-defence. This right is exercised only sparingly because of the obvious danger that if a United Nations force uses its weapons its impartiality is, however unfairly, called in question. This requirement sometimes demands exceptional restraint on the part of soldiers serving in United Nations peace-keeping forces.

Finally, it is essential that the operation should have a sound financial basis. The financing of peace-keeping has been one of its most controversial and least satisfactory aspects. Almost all operations are now financed by obligatory contributions levied on Member States. If the Member States do not pay their contributions promptly and in full, the Secretary–General lacks the financial resources needed to reimburse to the troop-contributing Governments the sums due to them. This means, in effect, that those Governments have to pay an unfairly high share of the cost of the operation in question, in addition to sending their soldiers to serve in unpredictable and sometimes dangerous situations.

Peace-keeping and Peace-making

Peace-keeping operations have usually been mounted only after hostilities have already broken out. However, the Charter of the United Nations aims at a system of international relations wherein the use of force as a means of foreign policy is eliminated altogether. Consequently, the Charter deals at length with the peaceful settlement of disputes. This may be achieved by various means, including multilateral diplomatic efforts within the framework of the Security Council, bilateral efforts of Member States, or through the good offices of the

---

c. [The Scandinavian states, plus Canada and Ireland, have often provided peacekeeping personnel. Ed.]

Secretary–General. These approaches to peace-making are by no means mutually exclusive. On the contrary, the Organization has been most successful when co-ordinated efforts were undertaken at all levels.

In recent years, there has been a marked increase in the demand for the Secretary–General's good offices, with a view to helping the parties to a conflict to compose their differences. In responding to these demands, the Secretary–General has usually been able to rely on a formal request of the Security Council or the General Assembly. In some cases, peace-keeping operations were established as a direct result of agreements reached through his and others' diplomatic efforts, and in some cases—West Irian and Namibia are the best examples—as part of complex arrangements for the final and, in the end, peaceful settlement of the conflict.

Peace-keeping operations are intended to be provisional and thus temporary measures. They can never, alone, resolve a conflict. Their tasks are essentially two: to stop or contain hostilities and thus help create conditions in which peace-making can prosper; or to supervise the implementation of an interim or final settlement which has been negotiated by the peace-makers. Ideally, peace-keeping should move in step with peace-making in a combined effort leading to the peaceful resolution of a conflict. In practice this ideal cannot always be attained. * * *

The Operations

United Nations peace-keeping operations can be divided into broad categories: observer missions, which consist largely of officers who are almost invariably unarmed; and peace-keeping forces, which consist of lightly armed infantry units, with the necessary logistic support elements. These categories are not, however, watertight. Observer missions are sometimes reinforced by infantry and/or logistic units, usually for a specific purpose and a brief period of time. Peace-keeping forces are often assisted in their work by unarmed military observers.

The first use of military personnel by the United Nations was in 1947, in two United Nations bodies: the Consular Commission in Indonesia and the Special Committee on the Balkans. Since the small officer groups worked as members of the national delegations comprising those bodies, and were not under the Secretary–General's authority, they cannot be considered as United Nations peace-keeping operations as the term has come to be used.

The international force in Korea was not a United Nations peace-keeping operation in the current sense of the term since the enforcement action was not carried out by the Organization, was not based on the consent of the parties, and involved the use of force.

The first peace-keeping operation established by the United Nations was an observer mission, the United Nations Truce Supervision Organization (UNTSO), which was set up in Palestine in June 1948. Later observer missions were: the United Nations Military Observer

Group in India and Pakistan (UNMOGIP) in 1949, the United Nations Observation Group in Lebanon (UNOGIL) in 1958, the United Nations Yemen Observation Mission (UNYOM) in 1963, the United Nations India–Pakistan Observation Mission (UNIPOM) in 1965, the Mission of the Representative of the Secretary–General in the Dominican Republic (DOMREP) in the same year, the United Nations Good Offices Mission in Afghanistan and Pakistan (UNGOMAP) in 1988, the United Nations Iran–Iraq Military Observer Group (UNIIMOG) also in 1988, the United Nations Angola Verification Mission (UNAVEM) in 1989 and the United Nations Observer Group in Central America (ONUCA) in 1990. Of these, UNTSO, UNMOGIP, UNIIMOG, UNAVEM and ONUCA are still in operation.[d]

[The first armed peace-keeping force] was the United Nations Emergency Force (UNEF I), which was in operation in the Egypt–Israel sector from November 1956 until May 1967. The United Nations Operation in the Congo (ONUC) was deployed in the Republic of the Congo (now Zaire) from July 1960 until June 1964. The United Nations Security Force in West Irian (UNSF) was in operation from its establishment in September 1962 until April 1963. The second United Nations Emergency Force (UNEF II) functioned between Egypt and Israel from October 1973 until July 1979. The United Nations Transition Assistance Group (UNTAG) was deployed in Namibia from March 1989 until March 1990. The other three forces, which are still in operation, are the United Nations Peace-keeping Force in Cyprus (UNFICYP), established in March 1964; the United Nations Disengagement Observer Force (UNDOF) established in the Syrian Golan Heights in May 1974; and the United Nations Interim Force in Lebanon (UNIFIL), established in March 1978.

OTHER PEACEKEEPING OPERATIONS

Within two years after the description above had been written, several other U.N. observer missions and peacekeeping operations were authorized. These include the U.N. Iraq–Kuwait Observation Mission (UNIKOM), established in April 1991 to monitor the demilitarized zone between Iraq and Kuwait; the U.N. Mission for the Referendum in Western Sahara (MINURSO), established in April 1991 to make arrangements for, and supervise, a referendum on the future political status of the Western Sahara; the U.N. Observer Mission in El Salvador (ONUSAL), established in May 1991 and expanded in January 1992, to monitor the peacemaking process between the FMLN rebels in El Salvador and the government there; the U.N. Angola Verification Mission (UNAVEM II), established in May 1991 to oversee implementa-

d. [UNIIMOG, ONUCA and the original UNAVEM have now been terminated. Ed.]

tion of the Angola peace accords; the U.N. Transitional Authority in Cambodia (UNTAC), begun as an advance mission in October 1991 and expanded in February 1992, involving thousands of military and civilian personnel to disarm the factions vying for control and to oversee transition to a new elected government; a large peacekeeping force (UNPROFOR) established in February 1992 to help maintain order in areas of Croatia where Serbian forces had taken control (later expanded to provide humanitarian relief in Bosnia-Herzegovina when the conflict spread to that new state, and then extended to a preventive deployment role in Macedonia); the U.N. Operation in Somalia (UNOSOM), established in April 1992 with the aim of overseeing a ceasefire in Mogadishu and providing humanitarian assistance; and the U.N. Operation in Mozambique (ONUMOZ), established in December 1992 to monitor a transition to normalcy after 14 years of civil war. The estimated aggregate annual cost of the peacekeeping operations in force at the end of 1992 was in the neighborhood of $3 billion.

MIXED RESULTS

Not all U.N. peacekeeping operations have been resounding successes. As these materials will indicate, serious problems arose in connection with UNEF I in Egypt and ONUC in what was then the Congo. A more recent operation, MINURSO, has had difficulties, in part because it has not been able to exercise freedom of movement in the Western Sahara. Another, UNTAC, has had trouble getting cooperation from the Khmer Rouge, a key player in the Cambodian drama. In other cases, such as UNFICYP in Cyprus, one could argue that the presence of U.N. peacekeepers has removed any sense of urgency from settlement efforts, thus prolonging the stalemate. An ongoing, serious problem has been lack of adequate financial support for some of the more ambitious peacekeeping efforts.

Despite financial and other difficulties, some operations have culminated in noteworthy successes. For example, UNTAG in Namibia, after a shaky start, helped generate enough stability to enable an independent state to come into being under a constitution embodying democratic principles and protection of human rights. As will appear later in this Chapter, ONUCA successfully disarmed the Nicaraguan contras as part of a Central American peace effort, and ONUVEN played a significant role in restoring the democratic process in Nicaragua.

STATUS–OF–FORCES AGREEMENTS

When peacekeeping forces are to be stationed on the territory of a state, arrangements need to be made between the U.N. and the state regarding such things as logistics, facilities, privileges and immunities of persons and property, dispute-settlement, etc. Beginning with the First United Nations Emergency Force in Egypt, these arrangements have been embodied in formal agreements between the U.N. and host governments. Drawing on this experience, in 1990 the Secretary-General (at the request of the General Assembly) prepared a model agreement to serve as a basis for drafting individual agreements, subject to modifications appropriate for particular cases. (Paragraphs 3 and 4, below, are alternatives to each other. Paragraph 3 is to be used if the host state is not a party to the General Convention on the Privileges and Immunities of the United Nations; paragraph 4 is to be used if it is a party. The agreement, as set forth below, has been edited to illustrate only its more important provisions.)

MODEL STATUS–OF–FORCES AGREEMENT FOR PEACE–KEEPING OPERATIONS

Oct. 9, 1990.
U.N. Doc. A/45/594.

* * *

III. Application of the Convention

3. The Convention on the Privileges and Immunities of the United Nations of 13 February 1946 shall apply to the United Nations peace-keeping operation subject to the provisions specified in the present Agreement.

or

4. The United Nations peace-keeping operation, its property, funds and assets, and its members, including the Special Representative/Commander, shall enjoy the privileges and immunities specified in the present Agreement as well as those provided for in the Convention, to which [host country] is a Party.

5. Article II of the Convention, which applies to the United Nations peace-keeping operation, shall also apply to the property, funds and assets of participating States used in connection with the United Nations peace-keeping operation.

IV. Status of the Peace-keeping Operation

6. The United Nations peace-keeping operation and its members shall refrain from any action or activity incompatible with the impartial and international nature of their duties or inconsistent with the spirit of the present arrangements. The United Nations peace-keeping operation and its members shall respect all local laws and regulations. The Special Representative/Commander shall take all appropriate measures to ensure the observance of those obligations.

7. The Government undertakes to respect the exclusively international nature of the United Nations peace-keeping operation.

* * *

Communications

10. The United Nations peace-keeping operation shall enjoy the facilities in respect to communications provided in article III of the Convention and shall, in co-ordination with the Government, use such facilities as may be required for the performance of its task. Issues with respect to communications which may arise and which are not specifically provided for in the present Agreement shall be dealt with pursuant to the relevant provisions of the Convention.

11. Subject to the provisions of paragraph 10:

(a) The United Nations peace-keeping operation shall have authority to install and operate radio sending and receiving stations as well as satellite systems to connect appropriate points within the territory of [host country/territory] with each other and with United Nations offices in other countries, and to exchange traffic with the United Nations global telecommunications network. * * *

(b) The United Nations peace-keeping operation shall enjoy, within the territory of [host country/territory], the right to unrestricted communication by radio (including satellite, mobile and hand-held radio), telephone, telegraph, facsimile or any other means, and of establishing the necessary facilities for maintaining such communications within and between premises of the United Nations peace-keeping operation * * *.

* * *

Travel and Transport

12. The United Nations peace-keeping operation and its members shall enjoy, together with its vehicles, vessels, aircraft and equipment, freedom of movement throughout the [host country/territory]. That freedom shall, with respect to large movements of personnel, stores or vehicles through airports or on railways or roads used for general traffic within the [host country/territory], be co-ordinated with the Government. The Government undertakes to supply the United Nations peace-keeping operation, where necessary, with maps and other information, including locations of mine fields and other dangers and impediments, which may be useful in facilitating its movements.

* * *

Privileges and Immunities of the United Nations Peace-keeping Operation

15. The United Nations peace-keeping operation, as a subsidiary organ of the United Nations, enjoys the status, privileges and immunities of the United Nations [as provided for in the present Agreement] [in accordance with the Convention].[e] The provision of article II of the

---

[e.] [The first bracketed phrase is to be used if the host state is not a party to the General Convention on Privileges and Immunities of the U.N.; the second is to be used if it is. Ed.]

Convention which applies to the United Nations peace-keeping operation shall also apply to the property, funds and assets of participating States used in [host country/territory] in connection with the national contingents serving in the United Nations peace-keeping operation, as provided for in paragraph 5 of the present Agreement. The Government recognizes the right of the United Nations peace-keeping operation in particular:

(a) To import, free of duty or other restrictions, equipment, provisions, supplies and other goods which are for the exclusive and official use of the United Nations peace-keeping operation or for resale in the commissaries provided for hereinafter;

* * *

(d) To re-export or otherwise dispose of such equipment, as far as it is still usable, all unconsumed provisions, supplies and other goods so imported or cleared ex customs and excise warehouse which are not transferred, or otherwise disposed of, on terms and conditions to be agreed upon, to the competent local authorities of the [host country/territory] or to an entity nominated by them.

* * *

V. FACILITIES FOR THE UNITED NATIONS PEACE-KEEPING OPERATION

Premises Required for Conducting the Operational and Administrative Activities of the United Nations Peacekeeping Operation and for Accommodating Members of the Peace-keeping Operation

16. The Government of [host country] shall provide without cost to the United Nations peace-keeping operation and in agreement with the Special Representative/Commander such areas for headquarters, camps or other premises as may be necessary for the conduct of the operational and administrative activities of the United Nations peace-keeping operation and for the accommodation of the members of the United Nations peace-keeping operation. Without prejudice to the fact that all such premises remain [host country] territory, they shall be inviolable and subject to the exclusive control and authority of the United Nations. Where United Nations troops are co-located with military personnel of the host country, a permanent, direct and immediate access by the United Nations peace-keeping operation to those premises shall be guaranteed.

* * *

19. The United Nations alone may consent to the entry of any government officials or of any other person not member of the United Nations peace-keeping operation to such premises.

Provisions, Supplies and Services, and Sanitary Arrangements

20. The Government undertakes to assist the United Nations peace-keeping operation as far as possible in obtaining equipment,

provisions, supplies and other goods and services from local sources required for its subsistence and operations.

* * *

VI. STATUS OF THE MEMBERS OF THE UNITED NATIONS PEACE-KEEPING OPERATION

Privileges and Immunities

24. The Special Representative, the Commander of the military component of the United Nations peace-keeping operation, the head of the United Nations civilian police, and such high-ranking members of the Special Representative/Commander's staff as may be agreed upon with the Government shall have the status specified in sections 19 and 27 of the Convention, provided that the privileges and immunities therein referred to shall be those accorded to diplomatic envoys by [national or international] law.

25. Members of the United Nations Secretariat assigned to the civilian component to serve with the United Nations peace-keeping operation remain officials of the United Nations entitled to the privileges and immunities of articles V and VII of the Convention.

26. Military observers, United Nations civilian police and civilian personnel other than United Nations officials whose names are for the purpose notified to the Government by the Special Representative/Commander shall be considered as experts on mission within the meaning of article VI of the Convention.

27. Military personnel of national contingents assigned to the military component of the United Nations peace-keeping operation shall have the privileges and immunities specifically provided for in the present Agreement.

28. Unless otherwise specified in the present Agreement, locally recruited members of the United Nations peace-keeping operation shall enjoy the immunities concerning official acts and exemption from taxation and national service obligations provided for in sections 18(a), (b) and (c) of the Convention.

* * *

Entry, Residence and Departure

32. The Special Representative/Commander and members of the United Nations peace-keeping operation shall, whenever so required by the Special Representative/Commander, have the right to enter into, reside in and depart from [host country/territory].

33. The Government of [host country/territory] undertakes to facilitate the entry into and departure from [host country/territory] of the Special Representative/Commander and members of the United Nations peace-keeping operation and shall be kept informed of such movement. For that purpose, the Special Representative/Commander and members of the United Nations peace-keeping operation shall be

exempt from passport and visa regulations and immigration inspection and restrictions on entering into or departing from [host country/territory]. They shall also be exempt from any regulations governing the residence of aliens in [host country/territory], including registration, but shall not be considered as acquiring any right to permanent residence or domicile in [host country/territory].

* * *

Military Police, Arrest and Transfer of Custody, and Mutual Assistance

40. The Special Representative shall take all appropriate measures to ensure the maintenance of discipline and good order among members of the United Nations peace-keeping operation, as well as locally recruited personnel. To this end personnel designated by the Special Representative/Commander shall police the premises of the United Nations peace-keeping operation and such areas where its members are deployed. Elsewhere such personnel shall be employed only subject to arrangements with the Government and in liaison with it in so far as such employment is necessary to maintain discipline and order among members of the United Nations peace-keeping operation.

41. The military police of the United Nations peace-keeping operation shall have the power of arrest over the military members of the United Nations peace-keeping operation. Military personnel placed under arrest outside their own contingent areas shall be transferred to their contingent Commander for appropriate disciplinary action. The personnel mentioned in paragraph 40 above may take into custody any other person on the premises of the United Nations peace-keeping operation. Such other person shall be delivered immediately to the nearest appropriate official of the Government for the purpose of dealing with any offence or disturbance on such premises.

42. Subject to the provisions of paragraphs 24 and 26, officials of the Government may take into custody any member of the United Nations peace-keeping operation:

(a) When so requested by the Special Representative/Commander; or

(b) When such a member of the United Nations peace-keeping operation is apprehended in the commission or attempted commission of a criminal offence. Such person shall be delivered immediately, together with any weapons or other item seized, to the nearest appropriate representative of the United Nations peace-keeping operation, whereafter the provisions of paragraph 47 shall apply *mutatis mutandis*.

43. When a person is taken into custody under paragraph 41 or paragraph 42(b), the United Nations peace-keeping operation or the Government, as the case may be, may make a preliminary interrogation but may not delay the transfer of custody. Following such trans-

fer, the person concerned shall be made available upon request to the arresting authority for further interrogation.

44. The United Nations peace-keeping operation and the Government shall assist each other in carrying out all necessary investigations into offences in respect of which either or both have an interest, in the production of witnesses and in the collection and production of evidence, including the seizure of and, if appropriate, the handing over of items connected with an offence. * * *

45. The Government shall ensure the prosecution of persons subject to its criminal jurisdiction who are accused of acts in relation to the United Nations peace-keeping operation or its members which, if committed in relation to the forces of the Government, would have rendered such acts liable to prosecution.

Jurisdiction

46. All members of the United Nations peace-keeping operation including locally recruited personnel shall be immune from legal process in respect of words spoken or written and all acts performed by them in their official capacity. Such immunity shall continue even after they cease to be members of or employed by the United Nations peace-keeping operation and after the expiration of the other provisions of the present Agreement.

47. Should the Government consider that any member of the United Nations peace-keeping operation has committed a criminal offence, it shall promptly inform the Special Representative/Commander and present to him any evidence available to it. Subject to the provisions of paragraph 24:

(a) If the accused person is a member of the civilian component or a civilian member of the military component, the Special Representative/Commander shall conduct any necessary supplementary inquiry and then agree with the Government whether or not criminal proceedings should be instituted. Failing such agreement, the question shall be resolved as provided in paragraph 53 of the present Agreement.

(b) Military members of the military component of the United Nations peace-keeping operation shall be subject to the exclusive jurisdiction of their respective participating States in respect of any criminal offences which may be committed by them in [host country/territory].

48. The Secretary–General of the United Nations will obtain assurances from Governments of participating States that they will be prepared to exercise jurisdiction with respect to crimes or offences which may be committed by members of their national contingents serving with the peace-keeping operation.

49. If any civil proceeding is instituted against a member of the United Nations peace-keeping operation before any court of [host country/territory], the Special Representative/Commander shall be notified

immediately, and he shall certify to the court whether or not the proceeding is related to the official duties of such member:

(a) If the Special Representative/Commander certifies that the proceeding is related to official duties, such proceeding shall be discontinued and the provisions of paragraph 51 of the present Agreement shall apply.

(b) If the Special Representative certifies that the proceeding is not related to official duties, the proceeding may continue. If the Special Representative/Commander certifies that a member of the United Nations peace-keeping operation is unable because of official duties or authorized absence to protect his interests in the proceeding, the court shall at the defendant's request suspend the proceeding until the elimination of the disability, but for not more than ninety days. Property of a member of the United Nations peace-keeping operation that is certified by the Special Representative/Commander to be needed by the defendant for the fulfilment of his official duties shall be free from seizure for the satisfaction of a judgment, decision or order. The personal liberty of a member of the United Nations peace-keeping operation shall not be restricted in a civil proceeding, whether to enforce a judgment, decision or order, to compel an oath or for any other reason.

* * *

VII. Settlement of Disputes

51. Except as provided in paragraph 53, any dispute or claim of a private law character to which the United Nations peace-keeping operation or any member thereof is a party and over which the courts of [host country/territory] do not have jurisdiction because of any provision of the present Agreement, shall be settled by a standing claims commission to be established for that purpose. One member of the commission shall be appointed by the Secretary–General of the United Nations, one member by the Government and a chairman jointly by the Secretary–General and the Government. If no agreement as to the chairman is reached within thirty days of the appointment of the first member of the commission, the President of the International Court of Justice may, at the request of either the Secretary–General of the United Nations or the Government, appoint the chairman. * * * The awards of the commission shall be final and binding, unless the Secretary–General of the United Nations and the Government permit an appeal to a tribunal established in accordance with paragraph 53. The awards of the commission shall be notified to the parties and, if against a member of the United Nations peace-keeping operation, the Special Representative/Commander or the Secretary–General of the United Nations shall use his best endeavours to ensure compliance.

52. Disputes concerning the terms of employment and conditions of service of locally recruited personnel shall be settled by the adminis-

trative procedures to be established by the Special Representative/Commander.

53. Any other dispute between the United Nations peace-keeping operation and the Government, and any appeal that both of them agree to allow from the award of the claims commission established pursuant to paragraph 51 shall, unless otherwise agreed by the parties, be submitted to a tribunal of three arbitrators. The provisions relating to the establishment and procedures of the claims commission shall apply, *mutatis mutandis*, to the establishment and procedures of the tribunal. The decisions of the tribunal shall be final and binding on both parties.

54. All differences between the United Nations and the Government of [host country/territory] arising out of the interpretation or application of the present arrangements which involve a question of principle concerning the Convention shall be dealt with in accordance with the procedure of section 30 of the Convention.[f]

* * *

X. Miscellaneous Provisions

* * *

60. The present Agreement shall remain in force until the departure of the final element of the United Nations peace-keeping operation from [host country/territory] except that:

(a) The provisions of paragraphs 46 and 53 [and 54] shall remain in force.

(b) The provisions of paragraph 51 shall remain in force until all claims have been settled that arose prior to the termination of the present Agreement and were submitted prior to or within three months of such termination.

RELATIONS WITH THE HOST STATE UNDER THE MODEL AGREEMENT

If the host state is not a party to the General Convention on Privileges and Immunities of the U.N., does paragraph 3 of the model agreement make it applicable, in toto, to the relations between the U.N. and the host state for purposes of the peacekeeping operation?

Does the model agreement strike the appropriate balance between the sovereign rights of a host state and the peacekeeping interests of the international community (as represented by the U.N.), under circumstances of a cease-fire between armed forces within the host state's territory? Note that in such cases, the armed forces of the parties to

---

f. [This provision is intended for use if the host state is a party to the General Convention. Ed.]

the conflict typically have much more firepower at their disposal than do any U.N. peacekeeping forces.

Some peacekeeping operations have had quite a long duration. In such cases, the provisions in the agreement on criminal and civil jurisdiction inevitably come into play. How do they work? For example, who has criminal jurisdiction to try a host state national, not a member of the peacekeeping operation, who enters premises mentioned in paragraph 16 and steals property belonging to individuals who are members of the operation? Who has criminal jurisdiction to try a civilian member of the peacekeeping operation who is off duty and steals property in the host state's territory, outside the paragraph 16 premises?

Why should military personnel be subject to the exclusive criminal jurisdiction of their own states? See paragraph 47(b). Does this undermine the international character of the peacekeeping operation?

For purposes of civil jurisdiction, are there adequate safeguards to ensure that essentially private disputes are not immunized from local proceedings under the cloak of official duties? See paragraph 49. If a private dispute is adjudicated in local proceedings, how could a judgment against a member of the peacekeeping operation be enforced? See paragraphs 49 and 51.

How would a dispute between a local merchant and the peacekeeping force over interpretation of a contract for the supply of goods be resolved? How about a dispute between host state officials and the peacekeeping force commander over areas in the territory of the host state where peacekeeping patrols could go? See paragraphs 51–54.

Are the dispute-settlement procedures adequate?

B. EARLY PATHBREAKING EFFORTS: UNEF AND ONUC

1. Creation and Terms of Reference

The First United Nations Emergency Force (UNEF I) was created in 1956 to keep the peace between Egypt and Israel, after Israel had invaded Egypt with the support of France and the United Kingdom. Although it was in one respect atypical (it was created by the General Assembly rather than by the Security Council, thus raising legal questions to be discussed later in this chapter), in many respects it became "the prototype for future U.N. peacekeeping operations."[a]

The United Nations Operation in the Congo (ONUC) was created in 1960 when internal security in the Congo (now Zaire) disintegrated after Belgium relinquished colonial control. By becoming embroiled in

---

[a] M. Browne, United Nations Peacekeeping: Historical Overview and Current Issues 22 (Congressional Research Service, 1990).

a civil war with outside intervention, ONUC demonstrated some of the problems one might expect in the 1990s as the U.N. tries to respond to centrifugal forces that threaten what has been regarded as the inviolate territorial integrity of existing states.

a. UNEF I

UNEF I was not the first U.N. peacekeeping effort in the Middle East, having been preceded by the U.N. Truce Supervision Organization (UNTSO) in 1948. In the narrative below by the U.N., note that the General Assembly asserted the authority to create UNEF I after the Security Council referred the matter to it on a contested procedural vote taken pursuant to the Uniting for Peace Resolution.[a] That General Assembly resolution, adopted when the Security Council was at an impasse during the Korean War, established a procedure for General Assembly consideration of matters affecting international peace and security if the use of the veto prevents the Security Council from acting.

THE BLUE HELMETS: A REVIEW OF UNITED NATIONS PEACEKEEPING
43–47 (2d ed. 1990).
U.N. Sales No. E.90.I.18.[*]

[Between the summers of 1955 and 1956,] relations between Egypt and Israel had been steadily deteriorating, despite the efforts of the Chief of Staff of UNTSO and the Secretary–General himself. Palestinian *fedayeen*, with the support of the Egyptian Government, had been launching frequent raids against Israel from their bases in Gaza, and these had been followed by increasingly strong reprisal attacks by Israeli armed forces. The decision taken by Egypt in the early 1950s to restrict Israeli shipping through the Suez Canal and the Strait of Tiran at the entrance to the Gulf of Aqaba, in contravention of a decision of the Security Council, remained a controversial and destabilizing issue. In the heightening tension, the control of armaments * * * had broken down, and Egypt and Israel were engaging in an intense arms race, with the East and the West supplying sophisticated weapons and equipment to the opposing sides.

On 19 July 1956, the United States Government decided to withdraw its financial aid for the Aswan Dam project on the Nile River. President Gamal Abdel Nasser announced the nationalization of the Suez Canal Company a week later and declared that Canal dues would be used to finance the Aswan project.

---

a. G.A. Res. 377, 5 GAOR Supp. (No. 20) at 10, U.N. Doc. A/1775 (1950). Because a Security Council vote to refer a matter to the General Assembly under the Uniting for Peace Resolution is procedural, a negative vote by a permanent member does not amount to a veto.

[*] Copyright 1990 United Nations. Reprinted by permission of the United Nations Department of Public Information.

[On September 26, 1956, the Security Council met. At the same time, there were negotiations among the U.K., France and Egypt with the good offices of the Secretary-General. The Security Council then adopted Resolution 118, setting forth a blueprint for settling the Suez question. The Security Council's plan was frustrated in October 1956 when Israel, in coordination with the British and French governments, attacked Egypt.]

The Israeli forces crossed the border on the morning of 29 October, advancing in three columns towards El Arish, Ismalia and the Mitla Pass. In the early hours of 30 October, the Chief of Staff of UNTSO * * * called for a cease-fire and requested Israel to pull its forces back to its side of the border. * * * On 31 October, France and the United Kingdom launched an air attack against targets in Egypt, which was followed shortly by a landing of their troops near Port Said at the northern end of the Canal.

General Assembly's First Emergency Special Session

The Security Council held a meeting on 30 October at the request of the United States, which submitted a draft resolution calling upon Israel immediately to withdraw its armed forces behind the established armistice lines. [S/3710.] It was not adopted because of British and French vetoes. A similar draft resolution [S/3713/Rev.1] sponsored by the Soviet Union was also rejected. The matter was then transferred to the General Assembly, on a proposal by Yugoslavia, in accordance with the procedure provided by Assembly resolution 377(V) of 3 November 1950 entitled "Uniting for peace". Thus, the first emergency special session of the General Assembly called under that resolution was convened on 1 November 1956.

In the early hours of the next day, the General Assembly adopted, on the proposal of the United States, resolution 997(ES-I), calling for an immediate cease-fire, the withdrawal of all forces behind the armistice lines and the reopening of the Canal. The Secretary-General was requested to observe and report promptly on compliance to the Security Council and to the General Assembly, for such further action as those bodies might deem appropriate in accordance with the United Nations Charter.

The resolution was adopted by 64 votes to 5, with 6 abstentions. The dissenters were Australia and New Zealand, in addition to France, Israel and the United Kingdom. In explaining Canada's abstention, Lester Pearson stated that the resolution did not provide for, along with the cease-fire and a withdrawal of troops, any steps to be taken by the United Nations for a peace settlement, without which a cease-fire would be only of a temporary nature at best.

Before the session, Pearson had had extensive discussions with [Secretary-General Dag] Hammarskjöld and he felt that it might be necessary to establish some sort of United Nations police force to help resolve the crisis. Pearson submitted to the General Assembly, when it reconvened the next morning, a draft resolution on the establishment of an emergency international United Nations force.

Enabling Resolutions of the United Nations Force

The Canadian proposal was adopted by the General Assembly on the same morning and became resolution 998(ES–I) of 4 November 1956, by which the Assembly:

"*Requests*, as a matter of priority, the Secretary-General to submit to it within forty-eight hours a plan for the setting up, with the consent of the nations concerned, of an emergency international United Nations Force to secure and supervise the cessation of hostilities in accordance with all the terms of the aforementioned resolution [997(ES–I)]."

The voting was 57 to none, with 19 abstentions. Egypt, France, Israel, the United Kingdom and the Soviet Union and Eastern European States were among the abstainers.

At the same meeting, the General Assembly also adopted resolution 999(ES–I), by which it reaffirmed resolution 997(ES–I) and authorized the Secretary-General immediately to arrange with the parties concerned for the implementation of the cease-fire and the halting of the movement of military forces and arms into the area.

On the same day, the Secretary-General submitted his first report on the plan for an emergency international United Nations Force [A/3302], in which he recommended certain preliminary steps, including the immediate setting up of a United Nations Command. All his recommendations were endorsed by the General Assembly and included in resolution 1000(ES–I) adopted on 5 November 1956, by which the Assembly:

— Established a United Nations Command for an emergency international Force to secure and supervise the cessation of hostilities in accordance with all the terms of General Assembly resolution 997(ES–I) of 2 November 1956;

— Appointed, on an emergency basis, the Chief of Staff of UNTSO, Major-General (later Lieutenant-General) E.L.M. Burns, as Chief of the Command;

— Authorized the Chief of the Command immediately to recruit, from the observer corps of UNTSO, a limited number of officers who were to be nationals of countries other than those having permanent membership in the Security Council, and further authorized him, in consultation with the Secretary-General, to undertake the recruitment directly, from various Member States other than the permanent members of the Security Council, of the additional number of officers needed;

— Invited the Secretary-General to take such administrative measures as might be necessary for prompt execution of the actions envisaged.

The resolution was adopted by 57 votes to none, with 19 abstentions. As with resolution 998(ES–I), Egypt, France, Israel, the United Kingdom, the Soviet Union and Eastern European States abstained.

On 6 November, the Secretary–General submitted to the General Assembly his second and final report on the plan for an emergency United Nations Force. In this report, Hammarskjöld defined the concept of the new Force and certain guiding principles for its organization and functioning.

SECOND AND FINAL REPORT OF THE SECRETARY–GENERAL ON THE PLAN FOR AN EMERGENCY UNITED NATIONS FORCE

U.N. Doc. A/3302, Nov. 6, 1956.
GAOR, First Emergency Special Sess., Annexes, at 19 (1956).

* * *

4. An emergency international United Nations Force can be developed on the basis of three different concepts:

(a) It can, in the *first* place, be set up on the basis of principles reflected in the constitution of the United Nations itself. This would mean that its chief responsible officer should be appointed by the United Nations, and that he, in his functions, should be responsible ultimately to the General Assembly and/or the Security Council. His authority should be so defined as to make him fully independent of the policies of any one nation. * * *

(b) A *second* possibility is that the United Nations charge a country, or a group of countries, with the responsibility to provide independently for an emergency international Force serving for purposes determined by the United Nations. In this case it would obviously be impossible to achieve the same independence in relation to national policies as would be established through the first approach;

(c) Finally, as a *third* possibility, an emergency international Force may be set up in agreement among a group of nations, later to be brought into an appropriate relationship to the United Nations. This approach is open to the same reservation as the second one, and possibly others.

* * *

5. In the decision on the establishment of the United Nations Command, on an emergency basis, which the General Assembly took on 5 November 1956, the Assembly chose to follow the first of the three types mentioned in paragraph 4 above. The second type was that followed in the case of the Unified Command in Korea. There is no precedent for the use of the third type * * *.

6. In its resolution 1000 (ES–I) on the United Nations Command, the General Assembly authorized the Chief of Command, in consultation with the Secretary–General, to recruit officers from the United

Nations Truce Supervision Organization, or directly from various Member States other than the permanent members of the Security Council. This recruitment procedure affords an important indication of the character of the Force to be set up. On the one hand, the independence of the Chief of Command in recruiting officers is recognized. On the other hand, the principle is established that the Force should be recruited from Member States other than the permanent members of the Security Council.

* * *

8. A closer analysis of the concept of the emergency international United Nations Force, based on what the General Assembly has stated in its resolution on the matter, indicates that the Assembly intends that the Force should be of a temporary nature, the length of its assignment being determined by the needs arising out of the present conflict. It is further clear that the General Assembly * * * has wished to reserve for itself the full determination of the tasks of this emergency Force and of the legal basis on which it must function in fulfilment of its mission. It follows from its terms of reference that there is no intent in the establishment of the Force to influence the military balance in the present conflict and, thereby, the political balance affecting efforts to settle the conflict. * * *

9. Functioning, as it would, on the basis of a decision reached under the terms of the resolution 337 (V) "Uniting for Peace", the Force, if established, would be limited in its operations to the extent that consent of the parties concerned is required under generally recognized international law. While the General Assembly is enabled to *establish* the Force with the consent of those parties which contribute units to the Force, it could not request the Force to be *stationed* or *operate* on the territory of a given country without the consent of the Government of that country. This does not exclude the possibility that the Security Council could use such a Force within the wider margins provided under Chapter VII of the United Nations Charter. I would not for the present consider it necessary to elaborate this point further, since no use of the Force under Chapter VII, with the rights in relation to Member States that this would entail, has been envisaged.

10. The point just made permits the conclusion that the setting up of the Force should not be guided by the needs which would have existed had the measure been considered as part of an enforcement action directed against a Member country. There is an obvious difference between establishing the Force in order to secure the cessation of hostilities, with a withdrawal of forces, and establishing such a Force with a view to enforcing a withdrawal of forces. It follows that while the Force is different in that, as in many other respects, from the observers of the United Nations Truce Supervision Organization, it is, although para-military in nature, not a Force with military objectives.

* * *

12. In the General Assembly resolution 998 (ES–I) the terms of reference are, as already stated, "to secure * * * the cessation of hostilities in accordance with all the terms" of resolution 997 (ES–I) of 2 November 1956. This resolution urges that "all parties now involved in hostilities in the area agree to an immediate cease-fire and, as part thereof, halt the movement of military forces and arms into the area;" and also "urges the parties to the armistice agreements promptly to withdraw all forces behind the armistice lines, to desist from raids across the armistice lines into neighbouring territory, and to observe scrupulously the provisions of the armistice agreements." These two provisions combined indicate that the functions of the United Nations Force would be, when a cease-fire is being established, to enter Egyptian territory with the consent of the Egyptian Government, in order to help maintain quiet during and after the withdrawal of non-Egyptian troops, and to secure compliance with the other terms established in the resolution of 2 November 1956. The Force obviously should have no rights other than those necessary for the execution of its functions, in co-operation with local authorities. It would be more than an observers' corps, but in no way a military force temporarily controlling the territory in which it is stationed; nor, moreover, should the Force have military functions exceeding those necessary to secure peaceful conditions on the assumption that the parties to the conflict take all necessary steps for compliance with the recommendations of the General Assembly. Its functions can, on this basis, be assumed to cover an area extending roughly from the Suez Canal to the armistice demarcation lines established in the armistice agreement between Egypt and Israel.

THE GENERAL ASSEMBLY'S RESPONSE

The General Assembly met the next day. It approved the principles and functions the Secretary–General had proposed.

GENERAL ASSEMBLY RESOLUTION ON PRINCIPLES AND FUNCTIONS OF UNEF

United Nations General Assembly, Nov. 7, 1956.
G.A. Res. 1001 (ES–I), GAOR First Emergency
Special Sess., Supp. No. 1 (A/3354), at 3.

The General Assembly,

* * *

1. *Expresses its approval* of the guiding principles for the organization and functioning of the emergency international United Nations Force as expounded in paragraphs 6 to 9 of the Secretary–General's report;

2. *Concurs* in the definition of the functions of the Force as stated in paragraph 12 of the Secretary-General's report;

3. *Invites* the Secretary-General to continue discussions with Governments of Member States concerning offers of participation in the Force, toward the objective of its balanced composition;

* * *

6. *Establishes* an Advisory Committee composed of one representative from each of the following countries: Brazil, Canada, Ceylon, Colombia, India, Norway and Pakistan, and requests this Committee, whose Chairman shall be the Secretary-General, to undertake the development of those aspects of the planning for the Force and its operation not already dealt with by the General Assembly and which do not fall within the area of the direct responsibility of the Chief of the Command;

7. *Authorizes* the Secretary-General to issue all regulations and instructions which may be essential to the effective functioning of the Force, following consultation with the Committee aforementioned, and to take all other necessary administrative and executive action;

* * *

9. *Decides* that the Advisory Committee, in the performance of its duties, shall be empowered to request, through the usual procedures, the convening of the General Assembly and to report to the Assembly whenever matters arise which, in its opinion, are of such urgency and importance as to require consideration by the General Assembly itself;

10. *Requests* all Member States to afford assistance as necessary to the United Nations Command in the performance of its functions, including arrangements for passage to and from the area involved.

THE LIMITS OF PEACEKEEPING AUTHORITY

The Soviet Union took the position that the General Assembly was acting beyond its Charter authority in establishing UNEF. See the Expenses Case, page 757 infra. For the present, it is enough to ask what plausible arguments might be made to justify peacekeeping measures using military forces under the authority of the General Assembly, rather than the Security Council. Possibilities that have been suggested include (a) the Uniting for Peace Resolution provides sufficient authority; (b) anything not expressly prohibited in the Charter is permitted; and (c) the combination of Charter articles *10, 11, 14 and 22* gave the Assembly the authority to act.[b]

Which of these, if any, is convincing? Is there a more convincing argument than any of these?

---

b. See 1 R. Higgins, United Nations Peacekeeping 1946–1967: Documents and Commentary 261–62 (1969). This multi-volume work is the definitive source of legal commentary on peacekeeping operations during the period covered.

In paragraph 9 of his report, the Secretary–General said that UNEF I "would be limited in its operations to the extent that consent of the parties concerned is required under generally recognized international law." What principle of international law did he have in mind? (These materials return later to the question whether the Security Council, rather than the General Assembly, could override the principle.)

How important was it that UNEF I be modeled on the first of the three concepts the Secretary–General outlined in paragraph 4? Does the U.N. Charter require that the first concept be used for all peacekeeping operations?

If, as the Secretary–General said in paragraph 12, a peacekeeping force is "in no way a military force temporarily controlling the territory," what good is it?

General Assembly Resolution 1001, supra, established an Advisory Committee of seven members from as many countries. The countries mentioned in paragraph 6 of the Resolution were selected because it was contemplated that they would provide troops, though not all of them ultimately did. Because the General Assembly is not in session continuously, and because it is such a large body, it made sense to establish a committee of member states to whom the Secretary–General could turn in order to get political support when difficult operational questions might arise. When the Security Council has authorized peacekeeping operations, the Secretary–General has simply turned to it for instructions and advice as the operations unfold.

Before we turn to the arrangements negotiated between the Secretary–General and Egypt for UNEF I operations, it is useful to compare the terms of reference of UNEF I with those of UNEF II. The Security Council established UNEF II in 1973, after the ceasefire in the war of that year between Israel and its neighbors. Its purpose was to supervise the ceasefire. Compare the terms of reference set out by Secretary–General Kurt Waldheim for UNEF II with those enunciated by Dag Hammarskjöld for UNEF I. The UNEF II terms of reference said:

REPORT OF THE SECRETARY–GENERAL ON THE IMPLEMENTATION OF SECURITY COUNCIL RESOLUTION 340

U.N. Doc. S/11052/Rev.1, Oct. 27, 1973.
28 SCOR Supp. for Oct., Nov. & Dec. 1973, at 91.

* * *

3. Three essential conditions must be met for the Force to be effective. Firstly, it must at all times have the full confidence and backing of the Security Council. Secondly, it must operate with the

full co-operation of the parties concerned. Thirdly, it must be able to function as an integrated and efficient military unit.

4. Having in mind past experience, I would suggest the following guidelines for the proposed Force:

(a) The Force will be under the command of the United Nations, vested in the Secretary–General, under the authority of the Security Council. The command in the field will be exercised by a Force Commander appointed by the Secretary–General with the consent of the Security Council. The Commander will be responsible to the Secretary–General.

The Secretary–General shall keep the Security Council fully informed of developments relating to the functioning of the Force. All matters which may affect the nature or the continued effective functioning of the Force will be referred to the Council for its decision.

(b) The Force must enjoy the freedom of movement and communication and other facilities that are necessary for the performance of its tasks. The Force and its personnel should be granted all relevant privileges and immunities provided for by the Convention on the Privileges and Immunities of the United Nations. The Force should operate at all times separately from the armed forces of the parties concerned. Consequently separate quarters and, wherever desirable and feasible, buffer zones will have to be arranged with the co-operation of the parties. Appropriate agreements on the Status of the Force will have to be concluded with the parties to cover the above requirements.

(c) The Force will be composed of a number of contingents to be provided by selected countries, upon the request of the Secretary–General. The contingents will be selected in consultation with the Security Council and with the parties concerned, bearing in mind the accepted principle of equitable geographic representation.

(d) The Force will be provided with weapons of a defensive character only. It shall not use force except in self-defence. Self-defence would include resistance to attempts by forceful means to prevent it from discharging its duties under the mandate of the Security Council. The Force will proceed on the assumption that the parties to the conflict will take all the necessary steps for compliance with the decisions of the Security Council.

(e) In performing its functions, the Force will act with complete impartiality and will avoid actions which could prejudice the rights, claims or positions of the parties concerned * * *.

THE COMPARISON

The Security Council established UNEF II for six-month, renewable terms. That became the norm for U.N. peacekeeping mandates, though there have been a few exceptions, such as the initial year-long mandate in 1992 for the peacekeeping operation in Yugoslavia.

How did the terms of reference for UNEF II differ from those for UNEF I? Do the differences seem significant?

One obvious difference was that the Security Council, rather than the General Assembly, established UNEF II. As it turned out, UNEF II established the pattern for the management of subsequent peacekeeping operations: day-to-day control by the Secretary-General, subject to regular consultations with members of the Security Council, leaving ultimate control with the Council.[c] Is this the optimal arrangement?

One very significant issue that arose for UNEF I had to do with the authority of Egypt to revoke its consent and, in effect, order UNEF to leave its territory. When the United Arab Republic (Egypt) did so in 1967, the Secretary-General (U Thant) responded without consulting either the General Assembly or the Security Council. As will appear later in these materials, he was severely criticized for that. Under the terms of reference for UNEF II, would the same procedure be followed if a host government ordered the U.N. troops out?

UNEF I IN EGYPT

When UNEF I was established on the territory of Egypt in 1956, a status-of-forces agreement was reached between the U.N. and Egypt not unlike the much later model agreement set forth at pages 723–30 supra, except that it was in the form of an exchange of letters.[d] There was also an aide-mémoire memorializing declarations by the government of Egypt and by the U.N., arising from the sensitivity of the operation. The aide-mémoire and its negotiating history took on great importance later, when the United Arab Republic in May 1967 "decided to terminate the presence" of UNEF on its territory in the prelude to the six-day war between Israel and its Arab neighbors.

AIDE-MÉMOIRE ON THE PRESENCE AND FUNCTIONING OF UNEF I
Nov. 20, 1956.
U.N. Doc. A/3375, Annex, 11 GAOR, Annexes, vol. II, Agenda item 66, at 9.

Noting that by telegram of 5 November 1956 addressed to the Secretary-General the Government of Egypt, in exercise of its sovereign rights, accepted General Assembly resolution 1000 (ES–I) of the same date establishing "a United Nations Command for an emergency international Force to secure and supervise the cessation of hostilities in accordance with all the terms of resolution 997 (ES–I) of the General Assembly of 2 November 1956";

Noting that the General Assembly in its resolution 1001 (ES–I) of 7 November 1956 approved the principle that it could not request the

---

c. See Jonah, The Management of UN Peacekeeping, in The United Nations and Peacekeeping 75, 76–77 (I. Rikhye & K. Skjelsbaek eds. 1990).

d. See the Exchange of Letters of Feb. 8, 1957, 260 U.N.T.S. 61.

Force "to be stationed or operate on the territory of a given country without the consent of the Government of that country" (A/3302, para. 9)

Having agreed on the arrival in Egypt of the United Nations Emergency Force (UNEF);

Noting that advance groups of UNEF have already been received in Egypt,

The Government of Egypt and the Secretary–General of the United Nations have stated their understanding on the basic points for the presence and functioning of UNEF as follows:

1. The Government of Egypt declares that, when exercising its sovereign rights on any matter concerning the presence and functioning of UNEF, it will be guided, in good faith, by its acceptance of General Assembly resolution 1000 (ES–I) of 5 November 1956.e

2. The United Nations takes note of this declaration of the Government of Egypt and declares that the activities of UNEF will be guided, in good faith, by the task established for the Force in the aforementioned resolutions; in particular, the United Nations, understanding this to correspond to the wishes of the Government of Egypt, reaffirms its willingness to maintain UNEF until its task is completed.

* * *

THE NEGOTIATING HISTORY

Several months after the U.N./Egypt aide-mémoire was agreed to, the Secretary–General, Dag Hammarskjöld, prepared another aide-mémoire (in the nature of a memorandum for his own files) setting out his view of the communications and negotiations that had led to it. In the second aide-mémoire, dated August 5, 1957, the Secretary–General chronicled the difference of opinion that had existed between Egyptian officials and himself on the conditions under which UNEF would be withdrawn from Egyptian territory if Egypt requested it.

As recounted in the August 1957 aide-mémoire, Mr. Hammarskjöld consistently took the position that Egyptian officials by endorsing General Assembly Resolution 1000 (ES–1) "had consented to the presence of the UNEF for certain tasks. They could thus not ask the UNEF to withdraw before the completion of the tasks without running up against their own acceptance of the resolution on the Force and its tasks." f Egypt, on the other hand, took the position that "It being agreed that consent of Egypt is indispensable for entry and presence of the UN Forces in any part of its [territory, if] such consent no longer

---

e. [See page 734 supra. Ed.]

f. Hammarskjöld aide-mémoire of Aug. 5, 1957, at 1, reprinted in 6 Int'l Legal Materials 595 (1967).

persists, those forces shall withdraw." [g] Mr. Hammarskjöld's August 1957 aide-mémoire continued:

In my effort to follow up the situation, which prevailed after the exchange in which different stands had been maintained by Egypt and by me, I was guided by the consideration that Egypt constitutionally had an undisputed right to request the withdrawal of the troops, even if initial consent had been given, but that, on the other hand, it should be possible on the basis of my own stand as finally tacitly accepted, to force them into an agreement in which they limited their freedom of action as to withdrawal by making a request for withdrawal dependent upon the completion of the task—a question which, in the UN, obviously would have to be submitted to interpretation by the General Assembly.

The most desirable thing, of course, would have been to tie Egypt by an agreement in which they declared, that withdrawal should take place only if so decided by the General Assembly. Put in this naked form, however, the problem could never have been settled. I felt that the same was true of an agreement to the effect that withdrawal should take place upon "agreement on withdrawal" between the UN and the Egyptian Government. However, I found it worthwhile to try a line, very close to the second one, according to which Egypt would declare to the United Nations that it would exert all its sovereign rights with regard to the troops on the basis of a good faith interpretation of the tasks of the Force. The United Nations should make a reciprocal commitment to maintain the Force as long as the task was not completed. If such a dual statement was introduced in an agreement between the parties, it would be obvious that the procedure in case of a request from Egypt for the withdrawal of UNEF would be as follows. The matter would at once be brought before the General Assembly. If the General Assembly found that the task was completed, everything would be all right. If they found that the task was not completed and Egypt, all the same, maintained its stand and enforced the withdrawal, Egypt would break the agreement with the United Nations. Of course Egypt's freedom of action could under no circumstances be limited but by some kind of agreement. The device I used meant only that instead of limiting their rights by a basic understanding requesting an agreement *directly concerning withdrawal,* we created an obligation to reach agreement on the fact that the tasks were completed and, thus, *the conditions for a withdrawal established.*

I elaborated a draft text for an agreement along the lines I had in mind during the night between 15 and 16 November in Capodachino. I showed the text to Fawzi [the Egyptian Foreign Minister] at our first talk on 16 November and I discussed practically only this issue with Nasser [the President of Egypt] for 7 hours in the

g. Id. at 596.

evening and night of 17 November. Nasser, in this final discussion, where the text I had proposed was approved with some amendments, showed that he very fully understood that, by limiting their freedom of action in the way I proposed, they would take a very serious step, as it would mean that the question of the extent of the task would become decisive for the relations between Egypt and the United Nations and would determine Egypt's political freedom of action. He felt, not without justification, that the definition given of the task in the UN texts was very loose and that, tying the freedom of action of Egypt to the concept of the task—which had to be interpreted also by the General Assembly—and doing so in a written agreement, meant that he accepted a far-reaching and unpredictable restriction. To shoot the text through in spite of Nasser's strong wish to avoid this, and his strong suspicion of the legal construction—especially of the possible consequences of differences of views regarding the task—I felt obliged, in the course of the discussion, to threaten three times, that unless an agreement of this type was made, I would have to propose the immediate withdrawal of the troops. If any proof would be necessary for how the text of the agreement was judged by President Nasser, this last mentioned fact tells the story.

It is obvious that, with a text of the content mentioned approved by Egypt, the whole previous exchange of views was superseded by a formal and explicit recognition by Egypt of the stand I had taken all through, in particular on 9 and 12 November. The previous exchange of cables cannot any longer have any interpretative value as only the text of the agreement was put before the General Assembly and approved by it with the concurrence of Egypt and as its text was self-contained and conclusive. All further discussion, therefore, has to start from the text of the agreement, which is to be found in Document A/3375. The interpretation of the text must be the one set out above.[h]

According to U Thant, the U.N. Secretary–General when the consent issue came to a head in 1967, Dag Hammarskjöld's August 1957 aide-mémoire was never made known to the Egyptian government.[i]

These materials return later to the circumstances surrounding UNEF's May 1967 withdrawal from Egypt, and the question whether the Secretary–General was obligated to withdraw them when Egypt withdrew its consent. For the moment, consider whether U.N. peacekeeping forces should be placed in a situation where their right to remain, if there is a future threat to the peace, is less than fully spelled out. Did Mr. Hammarskjöld do all he could, under the circumstances, to spell it out?

---

h. Id. at 600–02 (emphasis in the original); © American Society of International Law.

i. Statement of U Thant as reported in N.Y. Times, June 20, 1967, p. 19; reprinted in 6 Int'l Legal Materials 603 (1967).

In a situation involving potential threats to the peace from both sides of a border (here, from both Egypt and Israel), is it appropriate to station peacekeeping forces on only one side? (Israel had refused to allow U.N. forces on territory it occupied.)

In any event, UNEF I did take up positions in a buffer zone along the eastern border of Egypt and at Sharm-el-Sheikh on the Strait of Tiran. It conducted its business there until May 1967.

b. ONUC

THE BLUE HELMETS: A REVIEW OF UNITED NATIONS PEACEKEEPING

215–222 (2d ed. 1990).
U.N. Sales No. E.90.I.18.*

BACKGROUND

The United Nations Operation in the Congo (Opération des Nations Unies au Congo, or ONUC), which took place in the Republic of the Congo (now Zaire) from July 1960 until June 1964, [was] by far the largest peace-keeping operation ever established by the United Nations in terms of the responsibilities it had to assume, the size of its area of operation and the manpower involved. It included, in addition to a peace-keeping force which comprised at its peak strength nearly 20,000 officers and men, an important Civilian Operations component. Originally mandated to provide the Congolese Government with the military and technical assistance it required following the collapse of many essential services and the military intervention by Belgian troops, ONUC became embroiled by the force of circumstances in a chaotic internal situation of extreme complexity and had to assume certain responsibilities which went beyond normal peace-keeping duties. The policy followed by Secretary–General Dag Hammarskjöld in the Congo brought him into direct conflict with the Soviet Union and serious disagreement with some other Powers. The Operation cost the life of Hammarskjöld and led to a grave political and financial crisis within the United Nations itself.

With an area of some 2,345,000 square kilometres (about 1 million square miles), approximately the size of Western Europe, the Congo/Zaire is the third largest country in Africa, after the Sudan and Algeria. Encompassing the greatest part of the Congo basin in the very heart of Africa, the country has an important strategic position. The Congo is also exceptionally rich in minerals, much of them in the province of Katanga.

At the time of independence, the Congo had a population of about 14 million. The wind of change that had swept across Africa after the

---

* Copyright 1990 United Nations. Reprinted by permission of the United Nations Department of Public Information.

Second World War left the Territory largely untouched. The Belgian colonial administration practised a policy of paternalism which gave the indigenous population one of the highest living standards on the continent, but little political and educational advancement. Few Congolese studied beyond the secondary level and, at the time of independence, there were among them only 17 university graduates and no doctors, lawyers or engineers.

Little political activity was allowed the Congolese population until 1959. Early that year, the Belgian Government, confronted with increasing disturbances, announced its intention to prepare the Congo for independence, and soon embarked upon a radical decolonization plan. A charter granting freedom of speech, of the press and of association was put into effect in August 1959, and elections to municipal and territorial councils were held in December. In January 1960, at a round-table conference of Congolese leaders convened in Brussels, Belgium agreed to grant independence to the Congo as of 30 June that same year.

* * *

The [Congolese] Parliament convened in the early part of June and, by 23 June, after lengthy debate, the newly elected representatives worked out a compromise whereby the two rival dominant Congolese leaders were elected to the two key positions in the new political structure: Joseph Kasa–Vubu as President of the Republic and Patrice Lumumba as Prime Minister. Thus, the apparatus for the independent State was completed barely six days before independence.

On 29 June 1960, a treaty of friendship, assistance and cooperation between Belgium and the Congo was signed by the representatives of the two Governments (but never ratified). Under that treaty, most of the administrative and technical personnel of the colonial administration would remain in the Congo on secondment to the Congolese Government. The treaty also provided that the two military bases at Kamina and Kitona would be ceded to Belgium and that the Belgian Government could, at the request of the Congolese Government, call out the Belgian troops from the bases to assist the latter Government in maintaining law and order. Belgium hoped that with this massive assistance and the guarantees accompanying it, it would be possible to ensure a smooth transition from colonial status to independence. Its main hope lay in the *Force publique,* the 25,000–man security force which had maintained law and order in the country in a forceful and effective way during the colonial times and which would continue to be commanded by Belgium's Lieutenant–General Emile Janssens, with an all-Belgian officer corps.

[Dag Hammarskjöld was conscious of the potential problems ahead. He sent Ralph Bunche, his Under–Secretary for Special Political Affairs, to discuss with the Congolese authorities the technical assistance the U.N. could provide.]

Shortly after independence, Congolese soldiers of the *Force publique* became restive and petitioned for more promotion opportunity. Their petition was dismissed by General Janssens. He made it clear that so far as the *Force publique* was concerned, independence had changed nothing. On 5 July, a mutiny broke out in the Leopoldville garrison and spread to several other cities during the following days. As some mutineers attacked Belgians and other Europeans, and in some cases committed rape and other atrocities, most Belgian administrators and technicians fled the country, and this led to the collapse of a number of essential services throughout the country.

The Belgian Ambassador to the Congo repeatedly urged Prime Minister Lumumba to request the assistance of Belgian troops, under the friendship treaty, to maintain law and order, but Lumumba adamantly refused. Instead, he attempted to regain control of the *Force publique* by agreeing to the Congolese soldiers' demand for reform. He renamed the *Force publique* the *Armée nationale congolaise* (ANC), dismissed General Janssens and appointed Victor Lundula, a Congolese, as Commander of the Army with the rank of Major–General, and Joseph Mobutu, also a Congolese, as its Chief of Staff with the rank of Colonel. * * *

As disorder spread and intensified, Ralph Bunche, who was in Leopoldville [now Kinshasa] at the time, strongly advised the Belgian Ambassador not to call in Belgian troops without the prior agreement of the Congolese Government. At the same time, he was in close touch with the Congolese authorities and the Secretary–General in New York to work out a plan to help the Government control and strengthen the Congolese army through United Nations assistance. Hammarskjöld envisaged sending a large number of United Nations military advisers, experts and technicians for this purpose. He felt that if the Congolese Government were to request such military personnel as technical assistance of a military nature, rather than as military assistance, he could take immediate action on his own authority without referring the matter to the Security Council.

The Congolese Government agreed to this course of action and, on 10 July, submitted a formal request to the Secretary–General for technical assistance of a military nature, including military advisers, experts and technicians, to assist it in developing and strengthening the national army for the twin purposes of national defence and the maintenance of law and order.

Belgian Intervention and Security Council action

However, a new situation developed on the next day when the Belgian Government ordered its troops into the Congo without the agreement of the Congolese Government, for the declared purpose of restoring law and order and protecting Belgian nationals. Belgian troops landed at Leopoldville, Matadi, Luluabourg (now Kananga) and Elisabethville (now Lubumbashi), in Katanga. Their intervention, which was followed in some cases by heavy fighting with Congolese soldiers, further increased tension and disorder throughout the country. On 11 July, shortly after the arrival of Belgian troops in Elisabethville, Moïse Tshombé, the provincial president, proclaimed the independence of Katanga, the richest province of the Congo, which provided the country with more than half of its revenues.

On 12 July, President Kasa-Vubu and Prime Minister Lumumba sent a joint telegram to the Secretary-General requesting United Nations military assistance. [This telegram, and one they sent on 13 July, said in part:

[The Government of the Republic of the Congo requests urgent dispatch by the United Nations of military assistance. This request is justified by the dispatch to the Congo of metropolitan Belgian troops in violation of the treaty of friendship signed between Belgium and the Republic of the Congo on 29 June 1960. Under the terms of that treaty, Belgian troops may only intervene on the express request of the Congolese Government. No such request was ever made by the Government of the Republic of the Congo and we therefore regard the unsolicited Belgian action as an act of aggression against our country.

* * *

[In connexion with military assistance requested of the United Nations by the Republic of the Congo, the Chief of State and the Prime Minister of the Congo make the following clarification: (1) the purpose of the aid requested is not to restore the internal situation in Congo but rather to protect the national territory against acts of aggression committed by Belgian metropolitan troops.] [a]

On 13 July, Hammarskjöld, invoking Article 99 of the United Nations Charter—which empowers the Secretary-General to bring to the attention of the Security Council any matter which in his opinion may threaten international peace and security—requested an urgent meeting of the Council to consider the situation in the Congo [S/4381]. The Council met on the same evening. In an opening statement, Hammarskjöld outlined his ideas about the actions that the Council might take in response to the request of the Congolese Government. In essence, he recommended the establishment of a United Nations peacekeeping force to assist that Government in maintaining law and order until, with technical assistance from the United Nations, the Congolese national security forces were able fully to meet their tasks. He assumed that, were the United Nations to act as proposed, the Belgian Government would withdraw its forces from Congolese territory.

At the same meeting, during the night of 13/14 July, the Security Council adopted resolution 143 (1960), by which it called upon the Government of Belgium to withdraw its troops from the territory of the Congo and decided "to authorize the Secretary-General to take the

a. [Both telegrams are reprinted in U.N. Doc. S/4382 (1960). Ed.]

necessary steps, in consultation with the Government of the Republic of the Congo, to provide the Government with such military assistance as might be necessary until, through that Government's efforts with United Nations technical assistance, the national security forces might be able, in the opinion of the Government, to meet fully their tasks". It requested the Secretary-General to report to the Security Council as appropriate.

The Council resolution was adopted by 8 votes in favour (including the USSR and the United States) to none against, with 3 abstentions.

SECRETARY-GENERAL'S PRINCIPLES GOVERNING THE UNITED NATIONS FORCE

In his first report on the implementation of the resolution [S/4389], the Secretary-General outlined the principles which would govern the organization and activities of the United Nations Force in the Congo, its composition and the action he had taken or envisaged taking to establish it.

The proposals the Secretary-General set out for the Force were as follows:

(a) The Force was to be regarded as a temporary security force to be deployed in the Congo with the consent of the Congolese Government until the national security forces were able, in the opinion of that Government, to meet fully their tasks.

(b) Although dispatched at the request of the Congolese Government and remaining there with its consent, and although it might be considered as serving as an arm of the Congolese Government for the maintenance of law and order and protection of life, the Force was necessarily under the exclusive command of the United Nations, vested in the Secretary-General under the control of the Security Council. The Force was thus not under the orders of the Congolese Government and could not be permitted to become a party to any internal conflict.

(c) The host Government, when exercising its sovereign rights with regard to the presence of the United Nations Force in its territory, should be guided by good faith in the interpretation of the Force's purpose. Similarly, the United Nations should be so guided when it considered the question of the maintenance of the Force in the host country.

(d) The United Nations should have free access to the area of operation and full freedom of movement within that area as well as all the communications and other facilities required to carry out its tasks. A further elaboration of this rule obviously required an agreement with the Government specifying what was to be considered the area of operation.

(e) The authority granted to the United Nations Force could not be exercised within the Congo either in competition with the representatives of its Government or in co-operation with them in any joint operation. This principle applied also *a fortiori* to representatives and military units of Governments other than the host Government. Thus, the United Nations Operation must be separate and distinct from activities by any national authorities.

(*f*) The units of the Force must not become parties to internal conflicts. They could not be used to enforce any specific political solution of pending problems or to influence the political balance decisive for such a solution.

(*g*) The basic rules of the United Nations for international service were applicable to all United Nations personnel employed in the Congo Operation, particularly as regards loyalty to the aims of the Organization.

(*h*) The United Nations military units were not authorized to use force except in self-defence. They were never to take the initiative in the use of force, but were entitled to respond with force to an attack with arms, including attacks intended to make them withdraw from positions they occupied under orders from the Commander, acting under the authority of the Security Council. The basic element of influence in this principle was clearly the prohibition of any initiative in the use of armed force.

With regard to the composition of the Force, the Secretary-General reiterated the principle that, while the United Nations must preserve its authority to decide on this matter, it should take full account of the views of the host Government. He recalled that in order to limit the scope of possible differences of opinion with host Governments, the United Nations had in recent operations followed two principles: not to include units from any of the permanent members of the Security Council nor units from any country which, because of its geographical position or for other reasons, might be considered as having a special interest in the situation that had called for the operation. He indicated his intention to seek, in the first place, the assistance of African States for the United Nations Force in the Congo. The Force would be built around a core of military units from African States and should also include suitable units from other regions to give it a truly international character. In selecting the contingents, the Secretary-General would necessarily be guided by considerations of availability of troops, language and geographical distribution within the region.

* * *

As the responsibilities of the United Nations in the Congo expanded, the Secretary-General requested and obtained more battalions and support personnel. The Force reached a total of 19,828 at its peak strength by July 1961. From then on, as some of its responsibilities were fulfilled, the strength of the Force was progressively reduced. In addition to the military units, ONUC had a Civilian Operations component which employed some 2,000 experts and technicians to provide the Congolese Government with extensive assistance in the administrative, technical and humanitarian fields.

THE SECRETARY–GENERAL, THE SECURITY COUNCIL AND THE GENERAL ASSEMBLY

As mentioned in the excerpt above, Dag Hammarskjöld apparently felt, before Belgian troops entered the Congo, that he could have supplied military personnel as "technical assistance of a military nature," at the request of the Congolese government, without referring the matter to the Security Council. At that point there had been no Security Council resolution delegating any such authority to him. Where would the authority have come from? *Chapter XV* of the Charter?

Once the Belgian troops had arrived, Mr. Hammarskjöld felt that he could not send peacekeeping forces on his own authority. Instead, he took the matter to the Security Council under *article 99* of the Charter. An astute observer has remarked, "[I]t is fair to say that the Secretary–General essentially wrote the Congolese request for United Nations assistance, conceived the United Nations response, convened the Council, prompted the resolution by which he was empowered to act, and helped to ensure its adoption." [b] Was that proper? Would it be proper today?

The U.N. response was in Security Council Resolution 143, quoted at pages 748–49 supra. It authorized the Secretary–General to provide the Congolese government "with such military assistance as might be necessary until, through that Government's efforts with United Nations technical assistance, the national security forces might be able, in the opinion of the Government, to meet fully their tasks."

What tasks? [c] When Resolution 143 is read in conjunction with the Congolese government's request for U.N. assistance (page 748 supra), could the task be anything other than expelling Belgian troops from the Congo? But if that was the task, wouldn't the Security Council make it clear that it was taking enforcement action against Belgium under Chapter VII of the Charter? (Resolution 143 did not say what article of the Charter the Security Council was invoking.) Moreover, would the Secretary–General's principles governing the U.N. force (pages 749–50 supra) make sense?

On the other hand, if expelling Belgian troops was not the task, and the Security Council was authorizing military assistance to accomplish some other tasks not requested by the Congolese government, would there be a problem under *article 2(7)* of the Charter?

Was the Security Council wise to give such a vague mandate, or would it have been better not to act at all if no agreement could be

b. Franck, The Role and Future Prospects of the Secretary–General, in The Adaptation of Structures and Methods at the United Nations 81, 83 (Hague Acad.Colloq.1986).

c. T. Franck, Nation Against Nation 175 (1985), asks the same question.

reached among the permanent members on a more specific mandate? This question will come up again, in connection with the discussion later in this Section of some of the problems that developed in the Congo.

On July 22, the Security Council adopted Resolution 145, which said in part:

The Security Council,

Having considered the first report of the Secretary–General on the implementation of Security Council resolution 143 (1960) of 14 July 1960,

Appreciating the work of the Secretary–General and the support so readily and so speedily given to him by all Member States invited by him to give assistance,

* * *

Considering that the complete restoration of law and order in the Republic of the Congo would effectively contribute to the maintenance of international peace and security,

Recognizing that the Security Council recommended the admission of the Republic of the Congo to membership in the United Nations as a unit,

1. *Calls upon* the Government of Belgium to implement speedily Security Council resolution 143 (1960) on the withdrawal of its troops and authorizes the Secretary–General to take all necessary action to this effect;

2. *Requests* all States to refrain from any action which might tend to impede the restoration of law and order and the exercise by the Government of the Congo of its authority and also to refrain from any action which might undermine the territorial integrity and the political independence of the Republic of the Congo;

3. *Commends* the Secretary–General for the prompt action he has taken to carry out resolution 143 (1960) and for his first report;
* * *.

According to a leading analyst, the aim of Resolution 145 "was basically to maximize the pressure on Belgium in order to speed up the withdrawal of its troops from all parts of the Congo, including Katanga."[d]

Mr. Tshombé, the leader in Katanga, resisted entry of U.N. forces into the province. This led the U.N. special representative in the Congo, Dr. Ralph Bunche, to recommend against sending ONUC troops to Katanga under the circumstances then existing. He later wrote:

d. G. Abi–Saab, The United Nations (1978).
Operation in the Congo 1960–1964, at 27

While it was apparent that Katanga had no military force of consequence at that time, Mr. Tshombé was appealing by every means to the people of Katanga to resist United Nations entry. It would clearly put the United Nations Force in an untenable position if it had to fight the people of Katanga to enter that province and to remain there, for this would give it the posture of an army of occupation. * * * I greatly doubt that a United Nations peace force could be stationed for very long in any country if, even in self-defense, it would have to turn its guns on civilians rather than military forces.[e]

Do these words still ring true in the context of civil and ethnic strife in the 1990s? Do they have legal as well as political significance, when the Security Council has not authorized enforcement action under Chapter VII of the Charter?

In August 1960, Mr. Hammarskjöld returned to the Security Council. He noted the situation in the Congo and invited the Council "to clarify its views of the methods to be used," and said that the Council "may also wish to state explicitly what so far has been only implied, that is to say, that its resolutions apply fully and in all parts also to Katanga." He went on:

[The Security Council] should also find its way to formulate principles for the United Nations presence, which, in accordance with the Purposes and Principles of the Charter, would safeguard democratic rights and protect the spokesmen of all different political views within the large entity of the Congo so as to make it possible for them to make their voice heard in democratic forms; this is not an easy matter, because it will require a sensitive development of the United Nations activities, but I am sure it can be done, and I feel strongly that the United Nations would have failed in its mission if it maintained order while permitting democratic principles to be violated.[f]

Does this, too, ring true in the 1990s? Does it have legal as well as political significance?

On August 9, 1960, the Security Council adopted Resolution 146, which said in part:

The Security Council,

* * *

Noting with satisfaction the progress made by the United Nations in carrying out the Security Council resolutions in respect of the territory of the Republic of the Congo other than the province of Katanga,

e. Bunche, The United Nations Operation in the Congo, in The Quest for Peace 119, 130–31 (A. Cordier & W. Foote eds. 1965).

f. 15 SCOR, 884th meeting (S/PV.884), at 5 (1960).

Noting however that the United Nations had been prevented from implementing the aforesaid resolutions in the province of Katanga although it was ready, and in fact attempted, to do so,

* * *

1. *Confirms* the authority given to the Secretary–General by Security Council resolutions 143 (1960) and 145 (1960) and requests him to continue to carry out the responsibility placed on him thereby;

2. *Calls upon* the Government of Belgium to withdraw immediately its troops from the province of Katanga under speedy modalities determined by the Secretary–General and to assist in every possible way the implementation of the Council's resolutions;

3. *Declares* that the entry of the United Nations Force into the province of Katanga is necessary for the full implementation of the present resolution;

4. *Reaffirms* that the United Nations Force in the Congo will not be a party to or in any way intervene in or be used to influence the outcome of any internal conflict, constitutional or otherwise;

5. *Calls upon* all Member States, in accordance with Articles 25 and 49 of the Charter of the United Nations, to accept and carry out the decisions of the Security Council and to afford mutual assistance in carrying out measures decided upon by the Council;

6. *Requests* the Secretary–General to implement the present resolution and to report further to the Security Council as appropriate.

What article[s] of the Charter, if any, authorized Resolutions 143, 145 and 146? Consider *articles 24, 36, 39–42*.[g] Does paragraph 5 of Resolution 146 help to answer this question?

Did Resolutions 145 and 146 clarify the mandate of Resolution 143? If so, how?

On July 27, 1960, the Secretary–General and the Congolese government entered into an agreement on the presence and functioning of ONUC, based on the earlier agreement with Egypt on UNEF (page 742 supra). In it, the Congolese government said that "in the exercise of its sovereign rights with respect to any question concerning the presence and functioning of [ONUC], it will be guided, in good faith, by the fact that it has requested military assistance from the United Nations and by its acceptance of the resolutions of the Security Council of July 14 and 22, 1960 * * *." The next paragraph said that the U.N. would also be guided in good faith by those resolutions, and "reaffirms, considering it to be in accordance with the wishes of the Government of the Republic of the Congo, that it is prepared to maintain the United

---

g. See Miller (Schachter), Legal Aspects of the United Nations Action in the Congo, 55 Am.J.Int'l L. 1 (1961); Suy, Peace-keeping Operations, in A Handbook on International Organizations 379, 383 (R.–J. Dupuy ed. 1988).

Nations Force in the Congo until such time as it deems the latter's task to have been fully accomplished." h

Did this give the U.N. the authority unilaterally to define (and redefine later) its task? Would it, along with the Security Council resolutions, preclude the Congolese government from legitimately ordering ONUC out of its territory at some future time when the U.N. still did not deem its task to have been fully accomplished?

Should basic agreements like this and the one with Egypt be more specific about the content and duration of the peacekeeping force's mandate? More recent Security Council practice is to authorize peacekeeping forces only for limited but renewable periods, such as six months at a time. Does that solve the problem?

It did not take long for different interpretations of the U.N. mandate to develop between the central government of the Congo and Mr. Hammarskjöld. The government wanted help not just in expelling Belgian troops, but in establishing its authority over all of Katanga. The Secretary-General tried to maintain a line between those two objectives. He reported to the Security Council his differences with the Congolese government, saying in part that "it must be assumed that the Council would not authorize the Secretary-General to intervene with armed troops in an internal conflict, when the Council had not specifically adopted enforcement measures under Articles 41 and 42 of Chapter VII of the Charter." i

Could the Security Council lawfully authorize the Secretary-General to do what he assumed it would not authorize him to do?

In the summer and autumn of 1960, chaos prevailed in the Congo. Katanga's attempted secession gained momentum; tribal hostilities broke out on a scale that seemed to threaten the very existence of at least one ethnic group; troops of the Congolese army mutinied, looting villages and attacking civilians; the President, Mr. Kasavubu, summarily dismissed the Prime Minister, Mr. Lumumba, who in turn claimed to dismiss Mr. Kasavubu; the Parliament voted to annul the President's action. ONUC, with the subsequent approval of the Secretary-General, closed the radio station and the airports for several days in order to try to contain the situation.

In the Security Council, the Soviet Union and Poland castigated the ONUC actions, accusing the Secretary-General of taking sides in the conflict. The Soviet Union vetoed a proposed resolution that would have buttressed ONUC's authority "to act to restore and maintain law and order as necessary for the maintenance of international peace and security," and would have decided "that no assistance for military

h. U.N. Doc. S/4389/Add.5 (1960).

i. 15 SCOR, 887th meeting (S/PV.887), at 10 (1960).

purposes be sent to the Congo except as part of the United Nations action."[j] At that point the Security Council, over the objections of the Soviet Union and Poland, called an emergency special session of the General Assembly under the Uniting for Peace Resolution.[k]

The General Assembly met, and on September 20 adopted its Resolution 1474(ES–IV). Among other things, it expressed support for the previous Security Council resolutions, and requested the Secretary-General "to continue to take vigorous action in accordance with the terms of the aforesaid resolutions and to assist the Central Government of the Congo in the restoration and maintenance of law and order throughout the territory of the Republic of the Congo and to safeguard its unity, territorial integrity and political independence in the interests of international peace and security." It was apparent from the debate that this was intended to authorize ONUC to take measures to protect civilian life when necessary.[l]

Consider whether the General Assembly's mandate was consistent with the mandate as earlier expressed by the Security Council. Would the General Assembly have the authority under the U.N. Charter to expand or contract a peacekeeping mandate emanating originally from the Security Council?

Are Security Council Resolutions 145 and 146, plus General Assembly Resolution 1474(ES–IV), precedents for the proposition that whenever a state has been admitted to the U.N. as a unit, it is appropriate for the Security Council to send a peacekeeping force, at the behest of the central government, to prevent the secession of a province or region? (Note, inter alia, the reference to admission of the Congo as a unit, in the preamble to Resolution 145, and the reference in Resolution 1474(ES–IV) to safeguarding the unity of the Congo.)

The Security Council got back into the act in 1961, as the situation in the Congo continued to deteriorate. Some aspects of its 1961 resolutions are mentioned in the advisory opinion in the Expenses Case, below. These materials return later to the roles of the Security Council and the Secretary-General in the unravelling Congo situation in 1961 and thereafter. First, the materials examine the response of the International Court of Justice to questions about the legitimacy of U.N. peacekeeping in relation to UNEF I and ONUC.

2. Legitimacy

The legitimacy, under the U.N. Charter, of both UNEF I and ONUC was challenged when the Soviet Union, France and some other member states refused to pay the amounts the General Assembly assessed to them for the expenses of those operations. The General Assembly requested the International Court of Justice to give an

---

j. U.N. Doc. S/4523 (1960).

k. Because it was a procedural matter, the negative Soviet vote was not a veto.

l. See Miller (Schachter), supra note g, at 19–20.

advisory opinion on whether the expenses were "expenses of the organization" within the meaning of U.N. Charter *article 17(2)*. See pages 248–50 supra. Note particularly the Soviet argument at page 248 supra. The excerpts from the ICJ's advisory opinion, below, deal with the questions whether the General Assembly has the authority to undertake peacekeeping activities and whether peacekeeping is something other than enforcement action. They also deal with the specific authorizing measures for UNEF and ONUC.

CERTAIN EXPENSES OF THE UNITED NATIONS
International Court of Justice, Advisory Opinion, 1962.
[1962] I.C.J. 151, 162–167, 170–172, 175–177.

* * *

Article 17 is the only article in the Charter which refers to budgetary authority or to the power to apportion expenses, or otherwise to raise revenue, except for Articles 33 and 35, paragraph 3, of the Statute of the Court which have no bearing on the point here under discussion. Nevertheless, it has been argued before the Court that one type of expenses, namely those resulting from operations for the maintenance of international peace and security, are not "expenses of the Organization" within the meaning of Article 17, paragraph 2, of the Charter, inasmuch as they fall to be dealt with exclusively by the Security Council, and more especially through agreements negotiated in accordance with Article 43 of the Charter.

The argument rests in part upon the view that when the maintenance of international peace and security is involved, it is only the Security Council which is authorized to decide on any action relative thereto. It is argued further that since the General Assembly's power is limited to discussing, considering, studying and recommending, it cannot impose an obligation to pay the expenses which result from the implementation of its recommendations. This argument leads to an examination of the respective functions of the General Assembly and of the Security Council under the Charter, particularly with respect to the maintenance of international peace and security.

Article 24 of the Charter provides:

> "In order to ensure prompt and effective action by the United Nations, its Members confer on the Security Council primary responsibility for the maintenance of international peace and security . . ."

The responsibility conferred is "primary", not exclusive. This primary responsibility is conferred upon the Security Council, as stated in Article 24, "in order to ensure prompt and effective action". To this end, it is the Security Council which is given a power to impose an explicit obligation of compliance if for example it issues an order or command to an aggressor under Chapter VII. It is only the Security

Council which can require enforcement by coercive action against an aggressor.

The Charter makes it abundantly clear, however, that the General Assembly is also to be concerned with international peace and security. Article 14 authorizes the General Assembly to "recommend measures for the peaceful adjustment of any situation, regardless of origin, which it deems likely to impair the general welfare or friendly relations among nations, including situations resulting from a violation of the provisions of the present Charter setting forth the purposes and principles of the United Nations". The word "measures" implies some kind of action, and the only limitation which Article 14 imposes on the General Assembly is the restriction found in Article 12, namely, that the Assembly should not recommend measures while the Security Council is dealing with the same matter unless the Council requests it to do so. Thus while it is the Security Council which, exclusively, may order coercive action, the functions and powers conferred by the Charter on the General Assembly are not confined to discussion, consideration, the initiation of studies and the making of recommendations; they are not merely hortatory. Article 18 deals with "*decisions*" of the General Assembly "on important questions". These "decisions" do indeed include certain recommendations, but others have dispositive force and effect. Among these latter decisions, Article 18 includes suspension of rights and privileges of membership, expulsion of Members, "and budgetary questions". In connection with the suspension of rights and privileges of membership and expulsion from membership under Articles 5 and 6, it is the Security Council which has only the power to recommend and it is the General Assembly which decides and whose decision determines status; but there is a close collaboration between the two organs. Moreover, these powers of decision of the General Assembly under Articles 5 and 6 are specifically related to preventive or enforcement measures.

* * *

The argument supporting a limitation on the budgetary authority of the General Assembly with respect to the maintenance of international peace and security relies especially on the reference to "action" in the last sentence of Article 11, paragraph 2. This paragraph reads as follows:

> "The General Assembly may discuss any questions relating to the maintenance of international peace and security brought before it by any Member of the United Nations, or by the Security Council, or by a State which is not a Member of the United Nations in accordance with Article 35, paragraph 2, and, except as provided in Article 12, may make recommendations with regard to any such question to the State or States concerned or to the Security Council, or to both. Any such question on which action is necessary shall be referred to the Security Council by the General Assembly either before or after discussion."

The Court considers that the kind of action referred to in Article 11, paragraph 2, is coercive or enforcement action. This paragraph, which applies not merely to general questions relating to peace and security, but also to specific cases brought before the General Assembly by a State under Article 35, in its first sentence empowers the General Assembly, by means of recommendations to States or to the Security Council, or to both, to organize peacekeeping operations, at the request, or with the consent, of the States concerned. This power of the General Assembly is a special power which in no way derogates from its general powers under Article 10 or Article 14, except as limited by the last sentence of Article 11, paragraph 2. This last sentence says that when "action" is necessary the General Assembly shall refer the question to the Security Council. The word "action" must mean such action as is solely within the province of the Security Council. It cannot refer to recommendations which the Security Council might make, as for instance under Article 38, because the General Assembly under Article 11 has a comparable power. The "action" which is solely within the province of the Security Council is that which is indicated by the title of Chapter VII of the Charter, namely "Action with respect to threats to the peace, breaches of the peace, and acts of aggression". If the word "action" in Article 11, paragraph 2, were interpreted to mean that the General Assembly could make recommendations only of a general character affecting peace and security in the abstract, and not in relation to specific cases, the paragraph would not have provided that the General Assembly may make recommendations on questions brought before it by States or by the Security Council. Accordingly, the last sentence of Article 11, paragraph 2, has no application where the necessary action is not enforcement action.

* * *

It has further been argued before the Court that Article 43 of the Charter constitutes a particular rule, a *lex specialis,* which derogates from the general rule in Article 17, whenever an expenditure for the maintenance of international peace and security is involved. Article 43 provides that Members shall negotiate agreements with the Security Council on its initiative, stipulating what "armed forces, assistance and facilities, including rights of passage, necessary for the purpose of maintaining international peace and security", the Member State will make available to the Security Council on its call. According to paragraph 2 of the Article:

> "Such agreement or agreements shall govern the numbers and types of forces, their degree of readiness and general location, and the nature of the facilities and assistance to be provided."

The argument is that such agreements were intended to include specifications concerning the allocation of costs of such enforcement actions as might be taken by direction of the Security Council, and that it is only the Security Council which has the authority to arrange for meeting such costs.

With reference to this argument, the Court will state at the outset that, for reasons fully expounded later in this Opinion, the operations known as UNEF and ONUC were not *enforcement* actions within the compass of Chapter VII of the Charter and that therefore Article 43 could not have any applicability to the cases with which the Court is here concerned.

* * *

Moreover, an argument which insists that all measures taken for the maintenance of international peace and security must be financed through agreements concluded under Article 43, would seem to exclude the possibility that the Security Council might act under some other Article of the Charter. The Court cannot accept so limited a view of the powers of the Security Council under the Charter. It cannot be said that the Charter has left the Security Council impotent in the face of an emergency situation when agreements under Article 43 have not been concluded.

Articles of Chapter VII of the Charter speak of "situations" as well as disputes, and it must lie within the power of the Security Council to police a situation even though it does not resort to enforcement action against a State. The costs of actions which the Security Council is authorized to take constitute "expenses of the Organization within the meaning of Article 17, paragraph 2".

* * *

The expenditures enumerated in the request for an advisory opinion may conveniently be examined first with reference to UNEF and then to ONUC. In each case, attention will be paid first to the operations and then to the financing of the operations.

In considering the operations in the Middle East, the Court must analyze the functions of UNEF as set forth in resolutions of the General Assembly. Resolution 998 (ES–I) of 4 November 1956 requested the Secretary–General to submit a plan "for the setting up, with the consent of the nations concerned, of an emergency international United Nations Force to secure and supervise the cessation of hostilities in accordance with all the terms of" the General Assembly's previous resolution 997 (ES–I) of 2 November 1956. The verb "secure" as applied to such matters as halting the movement of military forces and arms into the area and the conclusion of a cease-fire, might suggest measures of enforcement, were it not that the Force was to be set up "with the consent of the nations concerned".

In his first report on the plan for an emergency international Force the Secretary–General used the language of resolution 998 (ES–I) in submitting his proposals. The same terms are used in General Assembly resolution 1000 (ES–I) of 5 November in which operative paragraph 1 reads:

"*Establishes* a United Nations Command for an emergency international Force to secure and supervise the cessation of hostilities in accordance with all the terms of General Assembly resolution 997 (ES–I) of 2 November 1956."

This resolution was adopted without a dissenting vote. In his second and final report on the plan for an emergency international Force of 6 November, [the] Secretary–General, in paragraphs 9 and 10, stated: [See page 736 supra.]

Paragraph 12 of the Report is particularly important because in resolution 1001 (ES–I) the General Assembly, again without a dissenting vote, "*Concurs* in the definition of the functions of the Force as stated in paragraph 12 of the Secretary–General's report". Paragraph 12 reads in part as follows: [See page 737 supra.]

It is not possible to find in this description of the functions of UNEF, as outlined by the Secretary–General and concurred in by the General Assembly without a dissenting vote, any evidence that the Force was to be used for purposes of enforcement. Nor can such evidence be found in the subsequent operations of the Force, operations which did not exceed the scope of the functions ascribed to it.

It could not therefore have been patent on the face of the resolution that the establishment of UNEF was in effect "enforcement action" under Chapter VII which, in accordance with the Charter, could be authorized only by the Security Council.

On the other hand, it is apparent that the operations were undertaken to fulfil a prime purpose of the United Nations, that is, to promote and to maintain a peaceful settlement of the situation. This being true, the Secretary–General properly exercised the authority given him to incur financial obligations of the Organization and expenses resulting from such obligations must be considered "expenses of the Organization within the meaning of Article 17, paragraph 2".

Apropos what has already been said about the meaning of the word "action" in Article 11 of the Charter, attention may be called to the fact that resolution 997 (ES–I), which is chronologically the first of the resolutions concerning the operations in the Middle East mentioned in the request for the advisory opinion, provides in paragraph 5:

"*Requests* the Secretary–General to observe and report promptly on the compliance with the present resolution to the Security Council *and* to the General Assembly, for such further *action as they may deem appropriate in accordance with the Charter.*"

The italicized words reveal an understanding that either of the two organs might take "action" in the premises. Actually, as one knows, the "action" was taken by the General Assembly in adopting two days later without a dissenting vote, resolution 998 (ES–I) and, also without a dissenting vote, within another three days, resolutions 1000 (ES–I) and 1001 (ES–I), all providing for UNEF.

The Court notes that these "actions" may be considered "measures" recommended under Article 14, rather than "action" recommended under Article 11. The powers of the General Assembly stated in Article 14 are not made subject to the provisions of Article 11, but only of Article 12. Furthermore, as the Court has already noted, the word "measures" implies some kind of action. So far as concerns the nature of the situations in the Middle East in 1956, they could be described as "likely to impair * * * friendly relations among nations", just as well as they could be considered to involve "the maintenance of international peace and security". Since the resolutions of the General Assembly in question do not mention upon which article they are based, and since the language used in most of them might imply reference to either Article 14 or Article 11, it cannot be excluded that they were based upon the former rather than the latter article.

* * *

The operations in the Congo were initially authorized by the Security Council in the resolution of 14 July 1960 which was adopted without a dissenting vote. The resolution, in the light of the appeal from the Government of the Congo, the report of the Secretary-General and the debate in the Security Council, was clearly adopted with a view to maintaining international peace and security. However, it is argued that that resolution has been implemented, in violation of provisions of the Charter inasmuch as under the Charter it is the Security Council that determines which States are to participate in carrying out decisions involving the maintenance of international peace and security, whereas in the case of the Congo the Secretary-General himself determined which States were to participate with their armed forces or otherwise.

[The Court recited five Security Council resolutions and one from the General Assembly, authorizing the Secretary-General to proceed and confirming what he had done.]

In the light of such a record of reiterated consideration, confirmation, approval and ratification by the Security Council and by the General Assembly of the actions of the Secretary-General in implementing the resolution of 14 July 1960, it is impossible to reach the conclusion that the operations in question usurped or impinged upon the prerogatives conferred by the Charter on the Security Council. The Charter does not forbid the Security Council to act through instruments of its own choice: under Article 29 it "may establish such subsidiary organs as it deems necessary for the performance of its functions"; under Article 98 it may entrust "other functions" to the Secretary-General.

It is not necessary for the Court to express an opinion as to which article or articles of the Charter were the basis for the resolutions of the Security Council, but it can be said that the operations of ONUC did not include a use of armed force against a State which the Security Council, under Article 39, determined to have committed an act of aggression or to have breached the peace. The armed forces which were utilized in the Congo were not authorized to take military action against any State. The operation did not involve "preventive or enforcement measures" against any State under Chapter VII and therefore did not constitute "action" as that term is used in Article 11.

For the reasons stated, financial obligations which, in accordance with the clear and reiterated authority of both the Security Council and the General Assembly, the Secretary-General incurred on behalf of the United Nations, constitute obligations of the Organization for which the General Assembly was entitled to make provision under the authority of Article 17.

THE ALLOCATION OF PEACEKEEPING AUTHORITY ACCORDING TO THE ICJ

Did the Court consider the General Assembly's authorization of UNEF to be a "decision" having "dispositive force and effect" (page 758 supra) or a recommendation? (*Could* it have been a "decision"? If not, did the General Assembly simply recommend to the Secretary-General that he set up UNEF?)

As a consequence of the Expenses Case, could the General Assembly establish a peacekeeping force whenever it deems it advisable to do so, even if the Security Council has not been blocked from acting by a veto? If there would be limits to this, what are they?

Could the General Assembly avoid the strictures of article 11 simply by saying that it is acting under article 14? See the Court's discussion of these articles at pages 758–59 supra.

When the Security Council establishes a peacekeeping operation, as it actually did with ONUC, could it order the U.N. forces into a member state's territory without the consent of the government? What article(s) of the U.N. Charter might it rely on? For example, could it do so without acting under article 42? (Note that these questions arise if more than one faction has a plausible claim to be the government, and not all factions consent. More than one faction did claim to be the government in the Congo for a time, but not until after ONUC had been established.)

The Court said at page 762 supra that "the operations of ONUC did not include a use of armed force against a State which the Security Council, under Article 39, determined to have committed an act of aggression or to have breached the peace." Is the key to this the assertion that ONUC was not directed against a state, or that the Security Council made no express determination under *article 39?* If the former, what about Belgium? If the latter, is this just form over substance?

The Court added that ONUC did not involve "preventive or enforcement measures" against any state under Chapter VII. But in portions of the Security Council resolution of February 21, 1961 (Resolution 161A) not mentioned by the Court, the Council said that it was "deeply concerned at * * * the threat to international peace and security," and urged the U.N. to take "all appropriate measures to prevent the occurrence of civil war in the Congo, including * * * the use of force, if necessary, in the last resort." This seems to have gone beyond the existing practice of authorizing the use of force only in self-defense. If so, could it be reconciled with *article 2(7)* if it did not involve preventive or enforcement measures under Chapter VII?[a]

The Court said that since UNEF and ONUC were not enforcement actions under Chapter VII, "Article 43 could not have any applicability * * *." Does this mean that if article 43 agreements were to be concluded with member states, they could not include arrangements for the use of their armed forces in peacekeeping operations? Does *article 43* itself preclude that?[b]

In the final analysis, can it be said that the Expenses Case is an example of substance over form, in that the Court upheld U.N. authority to engage in activities designed to restore peace in two troubled areas of the world, despite the lack of any explicit authority in the Charter for such peacekeeping operations, and in the process implicitly supplied a narrow interpretation of article 2(7) in peacekeeping situations?

Is the Expenses Case relevant today? Note that financing remains a serious problem, with payments slow to come in for burgeoning peacekeeping expenses in the 1990s, as ambitious operations are undertaken in such places as Cambodia and the former Yugoslavia. Most of those expenses are allocated to member states as part of the regular U.N. budget process.

3. *Difficulties and Controversies*

a. *UNEF I*

UNEF I operated on Egyptian territory for 10½ years, without serious incident until the spring of 1967. Then, after escalations in tension between Israel and its neighbors, including serious cross-border raids involving Israel, Syria and Jordan, political pressures on President Nasser of Egypt led him to reimpose a blockade of the Strait of Tiran that had been lifted since March 1957. The blockade was directed against Israeli-flag ships and strategic goods (including oil) bound for the Israeli port of Eilat on the Gulf of Aqaba. In addition, the Egyptian government withdrew its consent to the continued presence of UNEF on Egyptian territory and moved its armed forces into

---

[a] See G. Abi–Saab, The United Nations Operation in the Congo 1960–1964, at 106 (1978).

[b] See 1982 U.N. Juridical Y.B. 184.

the areas formerly patrolled by UNEF.[a] The six-day war ensued, with Israel gaining control of the Sinai, the Gaza Strip, the West Bank and the Golan Heights.

U Thant's decision to remove UNEF, as demanded by the United Arab Republic (Egypt), was highly controversial. The materials below show the sequence of events and the legal arguments on both sides regarding the decision.

SPECIAL REPORT OF THE SECRETARY-GENERAL ON REMOVAL OF UNEF FROM EGYPTIAN TERRITORY

U.N. Doc. A/6669, May 18, 1967.
Reissued in U.N. Doc. A/6730, GAOR, Fifth Emergency Special Sess., Agenda item 5 (1967).

[The report has been reorganized to set forth the events and communications in chronological order.]

At 2200 hours LT on 16 May Brigadier Eiz–El–Din Mokhtar [of the United Arab Republic] handed to General Rikhye, the Commander of UNEF, the following letter:

> To your information, I gave my instructions to all UAR Armed Forces to be ready for action against Israel the moment it might carry out any aggressive action against any Arab country. Due to these instructions our troops are already concentrated in Sinai on our eastern borders. For the sake of complete secure of all UN troops which install OPs along our borders, I request that you issue your orders to withdraw all these troops immediately. I have given my instructions to our Commander of the eastern zone concerning this subject. Inform back the fulfilment of this request. Yours, Farik Awal: (M. Fawzy) COS of UAR Armed Forces.

The Commander of UNEF replied that he had noted the contents of General Fawzy's letter and would report immediately to the Secretary-General for instructions, since he had no authority to withdraw any troops of UNEF, or in any other way to redeploy UNEF troops, except on instructions from the Secretary-General.

On learning of the substance of General Fawzy's letter to General Rikhye, the Secretary-General asked the Permanent Representative of the United Arab Republic to the United Nations to see him immediately. The Permanent Representative of the United Arab Republic came to the Secretary-General's office at 1845 hours on 16 May. The Secretary-General requested him to communicate with his Government with the utmost urgency and to transmit to them his views, of which the following is a summary:

---

a. For discussion of the events leading to the removal of UNEF, see I. Rikhye, The Sinai Blunder 1–86 (1980); Yost, The Arab–Israeli War: How it Began, 46 Foreign Affairs 304 (1968).

(i) The letter addressed to the Commander of UNEF was not right procedurally since the Commander of UNEF could not take orders affecting his command from a source other than the Secretary–General. General Rikhye was therefore correct in his insistence on taking no action until he received instructions from the Secretary–General.

(ii) The exact intent of General Fawzy's letter needed clarification. If it meant the temporary withdrawal of UNEF troops from the Line or from parts of it, it would be unacceptable because the purpose of the United Nations Force in Gaza and Sinai is to prevent a recurrence of fighting, and it cannot be asked to stand aside in order to enable the two sides to resume fighting. If it was intended to mean a general withdrawal of UNEF from Gaza and Sinai, the communication should have been addressed to the Secretary–General from the Government of the United Arab Republic and not to the Commander of UNEF from the Chief of Staff of the Armed Forces of the United Arab Republic.

(iii) If it was the intention of the Government of the United Arab Republic to withdraw the consent which it gave in 1956 for the stationing of UNEF on the territory of the United Arab Republic and in Gaza it was, of course, entitled to do so. Since, however, the basis for the presence of UNEF was an agreement made directly between President Nasser and Dag Hammarskjöld as Secretary–General of the United Nations, any request for the withdrawal of UNEF must come directly to the Secretary–General from the Government of the United Arab Republic. On receipt of such a request, the Secretary–General would order the withdrawal of all UNEF troops from Gaza and Sinai, simultaneously informing the General Assembly of what he was doing and why.

(iv) A request by the United Arab Republic authorities for a temporary withdrawal of UNEF from the Armistice Demarcation Line and the International Frontier, or from any parts of them, would be considered by the Secretary–General as tantamount to a request for the complete withdrawal of UNEF from Gaza and Sinai, since this would reduce UNEF to ineffectiveness.

The Secretary–General informed the Commander of UNEF of the position as outlined above, as explained to the Permanent Representative of the United Arab Republic, and instructed him to do all that he reasonably could to maintain all UNEF positions pending further instructions.

* * *

[On May 17, the Secretary–General gave the representative of the United Arab Republic an aide-mémoire which read in part:]

The Secretary-General of the United Nations requests the Permanent Representative of the United Arab Republic to the United Nations to convey to his Government the Secretary-General's most serious concern over the situation that has arisen with regard to the United Nations Emergency Force in the past twenty-four hours as a result of the demands upon it made by United Arab Republic military authorities and of certain actions of United Arab Republic troops in the area.

Before engaging in detail, the Secretary-General wishes to make the following general points entirely clear:

(a) He does not in any sense question the authority of the Government of the United Arab Republic to deploy its troops as it sees fit in United Arab Republic territory or territory under the control of the United Arab Republic.

(b) In the sectors of Gaza and Sinai, however, it must be recognized that the deployment of troops of the United Arab Republic in areas in which UNEF troops are stationed and carrying out their functions may have very serious implications for UNEF, its functioning and its continued presence in the area.

(c) The Commander of UNEF cannot comply with any requests affecting the disposition of UNEF troops emanating from any source other than United Nations Headquarters * * *.

(d) UNEF has been deployed in Gaza and Sinai for more than ten years for the purpose of maintaining quiet along the Armistice Demarcation Line and the International Frontier. It has served this purpose with much distinction. It went into the area and has remained there with the full consent of the Government of the United Arab Republic. If that consent should be withdrawn or so qualified as to make it impossible for the Force to function effectively, the Force, of course, will be withdrawn.

* * *

On 18 May 1967, at 12 noon, I received through the Permanent Representative of the United Arab Republic to the United Nations the following message from Mr. Mahmoud Riad, Minister for Foreign Affairs of the United Arab Republic:

The Government of the United Arab Republic has the honour to inform Your Excellency that it has decided to terminate the presence of the United Nations Emergency Force from the territory of the United Arab Republic and Gaza Strip.

Therefore, I request that the necessary steps be taken for the withdrawal of the Force as soon as possible.

* * *

Late in the afternoon of 18 May, I convened a meeting of the UNEF Advisory Committee, set up under the terms of paragraphs 6, 8 and 9 of resolution 1001 (ES–I) of 7 November 1956, and the representatives of three countries not members of the Advisory Committee but providing contingents to UNEF to inform them of developments and to consult them on the situation.

* * *

I replied to the [Egyptian] message in the early evening of 18 May as follows:

> I have the honour to acknowledge your letter to me of 18 May conveying the message from the Minister of Foreign Affairs of the United Arab Republic concerning the United Nations Emergency Force. Please be so kind as to transmit to the Foreign Minister the following message in reply:
>
> Dear Mr. Minister,
>
> Your message informing me that your Government no longer consents to the presence of the United Nations Emergency Force on the territory of the United Arab Republic, that is to say in Sinai, and in the Gaza Strip, and requesting that the necessary steps be taken for its withdrawal as soon as possible, was delivered to me by the Permanent Representative of the United Arab Republic at noon on 18 May.
>
> As I have indicated to your Permanent Representative on 16 May, the United Nations Emergency Force entered Egyptian territory with the consent of your Government and in fact can remain there only so long as that consent continues. In view of the message now received from you, therefore, your Government's request will be complied with and I am proceeding to issue instructions for the necessary arrangements to be put in train without delay for the orderly withdrawal of the Force, its vehicles and equipment and for the disposal of all properties pertaining to it. * * *
>
> Irrespective of the reasons for the action you have taken, in all frankness, may I advise you that I have serious misgivings about it for, as I have said each year in my annual reports to the General Assembly on UNEF, I believe that this Force has been an important factor in maintaining relative quiet in the area of its deployment during the past ten years and that its withdrawal may have grave implications for peace.

* * *

4. Instructions relating to the withdrawal of UNEF were cabled by me to the Force Commander in the evening of 18 May.

EVALUATING THE SECRETARY-GENERAL'S INITIAL RESPONSE

Leaving aside for the moment any definitive answer to the question whether the Secretary-General was legally obligated to order the withdrawal of UNEF at the request of the Egyptian government, but assuming that he was not completely without foundation for thinking so, was his initial response on May 16 the best a Secretary-General could do under the circumstances? (Does the answer have implications for possible future cases?)

It is not apparent from the record whether the U.N. Legal Counsel was consulted before the Secretary-General expressed his views on May 16. If he had been, what advice should he have given? (Of course, there was no time for any substantial legal research or for the preparation of an authoritative legal memorandum.)

When U Thant ordered the withdrawal of UNEF on May 18, he was immediately criticized. The arguments are well stated in a book written many years later by a leading authority on the law of the United Nations. The excerpt below picks up his account of the events following U Thant's receipt on May 18 of the message that Cairo had decided to terminate the presence of UNEF.

T. FRANCK, NATION AGAINST NATION
89–91 (1985).*

At this time the Secretary-General did go through the motions of consultation. Just before handing his reply to the Egyptian Permanent Representative, he met with his advisory committee on UNEF to inform them of the response he had drafted. He also told them that he would be reporting his actions to the General Assembly and Security Council immediately. At the meeting, it was reported, several government representatives suggested that the Secretary-General delay his offer to comply, asking instead for more time to consult with other interested parties, including Israel and the states contributing troops to UNEF. It was also proposed that the reply be delayed until after the Secretary-General could obtain the views of the General Assembly. Thant, however, said that, as he interpreted the relevant resolutions, agreements, and documents establishing UNEF and placing it in Egypt, it was not for the General Assembly to decide what to do in response to Cairo's unambiguous request. He adamantly insisted that he would

---

* From *Nation Against Nation: What Happened to the U.N. Dream and What the U.S. Can Do About It* by Thomas M. Franck. Copyright © 1985 by Oxford University Press, Inc. Reprinted by permission.

reply to Cairo that evening and report to the Assembly the next day.[68]

Thant did report on May 18, but merely gave his reasons for what had now become a *fait accompli*. To the Security Council, he observed—rather fatuously—that no "peace-keeping operation can be envisaged as permanent or semi-permanent. Each one must come to an end at some time or another."[69] By June 5 the six-day war had broken out. Some called it U Thant's war.

That the U.N. is not exactly gazelle-like in its response to most crises made the unaccustomed speed with which the Secretary–General responded to the demand for UNEF's withdrawal all the more controversial. In his own defense, Thant made two points. First, he argued, the legal basis for UNEF's presence on Egyptian soil made it clear that it could only remain for as long as the Cairo government consented to its presence. Second, at a practical level, there was no way to keep UNEF in place against the wishes of the vastly superior U.A.R. forces.

In support of the legal argument, it was said that UNEF had been created by the General Assembly under the Uniting for Peace resolution. Since such General Assembly actions are limited by the Charter to "recommendations" and are not mandatory, Egypt could not be bound to play host to the international force against its will.[70] Any delay, Thant argued, would be "putting in question the sovereign authority of the Government of the United Arab Republic within its own territory."[71]

There is ample evidence, however, that the Secretary–General need not have acted as he did and, in any event, that he need not have acted quite so expeditiously. After Secretary–General Hammarskjöld had flown to Egypt in 1956 to negotiate the presence of UNEF with President Nasser, he reported to the Assembly that " * * * the United Nations, understanding this to correspond to the wishes of the Government of Egypt, reaffirms its willingness to maintain UNEF until its task is completed."[72] In an *aide-mémoire* prepared by Hammarskjöld on August 5, 1957, the Secretary–General had recorded that, as a result of seven hours of discussion on November 17 with President Nasser, it had been agreed that the stationing of UNEF until its "task is completed" meant that the troops would remain until *both* Egypt and the U.N. agreed that they should leave.[73] On February 26, 1957, Hammarskjöld further stated that, prior to withdrawal of the Force, "an indicated procedure would be for the Secretary–General to inform the Advisory Committee of the UNEF, which would determine whether the matter should be brought to the attention of the Assembly."[74]

68. El–Araby, survey in [1] *N.Y.U. Jour. of Intl. Law,* 169–70. See also U.N. Doc. A/6730, 26 June 1967, pp. 7–8.

69. U.N. Doc. S/7896, 19 May 1967, p. 3.

70. U.N. Doc. A/6669, 18 May 1967, p. 9.

71. Ibid.

72. U.N. Doc. A/3375, Annex, 20 Nov. 1956, p. 1.

73. Letter of Ambassador Ernest Gross to the Editors, *New York Times,* May 26, 1967, p. 46.

74. Ibid.

The U.S. ambassador Ernest Gross, recalling in 1967 his personal involvement in the 1956 negotiations which had installed UNEF, concluded that it had at that time been the understanding of Hammarskjöld and Nasser that whether or not "the task" was, in fact, completed "would be a question which would have to be submitted to interpretation by the Assembly."[75] In the retrospective view of Egypt's legal expert and sometime ambassador to the U.N., Nabil El-Araby, the procedure agreed to in 1956 was as follows: "Egypt's request for the withdrawal of UNEF should be discussed in the Advisory Committee, which is empowered, at its discretion, to convene the General Assembly. If the Assembly should object to the withdrawal, it is submitted that Egypt's 1956 good faith commitment would obligate the Egyptian Government not to act contrary to the wishes of the Assembly."[76]

If these interpretations of the relevant legal documents by leading U.S. and Egyptian authorities are correct, U Thant had considerably more room for maneuver than he chose to employ. At a minimum, he could have postponed the drafting of his note of compliance with Egypt's demand until after thorough study of the options by the advisory committee. That could have taken a while, during which other negotiations might have been set in motion. Or he could have asked the committee to support the view that the task of UNEF had not been completed—a view he apparently did hold—and might then have proposed that the committee arrange to convene the Assembly to advise him, and, perhaps, to mediate between the views of his office and those of the U.A.R. Any of these approaches, at the very least, would have justified delay, which might have prevented the outbreak of war. These observations take on a greater validity if it is true—as Ambassador El-Araby believes—that while Nasser may have been maneuvering to impress the Syrians, who were taunting him for hiding behind UNEF's skirts, he did not intend to attack Israel.[77]

On the other hand, in practice the Secretary-General may not have had much room to maneuver. Troops which had been positioned to stand between the Israeli-Egyptian lines had suddenly found themselves *behind* the Egyptian forces, where they could do no good, but could easily come to harm.[78] Most persuasive is the Secretary-General's admission to the Security Council that "if the [Egyptian] request were not promptly complied with, the Force would quickly disintegrate due to the withdrawal of individual contingents."[79] The Egyptian government did not make its move on May 16 without the complicity of two governments that had provided contingents for UNEF. When Egyptian troops made their surprise deployment around U.N. lines, they did so in the areas occupied by forces of India and Yugoslavia. Had the three nations concerned not acted in some premeditated

75. Gross, *The United Nations*, 32.
76. El-Araby, survey in [1] *N.Y.U. Jour. of Intl. Law*, 165.
77. Interview with Ambassador Nabil El-Araby (New York, Oct. 3, 1982).
78. U.N. Doc. S/7906, 26 May 1967, p. 2.
79. Ibid.

fashion, the possibilities of accidental conflict would have been enormous.

* * *

Further light was shed by India's permanent representative, Ambassador Parthasarathi, when he made known his government's decision that "Indian troops could not remain part of UNEF without the United Arab Republic's approval." [81] Both India and Yugoslavia appear to have informed the Secretary-General that, were he to attempt to delay the withdrawal of the Force by taking the issue to the General Assembly, they would unilaterally withdraw their men. Rather than see his "army" fall apart publicly, Thant chose the path of least resistance.

THE WITHDRAWAL OF THE TROOPS

Professor Franck noted, at the end of the excerpt above, the apparent intervention by the governments of India and Yugoslavia on behalf of their own troops assigned to UNEF. Since that time, the U.N. has developed a model agreement for use with member states contributing personnel and equipment to peacekeeping operations.[b] Articles V, VI and IX provide in part:

V. AUTHORITY

During the period of their assignment * * *, the personnel made available by [the Participating State] shall remain in their national service but shall be under the command of the United Nations * * *. Accordingly, the Secretary-General * * * shall have full authority over the deployment, organization, conduct and direction of [the peacekeeping operation], including personnel made available by [the Participating State]. * * *

VI. INTERNATIONAL CHARACTER

The functions of [the peacekeeping operation] are exclusively international and personnel made available by [the Participating State] shall regulate their conduct with the interests of the United Nations only in view. Except on national administrative matters, they shall not seek or accept instructions in respect of the performance of their duties from any authority external to the United Nations, nor shall the Government of [Participating State] give such instructions to them.

The Government of [Participating State] may raise with the Secretary-General any matter relating to its personnel serving with [the peacekeeping operation].

* * *

---

81. SCOR, 22nd Year, 1343rd Mtg., 29 May 1967, p. 19.

b. U.N. Doc. A/46/185 (1991).

IX. NOTIFICATION OF WITHDRAWAL

The Government of [Participating State] shall not withdraw its personnel from [the peacekeeping operation] without giving adequate prior notification to the Secretary-General of the United Nations.

Would the conduct of India and Yugoslavia in May 1967 be consistent with these provisions?

Do the provisions permit a participating state to withdraw its contingent at will, subject only to prior notification? If so, is that a workable arrangement?

The model agreement provides in article VII that the government of the participating state is responsible for payment of whatever emoluments, allowances and benefits may be due to its personnel under national arrangements. In the case of troops, the United Nations is to reimburse the participating state at a standard rate established by the General Assembly. Beginning with UNEF, withholdings of assessed peacekeeping expenses by several member states have prevented the U.N. from providing reimbursement as contemplated. Is that likely to compromise the international character of peacekeeping forces in times of crisis, as in May 1967?

U Thant's decision to withdraw UNEF was based on practicalities as well as legalities. As a practical matter, did he have any choice?

In this connection, was convening the General Assembly a practical alternative? Was it a legally-required one?

As a matter of international law, was the U.A.R. (Egypt) within its rights to withdraw its consent unilaterally to the continued presence of UNEF on its territory?

If the answer is no, does it follow that the Secretary-General should have kept the Force in place regardless of the odds against its being able to fulfill its mandate?

Should agreements with host governments at the outset of peacekeeping operations be more explicit than the U.N.-Egypt aide-mémoire of November 20, 1956, regarding the conditions under which the host government could withdraw its consent? Is greater explicitness a practical option?

If a peacekeeping force, such as UNEF, is subject to withdrawal at the order of the host government, what good is it?

---

b. ONUC

We have already seen some of the difficulties that engulfed ONUC and Mr. Hammarskjöld from the very beginning. Turmoil in the Congo continued in the winter of 1960–61. Mr. Lumumba was arrested and sent to imprisonment in Katanga. In February 1961 he was assassinated. When news of his death reached New York, "there was an uproar in the United Nations."[a] The Soviet Union placed his death squarely at the door of Mr. Hammarskjöld, who in turn defended himself in the Security Council. Among other things, he reported steps he had taken, and steps he had been urged to take, to try to restore order. Thus, he said that instructions had "been given to the Force to protect the civilian population against attacks from armed units, whatever the authority under which they are acting." He acknowledged that this was "on the outer margin of the mandate of the United Nations, but * * * I felt that it must be considered as a natural part of the duties of the Organization, and I did not meet with any objections."[b]

Was protection of the civilian population against attacks from units of the Congolese army on or outside the outer margin of the Secretary-General's mandate? See the Security Council and General Assembly resolutions at pages 752–56 supra.

Could it legitimately be said that in any peacekeeping operation, protection of civilians from undisciplined indigenous armed troops is within the mandate unless specifically prohibited by the Security Council (or General Assembly, as the case may be)?

Mr. Hammarskjöld had been urged in February 1961 to go further. He indicated his qualms, on legal grounds, about doing so:

> It can be put in question whether the United Nations has the right to inspect trains and aircraft coming to the Congo so as to see to it that no arms are imported. The legal advice I have sought and obtained indicates that we may have no such right to search.
>
> * * *
>
> There is also the constitutional question. Already in the fall I pointed out the essential importance of getting [the Congolese] Parliament together as a basis for the reorganization of the political life of the nation. This attitude had a wide support, but what can the Organization do in this respect as obviously it has not so far claimed a right itself to convene Parliament? * * * [I]s the Council prepared to override the sovereign rights of the Republic of the Congo, and, in the interest of peace and security, to order the reconvening of Parliament?[c]

Was Mr. Hammarskjöld correct in thinking that ONUC could not lawfully search incoming trains and aircraft for arms? If so, could a new Security Council resolution authorize him—or the current Secretary-General under similar circumstances—to do so without contravening the U.N. Charter? (Later in 1961 the Security Council did so,

a. C. Narasimhan, The United Nations: An Inside View 108 (1988).

b. 16 SCOR, 935th meeting (S/PV.935), at 9 (1961).

c. Id. at 10.

without specifically mentioning searches of trains or aircraft. See Resolution 169, paragraph 5, page 779 infra.)

Mr. Hammarskjöld was obviously skeptical about the Security Council's authority to convene the legislative body of a member state. In the event, the Security Council merely "urged" the convening of the Congolese Parliament.[d] Could it properly order the convening of the domestic legislative body, when chaotic conditions in the member state prevent normal political processes from operating?

In response to Mr. Hammarskjöld's report in February 1961, the Security Council adopted Resolution 161A, which not only urged the convening of the Parliament, but also found a threat to international peace and security, and said that the Security Council:

> 1. *Urges* that the United Nations take immediately all appropriate measures to prevent the occurrence of civil war in the Congo, including arrangements for cease-fires, the halting of all military operations, the prevention of clashes, and the use of force, if necessary, in the last resort;
>
> 2. *Urges* that measures be taken for the immediate withdrawal and evacuation from the Congo of all Belgian and other foreign military and paramilitary personnel and political advisors not under the United Nations Command, and mercenaries * * *.

This appeared to include authority to go beyond mere self-defense, raising a question under article 2(7) of the Charter. See page 751 supra.

How broad a precedent was set regarding the use of force in U.N. peacekeeping operations?

Once a government consents to U.N. peacekeeping in its territory, does it have any further control over the manner in which the peacekeeping is conducted? Consider the position Mr. Hammarskjöld took, below, when the Congolese government reacted negatively to Resolution 161A, and forced U.N. troops to evacuate a position they had held at Matadi, near the capital of the Congo.

MESSAGE FROM THE SECRETARY–GENERAL TO THE PRESIDENT OF THE REPUBLIC OF THE CONGO

U.N. Doc. S/4775, March 8, 1961.
16 SCOR Supp. for Jan., Feb. & Mar. 1961, at 261, 262–63.

* * *

We are, of course, strongly aware of the fact that the initial action of the United Nations was undertaken in response to a request of the Government of the Republic of the Congo. But I am certain that you, on your side, are also aware of the fact that this action was taken

---

d. S.C. Res. 161B (1961).

because it was considered necessary in view of an existing threat to international peace and security. Thus, in its resolution of 22 July 1960, and subsequent resolutions, the Security Council expressly linked the maintenance of law and order in the Congo to the maintenance of international peace and security, and made it clear that the primary basis of the Security Council decision was the maintenance of international peace and security. The considerations ruling the relationship between the Republic of the Congo and the United Nations, therefore, should not be seen solely in the light of the request of the Government and what flows from that request. The status, rights and functions of the United Nations are basically determined by the fact that the action was taken in order to counteract an international threat to peace.

This becomes important especially to an interpretation of the undertaking entered into by the Government of the Republic of the Congo on 27 July 1960, [page 754 supra].

* * *

You will observe that the Government undertook "in the exercise of its sovereign rights with respect to any question concerning the presence and functioning of the United Nations Force" to be guided in good faith by its acceptance of the resolutions of the Security Council of 14 and 22 July 1960, and, specifically, to ensure the freedom of movement of the Force. This undertaking has obviously continued in legal force, and must be considered as precluding any actions of the Government which would make it impossible for the United Nations Force to function, under the resolutions, in the way called for as a means of eliminating the threat to international peace and security. This in particular refers to its freedom of movement.

As a further element of the legal situation you will have noted the explicit declaration by the Security Council in its resolution of 9 August 1960, that all Member States are bound in accordance with Articles 25 and 49 of the Charter to accept and carry out the decisions of the Council and, in particular, to afford mutual assistance in carrying out measures decided by the Council. This obviously precludes all Member States, including in this case the host State, from actions which render the United Nations operation ineffective for its declared purposes or hamper its successful continuation. In fact, Member States are under the obligation positively and actively to assist in the operation.

You will see from the references made that the relation between the United Nations and the Government of the Republic of the Congo is not merely a contractual relationship in which the Republic can impose its conditions as host State and thereby determine the circumstances under which the United Nations operates. It is rather a relationship governed by mandatory decisions of the Security Council. The consequence of this is that no Government, including the host Government, can by unilateral action determine how measures taken by the Security Council in this context should be carried out. Such a determination can be made only by the Security Council itself or on the basis of its explicit delegation of authority. It is of special importance that only the Security Council can decide on the discontinuance of the operation, and that, therefore, conditions which, by their effect on the operation, would deprive it of its necessary basis, would require direct consideration by the Security Council, which obviously could not be counted upon to approve of such conditions unless it were to find that the threat to peace and security had ceased.

THE SECURITY COUNCIL'S AUTHORITY

The Secretary-General relied in part on the undertaking by the government of the Congo on July 27, 1960, and in part on the Security Council's authority under the U.N. Charter. How did these two prongs of his argument mesh, in his view, to preclude the host government from restricting the freedom of movement of the U.N. peacekeeping force? Did he have a strong argument?

In another message to the President of the Republic of the Congo, dated March 12, 1961, Mr. Hammarskjöld said, "[W]hen the Congo has to adjust itself to circumstances and accept decisions of the Security Council in conformity with Chapter VII of the Charter, like any other State Member, there is no impairment of the wider interests of the country, as these can best be judged by the Council with its high authority under the Charter; nor is there any impairment of the sovereign rights of the Congo, other than within the limits accepted by all other Member States under a resolution like that adopted on 21 February." [e] Does this add anything to the earlier message? Is it disingenuous to lump the host state in with all other member states in a situation like this?

Could Mr. Hammarskjöld's argument apply to other peacekeeping operations involving a similar undertaking and a finding of a threat to international peace and security?

If so, would there be any limit to what the Security Council could authorize a peacekeeping force to do? Would governments be deterred from consenting to peacekeeping in the first place?

Could Mr. Hammarskjöld's argument have been used effectively by U Thant in 1967 to resist the Egyptian government's withdrawal of its consent to the stationing of UNEF I on Egyptian territory?

The rift with the central Congolese government was mended, temporarily, when ONUC troops in Katanga successfully resisted an offensive by secessionist forces led by foreign mercenaries. At Mr. Hammarskjöld's urging, the central government then formally request-

e. U.N. Doc. S/4775, 16 SCOR Supp. for Jan., Feb. & Mar. 1961, at 261, 269.

ed the U.N. to assist in expelling the foreign mercenaries from Katanga. The ensuing ONUC operation was partially successful, but a substantial number of mercenaries evaded capture and by September 1961 the situation in Katanga had again deteriorated. Another ONUC operation, designed to end the secession, failed to achieve its objective at the cost of much bloodshed. A few days later, Dag Hammarskjöld, trying to induce a cease-fire in the Congo, was killed when his plane crashed on the way to a meeting with the leader of Katanga, Mr. Tshombé.

A cease-fire agreement was nevertheless reached between the U.N. and Katanga, but it did not last. In October the central Congolese government began a new military campaign against Katanga. This resulted in the massacre of eleven ONUC members at the hands of renegade central government troops, and seemed to strengthen, rather than suppress, the movement toward secession in Katanga.

At this point the Security Council re-entered the fray with the resolution below.

SECURITY COUNCIL RESOLUTION 169
Nov. 24, 1961.
16 SCOR, Resolutions and Decisions 1961, at 3 (1965).

The Security Council,

* * *

Reaffirming the policies and purposes of the United Nations with respect to the Congo (Leopoldville) as set out in the aforesaid resolutions, namely:

(*a*) To maintain the territorial integrity and the political independence of the Republic of the Congo,

(*b*) To assist the Central Government of the Congo in the restoration and maintenance of law and order,

(*c*) To prevent the occurrence of civil war in the Congo,

(*d*) To secure the immediate withdrawal and evacuation from the Congo of all foreign military, paramilitary and advisory personnel not under the United Nations Command, and all mercenaries,

(*e*) To render technical assistance,

* * *

Deploring all armed action in opposition to the authority of the Government of the Republic of the Congo, specifically secessionist activities and armed action now being carried on by the provincial administration of Katanga with the aid of external resources and foreign mercenaries, and *completely rejecting* the claim that Katanga is "a sovereign independent nation",

Noting with deep regret the recent and past actions of violence against United Nations personnel,

Recognizing the Government of the Republic of the Congo as exclusively responsible for the conduct of the external affairs of the Congo,

Bearing in mind the imperative necessity for speedy and effective action to implement fully the policies and purposes of the United Nations in the Congo to end the unfortunate plight of the Congolese people, necessary in the interests both of world peace and international co-operation and of the stability and progress of Africa as a whole,

1. *Strongly deprecates* the secessionist activities illegally carried out by the provincial administration of Katanga with the aid of external resources and manned by foreign mercenaries;

2. *Further deprecates* the armed action against United Nations forces and personnel in the pursuit of such activities;

3. *Insists* that such activities shall cease forthwith, and *calls upon* all concerned to desist therefrom;

4. *Authorizes* the Secretary–General to take vigorous action, including the use of the requisite measure of force, if necessary, for the immediate apprehension, detention pending legal action and/or deportation of all foreign military and paramilitary personnel and political advisers not under the United Nations Command, and mercenaries, as laid down in paragraph 2 of Security Council resolution 161 A (1961) of 21 February 1961;

5. *Further requests* the Secretary–General to take all necessary measures to prevent the entry or return of such elements under whatever guise, and also of arms, equipment or other material in support of such activities;

6. *Requests* all States to refrain from the supply of arms, equipment or other material which could be used for warlike purposes, and to take the necessary measures to prevent their nationals from doing the same, and also to deny transportation and transit facilities for such supplies across their territories, except in accordance with the decisions, policies and purposes of the United Nations;

7. *Calls upon* all Member States to refrain from promoting, condoning, or giving support by acts of omission or commission, directly or indirectly, to activities against the United Nations often resulting in armed hostilities against the United Nations forces and personnel;

8. *Declares* that all secessionist activities against the Republic of the Congo are contrary to the *Loi fondamentale* and Security Council decisions and specifically *demands* that such activities which are now taking place in Katanga shall cease forthwith;

9. *Declares* full and firm support for the Central Government of the Congo and the determination to assist that Government, in accordance with the decisions of the United Nations, to maintain law and

order and national integrity, to provide technical assistance and to implement those decisions;

10. *Urges* all Member States to lend their support, according to their national procedures, to the Central Government of the Republic of the Congo, in conformity with the Charter and the decisions of the United Nations;

11. *Requests* all Member States to refrain from any action which may directly or indirectly impede the policies and purposes of the United Nations in the Congo and is contrary to its decisions and the general purposes of the Charter.

AN INTERVENTIONIST SECURITY COUNCIL?

Fighting continued between Katangese gendarmerie and ONUC troops until January 1963, when Katanga's attempted secession finally ended.

Did Resolution 169 authorize ONUC to use armed force in any greater magnitude, or for any further purposes, than did Resolution 161A, page 775 supra?

Paragraph 8 of Resolution 169 declared that the secessionist activities were contrary to the *Loi fondamentale* of the Congo. Is it the Security Council's business to determine what is or is not contrary to the domestic law of a state? What about *article 2(7)?*

During the debate leading to the adoption of Resolution 169, Mr. Tshombé sent a telegram to the Secretary–General, saying in part:

> Like all democratic nations, Katanga invokes the principle on which the very existence of the United Nations is based, according to which all peoples and all nations have the right of self-determination, namely, the right freely to determine their political, economic and cultural status.[f]

Was the Security Council's response in Resolution 169 a denial of the right of self-determination? Was it an intervention in the internal affairs of a member state by authorizing the broad use of force on behalf of one side in a civil war? It has been argued that it was neither, because (a) Mr. Tshombé's regime was not representative, since the Baluba people in Katanga (a significant tribal group) were opposed to secession, and (b) Mr. Tshombé's regime was made possible and maintained only through foreign intervention.[g] If these were the true facts, as appears to have been the case, does that settle the matter legally?

[f.] U.N. Doc. S/4988, 16 SCOR Supp. for Oct., Nov. & Dec. 1961, at 135.

[g.] G. Abi–Saab, The United Nations Operation in the Congo 1960–1964, at 167 (1978).

A leading international lawyer and scholar, who served as Dag Hammarskjöld's legal adviser during the Congo crisis, has said that "it is highly problematic whether a U.N. peacekeeping operation would or should be used to enforce 'law and order' at the request of the *de jure* government, in order to repress a movement for self-determination or autonomy."[h] As suggested above, it is arguable that Katanga's attempted secession was not a genuine movement for self-determination. But what would be? Would it require an entirely indigenous movement, with no dissenting group in the territory and with no material help from outside? Or would it be sufficient if the impetus for autonomy comes from a popular uprising or a democratically-elected body, regardless of dissent within the territory or external support?

In light of all this, what exactly is the precedent set by Resolution 169 for future peacekeeping operations?

As the Congo crisis played itself out, the Secretary–General was often left to decide the limits of his authority without specific guidance from either the Security Council or the General Assembly. The materials above have touched on some of the issues raised by the positions he took. Running through all of this were two possible sources of authority other than explicit empowerment by the Council or Assembly: tacit authorization by the Council, and *article 99* of the Charter.

The tacit authorization issue came to a head in the autumn of 1960, after ONUC had closed the radio station and the airports in the Congo. In a meeting of the Security Council on September 16, the Polish representative mentioned Dag Hammarskjöld's assertion that he had reported this action in an earlier meeting of the Council, which took no action, leading Mr. Hammarskjöld to conclude that his interpretation of his authority had been approved by a majority of the Council. The Polish representative continued:

> We express our grave concern over the Secretary–General's contention that his interpretation, which was used as a basis for action of far-reaching consequences, was approved by the majority of the Council when in fact there was no decision of the Council in that respect. Were this a practice to be followed in the future, it could bring us to abrogation of the Council's rights and therefore to complete departure from the Charter.[i]

Why shouldn't an assertion-acquiescence process operate when the Secretary–General has to make do with a peacekeeping mandate from the Security Council that does not cover every contingency, he reports what he has done to the Council, and the Council does not disapprove?

---

h. Schachter, Authorized Uses of Force by the United Nations and Regional Organizations, in Law and Force in the New International Order 65, 83–84 (L. Damrosch & D. Scheffer eds. 1991).

i. 15 SCOR, 904th meeting (S/PV.904), at 10 (1960).

Would the Polish representative's approach tie the Secretary-General's hands too much?

Is there a lesson to be learned here about the need for a reasonably specific mandate, or series of mandates, from the Security Council when a peacekeeping operation is injected into a chaotic situation such as existed in the Congo in 1960–1963?

Would it help to have an active Military Staff Committee involved in peacekeeping operations, as suggested by President Mitterand of France in 1992?[j] Secretary-General Boutros Boutros-Ghali thought not.[k] Would it make a difference if the composition of the Committee could be changed? See *article 47* of the Charter. What would be the optimal composition?

As for article 99, consider this passage from Dag Hammarskjöld's introduction to his annual report, submitted at the height of the Congo crisis in 1961:

> The forms used for executive action by the Security Council—or when the Council has not been able to reach decisions, in some cases, by the General Assembly—are varied and are to be explained by an effort to adjust the measures to the needs of each single situation. [Among other things,] police forces under the aegis of the United Nations have been organized for the assistance of the Governments concerned with a view to upholding the principles of the Charter. As these, or many of these, arrangements require centralized administrative measures, which cannot be performed by the Council or the General Assembly, Members have to a large extent used the possibility to request the Secretary-General to perform special functions by instructing him to take the necessary steps for implementation of the action decided upon. * * * The character of the mandates has, in many cases, been such that in carrying out his functions the Secretary-General has found himself forced also to interpret the decisions in light of the Charter, United Nations precedents and the aims and intentions expressed by the Members. When that has been the case, the Secretary-General has been under the obligation to seek guidance, to all possible extent, from the main organs; but when such guidance has not been forthcoming, developments have sometimes led to situations in which he has had to shoulder responsibility for certain limited political functions, which may be considered to be in line with the spirit of Article 99 but which legally have been based on decisions of the main organs themselves, under Article 98, and thus the exclusive responsibility of Member States acting through these

---

j. See U.N. Doc. S/PV.3046, at 18 (1992). As early as 1965, the Soviet Union had suggested a peacekeeping role for the Military Staff Committee. See U.N. Doc. A/5915, Annex I, in 19 GAOR Annex No. 21, at 26, 34 (1965). See generally B. Rivlin, The Rediscovery of the UN Military Staff Committee, Occasional Paper No. IV of The Ralph Bunche Institute on the United Nations (1991).

k. See U.N. Doc. A/47/277–S/24111, at 13 (1992).

organs. Naturally, in carrying out such functions the Secretariat has remained fully subject to the decisions of the political bodies.[1]

One scholar has recently taken issue with Mr. Hammarskjöld's view of article 99, as expressed in the excerpt above.

T. BOUDREAU, SHEATHING THE SWORD: THE U.N. SECRETARY-GENERAL AND THE PREVENTION OF INTERNATIONAL CONFLICT
56–57 (1991).*

Article 99 provides the Secretary-General with a preventive role and equips him with expertise and implied powers to help maintain international peace and security. The Article allows the Secretary-General to invoke the Security Council, if he believes it necessary to preserve the peace. Yet, the Article is silent on any duties of the Secretary-General once the Article is invoked. Presumably, once he has brought a matter to the attention of the Security Council, his political responsibilities under the Article cease. Once this Article is invoked, the legal basis for action by the Secretary-General—Executive or otherwise—inevitably shifts to incorporate the specific mandate of the Security Council; thus, Article 98 becomes the legal basis for further action by the Secretary-General, if the Security Council deems it necessary.

In short, no spirit of Article 99 lingers in the aftermath of the Article's invocation. The broad discretion of the Secretary-General to bring any matter before the Council should not be legally linked—even in spiritual, wraithlike form—to administrative and executive functions after the Article is invoked. To do so may lead to political difficulties—such as those that Hammarskjöld encountered in the Congo—that will have the inevitable result of diminishing the influence of the Secretary-General. If such linkage occurs, and then some action of the Secretary-General is seriously challenged or attacked—as in the Congo—then the preventive powers of the Secretary-General under Article 99 will be inevitably questioned or challenged. The outcome will be diminished discretionary power for the Secretary-General under this Article.

This discretionary power exists only before the Article's invocation. In particular, it cannot be invoked to justify executive action in peacekeeping operations. Reporting on such operations is inevitably requested by the Security Council; if a threat to the operation exists, it should be reported as part of the Secretary-General's mandate to administer the force. To link his discretionary powers under Article 99 to execu-

---

1. Introduction to the Annual Report of the Secretary-General on the Work of the Organization, 16 GAOR Supp. No. 1A (A/4800/Add.1), at 5 (1961).

* Reprinted by permission of Greenwood Publishing Group, Inc., Westport, CT, from Sheathing the Sword: The U.N. Secretary-General and the Prevention of International Conflict, by Thomas E. Boudreau. Copyright by Thomas E. Boudreau and published in 1991 by Greenwood Press.

tive actions in UN peacekeeping might be construed as allowing the Secretary–General an independent role in the use of UN military forces. Yet, he has no such role unless specifically provided for by the UN Security Council. He most certainly has no such residual role emerging from the spirit of Article 99.

This is not to argue that the possibility of executive action by the Secretary–General does not exist. A specific mandate of the Security Council (or General Assembly) under Article 98 may ask the Secretary–General to exercise his own judgment or good offices in a certain issue or area. * * * Yet, such executive action should never be linked to the Secretary–General's preventive role under Article 99. Once Hammarskjöld invoked Article 99 in the Congo crisis, the legal—and one might add, political—basis for his subsequent actions changed radically. By convening the Council, he had surrendered his discretionary powers as a watchman of the peace to become the Security Council's servant. At this point, any subsequent UN successes or failures, especially in the realm of UN peacekeeping, [become] the primary responsibility of the Council's members.

THE SECRETARY–GENERAL'S LATITUDE

What did Mr. Hammarskjöld mean by "the spirit of Article 99"? Was he asserting an independent right to determine how peacekeeping operations would be conducted, once the Security Council or General Assembly has established the peacekeeping force?

Would the Secretary–General have any latitude for interpreting and applying nonspecific Security Council peacekeeping instructions under Boudreau's approach? Were his objections essentially legal or political?

Would all problems regarding the Secretary–General's latitude be eliminated by more specific Security Council resolutions than were adopted in the Congo crisis? It has been asserted that:

> [C]ertain basic constitutional limitations can never be changed without the revision of the Charter itself. The most fundamental limitations on the Secretary–General with respect to the implementation of resolutions relates to the fact that he must carry them out. He is not a policy-making body. His role is to strive for the implementation of the decisions and recommendations of the deliberative organs. He cannot modify the resolutions by addition or deletion. It follows that when embarking on the implementation of a given resolution, the Secretary–General is bound by the text of that resolution.[m]

m. Elaraby, The Office of the Secretary–General and the Maintenance of International Peace and Security, in The United Nations and the Maintenance of International Peace and Security 177, 184 (UNITAR, 1987).

The same author concedes that some resolutions might not give the Secretary–General adequate guidelines, in which case he is forced to interpret the resolutions himself. But even the most specific Security Council resolution requires some interpretation when unforeseen or dimly-foreseen situations arise. Under the views expressed above, does the Secretary–General have to keep going back to the Security Council for authoritative interpretations before he acts? If not, how could he legally justify acting on his own interpretation when he has reason to think it might not be shared by all Security Council members?

C. STRIFE IN YUGOSLAVIA

As noted in Chapter 4, Serbs and Croats fought a devastating civil war in 1991 after Croatia declared its independence from Yugoslavia. Serbian irregulars, supported by Serb-commanded federal armed forces, gained control over areas in Croatia where Serbs constituted a majority, or a sizeable minority, of the local population. Fourteen cease-fires, brokered by the European Community, were observed only briefly if at all. When the fifteenth showed greater promise, the U.N. Secretary–General, in consultation with the Security Council, began planning a peacekeeping effort that could give the parties breathing room to negotiate their differences. Repeated efforts by the Secretary–General's personal envoy, Cyrus Vance, finally produced the consent of the President of Croatia, the Yugoslav Federal Presidency, and—grudgingly—the leader of the self-declared "Serbian Krajina Republic," a sizeable region in Croatia under Serbian control. Nevertheless, when Secretary–General Boutros–Ghali recommended in February 1992 that the Security Council establish the U.N. Protection Force (UNPROFOR), the situation in Croatia remained highly unstable. As it turned out, the situation in neighboring Bosnia–Herzegovina became even worse.

The Secretary–General set forth the basic concept of the peacekeeping plan for Croatia:

> United Nations troops and police monitors would be deployed in certain areas in Croatia, designated as "United Nations Protected Areas". These areas would be demilitarized; all armed forces in them would be either withdrawn or disbanded. The role of the United Nations troops would be to ensure that the areas remained demilitarized and that all persons residing in them were protected from fear of armed attack. The role of the United Nations police monitors would be to ensure that the local police forces carried out their duties without discriminating against persons of any nationality or abusing anyone's human rights. As the United Nations Force assumed its responsibilities in the United Nations Protected Areas (UNPAs), all JNA [Yugoslav People's Army] forces deployed elsewhere in Croatia would be relocated outside that republic. The United Nations Force would also, as appropriate, assist the humanitarian agencies of the United Nations in the return of all displaced persons who so desired to their homes in the UNPAs.

The UNPAs would be [three] areas in Croatia in which the Secretary–General judged that special arrangements were required during an interim period to ensure that a lasting cease-fire was maintained. They would be areas in which Serbs constitute the majority or a substantial minority of the population and where inter-communal tensions have led to armed conflict in the recent past.[a]

The Secretary–General recommended a force for Croatia of about 13,000 military personnel, 530 police personnel (regarded by the U.N. as civilians), and another civilian component to perform various political, legal, information and administrative functions. The key elements in the U.N. plan were demilitarization of the protected areas, including withdrawal of the federal armed forces; and the functioning of existing local authorities, including police, under U.N. supervision pending an overall political solution to the crisis.

The role of the U.N. military personnel was to ensure that the areas remained demilitarized and that all residents were protected from fear of armed attack. According to the plan, military units would patrol extensively inside the protected areas. "They would also investigate any complaints made to them about violations of the demilitarized status of the [areas]. Any confirmed violations would be taken up with the offending party and would, if necessary, be reported by the Secretary–General to the Security Council. If serious tension were to develop between nationalities in [an area], the United Nations Force would interpose itself between the two sides in order to prevent hostilities."[b]

The police monitors were to ensure that the local police carried out their duties without discrimination and without abusing anyone's human rights. Mr. Boutros–Ghali said that the U.N. role regarding local administration and maintenance of public order, pending negotiation of an overall settlement, would be:

(a) To identify * * * the existing arrangements for local administration and the maintenance of public order in each of the * * * protected areas, together with any existing regional structures;

(b) To confirm that the composition of the existing police forces reflects the national composition of the population which lived in the area concerned before the recent hostilities; and, in cases where that is not so, to arrange, in cooperation with the existing local authorities, any change that may be necessary;

(c) To monitor the work of the local police forces * * *;

(d) To use its good offices to ensure that any changes to the status quo as regards other aspects of local administration are

---

a. U.N. Doc. S/23280, at 16 (1991).   b. Id. at 17.

consistent with the spirit of the plan and pose no threat to public order.^c

According to the plan:

> The civilian police monitors would also be deployed throughout the [areas]. They would be unarmed. They would have no executive responsibility for the maintenance of public order but they would closely monitor the work of the local police forces. To this end, they would be co-located with police headquarters in each region and [subregion] and would accompany the local police on their patrols and in their performance of their other duties. They would investigate any complaints of discrimination or other abuse of human rights and would report to the Chief of the United Nations Force any confirmed cases of discrimination or abuse. They would require free and immediate access to all premises and facilities of, or under the control of, the local police forces.^d

Was this a fundamentally different peacekeeping situation from those involving UNEF and ONUC?

How effective could the U.N. military units be if they had to interpose themselves between two ethnic groups, harboring longstanding animosities toward each other, that are ready to resume fighting? Is that the U.N.'s lawful business, if there is no threat to the peace from outside the country?

Does a U.N. operation such as the one in Yugoslavia require, for its success, ultimate control of police functions by the U.N. within designated areas of a sovereign state? What remedies would be available to the U.N. if local police forces failed to maintain order, or did so at the expense of the fundamental human rights of one or another segment of the population?

When a question arose whether Croatian law would apply within the protected areas to such things as traffic, trade, banking, law and order, and the return of refugees, Mr. Boutros-Ghali asserted that this would be inconsistent with the U.N. plan. He recommended going forward on the basis of the Croatian President's assurances that these questions would be resolved in a status-of-forces agreement within the letter and spirit of the plan.

Presumably a status-of-forces agreement could cover civilian as well as military personnel in an operation such as the one in Yugoslavia. Would the civilian component (including the police personnel) enjoy privileges and immunities necessary for the performance of their functions, even if they were not covered by a status-of-forces agreement? The Secretary-General has said that under those circumstances they would have the status of experts on missions for the United Nations, under *section 22* of the General Convention on Privileges and

---

c. U.N. Doc. S/23592, at 4–5 (1992).   d. U.N. Doc. S/23280, at 18 (1991).

Immunities.ᵉ See the Mazilu Case, page 86 supra. If the civilians are experts on U.N. missions, would the military personnel be too?

In a situation such as that in Croatia or Bosnia–Herzegovina, civilian members of the peacekeeping operation, like the military members, are at risk of personal injury or death. The U.N. provides something akin to workers' compensation for military observers, and the Secretary–General has proposed extending it to civilian personnel. As of 1990, the maximum entitlement was $20,000, or twice the basic annual salary, whichever is greater. Payment would be made to the person's government, and would be the sole compensation payable by the U.N. for death, injury or illness.ᶠ Under the U.N. Reparations Case, page 7 supra, could the U.N. assert a claim on behalf of the injured or deceased civilian against Croatia if the injury or death could be attributed to a failure by local authorities in Croatia to fulfil an obligation to protect U.N. agents in the course of their duties? Note that civilian members of U.N. peacekeeping operations have no contractual relationship with the U.N. They are simply "placed at the disposal of, and under the authority of, the Secretary–General, following a formal request to their Government."ᵍ

Mr. Boutros–Ghali's predecessor, Javier Pérez de Cuéllar, had recommended that a civilian chief of mission be in charge of the overall operation in Croatia. But Mr. Boutros–Ghali said:

> I have come to the conclusion that the appointment of a very senior civilian representative of the Secretary–General in Yugoslavia would blur the distinction between the peace-keeping role of the United Nations, whose primary purpose is to create the conditions in which a political settlement can be negotiated, and the peacemaking role of the European Community, which is to conduct and mediate the necessary negotiations. I intend therefore to entrust the overall command of the United Nations operation to the Force Commander, who will be assisted in the political aspects of his duties by a senior civilian official * * *.ʰ

Since the European Community had begun its mediation effort several months earlier, and since the Community did not have armed forces at its disposal, there was obviously a basis for distinguishing between the Community's peacemaking efforts and the U.N.'s peacekeeping efforts. Although there was some question whether the European Community was well equipped to conduct peacemaking efforts, particularly outside its own membership, the only other regional organization with any prospect of doing so—the Conference on Security and

---

e. See U.N. Doc. A/45/502, at 5 (1990).
f. Id. at 6.
g. Id. at 5. On the extent of member states' obligation to protect U.N. agents, see pages 846–48 infra, relating to good offices missions.

h. U.N. Doc. S/23592, at 3–4 (1992).

Cooperation in Europe (CSCE)—had such rudimentary organs and diffuse centers of power that it could not effectively mediate.

Is there an optimal relationship between the U.N. and regional organizations in the peacekeeping/peacemaking field? Note that the U.N. Secretary-General's envoy engaged in some preliminary peacemaking in Yugoslavia, though the burden of mediating a lasting solution fell to the European Community. In recent years when the Security Council has authorized a U.N. peacekeeping operation, it has often also authorized the Secretary-General to appoint a special representative to conduct diplomacy while the peacekeeping forces try to keep a lid on the fighting.[i] Should this be done if there is a regional organization that could undertake the peacemaking burden?

One of the major concerns in establishing the peacekeeping operation in Croatia was that there be no repetition of UNEF I's demise before the job was finished. In particular, it was necessary to assure the Serbian population in the protected areas that the Croatian authorities would not simply order UNPROFOR out as soon as the Serbs had given up their weapons. Mr. Boutros-Ghali addressed this issue:

> [S]ubject to the Council's agreement, the United Nations Force would remain in Yugoslavia until a negotiated settlement [is] achieved. The Force will succeed only if there is confidence that this will indeed be the case. Fears that it might be precipitately withdrawn before the underlying problems had been peacefully resolved would have a most unsettling effect in the United Nations protected areas.
>
> The Security Council may therefore wish in the present case to decide to establish UNPROFOR for a period of 12 months in the first instance, with provision for its mandate to be renewed if necessary thereafter, in the event of a negotiated settlement not having been achieved. The Security Council could further build confidence by including in its resolution a provision that the Force could be withdrawn before the initial 12-month period was completed only if the Council took a specific decision to that effect.[j]

The Security Council responded:

SECURITY COUNCIL RESOLUTION 743
Feb. 21, 1992.
U.N. Doc. S/RES/743.

The Security Council,

* * *

---

i. See A. Norton & T. Weiss, UN Peacekeepers: Soldiers with a Difference 32 (Foreign Policy Ass'n Headline Series No. 292, 1990).

j. U.N. Doc. S/23592, at 7 (1992).

Noting the report of the Secretary–General of 15 February 1992 (S/23592) submitted pursuant to resolution 721 (1991) and the request of the Government of Yugoslavia (S/23240) of 26 November 1991 for a peace-keeping operation referred to in that resolution,

* * *

Concerned that the situation in Yugoslavia continues to constitute a threat to international peace and security as determined in resolution 713 (1991),

Recalling its primary responsibility under the Charter of the United Nations for the maintenance of international peace and security,

Recalling also the provisions of Article 25 and Chapter VIII of the Charter of the United Nations,

* * *

1. *Approves* the report of the Secretary–General of 15 February 1992 (S/23592);

2. *Decides* to establish, under its authority, a United Nations Protection Force (UNPROFOR) in accordance with the above-mentioned report and the United Nations peace-keeping plan and *requests* the Secretary–General to take the measures necessary to ensure its earliest possible deployment;

3. *Decides* that, in order to implement the recommendations in paragraph 30 of the report of the Secretary–General, the Force is established in accordance with paragraph 4 below, for an initial period of 12 months unless the Council subsequently decides otherwise;

4. *Requests* the Secretary–General immediately to deploy those elements of the Force which can assist in developing an implementation plan for the earliest possible full deployment of the force for approval by the Council and a budget which together will maximize the contribution of the Yugoslav parties to offsetting its costs and in all other ways secure the most efficient and cost-effective operation possible;

5. *Recalls* that, in accordance with paragraph 1 of the United Nations peace-keeping plan, the Force should be an interim arrangement to create the conditions of peace and security required for the negotiation of an overall settlement of the Yugoslav crisis;

* * *

8. *Urges* all parties and others concerned to comply strictly with the cease-fire arrangements signed at Geneva on 23 November 1991 and at Sarajevo on 2 January 1992, and to cooperate fully and unconditionally in the implementation of the peace-keeping plan;

9. *Demands* that all parties and others concerned take all the necessary measures to ensure the safety of the personnel sent by the

United Nations and of the members of the European Community Monitoring Mission;

10. *Calls again upon* the Yugoslav parties to cooperate fully with the Conference on Yugoslavia in its aim of reaching a political settlement consistent with the principles of the Conference on Security and Cooperation in Europe and *reaffirms* that the United Nations peacekeeping plan and its implementation is in no way intended to prejudge the terms of a political settlement; * * *.

THE UNPROFOR MANDATE AND ETHNIC CONFLICT

The United States and other Western members of the Security Council wanted Resolution 743 to be adopted under Chapter VII of the Charter, in order to deprive the Croatian authorities of any legal ground for ordering UNPROFOR out before a negotiated settlement was achieved. India and some other non-permanent members objected on the ground that this could set a precedent by imposing a peacekeeping operation on a state without its consent.[k] Apparently as a concession to India and those aligned with it, the draft resolution was amended to include the reference to Yugoslavia's request for a peacekeeping operation, in the first preambular paragraph set forth above.[l]

Did Resolution 743 have to be adopted under Chapter VII in order to achieve the U.S. objective?

Did India accurately identify the potential precedent?

In the end, was Resolution 743 adopted under Chapter VII?

In light of Resolution 743 as adopted, could Croatia lawfully order UNPROFOR out without the Security Council's approval?

To whom was paragraph 9 addressed? If it included such "parties" as Serb and Croat irregulars, did it purport to impose a duty on them under international law? *Can* the Security Council impose a duty on such persons? The President of the Security Council, Mr. Pickering of the United States, said just before Resolution 743 was adopted, "Article 25 of the Charter will apply to the decisions the Council will be taking in this resolution."[m] Does that answer these questions?

The "Yugoslav parties" mentioned in paragraph 10 presumably included at least the governments of Serbia and Croatia. Did it impose a duty on them to cooperate with the European Community-convened Conference on Yugoslavia? Note that they were not then members of the United Nations.

The likelihood of a successful peacekeeping effort is enhanced by advance agreement among the parties to a conflict on the peacekeeping modalities to be used. This can be a problem in multi-party conflicts,

---

k. See N.Y. Times, Feb. 22, 1992, p. 3, col. 4.

l. See U.N. Doc. S/PV.3055, at 3 (1992).

m. Id.

particularly when some of the parties are not states—as in Croatia, but also in the Middle East and some other conflict situations.[n] The Security Council has recognized the principle that peacekeeping should only be undertaken with the consent of host countries "and the parties concerned," which presumably includes nonstate parties.[o] Is this always feasible? Is it a legal or a political principle?

Brian Urquhart, who was for many years the chief career U.N. official in the peacekeeping arena, argued during the crisis in Croatia that something between traditional peacekeeping (on the UNEF model) and Chapter VII enforcement action is needed for civil war situations. The forces involved, like traditional peacekeeping forces, would be multinational and would not have military objectives as such. Unlike traditional peacekeeping forces, they would have to take some initiatives, and thus some combat risks, in bringing the violence under control.[p]

Secretary–General Boutros Boutros–Ghali seems to have picked up on this in his 1992 report to the Security Council, An Agenda for Peace:

> Cease-fires have often been agreed to but not complied with, and the United Nations has sometimes been called upon to send forces to restore and maintain the cease-fire. This task can on occasion exceed the mission of peace-keeping forces and the expectations of peace-keeping force contributors. I recommend that the Council consider the utilization of peace-enforcement units in clearly defined circumstances and with their terms of reference specified in advance. Such units from Member States would be available on call and would consist of troops that have volunteered for such service. They would have to be more heavily armed than peace-keeping forces and would need to undergo extensive preparatory training within their national forces. Deployment and operation of such forces would be under the authorization of the Security Council and would, as in the case of peace-keeping forces, be under the command of the Secretary–General. I consider such peace-enforcement units to be warranted as a provisional measure under Article 40 of the Charter. Such peace-enforcement units should not be confused with the forces that may eventually be constituted under Article 43 to deal with acts of aggression or with the military personnel which Governments may agree to keep on stand-by for possible contribution to peace-keeping operations.[q]

Do you agree that *article 40* authorizes this sort of peace-enforcement unit? If so, would it obviate any need for consent by the parties to the conflict? How about *article 24?*

n. See Wiseman, Peacekeeping in the International Political Context: Historical Analysis and Future Directions, in The United Nations and Peacekeeping 32, 40 (I. Rikhye & K. Skjelsbaek eds. 1990).

o. See, e.g., U.N. Doc. S/21323 (1990).

p. N.Y. Times, Dec. 29, 1991, § 4, p. 9, col. 2.

q. U.N. Doc. A/47/277–S/24111, at 13 (1992).

Was UNPROFOR a significant step in the direction contemplated by Mr. Urquhart and Secretary-General Boutros-Ghali?

Implementation of the U.N. plan for Croatia came slowly and with difficulty. At one point, UNPROFOR found that local Serbs were forcibly evacuating Croats from their homes in the protected areas, reflecting a pattern of systematic harassment. UNPROFOR protested, asked Serbian authorities in Belgrade to investigate, and increased its patrols in an effort to forestall further incidents.[r] Was that all UNPROFOR could lawfully do?

A thorny problem arose in "pink zones"—areas in Croatia outside the designated protected areas, where Serbian communities feared a return of unsupervised Croatian control. The authorities in Belgrade pressed to have the protected areas enlarged to include these communities, but Croatian authorities resisted any change in the boundaries. The Security Council, in Resolution 762, called on Croatia to withdraw its military forces from the pink zones and allow U.N. monitors in. Eventually the commander of UNPROFOR reached an agreement with the Croatian government and "the Serb authorities in the area"—the U.N. euphemism for the president of the "Serbian Krajina Republic" in Croatia—on the concept of a gradual transfer of the zones to Croatian authority under a joint commission.[s]

One might wonder whether U.N. willingness to deal with self-styled political entities such as the "Serbian Krajina Republic" endows them with international personality and thus legitimizes their claims to be subjects of international law. These materials return to that question in Section 4 of this chapter.

If the "Serbian Krajina Republic" was not a state or other international person under international law, the agreement would not amount to a treaty. If the "Republic" also did not have capacity under Croatian law, would such an agreement have any legal effect? (Is legal effect significant in a situation like this?)

With the disintegration of the former Yugoslav state into several states, some boundaries of the U.N. protected areas coincided with what became international boundaries (for example, between Croatia and Bosnia-Herzegovina). The Croatian government proposed that it be allowed to take control of the border entry points and establish customs and immigration procedures along these boundaries, as well as on other Croatian borders. The Secretary-General said that this would be inconsistent with the U.N. plan. This led him to consider the possibility of border control by UNPROFOR. He reported to the Security Council:

r. See U.N. Docs. S/23844, at 4, and S/24353, at 4–5 (1992).

s. U.N. Doc. S/24353, at 3 (1992); see also N.Y. Times, July 10, 1992, p. A6, col. 6.

The United Nations peace-keeping plan gives UNPROFOR explicit authority only to prevent movement of arms, ammunition and other war-like material into the UNPAs. If it was thought appropriate for the United Nations to respond to Croatia's concerns regarding border control, UNPROFOR's mandate would have to be further enlarged to give it powers to carry out immigration and customs functions on the international borders. In the case of Sector East, these would have to include controls required by the sanctions imposed by the Security Council on the Federal Republic of Yugoslavia (Serbia and Montenegro). For UNPROFOR's control to be effective, the Force would also need powers to designate authorized border crossing points and to intercept any persons who were discovered trying to cross the borders at other locations.[t]

Is the operation of a customs and immigration service a proper function for a U.N. peacekeeping operation? (Note that considerably broader governmental functions have been contemplated for UNTAC, the U.N. peacekeeping operation in Cambodia.) If there is serious doubt, is it resolved by the doctrine of functional necessity, dating back to the U.N. Reparations Case, page 7 supra?

Conflict in the former territory of Yugoslavia was by no means limited to Croatia. In March 1992, after Bosnia–Herzegovina had declared its independence, fighting broke out there among the resident Slavic Muslims, Serbs and Croats, with the Yugoslav People's Army supporting the resident Serbs. After the European Community and the United States recognized Bosnia–Herzegovina as an independent state, the fighting intensified. See page 691 supra. Massive destruction ensued, and hundreds of thousands of people fled from their homes. The goal of the resident Serbs apparently was to achieve "ethnic cleansing" by carving up Bosnia–Herzegovina into Serbian, Muslim and Croatian cantons. By the end of November 1992, the Serbs controlled about two-thirds of the territory in Bosnia–Herzegovina.

In April 1992 the President and Foreign Minister of Bosnia–Herzegovina requested the U.N. Secretary–General and his personal envoy to deploy U.N. peacekeeping forces. As summarized by the Secretary–General:

> My Personal Envoy informed President Izetbegovic and other interlocutors that, in light of all the factors bearing on the current situation in Bosnia–Hercegovina, the deployment of a peace-keeping force there was not feasible. Given the limitations on human, material and financial resources, and especially in view of the current widespread violence, he could not recommend to me such a course of action. I fully concur * * *. The sad fact is that the present conditions in Bosnia–Hercegovina make it impossible to

---

t. U.N. Doc. S/24353, at 7 (1992).

define a workable concept for a United Nations peace-keeping operation."

When the conflict intensified, President Izetbegovic "suggested the deployment of a 6,000 to 7,000–man United Nations infantry force to ensure the unblocking of road, rail and air transport in the Republic, to protect and keep open Sarajevo Airport and certain essential bridges and to keep the peace at 'neuralgic spots' where conflict was currently raging."ᵛ The Secretary–General's envoy conceded that such a role would be consistent with previous peacekeeping practice, but would require agreement among the principal parties to the conflict.ʷ No such agreement was then in sight; even if an agreement among leaders could be reached, it was not at all clear that they could get their forces to respect it. The Secretary–General concluded that several infantry battalions might be needed even if an agreement could be reached, and enforcement action under Chapter VII might be necessary.ˣ Nothing further was done at that time.

Could a peace-enforcement unit, of the sort contemplated by Messrs. Urquhart and Boutros–Ghali, have been sent in under article 40, in the absence of agreement among all parties?

The Secretary–General did decide to dispatch a small contingent of unarmed military observers from UNPROFOR to Bosnia–Herzegovina, ahead of the time they were supposed to go there under the original UNPROFOR plan. The President of the Security Council made a statement on behalf of the Council approving the decision. The President also said:

> The Council demands that all forms of interference from outside Bosnia–Hercegovina cease immediately. In this respect, it specifically calls upon Bosnia–Hercegovina's neighbours to exercise all their influence to end such interference.ʸ

What is the legal effect of such a statement? Obviously this one was directed primarily at Serbia, or the rump Yugoslavia of Serbia and Montenegro. Was it a decision of the Security Council for purposes of *article 25?*

If so, would it be binding on Serbia and Montenegro, whose status as successor to Yugoslavia's U.N. membership was in doubt (see page 601 supra)?

A few weeks later, in May 1992, the Security Council adopted Resolution 752, which formalized the Council's demands regarding outside interference, specifically naming the Yugoslav People's Army (as well as elements of the Croatian Army). Resolution 752 did not say that it was adopted under Chapter VII of the Charter. Assuming that it was intended to be binding, would it bind Serbia and Montenegro,

u. U.N. Doc. S/23836, at 6 (1992).
v. U.N. Doc. S/23900, at 5 (1992).
w. Id.
x. Id. at 9.
y. U.N. Doc. S/23842, at 2 (1992).

given their challenged status as the combined successor to Yugoslavia? Consider not only *articles 24* and *25,* but also *article 2(6).*

As has already been noted in this section, the U.N. and the European Community seemed at first to have played mutually supportive roles in the former Yugoslavia: the U.N. as peacekeeper and the E.C. as peacemaker. In July 1992 the distinction between those roles became blurred and the harmony between the organizations became tattered.

On July 17, 1992, the parties to the conflict in Bosnia–Herzegovina signed an agreement in London under the aegis of the E.C. Among other things, the parties asked the Security Council to make arrangements for international supervision of all their heavy weapons. The President of the Security Council promptly announced that the Council had decided in principle to do so.

The Secretary-General prepared a report for the Security Council, outlining the increase in UNPROFOR personnel strength and logistical support that would be required, as well as the necessity of cooperation from the parties. In an unusual move, he recommended against accepting the request that the Security Council had already accepted in principle. He referred not only to the practical problems of such an operation, but also to questions of principle concerning peacekeeping relationships between the U.N. and regional organizations:

> In the first place, the request contained in the London Agreement raises the question of the relationship between the United Nations and regional organizations in the maintenance of international peace and security. In "An Agenda for Peace" (S/24111), I have stated my view that their potential should be utilized in serving the functions of preventive diplomacy, peacemaking and peace-keeping. Chapter VIII of the Charter of the United Nations describes the role which such arrangements and agencies can play and lays down guidelines for their relationship with the United Nations and specifically with the Security Council. That Chapter underlines the primary responsibility of the Security Council in such matters, providing, for instance, that in certain circumstances it can "utilize" regional organizations or agencies. There is no provision for the reverse to occur. In other instances when the United Nations and a regional organization have both been involved in an international peace and security situation, care has been taken to ensure that the primacy of the world Organization has not been compromised.
>
> Secondly, the United Nations did not participate in the negotiation of the London Agreement. Only on the eve of its signature were my staff informed of the request it was likely to contain and given the opportunity to draw attention to the practical constraints on UNPROFOR's ability to carry out this task. It is most unusual for the United Nations to be asked to help implement a politico-military agreement in whose negotiation it has played no part.

The London Agreement is thus very different from the United Nations peace-keeping plan in Croatia which was negotiated by the Secretary–General's Personal Envoy, assisted by experienced staff from the Secretariat. As a matter of principle, I believe that such staff should be involved in the negotiation of any agreement which is likely to give rise to a peace-keeping role for the United Nations.[z]

Mr. Boutros–Ghali relied on *Chapter VIII* of the Charter. Did he accurately set forth the essence of Chapter VIII? Was the E.C. acting inconsistently with Chapter VIII in this instance?

Are there good reasons for Mr. Boutros–Ghali's second concern?

Is there a need for peacekeeping relationship agreements between the U.N. and regional organizations in order to clarify their functions when they deal with regional conflicts? Is it likely that such an agreement would have prevented the awkward situation that arose between the E.C. and Mr. Boutros–Ghali? (The ceasefire assumption underlying the London agreement did not hold, and the weapons-supervision plan was not put into effect. The Security Council did authorize an expansion of UNPROFOR's mandate and troop strength to protect shipments of food and medicine through the Sarajevo airport to the citizens of that city, and later, in Resolution 770 (1992), called upon all states to take "all measures necessary" to facilitate delivery of humanitarian assistance to Sarajevo and other parts of Bosnia–Herzegovina. See Section 2 of this Chapter.)

When Serbian military aircraft continued to operate over Bosnia–Herzegovina in the autumn of 1992, the United States pressed for a Security Council resolution banning the flights. By that time, British and French ground forces were attempting to get humanitarian supplies to Bosnian Muslim civilians under Resolution 770. The United States wanted a resolution with teeth in it, but the British and French governments were concerned that if a flight ban were enforced by the use of air power, the Serb forces in Bosnia would retaliate against their ground forces. Ultimately the United States agreed to the watered-down resolution below.

SECURITY COUNCIL RESOLUTION 781
Oct. 9, 1992.
U.N. Doc. S/RES/781.

The Security Council,

* * *

Determined to ensure the safety of humanitarian flights to Bosnia and Herzegovina,

* * *

---

z. U.N. Doc. S/24333, at 3 (1992).

Alarmed at reports that military flights over the territory of Bosnia and Herzegovina are * * * continuing,

* * *

Considering that the establishment of a ban on military flights in the airspace of Bosnia and Herzegovina constitutes an essential element for the safety of the delivery of humanitarian assistance and a decisive step for the cessation of hostilities in Bosnia and Herzegovina,

Acting pursuant to the provisions of resolution 770 (1992) aimed at ensuring the safety of the delivery of humanitarian assistance in Bosnia and Herzegovina,

1. *Decides* to establish a ban on military flights in the airspace of Bosnia and Herzegovina, this ban not to apply to United Nations Protection Force flights or to other flights in support of United Nations operations, including humanitarian assistance;

2. *Requests* the United Nations Protection Force to monitor compliance with the ban on military flights, including the placement of observers where necessary at airfields in the territory of the former Yugoslavia;

* * *

5. *Calls upon* States to take nationally or through regional agencies or arrangements all measures necessary to provide assistance to the United Nations Protection Force, based on technical monitoring and other capabilities, for the purposes of paragraph 2 above; * * *.

BANNING MILITARY FLIGHTS

Was paragraph 1 binding on all states and nonstate parties to the conflict, as a matter of international law?

The only enforcement mechanism in Resolution 781 involved monitoring under paragraphs 2 and 5. The latter paragraph contemplated such things as Airborne Warning and Control Systems (AWACS) surveillance under NATO command. In the ensuing months, the monitoring revealed persistent violations of the flight ban, but nothing could be done about it in the absence of a new Security Council resolution authorizing enforcement by military means.

Does it make sense for the Security Council to prohibit military activity in a conflict situation, without simultaneously establishing a meaningful enforcement mechanism? ("No-fly zones" over parts of Iraq were in effect at the time of Resolution 781, and were being enforced by military aircraft, but they were not directly established by a Security Council resolution. Instead, they were declared by the United States, United Kingdom and France. As of early January 1993, the United States had made some efforts to persuade its allies to support a Security Council resolution enforcing the restriction on military flights over Bosnia and Herzegovina, but the Security Council had not acted.)

When this was written, the book was not yet closed on U.N. peacekeeping in Croatia or in Bosnia. What was known was that the situation was volatile, marked by intractable ethnic conflict, with U.N. peacekeeping forces in precarious and often dangerous positions. Should the U.N. have kept out in the first place, in light of its experience years earlier with ONUC? Note that when the U.N. got itself into the Yugoslav situation, there was no regional organization in Europe with peacekeeping capabilities. As has been noted above, the European Community was attempting to perform a peacemaking function, but it had no armed forces for peacekeeping. The Western European Union (WEU), a loose organization designed to coordinate military activities among its nine members, was essentially dormant at that time.

In July 1992, after the U.N. effort was under way, the Conference on Security and Cooperation in Europe (CSCE) decided to establish its own peacekeeping capability, seeking the support on a case-by-case basis of the European Community, WEU and NATO.[a] CSCE is a large and quite loosely-structured organization consisting of virtually all the European states (including most of the former Soviet republics), Canada and the United States. Does this offer a more promising prospect for future peacekeeping involving ethnic conflicts in Europe than does UNPROFOR-style U.N. peacekeeping?

D. CIVIL STRIFE IN LIBERIA AND IN SOMALIA

INTRODUCTORY NOTE

In recent years priorities have had to be established for the creation of new U.N. peacekeeping operations—not because of the political stalemates familiar during the cold war, but because of financial limitations or the very absence, in some cases, of cold war incentives to become involved. Thus, while peacekeeping efforts in such places as Yugoslavia, Cambodia and the Western Sahara claimed the attention and resources of the U.N., some other destructive, but localized, conflicts remained at the margin of U.N. concern. Liberia fell into the latter category in the early 1990s. Somalia did too, until the humanitarian crisis there became so desperate that it captured the world's attention.

1. Liberia

From independence in 1847 until a coup d'état in 1980, Liberia was

[a]. Helsinki Summit Declaration, July 8, 1992, para. 20.

tightly controlled by descendants of former American slaves.[a] In the 1980 coup, Sergeant Samuel Doe took control. His authoritarian rule led to dissent and rebellion. In December 1989, a rebel group—the National Patriotic Front of Liberia (NPFL)—led by Charles Taylor invaded from Côte d'Ivoire, and within a matter of months gained control of a substantial part of the countryside. A breakaway rebel group led by Prince Johnson made some military gains of its own. Doe and his supporters were eventually cornered in the capital, Monrovia, where he was captured and killed. Large numbers of refugees fled to neighboring countries, and food supplies in Monrovia dwindled precipitously.

Neither the United Nations nor the Organization of African Unity made any move to mediate or to keep the peace. In this vacuum, the Economic Community of West African States (ECOWAS) decided to send ground and naval forces from five of its member states to try to establish peace in Liberia. ECOWAS is an organization of 16 West African states, including Liberia. As set forth in its constituent instrument, it was established "to promote co-operation and development in all fields of economic activity * * * for the purpose of raising the standard of living of its peoples, of increasing and maintaining economic stability, of fostering closer relations among its members and of contributing to the progress and development of the African continent."[b] A Protocol on Non-Aggression entered into force in 1981, prohibiting aggression among the member states, and calling on each of them to undertake to prevent foreigners on its territory from committing acts of aggression against other member states.[c] The ECOWAS peacekeeping force, ECOMOG, was created in reliance on this Protocol, even though the Protocol—like the U.N. Charter—is silent regarding peacekeeping operations.

ECOMOG arrived in Monrovia in August 1990. Initially, it adopted a passive posture, declining to respond even when attacked. Eventually, having failed to prevent arms and ammunition from reaching the rival groups and having taken some casualties, it mounted some offensive operations. Ultimately it became a force of about 7,000 members. An Extraordinary Session of the ECOWAS Heads of State and Government in November 1990 endorsed a peace plan for Liberia, including a cease-fire subject to ECOWAS monitoring; establishment of a broad-based interim government; and the holding of elections, to be observed by ECOWAS "and other international bodies."[d] A stalemate

a. Much of the factual material on Liberia in this section is based on Williams, Regional Peacemaking: ECOWAS and the Liberian Civil War, in The Diplomatic Record 1990–1991, at 213 (1992), and on N.Y. Times, Apr. 14, 1992, p. A3, col. 1.

b. Treaty of the Economic Community of West African States, May 28, 1975, art. 2(1), 1010 U.N.T.S. 17, 14 Int'l Legal Materials 1200 (1975).

c. Protocol of Non-Aggression, Apr. 22, 1978, reprinted in West Africa, May 25, 1981, at 1153.

d. Final Communique of the First Extraordinary Session of the [ECOWAS] Heads of State and Government, Nov. 27–28, 1990, in U.N. Doc. A/45/894–S/22025, Annex (1990).

ensued, in which Charles Taylor's faction established what amounted to its own government in almost 95 percent of Liberia.

The United Nations did not get into the picture until January 1991, when the Security Council met at the request of Côte d'Ivoire (acting for ECOWAS). The Security Council adopted no resolution, but its President made a statement on the Council's behalf, which said, inter alia:

> The members of the Security Council commend the efforts made by the ECOWAS Heads of State and Government to promote peace and normalcy in Liberia.
>
> The members of the Security Council call upon the parties to the conflict in Liberia to continue to respect the cease-fire agreement which they have signed and to cooperate fully with the ECOWAS to restore peace and normalcy in Liberia.[e]

In October 1991 an accord was reached among the Liberian parties (the Yamoussoukro Accord) looking toward normalization and disarmament. In April 1992 an ECOWAS consultative group met and issued a statement saying that the meeting agreed:

(a) That the buffer zone on the Liberia–Sierra Leone border envisioned by the Accord should be established without further delay. ECOMOG alone shall secure the zone. NPFL may send unarmed observers to the zone.

(b) That all entry and exit points into and out of Liberia, in particular the seaports and airports, shall be secured by ECOMOG. NPFL may maintain an unarmed administrative presence at these points through police, customs and immigration in the areas under its control.

(c) That the encampment and disarmament of all combatants shall be carried out by ECOMOG as envisioned in the Yamoussoukro Accord.

(d) That Mr. Charles Taylor may maintain a personal security of company strength equipped only with small arms * * *.[f]

As before, the President of the Security Council issued a statement on behalf of the Council commending the ECOWAS efforts and calling on all parties to respect and implement the accords they had reached.[g]

Was the ECOWAS peacekeeping effort consistent with *Chapter VIII* of the U.N. Charter?

Would the statements by the President of the Security Council remove any doubt on that score?

Was the Liberian situation better suited for regional peacekeeping than for a U.N. effort? If so, why? Does it have to do with *article 2(7)* of the U.N. Charter?

e. U.N. Doc. S/22110/Add.3, at 2 (1991).
f. U.N. Doc. S/23863, at 3 (1992).
g. U.N. Doc. S/23886 (1992).

If the situation was better suited for regional peacekeeping, why wouldn't the appropriate agency be the Organization of African Unity?

2. *Somalia*

After a tenuous cease-fire had been achieved in the 1991–92 civil conflict between rival clans for control of Somalia—a conflict that created a state of chaos in the capital, Mogadishu, with large numbers of civilian casualties and refugees—the U.N. Secretary-General proposed that the Security Council establish a monitoring mechanism to try to maintain stability and to ensure the delivery of humanitarian assistance to Mogadishu and other affected areas.[a] The Security Council decided to send a technical team to Somalia to seek agreement on the monitoring mechanism.[b] This led to a plan, submitted by the Secretary-General, to send a small team of military observers and a 500-member infantry force with armored cars, stationed on a ship off the Somali coast, to protect relief workers and escort aid deliveries.[c] Mainly because of United States objections to sending the infantry force, the Council initially authorized only a team of 50 military observers to monitor the cease-fire.[d] Apparently the factions in and around Mogadishu had consented to U.N. protection for the relief workers.

The United States had tried to persuade Saudi Arabia and other countries to finance the larger force, but most Security Council members resisted any financing plan that would bypass the regular peacekeeping assessment process (under which the United States is assessed about 30 percent of the cost). In an election year, the U.S. share of the $22 million estimated for the larger force might not sit well in Congress. Although the United States did not formally veto the larger force, there was little point in creating it until U.S. support was forthcoming.

In light of the Security Council's decision creating UNPROFOR in Croatia only two months earlier (at an estimated cost of about $630 million), could the Council's response to the situation in Somalia be justified? Was it consistent with *article 2(1)* of the Charter?

The cease-fire in Somalia did not hold, and the situation continued to deteriorate after the Security Council acted. The Secretary-General forcefully brought home to the Security Council the urgent need for assistance. The Security Council responded first by increasing the size of the U.N. Operation in Somalia (UNOSOM), and later by authorizing member states "to use all necessary means to establish as soon as possible a secure environment for humanitarian relief operations in Somalia." See Section 2(D), infra.

a. See U.N. Doc. S/23693 (1992).

b. S.C. Res. 746 (1992).

c. See U.N. Doc. S/23829 (1992).

d. S.C. Res. 751 (1992). For background, see Int'l Docs. Rev., 27 Apr. 1992, p. 5; N.Y. Times, Apr. 26, 1992, p. 15, col. 1.

Was the decision in April 1992 to send even a tiny observer force an important precedent? Note that it involved a form of peacekeeping in a situation that came as close to pure civil strife as one is likely to find in the late 20th Century. That is, the situation was essentially unencumbered by political or military intervention on the part of governments outside the country, with indigenous parties instead vying for control of the central government.

If it is a significant precedent, is it a salutary one?

E. PEACEKEEPING AND THE DEMOCRATIC PROCESS: NICARAGUA

INTRODUCTORY NOTE

The 1980s were turbulent times in Central America, with unrest in every country except Costa Rica. Armed hostilities between central governments and rebel forces were particularly intense in Nicaragua and El Salvador. The Nicaraguan rebels ("contras") received military and financial support from the United States, while in El Salvador the United States supported the central government. The Nicaraguan contras operated substantially from bases in neighboring Honduras, making incursions across the border into Nicaragua. No solution was in sight in either Nicaragua or El Salvador until the Presidents of five Central American governments joined in a peace plan in 1987, to be implemented by the United Nations and the Organization of American States.

The materials below explore the U.N. involvement in Nicaragua, focusing on a peacekeeping force, the United Nations Observer Group in Central America (ONUCA), and on an observer group, the United Nations Observer Mission to Verify the Electoral Process in Nicaragua (ONUVEN). ONUCA was a tiny operation compared to the U.N. operation in the Congo and to some other U.N. peacekeeping efforts, but it accomplished its mission effectively and in a reasonable time under continuing Security Council guidance. It was disbanded in January 1992. ONUVEN represented the first instance in which the U.N. monitored an electoral process in a sovereign state. It was important not only because it helped materially to ensure a fair election under volatile circumstances in Nicaragua, but also as a possible precedent for future U.N. participation in democratic processes in existing states.

1. ONUCA

THE BLUE HELMETS: A REVIEW OF UNITED NATIONS PEACEKEEPING
389-90, 392-93 (2d ed. 1990).
U.N. Sales No. E.90.I.18.*

Years of turmoil in Central America inspired peace initiatives by the Governments of Colombia, Mexico, Panama and Venezuela—known as the Contadora Group—in 1983, and then by the Presidents of Costa Rica, El Salvador, Guatemala, Honduras and Nicaragua. After preliminary consultations in Esquipulas, Guatemala, in 1986, Costa Rican President Oscar Arias Sánchez drafted a comprehensive regional peace plan, based on the principle of solving several interrelated problems simultaneously. The plan, for which President Arias was awarded the 1987 Nobel Peace Prize, was embodied in the final declaration of a summit of the five Central American Presidents held in Guatemala in August 1987.

ESQUIPULAS II AGREEMENT

The "Procedure for the Establishment of a Firm and Lasting Peace in Central America", known both as the Esquipulas II Agreement and the Guatemala Procedure, dealt with issues of national reconciliation; an end to hostilities; democratization; free elections; termination of aid to irregular forces and insurrectionist movements; non-use of the territory of one State to attack other States; negotiations on security, verification and the control and limitation of weapons; refugees and displaced persons; co-operation, democracy and freedom for peace and development; international verification and follow-up; and a timetable for the fulfilment of commitments.

[The peace process faltered over the next two years.]

TELA ACCORD

On 27 July 1989, in an effort to revive the momentum of the peace process, the Security Council unanimously adopted resolution 637 (1989). In it the Council, *inter alia,* expressed its firmest support for the Esquipulas II Agreement and subsequent joint declarations by the Presidents and called upon them "to continue their efforts to achieve a firm and lasting peace in Central America". It also lent the Security Council's full support to the Secretary-General to continue his mission of good offices.

Considerable progress was made at the summit held at Tela, Honduras, between 5 and 7 August 1989, when the Presidents issued a Declaration and a "Joint Plan for the voluntary demobilization, repatriation or relocation of the members of the Nicaraguan Resistance and their families, as well as assistance in the demobilization of all those involved in armed actions in the countries of the region when they voluntarily seek it". The support for this process would be provided by an International Support and Verification Commission (CIAV), which

---

* Reprinted by permission of the United Nations Department of Public Information.

the Secretaries–General of the United Nations and the OAS were requested to establish.

Among the functions assigned to CIAV, both those of a humanitarian nature and those relating to development would be entrusted to the United Nations High Commissioner for Refugees and the United Nations Development Programme. CIAV was also to be entrusted with receiving arms, equipment and military supplies from the members of the Nicaraguan Resistance and storing them until the five Presidents decided how they should be disposed of.

* * *

On 25 August, the Secretaries–General of the United Nations and the OAS, meeting at United Nations Headquarters, decided to establish CIAV with effect from 6 September 1989. On 1 September 1989, Secretary–General Pérez de Cuéllar appointed Assistant Secretary–General Alvaro de Soto as his Personal Representative for the peace process in Central America. On 21 September, he informed the President of the Security Council of the establishment of CIAV and expressed the view that the demobilization of the members of the Nicaraguan Resistance was an operation of a clearly military nature, which would have to be launched by the Security Council.

THE SECRETARY–GENERAL'S REPORT

On the basis of information gathered by a U.N. mission to Nicaragua, the Secretary–General submitted a report to the Security Council recommending that ONUCA be established.

REPORT OF THE SECRETARY–GENERAL ON ESTABLISHING ONUCA
Oct. 11, 1989.
U.N. Doc. S/20895.

* * *

5. As requested by the Central American Governments, the mandate of ONUCA would be to conduct on-site verification of:

(a) The cessation of aid to irregular forces and insurrectionist movements;

(b) The non-use of the territory of one State for attacks on other States.

* * *

8. It is also envisaged that in addition to its functions as observer and monitor, ONUCA would by its very presence perform a preventive function—and, as appropriate, a deterrent function—with regard to possible non-fulfilment of the commitments [in the Esquipulas II Agree-

ment.] Its commander would have the authority, on his own initiative or at the request of a party, to suggest follow-up action to the Secretary–General, who in turn might recommend it to the Security Council so as to assist the parties in properly fulfilling their commitments under the Guatemala Agreement, the Declaration of El Salvador and subsequent joint declarations.

9. If the Security Council decides to set up an observer group for these purposes, I recommend that it should be known as the United Nations Observer Group in Central America (ONUCA) and that it should be under the command of the United Nations, vested in the Secretary–General, under the authority of the Security Council. Command of ONUCA in the field would be entrusted to a Chief Military Observer (CMO) with the rank of Major–General, who would be appointed by the Secretary–General after consultation with the five Governments and with the consent of the Security Council. The CMO would be answerable to the Secretary–General, who would in turn report regularly to the Security Council on all matters relating to the scope and efficient functioning of ONUCA.

10. The five Central American Governments have expressed to me their desire that the co-operation of the Secretary–General of the Organization of American States (OAS) be enlisted for the purposes of the verification mission. With a view to establishing the details of such co-operation, I would initiate contacts with the Secretary–General of OAS, should the Security Council decide to establish ONUCA. The co-operation could take the form of the attachment to ONUCA headquarters, of a civilian liaison officer from the OAS secretariat.

* * *

[Because of the terrain, mobile teams of military observers would be needed. The observers would be grouped in verification centers near sensitive areas where violations of the undertakings on cessation of assistance and non-use of territory might be most likely to occur.]

13. In order to verify the fulfilment of the aforementioned undertakings, ONUCA would use all the means at its disposal. In particular, the mobile teams would carry out regular patrols, in so far as geographical conditions and their security permitted. The patrols would be by vehicle, by helicopter and, in the Gulf of Fonseca and certain other coastal areas and rivers, by patrol boats and light speedboats, account being taken of operational requirements and the desirability of minimizing expenditures. In addition to their regular patrols, the mobile teams would make spot checks on their own initiative. They would also be instructed to undertake immediate *ad hoc* inspections to investigate allegations of violations of the undertakings.

* * *

18. As in the case of other United Nations peace-keeping operations, the Governments concerned would undertake to grant to ONUCA all the facilities, privileges and immunities necessary for the implemen-

tation of its mandate in accordance with the Convention on the Privileges and Immunities of the United Nations. The Governments would also undertake to give ONUCA personnel full and unrestricted freedom of movement within their territories as well as across their land, sea and air borders. * * * All these undertakings would be recorded in an agreement, in the form of an exchange of notes on the status of ONUCA, which would be concluded between the United Nations and the five Governments when ONUCA was set up.

19. The military observers of ONUCA, like those of other such United Nations missions, would not be armed. In order to ensure their security and effectiveness, it would be desirable for the irregular forces and insurrectionist movements to co-operate with ONUCA or, at the very least, to abstain from the threat or use of force against its members. The ability of ONUCA to carry out its mandate effectively would, to a large extent, depend on such co-operation being obtained. Discussions have already been initiated to obtain such co-operation from the groups in question and will be pursued if the Council decides to set up ONUCA. In accordance with United Nations practice, contacts with such groups are informal in character and in no way imply recognition of them. * * *

21. At full deployment, ONUCA would require the following personnel to carry out the tasks described above:

(a) A total of 260 military observers;

(b) Air-crew and support personnel for the fixed-wing aircraft and helicopters, totalling about 115 personnel;

(c) Crew and support personnel for the naval unit, totalling about 50 personnel;

(d) Up to 14 medical personnel to staff a small medical unit;

(e) About 104 international staff of the United Nations to perform a variety of political and administrative functions;

(f) About 82 locally recruited civilians.

* * *

22. In accordance with the normal practice of United Nations peace-keeping operations, Governments of certain Member States would be asked to contribute the military element in ONUCA personnel. These would include the military observers, the naval personnel, the air personnel (except for those required for the fixed-wing aircraft who could be civilian personnel), the medical personnel (although these also could, as in the United Nations Transition Assistance Group (UNTAG), be civilians provided by a Government), and the military signals personnel who would be required during the ONUCA set-up phase. The Member States contributing to ONUCA would be selected by the Secretary–General, after consultation with the five Governments and with the approval of the Security Council. As already reported, the five Governments have expressed the wish that those Member

States should include Canada, the Federal Republic of Germany and Spain, together with one or more Latin American countries, it being understood that the Federal Republic of Germany would not be in a position to contribute military personnel. * * *

24. Having carefully studied the report of the reconnaissance mission, I recommend to the Security Council, without hesitation, that it should accept the request of the Presidents of Costa Rica, El Salvador, Guatemala, Honduras and Nicaragua and decide to establish forthwith an observer group on the lines described above. I further recommend that, in accordance with the Council's recent practice, ONUCA should be established for an initial period of six months. If the Council so decided, its mandate could thereafter be renewed for further periods, assuming of course that that was the wish of the five Governments concerned. Each renewal would provide an opportunity to make, in consultation with the Governments concerned, any changes which, in the light of experience, appeared to the Council to be necessary in the ONUCA mandate, method of operation, organization or size.

* * *

27. It is recommended that if the Council decides to set up ONUCA, its costs should be considered as expenses of the Organization to be borne by the Member States in accordance with Article 17, paragraph 2, of the Charter.

THE FIRST PHASE OF ONUCA

The Security Council, in Resolution 644 (1989), approved the report of the Secretary–General and established ONUCA for six months, in accordance with the report. ONUCA reached its contemplated strength on June 5, 1990, when it had 14 verification centers and three operational posts. Mobile teams patrolled from the verification centers. When a complaint was registered with ONUCA it was forwarded to the government complained against, with a request to cooperate in an investigation. ONUCA received only a few complaints.

As is often the case, the Security Council did not say which article of the U.N. Charter it was acting under. Which article authorized it to establish ONUCA?

In the Military and Paramilitary Activities Case (Nicaragua v. United States),[a] the International Court of Justice held, inter alia, that U.S. military aid to the Nicaraguan contras violated the customary international law obligation not to intervene in the affairs of another state. Could ONUCA lawfully have been established, with the mandate in paragraph 5 of the Secretary–General's report, in the absence of that holding?

a. [1986] I.C.J. 14, 146.

Given (a) ONUCA's mandate, (b) the consent of the Central American governments, and (c) the fact that the ONUCA observers were unarmed, was it necessary to go to the Security Council in order to establish ONUCA? Could the General Assembly have established it? Could the Secretary–General, on his own authority?

Note that the Central American governments wanted to involve the Organization of American States. See paragraph 10 of the Secretary–General's report. But note also the minor role contemplated for the OAS. In fact, ONUCA was very much a U.N. operation. One reason for the minimal OAS participation was the dominant presence of the United States—hardly a neutral party in Central American affairs in the 1980s—in the OAS. Even in the absence of a member with overall dominance in the organization, the party providing the most resources to a regional peacekeeping operation has tended to dominate the effort. Thus, it has been said, "there are advantages in using international rather than regional peacekeeping." [b] Could a regional organization such as the OAS ever play a significant role in peacekeeping? If so, under what circumstances?

In paragraphs 13 and 18 of the Secretary–General's report, he contemplated freedom of movement and freedom to make on-the-spot investigations, with the advance (blanket) consent of the governments. What if, say, the government of Honduras had consented to the peacekeeping operation on its territory, but insisted on a right to object to any individual investigation by a peacekeeping team? Could a peacekeeping operation effectively be undertaken on those terms? Could the Security Council override a government's right to object, once the government has consented to the operation in general?

Why would the U.N. send unarmed observers into a situation such as this? Note that contacts had been established with the rebel groups, but it does not appear that any binding agreement to cooperate had been reached with them. See paragraph 19. The rebel groups had not been disarmed at that point. Does the U.N. Charter require that observers (as distinguished from peacekeeping forces) be unarmed?

Were the costs of ONUCA, as assessed by the General Assembly in accordance with paragraph 27 of the report, proper expenses of the organization under the U.N. Expenses Case, page 248 supra?

In December 1989, the five Central American Presidents requested that ONUCA's mandate be expanded to include verification of any cessation of hostilities and demobilization of irregular forces. Before this could be done, elections were held in Nicaragua on February 25, 1990, under the watchful eye of ONUVEN. To the surprise of many, the National Opposition Union defeated the then-governing Sandinista party. On March 1, consultations began in Managua on ONUCA's role

b. Indar Jit Rikhye, interview in U.S. Institute of Peace J., June 1991, at 1, 3.

in the transition process to a new domestic order. These led to agreement in principle on the demobilization of the Nicaraguan contras, as indicated in the Secretary-General's report below.

REPORT OF THE SECRETARY-GENERAL ON THE NEED FOR EXPANSION OF ONUCA'S MANDATE
March 15, 1990.
U.N. Doc. S/21194.

* * *

7. The results of the consultations at Managua have been communicated to the Governments of Costa Rica and Honduras, which have agreed in principle to their territory being used, on a temporary basis, for the demobilization of members of the Nicaraguan resistance * * * and which will be asked to confirm their agreement as soon as the recommendations in the present report have been approved by the Security Council. * * *

8. It will be clear to the members of the Security Council that the role envisaged for ONUCA in this process goes beyond its existing mandate, which is to verify, on the spot, compliance by the five Central American Governments with the security undertakings contained in the Guatemala Agreement (also known as the "Esquipulas II agreements"), namely cessation of aid to irregular forces and insurrectionist movements operating in the region and the non-use of the territory of one State for attacking others. If the Security Council agrees, it may wish to approve this enlargement of ONUCA's mandate, as well as the temporary addition of armed personnel to its strength (all existing ONUCA personnel are unarmed). Armed personnel will be required to take delivery of the weapons, *matériel* and military equipment, including military uniforms, of the members of the Nicaraguan resistance, to transport them to secure locations, to ensure their safe custody there until their final disposal is decided upon by the five Central American Presidents and to ensure the security of the assembly points which will be temporarily established in Nicaragua.

* * *

10. * * * I envisage that ONUCA military observers will play a part both in assisting the demobilization process itself and, through constant patrolling, in maintaining a sense of confidence and security in those areas of Nicaragua to which the demobilized members of the Nicaraguan resistance will return.

* * *

16. The voluntary demobilization of the Nicaraguan resistance is an essential element in the Central American peace process. Specific provision was made for it in the Tela accord of 7 August 1989 whose objectives were reaffirmed in the Declaration signed by the five Central

American Presidents at San Isidro de Coronado on 12 December 1989. In recent days it has become clear that both the present Government and the Government-elect in Nicaragua attach importance to voluntary demobilization as part of the process of transferring power, following the elections in that country. If, as I fervently hope, it proves possible for all the parties concerned to reach early agreement on a plan based on the modalities described in the present report, the United Nations will have to move quickly to deploy the additional personnel and material resources which ONUCA will need to carry out the role envisaged for it. It is for this reason that I am asking the Security Council to approve now, on a contingency basis, this enlargement of ONUCA's mandate and the addition of armed personnel to its strength. This is on the clear understanding that, as already indicated in the present report, the additional troops will not actually be deployed until the necessary political conditions are fulfilled, namely an agreement by all concerned for the voluntary demobilization of the members of the Nicaraguan resistance.

THE PROCESS CONTINUES

The Security Council, in Resolution 650 (1990), approved the Secretary-General's report. The resolution authorized the enlargement of ONUCA's mandate and the addition of armed personnel, in accordance with the report.

In April the Secretary-General had further news for the Security Council, and another request for broadening of the mandate. The statement below was made in informal consultations with the Security Council on April 19.

STATEMENT BY THE SECRETARY-GENERAL ON THE NEED FOR FURTHER EXPANSION OF ONUCA'S MANDATE
April 19, 1990.
U.N. Doc. S/21259, Annex.

* * *

It gives me great pleasure to inform the members of the Security Council that early this morning in Managua, following an all night meeting, a series of agreements were signed which establish a cease-fire, security zones and a timetable for the voluntary demobilization of the members of the Nicaraguan Resistance. The participants in the meeting were the Government of Nicaragua, representatives of the President-elect, representatives of the northern, central and Atlantic fronts of the Nicaraguan Resistance and the Archbishop of Managua, Cardinal Obando Y Bravo. The Chief Military Observer of ONUCA and my alternate personal representative for the Central American peace process also took part but did not sign the agreements.

The main points in the agreements relating to the northern and central fronts are as follows:

(A) A cease-fire which came into effect at 12 noon local time today and which the parties wish to be monitored by ONUCA in cooperation with Cardinal Obando Y Bravo;

(B) The establishment of five security zones, to which the members of the Nicaraguan Resistance will move immediately * * *;

(C) Withdrawal of the military and security forces of the Government of Nicaragua from the security zones and from locations within 20 kilometres of the boundaries of the zones * * *;

(D) Provision of humanitarian aid by CIAV to the members of the Nicaraguan Resistance as soon as they reach the security zones;

(E) Complete demobilization of the members of the Nicaraguan Resistance by ONUCA during the period from 25 April to 10 June.

* * *

As [these arrangements] differ in certain respects from those envisaged in my report of 15 March (S/21194), I have thought it right to inform the members of the Council of the main differences. These are: first, the formal cease-fire and separation of forces; secondly, the fact that the security zones are to be considerably larger than the temporary assembly points envisaged in my report; and thirdly, the fact that CIAV will provide humanitarian assistance to the members of the Nicaraguan Resistance as soon as they arrive in the security zones, i.e., before demobilization is complete.

The functions which the Nicaraguan parties have asked that ONUCA should perform can be summarized as:

(A) Monitoring the cease-fire and the separation of forces which will result from withdrawal of the Nicaraguan Government's forces from the security zones and the surrounding areas;

(B) Taking delivery of, and destroying, the weapons, *matériel* and military equipment, including military uniforms of the members of the Nicaraguan Resistance as described in my previous reports to the Security Council.

The second of these functions is already included in the expanded mandate for ONUCA which was approved by the Security Council in resolution 650 (1990). The first, however, namely monitoring the cease-fire and the separation of forces, will constitute a further addition to ONUCA's mandate and will thus require the approval of the Security Council. * * *

THE EXPANDED MANDATE

Security Council Resolution 653 (1990) approved the new functions proposed by the Secretary-General.

Was Resolution 653 necessary, as a matter of law, in order to authorize the first of the functions the Secretary-General outlined in his statement of April 19, 1990? Or was his authority, as envisaged in paragraph 10 of his report of March 15, already adequate for those purposes?

If his authority was already adequate, would there be any reason to go back to the Security Council, as he did in his statement of April 19?

It is not clear that all of the Nicaraguan contras ultimately surrendered all of their arms to ONUCA. Could ONUCA lawfully have used force to disarm the recalcitrant contras, without further authorization from the Security Council?

If the military forces of the government of Nicaragua had refused to withdraw to locations 20 kilometers from the security zones, could ONUCA lawfully have used force to push them back, without further authorization from the Security Council?

If the answer to either of the two preceding questions is no, could the Security Council lawfully have authorized ONUCA to take the action contemplated?

Sometimes there is a disagreement in the field between U.N. peacekeepers and one or more parties to the conflict over interpretation or application of the relevant Security Council resolutions or of a ceasefire agreement. There appear to have been no serious disagreements of that sort involving ONUCA. But there have been in similar demilitarization situations in El Salvador and Cambodia, for example. In El Salvador, the U.N. peacekeeping force, ONUSAL, took the position that the government's failure to adopt clear legislation abolishing the Treasury Police and National Guard violated the U.N.-brokered peace agreement.[c] In Cambodia, the head of UNTAC said that the refusal of the Khmer Rouge to place its forces under U.N. supervision in June 1992 was a clear violation of the peace agreement among all of the Cambodian factions.[d]

Is it appropriate for officials in charge of peacekeeping operations in the field to make legal judgments of this sort?

At one point, representatives of the Nicaraguan contras proposed that ONUCA should collect weapons remaining in civilian hands in Nicaragua, train a new national police force, and verify a reduction in strength of the Nicaraguan army. The Secretary-General responded by saying that a decision on such matters would be up to the Security Council.[e] The Security Council did not act. Would it have been proper

---

c. See U.N. Doc. S/23999, at 5 (1992).

d. See N.Y. Times, June 15, 1992, p. A3, col. 4.

e. U.N. Doc. S/21341, at 2 (1990).

for the Security Council to adopt the contras' proposal either with or without the consent of the Nicaraguan government?

The Nicaraguan demobilization process proceeded without serious hitches. Eventually 19,614 members of the Nicaraguan Resistance were demobilized in Nicaragua and 2,759 in Honduras. A substantial cache of weaponry was handed over to ONUCA.[f]

2. ONUVEN

Before the creation of ONUVEN, the United Nations had quite a bit of experience in observing elections in partitioned territories and newly-independent states, as in Namibia, but it had never done so in an established, independent state such as Nicaragua. It was contemplated from the outset that ONUVEN would involve much more than simply observing the polling on election day. Instead, it would amount to overseeing the entire election process.

FIRST REPORT OF ONUVEN TO THE SECRETARY–GENERAL
Oct. 17, 1989.
U.N. Doc. A/44/642, at 2–4.

* * *

A. THE CENTRAL AMERICAN PEACE PROCESS AND THE NICARAGUAN REQUEST

1. In the Guatemala agreements (also known as the Esquipulas II agreements) signed on 7 August 1987 (A/42/521–S/19085), the Presidents of the five Central American countries undertook, *inter alia,* to promote the holding of free, pluralistic and fair elections in the Central American countries. The Governments concerned undertook to invite the United Nations and the Organization of American States (OAS) to send observers to verify the various electoral processes. The Guatemala agreements were reaffirmed in the San José Declaration of 16 January 1988. In a Declaration signed at La Paz, El Salvador, on 14 February 1989 (A/44/140–S/20491), the Central American Presidents stated that they had been informed by the President of Nicaragua that he was prepared to undertake a process of democratization and national reconciliation in the context of the Esquipulas II agreements and to hold elections in Nicaragua no later than 25 February 1990, and that international observers, in particular representatives of the Secretary–General of the United Nations and the Secretary–General of OAS, would be invited to be present in all electoral districts in order to verify that the electoral process was genuine. On 3 March 1989, the Minister for Foreign Affairs of Nicaragua sent a letter to the Secretary–General of the United Nations requesting the establishment of a group of

---

[f]. The Blue Helmets: A Review of United Nations Peacekeeping 400 (2d ed. 1990).

observers to verify that the Nicaraguan electoral process was genuine at every stage.

B. Establishment of the Mission

2. In his letter dated 5 April 1989 (A/44/210) addressed to the President of the General Assembly, the Secretary-General said that he intended to consider the request from the Government of Nicaragua on the understanding that, if the United Nations agreed to it, it would not be creating a precedent. He cited special factors, such as the fact that the request had the support of the Presidents of Costa Rica, El Salvador, Guatemala, Honduras and Nicaragua, in the context of Central American peace efforts. He also referred to General Assembly resolution 43/24 of 15 November 1988, in paragraph 6 of which the Assembly requested him "to afford the fullest possible support to the Central American Governments in their efforts to achieve peace, especially by taking the measures necessary for the development and effective functioning of the essential verification machinery". Lastly, he indicated that acceptance of that task, if it was to be carried out as seriously and exhaustively as would be required, would entail unanticipated expenditures * * *.

3. In his letter dated 6 June 1989 (A/44/304), the Secretary-General informed the President of the General Assembly that he had sent several missions to Nicaragua in the context of consideration of the Nicaraguan request, that an in-depth study had been made of legal instruments and that United Nations expert consultants had submitted a report to the Nicaraguan Government containing a number of suggestions. He also indicated that he considered General Assembly resolution 43/24 as giving him sufficient legislative basis to undertake observation of Nicaragua's electoral process.

4. On 6 July 1989, the Secretary-General informed the President of the General Assembly of his decision to establish a United Nations Observer Mission to verify the electoral process in Nicaragua (A/44/375) and attached an agreement reached by exchange of letters between the United Nations and the Government of Nicaragua. In his letter, the Secretary-General had explained that his decision should not, of course, be construed as any kind of value judgement as to the laws in force in Nicaragua governing the electoral process. He had also proposed that the Mission should have unrestricted freedom of movement within all electoral districts, unrestricted access to all polling stations and unimpeded contacts with all political parties. The agreement established the terms of reference of the Mission as including the following functions:

(a) To verify that political parties are equitably represented in the Supreme Electoral Council and its subsidiary bodies;

(b) To verify that political parties enjoy complete freedom of organization and mobilization, without hindrance or intimidation by anyone;

(c) To verify that all political parties have equitable access to State television and radio in terms of both the timing and the length of broadcasts;

(d) To verify that electoral rolls are properly drawn up;

(e) To inform the Supreme Electoral Council or its subsidiary bodies of any complaints received or any irregularities or interference observed in the electoral process in order to ensure that the process is conducted in the best possible manner. Where appropriate, the Mission could also request information on any remedial action that might be required;

(f) To submit reports to the Secretary-General, who shall in turn inform the Supreme Electoral Council where appropriate. Reports shall be factual and objective and shall include comments or conclusions that reflect the Mission's role in verifying the electoral process.

5. On 27 July 1989, the Security Council, in its resolution 637 (1989), noted with appreciation the efforts undertaken by the Secretary-General in support of the Central American peace process, particularly his agreement with Nicaragua to deploy a United Nations elections observer mission in that country. In that resolution, the Council lent its full support to the Secretary-General to continue his mission of good offices in consultation with the Council in support of the Central American Governments in their effort to achieve the goals set forth in the Guatemala Agreement.

6. As part of the planning process for the Mission, the Secretary-General of the United Nations wrote to the Secretary-General of OAS on 8 May 1989 suggesting that the two organizations might observe the elections jointly. The Secretary-General of OAS replied on 22 June that OAS had already begun the observation, but that he attached special importance to the exchange of views and the dialogue on the possible form and modalities of collaboration between the two organizations. He suggested that officials of the two organizations might meet to discuss the matter. [Meetings were held in Washington and in Nicaragua.]

7. The Mission has planned its functions in three stages. In the first stage (25 August–3 December 1989), which coincides with the stage of organization and mobilization of political parties envisaged in Nicaragua's electoral timetable, the Mission consists of 17 substantive international officials who, although mainly selected from among Secretariat staff, include three externally recruited advisers specialized in different aspects of electoral processes. The Mission also has the support of a distinguished group of international electoral experts who will visit Nicaragua at key periods in the electoral process. During the first stage, the Mission is based at Managua in order to establish and pursue contacts with the Supreme Electoral Council, political parties and other entities involved in the electoral process. Since it has an efficient transport and communications system, the Mission's regional observers travel constantly both to regional capitals and to municipali-

ties in each of the electoral regions to maintain contact with regional electoral councils and regional politicians and to familiarize themselves with the situation in individual regions.

8. The second stage (4 December 1989–20 February 1990) corresponds to the electoral campaign proper. The staff will be joined by an additional 22 officials so that permanent offices can be set up in electoral regions and the Managua headquarters can be reinforced.

9. The third stage covers the last five days of the electoral process and will centre on intensive observation of the elections themselves on 25 February 1990. Accordingly, there are plans to strengthen the Mission at this stage with some 120 international observers from the Secretariat, from programmes of the United Nations system in the region and, possibly, from other sources.

ONUVEN'S MISSION AND THE SECRETARY-GENERAL'S AUTHORITY

The Secretary-General designated Elliot Richardson, of the United States, as his Personal Representative to oversee ONUVEN's activities, and Igbal Riza, of Pakistan, as the Chief of Mission (the person in charge on a day-to-day basis).

The Secretary-General relied on General Assembly Resolution 43/24 (1988) for his authority to establish ONUVEN. See paragraphs 2 and 3. Was paragraph 6 of that resolution (quoted in paragraph 2 above) adequate authority, even though it did not come from the Security Council, and—as the Secretary-General noted in his earlier letter to the President of the General Assembly—the resolution contained no specific provision authorizing him to undertake observation of Nicaragua's electoral process?[a] Does the Expenses Case, page 248 supra, answer this question?

As the Report above noted in paragraph 5, the Security Council supported the Secretary-General's efforts after he had set ONUVEN in motion. Did that settle any lingering legal question about his authority?

In paragraph 4, the Secretary-General said that, "of course," his decision should not be construed as any value judgment regarding the electoral laws of Nicaragua. But doesn't any U.N. involvement in domestic elections involve a value judgment regarding either the electoral laws of the country or the likelihood that they will be applied evenhandedly?

Could U.N. involvement be justified under *article 2(7)* of the Charter, in the absence of a request from the recognized government, made at its own initiative and without any pressure from the outside?

---

a. See U.N. Doc. A/44/304, at 2 (1989).

As in the case of ONUCA, the plan for ONUVEN was to involve the Organization of American States. Is election monitoring a more promising field for coordinated efforts between the U.N. and a regional organization than is traditional peacekeeping?

The elections were held as scheduled, on February 25, 1990. The National Opposition Union defeated the incumbent Sandinista government. The polling was conducted under an elaborate system of voting controls and procedures adopted by the Supreme Electoral Council of Nicaragua, designed to ensure against the foreseeable forms of election fraud. On election day, 207 ONUVEN observers traveled around Nicaragua in teams, making assessments of the voting procedures and projecting the results before they were official. When it was over, Elliot Richardson, the Secretary-General's Personal Representative, reported that the election had been free and fair. He stressed three points in his letter transmitting ONUVEN's final report:

LETTER TRANSMITTING FINAL REPORT OF ONUVEN
March 22, 1990.
U.N. Doc. A/44/927, at 3–4.

* * *

[T]he likelihood that the United Nations is likely in the future to be called upon for similar assignments in other countries makes it appropriate that I offer some brief comments:

(a) First, the very fact that this was the first time the United Nations had been called upon to verify an election in an independent sovereign State makes it important to review carefully what was done and why. * * *

(b) Second, attention should be focused on the decision taken early in ONUVEN's history that responsibility for verification of the electoral process demanded more than merely recording the process, more than monitoring, and could not stop short of actively seeking to get corrected whatever substantial defects had been discovered. The very fact that the future of Nicaragua literally depended on the fairness and freedom of the elections would have made a purely passive role for ONUVEN morally unacceptable;

(c) Third, a comparably important decision—to make a judgement before election day as to whether or not, despite its deficiencies, the electoral process was on balance sufficiently fair so as to assure that voters would be able to exercise a free choice—is reflected in ONUVEN's fourth report (A/44/921). It had to be recognized, of course, that the election might be close, and in that event not to have done this, to have waited instead until after the votes had been counted, could have greatly complicated the effort to render a final verdict.

ONUVEN AS A PRECEDENT

Space does not permit a detailed exposition of ONUVEN's activities leading to the election. As indicated above, though, ONUVEN did far more than observe on election day. It worked hard in advance to ensure that the elections would not only be fair, but would be perceived to be fair by all interested parties. In this, it seems to have succeeded spectacularly.

Mr. Richardson referred, above, to "ONUVEN's precedent-setting performance." The Secretary–General, however, said at the outset that if the U.N. agreed to the request from the government of Nicaragua, "it would not be creating a precedent." He also cited "special factors" in establishing ONUVEN, such as the fact that the request had the support of the five Central American Presidents in the context of their peace efforts. See page 815 supra.

Did ONUVEN create a precedent? If so, precisely what is the precedent?

Why would the Secretary–General have said in the first place that it would not be creating a precedent?

Is there a promising future for U.N. election monitoring in existing states? Note that election monitoring cannot always be separated from the need for a larger U.N. role in ensuring peaceful political change within a member state. In February 1992, for example, the Security Council approved a far-reaching and very expensive plan for Cambodia, involving not only election preparation and monitoring and the disarming of rival factions (endeavors not unlike those undertaken in Nicaragua), but also the virtual administration of the country for 18 months.[b]

U.N. participation in electoral processes has been a rather controversial question, at least when it is not a direct outgrowth of a traditional peacekeeping operation, as the next subsection of these materials indicates.

F. THE PRINCIPLE OF PERIODIC AND GENUINE ELECTIONS

The Universal Declaration of Human Rights has this to say about a democratic form of government:

Article 21

1. Everyone has the right to take part in the government of his country, directly or through freely chosen representatives.

* * *

3. The will of the people shall be the basis of the authority of government; this will shall be expressed in periodic and genuine

---

b. S.C. Res. 745 (1992).

elections which shall be by universal and equal suffrage and shall be held by secret vote or by equivalent free voting procedures.

Similarly, the International Covenant on Civil and Political Rights says:

Article 25

Every citizen shall have the right and opportunity, without any of the distinctions mentioned in article 2 [race, sex, religion, political opinion, national origin, etc.] and without unreasonable restrictions:

(a) To take part in the conduct of public affairs, directly or through freely chosen representatives;

(b) To vote and to be elected at genuine periodic elections which shall be by universal and equal suffrage and shall be held by secret ballot, guaranteeing the free expression of the will of the electors * * *.

Despite these widely-accepted statements of political rights, many governments are wary of any international scrutiny designed to affect the way in which the principle of periodic and genuine elections is observed within their territories. In December 1990 the General Assembly asked the Secretary–General to solicit the views of member states concerning approaches that would permit the U.N. to respond to requests for electoral assistance. Set forth below is a small sample of the replies, indicating the range of views on the subject:

CHINA

1. The Government of China has always maintained that the political, social, legal, as well as electoral systems of a country are internal affairs of this country and should be established in accordance with the legislative procedure of the country. According to the purposes and principles of the Charter of the United Nations, the United Nations does not have the mandate and authority to intervene in the internal matters, including electoral matters, of its Member States.

2. Up to the present, the United Nations has only provided electoral assistance for related countries in special circumstances, such as in connection with decolonization and the resolution of conflicts that jeopardize world or regional peace and security, or at the invitation of individual sovereign States. Therefore, there is no universal need for the United Nations to provide assistance for the normal electoral matters of its Member States.

3. * * * The Chinese Government holds that it is the sovereign right of each Member State to decide whether to accept the electoral assistance of the United Nations, and such decision should be made by the Governments concerned. Only when a sovereign State has made a request can the United Nations begin to study

and decide on ways, means and methods of the assistance with this country.

PERU

1. It should be borne in mind that any action taken by the United Nations with regard to the holding of periodic and genuine elections must recognize and accept the existence of diverse cultures and political systems and diverse cultural characteristics and heritages, and must therefore be without prejudice to each people's sovereign right to choose its own system of government. On the other hand, the promotion of democracy also depends on an external environment that is conducive to economic development and social justice.

2. Similarly, the United Nations involvement in the holding of periodic and genuine elections should be governed by the same criteria as were applied to its participation in the supervision and observation of electoral processes in Nicaragua, Haiti and Namibia. Thus, it is useful to recall that such participation occurred in response to a request from the Government concerned and/or in the context of peace processes aimed at safeguarding international peace and security.

3. That being so, the Government of Peru reaffirms its conviction that the countries of a given region, which share a similar history, culture and level of development, are better placed to devise approaches that are in keeping with the particular characteristics of that region.

4. As regards the inter-American region, therefore, Peru considers the Organization of American States (OAS) to be the principal forum for an exhaustive study of the scope of the promotion of periodic and genuine elections, not only because OAS, unlike the United Nations, enshrines the principle of representative democracy in its Charter, but also because, bringing together as it does States that share similar political, economic and social conditions, it is able to carry out realistic and flexible analyses and action, the most recent instance being the process of peace and democratization in Central America.

* * *

6. The experience gained by the United Nations and OAS in the recent electoral processes in Nicaragua and Haiti could form the basis of a new era of cooperation between the two Organizations in matters relating to periodic and genuine elections and so lead to similar cooperation between the United Nations and other regional bodies.

* * *

UNITED STATES OF AMERICA

* * *

The Role of the United Nations in Electoral Assistance

* * *

3. The Charter provides firm legal bases for United Nations electoral assistance at the request of Member States. Article 1 outlines the purposes of the Organization, including the maintenance of international peace and security, friendly relations among nations based on respect for equal rights and self-determination of peoples, other appropriate measures to strengthen universal peace and international cooperation in promoting and encouraging respect for human rights and fundamental freedoms for all without distinction as to race, sex, language, or religion. United Nations electoral assistance at the request of a Member State can further these purposes.

4. Article 13 of the Charter sets out two relevant aspects of the General Assembly's mandate: (a) "promoting international cooperation in the political field", and (b) "assisting in the realization of human rights and fundamental freedoms for all without distinction as to race, sex, language, or religion".

5. Further, Article 55 of the Charter provides that the United Nations and its Member States shall promote universal respect for, and observance of, human rights and fundamental freedoms for all without distinction as to race, sex, language, or religion. United Nations electoral assistance, by promoting respect for the right of a citizen to participate in the Government of his or her country, fulfils the intent of the Charter in this regard, as well as the intent of Article 21 of the Universal Declaration of Human Rights and Article 25 of the International Covenant on Civil and Political Rights.

* * *

7. Article 39 of the Charter provides that the Security Council shall decide what measures shall be taken to maintain international peace and security. It is therefore appropriate that the Council consider authorizing United Nations electoral assistance in situations where a properly conducted election is likely to defuse international tensions, as it did in Nicaragua.

8. Chapters XI, XII and XIII of the Charter authorize the United Nations to oversee the administration by Member States of trust and Non–Self-Governing Territories. Many of the territories that had existed in 1945 have achieved self-determination, primarily through plebiscites and other elections conducted or monitored by visiting missions of the United Nations.

9. The United Nations has undertaken all of these activities at the request of countries and territories concerned. None of these activities can be viewed as conflicting with the provisions of Article 2, paragraph 7, of the Charter, which prevents the Organization from intervening in matters which are essentially within the domestic jurisdiction of any State.

* * *

Criteria for Responding to Requests for United Nations Electoral Assistance

11. As the United Nations is called upon to support electoral processes, it must have criteria to determine when it should and should not provide assistance. The United States believes that the following criteria are appropriate:

(a) Request of the Member State concerned. United Nations electoral assistance, in accordance with General Assembly resolution 45/150 and Article 2 of the Charter, must be at the request of the recipient Member State, in full respect for national sovereignty and the principle of non-interference in internal affairs, and must be supported by a broad spectrum of opinion within the requesting country;

(b) Full, unhindered electoral coverage. In cases in which a Member State asks the United Nations to assess the free and fair nature of an election, the Organization's observers must be able to cover the electoral process without hindrance, throughout the country and from beginning to end;

(c) Coordination with regional organizations. In keeping with the role of the United Nations to cooperate with regional organizations, the United Nations should coordinate its activities, where appropriate, with regional organizations, seeking to avoid duplication. The United Nations should focus primarily on providing assistance when regional organizations are unable to meet the need;

(d) Authorization by the appropriate United Nations body. The General Assembly should adopt a resolution granting the Secretary-General authority to respond to requests for technical assistance and observation of elections in exercise of its mandates to promote international cooperation in the political field and assist in the realization of human rights and fundamental freedoms. The Secretary-General should report annually to the General Assembly on the implementation of the resolution. In cases of threats to international peace and security, the Security Council would approve each mission.[a]

---

a. U.N. Doc. A/46/609/Add.1, at 15, 34–35, 42–44 (1991).

Governments concerned about external involvement in their political processes had little to worry about until democracy broke out all over, in the late 1980s and early 1990s. Until then, the United Nations paid no more than lip service to the principle of periodic and genuine elections. But with the proliferation of democracies, it became possible to consider whether a right of democratic governance exists in international law,[b] and if so, whether the United Nations should play an active role in ensuring its effectiveness through some form of observation or supervision of electoral processes within existing states. In Nicaragua, of course, it did so, at the request of the incumbent government. In December 1990, U.N. observers also joined forces with the OAS to monitor elections in Haiti, under the authorization of a General Assembly resolution responding to a request from the provisional government of Haiti.[c] In 1989, UNTAG played a vital role not only in the election of a Constituent Assembly in Namibia, but also in the demobilization of South African military forces there and in other steps toward Namibian independence.[d]

Drawing on this experience, in 1991 the General Assembly adopted a pair of resolutions on electoral processes. Resolution 46/137, on enhancing the principle of periodic and genuine elections, was adopted by a vote of 134 in favor, four opposed, and 13 abstaining. Resolution 46/130, on non-interference in the internal affairs of states in their electoral processes, was adopted by a vote of 102 in favor, 40 opposed, and 13 abstaining. Voting against it were all North American and European states except Yugoslavia.

RESOLUTION ON ENHANCING THE EFFECTIVENESS OF THE PRINCIPLE OF PERIODIC AND GENUINE ELECTIONS

United Nations General Assembly, Dec. 17, 1991.
G.A.Res. 46/137, 46 GAOR Supp. No. 49 (A/46/49), at 209.

The General Assembly,

* * *

Recalling that, under the Charter, all States enjoy sovereign equality and that each State, in accordance with the will of its people, has the right freely to choose and develop its political, social, economic and cultural systems,

Recognizing that there is no single political system or electoral method that is equally suited to all nations and their people and that the efforts of the international community to enhance the effectiveness of the principle of periodic and genuine elections should not call into question each State's sovereign right, in accordance with the will of its

---

b. See Franck, The Emerging Right to Democratic Governance, 86 Am.J.Int'l L. 46 (1992).

c. See G.A.Res. 45/2, 45 GAOR Supp. No. 49A (A/45/49), at 12 (1990).

d. See pages 385–86 supra.

people, freely to choose and develop its political, social, economic and cultural systems, whether or not they conform to the preferences of other States,

* * *

Taking note of the electoral assistance provided to Member States at their request by the Organization,

Affirming that electoral verification by the United Nations should remain an exceptional activity of the Organization to be undertaken in well-defined circumstances, *inter alia*, primarily in situations with a clear international dimension,

Taking note of the criteria contained in paragraph 79 of the Secretary-General's report which ought to be met before agreeing to requests for electoral verification,

1. *Takes note with appreciation* of the report of the Secretary-General on enhancing the effectiveness of the principle of periodic and genuine elections;

2. *Underscores* the significance of the Universal Declaration of Human Rights and the International Covenant on Civil and Political Rights, which establish that the authority to govern shall be based on the will of the people, as expressed in periodic and genuine elections;

3. *Stresses its conviction* that periodic and genuine elections are a necessary and indispensable element of sustained efforts to protect the rights and interests of the governed and that, as a matter of practical experience, the right of everyone to take part in the government of his or her country is a crucial factor in the effective enjoyment by all of a wide range of other human rights and fundamental freedoms, embracing political, economic, social and cultural rights;

4. *Declares* that determining the will of the people requires an electoral process that provides an equal opportunity for all citizens to become candidates and put forward their political views, individually and in cooperation with others, as provided in national constitutions and laws;

5. *Underscores* the duty of each Member State, in accordance with the provisions of the Charter of the United Nations, to respect the decisions taken by other States, in accordance with the will of their people, in freely choosing and developing their electoral institutions;

6. *Reaffirms* that apartheid must be abolished, that the systematic denial or abridgement of the right to vote on the grounds of race or colour is a gross violation of human rights and an affront to the conscience and dignity of mankind, and that the right to participate in a political system based on common and equal citizenship and universal franchise is essential for the exercise of the principle of periodic and genuine elections;

7. *Affirms* the value of the electoral assistance that the United Nations has provided at the request of some Member States, in the context of full respect for their sovereignty;

8. *Believes* that the international community should continue to give serious consideration to ways in which the United Nations can respond to the requests of Member States as they seek to promote and strengthen their electoral institutions and procedures;

9. *Endorses* the Secretary–General's view that he should designate a senior official in the Offices of the Secretary–General to act as a focal point, in addition to existing duties and in order to ensure consistency in the handling of requests of Member States organizing elections, who would assist the Secretary–General to coordinate and consider requests for electoral verification and to channel requests for electoral assistance to the appropriate office or programme, to ensure careful consideration of requests for electoral verification, to build on experience gained to develop an institutional memory, to develop and maintain a roster of international experts who could provide technical assistance as well as assist in the verification of electoral processes and to maintain contact with regional and other intergovernmental organizations to ensure appropriate working arrangements with them and the avoidance of duplication of efforts, and requests the Secretary–General to designate such an official to take on these tasks;

10. *Determines* that the designation of the senior official would neither pre-empt nor supersede ongoing arrangements regarding electoral assistance nor prejudice the operational arrangements for missions that the Organization may decide to undertake;

* * *

13. *Requests* the Secretary–General to notify the competent organ of the United Nations upon receipt of official requests by a Member State for electoral verification and, upon the direction of that organ, to provide appropriate assistance;

14. *Also requests* the Secretary–General to establish, in accordance with United Nations financial regulations, a voluntary trust fund for cases where the requesting Member State is unable to finance, in whole or in part, the electoral verification mission and to propose guidelines for disbursements therefrom;

15. *Affirms* the effectiveness of and the need for coordination with intergovernmental organizations, including regional organizations having international electoral assistance experience; * * *.

RESOLUTION ON RESPECT FOR NATIONAL SOVEREIGNTY AND NON-INTERFERENCE IN ELECTORAL PROCESSES

United Nations General Assembly, Dec. 17, 1991.
G.A.Res. 46/130, 46 GAOR Supp. No. 49 (A/46/49), at 202.

The General Assembly,

Reaffirming the purposes of the United Nations to develop friendly relations among nations based on respect for the principle of equal rights and self-determination of peoples and to take other appropriate measures to strengthen universal peace,

* * *

[*Recalling*] the principle enshrined in Article 2, paragraph 7, of the Charter of the United Nations, which establishes that nothing contained in the Charter shall authorize the United Nations to intervene in matters which are essentially within the domestic jurisdiction of any State or shall require the Members to submit such matters to settlement under the Charter,

* * *

Recognizing that the principles of national sovereignty and non-interference in the internal affairs of any State should be respected in the holding of elections,

Also recognizing that there is no single political system or single model for electoral processes equally suited to all nations and their peoples, and that political systems and electoral processes are subject to historical, political, cultural and religious factors,

* * *

1. *Reiterates* that, by virtue of the principle of equal rights and self-determination of peoples enshrined in the Charter of the United Nations, all peoples have the right, freely and without external interference, to determine their political status and to pursue their economic, social and cultural development, and that every State has the duty to respect that right in accordance with the provisions of the Charter;

2. *Reaffirms* that it is the concern solely of peoples to determine methods and to establish institutions regarding the electoral process, as well as to determine the ways for its implementation according to their constitutional and national legislation;

3. *Also reaffirms* that any activities that attempt, directly or indirectly, to interfere in the free development of national electoral processes, in particular in the developing countries, or that intend to sway the results of such processes, violate the spirit and letter of the principles established in the Charter and in the Declaration on Principles of International Law concerning Friendly Relations and Cooperation among States in accordance with the Charter of the United Nations;

4. *Recognizes* that there is no universal need for the United Nations to provide electoral assistance to Member States, except in special circumstances such as cases of decolonization, in the context of regional or international peace processes or at the request of specific sovereign States, by virtue of resolutions adopted by the Security Council or the General Assembly in each individual case, in strict conformity with the principles of sovereignty and non-interference in the internal affairs of States; * * *.

THE U.N., ELECTIONS AND SOVEREIGNTY

In light of article 21 of the Universal Declaration and article 25 of the Covenant on Civil and Political Rights, supra, can it legitimately be said—as Resolution 46/130 does—that it is the concern solely of peoples to determine matters regarding the electoral process, according to their constitutional and national legislation? What peoples would these be?

Is the principle of periodic and genuine elections, as embodied in Resolution 46/137, grounded in the human rights provisions of the Charter (*articles 1(3), 55* and *56*), or in a more general peacemaking authority which, as Brian Urquhart said about peacekeeping, "was discovered, like penicillin"? Or is it grounded in some mixture of the two? In this connection, note the legal justification given by the United States, at pages 822–23 supra.

Which provisions of Resolution 46/137 might raise issues under U.N. Charter *article 2(7)*? How serious are those issues?

Paragraph 4 of Resolution 46/130 reflects concerns of the sort voiced by China, and to some extent by Peru. Among other things, it says that there is no universal need for the United Nations to provide electoral assistance to member states. Does the other resolution—Resolution 46/137—assert (or assume) that there is such a universal need?

Peru expressed a preference for a regional response to the call for periodic and genuine elections, in cooperation with the U.N. So did the United States, when it said that the U.N. should focus primarily on providing assistance when regional organizations are unable to meet the need. Is this covered by *Chapter VIII* of the U.N. Charter? Is it a good idea? Did Resolution 46/137 heed this advice?

Resolution 46/137 took note of the criteria in paragraph 79 of the Secretary–General's report. That paragraph says:

79. While I consider it important for the United Nations to continue to use its discretion in deciding how to respond to requests for electoral verification and to decide on a case-by-case basis, I believe that certain criteria, along the lines of those I mentioned in my 1990 report on the work of the Organization, ought to be met before agreeing to such requests. Namely, requests should pertain

primarily to situations with a clear international dimension; the monitoring of an election or referendum should cover the entire electoral process in order to secure conditions of fairness and impartiality; where the induction of a United Nations presence in the electoral process of a State at a critical point in its political life is sought by the Government concerned, there must be broad public support in the State for the United Nations assuming such a role; and, finally, there should be approval by the competent organ of the United Nations.[e]

Compare the criteria set forth by the United States, at page 823 supra. Are those criteria and the Secretary-General's the same?

Both the Secretary-General and the preamble to Resolution 46/137 said that requests should pertain primarily to situations with a clear international dimension. What does that mean?

The United States suggested that the General Assembly give blanket authority to the Secretary-General to respond to requests for election observation unless there is a threat to international peace and security, in which case the Security Council would approve each mission. The Secretary-General simply said that "there should be approval by the competent organ of the United Nations." Did Resolution 46/137 give blanket approval for election monitoring in situations not involving threats to peace and security?

Could the Secretary-General be the "competent organ"? See U.N. Charter *article 7(1)*.

Between October 1, 1991 and September 30, 1992, the U.N. received 31 requests for technical assistance in organizing elections.[f] Could the Secretary-General respond favorably on his own authority to that type of request, not involving election monitoring, even if he were not the "competent organ" to approve a monitoring request?

Can the concerns of the proponents of Resolutions 46/130 and 46/137 be reconciled? If so, how?

In December 1991, the General Assembly adopted, without a vote, a resolution noting the assurances of the military government of Myanmar (Burma) to establish a democratic state, and urging it to "allow all citizens to participate freely in the political process in accordance with the principles of the Universal Declaration of Human Rights."[g] Is this what the proponents of Resolution 46/130 were concerned about? Did it contravene article 2(7)?

In "An Agenda for Peace," Secretary-General Boutros Boutros-Ghali noted the need for strong domestic institutions with participation of the people. "Promoting such institutions means promoting the empowerment of the unorganized, the poor, the marginalized." To further this end, he proposed strengthening U.N. activities in the field.

e. U.N. Doc. A/46/609, at 25 (1991).
f. See U.N. Doc. A/47/668 (1992).
g. G.A.Res. 46/132, 46 GAOR Supp. No. 49 (A/46/49), at 205 (1991).

He said, "The senior United Nations official in each country should be prepared to serve, when needed, and with the consent of the host authorities, as my Representative on matters of particular concern."[h] The Non-Aligned Movement responded: "The Secretary-General's idea that the senior U.N. official in each country would become his representative on matters of particular concern finds no support with the Movement."[i] Why not? Would there be a violation of sovereignty, even if the consent of host authorities is obtained?

What is the prognosis for U.N. participation in, and promotion of, national democratic processes?

G. PEACEMAKING, MAINLY BY THE SECRETARY-GENERAL

INTRODUCTORY NOTE

This Chapter has already examined several peacekeeping and peacemaking roles of the Secretary-General. These have ranged from the role of chief peacekeeping executive trying to maintain often-precarious ceasefires, to the role of organizer and supervisor of election monitoring teams in politically fragile settings. In all of these circumstances, questions have arisen as to the source and extent of his authority. Similar questions arise in connection with two additional roles that are likely to assume increasing importance in the 1990s and into the next century: fact-finding, on an ad hoc basis or as part of an early warning system, to try to head off international disputes or defuse them before they turn violent; and the use of good offices to try to help disputants find peaceful solutions. Sometimes these roles are performed in contexts other than peacemaking, as in the case of preparations for foreseeable natural disasters, but the focus in this Section is on the peacemaking function.

1. *Fact-Finding and Early Warning*

In Nicaragua, the Secretary-General engaged in preliminary fact-finding before he recommended establishment of the peacekeeping force (ONUCA), and again before he recommended establishment of the election observer mission (ONUVEN). He did much the same thing before the U.N. Transitional Authority in Cambodia (UNTAC) was established.[a] Similar efforts were undertaken by Cyrus Vance, his personal representative, in Yugoslavia in order to lay the groundwork for UNPROFOR.

On other occasions, he has sent fact-finding missions to trouble spots without necessarily contemplating the creation of a new U.N.

---

h. U.N.Doc. A/47/277–S/24111, at 23 (1992).

i. Informal paper of the Non-Aligned Movement, 3 Int'l Docs. Rev., No. 30, at 3, 6 (1992).

a. See Bourloyannis, Fact-Finding by the Secretary-General of the United Nations, 22 N.Y.U.J. Int'l L. & Pol. 641, 650–51 (1990).

operation. For example, in March 1992 he sent Mr. Vance to Armenia and Azerbaijan to gather information about the conflict in Nagorno–Karabakh. In each case he has obtained the consent of the host government before sending in his fact-finding representatives.

It has been said that when the Secretary–General investigates in order to provide a basis for settling an ongoing disturbance or crisis, his authority is based on U.N. Charter *article 99;* but when he gathers information for future U.N. activities he acts under *article 98*.[b] Does either of these articles, standing alone, authorize fact-finding missions? How about *article 97,* which designates him as the chief administrative officer of the Organization?

Early in U.N. practice, the question arose whether the Secretary–General's powers under article 99 included fact-gathering. In 1946, when the Security Council was discussing a proposal to establish a three-person commission to gather information regarding the Greek frontier situation, Secretary–General Trygve Lie said to the Council that if the proposal were not adopted, "I hope that the Council will understand that the Secretary–General must reserve his right to make such enquiries or investigations as he may think necessary, in order to determine whether or not he should consider bringing any aspect of this matter to the attention of the Council under the provisions of the Charter."[c] No member of the Security Council challenged him.[d]

Since then, Secretaries–General have "consistently asserted * * * the right to conduct fact-finding on [their] own authority pursuant to Article 99."[e] The Security Council has never objected.[f] Sometimes, however, the Security Council has taken the initiative and has itself authorized fact-finding missions. This can apply some pressure on parties to settle a dispute, by bringing home to them that the Council "is actively seized of the matter as a present or potential threat to international security."[g]

Is there any question about the Secretary–General's fact-finding authority under the terms of article 99? Note that it could lead to further fact-finding and other involvement by the Security Council, as indicated just above.

The Secretary–General gathers facts not only by sending his own representatives and missions on special assignments, but also by more

---

b. Id. at 650.

c. 1 SCOR, 2d ser., 70th mtg., at 404 (1946).

d. See S. Schwebel, The Secretary–General of the United Nations: His Political Power and Practice 90 (1952); T. Boudreau, Sheathing the Sword: The U.N. Secretary–General and the Prevention of International Conflict 33 (1991).

e. Elaraby, The Office of the Secretary–General and the Maintenance of International Peace and Security, in The United Nations and the Maintenance of International Peace and Security 177, 194 (UNITAR, 1987).

f. See Szasz, The Role of the U.N. Secretary–General: Some Legal Aspects, 24 N.Y.U.J. Int'l L. & Pol. 161, 187 (1991).

g. Boutros–Ghali, An Agenda for Peace, U.N. Doc. A/47/277–S/24111, at 7 (1992).

routine methods. U.N. Information Offices in cities around the world not only dispense information about the U.N. (their announced *raison d'être*), but also collect publicly-available information and forward it to U.N. headquarters in New York.[h] In addition, resident representatives of various U.N. bodies, such as UNICEF and the U.N. Development Program (UNDP) have supplied publicly-available information from their postings.

Under Javier Pérez de Cuéllar, an office was created at U.N. headquarters to enable staff members to collect the information systematically, and do such things as assess global trends, prepare country and regional profiles, provide early warning of situations requiring the Secretary–General's attention, keep track of possible refugee flows, and carry out research needed by the Secretary–General. These steps have been taken, in large part, in order to enable the Secretary–General to bring potentially dangerous situations to the attention of the Security Council under article 99.[i] They also serve as early warning systems for humanitarian emergencies, whether human-induced or not, and for the prevention or amelioration of natural disasters.[j]

Some of these information-compiling functions are potentially controversial. For example, some governments may be sensitive about having the Secretariat prepare politically-relevant profiles of their countries. It has been suggested that the solution is to prepare regional or subregional profiles, instead of country-specific ones, to ensure "that analysis of incoming information can proceed without violating Article 2, Paragraph 7, of the UN Charter."[k] Would the preparation of country-specific profiles violate *article 2(7)*? If so, would preparation instead of regional ones ensure that there is no violation?

Are the information-gathering activities of U.N. Information Offices legally justifiable when host governments originally consented to them as information-disseminating centers? What about the information-gathering activities of a resident UNDP representative, when the information has to do with a possible threat to the peace?

Is any legal objection obviated if these U.N. personnel gather only public information? Is any objection obviated by the silent acquiescence of host governments?

Secretaries–General have not considered the available channels of information adequate. Trygve Lie and Kurt Waldheim both proposed stationing U.N. ambassadors in the capitals of some member states,

h. Elaraby, supra note e, at 665–66.

i. See the 1982 Report of the Secretary–General on the Work of the Organization, 37 GAOR Supp. No. 1 (A/37/1), at 3, which foreshadowed the development of systematic fact-gathering and early-warning functions.

j. See generally B. Ramcharan, The International Law and Practice of Early–Warning and Preventive Diplomacy: The Emerging Global Watch (1991).

k. T. Boudreau, Sheathing the Sword: The U.N. Secretary–General and the Pre-

with a mandate to gather facts.[1] Javier Pérez de Cuéllar elaborated the need:

> In order to activate the potential of the Organization for averting wars, the necessity of earlier discussion of situations threatening to explode needs to be clearly recognized. Timely, accurate and unbiased information is a prerequisite for that purpose. At present, the pool of material available to the Secretary-General consists of information provided by government representatives supplemented by the collection and analyses of published reports and comments. This is manifestly insufficient in cases where more than anticipatory diplomacy is required. Even for such measures as the establishment of observation posts or the dispatch of fact-finding teams, not to speak of the appointment of military observer missions in situations where fighting appears imminent, the Secretary-General needs to have at his disposal information that is dependable *prima facie,* even though it might be subject to further inquiry or verification. Only then can he be in a position to assess whether and when an issue needs to be brought to the attention of the Security Council under Article 99 of the Charter. The invocation of this Article is discretionary and the discretion has to be exercised with a most careful consideration of its possible outcome. There are situations where quiet diplomacy can be more effective in moderating a conflict. In any case, the lack or paucity of objective information can have most deleterious results. But in a setting in which incipient conflicts are under a global watch, there will be less likelihood of confusion and, therefore, of indecision on the part of the Security Council in the matter of halting their escalation. Arrangements, for instance, could be made to receive information from space-based and other technical surveillance systems, which would enable the Secretariat to monitor potential conflict situations from a clearly impartial standpoint, but the question is whether the potential of modern technology can be placed in the service of peace.[m]

Whose space-based surveillance systems did he have in mind? If the Secretary-General would have to rely on the surveillance systems of the United States government (or of any other government), would U.N. Charter *article 100* be compromised?

Would consent have to be obtained from every state that might be monitored? Or could the Security Council adopt a resolution under *article 24,* making it mandatory under *article 25,* to the effect that this

vention of International Conflict 119 (1991).

l. See Franck, The Good Offices Function of the UN Secretary-General, in United Nations, Divided World 79, 92 (A. Roberts & B. Kingsbury eds. 1988).

m. Report of the Secretary-General on the Work of the Organization, 44 GAOR Supp. No. 1 (A/44/1), at 5 (1989).

type of surveillance shall be undertaken?" [n]

Without being specific, the General Assembly in 1992 encouraged the Secretary-General to set up an early-warning mechanism, and asked member states to provide him with any expertise and logistical resources he might need for preventive diplomacy.[o]

For several years the Special Committee on the Charter of the United Nations struggled with preparing a draft declaration on fact-finding, to be presented to the General Assembly for its adoption. Only after the cold war ended was the Special Committee able to reach a consensus. Finally, in 1991 it submitted a draft declaration which the General Assembly adopted.

DECLARATION ON FACT–FINDING BY THE UNITED NATIONS IN THE FIELD OF THE MAINTENANCE OF INTERNATIONAL PEACE AND SECURITY

United Nations General Assembly, Dec. 9, 1991.
G.A. Res. 46/59, Annex, 46 GAOR Supp. No. 49 (A/46/49), at 290.

The General Assembly,

* * *

Emphasizing that the ability of the United Nations to maintain international peace and security depends to a large extent on its acquiring detailed knowledge about the factual circumstances of any dispute or situation, the continuance of which might threaten the maintenance of international peace and security (hereinafter, "disputes or situations"),

* * *

Recognizing the need for States, in exercising their sovereignty, to cooperate with the relevant organs of the United Nations as regards fact-finding missions undertaken by them,

Seeking to contribute to the effectiveness of the United Nations, with a view to enhancing mutual understanding, trust and stability in the world,

Solemnly declares that:

I

1. In performing their functions in relation to the maintenance of international peace and security, the competent organs of the United

---

n. Secretary–General Boutros–Ghali, discussing fact-finding in his report to the Security Council, An Agenda for Peace, did not mention surveillance systems of the sort contemplated by former Secretary-General Pérez de Cuéllar. See U.N. Doc. A/47/277–S/24111, at 7–8 (1992).

o. G.A.Res. 47/120 (1992).

Nations should endeavour to have full knowledge of all relevant facts. To this end they should consider undertaking fact-finding activities.

2. For the purpose of the present Declaration fact-finding means any activity designed to obtain detailed knowledge of the relevant facts of any dispute or situation which the competent United Nations organs need in order to exercise effectively their functions in relation to the maintenance of international peace and security.

3. Fact-finding should be comprehensive, objective, impartial and timely.

4. Unless a satisfactory knowledge of all relevant facts can be obtained through the use of the information-gathering capabilities of the Secretary–General or other existing means, the competent organ of the United Nations should consider resorting to a fact-finding mission.

5. In deciding if and when to undertake such a mission, the competent United Nations organs should bear in mind that the sending of a fact-finding mission can signal the concern of the Organization and should contribute to building confidence and defusing the dispute or situation while avoiding any aggravation of it.

6. The sending of a United Nations fact-finding mission to the territory of any State requires the prior consent of that State, subject to the relevant provisions of the Charter of the United Nations.

II

7. Fact-finding missions may be undertaken by the Security Council, the General Assembly and the Secretary–General, in the context of their respective responsibilities for the maintenance of international peace and security in accordance with the Charter.

8. The Security Council should consider the possibility of undertaking fact-finding to discharge effectively its primary responsibility for the maintenance of international peace and security in accordance with the Charter.

9. The Security Council should, wherever appropriate, consider the possibility of providing in its resolutions for recourse to fact-finding.

10. The General Assembly should consider the possibility of undertaking fact-finding for exercising effectively its responsibilities under the Charter for the maintenance of international peace and security.

11. The General Assembly should, wherever appropriate, consider the possibility of providing for recourse to fact-finding in its resolutions relevant to the maintenance of international peace and security.

12. The Secretary–General should pay special attention to using the United Nations fact-finding capabilities at an early stage in order to contribute to the prevention of disputes and situations.

13. The Secretary–General, on his own initiative or at the request of the States concerned, should consider undertaking a fact-finding mission when a dispute or a situation exists.

14. The Secretary–General should prepare and update lists of experts in various fields who would be available for fact-finding missions. He should also maintain and develop, within existing resources, capabilities for mounting emergency fact-finding missions.

15. The Security Council and the General Assembly should, in deciding to whom to entrust the conduct of a fact-finding mission, give preference to the Secretary–General, who may, inter alia, designate a special representative or a group of experts reporting to him. Resort to an ad hoc subsidiary body of the Security Council or the General Assembly may also be considered.

16. In considering the possibility of undertaking a fact-finding mission, the competent United Nations organ should bear in mind other relevant fact-finding efforts, including those undertaken by the States concerned and in the framework of regional arrangements or agencies.

17. The decision by the competent United Nations organ to undertake fact-finding should always contain a clear mandate for the fact-finding mission and precise requirements to be met by its report. The report should be limited to a presentation of findings of a factual nature.

18. Any request by a State to a competent organ of the United Nations for the sending of a United Nations fact-finding mission to its territory should be considered without undue delay.

III

19. Any request by a competent organ of the United Nations for the consent of a State to receive a fact-finding mission within its territory should be given timely consideration by that State. That State should inform the organ of its decision without delay.

20. In the event a State decides not to admit a United Nations fact-finding mission to its territory, it should, if it deems it appropriate, indicate the reasons for its decision. It should also keep the possibility of admitting the fact-finding mission under review.

21. States should endeavour to follow a policy of admitting United Nations fact-finding missions to their territory.

22. States should cooperate with United Nations fact-finding missions and give them, within the limits of their capabilities, the full and prompt assistance necessary for the exercise of their functions and the fulfilment of their mandate.

23. Fact-finding missions should be accorded all immunities and facilities needed for discharging their mandate, in particular full confidentiality in their work and access to all relevant places and persons, it being understood that no harmful consequences will result to these

persons. Fact-finding missions have an obligation to respect the laws and regulations of the State in which they exercise their functions; such laws and regulations should not however be applied in such a way as to hinder missions in the proper discharge of their functions.

24. The members of fact-finding missions, as a minimum, enjoy the privileges and immunities accorded to experts on missions by the Convention on the Privileges and Immunities of the United Nations. Without prejudice to their privileges and immunities, members of fact-finding missions have an obligation to respect the laws and regulations of the State in the territory in which they exercise their functions.

25. Fact-finding missions have an obligation to act in strict conformity with their mandate and perform their task in an impartial way. Their members have an obligation not to seek or receive instructions from any Government or from any authority other than the competent United Nations organ. They should keep the information acquired in discharging their mandate confidential even after the mission has fulfilled its task.

26. The States directly concerned should be given an opportunity, at all stages of the fact-finding process, to express their views in respect of the facts the fact-finding mission has been entrusted to obtain. When the results of fact-finding are to be made public, the views expressed by the States directly concerned should, if they so wish, also be made public.

27. Whenever fact-finding includes hearings, appropriate rules of procedure should ensure their fairness.

IV

28. The Secretary-General should monitor the state of international peace and security regularly and systematically in order to provide early warning of disputes or situations which might threaten international peace and security. The Secretary-General may bring relevant information to the attention of the Security Council and, where appropriate, of the General Assembly.

29. To this end, the Secretary-General should make full use of the information-gathering capabilities of the Secretariat and keep under review the improvement of these capabilities.

V

30. The sending of a United Nations fact-finding mission is without prejudice to the use by the States concerned of inquiry or any similar procedure or of any means of peaceful settlement of disputes agreed by them.

31. Nothing in the present Declaration is to be construed as prejudicing in any manner the provisions of the Charter.

FACT–FINDING UNDER THE DECLARATION

Under paragraph 6 of the Declaration, a state would have to consent before a fact-finding mission could be sent into its territory, "subject to the relevant provisions of the Charter." What provisions might be relevant?

Do paragraphs 12 and 13 add anything to the Secretary–General's authority under U.N. Charter *article 99*?

Why should the Security Council and General Assembly give preference to the Secretary–General to conduct fact-finding missions (paragraph 15)?

In July 1992, the Security Council in Resolution 765 decided to send a special envoy to South Africa to investigate incidents of violence that had impeded negotiations aimed at creating a representative democracy in that country, and to make recommendations. Resolution 772, in August 1992, authorized the deployment of U.N. observers. Although there had been serious disturbances of the peace within townships in South Africa and charges of police complicity in the violence, the trouble appeared to be contained within South Africa and not instigated from outside. All interested parties in South Africa consented to the Security Council's decisions. That presumably took care of any article 2(7) problem. Did it remove all possible objections based on the Security Council's role as stated in *article 24(1)*: the maintenance of international peace and security? (Note also paragraph 8 of the General Assembly's Declaration.) Does *article 34* resolve this issue?

Paragraph 17 of the Declaration says that a fact-finding report "should be limited to a presentation of findings of a factual nature." Resolution 765 contemplated a report with recommendations as well as findings of fact. Is there any reason why fact-finding missions should be limited to "findings of a factual nature"? Do *articles 36–38* of the Charter contemplate more than that, when the Security Council gets involved?

Suppose the Security Council considers a situation, takes no action, and remains seized of it. If the General Assembly then requests a member state to receive a Secretariat fact-finding mission on that situation, could the state plausibly assert that the request does not come from a "competent organ," in light of U.N. Charter *article 12(1)*? Would such a request actually contravene that provision?

Does paragraph 20 place full discretion in a nonconsenting state to refuse to give reasons for its decision? Why should it have any discretion at all to withhold its reasons?

Under paragraph 23, fact-finding missions should be given access to all relevant persons, "it being understood that no harmful consequences will result to these persons." Is that adequate protection for persons who might have information tending to put their government in a bad light? Could anything further be done to protect them?

Suppose a fact-finding mission, having received the government's consent, becomes too intrusive to suit the government's taste. Could it order the mission out? See paragraphs 24 and 25, and see General Convention on the Privileges and Immunities of the United Nations, *section 22.*

Under paragraph 26, states directly concerned should be given an opportunity to express their views at all stages, which presumably would include the final stage when a report is being prepared. It has been argued that this will hinder the Secretary–General's fact-finding role, at least if the mission is being conducted under article 99 in order to help the Secretary–General form an opinion on whether there is a threat to international peace and security.[p] Why might that be so? Does basic fairness, or political reality, nevertheless dictate that governments be given the opportunity to express their views?

Do paragraphs 28 and 29 put to rest any legitimate objections by host governments to information-gathering by U.N. Information Offices or resident representatives of U.N. bodies?

What provisions of the Charter might have been "prejudiced," were it not for paragraph 31? *Could* any provisions of the Charter be prejudiced by a General Assembly resolution?

The Declaration on Fact–Finding sets out the purposes of fact-finding only in broad terms, in the preamble. Among the purposes would be assisting the Security Council to perform its dispute-settlement functions under Chapter VI of the Charter and, in some cases, assisting the General Assembly to perform its functions under *article 11.* Another purpose, as these materials have already indicated, could be to set the stage for a peacekeeping operation.

How would you expect U.N. fact-finding and early warning activities to develop in the foreseeable future? One area that has been suggested as appropriate for U.N. specialized fact-finding is disarmament, where U.N.-appointed multilateral inspection teams could provide a politically acceptable means of verifying compliance with arms-reduction agreements.[q]

Is the Declaration on Fact–Finding an important step in the development of fact-finding and early warning activities—and in the development of the peacemaking function of the United Nations?

---

p. Bourloyannis, supra note a, at 661.

q. See A Successor Vision: The United Nations of Tomorrow 98–99 (UNA–USA Panel Rep.1987).

2. Good Offices

Good offices by the Secretary–General are "the informal contacts and friendly suggestions made as far as circumstances allow by the Secretary–General which are designed to facilitate the settlement of a dispute between two or several of the Organization's Member States. * * * Good offices in a strict sense seek to reduce acute tensions, provide communication bridges, bring the parties to the negotiating table, and negotiate practical arrangements that would remove underlying causes of friction or alleviate the human suffering or material damage that all too often accompanies conflict." [a]

As put more recently by Javier Pérez de Cuéllar toward the end of his time in office:

> Good offices and related peace-making activities, such as special missions, constitute the fundamental means whereby the Secretary–General fulfils his political role. As such, they are intrinsic to the manner in which the Secretary–General carries out his responsibilities on a daily basis. Such activities by the Secretary–General are undertaken at the request of the Security Council or the General Assembly, at the request of States, or on the initiative of the Secretary–General within the framework of his responsibilities under Article 99 of the Charter. The fundamental objective of the Secretary–General in the discharge of his good offices is to assist States involved in disputes or conflicts to resolve their differences peacefully in accordance with the principles of the Charter of the United Nations and, wherever possible, to prevent conflicts from arising.[b]

Although the Charter does not spell out the good offices role, it was foreseen in the infancy of the organization. The Preparatory Commission, established at the end of the 1945 San Francisco Conference to begin making preparations for the new organization, had this to say:

> The Secretary–General may have an important role to play as a mediator and as an informal adviser of many governments, and will undoubtedly be called upon from time to time, in the exercise of his administrative duties, to take decisions which may justly be called political. Under Article 99 of the Charter, moreover, he has been given a quite special right which goes beyond any power previously accorded to the head of an international organization, viz: to bring to the attention of the Security Council any matter (not merely any dispute or situation) which, in his opinion, may threaten the maintenance of international peace and security. It is impossible to foresee how this Article will be applied; but the responsibility it confers upon the Secretary–General will require

---

a. V. Pechota, The Quiet Approach: A Study of the Good Offices Exercised by the United Nations Secretary–General in the Cause of Peace (UNITAR study, 1972), reprinted in Dispute Settlement Through the United Nations 577, 578 & 647 (K. Raman ed. 1977).

b. Medium–Term Plan for the Period 1992–1997, vol. I, 45 GAOR Supp. No. 6 (A/45/6/Rev.1), at 21–22 (1991).

the exercise of the highest qualities of political judgment, tact and integrity.[c]

In practice, the qualities mentioned in 1945 have proven to be essential to the good offices role. The Secretary–General has had to determine whether the political situation was such as to enable his good offices to be effective, before putting his position on the line. He has had to deal with governments sensitive about their sovereignty and about wrongs allegedly committed against them. And he has had to maintain absolute integrity, including impartiality in fact and in appearance.

Writing in 1972, a research fellow at the U.N. Institute for Training and Research (UNITAR) and former chair of the General Assembly's Sixth (Legal) Committee identified four ways in which the Secretary–General exercises his good offices function.

V. PECHOTA, THE QUIET APPROACH: A STUDY OF THE GOOD OFFICES EXERCISED BY THE UNITED NATIONS SECRETARY–GENERAL IN THE CAUSE OF PEACE

UNITAR Study, 1972.
Reprinted in Dispute Settlement Through the United Nations 577, 595–96 (K. Raman ed. 1977).*

The distinctive nature of the Secretary–General's good offices can best be illustrated by classifying them in the following ways. The first type comprises the most rudimentary forms of diplomatic assistance, such as informal contacts and consultations with a view to exposing each side to the other's attitudes and claims, and facilitating communications between them. This type of good offices could be regarded as a part of the harmonizing functions set out in Article 1, paragraph 4 of the Charter, which is applicable to all United Nations organs, including the Secretary–General. It is the least visible type and one which cannot easily be distinguished from the Secretary–General's day-to-day diplomatic activities, particularly those designed to maintain a certain level of political relations and interaction between the Secretary–General and individual Governments. Emphasis here is on understanding as the basis for action, particularly understanding among the permanent members of the Security Council.

* * *

The second type consists of diplomatic action designed to express international concern, to coax the parties into talks before a favourable atmosphere fades away or before they reach a point of no return, and to assist them in finding a suitable framework for settlement. This type of activity stands closest to the traditional concept of good offices. The

---

[c]. Report of the Preparatory Comm., U.N.Doc. PC/20, Ch. VIII, § 2, ¶ 16 (1945), reprinted in L. Gordenker, The UN Secretary–General and the Maintenance of Peace 343–44 (1967).

* Reprinted by permission of UNITAR.

assistance rendered by the Secretary–General is basically confined to moves essential to bringing the parties to a negotiating table and to help make their talks run smoothly.

The third type consists of all kinds of mediation, conciliation and co-ordination. This type of activity is not dissimilar to international mediation which consists in reconciling opposing claims and in appeasing feelings of resentment that might arise between States at variance. If circumstances warrant, the Secretary–General may take a further step and assume the role of international conciliator carrying out an impartial examination of claims and attempting to define the terms of settlement acceptable to the parties, or affording them any other aid they request in reaching a compromise. Also included in this category are various activities aimed at assisting the parties in alleviating human sufferings or easing other burdens such as refugee problems entailed in certain conflicts. Such activities can hardly be described as good offices in the usual meaning of the term.

The fourth type is fairly well defined and consists of enquiries, fact-finding, the supervision of plebiscites or other acts of choice and the determination of legal rights and duties in a specific issue. Most of these activities are executive in nature and introduce elements of international administration into a disputed situation. The Secretary–General must bring together a capable international team to perform these tasks and assume full responsibility for all of the political and administrative details.

SOME EXAMPLES

A close observer of the U.N. Secretariat has given illustrations of the Secretary–General's good offices role. Four of them are set forth in this excerpt:

FRANCK, THE GOOD OFFICES FUNCTION OF THE UN SECRETARY–GENERAL
United Nations, Divided World 79, 80–83
(A. Roberts & B. Kingsbury eds. 1988).*

1. Cyprus

In the more than twenty-year-old conflict between ethnic Turkish and Greek communities in Cyprus, the Secretary–General remains the only person currently engaged in active efforts to prevent a renewal of bloodshed. In addition, he has mediated between the parties in an effort to begin direct negotiations towards a constitutional formula that would resolve the communal crisis through an agreed-upon confederal structure of government. Early in 1986, after presenting a new set of

---

* Reprinted by permission of Oxford University Press.

proposals to the leaders of both communities, he appeared on the verge of success, at least to the extent that both parties' leaders accepted in principle the parameters for negotiating a confederal solution. That these were later repudiated by the second tier of the Greek Cypriot political establishment merely means that the effort will have to be resumed, for there is no alternative to a negotiated solution and no alternative to the Secretary–General as convener of such face-to-face negotiations.

2. THE RAINBOW WARRIOR DISPUTE

Quite a different facet of the "good offices" function is revealed by the role of the Secretary–General, in summer 1986, in resolving the *Rainbow Warrior* dispute between New Zealand and France. That conflict was occasioned by the role of French agents in the death of a Dutch citizen aboard the *Rainbow Warrior* and the demolition of that vessel as it was intending to make itself hostage to French Pacific nuclear tests in Mururoa Atoll. Two French agents were captured by New Zealand authorities and sentenced to ten-year prison terms. So acrimonious had the dispute become that it threatened to thwart European Common Market operations because of French retaliation against New Zealand agricultural products. New Zealand lambs' brains, for example, were being subject to extraordinary health checks by the French authorities. There were *sotto voce* threats to cut the New Zealand butter quota.

It was the Dutch government which proposed to the parties that they seek a solution on the 38th floor of the UN Secretariat. As a consequence, on 19 June 1986, the office of Secretary–General was inducted to arbitrate certain differences between the parties and, equally important, to legitimize the compromise that would terminate the dispute. In this instance, the Secretary–General acted as a quasi-arbitrator. The parties made a written submission in which they outlined the problem, the elements of a solution they had already negotiated, and indicated remaining aspects of the dispute which they had been unable to resolve. They also agreed, in advance, to treat the Secretary–General's decisions as binding. The Secretary–General then addressed written enquiries to the parties, and produced a written proposal which the parties, as agreed, have implemented.[1] It involved a formal apology by France to New Zealand, the payment of US$7 million in compensation, and the release of the two French agents to French custody on the understanding that they would serve three years "on assignment" to a totally isolated post on the French island of Hao in Polynesia. France was also to undertake not to try to restrict New Zealand butter, mutton, and goat meat trade with the European Community.

---

1. The text of the UN Secretary–General's ruling of 6 July 1986 on the *Rainbow Warrior* affair is published in *American Journal of International Law,* 81 (1987), p. 325.

This solution is not without critics in both countries, but it proved much more acceptable—precisely because of its unimpeachable source—than would have been the same, or any other, solution arrived at solely by the parties themselves. Neither government could now be accused by its internal critics of having yielded to the other. Thus, both arbitration and legitimization entered into the Secretary–General's role.

3. Western Sahara

Also in the summer of 1986, the Secretary–General illustrated the "quiet diplomacy" aspect of his good offices function by his visit to King Hassan II of Morocco. They discussed the ultimate discharge of Morocco's obligation to give self-determination to the people of the Western Sahara in accordance with the Charter, an advisory opinion of the International Court of Justice, and resolutions of the General Assembly. The Secretary–General's principal advisers, who accompanied him on this mission, returned feeling considerable optimism about the degree of agreement on future steps to resolve a conflict which has not only divided Morocco and Algeria, but which has traumatized the Organization of African Unity and continues to engender considerable loss of life. With the OAU effectively out of action on the issue, the Secretary–General has stepped into the void to resume negotiations, being, once again, the "only ballgame in town".

4. Afghanistan

In a somewhat different kind of diplomatic enterprise, the Secretary–General has appointed one of his Under–Secretaries–General, Diego Cordovez, to serve as his personal representative in negotiations between Pakistan, the Soviet Union, and Afghanistan on modalities for the removal of Soviet troops from Afghanistan. UN efforts towards a negotiated settlement have continued since 1980; and by 1986 the resulting "proximity talks" had drawn up an agreed framework for three of the projected four elements of a settlement. * * * The negotiations have been conducted by shuttling between the capitals of Afghanistan and Pakistan, and between separate rooms allotted to the parties, simultaneously, in the Geneva headquarters of the UN.[d]

THE LEGAL BASIS FOR GOOD OFFICES

As has been noted above, *article 99* has been cited as a source of the Secretary–General's good offices authority. Other sources have been

---

d. [After Professor Franck had written the above description of peace efforts in Afghanistan, a settlement was reached. An agreement between Afghanistan and Pakistan included this provision: "A representative of the Secretary-General of the United Nations shall lend his good offices to the Parties and in that context he will assist in the organization of the meetings and participate in them. He may submit to the Parties for their consideration and approval suggestions and recommendations for prompt, faithful and complete observance of the provisions of the instruments." U.N. Doc. S/19835, at 12 (1988). Ed.]

suggested as well: (a) diplomatic powers inherent in the office of Secretary–General necessarily give him discretion to preserve peace and security by assisting states to iron out their differences; (b) since the International Court of Justice said that U.N. members "by entrusting certain functions to [the U.N.], with the attendant duties and responsibilities, have clothed it with the competence required to enable those functions to be effectively discharged," [e] by analogy the members, having entrusted the Secretary–General with upholding the purposes and principles of the U.N., have clothed him with the competence required to enable him to discharge that function; (c) the parties to a dispute, seeking to settle it peacefully as contemplated by *article 33* of the Charter, may empower the Secretary–General to lend his good offices wholly apart from any authority the Charter might give him.[f]

Are all of these arguments, including the one based on article 99, sound?

There are occasions when the Secretary–General does not think it useful to get the Security Council involved. Consider U Thant's response to an assertion in 1970 that he had failed to consult the Security Council before offering his good offices in a dispute involving Bahrain:

> From time to time, as in the present case affecting Bahrain, Member States of the United Nations approach the Secretary–General directly asking for the exercise of his good offices on a delicate matter. They explain that they do so because they feel that a difference between them may be capable of an amicable solution if dealt with at an early stage quietly and diplomatically and, therefore, it would be inadvisable to take the particular matter before the Security Council or to consult its members individually on it. They express the wish to have the matter worked out through the good offices of the Secretary–General on a completely confidential basis. In all such cases the Secretary–General, naturally, examines the proposals carefully. If those proposals are fully consistent with the principles and purposes of the United Nations Charter, and if they in no way impinge upon the authority of the Security Council or any other organ of the United Nations, he unavoidably feels obligated to afford the Member States the assistance in the manner requested. To do otherwise would be to thwart a commendable effort by these Member States to abide by a cardinal principle of the Organization, namely, the peaceful settlement of disputes.[g]

In such cases, could the Secretary–General rely on article 99 for his authority? If not, which of the rationales above could he rely on? Does article 33 contemplate this role?

e. Supra page 9.
f. See V. Pechota, supra note a, at 585–89.
g. U.N. Doc. S/9738 (1970), in 25 SCOR, Supp. for April, May & June 1970, at 143, 144.

How could the Security Council know in such cases whether the proposals are consistent with the purposes and principles of the Charter, or whether they impinge on the authority of the Security Council? Is there any alternative to leaving the answers to these questions to the Secretary–General?

Would a solution to a conflict involving a distinct ethnic group that resides on both sides of a territorial boundary be inconsistent with the purposes and principles of the Charter if it takes no account of the group's demands for some sort of political autonomy? What should the Secretary–General do if he regarded such a solution, reached by the states parties in a particular case in which he has exercised his good offices, as inconsistent with the Charter?

The 1972 study by Vratislav Pechota concluded that:

[C]onstitutional balance within the United Nations will be maintained, if, in his relationship with the Security Council, the Secretary–General:

(i) Refrains, as a rule, from any action of his own while the Security Council is exercising, or is likely to exercise, the functions assigned to it by the Charter.

(ii) Seeks prior authorization by the Council, if the contemplated action relates to a situation which may require, at any stage of its development, action by the Council in accordance with Chapter VII of the Charter * * *.

(iii) Keeps the Council informed, and consults its members as appropriate, about any involvement in disputes the continuance of which is likely to endanger the maintenance of international peace and security, so that the Council, if it so decides, can take appropriate steps in accordance with Articles 33(2), 34, 36 and 38.

(iv) Reports to the Council, with or without a recommendation as to appropriate action, on the outcome of his involvement in the settlement of disputes under Chapter VI of the Charter * * *.[h]

Do these rules of thumb make sense today? Are they all legally necessary?

Under current circumstances, is there still a need for quiet diplomacy of the sort described above by U Thant?

Sometimes the Secretary–General can perform the good offices role without leaving U.N. headquarters. Often, though, he (or more likely, his personal representative) must travel to the scene of the dispute. When the dispute involves armed hostilities or the imminent threat of hostilities, such a visit can be personally dangerous. In fact, the leading ICJ judgment on the capacities of the U.N., the Reparations

---

h. V. Pechota, supra note a, at 619–20.
Reprinted by permission of UNITAR.

Case,[i] arose when Count Bernadotte, the Secretary-General's designated mediator in the Middle East in the late 1940s, was assassinated while performing his duties. The Reparations Case held that if harm comes to such a U.N. representative because of a failure by the state to perform obligations designed to protect U.N. agents in the performance of their duties, the U.N. has the capacity to bring an international claim against the state for reparations on account of damage to the U.N. itself and to the victim or his survivors. Among the reasons given was the pragmatic one: only if the U.N. agent can look to the U.N. for protection can he or she function entirely independently from any state. In other words, only then can he or she effectively perform the good offices or mediation function. Do you agree?

The Reparations Case did not decide what obligations, if any, a state is under to provide physical protection for such a U.N. agent. What obligations are there? See General Convention on the Privileges and Immunities of the United Nations, *sections 18, 19, 22*. Do these provisions answer the question? If not, one would have to look to such instruments as the Convention on the Prevention and Punishment of Crimes Against Internationally Protected Persons, Including Diplomatic Agents[j] and the Vienna Convention on Diplomatic Relations.[k]

The Convention on Crimes Against Internationally Protected Persons says in article 1(1)(b) that such persons include, inter alia, "any official or other agent of an international organization of an intergovernmental character who, at the time when and in the place where a crime against him * * * is committed, is entitled pursuant to international law to special protection from any attack on his person, freedom or dignity * * *." It also says, in article 4, that states parties shall take "all practicable measures to prevent preparations in their respective territories for the commission of [crimes enumerated in article 2, including murder or other attack on an internationally protected person]."

The Vienna Convention on Diplomatic Relations says in article 29, "The person of a diplomatic agent shall be inviolable. He shall not be liable to any form of arrest or detention. The receiving State shall treat him with due respect and shall take all appropriate steps to prevent any attack on his person, freedom or dignity." A diplomatic agent is defined in article 1(e) as the head of a mission or a member of the diplomatic staff of a mission.

How do these Conventions, taken together, affect the answer to the question regarding a receiving state's obligations to provide physical protection for a U.N. representative on a good offices mission? Does it matter whether the representative holds the rank of Assistant Secretary or its equivalent? Are the obligations different if he or she is not

i. [1949] I.C.J. 174, reprinted in part at page 7 supra.

j. Dec. 14, 1973, 28 U.S.T. 1975, T.I.A.S. 8532, 1035 U.N.T.S. 167.

k. Apr. 18, 1961, 23 U.S.T. 3227, T.I.A.S. 7502, 500 U.N.T.S. 95.

at the level of Assistant Secretary or higher, but qualifies as an expert on a mission? As to who qualifies as an expert on a mission, see the Mazilu Case, at page 86 supra.

In some cases, the Secretary-General may wish to offer his good offices to help resolve internal conflicts. This may raise questions about the propriety of doing so, and about the appropriate extent of his involvement. It has been said:

> [T]he Secretary-General could not regard internal situations with clear international repercussions as lying *a priori* outside the scope of his good offices, but he must take extra care to avoid charges of exceeding United Nations competence. He must endeavour to make it plain that the concern that motivated his involvement had been international and widely shared, and that the action taken by him was basically directed to those aspects of the situation which were predominantly international, and was not designed to interfere with the balance of forces at the domestic level.[l]

Do these standards obviate any *article 2(7)* problem? Are they practical?

In addition to internal conflicts, there have been a great many regional or subregional conflicts that have raised questions about the respective roles of the U.N. and regional organizations. Note the attempt in *article 52* of the U.N. Charter to sort that out. Does article 52 help? What matters "are appropriate for regional action" under article 52(1)?

Does article 52(2) and/or (3) attach an exhaustion-of-regional-remedies condition precedent to Security Council involvement? If so, does the same condition precedent apply to fact-finding or good offices efforts by the Secretary-General under article 99?

In practice, the answers to the last two questions seem to be no. At least in part, this seems to be because there has been no clear answer to the question about what matters are appropriate for regional action. The U.N. Secretary-General has sometimes deferred to regional organizations, even when they have not risen to the challenge, as in the case of the Nigerian civil war in 1968–1970. On other occasions, he has accepted the good offices mantle even though a regional organization was at least nominally available to act in much the same role. For example, he has sometimes acted when an extraregional state has been involved as more than an interested bystander.[m]

---

l. V. Pechota, supra note a, at 606.

m. For an example of such a case, where Spain was the extraregional state in a conflict in Equatorial Guinea, see id. at 622–23.

Would there be other types of cases where the Secretary-General should offer his good offices, or at least not decline to exercise them if requested, despite the existence of a regional organization with a mandate that would allow it to act? What role should article 52 play in determining the answer?"

It has been noted that there is a "steady increase in the demand for the Secretary-General's conciliatory activities which involve contacts with parties other than States." ° For example, the steadily-proliferating number and variety of nongovernmental organizations, many with special interests (human rights, environmental protection, etc.) that put them at odds with some governments, mean increasing opportunities for the Secretary-General's good offices to help resolve disputes, if it is proper to become involved when NGOs challenge governments. Under what circumstances is it appropriate for the Secretary-General to make available his good offices at the request, or demand, of a nongovernmental organization? Consider the example in this excerpt from Vratislav Pechota's 1972 study:

> Parties, which by any standard are non-governmental units and groups, may become a source of formidable international action, and to deprive them of the possibility of redress of grievances through international procedures of peaceful adjustment might adversely affect the international interest. The hijacking of a Trans World Airlines aircraft to Syria on 28 August 1969 is a case in point. The United Nations was urged [72] by the International Federation of Air Line Pilots Associations (IFALPA) "to take such measures as are necessary to secure the immediate release of the two passengers detained in Syria and, further, the imposition of suitable punishment of the hijackers". Expressing the hope that its appeal would be heard, the Federation added that if this action was unsuccessful, it would, taking into account the near-disastrous character of the incident, recommend that its members cease operations for a 24-hour period on a world-wide scale or carry out a series of such stoppages. The Secretary-General decided to meet IFALPA representatives in Geneva and discuss with them the issues involved in the problem of hijacking. The Secretary-General stated [73] his opinion that ceasing flight operations "would not produce the desired result" and informed the IFALPA representative that he had been in touch with the Government of Syria on the matter. The Secretary-General's contacts with the Federation

---

n. As of 1992, the Special Committee on the Charter of the United Nations and on the Strengthening of the Role of the Organization was considering the question of enhancing cooperation between the U.N. and regional organizations for the maintenance of peace and security.

o. V. Pechota, supra note a, at 634.

72. See *Official Records of the Security Council, Twenty-fourth Year, Supplement for July, August and September 1969*, document S/9428.

73. Ibid., Add. 1.

were a significant element in the chain of events leading to the eventual release of crew, passengers and aircraft.[p]

Which of the legal bases for the Secretary–General's good offices (see pages 844–45 would support what he did on that occasion?

Would the basis for his involvement be as strong if the dispute were, say, between a nongovernmental environmental organization and a government, with no risk of violence or threat to international peace and security?

Of course, nongovernmental organizations quite often are part of the solution rather than part of the problem. A leading example is the International Committee of the Red Cross, which has assumed a large share of the burden of providing humanitarian relief during armed conflicts. The ICRC's mission is to prevent and ameliorate unnecessary suffering in wartime, rather than to resolve the conflict itself, but in the course of providing the relief, the ICRC can facilitate a reduction of the conflict's intensity and thus may ease the U.N.'s attempts to resolve it.

Consider, finally, this assessment of the Secretary–General's good offices function:

V. PECHOTA, THE QUIET APPROACH: A STUDY OF THE GOOD OFFICES EXERCISED BY THE UNITED NATIONS SECRETARY–GENERAL IN THE CAUSE OF PEACE
UNITAR Study, 1972.
Reprinted in Dispute Settlement Through the United
Nations 577, 673–75 (K. Raman ed. 1977).*

It should be emphasized that the Secretary–General's good offices are not identical with those practised in ordinary diplomacy. They extend far beyond the limits set by international law for classical good offices, and include any conceivable method of conciliatory assistance which is in accordance with the United Nations Charter and reflects a realistic assessment of the potential and resources available to the Secretary–General.

The fundamental approach of the Secretary–General to the parties involved in a dispute conforms to the wisdom of Haemon's appeal to his intemperate royal father Creon in Sophocles' *Antigone*:

"Let not your first thought be your only thought. Think if there cannot be some other way."

To assist the parties when they have second thoughts is precisely the function of the Secretary–General's good offices. His intervention is, in

---

p. V. Pechota, supra note a, at 635. Reprinted by permission of UNITAR.

* Reprinted by permission of UNITAR.

many respects, indispensable to bring about just results. His presence provides a guarantee that the settlement process will take place on a basis of international legality and within the framework of the legitimate interests of the international community.

The main thrust of good offices is prevention—one of the most characteristic features of the Secretary-General's diplomatic functions in general. Most conflicts reach the collective organs at a point when it is too late for meaningful preventive action. The Secretary-General's good offices, on the contrary, as a result of their informality, total discretion and non-prejudicial nature, can be put into action even when the incipient character of a dispute does not qualify it as likely to endanger the maintenance of international peace and security.

* * *

The informality and non-prejudicial nature of good offices also make it possible for the Secretary-General to deal with issues which would pose difficult problems of competence or procedure if tackled by the collective political organs of the United Nations. The United Nations cannot lightly dissociate itself from such issues when raised before it, especially if some expectation of assistance has been encouraged by the Organization's resolute stands on the principles involved. A definite link can be seen between the progressive spread of United Nations interest over diverse fields and the steady increase in the demand for the Secretary-General's good offices, even in situations which originate within a State but which have definite international repercussions.

Some of the forms the Secretary-General's actions take go beyond what is usually expected of a diplomatic intermediary, and cut across the boundaries which separate his own diplomatic functions from his activities as co-ordinator of United Nations activities and head of an international administration. The positive impact of this is obvious. The possibility of mobilizing all the resources of the United Nations is bound to strengthen the mediatory potential of the Secretary-General's good offices, particularly in situations which require for their solution expertise and administrative skills that are non-partisan and truly international in character.

THE ASSESSMENT TODAY

Would Pechota's assessment hold true today, under circumstances that no longer involve the cold war rivalries and stalemates that existed when he wrote?

What future developments in the Secretary-General's peacemaking role can you foresee? Are U.N. Charter revisions needed, in order to accommodate the optimal role he might play?

SECTION 2. HUMANITARIAN INTERVENTION

INTRODUCTORY NOTE

The United Nations has offered or supported humanitarian relief in a variety of situations. Some of them have had human causes, as when superior force has been used against ethnically identifiable groups unable effectively to protect themselves; some have resulted from natural disasters, particularly in developing countries.

Some longstanding U.N. programs are designed to deal with recurring humanitarian needs. In particular, the U.N. High Commissioner for Refugees (UNHCR) has for many years provided relief for cross-border refugees around the world. UNHCR is a subsidiary organ of the General Assembly that provides emergency aid to refugees as well as attempting to educate governments about, and induce them to comply with, international law regarding refugees—in particular, the 1951 Convention on the Status of Refugees and its 1967 Protocol.[a]

To provide emergency relief, UNHCR works closely with other U.N. bodies that have mandates not limited to refugee assistance, including the World Food Program, UNICEF and the World Health Organization. It also works with nongovernmental organizations, such as the International Committee of the Red Cross.[b]

Once UNHCR became established, its normal operations have not engendered significant international law problems, though it has had more than its share of practical and financial difficulties. The focus of this section is on human-induced emergencies, and on novel U.N. responses that raise international law issues.

A. IRAQ, THE KURDS AND THE SHIITES

Among the after-effects of U.N. enforcement action against Iraq in 1991 were armed uprisings within Iraq by Kurds in the north and by Shiites in the south. After the uprisings enjoyed initial successes, they were forcibly quelled by Iraqi troops. Large numbers of Kurds and Shiites fled to inaccessible places in Iraq, to Turkey (in the case of the Kurds) or to Iran (in the case of the Shiites). The Kurds, in particular, feared bloody reprisals at the hands of the Iraqi authorities if they returned to their homes. They had some bitter experience on which to base their fears.

The Security Council tried to deal with the situation:

---

a. 19 U.S.T. 6223, 606 U.N.T.S. 267.

b. See generally Y. Beigbeder, The Role and Status of International Humanitarian Volunteers and Organizations 27–60 (1991).

UNHCR's annual report to the General Assembly appears as a Supplement to each year's GAOR. See, e.g., 46 GAOR Supp. No. 12 (A/46/12) (1991).

SECURITY COUNCIL RESOLUTION 688
April 5, 1991.
U.N. Doc. S/RES/688 (1991).

The Security Council,

Mindful of its duties and its responsibilities under the Charter of the United Nations for the maintenance of international peace and security,

Recalling Article 2, paragraph 7, of the Charter of the United Nations,

Gravely concerned by the repression of the Iraqi civilian population in many parts of Iraq, including most recently in Kurdish populated areas which led to a massive flow of refugees towards and across international frontiers and to cross border incursions, which threaten international peace and security in the region,

* * *

Reaffirming the commitment of all Member States to the sovereignty, territorial integrity and political independence of Iraq and of all States in the area,

* * *

1. *Condemns* the repression of the Iraqi civilian population in many parts of Iraq, including most recently in Kurdish populated areas, the consequences of which threaten international peace and security in the region;

2. *Demands* that Iraq, as a contribution to removing the threat to international peace and security in the region, immediately end this repression and expresses the hope in the same context that an open dialogue will take place to ensure that the human and political rights of all Iraqi citizens are respected;

3. *Insists* that Iraq allow immediate access by international humanitarian organizations to all those in need of assistance in all parts of Iraq and to make available all necessary facilities for their operations;

4. *Requests* the Secretary–General to pursue his humanitarian efforts in Iraq * * *;

5. *Requests further* the Secretary–General to use all the resources at his disposal, including those of the relevant United Nations agencies, to address urgently the critical needs of the refugees and displaced Iraqi population;

6. *Appeals* to all Member States and to all humanitarian organizations to contribute to these humanitarian relief efforts;

7. *Demands* that Iraq cooperate with the Secretary–General to these ends;

8. *Decides* to remain seized of the matter.

THE SECURITY COUNCIL AND HUMANITARIAN AID

There are Kurdish areas in Turkey and Iran, as well as in Iraq, with longstanding self-determination claims based on a greater Kurdistan that could span Iraq–Iran–Turkey borders. The governments of all three states have consistently, and quite forcefully, resisted those claims. Just before Resolution 688 was adopted, both Turkey and Iran sent letters to the U.N., complaining about the massing of Iraqi civilians on their borders and expressing apprehension that they were about to be forced across the borders.[a]

All of this gave credibility to the Security Council's assertion in Resolution 688 that Iraq's repression of its civilian population—at least of its Kurdish population—threatened international peace and security. Was that a legally important assertion for the Security Council to make, as a condition precedent to the operative provisions of the resolution? Or could the Security Council act any time a government represses a minority group, on the ground that human rights are no longer subject simply to the domestic jurisdiction of states, and severe human rights violations justify intervention by, or on the authority of, the U.N. organ best equipped to respond promptly and vigorously?[b]

If the latter, was there any reason for the Security Council to "recall" *article 2, paragraph 7* of the Charter? Three members of the Council—Cuba, Yemen and Zimbabwe—thought that the Council was acting inconsistently with the principle embodied in that Charter provision.[c]

Was Resolution 688 adopted under Chapter VII of the Charter? Under *article 24?* Would it make a difference?

The Cuban representative argued that this was a question falling within *Chapter IX* of the U.N. Charter ("International Economic and Social Cooperation"). He noted that *article 24(2)* does not mention Chapter IX among those granting specific powers to the Security Council. *Article 60,* which is in Chapter IX, vests responsibility for the functions set forth in that Chapter in the General Assembly and the Economic and Social Council. Consequently, he said, the Security Council should not act.[d] Did he have a good point? Note, among other things, the I.C.J.'s Namibia Advisory Opinion, at pages 501–02 supra.

An astute observer of the United Nations has said:

> Resolution 688 * * * established an important precedent. For the first time, the Security Council directed a member state to

---

a. U.N. Docs. S/22435 & S/22447 (1991).

b. Cf. Damrosch, Commentary on Collective Military Intervention to Enforce Human Rights, in Law and Force in the New International Order 215, 219 (L. Damrosch & D. Scheffer eds. 1991).

c. See U.N. Doc. S/PV.2982, at 27, 31, 44–45, 52 (1991).

d. Id. at 46.

stand aside and let international humanitarian agencies operate on its territory to assist citizens victimized by a government's repression. It stripped the Iraqi government of any right, under international law, to refuse admission to the humanitarian agencies. In fact, it obliged the government to make available "all necessary facilities for their operations." [e]

Is this correct? If so, exactly how broad is the precedent? Would it set the stage for similar Security Council measures any time a member state uses armed force to repress its own citizens? Would it apply if the need for humanitarian aid arose from a natural disaster, such as an earthquake?

The situation of the displaced Kurds in northern Iraq soon became desperate. When it appeared that neither the U.N. nor the international humanitarian organizations contemplated by Resolution 688 would be able to mount an effective relief operation in time to relieve their distress, the United States, the U.K. and France sent armed forces into northern Iraq to provide them with emergency assistance and to create a secure zone to which they could return. The allied forces did not meet armed resistance from Iraq. When they had established a reasonably secure zone to which most of the Kurds returned, and when a small, very lightly-armed contingent of U.N. guards had been put in place, they withdrew from Iraq to a border area within Turkey.

In the case of the S.S. Lotus, the Permanent Court of International Justice said:

> [T]he first and foremost restriction imposed by international law upon a State is that—failing the existence of a permissive rule to the contrary—it may not exercise its power in any form in the territory of another State.[f]

Arguably, customary international law provides a "permissive rule to the contrary" for certain types of humanitarian intervention, even without the benefit of a Security Council resolution.[g] Our question is whether the Security Council could, and did in this case, provide the permissive rule apart from any customary norm.

Was the U.S.–U.K.–French action in northern Iraq authorized by Security Council Resolution 688? By Resolution 678 or 687, pages 662 and 670 supra? Thomas R. Pickering, then the U.S. ambassador to the U.N., gave this legal justification:

> [Resolution 688] declared that the situation constituted a threat to international peace and security. It also called for member states to give assistance to the Secretary-General's humanitarian efforts. These two elements and the fact that Iraq was

---

e. Scheffer, Use of Force After the Cold War: Panama, Iraq, and the New World Order, in Right v. Might: International Law and the Use of Force 109, 146 (2d ed. 1991).

f. P.C.I.J. Ser. A, No. 10, at 18 (1927).

g. See, e.g., the Military and Paramilitary Activities Case (Nicaragua v. United States), [1986] I.C.J. 14, 124–25. Space does not permit examination here of state practice on this point.

a country already subject to Chapter VII enforcement, were enough to build a legal bridge for the coalition to provide relief and support for the Kurds. It was a space which was not challenged by those Permanent and other Council Members otherwise inclined to oppose a more direct approach on non-intervention grounds.[h]

Leaving aside the possible acquiescence by other Security Council members, was the "legal bridge" strong enough to justify the intervention?

Could the Security Council properly authorize such action, whether or not it actually did in this case? Consider whether the Security Council in the Rhodesian situation in 1965–66 may have provided a precedent.[i] As noted at pages 623–24 supra, after the Ian Smith government of Rhodesia declared its independence from the United Kingdom in a last-ditch effort to maintain white control by force in Rhodesia, the Security Council adopted several resolutions designed to force him to back down. One of them, Resolution 221, determined that there was a threat to the peace (though Rhodesia had not threatened to attack any other state), and called on the British government to prevent "by the use of force if necessary" the arrival by sea of oil destined for Rhodesia. If the Security Council could authorize the use of force by a member state in that situation, could it also authorize humanitarian intervention by a group of member states to prevent suffering by an identifiable ethnic group at the hands of the group's own government, even if it meant physical intervention within Iraqi territory?

In August 1992, reacting to mounting evidence of renewed Iraqi repression of Shiites in the southern part of the country, including air attacks on them, the United States, United Kingdom and France established a zone across southern Iraq over which Iraqi aircraft would be shot down if they dared venture. President Bush said, "This will provide coverage of the areas where a majority of the most significant recent violations of Resolution 688 have taken place."[j] The Iraqi representative to the U.N. said the "no-fly zone" was a violation of international law.[k]

Was the "legal bridge" cited by Ambassador Pickering in 1991 sufficient for this action as well? Would continuing Iraqi violations of Resolution 688, in themselves, justify the U.S.–British–French action? Or did the continuing authority of Resolution 678, page 662 supra, justify the action?

Did the apparent lack of effective challenge by other Security Council members establish the lawfulness of the interventions in Iraq, apart from any other legal justification?

h. Hearings on Relations in a Multipolar World, Before the Senate Comm. on Foreign Relations, 102d Cong., 1st Sess., at 69 (1991).

i. Cf. Damrosch, supra note b, at 218.

j. News conference, Aug. 26, 1992, as reported in N.Y. Times, Aug. 27, 1992, p. A14, col. 5.

k. Wash. Post, Aug. 27, 1992, p. A27, col. 1.

To return to mid-April 1991, the U.N. and Iraq by then had worked out an understanding by which the U.N. would take over the humanitarian effort within northern Iraq for a limited time. The government of Iraq agreed "to cooperate with the United Nations to have a humanitarian presence in Iraq, wherever such presence may be needed, and to facilitate it through the adoption of all necessary measures." [l] U.N. Humanitarian Centres were to be established in northern Iraq to facilitate the provision of food aid, medical care, shelter, etc. The Iraqi government was to establish a relief distribution and monitoring structure.

Did this understanding eliminate any legal objections to Resolution 688, insofar as it related to the Kurds? Did it affect the precedent set by that resolution?

The Secretary-General sent a lightly-armed contingent of U.N. guards into northern Iraq without any Security Council authorization other than Resolution 688. Apparently he thought at first that a new Security Council resolution would be required,[m] but ultimately he acted simply on the basis of consulting, and obtaining the consent of, the Iraqi government.[n] Could he have done so without Iraqi consent (and without a new Security Council resolution)? [o]

When the agreed term of the U.N. guards expired in 1992, Iraq declined to renew their mandate. They remained in place without any formal agreement, but their ranks dwindled through normal rotations home and the unavailability of new visas. Without the security of an agreement formalizing the U.N. presence, several private relief organizations pulled out of northern Iraq. At that point, the United States representative to the U.N., Edward Perkins, asserted that Iraq's failure to renew the agreement was hampering the relief operation and amounted to a violation of Resolution 688.[p] Eventually a shaky accommodation was reached.

Was Mr. Perkins correct about the violation of Resolution 688?

The situation in northern Iraq in 1991 led to an examination of the U.N.'s proper role in humanitarian emergencies. See below.

B. THE EVOLVING U.N. ROLE

In his report to the General Assembly on the work of the organization in 1991, Secretary-General Pérez de Cuéllar had this to say about the U.N. response to massive violations of human rights:

l. U.N.-Iraq Memorandum of Understanding, Apr. 18, 1991, U.N. Doc. S/22663 (1991), reprinted in 30 Int'l Legal Materials 860 (1991).

m. 2 Int'l Docs. Rev., No. 17, at 1 (1991).

n. U.N. Doc. S/22663, Annex (1991).

o. On the questions in this paragraph, see Schachter, United Nations Law in the Gulf Conflict, 85 Am.J.Int'l L. 452, 469 (1991); Malanczuk, The Kurdish Crisis and Allied Intervention in the Aftermath of the Second Gulf War, 2 Eur.J.Int'l L. 114, 129–30 (1991); O'Connell, Continuing Limits on UN Intervention in Civil War, 67 Ind.L.J. 903, 904–09 (1992).

p. See Washington Weekly Rep., 31 July 1992, at 3.

REPORT OF THE SECRETARY-GENERAL ON THE WORK OF THE ORGANIZATION
Sept. 13, 1991.
46 G.A.O.R. Supp. No. 1 (A/46/1), at 4–5.

[T]he fact must be squarely faced that the campaign for the protection of human rights has brought results mostly in conditions of relative normalcy and with responsive Governments. In other conditions, when human wrongs are committed in systematic fashion and on a massive scale—instances are widely dispersed over both time and place—the intergovernmental machinery of the United Nations has often been a helpless witness rather than an effective agent for checking their perpetration.

It would betray a callous or an overly bureaucratic attitude to expect the victims of these horrors to utilize the normal time-consuming procedures and mechanisms that are available for seeking redress.[a] The encouragement of respect for human rights becomes a vacuous claim if human wrongs committed on a major scale are met with lack of timely and commensurate action by the United Nations. To promote human rights means little if it does not mean to defend them when they are most under attack.

I believe that the protection of human rights has now become one of the keystones in the arch of peace. I am also convinced that it now involves more a concerted exertion of international influence and pressure through timely appeal, admonition, remonstrance or condemnation and, in the last resort, an appropriate United Nations presence, than what was regarded as permissible under traditional international law.

It is now increasingly felt that the principle of non-interference with the essential domestic jurisdiction of States cannot be regarded as a protective barrier behind which human rights could be massively or systematically violated with impunity. The fact that, in diverse situations, the United Nations has not been able to prevent atrocities cannot be cited as an argument, legal or moral, against the necessary corrective action, especially where peace is also threatened. Omissions or failures due to a variety of contingent circumstances do not constitute a precedent. The case for not impinging on the sovereignty, territorial integrity and political independence of States is by itself indubitably strong. But it would only be weakened if it were to carry the implication that sovereignty, even in this day and age, includes the right of mass slaughter or of launching systematic campaigns of decimation or forced exodus of civilian populations in the name of controlling civil strife or insurrection. With the heightened international interest in universalizing a regime of human rights, there is a marked and most

a. [The reference apparently is to the petitioning procedure under ECOSOC Res. 1503, discussed at page 970 infra. Ed.]

welcome shift in public attitudes. To try to resist it would be politically as unwise as it is morally indefensible. It should be perceived as not so much a new departure as a more focused awareness of one of the requirements of peace.

I would emphasize that novel doctrines are not only not required on this issue; they can also upset established understandings. It is possible that in the ongoing debate among legal experts and political theoreticians, new concepts may emerge and gain broad acceptance. However, at the intergovernmental level, what the present stage in international affairs demands, in the context of human rights as much as in any other, is not a process of theorizing but a higher degree of cooperation and a combination of common sense and compassion. We need not impale ourselves on the horns of a dilemma between respect for sovereignty and the protection of human rights. The last thing the United Nations needs is a new ideological controversy. What is involved is not the right of intervention but the collective obligation of States to bring relief and redress in human rights emergencies.

It seems to be beyond question that violations of human rights imperil peace, while disregard of the sovereignty of States would spell chaos. The maximum caution needs to be exercised lest the defence of human rights becomes a platform for encroaching on the essential domestic jurisdiction of States and eroding their sovereignty. Nothing would be a surer prescription for anarchy than an abuse of this principle.

Some caveats are, therefore, most necessary at this point. First, like all other basic principles, the principle of protection of human rights cannot be invoked in a particular situation and disregarded in a similar one. To apply it selectively is to debase it. Governments can, and do, expose themselves to charges of deliberate bias; the United Nations cannot. Second, any international action for protecting human rights must be based on a decision taken in accordance with the Charter of the United Nations. It must not be a unilateral act. Third, and relatedly, the consideration of proportionality is of the utmost importance in this respect. Should the scale or manner of international action be out of proportion to the wrong that is reported to have been committed, it is bound to evoke a vehement reaction, which, in the long run, would jeopardize the very rights that were sought to be defended.

THE SHAPE OF A NEW U.N. ROLE

The Secretary-General clearly had in mind the sort of human rights violations found in Iraq's treatment of the Kurds (and in the treatment of minorities in some other countries as well): systematic, massive human wrongs, rather than episodic violations.

The U.N. system already has some mechanisms for addressing persistent patterns of human rights violations. For example, the U.N.

Commission on Human Rights, a subsidiary body of the Economic and Social Council, on several occasions has appointed a Special Rapporteur to investigate alleged serious human rights abuses in individual countries (including Iraq), and to report back to the Commission. The reports are often critical of the governments involved, and provide an occasion for the mobilization of shame. Similarly, the Commission has appointed Experts to "assist" individual governments in improving their human rights practices. Through direct contacts with the governments, these Experts are able to exert some pressure for reform.

In addition, since 1970 there has been a petitioning procedure under Economic and Social Council Resolution 1503, designed to deal with "consistent pattern[s] of gross and reliably attested violations of human rights and fundamental freedoms." [b] Petitions are submitted through the U.N. Centre for Human Rights to the Sub–Commission on Prevention of Discrimination and Protection of Minorities for its review in nonpublic sessions. Petitions are screened by a Working Group, with those that appear admissible being referred to the full Sub–Commission. It, in turn, refers some of the petitions each year to its parent body, the Commission on Human Rights. The Commission has its own Working Group, which recommends the course of action the Commission should take on each situation referred to it. If a case gets that far, often the Commission appoints an Expert, or requests the U.N. Secretariat, to engage in direct contacts with the respondent government in order to persuade it to eliminate the pattern of gross violations. This cumbersome procedure may have produced some results, but one cannot easily tell whether it is responsible for any improvements in governments' human rights practices. It is incapable of responding quickly to the serious human rights situations it addresses. Little wonder that the Secretary–General called for a new U.N. approach to protect victims of massive human rights violations.

In the third paragraph of the excerpt quoted above, the Secretary–General mentioned "a concerted exertion of international influence and pressure through timely appeal, admonition, remonstrance or condemnation." Who would do the exerting? The Secretary–General? Does anything in the U.N. Charter authorize the Secretary–General to condemn a member government, in the absence of express authority to do so from the Security Council or another collective U.N. organ?

In the same paragraph, the Secretary–General referred to "an appropriate United Nations presence" as a last resort, and suggested that this might go further than "what was regarded as permissible under traditional international law." In the general debate during the General Assembly's 46th session in 1991, the Foreign Minister of Italy put the matter this way:

> As we have seen in the aftermath of the Gulf war, the right to intervene for humanitarian ends and for the protection of human

---

b. ECOSOC Res. 1503, 48 ECOSOC OR Supp. No. 1A (E/4832/Add.1), at 8 (1970). The 1503 procedure is examined in Chapter 6, infra.

rights is gaining ground. This type of intervention has become an *idée-force*, and the most truly innovative concept of the remaining decade of this century. This must be the focal point of our efforts through the United Nations, which is also the main forum of the new world order. Intervention that is primarily aimed at securing protection of human rights and respect for the basic principles of peaceful coexistence, is a prerogative of the international community, which must have the power to suspend sovereignty whenever it is exercised in a criminal manner.[c]

Does this *idée force* include sending armed U.N. forces to a member's territory, without its consent, to alleviate the suffering of oppressed groups, when the situation has not caused refugee flows across territorial boundaries? Would the Security Council have the authority to do that? Would the Secretary–General, acting on his own? Would a Charter revision be necessary?

Suggestions of this sort have caused unease among governments that might become unwilling recipients of humanitarian assistance. The concern was expressed by the representative of Zimbabwe:

> In the era we are entering, the Council will be called upon to deal more and more with conflicts and humanitarian situations of a domestic nature that could pose threats to international peace and stability. However, great care has to be taken to see that these domestic conflicts are not used as a pretext for the intervention of big Powers in the legitimate domestic affairs of small States, or that human rights issues are not used for totally different purposes of destabilizing other Governments. There is, therefore, the need to strike a delicate balance between the rights of States, as enshrined in the Charter, and the rights of individuals, as enshrined in the Universal Declaration of Human Rights.
>
> Zimbabwe supports very strongly both the Universal Declaration of Human Rights and the Charter on these issues. * * * However, we cannot but express our apprehension about who will decide when to get the Security Council involved in an internal matter and in what manner. In other words, who will judge when a threshold is passed that calls for international action? Who will decide what should be done, how it will be done and by whom? This clearly calls for a careful drawing up and drafting of general principles and guidelines that would guide decisions on when a domestic situation warrants international action, either by the Security Council or by regional organizations.[d]

Was Zimbabwe's concern legitimate? Did the Secretary–General's report, above, deal adequately with it?

[c] Statement of Mr. de Michelis, U.N. Doc. A/46/PV.12, at 32 (1991).

[d] U.N. Doc. S/PV.3046, at 131 (1992).

Was the Secretary-General correct in saying that there is no need to "impale ourselves on the horns of a dilemma between respect for sovereignty and the protection of human rights"?

Note the last paragraph quoted above from the Secretary-General's report. Is it realistic to suggest that the U.N. could avoid selectivity in the protection of human rights? Is even-handedness a legal concept in this context?

Did the Secretary-General, in that paragraph, imply that the U.S.-U.K.-French intervention on behalf of the Kurds in northern Iraq was in violation of the U.N. Charter? Or was he simply warning against future unilateral interventions when no competent U.N. organ has found a need for humanitarian assistance? If the former, what weight does such an opinion have?

In December 1991 the General Assembly authorized the Secretary-General to appoint a humanitarian aid coordinator to coordinate the assistance efforts of U.N. agencies in emergency situations (natural or human-made), and to represent the U.N. in its dealings with the governments of recipient states. The resolution was adopted without a vote. Consider, inter alia, whether the Guiding Principles in its Annex would satisfy the concern expressed by Zimbabwe.

RESOLUTION ON STRENGTHENING THE COORDINATION OF HUMANITARIAN EMERGENCY ASSISTANCE OF THE UNITED NATIONS

United Nations General Assembly, Dec. 19, 1991.
G.A. Res. 46/182, 46 GAOR Supp. No. 49 (A/46/49), at 49.

The General Assembly,

* * *

Deeply concerned about the suffering of the victims of disasters and emergency situations, the loss in human lives, the flow of refugees, the mass displacement of people and the material destruction,

Mindful of the need to strengthen further and make more effective the collective efforts of the international community, in particular the United Nations system, in providing humanitarian assistance,

* * *

1. *Adopts* the text contained in the annex to the present resolution for the strengthening of the coordination of emergency humanitarian assistance of the United Nations system;

* * *

Annex
I. *Guiding Principles*

1. Humanitarian assistance is of cardinal importance for the victims of natural disasters and other emergencies.

2. Humanitarian assistance must be provided in accordance with the principles of humanity, neutrality and impartiality.

3. The sovereignty, territorial integrity and national unity of States must be fully respected in accordance with the Charter of the United Nations. In this context, humanitarian assistance should be provided with the consent of the affected country and in principle on the basis of an appeal by the affected country.

4. Each State has the responsibility first and foremost to take care of the victims of natural disasters and other emergencies occurring on its territory. Hence, the affected State has the primary role in the initiation, organization, coordination, and implementation of humanitarian assistance within its territory.

5. The magnitude and duration of many emergencies may be beyond the response capacity of many affected countries. International cooperation to address emergency situations and to strengthen the response capacity of affected countries is thus of great importance. Such cooperation should be provided in accordance with international law and national laws. Intergovernmental and non-governmental organizations working impartially and with strictly humanitarian motives should continue to make a significant contribution in supplementing national efforts.

6. States whose populations are in need of humanitarian assistance are called upon to facilitate the work of these organizations in implementing humanitarian assistance, in particular the supply of food, medicines, shelter and health care, for which access to victims is essential.

7. States in proximity to emergencies are urged to participate closely with the affected countries in international efforts, with a view to facilitating, to the extent possible, the transit of humanitarian assistance.

* * *

III. Preparedness

* * *

Early Warning

19. On the basis of existing mandates and drawing upon monitoring arrangements available within the system, the United Nations should intensify efforts, building upon the existing capacities of relevant organizations and entities of the United Nations, for the systematic pooling, analysis and dissemination of early-warning information on natural disasters and other emergencies. In this context, the United Nations should consider making use as appropriate of the early-warning capacities of Governments and intergovernmental and non-governmental organizations.

20. Early-warning information should be made available in an unrestricted and timely manner to all interested Governments and concerned authorities, in particular of affected or disaster-prone countries. The capacity of disaster-prone countries to receive, use and disseminate this information should be strengthened. In this connection, the international community is urged to assist these countries upon request with the establishment and enhancement of national early-warning systems.

IV. Stand-by Capacity

* * *

Additional Measures for Rapid Response

27. The United Nations should, building upon the existing capacities of relevant organizations, establish a central register of all specialized personnel and teams of technical specialists, as well as relief supplies, equipment and services available within the United Nations system and from Governments and intergovernmental and non-governmental organizations, that can be called upon at short notice by the United Nations.

28. The United Nations should continue to make appropriate arrangements with interested Governments and intergovernmental and non-governmental organizations to enable it to have more expeditious access, when necessary, to their emergency relief capacities, including food reserves, emergency stockpiles and personnel, as well as logistic support.

* * *

VI. Coordination, Cooperation and Leadership
Leadership of the Secretary–General

33. The leadership role of the Secretary–General is critical and must be strengthened to ensure better preparation for, as well as rapid and coherent response to, natural disasters and other emergencies. This should be achieved through coordinated support for prevention and preparedness measures and the optimal utilization of, *inter alia,* an inter-agency standing committee, consolidated appeals, a central emergency revolving fund and a register of stand-by capacities.

34. To this end, and on the understanding that the requisite resources envisaged in paragraph 24 above [calling for a voluntary $50 million fund] would be provided, a high-level official, emergency relief coordinator, would be designated by the Secretary–General to work closely with and with direct access to him, in cooperation with the relevant organizations and entities of the system dealing with humanitarian assistance and in full respect of their mandates, without prejudice to any decisions to be taken by the General Assembly on the overall restructuring of the Secretariat of the United Nations. This high-level official should combine the functions at present carried out

in the coordination of United Nations response by representatives of the Secretary–General for major and complex emergencies, as well as by the United Nations Disaster Relief Coordinator.

35. Under the aegis of the General Assembly and working under the direction of the Secretary–General, the high-level official would have the following responsibilities:

(*a*) Processing requests from affected Member States for emergency assistance requiring a coordinated response;

(*b*) Maintaining an overview of all emergencies through, *inter alia*, the systematic pooling and analysis of early-warning information as envisaged in paragraph 19 above, with a view to coordinating and facilitating the humanitarian assistance of the United Nations system to those emergencies that require a coordinated response;

(*c*) Organizing, in consultation with the Government of the affected country, a joint inter-agency needs-assessment mission and preparing a consolidated appeal to be issued by the Secretary–General, to be followed by periodic situation reports including information on all sources of external assistance;

(*d*) Actively facilitating, including through negotiation if needed, the access by the operational organizations to emergency areas for the rapid provision of emergency assistance by obtaining the consent of all parties concerned, through modalities such as the establishment of temporary relief corridors where needed, days and zones of tranquility and other forms;

(*e*) Managing, in consultation with the operational organizations concerned, the central emergency revolving fund and assisting in the mobilization of resources;

(*f*) Serving as a central focal point with Governments and inter-governmental and non-governmental organizations concerning United Nations emergency relief operations and, when appropriate and necessary, mobilizing their emergency relief capacities, including through consultations in his capacity as Chairman of the Inter–Agency Standing Committee;

(*g*) Providing consolidated information, including early warning on emergencies, to all interested Governments and concerned authorities, particularly affected and disaster-prone countries, drawing on the capacities of the organizations of the system and other available sources;

* * *

Country-level Coordination

39. Within the overall framework described above and in support of the efforts of the affected countries, the resident coordinator should normally coordinate the humanitarian assistance of the United Nations system at the country level. He/She should facilitate the preparedness of the United Nations system and assist in a speedy transition from

relief to development. He/She should promote the use of all locally or regionally available relief capacities. The resident coordinator should chair an emergency operations group of field representatives and experts from the system.

* * *

HUMANITARIAN ASSISTANCE OR INTERFERENCE?

Under this resolution, does an affected state have to take the initiative by requesting assistance, or could the U.N. take the initiative? See especially paragraph 3.

Does paragraph 3 call for the consent of the affected government? To what extent does it purport to be mandatory?

If the U.N. could take the initiative, could the high-level coordinator (or the Secretary–General) do so without further authorization by the General Assembly or Security Council?

Does the resolution impose a duty on governments of affected states to cooperate with U.N. humanitarian efforts? If so, what does the duty entail? If the resolution does not impose such a duty, is it of any value as a humanitarian measure?

Does paragraph 19 authorize the U.N. to make use of national surveillance systems in outer space, as the Secretary–General proposed in a peacemaking context (page 833 supra)? Would this, or anything else in the Preparedness or Stand-by Capacity provisions, encroach on the sovereignty of states?

What is the significance, if any, of emphasizing in paragraph 35(d) two methods of facilitating emergency relief: establishing temporary relief corridors and days/zones of tranquility?

Does the U.N. have any advantage over nongovernmental organizations, such as the International Committee of the Red Cross, in providing humanitarian assistance? Do they complement each other?

In 1989 a group of experts on humanitarian assistance met in Harare, Zimbabwe, to discuss humanitarian assistance in African armed conflicts. They considered the creation of a new U.N. humanitarian support operation, involving three elements:

   1. The codification of evolving practices and ethics into a new international norm to guarantee the rights of civilians to have access to humanitarian relief;

   2. the willingness to call governments as well as insurgents publicly to task and thereby to use the U.N. to embarrass any party which denied humanitarian aid to civilians for any purpose;

   3. the operational military capacity to ensure delivery of such assistance when international pressure failed which, given the

potential risks, would probably require the establishment of a volunteer force under U.N. auspices.[e]

Resolution 46/182 did not expressly adopt these elements. Did it set the stage for them? Are they a good idea?

C. BOSNIA–HERZEGOVINA

The first major U.N. humanitarian relief operation after the adoption of the 1991 General Assembly Resolution on humanitarian assistance was the opening of the Sarajevo airport and delivery of airlifted food and medicine to the people of Sarajevo beginning in the summer of 1992. It did not come easily. Nor did later attempts to broaden the humanitarian operation in Bosnia.

In the late spring and early summer of 1992, Serb irregulars held the Sarajevo airport as part of a sustained Serbian siege of the city apparently designed to drive non-Serbs out. Food and medicine were not reaching the city by land, and existing supplies for civilians in Sarajevo had run dangerously low.

The Security Council tried to deal with the situation. On May 15, 1992, it adopted Resolution 752 in which it recited its primary responsibility under the Charter for maintaining peace and security, but did not mention Chapter VII. It went on to call upon all parties to cease forcible expulsions of persons and to ensure that conditions were established for the delivery of humanitarian assistance.

When that effort had no apparent effect, the Security Council adopted Resolution 757 (1992). Relying this time on Chapter VII, the Security Council said, inter alia, that it:

Demands that all parties and others concerned create immediately the necessary conditions for unimpeded delivery of humanitarian supplies to Sarajevo and other destinations in Bosnia and Herzegovina, including the establishment of a security zone encompassing Sarajevo and its airport and respecting [agreements designed to allow the airport to function].

Is humanitarian assistance for the purpose of relieving suffering primarily in a single city within the authority of the Security Council under the Charter? Is it within the scope of Chapter VII? If so, was the paragraph above from Resolution 757 binding on all parties to the Bosnian conflict, including Serbian irregulars?

Again, the Security Council's effort was without discernible effect. In early June it authorized Secretary–General Boutros–Ghali to enlarge UNPROFOR by at least 1,100 people, including a 1,000-member infantry battalion for security at the Sarajevo airport, if a lasting cease-fire could be achieved. Later in June, Serbian forces withdrew from the airport and a humanitarian airlift began. At that point the Security

[e]. As reported in Y. Beigbeder, The Role and Status of International Humanitarian Volunteers and Organizations 371 (1991).

Council adopted Resolution 761 (1992), authorizing the Secretary-General to proceed with the deployment of the infantry battalion. Resolution 764 (1992) later increased the force to 1,600, including a helicopter unit. Food and medical supplies arrived and were distributed.

Was the U.N. humanitarian effort in Sarajevo to that point consistent with (a) the Guiding Principles of General Assembly Resolution 46/182, page 862 supra, and (b) the final paragraph of the humanitarian relief segment of Secretary-General Pérez de Cuéllar's 1991 report, page 859 supra?

Secretary-General Boutros-Ghali expressed reservations on the even-handedness issue. He said, "My concern is that if the Security Council continues to concentrate its attention and resources to such an extent on Yugoslav problems, this will be at the expense of the Organization's ability to help resolve equally cruel and dangerous conflicts elsewhere, e.g. in Somalia." [a]

If even-handedness is, or is becoming, a legal requirement, what is the solution when the U.N. does not have the human and financial resources needed for fully effective peacekeeping and humanitarian relief in all conflict-ridden areas of the world?

The airlift to Sarajevo continued through the summer of 1992, but in fits and starts because of fighting in and around the city. Supplies ran short in other Bosnian cities as well, and fighting in those areas also frustrated relief efforts. Reports from Bosnia told of inhumane treatment of persons detained in camps maintained by Bosnian Serbs and of mass rapes. Political pressures rose in the United States and some European countries for more forceful efforts to get supplies through and to do something about the treatment of civilians and prisoners in the camps.

On August 13, 1992, the Security Council responded with two resolutions. In Resolution 770 (1992), the Security Council said that it was acting under Chapter VII of the Charter, and that it:

1. *Reaffirms* its demand that all parties and others concerned in Bosnia and Herzegovina stop the fighting immediately;

2. *Calls upon* all states to take nationally or through regional agencies or arrangements all measures necessary to facilitate in coordination with the United Nations the delivery by relevant United Nations humanitarian organizations and others of humanitarian assistance to Sarajevo and wherever needed in other parts of Bosnia and Herzegovina;

3. *Demands* that unimpeded and continuous access to all camps, prisons and detention centres be granted immediately to the International Committee of the Red Cross and other relevant

a. U.N. Doc. S/24333, at 4 (1992).

humanitarian organizations and that all detainees therein receive humane treatment, including adequate food, shelter and medical care * * *.

The reference in paragraph 2 to "coordination with the United Nations" was intended to ensure that the existing U.N. presence in Bosnia–Herzegovina remain in place, rather than being supplanted by national or regional forces. It was thought that any significant use of force under the resolution could subject the U.N. peacekeepers and relief agencies to attack by Serbian forces.[b]

The drafters of paragraph 2, above, drew on paragraph 2 of Resolution 678 (1990)—the authorization for the use of force against Iraq after its invasion of Kuwait. See page 662 supra. In each case the intent was clear to authorize the use of armed force if it was "necessary" to achieve the stated goal. The goal, of course, was not the same in each case. Is that a legally significant difference? Who would determine what measures were "necessary" under Resolution 770?

Other than the different goals, are there legally significant differences between the two paragraphs 2? Did either of them *require* member states to act?

Note the reference to regional agencies in paragraph 2 of Resolution 770. Although the Security Council did not mention *article 53* (in Chapter VIII of the Charter), was it acting under that article in this part of paragraph 2?

Would a provision such as paragraph 2 of Resolution 770, tying national action to coordination with the U.N., survive an order by the Secretary–General to pull U.N. forces out rather than have them become embroiled in combat?

Consider paragraph 3 of Resolution 770 in connection with Resolution 771, adopted on the same day. Resolution 771, among other things, demanded that all parties and others concerned in the former Yugoslavia, and all military forces in Bosnia and Herzegovina, desist from all breaches of international humanitarian law, including such actions as mass expulsion and deportation of civilians, abuse of civilians in detention centers and attacks on non-combatants. Paragraph 2 condemned any violations of international humanitarian law, including those involved in the practice of "ethnic cleansing" (the practice ascribed to Serbs in Bosnia of driving non-Serbs from large areas intended to be reserved for Serbs).

Paragraph 7 of Resolution 771 said that the Security Council:

> *Decides,* acting under Chapter VII of the Charter of the United Nations, that all parties and others concerned in the former Yugoslavia, and all military forces in Bosnia and Herzegovina, shall comply with the provisions of the present resolution, failing which

---

b. See N.Y. Times, Aug. 11, 1992, p. A1, col. 6.

the Council will need to take further measures under the Charter * * *.

Did paragraph 3 of Resolution 770 and paragraph 7 of Resolution 771 impose binding obligations on nonstates involved in the conflict? If so, what made it so?

Did Resolution 770 go significantly further than Resolution 688 (the 1991 resolution on humanitarian aid to the Iraqi civilian population)? See page 853 supra.

What precedent did Resolution 770 set, if any, for future cases of humanitarian intervention?

The four Geneva Conventions on the law of war supply humanitarian rules for conflicts among "high contracting parties" (states) and much more general norms in the common article 3 for conflicts "not of an international character." Article 3 requires each party to the conflict to treat noncombatants humanely and without distinction based on such things as race, sex or religion; in particular, article 3 prohibits murder, mutilation, cruel treatment and torture, the taking of hostages, outrages on personal dignity, and sentencing without proper judicial guarantees.

Protocol I to the Geneva Conventions supplements them for international armed conflicts, and Protocol II does so for non-international conflicts. Before Yugoslavia disintegrated, it became a party to all four Geneva Conventions and both Protocols. Croatia became a party to all of them in May 1992.

This is not the place for an analysis of the applicability of the Geneva Conventions and Protocols to the Bosnian conflict. Suffice it to say that the International Committee of the Red Cross obtained commitments from the parties to the conflict that they would implement the basic principles of the Conventions, and asserted that the Conventions "must be observed in their entirety." [c]

The former Yugoslavia also became a party to the Genocide Convention, which makes genocide an international crime. It defines genocide as any of the following, if committed "with intent to destroy, in whole or in part, a national, ethnical, racial or religious group, as such": killing members of the group; causing serious bodily or mental harm to them; deliberately inflicting on the group conditions of life calculated to bring about its physical destruction in whole or in part; imposing measures intended to prevent births within the group; or forcibly transferring children of the group to another group.

Also relevant to the situation in the former Yugoslavia would be the crimes defined in the post-World War II Charter of the Nuremberg Tribunal. These include (a) crimes against peace, including such things as waging a war of aggression; (b) war crimes, including such things as

---

c. See ICRC Bull., Special ed. on Yugoslavia 7 (1992); Int'l Rev. of the Red Cross, No. 290, at 492–93 (1992).

murder, ill-treatment or deportation of civilian population in occupied territory, murder or ill-treatment of prisoners of war, plunder of property, and wanton destruction of cities or devastation not justified by military necessity; and (c) crimes against humanity, including murder, extermination, enslavement, deportation and other inhumane acts committed against any civilian population.[d]

In the autumn of 1992, reports of atrocities in Bosnia, and to some extent in Croatia, became increasingly urgent. At the urging of the United States, the U.N. Security Council acted.

SECURITY COUNCIL RESOLUTION 780
Oct. 6, 1992.
U.N. Doc. S/RES/780 (1992).

The Security Council,

* * *

Recalling paragraph 10 of its resolution 764 (1992) of 13 July 1992, in which it reaffirmed that all parties are bound to comply with the obligations under international humanitarian law and in particular the Geneva Conventions of 12 August 1949, and that persons who commit or order the commission of grave breaches of the Conventions are individually responsible in respect of such breaches,

* * *

Expressing once again its grave alarm at continuing reports of widespread violations of international humanitarian law occurring within the territory of the former Yugoslavia and especially in Bosnia and Herzegovina, including reports of mass killings and the continuance of the practice of "ethnic cleansing",

1. *Reaffirms* its call, in paragraph 5 of resolution 771 (1992), upon States and, as appropriate, international humanitarian organizations to collate substantiated information in their possession or submitted to them relating to the violations of humanitarian law, including grave breaches of the Geneva Conventions being committed in the territory of the former Yugoslavia, and requests States, relevant United Nations bodies, and relevant organizations to make this information available within thirty days of the adoption of the present resolution and as appropriate thereafter, and to provide other appropriate assistance to the Commission of Experts referred to in paragraph 2 below;

2. *Requests* the Secretary–General to establish, as a matter of urgency, an impartial Commission of Experts to examine and analyse the information submitted pursuant to resolution 771 (1992) and the present resolution, together with such further information as the Com-

---

d. The four Geneva Conventions appear in 75 U.N.T.S. 31, 85, 135 and 287; Protocols I and II appear in 1125 U.N.T.S. 3 and 609; the Genocide Convention appears in 78 U.N.T.S. 277; the relevant part of the Nuremberg Charter appears in 22 Trial of the Major War Criminals Before the International Military Tribunal 413–14 (1948).

mission of Experts may obtain through its own investigations or efforts, of other persons or bodies pursuant to resolution 771 (1992), with a view to providing the Secretary-General with its conclusions on the evidence of grave breaches of the Geneva Conventions and other violations of international humanitarian law committed in the territory of the former Yugoslavia;

3. *Also requests* the Secretary-General to report to the Council on the establishment of the Commission of Experts;

4. *Further requests* the Secretary-General to report to the Council on the conclusions of the Commission of Experts and to take account of these conclusions in any recommendations for further appropriate steps called for by resolution 771 (1992);

5. *Decides* to remain actively seized of the matter.

THE SECRETARY-GENERAL'S RESPONSE

In accordance with paragraph 3 of Resolution 780, the Secretary-General submitted a report to the Security Council.

REPORT OF THE SECRETARY-GENERAL ON THE ESTABLISHMENT OF THE COMMISSION OF EXPERTS
Oct. 12, 1992.
U.N. Doc. S/24657, at 2–3.

* * *

5. In considering how best to proceed in regard to the request of the Security Council contained in paragraph 2 of resolution 780 (1992), I have noted that the request parallels and to some extent duplicates an initiative of another United Nations organ, the Commission on Human Rights.

6. Members of the Security Council will recall that at its first special session, on 14 August 1992, the Commission on Human Rights adopted resolution 1992/S–1/1, in which it requested its Chairman to appoint a special rapporteur to investigate firsthand the human rights situation in the territory of the former Yugoslavia, in particular within Bosnia and Herzegovina, and to receive relevant, credible information on the human rights situation there from Governments, individuals, intergovernmental and non-governmental organizations, on a continuing basis, and to avail himself or herself of the assistance of existing mechanisms of the Commission on Human Rights. The Special Rapporteur visited areas of interest in the former Yugoslavia, and in particular Bosnia and Herzegovina, from 21 to 26 August 1992 and issued his first report on 3 September 1992.

* * *

8. Pursuant to paragraph 2 of resolution 780 (1992) I have decided to establish a Commission of Experts to be composed, in the first instance, of five members, one of whom will be designated by me as its Chairman. In appointing the members of the Commission I shall, of course, pay due regard to their professional qualifications, in particular in the areas of human rights, humanitarian law as well as criminal law and prosecution, experience, integrity and absolute impartiality. I reserve the right to expand the membership of the Commission should this become necessary.

9. The members of the Commission will serve in their personal capacity.

10. The terms of reference of the Commission, as set out in resolution 780 (1992), will be to examine and analyse the information submitted by States, international humanitarian organizations, other persons or bodies pursuant to resolution 771 (1992), as well as such further information as the Commission may obtain through its own investigations or efforts, with a view to providing me with its conclusions on the evidence of grave breaches of the Geneva Conventions and other violations of international humanitarian law committed in the territory of the former Yugoslavia. I expect that the Special Rapporteur of the Commission on Human Rights will cooperate closely with the Commission of Experts and provide it with all the information at his disposal. I shall take the necessary administrative steps to ensure continuing collaboration of the secretariats of the two bodies.

11. The Commission will adopt its own rules of procedure. In the absence of consensus, decisions of the Commission will be taken by a majority of the members present and voting.

12. The Commission, which for reasons of economy and efficiency will be located at the United Nations Office at Geneva, will be assisted by a small secretariat to provide the necessary substantive, secretarial and administrative assistance. * * *

13. The expenses of the Commission of Experts will be met, as far as possible, from existing resources. I reserve, however, the right to seek new appropriations should circumstances make this necessary.

14. The Convention on the Privileges and Immunities of the United Nations of 13 February 1946 will apply to the Commission, its members and its secretariat. The members of the Commission will have the status of experts on missions within the meaning of article VI of the Convention and the staff of the secretariat will have the status of officials within the meaning of articles V and VII of the Convention.

THE COMMISSION OF EXPERTS

In accordance with paragraph 8 of his report, the Secretary-General appointed a five-member Commission of Experts. The members were Professor Fritz Kalshoven (the Netherlands), Professor Cherif Bassiouni (a law professor in the United States), Mr. William Fenrick (Canada), Judge Keba Mbaye (Senegal) and Professor Torkel Opsahl (Norway).

This was the first time the Security Council had authorized the creation of a body to investigate violations of international humanitarian law arising from an armed conflict. What was its authority in the Charter to do so? *Article 24? Article 29? Article 34? Chapter VII?*

As the Secretary–General pointed out, the U.N. Commission on Human Rights had already undertaken a similar investigation, using a single Rapporteur. In addition, the International Committee of the Red Cross had adopted a procedure to receive reports of alleged breaches of humanitarian law in the former Yugoslavia, and to forward them in confidence to the party concerned for further investigation and action, if necessary. Why was a Commission of Experts needed?

In paragraph 14 of his report, the Secretary–General said that the members of the Commission would have the status of experts under *article VI* of the General Convention on the Privileges and Immunities of the U.N., and that members of the secretariat would be officials under *article V* and article VII. Does his saying so make it so? Does article VI give members of such a commission adequate protection when many of the combatants in an ongoing conflict are not under the control of an established state?

Paragraph 10 of the report directed the Commission to provide the Secretary–General with its conclusions on evidence of grave breaches of the Geneva Conventions and other violations of international humanitarian law. In February 1993 the Security Council decided that it would go ahead with a war crimes tribunal. It declared that the reported violations of humanitarian law were a threat to international peace and security. Are grave breaches of humanitarian law threats to the peace? If so, does that establish the Security Council's authority to create a war crimes tribunal?

At this writing, the tribunal had not been set up, nor had its procedure been determined. How should a war crimes tribunal's members be chosen? Should such a tribunal be empowered to try accused war criminals even if they are not brought personally before it? What procedural safeguards should be attached to it?

Is this the time to give greater urgency than heretofore to the creation of a permanent international criminal court? There has been a great deal of discussion about creating such a court, and some preliminary steps have been taken toward it.[e] Presumably it would have jurisdiction over war crimes as well as other acts made criminal under international law. What are the strengths and weaknesses of the idea?

[e]. See, e.g., U.N. Doc. A/CN.4/442 (1992).

Did Resolution 780 set a precedent for U.N. investigation of war crimes in other conflicts? How about Iraq, where there have been allegations not only of violations during the Persian Gulf conflict, but also of attempted genocide against the Kurds? Or Somalia, where undisciplined warfare among clans resulted in attacks on humanitarian agencies and the mass starvation of civilians?

D. SOMALIA

In July 1992 the Security Council responded to the Secretary-General's forceful plea for aid to Somalia, by adopting Resolution 767. It authorized an airlift to help ward off mass starvation; in addition, it called on all the factions in Somalia to facilitate the deployment of U.N. personnel who would help secure the delivery of the supplies, and in paragraph 4 called on them to "otherwise assist in the general stabilization of the situation in Somalia. In the absence of such cooperation, the Security Council does not exclude other measures to deliver humanitarian assistance to Somalia."

The Secretary-General immediately dispatched a representative to arrange the concurrence of the most recalcitrant leader of the warring Somali clans for the deployment of armed U.N. guards to protect delivery of the supplies. After about two weeks, his consent was obtained. The Security Council then adopted Resolution 775, increasing the strength of the U.N. Operation in Somalia (UNOSOM).

Was the consent of the feuding parties—none of which could have been said to be the effective government of Somalia—legally required for the deployment of U.N. guards to protect delivery of humanitarian supplies? Note that the civil war was between local clans, with no armed threat from forces outside the country. The principal political implications outside Somalia arose from quite substantial refugee flows. Unlike the Kurdish refugees in Turkey after the Persian Gulf war, the Somali refugees did not seem to pose a threat to international peace. Resolution 775, however, said that the Security Council was "concerned that the situation in Somalia constitutes a threat to international peace and security." Does that amount to a finding of such a threat?

Resolution 775 did not solve the problem. Ships carrying supplies to Somalia were prevented from unloading for several days at a time. Armed gangs looted most of the food and other supplies that actually reached Somalia. Private donor agencies were forced to pay large amounts in protection money to try to get their supplies through, but even that did not prevent the looting. Anarchy prevailed in the country, with no central government in place.

Secretary-General Boutros Boutros-Ghali decided that the situation was intolerable. After the U.S. government announced that it would be willing to send a substantial marine force, as the major part of a joint task force (under U.S. command) to get supplies through, the

Secretary–General outlined five options in a report[a] to the Security Council: (1) UNOSOM could continue to be the U.N. body in Somalia, under traditional peacekeeping principles. This would mean that it would not deploy without the agreement of the de facto authorities at each location, and would use force only in self-defense. Mr. Boutros–Ghali dismissed this option as inadequate. (2) UNOSOM's military elements could be withdrawn, leaving the private humanitarian agencies to negotiate on their own with clan leaders. This would mean continuing to pay protection money and would do nothing to restore national harmony. (3) UNOSOM could undertake a show of force in Mogadishu, in the hope that this would deter factions there and elsewhere in Somalia from continuing their attacks on relief providers. This was rejected as insufficient in light of the weaponry available to the Somali clans. (4) A country-wide enforcement operation could be undertaken by a group of member states authorized to do so by the Security Council. This was the option favored by the United States. Mr. Boutros–Ghali noted that the Security Council could adopt various means of influencing the operation once it was established, rather than simply leaving it to the group of states. (5) A country-wide enforcement operation could be carried out under direct U.N. command and control. This could be exercised by the Secretary–General or by some other arrangement. Member states would have to provide troops for the field and personnel for U.N. headquarters, and would have to accept U.N. control over their troops. Mr. Boutros–Ghali concluded:

> The focus of the Council's immediate action should be to create conditions in which relief supplies can be delivered to those in need. Experience has shown that this cannot be achieved by a United Nations operation based on the accepted principles of peace-keeping. There is now no alternative but to resort to Chapter VII of the Charter. In parallel, there must also be action to promote national reconciliation and thus remove the main factors that have created the humanitarian emergency. If forceful action is taken, it should preferably be under United Nations command and control. If this is not feasible, an alternative would be an operation undertaken by Member States acting with the authorization of the Security Council. In either case the objectives of the operation would be precisely defined and limited in time, in order to prepare the way for a return to peace-keeping and post-conflict peace building.[b]

U.S. antipathy to Mr. Boutros–Ghali's preferred option made it "not feasible," so the Security Council adopted his alternative recommendation in the resolution below.

---

a. U.N. Doc. S/24868 (1992).   b. Id. at 6.

SECURITY COUNCIL RESOLUTION 794
Dec. 3, 1992.
U.N. Doc. S/RES/794 (1992).

The Security Council,

* * *

Recognizing the unique character of the present situation in Somalia and *mindful* of its deteriorating, complex and extraordinary nature, requiring an immediate and exceptional response,

Determining that the magnitude of the human tragedy caused by the conflict in Somalia, further exacerbated by the obstacles being created to the distribution of humanitarian assistance, constitutes a threat to international peace and security,

Gravely alarmed by the deterioration of the humanitarian situation in Somalia and *underlining* the urgent need for the quick delivery of humanitarian assistance in the whole country,

* * *

Responding to the urgent calls from Somalia for the international community to take measures to ensure the delivery of humanitarian assistance in Somalia,

Expressing grave alarm at continuing reports of widespread violations of international humanitarian law occurring in Somalia, including reports of violence and threats of violence against personnel participating lawfully in impartial humanitarian relief activities; deliberate attacks on non-combatants, relief consignments and vehicles, and medical and relief facilities; and impeding the delivery of food and medical supplies essential for the survival of the civilian population,

Dismayed by the continuation of conditions that impede the delivery of humanitarian supplies to destinations within Somalia, and in particular reports of looting of relief supplies destined for starving people, attacks on aircraft and ships bringing in humanitarian relief supplies, and attacks on the Pakistani UNOSOM contingent in Mogadishu,

* * *

Determined to establish as soon as possible the necessary conditions for the delivery of humanitarian assistance wherever needed in Somalia, in conformity with resolutions 751 (1992) and 767 (1992),

Noting the offer by Member States aimed at establishing a secure environment for humanitarian relief operations in Somalia as soon as possible,

Determined further to restore peace, stability and law and order with a view to facilitating the process of a political settlement under the auspices of the United Nations, aimed at national reconciliation in Somalia, and *encouraging* the Secretary-General and his Special Representative to continue and intensify their work at the national and regional levels to promote these objectives,

Recognizing that the people of Somalia bear ultimate responsibility for national reconciliation and the reconstruction of their own country,

1. *Reaffirms* its demand that all parties, movements and factions in Somalia immediately cease hostilities, maintain a cease-fire throughout the country, and cooperate with the Special Representative of the Secretary–General as well as with the military forces to be established pursuant to the authorization given in paragraph 10 below in order to promote the process of relief distribution, reconciliation and political settlement in Somalia;

2. *Demands* that all parties, movements and factions in Somalia take all measures necessary to facilitate the efforts of the United Nations, its specialized agencies and humanitarian organizations to provide urgent humanitarian assistance to the affected population in Somalia;

3. *Also demands* that all parties, movements and factions in Somalia take all measures necessary to ensure the safety of United Nations and all other personnel engaged in the delivery of humanitarian assistance, including the military forces to be established pursuant to the authorization given in paragraph 10 below;

4. *Further demands* that all parties, movements and factions in Somalia immediately cease and desist from all breaches of international humanitarian law including from actions such as those described above;

5. *Strongly condemns* all violations of international humanitarian law occurring in Somalia, including in particular the deliberate impeding of the delivery of food and medical supplies essential for the survival of the civilian population, and *affirms* that those who commit or order the commission of such acts will be held individually responsible in respect of such acts;

6. *Decides* that the operations and the further deployment of the 3,500 personnel of the United Nations Operation in Somalia (UNOSOM) authorized by paragraph 3 of resolution 775 (1992) should proceed at the discretion of the Secretary–General in the light of his assessment of conditions on the ground; and *requests* him to keep the Council informed and to make such recommendations as may be appropriate for the fulfilment of its mandate where conditions permit;

7. *Endorses* the recommendation by the Secretary–General in his letter of 29 November 1992 (S/24868) that action under Chapter VII of the Charter of the United Nations should be taken in order to establish a secure environment for humanitarian relief operations in Somalia as soon as possible;

8. *Welcomes* the offer by a Member State described in the Secretary–General's letter to the Council of 29 November 1992 (S/24868)

concerning the establishment of an operation to create such a secure environment;

9. *Welcomes also* offers by other Member States to participate in that operation;

10. *Acting* under Chapter VII of the Charter of the United Nations, *authorizes* the Secretary–General and Member States cooperating to implement the offer referred to in paragraph 8 above to use all necessary means to establish as soon as possible a secure environment for humanitarian relief operations in Somalia;

11. *Calls* on all Member States which are in a position to do so to provide military forces and to make additional contributions, in cash or in kind, in accordance with paragraph 10 above and *requests* the Secretary–General to establish a fund through which the contributions, where appropriate, could be channelled to the States or operations concerned;

12. *Authorizes* the Secretary–General and the Member States concerned to make the necessary arrangements for the unified command and control of the forces involved, which will reflect the offer referred to in paragraph 8 above;

13. *Requests* the Secretary–General and the Member States acting under paragraph 10 above to establish appropriate mechanisms for coordination between the United Nations and their military forces;

14. *Decides* to appoint an ad hoc commission composed of members of the Security Council to report to the Council on the implementation of this resolution;

15. *Invites* the Secretary–General to attach a small UNOSOM liaison staff to the Field Headquarters of the unified command;

16. Acting under Chapters VII and VIII of the Charter, *calls upon* States, nationally or through regional agencies or arrangements, to use such measures as may be necessary to ensure strict implementation of paragraph 5 of resolution 733 (1992);[c]

17. *Requests* all States, in particular those in the region, to provide appropriate support for the actions undertaken by States, nationally or through regional agencies or arrangements, pursuant to this and other relevant resolutions;

18. *Requests* the Secretary–General and, as appropriate, the States concerned to report to the Council on a regular basis, the first such report to be made no later than fifteen days after the adoption of this resolution, on the implementation of this resolution and the attainment of the objective of establishing a secure environment so as to enable the Council to make the necessary decision for a prompt transition to continued peace-keeping operations; * * *.

c. [Establishing the arms embargo on Somalia. Ed.]

HUMANITARIAN ASSISTANCE UNDER CHAPTER VII

Resolution 794 was a pathbreaking resolution. For the first time in U.N. history, the Security Council used Chapter VII to ensure the delivery of humanitarian relief in a civil strife situation. Was Chapter VII intended for this?

The Security Council determined that there was a threat to international peace and security, even though the only armed threat to non-Somalis was to the providers of humanitarian aid and to UNOSOM personnel. Can it now be said that there is a threat to international peace and security whenever internal turmoil creates a major humanitarian crisis? If so, why?

Did the Security Council's reliance on Chapter VII in paragraph 10 turn what it did into enforcement action? In the Expenses Case, at page 757 supra, the ICJ said:

> The armed forces which were utilized in the Congo were not authorized to take military action against any State. The operation did not involve "preventive or enforcement measures" against any State under Chapter VII and therefore did not constitute "action" as that term is used in Article 11.

If the operation authorized by Resolution 794 was not directed against any state, and thus was not an enforcement measure, would there be an *article 2(7)* (domestic jurisdiction) problem? Note the language of the proviso at the end of article 2(7). Does it supply an exception for all measures adopted under Chapter VII, or only for some of them—those qualifying as "enforcement measures"?

If the operation authorized by Resolution 794 was not legitimized by the proviso in article 2(7), was it nevertheless lifted from that article because it was not an intervention in the domestic jurisdiction of a state? Would the absence of a functioning government in Somalia be significant?

The "all necessary means" language of paragraph 10 was obviously based on the operative language in Resolution 678, authorizing the use of force against Iraq in the Persian Gulf situation. See page 662 supra. Did the Security Council, in paragraph 10 and the subsequent paragraphs of Resolution 794, impose more authority over the operation than it had in the Persian Gulf conflict? Was this a step toward future use of the Secretary-General's preferred option?

Did Resolution 794 contribute anything to the development of international humanitarian law? See the preamble and paragraphs 2–5.

Soon after Resolution 794 was adopted, a difference of opinion developed between the United States and the U.N. Secretary-General over the scope of the U.S.-led operation. The United States said that its mission would be limited to securing the delivery of humanitarian assistance; the Secretary-General said that the disarming of Somali factions was necessary. Did Resolution 794 provide support for the Secretary-General's position? Is the disarming of armed gangs within a state a proper Chapter VII function?

How broad is the precedent set by Resolution 794?

Mr. Boutros-Ghali envisioned something more than a return to a traditional peacekeeping operation once the U.S.-led forces pulled out of Somalia. He contemplated a peace-enforcement operation with more teeth than the normal peacekeeping force. See below. Was the Somalia operation an example of the third type of peacekeeping arrangement contemplated years earlier by Dag Hammarskjöld? See page 735 supra.

SECTION 3. BEYOND PEACEKEEPING

INTRODUCTORY NOTE

The previous section has illustrated one important step beyond traditional peacekeeping: the use of armed force to ensure that humanitarian relief gets through. This section briefly explores some other measures that have been discussed seriously and/or that are being tried for the first time.

A. PEACE ENFORCEMENT

In the context of Somalia and more generally, Secretary-General Boutros-Ghali has proposed the use of peace enforcement units to enforce ceasefires more aggressively than traditional peacekeeping units have. As he envisages it, a peace enforcement operation would be authorized by the Security Council. As in the case of peacekeeping, the troops would be supplied by member states and would be under the direct authority of the Secretary-General, but they would be deployed without the express consent of the parties and could use force to maintain the ceasefire (not just in self-defense).[a]

In his "Agenda for Peace" (reprinted in the Documents volume accompanying this book), Mr. Boutros-Ghali contemplated an enhanced peacekeeping capability for the United Nations. See particularly *paragraphs 51 and 52*. The Security Council has taken up the recommendations in those paragraphs, and has said in a statement issued in October 1992:

> The Security Council, in accordance with the recommendations contained in paragraph 51 of the Secretary-General's report, encourages Member States to inform the Secretary-General of their willingness to provide forces or capabilities to the United Nations for peace-keeping operations and the type of units or capabilities

[a]. See Boutros-Ghali, Empowering the United Nations, 72 Foreign Affairs, No. 5, at 89, 93–94 (1992/93).

that might be available at short notice, subject to overriding national defence requirements and the approval of the Governments providing them. It further encourages the Secretariat and those Member States which have indicated such willingness to enter into direct dialogue so as to enable the Secretary–General to know with greater precision what forces or capabilities might be made available to the United Nations for particular peace-keeping operations, and on what time-scale;

    The Security Council shares the view of the Secretary–General in paragraph 52 of his report concerning the need for an augmentation of the strength and capability of military staff serving in the Secretariat and of civilian staff dealing more generally with peace-keeping matters in the Secretariat. * * * The Secretary–General might also consider * * * the establishment in the Secretariat of an enhanced peace-keeping planning staff and an operations centre in order to deal with the growing complexity of initial planning and control of peace-keeping operations in the field. The Council further suggests to Member States that they consider making available to the Secretariat appropriately experienced military or civilian staff, for a fixed period of time, to help with work on peace-keeping operations.[b]

Would peace enforcement have to be authorized, case-by-case, under Chapter VII of the Charter? Would it fall within *article 42*?

Would peace enforcement have to be under the direct control of the Secretary–General, or could it be done by member states under their own command, as were the operations in Iraq and Somalia?

Could the Security Council's suggestions about peacekeeping, above, be extended to peace enforcement? If so, how could they be implemented? For example, would *article 43* agreements be appropriate for peace enforcement?

U.N. peacekeeping has traditionally declined to take sides between the parties. Could peace enforcement be neutral? If not, is it a legal problem? A political problem?

When this was written, peace enforcement was contemplated for Somalia (UNSOM II) and parts of the former Yugoslavia. Other deployments were foreseeable. Is traditional peacekeeping a thing of the past?

B. NEW FORMS OF TRUSTEESHIP

It has been suggested that the U.N. might establish conservatorships for "failed states"—states that have descended into anarchy or that are otherwise unable to sustain themselves.[a] Somalia in 1992 would be a case in point. The suggestion is that "the Security Council

---

b. U.N. Doc. S/24728, at 2 (1992).

a. See Helman & Ratner, Saving Failed States, Foreign Policy No. 39, at 3 (1992–93).

might set up a board of trustees for Somalia by resolution, specifying the terms of the plan, and appoint five countries (perhaps three from Africa on the recommendation of the Africa Group) as members. That procedure would be consistent with the precedent set by the General Assembly in creating the U.N. Council for Namibia, which originally had only 11 members." [b]

Of course, the U.N. Council for Namibia existed before Namibia became a member of the United Nations. It was justified, at least by some, as a trusteeship under *Chapter XII* of the Charter, with the U.N. as the trustee under *article 81*. Could a similar arrangement for Somalia or other "failed" U.N. member states be justified that way? See *article 78*.

Could the Security Council instead use its authority under *article 24* or *Chapter VII* to create conservatorships for "failed states"?

Would such conservatorships be palatable to the majority of U.N. members? If so, should the Charter be amended to provide specifically for them?

C. PREVENTIVE DEPLOYMENT

"An Agenda for Peace" contains a key section that ties together several of the strands covered in this chapter. It looks toward prevention of violence rather than seeking containment or cure once violence has broken out.

AN AGENDA FOR PEACE
Report by Secretary–General Boutros Boutros–Ghali, June 17, 1992.
U.N. Doc. A/47/277–S/24111, at 8–9.

* * *

Preventive Deployment

28. United Nations operations in areas of crisis have generally been established after conflict has occurred. The time has come to plan for circumstances warranting preventive deployment, which could take place in a variety of instances and ways. For example, in conditions of national crisis there could be preventive deployment at the request of the Government or all parties concerned, or with their consent; in inter-State disputes such deployment could take place when two countries feel that a United Nations presence on both sides of their border can discourage hostilities; furthermore, preventive deployment could take place when a country feels threatened and requests the deployment of an appropriate United Nations presence along its side of the border alone. In each situation, the mandate and composition of the United Nations presence would need to be carefully devised and be clear to all.

b. Id. at 19.

29. In conditions of crisis within a country, when the Government requests or all parties consent, preventive deployment could help in a number of ways to alleviate suffering and to limit or control violence. Humanitarian assistance, impartially provided, could be of critical importance; assistance in maintaining security, whether through military, police or civilian personnel, could save lives and develop conditions of safety in which negotiations can be held; the United Nations could also help in conciliation efforts if this should be the wish of the parties. * * *

30. In these situations of internal crisis the United Nations will need to respect the sovereignty of the State; to do otherwise would not be in accordance with the understanding of Member States in accepting the principles of the Charter. The Organization must remain mindful of the carefully negotiated balance of the guiding principles annexed to General Assembly resolution 46/182 of 19 December 1991. Those guidelines stressed, *inter alia*, principles of humanity, neutrality and impartiality; that the sovereignty, territorial integrity and national unity of States must be fully respected in accordance with the Charter of the United Nations; and that, in this context, humanitarian assistance should be provided with the consent of the affected country and, in principle, on the basis of an appeal by that country. The guidelines also stressed the responsibility of States to take care of the victims of emergencies occurring on their territory and the need for access to those requiring humanitarian assistance. In the light of these guidelines, a Government's request for United Nations involvement, or consent to it, would not be an infringement of that State's sovereignty or be contrary to Article 2, paragraph 7, of the Charter which refers to matters essentially within the domestic jurisdiction of any State.

31. In inter-State disputes, when both parties agree, I recommend that if the Security Council concludes that the likelihood of hostilities between neighbouring countries could be removed by the preventive deployment of a United Nations presence on the territory of each State, such action should be taken. The nature of the tasks to be performed would determine the composition of the United Nations presence.

32. In cases where one nation fears a cross-border attack, if the Security Council concludes that a United Nations presence on one side of the border, with the consent only of the requesting country, would serve to deter conflict, I recommend that preventive deployment take place. Here again, the specific nature of the situation would determine the mandate and the personnel required to fulfil it.

PREVENTIVE DEPLOYMENT UNDER THE CHARTER

Mr. Boutros–Ghali was obviously concerned about possible tension between his preventive deployment idea and the domestic jurisdiction sensitivities expressed in *article 2(7)* of the Charter. Note all the references to consent.

In paragraph 28 he said that in a time of national crisis there could be preventive deployment "at the request of the Government or all parties concerned, or with their consent." Would consent of the government, alone, do away with any legal qualms? Would it matter whether the government came to power in a free and fair election in which all the people had a right to participate?

Who would be deployed in the situations contemplated by paragraphs 28–30? Troops? Civilian police? Civilian relief workers? Would consent of the government be required for any and all of these? Would it be required if there is a possibility that the crisis could spill over an international border?

What would paragraph 31 add to present practice, if the Security Council proceeds as recommended?

Does paragraph 32 recommend a form of collective self-defense, with U.N. forces helping to defend a nation from a potential aggressor? Could that be done outside of Chapter VII? If it were done within Chapter VII, would the consent of any party be required?

Paragraph 32 refers to a "nation" that fears attack. Traditionally, "nations" are not necessarily states under international law. Does this contemplate U.N. defense of nonstates, such as the several "nations" within Russia or other Eastern European states?

Some of these questions were answered in December 1992, when the Security Council authorized preventive deployment for the first time. It involved the Republic of Macedonia, formerly a part of Yugoslavia. By December 1992 it was an independent state for all practical purposes, even though it had not been formally recognized as such by the European Community or the United States (out of deference to Greece, which objected to the use of the name "Macedonia" for an independent state in the Balkans). The President of Macedonia asked the U.N. Secretary–General to explore the possibility of establishing a small U.N. presence in Macedonia. In response, the Secretary–General sent a team of UNPROFOR personnel to discuss the situation with the Macedonian authorities. The nature of the problem and the team's assessment appear in the excerpts below from its report.

REPORT OF THE UNPROFOR EXPLORATORY MISSION TO MACEDONIA
Dec. 9, 1992.
U.N. Doc. S/24923, Annex.

* * *

I. REQUEST BY MACEDONIA FOR A UNITED NATIONS PRESENCE

* * *

7. * * * [T]he main concern [of the Macedonian authorities] was that, if conflict erupted in Kosovo,[a] the fighting would spill over into Macedonia. The mission was informed that Albania had stated that, in case of a conflict in Kosovo, it would intervene in support of the Albanians in Kosovo. To do this, its forces would have to go through Macedonia, since its road communications to Kosovo are through Macedonia. Albanians from Macedonia, it was surmised, would also enter the conflict. It was said that the western part of Macedonia would become a base for Albanian operations into Kosovo. It should be noted that ethnic Albanians form the majority of the population in the central and northern parts of the border areas with Albania, as well as in the western part of the border areas with the Federal Republic of Yugoslavia (Serbia and Montenegro).

8. In the view of the Macedonia authorities, the above developments could then set off a wider Balkan war. Albanian activities in Macedonia would provide a reason for the Yugoslav Army to enter Macedonia. Moreover, they expressed a general concern with regard to the possible territorial ambitions of the Federal Republic of Yugoslavia (Serbia and Montenegro) on Macedonia. Statements recently made by certain nationalist sectors in Belgrade were cited.

9. The particular vulnerability of Macedonia, should hostilities break out in the area, was emphasized. When the Yugoslav National Army had left, it had taken with it all heavy weaponry and aircraft, as well as all border-monitoring equipment. The Macedonian army was, therefore, very lightly armed and lacked the equipment to monitor the borders effectively.

10. Another concern was that, if conflict erupted in Kosovo, there would be an exodus of refugees from Kosovo into Macedonia. This would have a destabilizing effect. * * *

II. OBJECTIVES OF A POSSIBLE UNITED NATIONS PRESENCE

* * *

12. It emerged that what was sought was monitoring of the borders and reporting of any developments which could signify a threat to the territory of Macedonia. At the same time, a United Nations presence would serve as a deterrent to external aggression against Macedonia. Its presence would assist in keeping potentially conflicting parties separate and would thus strengthen security in the region.

13. The mission sought also to determine whether a role for the United Nations in helping to calm any internal ethnic tensions, especially in the border areas, was envisaged. The role which UNCIVPOL[b] could play in this respect was explained. The President stated that the internal situation was stable. Ethnic concerns were being dealt with

---

a. [A province within Serbia, consisting primarily of persons of Albanian descent. Ed.]

b. [U.N. Civilian Police. Ed.]

through dialogue and negotiation. He did not see any need for United Nations assistance in this respect. In subsequent discussions with government officials, however, it appeared that an UNCIVPOL monitoring presence along the border would be welcome.

14. The situation in the border areas was thus of particular interest to the mission. At a meeting with the Mayor and Deputy Mayor of Debar on the western border with Albania it became clear that there are ethnic tensions in the area, where Albanians trying to enter Macedonia illegally have been killed by Macedonian soldiers. Incidents of this type could build up tensions within the Albanian community in these border areas.

* * *

IV. THE MISSION'S ASSESSMENT

17. Taking the above-described meetings into account, the mission considers that a United Nations presence in the first instance should be deployed primarily in the northern and western border areas of Macedonia. Its objectives would be:

(a) To monitor the border areas and report to the Secretary-General, through the Force Commander, any developments which could pose a threat to Macedonia;

(b) By its presence, to deter such threats from any source, as well as help prevent clashes which could otherwise occur between external elements and Macedonian forces, thus helping to strengthen security and confidence in Macedonia.

18. An UNPROFOR presence should have military, civilian police and civilian components. * * *

V. MILITARY ASPECTS OF A UNITED NATIONS DEPLOYMENT IN MACEDONIA

19. The border with the Federal Republic of Yugoslavia (Serbia and Montenegro) is 240 km long and the border with Albania 182 km. Both borders are mountainous, more so to the west, with heights of 2,700 metres. * * *

21. The Macedonian authorities did not expect the United Nations to defend its borders. It was the presence of United Nations forces that was most important. Given the aims above, the deployment of United Nations forces mainly in the actual border areas would seem to be the most appropriate.

Options for deployment

22. To achieve the aims, it would be necessary to maintain a constant presence by manning observation posts on a 24-hour basis. Because of road and weather conditions, each manning team would have to live close to its observation post. The task could be done by military observers, but their numbers would need to be as high as if

soldiers were used, and trained and skilled officers would be occupied with tasks that could be done by soldiers. It is therefore recommended that a battalion-sized infantry force of up to 700 persons be deployed from Debar on the western border northwards and eastwards as far as the Bulgarian border. * * *

United Nations Military Observers

24. The border area south of Debar should be covered by United Nations Military Observers, with a small headquarters in that region. A small number of Military Observers should also be deployed in the northern border area and attached to the headquarters in Skopje. The total requirement for Military Observers would be 35.

* * *

VI. UNCIVPOL DEPLOYMENT

26. On the basis of an assessment of the organization of the local police and of the situation on the northern and western borders of Macedonia, it is considered that UNCIVPOL's mandate should essentially be to monitor the work of the local border police. On the western border, the UNCIVPOL presence would assist in calming any inter-ethnic tensions arising from perceptions that the Macedonian police had harassed or abused Albanians, mainly in the context of illegal border crossings.

* * *

PREVENTIVE DEPLOYMENT IN MACEDONIA

The Secretary–General recommended that the Security Council approve this enlargement of UNPROFOR's mandate. In Resolution 795 (1992), the Security Council authorized the Secretary–General to deploy the personnel immediately, except that the police monitors would be deployed only upon receiving the consent of the Macedonian government. The resolution cited Chapter VIII of the U.N. Charter, in recognition of the presence in Macedonia of a mission of the Conference on Security and Cooperation in Europe (CSCE), but it did not cite Chapter VII and did not make a finding of a threat to the peace.

Could the Security Council have enlarged UNPROFOR's mandate to include preventive deployment in Macedonia, without the consent of the Macedonian government?

If the U.N. forces were not expected to defend Macedonia's borders (paragraph 21 of the report), and did not have the personnel or firepower to do so, did they serve any real purpose?

Under the mandate of Resolution 795, would the U.N. forces have to leave Macedonia, as UNEF I left Egypt, if the host government withdrew its consent?

Has the time come to amend the Charter to provide specifically for preventive deployment? If so, should it be hinged on the consent of the government(s) involved?

SECTION 4. NONSTATES, THE U.N. AND INTERNATIONAL PERSONALITY

In its resolutions on Yugoslavia and Somalia, the Security Council has called upon "all parties" to cooperate with U.N. peacekeeping and relief efforts, and to cease hostilities. In Resolution 787 (1992), the Security Council condemned the refusal of (inter alia) the Bosnian Serb paramilitary forces to comply with its resolutions, and demanded that they and other concerned parties fulfill immediately "their obligations under those resolutions." UNPROFOR entered into an agreement with the "Serbian Krajina Republic" on the establishment of Croatian authority in its "pink zones." The U.N. representative in Somalia obtained the consent of the head of a feuding clan before the Security Council could feasibly authorize a traditional peacekeeping force to protect the delivery of humanitarian relief. In "An Agenda for Peace," the Secretary–General contemplated preventive deployment in times of national crisis, at the request of the government "or all parties concerned."

Obviously, not all of the "parties" in these real or contemplated situations are sovereign states or other orthodox subjects of international law, nor are they necessarily within the effective control of states. In Europe and Somalia in the early 1990s, they have been primarily armed ethnic groups or clans. If the Security Council and the Secretary–General are to have any hope of being effective peacemakers, peacekeepers or providers of humanitarian assistance, they must deal with such nonstate parties under the conditions of the 1990s.

International law for many years has recognized limited rights and obligations of combatant entities in noninternational conflicts. Traditionally, this was in the form of recognition of belligerency for certain organized and effective insurgents, as well as national governments, in civil war situations. This led to common article 3 of the four 1949 Geneva Conventions on the law of war, which sets forth basic humanitarian obligations toward noncombatants for parties to armed conflicts that are not of an international character. Not all of these parties, of course, are states. But common article 3 concludes by saying, "The application of the preceding provisions shall not affect the legal status of the Parties to the conflict." This, presumably, prevents article 3 from conferring international personality upon nonstate insurgents—at least for purposes beyond article 3.

A question raised by the recent U.N. action in such places as the former Yugoslavia and in Somalia is whether the United Nations is in the process of conferring international personality on nonstate parties to armed conflicts (whether internal or international). Is the U.N.

effectively creating new international persons in a sense that goes beyond common article 3 of the Geneva Conventions?

If so, are those persons full subjects of international law, with capacity (for example) to assert international claims against states or international organizations?

If the U.N. has created new international persons, are they so only during times of armed conflict? Would all nonstate parties in effective control of territory in an armed conflict have whatever measure of international personality the Security Council or Secretary–General has bestowed on those they have dealt with in the former Yugoslavia and in Somalia, or would international personality be reserved only for parties the Security Council or Secretary–General has actually addressed?

Where would any U.N. authority to create new international persons come from? Is it in the Charter?

Chapter 6

PROTECTING BASIC HUMAN RIGHTS IN THE UNITED NATIONS AND IN REGIONAL ORGANIZATIONS

SECTION 1. INTRODUCTION

The materials in the first five chapters of this book have paid attention to human rights in some discrete contexts. Human rights are the focus of the rule-making, dispute-settlement and enforcement activities of the International Labor Organization, studied in Chapters 3 and 4. The right of self-determination is squarely involved in the quasi-constitutive role of the U.N. General Assembly, examined in Chapter 3. Concern for basic human rights has triggered some of the U.N. enforcement action considered in Chapter 4. And Chapter 5 has dealt with the right to free elections, as well as humanitarian intervention.

This chapter examines human rights activities of international organizations rather more systematically. Of course, it is impossible in a single chapter to provide comprehensive coverage.[a] Thus attention will be given only to three organizations—the United Nations, the Organization of American States and the Council of Europe—and even then, quite selectively. We will see a sampling of the ways in which these organizations try to enforce some of the major human rights instruments, with an emphasis on the judicial and quasi-judicial mechanisms of their treaty supervisory bodies.

We start, however, with a brief introduction to what has been called the "international bill of rights," stemming from the U.N. Charter, the Universal Declaration of Human Rights and the two basic U.N. Covenants: the Covenant on Economic, Social and Cultural Rights, and the Covenant on Civil and Political Rights.

---

a. For comprehensive sourcebooks on international human rights, see R. Lillich, International Human Rights: Problems of Law, Policy and Practice (1991); F. Newman & D. Weissbrodt, International Human Rights (1990).

SECTION 2. THE UNITED NATIONS

A. MAKING HUMAN RIGHTS LAW THROUGH THE UNIVERSAL DECLARATION AND THE COVENANTS

From the inception of the United Nations, the promotion of respect for fundamental human rights has stood as one of the Organization's basic goals. See U.N. Charter *preamble* and *articles 1(3), 55, 56, 62* and *68.* Although these provisions are quite general, the International Court of Justice has held the Charter to be a source of specific human rights in at least two contexts. In its Advisory Opinion on Namibia, the ICJ said:

> To establish * * *, and to enforce, distinctions, exclusions, restrictions and limitations exclusively based on grounds of race, colour, descent or national or ethnic origin which constitute a denial of fundamental human rights is a flagrant violation of the purposes and principles of the Charter.[a]

In its Judgment on the Diplomatic and Consular Staff in Tehran, the Court said:

> Wrongfully to deprive human beings of their freedom and to subject them to physical constraint in conditions of hardship is in itself manifestly incompatible with the principles of the Charter of the United Nations, as well as with the fundamental principles enumerated in the Universal Declaration of Human Rights.[b]

The United Kingdom has taken the position that U.N. Charter articles 55 and 56 "impose on member Governments of the United Nations the positive obligation to pursue policies to promote human rights and to co-operate with the United Nations organs and instruments to that end." [c]

Despite these pronouncements, no proponent of an international system for the protection of human rights would assert that the U.N. Charter, alone or even in conjunction with the Universal Declaration of Human Rights, provides the necessary normative framework. Much more is needed. Nevertheless, the job of fashioning specific, enforceable rules with mechanisms capable of fair and effective determinations has proved to be a difficult one that is still unfinished. The problem has its roots in pre-World War II governmental attitudes toward sovereignty and domestic jurisdiction.

Until the formation of the United Nations, there was virtually no significant challenge to the proposition that what a government does to and for its own citizens within its own territory is its own business, in the absence of a specific treaty commitment to the contrary. As put by

---

[a.] Legal Consequences for States of the Continued Presence of South Africa in Namibia (South West Africa) Notwithstanding Security Council Resolution 276 (1970), [1971] I.C.J. 16, 57.

[b.] Case Concerning United States Diplomatic and Consular Staff in Tehran (United States v. Iran), [1980] I.C.J. 3, 42.

[c.] [1978] British Y.B.Int'l L. 367.

a leading British authority, "Under customary law no rule was clearer than that a state's treatment of its own nationals is a matter exclusively within the domestic jurisdiction of that state, i.e. is not controlled or regulated by international law." [d]

Even as to noncitizens within its own territory, customary international law was thought to subject a government only to a rather loose overriding set of principles designed to protect alien-owned property from confiscation, and to protect aliens themselves from blatant "denials of justice" at the hands of government officials or perpetrated with their acquiescence. Such a system fell far short of anything approaching an international bill of rights, and did not set the stage at all well for any meaningful human rights effort by an international organization representing such diverse values and cultures as those represented in the United Nations.

Despite this inauspicious setting, the U.N. began early in its existence to particularize the human rights principles it was to promote.[e] On February 16, 1946, the Economic and Social Council (ECOSOC) established the Commission on Human Rights. Its mandate, as amended at the second session of ECOSOC, was to submit proposals, recommendations and reports to ECOSOC regarding "(a) an international bill of rights; (b) international declarations or conventions on civil liberties, the status of women, freedom of information and similar matters; (c) the protection of minorities; (d) the prevention of discrimination on grounds of race, sex, language or religion; and (e) any other matter concerning human rights not covered by items (a), (b), (c) and (d)."

The Commission originally consisted of one representative from each of 18 U.N. members selected by ECOSOC. The number was later increased in stages to 53. The Commission meets annually, normally in February and March, for five or six weeks at a time. The meetings are usually open to observers from U.N. member governments, specialized agencies, nongovernmental organizations in consultative status with ECOSOC under U.N. Charter article 71, and regional intergovernmental organizations concerned with human rights. Decisions are made by a majority of the members present and voting.

In 1947 the Commission, chaired by Mrs. Eleanor Roosevelt, began drafting the document that became the Universal Declaration of Human Rights. The draft Declaration was approved by the Commission and forwarded through ECOSOC to the General Assembly, which referred it to its Third (Social, Humanitarian and Cultural) Committee. The Committee held 86 meetings, and its drafting subcommittee held 20 meetings, considering the text in detail and revising it. In Decem-

d. J. Brierly, The Law of Nations 291 (6th ed. 1963).

e. The following discussion is based on 13 Whiteman, Digest of International Law 660–63 (1968), and 5 id. 236–44 (1965). For a more complete description of U.N. human rights activities through 1988, see United Nations Action in the Field of Human Rights, U.N. Doc. ST/HR/2/Rev. 3 (1988).

ber 1948, the General Assembly finally adopted the revised Declaration, by a vote of 48 to none, with eight abstentions. It is reproduced in the Documents volume accompanying this book.

The motivation for the Universal Declaration was expressed by U.S. Secretary of State George Marshall at the opening of the General Assembly session in 1948:

> Systematic and deliberate denials of basic human rights lie at the root of most of our troubles and threaten the work of the United Nations. It is not only fundamentally wrong that millions of men and women live in daily terror of secret police, subject to seizure, imprisonment, or forced labor without just cause and without fair trial, but these wrongs have repercussions in the community of nations. Governments which systematically disregard the rights of their own people are not likely to respect the rights of other nations and other people and are likely to seek their objectives by coercion and force in the international field.[f]

Just before the General Assembly voted on the Universal Declaration, Mrs. Roosevelt, speaking as the Chairperson of the Commission on Human Rights and as a representative of the United States, said:

> In giving our approval to the declaration today, it is of primary importance that we keep clearly in mind the basic character of the document. It is not a treaty; it is not an international agreement. It is not and does not purport to be a statement of law or of legal obligation. It is a declaration of basic principles of human rights and freedoms, to be stamped with the approval of the General Assembly by formal vote of its members, and to serve as a common standard of achievement for all peoples of all nations.[g]

At about the same time, John Foster Dulles, then a member of the U.S. delegation to the General Assembly, analogized the Universal Declaration to the U.S. Declaration of Independence as a document of political, not legal, significance.[h]

Despite these views, it did not take long for the General Assembly to start citing the Universal Declaration in a manner that sounded as though normative force was being accorded to it. In April 1949, the General Assembly invoked articles 13 and 16 of the Declaration as support for the assertion that "measures which prevent or coerce the wives of citizens of other nationalities from leaving their country of origin with their husbands or in order to join them abroad, are not in conformity with the Charter * * *."[i] In the following month, the General Assembly invited "the Governments of India, Pakistan and the Union of South Africa to enter into discussions [on the treatment of people of Indian origin in South Africa], taking into consideration the

f. 19 Dep't State Bull. 432 (1948).
g. 19 Dep't State Bull. 751 (1948).
h. International Conciliation No. 445, at 584–85 (1948).
i. G.A.Res. 285 (III), 4th & 5th paras. (1949).

purposes and principles of the Charter of the United Nations and the Declaration of Human Rights." j

Since then, as a former Director of the U.N. Division of Human Rights has said, "The General Assembly and other organs of the United Nations and of the specialized agencies have invoked [the Declaration's] principles and have been guided by them in so many cases, including some of the most controversial issues of our time, that it would require a major effort of research to list them." k In one particularly prominent example, the General Assembly in 1963 unanimously adopted the United Nations Declaration on the Elimination of All Forms of Racial Discrimination, in which it said that "Every State shall * * * faithfully observe the provisions of the present Declaration, the Universal Declaration of Human Rights and the Declaration on the granting of independence to colonial countries and peoples." l

The trend continues in the 1990s. For example, in 1991 the Economic and Social Council approved a decision of the Commission on Human Rights to create a working group to investigate "cases of detention imposed arbitrarily or otherwise inconsistently with the relevant international standards as set forth in the Universal Declaration of Human Rights or in the relevant international legal instruments accepted by the States concerned * * *." m

International conferences of governments have followed suit. In May 1968, 84 governments at the International Conference on Human Rights adopted the Proclamation of Teheran, which says (inter alia) that the Universal Declaration "constitutes an obligation for the members of the international community." n The Helsinki Final Act of the 1975 Conference on Security and Cooperation in Europe says (inter alia), "In the field of human rights and fundamental freedoms, the participating states will act in conformity with the purposes and principles of the Charter of the United Nations and with the Universal Declaration of Human Rights." o

In the United States, the Court of Appeals for the Second Circuit, in Filartiga v. Pena–Irala,p has had this to say about the Universal Declaration:

> [A]lthough there is no universal agreement as to the precise extent of the "human rights and fundamental freedoms" guaranteed to all by the [U.N.] Charter, there is at present no dissent from

---

j. G.A.Res. 265 (III), 2d para. (1949).

k. Humphrey, The U.N. Charter and the Universal Declaration of Human Rights, in The International Protection of Human Rights 39, 51 (E. Luard ed. 1967).

l. G.A.Res. 1904 (XVIII), art. 11 (1963).

m. ECOSOC Dec. 1991/243.

n. Proclamation of Teheran, para. 2, U.N. Doc. A/CONF. 32/41, at 4 (1968), U.N. Yearbook on Human Rights for 1968, at 457.

o. Final Act, Aug. 1, 1975, Part 1(a), Sec. VII, in 14 Int'l Legal Materials 1292, 1295 (1975). For discussion, see Humphrey, The Universal Declaration of Human Rights: Its History, Impact and Juridical Character, in Human Rights: Thirty Years After the Universal Declaration 21 (B. Ramcharan ed. 1979).

p. 630 F.2d 876, 882–83 (2d Cir.1980).

the view that the guaranties include, at a bare minimum, the right to be free from torture. This prohibition has become part of customary international law, as evidenced and defined by the Universal Declaration of Human Rights, General Assembly Resolution 217 (III)(A) (Dec. 10, 1948) which states, in the plainest of terms, "no one shall be subjected to torture." [10] The General Assembly has declared that the Charter precepts embodied in this Universal Declaration "constitute basic principles of international law." G.A.Res. 2625 (XXV) (Oct. 24, 1970).

[The court also discussed the General Assembly's 1975 Declaration on the Protection of All Persons from Being Subjected to Torture.]

These U.N. declarations are significant because they specify with great precision the obligations of member nations under the Charter. Since their adoption, "[m]embers can no longer contend that they do not know what human rights they promised in the Charter to promote." Sohn, "A Short History of United Nations Documents on Human Rights," in *The United Nations and Human Rights, 18th Report of the Commission* (Commission to Study the Organization of Peace ed. 1968). Moreover, a U.N. Declaration is, according to one authoritative definition, "a formal and solemn instrument, suitable for rare occasions when principles of great and lasting importance are being enunciated." 34 U.N. ESCOR, Supp. (No. 8) 15, U.N. Doc. E/CN.4/1/610 (1962) (memorandum of Office of Legal Affairs, U.N. Secretariat). Accordingly, it has been observed that the Universal Declaration of Human Rights "no longer fits into the dichotomy of 'binding treaty' against 'non-binding pronouncement,' but is rather an authoritative statement of the international community." *E. Schwelb, Human Rights and the International Community* 70 (1964). Thus, a Declaration creates an expectation of adherence, and "insofar as the expectation is gradually justified by State practice, a declaration may by custom become recognized as laying down rules binding upon the States." 34 U.N. ESCOR, supra. Indeed, several commentators have concluded that the Universal Declaration has become, *in toto*, a part of binding, customary international law.

The court went on to hold that official torture is prohibited by the law of nations, without distinction between treatment of aliens and citizens.[q]

---

10. Eighteen nations have incorporated the Universal Declaration into their own constitutions. 48 *Revue Internationale de Droit Penal* Nos. 3 & 4, at 211 (1977).

q. Congress later enacted the Torture Victim Protection Act of 1991, Public Law 102–256, 28 U.S.C.A. § 1350 note, which provides a private right of action in U.S. courts for victims of foreign official torture, without requiring the court to find that the act was in violation of international law. For any act to qualify as torture under the Act's definition, however, it would almost certainly be in violation of international law as determined in the Filartiga case.

In Siderman de Blake v. Republic of Argentina, the Court of Appeals for the Ninth Circuit said that although the Universal Declaration is not an international agreement within the meaning of the U.S. Foreign Sovereign Immunities Act, "it is a powerful and authoritative statement of the customary international law of human rights." [r]

As the materials above suggest, there is now a substantial body of evidence and opinion that the Universal Declaration's specific provisions on civil and political rights, if not the Declaration as a whole, represent customary international law. No governments have verbally denounced its provisions.[s] On the other hand, it would be difficult to maintain that there has been consistent international practice in compliance with all of its provisions. Consider, for example, the extent of state practice supporting *articles 5, 7, 10 and 19*. Can those provisions legitimately be considered to reflect custom? [t]

Is it more satisfactory to treat the Universal Declaration as an authoritative interpretation of the U.N. Charter's human rights provisions? As an expression of "general principles of law recognized by civilized nations"? [u] As an embodiment of a higher moral order recognized as law by those to whom it is addressed?

Would it ever make a difference which of these juridical explanations is most convincing?

Why do you suppose the Universal Declaration wasn't drafted as a statement of legal obligations in the first place?

THE U.N. COVENANTS

The Universal Declaration has been implemented by the U.N. Covenant on Economic, Social and Cultural Rights and by the U.N. Covenant on Civil and Political Rights.[v] These Covenants, in the form of treaties submitted to states for ratification, provide greater legislative detail than does the Declaration. (They are set out in full in the Documents volume, along with the Optional Protocols to the Covenant on Civil and Political Rights.) The article below summarizes the Covenants and compares them with the Declaration.

---

r. 965 F.2d 699, 719 (9th Cir.1992).

s. Not all decisionmakers, though, treat the Declaration as an expression of law. In Belgium, for example, it apparently is treated only as a statement of principle. See De Meyer v. État Belge, Belgian Conseil d'État, Feb. 9, 1966, 47 Int'l L.Rep. 196, 197.

t. On the relationship between state practice and *opinio juris* in such sensitive areas as the protection of basic human rights, see O. Schachter, International Law in Theory and Practice 335–42 (1991); Kirgis, Custom on a Sliding Scale, 81 Am. J.Int'l L. 146 (1987).

u. ICJ Statute art. 38. See J. Castañeda, Legal Effects of United Nations Resolutions 193–96 (1969).

v. Both were adopted by G.A.Res. 2200 (XXI) of Dec. 16, 1966, 21 GAOR Supp. No. 16 (A/6316), at 49–58 (1967). The Covenant on Economic, Social and Cultural Rights appears at 993 U.N.T.S. 3; the Covenant on Civil and Political Rights appears at 999 U.N.T.S. 171.

AFTER 30 YEARS, AN INTERNATIONAL BILL OF HUMAN RIGHTS
13 U.N. Chronicle, No. 4, at 50–52 (April 1976).

* * *

The Covenant on Civil and Political Rights, which came into force on 23 March 1976, ensures the right to life, liberty, security and privacy of person and the right to be protected from torture and other cruel, inhuman or degrading treatment. It prohibits slavery and forced labour and asserts among other rights: the right to freedom of thought, conscience and religion; the right to freedom of expression, to freedom of movement, and to equality before the law.

Several rights set out in the Covenant may be limited under specified conditions such as the necessity to protect national security and public order. However, certain rights, including the right to life and to protection against torture, may not be derogated from under any circumstances, even under a state of emergency.

The Covenant on Economic, Social and Cultural Rights, which came into force on 3 January 1976, includes articles recognizing the right to freedom from hunger, to an adequate standard of living, to just conditions of work, and to health and education.

A major right set forth in both covenants is the right of all peoples to self-determination and the right to enjoy and fully and freely use their natural wealth and resources.

Because of the nature of the rights, the Covenant on Economic, Social and Cultural Rights can only be implemented progressively, depending on the resources available to the State Party. On the other hand, since the Covenant on Civil and Political Rights deals with legally enforceable rights, its obligations are meant, by and large, to be carried out immediately upon ratification by a State.

That difference also accounts for the variation between the covenants in measures of implementation—or methods for international review of the way in which States are putting into effect the provisions of the covenants.

The principal method of review for both covenants which ratifying States are obligated to carry out is a system of reporting. While the Covenant on Economic, Social and Cultural Rights assigns the function of examining States' reports to the Economic and Social Council, the Covenant on Civil and Political Rights entrusts such a task to a Human Rights Committee whose members serve in an individual capacity. [In 1985 ECOSOC delegated the function of examining reports under the former Covenant to a Committee on Economic, Social and Cultural Rights.] The latter Covenant also provides optional machinery for State-to-State complaints.

* * *

Rights in Declaration But Not in Covenants Listed

The keystone of the covenants is the Universal Declaration of Human Rights. Generally they elaborate on the rights set forth in that document. There are, however, exceptions. Rights set forth in the Declaration and not reflected in the covenants are: the right of everyone to own property alone as well as in association with others, and the prohibition of arbitrary deprivation of property; the right of everyone to seek and to enjoy in other countries asylum from persecution; the right of everyone to a nationality and the right not to be arbitrarily deprived of one's nationality. The Covenant on Civil and Political Rights, however, affirms the right of every child to acquire a nationality.

On the other hand, the covenants recognize some rights not contained in the Declaration, the most important of which is the right of peoples to self-determination and their right freely to dispose of their natural wealth and resources.

States parties to either Covenant specifically undertake to ensure "the equal rights of men and women" to the enjoyment of the rights set forth in each Covenant.

Under the Covenant on Economic, Social and Cultural Rights, a ratifying State accepts the responsibility to take steps individually and "through international assistance and co-operation" to achieve progressively the rights recognized in the Covenant. It thereby recognizes:

— the right to work, freely chosen (article 6);

— the right of everyone, without distinction, to just and favourable conditions of work (article 7);

— the right to form and join trade unions (article 8);

— the right to social security, including social insurance (article 9);

— the right of the family, mothers, children and young persons to protection and assistance; and the right of free consent to marriage (article 10).

In its final substantive clauses, the Covenant recognizes the right of everyone to an adequate standard of living (article 11), to the highest standard of physical and mental health (article 12), to education (article 13), to participation in cultural life and to enjoyment of the benefits of scientific progress (article 15).

Some rights are set out in considerable detail. An article on education, for example, calls for a plan for the progressive achievement of compulsory primary education, free to all (article 14). Under the comprehensive article on trade unions States parties undertake to ensure the right of everyone to form and join trade unions and the right to strike, provided it is exercised in conformity with national laws.

Covenant Prohibits Torture, Arbitrary Arrest

The substantive provisions of the Covenant on Civil and Political Rights afford protection of the traditional rights in those fields, as enunciated in the Universal Declaration of Human Rights. The Covenant thus protects the right to life (article 6); prohibits torture or cruel, inhuman or degrading treatment or punishment (article 7); prohibits slavery, the slave trade and forced labour (article 8); prohibits arbitrary arrest or detention (article 9); provides that all persons deprived of their liberty shall be treated with humanity (article 10); and that no one shall be imprisoned merely for inability to fulfil a contractual obligation (article 11).

In other articles, the Covenant:

— asserts the right to liberty of movement and the freedom to leave any country, including one's own, and states that no one shall be arbitrarily deprived of the right to enter his own country (article 12);

— sets limitations on the expulsion of aliens lawfully in the territory of a State Party (article 13);

— provides for equality before the courts and tribunals and for guarantees in civil and criminal procedures (article 14);

— prohibits retroactive criminal legislation (article 15);

— stipulates the right of everyone to recognition everywhere as a person before the law (article 16); and

— prohibits arbitrary or unlawful interference with privacy, family, home or correspondence and unlawful attacks on honour and reputation (article 17).

In two successive articles, the Covenant states the right to freedom of thought, conscience and religion (article 18); and the right to freedom of opinion and expression (article 19).

The Covenant requires States parties to prohibit by law any propaganda for war and any advocacy of national, racial or religious hatred that constitutes incitement to discrimination, hostility or violence (article 20). It recognizes the right of peaceful assembly (article 21), and the right to freedom of association (article 22); calls on States parties to take steps "to ensure equality of rights and responsibilities of spouses as to marriage, during marriage and at its dissolution" (article 23); provides that every child shall have the right to protection by his family, society and the State (article 24); and stipulates that all citizens shall have the right and the opportunity to take part in the conduct of public affairs, to vote and to be elected at genuine periodic elections held by secret ballot (article 25). The Covenant states that all persons are equal before the law and are entitled to its equal protection (article 26).

A final right set out in the Covenant concerns minorities (article 27), a subject not included in the Universal Declaration because the

General Assembly stated at the time that its complexity made a uniform solution difficult. The Covenant provides that persons belonging to ethnic, religious or linguistic minorities shall not be denied the right, in community with the other members of their group, to enjoy their own culture, to profess and practise their own religion or to use their own language.

PROTOCOL PROVIDES FOR RECEIPT OF COMMUNICATIONS

Under the [first Optional Protocol to the Civil and Political Covenant] a ratifying State recognizes the competence of the Human Rights Committee "to receive and consider communications from individuals, subject to its jurisdiction [nationals or residents], claiming to be the victims of a violation by that State Party of any of the rights set forth in the Covenant". Before communicating with the Committee, the individual concerned must first have exhausted all domestic remedies. An anonymous communication or one which the Committee considers to be an abuse of the right of petition or to be incompatible with the Covenant provisions is inadmissible. The Protocol also provides that no communication shall be considered by the Committee unless it has ascertained that the matter is not being investigated under another international investigatory or settlement procedure.

The Committee is required to bring any communication submitted to it under the Protocol to the attention of the State Party concerned which, on its part, undertakes to provide the Committee with a written explanation of the matter and the remedy, if any, that it might have taken.

Meeting in closed session, the Committee will consider individual communications "in the light of all written information made available to it by the individual and by the State Party concerned". The Committee is to forward its views to the State Party concerned and to the individual; and will provide the General Assembly annually with a summary of its activities under the Protocol.

STATUS OF THE COVENANTS AND THEIR EFFECT ON THE UNIVERSAL DECLARATION

Each Covenant now has more than 100 states parties. More than 60 states are parties to the first Optional Protocol to the Covenant on Civil and Political Rights. (Its second Optional Protocol, aiming at the abolition of the death penalty, entered into force on July 11, 1991, with 10 states parties.)

Do those provisions of the Universal Declaration that are covered in the Covenants have continuing significance of their own?

Have those provisions of the Declaration that are not covered in either Covenant lost whatever legal significance they would otherwise have? For example, does the absence from the Covenants of the right not to be deprived arbitrarily of one's nationality (Universal Declaration article 15(2)) cast doubt on the existence in international law of such a right?

B. THE COVENANTS AND THE UNITED STATES

On October 5, 1977, the United States signed both Covenants. (It has not signed either Optional Protocol to the Civil and Political Covenant.) When the Carter administration submitted the Covenants to the Senate, it proposed that they be ratified subject to several statements, understandings, declarations and reservations. That caused quite a bit of political and academic furor, which lapsed when it became evident that neither Covenant at that time would receive the Senate's advice and consent.

In November 1991 the Senate Foreign Relations Committee signaled its renewed interest in the Civil and Political Covenant by holding a hearing on it. The Bush administration submitted a package of understandings, declarations and reservations similar in many respects to those the Carter administration had proposed. In April 1992 the Senate gave its advice and consent to the Civil and Political Covenant, subject to the package plus a proviso offered by Senator Helms of North Carolina. The President then ratified the Covenant in that form. (There was no move to resuscitate U.S. consideration of the Covenant on Economic, Social and Cultural Rights.)

UNITED STATES RESERVATIONS, UNDERSTANDINGS, DECLARATIONS AND PROVISO TO THE COVENANT ON CIVIL AND POLITICAL RIGHTS
United States Senate, April 2, 1992.
138 Cong.Rec. S 4783–84.

Resolved (two-thirds of the Senators present concurring therein), That the Senate advise and consent to the ratification of the International Covenant on Civil and Political Rights, adopted by the United Nations General Assembly on December 16, 1966, and signed on behalf of the United States on October 5, 1977 (Executive E, 95–2), subject to the following Reservations, Understandings, Declarations and Proviso:

I. The Senate's advice and consent is subject to the following reservations:

(1) That Article 20 does not authorize or require legislation or other action by the United States that would restrict the right of free speech and association protected by the Constitution and laws of the United States.

(2) That the United States reserves the right, subject to its Constitutional constraints, to impose capital punishment on any person (other than a pregnant woman) duly convicted under existing or future laws permitting the imposition of capital punishment, including such punishment for crimes committed by persons below eighteen years of age.

(3) That the United States considers itself bound by Article 7 to the extent that "cruel, inhuman or degrading treatment or punishment" means the cruel and unusual treatment or punishment prohibited by the Fifth, Eighth and/or Fourteenth Amendments to the Constitution of the United States.

(4) That because U.S. law generally applies to an offender the penalty in force at the time the offense was committed, the United States does not adhere to the third clause of paragraph 1 of Article 15.

(5) That the policy and practice of the United States are generally in compliance with and supportive of the Covenant's provisions regarding treatment of juveniles in the criminal justice system. Nevertheless, the United States reserves the right, in exceptional circumstances, to treat juveniles as adults, notwithstanding paragraphs 2(b) and 3 [of] Article 10 and paragraph 4 of Article 14. The United States further reserves to these provisions with respect to individuals who volunteer for military service prior to age 18.

II. The Senate's advice and consent is subject to the following understandings, which shall apply to the obligations of the United States under this Covenant:

(1) That the Constitution and laws of the United States guarantee all persons equal protection of the law and provide extensive protections against discrimination. The United States understands distinctions based upon race, colour, sex, language, religion, political or other opinion, national or social origin, property, birth or any other status—as those terms are used in Article 2, paragraph 1 and Article 26—to be permitted when such distinctions are, at minimum, rationally related to a legitimate governmental objective. The United States further understands the prohibition in paragraph 1 of Article 4 upon discrimination, in time of public emergency, based "solely" on the status of race, color, sex, language, religion or social origin not to bar distinctions that may have a disproportionate effect upon persons of a particular status.

(2) That the United States understands the right to compensation referred to in Articles 9(5) and 14(6) to require the provision of effective and enforceable mechanisms by which a victim of an unlawful arrest or detention or a miscarriage of justice may seek and, where justified, obtain compensation from either the responsible individual or the appropriate governmental entity. Entitlement to compensation may be subject to the reasonable requirements of domestic law.

(3) That the United States understands the reference to "exceptional circumstances" in paragraph 2(a) of Article 10 to permit the imprisonment of an accused person with convicted persons where appropriate in light of an individual's overall dangerousness, and to permit accused persons to waive their right to segregation from convicted persons. The United States further understands that paragraph 3 of Article 10 does not diminish the goals of punishment, deterrence, and incapacitation as additional legitimate purposes for a penitentiary system.

(4) That the United States understands that subparagraphs 3(b) and (d) of Article 14 do not require the provision of a criminal defendant's counsel of choice when the defendant is provided with court-appointed counsel on grounds of indigence, when the defendant is financially able to retain alternative counsel, or when imprisonment is not imposed. The United States further understands that paragraph 3(e) does not prohibit a requirement that the defendant make a showing that any witness whose attendance he seeks to compel is necessary for his defense. The United States understands the prohibition upon double jeopardy in paragraph 7 to apply only when the judgment of acquittal has been rendered by a court of the same governmental unit, whether the Federal Government or a constituent unit, [which] is seeking a new trial for the same cause.

(5) That the United States understands that this Covenant shall be implemented by the Federal Government to the extent that it exercises legislative and judicial jurisdiction over the matters covered therein, and otherwise by the state and local governments; to the extent that state and local governments exercise jurisdiction over such matters, the Federal Government shall take measures appropriate to the Federal system to the end that the competent authorities of the state or local governments may take appropriate measures for the fulfillment of the Covenant.

III. The Senate's advice and consent is subject to the following declarations:

(1) That the United States declares that the provisions of Articles 1 through 27 of the Covenant are not self-executing.

(2) That it is the view of the United States that States Party to the Covenant should wherever possible refrain from imposing any restrictions or limitations on the exercise of the rights recognized and protected by the Covenant, even when such restrictions and limitations are permissible under the terms of the Covenant. For the United States, Article 5, paragraph 2, which provides that fundamental human rights existing in any State Party may not be diminished on the pretext that the Covenant recognizes them to a lesser extent, has particular relevance to Article 19, paragraph 3, which would permit certain restrictions on the freedom of expression. The United States declares that it will continue to adhere to the requirements and constraints of its Constitution in respect to all such restrictions and limitations.

(3) That the United States declares that it accepts the competence of the Human Rights Committee to receive and consider communications under Article 41 in which a State Party claims that another State Party is not fulfilling its obligations under the Covenant.

(4) That the United States declares that the right referred to in Article 47 may be exercised only in accordance with international law.

IV. The Senate's advice and consent is subject to the following proviso, which shall not be included in the instrument of ratification to be deposited by the President:

Nothing in this Covenant requires or authorizes legislation, or other action, by the United States of America prohibited by the Constitution of the United States as interpreted by the United States.

THE RESERVATIONS, UNDERSTANDINGS AND DECLARATIONS

For the most part, the Senate and the Executive branch seem to have been concerned with maintaining the status quo in domestic U.S. law while becoming a party to the Covenant. Is that an appropriate stance when a state becomes a party to a human rights treaty? Is it consistent with *article 2* of the Covenant?

Note the five U.S. reservations. Vienna Convention on the Law of Treaties *article 2(1)(d)* defines "reservation," and *article 19* establishes the latitude a party has in attaching reservations to its consent to be bound. Are all the U.S. reservations permissible under article 19? In this connection, consider what Amnesty International said about the second U.S. reservation:

> Amnesty International has serious objections to the reservation proposed in respect to Article 6 of the [Covenant]—a reservation that envisages the continued practice within the United States of the execution of juvenile offenders. Article 6 guarantees one of the most fundamental rights protected by the [Covenant]—the right to life—and its provisions are among those which may never be derogated from in any circumstances, according to Article 4(2). Indeed, there is a serious question as to whether a reservation to a non-derogable right would be considered null and void. The international consensus against the execution of juvenile offenders, which is also reflected in a number of other important international human rights standards, is overwhelming. Only a very few governments continue to execute juvenile offenders—besides the United States these include Bangladesh, Iran, Iraq, Nigeria and Pakistan.[a]

If Amnesty International was correct about the U.S. reservation to *article 6,* would the effect be—as Amnesty said—to render the reservation null and void, or would it be to preclude the United States from being considered a party to the Covenant? See below.

Vienna Convention on the Law of Treaties *article 19* says that a state may formulate a reservation unless, inter alia, it is incompatible with the object and purpose of the treaty. The Vienna Convention does not spell out the consequences of formulating an incompatible reservation. Before the ICJ rendered its Advisory Opinion in the Reservations

---

a. 138 Cong.Rec. S 4781 (Apr. 2, 1992).

to the Genocide Convention Case in 1951, it was thought that a reserving state could not become a party to a multilateral treaty, no matter how insignificant its reservation, unless all other parties consented to the reservation. The ICJ Advisory Opinion introduced the notion that a state could become a party to a treaty even though some other states parties object to its reservation. The ICJ said, however, that if a reservation were incompatible with the Genocide Convention the reserving state "cannot be regarded as being a party to the Convention." [b]

The European Court of Human Rights in the Belilos case [c] addressed the effect of a reservation that is incompatible with the object and purpose of the European Convention on Human Rights. Switzerland had attached a reservation to article 6(1) of that Convention, which requires a fair and public hearing of civil and criminal cases by an independent and impartial tribunal. The Swiss reservation said that this required only "ultimate control by the judiciary," and Switzerland thus continued to allow some minor offenses to be tried by nonjudicial bodies with only a possibility of a limited appeal to a court.

The European Court held the Swiss reservation invalid under *article 64* of the European Convention, because it was too indefinite and did not contain a brief statement of the laws concerned. The Court said that "it is beyond doubt that Switzerland is, and regards itself as, bound by the Convention irrespective of the validity of the [reservation]." [d] Switzerland had been a party to the Convention for 14 years at that point, and had participated actively in its supervisory system.

Who would decide whether the U.S. reservation to article 6 of the Covenant is permissible? Would the reactions of other states parties—acquiescing in, or objecting to, the reservation—be determinative?

Why should *any* reservations be permitted to human rights conventions? Note that states may not attach reservations to conventions concluded under the auspices of the International Labor Organization. See page 278 supra. Are those conventions significantly different from other human rights conventions?

Are any of the U.S. "understandings" or "declarations" really reservations? If not, do they have any legal significance?

What is gained by declaring that articles 1 through 27 are not self-executing? Absent that declaration, would they be self-executing, in the sense that they would provide rights for individuals under U.S. law, without the need for implementing legislation? Consider, inter alia, the effect of article 2 on the other articles, and note also *article 40*.

What is the effect of the proviso at the end of the Senate's advice-and-consent resolution? Would it neutralize the rule in Missouri v.

b. [1951] I.C.J. 15, 18.

c. Series A, No. 132 (1988).

d. Id. at 23.

Holland,[e] where the Supreme Court relied on a treaty to legitimize a federal regulatory statute that would arguably have violated the Tenth Amendment (states' rights) absent the treaty? (Missouri v. Holland concerned migratory birds, not human rights.) Would any of the rights in the Covenant be beyond the federal legislative power absent the Covenant?

The United States declared that it accepts the competence of the Human Rights Committee to consider communications under *article 41,* which allows one state party to complain that another is not fulfilling its obligations under the Covenant, if both states have made the necessary article 41 declarations. If prior experience is any guide, this is not a major undertaking. As of early 1992, no inter-state communications had been submitted under article 41, even though 33 states in addition to the United States had made declarations under it. The article 41 procedure is examined below, in Section C(2).

At this writing no serious effort was being made in the U.S. government to revive interest in ratifying the Covenant on Economic, Social and Cultural Rights. Unlike the Covenant on Civil and Political Rights, which is comparable to the Bill of Rights in the U.S. Constitution, the Economic, Social and Cultural Covenant finds little parallel in the Constitution. With its emphasis on a governmental role in promoting such things as adequate food, clothing, housing and employment, it has been regarded by some as a reflection of socialist values inappropriate for a free market system. Yet the 104 states parties to it are by no means limited to socialist or formerly socialist states. Of the 24 OECD member states, only Switzerland, Turkey and the United States were not parties to the Economic, Social and Cultural Covenant as of January 1, 1992.

United States foreign policy has, in several respects, endorsed or at least accepted the proposition that economic, social and cultural rights exist. As a member of the Conference on Security and Cooperation in Europe (CSCE), the United States has joined in several CSCE declarations that recognize these rights. For example, the Charter of Paris, adopted in November 1990 at a CSCE summit meeting, says that everyone "has the right * * * to enjoy his economic, social and cultural rights."[f] In addition, as a member of the ILO, the United States participates in an elaborate system of protection of worker and employer rights, examined in Chapters 3 and 4 of this book.

Would ratification of the Covenant impose any immediate obligations on the United States, beyond the reporting obligations in *articles 16–17?* See *article 2(1).* When the Carter administration

---

e. 252 U.S. 416, 40 S.Ct. 382, 64 L.Ed. 641 (1920).

f. Charter of Paris for a New Europe, Nov. 21, 1990, 30 Int'l Legal Materials 190, 194 (1991).

submitted the Covenant to the Senate in 1978, the President recommended that this understanding be adopted: "The United States understands paragraph (1) of Article 2 as establishing that the provisions of Articles 1 through 15 of this Covenant describe goals to be achieved progressively rather than through immediate implementation."[g] Would that be an understanding or a reservation?

Are there cogent reasons for U.S. nonratification in the 1990s? To what extent are the reasons essentially domestic, having to do with possible governmental encroachment on individual liberties? To what extent are they essentially external, having to do with pressures on the United States from parties to the Covenant with more expansive notions of the welfare state than are widely held in the United States?

Are there positive reasons in favor of U.S. ratification in the 1990s? If so, what are they?

C. THE ENFORCEMENT PROCEDURES OF THE COVENANTS

1. *The Covenant on Economic, Social and Cultural Rights*

The international protection of economic rights dates back to the inception of the International Labor Organization in 1919. It picked up steam in 1944 with the Declaration of Philadelphia, adopted as an annex to the revised Constitution of the ILO. The Declaration of Philadelphia (set out in full in the Documents volume) affirms that "all human beings, irrespective of race, creed or sex, have the right to pursue both their material well-being and their spiritual development in conditions of freedom and dignity, of economic security and equal opportunity." Note, too, that the Universal Declaration of Human Rights envisages economic, social and cultural rights in its *articles 22–27*.

In the years since the Declaration of Philadelphia was adopted, the ILO has implemented its principles with more than 170 labor conventions and 180 recommendations, supported by a system for articulating, interpreting and enforcing these economic rights.

Social and cultural matters have been part of the concern of UNESCO since its inception shortly after World War II. Several conventions on education and on preservation of cultural property have been adopted under UNESCO auspices. UNESCO, however, has not developed dispute-settlement or enforcement procedures to the extent that the ILO has.

Part IV of the Covenant on Economic, Social and Cultural Rights contains its own enforcement procedure. See *articles 16–25*. It is not nearly as well developed as the ILO's enforcement mechanism, which deals only with labor conventions and recommendations. The Cove-

[g] 1978 Digest of U.S. Practice in Int'l Law 449. But see Alston, U.S. Ratification of the Covenant on Economic, Social and Cultural Rights: The Need for an Entirely New Strategy, 84 Am.J.Int'l L. 365, 377–80 (1990).

nant's procedure consists solely of a reporting system, by which states parties report "on the measures which they have adopted and the progress made in achieving the observance of the rights recognized herein." Article 16(1). The reports are considered by the U.N. Economic and Social Council, through a subsidiary body whose composition and mandate have evolved over the years, as indicated below.

When the draft Covenant was being considered in the Third Committee of the General Assembly in 1966, the United States offered an amendment that would have required states to submit their reports to "a Committee on Economic, Social and Cultural Rights * * *, consisting of ten experts of high moral standing, acknowledged impartiality, and recognized competence in the field of economic, social and cultural rights, elected by the States Parties from among their nationals." They were to serve in their personal capacities, with no two of the members to be nationals of the same state.[a] The amendment was not well received, and was never pressed to a vote.[b]

Under the reporting system as originally established, states parties were to submit reports, in stages, on clusters of the Covenant's articles. First reports on articles 6–9 were due in 1977; on articles 10–12 in 1979; and on articles 13–15 in 1981. Second reports on the same clusters were also due on staggered dates. Initially, reports were considered by a working group of ECOSOC "with appropriate representation of States parties."[c] The working group proved to be an ineffective supervisory body. In 1982 ECOSOC renamed it the Sessional Working Group of Governmental Experts. The 15 members were still representatives of states parties, but were to be selected on the basis of their expertise.[d]

The revamped Working Group was not much more effective than its predecessor. In 1985 ECOSOC decided to inject some new life into the process:

ECOSOC RESOLUTION ESTABLISHING THE COMMITTEE ON ECONOMIC, SOCIAL AND CULTURAL RIGHTS

United Nations Economic and Social Council, May 28, 1985.
ECOSOC Res. 1985/17, 1985 ESCOR Supp. No. 1 (E/1985/85), at 15.

The Economic and Social Council,

* * *

Decides that:

[a]. Report of the Third Comm., U.N. Doc. A/6546, at 9–10 (1966).

[b]. See Schwelb, Some Aspects of the Measures of Implementation of the International Covenant on Economic, Social and Cultural Rights, 1 Revue des Droits de l'Homme 363, 366 (1968).

[c]. ECOSOC Res. 1988, 60 ESCOR Supp. No. 1 (E/5850), at 11 (1976).

[d]. ECOSOC Res. 1982/33, in 1982 ESCOR Supp. No. 1 (E/1982/82), at 25.

(a) The Working Group * * * shall be renamed "Committee on Economic, Social and Cultural Rights" (hereinafter referred to as "the Committee");

(b) The Committee shall have eighteen members who shall be experts with recognized competence in the field of human rights, serving in their personal capacity, due consideration being given to equitable geographical distribution and to the representation of different forms of social and legal systems; to this end, fifteen seats will be equally distributed among the regional groups, while the additional three seats will be allocated in accordance with the increase in the total number of States parties per regional group;

(c) The members of the Committee shall be elected by the Council by secret ballot from a list of persons nominated by States parties to the International Covenant on Economic, Social and Cultural Rights under the following conditions:

> (i) The members of the Committee shall be elected for a term of four years and shall be eligible for re-election at the end of their term, if renominated;

* * *

(d) The Committee shall meet annually for a period of up to three weeks, taking into account the number of reports to be examined by the Committee, with the venue alternating between Geneva and New York;

* * *

(f) The Committee shall submit to the Council a report on its activities, including a summary of its consideration of the reports submitted by States parties to the Covenant, and shall make suggestions and recommendations of a general nature on the basis of its consideration of those reports and of the reports submitted by the specialized agencies, in order to assist the Council to fulfil, in particular, its responsibilities under articles 21 and 22 of the Covenant; * * *.

THE NEW COMMITTEE

The Committee on Economic, Social and Cultural Rights has been a far more dynamic force than its predecessor was. To a considerable extent, that is attributable to changes made by Resolution 1985/17, above. Which changes would explain it?

The only vote in ECOSOC against Resolution 1985/17 was cast by the United States, which said that it was not convinced that conversion of the Working Group into a committee of experts was the most appropriate way for ECOSOC to fulfill its responsibility under the Covenant.[e] The new Committee, of course, bears a strong resemblance

---

e. See 1985 U.N.Y.B. 879.

to the committee the United States proposed in 1966. Could there be a principled explanation for the apparent inconsistency in the U.S. position?

Much of the new Committee's attention in its first few years was devoted to establishing its procedures. Among other things, it decided that the system of requiring reports on clusters of Covenant articles every three years was too burdensome for some governments. Thus it decided to require a single report from each state party every five years on all of the substantive Covenant articles (a "global" report). A question was raised whether this is consistent with *article 17(1)* of the Covenant.[f] Is it?

The Committee also decided to request ECOSOC to authorize a working group of five Committee members to meet for a week prior to each Committee session, in order to identify in advance the questions that would be stressed for each government scheduled to report at the upcoming session. As approved and later amended by ECOSOC, the working group's week-long meeting occurs several weeks before the Committee session, so governments will have time to prepare responses to the group's questions for presentation at the Committee session.

Each reporting government is given 15 minutes at the Committee session to introduce its report; 90 minutes are then devoted to questions by members of the Committee and observations by representatives of specialized agencies directly concerned with the matters being reported; the government then has 60 minutes, usually at a subsequent meeting, to respond; and Committee members then have 15 minutes for concluding questions and observations. In accordance with Resolution 1985/17, above, the Committee then includes a summary of its consideration of each government report in its own report to ECOSOC.

A member of the Committee has said:

> In general terms, the potential effectiveness of the reporting procedure clearly lies less in the formal exchanges between the Committee and the state party and more in the mobilization of domestic political and other forces to participate in monitoring government policies and providing a detailed critique (assuming that one is warranted) of the government's own assessment of the situation.[g]

Would this point be equally valid no matter what form of government a reporting state has?

There has been uncertainty within the Committee about the propriety of including in its report to ECOSOC conclusions as to violations of the Covenant by named governments. Would that be within the Committee's mandate under Resolution 1985/17? Would it be a good

---

f. See 1988 ESCOR Supp. No. 4 (E/1988/14), at 58–59.

g. Alston, U.S. Ratification of the Covenant on Economic, Social and Cultural Rights: The Need for an Entirely New Strategy, 84 Am.J.Int'l L. 365, 371 (1990).

idea, given the nature of the Covenant and the composition of the Committee?

Although the Committee's practice so far has been not to make findings that specific Covenant provisions have been violated, it has discreetly expressed its disapproval of some governmental practices covered by the reports it has considered. The sensitivity of governments even to such discreet criticism is illustrated by an exchange of letters between the Argentine Chargé d'affaires in Geneva and the Chair of the Committee. The exchange also raises a question about the fairness of the Committee's procedure.

LETTER FROM THE ARGENTINE CHARGE D'AFFAIRES IN GENEVA

May 4, 1990.
1991 ESCOR Supp. No. 3 (E/1991/23—E/C.12/1990/8), at 113.

To: Chairman, Committee on Economic, Social and Cultural Rights

I have the honour to address you on behalf of the Government of the Argentine Republic with reference to the concluding observations of the Committee on Economic, Social and Cultural Rights concerning the initial report of Argentina concerning the rights covered by articles 13 to 15 * * *.

My Government wishes to inform you that it has taken note with surprise of the Committee's conclusions (document E/1990/23, para. 254). It is stated therein that the Committee "regretted that the answers provided by the representative of the State party to the questions concerning the position of the indigenous minorities had not entirely dispelled the concern which the members might have in that regard. Likewise, the information given in reply to the questions concerning the distribution of national income, the situation of the 12 million Argentinians living below the poverty level and the employment opportunities for university graduates were not felt to have been entirely adequate".

The authorities of Argentina do not question the right of the Committee to reach conclusions regarding any aspect of their report * * *.

It is, however, surprising—and indeed contrary to the practice of all the committees set up under human rights treaties—that none of the experts expressed any dissatisfaction when the Argentine delegation concluded its replies to the questions put to it.

The dissatisfaction of the experts appear all the more odd in that the summary record of the meeting (see E/C.12/1990/SR.19, para. 38) shows that none of them asked the Chairman for the floor to express his concerns and thus give the Argentine representatives an opportunity to make the relevant clarifications.

It was only at the 20th meeting of 29 January 1990—and in the absence of the Argentine delegation—that the experts expressed their criticisms, a situation which the Chairman of the meeting himself considered inappropriate since he "drew attention to the fact that the debate had been declared closed at the previous meeting, held on Friday, 26 January, as members of the Committee had had no further questions or comments on the Argentine report, and that the statements which were now being made were reopening the discussion, whereas they should have taken place when the Argentine delegation had been present to respond. He considered that to be a departure from the Committee's normal procedure * * * "; * * *.

The procedure thus adopted ignored the principle of equality of opportunity which must necessarily be observed by all the supervisory bodies bearing in mind the eminently legal character of their tasks, with the aggravating circumstance in the present case that it meant ignoring the rights of a State party to the Covenant.

We also consider it unacceptable that the inclusion in the Committee's report of the critical paragraphs in question is largely due to a presentation by a non-governmental organization made subsequently to our statement. * * *

The Argentine Republic has a deep respect for the non-governmental organizations and more particularly for those working in the area of human rights. It would never venture to challenge their right to participate in the life of international organizations and to make any criticisms they consider appropriate regarding the action of States. * * *

[Because it is necessary that all views are heard,] we consider it inadmissible that a statement by a representative of a non-governmental organization should have sufficed to make the majority of the experts change their views regarding the Argentine report and—what is even more serious—without allowing our delegation its legitimate right of reply.

In this connection, my country cannot accept the argument put forward by [a member of the Committee] (see E/C.12/1990/SR.20, para. 33) to the effect that "States parties had the right to be present during the submission of the concluding observations on reports, and that they were even invited to do so", giving in that regard the example of Cyprus. The fact is that 29 January, when the concluding observations were discussed, was the date on which the forty-sixth session of the Commission on Human Rights began, which obviously made it difficult for the Argentine delegation to attend the meeting of the Committee. In any case, there was nothing to prevent the Committee, had it so wished, from requesting the attendance of the Argentine delegation for the purposes of the required clarifications—a request with which we would have immediately complied * * *.

* * *

Before concluding, I wish to inform you that in due course my Government will transmit to the Committee its response to all the concerns expressed by the experts, in compliance with its obligations under the International Covenant on Economic, Social and Cultural Rights and with a view to continuing a fluid dialogue with the body under your chairmanship.

At the same time, the authorities of my country cannot but draw attention to what they consider to be a serious breach of procedure by a body entrusted with monitoring the observance of a human rights treaty, inasmuch as that breach deprived a State party of its equality of opportunity to defend its position. This resulted in critical observations on the part of the Committee which we believe could have been avoided in large measure if we had been given an opportunity of furnishing the necessary explanations at the appropriate time and in the appropriate form.

* * *

(*Signed*) Gregorio DUPONT
Minister Plenipotentiary
Chargé d'affaires a.i.

REPLY FROM THE CHAIR OF THE COMMITTEE ON ECONOMIC, SOCIAL AND CULTURAL RIGHTS

Dec. 11, 1990.
1991 ESCOR Supp. No. 3 (E/1991/23—E/C.12/1990/8), at 116.

* * *

One of the issues arising from [your] letter concerns the methods of work of the Committee and, in particular, its practice of reflecting in its report any concluding observations that its members consider to be warranted at the conclusion of the examination of each State party's report. This procedure has been clearly laid down in the Committee's reports, and is reflected in the rules of procedure which were adopted by the Committee at its third session. As the Government will certainly appreciate, the Committee is obliged to retain its autonomy in such matters in order to ensure its effective functioning.

Another issue arising from the letter concerns the issue of indigenous minorities and the use by some members of the Committee of information provided to them by non-governmental organizations. The Committee notes that its rules of procedure provide for the use of all relevant sources of information to facilitate its work. The Committee attaches great importance to the need to ensure the proper application of its procedures and its members have always endeavoured to respect this principle. It is with considerable regret therefore that the Committee notes the view of the Government that, in this instance, its members failed to follow the correct procedures. * * *

(*Signed*) Valeri I. Kouznetsov
Chairman
Committee on Economic, Social
and Cultural Rights

SENSITIVITIES AND FAIRNESS

Does the fact that the Argentine government took this matter so seriously bear witness to the potency of the Committee's reporting system?

Did the Chair of the Committee respond to the points raised by the Argentine government?

The Committee, like other international supervisory bodies, must walk a narrow path between overzealous enforcement and excessive deference to governments' sensitivities. The trick is to induce governments to cooperate constructively with the Committee, and thus to achieve the maximum attainable level of voluntary compliance. Did the Committee stray from its path in this case?

Nongovernmental organizations (NGOs) play an important role in human rights enforcement, within the U.N. system and elsewhere. As in the situation above involving Argentina, NGOs often provide international supervisory bodies with information not found in governments' own reports. By mobilizing their own memberships and by their direct efforts to apply pressure to governments, they can influence governmental policies and practices deemed inconsistent with the relevant international norms. Significantly, the Argentine government did not challenge the participation of NGOs in the work of the Committee on Economic, Social and Cultural Rights, and very few governments today would. Argentina challenged only the timing of the NGO's participation and the willingness of the Committee to use the NGO-supplied information as the basis for criticism without giving the government a chance to reply.

There are few, if any, international constraints on NGOs. Nearly everyone, other than those they target for criticism and other pressures, acknowledges the useful functions they serve not only in enforcement of human rights, but also in such fields as protecting the environment. Should they be given virtually a free rein, or is there a need for international regulation of their methods and activities?

There is considerable overlap between the Covenant on Economic, Social and Cultural Rights (particularly *articles 6–9*) and the concerns of the International Labor Organization. Chapter 4 of this book has examined the ILO supervisory mechanism, involving its Committee of Experts, its Conference Committee and its annual Conference. It involves a reporting system much like that used under the Covenant. Chapter 3 has examined another ILO mechanism that is partly supervisory and partly concerned with dispute-settlement: the submission of trade union questions to the ILO Committee on Freedom of Association. For the many states that are members of ILO and parties to the Covenant, which supervisory mechanism is likely to be more effective? Is there inefficient overlap? (Note that the ILO participates as an observer when the Committee on Economic, Social and Cultural Rights considers governments' reports on Covenant articles dealing with labor issues.)

Any supervisory system that relies on self-generated governmental reports is likely to have difficulty with some governments that do not submit reports on time or at all. The ILO is no exception, and neither is the Covenant system. As of October 1, 1991, 28 states parties to the Covenant on Economic, Social and Cultural Rights were maximally delinquent: they had not submitted any reports at all.[h] Some of them had been parties to the Covenant for more than ten years.[i]

The usual remedies for failure to submit reports are, first, direct contacts with the nonreporting governments, and if that fails, attempts to mobilize shame by naming them in documents issued by the supervisory body. The Committee has tried these remedies with nonreporting states. But part of the problem may well be the limited capacity of some governments to respond to the detailed Committee guidelines for the form and content of reports.[j] What remedy is available for that?

In addition to considering governments' reports, the Committee at each session sets aside a day for a general discussion of a specific right or a particular article in the Covenant, "in order to develop in greater depth its understanding of the relevant issues."[k] Although the day of general discussion is designed to have its own intrinsic value, it also can lead to the preparation of relevant general comments for inclusion in the Committee's report, as indicated below.[l]

Beginning with its third session in 1989, the Committee has prepared "general comments based on the various articles and provisions of the Covenant with a view to assisting the States parties in fulfilling their reporting obligations. * * * The Committee [endeavors] through its general comments to make the experience gained so far through the examination of [States parties'] reports available for the benefit of all States parties in order to promote their further implementation of the Covenant; to draw the attention of the States parties to insufficiencies disclosed by a large number of reports; to suggest improvements in the reporting procedures and to stimulate the activities of the States parties, the international organizations and the specialized agencies

---

h. See U.N. Doc. E/C.12/1991/3, at 6.
i. See U.N. Doc. E/C.12/1991/2, at 4.
j. See the Committee's Revised Guidelines, U.N. Doc. E/C.12/1991/1.
k. Id. at 63.
l. See Alston & Simma, Second Session of the UN Committee on Economic, Social and Cultural Rights, 82 Am.J.Int'l L. 603, 608 (1988).

concerned in achieving progressively and effectively the full realization of the rights recognized in the Covenant." [m] The general comments are included in the Committee's annual report to ECOSOC, and are transmitted to the states parties and to the specialized agencies concerned for their observations.

In 1990 the Committee's general comments addressed the nature of states parties' obligations under *article 2(1)*.

GENERAL COMMENT NUMBER 3
Committee on Economic, Social and Cultural Rights, 1990.
1991 ESCOR Supp. No. 3 (E/1991/23—E/C.12/1990/8), at 83.

1. Article 2 is of particular importance to a full understanding of the Covenant and must be seen as having a dynamic relationship with all of the other provisions of the Covenant. It describes the nature of the general legal obligations undertaken by States parties to the Covenant. * * * In particular, while the covenant provides for progressive realization and acknowledges the constraints due to the limits of available resources, it also imposes various obligations which are of immediate effect. Of these, two are of particular importance in understanding the precise nature of States parties' obligations. One of these, which is dealt with in a separate General Comment, and which is to be considered by the Committee at its sixth session, is the "undertaking to guarantee" that relevant rights "will be exercised without discrimination * * *".

2. The other is the undertaking in article 2(1) "to take steps", which in itself, is not qualified or limited by other considerations. The full meaning of the phrase can also be gauged by noting some of the different language versions. In English the undertaking is "to take steps", in French it is "to act" ("s'engage à agir") and in Spanish it is "to adopt measures" ("a adoptar medidas"). Thus while the full realization of the relevant rights may be achieved progressively, steps towards that goal must be taken within a reasonably short time after the Covenant's entry into force for the States concerned. Such steps should be deliberate, concrete and targeted as clearly as possible towards meeting the obligations recognized in the Covenant.

3. The means which should be used in order to satisfy the obligation to take steps are stated in article 2(1) to be "all appropriate means, including particularly the adoption of legislative measures". The Committee recognizes that in many instances legislation is highly desirable and in some cases may even be indispensable. For example, it may be difficult to combat discrimination effectively in the absence of a sound legislative foundation for the necessary measures. In fields such as health, the protection of children and mothers, and education, as well as in respect of the matters dealt with in articles 6 to 9, legislation may also be an indispensable element for many purposes.

m. Revised Guidelines, U.N. Doc. E/C.12/1991/1, at 63–64.

4. The Committee * * * wishes to emphasize, however, that the adoption of legislative measures, as specifically foreseen by the Covenant, is by no means exhaustive of the obligations of States parties. Rather, the phrase "by all appropriate means" must be given its full and natural meaning. * * * [T]he ultimate determination as to whether all appropriate measures have been taken remains one for the Committee to make.

5. Among the measures which might be considered appropriate, in addition to legislation, is the provision of judicial remedies with respect to rights which may, in accordance with the national legal system, be considered justiciable. The Committee notes, for example, that the enjoyment of the rights recognized, without discrimination, will often be appropriately promoted, in part, through the provision of judicial or other effective remedies. Indeed, those States parties which are also parties to the International Covenant on Civil and Political Rights are already obligated (by virtue of arts. 2 (paras. 1 and 3), 3 and 26) of that Covenant to ensure that any person whose rights or freedoms (including the right to equality and non-discrimination) recognized in that Covenant are violated, "shall have an effective remedy" (art. 2(3)(*a*)). In addition, there are a number of other provisions in the International Covenant on Economic, Social and Cultural Rights, including articles 3, 7(*a*)(*i*), 8, 10(3), 13(2)(*a*), (3) and (4) and 15(3) which would seem to be capable of immediate application by judicial and other organs in many national legal systems. Any suggestion that the provisions indicated are inherently non-self-executing would seem to be difficult to sustain.

6. Where specific policies aimed directly at the realization of the rights recognized in the Covenant have been adopted in legislative form, the Committee would wish to be informed, *inter alia,* as to whether such laws create any right of action on behalf of individuals or groups who feel that their rights are not being fully realized. In cases where constitutional recognition has been accorded to specific economic, social and cultural rights, or where the provisions of the Covenant have been incorporated directly into national law, the Committee would wish to receive information as to the extent to which these rights are considered to be justiciable (i.e. able to be invoked before the courts). The Committee would also wish to receive specific information as to any instances in which existing constitutional provisions relating to economic, social and cultural rights have been weakened or significantly changed.

7. Other measures which may also be considered "appropriate" for the purposes of article 2(1) include, but are not limited to, administrative, financial, educational and social measures.

* * *

9. The principal obligation of result reflected in article 2(1) is to take steps "with a view to achieving progressively the full realization of the rights recognized" in the Covenant. The term "progressive realization" is often used to describe the intent of this phrase. The concept of

progressive realization constitutes a recognition of the fact that full realization of all economic, social and cultural rights will generally not be able to be achieved in a short period of time. In this sense the obligation differs significantly from that contained in article 2 of the International Covenant on Civil and Political Rights which embodies an immediate obligation to respect and ensure all of the relevant rights. Nevertheless, the fact that realization over time, or in other words progressively, is foreseen under the Covenant should not be misinterpreted as depriving the obligation of all meaningful content. It is on the one hand a necessary flexibility device, reflecting the realities of the real world and the difficulties involved for any country in ensuring full realization of economic, social and cultural rights. On the other hand, the phrase must be read in the light of the overall objective, indeed the raison d'être, of the Covenant which is to establish clear obligations for States parties in respect of the full realization of the rights in question. It thus imposes an obligation to move as expeditiously and effectively as possible towards that goal. Moreover, any deliberately retrogressive measures in that regard would require the most careful consideration and would need to be fully justified by reference to the totality of the rights provided for in the Covenant and in the context of the full use of the maximum available resources.

10. On the basis of the extensive experience gained by the Committee, as well as by the body that preceded it, over a period of more than a decade of examining States parties' reports the Committee is of the view that a minimum core obligation to ensure the satisfaction of, at the very least, minimum essential levels of each of the rights is incumbent upon every State party. Thus, for example, a State party in which any significant number of individuals is deprived of essential foodstuffs, of essential primary health care, of basic shelter and housing, or of the most basic forms of education is, *prima facie,* failing to discharge its obligations under the Covenant. If the Covenant were to be read in such a way as not to establish such a minimum core obligation, it would be largely deprived of its raison d'être. By the same token, it must be noted that any assessment as to whether a State has discharged its minimum core obligation must also take account of resource constraints applying within the country concerned. Article 2(1) obligates each State party to take the necessary steps "to the maximum of its available resources". In order for a State party to be able to attribute its failure to meet at least its minimum core obligations to a lack of available resources it must demonstrate that every effort has been made to use all resources that are at its disposition in an effort to satisfy, as a matter of priority, those minimum obligations.

11. The Committee wishes to emphasize, however, that even where the available resources are demonstrably inadequate, the obligation remains for a State party to strive to ensure the widest possible enjoyment of the relevant rights under the prevailing circumstances.
* * *

12. Similarly, the Committee underlines the fact that even in times of severe resources constraints whether caused by a process of adjustment, of economic recession, or by other factors the vulnerable members of society can and indeed must be protected by the adoption of relatively low-cost targeted programmes. * * *

13. A final element of article 2(1), to which attention must be drawn, is that the undertaking given by all States parties is "to take steps, individually and through international assistance and co-operation, especially economic and technical * * *". The Committee notes that the phrase "to the maximum of its available resources" was intended by the drafters of the Covenant to refer to both the resources existing within a State and those available from the international community through international co-operation and assistance. Moreover, the essential role of such co-operation in facilitating the full realization of the relevant rights is further underlined by the specific provisions contained in articles 11, 15, 22 and 23. * * *

14. The Committee wishes to emphasize that in accordance with Articles 55 and 56 of the Charter of the United Nations, with well-established principles of international law, and with the provisions of the Covenant itself, international co-operation for development and thus for the realization of economic, social and cultural rights is an obligation of all States. It is particularly incumbent upon those States which are in a position to assist others in this regard. * * *

PROGRESSIVE REALIZATION

Is it fair to say that General Comment No. 3 is an authoritative, unreviewable interpretation of the obligation imposed by *article 2(1)*? What could a state party do if it disagreed with any part of the Comment?

Does General Comment No. 3 give article 2(1) teeth? Is it faithful to the language of article 2(1), and to the object and purpose of the Covenant?

At the end of paragraph 5, the Committee said it would be difficult to sustain any suggestion that the enumerated provisions of the Covenant are inherently non-self-executing. Was the Committee saying that any declaration to the effect that the Covenant is non-self-executing, like the one the United States made regarding the Covenant on Civil and Political Rights, would be incompatible with the object and purpose of the Covenant? If it wasn't saying that, did it have any business giving its opinion as to the direct effect of the Covenant's provisions in the domestic law of states parties?

Is it appropriate for the Committee to establish criteria for *prima facie* violations of the Covenant, in the abstract? See paragraph 10. Is the scheme for determining violations in that paragraph fair and efficient?

In paragraphs 11 and 12, was the Committee saying that governments have an obligation under the Covenant, even in times of scarcity, to redistribute resources among segments of the society in order to ensure that the most vulnerable members are taken care of? How might compliance with such an obligation be determined? For example, would evidence of large income or capital disparities among segments of a society establish noncompliance?

Do paragraphs 13 and 14 stand for the proposition that well-to-do states have an obligation under international law to supply foreign assistance to less well-off states? If so, was the Committee saying that even non-parties to the Covenant, like the United States, have such an obligation? What weight would that opinion have, as a matter of international law?

The Committee's practice of formulating general comments is not unique within the human rights field. In fact, as will appear in the next subsection, the Human Rights Committee administering the Protocol on Civil and Political Rights established the practice before this Committee did. Is it a promising technique for inducing or assisting states to comply with the Covenant on Economic, Social and Cultural Rights?

2. *The Covenant on Civil and Political Rights*

INTRODUCTORY NOTE

The only mandatory compliance procedure for the Covenant on Civil and Political Rights is another reporting system, under *article 40*. There are also two optional procedures: the inter-state communications procedure under *articles 41* and *42*, and the individual communications procedure under the first Optional Protocol. All three compliance procedures make use of the Human Rights Committee constituted under *articles 28–39*.

The Committee consists of 18 human rights experts who are nationals of states parties to the Covenant, elected at meetings of the states parties for four-year renewable terms. They serve in their personal capacities, not as representatives of their governments.

The materials below begin with a brief look at the least used of the compliance procedures, the inter-state communications option. The materials then move to the first Optional Protocol, which by now has engendered a substantial body of case law. Then we turn to the mandatory reporting system, which serves not only as as the central mechanism for supervising compliance with the Covenant by all parties to it, but also as a mechanism for enforcing the Committee's decisions under the first Optional Protocol.

a. Inter-state Communications

As of January 1, 1992, 33 states parties had made declarations recognizing the competence of the Human Rights Committee to consider inter-state communications under article 41 from any other state party that has made the same declaration. Nevertheless, as has been noted in Subsection B above, no communications had been submitted to the Committee under that procedure. Why might that be?

As in the case of the complaints procedure under article 26 of the ILO Constitution, there is no requirement regarding standing to present claims, other than acceptance by the initiating state of the same obligation. Thus State A, if it has made the required declaration, may complain about State B's failure to fulfill its obligations under the Covenant in respect of a national of State B, or even a national of State C, if State B has made the necessary declaration. As in the case of the ILO, the rationale is that protection of human rights is a universal responsibility such that standing requirements based on a showing of harm to the initiating state should not apply. That leaves open, of course, the question whether "communications" by one state directed against another under this procedure will be based primarily on genuine concern for the human rights of the persons involved. Moreover, it leaves open the question whether states that might some day be called upon to explain themselves in a human rights matter will often wish to represent the international community by accusing another. Is the inter-state dispute-settlement and enforcement procedure a useful human rights tool in any case other than that in which the complaining state has a direct stake in the matter (when its nationals are the victims of the respondent state's alleged human rights violations)? To put it another way, should some stricter standing requirements be put into such enforcement provisions?

Why should there be an exhaustion-of-domestic-remedies requirement in *article 41(1)(c)*? The exhaustion-of-remedies rule was developed primarily in cases involving governmental interference with private property. Is it equally appropriate for all cases involving governmental deprivations of civil and political rights? (There is no exhaustion-of-remedies requirement in the comparable ILO procedure.)

Suppose State A alleges that it believes State B is holding a group of persons in prison without charges and incommunicado, in violation of *articles 9* and *14* of the Covenant. State B refuses to respond to requests from State A for information, and the government of State A does not know what remedies, if any, the prisoners have pursued within State B. Under article 41(1)(c), could the Committee proceed?

The entire thrust of the inter-state procedure, of course, is to enable the Committee to "make available its good offices to the States Parties concerned with a view to a friendly solution of the matter on the basis of respect for human rights and fundamental freedoms as recognized in this Covenant." Article 41(1)(e). If it succeeds, it is to report only a brief statement of the facts and of the solution reached.

Article 41(1)(h)(i). But what if a friendly settlement is reached between the states parties, yet the Committee is not so sure that it fully respects the human rights recognized in the Covenant? (Is that wholly unlikely when governments reach negotiated settlements?)

What if no settlement is reached? The Committee would issue a report under article 41(1)(h)(ii), which turns out to be virtually the same as the report when a satisfactory solution is reached. When the Covenant was still in the draft form prepared by the Commission on Human Rights, it would have empowered the Committee in such a case to state its opinion as to whether there had been a breach of the Covenant. That provision was changed to its present form in the General Assembly's Third Committee. The principal argument for the change appears to have been that to permit the Committee to voice an opinion as to violation of the Covenant would be to blur the important distinction between conciliation—the Committee's role—and adjudication. The U.S. representative argued that giving an opinion was "a quasi-judicial function for which the Committee was not equipped, and it might interfere with the informal negotiations by which the Committee was to promote agreement between the parties."[a] Is that a strong argument?

If the Committee reaches no satisfactory solution, it may appoint an ad hoc Conciliation Commission under article 42, provided that the states involved agree. Like the Human Rights Committee, the Commission strives for an amicable solution on the basis of respect for human rights, but if that is not reached it is to issue a report which "shall embody its findings on all questions of fact * * *, as well as its views on the possibilities of amicable solution of the matter." Article 42(7)(c). Under that provision, could the Conciliation Commission include its opinion that the respondent state had violated the Covenant?[b]

Does the obligation in article 42(7)(d) have any enforcement significance?

b. Individual Communications

As of January 1, 1992, 60 states were parties to the first Optional Protocol. Under the Protocol, an individual may submit a communication (petition) to the Human Rights Committee, claiming to be the victim of a violation of the Covenant. Communications may be submitted only if the respondent state is a party to the Protocol, and then only if the individual is "subject to its jurisdiction." The latter phrase apparently means "within its physical control or having its nationality."[a]

a. 18 GAOR, 3d Committee, 1273d Meeting, at 329 (1963).

b. See Schwelb, Civil and Political Rights: The International Measures of Implementation, 62 Am.J.Int'l L. 827, 857–60 (1968).

a. See the remarks of the Swedish representative, 21 GAOR, 3d Committee, 1439th mtg., at 367 (1966). A line of Hu-

In practice, most communications alleging human rights violations are simply sent to the United Nations. Each year the U.N. receives thousands of these communications. The U.N. Centre for Human Rights in Geneva screens them, and channels to the Human Rights Committee those that appear to be within *article 1* of the Protocol, if the state complained against is a party to the Protocol.[b]

The Committee considers individual communications in closed meetings. Protocol *article 5(3)*. A respondent government is not allowed to appoint an ad hoc Committee member even if the regular membership includes no person of its nationality. This is in contrast to the situation in the International Court of Justice, where ICJ Statute article 31 allows a party to choose an ad hoc judge if the bench includes no judge of its nationality. Why wouldn't the Protocol provide for ad hoc Committee members chosen by respondent states?

Under the Committee's two-stage procedure for considering petitions, it first determines whether a petition is admissible, i.e. whether the procedural requirements of Protocol *articles 1, 3* and *5(2)* have been met. If it finds the petition admissible, it proceeds to the merits.

The Committee's Provisional Rules of Procedure set forth the conditions of admissibility, based on the procedural requirements established by the Protocol:

1. With a view to reaching a decision on the admissibility of a communication, the Committee shall ascertain:

(a) that the communication is not anonymous and that it emanates from an individual, or individuals, subject to the jurisdiction of a State party to the Protocol;

(b) that the individual claims to be a victim of a violation by that State party of any of the rights set forth in the Covenant. Normally, the communication should be submitted by the individual himself or by his representative; the Committee may, however, accept to consider a communication submitted on behalf of an alleged victim when it appears that he is unable to submit the communication himself;

(c) that the communication is not an abuse of the right to submit a communication under the Protocol;

(d) that the communication is not incompatible with the provisions of the Covenant;

(e) that the same matter is not being examined under another procedure of international investigation or settlement;

man Rights Committee decisions supports this interpretation.

b. See D. McGoldrick, The Human Rights Committee: Its Role in the Development of the International Covenant on Civil and Political Rights 127 et seq. (1991). This book contains a thorough examination of the functions, methods and work product of the Committee.

(f) that the individual has exhausted all available domestic remedies.[c]

Is paragraph 1(b) consistent with Protocol article 1? Why might it be more lenient in granting standing than a strict reading of Protocol article 1 would allow? The Committee has accepted a close family connection to the alleged victim as sufficient for standing. Other petitioners have been heard if they give reason to believe that the alleged victim (a) would approve and (b) could not act on his or her own behalf.[d]

Applying Protocol article 1 and paragraphs 1(a) and 1(b) above, the Committee has held that a nongovernmental organization may not submit a petition on behalf of a victim.[e] Could it have held otherwise? Is there any way an NGO concerned with human rights could still become involved in the submission of a petition?

Consider a sample of the admissibility issues the Committee has faced, taken from its practice in 1991:

HUMAN RIGHTS COMMITTEE SUMMARY OF SOME PROCEDURAL ISSUES DECIDED IN 1991

Report of the Human Rights Committee for 1991.
46 GAOR Supp. No. 40 (A/46/40), at 164–68.

Competence of the Committee and incompatibility with the provisions of the Covenant (Optional Protocol, art. 3)

681. In its work under the Optional Protocol the Committee has been circumspect and has avoided extending the scope of its competence beyond what the drafters had intended. For example, in determining whether the provisions of article 14 of the Covenant concerning the minimum guarantees for a fair trial have been observed, the Committee has consistently avoided becoming a "fourth instance". In declaring communication No. 304/1988 (D.S. v. Jamaica) inadmissible, the Committee observed:

"With respect to the author's claims of an unfair trial, the Committee observes that it is generally for the appellate courts of States parties to the Covenant and not for the Committee to evaluate facts and evidence placed before domestic courts and to review the interpretation of domestic law by national courts. Similarly, it is for the appellate courts and not for the Committee to review specific instructions to the jury by the judge, unless it is apparent

---

c. Rule 90, 32 GAOR Supp. No. 44 (A/32/44), Annex II, at 48, 64 (1977).

d. Cf. D. McGoldrick, supra note b, at 170–71.

e. See de Zayas, Möller & Opsahl, Application of the International Covenant on Civil and Political Rights Under the Optional Protocol by the Human Rights Committee, 28 German Y.B. Int'l L. 9, 18 (1985). This article, which also appears in 1986 Canadian Human Rts. Y.B. 101, provides an excellent summary of the Committee's procedural and substantive jurisprudence up to 1985.

from the author's submission that the instructions to the jury were clearly arbitrary or tantamount to a denial of justice, or that the judge manifestly violated his obligation of impartiality. The author's allegations do not show that the judge's instructions or conduct of the trial suffered from such defects in the present case. In this respect, therefore, the author's claims as submitted do not come within the competence of the Committee and, in that sense, fall outside the scope of protections provided by article 14, paragraph 1, of the Covenant. Accordingly, this part of the communication is inadmissible as incompatible with the provisions of the Covenant, pursuant to article 3 of the Optional Protocol."

* * *

683. Case No. 419/1990 (O.J. v. Finland) concerned the expropriation by the State of certain real estate for the purpose of the construction of a road. In declaring the communication inadmissible, the Committee observed:

"that the author's claims relate primarily to an alleged violation of her right to property, which she indicates is guaranteed by the Constitution of Finland. The right to property, however, is not protected by the International Covenant on Civil and Political Rights. Thus, since the Committee is only competent to consider allegations of violations of any of the rights protected under the Covenant, the author's allegations with regard to expropriation are inadmissible *ratione materiae*, under article 3 of the Optional Protocol, as incompatible with the provisions of the Covenant."

684. Another case turned on the competence of the Committee to examine questions relating to the right of self-determination. In case No. 413/1990 (A.B. *et al.* v. Italy), the authors alleged that the right of self-determination of the people of South Tirol, Italy, had been violated by numerous acts and decrees adopted by the Italian Parliament. In declaring the communication inadmissible, the Committee observed:

"With regard to the issue of the authors' standing under the Optional Protocol, the Committee recalls its constant jurisprudence that pursuant to article 1 of the Optional Protocol it can receive and consider communications only if they emanate from individuals who claim that their individual rights have been violated by a State party to the Optional Protocol. While all peoples have the right of self-determination and the right freely to determine their political status, pursue their economic, social and cultural development, and may, for their own ends, freely dispose of their natural wealth and resources, the Committee has already decided that no claim concerning the question of self-determination may be brought under the Optional Protocol. Thus, the Committee is not required to decide whether the ethno-German population living in South Tirol constitute 'peoples' within the meaning of article 1 of the International Covenant on Civil and Political Rights."

685. Under article 3 of the Optional Protocol, the Committee shall declare inadmissible a claim which it considers to be an abuse of the right of submission. In communication No. 314/1988 (Z.P. v. Canada), the author complained about a violation of his right to adequate time and facilities for the preparation of his defence, although deficiencies in the preparation of the defence were to some degree attributable to himself. The Committee noted that:

> "the first time the author complained about the unavailability of the trial transcript was over two months after being denied leave to appeal by the Supreme Court. In the circumstances, he is estopped from invoking an *ex post facto* violation of his right to adequate time and facilities for the preparation of his defence. The Committee concludes that this part of the communication is inadmissible as an abuse of the right of submission, pursuant to article 3 of the Optional Protocol."

No simultaneous examinations of the same matter (Optional Protocol, art. 5, para. 2(a))

686. Article 5, paragraph 2(a), of the Optional Protocol precludes the Committee from considering a communication if the same matter is being examined under another procedure of international investigation or settlement. Only the simultaneous examination of a case is precluded, however, and the Committee is, in principle, competent to consider cases that have been examined elsewhere, unless the State party has made a reservation upon ratification of or accession to the Optional Protocol precluding consideration of the same matter. For instance, most European States parties to the Optional Protocol that are also members of the Council of Europe and parties to the European Convention on Human Rights have made such reservations (the Netherlands and Portugal have not). Thus, while the Committee has had to declare inadmissible, on the basis of pertinent reservation, cases examined by the European Commission of Human Rights * * *, it has considered a number of cases submitted against the Netherlands and previously examined by the European Commission * * *.

* * *

The requirement of exhaustion of domestic remedies (Optional Protocol, art. 5, para. 2(b))

687. Pursuant to article 5, paragraph 2(b), of the Optional Protocol, the Committee shall not consider any communication unless it has ascertained that the author has exhausted all available domestic remedies. However, the Committee has already established that the rule of exhaustion applies only to the extent that these remedies are effective and available. The State party is required to give "details of the remedies which it submitted that had been available to the author in the circumstances of his case, together with evidence that there would be a reasonable prospect that such remedies would be effective" (case No. 4/1977, Torres Ramírez v. Uruguay). The rule also provides that

the Committee is not precluded from examining a communication if it is established that the application of the remedies in question is unreasonably prolonged.

688. In several cases concerning Jamaica the Committee had to decide whether a petition for special leave to appeal to the Privy Council was an available remedy for purposes of article 5, paragraph 2(b), of the Optional Protocol. In declaring communication No. 315/1988 (R.M. v. Jamaica) inadmissible, the Committee observed [that a petition for special leave to appeal under the Jamaican constitution would not be a priori ineffective.]

689. In this connection, the Committee has had the opportunity to stress that the availability of legal aid is also an important consideration in determining whether domestic remedies can be said to be available and effective. In case No. 315/1988 (R.M. v. Jamaica) the Committee stated:

"With regard to the practical operation of the system of legal aid in Jamaica, the Committee stresses that article 14, paragraph 3(d), of the Covenant requires States parties to ensure proper legal assistance to persons accused of criminal offences at all stages of their trial and appeal, including appeals to the Judicial Committee of the Privy Council. In the light of article 6, paragraph 2, of the Covenant it is imperative that whenever legal aid is provided, it must be sufficient to ensure that the trial can be conducted fairly."

690. The requirement of exhaustion of domestic remedies applies not only with respect to alleged trial irregularities but also in cases of alleged ill-treatment. The Optional Protocol requires that authors make at least a reasonable effort to denounce the alleged violations to the authorities concerned. In declaring communication No. 302/1988 (A.H. v. Jamaica) inadmissible, the Committee observed:

"With respect to issues that could arise under article 10 of the Covenant, the Committee notes that the author has not indicated what steps, if any, he has taken to denounce his alleged ill-treatment to the competent prison authorities, and what investigations, if any, have been carried out. Accordingly, the Committee finds that in this respect, the author has failed to exhaust domestic remedies."

THE LIMITS OF ADMISSIBILITY

Translated into terms familiar to English-speaking lawyers, what is meant by "incompatible with the provisions of the Covenant"? In that connection, what was meant by "inadmissible *ratione materiae*" in the case against Finland?

What is meant by "an abuse of the right of submission"?

Why was the petition alleging violation of the right of self-determination inadmissible? That right is expressly set out in *article 1(1)* of the Covenant. If members of the ethno-German population living in South Tirol could not assert it before the Committee, who could? Did the Committee simply use its authority to limit admissibility as a way to duck a very sensitive political issue?

Neither the Protocol nor the Committee's Rules of Procedure contain any limitation period for the filing of a petition. The reason appears to be that some persons whose rights have been violated may be unable promptly to submit a petition or to have someone with standing do it for them, and any arbitrary limitation period would unfairly cut off their remedy. Could the Committee nevertheless use any of the admissibility hurdles in the Protocol to dismiss unduly tardy petitions?

A ground for inadmissibility, discussed in the Committee's summary above, is that the same matter is being examined concurrently under another international procedure. Protocol article 5(2)(a). But the Committee is not precluded from considering a matter that has previously been examined under another procedure, such as the regional ones in Europe or the Americas (unless, of course, the respondent state has established a reservation to the Protocol precluding the Committee from considering such cases—as many European states have done). Why should petitioners have a second chance under the U.N. system after they have elected to use a regional procedure and have been disappointed?

It is not always clear whether a matter before the Committee is "the same matter" that is concurrently before another international body. For example, Economic and Social Council Resolution 1503, examined later in this Chapter, creates a separate U.N. mechanism to consider petitions against governments, when there is "a consistent pattern of gross and reliably attested violations of human rights and fundamental freedoms." The objective is to deal with massive human rights violations in one proceeding, rather than providing a case-by-case remedy. The Human Rights Committee has said that a respondent state may not claim inadmissibility on the basis of concurrent examination of a complaint against it under Resolution 1503, because "this procedure is not concerned with the examination of the same matter, within the meaning of article 5(2)(a) of the Protocol, as a claim by an individual under the Protocol." [f] Does that make sense?

Finally, there is the familiar admissibility requirement under the Protocol that available domestic remedies be exhausted. The principle is to let the state resolve the matter within its own system, if possible, before activating the international supervisory mechanism. At the same time, the state should not be allowed to hide behind unreasonable or ineffective mechanisms in its own system, in order to preclude any international review. Did the Human Rights Committee adequately balance the competing interests in its cases summarized above?

f. Communication No. 1/1976, in 1 Selected Decisions of the Human Rights Committee Under the Optional Protocol, U.N. Doc. CCPR/C/OP/1, at 17 (1985).

We turn now to a few examples of the Committee's handling of substantive issues under the Covenant, once a communication has been found admissible.

KELLY v. JAMAICA
U.N. Human Rights Committee, 1991.
Communication No. 253/1987, 46 GAOR Supp. No. 40 (A/46/40), at 241.

1. The author of the communication * * * is Paul Kelly, a Jamaican citizen awaiting execution at St. Catherine District Prison, Jamaica. He claims to be the victim of a violation by Jamaica of articles 6, paragraph 2; 7; 9, paragraphs 3 and 4; 10; and 14, paragraphs 1 and 3(a) to (e) and (g), of the International Covenant on Civil and Political Rights. He is represented by counsel.

Facts as Submitted by the Author

2.1 The author was arrested and taken into custody on 20 August 1981. He was detained until 15 September 1981 without formal charges being brought against him. Following a statement to the police given on 15 September 1981, he was charged with having murdered Owen Jamieson on 2 July 1981. He was tried with a co-defendant, Trevor Collins, in the Westmoreland Circuit Court between 9 and 15 February 1983. He and Mr. Collins were found guilty of murder and sentenced to death. On 23 February 1983, the author appealed his conviction; on 28 April 1986, the Jamaican Court of Appeal dismissed his appeal without producing a reasoned judgement. On appeal, author's counsel merely stated that he found no merit in arguing the appeal. Because of the absence of a reasoned judgement of the Court of Appeal, the author has refrained from further petitioning the Judicial Committee of the Privy Council for special leave to appeal.

2.2 The evidence relied on during the trial was that on 1 July 1981 the author and Mr. Collins had sold a cow to Basil Miller and had given him a receipt for the sale. According to the prosecution, the cow had been stolen from Mr. Jamieson, who had visited Mr. Miller's home on the afternoon of 1 July and had identified the cow as his property. The accused had then purportedly killed Mr. Jamieson in the belief that he had obtained the receipt from Mr. Miller implicating them in the theft of the cow.

* * *

Complaint

3.1 The author alleges a violation of articles 7 and 14, paragraph 3(g), of the Covenant on the ground that he was threatened and beaten by the police, who tried to make him give and sign a confession. Although the police sought to dismiss his version during the trial, the author contends that several factors support his claim: his "voluntary confession" was not obtained until nearly four weeks after his arrest; no independent witness was present at the time when he purportedly confessed and signed his statement; and there were numerous inconsistencies in the prosecution's evidence relating to the manner in which his statement was obtained.

3.2 The author further notes that 26 days passed between his arrest (20 August 1981) and the filing of formal charges against him (15 September 1981). During this time, he claims, he was not allowed to contact his family nor to consult with a lawyer, in spite of his requests to meet with one. After he was charged, another week elapsed before he was brought before a judge. During this period, his detention was under the sole responsibility of the police, and he was unable to challenge it. This situation, he contends, reveals violations of article 9, paragraphs 3 and 4, in that he was not "brought promptly before a judge or other officer authorized by law to exercise judicial power", and because he was denied the means of challenging the lawfulness of his detention during the first five weeks following his arrest.

3.3 According to the author, the State party violated article 14, paragraph 3(a), because he was not informed promptly and in detail of the nature of the charges against him. Upon his arrest, he was held for several days at the central lock-up at Kingston, pending "collection" by the Westmoreland police, and merely told that he was wanted in connection with a murder investigation. Further details were not forthcoming even after his transfer to Westmoreland. It was only on 15 September 1981 that he was informed that he was charged with the murder of Owen Jamieson.

3.4 The author submits that article 14, paragraph 3(b), was violated in his case, since he was denied adequate time and facilities for the preparation of his defence, had no or little opportunity to communicate with counsel representing him at trial and on appeal, both before and during trial and appeal, and because he was unable to defend himself through legal assistance of his own choosing. In this context, he notes that he experienced considerable difficulty in obtaining legal representation. Counsel assigned to him during the trial did not meet with him until the opening day of the trial; moreover, this meeting lasted a mere 15 minutes, during which it was virtually impossible for counsel to prepare the author's defence in any meaningful way. During the trial, he could not consult with the lawyers for more than a total of seven minutes, which means that preparation of the defence prior to and during the trial was restricted to 22 minutes. He points out that the lack of time for the preparation of the trial was extremely prejudicial to him, in that his lawyer could not prepare proper submissions on his behalf in relation to the admissibility of his "confession statement", or prepare properly for the cross-examination of witnesses. As to the hearing of the appeal, the author contends that he never met with, or even instructed, his counsel, and that he was not present during the hearing of the appeal.

3.5 The author also alleges that article 14, paragraph 3(d), was violated. In this connection, he notes that, as he is poor, he had to rely on legal aid lawyers for the judicial proceedings against him. While he concedes that this situation does not in itself reveal a breach of article 14, paragraph 3(d), he submits that the inadequacy of the Jamaican legal aid system, which resulted in substantial delays in securing suitable legal representation, does amount to a breach of this provision. He further notes that as he did not have an opportunity to discuss his case with the lawyers assigned to his appeal, he could not possibly know that this lawyer intended to withdraw the appeal and thus could not object to his intentions. He adds that had he been apprised of the situation, he would have sought other counsel.

3.6 The author contends that he has been the victim of a violation of article 14, paragraph 3(c), in that he was not tried without undue delay. Thus, almost 18 months elapsed between his arrest and the start of the trial. During the whole period, he was in police custody. As a result, he was prevented from carrying out his own investigations, which might have assisted him in preparing his defence, given that court-appointed legal assistance was not immediately forthcoming.

* * *

3.8 Finally, the author affirms that he is the victim of a violation of article 10 of the Covenant, since the treatment he is subjected to on death row is incompatible with the respect for the inherent dignity of the human person. In this context, he encloses a copy of a report about the conditions of detention on death row at St. Catherine Prison, prepared by a United States non-governmental organization, which describes the deplorable living conditions prevailing on death row. More particularly, the author claims that these conditions put his health at considerable risk, adding that he receives insufficient food, of very low nutritional value, that he has no access whatsoever to recreational or sporting facilities and that he is locked in his cell virtually 24 hours a day. It is further submitted that the prison authorities do not provide for even basic hygienic facilities, adequate diet, medical or dental care, or any type of educational services. Taken together, these conditions are said to constitute a breach of article 10 of the Covenant.

* * *

Issues and Proceedings Before the Committee

5.1 On the basis of the information before it, the Human Rights Committee concluded that the conditions for declaring the communication admissible had been met, including the requirement of exhaustion of domestic remedies. In this respect, the Committee considered that a written judgement of the Court of Appeal of Jamaica was a prerequisite for a petition for special leave to appeal to the Judicial Committee of the Privy Council. It observed that in the circumstances, author's counsel was entitled to assume that any petition for special leave to appeal would inevitably fail because of the lack of a reasoned judgement from the Court of Appeal; it further recalled that domestic remedies need not be exhausted if they objectively have no prospect of success.

5.2 On 17 October 1989, the Human Rights Committee declared the communication admissible.

* * *

5.4 As to the substance of the author's allegations of violations of the Covenant, the Committee notes with concern that several requests for clarifications notwithstanding, the State party has confined itself to the observation that the facts as submitted seek to raise issues of facts and evidence that the Committee is not competent to evaluate; it has not addressed the author's specific allegations under articles 7, 9, 10 and 14, paragraph 3, of the Covenant. Article 4, paragraph 2, of the Optional Protocol enjoins a State party to investigate in good faith all the allegations of violations of the Covenant made against it and its judicial authorities, and to make available to the Committee all the information at its disposal. The summary dismissal of the author's allegations, in general terms, does not meet the requirements of article 4, paragraph 2. In the circumstances, due weight must be given to the author's allegations, to the extent that they have been sufficiently substantiated.

5.5 As to the claim under articles 7 and 14, paragraph 3(g), of the Covenant, the Committee notes that the wording of article 14, paragraph 3(g)—i.e., that no one shall "be compelled to testify against himself or to confess guilt"—must be understood in terms of the absence of any direct or indirect physical or psychological pressure from the investigating authorities on the accused, with a view to obtaining a confession of guilt. *A fortiori*, it is unacceptable to treat an accused person in a manner contrary to article 7 of the Covenant in order to extract a confession. In the present case, the author's claim has not been contested by the State party. It is, however, the Committee's duty to ascertain whether the author has sufficiently substantiated his allegation, notwithstanding the State party's failure to address it. After careful consideration of this material, and taking into account that the author's contention was successfully challenged by the prosecution in court, the Committee is unable to conclude that the investigating officers forced the author to confess his guilt, in violation of articles 7 and 14, paragraph 3(g).

5.6 In respect of the allegations pertaining to article 9, paragraphs 3 and 4, the State party has not contested that the author was detained for some five weeks before he was brought before a judge or judicial officer entitled to decide on the lawfulness of his detention. The delay of over one month violates the requirement, in article 9, paragraph 3, that anyone arrested on a criminal charge shall be brought "promptly" before a judge or other officer authorized by law to exercise judicial power. The Committee considers it to be an aggravating circumstance that, throughout this period, the author was denied access to legal representation and any contact with his family. As a result, his right under article 9, paragraph 4, was also violated, since he was not in due time afforded the opportunity to obtain, on his own initiative, a decision by the court on the lawfulness of his detention.

5.7 Inasmuch as the author's claim under article 10 is concerned, the Committee reaffirms that the obligation to treat individuals with respect for the inherent dignity of the human person encompasses the provision of, *inter alia*, adequate medical care during detention. The provision of basic sanitary facilities to detained persons equally falls within the ambit of article 10. The Committee further considers that the provision of inadequate food to detained individuals and the total absence of recreational facilities does not, save under exceptional circumstances, meet the requirements of article 10. In the author's case, the State party has not refuted the author's allegation that he has contracted health problems as a result of a lack of basic medical care, and that he is only allowed out of his cell for 30 minutes each day. As a result, his right under article 10, paragraph 1, of the Covenant has been violated.

5.8 Article 14, paragraph 3(a), requires that any individual under criminal charges shall be informed promptly and in detail of the nature and the charges against him. The requirement of prompt information, however, only applies once the individual has been formally charged with a criminal offence. It does not apply to those remanded in custody pending the result of police investigations; the latter situation is covered by article 9, paragraph 2, of the Covenant. In the present case, the State party has not denied that the author was not apprised in any detail of the reasons for his arrest for several weeks following his apprehension and that he was not informed about the facts of the crime in connection with which he was detained or about the identity of the victim. The Committee concludes that the requirements of article 9, paragraph 2, were not met.

5.9 The right of an accused person to have adequate time and facilities for the preparation of his defence is an important element of the guarantee of a fair trial and an important aspect of the principle of equality of arms. In cases in which a capital sentence may be pronounced on the accused, it is axiomatic that sufficient time must be granted to the accused and his counsel to prepare the defence for the trial. The determination of what constitutes "adequate time" requires an assessment of the individual circumstances of each case. The author also contends that he was unable to obtain the attendance of witnesses. It is to be noted, however, that the material before the Committee does not disclose whether either counsel or author complained to the trial judge that the time or facilities were inadequate. Furthermore, there is no indication that counsel decided not to call witnesses in the exercise of his professional judgement, or that, if a request to call witnesses was made, the trial judge disallowed it. The Committee therefore finds no violation of article 14, paragraph 3(b) and (e).

5.10 As to the issue of the author's representation, in particular before the Court of Appeal, the Committee recalls that it is axiomatic that legal assistance should be made available to a convicted prisoner under sentence of death. This applies to all the stages of the judicial proceedings. In the author's case, it is clear that legal assistance was assigned to him for the appeal. What is at issue is whether his counsel had a right to abandon the appeal without prior consultation with the author. The author's application for leave to appeal to the Court of Appeal, dated 23 February 1983, indicates that he did not wish to be present during the hearing of the appeal, but that he wished legal aid to be assigned for this purpose. Subsequently, and without previously consulting with the author, counsel opined that there was no merit in the appeal, thus effectively leaving the author without legal representation. The Committee is of the opinion that while article 14, paragraph 3(d), does not entitle the accused to choose counsel provided to him free of charge, measures must be taken to ensure that counsel, once assigned, provides effective representation in the interests of justice. This includes consulting with, and informing, the accused if he intends to withdraw an appeal or to argue before the appeals court that the appeal has no merit.

5.11 With respect to the claim of "undue delay" in the proceedings against the author, two issues arise. The author contends that his right, under article 14, paragraph 3(c), to be tried without "undue delay" was violated because almost 18 months elapsed between his arrest and the opening of the trial. While the Committee reaffirms, as it did in its general comment on article 14, that all stages of the judicial proceedings should take place without undue delay, it cannot conclude that a lapse of a year and a half between the arrest and the start of the trial constituted "undue delay", as there is no suggestion that pre-trial investigations could have been concluded earlier, or that the author complained in this respect to the authorities.

5.12 However, because of the absence of a written judgement of the Court of Appeal, the author has, for almost five years since the dismissal of his appeal in April 1986, been unable effectively to petition the Judicial Committee of the Privy Council * * *. This, in the Committee's opinion, entails a violation of article 14, paragraph 3(c), and article 14, paragraph 5. The Committee reaffirms that in all cases, and in particular in capital cases, the accused is entitled to trial and appeal proceedings without undue delay, whatever the outcome of these judicial proceedings may turn out to be.

* * *

5.14 The Committee is of the opinion that the imposition of a sentence of death upon the conclusion of a trial in which the provisions of the Covenant have not been respected constitutes, if no further appeal against the sentence is available, a violation of article 6 of the Covenant. As the Committee noted in its general comment 6(16), the provision that a sentence of death may be imposed only in accordance with the law and not contrary to the provisions of the Covenant implies that "the procedural guarantees therein prescribed must be observed, including the right to a fair hearing by an independent tribunal, the presumption of innocence, the minimum guarantees for the defence, and the right to review by a higher tribunal". In the present case, while a petition to the Judicial Committee is in theory still available, it would not be an available remedy within the meaning of article 5, paragraph 2(b), of the Optional Protocol, for the reasons indicated in paragraph [5.1] above. Accordingly, it may be concluded that the final sentence of death was passed without having met the requirements of article 14, and that as a result, the right protected by article 6 of the Covenant has been violated.

6. The Human Rights Committee, acting under article 5, paragraph 4, of the Optional Protocol to the International Covenant on Civil and Political Rights, is of the view that the facts before the Committee disclose violations of articles 6, 9, paragraphs 2 to 4, 10 and 14, paragraphs 3(c) and (d) and 5 of the Covenant.

7. It is the view of the Committee that, in capital punishment cases, States parties have an imperative duty to observe rigorously all the guarantees for a fair trial set out in article 14 of the Covenant. The Committee is of the view that Mr. Paul Kelly, victim of a violation of article 14, paragraphs 3(c) and (d) and 5 of the Covenant, is entitled to a remedy entailing his release.

8. The Committee would wish to receive information on any relevant measures taken by the State party in respect of the Committee's views.

Individual Opinion Submitted by Mr. Waleed Sadi Pursuant to Rule 94, Paragraph 3, of the Committee's Rules of Procedure

I respectfully submit hereafter a separate opinion to the views adopted by the Human Rights Committee on 8 April 1991 with regard to communication No. 253/1987, submitted by Paul Kelly against Jamaica. In the Committee's view, the complainant was a victim of a violation of, *inter alia,* article 14, paragraph 3(d), of the Covenant, in the sense that he was essentially deprived of effective representation, as called for in a said provision, because court-appointed counsel did not pursue Mr. Kelly's right of appeal properly by deciding against pursuing it without prior consultation with his client. The central issue which the Committee had to determine is whether any error of judgement by the complainant's legal counsel may be imputed to the State party, and therefore render it responsible for the alleged errors of counsel and accordingly serve as a ground to order the release of the victim from imprisonment and thus escape from the sentence imposed upon him by the Westmoreland Circuit Court for a murder committed on 2 July 1981.

While sharing the view of the Committee that in proceedings for serious crimes, especially capital punishment cases, a fair trial for accused persons must provide them with effective legal counsel if the accused are unable to retain private counsel, the responsibility of the State party in providing legal counsel may not go beyond the responsibility to act in good faith in assigning legal counsel to accused individuals. Any errors of judgement by court-appointed counsel cannot be attributed to the State party any more than errors by privately retained counsel can be. In an adversary system of litigation, it is unfortunate that innocent people go to the gallows for mistakes made by their lawyers, just as criminals may escape the gallows simply because their lawyers are clever. This flaw runs deep into the adversary system of litigation applied by the majority of States parties to the Covenant. If court-appointed lawyers are held accountable to a higher degree of responsibility than their private counterparts, and thus the State party is made accountable for any of their own errors of judgement, then, I am afraid, the Committee is applying a double standard.

I therefore beg to differ with the Committee's view that the author should be released on account of the alleged errors made by counsel assigned to him for the appeal. I would have been open to suggestions of other remedies to be granted to the complainant, including declaring a mistrial or calling for another judicial review of his case by the appellate court to determine the matter of alleged gross errors made by his counsel.

[The individual opinion of Mr. Bertil Wennergren, another member of the Committee, has been omitted.]

THE COMMITTEE'S APPLICATION OF THE COVENANT

The Committee had already declared the communication admissible (see paragraphs 5.1 and 5.2), yet it said that it could not find violations in all instances claimed by the petitioner. See paragraphs 5.5, 5.9 and 5.11. Was that just another way of saying that those claims were inadmissible as being incompatible with the provisions of the Covenant?

Who had the burden of persuasion before the Committee? See especially paragraphs 5.4 and 5.5. Was what the Committee did in paragraph 5.5 consistent with what it said in 5.4? Was its willingness to take Mr. Kelly's word for prison conditions (paragraph 5.7) consistent with what it did in paragraph 5.5?

If the petitioner's allegations about lack of time to prepare for trial, as summarized in paragraph 3.4, were not rebutted by the government, why did the Committee conclude in paragraph 5.9 that there was no violation of *article 14, paragraph 3(b)* and *(e)*?

The nub of the matter before the Committee was the question of inadequate representation of counsel on appeal, and other appellate irregularities, in a capital case. See paragraphs 5.10, 5.14 and 7, as well as the individual opinion of Mr. Waleed Sadi. Because United

States courts have considerable experience with inadequacy-of-counsel issues, it is instructive to look briefly at a couple of U.S. Supreme Court cases.

In Strickland v. Washington,[g] the defendant had been convicted in a Florida court of three gruesome murders. His court-appointed counsel "cut his efforts short" when he learned that, against his advice, the defendant had confessed to two of the murders. At the sentencing hearing, counsel, apparently out of a sense of hopelessness of the case, did not present evidence concerning the defendant's character or emotional state. The trial judge sentenced the defendant to death, and that was upheld on appeal. The defendant later sought collateral relief, submitting (inter alia) 14 affidavits from friends and relatives saying they would have testified as to his character had they been asked to do so. The Supreme Court held that the District Court had properly declined to issue a writ of habeas corpus. It said, in part:

> Judicial scrutiny of counsel's performance must be highly deferential. * * *
>
> [T]he court should keep in mind that counsel's function * * * is to make the adversarial testing process work in the particular case. At the same time, the court should recognize that counsel is strongly presumed to have rendered adequate assistance and made all significant decisions in the exercise of reasonable professional judgment. * * *
>
> [In addition] any deficiencies in counsel's performance must be prejudicial to the defense in order to constitute ineffective assistance under the Constitution. * * *
>
> The defendant must show that there is a reasonable probability that, but for counsel's unprofessional errors, the result of the proceeding would have been different. * * * When a defendant challenges a death sentence such as the one at issue in this case, the question is whether there is a reasonable probability that, absent the errors, the sentencer—including an appellate court, to the extent it independently reweighs the evidence—would have concluded that the balance of aggravating and mitigating circumstances did not warrant death.[h]

In Keeney v. Tamayo–Reyes,[i] the defendant had been charged with murder arising from a stabbing death in a bar. He spoke little or no English. He was provided with an attorney and a translator. His attorney recommended that he plead *nolo contendere* to first-degree manslaughter. In the state court plea hearing, the judge explained what he was pleading to, in English. The translator conveyed the explanation to him in Spanish, his native language. He affirmed his

---

g. 466 U.S. 668, 104 S.Ct. 2052, 80 L.Ed.2d 674 (1984).

h. 466 U.S. at 689–90, 692, 694–95, 104 S.Ct. at 2065–69, 80 L.Ed.2d at 694–96, 698.

i. ___ U.S. ___, 112 S.Ct. 1715, 118 L.Ed.2d 318 (1992).

plea, and was sentenced. He later brought a collateral attack in a state court proceeding, claiming in his petition that he had not understood what manslaughter meant. The translator said in a deposition that he had translated "manslaughter" only as "less than murder." Under previous Supreme Court cases that assertion, if true, would render his conviction unconstitutional. In the ensuing state court hearing, his attorney did not ask him whether the translator had translated "manslaughter" for him, and did not call witnesses who could have assessed the translator's performance. The state court dismissed his petition; the state Supreme Court affirmed.

Mr. Tamayo–Reyes then sought a writ of habeas corpus in federal district court. The district court declined to hold an evidentiary hearing, but the Ninth Circuit reversed. It held, relying on a previous U.S. Supreme Court case, that a federal evidentiary hearing was required on a claim that would, if proved, require overturning the conviction, unless the petitioner had deliberately bypassed the state court review procedure. The U.S. Supreme Court reversed by a 5–4 vote, holding that the petitioner would be entitled to a federal evidentiary hearing only if he could show adequate cause for his failure to develop the facts in the state court proceedings, and could also show actual prejudice resulting from that failure. The Court recognized a narrow exception to that cause-and-prejudice standard, mandating a federal hearing if the petitioner can show that a fundamental miscarriage of justice would otherwise result.

This restrictive approach to collateral review, the majority said, would contribute to the finality of convictions, encourage full factual development in state courts, serve judicial economy, and channel the resolution of inadequate representation claims to the most appropriate forum. The four dissenting Justices stressed that Mr. Tamayo–Reyes alleged that he pleaded *nolo contendere* to a crime he did not understand, had exhausted his state remedies, had committed no procedural default, and had properly presented his claim to the federal district court.

Are the approaches of the U.S. Supreme Court and the Human Rights Committee similar or dissimilar regarding collateral review of a claim of inadequate representation of counsel in a homicide case?

Does the Human Rights Committee perform the same function vis-à-vis the courts of a national state party that federal courts in the United States do vis-à-vis state courts in criminal cases? If not, what is the difference, and what explains it?

Why did Mr. Waleed Sadi dissent on the issue of inadequacy of counsel? Was his disagreement essentially with the majority or with the adversarial system found in common-law countries?

In paragraph 7, the Committee said that, because of Jamaica's violations of article 14, paragraphs 3(c), 3(d) and 5, it was of the view that Mr. Kelly was entitled to be released. Is it appropriate for the Committee to take a position on the remedy a national government should provide, when the Committee finds a violation of the Covenant? See *article 5(4)* of the Protocol. Could the Committee have said instead that Mr. Kelly should be given a new trial?

Did the Committee in this case provide fair and effective international supervision of the state's compliance with the Covenant, without intermeddling in the state's domestic criminal justice system?

We turn next to a noncriminal case, involving a claim of sex discrimination under the Covenant's "equal protection clause"—*article 26*. That article is particularly significant, not only because of the inherent importance of its subject matter, but also because—unlike the "equal protection clauses" in regional human rights systems—it goes further than simply prohibiting unwarranted interpersonal discrimination by governments. What *does* it require of governments? (The case below does not fully answer this question, but it sets the stage for future cases to delve more deeply into it.)

ZWAAN–de VRIES v. THE NETHERLANDS
U.N. Human Rights Committee, 1987.
Communication No. 182/1984, 2 Selected Decisions of the Human
Rights Committee Under the [First] Optional Protocol, U.N.
Doc. CCPR/C/OP/2, at 209 (1990).

[The author of the communication, Mrs. Zwaan-de Vries, was a Netherlands national residing in Amsterdam. In February 1979 she lost her job as a computer operator. Under the Dutch Unemployment Act she was granted unemployment benefits for eight months. She then applied for continued benefits under the Unemployment Benefits Act (WWV). Her application was denied on the basis of section 13, subsection 1(1) of the WWV, which provided for further benefits to married women only if they were breadwinners or permanently separated from their husbands. No comparable requirements applied to married men. Mrs. Zwaan-de Vries appealed all the way to the Dutch Central Board of Appeal, which confirmed the denial of her application.

[The author then submitted her communication to the Human Rights Committee, claiming a violation of article 26 of the Covenant since the only reasons for denying her unemployment benefits were her sex and marital status. The State party (the Dutch government) contested the admissibility of the petition. It conceded that Mrs. Zwaan-de Vries had exhausted her domestic remedies, but said that the right she was claiming was covered by the Covenant on Economic, Social and Cultural Rights, *article 9* in conjunction with *articles 2* and *3*. The only remedy for an alleged violation of those articles, said the State party, was examination by the U.N. Committee on Economic, Social and Cultural Rights under that Covenant's reporting system.

The Netherlands, as a party to that Covenant, had submitted reports to the Committee on Economic, Social and Cultural Rights.

[The Human Rights Committee first addressed the admissibility issue:]

6.2 Article 5, paragraph 2(a), of the Optional Protocol precludes the Committee from considering a communication if the same matter is being examined under another procedure of international investigation or settlement. In this connection the Committee observes that the examination of State reports, submitted under article 16 of the International Covenant on Economic, Social and Cultural Rights, does not, within the meaning of article 5, paragraph 2(a), constitute an examination of the "same matter" as a claim by an individual submitted to the Human Rights Committee under the Optional Protocol.

6.3 The Committee further observes that a claim submitted under the Optional Protocol concerning an alleged breach of a provision of the International Covenant on Civil and Political Rights is not necessarily incompatible with the provisions of that Covenant (see art. 3 of the Optional Protocol), because the facts also related to a right protected by the International Covenant on Economic, Social and Cultural Rights or any other international instrument. It still had to be tested whether the alleged breach of a right protected by the International Covenant on Civil and Political Rights was borne out by the facts.

[The Committee held the communication admissible.]

8.2 In discussing the merits of the case, the State party first elucidates the factual background as follows:

> When Mrs. Zwaan applied for WWV benefits in October 1979, section 13, subsection 1(1), was still applicable. This section laid down that WWV benefits could not be claimed by those married women who were neither breadwinners nor permanently separated from their husbands. * * * That the conditions for granting benefits laid down in section 13, subsection 1(1), of WWV applied solely to married women and not to married men is due to the fact that the provision in question corresponded to the then prevailing views in society in general concerning the roles of men and women within marriage and society. Virtually all married men who had jobs could be regarded as their family's breadwinner, so that it was unnecessary to check whether they met this criterion for the granting of benefits upon becoming unemployed. These views have gradually changed in later years. * * *
>
> The Netherlands is a member State of the European Economic Community (EEC). On 19 December 1978 the Council of the European Communities issued a directive on the progressive implementation of the principle of equal treatment for men and women in matters of social security * * *. Pursuant to this directive the Netherlands Government examined the criteria for the granting of benefits laid down in section 13, subsection 1(1), of WWV in the

light of the principle of equal treatment of men and women and in the light of the changing role patterns of sexes in the years since about 1960.

Since it could no longer be assumed as a matter of course in the early 1980s that married men with jobs should always be regarded as "breadwinners", the Netherlands amended section 13, subsection 1(1), of WWV to meet its obligations under the EEC directive. The amendment consisted of the deletion of section 13, subsection 1(1), with the result that it became possible for married women who were not breadwinners to claim WWV benefits, while the duration of the benefits, which had previously been two years, was reduced for people aged under 35.

In view of changes in the status of women—and particularly married women—in recent decades, the failure to award Mrs. Zwaan WWV benefits in 1979 is explicable in historical terms. If she were to apply for such benefits now, the result would be different.

8.3 With regard to the scope of article 26 of the Covenant, the State party argues, *inter alia,* as follows:

The Netherlands Government takes the view that article 26 of the Covenant does entail an obligation to avoid discrimination, but that this article can only be invoked under the Optional Protocol to the Covenant in the sphere of civil and political rights. Civil and political rights are to be distinguished from economic, social and cultural rights, which are the object of a separate United Nations Covenant, the International Covenant on Economic, Social and Cultural Rights.

The complaint made in the present case relates to obligations in the sphere of social security, which fall under the International Covenant on Economic, Social and Cultural Rights.

* * *

Should the Human Rights Committee take the view that article 26 of the International Covenant on Civil and Political Rights ought to be interpreted more broadly, thus that this article is applicable to complaints concerning discrimination in the field of social security, the Government would observe that in that case article 26 must also be interpreted in the light of other comparable United Nations conventions laying down obligations to combat and eliminate discrimination in the field of economic, social and cultural rights. The Government would particularly point to the International Convention on the Elimination of All Forms of Racial Discrimination and the Convention on the Elimination of All Forms of Discrimination against Women.

If article 26 of the International Covenant on Civil and Political Rights were deemed applicable to complaints concerning discriminatory elements in national legislation in the field of those conventions, this could surely not be taken to mean that a State party would be required to have eliminated all possible discriminatory elements from its legislation in those fields at the time of ratification of the Covenant. Years of work are required in order to examine the whole complex of national legislation in search of discriminatory elements. The search can never be completed, either, as distinctions in legislation which are justifiable in the light of social views and conditions prevailing when they are first made may become disputable as changes occur in the views held in society.

* * *

12.1 The State party contends that there is considerable overlapping of the provisions of article 26 with the provisions of article 2 of the International Covenant on Economic, Social and Cultural Rights. The Committee is of the view that the International Covenant on Civil and Political Rights would still apply even if a particular subject-matter is referred to or covered in other international instruments, for example the International Convention on the Elimination of All Forms of Racial Discrimination, the Convention on the Elimination of All Forms of Discrimination against Women, or, as in the present case, the International Covenant on Economic, Social and Cultural Rights. Notwithstanding the interrelated drafting history of the two Covenants, it remains necessary for the Committee to apply fully the terms of the International Covenant on Civil and Political Rights. The Committee observes in this connection that the provisions of article 2 of the International Covenant on Economic, Social and Cultural Rights do not detract from the full application of article 26 of the International Covenant on Civil and Political Rights.

12.2 The Committee has also examined the contention of the State party that article 26 of the International Covenant on Civil and Political Rights cannot be invoked in respect of a right which is specifically provided for under article 9 of the International Covenant on Economic, Social and Cultural Rights (social security, including social insurance). In so doing, the Committee has perused the relevant *travaux préparatoires* of the International Covenant on Civil and Political Rights, namely the summary records of the discussions that took place in the Commission on Human Rights in 1948, 1949, 1950 and 1952 and in the Third Committee of the General Assembly in 1961, which provide a "supplementary means of interpretation" (art. 32 of the Vienna Convention on the Law of Treaties). The discussions, at the time of drafting, concerning the question whether the scope of article 26 extended to rights not otherwise guaranteed by the Covenant, were inconclusive and cannot alter the conclusion arrived at by the ordinary means of interpretation referred to in paragraph 12.3 below.

12.3 For the purpose of determining the scope of article 26, the Committee has taken into account the "ordinary meaning" of each element of the article in its context and in the light of its object and purpose (art. 31 of the Vienna Convention on the Law of Treaties). The Committee begins by noting that article 26 does not merely duplicate the guarantees already provided for in article 2. It derives from the principle of equal protection of the law without discrimination, as contained in article 7 of the Universal Declaration of Human Rights, which prohibits discrimination in law or in practice in any field regulated and protected by public authorities. Article 26 is thus concerned with the obligations imposed on States in regard to their legislation and the application thereof.

12.4 Although article 26 requires that legislation should prohibit discrimination, it does not of itself contain any obligation with respect to the matters that may be provided for by legislation. Thus it does not, for example, require any State to enact legislation to provide for social security. However, when such legislation is adopted in the exercise of a State's sovereign power, then such legislation must comply with article 26 of the Covenant.

* * *

13. The right to equality before the law and to equal protection of the law without any discrimination does not make all differences of treatment discriminatory. A differentiation based on reasonable and objective criteria does not amount to prohibited discrimination within the meaning of article 26.

14. It therefore remains for the Committee to determine whether the differentiation in Netherlands law at the time in question and as applied to Mrs. Zwaan-de Vries constituted discrimination within the meaning of article 26. The Committee notes that in Netherlands law the provisions of articles 84 and 85 of the Netherlands Civil Code [impose] equal rights and obligations on both spouses with regard to their joint income. Under section 13, subsection 1(1), of the Unemployment Benefits Act (WWV) a married woman, in order to receive WWV benefits, had to prove that she was a "breadwinner"—a condition that did not apply to married men. Thus a differentiation which appears on one level to be one of status is in fact one of sex, placing married women at a disadvantage compared with married men. Such a differentiation is not reasonable, and this seems to have been effectively acknowledged even by the State party by the enactment of a change in the law on 29 April 1985 * * *.

15. [The Netherlands violated article 26] because she was denied a social security benefit on an equal footing with men.

16. The Committee notes that the State party had not intended to discriminate against women and further notes with appreciation that the discriminatory provisions in the law applied to Mrs. Zwaan-de Vries have, subsequently, been eliminated. Although the State party has thus taken the necessary measures to put an end to the kind of discrimination suffered by Mrs. Zwaan-de Vries at the time complained

of, the Committee is of the view that the State party should offer Mrs. Zwaan-de Vries an appropriate remedy.

NONDISCRIMINATION AND THE COVENANTS

If an economic discrimination issue involving a government that is a party to both U.N. Covenants is being examined by the Committee on Economic, Social and Cultural Rights in connection with the government's report to it, why shouldn't that preclude the Human Rights Committee from considering it under *article 5(2)(a)* of the Protocol?

What if the two Committees take different views as to what is discriminatory in the field of "social insurance" (*article 9* of the Covenant on Economic, Social and Cultural Rights)? Did the Human Rights Committee adequately consider this possibility in dismissing the Dutch government's argument that economic and social rights should be left to the Committee on Economic, Social and Cultural Rights?

Did the Human Rights Committee's interpretation of *article 26* of the Covenant on Civil and Political Rights (paragraphs 12.2 and 12.3 of the decision) show that, regardless of any possible overlap, article 26 was intended to cover this situation?

Article 2(1) of the Covenant on Economic, Social and Cultural Rights recognizes that states parties may not be able to implement all of the Covenant's requirements immediately. Thus it calls on them "to take steps * * * with a view to achieving progressively the full realization of the rights recognized in the present Covenant * * *." Article 2 of the U.N. Convention on the Elimination of All Forms of Discrimination Against Women [j] also contemplates progressive implementation, though it expresses a greater sense of urgency than does the Covenant on Economic, Social and Cultural Rights:

> States Parties condemn discrimination against women in all its forms, agree to pursue by all appropriate means and without delay a policy of eliminating discrimination against women and, to this end, undertake [several enumerated measures, including taking] all appropriate measures, including legislation, to modify or abolish existing laws, regulations, customs and practices which constitute discrimination against women * * *.

Did the Dutch government have a point when it argued that, even if article 26 of the Covenant on Civil and Political Rights covers sex discrimination in economic and social matters, it should be construed only to require implementation over a reasonable period of time as do these other U.N. conventions? Or is such an argument beside the point, in light of the express provisions of the Covenant on Civil and Political Rights?

j. Dec. 18, 1979, 1249 U.N.T.S. 13.

Paragraph 12.4 enunciated a principle familiar to American law: a legislative or administrative body may not have to provide certain benefits, but if it does so, it must do it without discrimination. Is that a proper reading of article 26?

Paragraph 13 left the door open for differentiation "based on reasonable and objective criteria." The Committee did not elaborate further, except to note that Dutch law imposes equal rights and obligations on both spouses with regard to their joint income (paragraph 14), while—at the time in question here—imposing unequal rights to unemployment benefits. That was unreasonable. Did the Committee adequately deal with the government's argument that the reasonableness of its treatment of spouses for unemployment benefit purposes in 1979 should be judged according to prevailing social attitudes toward husband-wife roles at that time? (This assumes that the Dutch government was correct about social attitudes in Western countries at that time. Query.)

Does this decision provide guidance for future application of article 26 when governments treat spouses differently?

In paragraph 16, the Committee said that "the State party should offer Mrs. Zwaan-de Vries an appropriate remedy." What might that be? Why would the Committee be so vague about the remedy here, when it was quite specific about the remedy Jamaica should provide for Mr. Kelly?

A final example of case law under the first Optional Protocol concerns security of the person—a recurring issue for international bodies supervising civil and political rights.

DELGADO PÁEZ v. COLOMBIA
U.N. Human Rights Committee, 1990.
Communication No. 195/1985, 45 GAOR Supp. No. 40, Vol. II (A/45/40), at 43.

1. The author of the communication is William Eduardo Delgado Páez, a Colombian national who resided in Bogotá, Colombia, at the time of submission. In May 1986 he left the country and sought political asylum in France, where he was granted refugee status.

Background

2.1 In March 1983, the author was appointed by the Ministry of Education as a teacher of religion and ethics at a secondary school in Leticia, Colombia. He was elected vice-president of the teachers' union. As an advocate of "liberation theology", his social views differed from those of the then Apostolic Prefect of Leticia.

2.2 In October 1983, the Apostolic Prefect sent a letter to the Education Commission withdrawing the support that the Church had given to Mr. Delgado. On 10 December 1983, the Apostolic Prefect wrote to the Police Inspector accusing Mr. Delgado of having stolen money from a student.

2.3 On 25 August 1984, the Circuit Court dismissed all charges against the author, having established that the accusation of theft was unfounded.

2.4 On 5 February 1984, Mr. Delgado was informed that he would no longer teach religion. Instead, a course in manual labour and handicrafts (*manualidades y artesanías*), for which he had no training or experience, was assigned to him. In order not to lose employment altogether, he endeavoured to teach these subjects.

2.5 On 29 May 1984, the author requested from the Ministry of Education two weeks' leave for the period from 26 June to 10 July 1984 to attend an advanced course at Bogotá to further his teaching qualifications. He and other teachers were admitted to the course on 5 July 1984, but Mr. Delgado was subsequently denied leave. He considered this to be unjustified discrimination and decided to attend the course, also taking into account that, as a result of a national strike (*paro nacional*), the teachers were, by decree of the Ministry of Education, on enforced vacation (*vacaciones forzosas*).

2.6 By administrative decisions of the Ministry of Education, dated 12 July, and 11 and 25 September 1984, he was suspended from his post for 60 days, and a six-months' salary freeze was imposed on him on grounds of having abandoned his post without permission from the Principal. On 27 November 1984, the author requested the annulment of these administrative decisions (*recurso de reposición*), arguing that he had not abandoned his post, but that the law allowed teachers to take such special courses and that he had been duly admitted to the course with the approval of the Ministry of Education. The action was dismissed. He then submitted an appeal, and on 3 December 1985, by decision of the Ministry of Education, the prior decisions of suspension and salary freeze were annulled.

2.7 Convinced that he was a victim of discrimination by the ecclesiastical and educational authorities of Leticia, the author took the following steps:

(a) On 17 May 1985, he submitted a complaint to the Office of the Regional Attorney on grounds of alleged irregularities committed by the Fondo Educativo Regional (Regional Education Fund) in his case;

(b) On 18 May 1985, he submitted a complaint to the penal court of Leticia, accusing the Apostolic Prefect of slander and abuse (*injuria y calumnia*);

(c) On 28 May, 4 June and 3 October 1985, he wrote to the Office of the Attorney General of the Republic, expressing concern about the denial of justice at the regional level, attributable to the alleged influence of the Apostolic Prefect;

(d) On 13 May 1986, he again wrote to the Attorney General describing the pressures he had been and was being subjected to in order to force him to resign. He indicated, *inter alia,* that on 23 November 1983 the Apostolic Prefect had written to the Secretary of Education asking the latter in specific and clear terms:

> "to bring pressure on me to resign from my post, and this in fact happened, for, on 2 December 1983, I was summoned to the office of the Secretary of Education and orally informed that the Monsignor was putting pressure on him and that I therefore had to resign from my post as a teacher, failing which criminal proceedings would be instituted against me. * * * I of course refused to resign, but the threat was carried out and criminal proceedings were instituted against me."

2.8 While at his residence in Bogotá, the author received anonymous phone calls threatening him with death if he returned to Leticia and did not withdraw his complaint against the Apostolic Prefect and the education authorities. He also received death threats at the teachers' residence at Leticia, which he reported to the military authorities at Leticia, the teachers' union, the Ministry of Education and the President of Colombia.

2.9 On 2 May 1986, a work colleague, Ms. Rubiela Valencia, was shot to death outside the teachers' residence in Leticia by unknown killers. On 7 May 1986, the author was himself attacked in the city of Bogotá, and, fearing for his own life, left the country and obtained political asylum in France in June 1986.

* * *

The Complaint

3.1 The author claims to be a victim of violations by Colombia of articles 14, 18, 19, 25 and 26 in conjunction with article 2 of the International Covenant on Civil and Political Rights.

* * *

3.6 He claims that he "found it absolutely essential to leave the country, as there are no guarantees for the protection of the most basic human rights, such as equality, justice and life, which the Colombian Government has a constitutional and moral obligation to protect". Allegedly, the threats on his life and on the lives of other teachers have not been duly investigated by the State party.

The State Party's Observations

* * *

4.2 [The State party] denies that Mr. Delgado's rights under the Covenant have been violated. In particular, it indicates that Mr. Delgado was cleared of all charges against him and contends that his complaints against various Colombian authorities were duly investigated:

"William Eduardo Delgado Páez has not been subjected to restrictions on his freedom of thought, conscience, religion, speech or expression, as is demonstrated by the steps he was able to take under the criminal law and in the administrative sphere throughout this investigation."

4.3 In the disciplinary action initiated by Mr. Delgado against various officials, the court of first instance of Leticia acquitted three persons and sanctioned two others with a suspension of 15 days without remuneration. Appeals are pending.

4.4 The criminal action against the Apostolic Prefect on grounds of slander and abuse was referred to the Apostolic Nuncius pursuant to the Concordat between the Republic of Colombia and the Vatican. The investigation was terminated upon the death of the Apostolic Prefect in 1990.

* * *

4.7 The State party does not address the author's allegations concerning death threats against himself and other teachers, the alleged assault on his person on 7 May 1986, nor the general situation of persecution against named journalists and intellectuals, amounting to a violation of the right of security of the person.

THE ISSUES AND PROCEEDINGS BEFORE THE COMMITTEE

* * *

5.2 On 4 April 1988, the Committee declared the communication generally admissible, without specifying articles of the Covenant. The Committee, however, requested the State party to address the issues raised in one of the author's submissions, which focused on the right of security of the person.

* * *

5.4 Although the author has not specifically invoked article 9 of the Covenant, the Committee notes that his submission of 14 September 1987, which was transmitted to the State party prior to the adoption of the Committee's decision on admissibility, raised important questions under this article. The Committee recalls that upon declaring the communication admissible, it requested the State party to address these issues. The State party has not done so.

5.5 The first sentence of article 9 does not stand as a separate paragraph. Its location as a part of paragraph one could lead to the view that the right to security arises only in the context of arrest and detention. The *travaux préparatoires* indicate that the discussions of the first sentence did indeed focus on matters dealt with in the other provisions of article 9. The Universal Declaration of Human Rights, in article 3, refers to the right to life, the right to liberty and the right to security of the person. These elements have been dealt with in separate clauses in the Covenant. Although in the Covenant the only reference to the right of security of person is to be found in article 9, there is no evidence that it was intended to narrow the concept of the right to security only to situations of formal deprivation of liberty. At the same time, States parties have undertaken to guarantee the rights enshrined in the Covenant. It cannot be the case that, as a matter of law, States can ignore known threats to the life of persons under their jurisdiction, just because he or she is not arrested or otherwise detained. States parties are under an obligation to take reasonable and appropriate measures to protect them. An interpretation of article 9 which would allow a State party to ignore threats to the personal security of non-detained persons within its jurisdiction would render totally ineffective the guarantees of the Covenant.

5.6 There remains the question of the application of this finding to the facts of the case under consideration. There appears to have been an objective need for Mr. Delgado to be provided by the State with protective measures to guarantee his security, given the threats made against him, including the attack on his person, and the murder of a close colleague. It is arguable that, in seeking to secure this protection, Mr. Delgado failed to address the competent authorities, making his complaints to the military authorities in Leticia, the teachers' union, the Ministry of Education and the President of Colombia, rather than to the general prosecutor or the judiciary. It is unclear to the Committee whether these matters were reported to the police. It does not know either with certainty whether any measures were taken by the Government. However, the Committee cannot but note that the author claims that there was no response to his request to have these threats investigated and to receive protection, and that the State party has not informed the Committee otherwise. * * * The pertinent factors in this case are that Mr. Delgado had been engaged in a protracted confrontation with the authorities over his teaching and his employment. Criminal charges, later determined unfounded, had been brought against him and he had been suspended, with salary frozen, in the circumstances indicated in paragraphs 2.2 to 2.6 above. Further, he was known to have instituted a variety of complaints against the ecclesiastical and scholastical authorities in Leticia (see para. 2.7 above). Coupled with these factors were threats to his life. If the State party neither denies the threats nor co-operates with the Committee to explain whether the relevant authorities were aware of them, and, if so, what was done about them, the Committee must necessarily treat as correct allegations that the threats were known and that nothing was done. Accordingly, while fully understanding the situation in Colombia, the Committee finds that the State party has not taken, or has been unable to take, appropriate measures to ensure Mr. Delgado's right to security of his person under article 9, paragraph 1.

5.7 With respect to article 18, the Committee is of the view that the author's right to profess or to manifest his religion has not been violated. The Committee finds, moreover, that Colombia may, without violating this provision of the Covenant, allow the Church authorities to decide who may teach religion and in what manner it should be taught.

5.8 Article 19 protects, *inter alia,* the right of freedom of expression and of opinion. This will usually cover the freedom of teachers to teach their subjects in accordance with their own views, without interference. However, in the particular circumstances of the case, the special relationship between Church and State in Colombia, exemplified by the applicable Concordat, the Committee finds that the requirement, by the Church, that religion be taught in a certain way does not violate article 19.

5.9 Although the requirement, by the Church authorities, that Mr. Delgado teach the Catholic religion in its traditional form does not violate article 19, the author claims that he continued to be harassed while teaching the non-religious subjects to which he had been assigned. The Committee must for the reasons elaborated in paragraph 5.6 above, accept the facts as presented by the author. This constant harassment and the threats against his person (in respect of which the State party failed to provide protection) made the author's continuation in public service teaching impossible. Accordingly, the Committee finds a violation of article 25, paragraph (c), of the Covenant.

5.10 Article 26 requires that all persons are entitled, without discrimination, to be equal before the law and to receive equal protection by the law. The Committee finds that neither the terms of Colombian law nor the application of the law by the courts or other authorities discriminated against Mr. Delgado, and finds that there was no violation of article 26.

6. The Human Rights Committee, acting under article 5, paragraph 4, of the Optional Protocol to the International Covenant on Civil and Political Rights, is of the view that the facts of the communication disclose violations of articles 9, paragraph 1, and 25, paragraph (c), of the Covenant.

7.1 In accordance with the provisions of article 2 of the Covenant, the State party is under an obligation to take effective measures to remedy the violations suffered by the author, including the granting of appropriate compensation, and to ensure that similar violations do not occur in the future.

7.2 The Committee would wish to receive information on any relevant measures taken by the State party in respect of the Committee's views.

SUA SPONTE PROTECTION OF SECURITY OF THE PERSON

The author of the petition in this case was an educated teacher of religion and ethics who obviously knew a thing or two about his legal rights. In his petition he alleged violations of several specific articles of the Covenant, not including *article 9*. Is it appropriate for an international adjudicatory body like the Human Rights Committee in such a case to raise, sua sponte, a serious charge like failure to protect the personal security of the petitioner?

Having raised the article 9 issue, the Committee acknowledged that its reference to security of the person is in the context of the treatment of arrested or detained persons. It also acknowledged that the preparatory work for the Covenant showed that discussions of the first sentence focused on personal security while under arrest or in detention.[k] See paragraph 5.5. Yet the Committee found that the first sentence of article 9 applies also to security of persons who are not under arrest or in detention. Can that be reconciled with *articles 31–32* of the Vienna Convention on the Law of Treaties—the treaty interpretation articles of the Vienna Convention, on which the Committee relied when it interpreted article 26 of the Covenant in the Zwaan-de Vries case?

Note the Committee's reference in paragraph 5.5 to article 3 of the Universal Declaration of Human Rights ("Everyone has the right to life, liberty and the security of person"). What was the relevance of that provision to the issue under article 9 of the Covenant?

Could paragraph 5.5 legitimately be criticized as the international equivalent of judicial legislation? Or could it be said to be a quintessential example of what wise adjudicators are supposed to do: plug gaps in legislative texts in such a way as to make the legislative scheme fair and sensible?

In paragraph 5.6 the Committee resorted to its familiar device of assuming plausible factual contentions to be true if the state party offers no rebuttal. But the issue was whether the government had ensured Mr. Delgado's personal security, and the Committee conceded that he may not have reported his situation to the authorities who might best have been able to protect him—the public prosecutor or the courts. Was it proper in such circumstances to find that Colombia had not taken appropriate measures to ensure his right to security of the person? Was there doubt about awareness of his situation on the part of governmental authorities who could have intervened in his behalf?

In light of all the harassment Mr. Delgado received, how could the Committee conclude that neither his right to manifest his religion nor his freedom of expression and of opinion were infringed? See paragraphs 5.7 and 5.8.

How could there be a violation of *article 25(c)* without a violation of *article 26* when the issue is one of failure of the state to protect a particular individual from harassment in the conduct of his public

---

k. The preparatory work for what became article 9(1) shows that virtually no attention was given to the possibility that "security of the person" might be removed from the context of a deprivation of liberty. See M. Bossuyt, Guide to the "Travaux Préparatoires" of the International Covenant on Civil and Political Rights 193–202 (1987).

service? Does article 26, first sentence, apply only to discrimination officially sanctioned by law?

Suppose there had been no threats against Mr. Delgado's person. If he had simply been assigned to teach a course in manual labor and handicrafts instead of religion because of his espousal of liberation theology (see paragraph 2.4), and the state had responded to his complaints as it said it did in paragraphs 4.2–4.4, would the Committee have found a violation of any of the articles he cited in paragraph 3.1? What if the state had simply dismissed him as a teacher because of his espousal of liberation theology, and the dismissal had been upheld as lawful by the Colombian courts?

Was the remedy in paragraph 7.1 appropriate? Note that it involved not only compensation, but also an obligation upon Colombia "to ensure that similar violations do not occur in the future." Note also the Committee's "wish" in paragraph 7.2 to receive information on any relevant measures taken by Colombia.

How is the Committee supposed to monitor state parties' compliance with decrees of this sort? It took steps to deal with this in 1990.

MEASURES TO MONITOR COMPLIANCE WITH THE COMMITTEE'S VIEWS UNDER THE FIRST OPTIONAL PROTOCOL
U.N. Human Rights Committee, 1990.
45 GAOR Supp. No. 40, Vol. II (A/45/40), Annex XI.

1. When, in its Views under the Optional Protocol, the Committee makes a finding of a violation, the State party concerned will be asked in the Views itself to inform the Committee of what action it has taken in relation to the case. The Committee often indicates what action it deems appropriate. A time-limit will be indicated for the receipt of such information. This time-limit shall be determined on the basis of the circumstances of each case; it shall not exceed 180 days.

2. States parties have undertaken, under article 2, paragraph 3, of the Covenant, to ensure effective remedies for violations of the Covenant. If no reply is received within the indicated time period, or if the reply shows that no remedy has been provided, this will henceforth be noted in the Committee's Annual Report. Equally, positive responses and co-operation from States parties will also be included in the Annual Report.

3. The Committee's Guidelines for the preparation of Reports, requesting States parties who are also parties to the Optional Protocol, and in respect of whom any finding of a violation had been made in the period under review, shall be amended to include a brief section indicating "the measures which they have adopted which give effect to the rights recognized therein" (art. 40 of the Covenant) in respect of the authors concerned. Because of the periodicity of Reports under article 40, this information is additional to, and does not replace, the informa-

tion that is to be given to the Committee under the time-limits specified above.

4. Should this information not be made available in the relevant periodic Report, questions relating to it will be included by the Committee in its List of Questions that it customarily prepares for a State party a few days prior to the examination of the Report, and the matter will be pursued in the dialogue with the State party.

5. The Committee will appoint a Special Rapporteur for the Follow–Up of Views.

The Special Rapporteur's duties are as follows:

(a) To recommend to the Committee action upon all letters of complaint henceforth received from individuals held, in the Views of the Committee under the Optional Protocol, to have been the victims of a violation, and who claim that no appropriate remedy has been provided;

(b) To communicate with States parties, and, if he deems appropriate, with victims, in respect of such letters already received by the Committee;

(c) To seek to provide information on any action taken by States parties in relation to views adopted by the Committee to date, when such information has not otherwise been made available. To this end the Special Rapporteur will communicate with all States parties and, if he deems appropriate, victims in respect of whom findings of violations have been made, in order to ascertain what action, if any, has been taken. This information, when collected, will also be made available in a future annual report; * * *.

ENFORCING THE COMMITTEE'S DECISIONS

The Committee's measures are designed to induce compliance with its decisions by means of direct contacts with states parties and, if necessary, mobilization of shame through questioning during the Covenant's reporting mechanism and publication in the Committee's Annual Report. The ILO, of course, uses similar tactics. Is this approach likely to be as effective (more effective?) under the aegis of the Human Rights Committee as it is under the aegis of the ILO?

Where does the Committee's authority to monitor compliance with its decisions come from? *Article 40(1)* of the Covenant? The doctrine of implied powers?

Is it a violation of state sovereignty for the Special Rapporteur to communicate directly with victims, in the absence of consent by the state party? Note that the decision to initiate this practice was made by the 18 independent members of the Committee, not by the states parties to the Protocol.

Can advances in human rights enforcement be made without some further erosion of traditional state sovereignty notions?

c. *The Reporting System*

All states parties to the Covenant are required, under *article 40,* "to submit reports [to the Human Rights Committee] on the measures they have adopted which give effect to the rights recognized herein and on the progress made in the enjoyment of those rights." The first report is to be submitted within one year of the entry into force of the Covenant for the party concerned, and later reports are due whenever the Committee requests. In 1981 the Committee decided that subsequent reports are to be submitted every five years.

The Committee might wish to receive additional, ad hoc reports if it is dissatisfied with one of the periodic reports of a government. Or it might wish to examine a government's justification for declaring a state of emergency and thus suspending certain rights under *article 4,* without waiting for the next periodic report.[a] Could it require ad hoc reports under article 40?

The Committee has adopted guidelines for the content of the periodic reports. These include consolidated guidelines used for the initial (general) part of states' reports under the various human rights instruments adopted under U.N. auspices, plus guidelines of its own for first reports and for subsequent ones. Its own guidelines are much less detailed than are those of the Committee on Economic, Social and Cultural Rights.

REVISED GUIDELINES FOR THE PREPARATION OF STATE PARTY REPORTS
U.N. Human Rights Committee, 1991.
46 GAOR Supp. No. 40 (A/46/40), Annex VII.

A. Consolidated Guidelines for the Initial Part of Reports of States Parties

Land and People

1. This section should contain information about the main ethnic and demographic characteristics of the country and its population, as well as such socio-economic and cultural indicators as per capita income, gross national product, rate of inflation, external debt, rate of unemployment, literacy rate and religion. * * *

General Political Structure

2. This section should describe briefly the political history and framework, the type of government and the organization of the executive, legislative and judicial organs.

---

a. See D. McGoldrick, The Human Rights Committee: Its Role in the Development of the International Covenant on Civil and Political Rights 69–71 (1991).

General Legal Framework Within Which Human Rights are Protected

3. This section should contain information on:

(a) Which judicial, administrative or other competent authorities have jurisdiction affecting human rights;

(b) What remedies are available to an individual who claims that any of his rights have been violated and what systems of compensation and rehabilitation exist for victims;

(c) Whether any of the rights referred to in the various human rights instruments are protected either in the constitution or by a separate bill of rights and, if so, what provisions are made in the constitution or bill of rights for derogations and in what circumstances;

(d) How human rights instruments are made part of the national legal system;

(e) Whether the provisions of the various human rights instruments can be invoked before, or directly enforced by, the courts, other tribunals or administrative authorities or whether they must be transformed into internal laws or administrative regulations in order to be enforced by the authorities concerned;

(f) Whether there exist any institutions or national machinery with responsibility for overseeing the implementation of human rights.

Information and Publicity

4. This section should indicate whether any special efforts have been made to promote awareness among the public and the relevant authorities of the rights contained in the various human rights instruments. * * *

B. Guidelines Regarding the Form and Contents of Initial Reports From States Parties

* * *

4. *The part of the report relating specifically to parts I, II and III of the Covenant* should describe in relation to the provisions of each article:

(a) The legislative, administrative or other measures in force in regard to each right;

(b) Any restrictions or limitations, even of a temporary nature, imposed by law or practice or any other manner on the enjoyment of the right;

(c) Any other factors or difficulties affecting the enjoyment of the right by persons within the jurisdiction of the State;

(d) Any other information on the progress made in the enjoyment of the right.

5. When a State party to the Covenant is also a party to the [first] Optional Protocol, and if in the period under review the Committee has

issued views finding that the State party has violated provisions of the Covenant, the report should include a section explaining what action has been taken relating to the communication concerned. In particular, the State party should indicate what remedy it has afforded the author of the communication whose rights the Committee found to have been violated.

6. The report should be accompanied by copies of the principal legislative and other texts referred to in the report.

* * *

C. Guidelines Regarding the Form and Contents of Periodic Reports From States Parties

* * *

6. *Information relating to each of the articles in parts I, II and III of the Covenant* should concentrate especially on:

(a) The completion of the information before the Committee as to the measures adopted to give effect to rights recognized in the Covenant, taking account of questions raised in the Committee on the examination of any previous report and including in particular additional information as to questions not previously answered or not fully answered;

(b) Information taking into account general comments which the Committee may have made under article 40, paragraph 4, of the Covenant;

(c) Changes made or proposed in the laws and practices relevant to the Covenant;

(d) Action taken as a result of experience gained in cooperation with the Committee;

(e) Factors affecting and difficulties experienced in the implementation of the Covenant;

(f) The progress made since the last report in the enjoyment of rights recognized in the Covenant.

7. [This paragraph repeats paragraph B.5 above, regarding States parties to the first Optional Protocol.]

8. It should be noted that the reporting obligation extends not only to the relevant laws and other norms, but also to the practices of the courts and administrative organs of the State party and other relevant facts likely to show the degree of actual enjoyment of rights recognized by the Covenant.

9. The report should be accompanied by copies of the principal legislative and other texts referred to in it.

* * *

THE REPORTING SYSTEM IN ACTION

Like the Committee on Economic, Social and Cultural Rights, the Human Rights Committee has had trouble persuading some governments to submit their article 40 reports on time, or at all. It does what it can to induce compliance: it sends reminders to delinquent states; it establishes direct contacts with the permanent representatives in New York of states parties to which two or more reminders have been sent; and it publishes in its annual report the names of delinquent states.

For reports that are submitted:

The Committee follows two distinct procedures in considering initial reports and periodic reports. In the case of initial reports, members of the Committee pose a series of questions concerning the implementation of most or all of the articles of the Covenant. Once all the questions have been raised, the representative of the State party responds *en bloc* to the questions that had been raised.

In considering periodic reports, the Committee entrusts a working group with responsibility for reviewing the reports and other relevant information in order to identify the matters requiring discussion with the State party representatives of the reporting State. The working group prepares a list of issues to be taken up with State party representatives during the report's consideration and such lists when approved by the Committee are transmitted to the representatives of the States parties concerned prior to their appearance before the Committee together with the appropriate explanations on the procedure to be followed. The lists of issues are not exhaustive, and members of the Committee are free to raise other matters or to request additional information. The various issues are discussed, one by one, with the State party's representatives providing immediate responses to members' questions in a process of dialogue.[b]

Committee members ask a great many questions of each representative of a reporting state party. The questions are often quite specific. Some questions tend to be asked of virtually all representatives, while others are tailored to the conditions reported in the particular country. An example of the former is the frequently-asked question whether the domestic legal system enforces the provisions of the Covenant directly, and if not, how the Covenant is made effective within the country. The questions are clustered in topics corresponding to the rights set forth in the Covenant. Typical clusters would be: constitutional and legal framework within which the Covenant is implemented; nondiscrimination and equality of the sexes; right to life; treatment of prisoners and

---

b. United Nations Action in the Field of Human Rights, U.N.Doc. ST/HR/2/Rev. 3, at 240 (1988).

other detainees; liberty and security of the person; right to a fair trial; freedom of movement and expulsion of aliens; right to privacy; freedom of religion and expression; freedom of assembly and association; protection of the family and children; right to participate in public affairs; and rights of minorities.

After all the questions to a representative have been asked and answered, Committee members make their concluding observations. Examples from the Committee's 1991 report illustrate how the Committee tries to induce compliance.

CONCLUDING OBSERVATIONS ON REPORTS BY SOME STATES PARTIES SUBMITTED UNDER ARTICLE 40 OF THE COVENANT
U.N. Human Rights Committee, 1991.
46 GAOR Supp. No. 40 (A/46/40), Chapter III.

Spain (third periodic report)

Members of the Committee expressed satisfaction with Spain's informative report and thanked the State party's delegation for engaging in a constructive and fruitful dialogue with the Committee, which had provided an opportunity to observe at first hand the progress of democratic Spain. The steady improvement in the human rights situation in Spain, particularly through the strengthening of the legal system and the judiciary, deserved respect and it could confidently be said that Spain was continuing to make progress on all fronts.

Nevertheless, members noted that there were a number of problems that still gave rise to concern, some of which were the same as had been expressed during the consideration of the second periodic report. Among such concerns were the number of offenses carrying the death penalty; the suspension of the rights of terrorist suspects under article 55(2) of the Constitution and the fact that circumstances had given rise to what amounted to permanent emergency legislation; the need to take action aimed at preventing cases of torture and ill-treatment, such as police and security force training, as recommended in the report of the People's Advocate; the military nature of the *Guardia Civil;* the excessive length of the pre-trial detention period and its linkage to the length of the maximum allowable sentence; and conscientious objection. Members also expressed the hope that future reports would include more information on factors and difficulties encountered in implementing the Covenant.

India (second periodic report)

Members of the Committee expressed their thanks to the representatives of the State party for their cooperation in presenting the second periodic report of India and for having engaged in a fruitful and constructive dialogue with the Committee. Although the report had been drafted in conformity with the Committee's guidelines regarding the form and contents of reports from States parties under article 40 of the Covenant, it failed to refer to practice and the specific implementation of legislative provisions and, in that respect, was deficient. Satisfaction was expressed over the improvements that had occurred since the consideration of the initial report of India * * *.

At the same time, the consideration of the second periodic report had also highlighted some of the difficulties India had faced in implementing the Covenant, partly as a result of the country's size, economic problems and demographic composition, and the concerns expressed by members of the Committee had not been entirely allayed. Furthermore, the reservations entered by the Government and the fact that the provisions of the Covenant had not been fully incorporated in the Constitution tended to make it difficult to identify clearly the extent to which the Covenant was actually implemented in India. In that connection, members pointed out that rights, other than those limited by a specific limitation clause in the Covenant, could only be restricted by means of a formal derogation under article 4 of the Covenant; and that several provisions of the Armed Forces (Special Powers) Act, the National Security (Amendment) Act, and the Terrorist and Disruptive Activities (Prevention) Act seemed to be incompatible with articles 6, 9 and 14 of the Covenant.

Concerns were also expressed with respect to a number of issues such as the implementation of the Covenant in "disturbed" areas; arbitrary killings and arrests in some states; police excesses and the mistreatment of detainees; the failure to bring proceedings against police offenders; the system of preventive detention; and problems relating to the implementation of articles 19 and 22 of the Covenant and of the rights of persons belonging to minorities. It was also felt that greater efforts should be made to eliminate discriminatory practices rooted in India's social and ethnic diversity. * * *

The representative of the State party assured members that there had been no misuse of the powers conferred under the Armed Forces (Special Powers) Act, the National Security (Amendment) Act, and the Terrorist and Disruptive Activities (Prevention) Act and that the third periodic report of India would contain updated information on those matters that were of concern to the Committee.

Sweden (third periodic report)

Members of the Committee commended the Swedish delegation for its report and for having engaged in a constructive dialogue with the Committee, noting that Sweden had one of the most outstanding human rights records in the world. At the same time, it was noted that some of the concerns expressed by members of the Committee had not been fully allayed. In common with many other States parties, Sweden had not incorporated the Covenant into its domestic legislation, as a result of which there were some gaps between the provisions of the Covenant and Swedish law. Concerns were also expressed about the absence of remedies for persons expelled from Swedish territory because of suspected terrorist involvement; the possibility of extended periods of solitary confinement; the procedure for admitting refugees to Swedish territory; and rules regarding the censorship of extreme violence in the media. The provisions of articles 16 and 17 of the Constitution, which did not bar discrimination based on the grounds of language, political opinion, property, birth or other status, did not appear to be compatible with the Covenant. It was also regretted that article 9(3) was not yet the basis of Swedish practice concerning bail. It was also not evident from the Swedish Constitution that the judiciary was completely separate from the legislative and executive branches.

Sudan (initial report)

[During the discussion of the Sudanese report, Committee members asked some very specific questions about the compatibility of several Sudanese policies and practices with particular articles of the Covenant. As summarized in the Committee's report, the Sudanese representative began his reply:]

Responding to questions raised and comments made by members of the Committee, the representative stated that his Government was willing to recognize shortcomings and take the necessary measures to respect the obligations contained in international instruments. However, human rights was a field in which there was a risk of partiality or double standards, particularly with regard to the treatment of a number of third world countries. Countries should be allowed freely to choose their legal system based on their convictions, traditions and customs. In the light of the renewed and increased emphasis being given in recent years by Islamic countries to the application of the Shariah, it would be desirable to submit the rights contained in international human rights instruments, which were adopted at an earlier stage, to a review.

* * *

[The Committee's concluding observations:]

In concluding the consideration of the initial report of the Sudan, members of the Committee expressed appreciation for the frankness and directness with which the delegation had replied to their questions. In connection with the priority given to Islamic law in the Sudan, members were of the view that Islam was a progressive religion that did not pose an obstacle to the implementation of the Covenant in Islamic countries. They pointed out that many States in the Islamic world had participated in the drafting of the Covenant and that if certain of its provisions had been deemed irreconcilable with Islamic law, States could have entered reservations. Furthermore, although a State might defend its culture and national religion, in doing so, it could not deviate from the fundamental common values elaborated in the Covenant, which were aimed at the development of the individual and which were applicable to the entire international community. Such values, moreover, should be reflected in domestic legislation. At the same time, members considered that it would be possible for the

Sudanese authorities and the Committee together to find a way to reconcile the Sudan's freedom to live within a social system of its own choosing with the Committee's duty to ensure respect for human rights.

Members also pointed out that the Committee was composed of independent experts and never applied double standards in considering reports from States parties. Its task was to assist all States parties in implementing the provisions of the Covenant and to promote the universal application of that instrument. With regard to the issue of a multi-party system, members noted that in the absence of political opposition, Governments were likely to exercise their powers in a non-democratic fashion and expressed the hope that the Sudan would soon practice democracy.

Additionally, in the view of members of the Committee, certain punishments under Sudanese law constituted cruel or degrading treatment; domestic provisions regarding the crime of apostasy were not compatible with articles 6 and 18 of the Covenant; and Constitutional Decree No. 2 had been drafted too vaguely with respect to the Government's power to limit political activities.

The representative of the State party reiterated that the Government attached great significance to the application of Islamic law in the country. The Government had agreed, in principle, to the establishment of a national human rights council and intended to request assistance from the Centre for Human Rights in that regard. * * *

[The Chairman] reaffirmed that, although the Committee sought, in interpreting the provisions of the Covenant, to take into account various cultural factors, it was obliged to apply the principles of the Covenant without any distinctions among States parties. He hoped that the second periodic report of Sudan would show evidence of progress in implementing the international standards set forth in the Covenant.

Iraq (third periodic report)

Members of the Committee said that while they had hoped that a constructive dialogue between the Committee and Iraq would be possible, unfortunately that had not proven to be the case. Rather, the representative of the State party had engaged in a kind of monologue or "stonewalling" and had sought constantly to evade certain issues and to avoid responding to the legitimate questions posed by members of the Committee. In the latter connection, they referred to questions they had raised regarding such important issues as disappearances, unlawful executions, including the execution of minors, torture and the existence of political prisoners, which had not received clear replies or had remained unanswered.

The report itself appeared largely to be an attempt by the Government to present its views on the Gulf crisis and its aftermath without addressing the real issue, that of Iraq's compliance with the Covenant. It did not cover the entire reporting period from 1 January 1986 nor did it address any human rights violations or issues subsequent to 2 August 1990. In the latter regard, the State party's claim that the Security Council's involvement with events that had occurred after 2 August 1990 had pre-empted the Committee's competence was clearly indefensible from a legal standpoint. The Security Council's involvement did not in any way absolve Iraq from the need to observe the provisions of the Covenant nor remove from the Committee the mandate entrusted to it under the Covenant for monitoring the implementation of those provisions. Members also disagreed with the implication in the report that the difficult situation concerning human rights in the country was due primarily to the Gulf war and to the sanctions that had been adopted against Iraq by the international community, noting in that connection the existence in Iraq of reliably attested human rights violations, including summary executions and arbitrary detention, well before the invasion of Kuwait on 2 August 1990. The failure of the report to address events in Kuwait after 2 August 1990, given Iraq's clear responsibility under international law for the observance of human rights during its occupation of that country, was a matter of particular concern to the Committee.

Members of the Committee also expressed deep concern with regard to the existence in Iraq of special courts, as well as death sentences without any possibility of appeal; the lack of protection of freedom of expression; the situation of the Shiites in the country; and the repressive action of the Government, particularly against the Kurds and the Shiites. Indeed, it was their overall impression that a situation of serious human rights violations that had already been very disturbing in 1987 had persisted and worsened throughout the intervening period.

REPORTS AND THE COMMITTEE

As these excerpts indicate, the Committee's concluding observations have been judgmental, even in the case of states with very good human rights records such as Sweden. *Article 40(4)* of the Covenant authorizes the Committee to transmit "such general comments as it may consider appropriate" to states parties. Is that an authorization to make observations assessing the degree of compliance by individual states parties with specific provisions of the Covenant? If not, where does the authorization come from?

The Committee has disavowed any intent to turn the reporting procedure into contentious or inquisitory proceedings, wishing instead to provide assistance to the reporting states.[c] Does it appear that the Committee has remained true to that intent?

In the case of India, as in some others not included in the above excerpts, the Committee has stressed that rights could only be restrict-

---

c. See 35 GAOR Supp. No. 40 (A/35/40), at 84–86 (1980).

ed by means of a formal derogation under *article 4*, unless the restriction falls within the exceptions set forth in such articles as *12(3), 18(3), 19(3), 21* and *22(2)*. Why would the Committee attach such importance to a formal proclamation under article 4?

The Indian representative's response to the Committee's observations—denying abuse of powers that might be open to abuse, and promising future cooperation—was fairly typical. It would also be typical if India's next report, like the current one, fell somewhat short of satisfying the Committee. What motivates governments to try to please the Committee?

The Sudanese representative's rather defensive posture framed an issue that has come up in other international supervisory bodies as well: Can human rights standards that are perceived as reflecting the values of post-enlightenment European political systems and their progeny be applied even-handedly to non-Western societies? During the cold war, the issue often arose in connection with the review of socialist legal/political systems. Currently, it seems most likely to arise as it did with Sudan: in the context of systems tied to non-Western religious values, or in the North–South context. The Committee's response to the Sudanese position was typical of international supervisory bodies, asserting the need to apply the standards across the board (while taking account of cultural factors) and defending the impartiality of the supervisory body. Can an instrument like the Covenant on Civil and Political Rights be applied even-handedly to cultures as dissimilar as those of Sudan and Sweden?

To what extent should a supervisory body such as the Human Rights Committee be sensitive to the cultural or religious values prevailing within each state party?

The Committee usually tries to be diplomatic in its concluding observations. But, as its observations regarding Iraq (and to some extent Sudan) attest, it can sometimes publicly express its loss of patience with uncooperative governments. Iraq, of course, had become an international pariah by 1991. As a practical matter, could the Committee be as forceful toward an uncooperative government that had not become such an outlaw? Would it be counterproductive to do so?

Iraq raised a legal issue regarding the Committee's competence when it argued that the Security Council's involvement since August 1990 pre-empted the Committee. The Committee summarily rejected that argument. Note, though, that there was some overlap between the Security Council's concerns toward Iraq and those of the Human Rights Committee. Security Council Resolution 688 (1991), supra page 853, condemned Iraqi repression of its civilian population, including the Kurds, and demanded that Iraq immediately end its repression. The Human Rights Committee "expressed deep concern" about (inter alia) the repressive action of the Iraqi government, particularly against the Kurds and the Shiites.

Did the Iraqi argument have any merit?

In 1980 the Human Rights Committee decided that it would start to formulate "general comments," distinct from its observations on individual reports, under article 40(4). Different views had been expressed within the Committee as to how general such comments had to be. Finally a consensus statement was reached:

CONSENSUS STATEMENT ON GENERAL COMMENTS UNDER ARTICLE 40(4)
U.N. Human Rights Committee, 1980.
36 GAOR Supp. No. 40 (A/36/40), Annex IV.

* * *

(b) In formulating general comments the Committee will be guided by the following principles:

They should be addressed to the States parties in conformity with article 40, paragraph 4 of the Covenant;

They should promote co-operation between States parties in the implementation of the Covenant;

They should summarize experience the Committee has gained in considering States' reports;

They should draw the attention of States parties to matters relating to the improvement of the reporting procedure and the implementation of the Covenant; and

They should stimulate activities of States parties and international organizations in the promotion and protection of human rights.

(c) The general comments could be related, *inter alia*, to the following subjects:

The implementation of the obligation to submit reports under article 40 of the Covenant;

The implementation of the obligation to guarantee the rights set forth in the Covenant;

Questions related to th   plication and the content of individual articles of the Covenant;

Suggestions concerning co-operation between States parties in applying and developing the provisions of the Covenant.

THE COMMITTEE'S GENERAL COMMENTS

The Committee began with general comments on the reporting obligations and procedures. It then moved to a series of general comments on specific provisions of the Covenant. In each case, the general comment has been directed at all states parties, rather than to any particular state.[d]

Space limitations allow the examination here of only one general comment. In 1990, the Committee adopted a general comment on *article 23,* dealing with family rights. In doing so, it had to face one of the issues raised above: what is to be done about differing social attitudes and cultural practices?

GENERAL COMMENT NUMBER 19, CONCERNING ARTICLE 23
U.N. Human Rights Committee, 1990.
45 GAOR Supp. No. 40 (A/45/40), Vol. I, at 175.

1. Article 23 of the International Covenant on Civil and Political Rights recognizes that the family is the natural and fundamental group unit of society and is entitled to protection by society and the State. Protection of the family and its members is also guaranteed, directly or indirectly, by other provisions of the Covenant. Thus, article 17 establishes a prohibition on arbitrary or unlawful interference with the family. In addition, article 24 of the Covenant specifically addresses the protection of the rights of the child, as such or as a member of a family. * * *

2. The Committee notes that the concept of the family may differ in some respects from State to State, and even from region to region within a State, and that it is therefore not possible to give the concept a standard definition. However, the Committee emphasizes that, when a group of persons is regarded as a family under the legislation and practice of a State, it must be given the protection referred to in article 23. Consequently, States parties should report on how the concept and scope of the family is construed or defined in their own society and legal system. Where diverse concepts of the family, "nuclear" and "extended", exist within a State, this should be indicated with an explanation of the degree of protection afforded to each. In view of the existence of various forms of family, such as unmarried couples and their children or single parents and their children, States parties should also indicate whether and to what extent such types of family and their members are recognized and protected by domestic law and practice.

3. Ensuring the protection provided for under article 23 of the Covenant requires that States parties should adopt legislative, administrative or other measures. * * *

4. Article 23, paragraph 2, of the Covenant reaffirms the right of men and women of marriageable age to marry and to found a family. Paragraph 3 of the same article provides that no marriage shall be entered into without the free and full consent of the intending spouses. States parties' reports should indicate whether there are restrictions or

---

d. See D. McGoldrick, supra note a, at 93–94.

impediments to the exercise of the right to marry based on special factors such as degree of kinship or mental incapacity. The Covenant does not establish a specific marriageable age either for men or for women, but that age should be such as to enable each of the intending spouses to give his or her free and full personal consent in a form and under conditions prescribed by law. * * *

5. The right to found a family implies, in principle, the possibility to procreate and live together. When States parties adopt family planning policies, they should be compatible with the provisions of the Covenant and should, in particular, not be discriminatory or compulsory. * * *

6. Article 23, paragraph 4, of the Covenant provides that States parties shall take appropriate steps to ensure equality of rights and responsibilities of spouses as to marriage, during marriage and at its dissolution.

7. With regard to equality as to marriage, the Committee wishes to note in particular that no sex-based discrimination should occur in respect of the acquisition or loss of nationality by reason of marriage. Likewise, the right of each spouse to retain the use of his or her original family name or to participate on an equal basis in the choice of a new family name should be safeguarded.

8. During marriage, the spouses should have equal rights and responsibilities in the family. This equality extends to all matters arising from their relationship, such as choice of residence, running of the household, education of the children and administration of assets. Such equality continues to be applicable to arrangements regarding legal separation or dissolution of the marriage.

9. Thus, any discriminatory treatment in regard to the grounds and procedures for separation or divorce, child custody, maintenance or alimony, visiting rights or the loss or recovery of parental authority must be prohibited, bearing in mind the paramount interest of the children in this connection. States parties should, in particular, include information in their reports concerning the provision made for the necessary protection of any children at the dissolution of a marriage or on the separation of the spouses.

FAMILY LAW UNDER THE COMMITTEE'S GENERAL COMMENT

Was General Comment No. 19 faithful to the Committee's consensus statement on general comments?

In paragraph 2, the Committee addressed the question of nontraditional families. It did not mention the preparatory work that led to the inclusion of article 23 in the Covenant. The preparatory work shows that article 23 was included as a result of a request by the Commission on the Status of Women that article 16 of the Universal Declaration of

Human Rights be incorporated in the Covenant.[e] The discussions leading to the adoption of article 23 focused on the traditional husband-wife family and on the children of such a family.[f] Should the Committee have considered the preparatory work? On treaty interpretation, see Vienna Convention on the Law of Treaties *articles 31–32.* Did the Committee apply the method of those articles, even though it didn't cite them? Should it?

If the Committee had considered the preparatory work, should it have limited its general comment to rights within the traditional family? Or should it interpret article 23, like article 26 in the Zwaan-de Vries case, in light of changing social attitudes? (Have social attitudes regarding nontraditional families changed everywhere?)

Is the effect of paragraph 2 to leave the definition of "family" to each state party, or even to each region within a state party? Is that consistent with the proposition, enunciated in connection with the Sudan's report, that the Committee is obliged to apply the principles of the Covenant without any distinctions among states parties?

Under the approach taken in the general comment, would a state party that does not prohibit consensual homosexual relationships be obligated to provide homosexual couples the same rights and responsibilities, mutatis mutandis, that it provides heterosexual married couples?

What did the Committee mean in paragraph 5 when it said that states' family planning policies "should be compatible with the provisions of the Covenant"?

Paragraphs 6 through 9 related to article 23(4). When the Covenant was being drafted, article 23 originally contained only the first three sections. When section 4 was proposed, concern was expressed in some quarters about the ability of traditional, male-oriented societies to comply immediately with its equality requirement. A Philippine amendment inserted the words "take appropriate steps to" (ensure equality) in section 4. On behalf of the 15 sponsors of the amended section 4, the Philippine representative said in the General Assembly's Third Committee that the text "might be interpreted as permitting Contracting States to take appropriate measures progressively to assure the equality of the spouses * * *."[g] Several subsequent speakers assumed that the amended text permitted progressive action.[h]

Does the Human Rights Committee's general comment put an end to any assertion that measures to ensure the equality of spouses could still be adopted only progressively?

e. See U.N. Doc. A/2929, 10 GAOR, Annexes, Agenda Item 28 (Part II), at 57 (1955).

f. See M. Bossuyt, Guide to the "Travaux Préparatoires" of the International Covenant on Civil and Political Rights 441–54 (1987).

g. U.N. Doc. A/C.3/SR.1094, at 169 (1961).

h. Id. at 169–72.

Article 23, on its face and as interpreted in the general comment, calls for affirmative, effective regulation by states parties of private conduct. Does the reporting system under the Covenant give the Committee an adequate means of ensuring that each state's legislation actually has eliminated sex-based discrimination in the family?

Is the purpose of the Committee's general comments simply to enhance the reporting system under the Covenant, or could the comments have relevance also to communications under the Optional Protocol?

What are the advantages and disadvantages of interpreting substantive provisions of human rights instruments through general comments, as distinguished from interpreting them on a case-by-case basis as actual controversies arise? Note that there is now a steady flow of cases under the first Optional Protocol to the Covenant on Civil and Political Rights, many of them raising questions of interpretation.

D. ENFORCEMENT PROCEDURES OF THE COMMISSION ON HUMAN RIGHTS AND ITS SUB-COMMISSION ON PREVENTION OF DISCRIMINATION

As we have seen, the United Nations Secretariat receives thousands of communications (petitions) each year from individuals all over the world asserting that their rights are being violated by authority of a government to which they are subject. At its first session, the Commission on Human Rights considered whether it could take any action regarding those assertions, and concluded that "it has no power to take any action in regard to any complaints concerning human rights."[a] ECOSOC approved that position, in ECOSOC Res. 75 (V) (1947). Something had to be done about all the individual communications, however, so ECOSOC took a miniscule step in 1959 and much longer ones in 1967 and 1970.

In 1959, ECOSOC reaffirmed that the Commission on Human Rights could not take action on petitions, but requested the Secretary-General to distribute to Commission members before each session a list containing a brief description of each communication, and to make available to Commission members, upon request, the originals of communications; to furnish member states with copies of communications referring explicitly to them; and to inform authors of communications that their petitions were being handled in that manner, but that the Commission could not act on any specific complaint. The author's name would not be divulged by the Secretary-General unless he or she stated that there was no objection to divulgence. ECOSOC Resolution 728F (XXVIII).

[a]. See Report of the Commission on Human Rights, 4 ECOSOC OR Supp. No. 3, at 6 (1947).

In 1967, ECOSOC adopted its Resolution 1235 (XLII), which authorized the Commission on Human Rights and its Sub–Commission on Prevention of Discrimination and Protection of Minorities "to examine information relevant to gross violations of human rights and fundamental freedoms, as exemplified by the policy of apartheid as practised in the Republic of South Africa * * * and racial discrimination as practised notably in Southern Rhodesia, contained in the communications listed by the Secretary–General pursuant to [ECOSOC] resolution 728F" and to "make a thorough study of situations which reveal a consistent pattern of violations of human rights * * *, and report, with recommendations thereon, to the Economic and Social Council * * *."

In 1970 ECOSOC took the next step with Resolution 1503 (XLVIII), establishing a procedure for dealing with communications relating to consistent patterns of gross violations of human rights. Unlike the petitioning mechanism under the first Optional Protocol to the Covenant on Civil and Political Rights, it applies to all member states of the United Nations. It is reproduced in the Documents volume accompanying this book.

The Sub–Commission on Prevention of Discrimination and Protection of Minorities considers petitions under Resolution 1503. It consists of 26 persons selected by the Commission on Human Rights to serve for three years, in their personal capacities rather than as representatives of states (although selection is subject to the consent of the appointees' governments). The Sub–Commission meets annually, for three weeks at a time. In addition to considering communications, it appoints special rapporteurs from among its members to conduct studies on various aspects of discrimination. The studies frequently lead to resolutions either adopted by the Sub–Commission or proposed by it for adoption by the Commission. The Sub–Commission submits a report on each session to the Commission.

In 1971, after much debate and compromise, the Sub–Commission adopted a provisional procedure under Resolution 1503, for dealing with the admissibility of communications referred to it. The provisional procedure is still in force. It is contained in Sub–Commission Resolution 1, reproduced in the Documents volume.

Resolution 1 is applied by a working group appointed pursuant to Resolution 1503, to determine (in a few days) which of the thousands of communications received in a year are "admissible" in the sense of being appropriate for consideration by the Sub–Commission. Most of these communications come from persons who have no lawyer and who probably are completely unaware that the 1503 procedure exists. They simply want whatever help the United Nations can give them. Are they likely to draft a petition that complies with *paragraph 3(a)* of Resolution 1? No wonder most communications found admissible come from nongovernmental human rights organizations acting under *paragraph 2(a)*.

Sub-Commission Resolution 1 does not stand out as a model of clarity, or even of internal consistency. Moreover, because the proceedings under ECOSOC Resolution 1503 are confidential until the Commission on Human Rights decides to open the record in a particular case—something it has done only a few times—there is little practice available to the outsider to aid in interpreting Resolution 1. There is some preparatory work,[b] but it does not provide a great deal of interpretive assistance.

Consider these questions about Resolution 1:

What is the source of the rights referred to in *paragraph 3(a)*?

What is meant by "a consistent pattern of gross violations of human rights"? (Is the procedure designed to help individual petitioners?)

What is meant by *paragraph 1(a)*? Consider, inter alia, *article 5* of the Covenant on Civil and Political Rights.

What is meant by "politically motivated stands contrary to the provisions of the Charter" (*paragraph 2(a)*)? Is it the same as "manifestly political motivations and its subject is contrary to the provisions of the Charter" (*paragraph 3(c)*)? The Sub-Commission debates leading to the adoption of Resolution 1 reflect concern on the part of many representatives that the procedure might be used for propaganda purposes, particularly by nongovernmental organizations.[c] Does that explain what was meant by "political motivation"?

Would a petitioner with some knowledge of violations meet the "direct knowledge" test in all cases except those in which the knowledge appears to be based exclusively on mass media reports (*paragraph 3(d)*)? Would it make a difference whether the petitioner is a human being or a nongovernmental organization such as Amnesty International or the International Commission of Jurists? Note the wording of *paragraph 2(c)*. The word "individual" was inserted at the request of a delegate who was skeptical of the motives of nongovernmental organizations and who said that his amendment "would accord special consideration to communications from individuals but would exclude communications from groups of individuals or organizations which did not have direct and reliable knowledge of violations." [d]

On the question of standing to complain, compare *paragraph 2* with *articles 1–3* of the first Optional Protocol to the Covenant on Civil and Political Rights. Which is broader?

A petition alleging the violation of rights expressly set forth in either of the two principal ILO freedom of association conventions (ILO

b. See U.N. Docs. E/CN.4/Sub.2/SR.613–629, 633 (1971), and E/CN.4/1070 (1971).

c. See e.g., U.N. Docs. E/CN.4/Sub.2/SR.615, at 35, 38; SR.616, at 52–53; SR. 621, at 105–06 (1971).

d. U.N.Doc. E/CN.4/Sub.2/SR.627, at 43 (1971).

Nos. 87 and 98) would normally be referred to the ILO for consideration under its freedom of association procedure, if the respondent state is an ILO member. As long as the matter is being considered by the ILO, the working group and Sub–Commission clearly would keep their hands off, under Resolution 1, *paragraph 4(a)*. The ILO Committee on Freedom of Association construes its mandate quite broadly. For example, it has found violations of such rights as that of an accused trade unionist to be informed promptly of charges against him (a right not spelled out in the ILO conventions). If a trade union member petitions the U.N., alleging that he and others have been detained at great length without being charged by the government of a state that is a member of both the U.N. and the ILO, would paragraph 4(a) render the petition inadmissible if the matter is not then being considered by the ILO?

Was it appropriate to include an exhaustion-of-remedies requirement, in light of the purpose of the petitioning procedure?

What does *paragraph 4(c)* mean? How can the issues it raises be resolved without extensive investigations?

Consider the position of the petitioner. He or she is told nothing about the fate of the petition once it is submitted to the Sub–Commission's working group. Neither the petitioner nor anyone representing him or her may attend the sessions at which the communication is considered. While the process is ongoing, the only information that gets out is by way of unauthorized leaks (which do occur).

If civil proceedings to vindicate gross human rights violations at the national level were conducted in this way, would the proceedings themselves violate the complainant's international human rights? See Universal Declaration *articles 8* and *10*, and Covenant on Civil and Political Rights *article 14*. How can such a procedure within the U.N. be justified?

Is there wasteful duplication of effort between the Resolution 1503 procedure and the first Optional Protocol to the Covenant on Civil and Political Rights, as to states parties to the Protocol? What purpose is served by each of the two procedures?

Despite the formidable barriers to admissibility and to participation by petitioners under the 1503 procedure, some petitions do reach not only the Sub–Commission, but even the Commission on Human Rights. In 1978 the Commission decided to make public the list of countries referred to it under the Resolution 1503 procedure. In a typical year, eight or ten countries will be before the Commission in this way. They are allowed to participate in the Commission's consideration of their cases. Some of them are held over each year and considered again in the following year(s). By September 1987, situations in 42 countries had been referred to the Commission on Human Rights under the 1503 procedure.[e]

e. See United Nations Action in the Field of Human Rights, U.N.Doc. ST/HR/2/Rev.3, at 319 (1988).

As of mid–1992, however, the remedies set out in Resolution 1503 remained virtually unused. The Commission only once had ordered a "thorough study" and report under *paragraph 6(a)*, and it had never initiated an ad hoc committee investigation under *paragraph 6(b)*. The U.N. Centre for Human Rights explains:

> Instead, the Commission has strived for establishing a meaningful dialogue with the Governments of the countries concerned, through direct contacts, conducted between Commission sessions, either by the Secretary-General or by special representatives or independent experts, who are appointed by the Commission and requested to report to the following session. Government cooperation in exercises of this nature has steadily grown through the years, as the procedure itself has become more readily accepted and recognized.[f]

The direct contact technique is reminiscent of one of the frequently-used ILO enforcement techniques. The ILO, like the Commission on Human Rights, proceeds discreetly with direct contacts. But unlike Resolution 1503, the ILO's governing instruments do not mandate confidentiality; indeed, the annual reports of its Committee of Experts on the Application of Conventions and Recommendations are published, naming member states and the situations that have engendered direct contact missions. Can direct contacts under the confidential procedure of Resolution 1503 be as effective as those conducted without confidentiality?

The one "thorough study" and report under the 1503 procedure involved the government of Equatorial Guinea, in 1979. It followed efforts by the Commission on Human Rights to establish confidential direct contacts with the government, which the government rejected. The Commission removed the case from its 1503 docket and appointed a Special Rapporteur to examine the situation and issue a report under the public procedure of ECOSOC *Resolution 1235*. The Special Rapporteur, Professor Fernando Volio Jiménez, of Costa Rica, was able to visit Equatorial Guinea after a coup deposed the uncooperative government. He found that arbitrary arrests, torture and political assassinations had been common in Equatorial Guinea under the deposed government.[g]

Although the Special Rapporteur for Equatorial Guinea was a direct outgrowth of a 1503 proceeding, his appointment and mandate were not unlike those of other Special Rapporteurs appointed by the Commission under the public procedure of Resolution 1235. Under that resolution, the Commission has appointed Special Rapporteurs or their equivalents to investigate serious human rights allegations in several countries, including Chile, Bolivia, El Salvador, Guatemala, Poland, Iran, Iraq, Afghanistan and Haiti. In some instances, the persons appointed are designated as Experts rather than as Special

---

f. Id. at 320.

g. His report appears in U.N. Doc. E/CN.4/1371 (1980).

Rapporteurs, the difference being that an Expert implements the Commission's "advisory services" and presumably is more an advisor than an investigator. In practice, the difference is not substantial.[h]

As has been noted above, most admissible communications under the 1503 procedure have come from nongovernmental organizations. NGOs also are responsible for initiating the proceedings that have produced many of the investigations by Special Rapporteurs mentioned above, without necessarily going through the 1503 procedure. In other words, an NGO contemplating a complaint to the U.N. against systematic human rights violations in a particular country has a choice whether to proceed under the confidential 1503 procedure or to go public at the outset under Resolution 1235. What considerations would dictate which route to take in any given case?

In addition to country-specific investigations, the Commission has from time to time taken up investigations of themes, or particular types of human rights problems. Since 1982 this has taken the form of appointment of a Special Rapporteur on a particular theme.[i] The first was on summary or arbitrary executions; in 1985, one was appointed on torture; and in 1986 one was established on intolerance and discrimination based on religion or belief. At first it was questionable whether such a Special Rapporteur's mandate included anything more than a general study of the theme, but the first Rapporteur, on summary or arbitrary executions, gradually established the practice of receiving complaints from individuals and following up on them with their governments. He also established the practice of reporting publicly on this sort of thing. Consequently the theme procedure has taken on some of the characteristics of Resolution 1235 proceedings within the ambit of the theme being pursued, along with the characteristics of general studies and reports.

The Commission on Human Rights, unlike the Human Rights Committee under the Covenant on Civil and Political Rights, is a political body. Its 53 members are representatives of their governments. (The 18 members of the Human Rights Committee serve in their personal capacity.) Politics plays a substantial role in the Commission on Human Rights, particularly when it comes to deciding which governments to investigate or, once investigated, to keep on the Commission's agenda. Is it healthy to entrust an important human rights monitoring role to such a political body? Or is it just inevitable?

---

h. Sometimes the Commission has requested the U.N. Secretariat to investigate the human rights situation in a country. The resulting reports have been milder and less informative than those of non-Secretariat Special Rapporteurs and Experts. See Van Boven, The Role of the United Nations Secretariat in the Area of Human Rights, 24 N.Y.U. J. Int'l L. & Pol. 69, 81–85 (1991).

i. See Weissbrodt, The Three "Theme" Special Rapporteurs of the UN Commission on Human Rights, 80 Am.J. Int'l L. 685 (1986).

Space does not permit examination of the several other U.N.-related bodies concerned with human rights. Some of them, like the Commission on the Status of Women, are like the Commission on Human Rights in that they are subsidiary bodies of the Economic and Social Council, but they are concerned with specific situations or the problems of specific bodies of people. Others, including the Committee on the Elimination of Racial Discrimination, the Committee on the Elimination of Discrimination Against Women and the Committee Against Torture, are like the Committee on Economic, Social and Cultural Rights and the Human Rights Committee in that they are treaty-monitoring bodies for human rights conventions, but each of those conventions deals with a narrower universe of problems than do the two broad U.N. Covenants examined in these materials. Still others, like a UNESCO committee that considers alleged violations relating to education, science, culture and information, are comparable in their own fields to the ILO supervisory systems covered in this book.

SECTION 3. THE INTER-AMERICAN SYSTEM

A. INTRODUCTION

It is plausible to assume that a system confined to a region in which nations have not only geographical proximity, but some common historical and cultural ties, might stand a better chance of formulating and protecting the rights of the individual than a global United Nations system that must reflect and respect widely varying cultures among nations as much as half a world apart in space. That assumption is put to the test in both the Organization of American States and the Council of Europe.

The OAS system is administered by the Inter-American Commission on Human Rights, described below and examined more closely in Subsection C. The Inter-American Court of Human Rights, a separate entity under the American Convention on Human Rights, is also mentioned below; it is examined in Subsection D.

The Ninth International Conference of American States, meeting in Bogotá in 1948, adopted the Charter of the Organization of American States.[a] It has since been amended by the Protocol of Buenos Aires in 1967 and by the Protocol of Cartagena de Indias in 1985. The original OAS Charter contained only very general references to human rights.

The 1948 Bogotá conference also adopted the American Declaration of the Rights and Duties of Man, but did not incorporate it into the

---

[a.] This historical account is based largely on the Introduction to Basic Documents Pertaining to Human Rights in the Inter-American System, OAS Doc. OEA/Ser.L.V/II.71, Doc. 6 rev. 1, at 1–15 (1988); Medina, The Inter-American Commission on Human Rights and the Inter-American Court of Human Rights: Reflections on a Joint Venture, 12 Human Rts. Q. 439–444 (1990); Buergenthal, The Inter-American System for the Protection of Human Rights, in 2 Human Rights in International Law: Legal and Policy Issues 439, 470–79 (T. Meron ed. 1984).

Charter. Like the Universal Declaration of Human Rights, in a formal sense it is simply a nonbinding resolution.

The Fifth Meeting of Consultation of OAS Ministers of Foreign Affairs met in Santiago in 1959. It adopted a resolution creating the Inter-American Commission on Human Rights, to be composed of seven members elected by the OAS Council (later changed to election by the OAS General Assembly). The members serve in their individual capacities. In 1960 the OAS Council approved the first Statute of the Commission and elected its first members.

The Statute said nothing about receiving individual petitions, and the Commission at its first session decided that it was not authorized to make individual decisions on complaints submitted to it. The Statute did authorize the Commission to prepare studies and reports on human rights, and to make recommendations to OAS governments. The Commission seized on this, launching a series of country studies focusing on large-scale human rights violations. Information was gathered from written complaints, statements of witnesses, and some on-site investigations. Reports critical of some member states were published.

In 1965 the Second Special Inter-American Conference revised the Commission's Statute, giving it the additional function of examining communications referred to it with particular attention being given to observance of the rights found in *Articles I, II, III, IV, XVIII, XXV* and *XXVI* of the American Declaration of the Rights and Duties of Man. This enabled the Commission to establish an individual petitioning system, but it had few teeth because it was based only on the 1965 resolution of the Inter-American Conference, rather than on any instrument binding upon OAS member states.

The 1967 Protocol of Buenos Aires, amending the OAS Charter, made the Inter-American Commission one of the principal organs of the OAS. When the Protocol entered into force in 1970, the Commission became a treaty-based body. In the meantime, OAS member states adopted the American Convention on Human Rights in 1969. It, too, formalized the role of the Inter-American Commission (including its quasi-adjudicative role regarding individual petitions), as well as establishing the Inter-American Court of Human Rights. The American Convention entered into force in 1978. This led the OAS General Assembly to adopt a new Statute of the Commission in 1979.

The new Statute had to take account of the fact that some OAS member states were parties to the American Convention on Human Rights, and some were not. (As of 1992, the United States still was not.) Thus, in its key provisions, *articles 18–20,* the Statute established somewhat different functions for the Commission, depending on whether or not it is dealing with a state party to the Convention. Basically, the difference is that the Commission applies the articles mentioned above from the American Declaration of the Rights and Duties of Man when it deals with a nonparty to the Convention, and applies all relevant provisions in the Convention when it deals with a party.

In 1980 the Commission adopted its Regulations, and later amended them. They implement its Statute, establishing different procedures for parties and nonparties to the Convention.

The Convention gives the Inter-American Court of Human Rights both contentious and advisory jurisdiction. Only the Commission and states parties may bring contentious cases. They may do so only after proceedings before the Commission have been completed, and only against a state party that has made a declaration accepting the Court's contentious jurisdiction.

The Court's advisory jurisdiction is quite broad, as will appear in Subsection D below. It extends even to requests by OAS member states, as well as by OAS organs.

The Court has seven judges. The OAS General Assembly elected the first ones in 1979. They took office in San José, Costa Rica, where the Court has its seat, in September 1979.

These materials stress the Inter-American system's adjudicative role: its capacity to consider individual petitions alleging human rights violations, as well as the Inter-American Court's capacity to issue advisory opinions. But it is important also to note the Inter-American Commission's broader authority, derived from article 18 of its Statute and spelled out in some detail in its Regulations, to investigate human rights situations in individual countries and to publish reports on its findings, even in the absence of a petition from someone claiming a violation. These investigations usually involve on-site visits, if the government consents. The Commission has published several reports on the human rights situations in individual countries. They are often quite detailed and judgmental.

To give just one example, in 1989 the Commission published a Report on the Situation of Human Rights in Panama,[b] covering the period when General Manuel Noriega was in power. The Commission concluded that the Panamanian government had violated several provisions of the American Convention on Human Rights, including provisions on the right to life, the right to humane treatment, the right to personal liberty and the requirements of due process. The Commission also made recommendations regarding specific steps the government should take to restore the civil and political rights of individuals and groups.

Reports of this sort are designed, in large part, to bring pressure to bear on governments through the mobilization of shame. This, of course, is a familiar technique in the enforcement of international law. Is it likely to be more successful in the hands of a regional human rights body, like the Inter-American Commission, than in the hands of

b. OEA/Ser.L/V/II.76, Doc. 16 rev. 2 (1989).

the U.N. Human Rights Committee or the U.N. Commission on Human Rights?

B. THE AMERICAN DECLARATION OF THE RIGHTS AND DUTIES OF MAN

The American Declaration of the Rights and Duties of Man enunciates a body of rights that is quite similar to those set forth in the Universal Declaration of Human Rights. The rights are not always expressed in precisely the same way. In some instances, the differences in expression are probably insignificant. But in others, there seems to be a substantive difference. For example, the right to freedom of expression in *article IV* of the American Declaration does not refer to the right (expressed in *article 19* of the Universal Declaration) to seek and receive information and ideas through any media and regardless of frontiers.

There are two particularly striking differences between the American and the Universal Declarations. One is the elaboration in the American Declaration of the principle that duties go hand in hand with rights, including an entire chapter on Duties. The other is the existence in the OAS of a petitioning procedure for allegations of violations of certain rights in the American Declaration; the U.N. system contains no comparable procedure relating to the Universal Declaration (as distinguished from procedures relating to individual conventions that have implemented many of the Universal Declaration's provisions).

The American Declaration is set out in the Documents volume accompanying this book.

The Inter-American Court of Human Rights has had an opportunity to focus on the normative significance of the American Declaration. It was asked to give an advisory opinion on its own competence to interpret the American Declaration under *article 64* of the American Convention on Human Rights (which gives the Court advisory jurisdiction to interpret certain "treaties"). In the course of its opinion, the Court had this to say:

> The Charter of the [OAS] refers to the fundamental rights of man in its Preamble ((paragraph three) and in Arts. 3(j), 16, 43, 47, 51, 112 and 150; Preamble (paragraph four), Arts. 3(k), 16, 44, 48, 52, 111 and 150 of the Charter revised by the Protocol of Cartagena de Indias), but it does not list or define them. The member states of the Organization have, through its diverse organs, given specificity to the human rights mentioned in the Charter and to which the Declaration refers.
>
> This is the case of Article 112 of the Charter (Art. 111 of the Charter as amended by the Protocol of Cartagena de Indias) [which

establishes the Inter-American Commission as an organ of the OAS].

Article 150 of the Charter provides as follows:

> Until the inter-American convention on human rights, referred to in Chapter XVIII (Chapter XVI of the Charter as amended by the Protocol of Cartagena de Indias), enters into force, the present Inter-American Commission on Human Rights shall keep vigilance over the observance of human rights.

These norms authorize the Inter-American Commission to protect human rights. These rights are none other than those enunciated and defined in the American Declaration. That conclusion results from Article 1 of the Commission's Statute, which was approved by Resolution No. 447, adopted by the General Assembly of the OAS * * *. That Article reads as follows:

> 1. The Inter-American Commission on Human Rights is an organ of the Organization of the American States, created to promote the observance and defense of human rights and to serve as consultative organ of the Organization in this matter.
>
> 2. For the purposes of the present Statute, human rights are understood to be:
>
> a. The rights set forth in the American Convention on Human Rights, in relation to the States Parties thereto;
> b. The rights set forth in the American Declaration of the Rights and Duties of Man, in relation to the other member states.

Articles 18, 19 and 20 of the Statute enumerate these functions.

The General Assembly of the Organization has also repeatedly recognized that the American Declaration is a source of international obligations for the member states of the OAS. For example, in Resolution 314 (VII–0/77) of June 22, 1977, it charged the Inter-American Commission with the preparation of a study to "set forth their obligation to carry out the commitments assumed in the American Declaration of the Rights and Duties of Man." In Resolution 371 (VIII–0/78) of July 1, 1978, the General Assembly reaffirmed "its commitment to promote the observance of the American Declaration of the Rights and Duties of Man," and in Resolution 370 (VIII–0/78) of July 1, 1978, it referred to the "international commitments" of a member state of the Organization to respect the rights of man "recognized in the American Declaration of the Rights and Duties of Man." The Preamble of the American Convention to Prevent and Punish Torture, adopted and signed at the Fifteenth Regular Session of the General Assembly in Cartagena de Indias (December, 1985), reads as follows:

> Reaffirming that all acts of torture or any other cruel, inhuman, or degrading treatment or punishment constitute an offense against human dignity and a denial of the principles set forth in the Charter of the Organization of American States and in the Charter of the United Nations and are violations of the fundamental human rights and freedoms proclaimed in the American Declaration of the Rights and Duties of Man and the Universal Declaration of Human Rights.
>
> Hence it may be said that by means of an authoritative interpretation, the member states of the Organization have signaled their agreement that the Declaration contains and defines the fundamental human rights referred to in the Charter.
>
> * * *
>
> For the member states of the Organization, the Declaration is the text that defines the human rights referred to in the Charter. Moreover, Articles 1(2)(b) and 20 of the Commission's Statute define the competence of that body with respect to the human rights enunciated in the Declaration, with the result that to this extent the American Declaration is for these States a source of international obligations related to the Charter of the Organization.[a]

The Court went on to say that it has the authority to render advisory opinions interpreting the American Declaration, insofar as it is acting within its jurisdiction to interpret the OAS Charter, the American Convention or other treaties concerning the protection of human rights in the American states.

Can the Court's statements about the normative significance of the American Declaration in relation to the OAS Charter be dismissed simply as justifications for its own advisory jurisdiction?[b] The Inter-American Commission has reached the same normative conclusion in a different context. It has relied on the human rights provisions in the OAS Charter to conclude that the American Declaration has acquired binding force, in the context of petitions challenging the administration of the death penalty in the United States.[c]

---

a. Interpretation of the American Declaration of the Rights and Duties of Man Within the Framework of Article 64 of the American Convention on Human Rights, Advisory Opinion OC–10/89 (1989), Series A: Judgments and Opinions, No. 10, paras. 39–43, 45.

b. The Court has broad authority to give advisory opinions interpreting relevant human rights treaties, but it was far from clear at the time of the above opinion that its authority could extend to the American Declaration. These materials examine the Court's advisory jurisdiction in Subsection D.1 infra.

c. See Case No. 2141 (United States), 1980–1981 Ann.Rep. of the Inter-American Comm'n on Human Rights 25, 38; Case No. 9647 (United States), 1986–1987 Ann. Rep. 147, 166.

The references to human rights in the OAS Charter are quite general, except for some references to economic, social and cultural rights. For example, article 3(j) (article 3(k) as revised by the Protocol of Cartagena de Indias) says, "The American States proclaim the fundamental rights of the individual without distinction as to race, nationality, creed, or sex[.]" Does the court's advisory opinion mean that for every member state of the OAS, each right in the American Declaration, as articulated in the Declaration, is a binding treaty obligation?

On the other hand, would it be necessary to distinguish which rights in the American Declaration are "fundamental" and which are not? (Note the references in both the Court's opinion and in article 3(j), above, to "fundamental rights." The Statute of the Inter-American Commission, to be considered below, emphasizes the rights contained in *articles I–IV, XVIII, XXV* and *XXVI*, and clearly contemplates that the Commission will seek to enforce them. Would that make those rights "fundamental," while others are not?)

Article 29(1) of the Universal Declaration says that everyone has duties to the community, but fails to define them. On the other hand, Chapter Two of the American Declaration sets forth 11 reasonably well-defined individual duties. Why the difference? Does Chapter Two of the American Declaration establish duties under regional international law?

There is no international mechanism by which to enforce such duties against an individual. Does it serve any practical purpose to have enunciated them?

C. THE INTER-AMERICAN COMMISSION ON HUMAN RIGHTS AND ITS COMMUNICATIONS PROCEDURE

As we have seen, the Inter-American Commission considers communications alleging human rights violations, under a procedure that antedates the comparable U.N. procedure. For OAS member states that are not parties to the American Convention on Human Rights—a group that at this writing included Canada and the United States—the Commission acts under *articles 18* and *20* of its Statute. For states parties to the American Convention, the Commission acts under *Chapter VII* of the Convention and under *articles 18–19* of the Commission's Statute. (As of early 1992, 23 states were parties to the American Convention.)

These instruments have been implemented in the Commission's Regulations, which—like the Convention and the Commission's Statute—are set out in part in the Documents volume. When the Commission considers the admissibility of a petition, its procedure under the Regulations is the same whether or not the respondent state is a party to the American Convention.

The Commission receives about 500 petitions a year from individuals and other nongovernmental entities.ᵃ Do the petitioners have to be the injured parties or their family members? See American Convention *article 44*. Why would the rule on standing to file a petition in the Inter–American system be closer to the one under ECOSOC Resolution 1503 than to the one under the first Optional Protocol to the U.N. Covenant on Civil and Political Rights?

The petitioning procedure under article 44 is not optional: states parties to the American Convention consent to it simply by ratifying the Convention. On the other hand, the procedure under *article 45* is optional: a state party may, but need not, declare that it recognizes the competence of the Commission to examine complaints against it by another state party that has made a similar declaration.

Under the [European] Convention for the Protection of Human Rights and Fundamental Freedoms, the situation is just the opposite: any state party may complain to the European Commission about any other state party's alleged violations (*article 24* of the European Convention), but an individual may petition the Commission only if the respondent state party has declared that it recognizes the Commission's competence to receive such petitions (*article 25*).

Why would the Inter–American and European systems differ diametrically on this point? ᵇ

As in the case of other human rights systems, petitions are sometimes prepared by nongovernmental organizations with considerable expertise, but often they come from individuals with no legal expertise who simply want relief. Strict "pleading" requirements could be a significant barrier in such cases. Would *article 32* of the Inter–American Commission's Regulations be such a barrier?

All human rights petitioning systems have requirements for the admissibility of petitions. They include common grounds for inadmissibility, though they differ in some details. For example, they all include an exhaustion-of-domestic remedies requirement. See American Convention *article 46*, and the Commission's Regulations *article 37*. Is this an onerous requirement in the Inter–American system? (Exhaustion of domestic remedies was an issue in the Velásquez Rodríguez case, set forth in the next section of these materials.)

Note *article 39* of the Commission's Regulations, on duplication of procedures. Is it the same as *article 5(2)(a)* of the first Optional Protocol to the U.N. Covenant on Civil and Political Rights? Does it strike an appropriate balance that avoids wasteful duplication of adjudicative effort, on one hand, and denial of a fair opportunity to be heard, on the other?

a. See Medina, The Inter–American Commission on Human Rights and the Inter–American Court of Human Rights: Reflections on a Joint Venture, 12 Human Rts. Q. 439, 448 (1990).

b. See Buergenthal, The American and European Conventions on Human Rights: Similarities and Differences, 30 Am. U.L.Rev. 155, 160 (1981).

Under *article 41(b)* of the Commission's Regulations, a petition is inadmissible when it "does not state facts that constitute a violation of rights" defined in the American Convention, in the case of states parties to the Convention. This language, which was taken almost verbatim from *article 47(b)* of the American Convention, means essentially the same thing as "incompatible with the provisions" of the Covenant, in the first Optional Protocol to the U.N. Covenant: a petition must allege facts that, if proved, amount to a violation of one or more rights set forth in the relevant instrument.

According to *article 52* of the Inter-American Commission's Regulations, the procedure in *articles 32* to *43* apply even to nonparties to the American Convention, such as the United States. Could the United States rely on *article 41(b)* when a petition is filed against it? If so, would the relevant rights be those in the American Convention or those in the American Declaration? The Commission dealt with these questions, seemingly without much difficulty, in a death penalty case against the United States:

CASE NO. 10,031 (UNITED STATES)
Inter-American Commission on Human Rights, 1989.
1989–1990 Annual Report of the Commission,
OEA/Ser.L/V/II.77 rev. 1, Doc. 7, at 62.

I. INTRODUCTION

A. Summary of the Facts and the Petitioner's Complaint

1. The petitioner Willie L. Celestine, an impoverished young black man was convicted, sentenced to death, and electrocuted by the State of Louisiana in the United States, for the rape and murder of an elderly white woman.

2. Willie L. Celestine was convicted and sentenced to death on December 10, 1982, in the Fifteenth Judicial District Court of Lafayette Parish, Louisiana. Celestine sought review of his sentence in state and federal courts, including the U.S. Supreme Court. Every court either affirmed his death sentence or denied review. Celestine was denied *certiorari* by the Supreme Court on three occasions. * * * Celestine was executed on July 20, 1987.

* * *

4. The central issue raised by the complaint, filed July 15, 1987, is whether the death penalty, when applied in a racially discriminatory fashion and in the absence of an impartial hearing and equal protection before the law, is a violation of the obligations of the United States under the American Declaration of the Rights and Duties of Man (hereinafter "American Declaration"). The petitioner [through two American attorneys] specifically alleges violations of Articles I, II, and XXVI of the American Declaration. The United States, in its response dated January 26, 1988, denies the allegations, asserting the lack of any

factual basis for the allegations and questioning the applicability of the American Declaration.

* * *

II. The Facts

6. The facts of the present case are not in dispute between the parties. Willie L. Celestine was convicted and sentenced to death for the brutal rape-murder of an eighty-one year old woman at her home. Celestine was under the influence of drugs and alcohol and had an I.Q. far below normal.

III. Submissions of the Parties
A. *The Petitioner*

* * *

9. The petitioner claims that he was subject to arbitrary deprivation of his right to life as guaranteed under Article I of the American Declaration because the death penalty in Louisiana is imposed in a racially discriminatory manner in violation of Article II of the American Declaration and Article 3 of the OAS Charter.

10. The petitioner claims that he was denied an impartial hearing as guaranteed under Article XXVI of the American Declaration because he was sentenced by a death-qualified jury.

11. The petitioner claims that he was denied equal treatment before the law as guaranteed under Article II of the American Declaration because he was denied the opportunity to be tried by an impartial jury as a result of the death qualification process.

* * *

14. The petitioner bases his claims on a recent multiple-regression analysis of the capital punishment system in North Carolina, which demonstrates that the race of the defendant is a significant factor in virtually all stages of the criminal justice system, from the prosecutor's decision to file a first-degree murder charge to the decision to submit the case to a jury trial. The study also reveals that at the verdict stage, it is the race of the victim rather than that of the defendant that is the most significant factor in determining whether or not the death penalty will be imposed. According to the study, a defendant charged with murdering a white victim is six times more likely to be convicted than a defendant charged with murdering a black victim:

> All other factors being equal, including the quality of the evidence and the seriousness of the offense, defendants in cases with white victims were six times more likely to be found guilty of first degree murder than defendants in cases with non-white victims.

The petitioner notes that these conclusions support the findings of the Baldus study presented by the plaintiffs in *McCleskey v. Kemp*, (107

S.Ct. 1756). Although the Supreme Court held that the study, even assuming its validity, did not amount to a constitutional violation, the petitioners contend that the racially discriminatory imposition of the death penalty in the United States, as evidenced by sound statistical analysis, is nevertheless a violation of the American Declaration.

15. The petitioner also cites two independent studies of capital sentencing in Louisiana to demonstrate that they reveal similar patterns to those in North Carolina. In the Louisiana studies it is shown that "capital defendants who kill white rather than black victims are three times as likely to receive a death sentence. More pointedly, whites who kill blacks *never* receive the death penalty in Louisiana. Both studies concluded that the factor that most determines whether a death sentence will be returned is the victim's race. The Times-Picayune study involved a computer analysis of Louisiana defendants eligible to receive the death penalty, and it took into account a number of non-racial factors. It concluded that all other things being equal, the victim's race proved the most influential factor in determining who did and did not receive the death penalty." [Petitioner's brief.]

* * *

17. * * * Petitioner maintains that the present U.S. rule of law requiring the defendant to prove racial discrimination in his trial is an unrealistic standard of review because no capital defendant has ever met that burden. Subtle, system-wide racial discrimination is most often evident only through large statistical studies. Petitioner concludes, therefore, that if reliable statistical studies demonstrate the likelihood of racial discrimination within the criminal justice system, the burden must shift to the Government to prove that the capital hearing was free of racial discrimination. To presume otherwise, would allow the United States to arbitrarily deprive black defendants of their right to life without meaningful review which is a violation of Articles I and II of the American Declaration.

* * *

19. Additionally, the petitioner alleges that Celestine was denied the right to an impartial hearing guaranteed by Article XXVI because he was sentenced by a death-qualified jury. Death qualification refers to the exclusion of jurors who indicate that they would automatically vote against imposition of the death penalty at the sentencing stage of the trial without regard to the evidence presented. The Supreme Court, in *Witherspoon v. Illinois,* (391 U.S. 510) (1968), upheld the constitutionality of this practice, noting the state's interest in having a single rather than a bifurcated trial, i.e., with respect to sentencing and guilt. The petitioner contends, however, that death qualification leads to conviction-prone juries and cites studies in support of this argument. Petitioner also asserts that death qualification further compromises the impartiality of the jury by removing a disproportionate number of blacks and women from the jury, since these segments of the population

tend to vote against the death penalty more often than other groups. Moreover, the absence of a similar procedure in non-capital cases results in the unequal treatment of the capital defendant before the law in violation of Article II of the American Declaration.

20. Petitioner requests that the Commission find that the execution of Willie L. Celestine violated Articles I, II, and XXVI of the American Declaration. Petitioner also requests that the Commission recommend a moratorium on the imposition of the death penalty in the United States, or, in the alternative, that the Commission recommend to the United States that when a capital defendant presents reliable statistical data indicating that a risk of racial discrimination exists, the evidentiary burden should be on the Government to demonstrate that in fact racial discrimination did not affect the imposition of the death sentence.

B. The Government

21. The Government urges the Commission to declare this case inadmissible on grounds that the case does not state facts which constitute a violation of the American Declaration. According to the U.S. the petitioner does not attempt to prove that Articles I, II, and XXVI of the American Declaration were in fact violated in Celestine's particular case by showing, for example, that his sentence was disproportionate or racially motivated or that his jury was biased. Instead, states the U.S., the petitioner relies on statistical studies and makes no attempt to explain their relevance to a capital sentencing in the state of Louisiana. * * *

22. The United States denies that Celestine's sentence was the result of racial prejudice citing the findings of the Louisiana Supreme Court which upheld his conviction. As regards the charge of jury partiality, the jury in the Celestine case considered the statutorily-enumerated aggravating and mitigating circumstances. In mitigation it considered that, at the time of the crime, Celestine was under the influence of disabling drugs and alcohol[;] however, "the jury unanimously recommended the death penalty on the grounds that three statutory aggravating circumstances were present: (1) commission of aggravated rape in the course of the murder, (2) previous conviction of an unrelated aggravated rape, and (3) committing the murder in an especially cruel manner." The U.S. states that it is important what the petitioner does *not* contend, for example, the petitioner does not contend that Celestine's sentence was disproportionate to his crime. Celestine brutally raped and killed an eighty-one year old woman at her home. In the course of the murder and rape, he strangled the victim, disfigured her face, and fractured seven ribs on both sides of her body. After his arrest, he voluntarily confessed to this rape as well as to two previous rapes. * * * In addition, the U.S. argues that the petitioner does *not* contend that the jury's decision in Celestine's particular case was racially-motivated or biased.

* * *

IV. ADMISSIBILITY

26. * * * [T]he Commission finds that the petitioner has no further domestic remedies to exhaust.

27. Despite the fact that the United States Supreme Court did not address petitioner's case the Court has [addressed] the issues of statistically proven racial discrimination and death-qualified juries in the past.

[The Commission discussed McCleskey v. Kemp,[c] where the U.S. Supreme Court rejected a claim of racial discrimination that relied solely on the use of statistical evidence of a disparity in the imposition of death sentences based on the defendant's race and the victim's race. The Commission also discussed Witherspoon v. Illinois,[d] where the Supreme Court said that the available statistical evidence was too tentative to show that jurors not opposed to the death penalty (death-qualified juries) tend to favor the prosecution in the determination of guilt.

[After reiterating the points at issue, the Commission concluded:]

45. Capital punishment has not yet been abolished by the federal government of the United States or by the states of the United States as a whole. The Commission is persuaded by the U.S. Government's argument that "An entire criminal justice system cannot be proved invalid by mere citations to statistical studies without more." In the opinion of the Commission, the petitioner has not provided sufficient evidence that the statistical studies presented make a *prima facie* case to prove the allegations of racial discrimination and partiality in the imposition of the death penalty such as to shift the burden of proof to the United States Government. In addition, the Commission finds that this is a poor case upon which to recommend a reversal of the U.S. criminal justice practice. Willie Celestine brutally raped and murdered an elderly woman, a crime punishable by death in the state of Louisiana. This was a particularly heinous crime and the jury which unanimously convicted and sentenced him contained several black members. His case was specifically reviewed for prejudice by the Louisiana Supreme Court. None was found and the conviction and sentence were affirmed. Based on the evidence presented by the petitioner, the Commission finds no violations of the American Declaration of the Rights and Duties of Man. In conformity with Articles 52 and 41 of the Commission's Regulations this case is declared inadmissible for failure to state facts that constitute a violation of the rights set forth in the American Declaration.

THE COMMISSION AND ITS PROCEDURE

The Commission held the petition inadmissible even though it involved issues covered by *articles I, II* and *XXVI* of the American

[c]. 481 U.S. 279, 107 S.Ct. 1756, 95 L.Ed.2d 262 (1987).

[d]. 391 U.S. 510, 88 S.Ct. 1770, 20 L.Ed.2d 776 (1968).

Declaration—right to life; equality before the law; and right to an impartial hearing. Was the infirmity really just a failure of proof? If so, should that be decided at the admissibility stage, or on the merits after a full hearing?

On the other hand, was the infirmity (in the eyes of the Commission) a misuse of the petitioning procedure, in the sense that the representatives of the petitioner were using a case in which no prejudice could be shown, in order to challenge the death penalty in the United States?

Would the petition have been admissible if the petitioner had requested only the alternative remedy in paragraph 20: the reversal of the burden of proof regarding racial discrimination? Of course, that remedy would not have done Mr. Celestine any good at the time of this case. Should that, alone, be a reason to hold the petition inadmissible?

Did the Commission show too much deference to the courts of the United States in rejecting the use of statistical evidence of racial bias?

Would it ever be appropriate for an international quasi-judicial body, like the Inter-American Commission or the U.N. Human Rights Committee, to get out in front of member states in giving credence to new and controversial forms of evidence, such as statistical surveys or data based on the use of new technology? What are the advantages and disadvantages of doing so?

This was not the only death penalty case the Commission had heard involving the United States. In Case No. 9647, decided in 1987, the ACLU and the International Human Rights Law Group brought petitions on behalf of two persons who had been convicted of murders committed while they were 17 years old and who had been sentenced to death. The petitioners alleged that the United States had violated article I (right to life), article VII (special protection of children) and article XXVI (prohibition of cruel, infamous or unusual punishment) of the American Declaration by allowing the execution of persons for crimes committed before their eighteenth birthday.

The Commission treated the American Declaration as binding upon the United States, and defined the issue to be "whether the absence of a federal prohibition within U.S. domestic law on the execution of juveniles, who committed serious crimes under the age of 18, is in violation of the American Declaration." [e] Although the American Convention on Human Rights, article 4(5), expressly prohibits capital punishment for crimes committed while the offender was under 18 years of age, the United States was not a party to the Convention and the American Declaration is not explicit regarding capital punishment. Thus the Commission considered whether *jus cogens* (a peremptory norm, from

---

e. Case No. 9647, in 1986–1987 Ann. Rep. of the Inter-American Commission on Human Rights 147, 172.

which no state could opt out) or custom could flesh out the Declaration on this point.

The Commission found that "in the member States of the OAS there is recognized a norm of *jus cogens* which prohibits the State execution of children."[f] The trouble was, there was no consensus as to whether a 17-year-old is a "child" within the meaning of that norm. Consequently the Commission accepted the U.S. government's argument that there did not yet exist even a norm of ordinary customary international law establishing 18 as the minimum age for the death penalty, though it said that "the norm is emerging."[g]

The Commission, however, noted that 13 states in the United States and the District of Columbia had abolished the death penalty entirely, while nine others had abolished it for offenders under the age of 18. Others retained it, even for some offenders under 18. The Commission then said:

> The Commission finds that the diversity of state practice in the U.S.—reflected in the fact that some states have abolished the death penalty, while others allow a potential threshold limit of applicability as low as 10 years of age—results in very different sentences for the commission of the same crime. The deprivation by the State of an offender's life should not be made subject to the fortuitous element of where the crime took place. Under the present system of laws in the United States, a hypothetical sixteen year old who commits a capital offense in Virginia may potentially be subject to the death penalty, whereas if the same individual commits the same offense on the other side of the Memorial Bridge, in Washington, D.C., where the death penalty has been abolished for adults as well as for juveniles, the sentence will not be death.
>
> For the federal Government of the United States to leave the issue of the application of the death penalty to juveniles to the discretion of state officials results in a patchwork scheme of legislation which makes the severity of the punishment dependent, not, primarily, on the nature of the crime committed, but on the location where it was committed. Ceding to state legislatures the determination of whether a juvenile may be executed is not of the same category as granting states the discretion to determine the age of majority for purposes of purchasing alcoholic beverages or consenting to matrimony. The failure of the federal government to preempt the states as regards this most fundamental right—the right to life—results in a pattern of legislative arbitrariness throughout the United States which results in the arbitrary deprivation of life and inequality before the law, contrary to Articles I and II of the American Declaration of the Rights and Duties of Man, respectively.[h]

f. Id. at 170.
g. Id. at 172.
h. Id. at 172–73.

Note that the Commission found a violation of article II, as well as article I, even though the petitioners did not allege a violation of article II. The petitioners also had not argued the *jus cogens* point, above, yet the Commission decided it. The Commission explained that it is not a judicial body and is not limited to considering only the submissions of the parties. Is that convincing?

If the Commission is not at least a quasi-judicial body, why does it have admissibility requirements for petitions? On the other hand, if the Commission sticks strictly to points raised by petitioners, would it adequately perform its function of promoting the observance of human rights in the Americas?[i]

Could the Commission's reasoning be applied to adults as well as to juveniles in a federal system? If so, is the entire capital punishment system in the United States contrary to articles I and II of the (binding) American Declaration, without regard to the statistical evidence presented in Case No. 10,031, supra?

Did the Commission make article II of the Declaration a federal equal protection clause in a country like the United States? To use the familiar language of U.N. Charter article 2(7), did it intervene in matters which are essentially within the domestic jurisdiction of a (federal) state?

Case No. 9893, decided in 1990, arose in quite a different context from the ones above. The petitioners, members of a national association of pensioners in Uruguay, alleged that the Uruguayan government had violated several provisions of Uruguayan and international law, including *article 24* of the American Convention (to which Uruguay is a party). The basis for the allegation was the increase in the amount of their annual pensions by substantially less than the increase in the Uruguayan average wage index for the relevant year (1985), and the fact that these pensioners, unlike some of their more affluent counterparts, lacked the technical assistance or wherewithal to appeal the decree establishing the pension payment. Uruguay enacted legislation equating pension increases with inflation for 1986 and later years, but did not correct the 1985 situation. Because the increase for any given year was based on the prior year's level, a failure to correct the 1985 situation had adverse effects on the petitioners not only for that year, but for all subsequent years.

The Inter-American Commission held the petition inadmissible for failure to exhaust domestic remedies. But it did not stop there. It went on to say:

---

i. On the Commission's role and methods, including a critique of its reasoning in this case, see Shelton, Improving Human Rights Protections: Recommendations for Enhancing the Effectiveness of the Inter-American Commission and Inter-American Court of Human Rights, 3 Am.U.J.Int'l L. & Pol'y 323 (1988).

Nevertheless, the Commission cannot fail to consider the moral dimensions of the problem in view of the special circumstances of the case, namely, the equality, social, and economic condition and number of those affected by a real situation of inequality. This matter deals with a sizable social group that is particularly sensitive and economically weak to which the society should extend special protection. Furthermore, attention should be paid to the practical implications entailed for the petitioners and for the courts of presenting the claims of 100,000 or 54,000 retired persons and pension beneficiaries, depending on whether you use the figures of the petitioners or the Government, respectively. Therefore, the Commission cannot fail to weigh these special circumstances in this report.

* * *

The Inter-American Commission on Human Rights:

Declares that the petition relating to Case 9893 * * * is formally inadmissible because available remedies under domestic law were not exhausted, as required by the provisions of Article 46.1.a of the Convention and Article 37 of the Regulations of the Commission.

States the satisfaction of the Commission for the passage of Law 15900 of October 21, 1987, while this claim was in process, which called for the setting of adjustments for retired persons and pensioners for the years 1986 and later as a function of the Average Wage Index (IMS).

Recommends to the Government of Uruguay that, for reasons of moral order and social justice and its statements that this is "an open question and one still pending solution," to the extent that the economic-financial resources of the state allow, it consider the adoption of legislative or other measures that revoke decree 137/85 and its effects and make it possible to set the adjustments of pension payments owed for 1985 as a function of the Average Wage Index to all retired and pensioned persons and that they be adjusted to the amounts received at present; and consequently, to incorporate a chapter with regard to the subject matter in the Annual Report that Article 42 of the Convention alludes to, in order to make possible a follow-up on the part of the Commission.[j]

Was it proper for the Commission, after declaring the petition inadmissible, to give its view regarding the moral dimensions of the problem? Is that contemplated by *articles 48–51* of the American Convention?

j. Case No. 9893 (Uruguay), in 1990–1991 Ann.Rep. of the Inter-American Comm'n on Human Rights 77, 89–91.

Could the Commission base what it did in this case on the grant of functions and powers to it in *article 41* of the Convention, as implemented by *article 18* of its Statute?

If members of the Commission had doubts about the way the death penalty is administered in United States courts in cases involving members of minority groups, would it have been proper for the Commission, after declaring inadmissible the petition against the United States in Case No. 10,031, above, to express its concern and make recommendations to the United States? (Note that article 18 of the Commission's Statute applies to all OAS member states, not just to parties to the American Convention.) Why do you suppose it didn't do so?

In the case against Uruguay, the Commission wound up by recommending that the government include a chapter with regard to pension indexing in the annual reports it submits under *article 42* of the American Convention, in order to make possible a follow-up by the Commission. In other words, the Commission planned to monitor Uruguay's performance, in order to see that the inequity in pension indexing was rectified. Did the Commission thus effectively satisfy the petitioners, without having to cast aspersions on the government—as it would have if it had held the petition admissible and had held on the merits in favor of the petitioners? Is there anything wrong with this?

When a petition is held admissible, the Commission proceeds to gather evidence. One tool available to it is the on-site investigation. *Article 44* of its Regulations sounds as though the respondent government is required to allow such an investigation if the Commission requests it. In practice, though, the Commission seeks the government's consent, usually successfully.[k] The Commission at this stage is not limited to investigating and adjudicating. *Article 45* of the Regulations contemplates an effort by the Commission to help the parties achieve a friendly settlement, but apparently the Commission has not done much in this direction. Thus it usually reaches a decision on the merits, prepares a report and transmits it to the government concerned. The Commission may eventually publish the report. See *articles 46–48*. Unless the Commission submits the case to the Inter-American Court of Human Rights, its only tools for obtaining a government's compliance are direct contacts and the mobilization of shame (through publishing the report).

The Commission has been slow to refer cases to the Court. If it does, and if the Court renders a judgment on the merits, *article 68* of the American Convention makes the judgment binding on the state

---

k. See A.G. Mower, Regional Human Rights: A Comparative Study of the West European and Inter-American Systems 77 (1991), on which some of the other information in this paragraph is also based.

party and provides a means of executing an award of compensatory damages in the courts of the respondent state.

D. THE INTER-AMERICAN COURT OF HUMAN RIGHTS

1. Advisory Opinions

Article 64 of the American Convention on Human Rights gives broad authority to the Inter-American Court to issue advisory opinions. Requests for advisory opinions may be submitted by any OAS member state (not just by a state party to the American Convention), and by any organ of the OAS, including the Inter-American Commission, within the sphere of its competence. Advisory opinions may interpret the American Convention or "other treaties concerning the protection of human rights in the American states." As will appear below, the quoted phrase has itself been the subject of an advisory opinion, and has been interpreted quite broadly.

The Inter-American Court's advisory jurisdiction comes closer to that of the International Court of Justice than to any other adjudicative body in the human rights field. (In fact, it is broader than that of the ICJ, since states may not request ICJ advisory opinions. See U.N. Charter *article 96*.) The U.N. Human Rights Committee has no advisory jurisdiction. The European Court of Human Rights has very limited advisory jurisdiction under Protocol No. 2 to the [European] Convention for the Protection of Human Rights and Fundamental Freedoms. Under the European system, only the Council of Europe's Committee of Ministers may request an advisory opinion, and it may not deal with the content or scope of the substantive rights or freedoms in the Convention, or with any other question that might have to be considered in contentious proceedings under the Convention. Not surprisingly, the European Court's advisory jurisdiction has not been utilized, while the Inter-American Court's has.

Why would the Inter-American and the European systems differ so substantially over their Courts' advisory jurisdiction?

Why would the Inter-American Court be given advisory jurisdiction regarding not only requests from OAS organs, but also from OAS member states? Should other international tribunals, such as the ICJ, be given that authority?

For several years after July 1978, when the American Convention entered into force, practically all of the Inter-American Court's work stemmed from requests for advisory opinions. There were a number of reasons. First, states parties were slow to make declarations under *article 62* accepting the jurisdiction of the Court in contentious cases—a prerequisite if the Court is to have jurisdiction over a state in such a case. (By early 1992, 14 states had made article 62 declarations.) In addition, the Commission at first was reluctant to submit contentious cases to the Court, perhaps because as an organ antedating the Court, it had settled into a work pattern that did not look to the Court as a contributor.[a]

Another significant factor is as relevant today as it was in the early years of the Court. Under *article 61* only states parties and the Commission (not individuals) have the right to submit a case to the Court, and only after proceedings before the Commission have been completed. Thus, individuals—the real parties in interest—may not invoke the Court's contentious jurisdiction.

One of the Court's early advisory opinions actually arose when the Commission declined to submit a case involving an individual under the contentious jurisdiction. The Commission had received a petition against Costa Rica from a journalist alleging violation of *article 13* of the Convention, on freedom of expression. The Commission decided by a divided vote in favor of Costa Rica. When the Commission declined to submit the case to the Court, the Costa Rican government—living up to a commitment it had made to the Inter-American Press Association—requested the Court to issue an advisory opinion. The Court issued its opinion to the effect that Costa Rica had violated article 13,[b] creating the anomaly of an unreversed Commission decision in Costa Rica's favor and an advisory opinion of the Court to the contrary.[c]

The Court scolded the Commission for failing to submit the case to it under its contentious jurisdiction. It said that because individuals have no standing to do so and a government that has won in proceedings before the Commission would have no incentive to do so, "the Commission has a special duty to consider the advisability of coming to the Court" when it has not been able to achieve a friendly settlement of the case, in order to ensure the effective functioning of the protective system established by the Convention.[d]

The relationship between the contentious and advisory jurisdiction of the Court took another twist in a case involving Guatemala, which at the time had become a party to the American Convention, but had not made a declaration accepting the Court's jurisdiction under article 62 of the Convention. The Commission had been attempting to persuade the Guatemalan government to stop executing persons convicted by special tribunals outside the regular Guatemalan judicial system. The death sentences were pronounced under a Guatemalan decree, adopted after Guatemala had become a party to the American Convention, which substituted the death penalty for prison terms upon conviction of several offenses (including, for example, kidnapping, aggravated arson,

a. See Frost, The Evolution of the Inter-American Court of Human Rights: Reflections of Present and Former Judges, 14 Human Rts.Q. 171, 176–79 (1992).

b. Advisory Opinion No. OC–5/85, Inter-American Court of Human Rights Series A, No. 5, reprinted in 1985 Ann.Rep. of the Inter-American Court of Human Rights 19.

c. See Medina, The Inter-American Commission on Human Rights and the Inter-American Court of Human Rights: Reflections on a Joint Venture, 12 Human Rts. Q. 439, 452–53 (1990).

d. Advisory Opinion OC–5/85, para. 26.

treason and various forms of attack that could be viewed as terrorism). The Guatemalan government took the position that a reservation it had attached to *article 4(4)* of the American Convention excepted it from the prohibition in *article 4(2)*, last sentence.[e] See below.

When an impasse was reached, the Commission requested an advisory opinion on the matter. The Guatemalan government argued that the Commission was simply trying to do through article 64 what it could not do through article 62.

RESTRICTIONS TO THE DEATH PENALTY
Inter–American Court of Human Rights Advisory Opinion OC–3/83, 1983.
Series A: Judgments and Opinions, No. 3.

I
STATEMENT OF THE ISSUES

8. Invoking Article 64(1) of the Convention, the Commission requested the Court, in communications of April 15 and 25, 1983, to render an advisory opinion on the following questions relating to the interpretation of Article 4 of the Convention:

1) May a government apply the death penalty for crimes for which the domestic legislation did not provide such punishment at the time the American Convention on Human Rights entered into force for said state?

2) May a government, on the basis of a reservation to Article 4(4) of the Convention made at the time of ratification, adopt subsequent to the entry into force of the Convention a law imposing the death penalty for crimes not subject to this sanction at the moment of ratification?

9. Article 4 of the Convention reads as follows:

1. Every person has the right to have his life respected. This right shall be protected by law and, in general, from the moment of conception. No one shall be arbitrarily deprived of his life.

2. In countries that have not abolished the death penalty, it may be imposed only for the most serious crimes and pursuant to a final judgment rendered by a competent court and in accordance with a law establishing such punishment, enacted prior to the commission of the crime. The application of such punishment shall not be extended to crimes to which it does not presently apply.

3. The death penalty shall not be re-established in states that have abolished it.

---

e. See the Commission's Report on the Situation of Human Rights in the Republic of Guatemala, OEA/Ser.L/V/II.61, Doc. 47 rev. 1 (1983), excerpted in 4 Human Rights: The Inter–American System, Part 3, Pamphlet 22.1 (T. Buergenthal & R. Norris eds. 1984).

4. In no case shall capital punishment be inflicted for political offenses or related common crimes.

* * *

10. In its explanation of the considerations giving rise to the request, the Commission informed the Court of the existence of certain differences of opinion between it and the Government of Guatemala concerning the interpretation of the last sentence of Article 4(2) of the Convention as well as on the effect and scope of Guatemala's reservation to the fourth paragraph of that article. That reservation reads as follows:

> The Government of the Republic of Guatemala, ratifies the American Convention on Human Rights, signed in San José, Costa Rica, on the 22nd of November of 1969, making a reservation with regard to Article 4, paragraph 4 of the same, inasmuch as the Constitution of the Republic of Guatemala, in its Article 54, only excludes from the application of the death penalty, political crimes, but not common crimes related to political crimes.

The specific legal problem presented by the Commission is whether a reservation drafted in the aforementioned terms can be invoked by a State Party to permit it to impose the death penalty for crimes to which such penalty did not apply at the time of its ratification of the Convention. That is, in particular, whether this reservation can be invoked, as the Government of Guatemala did before the Commission, in order to justify the application of the death penalty to common crimes connected with political crimes to which that penalty did not previously apply. During the public hearing, the Delegates of the Commission stated that the problem that had arisen with respect to Guatemala's reservation had been referred to the Court as an example in order to highlight the underlying legal problem.

11. In a telex addressed to the President of the Court by the Minister of Foreign Affairs of Guatemala, * * * the Government of Guatemala requested the Court to decline to render the requested opinion. The specific grounds upon which the Government based its plea are stated as follows:

> The Government of Guatemala respectfully requests the Honorable Inter-American Court of Human Rights to decline to render the advisory opinion requested by the Commission, since even if Article 64 of the Convention empowers the Commission, in general terms, to consult the Court on the interpretation of the Convention, the fact is that Article 62(3) of the Convention itself clearly states that:
>
> > The jurisdiction of the Court shall comprise all cases concerning the interpretation and application of the provisions of this Convention that are submitted to it, provided that the States Parties to the case recognize or have recognized such jurisdiction, whether by special declaration pursuant to the preceding paragraphs, or by a special agreement.

Since Guatemala has not declared, either upon depositing its instrument of ratification of the convention or at any subsequent time, that it recognizes as binding, ipso facto, and not requiring special agreement, the jurisdiction of the Court on all matters relating to the interpretation of the Convention, as provided in Article 62(1), it is obvious that the Court must decline to render the advisory opinion requested by the Commission for lack of jurisdiction.

* * *

III

OBJECTIONS TO THE JURISDICTION OF THE COURT

30. * * * [Guatemala] contends that, although Article 64(1) of the Convention and Article 19(d) of the Statute of the Commission authorize the latter to seek an advisory opinion from the Court regarding the interpretation of any article of the Convention, if that opinion were to concern a given State directly, as it does Guatemala in the present case, the Court could not render the opinion unless the State in question has accepted the tribunal's jurisdiction pursuant to Article 62(1) of the Convention. The Government of Guatemala argues accordingly that because of the form in which the Commission submitted the present advisory opinion request, linking it to an existing dispute between Guatemala and the Commission regarding the meaning of certain provisions of Article 4 of the Convention, the Court should decline to exercise its jurisdiction.

31. The Convention distinguishes very clearly between two types of proceedings: so-called adjudicatory or contentious cases and advisory opinions. The former are governed by the provisions of Articles 61, 62 and 63 of the Convention; the latter by Article 64.

* * *

32. In contentious proceedings, the Court must not only interpret the applicable norms, determine the truth of the acts denounced and decide whether they are a violation of the Convention imputable to a State Party; it may also rule "that the injured party be ensured the enjoyment of his right or freedom that was violated." (Convention, Art. 63(1).) The States Parties to such proceeding are, moreover, legally bound to comply with the decisions of the Court in contentious cases. (Convention, Art. 68(1).) On the other hand, in advisory opinion proceedings the Court does not exercise any fact-finding functions; instead, it is called upon to render opinions interpreting legal norms. Here the Court fulfills a consultative function through opinions that "lack the same binding force that attaches to decisions in contentious cases." [Citing a previous case.]

33. The provisions applicable to contentious cases differ very significantly from those of Article 64, which govern advisory opinions. Thus, for example, Article 61(2) speaks of "case" and declares that "in

order for the Court to hear a **case,** it is necessary that the procedures set forth in Articles 48 to 50 shall have been completed (emphasis added)." These procedures apply exclusively to "a petition or communication alleging violation of any of the rights protected by this Convention." (Convention, Art. 48(1).) Here the word "case" is used in its technical sense to describe a **contentious case** within the meaning of the Convention, that is, a dispute arising as a result of a claim initiated by an individual (Art. 44) or State Party (Art. 45), charging that a State Party has violated the human rights guaranteed by the Convention.

34. One encounters the same technical use of the word "case" in connection with the question as to who may initiate a contentious case before the Court, which contrasts with those provisions of the Convention that deal with the same issue in the consultative area. Article 61(1) provides that "only States Parties and the Commission shall have a right to submit a case to the Court." On the other hand, not only "States Parties and the Commission," but also all of the "Member States of the Organization" and the "organs listed in Chapter X of the Charter of the Organization of American States" may request advisory opinions from the Court. (Convention, Art. 64(1).) There is yet another difference with respect to the subject matter that the Court might consider. While Article 62(1) refers to "all matters relating to the interpretation and application of this Convention," Article 64 authorizes advisory opinions relating not only to the interpretation of the Convention but also to "other treaties concerning the protection of human rights in the American states." It is obvious, therefore, that what is involved here are very different matters, and that there is no reason in principle to apply the requirements contained in Articles 61, 62 and 63 to the consultative function of the Court, which is spelled out in Article 64.

35. Article 62(3) of the Convention—the provision Guatemala claims governs the application of Article 64—reads as follows:

> The jurisdiction of the Court shall comprise all **cases** concerning the interpretation and application of the provisions of this Convention that are submitted to it, provided that the States Parties to the **case** recognize or have recognized such jurisdiction, whether by special declaration pursuant to the preceding paragraphs, or by a special agreement [emphasis added by the Court].

It is impossible to read this provision without concluding that it, as does Article 61, uses the words "case" and "cases" in their technical sense.

* * *

37. The instant request of the Commission does not fall within the category of advisory opinion requests that need to be rejected [as defeating the purposes of the Convention] because nothing in it can be deemed to interfere with the proper functioning of the system or might be deemed to have an adverse effect on the interests of a victim. The Court has merely been asked to interpret a provision of the Convention

in order to assist the Commission in the discharge of the obligation it has as an OAS Charter organ "to promote the observance and protection of human rights and to serve as a consultative organ of the Organization in these matters." (OAS Charter, Art. 112.)

38. The powers conferred on the Commission require it to apply the Convention or other human rights treaties. In order to discharge fully its obligations, the Commission may find it necessary or appropriate to consult the Court regarding the meaning of certain provisions whether or not at the given moment in time there exists a difference between a government and the Commission concerning an interpretation, which might justify the request for an advisory opinion. If the Commission were to be barred from seeking an advisory opinion merely because one or more governments are involved in a controversy with the Commission over the interpretation of a disputed provision, the Commission would seldom, if ever, be able to avail itself of the Court's advisory jurisdiction. Not only would this be true of the Commission, but the OAS General Assembly, for example, would be in a similar position were it to seek an advisory opinion from the Court in the course of the Assembly's consideration of a draft resolution calling on a Member State to comply with its international human rights obligations.

39. The right to seek advisory opinions under Article 64 was conferred on OAS organs for requests falling "within their spheres of competence." This suggests that the right was also conferred to assist with the resolution of disputed legal issues arising in the context of the activities of an organ, be it the Assembly, the Commission, or any of the others referred to in Chapter X of the OAS Charter. It is clear, therefore, that the mere fact that there exists a dispute between the Commission and the Government of Guatemala regarding the meaning of Article 4 of the Convention does not justify the Court to decline to exercise its advisory jurisdiction in the instant proceeding.

40. This conclusion of the Court finds ample support in the jurisprudence of the International Court of Justice. That tribunal has consistently rejected requests that it decline to exercise its advisory jurisdiction in situations in which it was alleged that because the issue involved was in dispute the Court was being asked to decide a disguised contentious case. (See, e.g., Interpretation of Peace Treaties, [1950 I.C.J. 65]; Reservations to the Convention on Genocide, 1951 I.C.J. 15; Legal Consequences for States of the Continued Presence of South Africa in Namibia (South West Africa) notwithstanding Security Council Resolution 276 (1970), 1971 I.C.J. 16; Western Sahara, [1975 I.C.J. 12].) In doing so, the Hague Court has acknowledged that the advisory opinion might affect the interests of States which have not consented to its contentious jurisdiction and which are not willing to litigate the matter. The critical question has always been whether the requesting organ has a legitimate interest to obtain the opinion for the purpose of guiding its future actions. (Western Sahara, [supra], p. 27.)

41. The Commission, as an organ charged with the responsibility of recommending measures designed to promote the observance and protection of human rights, has a legitimate institutional interest in the interpretation of Article 4 of the Convention. The mere fact that this provision may also have been invoked before the Commission in petitions and communications filed under Articles 44 and 45 of the Convention does not affect this conclusion. Given the nature of advisory opinions, the opinion of the Court in interpreting Article 4 cannot be deemed to be an adjudication of those petitions and communications.

42. In The Effect of Reservations on the Entry into Force of the American Convention (Arts. 74 and 75) (I/A Court H.R., Advisory Opinion OC–2/82 of September 24, 1982, Series A No. 2), this Court examined in considerable detail the requirements applicable to OAS organs requesting advisory opinions under Article 64. The Court there explained that Article 64, in limiting the right of OAS organs to advisory opinions falling "within their spheres of competence," meant to restrict the opinions "to issues in which such entities have a legitimate institutional interest." (Ibid., para. 14.) After examining Article 112 and Chapter X of the OAS Charter, as well as the relevant provisions of the Statute of the Commission and the Convention itself, the Court concluded that the Commission enjoys, in general, a pervasive legitimate institutional interest in questions bearing on the promotion and protection of human rights in the inter-American system, which could be deemed to confer on it, as a practical matter, "an absolute right to request advisory opinions within the framework of Article 64(1) of the Convention." (Ibid., para. 16.) Viewed in this light, the instant request certainly concerns an issue in which the Commission has a legitimate institutional interest.

43. * * * Here it is relevant merely to emphasize that the Convention, by permitting Member States and OAS organs to seek advisory opinions, creates a parallel system to that provided for under Article 62 and offers an alternate judicial method of a consultative nature, which is designed to assist states and organs to comply with and to apply human rights treaties without subjecting them to the formalism and the sanctions associated with the contentious judicial process. It would therefore be inconsistent with the object and purpose of the Convention and the relevant individual provisions, to adopt an interpretation of Article 64 that would apply to it the jurisdictional requirements of Article 62 and thus rob it of its intended utility merely because of the possible existence of a dispute regarding the meaning of the provision at issue in the request.

* * *

45. The fact that this legal dispute bears on the scope of a reservation made by a State Party in no way detracts from the preceding conclusions. Under the Vienna Convention on the Law of Treaties (hereinafter cited as Vienna Convention), incorporated by reference into the Convention by its Article 75, a reservation is defined

as any "unilateral statement, however phrased or named, made by a State when signing, ratifying, accepting, approving or acceding to a treaty, whereby it purports to exclude or to modify the legal effect of certain provisions of the treaty in their application to that State." Art. 2(d). The effect of a reservation, according to the Vienna Convention, is to modify with regard to the State making it the provisions of the treaty to which the reservation refers to the extent of the reservation. Art. 21(1)(a). Although the provisions concerning reciprocity with respect to reservations are not fully applicable to a human rights treaty such as the Convention, it is clear that reservations become a part of the treaty itself. It is consequently impossible to interpret the treaty correctly, with respect to the reserving State, without interpreting the reservation itself. The Court concludes, therefore, that the power granted it under Article 64 of the Convention to render advisory opinions interpreting the Convention or other treaties concerning the protection of human rights in the American states of necessity also encompasses jurisdiction to interpret the reservations attached to those instruments.

[On the merits, the Court said that under article 4(2), the government of a state party cannot apply the death penalty to crimes for which it was not provided under the domestic law of the state when it became a party to the Convention; and "a reservation restricted by its own wording to Article 4(4) of the Convention does not allow the Government of a State Party to extend by subsequent legislation the application of the death penalty to crimes for which this penalty was not previously provided."]

ADVISORY OPINIONS ON DISPUTED MATTERS

In paragraphs 31–35, the Court painstakingly demonstrated the differences between its contentious and its advisory jurisdiction. How significant are those differences?

In paragraph 10, the Court noted the Commission's statement that the matter had been referred to the Court "as an example in order to highlight the underlying legal problem." Does that cut in favor of issuing the advisory opinion on a matter actively disputed between the Commission and a government, or against it?

In paragraph 45, the Court said that its conclusions were not affected by the fact that the dispute concerned a state party's reservation. Was its reasoning convincing? Did it give an opinion on the specific Guatemalan reservation, or more generally on the effect of reservations to article 4(4)?

In paragraph 40, the Court said that the critical question, when essentially the same jurisdictional issue has arisen in the ICJ, "has always been whether the requesting organ has a legitimate interest to obtain the opinion for the purpose of guiding its future actions."

Neither the ICJ nor its predecessor, the PCIJ, has declined to issue a requested advisory opinion since the Eastern Carelia Case in 1923. See pages 505–11 supra. In its first advisory opinion under the American Convention, the Inter-American Court said, "The Court must have compelling reasons founded in the conviction that the request exceeds the limits of its advisory jurisdiction under the Convention before it may refrain from complying with a request for an opinion." [f]

On the whole, is the Court's willingness to give such advisory opinions salutary, from the standpoint of protection of human rights in the Americas? (Apparently the mere prospect of issuing it had the desired effect in this case. Even before it was handed down, the Guatemalan government decided to re-examine and suspend, at least temporarily, the execution of persons convicted by its courts of special jurisdiction.[g])

In light of all this, and given what the Inter-American Court said in paragraph 42 above, is it conceivable that it would ever decline to give an advisory opinion on the ground that it relates to an actual dispute regarding human rights, when requested by the Inter-American Commission?

The Court's approach has not been quite the same when the request is made by a member state. In its first advisory opinion the Court said:

> [C]oncern has been expressed that the Court's advisory jurisdiction might be invoked by States for the specific purpose of impairing the effectiveness of the proceedings in a case being dealt with by the Commission "to avoid having to accept the contentious jurisdiction of the Court and the binding character of the Court's decision," * * * thus interfering with the proper functioning of the Convention and adversely affecting the interests of the victim.[h]

More recently, the Court has declined to give an advisory opinion requested by the government of Costa Rica. The Costa Rican legal system did not provide a right of appeal for persons convicted of relatively minor crimes. Beginning in 1984, the Inter-American Commission began to receive petitions from persons in Costa Rica claiming that this violated article 8(2)(h) of the American Convention (establishing the right to appeal a conviction to a higher court). Nine petitions were received in all. The Commission decided only one of them, calling on Costa Rica to conform its legislation to the Convention. It suspended consideration of the others, pending Costa Rica's compliance with its recommendation in the first case. It decided to refer the first case to the Court if Costa Rica did not comply within six months. At Costa

---

f. "Other Treaties" Subject to the Advisory Jurisdiction of the Court, Advisory Opinion OC–1/82 (1982), Series A: Judgments and Opinions, No. 1, para. 30.

g. See Medina, supra note c, at 452, n. 58.

h. "Other Treaties," supra note f, para. 24, quoting from C. Dunshee de Abranches, *La Corte Interamericana de Derechos Humanos,* in La Convención Americana de Derechos Humanos 117 (OAS 1980).

Rica's request, it granted several six-month extensions, and at the time of this advisory opinion it still had not referred the first contentious case to the Court.

Meanwhile, Costa Rica prepared draft legislation that would establish a Court of Criminal Appeal, which apparently still would not provide an appellate forum for at least some minor offenses. In February 1991 the government of Costa Rica asked the Court for an advisory opinion on whether its proposed Court of Criminal Appeal would satisfy article 8(2)(h) of the Convention. Declining to give the opinion, the Court said:

> The Court believes that a reply to the questions presented by Costa Rica, could produce, under the guise of an advisory opinion, a determination of contentious matters not yet referred to the Court, without providing the victims with the opportunity to participate in the proceedings. Such a result would distort the Convention system. Contentious proceedings provide, by definition, a venue where matters can be discussed and confronted in a much more direct way than in advisory proceedings. This is an opportunity which cannot be denied to individuals who do not participate in the latter proceedings. Whereas the interests of individuals in contentious proceedings are represented by the Commission, the latter may have different interests to uphold in advisory proceedings.
>
> Although it appears that the draft legislation might correct, as far as concerns the future, the problems that gave rise to the petitions against Costa Rica now before the Commission, a ruling by the Court could in the long run interfere with cases that should be fully processed by the Commission in the manner provided for by the Convention.[i]

The Court gave no indication that the Costa Rican government had requested the advisory opinion in bad faith. Why then did the Court decline to answer? If it has to do with giving the petitioners in the pending cases their day in court, what about the fact that they have no standing in the Inter–American Court?

Would the Court have declined if the OAS General Assembly had requested the opinion?

As noted at pages 978–80 supra, the Court has concluded that:

> Article 64(1) of the American Convention authorizes the Court, at the request of a member state of the OAS or any duly qualified OAS organ, to render advisory opinions interpreting the American Declaration of the Rights and Duties of Man, provided that in doing so the Court is acting within the scope and framework of its

---

i. Costa Rican Draft Legislation on the Right to Appeal, Advisory Opinion OC–12/91 (1991), Series A: Judgments and Opinions, No. 12, paras. 28–29.

jurisdiction in relation to the Charter and Convention or other treaties concerning the protection of the human rights in the American states.[j]

This reading of article 64(1) was controversial, since article 64(1) refers only to the interpretation of "treaties." The United States argued against the reading the Court ultimately gave:

> It is the position of the United States that the American Declaration is not a treaty, and that therefore the Court does not have jurisdiction under Article 64 to interpret it or determine its normative status within the inter-American human rights system.[k]

Taking into account the quote from the Court's opinion at pages 978–80 supra, was the Court's conclusion justifiable?

In an earlier advisory opinion, the Court responded to a request from the government of Peru for an interpretation of the phrase, "or of other treaties concerning the protection of human rights in the American states" in article 64. Specifically, the Peruvian government asked:

> Does this aforementioned phrase refer to and include:
>
> a) Only treaties adopted within the framework or under the auspices of the inter-American system? or
>
> b) The treaties concluded solely among the American states, that is, is the reference limited to treaties in which only American states are parties? or
>
> c) All treaties in which one or more American states are parties?[l]

After reviewing the text of article 64, the object and purpose of the American Convention, the restrictions regarding interpretation in *article 29* of the Convention, the practice of the Inter–American Commission invoking treaties not adopted under OAS auspices, and the preparatory work of the Convention, the Court concluded that "no good reason exists to hold, in advance and in the abstract, that the Court lacks the power to receive a request for, or to issue, an advisory opinion about a human rights treaty applicable to an American State merely because non-American States are also parties to the treaty or because the treaty has not been adopted within the framework or under the auspices of the inter-American system."[m]

The Court went on to address the two principal arguments that had been made against this conclusion:

---

j. Interpretation of the American Declaration of the Rights and Duties of Man Within the Framework of Article 64 of the American Convention on Human Rights, Advisory Opinion OC–10/89 (1989), Series A: Judgments and Opinions, No. 10, para. 48.

k. Id., para. 17.

l. "Other Treaties" Subject to the Advisory Jurisdiction of the Court, Advisory Opinion OC–1/82 (1982), Series A: Judgments and Opinions, No. 1, para. 8.

m. Id. para. 48.

The first is that a broad interpretation would authorize the Court to render opinions affecting States which have nothing to do with the Convention or the Court, and which cannot even be represented before it. As to that issue, the Court has already emphasized that, if a request for an advisory opinion has as its principal purpose the determination of the scope of, or compliance with, international commitments assumed by States outside the inter-American system, the Court is authorized to render a [reasoned] opinion refraining to pass on the issues submitted to it. The mere possibility that the event hypothesized in the above argument might arise, which can after all be dealt with on a case by case basis, is hardly a sufficient enough reason for concluding that the Court, a priori, lacks the power to render an advisory opinion interpreting the human rights obligations assumed by an American State merely because such obligations originate outside the framework of the inter-American system.

The other argument that has been advanced is that the extension of the limits of the Court's advisory jurisdiction might produce conflicting interpretations emanating from the Court and from those organs outside the inter-American system that might be called upon also to apply and interpret treaties concluded outside of that system. The Court believes that it is here dealing with one of those arguments which proves too much and which, moreover, is less compelling than it appears at first glance. It proves too much because the possibility of conflicting interpretations is a phenomenon common to all those legal systems that have certain courts which are not hierarchically integrated. Such courts have jurisdiction to apply and, consequently, interpret the same body of law. Here it is, therefore, not unusual to find that on certain occasions courts reach conflicting or at the very least different conclusions in interpreting the same rule of law. On the international law plane, for example, because the advisory jurisdiction of the International Court of Justice extends to any legal question, the UN Security Council or the General Assembly might ask the International Court to render an advisory opinion concerning a treaty which, without any doubt, could also be interpreted by this Court under Article 64 of the Convention. Even a restrictive interpretation of Article 64 would not avoid the possibility that this type of conflict might arise.

Moreover, the conflicts being anticipated, were they to occur, would not be particularly serious. It must be remembered, in this connection, that the advisory opinions of the Court and those of other international tribunals, because of their advisory character, lack the same binding force that attaches to decisions in contentious cases. (Convention, Art. 68). This being so, less weight need be given to arguments based on the anticipated effects that the Court's opinions might have in relation to States lacking standing to participate in the advisory proceedings here in question.

Viewed in this light, it is obvious that the possibility that the opinions of the Court might conflict with those of other tribunals or organs is of no great practical significance; there are no theoretical obstacles, moreover, that would bar accepting the possibility that such conflicts might arise.

Regarding the first argument, is it a sufficient answer to say that the Court could decline to issue an advisory opinion if the request for it has a principal purpose of determining the scope of, or compliance with, international commitments of states outside the inter-American system? What if the principal purpose were to determine the scope of a provision in the International Covenant on Civil and Political Rights, to which many OAS member states (and many others) are parties? An advisory opinion, of course, would not formally bind either the OAS states or the others, but does that dispose of the problem?

Regarding the second argument, it is certainly true that overlapping jurisdiction exists among the domestic courts of some countries, and to some extent in the international system. But in most domestic legal systems, there is a single high court that can straighten out at least the most serious conflicts among lower courts. And in the international system, to take the example the Court gave, is it likely that the U.N. Security Council or General Assembly would ask the ICJ to render an advisory opinion interpreting the OAS Charter or the American Convention on Human Rights? If not, hasn't the Inter-American Court created a possibility of conflict that, as a practical matter, did not otherwise exist?

Suppose an individual has a human rights complaint against the government of a state that is a party to both the American Convention and the first Optional Protocol to the International Covenant on Civil and Political Rights. (There are several such states.) If the complaint concerns rights covered by both the Convention and the Covenant, the individual has a choice whether to submit a petition to the Inter-American Commission or to the U.N. Human Rights Committee. If the person has a lawyer, he or she—like any good lawyer in any system with multiple forums—will forum shop in order to file in the one most likely to decide in the petitioner's favor. If that turns out to be the U.N. Human Rights Committee, and if the case is of some moment to the respondent government, is it unlikely that the government would try to seize the initiative by seeking an advisory opinion on the same issue from the Inter-American Court? (Would that cause the Human Rights Committee to declare the petition submitted to it inadmissible under *article 5(2)(a)* of the first Optional Protocol?)

Is the problem of possible conflicting interpretations more serious than the Inter-American Court thought?

In the final analysis, despite any of the problems discussed above, is it best for the protection of human rights to give international adjudicative bodies, like the Inter-American Court of Human Rights, the broadest feasible advisory jurisdiction, and simply give the adjudicative body the discretion to cull out any requests it shouldn't answer?

---

2. *Contentious Cases*

As has been noted above, the Inter-American Court had very few contentious cases in its early years. Even in recent years, it has not had many more. States have not wished to refer contentious cases to it, perhaps for fear of the binding adverse decision that could result. The Inter-American Commission has begun to refer some cases to it, though the number still is not large. As we have seen, individuals who suffer from human rights violations have no standing to bring cases to the Court. (As will appear in the next section, the European system has recently taken a step to allow individuals to bring their own cases before the European Court of Human Rights, but by mid–1992 no similar step had yet been taken in the Americas.)

The Commission referred the Velásquez Rodríguez case, below, to the Court. It is a particularly important case involving one of a series of "disappearances" of persons who were outspoken opponents of Latin American governments in the 1970s and 1980s. The case deals with exhaustion of domestic remedies, admission of evidence, burden of proof, interpretation of some fundamental human rights provisions in the American Convention, and remedies for human rights violations.

VELÁSQUEZ RODRÍGUEZ CASE
Inter-American Court of Human Rights, 1988.
Series C, Decisions and Judgments, No. 4.

[A petition had been filed with the Inter-American Commission under article 44 of the American Convention. The petition asserted that Manfredo Velásquez Rodríguez, a student at a university in Honduras, was forcibly abducted by members of the Honduran Office of Investigations and Honduran armed forces on September 12, 1981. The petition claimed that he had been taken to a station of the Public Security Forces, where he was accused of political crimes and subjected to torture. He was alleged to have been moved to an army facility a few days later, and had not been heard from since.

[The Commission requested information from the Honduran government. After receiving no reply, it applied article 42 of its Regulations, allowing it to presume as true the allegations in the petition. The government then asked the Commission to reconsider, and said that it had appointed a commission of its own to investigate the matter. The government also said that its domestic remedies had not been exhausted. The Inter-American Commission postponed a final decision, pending the receipt of additional information from the government.

[About two years later the Honduran government presented to the Inter–American Commission the report of its own commission. The Inter–American Commission deemed the report inadequate and found that "all evidence shows that Angel Manfredo Velásquez Rodríguez is still missing and that the Government of Honduras * * * has not offered convincing proof that would allow the Commission to determine that the allegations are not true." The Commission confirmed its earlier decision, but also referred the matter to the Inter–American Court of Human Rights.

[Honduras had filed a declaration under article 62 of the American Convention in 1981, accepting the jurisdiction of the Court on all matters relating to the interpretation or application of the Convention. The Court held that it had jurisdiction. It rendered a judgment on some of Honduras' preliminary objections in 1987. The judgment below, on the merits, was rendered in 1988.]

IV

50. The Government raised several preliminary objections that the Court ruled upon in its Judgment of June 26, 1987. There the Court ordered the joining of the merits and the preliminary objection regarding the failure to exhaust domestic remedies, and gave the Government and the Commission another opportunity to "substantiate their contentions" on the matter.

* * *

52. The Commission presented witnesses and documentary evidence on [the preliminary objection]. The Government, in turn, submitted some documentary evidence, including examples of writs of habeas corpus successfully brought on behalf of some individuals. The Government also stated that this remedy requires identification of the place of detention and of the authority under which the person is detained.

53. In addition to the writ of habeas corpus, the Government mentioned various remedies that might possibly be invoked, such as appeal, cassation, extraordinary writ of amparo, ad effectum videndi, criminal complaints against those ultimately responsible and a presumptive finding of death.

* * *

55. The Commission argued that the remedies mentioned by the Government were ineffective because of the internal conditions in the country during that period. It presented documentation of three writs of habeas corpus brought on behalf of Manfredo Velásquez that did not produce results. It also cited two criminal complaints that failed to lead to the identification and punishment of those responsible. In the Commission's opinion, those legal proceedings exhausted domestic remedies as required by Article 46(1)(a) of the Convention.

* * *

57. Article 46(1)(a) of the Convention provides that, in order for a petition or communication lodged with the Commission in accordance with Articles 44 or 45 to be admissible, it is necessary

> that the remedies under domestic law have been pursued and exhausted in accordance with generally recognized principles of international law.

58. The same article, in the second paragraph, provides that this requirement shall not be applicable when

> a. the domestic legislation of the state concerned does not afford due process of law for the protection of the right or rights that have allegedly been violated;
>
> b. the party alleging violation of his rights has been denied access to the remedies under domestic law or has been prevented from exhausting them; or
>
> c. there has been unwarranted delay in rendering a final judgment under the aforementioned remedies.

59. In its Judgment of June 26, 1987, the Court decided, inter alia, that "the State claiming non-exhaustion has an obligation to prove that domestic remedies remain to be exhausted and that they are effective" (Velásquez Rodríguez Case, Preliminary Objections, supra 23, para. 88).

60. Concerning the burden of proof, the Court did not go beyond the conclusion cited in the preceding paragraph. The Court now affirms that if a State which alleges non-exhaustion proves the existence of specific domestic remedies that should have been utilized, the opposing party has the burden of showing that those remedies were exhausted or that the case comes within the exceptions of Article 46(2). It must not be rashly presumed that a State Party to the Convention has failed to comply with its obligation to provide effective domestic remedies.

61. The rule of prior exhaustion of domestic remedies allows the State to resolve the problem under its internal law before being confronted with an international proceeding. This is particularly true in the international jurisdiction of human rights, because the latter reinforces or complements the domestic jurisdiction (American Convention, Preamble).

62. It is a legal duty of the States to provide such remedies * * *.

* * *

65. Of the remedies cited by the Government, habeas corpus would be the normal means of finding a person presumably detained by the authorities, of ascertaining whether he is legally detained and, given the case, of obtaining his liberty. The other remedies cited by the Government are either for reviewing a decision within an inchoate proceeding (such as those of appeal or cassation) or are addressed to other objectives. If, however, as the Government has stated, the writ of habeas corpus requires the identification of the place of detention and

the authority ordering the detention, it would not be adequate for finding a person clandestinely held by State officials, since in such cases there is only hearsay evidence of the detention, and the whereabouts of the victim is unknown.

66. A remedy must also be effective—that is, capable of producing the result for which it was designed. Procedural requirements can make the remedy of habeas corpus ineffective: if it is powerless to compel the authorities; if it presents a danger to those who invoke it; or if it is not impartially applied.

67. On the other hand, contrary to the Commission's argument, the mere fact that a domestic remedy does not produce a result favorable to the petitioner does not in and of itself demonstrate the inexistence or exhaustion of all effective domestic remedies. For example, the petitioner may not have invoked the appropriate remedy in a timely fashion.

68. It is a different matter, however, when it is shown that remedies are denied for trivial reasons or without an examination of the merits, or if there is proof of the existence of a practice or policy ordered or tolerated by the government, the effect of which is to impede certain persons from invoking internal remedies that would normally be available to others. In such cases, resort to those remedies becomes a senseless formality. The exceptions of Article 46(2) would be fully applicable in those situations and would discharge the obligation to exhaust internal remedies since they cannot fulfill their objective in that case.

* * *

74. The record before the Court shows that the following remedies were pursued on behalf of Manfredo Velásquez:

A. Habeas Corpus

[Relatives of Manfredo Velásquez brought three petitions for habeas corpus, all with no result.]

B. Criminal Complaints

i. Brought by the father and sister of Manfredo Velásquez before the First Criminal Court of Tegucigalpa on November 9, 1982. No result.

ii. Brought by Gertrudis Lanza González, joined by Zenaida Velásquez, before the First Criminal Court of Tegucigalpa against various members of the Armed Forces on April 5, 1984. The court dismissed this proceeding and the First Court of Appeals affirmed on January 16, 1986, although it left open the complaint with regard to General Gustavo Alvarez Martínez, who was declared a defendant in absence.

75. Although the Government did not dispute that the above remedies had been brought, it maintained that the Commission should

not have found the petition admissible, much less submitted it to the Court, because of the failure to exhaust the remedies provided by Honduran law, given that there are no final decisions in the record that show the contrary. It stated that the first writ of habeas corpus was declared void because the person bringing it did not follow through; regarding the second and third, the Government explained that additional writs cannot be brought on the same subject, the same facts, and based on the same legal provisions. As to the criminal complaints, the Government stated that no evidence had been submitted and, although presumptions had been raised, no proof had been offered and that the proceeding was still before Honduran courts until those guilty were specifically identified. It stated that one of the proceedings was dismissed for lack of evidence with respect to those accused who appeared before the court, but not with regard to General Alvarez Martínez, who was out of the country. Moreover, the Government maintained that dismissal does not exhaust domestic remedies because the extraordinary remedies of amparo, rehearing and cassation may be invoked and, in the instant case, the statute of limitations has not yet run, so the proceeding is pending.

76. The record contains testimony of members of the Legislative Assembly of Honduras, Honduran lawyers, persons who were at one time disappeared, and relatives of disappeared persons, which purports to show that in the period in which the events took place, the legal remedies in Honduras were ineffective in obtaining the liberty of victims of a practice of enforced or involuntary disappearances (hereinafter "disappearance" or "disappearances"), ordered or tolerated by the Government. The record also contains dozens of newspaper clippings which allude to the same practice. According to that evidence, from 1981 to 1984 more than one hundred persons were illegally detained, many of whom never reappeared, and, in general, the legal remedies which the Government claimed were available to the victims were ineffective.

* * *

79. The Government had the opportunity to call its own witnesses to refute the evidence presented by the Commission, but failed to do so. Although the Government's attorneys contested some of the points urged by the Commission, they did not offer convincing evidence to support their arguments. The Court summoned as witnesses some members of the armed forces mentioned during the proceeding, but their testimony was insufficient to overcome the weight of the evidence offered by the Commission to show that the judicial and governmental authorities did not act with due diligence in cases of disappearances. The instant case is such an example.

80. The testimony and other evidence received and not refuted leads to the conclusion that, during the period under consideration, although there may have been legal remedies in Honduras that theoretically allowed a person detained by the authorities to be found, those

remedies were ineffective in cases of disappearances because the imprisonment was clandestine; formal requirements made them inapplicable in practice; the authorities against whom they were brought simply ignored them, or because attorneys and judges were threatened and intimidated by those authorities.

81. Aside from the question of whether between 1981 and 1984 there was a governmental policy of carrying out or tolerating the disappearance of certain persons, the Commission has shown that although writs of habeas corpus and criminal complaints were filed, they were ineffective or were mere formalities. The evidence offered by the Commission was not refuted and is sufficient to reject the Government's preliminary objection that the case is inadmissible because domestic remedies were not exhausted.

V

82. The Commission presented testimony and documentary evidence to show that there were many kidnappings and disappearances in Honduras from 1981 to 1984 and that those acts were attributable to the Armed Forces of Honduras (hereinafter "Armed Forces"), which was able to rely at least on the tolerance of the Government. Three officers of the Armed Forces testified on this subject at the request of the Court.

83. Various witnesses testified that they were kidnapped, imprisoned in clandestine jails and tortured by members of the Armed Forces (testimony of Inés Consuelo Murillo, José Gonzalo Flores Trejo, Virgilio Carías, Milton Jiménez Puerto, René Velásquez Díaz and Leopoldo Aguilar Villalobos).

[The Court summarized each witness' testimony. Some of the Court's summaries are included below.]

95. The Court received testimony which indicated that somewhere between 112 and 130 individuals were disappeared from 1981 to 1984. A former member of the Armed Forces testified that, according to a list in the files of Battalion 316, the number might be 140 or 150 (testimony of Miguel Angel Pavón Salazar, Ramón Custodio López, Efraín Díaz Arrivillaga and Florencio Caballero).

96. The Court heard testimony from the President of the Committee for the Defense of Human Rights in Honduras regarding the existence of a unit within the Armed Forces which carried out disappearances. According to his testimony, in 1980 there was a group called "the fourteen" under the command of Major Adolfo Díaz, attached to the General Staff of the Armed Forces. Subsequently, this group was replaced by "the ten," commanded by Capt. Alexander Hernández, and finally by Battalion 316, a special operations group, with separate units trained in surveillance, kidnapping, execution, telephone tapping, etc. The existence of this group had always been denied until it was mentioned in a communiqué of the Armed Forces in

September 1986 (testimony of Ramón Custodio López. See also the testimony of Florencio Caballero).

* * *

98. The current Director of Honduran Intelligence testified that he learned from the files of his department that in 1984 an intelligence battalion called 316 was created, the purpose of which was to provide combat intelligence to the 101st, 105th and 110th Brigades. He added that this battalion initially functioned as a training unit, until the creation of the Intelligence School, to which all its training functions were gradually transferred, and that the Battalion was finally disbanded in September 1987. He stated that there was never any group called "the fourteen" or "the ten" in the Armed Forces or security forces (testimony of Roberto Núñez Montes).

99. According to testimony on the modus operandi of the practice of disappearances, the kidnappers followed a pattern: they used automobiles with tinted glass (which requires a special permit from the Traffic Division), without license plates or with false plates, and sometimes used special disguises, such as wigs, false mustaches, masks, etc. The kidnappings were selective. The victims were first placed under surveillance, then the kidnapping was planned. Microbuses or vans were used. Some victims were taken from their homes; others were picked up in public streets. On one occasion, when a patrol car intervened, the kidnappers identified themselves as members of a special group of the Armed Forces and were permitted to leave with the victim (testimony of Ramón Custodio López, Miguel Angel Pavón Salazar, Efraín Díaz Arrivillaga and Florencio Caballero).

* * *

101. The Government objected, under Article 37 of the Rules of Procedure, to the testimony of Florencio Caballero because he had deserted from the Armed Forces and had violated his military oath. By unanimous decision of October 6, 1987, the Court rejected the challenge and reserved the right to consider his testimony.

102. The current Director of Intelligence of the Armed Forces testified that intelligence units do not carry out detentions because they "get burned" (are discovered) and do not use pseudonyms or automobiles without license plates. He added that Florencio Caballero never worked in the intelligence services and that he was a driver for the Army General Headquarters in Tegucigalpa (testimony of Roberto Núñez Montes).

103. The former member of the Armed Forces confirmed the existence of secret jails and of specially chosen places for the burial of those executed. He also related that there was a torture group and an interrogation group in his unit, and that he belonged to the latter. The torture group used electric shock, the water barrel and the "capucha." They kept the victims nude, without food, and threw cold water on them. He added that those selected for execution were handed over to

a group of former prisoners, released from jail for carrying out executions, who used firearms at first and then knives and machetes (testimony of Florencio Caballero).

104. The current Director of Intelligence denied that the Armed Forces had secret jails, stating that it was not its modus operandi. He claimed that it was subversive elements who do have such jails, which they call "the peoples' prisons." He added that the function of an intelligence service is not to eliminate or disappear people, but rather to obtain and process information to allow the highest levels of government to make informed decisions (testimony of Roberto Núñez Montes).

105. A Honduran officer, called as a witness by the Court, testified that the use of violence or psychological means to force a detainee to give information is prohibited (testimony of Marco Tulio Regalado Hernández).

106. The Commission submitted many clippings from the Honduran press from 1981 to 1984 which contain information on at least 64 disappearances, which were apparently carried out against ideological or political opponents or trade union members. Six of those individuals, after their release, complained of torture and other cruel, inhuman and degrading treatment. These clippings mention secret cemeteries where 17 bodies had been found.

107. According to the testimony of his sister, eyewitnesses to the kidnapping of Manfredo Velásquez told her that he was detained on September 12, 1981, between 4:30 and 5:00 p.m., in a parking lot in downtown Tegucigalpa by seven heavily-armed men dressed in civilian clothes (one of them being First Sgt. José Isaías Vilorio), who used a white Ford without license plates (testimony of Zenaida Velásquez. See also testimony of Ramón Custodio López).

108. This witness informed the Court that Col. Leónidas Torres Arias, who had been head of Honduran military intelligence, announced in a press conference in Mexico City that Manfredo Velásquez was kidnapped by a special squadron commanded by Capt. Alexander Hernández, who was carrying out the direct orders of General Gustavo Alvarez Martínez (testimony of Zenaida Velásquez).

109. Lt. Col. Hernández testified that he never received any order to detain Manfredo Velásquez and had never worked in police operations (testimony of Alexander Hernández).

110. The Government objected, under Article 37 of the Rules of Procedure, to the testimony of Zenaida Velásquez because, as sister of the victim, she was a party interested in the outcome of the case.

111. The Court unanimously rejected the objection because it considered the fact that the witness was the victim's sister to be insufficient to disqualify her. The Court reserved the right to consider her testimony.

112. The Government asserted that her testimony was irrelevant because it did not refer to the case before the Court and that what she

related about the kidnapping of her brother was not her personal knowledge but rather hearsay.

113. The former member of the Armed Forces who claimed to have belonged to the group that carried out kidnappings told the Court that, although he did not take part in the kidnapping of Manfredo Velásquez, Lt. Flores Murillo had told him what had happened. According to this testimony, Manfredo Velásquez was kidnapped in downtown Tegucigalpa in an operation in which Sgt. José Isaías Vilorio, men using the pseudonyms Ezequiel and Titanio, and Lt. Flores Murillo himself, took part. The Lieutenant told him that during the struggle Ezequiel's gun went off and wounded Manfredo in the leg. They took the victim to INDUMIL (Military Industries) where they tortured him. They then turned him over to those in charge of carrying out executions who, at the orders of General Alvarez, Chief of the Armed Forces, took him out of Tegucigalpa and killed him with a knife and machete. They dismembered his body and buried the remains in different places (testimony of Florencio Caballero).

114. The current Director of Intelligence testified that José Isaías Vilorio was a file clerk of the DNI. He said he did not know Lt. Flores Murillo and stated that INDUMIL had never been used as a detention center (testimony of Roberto Núñez Montes).

* * *

VI

119. The testimony and documentary evidence, corroborated by press clippings, presented by the Commission, tend to show:

    a. That there existed in Honduras from 1981 to 1984 a systematic and selective practice of disappearances, carried out with the assistance or tolerance of the government;

    b. That Manfredo Velásquez was a victim of that practice and was kidnapped and presumably tortured, executed and clandestinely buried by agents of the Armed Forces of Honduras, and

    c. That in the period in which those acts occurred, the legal remedies available in Honduras were not appropriate or effective to guarantee his rights to life, liberty and personal integrity.

* * *

VII

122. Before weighing the evidence, the Court must address some questions regarding the burden of proof and the general criteria considered in its evaluation and finding of the facts in the instant proceeding.

123. Because the Commission is accusing the Government of the disappearance of Manfredo Velásquez, it, in principle, should bear the burden of proving the facts underlying its petition.

124. The Commission's argument relies upon the proposition that the policy of disappearances, supported or tolerated by the Government,

is designed to conceal and destroy evidence of disappearances. When the existence of such a policy or practice has been shown, the disappearance of a particular individual may be proved through circumstantial or indirect evidence or by logical inference. Otherwise, it would be impossible to prove that an individual has been disappeared.

125. The Government did not object to the Commission's approach. Nevertheless, it argued that neither the existence of a practice of disappearances in Honduras nor the participation of Honduran officials in the alleged disappearance of Manfredo Velásquez had been proven.

126. The Court finds no reason to consider the Commission's argument inadmissible. If it can be shown that there was an official practice of disappearances in Honduras, carried out by the Government or at least tolerated by it, and if the disappearance of Manfredo Velásquez can be linked to that practice, the Commission's allegations will have been proven to the Court's satisfaction, so long as the evidence presented on both points meets the standard of proof required in cases such as this.

127. The Court must determine what the standards of proof should be in the instant case. Neither the Convention, the Statute of the Court nor its Rules of Procedure speak to this matter. Nevertheless, international jurisprudence has recognized the power of the courts to weigh the evidence freely, although it has always avoided a rigid rule regarding the amount of proof necessary to support the judgment (Cfr. Corfu Channel, Merits, Judgment, I.C.J. Reports 1949; Military and Paramilitary Activities in and against Nicaragua (Nicaragua v. United States of America), Merits, Judgment, I.C.J. Reports 1986, paras. 29–30 and 59–60).

128. The standards of proof are less formal in an international legal proceeding than in a domestic one. The latter recognize different burdens of proof, depending upon the nature, character and seriousness of the case.

129. The Court cannot ignore the special seriousness of finding that a State Party to the Convention has carried out or has tolerated a practice of disappearances in its territory. This requires the Court to apply a standard of proof which considers the seriousness of the charge and which, notwithstanding what has already been said, is capable of establishing the truth of the allegations in a convincing manner.

130. The practice of international and domestic courts shows that direct evidence, whether testimonial or documentary, is not the only type of evidence that may be legitimately considered in reaching a decision. Circumstantial evidence, indicia, and presumptions may be considered, so long as they lead to conclusions consistent with the facts.

131. Circumstantial or presumptive evidence is especially important in allegations of disappearances, because this type of repression is

characterized by an attempt to suppress all information about the kidnapping or the whereabouts and fate of the victim.

132. Since this Court is an international tribunal, it has its own specialized procedures. All the elements of domestic legal procedures are therefore not automatically applicable.

133. The above principle is generally valid in international proceedings, but is particularly applicable in human rights cases.

134. The international protection of human rights should not be confused with criminal justice. States do not appear before the Court as defendants in a criminal action. The objective of international human rights law is not to punish those individuals who are guilty of violations, but rather to protect the victims and to provide for the reparation of damages resulting from the acts of the States responsible.

135. In contrast to domestic criminal law, in proceedings to determine human rights violations the State cannot rely on the defense that the complainant has failed to present evidence when it cannot be obtained without the State's cooperation.

136. The State controls the means to verify acts occurring within its territory. Although the Commission has investigatory powers, it cannot exercise them within a State's jurisdiction unless it has the cooperation of that State.

137. Since the Government only offered some documentary evidence in support of its preliminary objections, but none on the merits, the Court must reach its decision without the valuable assistance of a more active participation by Honduras, which might otherwise have resulted in a more adequate presentation of its case.

138. The manner in which the Government conducted its defense would have sufficed to prove many of the Commission's allegations by virtue of the principle that the silence of the accused or elusive or ambiguous answers on its part may be interpreted as an acknowledgment of the truth of the allegations, so long as the contrary is not indicated by the record or is not compelled as a matter of law. This result would not hold under criminal law, which does not apply in the instant case. The Court tried to compensate for this procedural principle by admitting all the evidence offered, even if it was untimely, and by ordering the presentation of additional evidence. This was done, of course, without prejudice to its discretion to consider the silence or inaction of Honduras or to its duty to evaluate the evidence as a whole.

* * *

VIII

140. In the instant case, the Court accepts the validity of the documents presented by the Commission and by Honduras, particularly

because the parties did not oppose or object to those documents nor did they question their authenticity or veracity.

* * *

146. Many of the press clippings offered by the Commission cannot be considered as documentary evidence as such. However, many of them contain public and well-known facts which, as such, do not require proof; others are of evidentiary value, as has been recognized in international jurisprudence (Military and Paramilitary Activities in and against Nicaragua, supra 127, paras. 62–64), insofar as they textually reproduce public statements, especially those of high-ranking members of the Armed Forces, of the Government, or even of the Supreme Court of Honduras, such as some of those made by the President of the latter. Finally, others are important as a whole insofar as they corroborate testimony regarding the responsibility of the Honduran military and police for disappearances.

IX

147. The Court now turns to the relevant facts that it finds to have been proven. They are as follows:

    a. During the period 1981 to 1984, 100 to 150 persons disappeared in the Republic of Honduras, and many were never heard from again (testimony of Miguel Angel Pavón Salazar, Ramón Custodio López, Efraín Díaz Arrivillaga, Florencio Caballero and press clippings).

    b. Those disappearances followed a similar pattern, beginning with the kidnapping of the victims by force, often in broad daylight and in public places, by armed men in civilian clothes and disguises, who acted with apparent impunity and who used vehicles without any official identification, with tinted windows and with false license plates or no plates (testimony of Miguel Angel Pavón Salazar, Ramón Custodio López, Efraín Díaz Arrivillaga, Florencio Caballero and press clippings).

    c. It was public and notorious knowledge in Honduras that the kidnappings were carried out by military personnel or the police, or persons acting under their orders (testimony of Miguel Angel Pavón Salazar, Ramón Custodio López, Efraín Díaz Arrivillaga, Florencio Caballero and press clippings).

    d. The disappearances were carried out in a systematic manner * * *.

    e. On September 12, 1981, between 4:30 and 5:00 p.m., several heavily armed men in civilian clothes driving a white Ford without license plates kidnapped Manfredo Velásquez from a parking lot in downtown Tegucigalpa. Today, nearly seven years later, he remains disappeared, which creates a reasonable presumption that he is dead (testimony of Miguel Angel Pavón Salazar, Ramón

Custodio López, Zenaida Velásquez, Florencio Caballero, Leopoldo Aguilar Villalobos and press clippings).

f. Persons connected with the Armed Forces or under its direction carried out that kidnapping (testimony of Ramón Custodio López, Zenaida Velásquez, Florencio Caballero, Leopoldo Aguilar Villalobos and press clippings).

g. The kidnapping and disappearance of Manfredo Velásquez falls within the systematic practice of disappearances referred to by the facts deemed proved in paragraphs a–d. * * *

148. Based upon the above, the Court finds that the following facts have been proven in this proceeding: (1) a practice of disappearances carried out or tolerated by Honduran officials existed between 1981 and 1984; (2) Manfredo Velásquez disappeared at the hands of or with the acquiescence of those officials within the framework of that practice; and (3) the Government of Honduras failed to guarantee the human rights affected by that practice.

X

* * *

[The Court turned to a discussion of the applicable law. Its references to "the Convention" are to the American Convention on Human Rights.]

153. International practice and doctrine have often categorized disappearances as a crime against humanity, although there is no treaty in force which is applicable to the States Parties to the Convention and which uses this terminology. * * *

154. Without question, the State has the right and duty to guarantee its security. It is also indisputable that all societies suffer some deficiencies in their legal orders. However, regardless of the seriousness of certain actions and the culpability of the perpetrators of certain crimes, the power of the State is not unlimited, nor may the State resort to any means to attain its ends. The State is subject to law and morality. Disrespect for human dignity cannot serve as the basis for any State action.

155. The forced disappearance of human beings is a multiple and continuous violation of many rights under the Convention that the States Parties are obligated to respect and guarantee. The kidnapping of a person [accused of a crime against state security] is an arbitrary deprivation of liberty, an infringement of a detainee's right to be taken without delay before a judge and to invoke the appropriate procedures to review the legality of the arrest, all in violation of Article 7 of the Convention which recognizes the right to personal liberty by providing that: [the Court quoted *Article 7*].

156. Moreover, prolonged isolation and deprivation of communication are in themselves cruel and inhuman treatment, harmful to the psychological and moral integrity of the person and a violation of the

right of any detainee to respect for his inherent dignity as a human being. Such treatment, therefore, violates Article 5 of the Convention, which recognizes the right to the integrity of the person by providing that: [the Court quoted *Article 5*]. In addition, investigations into the practice of disappearances and the testimony of victims who have regained their liberty show that those who are disappeared are often subjected to merciless treatment, including all types of indignities, torture and other cruel, inhuman and degrading treatment, in violation of the right to physical integrity recognized in Article 5 of the Convention.

157. The practice of disappearances often involves secret execution without trial, followed by concealment of the body to eliminate any material evidence of the crime and to ensure the impunity of those responsible. This is a flagrant violation of the right to life, recognized in Article 4 of the Convention, the first clause of which reads as follows:

> Every person has the right to have his life respected. This right shall be protected by law and, in general, from the moment of conception. No one shall be arbitrarily deprived of his life.

158. The practice of disappearances, in addition to directly violating many provisions of the Convention, such as those noted above, constitutes a radical breach of the treaty in that it shows a crass abandonment of the values which emanate from the concept of human dignity and of the most basic principles of the inter-American system and the Convention. The existence of this practice, moreover, evinces a disregard of the duty to organize the State in such a manner as to guarantee the rights recognized in the Convention, as set out below.

XI

* * *

160. [The Court must] examine the conditions under which a particular act, which violates one of the rights recognized by the Convention, can be imputed to a State Party thereby establishing its international responsibility.

161. Article 1(1) of the Convention provides:

Article 1. Obligation to Respect Rights

The States Parties to this Convention undertake to respect the rights and freedoms recognized herein and to ensure to all persons subject to their jurisdiction the free and full exercise of those rights and freedoms, without any discrimination for reasons of race, color, sex, language, religion, political or other opinion, national or social origin, economic status, birth, or any other social condition.

162. This article specifies the obligation assumed by the States Parties in relation to each of the rights protected. Each claim alleging that one of those rights has been infringed necessarily implies that Article 1(1) of the Convention has also been violated.

163. The Commission did not specifically allege the violation of Article 1(1) of the Convention, but that does not preclude the Court from applying it. The precept contained therein constitutes the generic basis of the protection of the rights recognized by the Convention and would be applicable, in any case, by virtue of a general principle of law, iura novit curia, on which international jurisprudence has repeatedly relied and under which a court has the power and the duty to apply the juridical provisions relevant to a proceeding, even when the parties do not expressly invoke them ("Lotus", Judgment No. 9, 1927, P.C.I.J., Series A, No. 10, p. 31 and Eur. Court H.R., Handyside Case, Judgment of 7 December 1976, Series A, No. 24, para. 41).

164. Article 1(1) is essential in determining whether a violation of the human rights recognized by the Convention can be imputed to a State Party. In effect, that article charges the States Parties with the fundamental duty to respect and guarantee the rights recognized in the Convention. Any impairment of those rights which can be attributed under the rules of international law to the action or omission of any public authority constitutes an act imputable to the State, which assumes responsibility in the terms provided by the Convention.

165. The first obligation assumed by the States Parties under Article 1(1) is "to respect the rights and freedoms" recognized by the Convention. The exercise of public authority has certain limits which derive from the fact that human rights are inherent attributes of human dignity and are, therefore, superior to the power of the State.

* * *

166. The second obligation of the States Parties is to "ensure" the free and full exercise of the rights recognized by the Convention to every person subject to its jurisdiction. This obligation implies the duty of the States Parties to organize the governmental apparatus and, in general, all the structures through which public power is exercised, so that they are capable of juridically ensuring the free and full enjoyment of human rights. As a consequence of this obligation, the States must prevent, investigate and punish any violation of the rights recognized by the Convention and, moreover, if possible attempt to restore the right violated and provide compensation as warranted for damages resulting from the violation.

167. The obligation to ensure the free and full exercise of human rights is not fulfilled by the existence of a legal system designed to make it possible to comply with this obligation—it also requires the government to conduct itself so as to effectively ensure the free and full exercise of human rights.

* * *

169. According to Article 1(1), any exercise of public power that violates the rights recognized by the Convention is illegal. Whenever a State organ, official or public entity violates one of those rights, this

constitutes a failure of the duty to respect the rights and freedoms set forth in the Convention.

170. This conclusion is independent of whether the organ or official has contravened provisions of internal law or overstepped the limits of his authority: under international law a State is responsible for the acts of its agents undertaken in their official capacity and for their omissions, even when those agents act outside the sphere of their authority or violate internal law.

171. This principle suits perfectly the nature of the Convention, which is violated whenever public power is used to infringe the rights recognized therein. If acts of public power that exceed the State's authority or are illegal under its own laws were not considered to compromise that State's obligations under the treaty, the system of protection provided for in the Convention would be illusory.

172. Thus, in principle, any violation of rights recognized by the Convention carried out by an act of public authority or by persons who use their position of authority is imputable to the State. However, this does not define all the circumstances in which a State is obligated to prevent, investigate and punish human rights violations, nor all the cases in which the State might be found responsible for an infringement of those rights. An illegal act which violates human rights and which is initially not directly imputable to a State (for example, because it is the act of a private person or because the person responsible has not been identified) can lead to international responsibility of the State, not because of the act itself, but because of the lack of due diligence to prevent the violation or to respond to it as required by the Convention.

* * *

174. The State has a legal duty to take reasonable steps to prevent human rights violations and to use the means at its disposal to carry out a serious investigation of violations committed within its jurisdiction, to identify those responsible, to impose the appropriate punishment and to ensure the victim adequate compensation.

175. This duty to prevent includes all those means of a legal, political, administrative and cultural nature that promote the protection of human rights and ensure that any violations are considered and treated as illegal acts, which, as such, may lead to the punishment of those responsible and the obligation to indemnify the victims for damages. It is not possible to make a detailed list of all such measures, since they vary with the law and the conditions of each State Party. Of course, while the State is obligated to prevent human rights abuses, the existence of a particular violation does not, in itself, prove the failure to take preventive measures. On the other hand, subjecting a person to official, repressive bodies that practice torture and assassination with impunity is itself a breach of the duty to prevent violations of the rights to life and physical integrity of the person, even if that particular

person is not tortured or assassinated, or if those facts cannot be proven in a concrete case.

* * *

177. In certain circumstances, it may be difficult to investigate acts that violate an individual's rights. The duty to investigate, like the duty to prevent, is not breached merely because the investigation does not produce a satisfactory result. Nevertheless, it must be undertaken in a serious manner and not as a mere formality preordained to be ineffective. An investigation must have an objective and be assumed by the State as its own legal duty, not as a step taken by private interests that depends upon the initiative of the victim or his family or upon their offer of proof, without an effective search for the truth by the government. This is true regardless of what agent is eventually found responsible for the violation. Where the acts of private parties that violate the Convention are not seriously investigated, those parties are aided in a sense by the government, thereby making the State responsible on the international plane.

178. In the instant case, the evidence shows a complete inability of the procedures of the State of Honduras, which were theoretically adequate, to carry out an investigation into the disappearance of Manfredo Velásquez, and of the fulfillment of its duties to pay compensation and punish those responsible, as set out in Article 1(1) of the Convention.

179. As the Court has verified above, the failure of the judicial system to act upon the writs brought before various tribunals in the instant case has been proven. Not one writ of habeas corpus was processed. No judge had access to the places where Manfredo Velásquez might have been detained. The criminal complaint was dismissed.

180. Nor did the organs of the Executive Branch carry out a serious investigation to establish the fate of Manfredo Velásquez. There was no investigation of public allegations of a practice of disappearances nor a determination of whether Manfredo Velásquez had been a victim of that practice. The Commission's requests for information were ignored to the point that the Commission had to presume, under Article 42 of its Regulations, that the allegations were true. The offer of an investigation in accord with Resolution 30/83 of the Commission resulted in an investigation by the Armed Forces, the same body accused of direct responsibility for the disappearances. This raises grave questions regarding the seriousness of the investigation. The Government often resorted to asking relatives of the victims to present conclusive proof of their allegations even though those allegations, because they involved crimes against the person, should have been investigated on the Government's own initiative in fulfillment of the State's duty to ensure public order. This is especially true when the allegations refer to a practice carried out within the Armed Forces, which, because of its nature, is not subject to private investigations. No proceeding was initiated to establish responsibility for the disap-

pearance of Manfredo Velásquez and apply punishment under internal law. All of the above leads to the conclusion that the Honduran authorities did not take effective action to ensure respect for human rights within the jurisdiction of that State as required by Article 1(1) of the Convention.

181. The duty to investigate facts of this type continues as long as there is uncertainty about the fate of the person who has disappeared. Even in the hypothetical case that those individually responsible for crimes of this type cannot be legally punished under certain circumstances, the State is obligated to use the means at its disposal to inform the relatives of the fate of the victims and, if they have been killed, the location of their remains.

182. The Court is convinced, and has so found, that the disappearance of Manfredo Velásquez was carried out by agents who acted under cover of public authority. However, even had that fact not been proven, the failure of the State apparatus to act, which is clearly proven, is a failure on the part of Honduras to fulfill the duties it assumed under Article 1(1) of the Convention, which obligated it to ensure Manfredo Velásquez the free and full exercise of his human rights.

183. The Court notes that the legal order of Honduras does not authorize such acts and that internal law defines them as crimes. The Court also recognizes that not all levels of the Government of Honduras were necessarily aware of those acts, nor is there any evidence that such acts were the result of official orders. Nevertheless, those circumstances are irrelevant for the purposes of establishing whether Honduras is responsible under international law for the violations of human rights perpetrated within the practice of disappearances.

184. According to the principle of the continuity of the State in international law, responsibility exists both independently of changes of government over a period of time and continuously from the time of the act that creates responsibility to the time when the act is declared illegal. The foregoing is also valid in the area of human rights although, from an ethical or political point of view, the attitude of the new government may be much more respectful of those rights than that of the government in power when the violations occurred.

185. The Court, therefore, concludes that the facts found in this proceeding show that the State of Honduras is responsible for the involuntary disappearance of Angel Manfredo Velásquez Rodríguez. Thus, Honduras has violated Articles 7, 5 and 4 of the Convention.

186. As a result of the disappearance, Manfredo Velásquez was the victim of an arbitrary detention, which deprived him of his physical liberty without legal cause and without a determination of the lawfulness of his detention by a judge or competent tribunal. Those acts directly violate the right to personal liberty recognized by Article 7 of the Convention and are a violation imputable to Honduras of the duties to respect and ensure that right under Article 1(1).

187. The disappearance of Manfredo Velásquez violates the right to personal integrity recognized by Article 5 of the Convention. First, the mere subjection of an individual to prolonged isolation and deprivation of communication is in itself cruel and inhuman treatment which harms the psychological and moral integrity of the person, and violates the right of every detainee under Article 5(1) and 5(2) to treatment respectful of his dignity. Second, although it has not been directly shown that Manfredo Velásquez was physically tortured, his kidnapping and imprisonment by governmental authorities, who have been shown to subject detainees to indignities, cruelty and torture, constitute a failure of Honduras to fulfill the duty imposed by Article 1(1) to ensure the rights under Article 5(1) and 5(2) of the Convention. The guarantee of physical integrity and the right of detainees to treatment respectful of their human dignity require States Parties to take reasonable steps to prevent situations which are truly harmful to the rights protected.

188. The above reasoning is applicable to the right to life recognized by Article 4 of the Convention. The context in which the disappearance of Manfredo Velásquez occurred and the lack of knowledge seven years later about his fate create a reasonable presumption that he was killed. Even if there is a minimal margin of doubt in this respect, it must be presumed that his fate was decided by authorities who systematically executed detainees without trial and concealed their bodies in order to avoid punishment. This, together with the failure to investigate, is a violation by Honduras of a legal duty under Article 1(1) of the Convention to ensure the rights recognized by Article 4(1). That duty is to ensure every person subject to its jurisdiction the inviolability of the right to life and the right not to have one's life taken arbitrarily. These rights imply an obligation on the part of States Parties to take reasonable steps to prevent situations that could result in the violation of that right.

XII

189. Article 63(1) of the Convention provides:

If the Court finds that there has been a violation of a right or freedom protected by this Convention, the Court shall rule that the injured party be ensured the enjoyment of his right or freedom that was violated. It shall also rule, if appropriate, that the consequences of the measure or situation that constituted the breach of such right or freedom be remedied and that fair compensation be paid to the injured party.

Clearly, in the instant case the Court cannot order that the victim be guaranteed the enjoyment of the rights or freedoms violated. The Court, however, can rule that the consequences of the breach of the rights be remedied and that just compensation be paid.

190. During this proceeding the Commission requested the payment of compensation, but did not offer evidence regarding the amount

of damages or the manner of payment. Neither did the parties discuss these matters.

191. The Court believes that the parties can agree on the damages. If an agreement cannot be reached, the Court shall award an amount. The case shall, therefore, remain open for that purpose. The Court reserves the right to approve the agreement and, in the event no agreement is reached, to set the amount and order the manner of payment.

A PATHBREAKING CASE

Note the Inter–American Commission's role in this case. First, it considered the petition, conducted an investigation, and reached a decision on the merits. Then it referred the matter to the Inter–American Court, becoming a party representing Mr. Velásquez Rodríguez. It presented evidence to the Court, and argued points of law. Is it appropriate for the Commission to be first, an investigator attempting to reach an impartial decision, and later, advocate for the petitioner? One knowledgeable commentator has argued that this could adversely affect the trust the Commission needs from states, as well as from victims, in order to play its larger role as the impartial overseer of human rights in the Americas.[a] Do you agree?

An alternative would have been to emulate a procedure used by the European Commission of Human Rights when it refers a matter to the European Court of Human Rights involving an individual petition. It allows the attorney for the petitioner, in effect, to conduct the case before the Court. Is that preferable?

Why do you suppose the Commission referred the matter to the Court, thus opening itself up to possible reversal?

Did the Inter–American Court act essentially as an appellate court in this case?

Consider the Court's treatment of the exhaustion-of-domestic-remedies issue. In paragraph 59, the Court said that the state has the burden of proving that domestic remedies remain to be exhausted and that they are effective. In paragraph 60, it said that if the state does so, the opposing party has the burden of showing that those remedies were exhausted or that the case comes within one of the exceptions.

> (a) Did the Court reject Honduras' preliminary objection on this point because (1) Honduras had failed to show that domestic remedies remained to be exhausted, (2) Honduras failed to show that they were effective, (3) the Commission showed that the remedies were exhausted, or (4) the Commission showed that the

---

[a]. Medina, The Inter–American Commission on Human Rights and the Inter–American Court of Human Rights: Reflections on a Joint Venture, 12 Human Rts.Q. 439, 460 (1990).

case came within one of the exceptions? (If the answer is (1) or (2), why did the Court put such stress on evidence offered by the Commission, in paragraphs 76–81? If the answer is (3) or (4), how did the Court get beyond the initial burden on Honduras when the government apparently presented no evidence on the effectiveness of its own remedies?)

(b) Is the Court's allocation of the burdens regarding exhaustion of domestic remedies a sensible one?

Would the outcome have been the same regarding exhaustion of domestic remedies if none of the efforts described in paragraph 74 had been made?

Several witnesses were called by the Court, rather than by the parties. That is consistent with the nonadversary civil law procedure found in Latin America and in continental Europe. Do you see any problem with it?

Consider the Court's evidentiary rulings. For example, was it relevant to consider evidence of the modus operandi of the practice of disappearances, rather than limiting it to evidence of this particular disappearance?

Did the Court admit hearsay? If so, was that proper?

Does it appear that the witnesses were reliable? What about the press clippings?

The Court said in paragraphs 127 and 128 that it had to determine what the standards of proof should be, and that the standards are less formal in an international case than in a domestic one. What standards did the Court decide on?

Were the Court's inferences and conclusions on the evidence justifiable, regarding (a) the pattern of disappearances, and (b) the particular disappearance of Manfredo Velásquez Rodríguez?

On the legal issues, did the Court make a convincing case for holding that government-sponsored disappearances violate articles 7, 5 and 4 of the Convention (paragraphs 155–158 of the judgment)?

If the answer to the previous question is yes, why did the Court have to wrestle with article 1(1) of the Convention (paragraphs 161–188)? What *is* the significance of article 1(1) in the eyes of the Court? (In paragraph 163 the Court noted that the Commission had not alleged a violation of that article. Why do you suppose the Commission didn't do so?)

What is the most important aspect of the Velásquez Rodríguez case for the future protection of human rights in the Americas?

Articles 7, 5, 4 and 1(1) of the American Convention have counterparts in the U.N. Covenant of Civil and Political Rights and in the [European] Convention for the Protection of Human Rights and Fundamental Freedoms, though the counterparts do not track the American Convention verbatim. What significance, if any, do you suppose the

Velásquez Rodríguez case would have if a comparable claim of disappearance were made under the petitioning procedures of the Optional Protocol to the Covenant or of the European Convention?

After the judgment on the merits was rendered in the Velásquez Rodríguez case, the Commission and the Honduran government entered into negotiations over the damages to be paid. They failed to agree on the amount. Consequently the Commission submitted the damages issue to the Court. The Court denied a request for punitive damages, saying that such damages are not contemplated by the expression "fair compensation" in article 63(1) of the American Convention, and are not recognized by current international law. As for compensatory damages, the Court held that they should be calculated (a) to cover the victim's lost earnings based on the income he would have received for the remainder of his life expectancy, reduced in a case like this—where the beneficiaries are the victim's family members—by an amount that takes account of the beneficiaries' own earning power; plus (b) "moral damages" for "harmful psychological impacts among his immediate family" (i.e. mental anguish, in common law terms). The Court came up with rather arbitrary figures of 500,000 Honduran lempiras for net lost earnings plus 250,000 lempiras for moral damages (a total of U.S. $375,000 at the official exchange rate).[b]

If there ever was a case that called for an international tribunal to award punitive damages, this would be it. Could the Court have interpreted *article 63(1)* to allow punitive damages?

Why *shouldn't* punitive damages be allowed in egregious cases like this? Does the fact that governments change—as the Honduran government did—supply an answer?

The Honduran government delayed paying the judgment. The Commission went back to the Court, seeking not only an award of interest for the eight months that had elapsed since the judgment became payable, but also an adjustment to compensate for the loss in real value of the lempira resulting from inflation in Honduras since that date. The Court, exercising its power to supervise compliance with its original judgment, granted the Commission's request.[c]

Is this latest judgment an important precedent?

In 1991 the Honduran government reported that it had established a trust fund in the amount of 562,500 lempiras on behalf of the children of Manfredo Velásquez Rodríguez, and had paid compensatory damages in the amount of 187,500 lempiras to his wife.[d]

---

b. Judgment of July 21, 1989, Series C, No. 7.

c. Judgment of Aug. 17, 1990, Series C, No. ___.

d. 1991 Ann.Rep. of the Inter-American Court of Human Rights, OAS Doc. OAS/Ser.L/V/III.25, at 9 (1992).

E. CHANGING THE RULES UNILATERALLY

In its advisory opinion on Restrictions to the Death Penalty, page 995 supra, the Inter-American Court said that a state party to the American Convention was precluded by the last sentence of *article 4(2)* from applying the death penalty to crimes to which the penalty did not apply when the state became a party to the Convention. That case involved Guatemala.

In the autumn of 1992, the Peruvian government wanted to have the option of seeking the death penalty against some leaders of the Sendero Luminoso guerrilla movement. Like Guatemala, Peru had become a party to the American Convention at a time when its domestic law would not have applied the death penalty to the crimes in question. To get around the problem of article 4(2), the Peruvian President, Alberto Fujimori, announced that Peru would withdraw from the American Convention, which it had ratified in 1980.[a] For the withdrawal provision in the Convention, see *article 78*.

Could Peru (or Guatemala) lawfully denounce the Convention under that provision, when the express purpose is to apply the death penalty to crimes not subject to it when the state became a party?

When the Peruvian government made its announcement, the Inter-American Commission on Human Rights issued a statement that withdrawal from the Convention "would not relieve Peru of its human rights obligations, since it will remain subject to the jurisdiction of the Commission" even as a nonparty to the Convention, and (as a member of the OAS) would still be subject to the American Declaration of the Rights and Duties of Man.[b] See *article 20* of the Statute of the Inter-American Commission.

If Peru (or any other party to the Convention) were to withdraw from the Convention and then introduce the death penalty for crimes not theretofore subject to it, would it be violating its international obligations as embodied in the American Declaration of the Rights and Duties of Man? Would it be proper for the Inter-American Commission to make a determination to that effect under article 20 of its Statute?

If Peru, or any other party, were to accede again to the Convention after withdrawing and enacting the death penalty, would it effectively get around the last sentence of Convention article 4(2)? Would it effectively avoid any death penalty problem under the American Declaration?

When a state first becomes a party to the American Convention, could it properly attach a reservation opting out of the last sentence of article 4(2)? See *article 75*. Would the answer be the same if the state had formerly been a party without such a reservation, then withdrew, and then acceded again with the reservation?

a. See Latin America Weekly Rep., Oct. 29, 1992, p. 2.

b. Agence France Presse dispatch, Oct. 28, 1992.

Could a state properly attach a reservation to *article 5(2)* of the Convention when it first becomes a party? If not, what would be the effect if it declines to withdraw the reservation?

Should the American Convention be amended to make it more difficult to withdraw from it and/or to attach reservations?

SECTION 4. THE EUROPEAN SYSTEM

A. INTRODUCTION

The [European] Convention for the Protection of Human Rights and Fundamental Freedoms was the first convention concluded among the member states of the Council of Europe, in November 1950. In the ensuing years, the protection of human rights has become the Council of Europe's most significant function, though it has others as well. Originally a Western European organization, the Council of Europe had 27 member states, including some from Eastern Europe, by mid–1992.

Membership in the Council of Europe does not automatically make a state a party to the Convention for the Protection of Human Rights and Fundamental Freedoms. In mid–1992, 24 Council of Europe members were parties to the Convention.

The genesis and structure of the Convention are summarized in the first excerpt below, which also outlines the substantive rights covered in four of the protocols to the Convention. The second excerpt, from the Council of Europe itself, describes the human rights monitoring and judicial bodies under the Convention.

P. VAN DIJK & G. VAN HOOF, THEORY AND PRACTICE OF THE EUROPEAN CONVENTION ON HUMAN RIGHTS
1–5 (2d ed. 1990).*

§ 1. THE GENESIS OF THE CONVENTION

1. The European Convention for the Protection of Human Rights and Fundamental Freedoms is a product of the period shortly after the Second World War, when the issue of international protection of human rights attracted a great deal of attention. These rights had been crushed by the atrocities of National Socialism, and the guarantee of their protection at the national level had proved completely inadequate.

2. As early as 1941 Churchill and Roosevelt, in the Atlantic Charter, launched their four freedoms: freedom of life, freedom of religion, freedom from want and freedom from fear. After the Second World War the promotion of respect for human rights and fundamental freedoms became one of the aims of the United Nations. Within that

---

* Reprinted by permission of Kluwer Law and Taxation Publishers.

framework the Universal Declaration of Human Rights, which was adopted on 10 December 1948 by the General Assembly of the United Nations, became a significant milestone.

3. Meanwhile, preliminary steps were also taken at the European level. In May 1948 the International Committee of the Movements for European Unity organized a "Congress of Europe" in The Hague. This initiative gave the decisive impetus to the foundation of the Council of Europe in 1949. At the Congress a resolution was adopted, the introductory part of which reads as follows:

The Congress:

Considers that the resultant union or federation should be open to all European nations democratically governed and which undertake to respect a Charter of Human Rights;

Resolves that a Commission should be set up to undertake immediately the double task of drafting such a Charter and of laying down standards to which a State must conform if it is to deserve the name of democracy.

These matters formed the subject of a discussion during the first session of the Consultative Assembly (at present called the Parliamentary Assembly) of the Council of Europe in August 1949. The Assembly charged its Committee on Legal and Administrative Questions to consider in more detail the matter of a collective guarantee of human rights.

4. From that moment onwards the Convention was drafted in a relatively short time. In September of the same year the Assembly adopted the Committee's report, in which ten rights were included that were to be the subjects of a collective guarantee, and the establishment of a European Commission of Human Rights and a European Court of Justice was proposed. In November of that year the Committee of Ministers of the Council of Europe decided to appoint a Committee of Government Experts, which was entrusted with the task of preparing a draft text on the basis of this report.

This Committee completed its work in the spring of 1950. It had made considerable headway, but it failed to find a solution to a number of political problems. The subsequently appointed Committee of Senior Officials was also forced to leave the ultimate decision on a number of matters to the Committee of Ministers, even though it reached agreement about the greater part of the text of the Committee of Experts.

On 7 August 1950 the Committee of Ministers approved a revised draft text, which went considerably less far than the original proposals on a number of points. For example, the system of individual applications and the jurisdiction of the Court were made optional. This draft text was not substantially altered afterwards.

5. On 4 November 1950 the Convention, which according to its preamble was framed "to take the first steps for collective enforcement

of certain rights stated in the Universal Declaration", was signed in Rome. It entered into force on 3 September 1953 * * *.

* * *

§ 2. The Structure of the Convention

1. Under Article 1 of the Convention the contracting States are bound to secure to everyone within their jurisdiction the rights and freedoms set forth in Section I of the Convention. To the extent that a State has ratified the First, Fourth, Sixth, or Seventh Protocol, this obligation also applies to the rights and freedoms laid down in these Protocols, since the latter are considered as supplementary articles of the Convention, to which all the provisions of the Convention apply in a similar way.

As stated above, the contracting States must secure these rights and freedoms to "everyone within their jurisdiction". These words of Article 1 do not imply any limitation as to nationality. Even those who are not nationals either of the State concerned or of any one of the other contracting States may claim this guarantee when they are in some respect subject to the jurisdiction of the State from which they claim that guarantee. Furthermore it is irrelevant whether they have their residence inside or outside the territory of that State.

2. Section I of the Convention contains the following rights and freedoms:

> Article 2: right to life;
> Article 3: freedom from torture and inhuman or degrading treatment;
> Article 4: freedom from slavery and forced or compulsory labour;
> Article 5: right to liberty and security of person;
> Article 6: right to a fair and public trial within a reasonable time;
> Article 7: freedom from retrospective effect of penal legislation;
> Article 8: right to respect for private and family life, home and correspondence;
> Article 9: freedom of thought, conscience and religion;
> Article 10: freedom of expression;
> Article 11: freedom of assembly and association;
> Article 12: right to marry and found a family.

The First Protocol has added the following rights:

> Article 1: right to peaceful enjoyment of possessions;
> Article 2: right to education and free choice of education;
> Article 3: right to free elections by secret ballot.

In the Fourth Protocol the following rights and freedoms have been included:

Article 1: prohibition of deprivation of liberty on the ground of inability to fulfil a contractual obligation;
Article 2: freedom to move within and freedom to choose residence in a country;
Article 3: prohibition of expulsion of nationals and right of nationals to enter the territory of the State of which they are nationals;
Article 4: prohibition of collective expulsion of aliens.

The Sixth Protocol has added the prohibition of the condemnation to and execution of the death penalty (Article 1).

The Seventh Protocol contains the following rights and freedoms:

Article 1: procedural guarantees in case of expulsion of aliens lawfully resident in the territory of a State;
Article 2: right of review by a higher tribunal in criminal cases;
Article 3: right to compensation to a person convicted of a criminal offence, on the ground that a new or newly discovered fact shows that there has been a miscarriage of justice;
Article 4: prohibition of new criminal proceedings for offences for which one has already been finally acquitted or convicted (*ne bis in idem*);
Article 5: equality of rights and responsibilities between spouses.

3. The other articles of Section I of the Convention contain general provisions concerning the enjoyment, the protection and the limitation of the rights and freedoms mentioned above. Article 13 stipulates that everyone whose rights and freedoms mentioned in the Convention are violated shall have an effective remedy before national authorities, notwithstanding the fact that the violation has been committed by persons acting in an official capacity. Article 14 requires the contracting States to secure the rights and freedoms without discrimination on any ground whatsoever. Article 15 allows States to derogate from a number of provisions of the Convention in time of war or any other public emergency threatening the life of the nation. Under Article 16 States are allowed to impose limitations on political activities of aliens notwithstanding Articles 10, 11 and 14 of the Convention, while Article 17 provides that nothing in the Convention may justify activities aimed at the destruction of any of the rights and freedoms set forth in the Convention or their limitation to a greater extent than is provided for in the Convention. Finally, Article 18 implies a prohibition of misuse of power (*détournement de pouvoir*) as to the right of contracting States to impose restrictions on the rights and freedoms guaranteed by the Convention.

4. Besides these substantive provisions, the European Convention also contains a number of provisions to ensure the observance by the

contracting States of their obligations under the Convention. In this connection it should be noted that the supervision of the implementation of the Convention rests primarily with the national authorities, in particular the national courts (at least in States where the Convention is directly applicable). This is also implied in Article 13. With regard to those cases where a national procedure is not available or does not provide for an adequate remedy, or in the last resort has not produced a satisfactory result in the opinion of the prejudiced party or of a contracting State, the Convention itself provides for a supervisory procedure. This system consists of two phases, *viz.* the procedure before the European Commission of Human Rights (Section III) and subsequently the procedure before the European Court of Human Rights (Section IV) or before the Committee of Ministers of the Council of Europe (Articles 30 and 31). In addition, the Secretary General of the Council of Europe also takes part in the supervision of the observance of the Convention (Article 57).

THE COUNCIL OF EUROPE AND THE PROTECTION OF HUMAN RIGHTS
10–16 (1990).
Pamphlet of the Directorate of Human Rights of the Council of Europe.

THE PROTECTION MACHINERY

Under the Convention, the task of protecting human rights is shared by two specially created bodies—the European Commission of Human Rights and the European Court of Human Rights—together with the Committee of Ministers, the decision-making body of the Council of Europe, which is composed of the Foreign Ministers of member states or their deputies. All three are based in Strasbourg.

The European Commission of Human Rights

The Commission's role is to examine complaints of alleged breaches of the Convention, to establish the facts and to try to obtain a friendly settlement of cases, failing which it expresses its opinion as to whether there has been a violation of the Convention.

The Commission is composed of as many members as the number of states that have ratified the Convention. Members must either possess the qualifications required for the appointment to high judicial office or be jurists of recognised competence. They are elected by the Committee of Ministers from a list of names submitted by each state's delegation to the Council of Europe's Parliamentary Assembly.

They hold office for six years and can be re-elected. As members of the Commission they are entirely independent and do not represent the state in respect of which they have been elected.

The Commission does not sit continuously but organises its sessions in the light of the case-load. The Commission is assisted in its functions by a permanent secretariat established in Strasbourg. The Commission's sessions are private and its records are confidential.

The European Court of Human Rights

The Court is called to give judgment in cases where the Commission has failed to secure a settlement and which have been referred to it by either the Commission or any state concerned.

The Court consists of a number of judges equal to that of member states of the Council of Europe. As with members of the Commission, the judges must either possess qualifications for appointment to high judicial office or be jurists of recognized competence.

They are elected for nine years by the Parliamentary Assembly of the Council of Europe. Each state puts forward a list of three candidates of whom at least two must be its own nationals. The judge elected need not be a national of the state filling the vacancy (in 1980 a Canadian lawyer was elected as the Liechtenstein judge at the Court). Like members of the Commission, the judges sit in their individual capacity and do not represent the country that nominated them. They enjoy complete independence in the performance of their duties.

The Court is renewed one-third at a time and judges can be reelected. Like the Commission, the Court does not sit permanently but convenes whenever necessary to consider cases brought before it. Cases are normally dealt with by a Chamber of nine judges, one of whom will be the Court's President or Vice-President. Included in the Chamber will be a judge who is a national of a state concerned in the case, or, if there is none, a person of its choice. The remaining judges are drawn by lot by the President. If a Chamber considers that a case raises a serious question of interpretation of the Convention, it may relinquish jurisdiction in favour of the full Court. While the Court deliberates in private, its hearings are normally open to the public and its judgments are always made public.

How The Machinery Works

Complaints of a violation of the Convention are made to the European Commission of Human Rights. Although one member state may bring proceedings against another—these are known as inter-state applications—the most frequent form of complaint is the individual application brought by a person, group of individuals or non-governmental organisation against a state within whose jurisdiction the alleged violation occurred. Before such cases can be lodged, the state concerned must have recognised by express declaration the right of individuals to lodge complaints against it.

The right of individual petition under Article 25 of the Convention was an important innovation in international law and is one of the most remarkable features of the enforcement machinery set up by the Convention.

Decision on Admissibility

On receipt of a complaint of an alleged violation of human rights, the Commission's first task is to decide whether it is admissible under the Convention. Each year the Commission receives some 4,000 letters and communications from individuals of which about 1,000 are registered as qualifying for examination as to their admissibility. For petitions to be declared admissible, the applicants must show that they have exhausted all possible remedies in the country where the alleged violation took place and the application must have been made within six months of a final decision by the courts or authorities of that state.

The applicant must not be anonymous, the complaint must not be the same as one already examined by the Commission or previously submitted to another international body, and it must be covered by the scope of the Convention.

Before a decision on admissibility is taken, the Commission will often ask the parties concerned for information or for their observations. Applicants may be granted legal aid to help present their case. The parties may also be asked to submit observations at a hearing. It is possible for the parties to agree to a solution before admissibility. The case will then be struck off the Commission's list of cases provided it does not raise any questions of general interest that require further examination.

Currently, of all the applications investigated by the Commission, about 10% are declared admissible. If a petition is rejected, the Commission's decision is final and there is no right of appeal against it.

Preparation of the Commission's Report

Once an application is declared admissible, the Commission's next task is to establish the facts. At this stage, the parties may be invited to submit further evidence, answer questions and give explanations. Hearings may be held or on-the-spot investigations conducted when witnesses and experts can be examined.

While seeking to establish the facts, the Commission is also under an obligation to put itself at the disposal of the parties with a view to securing a friendly settlement on the basis of respect for the human rights guaranteed in the Convention.

Where a settlement is reached, the Commission draws up a brief report on the case. This is sent to the state concerned, the Committee of Ministers and the Secretary General of the Council of Europe for publication.

If no settlement emerges, the Commission draws up a more detailed report in which it establishes the facts and expresses a legal opinion as to the question whether there has been a violation of the Convention. Each member of the Commission has a vote and separate opinions may be recorded. The report is sent only to the states involved and the

Committee of Ministers. It remains at this stage confidential and is not sent to the applicant or his or her lawyers.

After the Commission's Report

Within three months of the Commission's report being sent to the Committee of Ministers, the case may be referred to the European Court of Human Rights.

For a case to go to the Court, the defendant state must have accepted the compulsory jurisdiction of the Court or, failing that, agreed to accept the Court's jurisdiction in the particular case.

Only the Commission or any state concerned may refer a case to the Court. Individuals complaining of a breach of the Convention have, at present, no such right. However, with respect to those states which ratify the ninth protocol to the Convention—when it comes into force—individuals will themselves be able to seize the Court. Once the case is before the Court, they or their lawyers [are normally] permitted to present written and oral argument at the hearing and the complainant may also be asked to appear before the Court as a witness. Legal aid may be provided.

In presenting a case to the Court, the Commission does not act on behalf of either of the parties. The role of the Commission is to present the Commission's conclusions in a strictly impartial and objective way. Once a case has been referred to the Court, the Commission's report with its opinion on whether there has been a violation of the Convention is normally made public.

Procedure of the Court

The Court examines the case in the light of the report of the Commission together with any further written evidence or legal argument. There will also normally be a public hearing in Strasbourg when the delegate of the Commission and lawyers for the respondent government and the applicant will present or supplement their submissions and may be questioned about them by the judges.

Judgments are delivered in open court. * * * The judgment of the Court is final and there is no appeal. It is binding on the state concerned but the Court has no enforcement powers of its own. The Committee of Ministers of the Council of Europe supervises the implementation of the Court's judgments.

* * *

In appropriate circumstances, the Court can afford the victim of a violation "just satisfaction" which may, for example, include an award of compensation and an order for the reimbursement of costs.

Cases Not Referred to the Court

Where a case is not referred to the Court, the Committee of

Ministers of the Council of Europe decides, by a two-thirds majority,[a] whether or not there was a breach of the Convention and whether to publish the Commission's report. In addition, the Committee of Ministers can recommend that a state afford the victim of a violation "just satisfaction", the modalities of which are fixed in consultation with the Commission. Like those of the Court, decisions of the Committee of Ministers are final and member states undertake to regard them as binding.

DECLARATIONS AND PROTOCOLS

As of mid–1992, all 24 states parties to the European Convention had declared their recognition of the competence of the Commission to receive individual petitions, under *article 25*. All 24 had also made declarations under *article 46*, recognizing the competence of the European Court of Human Rights in matters concerning the interpretation and application of the Convention.

By mid–1992, ten protocols to the European Convention had been adopted. Eight were in force for varying numbers of states (for each protocol, those that had ratified it). The ninth, giving limited standing to individuals before the European Court, and the tenth, allowing the Committee of Ministers to act under *article 32(1)* by simple majority rather than two-thirds, were not yet in force for any states. The first, fourth, sixth and seventh, adding substantive rights to the Convention, are summarized in the first excerpt above. The second protocol gives the Court very limited competence to issue advisory opinions. Protocol number three eliminated a subcommission; in other respects, it has been superseded by the eighth protocol. The fifth protocol deals with the terms of office of members of the Commission and Court.

The eighth protocol made several procedural changes relating to the Commission and Court. In the Documentary volume accompanying these materials, the eighth protocol has been incorporated into the relevant articles of Sections III and IV of the Convention.

THE REPORTING SYSTEM

Before we turn to the roles of the Commission and the Court, mention should be made of the reporting system contemplated by *article 57* of the European Convention. It requires states parties, at the request of the Secretary–General of the Council of Europe, to explain the implementation of any provisions of the Convention in their internal law.

---

a. [This will be reduced to a simple majority when Protocol No. 10 enters into force. Ed.]

On five occasions so far the Secretary–General has requested reports from all states parties under article 57. In 1964 he requested them to explain how their legislation, courts and administrative practices ensured the implementation of the rights in the Convention and the first protocol. In 1970 he requested information on the implementation of article 5(5), which provides a right of compensation for anyone arrested or detained in contravention of the other provisions of that article. In 1975 he asked for reports on the implementation of articles 8 (right of privacy), 9 (freedom of thought, conscience and religion), 10 (freedom of expression) and 11 (freedom of assembly and of association). In 1983 he inquired into the situation of children who have been placed out of the parental home by administrative or judicial order. In 1988 he requested reports on implementation of article 6(1), concerning the right to a fair and public hearing within a reasonable time.

Not all governments have responded to these requests. The responses that have been received are brought to the attention of all contracting states and the Council of Europe's Parliamentary Assembly, though individual states may ask that parts of their data be withheld.[b]

Does article 57 require states parties to respond to the Secretary–General's requests? Once again we have the problem of inducing governments to submit their reports under a human rights monitoring system. Would they be more likely to submit their reports in a regional system than in a global one (like those operating under the two U.N. Covenants)?

Could the Secretary–General request reports from a single state, or a few states, under article 57? Compare International Covenant on Economic, Social and Cultural Rights *article 16*; Covenant on Civil and Political Rights *article 40*. Would it ever be useful to single out a state for a report?

If the Secretary–General is dissatisfied with the response he receives from any state, could he refer the matter to the European Commission or Court? See European Convention *articles 24, 25, 45, 48*. If not, what good is the reporting system?

B. APPLICATION OF THE CONVENTION BY THE EUROPEAN COMMISSION OF HUMAN RIGHTS

Under article 24 of the European Convention, any state party may refer to the Commission any alleged breach by another party. No consent by the respondent state, other than by ratification of the Convention, is required. ILO Constitution article 26 provides a similar complaints procedure. Article 41 of the U.N. Covenant on Civil and Political Rights and article 45 of the American Convention of Human

---

b. See P. van Dijk & G. van Hoof, Theory and Practice of the European Convention on Human Rights 210–11 (2d ed. 1990).

Rights are similar in that they do not require a demonstration of the complaining state's cognizable interest in a particular victim. They are dissimilar in that they do not apply unless the complaining and respondent states have made declarations that they recognize the inter-state procedure. One of the concerns expressed about the non-European inter-state complaint systems is that complaining states may be tempted to use them simply for political purposes, to embarrass respondent states. Would the concern be the same under article 24 of the European Convention?

The inter-state procedure has been used sparingly in Europe, as elsewhere. When it has been used, the complaining state has generally invoked it on behalf of its own nationals. On only two occasions in the first 38 years—once against Greece and once against Turkey—was it used as a kind of *actio popularis*, on behalf of non-nationals of the complaining states.

As has already been noted, the petitioning procedure for individuals under article 25 may be invoked only against a respondent state that has declared its recognition of the Commission's competence in such matters. These declarations have usually been made for limited but renewable periods (two, three or five years).

Under some international petitioning procedures, persons or non-governmental organizations other than the victims have standing to submit petitions. This is so under the ECOSOC Resolution 1503 procedure for petitions alleging "a consistent pattern of gross violations," and under *article 44* of the American Convention. Is it so under *article 25* of the European Convention?

Compare article 25 of the European Convention with *article 1* of the first Optional Protocol to the International Covenant on Civil and Political Rights, and note also the U.N. Human Rights Committee's application of article 1, page 925 supra. Could a financially dependent child or spouse of a wrongfully detained person successfully petition the European Commission, seeking the person's release or compensation for lost earnings during detention?[a] Would the practice of the Human Rights Committee be relevant?

A considerable amount of the work of the European Commission arises under *articles 26* and *27*, relating to the admissibility of petitions. Article 26 is the familiar exhaustion-of-domestic-remedies rule. Note that it applies both to inter-state cases under article 24 and to individual petitions (applications) under article 25. The grounds for inadmissibility under article 27, however, apply only to individual petitions—the bulk of the Commission's work.

In the American Convention on Human Rights, all grounds of inadmissibility, including those comparable to the grounds in article 27 of the European Convention, apply to communications regardless of

---

a. On "indirect victims," see Rogge, The "Victim" Requirement in Article 25 of the European Convention on Human Rights, in Protecting Human Rights: The European Dimension 539, 541 (F. Matscher & H. Petzold eds. 1988).

source (even to inter-state cases). See American Convention *articles 46–47*. Why would the two Conventions differ on this point?

As has already been noted, about 90 percent of the petitions in the European system have been held inadmissible. Most of the rejected petitions have been found deficient on one of three grounds: there had been no exhaustion of domestic remedies; the alleged violations were "incompatible with the provisions of the Convention" (i.e. did not relate to rights protected by the Convention); or the petition was "manifestly ill-founded" (i.e. did not make out a prima facie case that the alleged violations occurred).

The vast majority of the rejections are so obvious that the petitions are not even referred to the respondent governments. When the Commission holds an application inadmissible, with or without communicating it to the respondent government, there is no further review. Should there be?

A few illustrative Commission decisions on admissibility are given below. They are close cases, in which the views of all parties were sought and considered.[b]

BERBERICH v. FEDERAL REPUBLIC OF GERMANY

European Commission of Human Rights, Application No. 5874/72.
1974 Yearbook of the European Convention on Human Rights 386.*

The applicant is a German citizen, born in 1942 and at present detained in prison in Berlin. She is a lawyer by profession and is represented before the Commission by * * * barristers practising in Berlin.

The applicant was arrested in Berlin on 8 October 1970 and remanded in prison ["detention on remand," i.e. pre-trial confinement] on the authority of a warrant of arrest issued on 9 October 1970 by the District Court of Tiergarten in Berlin. She was suspected of having aided members of the so-called "Baader–Meinhof gang" to escape punishment, in particular the former barrister Mahler who was wanted for attempted murder, by hiding them in an apartment.

Furthermore, she was suspected of having participated in three bank holdups, committed on 29 September 1970 in Berlin. The Court stated that there was danger of the applicant trying to abscond because she was threatened with the possibility of a severe sentence of many

---

[b] The European Commission's decisions through 1974 are reported in European Commission of Human Rights, Collection of Decisions. Beginning in 1975, they are reported in a series called Decisions and Reports. Selected Commission decisions are reported in the Yearbook of the European Convention on Human Rights (which also publishes the opinions of the European Court of Human Rights). There is also a multi-volume Digest of Strasbourg Case–Law Relating to the European Convention on Human Rights, covering the cases of both the Commission and the Court. Particularly significant Commission decisions appear in the Human Rights Law Journal before they become available elsewhere.

* © 1976 by Martinus Nijhoff, The Hague, Netherlands. Reprinted by permission of Kluwer Academic Publishers.

years of imprisonment. The Court also pointed out that the applicant was in possession of a number of forged papers and had rented a second apartment under a false name. [The applicant complains to the Commission of a lack of a speedy trial.]

* * *

On 1 April 1971 the Investigating Judge of the Federal Court amended the District Court's warrant of arrest to the effect that, insofar as the applicant had been suspected of having aided persons who were wanted for attempted murder to escape punishment, she was now suspected of having been a member of a criminal organisation (Article 129 of the Criminal Code) namely the Baader–Meinhof gang.

The judge stated that, according to the result of these investigations, there was strong suspicion that this gang had committed several holdups and other crimes and that the applicant belonged to the inner circle of the gang. She had rented an apartment in Berlin under a false name which has served as a hiding place for the members of the gang. In September 1970 she had rented several cars by presenting stolen or forged documents to the hirers. The cars had then been used by the members of the gang and had not been given back. At her arrest the applicant was found in possession of a forged motor vehicle registration card. The car which was registered under the forged card was parked nearby. Furthermore, the applicant was carrying a loaded pistol.

The judge concluded that, in view of the applicant's close relationship with other members of the underground organisation who had not yet been arrested and in view of the gravity of the criminal acts of which she was suspected, there was danger that she would try to abscond. He was further of the opinion that the applicant's conduct in prison proved her intention to suppress evidence and to influence witnesses and her co-defendants in order to hinder the investigation proceedings.

On 23 April 1971 the Federal Court, after having heard the Attorney–General and the applicant's defence counsel, ordered the applicant's further detention. * * * The Court pointed out that it was likely that the applicant would, if she were released, receive forged papers from other gang members not yet arrested and that consequently the only way to prevent her absconding was to keep her in prison. In the Court's opinion a detention exceeding six months was justified because the case was extremely complex and very difficult to investigate.

* * *

On 29 July 1971 the Federal Court again ordered that the applicant's detention on remand should continue.

* * *

At the beginning of 1972 the applicant was re-transferred to a prison in Berlin and her case was on 1 February 1972 again taken over by the Public Prosecutor at the Berlin Regional Court.

By decisions of 9 March, 4 April and 27 April 1972, the competent judge stopped correspondence addressed to the applicant because the contents were considered to be objectionable.

On 25 February 1972 the Berlin Court of Appeal decided that the applicant's detention on remand should continue.

* * *

On 17 April 1972 the Public Prosecutor filed the indictment against the applicant and other alleged gang members. The applicant was accused of having been a member of a criminal organisation, of armed robbery committed with others and of illegal possession of weapons and ammunition.

By orders of 2 June 1972 and 6 September 1972 the Berlin Court of Appeal decided that the applicant must remain in prison.

The trial against the applicant and several co-defendants began on 24 November 1972. It is still pending [May 1974] but at present is in its final phase, the prosecution having made their final plea.

The respondent Government, in their written observations on admissibility and at the hearing before the Commission * * * submitted their reasons why the application should be declared inadmissible. They first argued that the applicant had not exhausted domestic remedies. It was admitted that the applicant had no remedy against the orders of the Berlin Court of Appeal. However, it was pointed out by the Government that the applicant had failed to lodge appeals against, *inter alia*, the warrant of arrest issued by the District Court of Tiergarten on 9 October 1970 and the orders of the investigating judge of the Federal Court. It was further pointed out that the applicant had the possibility of lodging a constitutional appeal against the orders of the Federal Court.

The Government argued that consequently the applicant had to a considerable extent failed to file such domestic remedies as could reasonably be expected of her and therefore had not exhausted all domestic remedies in the sense of Article 26 of the Convention.

The Government also submitted that the application constituted an abuse of the right to petition. It was stated in this respect that the applicant's submissions were inconsistent with her behaviour during the trial proceedings. If she was really concerned about speedy proceedings, she would not during the trial, both inside and outside the court-room, continuously and persistently have disturbed and delayed the proceedings. The applicant showed that she intended to upset the criminal proceedings in any way she possibly could. It was apparently for this purpose that she introduced her application before the European Commission of Human Rights, namely in order to achieve her unjustified release and thus to evade justice. The present application therefore served the purpose of frustrating criminal proceedings directed against her.

* * *

The Government finally asked the Commission to reject the application as being manifestly ill-founded. It denied that there had been any unreasonable delay of the investigations against the applicant or of her trial.

* * *

The Law

The applicant's sole complaint is that the period of her detention on remand constituted a violation of Article 5(3) of the Convention which provides that:

> Everyone arrested or detained in accordance with the provisions of paragraph 1(c) of this Article shall be brought promptly before a judge or other officer authorised by law to exercise judicial power and shall be entitled to trial within a reasonable time or to release pending trial. Release may be conditioned by guarantee to appear for trial.

1. The Commission has first considered the question whether the applicant has exhausted all domestic remedies as is required by Article 26 of the Convention.

The term "all remedies" in the text of this provision refers to the case where the domestic law provides against some measure or decisions a single series of remedies at various levels, such as appeal to a court of appeal, further appeal to a supreme court and possibly a constitutional appeal. In such a case where there is a single remedy it should be pursued up to the highest level. The position is not so certain where the domestic law provides a number of different remedies. In such cases the Commission tends to admit that Article 26 has been complied with if the applicant exhausts only the remedy or remedies which are reasonably likely to prove effective.

On the other hand, Article 26 does not have the scope attributed to it by the respondent Government in cases where the domestic law provides a single remedy against a particular measure, but allows the person in question to make use of this remedy as often as he feels inclined and at intervals left entirely, or to a great extent, to his discretion throughout the time the measure in question remains in force. Such, in fact, is the position in the present case. Under the rules of criminal procedure in the Federal Republic of Germany persons in detention on remand may at any time apply for provisional release. The Code on Criminal Procedure imposes no restrictions on the exercise of this remedy. Nor, on the other hand, does it require the detained person to make a minimum use of the remedy. Furthermore, the competent court of appeal must, in cases where detention on remand exceeds six months, decide *ex officio* and at regular intervals whether that detention should continue. There is no possibility of an appeal or a constitutional appeal against such decision if, as in the present case, it is given by the Berlin Court of Appeal. It follows that the Commission can not accept the respondent Government's submission that the conditions of Article 26 of the Convention are not met simply because the applicant has not appealed against this or that particular decision ordering her detention on remand or the continuation of such detention. Nor can the Government rely on the fact that the applicant has not taken advantage of the possibility temporarily open to her of bringing the matter before the [Federal] constitutional court. In fact she was later deprived of this possibility by the retransfer of her case to the West Berlin prosecuting authorities.

It was sufficient for the purposes of Article 26 of the Convention that the applicant exhausted at any time she thought fit the domestic remedies existing at that time. This requirement is entirely satisfied. Prior to the lodging of the present application with the Commission on 9 October 1972, the Berlin Court of Appeal had, in three decisions not subject to appeal, refused to order the applicant's provisional release. The last of those decisions was taken on 6 September 1972.

2. The Commission next considered the respondent Government's submission that the application was inadmissible under Article 27(2) as being an abuse of the right of petition. The Commission does not accept this submission. According to the Commission's case-law an abuse can be seen in the use by the applicant of, e.g.:

— insulting remarks;

— completely specious arguments;

— false statements intended to mislead the Commission;

— completely unfounded allegations whose purpose was to escape consequences of a conviction.

None of these grounds appears in the present case. It is true that the applicant has, according to the undisputed statements made at the oral hearing by the representatives of the respondent Government, behaved in an objectionable manner at her trial. However, her submissions to the Commission were not objectionable and her behaviour before the trial court cannot be considered to constitute an element of abuse in the context of her complaint, under Article 5(3) of the Convention, that she was not brought to trial within a reasonable time.

The respondent Government also argued that the applicant was attempting by every means to frustrate the prosecution directed against her and that it was apparently for this purpose that she lodged an application with the Commission, her intention being to obtain an unjustified release as a means of escaping prosecution.

It is obvious that the danger of the prisoner absconding is one of the principal justifications for her detention on remand. Nevertheless, the existence of such a danger cannot justify the continuation of detention beyond the reasonable time mentioned in Article 5(3) of the Convention. Therefore, the applicant was not abusing her right of petition in asking the Commission to examine the question whether the period of her detention pending trial was reasonable within the meaning of this provision.

The Commission finds therefore that the application can not be declared inadmissible as being an abuse of the right of petition under Article 27(2) of the Convention.

3. According to the case-law of the European Court of Human Rights, the period with which Article 5(3) is concerned starts with a person's arrest and ends with the day on which the charge levelled against him is determined by a court of first instance. According to the respondent government, the trial court's decision in the applicant's case will be given in the near future, the taking of evidence having been concluded and the prosecution having made their final plea.

The period in question consequently amounts to a little more than three years and seven months. This is undoubtedly an exceptionally long period of detention on remand. However, the length of detention on remand is not by itself decisive in the context of Article 5(3) because the concept of a "reasonable time" can not be translated into a fixed number of months or years. The reasonableness of an accused person's continued detention must rather be assessed in each case according to its special features and the Commission has to judge whether the reasons given by the national authorities to justify the applicant's continued detention were relevant and sufficient to show that detention was not unreasonably prolonged.

The German courts based their decisions, ordering the applicant's original arrest and subsequently her detention, on the ground that there was a danger of her absconding if she were left at liberty. They pointed out in this respect that the applicant might expect a heavy sentence and that, at her arrest, she was in possession of forged papers and had rented an apartment under a false name. The latter findings were not contested by the applicant before the Commission. At the oral hearing it was furthermore mentioned by the Agent of the respondent Government that other alleged members of the so-called Baader–Meinhof group had succeeded in being released pending their trial and had taken advantage of this opportunity to abscond. It was further pointed out in this connection that Baader himself had already once been liberated in 1970 by way of armed attack. These statements were likewise not contested by the applicant's representatives who denied, however, that there was danger of her absconding. It was alleged that there was not enough evidence to convict the applicant of the crimes of which she was charged and that consequently her sentence would be in no relation to the length of her detention. Furthermore, it was pointed out by the applicant that she had a profession and a fixed residence.

The Commission does not find that the reasons given by the German judicial authorities were invalidated by the applicant's submissions. The Commission notes in this context that, when the applicant was arrested together with other group members, she undisputedly carried a loaded pistol and possessed forged papers. During her trial she manifested her solidarity with the group, approved criminal acts of other group members and also manifested her sympathy with a terrorist organisation which had attacked an embassy. This attitude confirmed the statements of the German judicial authorities and the Commission is of the opinion that it was not possible for the German authorities to obtain from the applicant valid guarantees which would have ensured her appearance at the trial if she had been released. It holds therefore that the arrest and detention were valid under Article 5(1)(c) of the Convention.

The Commission could, furthermore, not find that the exceptional length of the investigation and the trial was caused by an objectionable conduct of the case on the part of the German judicial authorities.

The Commission first notes in this respect that the investigation and the trial did not only concern the applicant but also several co-accused whose carefully planned activities were not restricted to West Berlin but covered also different parts of Western Germany. The result of the investigation filled several files. Originally the prosecution had named more than 300 witnesses and more than 20 experts to be heard by the trial court. There can therefore be no doubt that the applicant's case was of an exceptional complexity, and that the investigations were extremely difficult. This explains the length of the investigations from 8 October 1970 until the filing of the indictment on 17 April 1972.

* * *

As to the trial itself the applicant's counsels admitted themselves that it was of such complexity as to make it nearly impossible for someone not having participated in it to find out what caused the delays in this trial. The applicant's counsels even argued that it was legitimate for the defendants to disturb the proceedings in order to be excluded from it as the court would otherwise not have respected their desire not to attend the trial.

It has in fact to be noted that the applicant and her co-accused contributed a great deal to the delay of the proceedings by refusing to answer questions, behaving improperly, throwing objects at judges or the representatives of the prosecution, making insulting remarks, going on a hunger strike, and even provoking an explosion of a ballpoint pen filled with sulphur taken from matches.

The defence also caused a delay in the proceedings. For example, eight motions to replace judges or lay judges necessitated interruptions of the trial before being rejected as being unfounded. Although the taking of evidence had been terminated and the trial had come to its final phase, i.e. the conclusions of the prosecution and the defence, the defence requested the trial court in April 1974 to hear 49 further witnesses and one expert.

On the other hand, it has to be noted that the prosecution dropped several charges against the applicant and renounced the hearing of about 100 witnesses in order to speed up the proceedings.

* * *

In the light of all these circumstances the Commission finds that there is no appearance of a violation of Article 5(3).

It follows that the application is manifestly ill-founded within the meaning of Article 27(2) of the Convention.

For these reasons the Commission therefore

Declares this application inadmissible.

THE BERBERICH CASE AND ADMISSIBILITY

If in fact the applicant could have appealed her detention orders—and thus possibly obtained her release—before the case was retransferred to Berlin, why had she not failed to exhaust her domestic remedies? Would the result have been the same if German law had not required periodic reviews by the competent court of appeal?

Note that article 26, on exhaustion of remedies, refers to "the generally recognized rules of international law." This incorporates the international law rule that domestic remedies need not be pursued if they would be likely to be ineffectual or inadequate.[c]

How would you define "abuse of the right of petition" on the basis of this case? Does the concept refer only to what is said in the petition?

Under the petitioning procedure of ECOSOC Resolution 1503, administered by the U.N. Sub-Commission on Discrimination, petitions are inadmissible if their language is abusive or insulting—unless the abusive language can be deleted, leaving an otherwise admissible petition. Under the case law of the European Commission, mentioned in the Berberich case, the use of insulting remarks in a petition could be an abuse of the right. Why should human rights petitioning procedures get hung up on abusive language in petitions? Should the European Commission find the right of petition not abused if it can clean up the petition by deleting the offensive language?

As the Ringeisen case, infra, demonstrates, the Commission does not always find that petitions are inadmissible when they are based on claims of unreasonable detention before conviction. In that case, the petitioner had been imprisoned for about two years before and during

---

c. See the Commission's decisions in Greece v. United Kingdom, Application No. 299/57, in 1958–59 Yearbook of the European Convention on Human Rights 186, 192–94; Donnelly v. United Kingdom, Application Nos. 5577–5583/72, in 1973 Yearbook 212, 260–62.

criminal proceedings against him for fraudulent dealings in real estate and fraudulent bankruptcy, since there was reason to believe that he had concealed large sums of money and might abscond if released. On several occasions, he had petitioned the appropriate domestic courts for release and had been turned down. His petition to the European Commission was held admissible, and the petitioner ultimately won on the merits. Yet the Berberich petition was held inadmissible despite her imprisonment for three years and seven months between arrest and verdict. In a situation like the one in the Berberich case, how strict can the Commission be in applying article 5(3) against the respondent government?

Should the reasonableness test of article 5(3) be applied in a case such as Berberich at the preliminary (admissibility) stage, where there is no further avenue of review if the decision goes against the applicant?

X, Y AND Z v. AUSTRIA
European Commission of Human Rights, Application No. 5049/71.
1973 Yearbook of the European Convention on Human Rights 112.*

[The applicants were West German citizens charged in a West German court with murder during World War II, when they were Gestapo agents. In the course of the pretrial proceedings, the German court requested an Austrian court (the Regional Court of Krems) to take on its behalf the testimony of a witness then incarcerated in Krems. Counsel for the applicants asked to be present at the interrogation in the Austrian court. This request was denied by the Austrian authorities. (A previous request by the same counsel in relation to another Austrian witness had also been denied, and an appeal from that denial had failed.) The witness was examined without the applicants' counsel being present, but a copy of the transcribed testimony was furnished to him. Counsel then submitted questions he wished asked of the witness. The Austrian court complied with this request, but again outside the presence of counsel.]

The applicants have complained to the Commission that the Austrian Government have refused to allow their counsel to participate in the hearing on commission by a judge of the Krems Regional Court of a witness against them. They allege that, thereby, they were prevented from putting questions to this witness through counsel and that, consequently, their rights under Article 6(3)(d) of the Convention were violated.

The Commission, in this respect, has first examined the question whether the applicants' complaint raises an issue in connection with the right to a fair trial within the meaning of Article 6(1) of the Convention. This provides that "in the determination of * * * any

---

* © 1975 by Martinus Nijhoff, The Hague, Netherlands. Reprinted by permission of Kluwer Academic Publishers.

criminal charge against him, everyone is entitled to a fair and public hearing * * * ". However, having had regard to the particular features of the proceedings in question, the Commission finds that this hearing on commission of the witness against the applicants did not form part of the criminal proceedings whereby the charges against the applicants were determined. This provision of Article 6(1) is, consequently, not applicable to the above hearing and is irrelevant to the applicants' complaint.

For this reason, the applicants' complaint, as regards any such question of a fair hearing, is incompatible *ratione materiae* with the provisions of the Convention within the meaning of Article 27(2) of the Convention.

The Commission has then had regard to the terms of Article 6(3)(d) of the Convention which provides that "everyone charged with a criminal offence has the following minimum rights * * * (d) to examine or have examined witnesses against him and to obtain the attendance and examination of witnesses on his behalf under the same conditions as witnesses against him". In this respect it notes the respondent Government's objection that this provision is not applicable in the circumstances of the present case since the applicants were not charged before an Austrian court. The Commission has accordingly first examined the question whether it has competence *ratione personae* to deal with the applicants' complaint which was brought against the Austrian Government. In this respect it finds that the Austrian authorities were fully responsible for the form and conduct of this hearing on commission, including the question of who should participate at the hearing. Indeed, this hearing was exclusively governed by the rules of the Austrian Code of Criminal Procedure and their interpretation by the Austrian authorities. The Commission therefore decides that it cannot reject the applicants' complaint as being incompatible *ratione personae* with the Convention.

The Commission has already found that the provisions of Article 6(1) did not apply to the present applicants, since their complaints were not related to that stage of the criminal proceedings whereby the charges against them were determined. This finding, however, does not affect the applicability of Article 6(3)(d) to these complaints since its provisions expressly apply to "everyone charged with a criminal offence" and, consequently, to the present applicants who were charged with a criminal offence, albeit before the German courts. Their complaints cannot therefore be rejected on the ground that they fall outside the scope of Article 6(3)(d). The Commission consequently finds that the Austrian authorities were in the present case bound to observe the said provisions of Article 6(3)(d) of the Convention.

The Commission, having established that Article 6(3)(d) is applicable to the applicants' complaint against Austria, has then examined the question whether or not this provision was in fact respected by the Krems Regional Court. Having had regard to the course of the proceedings and, in particular, to the circumstance that the witness against the applicants was, on their request, reheard on commission after the applicants had studied the record of his first examination, the Commission finds that the applicants' complaint under Article 6(3)(d) is manifestly ill-founded under Article 27(2) of the Convention since their right "to examine or have examined witnesses" has been respected by the Austrian authorities.

For these reasons, the Commission

Declares this application inadmissible.

INCOMPATIBLE AND/OR ILL-FOUNDED

Note first of all that the Commission raised, on its own, the question of possible violation of article 6(1). That is not an unusual occurrence, as the Commission has considered it incumbent upon itself to examine all possible violations once it is properly seized of a colorable claim of a single violation. Other human rights monitoring bodies have done the same thing.

Why was any complaint under article 6(1) rejected as incompatible with the Convention, while the complaint under article 6(3)(d) was rejected as manifestly ill-founded?

If the applicants had joined the West German government as a respondent, would the application as to it have been held incompatible *ratione personae?*

Both of the above cases involved petitions claiming that specific governmental acts directed uniquely against the petitioner(s) violated the Convention, rather than claims of massive violations of the rights of large numbers of people. In that connection, compare article 25 of the European Convention—which aims at the individual violation—with the U.N. petitioning procedure under ECOSOC Resolution 1503—which aims at the consistent pattern of gross violations. The question arises whether, under the European Convention, an individual petitioner may in effect bring a class action in cases involving consistent patterns of violations affecting not only himself but others not joined in the petition. Such a case was Donnelly v. United Kingdom.[d] Seven applicants alleged that they had been tortured by British security officers in Northern Ireland, as part of a general administrative practice directed at those taken into custody for activities in connection with the civil strife there. The respondent state argued, inter alia, that the article 24 inter-state procedure was intended to deal with challenges to official government policies, but that was not the purpose of the individual

---

d. Application Nos. 5577–5583/72, in 1973 Yearbook of the European Convention on Human Rights 212.

petitioning procedure under article 25.[e] The Commission said:[f]

> The Commission first observes that, under Article 25 of the Convention, it may only receive petitions from a person, organisation or group of individuals "claiming to be the victim of a violation by one of the High Contracting Parties of the rights set forth in this Convention". It follows that the Commission can only consider the present applications insofar as they have been brought by the seven applicants on their own behalf and the Commission cannot, within the framework of the present case, examine whether or not there has been a violation of the rights under the Convention of any other individuals. However, neither Article 25, nor any other provisions in the Convention, *inter alia* Article 27(1)(b), prevent an individual applicant from raising before the Commission a complaint in respect of an alleged administrative practice in breach of the Convention provided that he brings *prima facie* evidence of such a practice and of his being a victim of it.*

How bold can the Commission be in considering, and upholding on the merits, individual petitions challenging not just isolated acts by officials of governments, but official government policies?[g]

Would any of the cases examined so far in this Subsection have been found admissible under the U.N. petitioning procedure, as embodied in ECOSOC Resolution 1503 and Resolution 1 of the Human Rights Sub-Commission? Under the first Optional Protocol to the U.N. Covenant on Civil and Political Rights? (Assume that in each case the alleged governmental acts were reliably attested by persons with direct knowledge of them, that the petitions contained no insulting or abusive language, and that they had not previously been submitted to the European Commission. The Resolutions and Protocol are in the Documents volume.)

Two 1991 cases involving alleged human rights violations on Cyprus demonstrate some of the difficulties that may arise as the Council of Europe expands to include states that may not be as politically stable as the Western European states have been after World War II. One of the cases raises significant questions concerning the Commission's role in interpreting and applying an article 25 declaration that purports to

---

e. See Boyle & Hannum, Individual Applications under the European Convention on Human Rights and the Concept of Administrative Practice: The Donnelly Case, 68 Am.J.Int'l L. 440 (1974), discussing not only this point but exhaustion of domestic remedies.

f. 1973 Yearbook, supra note d, at 260.

* © 1975 by Martinus Nijhoff, The Hague, Netherlands. Reprinted by permission of Kluwer Academic Publishers.

g. For discussion of the Commission's later decision backtracking somewhat from the 1973 decision, see Hannum & Boyle, The Donnelly Case, Administrative Practice and Domestic Remedies Under the European Convention: One Step Forward and Two Steps Back, 71 Am.J.Int'l L. 316 (1977).

limit the declaring state's exposure. The cases may also be relevant to human rights monitoring procedures in other organizations, such as the U.N. and OAS, that face questions arising in newly-proclaimed states, in occupied territories, or in territories otherwise not under the effective control of a central government.

Both cases involve northern Cyprus. Turkey invaded Cyprus in 1974 after a coup led by officers from Greece overthrew the Cypriot government of Archbishop Makarios. Turkey established control in northern Cyprus, which is heavily populated by people of Turkish descent. The island was effectively partitioned, with Turkish control in the north, Greek Cypriot control in the south, and a U.N. buffer zone in between. In 1983 the northern area proclaimed itself an independent state, the Turkish Republic of Northern Cyprus. It was not recognized by other states, within the Council of Europe or elsewhere. The situation remained at an impasse when these cases were brought.

Turkey's article 25 declaration, under which the first case was brought, stems from an earlier proceeding before the Commission. In the mid–1980s France, Norway, Denmark, Sweden and the Netherlands had brought an inter-state proceeding against Turkey under article 24. They alleged pervasive human rights violations in Turkey proper during the period 1980–1982, when Turkey was under martial law. That case culminated in a "friendly settlement" under *articles 28* and *30*. Part of the settlement required Turkey to submit a series of reports to the Commission on measures it would take to rectify the situation. The final report was due on February 1, 1987. Just before it was due Turkey filed a declaration recognizing the right of individual petition under article 25, apparently as a demonstration of its good faith effort to improve its human rights record. The declaration said that it extended only to acts and omissions in Turkey. It is quoted in the decision below, which considers the validity and effect of the territorial limitation.

CHRYSOSTOMOS v. TURKEY

European Commission of Human Rights, Application No. 15299/89.
12 Human Rights L.J. 113 (1991).*

THE FACTS

[Three Cypriots brought petitions against Turkey alleging that they were physically abused and detained by Turkish troops and Turkish Cypriot armed police in the buffer area of Cyprus and in Northern Cyprus. The alleged violations occurred when they were forcibly removed from demonstrations opposing the continuing partition of Cyprus.

[After setting forth the applicants' complaints and the Turkish government's denial, the Commission continued:]

* Reprinted by permission of N.P. Engel Verlag.

II. Turkey's Declaration Under Article 25 of the Convention:

1. On 28 January 1987 the Government of Turkey deposited the following declaration with the Secretary General of the Council of Europe pursuant to Article 25 of the Convention:

> The Government of Turkey, acting pursuant to Article 25(1) of the Convention * * *, hereby declares to accept the competence of the European Commission of Human Rights to receive petitions according to Article 25 of the Convention subject to the following:
>
> (i) the recognition of the right of petition extends only to allegations concerning acts and omissions of public authorities in Turkey performed within the boundaries of the territory to which the Constitution of the Republic of Turkey is applicable;
>
> [Subparagraphs (ii) through (v) set forth additional limitations.]

2. On 29 January 1987 the Secretary General of the Council of Europe transmitted the above declaration to the other High Contracting Parties to the Convention and added:

> At the time this declaration was deposited, I drew the Turkish authorities' attention to the fact that this notification made pursuant to Article 25(3) of the Convention in no way prejudges the legal questions which might arise concerning the validity of the said declaration.

[The government of Greece objected to the limitations in the Turkish declaration. The governments of Sweden, Luxembourg, Denmark, Norway and Belgium reserved their right to object. The government of Turkey replied that the conditions attached to its declaration did not amount to reservations within the meaning of Vienna Convention on the Law of Treaties *article 2(1)(d)* because they "do not purport to modify or to exclude any of the legal provisions of the Convention. The 'conditions' have the only purpose to define and limit the granting of additional power and authority which Turkey as a Contracting State has on its own volition bestowed upon the Commission." Turkey also pointed out that article 25 does not expressly prohibit conditions.

[The Commission continued:]

The Law

I. The Commission's Competence in Relation to the Declaration Made by Turkey Under Article 25 of the Convention:

* * *

3. The applicants claim to be victims of violations of the Convention by Turkey in the "buffer zone" and the northern part of Cyprus. The respondent Government, invoking the territorial limitation in paragraph (i) of their declaration of 28 January 1987, submit that Turkey has not recognised the Commission's competence to examine the present applications, which lie outside the territorial framework specified in the declaration. The applicants contest the validity of this

territorial limitation and its applicability to the present case. The respondent Government state that the declaration has been conceived as a whole and that the rejection of any of the conditions contained therein would make the declaration inexistent.

4. The Commission must first determine the validity of Turkey's declaration and its scope. Its competence for this determination has expressly been recognised by Turkey in earlier correspondence (letter of 26 June 1987 to the Secretary General) and at the hearing before the Commission. Moreover, the Secretary General of the Council of Europe has on 28 January 1987, when Turkey deposited her declaration, drawn the Turkish authorities' attention to the fact that the notification of the declaration to the other High Contracting Parties "in no way prejudges the legal questions which might arise concerning the validity of the said declaration".

(a) The Meaning of the Territorial Limitation in Para. (i) of Turkey's Declaration

* * *

7. The Commission finds that the territorial restriction in Turkey's declaration of 28 January 1987 must be interpreted in the light of its clear object and purpose in view of the previous Inter-State cases brought by Cyprus against Turkey. The applicants have stated earlier: "It is generally recognised that this restriction has the exclusive purpose of seeking to avoid the responsibility of Turkey for breaches of the European Convention arising from Turkish actions in the Turkish occupied area of Cyprus."

8. The Commission finds on the basis of the above interpretation that the acts complained of in the present applications come within the scope of the territorial restriction in Turkey's declaration of 28 January 1987. The Commission must therefore determine whether its jurisdiction is limited by this clause.

(b) The Validity of the Limitations in Paras. (i) to (v) of Turkey's Declaration

* * *

11. The * * * limitations contained in paras. (i) to (v) of Turkey's declaration * * * are not, like temporal restrictions, covered by paragraph 2 of Article 25 but, as limitations of a different character (ratione loci, ratione materiae and ratione personae), not expressly authorised in this Article. The Commission has examined whether they are nevertheless compatible with Article 25, as claimed by the respondent Government.

12. Article 31 para. 1 of the Vienna Convention on the Law of Treaties provides that a treaty shall be interpreted in good faith in accordance with "the ordinary meaning to be given to the terms of the treaty in their context and in the light of its object and purpose".

13. As regards the ordinary meaning of Article 25 para. 1 of the European Convention on Human Rights, the Commission considers that the wording "the rights set forth in this Convention" presupposes total, not partial recognition. Otherwise the Convention would in Article 25 para. 1 have referred to "any" or "some" rights.

14. The Commission has next considered Article 25 in the context of the Convention as a whole.

15. It notes that, under Article 64 para. 1 first sentence, any State may, when signing the Convention or when depositing its instrument of ratification, make a reservation in respect of any particular provision of the Convention to the extent that any law then in force in its territory is not in conformity with the provision. It follows from the clear wording of this provision ("when signing the Convention or when depositing its instrument of ratification") that a High Contracting Party may not, when at a latter stage recognising the right of individual petition, substantially modify its Convention obligations for the purpose of proceedings under Article 25. The respondent Government have repeatedly stated that the additional clauses in their declaration under Article 25 are not to be considered as "reservations" in the sense of international treaty law.

* * *

19. The Commission has further examined the five conditions in paras. (i) to (v) of Turkey's declaration under Article 25 in the light of the object and purpose of the Convention.

* * *

22. The Commission finds in the present case that the character of the Convention, as a constitutional instrument of European public order in the field of human rights, excludes application by analogy, as suggested by the respondent Government, of the State practice under Article 36 para. 3 of the Statute of the International Court of Justice. Declarations under this clause create mere reciprocal agreements between contracting States. The Commission notes that Article 36 para. 3 of the Statute does not, like Article 25 of the European Convention on Human Rights, concern petitions brought by individuals but applications by States. State applications are in the Convention regulated by Article 24.

* * *

[The Commission also examined the practice of other parties to the European Convention, in accordance with *article 31(3)* of the Vienna Convention on the Law of Treaties. It concluded that the practice did not support Turkey's position.]

30. The Commission has finally examined the territorial restriction in para. (i) of Turkey's declaration in the light of Articles 1 and 63 of the Convention, as applied by the Convention organs in the determination of their competence ratione loci.

31. Article 1 of the Convention provides:

The High Contracting Parties shall secure to everyone within their jurisdiction the rights and freedoms defined in Section 1 of this Convention.

32. The applicants claim that the alleged actions of Turkish military forces in Cyprus, and of persons acting under their authority, fall within Turkey's jurisdiction within the meaning of Article 1. The Commission recalls that the application of the Convention extends beyond the national frontiers of the High Contracting Parties and includes acts of State organs abroad. It has previously stated in Applications Nos. 6780/74 and 6950/75 (Cyprus v. Turkey, Dec. 26.5.75, D.R. 2 p. 125 at pp. 136–137), in inter-State proceedings instituted under Article 24 of the Convention:

In Article 1 of the Convention, the High Contracting Parties undertake to secure the rights and freedoms defined in Section 1 to everyone 'within their jurisdiction' (in the French text: 'relevant de leur juridiction'). The Commission finds that this term is not, as submitted by the respondent Government, equivalent to or limited to the national territory of the High Contracting Party concerned. It is clear from the language, in particular of the French text, and the object of this Article, and from the purpose of the Convention as a whole, that the High Contracting Parties are bound to secure the said rights and freedoms to all persons under their actual authority and responsibility, whether that authority is exercised within their territory or abroad. * * *

It follows from the above interpretation of Article 1 that the Commission's competence to examine the applications, insofar as they concern alleged violations of the Convention in Cyprus, cannot be excluded on the grounds that Turkey, the respondent Party in the present case, has neither annexed any part of Cyprus nor, according to the respondent Government, established either military or civil government there.

It remains to be examined whether Turkey's responsibility under the Convention is otherwise engaged because persons or property in Cyprus have in the course of her military action come under her actual authority and responsibility at the material times. In this respect it is not contested by the respondent Government that Turkish armed forces have entered the island of Cyprus, operating solely under the direction of the Turkish Government and under established rules governing the structure and command of these armed forces including the establishment of military courts. It follows that these armed forces are authorised agents of Turkey and that they bring any other persons or property in Cyprus 'within the jurisdiction' of Turkey, in the sense of Article 1 of the Convention, to the extent that they exercise control over such persons or property. Therefore, insofar as these armed forces, by their acts or omissions, affect such persons' rights or freedoms under the Convention, the responsibility of Turkey is engaged.

33. The above view has been confirmed and further developed by the Commission in Application No. 8007/77 (Cyprus v. Turkey, Dec. 10.7.78, D.R. 13 p. 85 at pp. 148–150), in the following terms:

> The Commission * * * is bound to observe [that Cyprus] has since 1974 been prevented from exercising its jurisdiction in the northern part of its territory by the presence there of armed forces of another High Contracting Party, namely Turkey; that the recognition by Turkey of the Turkish Cypriot administration in that area as 'Turkish Federated State of Cyprus' does not, according to the respondent Government's own submissions, affect the continuing existence of the Republic of Cyprus as a single State and High Contracting Party to the Convention; and that, consequently, the 'Turkish Federated State of Cyprus' cannot be regarded as an entity which exercises 'jurisdiction', within the meaning of Article 1 of the Convention, over any part of Cyprus.
>
> The Commission concludes that Turkey's jurisdiction in the north of the Republic of Cyprus, existing by reason of the presence of her armed forces there which prevents exercise of jurisdiction by the applicant Government, cannot be excluded on the ground that jurisdiction in that area is allegedly exercised by the 'Turkish Federated State of Cyprus'.

34. Article 1 of the Convention, as interpreted above, supports the view that the territorial restriction in Turkey's declaration is not permitted under Article 25.

35. As to the question whether Article 63 could be invoked in respect of the view that certain territorial limitations may validly be added to declarations made under Article 25 the Commission observes the following.

36. Article 63 paras. 1 and 4 provide:

"(1) Any State may at the time of its ratification or at any time thereafter declare by notification addressed to the Secretary General of the Council of Europe that the present Convention shall extend to all or any of the territories for whose international relations it is responsible."

"(4) Any State which has made a declaration in accordance with paragraph 1 of this Article may at any time thereafter declare on behalf of one or more of the territories to which the declaration relates that it accepts the competence of the Commission to receive petitions from individuals, non-governmental organisations or groups of individuals in accordance with Article 25 of the Convention."

37. The Commission observes that Article 63 cannot be applied directly in the present case. The northern part of Cyprus is not a territory for whose international relations Turkey is responsible in the

sense of this Article. Application of Article 63 para. 4 by analogy—in the sense that a High Contracting Party may validly exclude the application of a declaration recognising the right of individual petition to territories which do not clearly form part of its own metropolitan territory—is not suggested by the respondent Government who leave this issue to the Commission's determination. The applicants, who contest the legality of Turkey's presence in the north of Cyprus, deny the applicability of Article 63 in the present case.

38. The Commission has considered whether application by analogy of Article 63 para. 4 of the Convention to other non-metropolitan territories would in the circumstances of the present case be compatible with the object and purpose of the Convention.

39. The applicants submit that such application of Article 63 to Turkish acts in Northern Cyprus would be illegitimate, given the illegality under international law of Turkey's presence in that area. The respondent Government submit, as regards control of the implementation of the Convention by Turkey, that Turkey may be challenged before the Commission for alleged non-observance of the provisions of the Convention in the framework of Article 24.

40. The Commission has again had regard to the character of the Convention, as described above, and to the principle, reflected in its case-law under Article 1, that application of the Convention extends beyond the national frontiers of the High Contracting Parties and includes acts of State organs abroad (cf. paras. 32 and 33 above). The Commission also recalls that the Convention is intended to guarantee "not rights that are theoretical or illusory but rights that are practical and effective" (Eur. Court H.R., Artico judgment of 13 May 1980, Series A no. 37 p. 34 para. 33). The principle that Convention rights should serve a practical purpose ("effet utile") applies in the Commission's view not only to the rights defined in Section I of the Convention but also to the fundamental procedural right of individual petition under Article 25 as soon as a State has recognised that right. The Commission finally refers to its earlier observations at para. 9 of its decision of 26 May 1975 (reproduced at para. 32 above) concerning the purpose of Article 63, and at paras. 23 and 24 of its decision of 10 July 1978 (reproduced at para. 33 above) concerning the restriction, resulting from the presence of Turkish armed forces in the north of Cyprus, on the exercise of jurisdiction by Cyprus, a High Contracting Party to the Convention. While not called upon to pronounce on the legality under international law of Turkey's presence in the north of Cyprus the Commission finds that application by analogy of Article 63 would be incompatible with the specific situation in that area.

41. The Commission finds that application by analogy of Article 63 para. 4 would in the circumstances of the present applications be incompatible with the object and purpose of the Convention.

42. The Commission finds that the restrictions contained in paras. (i) to (v) of Turkey's declaration under Article 25 of 28 January 1987 are not permitted by this Article.

* * *

c) The Validity of Turkey's Recognition of the Right of Individual Petition

43. [Turkey argued that the territorial limitation in its declaration was an essential condition to its willingness to submit to individual petitions. If the limitation was rejected, Turkey's recognition of the right of individual petition would no longer exist.]

44. The Commission recalls that its competence to determine the scope and validity of Turkey's declaration under Article 25 has expressly been recognised by Turkey (cf. para. 4 above) and that Turkey has repeatedly stated that the restrictions contained in paras. (i) to (v) of the declaration "cannot be considered as 'reservations' in the sense of international treaty law".

45. The Commission must interpret Turkey's intention, when she made her declaration on 28 January 1987, as expressed at that time. It recalls that the declaration was deposited after a friendly settlement had been reached in proceedings brought against Turkey by France, Norway, Denmark, Sweden and the Netherlands (Applications Nos. 9940–9944/82 = 6 HRLJ 331 (1985)) and shortly before the expiry, on 1 February 1987, of the period provided for the reporting procedure agreed in the settlement (see Comm. Report 7.12.85, D.R. 44 pp. 31, 38f.). By making the declaration under Article 25 Turkey then manifested her will to be bound by the Convention system also as regards individual applications under Article 25.

46. Where a State has clearly expressed the intention to be bound under Article 25, but has added restrictions to its declaration which are incompatible with the Convention, the main intention of the State must prevail. The Commission finds Turkey's present statement, accepting to be bound by its declaration under Article 25 only if all conditions contained therein are valid, to be incompatible both with her above earlier statements and with the object and purpose of the Convention. It therefore cannot prevail within the framework of this instrument.

47. The Commission recalls that the Court, when finding that an interpretative declaration by Switzerland did not satisfy two of the requirements of Article 64 of the Convention, "with the result that it must be held to be invalid", found it at the same time "beyond doubt that Switzerland is, and regards itself as, bound by the Convention irrespective of the validity of the declaration" (Belilos judgment of 29 April 1988, Eur. Court H.R., Series A no. 132 p. 28 para. 60). The Commission notes in this context a principle frequently applied in the interpretation of legal instruments where parts are found to be invalid. This rule is expressed in the Latin phrase "ut res magis valeat quam pereat" [that the thing may have effect rather than be destroyed].

48. It follows from the above considerations that, by her declaration of 28 January 1987, Turkey has validly, and with a temporal limitation only, recognised the right of individual petition under Article 25 of the Convention.

49. The Commission therefore finds that it is competent ratione loci, under Turkey's declaration under Article 25 of the Convention of 28 January 1987, to deal with the present applications.

TURKEY'S DECLARATION

Did the Commission decide, in effect if not in so many words, that Turkey's restriction under *article 25* amounted to a reservation, despite Turkey's disclaimers?

Did the Commission do justice to Turkey's arguments based on *articles 25* and *63* of the Convention? During the Convention's drafting process, the article that became article 63 was called the "Colonial Clause." [h] If that accurately describes the intended coverage, does it affect Turkey's argument?

What was wrong with the analogy to ICJ Statute *article 36(2)* declarations, which clearly may be loaded down with territorial and other limitations?

Under *article 32* of the Vienna Convention on the Law of Treaties, the Commission presumably could have examined the preparatory work to article 25 of the European Convention. It would not have learned much. The preparatory work does not reveal that any attention was given to possible territorial or other limitations to article 25 declarations. The focus seems to have been on the question whether states should be subject to the right of petition simply by becoming parties to the Convention.[i] The compromise text that became article 25 answered that question in the negative.

If the territorial limitation attached to Turkey's declaration was tantamount to an impermissible reservation, why wouldn't the effect be that Turkey's declaration becomes a nullity? Turkey had argued, in effect, that without the territorial limitation (and the other restrictions it attached to its declaration), it would not have consented to subject itself to individual petitions. Consider also the discussion of reservations at pages 905–06 supra.

At the time of the Chrysostomos decision, Turkey recognized the Turkish Republic of Northern Cyprus as an independent state, though other governments did not. If it was not an independent state, it was

---

h. See 5 Collected Edition of the "Travaux Préparatoires" of the European Convention on Human Rights 104, 110 (1979).

i. See 2 id. at 280; 5 id. at 8, 63–64, 68, 98, 102–04, 108–16. There was some discussion about limiting the right of petition to nationals of the respondent state, if the right were to apply automatically to all states parties. 5 id. at 108–14.

part of the state of Cyprus, not of Turkey, and the Turkish armed forces in northern Cyprus would be an occupying force. The Fourth Geneva Convention, on the protection of civilians, imposes detailed obligations on occupying forces, though several of the protective provisions cease to apply a year after the close of active military operations. Protocol I to the Geneva Conventions imposes additional obligations for states parties to it, including obligations applying to occupied territory until the occupation ceases. The Geneva Conventions do not create supervisory bodies comparable to those established by the European Convention, although Protocol I has an optional provision for an International Fact–Finding Commission with authority not only to investigate, but also to make recommendations. Turkey is a party to the Geneva Conventions, but was not a party to Protocol I at the time of the Chrysostomos decision. The International Committee of the Red Cross does its best to see that the obligations in the Geneva Conventions and Protocol I are observed, mainly through quiet and unofficial diplomacy, but also through mobilization of shame in extreme cases. Does all this shed any light on the Commission's determination that non-Turkish citizens in northern Cyprus were "within Turkey's jurisdiction" under *article 1* of the European Convention? Which way does it cut?

Under the Commission's decision in this case, would all civilians in any territory temporarily occupied by the armed forces of a state party to the European Convention be "within its jurisdiction" under article 1, even if the occupied territory is not part of another state party to the Convention?

Does the decision in the Chrysostomos case create a risk that states parties to human rights conventions may decline to subject themselves to the petitioning process if and when they have a choice?

When this was written, the Chrysostomos case was still before the European Commission on the merits. The Council of Europe's Committee of Ministers had taken the unusual step of publicly urging Turkey to cooperate with the Commission.[j] Inevitably, there will be more to be said about the case than has been said here.

AN v. CYPRUS
European Commission of Human Rights, Application No. 18270/91.
13 Human Rights L.J. 153 (1992).[*]

THE FACTS

* * *

The applicants are the Turkish Cypriot members of a movement for an independent and federal Cyprus, an unregistered association of Turkish and Greek Cypriots. The movement has a Turkish Cypriot co-ordinating committee in the North and a Greek Cypriot co-ordinating

---

[j] Committee of Ministers Res. DH (91) 41 (1991).

[*] Reprinted by permission of N.P. Engel Verlag.

committee in the South of Cyprus. In general, the Turkish Cypriot authorities do not permit the Turkish Cypriot members of the movement to visit the buffer zone or Southern Cyprus and to return to the North. Only occasionally and on an arbitrary basis are such permits granted. Thus, out of 52 requests for permission to visit the buffer zone or Southern Cyprus only 14 were granted during the last 17 months.

The present application is confined to the restrictions on the applicants' freedom of movement during the last six months before the introduction of the application.

2. *Relevant Domestic Law and Practice*

The applicants submit that in Northern Cyprus there is no law regulating the restrictions which may reasonably be imposed, in a democratic society, on the freedom of movement within Cyprus. The relevant decree of 11 July 1986 is unconstitutional.

In order to get permission for crossing over to the buffer zone, the applicants usually submit to the competent Turkish Cypriot authority a written application, giving reasons, but they never receive a written reply or written permit. Occasionally, when permission is granted for crossing over, the authority sends a circular to the police stationed at the control point at the Ledra Palace Gate, Nicosia, containing a list of individuals permitted to cross over to the South and to return to the North. Where an application for a permit is rejected—which is usually the case—no written reply is issued; the police at the control point simply do not permit the passage as they have not received the necessary circular.

Protests against this state of affairs and discussions with the Turkish Cypriot authorities have been to no avail.

The applicants further observe that the entry-exit point at the Ledra Palace Gate is within "the first Degree Militarily Prohibited Region". Therefore the military authorities "have a say in granting the permits for crossing over. * * * The Turkish Cypriot Military, Security and Police Authorities are in practice under the command of Cyprus-Turkish Peace Keeping Force of Turkey which is stationed in Northern Cyprus."

The possibility of getting local redress in Northern Cyprus is uncertain because the Turkish Cypriot courts are likely to treat the freedom of movement from Northern to Southern Cyprus or vice versa as a political matter not judicially reviewable and therefore will decline to assume jurisdiction; their decision will not be binding on the military authorities of Turkey.

COMPLAINT

The applicants invoke the freedom of movement guaranteed in Article 2 of Protocol No. 4 to the Convention.

The Law

Article 1 of the Convention provides that the High Contracting Parties shall secure "to everyone within their jurisdiction" the rights and freedoms defined in Section 1. The Commission has considered whether, in the light of the situation which has been prevailing in the north of Cyprus since 1974, the Republic of Cyprus can be held responsible for the acts of the Turkish Cypriot authorities complained of in the present application.

The Commission has previously observed that "the European Convention on Human Rights continues to apply to the whole of the territory of the Republic of Cyprus" and that the recognition by Turkey of the Turkish Cypriot administration in the north of Cyprus as "Turkish Federated State of Cyprus" does not affect "the continuing existence of the Republic of Cyprus as a single State and High Contracting Party to the Convention" (No. 8007/77, Cyprus v. Turkey, Dec. 10.7.78, D.R. 13, p. 85 at pp. 149–150).

At the same time, however, the Commission has also found that the Government of the Republic of Cyprus "have since 1974 been prevented from exercising their jurisdiction in the north of the island. This restriction on the actual exercise of jurisdiction * * * is due to the presence of Turkish armed forces" (ibid.).

The Commission now finds that the authority of the respondent Government is in fact still limited to the southern part of Cyprus. It follows that the Republic of Cyprus cannot be held responsible under Article 1 of the Convention for the acts of Turkish Cypriot authorities in the north of Cyprus of which the present applicants complain.

The Commission concludes that the application is incompatible with the provisions of the Convention.

WITHIN THE TERRITORY BUT NOT WITHIN THE JURISDICTION

If there is a single state of Cyprus to which the European Convention applies, how could the Commission hold that events in northern Cyprus are not "within the jurisdiction" of the Republic of Cyprus? Could *article 1* of the European Convention be read to impose strict responsibility on each contracting party for the acts of public authorities in any part of its territory, whether or not it effectively controls the authorities there?

Suppose a state party to the European Convention loses control over part of its territory, not because of an invasion from another state, but because an indigenous group has effectively seized control under a claim of self-determination. If the indigenous group exercises governmental functions within its area, would the central government be responsible for what goes on there, under article 1? Would it matter whether or not the central government had tried unsuccessfully to maintain control over the area by force?

To what extent are these Cyprus cases likely to be useful to monitoring bodies of other human rights systems outside Europe? Are the U.N. and regional systems designed to deal with situations involving a loss of control by a central government over part of its territory?

If the European Commission finds a petition admissible, it is directed by *article 28* of the European Convention to perform essentially a conciliation function. Would you expect that function to be hampered by its exercise of an adjudicative function at the admissibility stage?[k]

If no friendly settlement is reached, the Commission's report includes its opinion on whether the respondent state has violated the Convention. The report is submitted not only to the Committee of Ministers, but to the state concerned. The state is not at liberty to publish it, though the Committee of Ministers may (and usually does). See *articles 31–32*. What calls for the prohibition against publication by states?

C. THE ROLE OF THE COMMITTEE OF MINISTERS

When the Commission submits a report on the merits to the state concerned and to the Committee of Ministers, a three-month period ensues during which the Commission or any of the states mentioned in *article 48* may refer the case to the European Court. If a case is to be referred to the Court, it is usually by the Commission. It refers more cases to the Court than it leaves in the hands of the Committee of Ministers.[a] If the case is not referred to the Court, the Committee of Ministers decides whether the respondent state has violated the Convention.

The petitioner has no standing before the Committee of Ministers, and may not submit a written statement unless the Committee requests one. As things currently stand, the Commission's report is not even sent to the petitioner unless the Committee of Ministers decides to do so after obtaining the consent of the respondent state.[b] However, if and when Protocol No. 9 enters into force, the Commission's report will be

---

k. As of January 1, 1989, 77 cases before the Commission had resulted in friendly settlement; 78 cases had been decided by the Committee of Ministers under *article 32*. Council of Europe, Stock-taking on the European Convention on Human Rights, Supp.1988, at 108, 112.

a. See A.G. Mower, Regional Human Rights: A Comparative Study of the West European and Inter-American Systems 98 (1991).

b. See P. van Dijk & G. van Hoof, Theory and Practice of the European Convention on Human Rights 196–97 (2d ed. 1990).

sent to the petitioner when it is sent to the respondent state.^c

In practice, the Committee of Ministers almost always agrees with the Commission's determination on the merits, and makes a formal decision to that effect. If it decides that there has been a violation, it considers the appropriate remedy—usually in the same formal resolution, without prescribing a period during which the respondent state is to take measures prescribed by the Committee. If the respondent state has taken steps to correct the offending practice for the future, and if the petitioner can show no out-of-pocket losses, the Committee is inclined to take no further action. Until recently, under one of its rules of procedure, if it decided that compensation was due, it recommended that the respondent government pay the petitioner a designated amount.

This practice was put to the test when Italy failed to make the Committee's recommended payments to petitioners who had successfully challenged the long delays in adjudicating their rights in Italian courts. The Committee had agreed with the Commission that Italy was in violation of article 6(1), which requires "a fair and public hearing within a reasonable time" in civil and criminal cases, and had recommended that Italy pay substantial compensatory damages to the petitioners. When Italy ignored the Committee's remonstrances, the Committee finally revoked its rule contemplating "recommended" damage payments.

In the cases against Italy, the Committee then adopted resolutions in which it "Holds, in accordance with Article 32, paragraph 2, of the Convention, that the Government of Italy is to pay to the applicant before [a designated date] the sum of [a specific amount] in respect of just satisfaction." [d]

Was the Committee's former practice consistent with *article 32*? Is its present practice?

One might wonder whether the transformation of recommendations into commands has any practical consequences. Article 3 of the Statute of the Council of Europe [e] requires every member to accept the principles of the rule of law and "the enjoyment by all persons within its jurisdiction of human rights and fundamental freedoms," and to collaborate in the realization of the aim of the Council (to achieve unity among its members in order to realize the ideals representing their common heritage). Article 8 authorizes the Committee of Ministers to suspend the right of representation of any member that has "seriously violated" article 3, and to request the member to withdraw from the organization. If the member fails to comply with the request, the Committee may expel it. Is the Committee likely to suspend or expel Italy or any other member for such things as the member's failure to

c. Protocol No. 9 appears in 30 Int'l Legal Materials 693 (1991).

d. See Committee of Ministers Resolutions DH (92) 2 and DH (92) 3 of Feb. 20, 1992, in 13 Human Rts. L.J. 181, 182 (1992).

e. May 5, 1949, 87 U.N.T.S. 103.

comply with commands relating to compensation for delays in its courts?

Would the Committee of Ministers' commands have greater practical significance than its recommendations, short of suspension or expulsion of a member state?

Occasionally the Committee of Ministers has been unable to muster the required two-thirds majority to make a decision under article 32(1). For example, in Huber v. Austria, the Commission had found a violation of article 6(1) and submitted its report to the Committee of Ministers. When the Committee was unable to obtain a two-thirds majority upholding the Commission, it decided to publish the Commission's report and took no further action.[f] To alleviate this problem, Protocol No. 10 to the European Convention was adopted in March 1992, enabling the Committee to act by a simple majority of the members entitled to sit.[g] At this writing the protocol had not entered into force.

Under *article 32(4)*, it is the Committee of Ministers' decision, not the Commission's, that is binding if a case is not referred to the Court. The Committee of Ministers is a political body composed of the Foreign Ministers, or their deputies, of the Council of Europe's member states. This essentially judicial function was given to the Committee of Ministers as a result of a compromise during the preparation of the Convention. States were not ready to submit to the European Court's jurisdiction simply by becoming parties to the Convention, but wanted some means for review of the Commission that would result in binding decisions.[h]

By now, states parties to the European Convention have become comfortable with the Commission and Court. Recall that all of them had accepted both the right of individual petition and the Court's jurisdiction as of mid-1992. Is there any reason to leave binding adjudicative authority in the Committee of Ministers?

If not, should the Commission's decisions on the merits be binding in the absence of a referral to the Court? Note that its determination that a petition is inadmissible is already effectively binding, since petitioners have no recourse under the Convention in such cases.

The Committee of Ministers plays a role not only when the Commission issues a report, but also when the European Court of Human Rights has rendered a judgment. These materials turn briefly to the latter role at the end of the next subsection.

---

f. See 1975 Y.B. of the European Convention on Human Rights 324.

g. Protocol No. 10 appears in 13 Human Rts. L.J. 182 (1992).

h. P. van Dijk & G. van Hoof, supra note b, at 192.

D. THE EUROPEAN COURT OF HUMAN RIGHTS

The caseload of the European Court of Human Rights has become quite substantial. In 1991, 93 contentious cases were referred to the Court—three times as many as in 1989, and more than twice as many as were referred to it from its inception through 1981.[a] The Court's advisory jurisdiction is another story.

As has already been noted, the European Court has only a very limited advisory jurisdiction under Protocol No. 2. It does not extend to the content or scope of the substantive rights in the Convention, or to any other question that might be considered in contentious proceedings. Only the Committee of Ministers may request an advisory opinion. So far, it has not done so.

The Court has created for itself a partial substitute for an advisory jurisdiction. In contentious cases, sometimes an individual petitioner, or the state involved, or even the Commission may request the Court to strike the case from its list. A "friendly settlement" between the parties may have occurred, or the petitioner for some other reason may have decided to drop the matter, or the respondent state may claim that it has provided full redress so the matter is moot. The Court's rules permit, but do not require, it to strike the case from its list in such instances. The Court has consistently reserved the right to proceed, on the ground that its "judgments in fact serve not only to decide those cases brought before the Court but, more generally, to elucidate, safeguard and develop the rules instituted by the Convention, thereby contributing to the observance by the States of the engagements undertaken by them as Contracting Parties."[b] Even when the Court does strike a case, it is careful to point out that it has found no reason of public policy to continue with it.[c]

Is this approach an adequate substitute for a useable, formal advisory jurisdiction? If not, should a new advisory jurisdiction be modeled on the Inter-American Court's?

A contentious case may be referred to the European Court of Human Rights by the Commission or by the states described in *article 48*, but only if all states concerned have accepted the Court's jurisdiction under *article 46* or if they have consented for purposes of the particular case. As things currently stand, an individual may not refer a matter to the Court. The explanation is that European states were not ready in 1950 to depart from the traditional rule that individuals are not proper parties before international tribunals, especially in

---

a. See Council of Europe, European Court of Human Rights: Survey of Activities 1959–1991, at 13 (1992). See also A.G. Mower, Regional Human Rights: A Comparative Study of the West European and Inter-American Systems 138 (1991).

b. Ireland v. United Kingdom, European Ct. of Human Rts. Series A, No. 25, at 62 (1978). This approach is not limited to inter-state cases. See the Guzzardi Case, Series A, No. 39, at 31 (1980).

c. See Owners' Services Ltd. v. Italy, European Ct. of Human Rts. Series A, No. 208, at 8 (1991).

matters as sensitive as those involving treatment by a government of its own nationals. The new optional petitioning procedure before what was then considered a nonadjudicative body (the Commission) was thought to be revolutionary enough.

A recent protocol, discussed below, will give individuals a qualified right to bring a case before the Court when the protocol enters into force. In the meantime, there are two back doors through which individuals may obtain access to the Court when the Commission finds against them on the merits. First, if the petitioner is a national of a member state other than the respondent, the state of nationality could refer the case to the Court under article 48(b). In addition, the Commission itself sometimes considers a matter sufficiently debatable and important to justify referring its own decision to the Court even though the decision has gone against the applicant.

Once a case has been referred to the Court by one of the parties mentioned in article 48, the applicant's position improves. Rule 30 of the Court's Revised Rules says in part:

> The applicant shall be represented by an advocate authorised to practise in any of the Contracting States and resident in the territory of one of them, or by any other person approved by the President [of the Court]. The President may, however, give leave to the applicant to present his own case, subject, if need be, to his being assisted by an advocate or other person as aforesaid.[d]

In practice, the applicant (or the applicant's counsel) participates fully in the proceedings. Contrast the much more limited role for the individual before the Inter-American Court of Human Rights. See page 1026 supra.

Protocol No. 9, adopted in November 1990 but not yet in force when this was written, would amend articles 44, 45 and 48 by adding "persons, non-governmental organisations or groups of individuals having submitted a petition under Article 25" to the list of parties with standing to bring a case before the Court. But it would also add this to article 48:

> If a case is referred to the Court only [by an article 25 petitioner], it shall first be submitted to a panel composed of three members of the Court. There shall sit as an *ex-officio* member of the panel the judge who is elected in respect of the High Contracting Party against which the complaint has been lodged, or, if there is none, a person of its choice who shall sit in the capacity of judge. If the complaint has been lodged against more than one High Contracting Party, the size of the panel shall be increased accordingly.
>
> If the case does not raise a serious question affecting the interpretation or application of the Convention and does not for

---

d. Revised Rules of Court, Nov. 24, 1982, Rule 30(1), in European Convention on Human Rights, Collected Texts 151, 162 (1987).

any other reason warrant consideration by the Court, the panel may, by a unanimous vote, decide that it shall not be considered by the Court. In that event, the Committee of Ministers shall decide, in accordance with the provisions of Article 32, whether there has been a violation of the Convention.[e]

Does this go far enough to provide standing to an individual petitioner? Too far?

Would a similar approach be feasible and desirable in the Inter-American system?

As we have seen, the Court normally sits in chambers of nine judges. The Commission's report is the basic document in the case, but the Court is not bound by the Commission's findings of fact or conclusions. The Court may take new evidence, orally or in writing. Witnesses may be examined by all parties to the case, including the Commission, and the judges may question them. But these powers are rarely used. In practice, the Court normally leaves fact-finding to the Commission. Compare the evidentiary proceedings before the Inter-American Court in the Velásquez Rodríguez case, supra page 1007. What would explain the difference?

We will look at just one substantive doctrine that has been developed in the European Court's jurisprudence. In several cases the Court has considered how much leeway it should give to local or national mores, customs and attitudes when it reviews the types of violation that occur most often in the Council of Europe countries: delays in civil proceedings, long pre-trial detentions in criminal cases, governmental invasions of privacy or restrictions on freedom of expression, rather than atrocities against the life, safety or fundamental dignity of the human person.

The case below deals with this "margin of appreciation" issue in the context of European Convention *article 10* (on freedom of expression).

OBERSCHLICK v. AUSTRIA
European Court of Human Rights, 1991.
Series A, No. 204.

[The applicant, Gerhard Oberschlick, was a journalist in Vienna. The case arose out of his publication in an Austrian periodical, *Forum,* of the text of a criminal information he and others had filed with the Vienna public prosecutor against Walter Grabher–Meyer. Mr. Grabher–Meyer was a politician who had made a public statement during an election campaign, to the effect that public family allowances for Austrian women should be increased by 50% in order to obviate any

---

e. Protocol No. 9, Nov. 6, 1990, 30 Int'l Legal Materials 693 (1991).

financial necessity for them to seek abortions, but the family allowances for immigrant women should be reduced by 50%.

[Mr. Oberschlick's criminal information, as published in *Forum*, alleged that Mr. Grabher–Meyer's statement was intended to place women in migrant workers' families and their unborn children in an inferior light, making it in the interests of the Austrian people that they have abortions. It was also alleged that this violated the Austrian constitutional law suppressing the National Socialist Party (NSDAP, or Nazi, party), because the statement corresponded with one of the basic Nazi objectives as stated in its 1920 Manifesto: to prevent further immigration into Germany and to expel all non-Germans who had immigrated since August 1914.

[The Vienna public prosecutor declined to prosecute Mr. Grabher–Meyer, who turned around and brought a private prosecution for defamation against Mr. Oberschlick. The Vienna Regional Court convicted him of defamation, and the Vienna Court of Appeal dismissed his appeal. It held that for the average reader, the publication would instill an attitude of contempt toward Mr. Grabher–Meyer; Mr. Oberschlick had disregarded the standards of fair journalism by insinuating motives that Mr. Grabher–Meyer had not expressed, in particular by suggesting that he had been guided by Nazi attitudes. A fine of 4,000 Austrian schillings was levied against Mr. Oberschlick.

[After exhausting his domestic remedies, Mr. Oberschlick submitted an application to the European Commission of Human Rights, in accordance with the petitioning procedure in the European Convention. The Commission found, inter alia, that Austria had violated article 10. The Austrian government took the case to the European Court of Human Rights, under articles 45 and 48 of the Convention.

[After disposing of a preliminary issue, as well as an issue about the fairness of Mr. Oberschlick's trial, the Court turned to freedom of expression as set forth in article 10 of the Convention. References in the judgment to the applicant are to Mr. Oberschlick.]

54. It was not disputed that the applicant's conviction by the Vienna Regional Court on 11 May 1984 * * *, as upheld by the Vienna Court of Appeal on 17 December 1984 * * *, constituted an "interference" with his right to freedom of expression.

Nor was it contested that this interference was "prescribed by law", namely Article 111 of the Criminal Code * * *, and was aimed at protecting the "reputation or rights of others" within the meaning of Article 10 § 2 of the Convention.

Argument before the Court concentrated on the question whether the interference was "necessary in a democratic society" to achieve that aim.

55. The applicant stressed that in a democratic society the role of periodicals like *Forum* included critical comment on social or legal policy proposals made by politicians. In this regard the press should be

free to choose the form of comment it thought most appropriate to its aim. In the present case he had limited himself to reporting and giving his own interpretation of Mr. Grabher–Meyer's proposal with regard to family allowances for foreigners. The Austrian courts had denied him the right not only of giving his opinion as to whether the proposal constituted a revival of National Socialism, but also of making historical comparisons on the basis of present facts.

The applicant's complaint was accepted by the Commission.

56. According to the Government, Mr. Oberschlick had overstepped the limits of justifiable and reasonable criticism. The impugned publication amounted, according to the Austrian courts, to an accusation that Mr. Grabher–Meyer held National Socialist ideas, the impact of this accusation being strengthened by the form chosen. They held that the applicant had not been able to prove that his accusation was well-founded and that he was therefore guilty of defamation.

In the opinion of the Government, it was not for the European Court to decide whether this reasoning of the Austrian courts was correct; this followed from the margin of appreciation to be left to the national authorities: they were better placed than the international judge to determine what matters should be regarded as defamatory, since this depended to a certain extent on national conceptions and legal culture.

B. General Principles

57. The Court recalls that freedom of expression, as secured in paragraph 1 of Article 10, constitutes one of the essential foundations of a democratic society and one of the basic conditions for its progress and for each individual's self-fulfilment. Subject to paragraph 2, it is applicable not only to "information" or "ideas" that are favourably received or regarded as inoffensive or as a matter of indifference, but also to those that offend, shock or disturb; such are the demands of that pluralism, tolerance and broadmindedness without which there is no "democratic society" (see, *inter alia*, the Handyside judgment of 7 December 1976, Series A no. 24, p. 23, § 49, and the Lingens judgment of 8 July 1986, Series A no. 103, p. 26, § 41).

Article 10 protects not only the substance of the ideas and information expressed, but also the form in which they are conveyed.

58. These principles are of particular importance with regard to the press. Whilst it must not overstep the bounds set, *inter alia*, for "the protection of the reputation of others", its task is nevertheless to impart information and ideas on political issues and on other matters of general interest (see, *mutatis mutandis*, the *Sunday Times* judgment of 26 April 1979, Series A no. 30, p. 40, § 65, and the above-mentioned Lingens judgment, loc. cit.).

Freedom of the press affords the public one of the best means of discovering and forming an opinion of the ideas and attitudes of political leaders. This is underlined by the wording of Article 10 where the public's right to receive information and ideas is expressly mentioned. More generally, freedom of political debate is at the very core of the concept of a democratic society which prevails throughout the Convention * * *.

59. The limits of acceptable criticism are accordingly wider with regard to a politician acting in his public capacity than in relation to a private individual. The former inevitably and knowingly lays himself open to close scrutiny of his every word and deed by both journalists and the public at large, and he must display a greater degree of tolerance, especially when he himself makes public statements that are susceptible of criticism.

A politician is certainly entitled to have his reputation protected, even when he is not acting in his private capacity, but the requirements of that protection have to be weighed against the interests of open discussion of political issues * * *.

60. The Court's task in this case has to be seen in the light of these principles. What are at stake are the limits of acceptable criticism in the context of public debate on a political question of general interest. In such cases the Court has to satisfy itself that the national authorities did apply standards which were in conformity with these principles and, moreover, that in doing so they based themselves on an acceptable assessment of the relevant facts.

* * *

C. APPLICATION OF THESE PRINCIPLES

61. * * *

The Court agrees with the Commission that the insertion of the text of the [criminal] information in *Forum* contributed to a public debate on a political question of general importance. In particular, the issue of different treatment of nationals and foreigners in the social field has given rise to considerable discussion not only in Austria but also in other member States of the Council of Europe.

Mr. Oberschlick's criticisms, as the Commission pointed out, sought to draw the public's attention in a provocative manner to a proposal made by a politician which was likely to shock many people. A politician who expresses himself in such terms exposes himself to a strong reaction on the part of journalists and the public.

62. In its judgment of 11 May 1984 the Regional Court found that the article in question, "despite its designation as a criminal information, gives the impression of being intended to condemn" the character of the politician. It therefore held that Mr. Oberschlick's allegations against him came under the general rule (Article 111 § 3 of the Criminal Code * * *) that a person making a defamatory statement through the media incurs criminal liability unless he proves that it is true. Since, in the Regional Court's opinion, Mr. Grabher–Meyer's proposal [was] "inconclusive" evidence of his alleged National Socialist

attitude and criminal behaviour and since no further evidence had been submitted, it found that the applicant had failed to prove his allegations and was therefore guilty * * *.

In its decision of 17 December 1984 the Vienna Court of Appeal basically confirmed these assessments * * *.

63. The Court, however, cannot subscribe to them. The information, as published by Mr. Oberschlick, began by * * * reporting Mr. Grabher–Meyer's statements. It is undisputed that this part of the information was factually correct. What followed was an analysis of these statements, on the basis of which the authors of the information concluded that this politician had knowingly expressed ideas that corresponded to those professed by the Nazis.

The Court can regard the latter part of the information only as a value-judgment, expressing the opinion of the authors as to the proposal made by this politician, which opinion was clearly presented as derived solely from a comparison of this proposal with texts from the National Socialist Party Manifesto.

It follows that Mr. Oberschlick had published a true statement of facts followed by a value-judgment as to those facts. The Austrian courts held, however, that he had to prove the truth of his allegations. As regards value-judgments this requirement is impossible of fulfilment and is itself an infringement of freedom of opinion * * *.

As to the form of the publication, the Court accepts the assessment made by the Austrian courts. It notes that they did not establish that "the presentation of the article in the form of a criminal information" was misleading in the sense that, as a consequence thereof, a significant number of the readers were led to believe that a public prosecution had been instituted against Mr. Grabher–Meyer or even that he had already been convicted. The Austrian courts said no more than that this particular form of presentation was intended to ensure that what in their eyes was an accusation as to his character would have "a particularly telling effect on the average reader". In the opinion of the Court, however, in view of the importance of the issue at stake (see paragraph 61 above), Mr. Oberschlick cannot be said to have exceeded the limits of freedom of expression by choosing this particular form.

64. It follows from the foregoing that the interference with Mr. Oberschlick's exercise of his freedom of expression was not "necessary in a democratic society * * * for the protection of the reputation * * * of others".

There has, accordingly, been a violation of Article 10 of the Convention.

IV. Application of Article 50

65. Under Article 50 of the Convention,

"If the Court finds that a decision or a measure taken by a legal authority or any other authority of a High Contracting Party is completely or partially in conflict with the obligations arising from the ... Convention, and if the internal law of the said Party allows only partial reparation to be made for the consequences of this decision or measure, the decision of the Court shall, if necessary, afford just satisfaction to the injured party."

The applicant requested the Court to direct the Government of Austria: (a) to rehabilitate him and formally set aside the judgment of 17 December 1984; and (b) to annul the seizure of issue no. 352/353 of *Forum*.

The Court, however, is not empowered to make directions of this kind (see, *mutatis mutandis*, the Hauschildt judgment of 24 May 1989, Series A no. 154, p. 23, § 54).

Mr. Oberschlick also sought compensation for pecuniary and non-pecuniary damage, as well as the reimbursement of costs and expenses.

* * *

A. Pecuniary Damage

66. The applicant sought firstly sums corresponding to the fine imposed (4,000 schillings) and the costs awarded to the private prosecutor (14,123.84 schillings) by the Austrian courts. Having regard to the direct link between these items and the violation of Article 10 found by the Court, he is, as the Government agreed, entitled to recover the full amount of 18,123.84 schillings.

* * *

B. Non-pecuniary Damage

68. The applicant sought 70,000 schillings for non-pecuniary damage, on account of the perplexity, anxiety and uncertainty occasioned by the prosecution for defamation.

The Government contested both the existence of any such damage and the amount claimed.

69. The Court does not exclude that the applicant may have sustained some prejudice of the kind alleged as a result of the breaches of Articles 6 § 1 and 10. It considers, however, that in the circumstances of the case the findings of violation in this judgment constitute of themselves sufficient just satisfaction.

C. Costs and Expenses

[The Court awarded Mr. Oberschlick his own out-of-pocket costs and expenses.]

PARTLY DISSENTING OPINION OF JUDGE THÓR VILHJÁLMSSON

To my regret I have found it unavoidable to part company with the majority of the Court on the question of Article 10. I have voted for nonviolation of that Article and would like to explain briefly my point of view.

The idea or ideal underlying the European Convention on Human Rights is that the individual should be protected vis-à-vis the State. The protection afforded to freedom of expression by Article 10 of our Convention clearly has this aim. The Lingens judgment shows that very harsh words expressed in the context of political debate enjoy this protection. However, as is stated at the beginning of paragraph 2 of this Article, the exercise of this freedom "carries with it duties and responsibilities". In this context one often has to keep in mind Article 8 of the Convention,[f] concerning the right to respect for private life, as well as what is said in paragraph 2 of Article 10 on the protection of the reputation or rights of others. The two principles enshrined in Articles 8 and 10 must both be respected in every democratic society worthy of that name. In our time and our part of the world, the application of rules intended to protect these principles is marked by the power of the media and the inability of the individual to protect his reputation. Legal rules have frequently proved not to be an effective tool in this respect, but this fact—as I consider it to be—should not influence our Court when it applies the Convention. The Austrian legislation * * * is an example of a set of rules enacted by a member State in order to meet the obligations flowing from Article 8 of our Convention.

The present case should be decided by an interpretation of Article 10 which takes into account the principle enshrined in Article 8. I am not of the opinion that the decisive question is whether or not a value-judgment is involved. Neither do I agree with the majority when it says that it regards "the latter part of the information only as a value-judgment".

The applicant had, of course, a right to voice strong disagreement with the statements of Mr. Grabher–Meyer, as reported in a television programme on 29 March 1983. This he could do without breaching Austrian law. He chose, however, to print in full a "criminal information"—a kind of private criminal summons—laid by himself and others, in which Mr. Grabher–Meyer was said to be suspected of contravening three provisions of Austrian penal law. The criminal-law setting thus given to his criticism took it out of the sphere of mere political debate and carried it into the arena of personal attack, thereby impinging on private life. The contents of the document printed were also, in my opinion, characterised by exaggerations. Here I have especially in mind the strong words to the effect that the statement corresponded to the aims of the Nazis or extolled measures applied by them. These very same words found in the text published by the applicant also, it seems to me, fall outside the ambit of value-judgments. The pro-

---

f. [Article 8 says, "Everyone has the right to respect for his private and family life, his home and his correspondence," subject to exceptions comparable to those in article 10(2). Ed.]

gramme and the acts of the Nazis constitute a set of facts and the statement is another fact. Whether or not that statement reflected that programme and those acts is a question of factual assessment and my own conclusion is that it did not. The applicant, in my opinion, transgressed the limits of freedom of expression and violated the rules on respect for the reputation of the person concerned that are necessary in a democratic society.

* * *

PARTLY DISSENTING OPINION OF JUDGE MATSCHER, APPROVED BY JUDGE BINDSCHEDLER-ROBERT

* * *

2. I fully endorse the reasoning in the Lingens judgment (Series A no. 103, p. 26, § 42), reiterated in the present judgment, to the effect that the limits of acceptable criticism are wider as regards a politician as such than as regards a private individual.

Criticism of political conduct may be expressed in press articles, in other publications or through other media, or again in a political debate. If the applicant, as a journalist, had had recourse to one of these means, criticism, even if it were harsh and bitter—but not going beyond the limits of decency—, would have been acceptable and his conviction for such criticism would indeed have constituted an interference with his freedom of expression which would not be covered by paragraph 2 of Article 10.

However, in the present case, the applicant did not engage in criticism of this type. He chose to proceed by another means, namely to lodge with the competent authority, and the very day on which his review appeared, a criminal information against X—in which he accused the person in question of very serious crimes—and to reproduce this information in that review, thereby giving the impression, at least to the average reader, that criminal proceedings had actually been instituted against X. This is a very important aspect of the case to which, regrettably, the majority of the Court has not thought right to accord the weight which in my view it merited.

In so acting, the applicant did not confine himself to permissible criticism, but perpetrated a treacherous attack on the reputation of a politician. Thus he did not respect the "duties and responsibilities" which freedom of expression carries with it; his conviction cannot therefore be regarded as a measure which was unnecessary and disproportionate for the purposes of this provision.

The majority of the Court also found a violation in the fact that the Austrian court had supposedly required Mr. Oberschlick to prove his accusations, proof which the majority regarded as impossible to establish since the criminal information constituted a value-judgment. I am, on the other hand, of the opinion that this information was merely an affirmation of certain facts—moreover an unfounded affirmation—, facts which in themselves were susceptible to proof. The Austrian court's judgment did not therefore infringe freedom of expression by regarding them as such.

THE MARGIN OF APPRECIATION

The Austrian government argued that there is a "margin of appreciation to be left to the national authorities," who are in a better position to judge what is defamatory, based on national cultural standards, than are international judges (paragraph 56 of the judgment). The jurisprudence of the European Court of Human Rights does establish a "margin of appreciation" for national or local discretion in certain cases, including those dealing with freedom of expression. The idea is to provide a certain latitude for local mores and cultures to develop on their own terms. But the size of the margin varies from case to case, depending on the facts.[g]

In Austria or Germany, to suggest that a prominent person is of a like mind with Nazis is a particularly serious and sensitive matter. In light of that, should the Court have accepted the Austrian government's argument?

Does the European Court's opinion differ significantly from the opinion you would expect the United States Supreme Court to deliver in a case involving alleged media defamation of a public person? Compare New York Times v. Sullivan,[h] where the Supreme Court said, "The constitutional guarantees require, we think, a federal rule that prohibits a public official from recovering damages for a defamatory falsehood relating to his official conduct unless he proves that the statement was made with 'actual malice'—that is, with knowledge that it was false or with reckless disregard of whether it was false or not." There is considerable dissatisfaction with Sullivan in the United States, but it remains the law.

The dissenting judges in the Oberschlick case readily conceded that harsh criticism in a political context would be protected, yet they thought that the applicant went too far in this case. What do you suppose underlay their concerns?

Mr. Oberschlick requested the Court not only to award money damages, but to set aside the Austrian judgment against him and to annul the seizure of the periodical in which his article appeared. The Court replied that it had no power to award these remedies. Does *article 50* of the Convention preclude such remedies? If not, should an

---

g. See Macdonald, The Margin of Appreciation in the Jurisprudence of the European Court of Human Rights, 1 Collected Courses of the Academy of European Law, Book 2, at 95 (1992).

h. 376 U.S. 254, 279–80, 84 S.Ct. 710, 726, 11 L.Ed.2d 686, 706 (1964).

international human rights tribunal, such as the European Court, award them?[i]

The applicant was awarded his out-of-pocket damages, but he received nothing for mental anguish. Why did "the findings of violation in this judgment constitute of themselves sufficient just satisfaction" (paragraph 69)?

Another freedom of expression context—obscenity—has provided the European Court with opportunities to develop the "margin of appreciation" idea. In Müller v. Switzerland,[j] the European Court found no violation of article 10 in the confiscation of allegedly obscene paintings by local authorities in Fribourg, Switzerland, and the imposition by a Swiss court of a fine of 300 Swiss francs on the artist. These measures were taken under article 204 of the Swiss Criminal Code, which provided in part:

> Anyone who makes or has in his possession any * * * items which are obscene with a view to trading in them, distributing them or displaying them in public * * * shall be imprisoned or fined. * * * The court shall order the destruction of the items.

The European Court held that the measures taken against Mr. Müller were within the margin of appreciation afforded national and local cultures. The paintings, by a well-known Swiss artist, explicitly depicted such acts as sodomy and bestiality. They were part of an exhibit, open to the public without charge, celebrating the 500th anniversary of Fribourg's entry into the Swiss Confederation.

The Court in the Müller case addressed the issues:

> The need to avoid excessive rigidity and to keep pace with changing circumstances means that many laws are inevitably couched in terms which, to a greater or lesser extent, are vague * * *. Criminal-law provisions on obscenity fall within this category.
>
> In the present instance, it is also relevant to note that there were a number of consistent decisions by the [Swiss] Federal Court on the "publication" of "obscene" items * * *. These decisions, which were accessible because they had been published and were followed by the lower courts, supplemented the letter of Article 204 § 1 of the Criminal Code.

* * *

> The applicant's conviction * * * was intended to protect morals. Today, * * * it is not possible to find in the legal and social orders of the Contracting States a uniform European conception of

---

i. Some states parties to the European Convention now allow an applicant in certain circumstances to have his or her case reopened if the European Court has decided that the domestic court's judgment violated the Convention. See Ryssdal, Cooperation Between Courts and Tribunals of Member States and The European Court of Human Rights 4 (Council of Europe Doc. Cour (92) 135, 1992).

j. European Ct. of Human Rts. Series A, No. 133 (1988).

morals. The view taken of the requirements of morals varies from time to time and from place to place, especially in our era, characterised as it is by a far-reaching evolution of opinions on the subject. By reason of their direct and continuous contact with the vital forces of their countries, State authorities are in principle in a better position than the international judge to give an opinion on the exact content of these requirements as well as on the "necessity" of a "restriction" or "penalty" intended to meet them. * * * In the circumstances, having regard to the margin of appreciation left to them under Article 10 § 2, the Swiss courts were entitled to consider it "necessary" for the protection of morals to impose a fine on the applicant for publishing obscene material.

Why was the margin of appreciation wide enough for Switzerland to punish the artist in this case, but not for Austria to punish the writer in the Oberschlick case?

The prevailing obscenity test in the United States was set forth in Miller v. California,[k] a case involving unsolicited mailing of sexually explicit, illustrated advertising brochures:

> The basic guidelines for the trier of fact must be: (a) whether "the average person, applying contemporary community standards" would find that the work, taken as a whole, appeals to the prurient interest ...; (b) whether the work depicts or describes, in a patently offensive way, sexual conduct specifically defined by the applicable state law; and (c) whether the work, taken as a whole, lacks serious literary, artistic, political, or scientific value.

In Pope v. Illinois,[l] the Supreme Court held that the third prong of the test in Miller v. California does not vary from community to community. "The proper inquiry is not whether an ordinary member of any given community would find serious literary, artistic, political, or scientific value in allegedly obscene material, but whether a reasonable person would find such value in the material, taken as a whole."

If the European Court were to adopt the U.S. Supreme Court's approach, how would Müller v. Switzerland come out?

Would the Supreme Court's approach be appropriate in Europe?

In the Oberschlick case, the Court decided the damages issue at the same time it decided the merits. In some cases the damages issue has been separated from the merits: once the merits have been decided in favor of the applicant, a separate phase of the case begins regarding the damages to be awarded. One of the early cases establishing this procedure was the Ringeisen case, below.

k. 413 U.S. 15, 24, 93 S.Ct. 2607, 2615, 37 L.Ed.2d 419, 431 (1973).

l. 481 U.S. 497, 500–01, 107 S.Ct. 1918, 1921, 95 L.Ed.2d 439, 445 (1987).

RINGEISEN v. AUSTRIA
European Court of Human Rights, 1972.
Series A, No. 15.

[The Court decided in a previous phase of the proceedings that Austria had violated the applicant's rights under article 5(3), which gives a person arrested on a criminal charge a right to be brought promptly before a judge and to be tried within a reasonable time or released pending trial. Mr. Ringeisen had been held in pre-trial detention ("detention while on remand") for what the Court had found to be an unreasonable time. The Commission referred the damages issue to the Court.

[Referring to its previous judgment (of 16 July 1971) in the same case, the Court said:]

11. That judgment concerned, inter alia, the detention of Ringeisen while on remand from 5 August to 23 December 1963, that is four months and eighteen days, and from 15 March 1965 to 20 March 1967, that is two years and five days.

12. Ringeisen's lawyer wrote, on 23 July 1971, to the Austrian Federal Minister of Justice requesting him, with reference to the judgment of 16 July and to Articles 5 § 5 and 50 of the Convention, to make proposals for the reparation of the damage allegedly sustained by the applicant. It was claimed that the applicant had, "as a result of his unjustified detention", suffered over and above the loss of his fortune irremediable damage to his health which reduced his life expectancy and made constant medical care necessary. The applicant's lawyer therefore requested the Minister to advance on account the sum of 50,000 German marks (DM). In a reminder dated 2 August, he insisted that the matter should be dealt with promptly, having regard, in particular, to Ringeisen's state of health.

On 10 September 1971, the Minister replied that in view of his Ministry's competence under the Constitution it was not in a position to deal with the matter.

* * *

The applicant has set out more particulars of his claims in letters which he and his wife sent to the Commission on 24 November 1971, 10 December 1971, 21 January 1972 and 8 February 1972. He alleges that he has sustained considerable material damage resulting, inter alia, from interference with the conduct of his business and from loss of property and rents in Austria and for this he claims some 100 million schillings. Furthermore, he states that he is entitled to compensation, in an amount which he leaves the Court to assess: for personal injury, for damage to his reputation and "for detention".

As to the Law
I. *On the Admissibility of the Applicant's Claim*

[The Court rejected the Austrian government's argument that a claim for damages had to start with a new petition under article 25.

The Court said that the bifurcated merits/damages procedure used in this case had been "inspired by a desire to take account as far as possible of the wishes of respondent States: they may be reluctant to argue the consequences of a violation the existence of which they dispute; and they may wish, in the event of a finding of a violation, to maintain the possibility of settling the issue of reparation directly with the injured party without the Court being further concerned."]

II. As to the Fulfilment of the Conditions for the Application of Article 50

20. The Government submits that the conditions for the application of Article 50 are not fulfilled

(1) since it was possible to make full reparation in internal law for the consequences of the violation of Article 5 § 3 and this was in fact done by the decision of the Linz Regional Court on 24 April 1968 to reckon the entire time spent in detention on remand as part of the prison sentence;

(2) since, even assuming that that decision did not make *restitutio in integrum* to Ringeisen and the violation of Article 5 § 3 had caused him other damage, he could exercise several remedies.

21. The Court is unable to accept the first submission. The fact of deducting the time spent in detention on remand from the prison sentence imposed on a person must no doubt be taken into consideration in assessing the extent of the damage flowing from the excessive duration of that detention; but it does not in any way thus acquire the character of *restitutio in integrum,* for no freedom is given in place of the freedom unlawfully taken away.

The consequence of the Government's reasoning would be to deprive Article 5 § 3 of much of its effectiveness, at least in cases where the person detained on remand for more than a reasonable time is found guilty afterwards: in such cases it would suffice, in order to avoid the application of Article 50, that the time spent in detention on remand should be less than the term of the prison sentence pronounced later and should be deducted from it.

* * *

22. In its second submission, the Government maintains that even if Ringeisen was entitled to claim other reparation for damage caused by his excessive detention on remand, Austrian law provided him with various means of obtaining it but he confined himself to writing to the Minister of Justice who had no competence to deal with the claim.

[The Court relied on a previous case [m] for the proposition that the applicant, having made an unsuccessful request for compensation from the government (in this case, from the Austrian Minister of Justice), was not required to proceed through the domestic judicial system. To

---

m. The De Wilde, Ooms and Versyp Cases, Series A, No. 14 (1972).

require that would prevent the European Court "from speedily affording reparation for the damage caused by the violation it found."]

III. As to the Question of Affording Just Satisfaction

[The Court said that Mr. Ringeisen had failed to prove his claimed out-of-pocket losses and health deterioration.]

26. There remains the fact that Ringeisen's detention on remand exceeded by more than twenty-two months, as found by the Court in its judgment of 16 July 1971, the limits of a reasonable time referred to in Article 5 § 3.

The Court does not overlook that Ringeisen was found guilty and sentenced to a term of imprisonment longer than the time he had spent in detention on remand, that his time in detention was reckoned in full to his advantage as part of the sentence, and that he was subject in detention to a regime less severe than that which the prison sentence would have entailed.

These circumstances go some way to compensate the damage of which he complains.

However, the applicant protested his innocence and certainly felt such excessive detention on remand to be a great injustice. The detention must have been all the more hard to bear in that it inevitably made it much more difficult for him to conclude a composition for the termination of his bankruptcy.

Assessing these various factors, the Court considers that Ringeisen should be afforded just satisfaction and fixes at twenty thousand German marks (20,000 DM) the overall sum to be paid to him in this regard.

JUDICIAL REMEDIES UNDER THE CONVENTION

Is the separation of proceedings on damages from the proceedings on the merits a sound procedure from the standpoints of (a) efficiency, (b) fairness to the person whose rights were violated, and (c) sensitivity to the relationship between the Court and the respondent government? Is it contemplated by article 50 of the Convention?

[T]he exhaustion of remedies rule of article 26 clearly applies only to the initial referral of a matter to the Commission, not to claims for damages after the Court has found a violation. But what about article 50? Doesn't it contemplate damages only if the domestic system of the respondent state does not afford full compensation? Is it appropriate to proceed under article 50 if the applicant has simply claimed compensation through the Ministry of Justice in the respondent state and has been turned down?

How did the Court in the Ringeisen case determine that the amount of damages to be awarded was 20,000 marks?

Under *article 63(1)* of the American Convention on Human Rights, could the Inter-American Court of Human Rights award "non-material" (or "non-pecuniary") damages, as the European Court did in the Ringeisen case? Is that what the Inter-American Court did when it awarded "moral damages" in the Velásquez Rodríguez case? See page 1028 supra.

The Austrian government ultimately paid Mr. Ringeisen the full amount.[n] In fact, European governments routinely comply with the judgments of the European Court of Human Rights. In such cases the Committee of Ministers publishes information from the respondent government regarding its compliance with the judgment, and declares the case closed.[o]

Suppose, however, that the Austrian government had refused to pay Mr. Ringeisen. Under *article 53*, the Court's decision was binding on it, but nothing in the Convention gives it the effect of an enforceable domestic judgment in the member states. Instead, the Court's judgment is transmitted to the Committee of Ministers, "which shall supervise its execution." *Article 54*. The Committee of Ministers invites the respondent government to inform it of the measures taken in consequence of the judgment, and reminds the government of its obligations under article 53. If the Committee of Ministers considered the government's response deficient, it could call on the government to comply and presumably could request another report. In an extreme case, it could suspend or expel the respondent state from the Council of Europe. Is this enforcement procedure likely to be fair and effective? Is it the best that could realistically be expected?

Compare *article 68(2)* of the American Convention on Human Rights: a judgment of the Inter-American Court of Human Rights that stipulates compensatory damages "may be executed in the country concerned in accordance with domestic procedure governing the execution of judgments against the state." Is that an improvement over the European enforcement system? Would it be feasible in Europe?

As we have seen, the European Court views its mission not only as one of providing redress for violations of individual rights, but also as one of law reform. Some international human rights systems are weighted toward redress for individual violations (the regional systems, for the most part, and the Optional Protocol to the Covenant on Civil and Political Rights), and some toward law reform (ECOSOC Resolution 1503, concerned with consistent patterns of gross violations). Can the

---

n. See McNulty, Stock-Taking on the European Convention on Human Rights 17 (Council of Europe Doc. DH (74) 6, 1974).

o. See the periodic Council of Europe Information Sheets on Human Rights, and Collection of Resolutions Adopted by the Committee of Ministers in Application of Articles 32 and 54 of the European Convention on Human Rights, Supplements.

two objectives coexist successfully in the same system, administered by the same institutions?

E. OVERLAP WITH GLOBAL HUMAN RIGHTS CONVENTIONS

There is a great deal of overlap between the rights covered by the European Convention and the U.N. Covenant on Civil and Political Rights, and some overlap with other global human rights treaties.[a] Most of our attention in this section will be on overlap with the Covenant.

In some instances, the Covenant on Civil and Political Rights goes further than the Convention and in some instances essentially the same right is expressed somewhat differently in the two instruments. As substantive protocols—especially Protocol No. 7—have been added to the European Convention, the gaps have been narrowed, but they have not been entirely eliminated.

At various times, the Council of Europe has addressed the potential problems created by the overlap and by the existence of separate supervisory bodies under the two instruments—the Human Rights Committee under the Covenant, and the "Strasbourg organs" (the European Commission, Court and Committee of Ministers) under the European Convention. The problems, and some of the experience in dealing with them, are summarized in the Council of Europe Secretariat memorandum below.

EFFECTS OF THE VARIOUS HUMAN RIGHTS INSTRUMENTS

Memorandum prepared by the Council of Europe's
Directorate of Human Rights, Feb. 1, 1985.
Council of Europe Doc. H (85) 3, at 7–12.

* * *

18. For Contracting Parties to the European Convention on Human Rights, the coexistence of the European Convention and the United Nations Covenant on Civil and Political Rights is likely to raise a number of problems, including risks of conflict resulting either from the lack of conformity between the definitions of the rights guaranteed, or from differences in international procedure in the protection of human rights, which sometimes even could lead to opposite results. Under the European Convention and its Protocols, 19 different rights are safeguarded compared with 23 in the United Nations Covenant. As

---

[a]. For comprehensive treatment of overlapping human rights instruments, see A. Cançado Trindade, Co-existence and Coordination of Mechanisms of International Protection of Human Rights, 202 Hague Academy, Recueil des Cours 9 (1987–II).

might be expected, a number of rights protected by both instruments are the same and their definitions are broadly similar. There are nevertheless cases where, although the same rights are concerned, their definitions differ appreciably; such differences are of considerable importance for the states parties to both instruments or those intending to accede to them.

* * *

22. As far as differences in systems of control are concerned, the problems appear much more complex. In the case of inter-state complaints, problems could result from the coexistence of the United Nations procedure and the European procedure, in the case of states accepting the optional procedure provided under Article 41 of the Covenant.

As regards the question whether there would be a choice between the two procedures, it should be noted that Article 44 of the UN Covenant states that its provisions for implementation shall not prevent states parties from having recourse to other procedures for settling a dispute, while under Article 62 of the European Convention, the Contracting Parties have agreed that, except by special agreement, they will not submit a dispute arising out of the interpretation or application of the Convention to a means of settlement other than as provided for in the Convention. It should also be noted in this connection that Article 33 of the United Nations Charter approves the principle of the regional settlement of inter-state disputes.

In the case of inter-state complaints between Contracting Parties to the European Convention which could be submitted either to the United Nations procedure or to that of the Council of Europe, the procedure instituted by the European Convention should normally be preferred.

It would, on the other hand, be undesirable that states which had brought a case before the Strasbourg organs under the European Convention unsuccessfully should refer the same matter subsequently to the UN Committee. Even though the issue raised in New York would be, technically speaking, a different issue (because the complaint is of violation of the terms of a different treaty), this might create the impression of an "appeal" from the European organs to the UN Committee and this might undermine, or at least weaken, the authority of those organs; this would be contrary to the general sense of Articles 32 and 52 of the European Convention, which provide that decisions of the Committee of Ministers and the Court shall be final.

In Resolution (70) 17, the Committee of Ministers of the Council of Europe declared that, "as long as the problem of interpretation of Article 62 of the European Convention is not resolved, states parties to the Convention which ratify the UN Covenant on Civil and Political Rights and make a declaration under Article 41 of that Covenant should normally utilise only the procedure established by the European

Convention in respect of complaints against another Contracting Party to the European Convention relating to an alleged violation of a right which in substance is covered both by the European Convention (or its Protocols) and by the UN Covenant on Civil and Political Rights, it being understood that the UN procedure may be invoked in relation to rights not guaranteed in the European Convention or in relation to states which are not parties to the European Convention".

23. With regard to individual applications, it must be conceded that the coexistence of the two sets of implementation measures raise in particular the questions whether an individual applicant, if the state concerned has accepted both Article 25 of the European Convention and the [first] UN Optional Protocol, can choose between the two systems and whether he can use both of them in turn.

The acceptance of the UN Optional Protocol by states which have accepted the right of individual petition under Article 25 of the European Convention would produce the result that an individual who alleges violation of a right guaranteed both by the European Convention and by the UN Covenant would have a choice to initiate proceedings under either procedure.

This choice would have to be accepted, though it might cause difficulties, in particular by reason of possible divergencies in the case-law of the two systems. On the other hand, in principle an applicant should not be able to bring the same case under both procedures either at the same time or successively. On this question, the following provisions of the two instruments are relevant:

Article 27, paragraph 1(b) of the European Convention provides as follows:

"The Commission shall not deal with any petition submitted under Article 25 which:

* * *

(b) is substantially the same as a matter which has already been examined by the Commission or has already been submitted to another procedure of international investigation or settlement and if it contains no relevant new information".

Article 5, paragraph 2 of the Optional Protocol provides as follows:

"The committee shall not consider any communication from an individual unless it has ascertained that:

(a) the same matter is not being examined under another procedure of international investigation or settlement.
* * *

It may be argued that the European Commission will be prevented from considering a complaint previously lodged with the UN Committee (unless new information is produced), but the UN Committee could entertain a case previously heard in Strasbourg once the European proceedings are terminated.

* * *

24. In order to prevent the possibility of successive applications to the European Commission and the UN Committee, member states of the Council of Europe which sign or ratify the Optional Protocol might wish to make a declaration, at the moment of signing or ratifying, whose effect would be that the competence of the UN Human Rights Committee would not extend to receiving and considering individual complaints relating to cases which are being or already have been examined under the procedure provided for by the European Convention. Such a declaration should only cover complaints of violation of rights which in substance are covered by the two instruments, and not complaints of violation of rights not guaranteed in the European Convention.

[As of December 31, 1990, each Council of Europe member state that had become a party to the first Optional Protocol, except Portugal and the Netherlands,[1] had made a reservation along the above lines.]

25. Some doubts have been expressed on the immunity conferred by reservations of this kind.

At an important sitting of the Federal German Bundestag, it was suggested that the United Nations Committee might take discrepancies in the definition of rights guaranteed in both instruments as a pretext for insisting on its own jurisdiction. The Federal Government shared the Bundestag Committee's view and declared that, as far as the Federal Republic was concerned, there was no objection of principle to ratification of the Optional Protocol, provided that the two protection systems did not interfere with each other. In this connection, the reservation proposed by the Committee of Ministers was not sufficient, "in its present abstract form", to dispel all anxiety and did not "rule out the danger of a duplication of individual petitions in the case of rights covered both by the European Convention and the United Nations Covenant".[2]

The German Government also wonders whether the reservation suggested by the Committee of Ministers will be regarded as valid. On this point, the Committee of Experts on Human Rights first noted, in its report on problems arising from the coexistence of the two control systems, that the Protocol made no provision for reservations and went

---

1. The explanatory memorandum * * * of the Netherlands states that, although "for practical reasons, it is undesirable that a single case should be submitted to two different procedures", the Netherlands Government has nonetheless decided that "this argument is insufficient to prevent individuals from approaching the Covenant Committee after approaching the European Commission of Human Rights". The government adds that "this method of making declarations could be followed in other regional contexts, undermining the world-wide system for the protection of human rights". [Footnote in the original.]

2. Extracts from the "Deutscher Bundestag", 7 Wahlperiode, Drucksache 7/3076, 15.1.1975. [Footnote in the original.]

on to conclude that this did not preclude reservations, but that the matter should be determined by the general rules of international law.

26. As for the relevant practice of the two bodies concerned, the European Commission of Human Rights and the United Nations Human Rights Committee, it is interesting to note that no application has yet been rejected by the European Commission under Article 27(1)(b) of the European Convention and that, whenever the Secretariat of the Commission has learned that the same case has already been brought before the United Nations Committee, the applicant has been advised of the content of Article 27(1)(b).

27. The United Nations Committee, for its part, has taken two decisions—Communication No. 75/1980, Fanali v. Italy, and Communication No. R 26/121, A M v. Denmark—in which the problems referred to above were raised. * * *

28. The extent to which the application before the Commission and the communication before the committee were the same was considered by the committee in the case of Fanali v. Italy.

The applicant and other well-known figures had been brought before the Italian Constitutional Court following the discovery of certain secret payments made in connection with the purchase of military equipment (the "Lockheed scandal"); there is no domestic remedy against a criminal sentence imposed by this court. Some of the convicted had approached the European Commission,[3] but Mr. Fanali preferred to submit a communication to the committee. The Italian Government argued that this communication was inadmissible, since it concerned the "same question" as that before the Commission. The committee ruled, however, that the "same question" must be understood as meaning the same application, concerning the same individual, brought by him or someone entitled to act on his behalf before the other international authority. The committee thus insists that both the object of the communication and the parties to the case must be the same. Its interpretation accordingly suggests that it will have jurisdiction whenever the applicant has not himself seized the European Commission. At first sight, this can only apply to situations such as that in the Fanali case, in which other individuals took action solely on their own account within the European context. Another possibility is suggested, however, by certain decisions given by the committee in cases which had previously come before the Inter–American Commission on Human Rights, which may hear collective cases brought not only by the victims themselves, but also by third parties acting on their behalf but without their instructions. When a collective case is being examined by the Inter–American Commission, may an individual involved in the case approach the committee separately, or is his communication inadmissible because it concerned the "same question"? The

---

3. Applications Nos. 8603/79, 8722/79, 8723/79 and 8729/79—Crociani and others v. Italy, in "Decisions and Reports of the European Commission of Human Rights", Vol. 22. * * * [Footnote in the original; renumbered.]

committee has always ruled that a communication of this kind is not inadmissible, because it does not raise the "same question" as the collective case.

29. The reservations made by the European states should take effect in the case of communications concerning matters which are being or have been examined by another procedure of international investigation or settlement. These reservations are unquestionably aimed at applications whose merits have been examined by the European Convention bodies. Can the same be said, however, of applications which the European Commission has declared inadmissible? The case of A M v. Denmark gave the United Nations Committee an opportunity to answer this question [see below].

A.M. v. DENMARK
U.N. Human Rights Committee, 1982.
Communication No. R.26/121.
37 GAOR Supp. No. 40 (A/37/40), at 212.

[The petitioner was a Pakistani national serving a prison term in Denmark for inflicting bodily injuries during a fight. The Danish authorities had notified him that he would be deported when his prison term was completed. His petition claimed, inter alia, that he had been denied a fair trial and that the deportation order amounted to degrading punishment.]

4. It appears from the communication that the author has submitted the same matter to the European Commission of Human Rights. His application before that body was declared inadmissible on 1 March 1982 as manifestly ill-founded.

5. Before considering any claims contained in a communication, the Human Rights Committee must decide whether the communication is admissible under the Optional Protocol to the International Covenant on Civil and Political Rights. The Committee observes in this connexion that when ratifying the Optional Protocol and recognizing the competence of the Committee to receive and consider communications from individuals subject to its jurisdiction, the State party Denmark, made a reservation, with reference to article 5(2)(a) of the Optional Protocol, in respect of the competence of the Committee to consider a communication from an individual if the matter has already been considered under other procedures of international investigation.

6. In the light of the above-mentioned reservation and observing that the same matter has already been considered by the European Commission of Human Rights and therefore by another procedure of international investigation within the meaning of article 5(2)(a) of the Optional Protocol to the International Covenant on Civil and Political Rights, the Committee concludes that it is not competent to consider the present communication.

APPENDIX

Individual Opinion

Mr. Bernhard Graefrath, member of the Human Rights Committee, submits the following individual opinion relating to the admissibility of communication No. R.26/121 (A.M. v. Denmark):

I concur in the decision of the Committee that the communication is inadmissible. However, in my view the communication is inadmissible in accordance with article 3 of the Optional Protocol. The claims of the author do not raise issues under any of the provisions of the Covenant.

I cannot, however, share the view that the Committee is barred from considering the communication by the reservation of Denmark relating to article 5(2)(a) of the Optional Protocol. That reservation refers to matters that have already been considered under other procedures of international investigation. It does not in my opinion refer to matters, the consideration of which has been denied under any other procedure by a decision of inadmissibility.

In the case of the author of communication R.26/121, the European Commission of Human Rights has declared his application inadmissible as being manifestly ill-founded. It has thereby found that it has no competence to consider the matter within the legal framework of the European Convention. An application that has been declared inadmissible has not, in the meaning of the reservation, been "considered" in such a way that the Human Rights Committee is precluded from considering it.

The reservation aims at preventing the Human Rights Committee from reviewing cases that have been considered by another international organ of investigation. It does not seek to limit the competence of the Human Rights Committee to deal with communications merely on the ground that the rights of the Covenant allegedly violated may also be covered by the European Convention and its procedural requirements. If that had been the aim of the reservation, it would, in my opinion, have been incompatible with the Optional Protocol.

* * *

An application that has been declared inadmissible under the system of the European Convention is not necessarily inadmissible under the system of the Covenant and the Optional Protocol, even if it refers to the same facts. This is also true in relation to an application that has been declared inadmissible by the European Commission as being manifestly ill-founded. The decision that an application is manifestly ill-founded can necessarily be taken only in relation to rights set forth in the European Convention. These rights, however, differ in substance and in regard to their implementation procedures from the rights set forth in the Covenant. They, as well as the competence of the European Commission, derive from a separate and independent international instrument. A decision on non-admissibility of the European Commission, therefore, has no impact on a matter before the Human Rights Committee and cannot hinder the Human Rights Committee from reviewing the facts of a communication on its own legal basis and under its own procedure and from ascertaining whether they are compatible with the provisions of the Covenant. This might lead to a similar result as under the European Convention, but not necessarily so.

The reservation of Denmark was intended to avoid the same matter being considered twice. It did not aim at closing the door for a communication that might be admissible under the Optional Protocol despite the fact that it has been declared inadmissible by the European Commission.

MINIMIZING THE OVERLAP

Consider first the overlapping interstate procedures. The Committee of Ministers of the Council of Europe said in the first excerpt above that "as long as the problem of interpretation of Article 62 of the European Convention is not resolved," states parties should normally use only the interstate procedure under the European Convention against other European states parties. What is the ambiguity in *article 62* that led the Committee of Ministers to take that stance?

What is wrong with giving a party to the European Convention that also becomes a party to the Covenant and accepts its *article 41* a choice whether to allege a human rights violation against a similarly-situated state under the Covenant or the European Convention, if article 62 of the Convention allows it?

Note the slightly different point raised in paragraph 22, fourth subparagraph of the excerpt from the memorandum of the Directorate of Human Rights. It evokes images of the res judicata doctrine in domestic law. Would the opposite view tend to defeat the integrity of the European human rights system? Would the second proceeding (under the Covenant) be barred by *articles 32* and *52* of the European Convention?

With respect to individual petitions, note the difference between *article 27(1)(b)* of the European Convention and *article 5(2)* of the first Optional Protocol. Is it clear that the European Commission could not consider a matter that has already been considered under another procedure, while the U.N. Human Rights Committee could?

The Netherlands made no reservation to article 5(2) when it became a party to the Optional Protocol. Suppose an individual petition against the Netherlands were considered on the merits by the European Commission and rejected, with the Committee of Ministers concurring. If the same matter were then considered by the Human Rights Committee and found meritorious under the Covenant, could the

Dutch government rely on the European outcome to avoid responsibility?

As indicated in the excerpt from the memo of the Directorate of Human Rights, the German government was unsure about either the efficacy or the validity of the standard reservation made by most European governments to article 5(2) of the Optional Protocol. In the excerpt from A.M. v. Denmark, however, the U.N. Human Rights Committee honored the Danish reservation and applied it even to a matter that had been found inadmissible under the European Convention. What policy, if any, was served by applying the reservation to such a case?

Do you agree with Mr. Graefrath's individual opinion in A.M. v. Denmark that a reservation limiting the competence of the Human Rights Committee to deal with any matter, simply on the ground that it is covered by the European Convention, would be incompatible with the object and purpose of the Optional Protocol?

Note also Fanali v. Italy, summarized in the excerpt from the memo of the Directorate of Human Rights. Did the Human Rights Committee lean too far in favor of the individual petitioner, who asserted the same claim others in his shoes were asserting before the European Commission? Was he simply forum shopping? (Is anything wrong with that?)

We turn briefly to an overlap with a global convention other than the Covenant on Civil and Political Rights. Article 11(1) of the European Convention is quite similar to article 2 of International Labor Organization Convention No. 87, on freedom of association. Both give workers the right to join trade unions of their own choosing, though they do not use precisely the same language. Both contain exceptions. Convention No. 87, article 9(1) says, "The extent to which the guarantees provided for in this Convention shall apply to the armed forces and the police shall be determined by national laws or regulations." European Convention article 11(2) says in part, "This Article shall not prevent the imposition of lawful restrictions on the exercise of these rights by members of the armed forces, of the police or of the administration of the State."

In Chapter 4, these materials have examined the complaint the British Trades Union Congress (TUC) brought before the ILO Committee on Freedom of Association in 1984. The TUC claimed that the British government had deprived the civil servants at the Cheltenham Government Communications Headquarters (GCHQ) of the right to belong to a trade union. The British government argued, inter alia, that the case came within the exception in Convention No. 87, article 9(1), above. The Committee on Freedom of Association rejected the British argument and found that the British government had violated article 2 of Convention No. 87. The matter was later taken up by the ILO Committee of Experts (which agreed with the Committee on Freedom of Association) and the ILO Conference Committee (which reached an inconclusive result). See pages 536–47 supra.

In 1985 the British Council of Civil Service Unions (a member of the TUC) and six present or former civil servants petitioned the European Commission of Human Rights, claiming that the British government's GCHQ policy violated article 11(1) of the European Convention. The Commission considered whether the application was substantially the same as the complaint before the ILO, within the meaning of article 27(1)(b) of the European Convention. No, said the Commission:

> It is true that the rights mentioned in Article 2 of [ILO Convention No. 87] resemble to an extent the rights guaranteed in Article 11 para. 1 of the [European] Convention. However, the Commission finds that the present applicants * * * are not identical with the complainant before the ILO organs concerned. Rather the complaints before the ILO were brought by the Trades Union Congress, through its General Secretary, on its own behalf. Indeed, the six individual applicants before the Commission would not have been able to bring such complaints since the [ILO] Committee on Freedom of Association was set up to examine complaints from organisations of workers and [employers], as opposed to individual complainants.[b]

Since the British Trades Union Congress represents individual British unions, including the one involved in this case, and indirectly represents the members of unions, how could it be said that this was not substantially the same as the matter considered by the ILO? Was the Commission using a technicality to protect its own turf?

By the time the European Commission made its decision on admissibility, the ILO Committee on Freedom of Association and the ILO Committee of Experts had both decided against the U.K. under ILO Convention No. 87. The European Commission, however, found that the application was "manifestly ill-founded" and thus inadmissible, because the British measures were "lawful restrictions on the exercise of [trade union] rights by members * * * of the administration of the State," within the meaning of article 11(2) of the European Convention, above. The European Commission did not mention the ILO proceedings in this part of its decision. Should it have considered those proceedings? If so, what weight should they have been given?

Is consideration by a regional and a global human rights body of essentially the same complaint, with different complainants asserting rights under similar but distinct treaties, a good or a bad thing from the standpoint of effective protection of human rights?

---

b. Council of Civil Service Unions and others v. the United Kingdom, Application No. 11603/85, European Commission of Human Rights Decisions and Reports No. 50, at 228, 237 (1987).

F. REFORM OF THE EUROPEAN SYSTEM

When this was written, attention was being given in Europe to reform of the human rights enforcement machinery. This is largely an outgrowth of the rapidly increasing workload of both the Commission and the Court, with the corresponding increase in demands on the members of those two institutions and in delays experienced by petitioners. In 1991 the President of the Court gave some of his personal views about possible reforms.

RYSSDAL, FORTY YEARS OF THE EUROPEAN CONVENTION ON HUMAN RIGHTS
Address given in Vienna, Jan. 18, 1991.
Council of Europe Doc. Cour (91) 61, at 13–14.

It is important to make it possible for the complex Strasbourg system for the protection of human rights with its two independent institutions to give an answer within a reasonable time to applications lodged by citizens which have usually already been the subject of proceedings in the national courts lasting many years. There are I believe at present essentially three possible solutions:

— *firstly:* to make the Commission and the Court permanent [i.e. full time] without altering their functions as provided for in the Convention;

— *secondly:* to make the Commission a court of first instance, the Court thereby acquiring appellate jurisdiction;

— *thirdly:* to set up a *permanent* European Court of Human Rights to determine the admissibility *and* substance of European human rights' complaints, as opposed to the present system of two independent institutions, the Commission and the Court, where admissibility falls to be determined by the former.

* * *

It does at least seem to be clear in my view that we are moving towards a permanent Commission and Court, since judges must already set aside on average 135 days per year to deal with the work in Strasbourg. The office of judge can no longer be regarded as a part-time activity. However, the question arises as to whether it is advisable in the interests of an effective protection of rights to set up one permanent European institution for the preliminary examination of European human rights complaints and another for the decision on the merits of the case—each with twenty-three, shortly perhaps thirty highly qualified lawyers and the corresponding number of legal and other staff.

The alternative would surely be a permanent European Court which, following the example of judicial organisation in Europe would have to decide on the admissibility and the merits of complaints. In this connection it would however have to be considered whether and how the present function of the Commission, in assisting the Court through expressing an opinion on the legal issues, can be preserved in such a system.

Nevertheless I have serious misgivings about the proposal to set up two levels of jurisdiction in the protection system of the Convention. Let us not forget that the applicant cannot lodge an application in Strasbourg until he has exhausted all the remedies available to him under domestic law. Thus his application has usually been examined by two, sometimes three or even four national courts and in most of the Convention States already in the light of the Convention. In these circumstances, whatever the scope of the investigation of the facts to be carried out in Strasbourg, the introduction of a European appeals system and the setting up of a "first instance" organ and a separate organ to hear appeals on questions of law does not seem to me appropriate in relation to European human rights complaints any more than it is for constitutional complaints as provided for in various Convention States. A second European level of jurisdiction, an appellate jurisdiction, would in any case mean further delay for the final determination of the case and consequently a clear loss of effectiveness with regard to the protection of rights. In so far as this proposal expressed the concern that with only one European level of jurisdiction—whether in the present form or in the form of a single permanent court—the protection of fundamental rights in Europe can be only incompletely guaranteed, it must be remembered that the protection of the rights and freedoms secured in the Convention is first and foremost the duty of the Contracting States, their authorities and in particular their courts. The system for the protection of rights of the Convention is—as the Court has repeatedly stressed—subsidiary in nature. In this respect the system depends on a kind of cooperation between the national courts and the European court, which can be especially effective where the national courts themselves have to apply the Convention. For the Convention to be firmly anchored in the national system is therefore the necessary corollary of any reform of the Strasbourg institutions. The more natural it becomes for national courts to refer to the European Convention on Human Rights, the greater the restraint which it will be possible for the European Court to show in carrying out its review.

THE ALTERNATIVES

As the caseload of the European human rights organs has continued to grow exponentially, discussion of restructuring the system has taken on greater urgency than it had at the time of Judge Ryssdal's remarks above. Are his three alternatives the only feasible ones?

As Judge Ryssdal has made clear in more recent remarks,[a] he favored the third alternative. It was explored in a 1989 study by a committee of experts reporting to the Council of Europe.

REPORT OF THE COMMITTEE OF EXPERTS ON THE IMPROVEMENT OF HUMAN RIGHTS PROCEDURES
May 2, 1989.
Council of Europe Doc. H (89) 2, at 7–10, 12–13.

* * *

14. For cases that are ultimately referred to the Court, the existing two-stage procedure undeniably displays a *considerable degree of overlapping*. This is not unduly evident as regards fact-finding and the question of admissibility, though issues of fact and admissibility can be, and are on occasion, raised at the level of the Court. However, in respect of examination of the merits, the duplication of work may be very significant: two sets of written pleadings, two sets of hearings and a twofold analysis of the issues raised under the Convention.

15. A merger of the Commission and Court would prevent such duplication of work. It would also avoid certain other time-consuming elements inherent in the present supervisory machinery e.g. the delays involved at the referral stage. On the basis of current experience, it is claimed that the simplification of procedure arising out of a merger should of itself shorten the length of proceedings by some 18 months to two years.

16. However, the view is held by some that in practice a merger might not lead to an appreciable reduction in the length of proceedings, since a single body system would inevitably possess many of the features of the present system (e.g. a filter function and friendly settlement procedures) and possibly certain additional ones (e.g. conclusions of an Advocate–General).

17. Further, although certainly a lengthy process, it has been argued that a *two-fold examination of the merits offers advantages* which one should not give up.

It ensures first of all that the important matters involved in cases arising under the Convention are examined with the greatest care. Against this position it might be argued that the Convention issues in cases submitted to Strasbourg will in principle already have been examined at national level in the course of the exhaustion of domestic remedies. However, this is not necessarily so as regards cases from countries which have not incorporated the Convention into domestic law; and even as regards cases from countries in which the Convention is part of domestic law, arguments based on the Convention are on occasion not dealt with exhaustively by the national courts.

a. See, e.g., Ryssdal, European Human Rights Protection in the Year 2000, at 22– 23 (Council of Europe Doc. Cour (92) 173, 1992).

In addition, the existing system, it is argued, means that States are given timely warning, through the Commission's procedure, of the possibility of a breach of the Convention, thereby assisting governments to assimilate any necessary changes highlighted by the case in question. However, the view has been expressed too that the procedure of a single body would also give such a timely warning, in particular through friendly settlement negotiations.

* * *

20. In addition to its alleged ability to overcome the problems arising from the overburdening of the supervisory machinery, certain advocates of a merger see it as a means of removing what they consider to be anomalies in the design of that machinery, anomalies which had their reason at the time of its creation but which are no longer justified. The arguments in this context centre on the role played by the Committee of Ministers within the supervisory machinery.

* * *

22. The *giving to a political body of a function which is judicial in character,* namely to decide whether or not in a given case there has been a violation of the Human Rights Convention, has been criticised in certain quarters. Such a decision, it is argued, should be based exclusively on legal considerations, whereas within the Committee of Ministers it was inevitable that considerations of political expediency would also enter into play. Moreover, the point is made that the procedure of the Committee of Ministers when acting under Article 32 of the Convention reflects that body's political nature and does not meet even the most rudimentary criteria of a fair hearing; indeed, the individual concerned is totally excluded from the consideration of the case.

23. A merger of the Commission and Court into a single body of a judicial nature would dispense with the participation of the Committee of Ministers in the decision-making process under the Convention (at least insofar as individual applications are concerned) and by the same token would respect the individual's right of access to a tribunal. It is considered that such a step forward should be possible, especially now that practically all the Contracting Parties have both recognised the Court's jurisdiction and accepted the right of individual petition.

24. However, the position is also advanced that a merger—at least into a single Court system—would be undesirable. The present control system, it is argued, reflects the view held by some States that *an international system for the enforcement of human rights should not follow a wholly judicial approach.* It represents a carefully worked-out balance of non-judicial and judicial elements, a balance which clearly would be upset by the reform proposed. The point is made in this context that a purely judicial approach is—as experience had shown—not always the best way of solving human rights problems at the international level.

* * *

26. Moreover, it is feared that *a merger into a single Court system would prejudice the role of conciliation* within the supervisory machinery. Although there is no fundamental objection to the presence of provisions for conciliation in the framework of a judicial body, it is felt that it would be difficult to maintain a procedure for *actively* promoting friendly settlements similar to that currently operated by the Commission. The latter, by virtue of the particular position it holds under the existing control system as well as the confidential and informal character of its proceedings, is very well-suited to perform the function of conciliator, and in particular could use the device of a provisional opinion on the merits to stimulate interest for a settlement. A single judicial body, to which it might fall in due course to give a binding decision on a case, could hardly act in the same manner.

On the other hand, the view is also expressed that the function of conciliator within a single Court system could be satisfactorily performed by an Advocate General.

* * *

36. The Convention's provisions concerning the admissibility of petitions act as a sort of filter or screen through which a petition must pass before it is awarded the benefit of a thorough examination; they are designed to prevent the Convention's machinery from becoming overburdened with worthless petitions or from being exploited for purposes alien to the protection of human rights.

All experts agreed that this filter function should be retained in the event of a merger.

37. As regards the *means of operating the filter function* within the framework of the new Court, some experts felt that the precedent of Protocol No. 8 should be followed, i.e. groups of at least three members could be set up with the power to reject by unanimous decision manifestly inadmissible petitions; petitions not rejected at this stage would be referred to a Chamber of the Court for a decision as to their admissibility.

Other experts considered that somewhat larger groups of, for example, five to seven members might be established with power to settle the question of admissibility (i.e. to declare a petition inadmissible or admissible) by majority decision; consequently, the issue of admissibility would be dealt with by one body.

* * *

42. There was general agreement that *examination by a Chamber* should remain the principle, with the *possibility of relinquishment to the plenary Court* of cases raising serious questions of interpretation of the Convention. As regards the size of the Chambers, it was felt that the figure of 9 judges already provided for by Protocol No. 8 was the best approach; in this way Chambers would be reasonably representa-

tive of the Court as a whole, thereby avoiding an excessive number of relinquishments. * * *

TOWARD A MERGED COMMISSION AND COURT

In October 1992, the Parliamentary Assembly of the Council of Europe proposed that the Commission and Court be merged, with petitions being submitted directly to the Court.[b] At this writing, the Committee of Ministers had not yet acted on the proposal.

Is the merger a good idea?

If so, should states parties to the European Convention retain the option whether or not to submit themselves to petitions by individuals? Should they be given the option whether or not to submit themselves to complaints from other states parties? Or should both procedures be mandatory for all states parties?[c]

What is the optimal future structure of international human rights enforcement machinery? Should there be closer coordination between the United Nations machinery and those of the regional organizations? Should there be a United Nations Court of Human Rights, perhaps modeled on the European or Inter–American Court? If so, which model would be preferable? Or should it be some combination of the two?

[b.] The Reuter Library Rep., Oct. 6, 1992.

[c.] On these and other issues, see Golsong, On the Reform of the Supervisory System of the European Convention on Human Rights, 13 Human Rights L.J. 265 (1992).

Index

References are to pages

ACHESON, D.
Rhodesian sanctions, position on, 628

ADMINISTRATIVE UNIONS
Postal and telegraphic unions, 5–6
River commissions, 5

AFGHANISTAN
Good offices mission to, 844

AGENDA FOR PEACE
Text in Documents volume; see also Boutros-Ghali, Boutros this index

AGO, R.
ICJ and international organizations, 516–517

AMERICAN CONVENTION ON HUMAN RIGHTS
See also Documents volume; Inter-American Commission on Human Rights; Inter-American Court of Human Rights
European Convention, admissibility requirements compared, 1040–1041
Optional procedures, European Convention compared, 982
Parties and nonparties, distinction, 981
Petitions, standing to file, 982
Reservations to, 1029–1030
Withdrawal from, 1029–1030

AMERICAN DECLARATION OF RIGHTS AND DUTIES OF MAN
Text in Documents volume
Death penalty, 988–990, 1029
Duties of individuals, 981
Fundamental rights, 981
Legal significance,
  Inter-American Commission opinion, 988–990
  Inter-American Court opinion, 978–981
  United States, 988–990
Universal Declaration compared, 978, 981

AMNESTY INTERNATIONAL
Objection to U.S. human rights reservation, 905

ARAB LEAGUE
Iraqi invasion of Kuwait, 643, 709
Libya and Lockerbie incident, 703, 709

ARGENTINA
Committee on Economic, Social and Cultural Rights, correspondence with, 912–915

AUSTRIA
European human rights proceedings against,
  Criminal procedure, fairness, 1049–1051
  Freedom of political expression, 1070–1078
  Prompt criminal trial, damages for failure to provide, 1081–1084

BELGIUM
Congo, role in, 745–749, 752

BOSNIA-HERZEGOVINA
See also Humanitarian Assistance; Yugoslavia (Current and Former)
Ethnic composition, 691
UNPROFOR, expansion to, 794–795, 797

BOUDREAU, T.
Secretary–General, article 99 authority, 783–784

BOUTROS-GHALI, BOUTROS
Agenda for Peace, text in Documents volume
Democratic institutions, views on, 829–830
Peace enforcement proposal, 792
Preventive deployment, 883–885
Regional organizations and peacekeeping, 796–797
Somalia, options for assistance, 875–876
UNPROFOR guiding principles (Croatia), 785–789

BUERGENTHAL, T.
ICAO description, 302–303
ICAO dispute settlement, 443–444

BURMA
See Myanmar (Burma)

CAMBODIA
Khmer, Rouge, Security Council action, 713–715
United Nations, representation in, 181–184
UNTAC, 722, 813

CANADA
ILO Freedom of Association report on public employees, 421–425

INDEX

References are to pages

CASTAÑEDA, J.
Effect of U.N. resolutions, 335–336

CHICAGO CONVENTION
See International Civil Aviation Organization

CHINA
Chinese Translators Case, 123–135
Electoral assistance, views on, 820–821
FAO, representation in, 186–188
Security Council permanent membership, 189
Tiananmen Square incident,
 IBRD loans, effect on, 572
 ILO Freedom of Association report, 415–421
U.N., representation in, 176–181, 185

COMORO ISLANDS
Relationship with France (U.N.), 195–202

CONFERENCE ON SECURITY AND COOPERATION IN EUROPE
Member, suspension of, 619–620
Peacekeeping capability, 799

CONFERENCE SYSTEM
Congress of Vienna, 2–3
Peace conferences, 3–4

CONGO
See Zaire

CONSULTATION
Expulsion of U.N. representative, 93–97
GATT requirements, 584–585
IMF and exchange arrangements, 532–533, 584
Shared natural resources, 360–365

CONVENTION FOR THE PROTECTION OF HUMAN RIGHTS AND FUNDAMENTAL FREEDOMS
See European Convention for the Protection of Human Rights and Fundamental Freedoms

CONVENTION ON PRIVILEGES AND IMMUNITIES OF U.N.
See United Nations, Privileges and immunities

COSTA RICA
Inter-American human rights system,
 Criminal appeals case, 1002–1003
 Freedom of expression case, 994

COUNCIL OF EUROPE
See also European Convention for the Protection of Human Rights and Fundamental Freedoms
Committee of Ministers,
 Human rights role,
  Examined, 1065–1067, 1084
  Summarized, 1036–1038
 Voting procedure, 1067

COVENANT ON CIVIL AND POLITICAL RIGHTS
See International Covenant on Civil and Political Rights

COVENANT ON ECONOMIC, SOCIAL AND CULTURAL RIGHTS
See International Covenant on Economic, Social and Cultural Rights

CROATIA
See also Yugoslavia (Current and Former)
Border control, 793–794
Pink zones, 793
"Serbian Krajina Republic," 793
UNPROFOR guiding principles, 785–791

CUBA
Missile crisis, 710–711
OAS, relations with, 617–619

CYPRUS
European Commission of Human Rights proceedings involving, 1052–1065
Good offices missions to, 842–843

CZECHOSLOVAKIA
ILO Committee under article 24, Charter 77 case, 409–412

DANUBE RIVER
Navigation rights and Security Council sanctions, 698–699

DECISION-MAKING
Consensus, 214–222, 237–238
Majority, special, 236–237
Nongovernmental voting parties, 238
Secretariats, role of, 238, 519–520
Security Council, 191–202, 492–493
Structures for, 223–233
U.N. budget, 233–235
Weighted voting, 237

DIPLOMATIC RELATIONS ACT
See United States

EARLY WARNING
See Humanitarian Assistance; Secretary-General (U.N.)

ECONOMIC AND SOCIAL COUNCIL (U.N.)
Committee on Economic, Social and Cultural Rights, see International Covenant on Economic, Social and Cultural Rights
Petitioning procedure (Resolutions 1235 and 1503), see United Nations Commission on Human Rights
Reform proposals,
 Nordic countries, 229–232
 Secretary-General, 232–233
 United Nations Association, 225–229
Resolution 1503,
 Procedure, 860
Sessions, how organized, 224

ECONOMIC AND SOCIAL COUNCIL (U.N.)
—Cont'd
Size, 223
Structural problems, 223–224

ECONOMIC COMMUNITY OF WEST AFRICAN STATES
Liberia, role in, 711–713, 800–801

EGYPT
Tiran, blockade of, 764
United Nations Emergency Force (UNEF), see Peacekeeping

EL SALVADOR
ONUSAL, 813

ELECTIONS
Electoral assistance, sovereignty issue,
  China, views on, 820–821
  General Assembly resolution, 827–828
  Non-Aligned Movement, views on, 830
  Peru, views on, 821
  U.S.A., views on, 822–823
Monitoring by U.N.,
  Criteria, 823, 828–829
  Haiti, 824
  Namibia, 386, 824
  Nicaragua, 814–819, 824
  Resident representatives, role of, 829–830
  Secretary-General, authority, 829
Periodic and genuine elections,
  General Assembly resolution, 824–826
  Myanmar (Burma), 829
  Origin of principle, 828
  Regional organizations, role of, 821, 823, 828
Universal Declaration of Human Rights, 819–820

ENFORCEMENT ACTION
See Security Council (U.N.)

ENVIRONMENT
Persian Gulf war, 665, 674, 682
Shared natural resources, 360–365
UNEP privileges and immunities, 26–34

EQUATORIAL GUINEA
ECOSOC Resolution 1503 proceedings, 973

EUROPEAN BANK FOR RECONSTRUCTION AND DEVELOPMENT
Loan policy, 574–575

EUROPEAN COMMISSION OF HUMAN RIGHTS
Friendly settlement function, 1065
Merger with Court, proposed, 1097–1100
Petitions, admissibility,
  Abuse of right of petition, 1043–1044, 1045–1046, 1048
  Exhaustion of remedies, 1040, 1043–1045, 1048
  Incompatible with Convention, 1049–1050, 1051

EUROPEAN COMMISSION OF HUMAN RIGHTS—Cont'd
Petitions, admissibility—Cont'd
  Manifestly ill-founded, 1044, 1046–1049, 1050–1051
  Other procedures compared, 1052
Role and procedure summarized, 1034–1035, 1036–1037
Standing to submit petitions, 1040

EUROPEAN COMMUNITIES (INCLUDING EEC)
FAO, application for membership, 164–166
U.N., possible membership in, 166
Yugoslavia, role regarding, 788, 796–797

EUROPEAN CONVENTION FOR THE PROTECTION OF HUMAN RIGHTS AND FUNDAMENTAL FREEDOMS
  Text in Documents volume; European Commission of Human Rights; European Court of Human Rights
American Convention, admissibility requirements compared, 1040–1041
Article 25 declarations,
  Restrictions contained in, compatibility with Convention, 1053–1060
  Validity if restrictions rejected, 1060–1061
Class actions, 1051–1052
Committee of Ministers, see Council of Europe
Covenant on Civil and Political Rights, overlap with,
  Inter-state proceedings, 1086–1087, 1092
  Petitions of individuals, 1087–1093
  Reservations by European parties to Protocol, 1088, 1090–1093
  Rights, similarity, 1085–1086
Cyprus, northern, application to, 1052–1065
History, 1030–1032
ILO Convention on Freedom of Association, overlap with, 1093–1094
Inter-state procedure, 1039–1040, 1053
Law reform function, 1051–1052, 1068, 1084–1085
Occupied territory, application in, 1061–1065
Optional procedures, American Convention compared, 982
Protocols summarized, 1032–1033, 1038
Reform of system, 1095–1100
Reporting procedure, 1038–1039
Reservation to, 906
Summarized, 1032–1038
Territorial scope, 1057–1059, 1061–1065

EUROPEAN COURT OF HUMAN RIGHTS
Advisory jurisdiction,
  Described, 1068
  Inter-American system compared, 993

EUROPEAN COURT OF HUMAN RIGHTS
—Cont'd
European Convention on Human Rights, opinion on reservation to, 906
Fact-finding by, 1070
Judgments, enforcement, 1084
Margin of appreciation doctrine,
    Freedom of political expression, 1070–1079
    Obscenity, 1079–1080
    U.S. approach compared, 1078, 1080
Reform, proposed, 1095–1100
Remedies,
    Nature of, 1074–1075, 1078–1079, 1083–1084
    Procedure, 1080–1083
Role and procedure summarized, 1035, 1037
Standing, individuals, 1068–1070

EXCHANGE CONTROLS AND RATES
See International Monetary Fund

FACT-FINDING
    See also General Assembly (U.N.); Secretary-General (U.N.); Security Council (U.N.)
Consent requirement, 835, 838
Disarmament, role in, 839
Host states, expression of views by, 837, 839
Purposes, 834, 839
Recommendations by fact-finders, 838
Secretary-General, role of, 836, 838

FEDERAL JURISDICTION
See United States

FOOD AND AGRICULTURE ORGANIZATION
China, representation in, 186–188
Dues, withholding of, 270–273
European Economic Community, application for membership, 164–166
Immunities, 33
Membership eligibility, 149, 153
Namibia, application for membership, 153
Palestinian people, assistance to, 270–273
Voting rights, United States, 564
Withdrawal from, 186–188, 259

FRANCE
Comoro Islands, voting in Security Council, 195–202
United Nations,
    Dues, withholding of, 247–251
    Voting rights, 558–563

FRANCK, T.
Secretary-General, good offices, 842–844
UNEF, withdrawal of, 769–772

GENERAL AGREEMENT ON TARIFFS AND TRADE (GATT)
Consultation requirements, 584–585
Retaliation sanction, 555–557

GENERAL ASSEMBLY (U.N.)
Article 11 (U.N. Charter), 758–759
Article 12 (U.N. Charter), 695–696
Article 14 (U.N. Charter), 758, 762
Charter of Economic Rights and Duties, 355–356
Declarations, effect of, 339–340, 349–350
Determinations, power to make, 500
Expenses of U.N.,
    Budget process, 234–235
    Power to apportion, 757–764
General debate, right of reply, 168–169
League of Nations mandates, authority over, 371–372
Observer status, 166–170
Quasi-judicial role, 499–500, 512–513
Palestine,
    Committee on Inalienable Rights of Palestinian People, 374
    Partition resolution, 368–370, 379
    Statehood issue, 159, 373–380
Participation in,
    Israel, 598–600
    South Africa, 590–597
    Yugoslavia, 600–603
Peacekeeping, this index
Permanent Sovereignty, Declaration on, 352–353
Precedents, how established, 170
Representation,
    Cambodia, 181–184
    China, 176–181
    Effect on other U.N. bodies, 184–185
Resolutions,
    See also Declarations; Determinations; titles of individual resolutions
    Arbitral tribunals, consideration by, 357–359
    Effect of, 334–351, 758, 763
    Elections, periodic and genuine, 824–826
    Electoral process, non-interference, 827–828
    Expenses of U.N., 757–764
    Expropriation, 351–360
    Fact-finding by U.N., 834–837
    Humanitarian assistance, 862–866
    Human rights, 349
    Judicial review of, 497–500
    Law-declaring and law-developing, 350–351
    Shared natural resources, 360–365
    Ultra vires, 250, 497
    Use of force, 349–350
Security Council,
    Failure to elect members of, 202–205
    Relationship to, 758–759, 762–763, 838
Self-determination, recognition of right, 374
South West Africa Mandate, termination of, 489–490
Treaties, convening conferences to adopt, 334

GENERAL ASSEMBLY (U.N.)—Cont'd
Voting,
  Consensus as substitute for, 214–222
  Important questions, 179–180, 212–214
  Law of Sea Conference as a model, 216–222

GENERAL CONVENTION ON PRIVILEGES AND IMMUNITIES OF U.N.
See United Nations, Privileges and immunities

GERMANY
Pre-trial detention and trial delays, European Commission of Human Rights proceeding, 1041–1049

GHANA
ILO Commission of Inquiry, case involving, 390–393

GOOD OFFICES
See Secretary–General (U.N.)

GROSS, E.
South West Africa Case, 485–489

GUATEMALA
Death penalty and Inter–American human rights system, 994–1001

HAITI
Elections monitoring, 824
OAS and democratic government, 711

HAMMARSKJÖLD, DAG
Article 99 (U.N. Charter), use of, 748, 751, 781–785
Headquarters Agreement, U.S. security reservation, 117–118
ONUC,
  Authority of Secretary–General, 781–785
  Civilian protection, mandate, 774
  Congolese government, disagreement with, 775–777
  Democratic rights, safeguarding, 753, 774
  Guiding principles, 749–750
  Katanga, 755, 774, 777–778
  Proposals, initial, 748
UNEF I,
  Aide-mémoire on negotiations with Egypt, 742–744
  Guiding principles, 735–737

HENRY, C.
Carriage of dangerous goods by sea, 319–324

HIGGINS, R.
Role of resolutions, 341–345

HONDURAS
Disappearances, Inter–American Court judgment, 1007–1028

HUMAN RIGHTS
See also names of instruments, organizations and organs concerned with human rights
Conventions, reservations to, 906
Custom as source, 893, 897
International bill of rights, 898–901
U.N. Charter as source, 892

HUMAN RIGHTS COMMISSION
See United Nations Commission on Human Rights

HUMANITARIAN ASSISTANCE
African conflicts, 866–867
Bosnia–Herzegovina,
  Delivery measures, 868–869
  Sarajevo, 867–868
  Security Council measures, 797–799, 867, 868–870
Chapter VII (U.N. Charter), relationship to, 877–881
Chapter IX (U.N. Charter), relationship to, 854
Early warning, 863–864, 866
Enforcement action, relationship to, 701, 854–855
Even-handedness, 859, 868
Facilitation of, 865–866
General Assembly resolution on coordination, 862–866
Humanitarian aid coordinator, 862, 864–866
Human rights violations and humanitarian assistance, 858–862
International peace and security, threat as basis for action, 854
Iraq,
  Exemptions from sanctions, 675, 683–684
  Kurds, 852–857
  Security Council Resolution 688,
    No-fly zone, 856
    Text, 853
    U.N. guards, 857
  Shiites, 856
Nongovernmental organizations, 866
Security Council,
  Authority, 853–856, 861, 869, 877–881
  Authorization of national intervention, 855–856, 868–869
Somalia,
  Clans, consent, 875
  Operation, scope of, 880–881
  Options for assistance, 875–876
  Security Council authorization, Chapter VII, 877–881
  Starvation in, 875
Sovereignty issues, 858–867, 875, 880

HUMANITARIAN LAW OF WAR
International criminal court, 874
Persian Gulf conflict, 644, 659–661, 664–666
Somalia, 878, 880

HUMANITARIAN LAW OF WAR—Cont'd
Yugoslavia (former),
    Commission of Experts, creation, 871–874
    Security Council demand that breaches cease, 869–870
    War crimes tribunal, preparations for, 870–874
War crimes defined, 870–871

INDIA
Human Rights Committee observations on, 959–960
ICAO dispute settlement, 443–444, 448–468

INSTITUTE OF INTERNATIONAL LAW
Commission report on General Assembly resolutions, 350

INTER-AMERICAN COMMISSION ON HUMAN RIGHTS
American Convention, parties and nonparties, distinction, 981
American Declaration, application of, 983–990
Compliance mechanisms, 992
Death penalty cases, 983–990
Domestic jurisdiction issue, 990
Evidence,
    On-site investigation, 992
    Statistical, 987–988
Fact-finding, respondent's nonparticipation, 1007
Friendly settlement authority, 992
Inter-American Court, right to request advisory opinions from, 993, 1000
Investigations by, 977–978
Jus cogens, 989–990
Juveniles, death penalty, 989–990
OAS, principal organ of, 976
Origin and development, 976–977
Petitions, admissibility,
    Exhaustion of remedies, 982, 990
        See also Inter-American Court of Human Rights
    Failure to state facts constituting a violation, 983–988
Pleading requirements, 982
Procedures, duplication, Optional Protocol to Covenant compared, 982
Recommendations despite inadmissibility of petition, 990–992
United States, cases against, 983–990

INTER-AMERICAN COURT OF HUMAN RIGHTS
Advisory jurisdiction,
    American Declaration, interpretation of, 978–980, 1003–1004
    Contentious jurisdiction, relationship to, 993–1003
    European system compared, 993
    ICJ discretion compared, 999, 1001–1002
    Standing to request opinion, 993

INTER-AMERICAN COURT OF HUMAN RIGHTS—Cont'd
Advisory jurisdiction—Cont'd
    Treaties with non-American parties, 1004–1006
Contentious jurisdiction,
    Disappearances, violation of Convention, 1019–1025, 1027
    Evidentiary matters, 1011–1018, 1027
    Exhaustion of remedies, 1008–1011, 1026–1027
    Fact-finding, respondent's nonparticipation, 1017
    Inter-American Commission's role, 993–994, 1026
    Petitioner, representation of, 1026
    Proof, standards of, 1015–1017, 1027
    Remedies, 1025–1026, 1028
Judgments,
    Execution, European system compared, 1084
    Precedential value outside Americas, 1027–1028
Jurisdiction, generally, 977
Origin, 976

INTER-AMERICAN DEVELOPMENT BANK
Immunities, waiver, 39–43

INTERNATIONAL ATOMIC ENERGY AGENCY
Assistance to states, withholding of, 575, 581–583
Authority of Director General, 16–18
Decision-making process, 236
Iraq, relations with,
    Inspections of facilities, 673–674, 679–682
    NPT breach, condemnation of, 549–550, 679
Israel, relations with,
    Credentials, rejection of, 610
    Suspension, attempt to, 610
    Withholding of assistance to, 581–583
Membership, continuation of, 603
NPT, inspections under, 681
Safeguard system, 14
Treaty-making capacity, 14–18
United Nations, relationship agreement with, 583
Yugoslavia, relations with, 603

INTERNATIONAL BANK FOR RECONSTRUCTION AND DEVELOPMENT
European Bank for Reconstruction and Development, comparison with, 574–575
Executive Directors, status, 573
Immunities, 35–51, 53
    Waiver, 39–51, 53
Loan agreements, 569–570
Loan policy,
    Expropriations by borrowing states, 570–571

INTERNATIONAL BANK FOR RECON-STRUCTION AND DEVELOPMENT —Cont'd
Loan policy—Cont'd
Human rights patterns of borrowing states, 571–574
Membership eligibility, 149

INTERNATIONAL CIVIL AVIATION ORGANIZATION
Air Navigation Commission, 305, 309–312
Air traffic control clearances, 306–307
Chicago Convention,
Amendment of, 316–318
Article 3 bis, 317–318, 471, 653, 655
Dispute settlement, formal,
Council, role of, 443–455
ICJ, role of, 455–468
ILO compared, 455
India–Pakistan, 443–444, 448–468
Procedural matters, 444–447, 454–455
Transit agreement, complaint under, 467–468
Dispute settlement, informal,
Council, role of, 469–474, 479
ICJ, role of, 475–478
Iran airbus incident, 471–478
Korean airliner incident, 469–471
Secretariat, role of, 469–470, 472–473, 474
Interception of aircraft, rules on, 309–315
International standards and recommended practices, 303–315
Iraq air embargo, position on, 655
Korean airliner incident, 309, 469–471
Legal Bureau Director, role of, 311, 314
Legal Committee, 303
Membership eligibility, 149
NOTAM, 472–473, 478
Rules of the Air, 305, 308–309
South Africa, withholding of benefits from, 575
Spain, suspension of participation, 268
State aircraft, 310–314
Technical assistance and norm enforcement, 531
U.N. Convention on Law of Sea, relationship to, 308–309
Voting rights, loss of, 563
Withdrawal from, 259

INTERNATIONAL COURT OF JUSTICE
Advisory jurisdiction,
Ad hoc judges, 492, 495–496, 512
Binding opinions, 515–517
Contentious jurisdiction, relationship to, 494–495, 505–512
Discretion to decline, 494–496
Judicial review, 497–500, 512, 513
Regional organizations, requests by or for, 515
Secretary-General, authority to request advisory opinions, 511–512

INTERNATIONAL COURT OF JUSTICE —Cont'd
Advisory jurisdiction—Cont'd
U.N. Administrative Tribunal, appeals from, 135–136
Contentious jurisdiction,
International organizations as parties, 18–19, 516–518
Lockerbie Incident Case, 703, 707–708
South West Africa Case, 485–489
Enforcement action, meaning, 759, 761–763
Expenses of U.N., 757–764
Experts on missions, meaning, 86–90
Force, adjudication regarding, 518–519
General Assembly powers, views on, 497–500, 512–513, 757–764
ICAO dispute settlement, role in, 455–468, 475–478
Montreal Convention, jurisdiction under, 703–704, 708
Namibia, termination of mandate, 491–505, 512–515
Privileges and Immunities Convention, interpretation of, 507–510
Provisional measures, 707–708
Security Council,
Powers, views on, 501–503, 513–515, 757–758
Relationship to, 518–519, 707–708
U.N., implied powers, 11
Western Sahara, status of, 506

INTERNATIONAL COVENANT ON CIVIL AND POLITICAL RIGHTS
Economic, social and political rights, relationship to, 941–946
Family rights provision, 966–969
Human Rights Committee,
Admissibility issues,
Abuse of right of submission, 927, 928
Exhaustion of remedies, 927–928, 929
Incompatibility with Covenant, 925–926, 928
Simultaneous examination of same matter, 927, 929
Competence, 923–924
Decisions, monitoring compliance with, 953–954
Fact-finding, respondent's nonparticipation, 933, 934, 937, 950, 952
General comments,
Family rights, example, 966–969
Guidelines, 965
Purpose, 969
Persuasion, burden of, 937
Procedure, 924–925
Remedies, 936, 939–940, 944–945, 946, 951, 953
Reporting system, see below
Special Rapporteur, 954
Sua sponte raising of issues, 951–952

INTERNATIONAL COVENANT ON CIVIL AND POLITICAL RIGHTS—Cont'd
Human Rights Committee—Cont'd
   Substantive rights, examples,
      Criminal procedure, fairness, 930–940
      Personal security, protection, 946–953
      Sex discrimination, prohibition, 940–946
   U.S. Supreme Court approach, comparison, 938–939
Inter-state procedure,
   Exhaustion of remedies, 922
   Nonuse of, 907, 922
   Solutions available, 922–923
   Standing of complainants, 922
   U.S. acceptance, 907
Optional Protocol (first),
   Human Rights Committee, see above
   Summarized, 901
Procedures, duplication, Inter-American system compared, 982
Reporting system,
   Even-handedness, 964
   Guidelines, 955–957
   Observations, examples,
      India, 959–960
      Iraq, 962–963
      Spain, 959
      Sudan, 961–962
      Sweden, 960–961
   Observations, nature of, 963–964
   Procedures, 958–959
   Security Council, relationship to, 964
Rights summarized, 900–901
Self-determination, 926, 928–929
U.S. reservations, understandings, declarations, 902–907

INTERNATIONAL COVENANT ON ECONOMIC, SOCIAL AND CULTURAL RIGHTS
Committee on Economic, Social and Cultural Rights,
   Article 2(1), Committee's comments on, 917–921
   Creation, 909–910
   General comments,
      Article 2(1), example, 917–921
      Purpose, 916–917
   Governments, criticism of, 911–915
   Prima facie violations, views on, 919–920
   Procedure, 911
   Supervisory system, 916–917
   U.S. position, 910–911
Protection of rights, history, 908
Rights summarized, 899
U.S. position, 907–908

INTERNATIONAL CRIMINAL COURT
   See also Humanitarian Law of War
War crimes, jurisdiction, 874

INTERNATIONAL LABOR ORGANIZATION
British trade union case, 536–548
Commissions of Inquiry,
   Appeals from, 406–407
   Binding decisions, 407
   Freedom of association, views on, 399–404
   Ghana–Portugal, 390–393
   Poland, 394–406
   Portugal–Liberia, 393–394
   Procedure, 390–392, 396–398
   Rules for Conciliation of Disputes, relationship to, 407–408
Committee of Experts,
   Composition, 525
   Conclusions, legal effect, 546
   Direct contact procedure, 526, 528–532
   Legitimacy, 527
   Procedure, 526
   Quasi-judicial role, 545
   Requests to governments, 526, 528
   Treaty interpretation methods, 541, 545–546
   United Kingdom and public employees, 538–539, 547–548
Committee on Application of Conventions and Recommendations,
   See Committee on Application of Standards, below
Committee on Application of Standards,
   Effectiveness, 548
   Even-handedness, 547
   Procedure, 526–527, 533–536, 546
   Reports on application of conventions, 535–536
   Special list, 533–535
   Special paragraphs, 536, 543–544, 547
   United Kingdom and public employees, 539–544, 546–547
Committee on Freedom of Association,
   Canada and public employees, 421–425
   China and Tiananmen Square incident, 415–421
   Domestic courts, relationship to, 425
   ICAO dispute settlement, comparison with, 455
   Procedure, 414–415
   Right to organize, 536–538
   Right to strike, 419, 421–425
   Sources of substantive law, 420
   United Kingdom and public employees, 536–538
Conference Committee,
   See Committee on Application of Standards, above
Constitution, amendment of, 294–295
Conventions,
   Adoption procedure, 276, 280
   Construction safety convention, 285–288, 290–291
   Denunciation, 290–291
   Equal remuneration convention, 281–282, 292
   Flexibility clauses, 279–280, 290, 294

INTERNATIONAL LABOR ORGANIZATION
—Cont'd
Conventions—Cont'd
Proliferation, 293–294
Reservations, 278–280
Decision-making,
Nongovernmental voting delegates, 238
Declaration of Philadelphia, 908
Director–General, role of, 150–152
Duty-specific instruments defined, 278
Free City of Danzig application for membership, 155–156, 158
Freedom of association,
British trade union case, 536–548, 1093–1094
Commission of Inquiry, views of, 399–404
Committee on Freedom of Association, see above
Fact-Finding and Conciliation Committee, 413–414
International Court of Justice,
Appeals from Commission of Inquiry to, 406–407
Interpretation of labor conventions, 426–427, 430, 541, 546
International Labor Office,
Convention No. 111, interpretation of, 427–429
Interpretation of conventions by, 426–431
Preparatory work, use of, 428–429
International labor standards, 276–277
Membership eligibility, 149, 153–158
Namibia application for membership, 153–158
Nongovernmental organizations, role of, 548–549
PLO observer status in, 176
Promotional instruments defined, 278
Recommendations,
Adoption procedure, 276
Construction safety recommendation, 288–290
Conventions, relationship to, 284, 291–292
Equal remuneration recommendation, 282–284
Reports by members on conventions and recommendations, 524–525, 548
Representations under article 24,
Czechoslovakia and Charter 77 Manifesto, 409–412
Governing Body committee, 408
Relationship to article 26, 412
Soviet Union,
Application for membership, 150–152
Special list, inclusion in, 534–535
Technical assistance, role of, 530–531
Voting rights, loss of, 563
Withdrawal from, 259–263

INTERNATIONAL LAW ASSOCIATION
Declaration on new international economic order, 359–360

INTERNATIONAL LAW COMMISSION
Composition, 13, 333
Functions, 333
Jurisdictional immunities of states, 51–53
Immunities of members, 91
States and international organizations, project on relations between, 13–14
Watercourses, articles on, 365

INTERNATIONAL MARITIME ORGANIZATION
Assembly, dispute-settlement role, 479–480
COLREG, 319, 321–322
IMDG Code, 319–324
Marine Environmental Protection Committee, 318, 479–480
Maritime Safety Committee, 318, 479–480
MARPOL,
Amendments to Annexes and Appendices, 325–329
Description, 325
U.N. Convention on Law of Sea, relationship to, 332
Membership, expulsion, 604
Recommendations,
Adoption procedure, 324–325
Role of, 319–325
SOLAS, 319, 321
U.N. Convention on Law of Sea, relationship to, 329–332
UNEP dispute settlement, comparison to, 480–481
Voting rights, loss of, 563–564

INTERNATIONAL MONETARY FUND
Agreement, amendment of, 302
Code of conduct for members, 295
Conditionality, 566–569
Consultations with members, 532–533, 584
Enforcement techniques, nonpublic nature, 549
Exchange rates,
Description of system, 296–297
Floating, Fund response, 301
Fund surveillance, 298–301
Executive Board,
Interpretation of article VIII, section 2(b), 437–443
Interpretation of Fund Agreement, binding effect, 432–436
Firm surveillance, 533
Foreign Sovereign Immunities Act (U.S.) and exchange controls, 442–443
Immunities, 42
Income distribution, relevance of, 568
Interpretation of Fund Agreement,
Choice of law, 437–443
Dispute, existence of, 436–437
Effect internationally, 433–434, 435
Effect within U.S., 432–443
Exchange contracts, 437–443

References are to pages

INTERNATIONAL MONETARY FUND—Cont'd
Membership,
  Eligibility, 149
  Expulsion, 603
Performance criteria, 567–569
Quotas, 565
Resources,
  Charges for use, 583–584
  Ineligibility to use, 565–566
Special drawing rights, 295
Suspension of Fund Agreement provisions, 301
Tranches, use of, 565–568
Weighted voting, 295, 432

INTERNATIONAL ORGANIZATIONS IMMUNITIES ACT
See United States

INTERNATIONAL PERSONALITY
Attributes, 9
International claims, 7–13
Nonstates, 889–890
Treaty-making capacity, 14–18
United Nations, 9

INTERNATIONAL TELECOMMUNICATION UNION
Israeli rights, attempt to exclude, 610–616
Membership eligibility, 149
Sanctions, 612–614
South African rights, exclusion, 616

IRAN
Airbus incident, 471–478

IRAQ
  See also Security Council (U.N.); Humanitarian Assistance
Armed force, use against, 662–669
Compensation for damage caused by, 674–675, 682–684, 686–688
Human Rights Committee observations on, 962–963
Humanitarian law of war issues, 644, 659–661
Kuwait,
  Boundary, 649, 671–672, 676–678
  Grievances against, 642
  History of relations with, 647–650
  Invasion and occupation of, 642–644, 659
Nuclear Nonproliferation Treaty, breach of,
  IAEA condemnation, 549–550, 679
  Security Council condemnation, 679
Nuclear weapon development, measures against, 673–674, 678–682
Oil exports, Security Council regulation, 683–684
Resolution 687, acceptance of, 676, 677, 682
Self-defense, 678
Sovereignty, 676, 678, 684
Weapons destruction, 672, 678

IRAQ—Cont'd
Withdrawal from U.N. (hypothetical), 246

ISRAEL
History, 366–371
IAEA,
  Rejection of credentials by, 610
  Suspension attempt by, 610
  Withholding of assistance by, 581–583
Iraqi nuclear reactor, attack on, 581
ITU, attempt to exclude rights by, 610–616
Statehood, 368–371
UNESCO,
  Suspension of participation in, 268, 578–581
  Withholding of assistance by, 575–581
United Nations, credentials dispute, 598–600
WHO, relationship with, 550–554, 564

ITALY
Council of Europe, Committee of Ministers, action regarding delays in Italian courts, 1066

JENKS, C.W.
Decision-making in international organizations, 214–215, 236–237
ILO Commissions of Inquiry, 390–394

KAMPUCHEA
See Cambodia

KHALIDI, R.
Palestine National Council resolutions, 377–378

KIRGIS, F.
Prior consultation and natural resources, 361–364

KOREA
Airliner incident, 309, 469–471

KUWAIT
  See also Security Council (U.N.)
Iraq,
  Boundary, 649, 671–672, 676–678
  Environmental harm caused by, 665, 674, 682
  History of relations with, 647–650
Map, 643

LEAGUE OF NATIONS
Mandates, Council authority over, 371
Palestine Mandate, 366–367
South West Africa Mandate, 380–381

LEGISLATIVE ACTS
Defined, 275

LIBERIA
Civil war, 711–713, 799–802
ILO Commission of Inquiry, case involving, 393–394

INDEX

References are to pages

LIBYA
Lockerbie incident,
  Description, 701–702
  ICJ proceedings, 703–704, 707–708
  Security Council action, 702–706

LIE, TRYGVE
Fact-finding authority, views on, 831
Representation in U.N., memorandum on, 177–178

LUARD, E.
International labor standards, 293–294
Norm compliance, 522–523

MACEDONIA
U.N. preventive deployment,
  Military aspects, 887–888
  Objectives, 886–887
  Police aspects, 888
  Request by, 885–886
  Security Council authorization, 888

MALAWI
Governance and IBRD policy toward, 574

MILDE, M.
Aircraft, interception of, 309–314

MILITARY STAFF COMMITTEE
See Security Council (U.N.)

MONTREAL CONVENTION
ICJ jurisdiction, 703–704, 708

MOROCCO
Good offices mission to, 844
ICJ Advisory Opinion on Western Sahara, 506

MYANMAR (BURMA)
General Assembly resolution on political process in, 829

NAMIBIA
Constitution, 386–387
Council for Namibia,
  Creation, 381–382
  Decree No. 1, 383–385
International Court of Justice,
  Advisory proceedings, 491–506, 512–515
  Contentious proceedings, 485–489
SWAPO, 386
UNTAG, 385–386, 722, 824

NICARAGUA
Conflict with contras, 803
ONUCA, see Peacekeeping
ONUVEN, see Peacekeeping

NONGOVERNMENTAL ORGANIZATIONS
Amnesty International, 905
Enforcement of norms, role in, 548–549
Good offices, role in, 849–850
Human rights enforcement, role in, 915, 971, 974
Humanitarian assistance and U.N. role, 866

NONGOVERNMENTAL ORGANIZATIONS
—Cont'd
International Committee of the Red Cross, 868–870

NONSTATE ENTITIES
International personality, 889–890
Membership in international organizations, 164–166
Obligations to U.N., 91–92

NUCLEAR NONPROLIFERATION TREATY
Breach as threat to peace, 681
IAEA inspections, 681
Iraqi breach,
  IAEA condemnation, 549–550, 679

OBSERVER MISSIONS
See Peacekeeping

OPTIONAL PROTOCOL
See International Covenant on Civil and Political Rights

ORGANIZATION OF AFRICAN UNITY
Liberian civil war, 800, 802

ORGANIZATION OF AMERICAN STATES
  See also Inter-American Commission on Human Rights
Cuban government, exclusion of, 617–619
Cuban missile crisis, 710–711
Haiti, measures involving, 711
History, 4
Human rights, development of system, 975–977
Nicaragua,
  Election monitoring role, 816, 818
  Peacekeeping, minimal role, 809
Treaty-making capacity, 15–16

ORGANIZATIONS, PERSONNEL OF
Employment contracts, disputes regarding, 36–37, 43–53

PAKISTAN
ICAO dispute settlement, 443–444, 448–468

PALESTINE
General Assembly acknowledgment of statehood proclamation, 159
General Assembly partition resolution, 368–370
History, 366–368, 372–373
Intifadeh, 375
Statehood claim, 159–163, 372–380
United Nations Emergency Force (UNEF), see Peacekeeping
WHO membership, application for, 158–164, 268–270

PALESTINE LIBERATION ORGANIZATION
Arafat, Yasir, denial of visa to, 113–121
Governmental indicia, 380
History, 373
ILO, observer status in, 176

PALESTINE LIBERATION ORGANIZATION—Cont'd
U.N.,
  Observer mission to, 104–113
  Observer status in, 166–175, 373
  Self-representation in, 173–175

PALESTINE NATIONAL COUNCIL
Proclamation of independence, 159, 375–378

PEACE ENFORCEMENT
Chapter VII (U.N. Charter), relationship to, 882
Proposals for, 792, 881
Security Council response, 881–882
Staffing needs, 882

PEACEKEEPING
Article 99 (U.N. Charter), 781–785
Border control, 793–794
Chapter VII as authority for, 791
Characteristics, 718–719, 792
Civilians, relationship to, 753
Command of forces, 719
Consent of parties, 736, 739, 767–773, 790–792, 817
Definition, 717
Democratic principles, respect for, 753, 774–775
Dispute settlement, authority of field officials, 813
Election monitoring, see ONUVEN, below
Enforcement action distinguished, 758–759, 761–764
Force, use of, 775, 813
Funding problem, 773
General Assembly, role of, 733–734, 737–738, 756–764, 815, 817
Internal conflicts, role in, 755
Military Staff Committee, proposal, 782
Nonstate parties to conflict, 791–792
Observer missions, 720
ONUC (Congo),
  Composition, 750
  Congolese government,
    Agreement with, 754–755
    Disagreement with, 775–777
  Creation, 731, 745–749
  Katanga, role in, 752–753, 755, 774, 777–780
  Legitimacy, 756–764
  Terms of reference, 749–751
ONUCA (Nicaragua),
  Assessed expenses, 809
  Creation and events leading to it, 804–808
  OAS, relationship to, 809
  Terms of reference, 805–808, 810–813
ONUSAL, relations with El Salvador government, 813
ONUVEN,
  Assessment, 818–819
  Creation and events leading to it, 814–816

PEACEKEEPING—Cont'd
ONUVEN—Cont'd
  General Assembly authority, 815, 817
  Precedent, 815, 819
  Stages, 816–817
Operations listed, 720–722
Origin, 716–717
Participating states, agreements with, 772–773
Peace enforcement, relationship to, 792, 881–882
Regional organizations, relationship with, 788–789, 796–797, 801, 809, 816, 818
Search, authority to, 774–775
Secretary–General, limits of authority, 781–783, 813–814
Security Council,
  Acquiescence in Secretary–General's acts, 781
  Authority, 776–777, 791
Self-determination, relationship to, 780–781
Status of forces agreements, 722–731, 754–755
Structure, alternatives, 735
UNEF I,
  Advisory Committee, 738–739
  Aides-mémoires, 741–744
  Creation, 731–738
  Egypt, agreement with, 741–742
  Legitimacy, 756–764
  Terms of reference, 736–737
  Withdrawal of, 741–744, 764–773
UNEF II,
  Creation, 739
  Terms of reference, 739–741
UNIKOM (Iraq-Kuwait), 678
UNOSOM,
  See also Humanitarian Assistance
  Creation, 802–803
UNPROFOR,
  Border control by, 793–794
  Bosnia-Herzegovina, expansion to, 794–795, 797
  Creation, 785–791
  European organizations, relationship to, 788–789
  Pink zones, 793
  Terms of reference, original, 785–788
UNTAC, relations with Khmer Rouge, 813
Weapons disposal role, 810, 812–813

PEACEMAKING
See Secretary–General (U.N.)

PECHOTA, V.
Secretary–General, good offices role of, 840, 841–842, 845, 846, 848, 849–851

PEREZ DE CUÉLLAR, JAVIER
Dues, unpaid, proposal for interest on, 584
Election monitoring, views on, 828–829
Good offices, views on, 840
Human rights, massive violations and U.N. role, 858–859

INDEX

References are to pages

PEREZ DE CUÉLLAR, JAVIER—Cont'd
Information-gathering methods and proposals, 832–833
ONUCA guiding principles, 805–808, 810–813
ONUVEN guiding principles, 815–816
U.S. travel restrictions, position on, 99–100

PERIODIC AND GENUINE ELECTIONS
See Elections

PERSIAN GULF WAR
See Iraq; Kuwait; Security Council (U.N.)

PERSONNEL
See Organizations, Personnel of

PERU
American Convention on Human Rights, death penalty issue, 1029
Electoral assistance, views on, 821

POLAND
ILO Commission of Inquiry, Solidarity case, 395–406

PORTUGAL
ILO Commissions of Inquiry, cases involving, 390–394

PREVENTIVE DEPLOYMENT
Consent, 883–885, 888
Macedonia,
  Military aspects, 887–888
  Objectives, 886–887
  Police aspects, 888
  Request by, 885–886
  Security Council authorization, 888
Meaning, 883–885
Uses, 883–884, 888

PRIVILEGES AND IMMUNITIES
Automobile accidents, 70–79
Diplomatic immunities, 53–55, 64–65, 67–68, 69–70, 71–74
Experts, 84–92, 873–874
Functional immunities, 68–79
International Law Commission members, 91
Internationally protected persons, 55, 59–60
Missions to U.N.,
  Bank accounts, 68–70
  Eviction, 61–68
  Protection, 56–61
Nonstates, obligations of, 91–92
Peacekeeping forces, 726, 728–729, 731
Rapporteurs, 84–85, 88–91
United Nations,
  Capacity in domestic courts, 20
  Commission of Experts (Yugoslavia), 873–874
  Dinh Ba Thi incident, 92–98
  Immunity from execution, 34
  Immunity from suit, 28–29
  Mazilu incident, 84–91

PRIVILEGES AND IMMUNITIES—Cont'd
United Nations—Cont'd
  Officials of U.N., 77–78, 80–81
  Waiver of immunity, 32–34, 78
  Wesolowska incident, 79–83
Waiver of immunity,
  Inter-American Development Bank, 39–43
  International Bank for Reconstruction and Development, 39–51, 53
  United Nations, 32–34, 78

REGIONAL ORGANIZATIONS
See also names of individual organizations
Advisory opinions, requests by or for, 515
Election monitoring, role in, 816, 818, 821, 823, 828
Enforcement action by, 709–713
Good offices, role in, 848–849
Membership in universal organizations, 164–166
Peaceful dispute-settlement, role in, 708–709
Peacekeeping, role in, 788–789, 796–797, 799, 800–802, 809
Suspension or expulsion of members, 619–620

REPRISAL
Argument for withholding dues, 269

RESOLUTION 1503
See Economic and Social Council (U.N.)

RHODESIA
See also Zimbabwe
U.N. enforcement action against, 621–636

ROMANIA
Mazilu Case, 86–90, 507–511

RUSSIA
See also Soviet Union
Admission to U.N. membership, 146–147
Security Council permanent membership, 188–191

SAN FRANCISCO CONFERENCE
See United Nations

SANCTIONS
See Security Council (U.N.)

SCHREUER, C.
Recommendations and international law, 345–347

SCHWEBEL, S.
General Assembly resolutions and custom, 337–341

SCHWELB, E.
Indonesian withdrawal from U.N., 244–245

SEA, LAW OF
See also United Nations Convention on the Law of the Sea

SEA, LAW OF—Cont'd
Nationality of vessel, Security Council authority to determine, 697, 699
Navigation rights, Security Council action, 699

SECRETARIAT (U.N.)
Interpretation and dispute settlement, 519–521

SECRETARY-GENERAL (U.N.)
See also names of Secretaries-General
Advisory opinions, authority to request, 511–512
Article 97 (U.N. Charter), 831
Article 98 (U.N. Charter), 831
Article 99 (U.N. Charter), 751, 781–785, 831, 838, 840, 844–845
Early warning methods,
  Information Offices and resident representatives, 832–833
  Space-based surveillance, 833
ECOSOC, views on, 232–233
Election monitoring, authority to respond, 829
Fact-finding declaration (General Assembly), 834–837
Fact-finding missions,
  Armenia and Azerbaijan, 831
  Authority for, 831
  Cambodia, 830
  Consent requirement, 835, 838
  Nicaragua, 830
  Yugoslavia, 830
Good offices,
  Afghanistan, 844
  Assessment of, 850–851
  Authority for, 844–846
  Confidentiality, occasional need for, 845
  Cyprus, 842
  Definition, 840
  Internal conflicts, 848
  Missions, protection for, 846–848
  Nongovernmental organizations, role of, 849–850
  Rainbow Warrior dispute, 843–844
  Regional organizations, relations with, 848–849
  Role, 841–844
  San Francisco Conference foresight, 840–841
  Security Council, relationship with, 845–846
  Western Sahara, 844
Information-gathering methods, 831–833, 839
Legal issues, determination of, 519–520
Namibia, role in administering oath of office, 387–388
Peacekeeping role,
  Forces, commander of, 719
  Host government, relations with, 764–773, 775–777

SECRETARY-GENERAL (U.N.)—Cont'd
Peacekeeping role—Cont'd
  Security Council, relationship with, 751, 753, 755–756, 762, 781–783, 813–814
Peacemaking role,
  Good offices, relationship to peacekeeping, 720
Security Council,
  Acquiescence as source of Secretary-General's authority, 781–782
  Resolutions, limited by, 784–785
Security reservation, U.S., position on, 118
Travel restrictions by host country, position on, 99–100
U.N. Information Offices as listening posts, 832, 839

SECURITY COUNCIL (U.N.)
Article 24 (U.N. Charter), 501–502, 513–515, 684, 708, 757
Article 25, meaning, 629, 684
Article 43 agreements, 663–664, 668–669, 759–760
Article 50, effectiveness, 634–635, 656–657
Boundary-setting by, 671–672, 676–677
Chapter VI of the Charter,
  Chapter VII, relationship to, 685–686
  Resolutions, effect of, 685
  Voting, 193–201
China, representation in, 185, 189
Compensation Commission, Iraq, 674–675, 686–688
Composition, future,
  European Community as possible member, 211
  Membership increase, 206–211
  Veto power, 208, 210–211
Domestic legal systems, determinations affecting, 675, 684, 687–688, 694
Enforcement action,
  Armed force, 662–669, 688
  Arms embargoes,
    Liberia, 712
    Libya, 705
    Somalia, 700–701
    South Africa, 638–642
    Yugoslavia, 689–691
  Authority, lack of specificity, 662–663, 676
  Beira, oil tanker incident, 624, 856
  Civil war situations, 689–691
  Compliance measures,
    Air embargo, 653–656
    Danube traffic (Yugoslavia), 698–699
    Interdiction at sea, 623–624, 650–653, 698–699
    Monitoring trade, 629–630
    Port state measures, 655–656
  Diplomatic sanctions, Libya, 705
  Economic sanctions,
    Coverage of, 624–626, 645–646, 692–694, 705
    Effectiveness, 635–636, 657–659

INDEX

References are to pages

SECURITY COUNCIL (U.N.)—Cont'd
Enforcement action—Cont'd
  Economic sanctions—Cont'd
    Force majeure determination, 675, 684, 694
    Humanitarian exceptions, 646–647
    Nonmember states, effect on, 646
    Participating states, burdens on, 634–635, 656–657
    Purposes of, 657–659, 668, 695
    Termination of, 635–638
  Humanitarian assistance, relationship to, 701, 797–799, 877–881
  Iraq,
    See also separate heading
    Armed force against, 662–669
    Effect of economic sanctions on, 657–659
    Post-war measures, 670–688
    Resolutions adopting sanctions, 645–646, 662
    Sanctions against, goals of, 657–659, 668
  Liberia,
    See also separate heading
    ECOWAS and Security Council, 711–713
  Libya,
    See also separate heading
    ICJ and Security Council, 704–708
  Meaning of, 759, 761–764, 880
  Quasi-enforcement action, 713–715
  Regional organizations, relationship to, 710–713
  Rhodesia,
    Humanitarian intervention, precedent for, 856
    Resolutions adopting sanctions, 624–626
    Termination of sanctions, 635–638
    U.S. position, 626–629, 630–634
  Threats to international peace, controversial findings,
    Iraq, 683
    Rhodesia, 626–629
    Somalia, 700–701, 877–881
    South Africa, 640–641
    Yugoslavia, 690–691
  Weapons of mass destruction as basis for action, 715
  Yugoslavia,
    Enforcement of sanctions against, 696–699
    Resolutions adopting sanctions, 689–690, 692–698
    Vessels, ownership of, 697, 699
Fact-finding missions, 838
General Assembly, relationship to, 758–759, 762–763, 838
Good offices, relationship with Secretary-General, 845–846
Human Rights Committee, relationship to, 964
Humanitarian assistance, this index

SECURITY COUNCIL (U.N.)—Cont'd
ICJ, relationship to, 707–708
Khmer Rouge, 713–715
Korean War precedent, 662–663, 667–668
Meetings, open or private, 666–667
Members,
  Future, 206–211
  Nonpermanent, election by General Assembly, 202
  Shortfall, 202–205
Military Staff Committee, 662, 664
Namibia, resolution on illegality of South African presence, 490–491, 501–503
Nonstates, relationship with, 889–890
NPT, breach as threat to peace, 681
Peacekeeping, this index
PLO,
  Observer status in, 170–175
  Self-representation in, 173–175
Presidency of, 661
Quasi-judicial determinations, 659–661, 669–670, 674, 675, 682–684, 697–698, 702, 706
Resolutions,
  See also individual subjects
  Binding outside of Chapter VII, 502–503, 514–515
  Resolution 678, text, 662
    Questions regarding, 662–663
  Resolution 687, text, 670–676
    Questions regarding, 676–685
Rules 37 & 39, 170–175
Russia as permanent member, 188–191
Sanctions Committee,
  Iraq, 646, 654, 675
  Rhodesia, 629–630
Statements, effect of, 795
Terrorism, measures against, 676, 685, 702–706
Voting,
  Abstention as concurring vote, 192–193, 492–493, 505
  Chapter VII of the Charter, 201–202
  Comoro Islands matter, 195–202
  Dispute, definition, 193–195
  Dispute, party to, 193–202, 493, 504
  Panama Canal matter, 198–199, 201
  Procedural matters, 192, 492–493, 504–505
  Suez Canal matter, 194–195
War crimes, measures regarding,
  Persian Gulf conflict, 659–661
  Yugoslavia, 871–874
Weapons of mass destruction, position on, 715

SERBIA
See Yugoslavia

SOMALIA
Humanitarian assistance,
  Enforcement action, relationship to, 701, 877–881
  Operation, scope of, 880–881

INDEX

References are to pages

SOMALIA—Cont'd
Humanitarian assistance—Cont'd
  Options considered, 875–876
  UNOSOM, creation, 802–803
Power struggle, 699–700

SOUTH AFRICA
IAEA, exclusion from General Conference, 607
ICAO, access to meetings and documents, 575
ITU, exclusion of rights in, 616
Namibia, termination of Mandate, 485–505, 512–513
U.N.,
  Arms embargo, 638–642
  Fact-finding mission, 838
  Rejection of credentials, 585–597
UPU, expulsion from, 607–609
WMO, suspension from, 604–607

SOUTH WEST AFRICA
See Namibia

SOVEREIGN IMMUNITY
See United States

SOVIET UNION
  See also Russia
International Labor Organization,
  Admission to, 150–152
  Special list, inclusion in, 534–535
Korean airliner incident, 309, 469–471
United Nations,
  Dues, withholding of, 247–251
  Mission, size of, 103–104
  Voting rights, 558–563

SPAIN
Human Rights Committee observations on, 959
Western Sahara dispute, 506

STATEHOOD
Country or nation compared, 149–150
Defined, 139, 154, 160–161
Palestine, claim by, 159, 162–163

SUCCESSION OF STATES
India–Pakistan, 190–191
Sixth Committee view regarding membership, 191
Soviet Union–Russia, 188–191
Treaties, 189–190

SUDAN
Human Rights Committee observations on, 961–962

SWEDEN
Human Rights Committee observations on, 960–961

SWITZERLAND
Regulation of obscenity, European Court of Human Rights proceeding, 1079–1080

TECHNICAL ASSISTANCE
Enforcement measures, relationship to, 530–531

TERRORISM
ICJ and Security Council, 707–708
Lockerbie incident, 701–702
Security Council measures, 676, 685, 702–706

THANT, U
Good offices, occasional need for confidentiality, 845
UNEF I, withdrawal of, 765–773

TREATIES, LAW OF
Breach, determination by international organization, 679
Change of circumstances, 253
Coercion, 677
Desuetude, 252
International organizations, capacity, 15
Interpretation rules, 429, 483–484, 943–944, 949–950, 952, 967–968, 1055–1056, 1061
Material breach, 253, 269, 498
Ratification, Iraq–Kuwait, 677
Reservations,
  Constituent instruments, 150–152
  Covenant on Civil and Political Rights, 902–906
  Labor conventions, 278–280
  WHO regulations, 315
Self-executing, see United States
Succession of states, 189–190
Withdrawal from organization, 245

TRUSTEESHIP
Namibia, 384, 883
New form, 882–883
Somalia proposal, 882–883

TURKEY
Cyprus, northern, responsibility for human rights violations on, 1052–1062

UNESCO
Assessments during noncooperation, 257
Dispute settlement by, 479
Israel,
  Suspension of participation, 268, 578–581
  Withholding of assistance, 576–581
Membership, suspension and expulsion from, 603–604
Reporting system, difficulties, 548
Voting rights, loss of, 563
Withdrawal from, 256–257, 258–259, 263–268

UNITED KINGDOM
Beira incident and Rhodesian sanctions, 624

INDEX

References are to pages

UNITED KINGDOM—Cont'd
Cheltenham Government Communications Headquarters, employees' right to organize,
    European Commission of Human Rights proceedings, 1093–1094
    ILO proceedings, 536–548
Equal Remuneration Convention (ILO), 292
Lancaster House Conference (Rhodesia/Zimbabwe), 637
Termination of sanctions against Rhodesia, 637–638

UNITED NATIONS
Admission to membership,
    Angola, 145–146
    Bangladesh, 144–145
    Conditions attached to vote, 140–142
    Divided states, 143
    General Assembly, role of, 148
    Korea, 143
    Obligations of, 143–146
    Pakistan, 190–191
    Russia, 146–147, 188–191
    Security Council, role of, 148–149
    Statehood, 139
    Viet-Nam, 143, 146
    Yugoslavia, 147, 602
Budget process, 233–235
Charter interpretation,
    ICJ, role of, 491–505, 512–515
    Organs, interpretation by, 482–484, 505
    Plain meaning rule, 483–484
Committee on Relations with Host Country, 92–96, 101–103
Cooperation agreements, 17–18
Credentials of members,
    Procedure for examining, 586
    Rejection of, 585–600
Dues,
    Interest on, proposal, 584
    Withholding of, 247–254
Economic and Social Council, this index
Economic and Social functions, reform of, 225–233
Enforcement action, see Security Council (U.N.)
Expenses of the Organization, 248–250
Experts, 84–92, 871–874
Expulsion of members, 588–589
General Assembly, this index
Headquarters Agreement,
    See United Nations Headquarters Agreement
Headquarters District, tort liability, 34–35
Implied powers, 11
International personality, 7–9, 13
Israel, this index
Legal Counsel, role of, 94–95, 97
Membership, questions of succession to,
    Pakistan, 190–191
    Russia, 146–147, 188–191
    Yugoslavia, 147, 600–603
Namibia, this index

UNITED NATIONS—Cont'd
Nonmembers, 12–13
Observer status, implications of, 167–169
Palestine, this index
Peacekeeping, this index
Privileges and immunities,
    Generally, 26–35
    Capacity in domestic courts, 20
    Commission of Experts (Yugoslavia), 873–874
    Dinh Ba Thi incident, 92–98
    Immunity from execution, 34
    Immunity from suit, 28–29
    Mazilu incident, 84–91
    Officials, 77–78, 80–81
    Waiver of immunity, 32–34, 78
    Wesolowska incident, 79–83
Rapporteurs, 84–85, 88–91
Reparations, 7–13, 83, 846–847
Representation in, legal aspects, 177–179
San Francisco Conference, 28–29, 138–139, 239–241, 482–483, 561, 840–841
Secretariat, this index
Secretary–General, this index
Security Council, this index
Sixth (Legal) Committee, 191
South Africa, this index
Staff members,
    Career appointment, right to, 129–132, 134
    Custody, right to visit, 79–83
    Secondment, 128–129, 134
Suspension of members, 590–597
Voting rights, loss of, 558–563
Withdrawal from,
    Assessments during nonparticipation, 243–246
    "Cessation of cooperation," 243–246
    Exceptional circumstances, 240, 242, 244–246
    Indonesia, 241–246
    San Francisco Conference, 239–241

UNITED NATIONS ADMINISTRATIVE TRIBUNAL
Composition and competence, 122
ICJ, appeal to, 135–136
Remedies for successful applicants, 132, 135
Right to career appointment, views on, 129–132
Secondment, views on, 128–129
Secretary–General's discretion, views on, 129–132
Status of, 133–134

UNITED NATIONS COMMISSION ON HUMAN RIGHTS
Investigations, 974
Mandate and composition, 893
Petitioning procedure,
    Covenant Protocol, relationship to, 972
    ECOSOC Resolutions 1235 and 1503, Compared, 973–974

UNITED NATIONS COMMISSION ON HUMAN RIGHTS—Cont'd
Petitioning procedure—Cont'd
    ECOSOC Resolutions 1235 and 1503
      —Cont'd
      Summaries, 970
      Equatorial Guinea proceeding, 973
      History, 969–970
      NGO role, 971, 974
      Results, 972–974
      Sub–Commission Resolution 1,
        ILO proceedings, relationship to, 971–972
        Meaning and procedure, 970–972
        Standing, Covenant Protocol compared, 971
Political character, 974
Special Rapporteurs and Experts, 859–860, 973–974

UNITED NATIONS CONFERENCE ON ENVIRONMENT AND DEVELOPMENT
Principle on prior notification and consultation, 365

UNITED NATIONS CONFERENCE ON THE LAW OF THE SEA
Decision-making, relevance to U.N. General Assembly, 216–222

UNITED NATIONS CONVENTION ON THE LAW OF THE SEA
ICAO standards, relationship to, 308–309
IMO standards, relationship to, 329–332

UNITED NATIONS EDUCATIONAL, SCIENTIFIC AND CULTURAL ORGANIZATION
See UNESCO

UNITED NATIONS ENVIRONMENT PROGRAM
Dispute-settlement role, 480–481
Immunities, 26–34
Structure, 26

UNITED NATIONS HEADQUARTERS AGREEMENT
Duty to arbitrate under, 105, 107–108
Headquarters District, 34–35
Security reservation, U.S.,
    Legislative history, 115–116
    Interpretation,
      U.N., 116–117, 118–121
      U.S., 117–118
Third party beneficiaries, 103

UNITED NATIONS HIGH COMMISSIONER FOR REFUGEES
Functions, 852

UNITED STATES
Anti–Terrorism Act, 104–113
Arafat, Yasir, denial of visa to, 113–121
Death penalty, 902, 905, 983–990
Diplomatic Relations Act, 72–74
Dues, position on duty to pay, 251–252, 269

UNITED STATES—Cont'd
ECOSOC Committee on Economic, Social and Cultural Rights, position regarding, 910–911
Expulsion of foreign representative to U.N., 92–98
FAO, withholding of dues from, 270–273, 564
Federal jurisdiction, 20–26, 27
First Amendment, 60–61
Foreign sovereign immunity in U.S. courts, 29–32, 53, 62–63, 67, 70, 442–443
Goldberg reservation, 250–251, 253, 561–562
Headquarters Agreement, security reservation, 114–121
Host country to U.N., 34–35, 56–70, 92–121
Human rights policy and support for IBRD loans, 571–572
ICAO standard on interception of aircraft, position on, 314–315
ILO, withdrawal from, 260–263, 267–268
Inter–American Commission on Human Rights, proceedings before, 983–990
Inter–American Court of Human Rights, advisory opinion interpreting American Declaration, position on, 1004
International Covenant on Civil and Political Rights, reservations to, 902–906
International Covenant on Economic, Social and Cultural Rights, position regarding, 907–908
International Organizations Immunities Act,
    Capacities of organizations, 20–22
    Functional immunities of personnel, 75
    Immunities of specialized agencies, 35–53
    Immunity of U.N., 29
    Relationship to FSIA, 35–38
Iran airbus incident, 471–478
Iraq,
    Collective self-defense against, 650–652, 661
    Humanitarian intervention in, 855–856
Judicial authority, delegation of, 443
Legislative authority, delegation of, 315, 443
Missions of foreign governments, size, 103–104
Nicaraguan contras, aid to, 808
Palestine, position on statehood, 160–161
PLO Observer mission, attempt to close, 104–113
Rhodesian sanctions, position on, 626–629, 630–634
Self-executing treaties, 19, 70, 75, 290, 634
Somalia, role in, 876–881
Statute and international obligation, conflict between, 109–113
Supreme Court in criminal cases, comparison with U.N. Human Rights Committee, 938–939

INDEX

UNITED STATES—Cont'd
Travel restrictions upon mission personnel and U.N. employees, 98–103
Treaties,
    Constitution, relation to, 905, 906–907
    Self-executing, 19, 70, 75, 290, 634, 904, 906
U.N. dues,
    Interest on, objection to proposal, 584
    Withholding of, 233, 247, 251–254
UNESCO,
    Withdrawal from, 263–268
    Withholding of dues from, 579
WHO,
    Withdrawal from, threat, 564
    Withholding dues from, threat, 268–270

UNIVERSAL DECLARATION OF HUMAN RIGHTS
Text in Documents volume
American Declaration compared, 978, 981
Covenants compared, 899, 901–902
Democratic form of government, 819–820
Nonbinding nature, 894
Preparation of, 893–894
Source of international law, 892, 894–897
Torture, source of law on, 895–896

UNIVERSAL POSTAL UNION
Membership eligibility, 149, 607
Retaliation sanction, 557
South Africa, expulsion of, 607–609

URQUHART, B.
Peace enforcement proposal, 792

URUGUAY
Inter-American Commission, proceeding on pensioners, 990–992

VALTICOS, N.
ILO formulation of standards, 276-278
ILO supervisory system, 524–527

VIENNA CONVENTION ON THE LAW OF TREATIES
See Treaties, Law of

VOTING
See Decision–Making

WALDHEIM, KURT
UNEF II guiding principles, 739–740

WAR CRIMES
See Humanitarian Law of War; International Criminal Court

WESTERN SAHARA
Good offices mission to Morocco, 844
ICJ Advisory Opinion, 506

WOMEN, DISCRIMINATION AGAINST
U.N. Human Rights Committee, decision on sex discrimination, 940–945

WORLD BANK
See International Bank for Reconstruction and Development

WORLD COURT
See International Court of Justice

WORLD HEALTH ORGANIZATION
Assessments during nonparticipation, 255–256
Assistance to member states, withholding of, 575
Dispute settlement by, 479
Dues, U.S. threat to withhold, 268–270
Health Regulations, interpretation of, 431
Israel, condemnation of, 550–554
Membership eligibility, 149
Palestine application for membership, 158–164, 268–270
Standard-setting authority, 315–316
Ultra vires issues, 552–554
U.N., relationship agreement with, 164, 553
Voting rights, loss of, 563–564
Withdrawal from, 254–255

WORLD METEOROLOGICAL ORGANIZATION
Membership, suspension of, 604–607
Technical assistance and norm enforcement, 531
Voting rights, loss of, 563

YUGOSLAVIA (CURRENT AND FORMER)
    See also Bosnia–Herzegovina; Croatia; Humanitarian Assistance; Macedonia; Peacekeeping
Arms embargo against, 689–691
CSCE membership, 619–620
Economic sanctions, 692–699
"Ethnic cleansing," 697–698, 871
Humanitarian law of war,
    Commission of Experts, creation, 871–874
    Security Council demand that breaches cease, 869–870
    War crimes tribunal, preparations for, 870–874
IAEA membership, 603
JNA, 691
Security Council, effect of decisions by, 795–796
U.N. membership, 147, 600–603, 695
War crimes, see Humanitarian law of war, above

ZAIRE
United Nations Operation in Congo (ONUC), see Peacekeeping

ZIMBABWE
    See also Rhodesia
Humanitarian assistance, sovereignty concerns, 861
Independence of, 637–638